THE
GUINNESS
ENCYCLOPEDIA
OF
INTERNATIONAL
SPORTS RECORDS
AND RESULTS

4th Edition

PETER MATTHEWS

GUINNESS PUBLISHING

THE AUTHOR

Peter Matthews is Editor of *The New Guinness Book of Records*, having previously been its sports editor for ten years. He takes a wide interest in all sports and commentates on his speciality, athletics, for ITV. He has been a member of the Association of Track & Field Statisticians since 1970 and has edited their *International Athletics Annual* since 1984. His other works include *Who's Who in British Athletics* (1990) and *All-time Greats of British and Irish Sport* (co-written with Ian Buchanan), published by Guinness in October 1995.

Peter Matthews and Ian Buchanan wrote, with Bill Mallon MD, the *Guinness International Who's Who of Sport*, first published in 1993, and Peter Mathews wrote, with Robert Brooke, the *Guinness Book of Cricket Firsts*.

4th edition
First published 1995
Reprint 10 9 8 7 6 5 4 3 2 1 0

Published in Great Britain by Guinness Publishing Ltd, 33 London Road, Enfield, Middlesex

Illustrations courtesy of Allsport UK Ltd

Cover design by Ad Vantage

Typeset in Palatino and Helvetica

Printed and bound in Great Britain by The Bath Press, Bath, Avon

'GUINNESS' is a registered trademark of Guinness Publishing Ltd

A catalogue record for this book is available friom the British Library

ISBN 0-85112-686-3

Contents

Introduction

My aim for this book, as with the previous three editions, has been to gather a comprehensive collection of the records, results and statistics of international sport. In the two and a half years since the third edition was published there has been extensive sporting competition all over the world, and the details contained in previous editions have been thoroughly updated, with several new categories added as newly important events have been established.

There are concise introductions to the individual sports and to the leading events within those sports, with detailed lists of records and winners. Comprehensive coverage is given to world championships and major international events within each sport, as well as to major national events in the UK, USA, Australia and elsewhere.

While maintaining the same number of pages my publisher and I have managed to pack yet more details into this book, adding the events of recent years – up to near the end of July 1995 – and also to amplify certain tables, such as world champions at skiing and winners of cycling classics .

Nonetheless, such is the magnitude of this task, that to contain the extent of this book in a reasonable size I have had to face difficult decisions on what to include and what to leave out. There are many sports that are practiced in different parts of the world, but I have tried to include as many as possible, and in particular all those that are widespread.

In lists of team champions I have summarised the wins by each team. In these and other lists I have shown consecutive wins as, e.g. 1983-7, for wins in each year from 1983 to 1987. Seasons that encompass two calendar years have been shown in the style 1994/5. Country abbreviations have been used throughout as shown in the list opposite.

Space has not always permitted the inclusion of complete lists for long-established events, but where such lists have been restricted to more recent winners I have given summaries to include the champions who have won most titles, thus ensuring that the 'greats' of the past are recognised. Complete lists of Olympic champions are included, but under each sport rather than in the separate Olympic section.

I have been collecting sports records since the age of eight, when my first sporting memories include England's regaining the Ashes at The Oval in 1953. I could just make out, on a very poor television picture at my grand-parents' home in Hampshire, the scenes of delight, with Compton and Edrich in action, as the runs were scored that took England to an epic victory. That year , too, I first 'devoured' my father's run of *Wisden's*. In the years since then many notebooks have been filled with data from a wide range of sources, and in the past 13 years the information has also gone into a series of wonderful Apple computers.

I have been fortunate, indeed, that my long-standing hobby has, over the years, become more and more my job, so that I have been able to go to five Olympic Games, to Commonwealth Games and to all the major events in athletics. My own sporting abilities as leg-spin bowler, half-back at hockey or slow marathon runner – have been modest in the extreme, but like many readers I remain hugely enthusiastic about sport, its important place in our culture, and the pleasure it brings to so many people – even those who like to moan about its problems.

For the data in this book, my thanks are due to myriad sources of information around the world, books, newspapers, specialist magazines and television and radio, and to all who have responded to requests for help, especially, of course, Ian Morrison, who helped me compile the first two editions of this Encyclopedia.

Peter Matthews
July 1995

Acknowledgements

Information for this book has come from a huge range of sources. The list that follows includes many experts and officials of governing bodies that I have consulted.

To them and to others that I (or Ian Morrison for the first edition) have contacted over the four editions of this book, go my very grateful thanks.

Howard Bass, winter sports

John Beeton, International Trampoline Federation

Paul Campion, croquet

Marion Collin, women's cricket

Pat Davis, Badminton

Albert Dormer, World Bridge Federation

Gavin Ehringer, Professional Rodeo Cowboys Association

Keith Escott, chess

Clive Everton, billiardes and snooker

Paulette Foyle, TT racing

Jane Fuller, Rugby Fives Association

Rulon I Hancock, United States National Archery Association

Col.Harper, the Hurlingham Polo Association

Valerie Harper, PGA European Tour

Jodi Herb, PGA tour

Elisabeth Hussey, skiing

Victor H Isaacs, One Day Cricket

Sir Peter Johnson, yachting

Ken Knelly, Thoroughbred Racing Association

Lennart Levin, International Orienteering Federation

Peter Lunn, skiing

Bob Mason, hockey

Mark Miller, American Bowling Congress

Andy Milroy, ultra-distance running

John Moody, powerlifting

Anthony Needell, powerboating

Joseph and Pauline New, National Skating Association of Great Britain

Irmgard Nienstedt, Fédération Equestre Internationale

Mike Powell, Eton Fives Association

Paul Ramlow, US Trotting Association

John Randall, horse racing

Chris Rhys, rugby union

Barry Rolfe, British Gliding Association

Jack Rollin, soccer

Renee Schlitz, Women's International Bowling Congress

Greg Sharko, ATP tour

Len Smith, Australian harness racing

Mike Thomson, World Curling Federation

Steve Trew, triathlon

Dr Roy Wheatley, National Roller Hockey Association of Great Britain

Rick Wilson, British Hang Gliding Association

Toni Woods, Women's Tennis Association

Hugh Wrampling, pétanque

Ian Wright, racketball and squash

Also to Paulo Abbiati, Edward Abelson, Naomi Beinart, Ian Buchanan, Cris Freddi, Stan Greenberg, Paul Jenes, Bill Mallon, Mike Messerole, Jean-Jacques Tissier and those listed in previous editions of the book. And especially to Ove Karlsson, Ian Morrison and Mark Young.

Abbreviations

Measurements

ave.	average
cc	cubic capacity
d	days
hr	hours
kg	kilograms
km	kilometres
km/h	kilometres per hour
m	metres
min	minutes
mph	miles per hour
m/s	metres per second
sec	seconds
y	yards
yr	years

In dates, months are usually abbreviated to their first three digits.

Countries

Alb	Albania
Alg	Algeria
Ant	Antigua
Arg	Argentina
Arm	Armenia
Aus	Australia
Aut	Austria
Bah	Bahamas
Ban	Bangladesh
Bar	Barbados
Bel	Belgium
Ber	Bermuda
Bhn	Bahrain * (BRN)
Bls	Belarus (BLR)
Bra	Brazil
Bul	Bulgaria
Bur	Burma (now Myanmar) * (MYA)
Cam	Cameroon * (CMR)
Can	Canada
Chl	Chile * (CHI)
Chn	China (People's Republic)
Col	Colombia
Con	Congo * (CGO)
Cro	Croatia
Cs	Czechoslovakia * (TCH)
Cub	Cuba
Cyp	Cyprus
Cze	Czech Republic
Den	Denmark
Dji	Djibouti
Dom	Dominican Republic
Ecu	Ecuador
Egy	Egypt
Eng	England
Est	Estonia
Eth	Ethiopia
Fij	Fiji
Fin	Finland
Fra	France
FRG	Federal Republic of Germany
Gab	Gabon
Gam	The Gambia
GDR	German Democratic Republic
Geo	Georgia
Ger	Germany
Gha	Ghana
Gre	Greece
Gua	Guatemala
Guy	Guyana
Haw	Hawaii
HK	Hong Kong * (HKG)
Hol	Holland/Netherlands (NED)
Hun	Hungary
Ice	Iceland * (ISL)
Ina	Indonesia
Ind	India
IOM	Isle of Man
Ire	Ireland * (IRL)
Irn	Iran
Irq	Iraq
Isr	Israel
Ita	Italy
IvC	Ivory Coast/Côte d'Ivoire * (CIV)
Jam	Jamaica
Jap	Japan * (JPN)
Ken	Kenya
Kgz	Kyrgyzstan
Kuw	Kuwait
Kzk	Kazakhstan
Lat	Latvia
Lie	Liechtenstein
Lit	Lithuania
Lux	Luxembourg
Mal	Malaysia
Maw	Malawi
Mex	Mexico
Mgl	Mongolia
Mlt	Malta
Mol	Moldova
Mon	Monaco
Mor	Morocco * (MAR)
NI	Northern Ireland
Nic	Nicaragua * (NCA)
Nig	Nigeria * (NGR)
NKo	North Korea (Korean DPR) * (PRK)
Nor	Norway
NZ	New Zealand * (NZL)
Pak	Pakistan
Pan	Panama
Par	Paraguay
Per	Peru
Phi	Philippines
PNG	Papua New Guinea
Pol	Poland
Por	Portugal
PR	Puerto Rico * (PUR)
Qat	Qatar
Rho	Rhodesia
Rom	Romania
Rus	Russia
SAf	South Africa (RSA)
Sco	Scotland
Sen	Sénégal
Sin	Singapore
SKo	Korea (South) * (KOR)
Slo	Slovenia
Som	Somalia
Spa	Spain * (ESP)
SRho	Southern Rhodesia (now Zimbabwe)
Sri	Sri Lanka
Sud	Sudan
SVI	St Vincent
Svk	Slovakia
Sur	Surinam
Swe	Sweden
Swi	Switzerland * (SUI)
Syr	Syria
Tai	Taiwan (Chinese Taipeh) * (TPE)
Tan	Tanzania
Tha	Thailand
Tjk	Tadjikstan
Tkm	Turkmenistan
Tri	Trinidad & Tobago
Tun	Tunisia
Tur	Turkey
Uga	Uganda
UK	United Kingdom of Great Britain & N.Ireland * (GBR)
Ukr	Ukraine
Uru	Uruguay
USA	United States
USSR	Soviet Union * (URS) 1917-91
Uzb	Uzbekistan
Ven	Venezuela
Wal	Wales
WI	West Indies
Yug	Yugoslavia
Zai	Zaire
Zam	Zambia
Zim	Zimbabwe (formerly Rhodesia)

* These abbreviations differ in some cases from those used by the IOC (which are shown in brackets). The latter are always three digits and often French language based; I have preferred English or those of the countries concerned.

Governing Bodies and Sports Organisations

Specified here in English - see relevant sports for actual titles and dates of founding.

AAA	Amateur Athletic Association (UK)
AAU	Amateur Athletic Union (USA)
AIBA	International Amateur Boxing Federation
ATP	Association of Tennis Professionals
FAI	International Aeronautics Federation
FEI	International Equestrian Federation
FIA	International Automobile Association
FIAC	International Amateur Cycling Federation
FIBA	International Basketball Federation
FIBT	International Bobsleigh and Tobogganing Federation
FIC	International Canoeing Federation
FIDE	International Chess Federation
FIE	International Fencing Federation
FIFA	International Association Football Federation
FIG	International Gymnastic Federation
FIH	International Hockey Federation
FIL	International Luge Federation
FILA	International Amateur Wrestling Federation
FIM	International Motorcycling Federation
FINA	International Amateur Swimming Federation
FIQ	International Bowling Federation
FIRA	International Amateur Rugby Federation
FIRS	International Roller Skating Federation
FIS	International Ski Federation
FISA	International Rowing Federation
FIT	International Trampoline Federation
FITA	International Archery Federation
FIVB	International Volleyball Federation
GAA	Gaelic Athletic Association
IAAF	International Amateur Athletic Federation
IBA	International Baseball Federation
IBF	International Badminton Federation
	International Boxing Federation
IBSF	International Billiards & Snooker Federation
ICF	International Curling Federation
IHF	International Handball Federation
IIHF	International Ice Hockey Federation
IJF	International Judo Federation
IOF	International Orienteering Federation
IRF	International Racketball Federation
IRFB	International Rugby Football Board
ISF	International Softball Federation
ISRF	International Squash Rackets Federation
ISU	International Skating Union
ITF	International Tennis Federation
ITTF	International Table Tennis Federation
IWF	International Weightlifting Federation
IWSF	International Water Ski Federation
IYRU	International Yacht Racing Union
LPGA	Ladies Professional Golfers Association
MCC	Marylebone Cricket Club
NBA	National Basketball Federation (USA)
NBL	National Basketball League (USA)
NCAA	National Collegiate Athletic Association (USA)
NFL	National Football League (USA)
NHL	National Hockey League (USA)
PGA	Professional Golfers Association
PRCA	Professional Rodeo Cowboys Association
TCCB	Test and County Cricket Board
UCI	International Cycling Union
UIPMB	International Union of Modern Pentathlon and Biathlon
UIT	International Shooting Union
WBA	World Boxing Association
WBC	World Boxing Council
WBO	World Boxing Organisation
WSF	World Squash Federation
WTF	World Taekwan-Do Federation
WWSU	World Water Skiing Union

Other abbreviations for sports bodies are given under their respective sports.

American Football

American Football evolved from the British games of soccer and rugby in the latter part of the 19th century. There were conflicting versions of football, but an important development was the first match under Harvard Rules by Harvard University against McGill University, Montreal in May 1874. In 1876 the Intercollegiate Football Association was formed, and in that year Harvard agreed to reduce the number of players per side from 15 to 11, which it is today. The first professional game was between Latrobe and Jeanette in Pennsylvania on 31 Aug 1895, and by the end of the century it had become the national game, although exceptionally rough at the time. After many fatalities in the early part of the 20th century considerable modifications were made to the rules, including the introduction of the forward pass in 1906. The first Rose Bowl game between the leading college teams was held in 1902.

The American Professional Football Association was formed in 1920 and twelve teams contested the first league season, with Akron Pros designated the first champions. The association became the National Football League (NFL) in 1922.

National Football League Champions

There was just one league to 1932. *Champions*:

1921	Chicago Staleys
1922	Canton Bulldogs (Ohio)
1923	Canton Bulldogs (Ohio)
1924	Cleveland Bulldogs
1925	Chicago Cardinals
1926	Frankford Yellow Jackets
1927	New York Giants
1928	Providence Steam Roller
1929	Green Bay Packers
1930	Green Bay Packers
1931	Green Bay Packers
1932	Chicago Bears

From 1933 the NFL was divided into two divisions, Eastern and Western, with the respective winners playing off for the NFL Championship. In 1950-2 the divisions were named American Conference (Eastern) and National Conference (Western). Between 1953-9 they were known as the Eastern and Western Conferences.

NFL Championship 1933–59

Year	Eastern	Western	Championship Game
1933	New York Giants	Chicago Bears	Chicago 23 New York 21
1934	New York Giants	Chicago Bears	New York 30 Chicago 13
1935	New York Giants	Detroit Lions	Detroit 26 New York 7
1936	Boston Redskins	Green Bay Packers	Green Bay 21 Boston 6
1937	Washington Redskins	Chicago Bears	Washington 28 Chicago 21
1938	New York Giants	Green Bay Packers	New York 23 Green Bay 17
1939	New York Giants	Green Bay Packers	Green Bay 27 New York 0
1940	Washington Redskins	Chicago Bears	Chicago 73 Washington 0
1941	New York Giants	Chicago Bears	Chicago 37 New York 9
1942	Washington Redskins	Chicago Bears	Washington 14 Chicago 6
1943	Washington Redskins	Chicago Bears	Chicago 41 Washington 21
1944	New York Giants	Green Bay Packers	Green Bay 14 New York 7
1945	Washington Redskins	Cleveland Rams	Cleveland 15 Washington 14
1946	New York Giants	Chicago Bears	Chicago Bears 24 New York 14
1947	Philadelphia Eagles	Chicago Cardinals	Chicago Cardinals 28 Philadelphia 21
1948	Philadelphia Eagles	Chicago Cardinals	Philadelphia 7 Chicago Cardinals 0
1949	Philadelphia Eagles	Los Angeles Rams	Philadelphia 14 Los Angeles 0
1950	Cleveland Browns	Los Angeles Rams	Cleveland 30 Los Angeles 28
1951	Cleveland Browns	Los Angeles Rams	Los Angeles 24 Cleveland 17
1952	Cleveland Browns	Detroit Lions	Detroit 17 Cleveland 7
1953	Cleveland Browns	Detroit Lions	Detroit 17 Cleveland 16
1954	Cleveland Browns	Detroit Lions	Cleveland 56 Detroit 10
1955	Cleveland Browns	Los Angeles Rams	Cleveland 38 Los Angeles 14
1956	New York Giants	Chicago Bears	New York 47 Chicago 7
1957	Cleveland Browns	Detroit Lions	Detroit 59 Cleveland 14
1958	New York Giants	Baltimore Colts	Baltimore 23 New York 17
1959	New York Giants	Baltimore Colts	Baltimore 31 New York 16

The American Football League (AFL) was formed in 1960 as a rival to the NFL. It had Eastern and Western Divisions while the NFL still had its Eastern and Western Conferences. Both the AFL and NFL had end of season Championships and at the end of the 1966 season the AFL and NFL champions met for the first Super Bowl (played January 1967). *Divisional winners and championship game results 1960-9:*

American Football League

Year	Eastern winners	Western winners	Playoff
1960	Houston Oilers	Los Angeles Chargers	Houston 24 Los Angeles 16
1961	Houston Oilers	San Diego Chargers	Houston 10 San Diego 3
1962	Houston Oilers	Dallas Texans	Dallas 20 Houston 17
1963	Boston Patriots	San Diego Chargers	San Diego 51 Boston 10
1964	Buffalo Bills	San Diego Chargers	Buffalo 20 San Diego 7
1965	Buffalo Bills	San Diego Chargers	Buffalo 23 San Diego 0
1966	Buffalo Bills	Kansas City Chiefs	Kansas City 31 Buffalo 7
1967	Houston Oilers	Oakland Raiders	Oakland 40 Houston 7
1968	New York Jets	Oakland Raiders	New York Jets 27 Oakland 23
1969	New York Jets	Oakland Raiders	Kansas City Chiefs 17 Oakland 7

In 1969 the top two in each division qualified for AFL play-offs.

National Football League

Year	Eastern winners	Western winners	Playoff
1960	Philadelphia Eagles	Green Bay Packers	Philadelphia 17 Green Bay 13
1961	New York Giants	Green Bay Packers	Green Bay 37 New York 0
1962	New York Giants	Green Bay Packers	Green Bay 16 New York 7
1963	New York Giants	Chicago Bears	Chicago 14 New York 10
1964	Cleveland Browns	Baltimore Colts	Cleveland 27 Baltimore 0
1965	Cleveland Browns	Green Bay Packers	Green Bay 23 Cleveland 12
1966	Dallas Cowboys	Green Bay Packers	Green Bay 34 Dallas 27
1967	(a) Dallas Cowboys	(c) Los Angeles Rams	
	(b) Cleveland Browns	(d) Green Bay Packers	Green Bay 21 Dallas 17
1968	(a) Dallas Cowboys	(c) Baltimore Colts	
	(b) Cleveland Browns	(d) Minnesota Vikings	Baltimore 34 Cleveland 0
1969	(a) Dallas Cowboys	(c) Los Angeles Rams	
	(b) Cleveland Browns	(d) Minnesota Vikings	Minnesota 27 Cleveland 7

(a) Capitol Division, (b) Century Division, (c) Coastal Division, (d) Central Division

In 1970 the NFL and AFL merged under the National Football League banner and divided into two conferences, American (AFC) and National (NFC), each with three divisions, Eastern, Central and Western. End of season play-offs culminate in the American and National Conference Championship games with the two winners meeting in the Super Bowl.

AFC Divisional champions

	Eastern	Central	Western
1970	Baltimore Colts	Cincinnati Bengals	Oakland Raiders
1971	Miami Dolphins	Cleveland Browns	Kansas City Chiefs
1972	Miami Dolphins	Pittsburgh Steelers	Oakland Raiders
1973	Miami Dolphins	Cincinnati Bengals	Oakland Raiders
1974	Miami Dolphins	Pittsburgh Steelers	Oakland Raiders
1975	Baltimore Colts	Pittsburgh Steelers	Oakland Raiders
1976	Baltimore Colts	Pittsburgh Steelers	Oakland Raiders
1977	Baltimore Colts	Pittsburgh Steelers	Denver Broncos
1978	New England Patriots	Pittsburgh Steelers	Denver Broncos
1979	Miami Dolphins	Pittsburgh Steelers	San Diego Chargers
1980	Buffalo Bills	Cleveland Browns	San Diego Chargers
1981	Miami Dolphins	Cincinnati Bengals	San Diego Chargers
1983	Miami Dolphins	Pittsburgh Steelers	Los Angeles Raiders
1984	Miami Dolphins	Pittsburgh Steelers	Denver Broncos
1985	Miami Dolphins	Cleveland Browns	Los Angeles Raiders
1986	New England Patriots	Cleveland Browns	Denver Broncos
1987	Indianapolis Colts	Cleveland Browns	Denver Broncos
1988	Buffalo Bills	Cincinnati Bengals	Seattle Seahawks
1989	Buffalo Bills	Cleveland Browns	Denver Broncos
1990	Buffalo Bills	Cincinnati Bengals	Los Angeles Raiders
1991	Buffalo Bills	Houston Oilers	Denver Broncos
1992	Miami Dolphins	Pittsburgh Steelers	San Diego Chargers
1993	Buffalo Bills	Houston Oilers	Kansas City Chiefs
1994	Miami Dolphins	Pittsburgh Steelers	San Diego Chargers

AFC Championship Games

1970	Baltimore 27 Oakland 17
1971	Miami 21 Baltimore 0
1972	Miami 21 Pittsburgh 17
1973	Miami 27 Oakland 10
1974	Pittsburgh 24 Oakland 13
1975	Pittsburgh 16 Oakland 10
1976	Oakland 24 Pittsburgh 7
1977	Denver 20 Oakland 17
1978	Pittsburgh 34 Houston 5
1979	Pittsburgh 27 Houston 13
1980	Oakland 34 San Diego 27
1981	Cincinnati 27 San Diego 7
1982	Miami 14 New York Jets 0
1983	Los Angeles 30 Seattle 14
1984	Miami 45 Pittsburgh 28
1985	New England 31 Miami 14
1986	Denver 23 Cleveland 20
1987	Denver 38 Cleveland 33
1988	Cincinnati 21 Buffalo 10
1989	Denver 37 Cleveland 21
1990	Buffalo 51 Los Angeles 3
1991	Buffalo 10 Denver 7
1992	Buffalo 29 Miami 10
1993	Buffalo 30 Kansas City 13
1994	San Diego 17 Pittsburgh 13

NFC Divisional champions

	Eastern	*Central*	*Western*
1970	Dallas Cowboys	Minnesota Vikings	San Francisco 49ers
1971	Dallas Cowboys	Minnesota Vikings	San Francisco 49ers
1972	Washington Redskins	Green Bay Packers	San Francisco 49ers
1973	Dallas Cowboys	Minnesota Vikings	Los Angeles Rams
1974	St Louis Cardinals	Minnesota Vikings	Los Angeles Rams
1975	St Louis Cardinals	Minnesota Vikings	Los Angeles Rams
1976	Dallas Cowboys	Minnesota Vikings	Los Angeles Rams
1977	Dallas Cowboys	Minnesota Vikings	Los Angeles Rams
1978	Dallas Cowboys	Minnesota Vikings	Los Angeles Rams
1979	Dallas Cowboys	Tampa Bay Buccaneers	Los Angeles Rams
1980	Philadelphia Eagles	Minnesota Vikings	Atlanta Falcons
1981	Dallas Cowboys	Tampa Bay Buccaneers	San Francisco 49ers
1983	Washington Redskins	Detroit Lions	San Francisco 49ers
1984	Washington Redskins	Chicago Bears	San Francisco 49ers
1985	Dallas Cowboys	Chicago Bears	Los Angeles Rams
1986	New York Giants	Chicago Bears	San Francisco 49ers
1987	Washington Redskins	Chicago Bears	San Francisco 49ers
1988	Philadelphia Eagles	Chicago Bears	San Francisco 49ers
1989	New York Giants	Minnesota Vikings	San Francisco 49ers
1990	New York Giants	Chicago Bears	San Francisco 49ers
1991	Washington Redskins	Detroit Lions	New Orleans Saints
1992	Dallas Cowboys	Minnesota Vikings	San Francisco 49ers
1993	Dallas Cowboys	Detroit Lions	San Francisco 49ers
1994	Dallas Cowboys	Minnesota Vikings	San Francisco 49ers

NFC Championship Games

1970	Dallas 17 San Francisco 10
1971	Dallas 14 San Francisco 3
1972	Washington 26 Dallas 3
1973	Minnesota 27 Dallas 10
1974	Minnesota 14 Los Angeles 10
1975	Dallas 37 Los Angeles 7
1976	Minnesota 24 Los Angeles 13
1977	Dallas 23 Minnesota 6
1978	Dallas 28 Los Angeles 0
1979	Los Angeles 9 Tampa Bay 0
1980	Philadelphia 20 Dallas 7
1981	San Francisco 28 Dallas 27
1982	Washington 31 Dallas 17
1983	Washington 24 San Francisco 21
1984	San Francisco 23 Chicago 0
1985	Chicago 24 Los Angeles Rams 0
1986	New York 17 Washington 0
1987	Washington 17 Minnesota 10
1988	San Francisco 28 Chicago 3
1989	San Francisco 30 Los Angeles Rams 3
1990	New York 15 San Francisco 13
1991	Washington 41 Detroit 10
1992	Dallas 30 San Francisco 20
1993	Dallas 38 San Francisco 21
1994	San Francisco 38 Dallas 28

In 1982 a players' strike shortened the season and the top eight teams in each Conference played-off to decide the championship.

American Football - positions

DE	Defensive end
DT	Defensive tackle
LB	Linebacker
Q	Quarterback
RB	Running back
S	Safety
WR	Wide receiver

Super Bowl

Inaugurated in 1966 the Super Bowl, the contest between the AFC and NFC champions, has become America's greatest sporting event.

Tickets for the game are highly prized and record television audiences are regularly attracted to the game, held in January each year at the end of the regular season.

Traditionally numbered by Roman numerals, the January 1995 game was Super Bowl XXVIII.

San Francisco's Jerry Rice - his first touchdown in the 1995 Super Bowl which the 49ers won 49-26

Results:

Year	Venue	Winners	Runners-up	Attendance
1967	Los Angeles	Green Bay Packers 35	Kansas City Chiefs 10	61,946
1968	Miami	Green Bay Packers 33	Oakland Raiders 14	75,546
1969	Miami	New York Jets 16	Baltimore Colts 7	75,389
1970	New Orleans	Kansas City Chiefs 23	Minnesota Vikings 7	80,562
1971	Miami	Baltimore Colts 16	Dallas Cowboys 13	79,204
1972	New Orleans	Dallas Cowboys 24	Miami Dolphins 3	81,023
1973	Los Angeles	Miami Dolphins 14	Washington Redskins 7	90,182
1974	Houston	Miami Dolphins 24	Minnesota Vikings 7	71,882
1975	New Orleans	Pittsburgh Steelers 16	Minnesota Vikings 6	80,997
1976	Miami	Pittsburgh Steelers 21	Dallas Cowboys 17	80,187
1977	Pasadena	Oakland Raiders 32	Minnesota Vikings 14	103,438
1978	New Orleans	Dallas Cowboys 27	Denver Broncos 10	75,583
1979	Miami	Pittsburgh Steelers 35	Dallas Cowboys 31	79,484
1980	Pasadena	Pittsburgh Steelers 31	Los Angeles Rams 19	103,985
1981	New Orleans	Oakland Raiders 27	Philadelphia Eagles 10	76,135
1982	Pontiac	San Francisco 49ers 26	Cincinnati Bengals 21	81,270
1983	Pasadena	Washington Redskins 27	Miami Dolphins 17	103,667
1984	Tampa	Los Angeles Raiders 38	Washington Redskins 9	72,920
1985	Stanford	San Francisco 49ers 38	Miami Dolphins 16	84,059
1986	New Orleans	Chicago Bears 46	New England Patriots 10	73,818
1987	Pasadena	New York Giants 39	Denver Broncos 20	101,063
1988	San Diego	Washington Redskins 42	Denver Broncos 10	73,302
1989	Miami	San Francisco 49ers 20	Cincinnati Bengals 16	75,179
1990	New Orleans	San Francisco 49ers 55	Denver Broncos 10	72,191
1991	Tampa	New York Giants 20	Buffalo Bills 19	73,818
1992	Minneapolis	Washington Redskins 37	Buffalo Bills 24	63,130
1993	Pasadena	Dallas Cowboys 52	Buffalo Bills 19	98,374
1994	Atlanta	Dallas Cowboys 30	Buffalo Bills 13	72,817
1995	Miami	San Francisco 49ers 49	San Diego Chargers 26	74,107

Most wins: 5 San Francisco 49ers, 4 Pittsburgh Steelers, Dallas Cowboys

Super Bowl career records

Most games (player):
5 Marv Fleming (Green Bay 1967-8, Miami 1972-4)
5 Larry Cole (Dallas 1971-2, 1976, 1978-9)
5 Cliff Harris (Dallas 1971-2, 1976, 1978-9)
5 D D Lewis (Dallas 1971-2, 1976, 1978-9)
5 Preston Pearson (Baltimore 1969, Pittsburgh 1975, Dallas 1976, 1978-9)
5 Charlie Waters (Dallas 1971-2, 1976, 1978-9)
5 Rayfield Wright (Dallas 1971-2, 1976, 1978-9)
Most games (coach): 6 Don Shula (Baltimore 1969, Miami 1972-4, 1983, 1985)

Most points: 42 Jerry Rice (San Francisco 1989-95)
Most touchdowns: 7 Jerry Rice (San Francisco 1989-95)
Most touchdown passes: 11 Joe Montana (San Francisco 1982-90)
Most yards gained passing: 1142 Joe Montana (San Francisco 1982-90)
Most passes completed: 83 Joe Montana (San Francisco 1982-90)
Most pass receptions: 28 Jerry Rice (San Francisco 1989-95)

Most yards gained receiving: 512 Jerry Rice (San Francisco 1989-95)

Most yards gained rushing: 354 Franco Harris (Pittsburgh 1975-80)

Most field goals: 5 Ray Wersching (San Francisco 1982-5)

Super Bowl single game records

Most points: 18 Roger Craig (San Francisco 1985), Jerry Rice (San Francisco 1990)

Most touchdowns: 3 Roger Craig (San Francisco 1985), 3 Jerry Rice (San Francisco 1990 and 1995), Ricky Walters (San Francisco 1995)

Touchdown passes: 6 Steve Young (San Francisco 1995)

Yards gained passing: 357 Joe Montana (San Francisco 1989)

Passes completed: 31 Jin Kelly (Buffalo 1994)

Pass receptions: 11 Dan Ross (Cincinnati 1982), Jerry Rice (San Francisco 1989)

Yards gained receiving: 215 Jerry Rice (San Francisco 1989)

Yards gained rushing: 204 Timmy Smith (Washington 1988)

Most field goals: 4 Don Chandler (Green Bay v Oakland, 1968), Ray Wersching (San Francisco v Cincinnati, 1982)

Super Bowl MVPs

1967	Bart Starr (QB), Green Bay Packers
1968	Bart Starr (QB), Green Bay Packers
1969	Joe Namath (QB), New York Jets
1970	Len Dawson (QB), Kansas City
1971	Chuck Howley (LB), Dallas Cowboys
1972	Roger Staubach (QB), Dallas Cowboys
1973	Jake Scott (S), Miami Dolphins
1974	Larry Csonka (RB), Miami Dolphins
1975	Franco Harris (RB) Pittsburgh Steelers
1976	Lynn Swann (WR), Pittsburgh Steelers
1977	Fred Biletnikoff (WR), Oakland Raiders
1978	Randy White (DT) & Harvey Martin (DE), Dallas
1979	Terry Bradshaw (QB), Pittsburgh Steelers
1980	Terry Bradshaw (QB), Pittsburgh Steelers
1981	Jim Plunkett (QB), Oakland Raiders
1982	Joe Montana (QB), San Francisco 49ers
1983	Joe Riggins (RB), Washington Redskins
1984	Marcus Allen (RB), Los Angeles Raiders
1985	Joe Montana (QB), San Francisco 49ers
1986	Richard Dent (DE), Chicago Bears
1987	Phil Simms (QB), New York Giants
1988	Doug Williams (QB), Washington Redskins
1989	Jerry Rice (WR), San Francisco 49ers
1990	Joe Montana (QB), San Francisco 49ers
1991	Ottis Anderson (RB), New York Giants
1992	Mark Rypien (QB), Washington Redskins
1993	Troy Aikman (QB), Dallas Cowboys
1994	Emmitt Smith (RB), Dallas Cowboys
1995	Steve Young (QB), San Francisco 49ers

Major NFL Records

General

Most games: 340 George Blanda (Chicago Bears, Baltimore, Houston, Oakland) 1949-75

Most seasons as head coach: 40 George Halas (Chicago Bears) 1920-9, 1933-42, 1946-55, 1958-67 (record 325 wins)

Scoring

Most points (career): 2002 George Blanda (Chicago Bears, Baltimore, Houston, Oakland) 1949-75

Most points (season): 176 Paul Hornung (Green Bay) 1960

Most points (game): 40 Ernie Nevers (Chicago Cardinals v Chicago Bears) 28 Nov 1929

Most touchdowns (career): 139 Jerry Rice (San Francisco 49ers) 1985-94

Most touchdowns (season): 24 John Riggins (Washington) 1983

Most touchdowns (game)

6 Ernie Nevers (Chicago Cardinals v Chicago Bears) 28 Nov 1929

6 William Jones (Cleveland v Chicago Bears) 25 Nov 1951

6 Gale Sayers (Chicago v San Francisco) 12 Dec 1965

Most field goals (career): 373 Jan Stenerud (Kansas City, Green Bay, Minnesota) 1967-85

Most field goals (season): 35 Ali Haji-Sheikh (New York Giants) 1983

Most field goals (game)

7 Jim Bakken (St Louis v Pittsburgh) 24 Sep 1967

7 Rich Karlis (Minnesota v Los Angeles Rams) 5 Nov 1989

Rushing

Most yards gained (career): 16,726 Walter Payton (Chicago) 1975-87

Most yards gained (season): 2105 Eric Dickerson (Los Angeles Rams) 1984

Most yards gained (game): 275 Walter Payton (Chicago v Minnesota) 20 Nov 1977

Passing

Most passes completed (career): 3686 Fran Tarkenton (Minnesota, New York Giants) 1961-78

Most passes completed (season): 404 Warren Moon (Houston Oilers) 1991 (from record 655 attempts)

Most passes completed (game): 42 Richard Todd (New York Jets v San Francisco) 21 Sep 1980

Most yards gained (career): 47,003 Fran Tarkenton (Minnesota, New York Giants) 1961-78

Most yards gained (season): 5084 Dan Marino (Miami) 1984

Most yards gained (game): 554 Norm Van Brocklin (Los Angeles v New York Yanks) 28 Sep 1951

Franchise changes

Since the formation of the AFL in 1960 the following teams have changed their franchise:

	From	To
1960	Chicago Cardinals	St Louis Cardinals
1961	Los Angeles Chargers	San Diego Chargers
1963	Dallas Texans	Kansas City Chiefs
1971	Boston Patriots	New England Patriots
1982	Oakland Raiders	Los Angeles Raiders
1984	Baltimore Colts	Indianapolis Colts
1988	St Louis Cardinals	Phoenix Cardinals
1988	Phoenix Cardinals	Arizona Cardinals

New franchises

1995   Carolina Cougars (Charlotte) and Jacksonville Jaguars

All time Top Tens
(as at end of 1994 season)

Most points

George Blanda	2002
Jan Stenerud	1699
Nick Lowery	1559
Pat Leahy	1470
Jim Turner	1439
Mark Moseley	1382
Jim Bakken	1380
Fred Cox	1365
Eddie Murray	1359
Lou Groza	1349

Most touchdowns

Jerry Rice	139
Jim Brown	126
Walter Payton	125
Marcus Allen	120
John Riggins	116
Lenny Moore	113
Don Hutson	105
Steve Largent	101
Franco Harris	100
Eric Dickerson	96

Most passes completed

Fran Tarkenton	3686
Dan Marino	3604
Joe Montana	3409
Dan Fouts	3297
John Elway	3030
Warren Moon	3003
Steve DeBerg	2844
Johnny Unitas	2830
Ken Anderson	2654
Jim Hart	2593

Most yards gained passing

Fran Tarkenton	47,003
Dan Marino	45,173
Dan Fouts	43,040
Joe Montana	40,551
Johnny Unitas	40,239
Warren Moon	37,949
John Elway	37,736
Jim Hart	34,665
Steve DeBerg	33,872
John Hadl	33,503
Phil Simms	33,462

Most yards gained rushing

Walter Payton	16,726
Eric Dickerson	13,259
Tony Dorsett	12,739
Jim Brown	12,312
Franco Harris	12,120
John Riggins	11,352
O J Simpson	11,236
Ottis Anderson	10,273
Marcus Allen	10,108
Earl Campbell	9,407

Fewest games to reach 10,000 yards rushing:

Eric Dickerson	91
O J Simpson	110
Walter Payton	113

College Football

More than 650 colleges, affiliated to the National Collegiate Athletic Association, compete throughout the United States each year; now divided into four divisions: 1-A, 1-AA, II, III. The ultimate aim of them all is to reach one of the many Bowl finals held at the end of the season.

National College Football Champions

At the end of December each year, journalists throughout the United States engage in a national poll to vote for the outstanding college team of the year. The Associated Press poll has been conducted since 1936 and United Press, now UPI, introduced a coaches' poll in 1950. Where the two polls differ, both teams are shown, with the AP winner first and the UPI winner second.

1936	Minnesota
1937	Pittsburgh
1938	Texas Christian
1939	Texas A & M
1940-1	Minnesota
1942	Ohio State
1943	Notre Dame
1944-5	Army
1946-7	Notre Dame
1948	Michigan
1949	Notre Dame
1950	Oklahoma
1951	Tennessee
1952	Michigan State
1953	Maryland
1954	Ohio State & UCLA
1955-6	Oklahoma
1957	Auburn & Ohio State
1958	Louisiana State
1959	Syracuse
1960	Minnesota
1961	Alabama
1962	South Carolina
1963	Texas
1964	Alabama
1965	Alabama & Michigan State
1966	Notre Dame
1967	South Carolina
1968	Ohio State
1969	Texas
1970	Texas & Nebraska
1971	Nebraska
1972	South Carolina
1973	Notre Dame
1974	Oklahoma & Southern California
1975	Oklahoma
1976	Pittsburgh
1977	Notre Dame
1978	Alabama & Southern California
1979	Alabama
1980	Georgia
1981	Clemson
1982	Penn State
1983	Miami (Florida)
1984	Brigham Young
1985	Oklahoma
1986	Penn State
1987	Miami (Florida)
1988	Notre Dame
1989	Miami (Florida)
1990	Colorado & Georgia Tech
1991	Miami & Washington
1992	Alabama
1993	Florida State
1994	Nebraska

Most wins: 8 Notre Dame

Bowl Games

The highlight of the College season comes with the end of season Bowl Games. The 'Big Four' are the Rose Bowl (first played 1902), Orange Bowl (1935), Sugar Bowl (1935), and Cotton Bowl (1937). Most wins in each have been as follows:

Rose Bowl
19 Southern California (USC),
7 Michigan, 6 Washington,
5 Alabama, Stanford, Ohio State,
UCLA; 3 Illinois, Michigan State

Orange Bowl
11 Oklahoma, 6 Miami, Nebraska;
4 Alabama, 3 Georgia Tech, Penn
State; 2 Duquesne, Georgia,
Louisiana State, Texas, Clemson,
Notre Dame, Florida State

Sugar Bowl
8 Alabama, 5 Mississippi,
4 Georgia Tech, Oklahoma,
Tennessee; 3 Louisiana State,
Nebraska; 2 Texas Christian, Santa
Clara, Georgia, Pittsburgh,
Auburn, Notre Dame, Florida
State

Cotton Bowl
9 Texas, 5 Notre Dame, 4 Texas A
& M, 3 Rice, Louisiana State,
Southern Methodist; 2 Texas
Christian, Alabama, Arkansas,
Georgia, Penn State, Houston,
Tennessee

Bowl Records
Most 'Big Four' appearances:
31 Alabama, 28 USC, 23 Nebraska,
22 Texas, 21 Oklahoma,
18 Louisiana State

Most 'Big Four' wins
20 USC, 18 Alabama,
15 Oklahoma, 12 Texas

Alabama, Georgia, Georgia Tech
and Notre Dame have won all four
major Bowls

NCAA Div 1-A career records

Most points scored: 423 Roman Anderson (Houston) 1988-91
Most touchdowns: 65 Anthony Thompson (Indiana) 1986-9
Most field goals: 80 Jeff Jaeger (Washington) 1983-6
Most yards gained rushing:
6082 Tony Dorsett (Pittsburgh) 1973-6

Most yards gained passing:
15,031 Ty Detmer (Brigham Young) 1988-91
Most passes completed: 958 Ty Detmer (Brigham Young) 1988-91

Heisman Trophy

Awarded annually since 1935 by the Downtown Athletic Club of New York to the top college footballer as determined by a poll of journalists. It was originally called the D.A.C. Trophy but its name was changed in 1936. Its full title is the John W Heisman Memorial Trophy and is named after the first athletic director of the Downtown club.

Winners:

1935 Jay Berwanger (Chicago)
1936 Larry Kelley (Yale)
1937 Clint Frank (Yale)
1938 Davey O'Brien (Texas Christian)
1939 Nile Kinnick (Iowa)
1940 Tom Harmon (Michigan)
1941 Bruce Smith (Minnesota)
1942 Frank Sinkwich (Georgia)
1943 Angelo Bertelli (Notre Dame)
1944 Les Horvath (Ohio State)
1945 Doc Blanchard (Army)
1946 Glenn Davis (Army)
1947 John Lujack (Notre Dame)
1948 Doak Walker (Southern Methodist)
1949 Leon Hart (Notre Dame)
1950 Vic Janowicz (Ohio State)
1951 Dick Kazmaier (Princeton)
1952 Billy Vessels (Oklahoma)
1953 John Lattner (Notre Dame)
1954 Alan Ameche (Wisconsin)
1955 Howard Cassady (Ohio State)
1956 Paul Hornung (Notre Dame)
1957 John Crow (Texas A & M)
1958 Pete Dawkins (Army)
1959 Billy Cannon (Louisiana State)
1960 Joe Bellino (Navy)
1961 Ernie Davis (Syracuse)
1962 Terry Baker (Oregon State)
1963 Roger Staubach (Navy)
1964 John Huarte (Notre Dame)
1965 Mike Garrett (USC)
1966 Steve Spurrier (Florida)
1967 Gary Beban (UCLA)
1968 O J Simpson (USC)
1969 Steve Owens (Oklahoma)
1970 Jim Plunkett (Stanford)
1971 Pat Sullivan (Auburn)
1972 Johnny Rogers (Nebraska)
1973 John Cappelletti (Penn State)
1974 Archie Griffin (Ohio State)
1975 Archie Griffin (Ohio State)
1976 Tony Dorsett (Pittsburgh)
1977 Earl Campbell (Texas)
1978 Billy Sims (Oklahoma)
1979 Charles White (USC)
1980 George Rogers (South Carolina)
1981 Marcus Allen (USC)
1982 Herschel Walker (Georgia)
1983 Mike Rozier (Nebraska)
1984 Doug Flutie (Boston College)
1985 Bo Jackson (Auburn)
1986 Vinny Testaverde (Miami)
1987 Tim Brown (Notre Dame)
1988 Barry Sanders (Oklahoma)
1989 Andre Ware (Houston)
1990 Ty Detmer (Brigham Young)
1991 Desmond Howard (Michigan)
1992 Gino Torretta (Miami)
1993 Charlie Ward (Florida State)
1994 Rashaan Salaam (Colorado)

World League

Inaugurated in 1991 as the World League of American Football by the NFL as an international spring league. Franchises were granted to teams in the USA, Canada, Mexico, Britain, Germany, Italy and Spain and the event was contested for two years.

The NFL agreed at the end of 1993 to end the World League, but to create an all-European league from 1995, with the return of the World Bowl as its final.

World Bowl (final)
1991 London Monarchs beat Barcelona Dragons 21-0
1992 Sacramento Surge beat Orlando Thunder 21-17
1995 Frankfurt Galaxy beat Amsterdam Admirals 26-22

Eurobowl Winners

1986	Taft Vantaa (Fin)
1988	Helsinki Roosters (Fin)
1989	Legnano Frogs (Ita)
1990	Manchester Spartans (UK)
1991-2	Amsterdam Crusaders (Hol)
1993-4	London Olympians (UK)

Canadian Football League

Canadian football differs in severaf respects from American football, including having teams of 12 rather than 11 players.

The earliest recorded game of football in Canada was between students at the University of Toronto in 1861. In 1909 Earl Grey, the Governor-General of Canada, donated a trophy to be awarded annually to the Canadian rugby football champion. From 1954 however, the Earl Grey Cup was awarded to the champion of the Canadian Football League (CFL), founded as a professional organisation in 1958.

Grey Cup wins

12 Toronto Argonauts 1914, 1921, 1933, 1937-8, 1945-7, 1950, 1952, 1983, 1991

12 Hamilton Tigers (Tiger-Cats from 1953) 1913, 1915, 1928-9, 1932, 1953, 1957, 1963, 1965, 1967, 1972, 1986

11 Edmonton Eskimos 1954-6, 1975, 1978-82, 1987, 1993 (most CFL wins)

9 Winnipeg Blue Bombers 1939, 1941, 1958-9, 1961-2, 1984, 1988, 1990

7 Ottawa Senators 1925-6, 1960, 1968-9, 1973, 1976

4 Montreal Alouettes 1949, 1970, 1974, 1977

4 University of Toronto 1909-11, 1920

3 Queen's University 1922-4

3 Calgary Stampeders 1948, 1971, 1992

3 British Columbia Lions 1964, 1985, 1994

2 Ottawa Rough Riders 1940, 1951

2 Sarnia Imperials 1934, 1936

2 Sasketchewan Roughriders 1966, 1989

2 Toronto Balmy Beach 1927, 1930

1 Hamilton Alerts 1912,

1 Montreal AAA Winged Wheelers 1931

1 Winnipeg 1935

1 Toronto Hurricanes 1942

1 Hamilton Flying Wildcats 1943

1 St Hyacinthe-Donnacona Navy 1944

CFL Most Outstanding Player:

Most wins: 4 Doug Flutie (Calgary, QB) 1991-4; 3 Jackie Parker (Edmonton, QB) 1957-8, 1960.

Angling

Angling is the art of catching fish with rod, line and hook. Such an activity naturally dates back to civilised man's earliest days. The oldest club still in existence is the Ellem fishing club in Scotland, formed in 1829. English national championships were first held in 1906 and the International Confederation of Anglers (CIPS - see below) was formed in Rome in 1952.

World Championships

The first World Fresh Water Championship was held in 1957, three years after the staging of the first European championships.
Winners:

Individual		*Team*
1957	Mandeli (Ita)	Italy
1958	Garroit (Bel)	Belgium
1959	Robert Tesse (Fra)	France
1960	Robert Tesse (Fra)	Belgium
1961	Ramon Legogue (Fra)	GDR
1962	Raimondo Tedasco (Ita)	Italy
1963	William Lane (Eng)	France
1964	Joseph Fontanet (Fra)	France
1965	Robert Tesse (Fra)	Romania
1966	Henri Guiheneuf (Fra)	France
1967	Jacques Isenbaert (Bel)	Belgium
1968	Günter Grebenstein (FRG)	France
1969	Robin Harris (Eng)	Holland
1970	Marcel Van den Eynde (Bel)	Belgium
1971	Dino Bassi (Ita)	Italy
1972	Hubert Levels (Hol)	France
1973	Pierre Michiels (Bel)	Belgium
1974	Aribert Richter (FRG)	France
1975	Ian Heaps (Eng)	France
1976	Dino Bassi (Ita)	Italy
1977	Jean Mainil (Bel)	Luxembourg
1978	Jean-Pierre Fouquet (Fra)	France
1979	Gérard Heulard (Fra)	France
1980	Wolf-Rüdiger Kremkus (FRG)	FR Germany
1981	Dave Thomas (Eng)	France
1982	Kevin Ashurst (Eng)	Holland
1983	Wolf-Rüdiger Kremkus (FRG)	Belgium
1984	Bobby Smithers (Ire)	Luxembourg
1985	Dave Roper (Eng)	England
1986	Lud Wever (Hol)	Italy
1987	Clive Branson (Wal)	England
1988	Jean-Pierre Fouquet (Fra)	England
1989	Tom Pickering (Eng)	Wales
1990	Bob Nudd (Eng)	France
1991	Bob Nudd (Eng)	England
1992	David Wesson (Aus)	Italy
1993	Mario Barros (Por)	Italy
1994	Bob Nudd (Eng)	England

Most individual wins: 3 Robert Tesse, Bob Nudd
Most team wins: 12 France

Women's World Championships
First held in 1994.
Winners:

1994	Astrid Block (Ger)	Italy

World Fly Fishing Championships

The first world fly fishing championship was held in 1981, organised by the Confédération Internationale de la Pêche Sportive (CIPS).

Year	Venue	Individual winner	Team winner
1981	Lake Echternach (Lux)	C Wittkamp (Hol)	Netherlands
1982	Narcea River (Spa)	Viktor Diez y Diez (Spa)	Italy
1983	Sesia River (Ita)	Segismondo Fernandez (Spa)	Italy
1984	Tormes River (Spa)	Tony Pawson (Eng)	Italy
1985	San River (Pol)	Leslaw Frasik (Pol)	Poland
1986	Ourthe River (Bel)	Slivoj Svoboda (Cs)	Italy
1987	Various locations (Eng)	Brian Leadbetter (Eng)	England
1988	Tasmania (Aus)	John Pawson (Eng)	England
1989	Kuusinski and Kitka Rivers (Fin)	Wladyslaw Trzebuinia (Pol)	Poland
1990	River Dee and Llyn Brenig (Wal)	Franciszek Szajnik (Pol)	Czechoslovakia
1991	Roturua, New Zealand	Brian Leadbetter (Eng)	New Zealand
1992	Three rivers in Italy	Pierluigi Cocito (Ita)	Italy
1993	Lakes in Kamloops area (Can)	Russell Owen (Wal)	England
1994	Ringebu & Lillehammer (Nor)	Pascal Cognard (Fra)	Czech Republic

Archery

From the use of bow and arrow in hunting and in warfare, archery developed as one of man's earliest known organised sports. The world governing body is the Fédération Internationale de Tir á l'Arc (FITA), which was founded in 1931, and whose membership reached 100 nations in 1994. Practitioners can remain at the top for a long time. A most notable example is that of Alice Blanche Legh who won a record 23 British ladies' titles between 1881 and 1922, when she was 67.

World Championships

World target archery championships were first staged in 1931 and are now held biennially. From 1957 to 1985 the contests were over Double FITA rounds of 36 arrows at 90m, 70m, 50m and 30m for men; 70m, 60m, 50m and 30m for women; scores are given for these. From 1987 the championships were conducted on a knock-out basis with scores not being accumulated over the rounds, and the scores given are for the final round of 36 arrows. From 1993 there has been a knock-out head-to-head competition for the top 32 from the open FITA round of 144 arrows.

Winners:

Men's Individual
1931 Michal Sawicki (Pol)
1932 Laurent Reith (Bel)
1933 Donald Mackenzie (USA)
1934 Henry Kjellson (Swe)
1935 Adriaan van Kohlen (Bel)
1936 Emil Heilborn (Swe)
1937 George De Rons (Bel)
1938 Frantisek Hadas (Cs)
1939 Roger Beday (Fra)
1946 Einar Tang Holbek (Den)
1947-50 Hans Deutgen (Swe)
1952 Stellan Andersson (Swe)
1953 Bror Lundgren (Swe)
1955 Nils Andersson (Swe)
1957 Ozziek Smathers (USA) 2231
1958 Stig Thysell (Swe) 2101
1959 James Caspers (USA) 2247
1961 Joseph Thornton (USA) 2310
1963 Charles Sandlin (USA) 2332
1965 Matti Haikonen (Fin) 2313
1967 Ray Rogers (USA) 2298
1969 Hardy Ward (USA) 2423
1971 John Williams (USA) 2445
1973 Viktor Sidoruk (USSR) 2185
1975 Darrell Pace (USA) 2548
1977 Richard McKinney (USA) 2501
1979 Darrell Pace (USA) 2474
1981 Kyösti Laasonen (Fin) 2541
1983 Richard McKinney (USA) 2617
1985 Richard McKinney (USA) 2601
1987 Vladimir Yesheyev (USSR) 329
1989 Stanislav Zabrodskiy (USSR) 332
1991 Simon Fairweather (Aus) 334
1993 Park Kyung-mo (SKo)

Most wins:
4 Deutgen, 3 McKinney

Men's Team
14	USA	1957, each title from 1959-83
5	Sweden	1934, 1948, 1952-3, 1955
4	Czechoslovakia	1936, 1938, 1947, 1949
3	France	1931, 1939, 1993
2	Poland	1932, 1937

Kim Soo-nyung

Sébastien Flute

2	Belgium	1933, 1935
2	Denmark	1946, 1950
2	South Korea	1985, 1991
1	Finland	1958
1	F R Germany	1987
1	USSR	1989

Women's Individual
1931-4 Janina Kurkowska (Pol)
1935 Ina Catani (Swe)
1936 Janina Kurkowska (Pol)
1937 Ingo Simon (UK)
1938 Nora Weston Martyr (UK)
1939 Janina Kurkowska (Pol)
1946 Nilla de Wharton Burr (UK)
1947 Janina Kurkowska (Pol)
1948 Nilla de Wharton Burr (UK)
1949 Barbara Waterhouse (UK)
1950 Jean Lee (USA)
1952 Jean Lee (USA)
1953 Jean Richards (USA)
1955 Katarzyna Wisniowska (Pol)

1957 Carole Meinhart (USA) 2120
1958 Sigrid Johansson (Swe) 2053
1959 Ann Corby (née Weber) (USA) 2023
1961 Nancy Vanderheide (USA) 2173
1963 Victoria Cook (USA) 2253
1965 Maire Lindholm (Fin) 2214
1967 Maria Maczynska (Pol) 2240
1969 Dorothy Lidstone (Can) 2361
1971 Emma Gapchenko (USSR) 2380
1973 Linda Myers (USA) 2204
1975 Zebiniso Rustamova (USSR) 2465
1977 Luann Ryon (USA) 2515
1979 Kim Jin-ho (SKo) 2507
1981 Natalya Butuzova (USSR) 2514
1983 Kim Jin-ho (SKo) 2616
1985 Irina Soldatova (USSR) 2595
1987 Ma Xiagjun (Chn) 330

1989 Kim Soo-nyung (SKo) 338
1991 Kim Soo-nyung (SKo) 333
1993 Kim Hyo-jung (Sko)
Most wins: 7 Janina Kurkowska (née Spychajowa)

Women's Team
8	USA	1952, 1957-9, 1961, 1963, 1965, 1977
7	Poland	1933-4, 1936, 1938-9, 1967, 1971
6	USSR	1969, 1973, 1975, 1981, 1985, 1987
5	United Kingdom	1935, 1937, 1946, 1949, 1955
5	South Korea	1979, 1983, 1989, 1991, 1993
2	Finland	1950, 1953
1	Denmark	1947
1	Czechoslovakia	1948

Olympic Games

The sport was included in the Olympic Games from 1900 to 1908, then again in 1920 (at the Belgian style of shooting) and was reintroduced in 1972. Scores for 1972 to 1984 were for double FITA rounds, while in 1988 there was an open FITA round, then a series of elimination rounds with nine arrows shot at each distance. In 1992 the system was changed again, as after the open FITA round of 144 arrows, the top 32 met in head-to-head knock-out competition. *Winners:*

Year	Men	Women
1972	John Williams (USA) 2528	Doreen Wilber (USA) 2424
1976	Darrell Pace (USA) 2571	Luann Ryon (USA) 2499
1980	Tomi Poikolainen (Fin) 2455	Keto Lossaberidze (USSR) 2491
1984	Darrell Pace (USA) 2616	Seo Hyang-soon (SKo) 2568
1988	Jay Barrs (USA) 338	Kim Soo-nyung (SKo) 344
1992	Sébastien Flute (Fra)	Cho Youn-jeong (SKo)

Team events for men and women were contested from 1988. *Winners:*

Year	Men	Women
1988	South Korea 986	South Korea 982
1992	Spain	South Korea

Conducted on knock-out basis in 1992

Olympic records for Double FITA rounds:
Men   Darrell Pace (USA) 2616 in 1984
Women Kim Soo-nyung (SKo) 2683 in 1988

Most medals
Hubert van Innis (Bel) won a record six gold and three silver medals: two gold, one silver 1900, the rest in 1920.

World Records

For single FITA rounds (maximum 360 points for each set).
Men
FITA	1354	Han Seung-hoon (SKo) 1994
90m	330	Vladimir Yesheyev (USSR) 1990
70m	344	Hiroshi Yamamoto (Jap) 1990
50m	348	Han Seung-hoon (SKo) 1994
30m	360	Han Seung-hoon (SKo) 1994
Final	345	Vladimir Yesheyev (USSR) 1990
Team	4035	South Korea (Park Kyung-mo, Kim Kyung-ho, Han Soong-nam) 1993
Final	1006	South Korea (Park Kyung-mo, Kim Kyung-ho, Kim Byung-nam) 1993

Women
FITA	1375	Cho Youn-jeong (SKo) 1992
70m	338	Cho Youn-jeong (SKo) 1992
	341u	Kim Soo-nyung (SKo) 1990 (unofficial)
60m	349	Ying He (Chn) 1995
50m	340	Lim Jung (SKo) 1994
30m	357	Joanne Edens (UK) 1990
Final	346	Kim Soo-nyong (SKo) 1989
Team	4094	South Korea (Cho Youn-jeong, Kim Soo-nyung, Lee Eun-kyung) 1992
Final	1030	South Korea (Kim Soo-nyung, Lee Eun-kyung, Lee Seon-hee) 1991

World Indoor Championships

First held in 1991. *Winners:*
Men freestyle
1991   Sébastien Flûte (Fra)
1993   Gennadiy Metrofanov (Rus)
1995   Magnus Pattersson (Swe)

Men compound bow
1991   Joe Asay (USA)
1993   Kirk Ethridge (USA)
1995   Mike Hendrikse (USA)

Women freestyle
1991   Natalya Valeyeva (USSR)
1993   Jennifer O'Donnell (USA)
1995   Natalya Valeyeva (Mol)

Women compound bow
1991   Lucia Panico (Ita)
1993   Inga Low (USA)
1995   Glenda Penaz (USA)

World Indoor Records
Indoor FITA Rounds, maximum score 600
Men
18m   596   Magnus Pattersson (Swe) 1995
25m   593   Magnus Pattersson (Swe) 1993

Women
18m   590   Natalya Valeyeva (Mol) 1995
25m   592   Petra Ericsson (Swe) 1991

World Field Archery Championships

Held in 1969, 1971 and biennially from 1972 at bare bow and
freestyle categories for men and women.
Most wins: 4 Anders Rosenberg (Swe) men's bare
bow 1978, 1980, 1982 - and 1992

World Flight Records

The following have been recognised as records by the
United States National Archery Association at unlimited
weight categories (or at weight categories shown in brackets
if superior):

Regular Flight

Bow type	Metres	Name	Year
Men			
Recurve Bow	1222.01	Don Brown	1987
Compound Bow	1207.39	Kevin Strother	1992
Longbow	325.87	Don Brown	1989
Primitive Bow	259.56	Daniel Perry	1988
Unlimited Footbow	1854.40	Harry Drake	1971
Conventional Footbow	1410.87	Harry Drake	1979
Crossbow	1871.84	Harry Drake	1988
Women			
Recurve Bow	950.39	April Moon	1981
Compound Bow (25kg)	826.73	April Moon	1989
Longbow	199.11	April Moon	1989
Conventional Footbow	1018.48	Arylne Rhode	1978

Broadhead Flight

Bow type	Metres	Name	Year
Men			
Compound Bow	717.72	Bert McCune Jr	1992
Recurve Bow	481.10	Don Brown	1988
Longbow	304.19	Don Brown	1992
Primitive Bow	223.81	Daniel Perry	1990
Women			
Compound Bow	440.01	April Moon	1989
Recurve Bow	332.95	April Moon	1987
Longbow	217.40	April Moon	1992
Primitive Bow (50lb)	119.09	Gwen Perry	1990

Bow types
Longbows are of a minimum length of 68 inches for men
and 66 inches for women.
Primitive bows are totally constructed of natural materials,
plant or animal.
Standard recurve bows are of the type normally used for
hunting purposes or field events.
Compound bows are so constructed that a mechanical
advantage is obtained by the use of accessory limbs, levers,
pulleys etc..

Athletics

Competition in running, jumping or throwing naturally
dates back into pre-history. The earliest evidence we have of
organised running is from about 3800BC in Egypt, and athletic achievements were particularly prized at the ancient
Olympic Games in Greece. Those Games were more than
just sporting contests, for they were also great artistic and
cultural festivals maintaining the Greek ideal of perfection of
mind and body. They provided the inspiration for the modern Olympic Games, which have provided the focus for athletics, since their reintroduction in 1896. At least that is until
recently, for separate world championships for all events
were instituted in 1983, and nowadays there is a plethora of
top-class competition.

The first national championships were those of England in
1866, organised by the Amateur Athletic Club. These preceded
the formation of the Amateur Athletic Association in 1880.

International governing body: The International Amateur
Athletic Federation (IAAF), formed in 1912 initially with 17
members. It ratified the first list of world records in 1914. By
the end of 1994 the IAAF had 206 nations affiliated to it,
more than any other international organisation, sporting or
otherwise.

Note that times are given in minutes: seconds; distances in
metres.

Olympic Games

The first Olympic Games of the modern era were staged in Athens, Greece from the 6th to 15th April 1896, when just 59 athletes from ten nations contested the athletics events. The 1900 and 1904 Games were also small-scale affairs, with just over 100 athletes at each, but from 1908 the Games grew rapidly in importance to true world championships.

Women's events were first included in 1928, and the number of contestants in athletics passed 1000 for the first time at the 1960 Games.

Note that automatic timing was first used at the Olympic Games in 1932. In this list of champions, automatic times are given, where known, for proper comparisons.

Olympic records are shown by OR.

Linford Christie – Olympic, World, European and Commonwealth champion – wins at 100 metres at Barcelona in 1992

Men

100 metres
1896 Thomas Burke (USA) 12.0
1900 Francis Jarvis (USA) 11.0
1904 Archie Hahn (USA) 11.0
1906 Archie Hahn (USA) 11.2
1908 Reginald Walker (SAf) 10.8
1912 Ralph Craig (USA) 10.8
1920 Charles Paddock (USA) 10.8
1924 Harold Abrahams (UK) 10.6
1928 Percy Williams (Can) 10.8
1932 Eddie Tolan (USA) 10.38
1936 Jesse Owens (USA) 10.3
1948 Harrison Dillard (USA) 10.3
1952 Lindy Remigino (USA) 10.79
1956 Bobby Morrow (USA) 10.62
1960 Armin Hary (FRG) 10.32
1964 Robert Hayes (USA) 10.06
1968 James Hines (USA) 9.95
1972 Valeriy Borzov (USSR) 10.14
1976 Hasely Crawford (Tri) 10.06
1980 Allan Wells (UK) 10.25
1984 Carl Lewis (USA) 9.99
1988 Carl Lewis (USA) 9.92 OR
1992 Linford Christie (UK) 9.96

200 metres
1900 Walter Tewksbury (USA) 22.2
1904 Archie Hahn (USA) 21.6
1908 Robert Kerr (Can) 22.6
1912 Ralph Craig (USA) 21.7
1920 Allen Woodring (USA) 22.0
1924 Jackson Scholz (USA) 21.6
1928 Percy Williams (Can) 21.8
1932 Eddie Tolan (USA) 21.12
1936 Jesse Owens (USA) 20.7
1948 Melvin Patton (USA) 21.1
1952 Andrew Stanfield (USA) 20.81
1956 Bobby Morrow (USA) 20.75
1960 Livio Berruti (Ita) 20.62
1964 Henry Carr (USA) 20.36
1968 Tommie Smith (USA) 19.83
1972 Valeriy Borzov (USSR) 20.00
1976 Donald Quarrie (Jam) 20.22
1980 Pietro Mennea (Ita) 20.19
1984 Carl Lewis (USA) 19.80
1988 Joe DeLoach (USA) 19.75
1992 Michael Marsh (USA) 20.01 (19.73 OR semi)

400 metres
1896 Thomas Burke (USA) 54.2
1900 Maxie Long (USA) 49.4
1904 Harry Hillman (USA) 49.2
1906 Paul Pilgrim (USA) 53.2
1908 Wyndham Halswelle (UK) 50.0
1912 Charles Reidpath (USA) 48.2
1920 Bevil Rudd (SAf) 49.6
1924 Eric Liddell (UK) 47.6
1928 Ray Barbuti (USA) 47.8
1932 Bill Carr (USA) 46.28
1936 Archie Williams (USA) 46.66
1948 Arthur Wint (Jam) 46.2
1952 George Rhoden (Jam) 46.09
1956 Charles Jenkins (USA) 46.86
1960 Otis Davis (USA) 45.07
1964 Michael Larrabee (USA) 45.15
1968 Lee Evans (USA) 43.86
1972 Vincent Matthews (USA) 44.66
1976 Alberto Juantorena (Cub) 44.26
1980 Viktor Markin (USSR) 44.60
1984 Alonzo Babers (USA) 44.27
1988 Steve Lewis (USA) 43.87
1992 Quincy Watts (USA) 43.50 OR

800 metres
1896 Edwin Flack (Aus) 2:11.0
1900 Alfred Tysoe (UK) 2:01.2
1904 James Lightbody (USA) 1:56.0
1906 Paul Pilgrim (USA) 2:01.5
1908 Mel Sheppard (USA) 1:52.8
1912 James Meredith (USA) 1:51.9
1920 Albert Hill (UK) 1:53.4
1924 Douglas Lowe (UK) 1:52.4
1928 Douglas Lowe (UK) 1:51.8
1932 Tom Hampson (UK) 1:49.70
1936 John Woodruff (USA) 1:52.9
1948 Malvin Whitfield (USA) 1:49.2
1952 Malvin Whitfield (USA) 1:49.34

1956 Thomas Courtney (USA) 1:47.75
1960 Peter Snell (NZ) 1:46.48
1964 Peter Snell (NZ) 1:45.1
1968 Ralph Doubell (Aus) 1:44.40
1972 David Wottle (USA) 1:45.86
1976 Alberto Juantorena (Cub) 1:43.50
1980 Steven Ovett (UK) 1:45.40
1984 Joaquim Cruz (Bra) 1:43.00 OR
1988 Paul Ereng (Ken) 1:43.45
1992 William Tanui (Ken) 1:43.66

1500 metres
1896 Edwin Flack (Aus) 4:33.2
1900 Charles Bennett (UK) 4:06.2
1904 James Lightbody (USA) 4:05.4
1906 James Lightbody (USA) 4:12.0
1908 Mel Sheppard (USA) 4:03.4
1912 Arnold Jackson (UK) 3:56.8
1920 Albert Hill (UK) 4:01.8
1924 Paavo Nurmi (Fin) 3:53.6
1928 Harri Larva (Fin) 3:53.2
1932 Luigi Beccali (Ita) 3:51.20
1936 Jack Lovelock (NZ) 3:47.8
1948 Henry Eriksson (Swe) 3:49.8
1952 Josef Barthel (Lux) 3:45.28
1956 Ron Delany (Ire) 3:41.49
1960 Herbert Elliott (Aus) 3:35.6
1964 Peter Snell (NZ) 3:38.1
1968 Kipchoge Keino (Ken) 3:34.91
1972 Pekka Vasala (Fin) 3:36.33
1976 John Walker (NZ) 3:39.17
1980 Sebastian Coe (UK) 3:38.40
1984 Sebastian Coe (UK) 3:32.53 OR
1988 Peter Rono (Ken) 3:35.96
1992 Fermin Cacho (Spa) 3:40.12

5000 metres
1912 Hannes Kolehmainen (Fin) 14:36.6
1920 Joseph Guillemot (Fra) 14.55.6
1924 Paavo Nurmi (Fin) 14:31.2
1928 Ville Ritola (Fin) 14:38.0
1932 Lauri Lehtinen (Fin) 14:29.91
1936 Gunnar Höckert (Fin) 14.22.2
1948 Gaston Reiff (Bel) 14:17.6
1952 Emil Zátopek (Cs) 14:06.72
1956 Vladimir Kuts (USSR) 13:39.86
1960 Murray Halberg (NZ) 13:43.4
1964 Robert Schul (USA) 13:48.8
1968 Mohamed Gammoudi (Tun) 14:05.0
1972 Lasse Viren (Fin) 13:26.42
1976 Lasse Viren (Fin) 13:24.76
1980 Miruts Yifter (Eth) 13.20.91
1984 Saïd Aouita (Mor) 13:05.59 OR
1988 John Ngugi (Ken) 13:11.70
1992 Dieter Baumann (Ger) 13:12.52

10 000 metres
1912 Hannes Kolehmainen (Fin) 31:20.8
1920 Paavo Nurmi (Fin) 31:45.8
1924 Ville Ritola (Fin) 30:23.2
1928 Paavo Nurmi (Fin) 30:18.8
1932 Janusz Kusocinski (Pol) 30:11.4
1936 Ilmari Salminen (Fin) 30:15.4

Vladimir Kuts – brilliant distance running to become double Olympic champion in Melbourne, 1956

1948 Emil Zátopek (Cs) 29:59.6
1952 Emil Zátopek (Cs) 29:17.0
1956 Vladimir Kuts (USSR) 28:45.60
1960 Pyotr Bolotnikov (USSR) 28:32.18
1964 William Mills (USA) 28:24.4
1968 Naftali Temu (Ken) 29:27.4
1972 Lasse Viren (Fin) 27:38.35
1976 Lasse Viren (Fin) 27:40.38
1980 Miruts Yifter (Eth) 27:42.69
1984 Alberto Cova (Ita) 27:47.54
1988 Brahim Boutayeb (Mor) 27:21.46 OR
1992 Khalid Skah (Mor) 27:46.70

Marathon (42.295km)
1896 Spyridon Louis (Gre) 2:58:50.0 (40km)
1900 Michel Théato (Lux) 2:59:45.0 (40.26km)
1904 Thomas Hicks (USA) 3:28:35.0 (40km)
1906 William Sherring (Can) 2:51:23.6 (41.86km)
1908 John Hayes (USA) 2:55:18.4
1912 Kenneth McArthur (SAf) 2:36:54.8 (40.2km)
1920 Hannes Kolehmainen (Fin) 2:32:35.8 (42.75km)
1924 Albin Stenroos (Fin) 2:41:22.6
1928 Mohamed Boughéra El Ouafi (Fra) 2:32:57.0
1932 Juan Carlos Zabala (Arg) 2:31:36.0
1936 Kitei Son (Jap)* 2:29:19.2
* *Actually the Korean Sohn Kee-chung*
1948 Delfo Cabrera (Arg) 2:34:51.6
1952 Emil Zátopek (Cs) 2:23:03.2
1956 Alain Mimoun (Fra) 2:25:00.0
1960 Abebe Bikila (Eth) 2:15:16.2
1964 Abebe Bikila (Eth) 2:12:11.2
1968 Mamo Wolde (Eth) 2:20:26.4
1972 Frank Shorter (USA) 2:12:19.8

1976 Waldemar Cierpinski (GDR) 2:09:55
1980 Waldemar Cierpinski (GDR) 2:11:03
1984 Carlos Lopes (Por) 2:09:21 OR
1988 Gelindo Bordin (Ita) 2:10:32
1992 Hwang Young-cho (SKo) 2:13:23

110 metres hurdles
1896 Thomas Curtis (USA) 17.6
1900 Alvin Kraenzlein (USA) 15.4
1904 Fred Schule (USA) 16.0
1906 Robert Leavitt (USA) 16.2
1908 Forrest Smithson (USA) 15.0
1912 Fred Kelly (USA) 15.1
1920 Earl Thomson (Can) 14.8
1924 Daniel Kinsey (USA) 15.0
1928 Sydney Atkinson (SAf) 14.8
1932 George Saling (USA) 14.57
1936 Forrest Towns (USA) 14.2
1948 William Porter (USA) 13.9
1952 Harrison Dillard (USA) 13.91
1956 Lee Calhoun (USA) 13.70
1960 Lee Calhoun (USA) 13.98
1964 Hayes Jones (USA) 13.67
1968 Willie Davenport (USA) 13.33
1972 Rodney Milburn (USA) 13.24
1976 Guy Drut (Fra) 13.30
1980 Thomas Munkelt (GDR) 13.39
1984 Roger Kingdom (USA) 13.20
1988 Roger Kingdom (USA) 12.98 OR
1992 Mark McKoy (Can) 13.12

400 metres hurdles
1900 Walter Tewksbury (USA) 57.6
1904 Harry Hillman (USA) 53.0
1908 Charles Bacon (USA) 55.0
1920 Frank Loomis (USA) 54.0
1924 Morgan Taylor (USA) 52.6
1928 Lord Burghley (UK) 53.4
1932 Robert Tisdall (Ire) 51.67
1936 Glenn Hardin (USA) 52.4
1948 Roy Cochran (USA) 51.1
1952 Charles Moore (USA) 51.06
1956 Glenn Davis (USA) 50.29
1960 Glenn Davis (USA) 49.51
1964 Rex Cawley (USA) 49.69
1968 David Hemery (UK) 48.12
1972 John Akii-Bua (Uga) 47.82
1976 Edwin Moses (USA) 47.63
1980 Volker Beck (GDR) 48.70
1984 Edwin Moses (USA) 47.75
1988 Andre Phillips (USA) 47.19
1992 Kevin Young (USA) 46.78 OR

Steeplechase
1900 George Orton (Can) 7:34.4 (2500m)
1900 John Rimmer (UK) 12:58.4 (4000m)
1904 James Lightbody (USA) 7:39.6 (2590m)
1908 Arthur Russell (UK) 10:47.8 (3200m)

3000 metres steeplechase
1920 Percy Hodge (UK) 10:00.4
1924 Ville Ritola (Fin) 9:33.6
1928 Toivo Loukola (Fin) 9:21.8

1932 Volmari Iso-Hollo (Fin) 10:33.4*
1936 Volmari Iso-Hollo (Fin) 9:03.8
1948 Tore Sjöstrand (Swe) 9:04.6
1952 Horace Ashenfelter (USA) 8:45.68
1956 Christopher Brasher (UK) 8:41.35
1960 Zdzislaw Kryszkowiak (Pol) 8:34.31
1964 Gaston Roelants (Bel) 8:30.8
1968 Amos Biwott (Ken) 8:51.0
1972 Kipchoge Keino (Ken) 8:23.64
1976 Anders Gärderud (Swe) 8:08.02
1980 Bronislaw Malinowski (Pol) 8:09.70
1984 Julius Korir (Ken) 8:11.80
1988 Julius Kariuki (Ken) 8:05.51 OR
1992 Matthew Birir (Ken) 8:08.94
* *due to lap counting error distance was 3460 metres*

High jump
1896 Ellery Clark (USA) 1.81
1900 Irving Baxter (USA) 1.90
1904 Samuel Jones (USA) 1.80
1906 Con Leahy (UK/Ire) 1.77
1908 Harry Porter (USA) 1.90
1912 Alma Richards (USA) 1.93
1920 Richard Landon (USA) 1.94
1924 Harold Osborn (USA) 1.98
1928 Robert King (USA) 1.94
1932 Duncan McNaughton (Can) 1.97
1936 Cornelius Johnson (USA) 2.03
1948 John Winter (Aus) 1.98
1952 Walter Davis (USA) 2.04
1956 Charles Dumas (USA) 2.12
1960 Robert Shavlakadze (USSR) 2.16
1964 Valeriy Brumel (USSR) 2.18
1968 Dick Fosbury (USA) 2.24
1972 Jüri Tarmak (USSR) 2.23
1976 Jacek Wszola (Pol) 2.25
1980 Gerd Wessig (GDR) 2.36
1984 Dietmar Mögenburg (FRG) 2.35
1988 Gennadiy Avdeyenko (USSR) 2.38 OR
1992 Javier Sotomayor (Cub) 2.34

Pole vault
1896 William Hoyt (USA) 3.30
1900 Irving Baxter (USA) 3.30
1904 Charles Dvorak (USA) 3.50
1906 Fernand Gonder (Fra) 3.40
1908 Edward Cooke & Alfred Gilbert (USA) 3.71
1912 Harry Babcock (USA) 3.95
1920 Frank Foss (USA) 4.09
1924 Lee Barnes (USA) 3.95
1928 Sabin Carr (USA) 4.20
1932 Bill Miller (USA) 4.31
1936 Earle Meadows (USA) 4.35
1948 Guinn Smith (USA) 4.30
1952 Robert Richards (USA) 4.55
1956 Robert Richards (USA) 4.56
1960 Donald Bragg (USA) 4.70
1964 Frederick Hansen (USA) 5.10
1968 Bob Seagren (USA) 5.40
1972 Wolfgang Nordwig (GDR) 5.50
1976 Tadeusz Slusarski (Pol) 5.50
1980 Wladyslaw Kozakiewicz (Pol) 5.78

1984 Pierre Quinon (Fra) 5.75
1988 Sergey Bubka (USSR) 5.90 OR
1992 Maksim Tarasov (CIS/Rus) 5.80

Long jump
1896 Ellery Clark (USA) 6.35
1900 Alvin Kraenzlein (USA) 7.18
1904 Myer Prinstein (USA) 7.34
1906 Myer Prinstein (USA) 7.20
1908 Francis Irons (USA) 7.48
1912 Albert Gutterson (USA) 7.60
1920 William Pettersson (Swe) 7.15
1924 William De Hart Hubbard (USA) 7.44
1928 Edward Hamm (USA) 7.73
1932 Edward Gordon (USA) 7.64
1936 Jesse Owens (USA) 8.06
1948 William Steele (USA) 7.82
1952 Jerome Biffle (USA) 7.57
1956 Gregory Bell (USA) 7.83
1960 Ralph Boston (USA) 8.12
1964 Lynn Davies (UK) 8.07
1968 Bob Beamon (USA) 8.90 OR
1972 Randy Williams (USA) 8.24
1976 Arnie Robinson (USA) 8.35
1980 Lutz Dombrowski (GDR) 8.54
1984 Carl Lewis (USA) 8.54
1988 Carl Lewis (USA) 8.72
1992 Carl Lewis (USA) 8.67

Triple jump
1896 James Connolly (USA) 13.71
1900 Myer Prinstein (USA) 14.47
1904 Myer Prinstein (USA) 14.35
1906 Peter O'Connor (UK/Ire) 14.07
1908 Tim Ahearne (UK/Ire) 14.91
1912 Gustaf Lindblom (Swe) 14.76
1920 Vilho Tuulos (Fin) 14.50
1924 Anthony Winter (Aus) 15.52
1928 Mikio Oda (Jap) 15.21
1932 Chuhei Nambu (Jap) 15.72
1936 Naoto Tajima (Jap) 16.00
1948 Arne Åhman (Swe) 15.40
1952 Adhemar Ferreira da Silva (Bra) 16.22
1956 Adhemar Ferreira da Silva (Bra) 16.35
1960 Jozef Schmidt (Pol) 16.81
1964 Jozef Schmidt (Pol) 16.85
1968 Viktor Saneyev (USSR) 17.39
1972 Viktor Saneyev (USSR) 17.35
1976 Viktor Saneyev (USSR) 17.29
1980 Jaak Uudmäe (USSR) 17.35
1984 Al Joyner (USA) 17.26
1988 Khristo Markov (Bul) 17.61
1992 Mike Conley (USA) 18.17w (& 17.63) OR

Shot
1896 Robert Garrett (USA) 11.22
1900 Richard Sheldon (USA) 14.10
1904 Ralph Rose (USA) 14.80
1906 Martin Sheridan (USA) 12.32
1908 Ralph Rose (USA) 14.21
1912 Patrick McDonald (USA) 15.34
1920 Ville Pörhölä (Fin) 14.81
1924 Clarence Houser (USA) 14.99

1928 John Kuck (USA) 15.87
1932 Leo Sexton (USA) 16.00
1936 Hans Woellke (Ger) 16.20
1948 Wilbur Thompson (USA) 17.12
1952 Parry O'Brien (USA) 17.41
1956 Parry O'Brien (USA) 18.57
1960 William Nieder (USA) 19.68
1964 Dallas Long (USA) 20.33
1968 Randy Matson (USA) 20.54
1972 Wladyslaw Komar (Pol) 21.18
1976 Udo Beyer (GDR) 21.05
1980 Vladimir Kiselyov (USSR) 21.35
1984 Alessandro Andrei (Ita) 21.26
1988 Ulf Timmermann (GDR) 22.47 OR
1992 Mike Stulce (USA) 21.70

Discus
1896 Robert Garrett (USA) 29.15
1900 Rudolf Bauer (Hun) 36.04
1904 Martin Sheridan (USA) 39.28
1906 Martin Sheridan (USA) 41.46
1908 Martin Sheridan (USA) 40.89
1912 Armas Taipale (Fin) 45.21
1920 Elmer Niklander (Fin) 44.68
1924 Clarence Houser (USA) 46.15
1928 Clarence Houser (USA) 47.32
1932 John Anderson (USA) 49.49
1936 Ken Carpenter (USA) 50.48

Mike Conley – triple jumped 18.17m in Barcelona, but had a wind just 0.1 m/s over the limit for records.

1948 Adolfo Consolini (Ita) 52.78
1952 Sim Iness (USA) 55.03
1956 Al Oerter (USA) 56.36
1960 Al Oerter (USA) 59.18
1964 Al Oerter (USA) 61.00
1968 Al Oerter (USA) 64.78
1972 Ludvik Danek (Cs) 64.40
1976 Mac Wilkins (USA) 67.50
1980 Viktor Rashchupkin (USSR) 66.64
1984 Rolf Danneberg (FRG) 66.60
1988 Jürgen Schult (GDR) 68.82 OR
1992 Romas Ubartas (Lit) 65.12

Hammer
1900 John Flanagan (USA) 49.73
1904 John Flanagan (USA) 51.23
1908 John Flanagan (USA) 51.92
1912 Matt McGrath (USA) 54.74
1920 Patrick Ryan (USA) 52.87
1924 Fred Tootell (USA) 53.29
1928 Patrick O'Callaghan (Ire) 51.39
1932 Patrick O'Callaghan (Ire) 53.92
1936 Karl Hein (Ger) 56.49
1948 Imre Németh (Hun) 56.07
1952 József Csermak (Hun) 60.34
1956 Harold Connolly (USA) 63.19
1960 Vasiliy Rudenkov (USSR) 67.10
1964 Romuald Klim (USSR) 69.74
1968 Gyula Zsivótzky (Hun) 73.36
1972 Anatoliy Bondarchuk (USSR) 75.50
1976 Yuriy Sedykh (USSR) 77.52
1980 Yuriy Sedykh (USSR) 81.80
1984 Juha Tiainen (Fin) 78.08
1988 Sergey Litvinov (USSR) 84.80 OR
1992 Andrey Abduvaliyev (CIS/Tjk) 82.54

Javelin
1906 Erik Lemming (Swe) 53.90
1908 Erik Lemming (Swe) 54.82
1912 Erik Lemming (Swe) 60.64
1920 Jonni Myyrä (Fin) 65.78
1924 Jonni Myyrä (Fin) 62.96
1928 Erik Lundkvist (Swe) 66.60
1932 Matti Järvinen (Fin) 72.71
1936 Gerhard Stöck (Ger) 71.84
1948 Tapio Rautavaara (Fin) 69.77
1952 Cyrus Young (USA) 73.78
1956 Egil Danielsen (Nor) 85.71
1960 Viktor Tsibulenko (USSR) 84.64
1964 Pauli Nevala (Fin) 82.66
1968 Janis Lusis (USSR) 90.10
1972 Klaus Wolfermann (FRG) 90.48
1976 Miklós Németh (Hun) 94.58 OR
1980 Dainis Kula (USSR) 91.20
New specification javelin
1984 Arto Harkönen (Fin) 86.76
1988 Tapio Korjus (Fin) 84.28
1992 Jan Zelezny (Cs) 89.66 OR

Decathlon (points re-scored on 1984 tables)
1912 Jim Thorpe (USA) 6564 #
1920 Helge Lövland (Nor) 5804
1924 Harold Osborn (USA) 6476

1928 Paavo Yrjölä (Fin) 6587*
1932 James Bausch (USA) 6735*
1936 Glenn Morris (USA) 7254
1948 Robert Mathias (USA) 6628
1952 Robert Mathias (USA) 7592
1956 Milton Campbell (USA) 7614
1960 Rafer Johnson (USA) 7926
1964 Willi Holdorf (FRG) 7794 estimated
1968 Bill Toomey (USA) 8144
1972 Nikolay Avilov (USSR) 8466
1976 Bruce Jenner (USA) 8634
1980 Daley Thompson (UK) 8522
1984 Daley Thompson (UK) 8847 OR
1988 Christian Schenk (GDR) 8488
1992 Robert Zmelík (Cs) 8611
 # disqualified for professionalism, and gold given to Hugo Weislander (Swe) 5965, but Thorpe posthumously re-instated in 1982
* On the 1984 tables, the second placed Akilles Järvinen scored 6645 in 1928 and 6879 in 1932!

20 000 metres walk
1956 Leonid Spirin (USSR) 1:31:27.4
1960 Vladimir Golubnichiy (USSR) 1:34:07.2
1964 Kenneth Matthews (UK) 1:29:34.0
1968 Vladimir Golubnichiy (USSR) 1:33:58.4
1972 Peter Frenkel (GDR) 1:26:42.4
1976 Daniel Bautista (Mex) 1:24:40.6
1980 Maurizio Damilano (Ita) 1:23:35.5
1984 Ernesto Canto (Mex) 1:23:13
1988 Jozef Pribilinec (Cs) 1:19:57 OR
1992 Daniel Plaza (Spa) 1:21:45

50 000 metres walk
1932 Thomas Green (UK) 4:50:10.0
1936 Harold Whitlock (UK) 4:30:41.1
1948 John Ljunggren (Swe) 4:41:52.0
1952 Giuseppe Dordoni (Ita) 4:28:07.8
1956 Norman Read (NZ) 4:30:42.8
1960 Don Thompson (UK) 4:25:30.0
1964 Abdon Pamich (Ita) 4:11:12.4
1968 Christophe Höhne (GDR) 4:20:13.6
1972 Bernd Kannenberg (GDR) 3:56:11.6
1980 Hartwig Gauder (GDR) 3:49:24
1984 Raúl Gonzales (Mex) 3:47:26
1988 Vyacheslav Ivanenko (USSR) 3:38.29 OR
1992 Andrey Perlov (CIS/Rus) 3:50:13

4x100 metres relay
1912 UK 42.4
1920 USA 42.2
1924 USA 41.0
1928 USA 41.0
1932 USA 40.1
1936 USA 39.8
1948 USA 40.6
1952 USA 40.26
1956 USA 39.59
1960 F R Germany 39.66
1964 USA 39.06
1968 USA 38.23
1972 USA 38.19
1976 USA 38.83

1980 USSR 38.26
1984 USA 37.83
1988 USSR 38.19
1992 USA 37.40 OR

Medley relay
(200m, 200m, 400m, 800m)
1908 USA 3:29.4

4x400 metres relay
1912 USA 3:16.6
1920 UK 3:22.2
1924 USA 3:16.0
1928 USA 3:14.2
1932 USA 3:08.14
1936 UK 3:09.0
1948 USA 3:10.4
1952 Jamaica 3:04.04
1956 USA 3:04.80
1960 USA 3:02.37
1964 USA 3:00.71
1968 USA 2:56.16
1972 Kenya 2:59.83
1976 USA 2:58.66
1980 USSR 3:01.08
1984 USA 2:57.91
1988 USA 2:56.16
1992 USA 2:55.74 OR

Women

100 metres
1928 Elizabeth Robinson (USA) 12.2
1932 Stanislawa Walasiewicz (Pol) 11.9
1936 Helen Stephens (USA) 11.5
1948 Fanny Blankers-Koen (Hol) 11.9
1952 Marjorie Jackson (Aus) 11.65
1956 Betty Cuthbert (Aus) 11.82
1960 Wilma Rudolph (USA) 11.18w
1964 Wyomia Tyus (USA) 11.49
1968 Wyomia Tyus (USA) 11.08
1972 Renate Stecher (GDR) 11.07
1976 Annegret Richter (FRG) 11.08
1980 Lyudmila Kondratyeva (USSR) 11.06
1984 Evelyn Ashford (USA) 10.97
1988 Florence Griffith-Joyner (USA) 10.54w
    (10.62 OR in quarter-final)
1992 Gail Devers (USA) 10.82

200 metres
1948 Fanny Blankers-Koen (Hol) 24.4
1952 Marjorie Jackson (Aus) 23.89
1956 Betty Cuthbert (Aus) 23.55
1960 Wilma Rudolph (USA) 24.03
1964 Edith Maguire (USA) 23.05
1968 Irena Szewinska (Pol) 22.58
1972 Renate Stecher (GDR) 22.40
1976 Bärbel Eckert (GDR) 22.37
1980 Bärbel Wöckel (née Eckert) (GDR) 22.03
1984 Valerie Brisco-Hooks (USA) 21.81
1988 Florence Griffith-Joyner (USA) 21.34 OR
1992 Gwen Torrence (USA) 21.81

Gwen Torrence wins Olympic gold at 200m in 1992

400 metres
1964 Betty Cuthbert (Aus) 52.01
1968 Colette Besson (Fra) 52.03
1972 Monika Zehrt (GDR) 51.08
1976 Irena Szewinska (Pol) 49.29
1980 Marita Koch (GDR) 48.88
1984 Valerie Brisco-Hooks (USA) 48.83
1988 Olga Bryzgina (USSR) 48.65 OR
1992 Marie-José Pérec (Fra) 48.83

800 metres
1928 Lina Radke (Ger) 2:16.8
1960 Lyudmila Shevtsova (USSR) 2:04.50
1964 Ann Packer (UK) 2:01.1
1968 Madeline Manning (USA) 2:00.92
1972 Hildegard Falck (FRG) 1:58.55
1976 Tatyana Kazankina (USSR) 1:54.94
1980 Nadezhda Olizarenko (USSR) 1:53.43 OR
1984 Doina Melinte (Rom) 1:57.60
1988 Sigrun Wodars (GDR) 1:56.10
1992 Ellen van Langen (Hol) 1:55.54

1500 metres
1972 Lyudmila Bragina (USSR) 4:01.38
1976 Tatyana Kazankina (USSR) 4:05.48
1980 Tatyana Kazankina (USSR) 3:56.56
1984 Gabriella Doria (Ita) 4:03.25
1988 Paula Ivan (Rom) 3:53.96 OR
1992 Hassiba Boulmerka (Alg) 3:55.30

3000 metres
1984 Maricica Puica (Rom) 8:35.96
1988 Tatyana Samolenko (USSR) 8:26.53 OR
1992 Yelena Romanova (CIS/Rus) 8:46.04

10 000 metres
1988 Olga Bondarenko (USSR) 31:05.21 OR
1992 Derartu Tulu (Eth) 31:06.02

Marathon
1984 Joan Benoit (USA) 2:24:52 OR
1988 Rosa Mota (Por) 2:25:40
1992 Valentina Yegorova (CIS/Rus) 2:32:41

80 metres hurdles
1932 Mildred Didrikson (USA) 11.7
1936 Trebisonda Valla (Ita) 11.75
1948 Fanny Blankers-Koen (Hol) 11.2
1952 Shirley Strickland (Aus) 11.03
1956 Shirley Strickland (Aus) 10.96

1960 Irina Press (USSR) 10.94
1964 Karin Balzer (GDR) 10.54
1968 Maureen Caird (Aus) 10.39

100 metres hurdles
1972 Annelie Ehrhardt (GDR) 12.59
1976 Johanna Schaller (GDR) 12.77
1980 Vera Komisova (USSR) 12.56
1984 Benita Fitzgerald-Brown (USA) 12.84
1988 Yordanka Donkova (Bul) 12.38 OR
1992 Paraskevi Patoulidou (Gre) 12.64

400 metres hurdles
1984 Nawal El Moutawakil (Mor) 54.61
1988 Debbie Flintoff-King (Aus) 53.17 OR
1992 Sally Gunnell (UK) 53.23

High jump
1928 Ethel Catherwood (Can) 1.59
1932 Jean Shiley (USA) 1.65
1936 Ibolya Csák (Hun) 1.60
1948 Alice Coachman (USA) 1.68
1952 Esther Brand (SAf) 1.67
1956 Mildred McDaniel (USA) 1.76
1960 Iolanda Balas (Rom) 1.85
1964 Iolanda Balas (Rom) 1.90
1968 Miloslava Rezková (Cs) 1.82
1972 Ulrike Meyfarth (FRG) 1.92
1976 Rosemarie Ackermann (GDR) 1.93
1980 Sara Simeoni (Ita) 1.97
1984 Ulrike Meyfarth (FRG) 2.02
1988 Louise Ritter (USA) 2.03 OR
1992 Heike Henkel (Ger) 2.02

Long jump
1948 Olga Gyarmati (Hun) 5.69
1952 Yvette Williams (NZ) 6.24
1956 Elzbieta Krzesinska (Pol) 6.35
1960 Vyera Krepkina (USSR) 6.37
1964 Mary Rand (UK) 6.76
1968 Viorica Viscopoleanu (Rom) 6.82
1972 Heide Rosendahl (FRG) 6.78
1976 Angela Voigt (GDR) 6.72
1980 Tatyana Kolpakova (USSR) 7.06
1984 Anisoara Stanciu (Rom) 6.96
1988 Jackie Joyner-Kersee (USA) 7.40 OR
1992 Heike Drechsler (Ger) 7.14

Shot
1948 Micheline Ostermeyer (Fra) 13.75
1952 Galina Zybina (USSR) 15.28
1956 Tamara Tishkyevich (USSR) 16.59
1960 Tamara Press (USSR) 17.32
1964 Tamara Press (USSR) 18.14
1968 Margitta Gummel (GDR) 19.61
1972 Nadezhda Chizhova (USSR) 21.03
1976 Ivanka Khristova (Bul) 21.16
1980 Ilona Slupianek (GDR) 22.41 OR
1984 Claudia Losch (FRG) 20.48
1988 Natalya Lisovskaya (USSR) 22.24
1992 Svetlana Krivelyova (CIS/Rus) 21.06

Jackie Joyner-Kersee - the greatest all-round woman athlete of the modern era.

Discus
1928 Helena Konopacka (Pol) 39.62
1932 Lillian Copeland (USA) 40.58
1936 Gisela Mauermayer (Ger) 47.63
1948 Micheline Ostermeyer (Fra) 41.92
1952 Nina Ponomaryeva (USSR) 51.42
1956 Olga Fikotová (Cs) 53.69
1960 Nina Ponomaryeva (USSR) 55.10
1964 Tamara Press (USSR) 57.27
1968 Lia Manoliu (Rom) 58.28
1972 Faina Melnik (USSR) 66.62
1976 Evelin Schlaak (GDR) 69.00
1980 Evelin Jahl (née Schlaak) (GDR) 69.96
1984 Ria Stalmach (Hol) 65.36
1988 Martina Hellmann (GDR) 72.30 OR
1992 Maritza Martén (Cub) 70.06

Javelin
1932 Mildred Didrikson (USA) 43.68
1936 Tilly Fleischer (Ger) 45.18
1948 Herma Bauma (Aut) 45.57
1952 Dana Zátopková (Cs) 50.47
1956 Inese Jaunzeme (USSR) 53.86
1960 Elvira Ozolina (USSR) 55.98
1964 Mihaela Penes (Rom) 60.54
1968 Angéla Németh (Hun) 60.36
1972 Ruth Fuchs (GDR) 63.88
1976 Ruth Fuchs (GDR) 65.94

1980 Maria Caridad Colón (Cub) 68.40
1984 Tessa Sanderson (UK) 69.56
1988 Petra Felke (GDR) 74.68 OR
1992 Silke Renk (Ger) 68.34

Pentathlon
80m hurdles, high jump, shot, long jump, 200m 1964-8.
100m hurdles replaced 80m hurdles from 1972 and
800m replaced 200m from 1976. All scored on 1971
tables.
1964 Irina Press (USSR) 4702
1968 Ingrid Becker (FRG) 4559
1972 Mary Peters (UK) 4801
1976 Sigrun Siegl (GDR) 4745
1980 Nadezhda Tkachenko (USSR) 5083

Heptathlon
1984 Glynis Nunn (Aus) 6387
1988 Jackie Joyner-Kersee (USA) 7291 OR
1992 Jackie Joyner-Kersee (USA) 7044

10 kilometres walk
1992 Chen Yueling (Chn) 44:32

4x100 metres relay
1928 Canada 48.4
1932 USA 46.86
1936 USA 46.9
1948 Netherlands 47.5
1952 USA 46.14
1956 Australia 44.65
1960 USA 44.72
1964 Poland 43.69
1968 USA 42.87
1972 FR Germany 42.81
1976 GDR 42.55
1980 GDR 41.60 OR
1984 USA 41.65
1988 USA 41.98
1992 USA 42.11

4x400 metres relay
1972 GDR 3:22.95
1976 GDR 3:19.23
1980 USSR 3:20.12
1984 USA 3:18.29
1988 USSR 3:15.18 OR
1992 CIS United team 3:20.20

Other discontinued men's events

60 metres
1900 Alvin Kraenzlein (USA) 7.0
1904 Archie Hahn (USA) 7.0

5 miles
1906 Henry Hawtrey (UK) 26:11.8
1908 Emil Voigt (UK) 25:11.2

Team race
1900 Great Britain (5000m)
1908 Great Britain (3 Miles)
1912 USA (3000m)
1920 USA (3000m)
1924 Finland (3000m)

Cross-country individual
1912 Hannes Kolehmainen (Fin) 45:11.6 (12 000m)
1920 Paavo Nurmi (Fin) 27:15.0 (8000m)
1924 Paavo Nurmi (Fin) 32:54.8 (10 000m)

Cross-country team
1904 USA
1912 Sweden
1920 Finland
1924 Finland

200 metres hurdles
1900 Alvin Kraenzlein (USA) 25.4
1904 Harry Hillman (USA) 24.6

Pentathlon
1906: standing long jump, Greek style discus, javelin, 192m
race and Greco-Roman wrestling.
1912-24: long jump, javelin, 200m, discus and 1500m.

1906 Hjalmar Mellander (Swe)
1912 Jim Thorpe (USA)*
      Ferdinand Bie (Nor)
1920 Eero Lehtonen (Fin)
1924 Eero Lehtonen (Fin)
* *posthumously reinstated as winner*

Standing high jump
1900 Ray Ewry (USA) 1.655
1904 Ray Ewry (USA) 1.50
1906 Ray Ewry (USA) 1.565
1908 Ray Ewry (USA) 1.575
1912 Platt Adams (USA) 1.63

Standing long jump
1900 Ray Ewry (USA) 3.21
1904 Ray Ewry (USA) 3.476
1906 Ray Ewry (USA) 3.30
1908 Ray Ewry (USA) 3.335
1912 Konstantin Tsiklitiras (Gre) 3.37

Standing triple jump
1900 Ray Ewry (USA) 10.58
1904 Ray Ewry (USA) 10.55

56lb weight
1904 Etienne Desmarteau (Can) 10.465
1920 Patrick McDonald (USA) 11.265

Stone (6.4kg) put
1906 Nicolaos Georgantas (Gre) 19.925

Shot - both hands
(aggregate of throws with right and left hands)
1912 Ralph Rose (USA) 27.70

Discus - Greek style
1906 Werner Järvinen (Fin) 35.17
1908 Martin Sheridan (USA) 38.00

Discus - both hands
1912 Armas Taipale (Fin) 82.86

Javelin - free style
1908 Erik Lemming (Swe) 54.445

Javelin - both hands
1912 Julius Saaristo (Fin) 109.42

1500 metres walk
1906 George Bonhag (USA) 7:12.6

3000 metres walk
1906 György Sztantics (Hun) 15:13.2
1920 Ugo Frigerio (Ita) 13:14.2

3500 metres walk
1908 George Larner (UK) 14:55.0

10 000 metres walk
1912 George Goulding (Can) 46:28.4
1920 Ugo Frigerio (Ita) 48:06.2
1924 Ugo Frigerio (Ita) 47:49.0
1948 John Mikaelsson (Swe) 45:13.2
1952 John Mikaelsson (Swe) 45:02.8

10 miles walk
1908 George Larner (UK) 1:15:57.4

Most Medals
G - Gold, S - Silver, B - Bronze

Men	G	S	B	Years
12 Paavo Nurmi (Fin)	9	3	-	1920-8
10 Raymond Ewry (USA)	10	-	-	1900-8
9 Carl Lewis (USA)	8	1	-	1984-92
9 Martin Sheridan (USA)	5	3	1	1906-8
8 Ville Ritola (Fin)	5	3	-	1924-8
7 Erik Lemming (Swe)	4	-	3*	1906-12

including one for tug of war

Others to win four gold medals:
Alvin Kraenzlein (USA) 1900
Archie Hahn (USA) 1904-06
James Lightbody (USA) 1904-06
Myer Prinstein (USA) 1900-06
Mel Sheppard (USA) 1908-12
Hannes Kolehmainen (Fin) 1912-20
Jesse Owens (USA) 1936
Emil Zátopek (Cs) 1948-52
Harrison Dillard (USA) 1948-52
Al Oerter (USA) 1956-68

Lasse Viren (Fin) 1972-76

Women	G	S	B	Years
7 Shirley de la Hunty (Aus)	3	1	3	1948-56
7 Irena Szewinska (Pol)	3	2	2	1964-76

Four gold medals:
Fanny Blankers-Koen (Hol) 1948
Betty Cuthbert (Aus) 1956-64
Bärbel Wöckel (GDR) 1976-80
Evelyn Ashford (USA) 1984-92

Most gold medals at one Games
Men:
5 Paavo Nurmi (Fin) 1924
4 Alvin Kraenzlein (USA) 1900
4 Ville Ritola (Fin) 1924
4 Jesse Owens (USA) 1936
4 Carl Lewis (USA) 1984.
Women
4 Fanny Blankers-Koen (Hol) 1948.

Most medals at one Games
6 Ville Ritola (Fin) 4 gold, 2 silver 1924

Oldest gold medallists
Men 42 years 23 days Pat McDonald (USA) 56lb weight 1920
Women 36 years 176 days Lia Manoliu (Rom) discus 1968.

Oldest medallists
Men 48y 115d Tebbs Lloyd Johnson (UK) 3rd 50km walk 1948
Women 37 years 348 days Dana Zátopková (Cs) 2nd javelin 1960.

Youngest gold medallists
Men: 17y 263d Bob Mathias (USA) decathlon 1948
Women: 15y 123d Barbara Pearl Jones (USA) 4x100m relay 1952

Most Games contested
6 Lia Manoliu (Rom) 1952-72, women's discus, successively 6th, 9th, 3rd, 3rd, 1st, 9th.

Medal table of leading nations (including 1906 Games)

Nation	Men Gold	Silver	Bronze	Women Gold	Silver	Bronze	Total Medals
USA	249	183	159	36	24	14	665
USSR/CIS	37	37	42	34	29	35	214
United Kingdom	42	54	41	5	20	13	175
GDR	14	19	14	25	28	24	124
Germany *	12	25	36	14	13	15	115
Finland	47	33	29	-	2	-	111
Sweden	17	25	41	-	-	3	86
Australia	6	9	12	11	8	12	58
Canada	10	10	16	2	5	7	50
France	7	19	17	4	1	2	50
Italy	13	7	19	3	4	2	48
Poland	9	7	5	6	8	7	42

Nation	Men Gold	Silver	Bronze	Women Gold	Silver	Bronze	Total Medals
Hungary	6	13	16	3	1	2	41
Kenya	12	12	8	-	-	-	30
Czechoslovakia	8	7	3	3	2	2	25
Jamaica	4	10	4	-	3	4	25
Romania	-	-	1	9	9	6	25
Greece	3	8	12	1	-	-	24

In all 68 nations have won medals at track and field sports, with Algeria, Bahamas, Colombia, Korea, Lithuania, Namibia and Qatar added to the list in 1992.

Germany 1896-1952 and 1992, Federal Republic of Germany 1956-88. Medals won by the combined German teams of 1956, 1960 and 1964 have been allocated to FRG or GDR according to the athlete's origin.

World Championships

Athletics events at the Olympic Games have had world championship status, but the first championships for athletics alone were staged in the Olympic Stadium, Helsinki, Finland in 1983. The second world championships were held in Rome in September 1987, and the third in Tokyo in 1991. They are now held biennially. *Champions:*

Men

100 metres
1983 Carl Lewis (USA) 10.07
1987 Carl Lewis (USA) 9.93 *
1991 Carl Lewis (USA) 9.86
1993 Linford Christie (UK) 9.87

*Ben Johnson (Can) won in 9.83, but following his admission of drug taking had his world record and title stripped from him by the IAAF.

200 metres
1983 Calvin Smith (USA) 20.14
1987 Calvin Smith (USA) 20.16
1991 Michael Johnson (USA) 20.01
1993 Frank Fredericks (Nam) 19.85

400 metres
1983 Bert Cameron (Jam) 45.05
1987 Thomas Schönlebe (GDR) 44.33
1991 Antonio Pettigrew (USA) 44.57
1993 Michael Johnson (USA) 43.65

800 metres
1983 Willi Wülbeck (FRG) 1:43.65
1987 Billy Konchellah (Ken) 1:43.06
1991 Billy Konchellah (Ken) 1:43.99
1993 Paul Ruto (Ken) 1:44.71

1500 metres
1983 Steve Cram (UK) 3:41.59
1987 Abdi Bile (Som) 3:36.80
1991 Noureddine Morceli (Alg) 3:32.84
1993 Noureddine Morceli (Alg) 3:34.24

5000 metres
1983 Eamonn Coghlan (Ire) 13:28.53
1987 Saïd Aouita (Mor) 13:26.44
1991 Yobes Ondieki (Ken) 13:14.45
1993 Ismael Kirui (Ken) 13:02.75

10 000 metres
1983 Alberto Cova (Ita) 28:01.04
1987 Paul Kipkoech (Ken) 27:38.63
1991 Moses Tanui (Ken) 27:38.74
1993 Haile Gebrselassie (Eth) 27:46.02

Marathon
1983 Rob de Castella (Aus) 2:10:03
1987 Douglas Wakiihuri (Ken) 2:11:48
1991 Hiromi Taniguchi (Jap) 2:14:57
1993 Mark Plaatjes (USA) 2:13:57

3000 metres steeplechase
1983 Patriz Ilg (FRG) 8:15.06
1987 Francesco Panetta (Ita) 8:08.57
1991 Moses Kiptanui (Ken) 8:12.59
1993 Moses Kiptanui (Ken) 8:06.36

110 metres hurdles
1983 Greg Foster (USA) 13.42
1987 Greg Foster (USA) 13.21
1991 Greg Foster (USA) 13.06
1993 Colin Jackson (UK) 12.91

400 metres hurdles
1983 Edwin Moses (USA) 47.50
1987 Edwin Moses (USA) 47.46
1991 Samuel Matete (Zam) 47.64
1993 Kevin Young (USA) 47.18

High jump
1983 Gennadiy Avdeyenko (USSR) 2.32
1987 Patrik Sjöberg (Swe) 2.38
1991 Charles Austin (USA) 2.38
1993 Javier Sotomayor (Cub) 2.40

Pole vault
1983 Sergey Bubka (USSR) 5.70
1987 Sergey Bubka (USSR) 5.85
1991 Sergey Bubka (USSR) 5.95
1993 Sergey Bubka (Ukr) 6.00

Long jump
1983 Carl Lewis (USA) 8.55
1987 Carl Lewis (USA) 8.67

Maria Mutola – unbeaten at 800m from 1992 to 1995

1991 Mike Powell (USA) 8.95
1993 Mike Powell (USA) 8.59

Triple jump
1983 Zdzislaw Hoffmann (Pol) 17.42
1987 Khristo Markov (Bul) 17.92
1991 Kenny Harrison (USA) 17.78
1993 Mike Conley (USA) 17.86

Shot
1983 Edward Sarul (Pol) 21.39
1987 Werner Günthör (Swi) 22.23
1991 Werner Günthör (Swi) 21.67
1993 Werner Günthör (Swi) 21.97

Discus
1983 Imrich Bugár (Cs) 67.72
1987 Jürgen Schult (GDR) 68.74
1991 Lars Riedel (Ger) 66.20
1993 Lars Riedel (Ger) 67.72

Hammer
1983 Sergey Litvinov (USSR) 82.68
1987 Sergey Litvinov (USSR) 83.06
1991 Yuriy Sedykh (USSR) 81.70
1993 Andrey Abduvaliyev (Tjk) 81.64

Javelin
1983 Detlef Michel (GDR) 89.48 (old spec.)
1987 Seppo Räty (Fin) 83.54

1991 Kimmo Kinnunen (Fin) 90.82
1993 Jan Zelezny (Cze) 85.98

Decathlon
1983 Daley Thompson (UK) 8714
1987 Torsten Voss (GDR) 8680
1991 Dan O'Brien (USA) 8812
1993 Dan O'Brien (USA) 8817

4x100 metres relay
1983 USA 37.86
1987 USA 37.90
1991 USA 37.50
1993 USA 37.48 (37.40 sf CBP)

4x400 metres relay
1983 USSR 3:00.79
1987 USA 2:57.29
1991 Great Britain 2:57.53
1993 USA 2:54.29

20 kilometres walk
1983 Ernesto Canto (Mex) 1:20:49
1987 Maurizio Damilano (Ita) 1:20:45
1991 Maurizio Damilano (Ita) 1:19:37
1993 Valentin Massana (Spa) 1:22:31

50 kilometres walk
1983 Ronald Weigel (GDR) 3:43:08
1987 Hartwig Gauder (GDR) 3:40:53
1991 Aleksandr Potashov (USSR) 3:53:09
1993 Jesús Angel Garcia (Spa) 3:41:41

Women

100 metres
1983 Marlies Göhr (GDR) 10.97
1987 Silke Gladisch (GDR) 10.90
1991 Katrin Krabbe (Ger) 10.99
1993 Gail Devers (USA) 1`0.82

200 metres
1983 Marita Koch (GDR) 22.13
1987 Silke Gladisch (GDR) 21.74
1991 Katrin Krabbe (Ger) 22.09
1993 Merlene Ottey (Jam) 21.98

400 metres
1983 Jarmila Kratochvílová (Cs) 47.99
1987 Olga Bryzgina (USSR) 49.38
1991 Marie-José Pérec (Fra) 49.13
1993 Jearl Miles (USA) 49.82

800 metres
1983 Jarmila Kratochvílová (Cs) 1:54.68
1987 Sigrun Wodars (GDR) 1:55.26
1991 Lilia Nurutdinova (USSR) 1:57.50
1993 Maria Mutola (Moz) 1:55.43

1500 metres
1983 Mary Decker (USA) 4:00.90
1987 Tatyana Samolenko (USSR) 3:58.56
1991 Hassiba Boulmerka (Alg) 4:02.21
1993 Liu Dong (Chn) 4:00.50

3000 metres
1983 Mary Decker (USA) 8:34.62
1987 Tatyana Samolenko (USSR) 8:38.73
1991 Tatyana Dorovskikh (née Samolenko) (USSR) 8:35.82
1993 Qu Yunxia (Chn) 8:28.71

5000 metres
Replaces the 3000m in 1995.

10 000 metres (first held 1987)
1987 Ingrid Kristiansen (Nor) 31:05.85
1991 Liz McColgan (UK) 31:14.31
1993 Wang Junxia (Chn) 30:49.30

Marathon
1983 Grete Waitz (Nor) 2:28:09
1987 Rosa Mota (Por) 2:25:17
1991 Wanda Panfil (Pol) 2:29:53
1993 Junko Asari (Jap) 2:30:03

100 metres hurdles
1983 Bettine Jahn (GDR) 12.35
1987 Ginka Zagorcheva (Bul) 12.34
1991 Lyudmila Narozhilenko (USSR) 12.59
1993 Gail Devers (USA) 12.46

400 metres hurdles
1983 Yekaterina Fesenko (USSR) 54.14
1987 Sabine Busch (GDR) 53.62
1991 Tatyana Ledovskaya (USSR) 53.11
1993 Sally Gunnell (UK) 52.74

High jump
1983 Tamara Bykova (USSR) 2.01
1987 Stefka Kostadinova (Bul) 2.09
1991 Heike Henkel (Ger) 2.05
1993 Ioamnet Quintero (Cub) 1.99

Long jump
1983 Heike Daute (GDR) 7.27w
1987 Jackie Joyner-Kersee (USA) 7.36
1991 Jackie Joyner-Kersee (USA) 7.32
1993 Heike Drechsler (née Daute) (Ger) 7.11

Triple jump (first held 1993)
1993 Ana Biryukova (Rus) 15.09

Shot
1983 Helena Fibingerová (Cs) 21.05
1987 Natalya Lisovskaya (USSR) 21.24
1991 Huang Zhihong (Chn) 20.83
1993 Huang Zhihong (Chn) 20.57

Discus
1983 Martina Opitz (GDR) 68.94
1987 Martina Hellmann (née Opitz) (GDR) 71.62
1991 Tsvetanka Khristova (Bul) 71.02
1993 Olga Burova (Rus) 67.40

Javelin
1983 Tiina Lillak (Fin) 70.82
1987 Fatima Whitbread (UK) 76.64
1991 Xu Demei (Chn) 68.78
1993 Trine Hattestad (Nor) 69.18

Heptathlon
1983 Ramona Neubert (GDR) 6770
1987 Jackie Joyner-Kersee (USA) 7128
1991 Sabine Braun (Ger) 6672
1993 Jackie Joyner-Kersee (USA) 6837

10 kilometres walk (first held 1987)
1987 Irina Strakhova (USSR) 44:12
1991 Alina Ivanova (USSR) 42:57
1993 Sari Essayah (Fin) 42:59

4x100 metres relay
1983 GDR 41.76
1987 USA 41.58
1991 Jamaica 41.94
1993 Russia 41.49

4x400 metres relay
1983 GDR 3:19.73
1987 GDR 3:18.63
1991 USSR 3:18.43
1993 USA 3:16.79

Winners of the most medals
10 Carl Lewis (USA) gold 100m, long jump, 100m & 4x100m relay 1983; long jump & 4x100m relay 1987, long jump & 4x100m relay 1991; silver 100m 1987, long jump 1991; bronze 200m 1993
10 Merlene Ottey (Jam) gold 4x100mR 1991, 200m 1993; silver 200m 1983, 100m 1993; bronze 4x100mR 1983, 100m & 200m 1983 & 1987, 4x100mR 1993
6 Heike Daute/Drechsler (GDR/Ger) gold long jump 1983 & 1993; silver 100m 1987, LJ 1991; bronze LJ 1987, 4x100mR 1991
6 Gwen Torrence (USA) gold 4x400mR 1993; silver 100m 1991, 200m 1991 & 1993, 4x100mR 1993; bronze 100m 1993

World Indoor Championships

First held as World Indoor Games at Bercy, Paris, France 19-20 January 1985. Official Championships are now staged biennially. *Winners:*

Men

60 metres
1985 Ben Johnson (Can) 6.62
1987 Lee McRae USA 6.50
1989 Andrés Simon (Cub) 6.52
1991 Andre Cason (USA) 6.54
1993 Bruny Surin (Can) 6.50
1995 Bruny Surin (Can) 6.46
original winner Ben Johnson (Can) 6.41 was later disqualified after he had admitted long-term drug use.

200 metres
1985 Aleksandr Yakovlyev (USSR) 20.95
1987 Kirk Baptiste (USA) 20.73
1989 John Regis (UK) 20.54
1991 Nikolai Antonov (Bul) 20.67
1993 James Trapp (USA) 20.63
1995 Geir Moen (Nor) 20.58

400 metres
1985 Thomas Schönlebe (GDR) 45.60
1987 Antonio McKay (USA) 45.98
1989 Antonio McKay (USA) 45.59
1991 Devon Morris (Jam) 46.17
1993 Butch Reynolds (USA) 45.26
1995 Darnell Hall (USA) 46.17

800 metres
1985 Colomán Trabado (Esp) 1:47.42
1987 José Luiz Barbosa (Bra) 1:47.49
1989 Paul Ereng (Ken) 1:44.84
1991 Paul Ereng (Ken) 1:47.08
1993 Tom McKean (UK) 1:47.29
1995 Clive Terrelonge (Jam) 1:47.30

1500 metres
1985 Mike Hillardt (Aus) 3:40.27
1987 Marcus O'Sullivan (Ire) 3:39.04
1989 Marcus O'Sullivan (Ire) 3:36.64
1991 Noureddine Morceli (Alg) 3:41.57
1993 Marcus O'Sullivan (Ire) 3:45.00
1995 Hicham El Guerrouj (Mar) 3:44.54

3000 metres
1985 João Campos (Por) 7:57.63
1987 Frank O'Mara (Ire) 8:03.32
1989 Saïd Aouita (Mor) 7:47.94
1991 Frank O'Mara (Ire) 7:41.14
1993 Gennaro Di Napoli (Ita) 7:50.26
1995 Gennaro Di Napoli (Ita) 7:50.89

60 metres hurdles
1985 Stéphane Caristan (Fra) 7.67
1987 Tonie Campbell (USA) 7.51
1989 Roger Kingdom (USA) 7.43
1991 Greg Foster (USA) 7.45
1993 Mark McKoy (Can) 7.41
1995 Allen Johnson (USA) 7.39

High jump
1985 Patrik Sjöberg (Swe) 2.32
1987 Igor Paklin (USSR) 2.38
1989 Javier Sotomayor (Cub) 2.43
1991 Hollis Conway (USA) 2.40
1993 Javier Sotomayor (Cub) 2.41
1995 Javier Sotomayor (Cub) 2.38

Gennaro Di Napoli – sprint finish to two world titles

Ivan Pedroso – twice world indoor champion

Pole vault
1985 Sergey Bubka (USSR) 5.75
1987 Sergey Bubka (USSR) 5.85
1989 Rodion Gataullin (USSR) 5.85
1991 Sergey Bubka (USSR) 6.00
1993 Rodion Gataullin (Rus) 5.90
1995 Sergey Bubka (Ukr) 5.90

Long jump
1985 Jan Leitner (Cs) 7.96
1987 Larry Myricks (USA) 8.23
1989 Larry Myricks (USA) 8.37
1991 Dietmar Haaf (Ger) 8.15
1993 Ivan Pedroso (Cub) 8.23
1995 Ivan Pedroso (Cub) 8.51

Triple jump
1985 Khristo Markov (Bul) 17.22
1987 Mike Conley (USA) 17.54
1989 Mike Conley (USA) 17.65
1991 Igor Lapshin (USSR) 17.31
1993 Pierre Camara (Fra) 17.59
1995 Brian Wellman (Ber) 17.72

Shot
1985 Remigius Machura (Cs) 21.22
1987 Ulf Timmermann (GDR) 22.24
1989 Ulf Timmermann (GDR) 21.75
1991 Werner Günthör (Swi) 21.17
1993 Mike Stulce (USA) 21.27
1995 Mika Halvari (Fin) 20.74

5000 metres walk (discontinued)
1985 Gérard Lélièvre (Fra) 19:06.22
1987 Mikhail Shchennikov (USSR) 18:27.79
1989 Mikhail Shchennikov (USSR) 18:27.10
1991 Mikhail Shchennikov (USSR) 18:23.55
1993 Mikhail Shchennikov (USSR) 18:32.10

4x400 metres relay
1991 Germany 3:03.05
1993 USA 3:04.20
1995 USA 3:07.37

Heptathlon (official from 1995)
1993 Dan O'Brien (USA) 6476
1995 Christian Plaziat (Fra) 6246

Women

60 metres
1985 Silke Gladisch (GDR) 7.20
1987 Nellie Fiere-Cooman (Hol) 7.08
1989 Nellie Cooman (Hol) 7.05
1991 Irina Privalova (USSR) 7.02
1993 Gail Devers (USA) 6.95
1995 Merlene Ottey (Jam) 6.97

200 metres
1985 Marita Koch (GDR) 23.09
1987 Heike Drechsler (GDR) 22.27
1989 Merlene Ottey (Jam) 22.34
1991 Merlene Ottey (Jam) 22.24
1993 Irina Privalova (Rus) 22.15
1995 Melinda Gainsford (Aus) 22.64

400 metres
1985 Diane Dixon (USA) 53.35
1987 Sabine Busch (GDR) 51.66
1989 Helga Arendt (FRG) 51.52
1991 Diane Dixon (USA) 50.64
1993 Sandie Richards (Jam) 50.93
1995 Irina Privalova (Rus) 50.23

800 metres
1985 Cristieana Cojocaru (Rom) 2:04.22
1987 Christine Wachtel (GDR) 2:01.32
1989 Christine Wachtel (GDR) 1:59.24
1991 Christine Wachtel (Ger) 2:01.51
1993 Maria Mutola (Moz) 1:57.55
1995 Maria Mutola (Moz) 1:57.62

1500 metres
1985 Elly van Hulst (Hol) 4:11.41
1987 Doina Melinte (Rom) 4:05.68
1989 Doina Melinte (Rom) 4:04.79
1991 Lyudmila Rogachova (USSR) 4:05.09
1993 Yekaterina Podkopayeva (Rus) 4:09.29
1995 Regina Jacobs (USA) 4:12.61

3000 metres
1985 Debbie Scott (Can) 9:04.99
1987 Tatyana Samolenko (USSR) 8:46.52
1989 Elly van Hulst (Hol) 8:33.82
1991 Marie-Pierre Duros (Fra) 8:50.69
1993 Yvonne Murray (UK) 8:50.55
1995 Gabriela Szabo (Rom) 8:54.50

Irina Privalova - world class from 60m to 400m

60 metres hurdles
1985 Xénia Siska (Hun) 8.03
1987 Cornelia Oschkenat (GDR) 7.82
1989 Yelisaveta Chernyshova (USSR) 7.82
1991 Lyudmila Narozhilenko (USSR) 7.88
1993 Julie Baumann (Swi) 7.96
1995 Aliuska López (Cub) 7.92

High jump
1985 Stefka Kostadinova (Bul) 1.97
1987 Stefka Kostadinova (Bul) 2.05
1989 Stefka Kostadinova (Bul) 2.02
1991 Heike Henkel (Ger) 2.00
1993 Stefka Kostadinova (Bul) 2.02
1995 Alina Astafei (Ger) 2.01

Long jump
1985 Helga Radtke (GDR) 6.86
1987 Heike Drechsler (GDR) 7.10
1989 Galina Chistyakova (USSR) 6.98
1991 Larisa Berezhnaya (USSR) 6.84
1993 Marieta Ilcu (Rom) 6.84
1995 Lyudmila Galkina (Rus) 6.95

Triple Jump (Demonstration event 1991)
1991 Inessa Kravets (USSR) 14.44
1993 Inessa Kravets (USSR) 14.47
1995 Yolanda Chen (Rus) 15.03

Shot
1985 Natalya Lisovskaya (USSR) 20.07

1987 Natalya Lisovskaya (USSR) 20.52
1989 Claudia Losch (FRG) 20.45
1991 Sui Xinmei (Chn) 20.54
1993 Svetlana Krivelyova (Rus) 19.57
1995 Larisa Peleshenko (Rus) 19.93

Pentathlon (official from 1995)
1993 Liliana Nastase(Rom) 4686.
1995 Svetlana Moskalets (Rus) 4834
Original winner, Irina Belova (Rus) 4787, was disqualified following a positive drugs test.

3000 metres walk (discontinued)
1985 Giuliana Salce (Ita) 12:53.42
1987 Olga Krishtop (USSR) 12:05.49
1989 Kerry Saxby (Aus) 12:01.65
1991 Beate Anders (Ger) 11:50.90
1993 Yelena Nikolayeva (Rus) 11:49.73

4x400 metres relay
1991 Germany 3:27.22
1993 Jamaica 3:32.32
1995 Russia 3:29.29
Original winners Russia 3:28.90 disqualified following a postive drugs test.

IAAF World Cup

First held in 1977. The competing teams represent each of the five continents, with national teams from the USA and the top two men's and women's teams from the European Cup. Host nations Italy and Spain competed as ninth teams in 1981 and 1989. Each team enters one competitor per event. From 1994 the event is to be staged every four years.
Winners:

Year	Venue	Men	Women
1977	Düsseldorf	GDR	Europe
1979	Montreal	USA	GDR
1981	Rome	Europe	GDR
1985	Canberra	USA	GDR
1989	Barcelona	USA	GDR
1992	Havana	Africa	CIS
1994	London	Africa	Europe

Individual event winners

Men

100 metres
1977 Steve Williams (USA) 10.13
1979 James Sanford (USA) 10.17
1981 Allan Wells (Eur/UK) 10.20
1985 Ben Johnson (Ame/Can) 10.00
1989 Linford Christie (UK) 10.10
1992 Linford Christie (UK) 10.21
1994 Linford Christie (UK) 10.21

200 metres
1977 Clancy Edwards (USA) 20.17
1979 Silvio Leonard (Ame/Cub) 20.34
1981 Mel Lattany (USA) 20.21
1985 Robson da Silva (Ame/Bra) 20.44
1989 Robson da Silva (Ame/Bra) 20.00
1992 Robson da Silva (Ame/Bra) 20.56
1994 John Regis (UK) 20.45

400 metres
1977 Alberto Juantorena (Ame/Cub) 45.36
1979 Hassan El Kashief (Afr/Sud) 45.39
1981 Cliff Wiley (USA) 44.88
1985 Mike Franks (USA) 44.47
1989 Roberto Hernández (Ame/Cub) 44.58
1992 Sunday Bada (Afr/Ngr) 44.99
1994 Antonio Pettigrew (USA) 45.26

800 metres
1977 Alberto Juantorena (Ame/Cub) 1:44.04
1979 James Maina (Afr/Ken) 1:47.69
1981 Sebastian Coe (Eur/UK) 1:46.16
1985 Sammy Koskei (Afr/Ken) 1:45.14
1989 Tom McKean (UK) 1:44.95
1992 David Sharpe (UK) 1:46.06
1994 Mark Everett (USA) 1:46.02

1500 metres
1977 Steve Ovett (Eur/UK) 3:34.45
1979 Thomas Wessinghage (Eur/FRG) 3:46.00
1981 Steve Ovett (Eur/UK) 3:34.95
1985 Omer Khalifa (Afr/Sud) 3:41.16
1989 Abdi Bile (Afr/Som) 3:35.56
1992 Mohamed Suleiman (Asi/Qat) 3:39.37
1994 Noureddine Morceli (Afr/Alg) 3:34.70

5000 metres
1977 Miruts Yifter (Afr/Eth) 13:13.82
1979 Miruts Yifter (Afr/Eth) 13:35.9
1981 Eamonn Coghlan (Eur/Ire) 14:08.39
1985 Doug Padilla (USA) 14:04.11
1989 Saïd Aouita (Afr/Mor) 13:23.14
1992 Fita Bayissa (Afr/Eth) 13:41.23
1994 Brahim Lahlafi (Afr/Mar) 13:27.96

10 000 metres
1977 Miruts Yifter (Afr/Eth) 28:32.3
1979 Miruts Yifter (Afr/Eth) 27:53.07
1981 Werner Schildhauer (GDR) 27:38.43
1985 Woldajo Bulti (Afr/Eth) 29:22.96
1989 Salvatore Antibo (Eur/Ita) 28:05.26
1992 Addis Abebe (Afr/Eth) 28:44.38
1994 Khalid Skah (Afr/Mar) 27:38.74

3000 metres steeplechase
1977 Michael Karst (FRG) 8:21.6
1979 Kiprotich Rono (Afr/Ken) 8:25.97
1981 Boguslaw Maminski (Eur/Pol) 8:19.89
1985 Julius Kariuki (Afr/Ken) 8:39.51
1989 Julius Kariuki (Afr/Ken) 8:20.84
1992 Phillip Barkutwo (Afr/Ken) 8:26.81
1994 Moses Kiptanui (Afr/Ken) 8:28.28

110 metres hurdles
1977 Thomas Munkelt (GDR) 13.41
1979 Renaldo Nehemiah (USA) 13.39
1981 Greg Foster (USA) 13.32
1985 Tonie Campbell (USA) 13.35w
1989 Roger Kingdom (USA) 12.87w
1992 Colin Jackson (UK) 13.07
1994 Tony Jarrett (UK) 13.23

400 metres hurdles
1977 Ed Moses (USA) 47.58
1979 Ed Moses (USA) 47.53
1981 Ed Moses (USA) 47.37
1985 Andre Phillips (USA) 48.42
1989 David Patrick (USA) 48.74
1992 Samuel Matete (Afr/Zam) 48.88
1994 Samuel Matete (Afr/Zam) 48.77

High jump
1977 Rolf Beilschmidt (GDR) 2.30
1979 Franklin Jacobs (USA) 2.27
1981 Tyke Peacock (USA) 2.28
1985 Patrik Sjöberg (Eur/Swe) 2.31
1989 Patrik Sjöberg (Eur/Swe) 2.34
1992 Yuriy Sergiyenko (CIS/Ukr) 2.29
1994 Javier Sotomayor (Ame/Cub) 2.40

Pole vault
1977 Mike Tully (USA) 5.60
1979 Mike Tully (USA) 5.45
1981 Konstantin Volkov (USSR) 5.70
1985 Sergey Bubka (USSR) 5.85
1989 Philippe Collet (Eur/Fra) 5.75
1992 Igor Potapovich (CIS/Kzk) 5.60
1994 Okkert Brits (Afr/SAf) 5.90

Long jump
1977 Arnie Robinson (USA) 8.19
1979 Larry Myricks (USA) 8.52
1981 Carl Lewis (USA) 8.15
1985 Mike Conley (USA) 8.20
1989 Larry Myricks (USA) 8.29
1992 Ivan Pedroso (Ame/Cub) 7.97
1994 Fred Salle (UK) 8.10

Triple jump
1977 João de Oliveira (Ame/Bra) 16.68
1979 João de Oliveira (Ame/Bra) 17.02
1981 João de Oliveira (Ame/Bra) 17.37
1985 Willie Banks (USA) 17.58
1989 Mike Conley (USA) 17.49
1992 Jonathan Edwards (UK) 17.34
1994 Yoelbi Quesada (Ame/Cub) 17.61

Shot
1977 Udo Beyer (GDR) 21.74
1979 Udo Beyer (GDR) 20.45
1981 Udo Beyer (GDR) 21.40
1985 Ulf Timmermann (GDR) 22.00
1989 Ulf Timmermann (GDR) 21.68
1992 Mike Stulce (USA) 21.34
1994 C J Hunter (USA) 19.92

Discus
1977 Wolfgang Schmidt (GDR) 67.14
1979 Wolfgang Schmidt (GDR) 66.02
1981 Armin Lemme (GDR) 66.38
1985 Gennadiy Kolnootchenko (USSR) 69.08
1989 Jürgen Schult (GDR) 67.12
1992 Tony Washington (USA) 64.86
1994 Vladimir Dubrovshchik (Eur/Bls) 64.54

Khalid Skah – World Cup winner, Olympic champion and world titles on road and cross-country

Hammer
1977 Karl-Hans Riehm (FRG) 75.64
1979 Sergey Litvinov (USSR) 78.70
1981 Yuriy Sedykh (USSR) 77.42
1985 Jüri Tamm (USSR) 82.12
1989 Heinz Weis (Eur/FRG) 77.68
1992 Tibor Gécsek (Eur/Hun) 80.44
1994 Andrey Abduvaliyev (Asi/Tjk) 81.72

Javelin
1977 Michael Wessing (FRG) 87.46
1979 Wolfgang Hanisch (GDR) 86.48
1981 Dainis Kula (USSR) 89.74
1985 Uwe Hohn (GDR) 96.96
1989 Steve Backley (UK) 85.90
1992 Jan Zelezny (Eur/Cs) 88.26
1994 Steve Backley (UK) 85.02

4 x 100 metres relay
1977 USA 38.03
1979 Americas 38.70
1981 Europe 38.73
1985 USA 38.10
1989 USA 38.29
1992 USA 38.48
1994 UK 38.46

4 x 400 metres relay
1977 F R Germany 3:01.34
1979 USA 3:00.70
1981 USA 2:59.12

1985 USA 3:00.71
1989 Americas 3:00.65
1992 Africa 3:02.14
1994 UK 3:01.34

Women

100 metres
1977 Marlies Oelsner (GDR) 11.16
1979 Evelyn Ashford (USA) 11.06
1981 Evelyn Ashford (USA) 11.02
1985 Marlies Göhr (née Oelsner) (GDR) 11.10
1989 Sheila Echols (USA) 11.18
1992 Natalya Voronova (CIS/Rus) 11.33
1994 Irina Privalova (Eur/Rus) 11.32

200 metres
1977 Irena Szewinska (Eur/Pol) 22.72
1979 Evelyn Ashford (USA) 21.83
1981 Evelyn Ashford (USA) 22.18
1985 Marita Koch (GDR) 21.90
1989 Silke Möller (GDR) 22.46
1992 Marie-José Pérec (Eur/Fra) 23.07
1994 Merlene Ottey (Ame/Jam) 22.23

400 metres
1977 Irena Szewinska (Eur/Pol) 49.52
1979 Marita Koch (GDR) 48.97
1981 Jarmila Kratochvílová (Eur/Cs) 48.61
1985 Marita Koch (GDR) 47.60
1989 Ana Quirot (Ame/Cub) 50.60
1992 Jearl Miles (USA) 50.64
1994 Irina Privalova (Eur/Rus) 50.62

800 metres
1977 Totka Petrova (Eur/Bul) 1:59.20
1979 Nikolina Shtereva (Eur/Bul) 2:00.52
1981 Lyudmila Veselkova (USSR) 1:57.48
1985 Christine Wachtel (GDR) 2:01.57
1989 Ana Quirot (Ame/Cub) 1:54.44
1992 Maria Mutola (Afr/Moz) 2:00.47
1994 Maria Mutola (Afr/Moz) 1:58.27

1500 metres
1977 Tatyana Kazankina (USSR) 4:12.7
1979 Totka Petrova (Eur/Bul) 4:06.46*
1981 Tamara Sorokina (USSR) 4:03.33
1985 Hildegard Körner (GDR) 4:10.86
1989 Paula Ivan (Eur/Rom) 4:18.60
1992 Yekaterina Podkopayeva (CIS/Rus) 4:17.60
1994 Hassiba Boulmerka (Afr/Alg) 4:01.05

3000 metres
1977 Grete Waitz (Eur/Nor) 8:43.5
1979 Svyetlana Ulmasova (USSR) 8:36.32
1981 Angelika Zauber (GDR) 8:54.89
1985 Ulrike Bruns (GDR) 9:14.65
1989 Yvonne Murray (Eur/UK) 8:44.32
1992 Derartu Tulu (Afr/Eth) 9:05.89
1994 Robyn Meagher (Can) 9:05.81
#Yvonne Murray (UK) won the race in 8:56.81, but the UK team were later ruled ineligible to compete.

10 000 metres
1985 Aurora Cunha (Por) 32:07.50
1989 Kathrin Ullrich (GDR) 31:33.92
1992 Derartu Tulu (Afr/Eth) 33:38.97
1994 Elana Meyer (Afr/SAf) 30:52.51

100 metres hurdles
1977 Grazyna Rabsztyn (Eur/Pol) 12.70
1979 Grazyna Rabsztyn (Eur/Pol) 12.67
1981 Tatyana Anisimova (USSR) 12.85
1985 Cornelia Oschkenat (GDR) 12.71
1989 Cornelia Oschkenat (GDR) 12.60
1992 Aliuska López (Ame/Cub) 13.06
1994 Aliuska López (Ame/Cub) 12.91

400 metres hurdles
1979 Barbara Klepp (GDR) 55.83
1981 Ellen Neumann (GDR) 54.82
1985 Sabine Busch (GDR) 54.45
1989 Sandra Farmer-Patrick (USA) 53.84
1992 Sandra Farmer-Patrick (USA) 55.38
1994 Silvia Rieger (Ger) 56.14
#Sally Gunnell (UK) won the race in 54.80, but the UK team were later ruled ineligible to compete.

High jump
1977 Rosemarie Ackermann (GDR) 1.98
1979 Debbie Brill (Ame/Can) 1.96
1981 Ulrike Meyfarth (Eur/FRG) 1.96
1985 Stefka Kostadinova (Eur/Bul) 2.00
1989 Silvia Costa (Ame/Cub) 2.04
1992 Ioamnet Quintero (Ame/Cub) 1.94
1994 Britta Bilac (Eur/Slo) 1.91

Long jump
1977 Lynette Jacenko (Oce/Aus) 6.54
1979 Anita Stukane (USSR) 6.64
1981 Sigrid Ulbricht (GDR) 6.80
1985 Heike Drechsler (GDR) 7.27
1989 Galina Chistyakova (USSR) 7.10
1992 Heike Drechsler (Ger) 7.16
1994 Inessa Kravets (Eur/Ukr) 7.00

Triple jump
1992 Li Huirong (Asi/Chn) 13.88
1994 Ana Biryukova (Eur/Rus) 14.46

Shot
1977 Ilona Slupianek (GDR) 20.93 *
1979 Ilona Slupianek (GDR) 20.98
1981 Ilona Slupianek (GDR) 20.60
1985 Natalya Lisovskaya (USSR) 20.69
1989 Huang Zhihong (Asi/Chn) 20.73
1992 Belsy Laza (Ame/Cub) 19.19
1994 Huang Zhihong (Asi/Chn) 19.45

Discus
1977 Faina Melnik (USSR) 68.10
1979 Evelin Jahl (GDR) 65.18
1981 Evelin Jahl (GDR) 66.70
1985 Martina Opitz (GDR) 69.78
1989 Ilke Wyludda (GDR) 71.54
1992 Maritza Martén (Ame/Cub) 69.30
1994 Ilke Wyludda (Ger) 65.30

Javelin
1977 Ruth Fuchs (GDR) 62.36
1979 Ruth Fuchs (GDR) 66.10
1981 Antoaneta Todorova (Eur/Bul) 70.08

1985 Olga Gavrilova (USSR) 66.80
1989 Petra Felke (GDR) 70.32
1992 Tessa Sanderson (Eur/GBR) 61.86
1994 Trine Hattestad (Eur/Nor) 66.48

4 x 100 metres relay
1977 Europe 42.51
1979 Europe 42.19
1981 GDR 42.22
1985 GDR 41.37
1989 GDR 42.21
1992 Asia (Chn) 43.63
1994 Africa (Nig) 42.92

4 x 400 metres relay
1977 GDR 3:24.04
1979 GDR 3:20.38
1981 GDR 3:20.62
1985 GDR 3:19.49
1989 Americas 3:23.05
1992 Americas 3:29.73
1994 Germany 3:27.59

*Great Britain & NI won the race in 3:27.36, but the UK team were later ruled ineligible to compete.

Most individual event wins

Men: 4 Miruts Yifter (Afr/Eth); 3 Ed Moses (USA), João de Oliveira (Ame/Bra), Udo Beyer (GDR), Robson da Silva (Ame/Bra), Linford Christie (UK)

Women: 4 Evelyn Ashford (USA); 3 Ilona Slupianek* (GDR), Marita Koch (GDR)

* subsequently disqualified for infringing the doping regulations, Slupianek at the preceding European Cup

IAAF World Race Walking Cup

This competition is held biennially for the Lugano Trophy (men) and the Eschborn Cup (women). It has been officially recognised by the IAAF with the above name since 1977.

Lugano Cup
Contested by men's national teams walking over 20km and 50 km *Wins:*

5	GDR	1965, 1967, 1970, 1973, 1985
4	USSR	1975, 1983, 1987, 1989
4	Mexico	1977, 1979, 1993, 1995
2	United Kingdom	1961, 1963
2	Italy	1981, 1991

Individual winners - 20 kilometres
1961 Ken Matthews (UK) 1:30:54
1963 Ken Matthews (UK) 1:30:10
1965 Dieter Lindner (GDR) 1:29:10
1967 Nikolay Smaga (USSR) 1:28:39
1970 Hans-Georg Reimann (GDR) 1:26:55
1973 Hans-Georg Reimann (GDR) 1:29:31
1975 Karl-Heinz Stadtmüller (GDR) 1:26:12
1977 Daniel Bautista (Mex) 1:24:03
1979 Daniel Bautista (Mex) 1:18:49
1981 Ernesto Canto (Mex) 1:23:52
1983 Jozef Pribilinec (Cs) 1:19:30
1985 José Marin (Spa) 1:21:42
1987 Carlos Mercenario (Mex) 1:19:24
1989 Frants Kostyukevich (USSR) 1:20:21

Carlos Mercenario has won World Cup races at 20km and 50km to maintain the Mexican walking tradition.

1991 Mikhail Shchennikov (USSR) 1:20:43
1993 Daniel Garcia (Mex) 1.24.26
1995 Li Zewen (Chn) 1:19:44

Individual winners - 50 kilometres
1961 Abdon Pamich (Ita) 4:25:38
1963 István Havasi (Hun) 4:17:16
1965 Christoph Höhne (GDR) 4:03:14
1967 Christoph Höhne (GDR) 4:09:09
1970 Christoph Höhne (GDR) 4:04:36
1973 Bernard Kannenberg (FRG) 3:56:51
1975 Yevgeniy Lyungin (USSR) 4:03:42
1977 Raúl Gonzalez (Mex) 4:04:17
1979 Martín Bermudez (Mex) 3:43:36
1981 Raúl Gonzalez (Mex) 3:48:30
1983 Raúl Gonzalez (Mex) 3:45:37
1985 Hartwig Gauder (GDR) 3:47:31
1987 Ronald Weigel (GDR) 3:42:52
1989 Simon Baker (Aus) 3:43:13
1991 Carlos Mercenario (Mex) 3:42:03
1993 Carlos Mercenario (Mex) 3:50:28
1995 Zhao Yongsheng (Chn) 3:41:20

Eschborn Cup
Contested by women's national teams walking over 10km (5km 1979-81). *Wins:*

4	USSR	1981, 1987, 1989, 1991
3	China	1983, 1985, 1995
1	United Kingdom	1979
1	Italy	1993

Individual winners

5 kilometres

1979 Marion Fawkes (UK) 22:51
1981 Siw Gustavsson (Swe) 22:57

10 kilometres

1983 Xu Yongjiu (Chn) 45:14
1985 Yan Hong (Chn) 46:22
1987 Olga Krishtop (USSR) 43:22
1989 Beate Anders (GDR) 43:08
1991 Irina Strakhova (USSR) 43:55
1993 Wang Yan (Chn) 45:10
1995 Gao Hongmiao (Chn) 42:19

IAAF World Cup Marathon

Staged biennially from the first at Hiroshima, Japan in 1985. From 1997 the event will be incorporated with the marathon race in the World Championships. *Winners:*

Men's team

1985 Djibouti, 1987 Italy, 1989 Ethiopia, 1991 UK
1993 Ethiopia, 1995 Italy

Men's individual

1985 Ahmed Salah (Dji) 2:08:09
1987 Ahmed Salah (Dji) 2:10:55
1989 Metaferia Zeleke (Eth) 2:10:28
1991 Yakov Tolstikov (USSR) 2:09:17
1993 Richard Nerurkar (UK) 2:10:03
1995 Douglas Wakiihuri (Ken) 2:12:01

Women's team

1985 Italy, 1987 USSR, 1989 USSR, 1991 USSR
1993 China, 1995 Romania

Women's individual

1985 Katrin Dörre (GDR) 2:33:30
1987 Zoya Ivanova (USSR) 2:30:39
1989 Sue Marchiano (USA) 2:30:48
1991 Rosa Mota (Por) 2:26:14
1993 Wang Junxia (Chn) 2:28:16
1995 Anuta Catuna (Rom) 2:31:10

IAAF Women's World Road Race Championship

Held at 10km 1983-4 and 15km 1985-91. Then replaced by half marathon championship. *Winners:*

	Team	Individual
1983	USA	Wendy Sly (UK) 32:23
1984	UK	Aurora Cunha (Por) 33:04
1985	UK	Aurora Cunha (Por) 49:17
1986	USSR	Aurora Cunha (Por) 48:31
1987	Portugal	Ingrid Kristiansen (Nor) 47:17
1988	USSR	Ingrid Kristiansen (Nor) 48:24
1989	China	Wang Xiuting (Chn) 49:34
1990	Portugal	Iulia Negura (Rom) 50:12
1991	Germany	Iulia Negura (Rom) 48:42

IAAF World Half Marathon Championships

First held 1992 and to be held annually to 1996, from when the Half Marathon will alternate every two years with the World Road Race Championships. *Winners:*

	Team	Individual

Men

1992	Kenya	Benson Masya (Ken) 60:24
1993	Kenya	Vincent Rousseau (Bel) 61:06
1994	Kenya	Khalid Skah (Mor) 60:27

Women

1992	Japan	Liz McColgan (UK) 68:53
1993	Romania	M Conceição Ferreira (Por) 70:07
1994	Romania	Elana Meyer (SAf) 68:36

IAAF World Road Relay Championship

First held in 1992, with relay teams of five men (six in 1992) and six women combining for the marathon distance of 42.195km. *Winners:*

Men

1992 Kenya 2:00:02
1994 Morocco 1:57:56

Women

1992 Portugal 2:20:14
1994 Russia 2:17:19

Commonwealth Games

See Commonwealth Games section for all winners.

Most gold medals

Men

6 Don Quarrie (Jam) 1970-8

Women

7 Marjorie Nelson (née Jackson) (Aus) 1950-4
7 Raelene Boyle (Aus) 1970-82
6 Pam Kilborn/Ryan (Aus) 1962-70

Most wins at one event

Men

3 Howard Payne (Eng) Hammer 1962, 1966, 1970
3 Don Quarrie (Jam) 100m 1970, 1974, 1978
3 Daley Thompson (Eng) Decathlon 1978, 1982, 1986

Women

3 Valerie Young (NZ) Shot 1962, 1966, 1970
3 Pam Ryan (Aus) 80mh 1962, 1966, 100mh 1970
3 Jennifer Lamy (Aus) 4x100m relay 1966, 1970, 1974
3 Kathy Cook (Eng) 4x100m relay 1978, 1982, 1986
3 Tessa Sanderson (Eng) Javelin 1978, 1986, 1990

Most Medals G - Gold, S - Silver, B - Bronze

Men		G	S	B	Years
6	Don Quarrie (Jam)	6	-	-	1970-78
6	Harry Hart (SAf)	4	1	1	1930-34
6	Allan Wells (Sco)	4	1	1	1978-82
Women					
9	Raelene Boyle (Aus)	7	2	-	1970-82
8	Denise Boyd (Aus)	2	3	3	1974-82
7	Marjorie Jackson (Aus)	7	-	-	1950-4
7	Valerie Young (NZ)	5	1	1	1958-74

7	Kathy Cook (Eng)	3	3	1	1978-86
7	Debbie Flintoff (Aus)	3	3	1	1982-90
7	Angella Issajenko (Can)	3	2	2	1982-6

Boyd née Robertson, Young née Sloper, Cook née Smallwood, Issajenko née Taylor, Ryan née Kilborn

Most medals at one Games

| 5 | Decima Norman (Aus) | 5 | - | - | 1938 |
| 5 | Shirley Strickland (Aus) | 3 | 2 | - | 1950 |

European Cup

The European Cup has been contested biennially by European nations, with each team entering one athlete per event and one team in each relay. From 1994 the event is to be staged annually. The Cup is dedicated to the memory of Dr Bruno Zauli, the former President of the European Committee of the IAAF, who died suddenly in 1963 soon after the decision had been made to start this competition.

From 1965 until 1981 the competition was staged with a qualifying round, semifinals and final, but from 1983 the nations have been arranged into groups according to strength, with eight men's and eight women's teams in A and B groups, with additional nations in C1 and C2 groups. There is two up and two down promotion and relegation between the groups (one up and down between A and B prior to 1989). The groups for 1991 were rearranged with the merging of the FRG and GDR teams into a combined Germany and in 1993 to take account of the ex-Soviet and Yugoslav republics. In 1993 the top group was renamed as the Super League, with a First League and three groups in the Second League and the competition became an annual one.

Men's final wins

6	GDR	1970, 1975, 1977, 1979, 1981, 1983
6	USSR	1965, 1967, 1973, 1985, 1987, 1991
2	Germany	1994-5
1	UK 1989, Russia 1993	

Women's final wins

9	GDR	1970, 1973, 1975, 1977, 1979, 1981, 1983, 1987, 1989
3	USSR	1965, 1967, 1985
2	Germany	1991, 1994
2	Russia	1993, 1995

Most individual event wins in finals

Men

9 Linford Christie GBR 100m 1987, 1989, 1991, 1993-5; 200m 1987, 1994-5
5 Harald Schmid (FRG) 400m 1979, 400mh 1979, 1983, 1985, 1987

Women

6 Marlies Göhr (GDR) 100m 1977, 1979, 1981, 1983, 1985, 1987
6 Heike Drechsler (GDR/Ger) Long jump 1983, 1987, 1991, 1993-5
5 Renate Stecher (GDR) 100m 1973, 1975, 200m 1970, 1973, 1975

European Combined Events Cup

Held biennially at decathlon for men and heptathlon (pentathlon 1973-9) for women since 1973. As with the European

Cup, nations are now divided into A, B, C1 and C2 groups. *Wins:*

Men

3	USSR	1975, 1977, 1985
3	GDR	1979, 1987, 1989
2	FR Germany	1981, 1983
2	France	1993-4
1	Poland 1973, Germany 1991	

Women

6	GDR	1973, 1975, 1979, 1981, 1983, 1985
3	USSR	1977, 1987, 1989
2	Russia	1993, 1994
1	Germany	1991

European Marathon Cup

Held four times. Held with European Championships (qv) in 1994. *Winners:*

Men's individual

1981 Massimo Magnani (Ita) 2:13:29
1983 Waldemar Cierpinski (GDR) 2:12:26
1985 Michael Heilmann (GDR) 2:11:28
1988 Ravil Kashapov (USSR) 2:11:30

Men's team

1981 Italy, 1983 GDR, 1985 GDR, 1988 USSR
1994 Spain

Women's individual

1981 Zoya Ivanova (USSR) 2:38:58
1983 Nadezhda Gumerova (USSR) 2:38:36
1985 Katrin Dörre (GDR) 2:30:11
1988 Katrin Dörre (GDR) 2:28:28

Women's team

1985 GDR, 1988 USSR, 1994 Italy

IAAF/Mobil Grand Prix

Introduced in 1986, half the standard men's and women's events are contested each year for individual events Grand Prix and an overall Grand Prix over a series of international meetings throughout the world. *Overall champions:*

Year	Men	Women
1985	Doug Padilla (USA)	Mary Slaney (USA)
1986	Saïd Aouita (Mor)	Yordanka Donkova (Bul)
1987	Tonie Campbell (USA)	Merlene Ottey (Jam)
1988	Saïd Aouita (Mor)	Paula Ivan (Rom)
1989	Saïd Aouita (Mor)	Paula Ivan (Rom)
1990	Leroy Burrell (USA)	Merlene Ottey (Jam)
1991	Sergey Bubka (USSR)	Heike Henkel (Ger)
1992	Kevin Young (USA)	Heike Drechsler (Ger)
1993	Sergey Bubka (Ukr)	Sandra Farmer-Patrick (USA)
1994	Noureddine Morceli (Alg)	Jackie Joyner-Kersee (USA)

European Championships

The first European Championships were staged at the Stadio Communale, Turin in 1934 for men only. Women's championships were held separately in 1938, but men's and women's events were combined at one venue from 1946. The championships are held at four-yearly intervals, although there was a break in that pattern when they were held in 1969 and 1971.

Winners at the championships since 1978, championships bests (CBP), and athletes to have won a particular event twice:

Men

100 metres
1978 Pietro Mennea (Ita) 10.27
1982 Frank Emmelmann (GDR) 10.21
1986 Linford Christie (UK) 10.15
1990 Linford Christie (UK) 10.00w
1994 Linford Christie (UK) 10.14 (10.08 h CBP)
Most: 3 Valeriy Borzov (USSR) 1969, 1971, 1974; Christie

200 metres
1978 Pietro Mennea (Ita) 20.16
1982 Olaf Prenzler (GDR) 20.46
1986 Vladimir Krylov (USSR) 20.52
1990 John Regis (UK) 20.11 CBP
1994 Geir Moen (Nor) 20.30
Most: 2 Mennea 1974, 1978

400 metres
1978 Franz-Peter Hofmeister (FRG) 45.73
1982 Hartmut Weber (FRG) 44.72
1986 Roger Black (UK) 44.59 CBP
1990 Roger Black (UK) 45.08
1994 Du'aine Ladejo (UK) 45.09
Most: 2 Black

800 metres
1978 Olaf Beyer (GDR) 1:43.84 CBP
1982 Hans-Peter Ferner (FRG) 1:46.33
1986 Sebastian Coe (UK) 1:44.50
1990 Tom McKean (UK) 1:44.76
1994 Andrea Benvenuti (Ita) 1:46.12
Most: 2 Manfred Matuschewski (GDR) 1962, 1966

1500 metres
1978 Steve Ovett (UK) 3:35.59
1982 Steve Cram (UK) 3:36.49
1986 Steve Cram (UK) 3:41.09
1990 Jens-Peter Herold (GDR) 3:38.25
1994 Fermin Cacho (Spa) 3:35.27 CBP
Most: 2 Cram

5000 metres
1978 Venanzio Ortis (Ita) 13:28.57
1982 Thomas Wessinghage (FRG) 13:28.90
1986 Jack Buckner (UK) 13:10.15 CBP
1990 Salvatore Antibo (Ita) 13:22.00
1994 Dieter Baumann (Ger) 13:36.93

10 000 metres
1978 Martti Vainio (Fin) 27:30.99 CBP
1982 Alberto Cova (Ita) 27:41.03
1986 Stefano Mei (Ita) 27:56.79
1990 Salvatore Antibo (Ita) 27:41.27
1994 Abel Antón (Spa) 28:06.03
Most: 2 Ilmari Salminen (Fin) 1934, 1938; Emil Zátopek (Cs) 1950, 1954; Jürgen Haase (GDR) 1966, 1969

Marathon
1978 Leonid Moseyev (USSR) 2:11:58
1982 Gerard Nijboer (Hol) 2:15:16
1986 Gelindo Bordin (Ita) 2:10:54
1990 Gelindo Bordin (Ita) 2:14:02
1994 Martin Fíz (Spa) 2:10:31 CBP
Most: 2 Bordin

3000 metres steeplechase
1978 Bronislaw Malinowski (Pol) 8:17.08
1982 Patriz Ilg (FRG) 8:18.52
1986 Hagen Melzer (GDR) 8:16.65
1990 Francesco Panetta (Ita) 8:12.66 CBP
1994 Alessandro Lambruschini (Ita) 8:22.40
Most: 2 Malinowski 1974 , 1978

110 metres hurdles
1978 Thomas Munkelt (GDR) 13.54
1982 Thomas Munkelt (GDR) 13.41
1986 Stéphane Caristan (Fra) 13.20
1990 Colin Jackson (UK) 13.18
1994 Colin Jackson (UK) 13.08 (13.04 sf CBP)
Most: 2 Eddy Ottoz (Ita) 1966, 1969; Munkelt, Jackson

400 metres hurdles
1978 Harald Schmid (FRG) 48.51
1982 Harald Schmid (FRG) 47.48 CBP
1986 Harald Schmid (FRG) 48.65
1990 Kriss Akabusi (UK) 47.92
1994 Oleg Tverdokhleb (Ukr) 48.06
Most: 3 Schmid

4 x 100 metres relay
1978 Poland 38.53
1982 USSR 38.60
1986 USSR 38.29
1990 France 37.79 CBP
1994 France 38.57

4 x 400 metres relay
1978 FR Germany 3:02.03
1982 FR Germany 3:00.51
1986 United Kingdom 2:59.84
1990 United Kingdom 2:58.22 CBP
1994 United Kingdom 2:59.13

20 kilometres walk
1978 Roland Wieser (GDR) 1:23:12

Dieter Baumann wins the 1992 Olympic title – he added the European 5000m two years later.

1982 José Marin (Spa) 1:23:43
1986 Jozef Pribilinec (Cs) 1:21:15 CBP
1990 Pavol Blazek (Cs) 1:22:05
1994 Mikhail Shchennikov (Rus) 1:18:45

50 kilometres walk
1978 Jordi Llopart (Spaq) 3:53:30
1982 Reima Salonen (Fin) 3:55:29
1986 Hartwig Gauder (GDR) 3:40:55 CBP
1990 Andrey Perlov (USSR) 3:54:36
1994 Valeriy Spitsyn (Rus) 3:41:07
Most: 2 Abdon Pamich (Ita) 1962, 1966; 2 Christoph Höhne (GDR) 1969, 1974

High jump
1978 Vladimir Yashchenko (USSR) 2.30
1982 Dietmar Mögenburg (FRG) 2.30
1986 Igor Paklin (USSR) 2.34 CBP
1990 Dragutin Topic (Yug) 2.34
1994 Steinar Hoen (Nor) 2.35 CBP

Pole vault
1978 Vladimir Trofimenko (USSR) 5.55
1982 Aleksandr Krupskiy (USSR) 5.60
1986 Sergey Bubka (USSR) 5.85
1990 Rodion Gataullin (USSR) 5.85
1994 Rodion Gataullin (Rus) 6.00 CBP
Most: 3 Wolfgang Nordwig (GDR) 1966, 1969, 1971
2 Eeles Landström (Fin) 1954, 1958; Gataullin

Long jump
1978 Jacques Rousseua (Fra) 8.18
1982 Lutz Dombrowski (GDR) 8.41w
1986 Robert Emmiyan (USSR) 8.41 CBP
1990 Dietmar Haaf (FRG) 8.25
1994 Ivailo Mladenov (Bul) 8.09
Most: 3 Igor Ter-Ovanesyan (USSR) 1958, 1962, 1969;
2 Wilhelm Leichum (Ger) 1934, 1938

Triple jump
1978 Milos Srejovic (Yug) 16.94
1982 Keith Connor (UK) 17.29
1986 Khristo Markov (Bul) 17.66
1990 Leonid Voloshin (USSR) 17.74 CBP
1994 Denis Kapustin (Rus) 17.62
Most: 2 Leonid Shcherbakov (USSR) 1950, 1954;
2 Jozef Schmidt (Pol) 1958, 1962; 2 Viktor Saneyev (USSR) 1969, 1974

Shot
1978 Udo Beyer (GDR) 21.08
1982 Udo Beyer (GDR) 21.50
1986 Werner Günthör (Swi) 22.22 CBP
1990 Ulf Timmermann (GDR) 21.32
1994 Aleksandr Klimenko (Ukr) 20.78
Most: 2 Gunnar Huseby (Ice) 1946, 1950; Vilmos Varju (Hun) 1962, 1966; Hartmut Briesenick (GDR) 1971, 1974; Beyer

Discus
1978 Wolfgang Schmidt (GDR) 66.82 (CBP 67.20 qual)
1982 Imrich Bugár (Cs) 66.64
1986 Romas Ubartas (USSR) 67.08
1990 Jürgen Schult (GDR) 64.58
1994 Vladimir Dubrovshchik (Bls) 64.78

Most: 3 Adolfo Consolini (Ita) 1946, 1950, 1954

Hammer
1978 Yuriy Sedykh (USSR) 77.28
1982 Yuriy Sedykh (USSR) 81.66
1986 Yuriy Sedykh (USSR) 86.74 CBP
1990 Igor Astapkovich (USSR) 84.14
1994 Vasiliy Sidorenko (Rus) 81.10
Most: 3 Sedykh

Javelin (new specification from 1986)
1978 Michael Wessing (FRG) 89.12
1982 Uwe Hohn (GDR) 91.34
1986 Klaus Tafelmeier (FRG) 84.76
1990 Steve Backley (UK) 87.30 CBP
1994 Steve Backley (UK) 85.20
Most: 4 Janis Lusis (USSR) 1962, 1966, 1969 (CBP old javelin 91.52), 1971; 2 Matti Järvinen (Fin) 1934, 1938; Janusz Sidlo (Pol) 1954, 1958; Backley

Decathlon
1978 Aleksandr Grebenyuk (USSR) 8340
1982 Daley Thompson (UK) 8744
1986 Daley Thompson (UK) 8811 CBP
1990 Christian Plaziat (Fra) 8574
1994 Alain Blondel (Fra) 8453
Most: 3 Vasiliy Kuznetsov (USSR) 1954, 1958, 1962;
2 Joachim Kirst (GDR) 1969, 1971; Thompson

Women

100 metres
1978 Marlies Göhr (GDR) 11.13
1982 Marlies Göhr (GDR) 11.01
1986 Marlies Göhr (GDR) 10.91
1990 Katrin Krabbe (GDR) 10.89 CBP
1994 Irina Privalova (Rus) 11.02
Most: 3 Göhr

200 metres
1978 Lyudmila Kondratyeva (USSR) 22.52
1982 Bärbel Wöckel (GDR) 22.04
1986 Heike Drechsler (GDR) 21.71 CBP
1990 Katrin Krabbe (GDR) 21.95
1994 Irina Privalova (Rus) 22.32
Most: 2 Irena Szewinska (Pol) 1966, 1974

400 metres
1978 Marita Koch (GDR) 48.94
1982 Marita Koch (GDR) 48.15 CBP
1986 Marita Koch (GDR) 48.22
1990 Grit Breuer (GDR) 49.50
1994 Marie-José Pérec (Fra) 50.33
Most: 3 Koch; 2 Mariya Itkina (USSR) 1958, 1962

800 metres
1978 Tatyana Providokhina (USSR) 1:55.80
1982 Olga Mineyeva (USSR) 1:55.41 CBP
1986 Nadezhda Olizarenko (USSR) 1:57.15
1990 Sigrun Wodars (GDR) 1:55.87
1994 Lyubov Gurina (Rus) 1:58.55
Most: 2 Vera Nikolic (Yug) 1966, 1971

1500 metres
1978 Giana Romanova (USSR) 3:59.01
1982 Olga Dvirna (USSR) 3:57.80 CBP

1986 Ravilya Agletdinova (USSR) 4:01.19
1990 Snezana Pajkic (Yug) 4:08.12
1994 Lyudmila Rogachova (Rus) 4:18.93

3000 metres
1978 Svetlana Ulmasova (USSR) 8:33.16
1982 Svetlana Ulmasova (USSR) 8:30.28 CBP
1986 Olga Bondarenko (USSR) 8:33.99
1990 Yvonne Murray (UK) 8:43.06
1994 Sonia O'Sullivan (Ire) 8:31.84
Most: 2 Ulmasova

10 000 metres
1986 Ingrid Kristiansen (Nor) 30:23.25 CBP
1990 Yelena Romanova (USSR) 31:46.83
1994 Fernanda Ribeiro (Por) 31:08.75

Marathon
1982 Rosa Mota (Por) 2:36:04
1986 Rosa Mota (Por) 2:28:38 CBP
1990 Rosa Mota (Por) 2:31:27
1994 Manuela Machado (Por) 2:29:54
Most: 3 Mota

100 metres hurdles
1978 Johanna Klier (GDR) 12.62
1982 Lucyna Kalek (Pol) 12.45
1986 Yordanka Donkova (Bul) 12.38 CBP
1990 Monique Ewanje-Épée (Fra) 12.79
1994 Svetla Dimitrova (Bul) 12.72

Sonia O'Sullivan – a great year in 1994

Most: 3 Karin Balzer (GDR) 1966 (80mh), 1969, 1971;
2 Fanny Blankers-Koen (Hol) 1946, 1950 (both at 80mh)

400 metres hurdles
1978 Tatyana Zelentsova (USSR) 54.89
1982 Ann-Louise Skoglund (Swe) 54.58
1986 Marina Styepanova (USSR) 53.32 CBP
1990 Tatyana Ledovskaya (USSR) 53.62
1994 Sally Gunnell (UK) 53.33

4 x 100 metres relay
1978 USSR 42.54
1982 GDR 42.19
1986 GDR 41.84
1990 GDR 41.68 CBP
1994 Germany 42.90

4 x 400 metres relay
1978 GDR 3:21.20
1982 GDR 3:19.05
1986 GDR 3:16.87 CBP
1990 GDR 3:21.02
1994 France 3:22.34

10 kilometres walk
1986 Maria Cruz Diaz (Spa) 46:09
1990 Anna Rita Sidoti (Ita) 44:00
1994 Sari Essayah (Fin) 42:37 CBP

High jump
1978 Sara Simeoni (Ita) 2.01
1982 Ulrike Meyfarth (FRG) 2.02 CBP
1986 Stefka Kostadinova (Bul) 2.00
1990 Heike Henkel (FRG) 1.99
1994 Britta Bilac (Slo) 2.00
Most: 2 Iolanda Balas (Rom) 1958, 1962

Long jump
1978 Vilma Bardauskiené (USSR) 6.88
1982 Vali Ionescu (Rom) 6.79
1986 Heike Drechsler (GDR) 7.27
1990 Heike Drechsler (GDR) 7.30 CBP
1994 Heike Drechsler (GDR) 7.14
Most: 3 Drechsler

Triple jump
1994 Ana Biryukova (Rus) 14.89

Shot
1978 Ilona Slupianek (GDR) 21.41
1982 Ilona Slupianek (GDR) 21.59 CBP
1986 Heidi Krieger (GDR) 21.10
1990 Astrid Kumbernuss (GDR) 20.38
1994 Viktoriya Pavlysh (Ukr) 19.61
Most: 4 Nadezhda Chizhova (USSR) 1966, 1969, 1971, 1974; 2 Slupianek

Discus
1978 Evelin Jahl (GDR) 66.98
1982 Tsvetanka Khristova (Bul) 68.34
1986 Diane Sachse (GDR) 71.36 CBP
1990 Ilke Wyludda (GDR) 68.46
1994 Ilke Wyludda (Ger) 68.72
Most: 2 Nina Dumbadze (USSR) 1946, 1950; Tamara Press (USSR) 1958, 1962; Faina Melnik (USSR) 1971, 1974; Wyludda

Javelin
1978 Ruth Fuchs (GDR) 69.16
1982 Anna Verouli (Gre) 70.02
1986 Fatima Whitbread (UK) 76.32 (77.44 CBP qual)
1990 Päivi Alafranti (Fin) 67.68
1994 Trine Hattestad (Nor) 68.00
Most: 2 Dana Zátopková (Cs) 1954, 1958; Fuchs 1974, 1978

Heptathlon
1978 Margit Papp (Hun) 4655 (Pentathlon)
1982 Ramona Neubert (GDR) 6664
1986 Anke Behmer (GDR) 6717 CBP
1990 Sabine Braun (FRG) 6688
1994 Sabine Braun (Ger) 6419
Most: 2 Galina Bystrova (USSR) at pentathlon 1958, 1962; Braun

Most gold medals at all events
Men
5 Harald Schmid (FRG) 1978-86
5 Roger Black (UK) 1986-94
4 Janis Lusis (USSR) 1962-71
4 Valeriy Borzov (USSR) 1969-74
Women
6 Marita Koch (GDR) 1978-86
5 Fanny Blankers-Koen (Hol) 1946-50
5 Irena Szewinska (Pol) 1966-74
5 Marlies Göhr (GDR) 1978-86
4 Maria Itkina (USSR) 1954-62
4 Nadezhda Chizhova (USSR) 1966-74
4 Renate Stecher (GDR) 1969-74
4 Heike Drechsler (GDR/GER) 1986-90

Most medals: Gold, Silver, Bronze

Men	G	S	B	Years
6 Harald Schmid (FRG)	5	1	-	1978-86
6 Pietro Mennea (Ita)	3	2	1	1971-74
6 Roger Black (UK)	5	1	-	1986-94

Women	G	S	B	Years
10 Irena Szewinska (Pol)	5	1	4	1966-78
8 Fanny Blankers-Koen (Hol)	5	1	2	1938-50
8 Renate Stecher (GDR)	4	4	-	1969-74
7 Marlies Göhr (GDR)	5	1	1	1978-86
6 Yevgeniya Sechenova (USSR)	2	2	2	1946-50
6 Marita Koch (GDR)	6	-	-	1978-86

Most medals at one event: (long jump)
5 Igor Ter-Ovanesyan (USSR)   3   2   -   1966-71

Most medals at one Championships:
Men
4 John Regis (UK)   2   1   1   1990
Women
4 Fanny Blankers-Koen (Hol)   3   1   -   1950
4 Irena Kirszenstei/Szewinska
   (Pol)   3   1   -   1966
4 Stanislawa Walasiewicz (Pol)   2   2   -   1938

European Indoor Championships
European Indoor Games were held for the first time on 27 Mar 1966 at the Westfallenhalle in Dortmund. From 1970 they received IAAF sanction as the official European Indoor Championships and were held annually until 1990, simce when they have been biennial.

Most wins:
Men
7 Valeriy Borzov (USSR) 60m 1970-1, 1974-7; 50m 1972
6 Viktor Saneyev (USSR) triple jump 1970-2, 1975-7
5 Marian Woronin (Pol) 60m 1979-82, 1987
5 José Luis González (Spa) 1500m 1982, 1985-6; 3000m 1987-8
5 Dietmar Mögenburg (FRG) high jump 1980, 1982, 1984, 1986, 1989
Women
8 Helena Fibingerová (Cs) shot 1973-4, 1977-8, 1980, 1983-5
6 Nellie Cooman/Fiere (Hol) 60m 1985-9, 1994
5 Karin Balzer (GDR) 50m hurdles 1967-9, 60m hurdles 1970-1
5 Nadezhda Chizhova (USSR) shot 1967-8, 1970-2
5 Marlies Göhr (GDR) 60m 1977-9, 1982-3

World Records
World records for athletics were first officially recognised by the IAAF in 1913. Initially records were accepted for 96 men's events, and this list has been reduced at various times, including the elimination of Imperial distances, except the 1 mile, in 1977. From 1977 all records at sprint distances up to 400 metres have been accepted only if timed fully automatically. Prior to that date the best hand times have been listed.

Records are shown for each of the currently recognised events, with the records at 15-year intervals, and all those from 1990. Pre-1900 performances and those indicated by (u) were not, for various reasons, ratified by the IAAF, but they are considered as the best acceptable. Also listed are those athletes to have set most records at each event.
A = set at high altitude (over 1000m).

Men

100 metres
1900	10.8	Luther Cary (USA) 4 Jul 1891
	10.8	eight other men
1915	10.5 u	Emil Ketterer (Ger) 9 Jul 1911
	10.5 u	Richard Rau (Ger) 13 Aug 1911
1930	10.2 u	Charles Paddock (USA) 18 Jun 1921
1945	10.2	also Jesse Owens (USA) 20 Jun 1936
	10.2	Hal Davis (USA) 6 Jun 1941
	10.2u	Lloyd La Beach (Pan) 8 Aug 1943
1960	10.0	Armin Hary (FRG) 21 Jun 1960 (10.25 auto)
	10.0	Harry Jerome (Can) 15 Jul 1960
1975	9.9 *hand*	by seven men
	9.95A	Jim Hines (USA) 14 Oct 1968
1990	9.92	Carl Lewis (USA) 24 Sep 1988
	9.83	Ben Johnson (Can) 30 Aug 1987

Johnson's time was officially ratified but later dropped after his admission of taking steroids for many years. He ran 9.79 in the Olympic Games at Seoul on 24 Sep 1988 but was disqualified on that occasion for a positive drugs test.

	9.90	Leroy Burrell (USA) 14 Jun 1991
	9.86	Carl Lewis (USA) 25 Aug 1991
	9.85	Leroy Burrell (USA) 6 Jul 1994

Most officially ratified: 4 Steve Williams (USA) all at 9.9 1974-6

200 metres (y = 220 yards)

1900	21.2y #	Bernie Wefers (USA) 30 May 1896
1915	21.2y	William Applegarth (UK) 4 Jul 1914
	20.8y #	Albert Robinson (USA) 2 May 1913
1930	21.0 u	Helmut Körnig (Ger) 26 Aug 1928
	20.6 #	Roland Locke (USA) 1 May 1926
1945	20.6y u	James Carlton (Aus) 18 Jun 1932
	20.3y #	Jesse Owens (USA) 25 May 1935
1960	20.5y	Peter Radford (UK) 28 May 1960
	20.5	Stonewall Johnson (USA) 2 Jul 1960
	20.5	Ray Norton (USA) 2 Jul 1960
	20.5	Livio Berruti (Ita) 3 Sep 1960 (20.62 auto)
	20.0 #	Dave Sime (USA) 9 Jun 1956
1975	19.83A	Tommie Smith (USA) 16 Oct 1968
	19.5 #	Tommie Smith (USA) 7 May 1966
1990	19.72A	Pietro Mennea (Italy) 12 Sep 1979

Best time at low altitude: 19.73 Michael Marsh (USA) 5 Aug 1992

 # Straight track (c.0.3 - 0.4.sec faster) - prior to 1951 records could be set on any type of course, from 1951 to 1975 separate records were maintained for straight and turn, thereafter all records must be made around a full turn.

Most: 5 Ray Norton (USA) 20.6 - 20.5 (1959-60)

400 metres (y = 440 yards)

1900	47.8y	Maxie Long (USA) 29 Sep 1900
1915	47.8y	as above
1930	47.0	Emerson Spenser (USA) 12 May 1928
1945	46.0	Rudolf Harbig (Ger) 12 Aug 1939
	46.0	Grover Klemmer (USA) 29 Jun 1941
1960	44.9	Otis Davis (USA) 6 Sep 1960
	44.9	Carl Kaufmann (FRG) 6 Sep 1960 (auto times: 45.07 Davis, 45.08 Kaufmann)
1975	43.86A	Lee Evans (USA) 18 Oct 1968
1990	43.29	Butch Reynolds (USA) 17 Aug 1988

Most: 4 Herb McKenley (Jam) 46.2y - 45.9 (1946-8)

800 metres (y = 880 yards)

1900	1:53.4y	Charles Kilpatrick (USA) 21 Sep 1895
1915	1:51.9	Ted Meredith (USA) 8 Jul 1912
1930	1:50.6	Séraphin Martin (Fra) 14 Jul 1928
1945	1:46.6	Rudolf Harbig (Ger) 15 Jul 1939
1960	1:45.7	Roger Moens (Bel) 3 Aug 1955
1975	1:43.7	Marcello Fiasconaro (Ita) 27 Jun 1973
	1:44.1y	Rick Wohlhuter (USA) 8 Jun 1974
1990	1:41.73	Sebastian Coe (UK) 10 Jun 1981

Most: 5 Lawrence 'Lon' Myers (USA) 1:56.2y - 1:55.4y (1880-5)

1000 metres

1900	2:36.8	Henri Deloge (Fra)10 Jun 1900
1915	2:31.0 u	Emilio Lunghi (Ita) 31 May 1908
1930	2:23.6	Jules Ladoumègue (Fra) 19 Oct 1930
1945	2:21.5	Rudolf Harbig (Ger) 24 May 1941
1960	2:16.7	Siegfried Valentin (GDR) 29 Jul 1960
1975	2:13.9	Rick Wohlhuter (USA) 30 Jul 1974
1990	2:12.18	Sebastian Coe (UK) 11 Jul 1981

Most: 3 Auden Boysen (Nor) 2:20.4 - 2:19.0 (1953-5)

1500 metres

1900	4:06.2	Charles Bennett (UK) 15 Jul 1900
1915	3:55 est	Norman Taber (USA) 16 Jul 1915
1930	3:49.2	Jules Ladoumègue (Fra) 5 Oct 1930
1945	3:43.0	Gunder Hägg (Swe) 7 Jul 1944
1960	3:35.6	Herb Elliott (Aus) 6 Sep 1960
1975	3:32.16	Filbert Bayi (Tan) 2 Feb 1974
1990	3:29.46	Saïd Aouita (Mor) 23 Aug 1985
	3:28.86	Noureddine Morceli (Alg) 6 Sep 1992
	3:27.37	Noureddine Morceli (Alg) 12 Jul 1995

Most: 3 Abel Kiviat (USA) 3:59.2 - 3:55.8 (1912)
3 Gunder Hägg (Swe) 3:47.6 - 3:43.0 (1941-4)
3 Steve Ovett (UK) 3:32.09 - 3:30.77 (1980-3)

1 mile

1900	4:12 $^3/_4$	Walter George (UK) 23 Aug 1886 (pro)
	4:15.6	Thomas Conneff (USA) 30 Aug 1895
1915	4:12.6	Norman Taber (USA) 16 Jul 1915
1930	4:10.4	Paavo Nurmi (Fin) 23 Aug 1923
1945	4:01.3	Gunder Hägg (Swe) 17 Jul 1945
1960	3:54.5	Herb Elliott (Aus) 6 Aug 1958
1975	3:49.4	John Walker (NZ) 12 Aug 1975
1990	3:46.32	Steve Cram (UK) 27 Jul 1985
	3:44.39	Noureddine Morceli (Alg) 5 Sep 1993

Most: 3 Gunder Hägg (Swe) 4:06.1 - 4.01.3 (1942-5)
3 Arne Andersson (Swe) 4:06.2 - 4:01.6 (1942-4)
3 Sebastian Coe (UK) 3:48.95 - 3:47.33 (1979-81)

2000 metres

1900	5:38.8*	Thomas Conneff (USA) 2 Sep 1895
1915	5:37.0*	Alfred Shrubb (UK) 11 Jun 1904
1930	5:23.4	Eino Borg (Purje) (Fin) 9 Aug 1927
1945	5:11.8	Gunder Hägg (Swe) 23 Aug 1942
1960	5:02.2	István Rozsavölgyi (Hun) 2 Oct 1955
1975	4:56.2	Michel Jazy (Fra) 12 Oct 1966
1990	4:50.81	Saïd Aouita (Mor) 16 Jul 1987
	4:47.88	Noureddine Morceli (Alg) 3 Jul 1995

* time at $1^1/_4$ Mile (2011.68m)

3000 metres

1900	9:18.2	Henri Deloge (Fra) Paris 22 Oct 1895
1915	8:36.9	Hannes Kolehmainen (Fin) 12 Jul 1912
1930	8:20.4	Paavo Nurmi (Fin) 13 Jul 1926
1945	8:01.2	Gunder Hägg (Swe) 28 Aug 1942
1960	7:52.8	Gordon Pirie (UK) 4 Sep 1956
1975	7:35.2	Brendan Foster (UK) 3 Aug 1974
1990	7:29.45	Saïd Aouita (Mor) 20 Aug 1989
	7:28.96	Moses Kiptanui (Ken) 16 Aug 1992
1994	7:25.11	Noureddine Morceli (Alg) 2 Aug

Most: 4 Paavo Nurmi (Fin) 8:28.6 - 8:20.4 (1922-6)

5000 metres

1900	15:20.0	Charles Bennett (UK) 22 Jul 1900
1915	14:36.6	Hannes Kolehmainen (Fin) 10 Jul 1912
1930	14:28.2	Paavo Nurmi (Fin) 19 Jun 1924
1945	13:58.1	Gunder Hägg (Swe) 20 Sep 1942
1960	13:35.0	Vladimir Kuts (USSR) 13 Oct 1957
1975	13:13.0	Emiel Puttemans (Bel) 20 Sep 1972

1990	12:58.39	Saïd Aouita (Mor) 22 Jul 1987
	12:56.96	Haile Gebrselassie (Eth) 4 Jun 1994
	12:55.30	Moses Kiptanui (Ken) 8 Jun 1995
Most:	4 Vladimir Kuts (USSR) 13:56.6-13:35.0 (1954-7)	
	4 Ron Clarke (Aus) 13:34.4 - 13:16.6 (1965-6)	

10 000 metres

1900	31:40.0	Walter George (UK) 28 Jul 1884
1915	30:58.8	Jean Bouin (Fra) 16 Nov 1911
1930	30:06.1	Paavo Nurmi (Fin) 31 Aug 1924
1945	29:35.4	Viljo Heino (Fin) 25 Aug 1944
1960	28:18.8	Pyotr Bolotnikov (USSR) 5 Oct 1960
1975	27:30.80	David Bedford (UK) 13 Jul 1973
1990	27:08.23	Arturo Barrios (Mex) 18 Aug 1989
	27:07.91	Richard Chelimo (Ken) 5 Jul 1993
	26:58.38	Yobes Ondieki (Ken) 10 Jul 1993
	26:52.23	William Sigei (Ken) 22 Jul 1994
	26:43.53	Haile Gebrselassie (Eth) 5 Jun 1995
Most:	5 Emil Zátopek (Cs) 29:28.2 - 28:54.2 (1949-54)	

Marathon

Note that records are not officially recognised for the marathon, for which times are affected by the nature of the road courses. The distance of 26 miles 385 yards (42.195 km) was that used for the race at the 1908 Olympic Games, run from Windsor to the White City stadium, and which became standard from 1924. *Best times:*

1915	2:36:06.6	Alexis Ahlgren (Swe) 31 May 1913
1930	2:29:01.8	Al Michelsen (USA) 12 Oct 1925
1945	2:26:42	Sohn Kee-chung (Kor) 3 Nov 1935
1960	2:15:16.2	Abebe Bikila (Eth) 10 Sep 1960
1975	2:08:33.6	Derek Clayton (Aus) 30 May 1969
1990	2:06:50	Belayneh Dinsamo (Eth) 17 Apr 1988
Most:	4 Jim Peters (UK) 2:20:42.2 - 2:17:39.4 (1952-4)	

3000 metres steeplechase

1930	9:21.8 u	Toivo Loukola (Fin) 4 Aug 1928
1945	8:59.6 u	Erik Elmsäter (Swe) 4 Aug 1944
1960	8:31.4	Zdzislaw Krzyszkowiak (Pol) 26 Jun 1960
1975	8:09.70	Anders Gärderud (Swe) 1 Jul 1975
1990	8:05.35	Peter Koech (Ken) 4 Jul 1989
	8:02.08	Moses Kiptanui (Ken) 19 Aug 1992
Most:	4 Anders Gärderud (Swe) 8:20.7 - 8:08.02 (1972-6)	

110 metres hurdles (y = 120 yards 109.73m time)

1900	15.4y	Stephen Chase (USA) 28 Sep 1895
1915	15.0	Forrest Smithson (USA) 25 Jul 1908
1930	14.4y	Earl Thomson (USA) 29 May 1920
	14.4	Eric Wennström (Swe) 25 Aug 1929
	14.4y	Stephen Anderson (USA) 23 Aug 1930
1945	13.7	Forrest Towns (USA) 27 Aug 1936
	13.7	Fred Wolcott (USA) 29 Jun 1941
1960	13.2	Martin Lauer (FRG) 7 Jul 1959 (13.56 auto)
	13.2	Lee Calhoun (USA) 21 Aug 1960
1975	13.0y	Rod Milburn (USA) 25 Jun 1971
		Rod Milburn (USA) 20 Jun 1973
	13.0	Guy Drut (Fra) 22 Aug 1975

	13.24	Rod Milburn (USA) 7 Sep 1972
1990	12.92	Roger Kingdom (USA) 16 Aug 1989
	12.91	Colin Jackson (UK) 20 Aug 1993
Most:	6 Forrest Towns (USA) 14.1 - 13.7 (1936)	
	6 Rod Milburn (USA) 13.2 - 13.0y/13.24 (1971-5)	

400 metres hurdles (y = 440 yards time)

1900	57.2	Godfrey Shaw (UK) 12 Aug 1891
1915	54.6y u	William Meanix (USA) 16 Jul 1915
1930	52.0	F Morgan Taylor (USA) 5 Jul 1928
1945	50.6	Glenn Hardin (USA) 26 Jul 1934
1960	49.2	Glenn Davis (USA) 6 Aug 1958
	49.3y	Gert Potgieter (SAf) 16 Apr 1960
1975	47.82	John Akii-Bua (Uga) 2 Sep 1972
1990	47.02	Edwin Moses (USA) 31 Aug 1983
	46.78	Kevin Young (USA) 6 Aug 1992
Most:	4 Edwin Moses (USA) 47.63 - 47.02 (1976-83)	

High jump

1900	1.97m	Michael Sweeney (USA) 21 Sep 1895
1915	2.01m	Edward Beeson (USA) 2 May 1914
1930	2.03m	Harold Osborn (USA) 27 May 1924
1945	2.11m	Lester Steers (USA) 17 Jun 1941
1960	2.22m	John Thomas (USA) 1 Jul 1960
1975	2.30m	Dwight Stones (USA) 11 Jul 1973
1990	2.44m	Javier Sotomayor (Cub) 29 Jul 1989
	2.45m	Javier Sotomayor (Cub) 27 Jul 1993
Most:	6 Valeriy Brumel (USSR) 2.23 - 2.28 (1961-3)	
	4 John Thomas (USA) 2.17 - 2.22 (1960)	

Pole vault

1900	3.62m	Raymond Clapp (USA) 16 Jun 1898
1915	4.02m	Marcus Wright (USA) 8 Jun 1912
1930	4.30m	Lee Barnes (USA) 28 Apr 1930
1945	4.77m	Cornelius Warmerdam (USA) 23 May 1942 (and 4.78m indoors 20 Mar 1943)
1960	4.82m u	Bob Gutowski (USA) 15 Jun 1957
	4.80m	Don Bragg (USA) 2 Jul 1960
1975	5.65m	Dave Roberts (USA) 28 Mar 1975
1990	6.06m	Sergey Bubka (USSR) 10 Jul 1988
	6.07m	Sergey Bubka (USSR) 6 May 1991
	6.08m	Sergey Bubka (USSR) 9 Jun 1991
	6.10m	Sergey Bubka (USSR) 5 Aug 1991
	6.11m	Sergey Bubka (Ukr) 13 Jun 1992
	6.12m	Sergey Bubka (Ukr) 30 Aug 1992
	6.13m	Sergey Bubka (Ukr) 19 Sep 1992
	6.14m	Sergey Bubka (Ukr) 31 Jul 1994
Most:	17 Sergey Bubka (USSR) 5.85 - 6.14 (1984-94)	
	9 John Pennel (USA) 4.95 - 5.44 (1963-9) (five u)	
	7 Cornelius Warmerdam (USA) 4.57 - 4.77 (1940-2)	
	6 Bob Seagren (USA) 5.32 - 5.63 (1966-72)	
	5 Thierry Vigneron (Fra) 5.75 - 5.91 (1980-4)	

Long jump

1900	7.51m	Peter O'Connor (Ire) 29 Aug 1900
1915	7.61m	Peter O'Connor (Ire) 5 Aug 1901
1930	7.93m	Silvio Cator (Haiti) 9 Sep 1928
1945	8.13m	Jesse Owens (USA) 25 May 1935
1960	8.21m	Ralph Boston (USA) 12 Aug 1960

1975	8.90mA	Bob Beamon (USA) 18 Oct 1968
1990		as above
	8.95m	Mike Powell (USA) 30 Aug 1991
	8.96mA	Iván Pedroso (Cub) 29 Jul 1995
Most:	6 Ralph Boston (USA) 8.21 - 8.35 (1960-5)	
	5 Peter O'Connor (Ire) 7.51 - 7.61 (1900-1)	

Triple jump

1900	14.78m	Edwin Bloss (USA) 16 Sep 1893
1915	15.52m	Daniel Ahearne (USA) 30 May 1911
1930	15.52m	also Anthony Winter (Aus) 12 Jul 1924
1945	16.00m	Naoto Tajima (Jap) 6 Aug 1936
1960	17.03m	Jozef Schmidt (Pol) 5 Aug 1960
1975	17.89mA	João Carlos de Oliveira (Bra) 15 Oct 1975
1990	17.97m	Willie Banks (USA) 16 Jun 1985
	17.98m	Jonathan Edwards (UK) 18 Jul 1995
Most:	5 Adhemar Ferreira da Silva (Bra) 16.00 - 16.56 (1951-5)	

Shot

1900	14.75m	George Gray (Can) 1 Aug 1898
1915	15.54m	Ralph Rose (USA) 21 Aug 1909
1930	16.04m	Emil Hirschfeld (Ger) 26 Aug 1928
1945	17.40m	Jack Torrance (USA) 5 Aug 1934
1960	20.06m	Bill Nieder (USA) 12 Aug 1960
1975	22.86m	Brian Oldfield (USA) 10 May 1975 (professional)
	22.02m	George Woods (USA) 8 Feb 1974 (indoors)
	21.82m	Al Feuerbach (USA) 5 May 1973
1990	23.12m	Randy Barnes (USA) 19 May 1990
Most:	15 Parry O'Brien (USA) 18.00 - 19.30 (1953-9)	
	10 Dallas Long (USA) 19.25 - 20.68 (1959-64)	
	7 George Gray (USA) 13.76 - 14.75 (1889-98)	
	7 Ralph Rose (USA) 14.81 - 15.54 (1904-9)	
	5 Jack Torrance (USA) 16.30 - 17.40 (1934)	

Discus

1915	47.85mu	Armas Taipale (Fin) 20 Jul 1913
1930	51.73m	Paul Jessup (USA) 23 Aug 1930
1945	53.34m	Adolfo Consolini (Ita) 26 Oct 1941
1960	59.91m	Edmund Piatkowski (Pol) 14 Jun 1959
	59.91m	Rink Babka (USA) 12 Aug 1960
1975	69.08m	John Powell (USA) 4 May 1975
	70.38mu	Jay Silvester (USA) 16 May 1971
1990	74.08m	Jürgen Schult (GDR) 6 Jun 1986
Most:	6 Jay Silvester (USA) 60.56 - 70.38 (1961-71)	
	5 Martin Sheridan (USA) from 2.5m circle 36.77 - 43.69 (1901-5)	
	4 Fortune Gordien (USA) 56.46 - 59.28 (1949-53)	
	4 Al Oerter (USA) 61.10 - 62.94 (1962-4)	
	4 Mac Wilkins (USA) 69.18 - 70.86 (1976)	

Hammer

1900	51.61m	John Flanagan (USA) 29 Sep 1900
1915	57.77m	Pat Ryan (USA) 17 Aug 1913
1930	as above	
1945	59.00m	Erwin Blask (Ger) 27 Aug 1938
	59.55mu	Pat O'Callaghan (Ire) 22 Aug 1937
1960	70.33m	Hal Connolly (USA) 12 Aug 1960

1975	79.30m	Walter Schmidt (FRG) 14 Aug 1975
1990	86.74m	Yuriy Sedykh (USSR) 30 Aug 1986
Most:	19 John Flanagan (USA) 44.46 - 56.19 (1895-1909)	
	7 Hal Connolly (USA) 66.71 - 71.26 (1956-65)	
	7 Mikhail Krivonosov (USSR) 63.34 - 67.32 (1954-6)	
	7 James Mitchell (USA) 36.40 - 44.21 (1886-92)	
	6 Yuriy Sedykh (USSR) 80.38 - 86.74 (1980-6)	

Javelin - old specification

1900	49.32m	Eric Lemming (Swe) 18 Jun 1899
1915	64.81mu	Jonni Myyrä (Fin) 18 Jul 1915
1930	72.93m	Matti Järvinen (Fin) 14 Sep 1930
1945	78.70m	Yrjö Nikkanen (Fin) 11 Oct 1938
1960	86.04m	Albert Cantello (USA) 5 Jun 1959
1975	94.08m	Klaus Wolfermann (FRG) 5 May 1973
Last	104.80m	Uwe Hohn (GDR) 20 Jul 1984
Most:	10 Matti Järvinen (Fin) 71.57 - 77.23 (1930-6)	
	9 Eric Lemming (Swe) 49.32 - 62.32 (1899- 1912)	
	5 Jonni Myrrä(Fin) 63.29 - 68.56 (1914-25)	

- new specification introduced 1987

1990	89.58m	Steve Backley (UK) 2 Jul 1990
	89.66mR	Jan Zelezny (Cs) 14 Jul 1990
	90.98mR	Steve Backley (UK) 20 Jul 1990
	91.98mR	Seppo Räty (Fin) 6 May 1991
	96.96mR	Seppo Räty (Fin) 2 Jun 1991

Performances marked R were made with a javelin with a roughened surface, banned in 1991, when Backley's 89.58 was reinstated as the world record.

	91.46m	Steve Backley (UK) 25 Jan 1992
	94.74m *	Jan Zelezny (Cs) 4 Jul 1992
	95.54m	Jan Zelezny (Cze) 6 Apr 1993
	95.66m	Jan Zelezny (Cze) 26 Aug 1993

* not recognised due to javelin specification

Decathlon - all rescored on the 1984 Tables

1915	6564u	Jim Thorpe (USA) 13/15 Jul 1912
1930	6865	Akilles Järvinen (Fin) 19/20 Jul 1930
1945	7254	Glenn Morris (USA) 7/8 Aug 1936
1960	7982	Rafer Johnson (USA) 8/9 Jul 1960
1975	8420	Bruce Jenner (USA) 9/10 Aug 1975
1990	8847	Daley Thompson (UK) 8/9 Aug 1984
	8891	Dan O'Brien (USA) 4/5 Sep 1992

(100m: 10.43w, long jump: 8.08m, shot: 16.69m, high jump: 2.07m, 400m: 48.51, 110m hurdles: 13.98, discus: 48.56m, pole vault: 5.00m, javelin: 62.58m, 1500m: 4:42.10)

| **Most:** | 4 Paavo Yrjölä (Fin) 6460 - 6700 (1926-30) | |
| | 4 Daley Thompson (UK) 8648 - 8847 (1980-4) | |

4 x 100 metres relay

1915	42.3	Germany 8 Jul 1912
1930	40.8	Germany 2 Sep 1928
	40.8	four other times
1945	39.8	USA 9 Aug 1936
1960	39.59	USA 1 Dec 1956
1975	38.19	USA 10 Sep 1972
1990	37.79	France 1 Sep 1990
	37.79	Santa Monica TC (USA) 3 Aug 1991
	37.67	USA 7 Aug 1991
	37.50	USA 1 Sep 1991

37.40   USA 8 Aug 1992
(Michael Marsh, Leroy Burrell, Dennis
Mitchell, Carl Lewis)
37.40   USA 21 Aug 1993
(Jon Drummond, Andre Cason, Dennis
Mitchell, Leroy Burrell)

4 x 400 metres relay

1915	3:16.6	USA 15 Jul 1912
1930	3:14.2	USA 5 Aug 1928
1945	3:08.2	USA 7 Aug 1932
1960	3:02.37	USA 8 Sep 1960
1975	2:56.16A	USA 20 Oct 1968
1990	2:56.16	USA 1 Oct 1988
	2:55.74	USA 8 Aug 1992

(Andrew Valmon, Quincy Watts, Michael
Johnson, Steve Lewis)
2:54.29   USA 22 Aug 1993
(Andrew Valmon, Quincy Watts, Butch
Reynolds, Michael Johnson)

Other current relay world records

4 x 200m   1:18.68 Santa Monica Track Club (USA)
               17 Apr 1994
(Michael Marsh, Leroy Burrell, Floyd Heard, Carl Lewis)
4 x 800m   7:03.89 UK 30 Aug 1982
(Peter Elliott, Garry Cook, Steve Cram, Sebastian Coe)
4 x 1500m 14:38.8 FR Germany 17 Aug 1977
(Thomas Wessinghage, Harald Hudak, Michael
Lederer, Karl Fleschen)

Women

Women's athletics effectively started in the 1920s, but
1915 'records' are shown for some events, recognising
the efforts of dedicated early pioneers. Women's
records were first accepted by the Féderation Sportive
Féminine Internationale (FSFI), from its formation in
1921. The FSFI merged with the IAAF in 1936.

Women's records at distances from 1500m upwards
have only been added to the official lists over the past
two decades. The years that the IAAF first officially
recognised records for such events are shown as IAAF
19... (e.g. 1984 for 1000m).

100 metres

1915	13.1	Nina Popova (Russia) 22 Aug 1913
1930	12.0	Elizabeth Robinson (USA) 2 Jun 1928
	12.0	Myrtle Cook (Can) 2 Jul 1928
	12.0	Tollien Schuurman (Hol) 31 Aug 1930
1945	11.5 u	Helen Stephens (USA) 15 May 1936
	11.5	Helen Stephens (USA) 10 Aug 1936
1960	11.3	Shirley Strickland (Aus) 4 Aug 1955
	11.3	Vera Krepkina (USSR) 13 Sep 1958
1975	10.8	Renate Stecher (GDR) 20 Jul 1973
	11.07	Renate Stecher (GDR) 2 Sep 1972
1990	10.49	Florence Griffith-Joyner (USA) 16 Jul 1988

Most: 10 Stanislawa Walasiewicz* (Pol) 11.9 - 11.6
          (1932-7)
        9 Renate Stecher (née Meissner) (GDR) 11.0 -
          10.8 (1970-3)

* Walasiewicz's femininity has subsequently been questioned.

200 metres (y = 220 yards time)

1930	25.2y	Nellie Halstead (UK) 16 Aug 1930
	24.7 #	Kitomi Hitomi (Jap) 19 May 1929
1945	24.1	Helen Stephens (USA) 19 Aug 1936
	23.6	Stanislawa Walasiewicz* (Pol) 4 Aug 1935
1960	22.9	Wilma Rudolph (USA) 9 Jul 1960
1975	22.21	Irena Szewinska (Pol) 13 Jun 1974 (22.0 hand)
1990	21.34	Florence Griffith-Joyner (USA) 29 Sep 1988

Most: 4 Irena Szewinska (née Kirszenstein) (Pol)
        22.7 - 22.21 1965-74
      4 Marita Koch (GDR) 22.06 - 21.71 (1978-84)
      4 Eileen Edwards (UK) 26.2y = 25.3 (1924-7)

 # straight track

400 metres IAAF 1957 (y = 440 yards time)

1930	59.0 #	Kinue Hitomi (Jap) 5 May 1928
	59.2y	Marion King (USA) 13 Jul 1929
1945	56.8y	Nellie Halstead (UK) 9 Jul 1932
1960	53.0 u	Shin Keum Dan (NKo) 22 Oct 1960
	53.4	Mariya Itkina (USSR) 12 Sep 1959
1975	49.9	Irena Szewinska (Pol) 22 Jun 1974
	50.14	Riitta Salin (Fin) 4 Sep 1974
1990	47.60	Marita Koch (GDR) 6 Oct 1985

Most: 7 Marita Koch (GDR) 49.19 - 47.60 (1978-85)
      5 Shin Keum Dan (NKo) 53.0 - 51.2 (1962-4)

 # nearly straight track

800 metres (y = 880 yards time)

1930	2:18.2y	Gladys Lunn (UK) 16 Aug 1930
1945	2:12.0 u	Yekdokiya Vasilyeva (USSR) 5 Aug 1943
1960	2:04.3	Lyudmila Lysenko/Shevtsova (USSR) 3 Jul 1960
		Lyudmila Lysenko/Shevtsova (USSR) 7 Sep 1960
1975	1:57.48	Svetla Zlateva (Bul) 24 Aug 1973
1990	1:53.28	Jarmila Kratochvílová (Cs) 26 Jul 1983

Most: 7 Nina Otkalenko (née Pletnyova) 2:12.0 -
      2:05.0 (1951-5)

1000 metres IAAF 1984

| 1990 | 2:30.6 | Tatyana Providokhina (USSR) 20 Aug 1978 |
| | 2:30.67 | Christine Wachtel (GDR) 17 Aug 1990 |

1500 metres IAAF 1967

1930	5:18.2	Anna Mushkina (USSR) 19 Aug 1927
1945	4:38.0	Yevdokiya Vasilyeva (USSR) 17 Aug 1944
1960	4:25.0 u	Diane Leather (UK) 21 Sep 1955
1975	4:01.38	Lyudmila Bragina (USSR) 9 Sep 1972
1990	3:52.47	Tatyana Kazankina (USSR) 13 Aug 1980
	3:50.46	Qu Yunxia (Chn) 11 Sep 1993

Most: 4 Lyudmila Bragina (USSR) 4:06.9 - 4:01.38
      (1972)

1 mile   IAAF 1967
1945	5:15.3	Evelyne Forster (UK) 22 Jul 1939
1960	4:45.0	Diane Leather (UK) 21 Sep 1955
1975	4:28.5 ind	Francie Larrieu (USA) 3 Mar 1975
	4:28.8 u	Adrienne Beames (Aus) 7 Jan 1972
	4:29.5	Paola Pigni (Ita) 8 Aug 1973
1990	4:15.61	Paula Ivan (Rom) 10 Jul 1989

Most: 5 Diane Leather (UK) 5:07.6 - 4:45.0 (1953-5)

2000 metres   IAAF 1984
| 1990 | 5:28.69 | Maricica Puica (Rom) 11 Jul 1986 |
| | 5:25.36 | Sonia O'Sullivan (Ire) 8 Jul 1994 |

3000 metres   IAAF 1974
1975	8:46.6	Grete Waitz (Nor) 24 Jun 1975
1990	8:22.62	Tatyana Kazankina (USSR) 26 Aug 1984
	8:22.06	Zhang Linli (Chn) 12 Jun 1993
	8:12.19	Wang Junxia (Chn) 12 Sep 1993
	8:06.11	Wang Junxia (Chn) 13 Sep 1993

Most: 4 Paola Cacchi (née Pigni) (Ita) 9:42.8- 9:09.4 (1969-72)
7 3 Lyudmila Bragina (USSR) 8:53.0 - 8:27.12 (1972-6)

5000 metres   IAAF 1981
1975	15:48.5u	Adrienne Beames (Aus) 5 Jan 1972
1990	14:37.33	Ingrid Kristiansen (Nor) 5 Aug 1986
	14:36.45	Fernanda Ribeiro (Por) 15 Jul 1995

Most: 3 Ingrid Kristiansen (Nor) 15:28.43 -14:37.33 (1981-6)

10 000 metres   IAAF 1981
1975	34:01.4	Christa Vahlensieck (FRG) 20 Aug 1975
1990	30:13.74	Ingrid Kristiansen (Nor) 5 Jul 1986
	29:31.78	Wang Junxia (Chn) 8 Sep 1993

Marathon
Note that records are not officially recognised for the marathon, for which times are affected by the nature of the road courses. Best times:
1960	3:40:22	Violet Piercy (UK) 3 Oct 1926
1975	2:38:19	Jackie Hansen (USA) 1 Dec 1974
1990	2:21:06	Ingrid Kristiansen (Nor) 21 Apr 1985

Most: 4 Grete Waitz (Nor) 2:32:30 - 2:25:29 (1978-83)

80 metres hurdles
The standard women's hurdles distance was 80 metres, over seven flights of 2ft 6in (76cm) hurdles from 1927 until replaced by the 100m over eight flights of 2ft 9in (84cm) hurdles in 1969.
1930	12.1	Maj Jacobsson (Swe) 2 Sep 1930
1945	11.3	Claudia Testoni (Ita) 23 Jul 1939
	11.3	Claudia Testoni (Ita) 13 Aug 1939
	11.3	Fanny Blankers-Koen (Hol) 20 Sep 1942
1960	10.5	Gisela Birkmeyer (GDR) 24 Jul 1960
1969	10.2	Vera Korsakova (USSR) 16 Jun 1968
(auto)	10.39	Maureen Caird (Aus) 18 Oct 1968

Most: 6 Irina Press (USSR) 10.6 - 10.3 (1960-5)
5 Claudia Testoni (Ita) 11.6 - 11.3 (1938-9)

100 metres hurdles
Replaced the 80 metres hurdles in 1969
1975	12.3/12.68	Annelie Ehrhardt (GDR) 22 Jul 1973
	12.59	Annelie Ehrhardt (GDR) 8 Sep 1972
1990	12.21	Yordanka Donkova (Bul) 20 Aug 1988

Most: 6 Karin Balzer (GDR) 13.3 - 12.6 (1969-71)
5 Yordanka Donkova (Bul) 12.36 - 12.21 (1986-8)

400 metres hurdles   IAAF 1974
1975	56.51	Krystyna Kacperczyk (Pol) 13 Jul 1974
1990	52.94	Marina Styepanova (USSR) 17 Sep 1986
	52.74	Sally Gunnell (UK) 19 Aug 1993

Most: 3 Marina Styepanova (née Makeyeva) (USSR) 54.78 - 52.94 1979-86

High jump
1915	1.47m *	Margaret Belasco (UK) 6 Jun 1914
1930	1.625m *	Joan Belasco (UK) 27 May 1920
	1.60m	Carolina Gisolf (Hol) 18 Aug 1929
1945	1.71m	Fanny Blankers-Koen (Hol) 30 May 1943
1960	1.86m	Iolanda Balas (Rom) 10 Jul 1960
1975	1.95m	Rosemarie Witschas (GDR) 8 Sep 1974
1990	2.09m	Stefka Kostadinova (Bul) 30 Aug 1987

Most: 14 Iolanda Balas (Rom) 1.75 - 1.91 (1956-61)
7 Rosemarie Ackermann (née Witschas) (GDR) 1.94 - 2.00 (1974-7)

* in schools meetings, not subject to official measurements

Pole vault   IAAF 1995
	4.00mu	Zhang Chunzhen (Chn) 24 Mar 1991
	4.02mu	Zhang Chunzhen (Chn) 5 Jun 1991
	4.05mu	Zhang Chunzhen (Chn) 10 Aug 1991
	4.05m	Sun Caiyun (Chn) 21 May 1992
	4.11mu	Sun Caiyun (Chn) 21 Mar 1993
	4.12mu	Sun Caiyun (Chn) 22 Oct 1994
	4.12mu	Sun Caiyun (Chn) 24 Nov1994
	4.06m	Sun Caiyun (Chn) 26 May 1995
	4.07m	Cai Weiyun (Chn) 29 Apr 1995
	4.08m	Zhong Guiqing (Chn) 18 May 1995
	4.08m	Sun Caiyun (Chn) 18 May 1995
	4.10m	Dániela Bartová (Cze) 21 May 1995
	4.12m	Dániela Bartová (Cze) 18 Jun 1995
	4.13m	Dániela Bartová (Cze) 24 Jun 1995
	4.14m	Dániela Bartová (Cze) 2 Jul 1995
	4.15m	Dániela Bartová (Cze) 9 Jul 1995
	4.16m	Dániela Bartová (Cze) 14 Jul 1995
	4.17m	Dániela Bartová (Cze) 15 Jul 1995

Long jump
1915	5.00m	Ellen Hayes (USA) 7 Apr 1913
1930	5.98m	Kinue Hitomi (Jap) 20 May 1928
1945	6.25m	Fanny Blankers-Koen (Hol) 19 Sep 1943
1960	6.40m	Hildrun Claus (FRG) 7 Aug 1960
1975	6.84m	Heide Rosendahl (FRG) 3 Sep 1970
1990	7.52m	Galina Chistyakova (USSR) 11 Jun 1988

Most: 4 Tatyana Shchelkanova (USSR) 6.48 - 6.70 (1962-4)
4 Anisoara Cusmir (Rom) 7.15 - 7.43 (1982-3)

Triple jump

Official recognition from 1990.

1990	14.54m	Li Huirong (Chn) 25 Aug 1990
	14.95m	Inessa Kravets (Ukr) 10 Jun 1991
	14.97m	Yolanda Chen (Rus) 18 Jun 1993
	15.09m	Anna Biryukova (Rus) 21 Aug 1993

Shot

1930	12.85m	Grete Heublein (Ger) 21 Jul 1929
1945	14.89m	Tatyana Sevryukova (USSR) 14 Oct 1945
1960	17.78m	Tamara Press (USSR) 13 Aug 1960
1975	21.60m	Marianne Adam (GDR) 6 Aug 1975
1990	22.63m	Natalya Lisovskaya (USSR) 7 Jun 1987

Most: 14 Galina Zybina (USSR) 15.19 - 16.76 (1952-6)
10 Nadezhda Chizhova (USSR) 18.67 - 21.45 (1968-73)
9 Grete Heublein (Ger) 10.86 - 13.70 (1927-31)
6 Tamara Press (USSR) 17.25 - 18.59 (1959-65)
5 Ruth Lange (Ger) 10.84 - 11.52 (1927-8)

Discus

1930	39.62m	Halina Konopacka (Pol) 31 Jul 1928
1945	49.88m	Nina Dumbadze (USSR) 14 Aug 1944
1960	57.15m	Tamara Press (USSR) 12 Sep 1960
1975	70.20m	Faina Melnik (USSR) 20 Aug 1975
1990	76.80m	Gabriele Reinsch (GDR) 9 Jul 1988

Most: 11 Faina Melnik (USSR) 64.22 - 70.50 (1971-6)
10 Gisela Mauermayer (Ger) 44.34 - 48.31 (1935-6)
9 Jadwiga Wajsowna (Pol) 40.34 - 44.19 (1932-4)
7 Nina Dumbadze (USSR) 49.11 - 57.04 (1939-52)
6 Halina Konopacka (Pol) 31.24 - 39.62 (1925-8)
6 Tamara Press (USSR) 57.15 - 59.70 (1960-5)

Hammer IAAF 1995

61.96m	Larisa Baranova (Rus) 11 Feb 1990
64.44m	Alla Fyodorova (Rus) 24 Feb 1991
65.40m	Olga Kuzenkova (Rus) 4 Jun 1992
66.84m	Olga Kuzenkova (Rus) 23 Feb 1994
67.34mu	Svetlana Sudak (Bls) 5 Jun 1994
66.86m	Mihaela Melinte (Rom) 4 Mar 1995
67.08m	Olga Kuzenkova (Rus) 24 May 1995
68.16m	Olga Kuzenkova (Rus) 5 Jun 1995
68.16m	Olga Kuzenkova (Rus) 17 Jun 1995

Javelin

1930	42.32m	Elisabeth Schumann (Ger) 8 Aug 1930
1945	48.39mu	Lyudmila Anokina (USSR) 15 Sep 1945
1960	59.55m	Elvira Ozolina (USSR) 4 Jun 1960
1975	67.22m	Ruth Fuchs (GDR) 3 Sep 1974
1990	80.00m	Petra Felke (GDR) 9 Sep 1988

Most: 6 Ruth Fuchs (GDR) 65.06 - 69.96 (1972-80)
4 Elvira Ozolina (USSR) 57.92 - 61.38 (1960-4)

Heptathlon - scored on the 1984 Tables

1990   7291   Jackie Joyner (USA) 23/24 Sep 1988 (100m hurdles: 12.69, high jump: 1.86m, shot: 15.80m, 200m: 22.56, long jump: 7.27m, javelin: 45.66m, 800m: 2:08.51)

Most: 4 Ramona Neubert (GDR) 6670 - 6935 (1981-3)
4 Jackie Joyner-Kersee (USA) 7148 - 7291 (1986-8)

The heptathlon has been the standard women's multi-event competition since 1981.

Pentathlon

Until 1980 the pentathlon was the standard competition. The events changed several times, and the totals given are all rescored on the 1984 tables.

Most: 8 Irina Press (USSR) 4121 - 4602 (1959-64)
5 Aleksandra Chudina (USSR) 3564 - 4024 (1947-55)

4 x 100 metres relay

1930	48.4	Canada 5 Aug 1928
1945	46.4	Germany 8 Aug 1936
1960	44.51	USA 7 Sep 1960
1975	42.51	GDR 8 Sep 1974
1990	41.37	GDR 6 Oct 1985

(Silke Gladisch, Sabine Rieger, Ingrid Auerswald, Marlies Göhr)

4 x 400 metres relay IAAF 1969

1975	3:22.95	GDR 10 Sep 1972
1990	3:15.17	USSR 1 Oct 1988

(Tatyana Ledovskaya, Olga Nazarova, Maria Pinigina, Olga Bryzgina)

Other current relay world records

4 x 200m   1:28.15   GDR 9 Aug 1980
(Marlies Göhr, Romy Müller, Bärbel Wöckel, Marita Koch)
4 x 800m   7:50.17   USSR 5 Aug 1984
(Nadezhda Olizarenko, Lyubov Gurina, Lyudmila Borisova, Irina Podyalovskaya)

Marita Koch – perhaps the greatest woman athlete

World Indoor records

World indoor records have been recognized by the IAAF since 1 Jan 1987. Track performances around a turn must be made on a track no larger than 200 metres.

Event	Mark	Athlete (Nation)	Venue	Date
Men				
50 metres	5.61	Manfred Kokot (GDR)	Berlin	4 Feb 1973
	5.61	James Sanford (USA)	San Diego	20 Feb 1981
	5.55 #	Ben Johnson (Can)	Ottawa	31 Jan 1987
60 metres	6.41	Andre Cason (USA)	Madrid	14 Feb 1992
	6.41 #	Ben Johnson (Can)	Indianapolis	7 Mar 1987
200 metres	20.25	Linford Christie (UK)	Liévin	19 Feb 1995
400 metres	44.63	Michael Johnson (USA)	Atlanta	4 Mar 1995
800 metres	1:44.84	Paul Ereng (Ken)	Budapest	4 Mar 1989
1000 metres	2:15.26	Noureddine Morceli (Alg)	Birmingham	22 Feb 1992
1500 metres	3:34.16	Noureddine Morceli (Alg)	Seville	28 Feb 1991
1 mile	3:49.78	Eamonn Coghlan (Ire)	East Rutherford	27 Feb 1983
3000 metres	7:35.15	Moses Kiptanui (Ken)	Ghent	12 Feb 1995
5000 metres	13:20.4	Suleiman Nyambui (Tan)	New York	6 Feb 1981
50 metres hurdles	6.25	Mark McKoy (Can)	Kobe	5 Mar 1986
60 metres hurdles	7.30	Colin Jackson (UK)	Sindelfingen	6 Mar 1994
High jump	2.43	Javier Sotomayor (Cub)	Budapest	4 Mar 1989
Pole vault	6.15	Sergey Bubka (USSR)	Donetsk	21 Feb 1993
Long jump	8.79	Carl Lewis (USA)	New York	27 Jan 1984
Triple jump	17.77	Leonid Voloshin (Rus)	Grenoble	6 Feb 1994
Shot	22.66	Randy Barnes (USA)	Los Angeles	20 Jan 1989
35 lb weight	25.86	Lance Deal (USA)	Atlanta	4 Mar 1995
5000m walk	18:07.08	Mikhail Shchennikov (Rus)	Moscow	14 Feb 1995
4 x 200m relay	1:22.11	United Kingdom	Glasgow	3 Mar 1991
		(Linford Christie, Darren Braithwaite, Ade Mafe, John Regis)		
4 x 400m relay	3:03.05	Germany	Seville	10 Mar 1991
		(Rico Lieder, Jens Carlowitz, Karsten Just, Thomas Schönlebe)		
Heptathlon	6476	Dan O'Brien (USA)	Toronto	13/14 Mar 1993
		(6.67 60m, 7.84 LJ, 16.02 SP, 2.13 HJ, 7.85 60mh, 5.20 PV, 2:57.96 1000m)		
Women				
50 metres	5.96	Irina Privalova (Rus)	Madrid	9 Feb 1995
60 metres	6.92	Irina Privalova (Rus)	Madrid	11 Feb 1993
	6.92	Irina Privalova (Rus)	Madrid	9 Feb 1995
200 metres	21.87	Merlene Ottey (Jam)	Liévin	13 Feb 1993
400 metres	49.59	Jarmila Kratochvilová (Cs)	Milan	7 Mar 1982
800 metres	1:56.40	Christine Wachtel (GDR)	Vienna	13 Feb 1988
1000 metres	2:33.93u	Inna Yevseyeva (Ukr)	Moscow	7 Feb 1992
1500 metres	4:00.27	Doina Melinte (Rom)	East Rutherford	9 Feb 1990
1 mile	4:17.14	Doina Melinte (Rom)	East Rutherford	9 Feb 1990
3000 metres	8:33.82	Elly van Hulst (Hol)	Budapest	4 Mar 1989
5000 metres	15:03.17	Liz McColgan (UK)	Birmingham	22 Feb 1992
50 metres hurdles	6.58	Cornelia Oschkenat (GDR)	East Berlin	20 Feb 1988
60 metres hurdles	7.69	Lyudmila Narozhilenko (USSR)	Chelyabinsk	4 Feb 1990
	drugs dq 7.63	Lyudmila Narozhilenko (Rus)	Seville	4 Mar 1993
High jump	2.07	Heike Henkel (Ger)	Karlsruhe	9 Feb 1992
Pole vault	4.15	Sun Caiyun (China)	Erfurt	15 Feb 1995
Long jump	7.37	Heike Drechsler (GDR)	Vienna	13 Feb 1988
Triple jump	15.03	Yolanda Chen (Rus)	Barcelona	11 Mar 1995
Shot	22.50	Helena Fibingerová (Cs)	Jablonec	19 Feb 1977
3000m walk	11:44.00	Alina Ivanova (Ukr)	Moscow	7 Feb 1992
4 x 200m relay	1:32.55	SC Eintracht Hamm (FRG)	Dortmund	20 Feb 1988
		(Helga Arendt, Silke-Beate Knoll, Mechthild Kluth, Gisela Kinzel)		
4 x 400m relay	3:27.22	Germany	Seville	10 Mar 1991
		(Sandra Seuser, Katrin Schreiter, Annett Hesselbarth, Grit Breuer)		
Pentathlon	4991	Irina Belova (Rus)	Berlin	14/15 Feb 1992
		(8.22 60mh, 1.93 HJ, 13.25 SP, 6.67 LJ, 2:10.26 800m)		

u - unratified mark

 # The IAAF stripped Johnson of his records in January 1990, after he had admitted long-term steroid use

World Records and Bests – Long Distance Track Events – Men

	hr:min:sec	Name	Venue	Date
15 km	42:34.0	Arturo Barrios (Mex)	La Flèche	30 Mar 1991
10 miles	45:57.6	Jos Hermens (Hol)	Papendal	14 Sep 1975
20 km	56:55.6	Arturo Barrios (Mex)	La Flèche	30 Mar 1991
15 miles	1:11:43.1	Bill Rodgers (USA)	Saratoga, Cal.	21 Feb 1979
25 km	1:13:55.8	Toshihiko Seko (Jap)	Christchurch, NZ	22 Mar 1981
30 km	1:29:18.8	Toshihiko Seko (Jap)	Christchurch, NZ	22 Mar 1981
20 miles	1:39:14.4	Jack Foster (NZ)	Hamilton, NZ	15 Aug 1971
30 miles	2:42:00	Jeff Norman (UK)	Timperley, Cheshire	7 Jun 1980
50 km	2:48:06	Jeff Norman (UK)	Timperley, Cheshire	7 Jun 1980
40 miles	3:48:35	Don Ritchie (UK)	Hendon, London	16 Oct 1982
50 miles	4:51:49	Don Ritchie (UK)	Hendon, London	12 Mar 1983
100 km	6:10:20	Don Ritchie (UK)	Crystal Palace	28 Oct 1978
150 km	10:36:42	Don Ritchie (UK)	Crystal Palace	15 Oct 1977
100 miles	11:30:51	Don Ritchie (UK)	Crystal Palace	15 Oct 1977
200 km	15:11:10#	Yiannis Kouros (Gre)	Montauban, Fra	15-16 Mar 1985
200 miles	27:48:35	Yiannis Kouros (Gre)	Montauban, Fra	15-16 Mar 1985
500 km	60:23.00	Yiannis Kouros (Gre)	Colac, Aus	26-29 Nov 1984
500 miles	105:42:09	Yiannis Kouros (Gre)	Colac, Aus	26-30 Nov 1984
1000 km	136:17:00	Yiannis Kouros (Gre)	Colac, Aus	26-31 Nov 1984
1500 km	12d 21:06:43	Gary Parsons (Aus)	Nanango, Qld	10-23 Mar 1994
1000 mile	13d 17:37:21	Gary Parsons (Aus)	Nanango, Qld	10-24 Mar 1994

	kilometres			
1 hour	21.101	Arturo Barrios (Mex)	La Flèche	30 Mar 1991
2 hrs	37.994	Jim Alder (UK)	Walton-on-Thames	17 Oct 1964
24 hrs	285.362	Yiannis Kouros (Gre)	Surgères, Fra	6-7 May 1995
48 hrs	470.781	Yiannis Kouros (Gre)	Surgères, Fra	6-8 May 1995
6 days	1030.000	Jean-Gilles Bousiquet (Fra)	La Rochelle (indoors)	16-23 Nov 1992
Outdoors	1023.200	Yiannis Kouros (Gre)	Colac, Aus	26 Nov-1 Dec 1984

 # Running watch time, no stopped times taken.

Long Distance Road Bests

Where superior to track bests and run on properly measured road courses

	hr:min:sec	Name	Venue	Date
10 miles	45.38	Ismael Kirui (Ken)	Washington, DC	9 Apr 1995
15 km	42:22	Todd Williams (USA)	Washington, DC	11 Mar 1995
Half mar	59:47	Moses Tanui (Ken)	Milan	3 Apr 1993
30 km	1:28:40	Steve Jones (UK)	Chicago	10 Oct 1985
20 miles	1:35:22	Steve Jones (UK)	Chicago	10 Oct 1985
30 miles	2:37:31	Thompson Magawana (RSA)	Claremont-Kirstenbosch	12 Apr 1988
50km	2:43:38	Thompson Magawana (RSA)	Claremont-Kirstenbosch	12 Apr 1988
40 miles	3:45:39	Andy Jones (Can)	Houston	23 Feb 1991
50 miles	4:50:21	Bruce Fordyce (RSA)	London-Brighton	25 Sep 1983
1000 miles	10d:10:30:35	Yiannis Kouros (Gre)	New York	21-30 May 1988

	kilometres			
24 hours	286.463	Yiannis Kouros (Gre)	New York	28-29 Sep 1985
6 days	1028.370	Yiannis Kouros (Gre)	New York	21-26 May 1988

It should be noted that road times must be assessed with care as course conditions can vary considerably.

Uncertain measurement

10 miles	45:13	Ian Stewart (UK)	Stoke-on-Trent	8 May 1977

World records and bests – Long Distance Track Events – Women

	hr:min:sec	Name	Venue	Date
15 km	49:44.0	Silvana Cruciata (Ita)	Rome	4 May 1981
10 miles	54:21.8	Lorraine Moller (NZ)	Auckland	9 Jan 1993
20 km	1:06:48.8	Isumi Maki (Jap)	Amagasaki	19 Sep 1993
25 km	1:29:29.2	Karolina Szabó (Hun)	Budapest	23 Apr 1988
30 km	1:47:05.6	Karolina Szabó (Hun)	Budapest	23 Apr 1988
20 miles	1:59:09 #	Chantal Langlacé (Fra)	Amiens	3 Sep 1983

30 miles	3:19:41	Carolyn Hunter-Rowe (UK)	Barry, Wales	7 Mar 1993
50 km	3:20:23	Ann Trason (USA)	Santa Rosa, Cal.	18 Mar 1995
40 miles	4:26:43	Carolyn Hunter-Rowe (UK)	Barry, Wales	7 Mar 1993
50 miles	6:07:58	Linda Meadows (Aus)	Burwood, Vic	18 Jun 1994
100 km	7:50:09	Ann Trason (USA)	Hayward, Cal.	3-4 Aug 1991
100 miles	14:29:44	Ann Trason (USA)	Santa Rosa, Cal.	18-19 Mar 1989
200 km	19:28:48	Eleanor Adams (UK)	Melbourne	19-20 Aug 1989
200 miles	39:09:03	Hilary Walker (UK)	Blackpool	5-7 Nov 1988
500 km	77:53:46	Eleanor Adams (UK)	Colac, Aus.	13-15 Nov 1989
500 miles	130:59:58	Sandra Barwick (NZ)	Campbelltown, Aus	18-23 Nov 1990
	kilometres			
1 hour	18.084	Silvana Cruciata (Ita)	Rome	4 May 1981
2 hrs	32.652	Chantal Langlacé (Fra)	Amiens	3 Sep 1983
24 hrs	240.169	Eleanor Adams (UK)	Melbourne	19-20 Aug 1989
48 hrs	366.512	Hilary Walker (UK)	Blackpool	5-7 Nov 1988
6 days	883.631	Sandra Barwick (NZ)	Campbelltown, NSW	18-24 Nov 1990

Timed on one running watch only

Indoors where superior to track best

200 km	19:00:31	Eleanor Adams (UK)	Milton Keynes	3/4 Feb 1990

Long Distance Road Bests

Run on properly measured road courses.

	hr:min:sec	*Name*	*Venue*	*Date*
10 km	30:38	Liz McColgan (UK)	Orlando	12 Feb 1989
15 km	46:57	Elana Meyer (SAf)	Cape Town	2 Nov 1991
10 miles	51:40	Rose Cheruiyot (Ken)	Washington	9 Apr 1995
	50:31 u	Ingrid Kristiansen (Nor)	Amsterdam	11 Oct 1989
Half mar	1:07:11	Liz McColgan (UK)	Tokyo (33m drop)	26 Jan 1992
	1:06:40u	Ingrid Kristiansen (Nor)	Sandnes	5 Apr 1987
25 km	1:21:21	Ingrid Kristiansen (Nor)	London	10 May 1987
30 km	1:38:27	Ingrid Kristiansen (Nor)	London	10 May 1987
20 miles	1:46:04	Ingrid Kristiansen (Nor)	London	10 May 1987
30 miles	3:01:16	Frith van der Merwe (SAf)	Claremont - Kirstenbosch	25 Mar 1989
50 km	3:08:13	Frith van der Merwe (SAf)	Claremont - Kirstenbosch	25 Mar 1989
40 miles	4:26:13	Ann Trason (USA)	Houston	23 Feb 1991
50 miles	5:40:18	Ann Trason (USA)	Houston	23 Feb 1991
100 km	7:09:44	Ann Trason USA	Amiens	27 Sep 1993
100 miles	13:47.41	Ann Trason (USA)	New York	4 May 1991
200 km	19:08:21 *	Sigrid Lomsky (Ger)	Basel	1-2 May 1993
500 km	82:10 #	Annie van der Meer (Hol)	Paris-Colmar	8-11 Jun 1983
1000 km	7d 01:11:00	Sandra Barwick (NZ)	New York	16-23 Sep 1991
1000 miles	12d 14:38:40	Sandra Barwick (NZ)	New York	16-29 Sep 1991
	kilometres			
24 hours	243.657	Sigrid Lomsky (Ger)	Basel	1-2 May 1993

* *time at 201km)on one running watch, # for 518km*

It should be noted that road times must be assessed with care as course conditions can vary considerably.

Walking

The IAAF currently ratify records at just four track walking events - at 20, 30 and 50 kilometres and at 2 hours. At one time their list embraced a large number of distances, but the shorter distance records were dropped due in particular to difficulties in judging whether walkers were maintaining the strict disciplines of the event. The standard road walking events have become established at 20 and 50 kilometres.

World Records and Bests – Men's Track Walks

	hr:min:sec			
1500m	5:12.0	Antanas Grigaliunas (Lit)	Vilnius	12 May 1990
1 mile	5:33.53i	Tim Lewis (USA)	New York	5 Feb 1988
	5:36.9	Antanas Grigaliunas (Lit)	Vilnius	12 May 1990
3000m	10:47.11	Giovanni De Benedictis (Ita)	San Giovanni Valdermo	19 May 1990
5000m	18:07.08i	Mikhail Shchennikov (Rus)	Moscow	14 Feb 1995
	18:17.22	Robert Korzeniowski (Pol)	Reims	3 Jul 1992

10 km	38:02.60	Jozef Pribilinec (Cs)	Banská Bystrica	30 Aug 1985
15 km	58:22.4	Jozef Pribilinec (Cs)	Hildesheim	6 Sep 1986
20 km	1:17:25.6	Bernardo Segura (Mex)	Fana	7 May 1994
25 km	1:44:54.0	Maurizio Damilano (Ita)	San Donato Milanese	5 May 1985
30 km	2:01:44.1	Maurizio Damilano (Ita)	Cuneo, Italy	4 Oct 1992
40 km	2:55:54.0	Raúl Gonzales (Mex)	Fana	2 May 1980
50 km	3:41:28.2	René Piller (Fra)	Fana	7 May 1994
100 km	9:16:32.3	Fréderic Marie (Fra)	Etrechy	19 Apr 1987
	kilometres			
1 hour	15.577	Bernardo Segura (Mex)	Fana	7 May 1994
2 hrs	29.572	Maurizio Damilano (Ita)	Cuneo, Italy	4 Oct 1992

*i indoors, * unratified*

World Bests – Road Walks

Where superior to track bests and walked on properly measured road courses.

	hr:min:sec			
25 km	1:42:14	Andrey Perlov (USSR)	Sochi	19 Feb 1989
35 km	2:28:30	Robert Korzeniowski (Pol)	Eschborn	12 Jun 1993
40 km	2:53:59	Andrey Perlov (USSR)	Leningrad	5 Aug 1989
50 km	3:37:41	Andrey Perlov (USSR)	Leningrad	5 Aug 1989
100 km	8:58:12	Gérard Lelièvre (Fra)	Laval	7 Oct 1984
200 km	19:55:07	Zbigniew Klapa (Pol)	Chapelle	22-23 Oct 1983
	kilometres			
24 hours	228.930	Jesse Casteneda (USA)	Albuquerque	18-19 Sep 1976

Women's World Records and Bests – Track Walks

The IAAF have ratified records for women's track walking at 5000m and 10,000m since 1981.

	hr:min:sec			
1500m	5:50.51	Kerry Saxby (Aus)	Sydney	20 Jan 1991
1 mile	6:16.72i	Sada Eidikite (Lit)	Kaunas	24 Feb 1990
	6:19.39	Ileana Salvador (Ita)	Siderno	15 Jun 1991
3000m	11:48.24	Ileana Salvador (Ita)	Padova	29 Aug 1993
5000m	20.07.52	Beate Anders (GDR)	Rostock	23 Jun 1990
10 000m	41:56.23	Nadezhda Ryashkina (USSR)	Seattle	24 Jul 1990
15 000m	1:15:37.9	Ann Jansson (Swe)	Stockholm	25 Oct 1987
20 000m	1:35:29.5	Madeleine Svensson (Swe)	Borås	10 Jul 1991
100 km	11:17:42	Sandra Brown (UK)	Etrechy, Fra	27-28 Oct 1990
	kilometres			
1 hour	13.194	Victoria Herazo (USA)	Santa Monica	12 May 1992
2 hours	22.239	Jana Zarubová (Cs)	Prague	12 Oct 1985
24 hours	193.306	Sandra Brown (UK)	Etrechy, Fra	27-28 Oct 1990

i indoors, # in mixed race (men and women), disallowed for record purposes

Women's World Bests – Road Walks – Where superior to track bests

10 km	41:29	LarisaRamazonova (Rus)	Izhevsk	8 Jun 1995
15 km	1:09:33	Kerry Saxby (Aus)	Canberra	13 Jul 1985
20 km	1:29:40	Kerry Saxby (Aus)	Värnamo	13 May 1988
25 km	2:12:38	Sue Cook (Aus)	Canberra	20 Jun 1981
30 km	2:42:46	Lynda Brusbaker (USA)	Atlanta	31 Oct 1993
40 km	3:39:43	Ann Jansson (Swe)	New York	27 Oct 1985
50 km	4:50:28	Kora Sommerfeld (Aus)	Neuilly-sur-Marne	26 Sep 1993
50 miles	7:54:54	Sandra Brown (UK)	Manchester-Blackpool	27 Jul 1991
100 km	10:57:50	Annie van den Meer (Hol)	Rouen	10 May 1986
200km	24:04:20	Sandra Brown (UK)	Vallorbe, Switzerland	20/21 Sep 1991
	kilometres			
24 hours	211.250	Annie van den Meer (Hol)	Rouen	10-11 May 1986

Major Marathon Races

The marathon distance is 26 miles 385 yards (42.195km), the distance for the race at the 1908 Olympic Games, run from Windsor to the White City Stadium, London. That distance became standard from 1924.

Boston

The Boston marathon is the world's oldest annual race. It was first run by 15 men on 19 Apr 1897 over a distance of 24 miles 1232 yards (39.75km). Since then it has been run every year on or about the 19th April, Patriot's Day, which honours the famed ride of Paul Revere through Boston. The full marathon distance was first run in 1927.

Kathy Switzer (USA) contested the race in 1967, although the race director tried to prevent her, but her pioneering efforts helped force the acceptance of women runners, and they were admitted officially for the first time in 1972. *Winners from 1970:*

Men

1970	Ron Hill (UK)	2:10:30
1971	Alvaro Mejia (Col)	2:18:45
1972	Olavi Suomalainen (Fin)	2:15:39
1973	Jon Anderson (USA)	2:16:03
1974	Neil Cusack (Ire)	2:13:39
1975	Bill Rodgers (USA)	2:09:55
1976	Jack Fultz (USA)	2:20:19
1977	Jerome Drayton (Can)	2:14:46
1978	Bill Rodgers (USA)	2:10:13
1979	Bill Rodgers (USA)	2:09:27
1980	Bill Rodgers (USA)	2:12:11
1981	Toshihiko Seko (Jap)	2:09:26
1982	Alberto Salazar (USA)	2:08:51
1983	Greg Meyer (USA)	2:09:01
1984	Geoff Smith (UK)	2:10:34
1985	Geoff Smith (UK)	2:14:05
1986	Rob de Castella (Aus)	2:07:51
1987	Toshihiko Seko (Jap)	2:11:50
1988	Ibrahim Hussein (Ken)	2:08:43
1989	Abebe Mekonnen (Eth)	2:09:06
1990	Gelindo Bordin (Ita)	2:08:19
1991	Ibrahim Hussain (Ken)	2:11:06
1992	Ibrahim Hussain (Ken)	2:08:14
1993	Cosmas Ndeti (Ken)	2:09:33
1994	Cosmas Ndeti (Ken)	2:07:15
1995	Cosmas Ndeti (Ken)	2:09:22

Most wins: 7 Clarence De Mar (USA) 1911, 1922-4, 1927-8, 1930; 4 Gérard Coté (Can) 1940, 1943-4, 1948; 4 Bill Rodgers (USA) 1975, 1978-80

Women

1972	Nina Kuscsik (USA)	3:08:58
1973	Jackie Hansen (USA)	3:05:59
1974	Miki Gorman (USA)	2:47:11
1975	Liane Winter (FRG)	2:42:24
1976	Kim Merritt (USA)	2:47:10
1977	Miki Gorman (USA)	2:48:33
1978	Gayle Barron (USA)	2:44:52
1979	Joan Benoit (USA)	2:35:15
1980	Jacqueline Gareau (Can)	2:34:28
1981	Allison Roe (NZ)	2:26:46
1982	Charlotte Teske (FRG)	2:29:33
1983	Joan Benoit (USA)	2:22:43
1984	Lorraine Moller (NZ)	2:29:28
1985	Lisa Weidenbach (USA)	2:34:06
1986	Ingrid Kristiansen (Nor)	2:24:55
1987	Rosa Mota (Por)	2:25:21
1988	Rosa Mota (Por)	2:24:30
1989	Ingrid Kristiansen (Nor)	2:24:35
1990	Rosa Mota (Por)	2:25:24
1991	Wanda Panfil (Pol)	2:24:18
1992	Olga Markova (Rus)	2:23:43
1993	Olga Markova (Rus)	2:25:27
1994	Uta Pippig (Ger)	2:21:45
1995	Uta Pippig (Ger)	2:25:11

Most wins: 3 Rosa Mota; 2 Miki Gorman, Joan Benoit, Ingrid Kristiansen

Chicago

First held in 1977 as the Mayor Daley Marathon, world class fields were attracted from 1983, and there have been large prize funds, especially rewarding for the world records for both men and women in 1985. Not held in 1987 and held with substantially reduced prize money from 1991. *Winners from 1983:*

Men

1983	Joseph Nzau (Ken)	2:09:45
1984	Steve Jones (UK)	2:08:05
1985	Steve Jones (UK)	2:07:13
1986	Toshihiko Seko (Jap)	2:08:27
1988	Alejandro Cruz (Mex)	2:08:57
1989	Paul Davies-Hale (UK)	2:11:25
1990	Martin Pitayo (Mex)	2:09:41
1991	Joseildo Silva (Bra)	2:14:33
1992	José Cesar Souza (Bra)	2:16:14
1993	Luiz dos Santos (Bra)	2:13:14
1994	Luiz dos Santos (Bra)	2:11:16

Women

1983	Rosa Mota (Por)	2:31:12
1984	Rosa Mota (Por)	2:26:01
1985	Joan Benoit (USA)	2:21:21
1986	Ingrid Kristiansen (Nor)	2:27:08
1988	Lisa Weidenbach (USA)	2:29:17
1989	Lisa Weidenbach (USA)	2:28:15
1990	Aurora Cunha (Por)	2:30:11
1991	Midde Hamrin (Swe)	2:36:21
1992	Linda Somers (USA)	2:37:14
1993	Ritva Lemettinen (Fin)	2:33:18
1994	Kristy Johnston (USA)	2:31:34

Fukuoka

The Asahi marathon was first run in 1947 at Kumamoto. It was first held at Fukuoka in 1951, and the race has been held there every year since 1964 in early December. Over the past 20 years it has consistently attracted world class men's fields. Winners from 1967, when Derek Clayton set a world record to win the race:

1967	Derek Clayton (Aus)	2:09:37
1968	Bill Adcocks (UK)	2:10:48
1969	Jerome Drayton (Can)	2:11:13
1970	Akio Usami (Jap)	2:10:38
1971	Frank Shorter (USA)	2:12:51

1972	Frank Shorter (USA) 2:10:30
1973	Frank Shorter (USA) 2:11:45
1974	Frank Shorter (USA) 2:11:32
1975	Jerome Drayton (Can) 2:10:09
1976	Jerome Drayton (Can) 2:12:25
1977	Bill Rodgers (USA) 2:10:56
1978	Toshihiko Seko (Jap) 2:10:21
1979	Toshihiko Seko (Jap) 2:10:35
1980	Toshihiko Seko (Jap) 2:09:45
1981	Rob de Castella (Aus) 2:08:18
1982	Paul Ballinger (NZ) 2:10:15
1983	Toshihiko Seko (Jap) 2:08:52
1984	Takeyuki Nakayama (Jap) 2:10:00
1985	Masanari Shintaku (Jap) 2:09:51
1986	Juma Ikangaa (Tan) 2:10:06
1987	Takeyuki Nakayama (Jap) 2:08:18
1988	Toshihiru Shibutani (Jap) 2:11:04
1989	Manuel Matias (Por) 2:12:54
1990	Belayneh Dinsamo (Eth) 2:11:35
1991	Shuichi Morita (Jap) 2:10:58
1992	Tena Negere (Eth) 2:09:04
1993	Dionicio Ceron (Mex) 2:08:51
1994	Boay Akonay (Tan) 2:09:45

Most wins: 4 Frank Shorter, Toshihiko Seko

London

The first London marathon was run on 29 Mar 1981. Organised and inspired by the 1956 Olympic steeplechase gold medallist, Chris Brasher, it caught the public's imagination and was a great success, 7055 runners started and 6418 finished. There were 15,011 finishers in 1982 and new records each year to 24,953 finishers in 1990, with further records at 25,194 in 1994 and 25,320 in 1995. *Winners:*

Men

1981	Dick Beardsley (USA) & Inge Simonsen (Nor) 2:11:48
1982	Hugh Jones (UK) 2:09:24
1983	Mike Gratton (UK) 2:09:43
1984	Charlie Spedding (UK) 2:09:57
1985	Steve Jones (UK) 2:08:16
1986	Toshihiko Seko (Jap) 2:10:02
1987	Hiromi Taniguchi (Jap) 2:09:50
1988	Henrik Jørgensen (Den) 2:10:20
1989	Douglas Wakiihuri (Ken) 2:09:03
1990	Allister Hutton (UK) 2:10:10
1991	Yakov Tolstikov (USSR) 2:09:17
1992	António Pinto (Por) 2:10:02
1993	Eamonn Martin (UK) 2:10:50
1994	Dionicio Ceron (Mex) 2:08:53
1995	Dionicio Ceron (Mex) 2:08:30

Women

1981	Joyce Smith (UK) 2:29:57
1982	Joyce Smith (UK) 2:29:43
1983	Grete Waitz (Nor) 2:25:29
1984	Ingrid Kristiansen (Nor) 2:24:26
1985	Ingrid Kristiansen (Nor) 2:21:06
1986	Grete Waitz (Nor) 2:24:54
1987	Ingrid Kristiansen (Nor) 2:22:48
1988	Ingrid Kristiansen (Nor) 2:25:41
1989	Véronique Marot (UK) 2:25:56
1990	Wanda Panfil (Pol) 2:26:31
1991	Rosa Mota (Por) 2:26:14
1992	Katrin Dörre (Ger) 2:29:39
1993	Katrin Dörre (Ger) 2:27:09
1994	Katrin Dörre (Ger) 2:32:34
1995	Malgorzata Sobanska (Pol) 2:27:43

New York

Fred Lebow has organised the New York marathon annually from 1970. The race was run in Central Park until 1976, when, to celebrate the US Bicentennial the course was changed to a route through all five boroughs of the city. From that year, when there were 2090 runners, the race has become one of the world's great sporting occasions, and in 1994 there were a record 29,543 finishers. *Winners since 1976:*

Men

1976	Bill Rodgers (USA) 2:10:10
1977	Bill Rodgers (USA) 2:11:29
1978	Bill Rodgers (USA) 2:12:12
1979	Bill Rodgers (USA) 2:11:42
1980	Alberto Salazar (USA) 2:09:41
1981	Alberto Salazar (USA) 2:08:13
1982	Alberto Salazar (USA) 2:09:29
1983	Rod Dixon (NZ) 2:08:59
1984	Orlando Pizzolato (Ita) 2:14:53
1985	Orlando Pizzolato (Ita) 2:11:34.
1986	Gianni Poli (Ita) 2:11:06
1987	Ibrahim Hussein (Ken) 2:11:01
1988	Steve Jones (UK) 2:08:20
1989	Juma Ikangaa (Tan) 2:08:01
1990	Douglas Wakiihuri (Ken) 2:12:39
1991	Salvador Garcia (Mex) 2:09:24
1992	Willie Mtolo (SAf) 2:09:29
1993	Andrés Espinosa (Mex) 2:10:04
1994	German Silva (Mex) 2:11:21

Women

1976	Miki Gorman (USA) 2:39.11
1977	Miki Gorman (USA) 2:43.10
1978	Grete Waitz (Nor) 2:32:30
1979	Grete Waitz (Nor) 2:27:33
1980	Grete Waitz (Nor) 2:25:41
1981	Allison Roe (NZ) 2:25:29
1982	Grete Waitz (Nor) 2:27:14
1983	Grete Waitz (Nor) 2:27:00
1984	Grete Waitz (Nor) 2:29:30
1985	Grete Waitz (Nor) 2:28:34
1986	Grete Waitz (Nor) 2:28:06
1987	Priscilla Welch (UK) 2:30:17
1988	Grete Waitz (Nor) 2:28:07
1989	Ingrid Kristiansen (Nor) 2:25:30
1990	Wanda Panfil (Pol) 2:30:45
1991	Liz McColgan (UK) 2:27:32
1992	Lisa Ondieki (Aus) 2:24:40
1993	Uta Pippig (Ger) 2:26:24
1994	Tecla Lorupe (Ken) 2:27:37

The course used from 1981 to 1983 was found to be 170 yards (155m) short, equivalent to about 30 seconds at top men's pace. That meant that the world best times set by Alberto Salazar and Alison Roe in 1981 were invalidated.

Rotterdam

Since its inception in 1981 Rotterdam has attracted élite fields for men. Women also run, but the field has usually not matched the men's for quality. *Winners:*

Men
1981 John Graham (UK) 2:09:28
1982 Rodolfo Gomez (Mex) 2:11:57
1983 Rob de Castella (Aus) 2:08:37
1984 Gidamis Shahanga (Tan) 2:11:12
1985 Carlos Lopes (Por) 2:07:12
1986 Abebe Mekonnen (Eth) 2:09:08
1987 Belayneh Dinsamo (Eth) 2:12:58
1988 Belayneh Dinsamo (Eth) 2:06:50
1989 Belayneh Dinsamo (Eth) 2:08:39
1990 Hiromi Taniguchi (Jap) 2:10:56
1991 Rob de Castella (Aus) 2:09:42
1992 Salvador Garcia (Mex) 2:09:16
1993 Dionicio Ceron (Mex) 2:11:06
1994 Vincent Rousseau (Bel) 2:07:51
1995 Martin Fíz (Spa) 2:08:57

Women
1983 Rosa Mota (Por) 2:32:27
1984 Carla Beurskens (Hol) 2:34:56
1985 Wilma Rusman (Hol) 2:35:32
1986 Ellinor Ljungros (Swe) 2:41:06
1987 Nelly Aerts (Bel) 2:41:24
1988 Xiao Hong-yan (Chn) 2:37:46
1989 Elena Murgoci (Rom) 2:32:03
1990 Carla Beurskens (Hol) 2:29:47
1991 Joke Kleyweg (Hol) 2:34:18
1992 Aurora Cunha (Por) 2:29:15
1993 Anne van Schuppen (Hol) 2:34:15
1994 Miyoko Asahina (Jap) 2:25:52
1995 Monica Pont (Spa) 2:30:34

Cross-Country Running

World Cross-Country Championships

The International Cross-country Championships were first held at Hamilton Park Racecourse, Glasgow in 1903 over 8 miles (12.87km), contested by the four countries from the British Isles. The race was held annually, with France first entering in 1907, Belgium in 1923, and thereafter the event steadily gained in international prestige. A junior race was first added in 1961, although there had been an international race for juniors between England, France and Belgium in 1940, and the first women's race held in 1967. There were two women's races in 1970; included here is the one in the USA, the other, in France, was won by Paula Pigni (Ita), with the Netherlands team winners. The event has had official world championship status from 1973, when the IAAF took control of the event from the International Cross-Country Union. A junior women's race was run for the first time in 1989.

The distances raced now are:
Men 12km, women 5km, junior men 8km, junior women 4km. Men's teams are of nine runners, with six to score; women and juniors of six runners, four to score. *Winning senior teams:*

Men's Team
45	England	1903-14, 1920-1, 1924-5, 1930-8, 1951, 1953-5, 1958-60, 1962, 1964-72, 1976, 1979-80
14	France	1922-3, 1926-9, 1939, 1946-7, 1949-50, 1952, 1956, 1978
10	Kenya	1986-95
7	Belgium	1948, 1957, 1961, 1963, 1973-4, 1977
5	Ethiopia	1981-5
1	New Zealand	1975

Women's Team
8	USA	1968-9, 1975, 1979, 1983-5, 1987
8	USSR	1976-7, 1980-2, 1988-90
7	England	1967, 1970-74, 1986
4	Kenya	1991-3, 1995
1	Romania	1978
1	Portugal	1994

There were record fields in 1986, when the number of finishers were: 328 men, 171 junior men and 161 women; with 39, 29 and 28 teams respectively placing.

Men's winners – International
1903-4 Alfred Shrubb (Eng)
1905 Albert Aldridge (Eng)
1906 Charles Straw (Eng)
1907 Adam Underwood (Eng)
1908 Archie Robertson (Eng)
1909-10 Edward Wood (Eng)
1911-3 Jean Bouin (Fra)
1914 Arthur Nicholls (Eng)
1920 James Wilson (Sco)
1921 Walter Freeman (Eng)
1922 Joseph Guillemot (Fra)
1923 Charles Blewitt (Eng)
1924 William 'Joe' Cotterell (Eng)
1925 Jack Webster (Eng)
1926 Ernest Harper (Eng)
1927 Lewis Payne (Eng)
1928 Harry Eckersley (Eng)
1929 William 'Joe' Cotterell (Eng)
1930 Thomas Evenson (Eng)
1931 Tim Smythe (Ire)
1932 Thomas Evenson (Eng)
1933-5 Jack Holden (Eng)
1936 William Eaton (Eng)
1937 James Flockhart (Sco)
1938 John Emery (Eng)
1939 Jack Holden (Eng)
1946-7 Raphael Pujazon (Fra)
1948 John Doms (Bel)
1949 Alain Mimoun (Fra)
1950 Lucien Theys (Bel)
1951 Geoffrey Saunders (Eng)
1952 Alain Mimoun (Fra)
1953 Franjo Mihalic (Yug)
1954 Alain Mimoun (Fra)
1955 Frank Sando (Eng)
1956 Alain Mimoun (Fra)
1957 Frank Sando (Eng)
1958 Stan Eldon (Eng)
1959 Fred Norris (Eng)
1960 Rhadi ben Abdesselem (Mor)
1961 Basil Heatley (Eng)
1962 Gaston Roelants (Bel)
1963 Roy Fowler (Eng)
1964 Francesco Arizmendi (Spa)
1965 Jean Fayolle (Fra)
1966 Ben Assou El Ghazi (Mor)
1967 Gaston Roelants (Bel)
1968 Mohammed Gammoudi (Tun)
1969 Gaston Roelants (Bel)
1970 Michael Tagg (Eng)
1971 David Bedford (Eng)
1972 Gaston Roelants (Bel)

Men – IAAF World Champions
1973 Pekka Paivarinta (Fin)
1974 Eric De Beck (Bel)
1975 Ian Stewart (Sco)
1976 Carlos Lopes (Por)

1977	Leon Schots (Bel)
1978	John Treacy (Ire)
1979	John Treacy (Ire)
1980	Craig Virgin (USA)
1981	Craig Virgin (USA)
1982	Mohamed Kedir (Eth)
1983	Bekele Debele (Eth)
1984	Carlos Lopes (Por)
1985	Carlos Lopes (Por)
1986	John Ngugi (Ken)
1987	John Ngugi (Ken)
1988	John Ngugi (Ken)
1989	John Ngugi (Ken)
1990-1	Khalid Skah (Mor)
1992	John Ngugi (Ken)
1993-4	William Sigei (Ken)
1995	Paul Tergat (Ken)

Most wins: 5 John Ngugi (Ken), 4 Jack Holden (Eng), Alain Mimoun (Fra), Gaston Roelants (Bel).
Most placings in first three:
7 Gaston Roelants four wins, three second 1960-72
Most placings in first ten:
10 Jack Holden 1930-46
Most appearances:
20 Marcel Van de Wattyne 1946-65

Women - International
1967-71	Doris Brown (USA)
1972	Joyce Smith (Eng)

Women - IAAF World Champions
1973	Paola Cacchi (Ita)
1974	Paola Cacchi (Ita)
1975	Julie Brown (USA)
1976	Carmen Valero (Spa)
1977	Carmen Valero (Spa)
1978	Grete Waitz (Nor)
1979	Grete Waitz (Nor)
1980	Grete Waitz (Nor)
1981	Grete Waitz (Nor)
1982	Maricica Puica (Rom)
1983	Grete Waitz (Nor)
1984	Maricica Puica (Rom)
1985	Zola Budd (Eng)
1986	Zola Budd (Eng
1987	Annette Sergent (Fra)
1988	Ingrid Kristiansen (Nor)
1989	Annette Sergent (Fra)
1990-2	Lynn Jennings (USA)
1993	Albertina Dias (Por)

1994	Helen Chepngeno (Ken)
1995	Derartu Tulu (Eth)

Most wins: 5 Doris Brown (USA), Grete Waitz (Nor).
Most placings in first three:
7 Grete Waitz five wins, two third 1978-84
Most placings in first ten:
7 Grete Waitz 1978-84
Most appearances:
16 Jean Lochhead (Wal) 1967-84
Greatest winning margins
Men: 56 sec Jack Holden (Eng) 1934
Women: 40 sec Grete Waitz (Nor) 1980

English National Cross-Country Championship

The 'National' is the oldest and largest of all national cross-country championships. It was first held in 1876, when all 32 runners went off course and the race was declared void. Held annually since then, apart from the war years, there was a peak field in the senior race in 1990, when 2195 men finished and 250 teams of six runners scored.
Winners: from 1980:

Men's Individual
1980	Nick Rose
1981	Julian Goater
1982	David Clarke
1983	Tim Hutchings
1984	Eamonn Martin
1985	David Lewis
1986	Tim Hutchings
1987-8	David Clarke
1989	David Lewis
1990-1	Richard Nerurkar
1992	Eamonn Martin
1993	Richard Nerurkar
1994	David Lewis
1995	Spencer Duva

Most wins: 4 Percy Stenning 1877-80, Alfred Shrubb 1901-4; 3 Edward Parry 1888-9, 1891; Jack Holden 1938-9, 1946; Frank Aaron 1949-51, Gordon Pirie 1953-5, Basil Heatley 1960-1, 1963; David Lewis

Men's Team
1980-2	Tipton Harriers
1983-5	Aldershot, Farnham & D
1986	Tipton Harriers
1987	Gateshead Harriers
1988	Birchfield Harriers
1989	Tipton Harriers
1990	Valli Harriers
1991	Bingley Harriers
1992	Tipton Harriers
1993	Bingley Harriers
1994-5	Blackheath Harriers

Most wins
29 Birchfield Harriers, 8 Tipton Harriers, 6 Salford Harriers, Gateshead Harriers

The Women's National was first held in 1927. *Winners: from 1980*

Women's Individual
1980	Ruth Smeeth
1981	Wendy Smith
1982	Paula Fudge
1983	Christine Benning
1984	Jane Furniss
1985	Angela Tooby
1986	Carole Bradford
1987	Jane Shields
1988	Helen Titterington
1989	Angela Pain
1990-1	Andrea Whitcombe
1992	Lisa York
1993	Gillian Stacey
1994	Paula Radcliffe
1995	Kate McCandless (USA)

Most wins: 6 Lillian Styles 1928-30, 1933-4, 1937; 5 Rita Ridley 1969-72, 1974; 4 Diane Leather 1953-6, Pam Davies 1965-8

Women's Team
1980	Birchfield Harriers
1981-3	Sale Harriers
1984	Aldershot, Farnham & D
1985	Crawley
1986-7	Sale Harriers
1988	Birchfield Harriers
1989-95	Parkside

Most wins: 13 Birchfield Harriers, 7 London Olympiades, Parkside; 6 Ilford, Sale Harriers

Australian Rules Football

A predominantly kicking game, played by teams of 18-a-side. Its principal initiators were Henry Colden Harrison and Thomas Wills, who helped to form the Melbourne Football Club in 1858. In 1877 the Victorian Football Association was founded, from which eight clubs broke away to form the Victorian Football League (VFL). Four more teams had been admitted by 1925, and in 1987 teams from Queensland and Western Australia joined the league, which was renamed the Australian Football League in 1990.

Australian Football League

Australia's premier game is the Grand Final, played annually since 1897 at the Melbourne Cricket Ground, except in 1945 when it was staged at North Carlton. The attendance record is 121,696 in 1970. *Most premierships (winning Grand Final):*

15	Carlton	1906-8, 1914-5, 1938, 1945, 1947, 1968, 1970, 1972, 1979, 1981-2, 1987
15	Essendon	1897, 1901, 1911-2, 1923-4, 1942, 1946, 1949-50, 1962, 1965, 1984-5, 1993
14	Collingwood	1902-3, 1910, 1917, 1919, 1927-30, 1935-6, 1953, 1958, 1990
12	Melbourne	1900, 1926, 1939-41, 1948, 1955-7, 1959-60, 1964
10	Richmond	1920-1, 1932, 1934, 1943, 1967, 1969, 1973-4, 1980
9	Hawthorn	1961, 1971, 1976, 1978, 1983, 1986, 1988-9, 1991
8	Fitzroy	1898-9, 1904-5, 1913, 1916, 1922, 1944
6	Geelong	1925, 1931, 1937, 1951-2, 1963
3	South Melbourne	1909, 1918, 1933
2	North Melbourne	1975, 1977
2	West Coast	1992, 1994
1	Footscray	1954, St Kilda 1966

In 1992 West Coast Eagles of Perth became the first non-Victorian winners.

Most premierships

South Australia: 32 Port Adelaide 1884-1994
Western Australia: 29 East Fremantle 1900-94

Badminton

The name of the game comes from its playing at Badminton House in England by the family and guests of the Duke of Beaufort in the 19th century. Its origins, however, are most directly from the children's game of battledore and shuttle-cock, and a similar game was played in China over 2000 ago. Badminton was played considerably by Army officers in the 1870s in India, where the first modern rules were codified.

The Badminton Association was founded in England in 1893. The world governing body is the International Badminton Federation, formed in 1934, with 113 affiliated member nations (and 9 associates) in 1994.

AFL: Records

Highest aggregate score: 345 St Kilda beat Melbourne 204-141, 6 May 1978
Team score: 239 (37 goals, 17 behinds) Geelong v Brisbane 3 May 1992
Record margin in Grand Final: 96 Hawthorn beat Melbourne 152 to 56 on 24 Sep 1988
Goals in career: 2191 Peter Hudson 1963-81
Goals in season: 150 Bob Pratt (South Melbourne) 1934, Peter Hudson (Hawthorn) 1971
Goals in Grand Final: 9 Gordon Coventry for Collingwood v Richmond 1928
9 Gary Ablett for Geelong v Hawthorn 1989
Most matches: 426 Michael Tuck (Hawthorn) 1972-91
Greatest attendance: 121,696 for the Grand Final on 26 Sep 1970.

Australian National Football League Championship

The first inter-state game was between Victoria and South Australia in 1879 and the first inter-state carnival in 1908. *Winners:*

17	Victoria	1908, 1914, 1924, 1927, 1930, 1933, 1937, 1947, 1950, 1953, 1956, 1958, 1966, 1969, 1972, 1980, 1989
6	Western Australia	1921, 1961, 1979, 1983, 1984, 1986
4	South Australia	1911, 1985, 1987-8

National Football League

Contested by the leading teams from all over Australia. Held from 1976 to 1986, but Victoria withdrew in 1977-8, when it ran its own Premiership series (winners: 1977 Hawthorn, 1978 Fitzroy). *Winners:*

1976	Hawthorn (Vic)
1977	Norwood (SA)
1978	South Adelaide (SA)
1979	Collingwood (Vic)
1980	North Melbourne (Vic)
1981	Essendon (Vic)
1982	Sydney Swans (NSW)
1983	Carlton (Vic)
1984	Essendon (Vic)
1985-6	Hawthorn (Vic)

Men's World Team Championships (Thomas Cup)

For men's teams of six players who play five singles and four doubles in each contest, held every three years until 1982 when it became a biennial event. The cup was donated in 1940 by Sir George Thomas, winner of 21 All-England titles, but the competition could not start until after the war. *Winners:*

9	Indonesia	1958, 1961, 1964, 1970, 1973, 1976, 1979, 1984, 1994
5	Malaysia	Malaya 1949, 1952, 1955, Malaysia 1967, 1992
4	China	1982, 1986, 1988, 1990

Women's World Team Championships (Uber Cup)

The women's equivalent of the Thomas Cup, it was also contested triennially until 1984 when it became a biennial event. The cup was presented by Betty Uber who represented England a then-record 37 times between 1926 and 1951. Each tie consists of three singles and four doubles. *Winners:*

5	Japan	1966, 1969, 1972, 1978, 1981
5	China	1984, 1986, 1988, 1990, 1992
3	United States	1957, 1960, 1963
2	Indonesia	1975, 1994

World Championships

Individual championships were instituted in 1977; initially they were held every three years, but now biennially. *Winners:*

	Men's singles	Women's singles
1977	Flemming Delfs (Den)	Lene Köppen (Den)
1980	Rudy Hartono (Ina)	Wiharjo Verawaty (Ina)
1983	Icuk Sugiarto (Ina)	Li Lingwei (Chn)
1985	Han Jian (Chn)	Han Aiping (Chn)
1987	Yang Yang (Chn)	Han Aiping (Chn)
1989	Yang Yang (Chn)	Li Lingwei (Chn)
1991	Zhao Jianhua (Chn)	Tang Jiuhong (Chn)
1993	Joko Suprianto (Ina)	Susi Susanti (Ina)
1995	Heryanto Arbi (Ina)	Ye Zhaoying (Chn)

Men's doubles

1977 Johan Wahjudi & Tjun Tjun (Ina)
1980 Ade Chandra & Hadinata Christian (Ina)
1983 Steen Fladberg & Jesper Helledie (Den)
1985 Park Joo-bong & Kim Moon-soo (SKo)
1987 Li Yongbo & Tian Bingyi (Chn)
1989 Li Yongbo & Tian Bingyi (Chn)
1991 Kim Moon-soo & Park Joo-bong (SKo)
1993 Ricky Subagya & Rudy Gunawan (Ina)
1995 Rexy Mainaky & Ricky Subagya (Ina

Women's doubles

1977 Etsuko Tuganoo & Emiko Vero (Jap)
1980 Nora Perry & Jane Webster (UK)
1983 Lin Ying & Wu Dixi (Chn)
1985 Han Aiping & Li Lingwei (Chn)
1987 Lin Ying & Guan Weizhen (Chn)
1989 Lin Ying & Guan Weizhen (Chn)
1991 Guan Weizhen & Nong Qunhua (Chn)
1993 Nong Qunhua & Zhou Lei (Chn)
1995 Gil Young-ah & Jang Hye-ock (SKo)

Mixed doubles

1977 Steen Stovgaard & Lene Köppen (Den)

Suzi Susanti – the top woman player of the 1990s

1980 Hadinata Christian & Imelda Wigoeno (Ina)
1983 Thomas Kihlström (Swe) & Nora Perry (UK)
1985 Park Joo-bong & Yoo Sang-hee (SKo)
1987 Wang Pengrin & Shi Fagjing (Chn)
1989 Park Joo-bong & Chung Myung-hee (SKo)
1991 Park Joo-bong & Chung Myung-hee (SKo)
1993 Thomas Lund (Den) & Catrine Bengtsson (Swe)
1995 Thomas Lund & Marlene Thomsen (Den)

Team (mixed) - for the Sudirman Trophy

1989 Indonesia	1993 South Korea
1991 South Korea	1995 China

Olympic Games

Badminton was played as a demonstration sport in 1972 and 1988, and it became a medal sport in 1992, when the winners were:

Men's singles: Alan Budi Kusuma (Ina)
Women's singles: Susi Susanti (Ina)
Men's doubles: Kim Moon-soo & Park Joo-bong (SKo)
Women's doubles: Hwang Hye-young & Chung So-young (SKo)

All-England Championships

First played in 1899, until the advent of the World Championships this was the premier tournament in the world.

Men's singles					
1900	Sydney Smith (Eng)	1924	'Curly' Mack (Ire)	1947	Conny Jepsen (Swe)
1901	H Davies (Eng)	1925-9	Frank Devlin (Ire)	1948	Jørn Skaarup (Den)
1902-3	Ralph Watling (Eng)	1930	Donald Hume (Eng)	1949	Dave Freeman (USA)
1904-5	Henry Marrett (Eng)	1931	Frank Devlin (Ire)	1950-2	Wong Peng Soon (Mal)
1906-7	Norman Wood (Eng)	1932	Ralph Nichols (Eng)	1953-4	Eddie Choong (Mal)
1908	Henry Marrett (Eng)	1933	Raymond White (Eng)	1955	Wong Peng Soon (Mal)
1909-10	Frank Chesterton (Eng)	1934	Ralph Nichols (Eng)	1956-7	Eddie Choong (Mal)
1911-2	George Sautter (Eng)	1935	Raymond White (Eng)	1958	Erland Kops (Den)
1920	George Thomas (Eng)	1936-8	Ralph Nichols (Eng)	1959	Tan Joe Hok (Ina)
		1939	Tage Madsen (Den)	1960-3	Erland Kops (Den)

1964	Knud Nielsen (Den)	1906	Ethel Thomson (Eng)	1960	Judy Devlin (USA)
1965	Erland Kops (Den)	1907-10	Meriel Lucas (Eng)	1961-4	Judy Hashman (née
1966	Tan Aik Huang (Mal)	1911	Margaret Larminie (Eng)		Devlin) (USA)
1967	Erland Kops (Den)	1912	Margaret Tragett (née	1965	Ursula Smith (Eng)
1968-74	Rudy Hartono (Ina)		Larminie) (Eng)	1966-7	Judy Hashman (USA)
1975	Svend Pri (Den)	1913-4	Lavinia Radeglia (Eng)	1968	Eva Twedberg (Swe)
1976	Rudy Hartono (Ina)	1920-2	Kitty McKane (Eng)	1969	Hiroe Yuki (Jap)
1977	Flemming Delfs (Den)	1923	Lavinia Radeglia (Eng)	1970	Etsuko Takenaka (Jap)
1978-9	Liem Swie King (Ina)	1924	Kitty McKane (Eng)	1971	Eva Twedberg (Swe)
1980	Prakash Padukone (Ina)	1925	Margaret Stocks (Eng)	1972	Noriko Nakayama (Jap)
1981	Liem Swie King (Ina)	1926-7	Marjorie Barrett (Eng)	1973	Margaret Beck (Eng)
1982	Morten Frost (Den)	1928	Margaret Tragett (Eng)	1974-5	Hiroe Yuki (Jap)
1983	Luan Jin (Chn)	1929-31	Marjorie Barrett (Eng)	1976	Gillian Gilks (Eng)
1984	Morten Frost (Den)	1932	Leonie Kingsbury (Eng)	1977	Hiroe Yuki (Jap)
1985	Zhao Jianhua (Chn)	1933	Alice Woodroffe (Eng)	1978	Gillian Gilks (Eng)
1986-7	Morten Frost (Den)	1934	Leonie Kingsbury (Eng)	1979-80	Lene Køppen (Den)
1988	Ib Frederiksen (Den)	1935	Betty Uber (Eng)	1981	Sun Ai-hwang (SKo)
1989	Yang Yang (Chn)	1936-7	Thelma Kingsbury (Eng)	1982-3	Zang Ailing (Chn)
1990	Zhao Jianhua (Chn)	1938	Daphne Young (Eng)	1984	Li Lingwei (Chn)
1991	Ardy Wiranata (Ina)	1939	Dorothy Walton (Can)	1985	Han Aiping (Chn)
1992	Liu Jun (Chn)	1947	Marie Ussing (Den)	1986	Kim Yun-ja (SKo)
1993-4	Heryanto Arbi (Ina)	1948	Kirsten Thorndahl (Den)	1987	Kirsten Larsen (Den)
1995	Poul-Erik Hoyer Larsen	1949	Aase Jacobsen (Den)	1988	Gu Jiaming (Chn)
	(Den)	1950	Tonny Olsen-Ahm (Den)	1989	Li Lingwei (Chn)
		1951	Aase Jacobsen (Den)	1990-1	Susi Susanti (Ina)

Most wins: 8 Rudy Hartono (Ina)

1952	Tonny Olsen-Ahm (Den)	1992	Tang Jiuhong (Chn)
1953	Marie Ussing (Den)	1993-4	Susi Susanti (Ina)
1954	Judy Devlin (USA)	1995	Lim Xiaoqing (Swe)

Women's singles

1900-1	Ethel Thomson (Eng)	1955-6	Margaret Varner (USA)
1902	Meriel Lucas (Eng)	1957-8	Judy Devlin (USA)
1903-4	Ethel Thomson (Eng)	1959	Heather Ward (Eng)
1905	Meriel Lucas (Eng)		

Most wins: 10 Judy Hashman (née Devlin) (USA)

Men's doubles

1899	D Oakes & Stewart Massey (Eng)	1950	Preben Dabelsteen & Jørn Skaarup (Den)
1900-2	H Mellersh & F Collier (Eng)	1951-3	Eddie Choong & David Choong (Mal)
1903	Stewart Massey & E Huson (Eng)	1954	Ooi Teik Hock & Ong Poh Lim (Mal)
1904	Albert Prebble & Henry Marrett (Eng)	1955-6	Finn Kobbero & Jørgen Hammergaard Hansen (Den)
1905	Stewart Massey & C Barnes (Eng)	1957	Joseph Alston (USA) & Hock Aun Heah (Mal)
1906	George Thomas & Henry Marrett (Eng)	1958	Erland Kops & Per Nielsen (Den)
1907	Albert Prebble & Norman Wood (Eng)	1959	Lim Say Hup & Teh Kew San (Mal)
1908	George Thomas & Henry Marrett (Eng)	1960	Finn Kobbero & Per Neilsen (Den)
1909	Albert Prebble & Frank Chesterton (Eng)	1961-4	Finn Kobbero & Jørgen Hammergaard Hansen (Den)
1910	George Thomas & Henry Marrett (Eng)		
1911	P Fitton & Edward Hawthorn (Eng)	1965-6	Ng Boon Bee & Tan Yee Khan (Mal)
1912	George Thomas & Henry Marrett (Eng)	1967-9	Erland Kops & Henning Borch (Den)
1913-4	George Thomas & Frank Chesterton (Eng)	1970	Tom Backer & Paul Petersen (Den)
1920	Alfred Engelbach & Robert du Roveray (Eng)	1971	Ng Boon Bee & Punch Gunalan (Mal)
1921	George Thomas & Francis Hodge (Eng)	1972-3	Hadinata Christian & Ade Chandra (Ina)
1922	Frank Devlin (Ire) & George Sautter (Eng)	1974-5	Tjun Tjun & Johan Wahjudi (Ina)
1923	Frank Devlin & 'Curly' Mack (Ire)	1976	Bengt Froman & Thomas Kihlström (Swe)
1924	George Thomas & Francis Hodge (Eng)	1977-80	Tjun Tjun & Johan Wahjudi (Ina)
1925	Herbert Huber & A Jones (Eng)	1981	Hariamanto Kartono & Rudy Heryanto (Ina)
1926-7	Frank Devlin & 'Curly' Mack (Ire)	1982	Razif Sidek & Jalaini Sidek (Mal)
1928	George Thomas & Francis Hodge (Eng)	1983	Stefan Karlsson & Thomas Kihlström (Swe)
1929-31	Frank Devlin & 'Curly' Mack (Ire)	1984	Hariamanto Kartono & Rudy Heryanto Ina)
1932-5	Donald Hume & Raymond White (Eng)	1985-6	Kim Moon-soo & Park Joo-bong (SKo)
1936-8	Ralph Nichols & Leslie Nichols (Eng)	1987-8	Li Yongbo & Tian Bingyi (Chn)
1939	Tom Boyle & James Rankin (Ire)	1989	Lee Sang-bok & Park Joo-bong (SKo)
1947	Tage Madsen & Poul Holm (Den)	1990	Kim Moon-soo & Park Joo-bong (SKo)
1948	Preben Dabelsteen & Borge Fredricksen (Den)	1991	Li Yongbo & Tian Bingyi (Chn)
1949	Ooi Teik Hock & Teoh Seng Khoon (Mal)	1992	Rudy Gunawan & Eddy Hartono (Ina)

1993	Jon Holst-Christensen & Thomas Lund (Den)
1994	Rudy Gunawan & Bambang Suprianto (Ina)
1995	Rexy Mainaky & Ricky Subagya (Ina)

Women's doubles

1899-1900	Meriel Lucas & Miss Graeme (Eng)
1901	Miss St John & E Moseley (Eng)
1902	Meriel Lucas & Ethel Thomson (Eng)
1903	M Hardy & Dorothea Douglass (Eng)
1904-6	Meriel Lucas & Ethel Thomson (Eng)
1907-9	Meriel Lucas & G Murray (Eng)
1910	Mary Bateman & Meriel Lucas (Eng)
1911-2	Alice Gowenlock & Dorothy Cundall (Eng)
1913	Hazel Hogarth & Mary Bateman (Eng)
1914	Margaret Tragett (née Larminie) & Eveline Peterson (Eng)
1920	Lavinia Radeglia & Violet Elton (Eng)
1921	Kitty McKane & Margaret McKane (Eng)
1922-3	Margaret Tragett & Hazel Hogarth (Eng)
1924	Margaret Stocks (née McKane) & Kitty McKane (Eng)
1925	Margaret Tragett & Hazel Hogarth (Eng)
1926	A Head & Violet Elton (Eng)
1927	Margaret Tragett & Hazel Hogarth (Eng)
1928-30	Marjorie Barrett & Violet Elton (Eng)
1931	Betty Uber & Marianne Horsley (Eng)
1932	Marjorie Barrett & Leonie Kingbury (Eng)
1933-6	Thelma Kingsbury & Marjorie Bell-Henderson (Eng)
1937-8	Betty Uber & Diana Doveton (Eng)
1939	Ruth Dalsgard & Tonny Olsen (Den)
1947-8	Tonny Olsen-Ahm & Kirsten Thorndahl (Den)
1949	Betty Uber & Queenie Allen (Eng)
1950-1	Tonny Olsen-Ahm & Kirsten Thorndahl (Den)
1952	Tonny Olsen-Ahm & Aase Jacobsen (Den)
1953	Iris Cooley & June White (Eng)
1954	Judy Devlin & Susan Devlin (USA)
1955	Iris Cooley & June White (Eng)
1956	Judy Devlin & Susan Devlin (USA)
1957	Kirsten Granlund (née Thorndahl) & Ami Hammergaard Hansen (Den)
1958	Margaret Varner (USA) & Heather Ward (Eng)
1959	Iris Cooley-Rogers & June White-Timperley (Eng)
1960	Judy Devlin & Susan Devlin (USA)
1961	Judy Hashman (née Devlin) (USA) & Susan Peard (née Devlin) (Ire)
1962	Judy Hashman (USA) & Tonny Holst-Christensen (Den)
1963	Judy Hashman (USA) & Susan Peard (Ire)
1964-5	Karen Jorgensen & Ulla Rasmussen (Den)
1966	Judy Hashman (USA) & Susan Peard (Ire)
1967	Irme Rietveld (Hol) & Ulla Strand (née Rasmussen) (Den)
1968	Retno Koestijah & Miss Minarni (Ina)
1969-70	Margaret Boxall & Sue Whetnall (Eng)
1971	Noriko Takagi & Hiroe Yuki (Jap)
1972-3	Machiko Aizawa & Etsuko Takenaka (Jap)
1974	Margaret Beck & Gillian Gilks (Eng)
1975	Machiko Aizawa & Etsuko Takenaka (Jap)
1976	Gillian Gilks & Sue Whetnall (Eng)
1977	Etsuko Tuganoo (née Takenaka) & Emiko Ueno (Jap)

1978	Atsuko Tokuda & Mikiko Takada (Jap)
1979	Wiharjo Verawaty & Imelda Wigoeno (Ina)
1980	Gillian Gilks & Nora Perry (Eng)
1981	Nora Perry & Jane Webster (Eng)
1982	Lin Ying & Wu Dixi (Chn)
1983	Xu Rong & Wu Jianqiu (Chn)
1984	Liu Ying & Wu Dixi (Chn)
1985	Li Lingwei & Han Aiping (Chn)
1986-7	Chung Myung-hee & Hwang Hye-young (SKo)
1988	Chung So-young & Kim Jun-ja (SKo)
1989	Chung Myung-hee & Chung So-young (SKo)
1990	Chung Myung-hee & Hwang Hye-young (SKo)
1991	Chung So-young & Hwang Hye-young (SKo)
1992	Lin Yanfen & Yao Fen (Chn)
1993-4	Chung So-young & Gil Young-ah (SKo)
1995	Gil Young-ah & Jang Hye-ock (SKo)

Mixed doubles

1899-1900	D Oakes & Miss St John (Eng)
1901	F Collier & Miss E Stawell-Brown (Eng)
1902	L Ransford & Miss E Moseley (Eng)
1903	George Thomas & Ethel Thomson (Eng)
1904	Henry Marrett & Dorothea Douglass (Eng)
1905	Henry Marrett & Hazel Hogarth (Eng)
1906	George Thomas & Ethel Thomson (Eng)
1907	George Thomas & Miss G Murray (Eng)
1908	Norman Wood & Meriel Lucas (Eng)
1909	Albert Prebble & Dora Boothby (Eng)
1910	George Sautter & Dorothy Cundall (Eng)
1911	George Thomas & Margaret Larminie (Eng)
1912	Edward Hawthorn & Hazel Hogarth (Eng)
1913	George Sautter & Miss M Mayston (Eng)
1914	George Thomas & Hazel Hogarth (Eng)
1920-2	George Thomas & Hazel Hogarth (Eng)
1923	'Curly' Mack (Ire) & Margaret Tragett (née Larminie) (Eng)
1924-5	Frank Devlin (Ire) & Kitty McKane (Eng)
1926-7	Frank Devlin (Ire) & Eveline Peterson (Eng)
1928	A Harbot & Margaret Tragett (Eng)
1929	Frank Devlin (Ire) & Marianne Horseley (Eng)
1930-2	Herbert Uber & Betty Uber (Eng)
1933-6	Donald Hume & Betty Uber (Eng)
1937	Ian Maconachie (Ire) & Thelma Kingsbury (Eng)
1938	Raymond White & Betty Uber (Eng)
1939	Ralph Nichols & Bessie Staples (Eng)
1947	Poul Holm & Tonny Olsen-Ahm (Den)
1948	Jørn Skaarup & Kirsten Thorndahl (Den)
1949	Cliton Stephens & Patsey Stephens (USA)
1950-2	Poul Holm & Tonny Olsen-Ahm (Den)
1953	Eddie Choong (Mal) & June White (Eng)
1954	John Best & Iris Cooley (Eng)
1955	Finn Kobbero & Kirsten Thorndahl (Den)
1956	Tony Jordan & June Timperley (née White) (Eng)
1957	Finn Kobbero & Kirsten Granlund (née Thorndahl) (Den)
1958	Tony Jordan & June Timperley (Eng)
1959	Per Nielsen & Inge Birgit Hansen (Den)
1960-1	Finn Kobbero & Kirsten Granlund (Den)
1962-3	Finn Kobbero & Ulla Ramussen (Den)
1964	Tony Jordan & Jennifer Pritchard (Eng)
1965-6	Finn Kobbero & Ulla Strand (née Ramussen) (Den)

1967	Svend Andersen & Ulla Strand (Den)
1968	Tony Jordan & Sue Pound (Eng)
1969	Roger Mills & Gillian Perrin (Eng)
1970	Per Walsöe & Pernille Mölgaard Hansen (Den)
1971-2	Svend Pri & Ulla Strand (Den)
1973	Derek Talbot & Gillian Gilks (Eng)
1974	David Eddy & Sue Whetnall (Eng)
1975	Elliott Stuart & Nora Gardner (Eng)
1976-7	Derek Talbot & Gillian Gilks (Eng)
1978	Mike Tredgett & Nora Perry (née Gardner) (Eng)
1979	Hadinata Christian & Imelda Wigoeno (Ina)
1980-1	Mike Tredgett & Nora Perry (Eng)
1982	Martin Dew & Gillian Gilks (Eng)
1983	Thomas Kihlstrom (Swe) & Nora Perry (Eng)
1984	Martin Dew & Gillian Gilks (Eng)
1985	Billy Gillibrand & Nora Perry (Eng)
1986	Park Joo-bong & Chung Myung-hee (SKo)
1987	Lee Deuk-choon & Chung Myung-hee (SKo)
1988	Wang Pengren & Shi Fangjing (Chn)
1989-91	Park Joo-bong & Chung Myung-hee (SKo)
1992	Thomas Lund & Pernille Dupont (Den)
1993	Jon Holst-Christensen & Grethe Morgensen (Den)
1994	Nick Ponting & Joanne Wright (UK)
1995	Thomas Lund & Marlene Thomsen (Den)

Most titles

Men

21 George Thomas 4 singles, 9 men's doubles, 8 mixed doubles 1903-28

18 Frank Devlin 6 singles, 7 men's doubles, 5 mixed doubles 1922-31

Women

17 Meriel Lucas 6 singles, 10 women's doubles, 1 mixed doubles 1899-1910

17 Judy Hashman (née Devlin) 10 singles, 7 women's doubles 1954-67

Badminton champions who won Wimbledon titles at Lawn Tennis:

Men: Sydney Smith 1900-6

Women: Ethel Larcombe (née Thomson) 1900-14; Dorothea Lambert Chambers (née Douglass) 1903-14; Dora Boothby 1909-13; Kitty Godfree (née McKane) 1920-6

European Championships

The European Badminton Union was formed in 1967, and has staged biennial championships from 1968.

Men's singles champions
1968 Sture Johnsson (Swe)
1970 Sture Johnsson (Swe)
1972 Wolfgang Bochow (FRG)
1974 Sture Johnsson (Swe)
1976 Flemming Delfs (Den)
1978 Flemming Delfs (Den)
1980 Flemming Delfs (Den)
1982 Jens Peter Nierhoff (Den)
1984 Morten Frost (Den)
1986 Morten Frost (Den)
1988 Darren Hall (Eng)
1990 Steve Baddeley (Eng)
1992 Poul-Erik Høyer-Larsen (Den)
1994 Poul-Erik Høyer-Larsen (Den)

Women's singles champions
1968 Irmgard Latz (FRG)
1970 Eva Twedberg (Swe)
1972 Margaret Beck (Eng)
1974 Gillian Gilks (Eng)
1976 Gillian Gilks (Eng)
1978 Lene Køppen (Den)
1980 Liselotte Blumer (Swi)
1982 Lene Køppen (Den)
1984 Helen Troke (Eng)
1986 Helen Troke (Eng)
1988 Kirsten Larsen (Den)
1990 Pernille Nedergaard (Den)
1992 Pernille Nedergaard (Den)
1994 Lim Xiaoqing (Swe)

European team champions
England   1974, 1978, 1982, 1984
Denmark 1976, 1980, 1986, 1988, 1990
Sweden   1992, 1994

Most doubles titles
10 Gillian Gilks (Eng) Women's 1972, 1974, 1976, 1982, Mixed 1972, 1974, 1976, 1982, 1984, 1986
6 Mike Tredgett (Eng) Men's 1976, 1978, 1984, Mixed 1978, 1980
5 Sue Whetnall (Eng) Women's 1968, 1970, 1976, Mixed 1968, 1970

World Cup

Men's singles
1991 Ardy B Wiranata (Ina)
1992 Joko Suprianto (Ina)
1993 Alan Budi Kusuma (Ina)
1994 Heryanto Arbi (Ina)

Women's singles
1991 Huang Hwa (Chn)
1992 Tang Jiuhong (Chn)
1993-4 Susi Susanti (Ina)

Bandy

Bandy is an 11-a-side game similar to hockey, but played on an ice rink, between 90 and 110m long and 45-65m wide. Unlike ice hockey, however, bandy is played with a ball rather than a puck. It may have originated in England c.1790, and Bury Fen Bandy Club in the North East of England is the original home of the modern game. Some well-known soccer clubs, such as Sheffield United and Nottingham Forest, originally had Bandy in their titles as well as Football. The game is now played principally in the Baltic regions, with more than half a million players in the USSR, Finland, Norway and Sweden. The National Bandy Association was formed in England in 1891, but soon the game was forced into the background by ice hockey. The game was introduced into Sweden in 1894 by C G Tebbutt of Bury Fen, who had also organised the first international match, between Bury Fen and Haarlem (Hol) in 1891. The first Swedish club was established in Stockholm in 1895. Bandy was first played in Russia in 1898.

The International Bandy Federation was formed in 1955.

Bandy was included as a demonstration sport at the 1952 Winter Olympics in Oslo, with Sweden the winners.

World Championships

These are held for men's teams, first in 1957, then every two years from 1961. *Champions:*

14 USSR   1957, 1961, 1963, 1965, 1967, 1969, 1971, 1973, 1975, 1977, 1979, 1985, 1989, 1991

4 Sweden 1981, 1983, 1987, 1993

The record score in a World Championship match: USSR beat USA 21-1 at Skövde, Sweden on 1 Feb 1987. Most gold medals by an individual: 8 Valeriy Maslov (USSR) 1961, 1963, 1965, 1967, 1971, 1973, 1975, 1977.

Baseball

A special commission sponsored by Albert G Spalding was set up in the United States in 1907 to establish the true 'birth' of baseball, and a year later they concluded that Abner Doubleday, a West Point cadet, had invented the game at Cooperstown, New York in 1839. This legend has become deeply embedded in American folklore, but is doubted by sports historians, who argue that the game evolved from such English games as cricket, paddleball, trap ball and rounders. Printed references to 'base ball' in England date to 1700 and in the United States to the mid-18th century.

The first rules of the modern game were drawn up by Alexander Cartwright Jr in 1845 and the first match under these rules was played on 19 June 1846, when the New York Nine defeated a team from the sport's first organised club, the New York Knickerbockers, 23-1 in four innings. In 1871 the National Association of Professional Base Ball Players was formed, the first professional league.

World Series

There are two baseball leagues in America, the National League (NL) which was formed in 1876 and the American League (AL) which was formed in 1900 and officially founded in 1901. A total of 26 teams made up the two leagues (until two expansion francises were granted at the end of the 1992 season to bring the total to 28) and after a regular season of 162 matches against other teams in their own league, a series of play-offs decided the teams to represent each league in the best-of-seven game World Series played each October.

In 1994 the AL and NL were realigned so that each had three divisions: East and Central, each with five teams, and West divisions of four teams. The three divisional winners plus the runner-up with the best record play-off for the right to contest the World Series.

Year	Winners	Runners-up	Score
1903	Boston Red Sox (AL)	Pittsburgh Pirates (NL)	5-3
1904	Not held		
1905	New York Giants (NL)	Philadelphia Athletics (AL)	4-1
1906	Chicago White Sox (AL)	Chicago Cubs (NL)	4-2
1907	Chicago Cubs (NL)	Detroit Tigers (AL)	4-0*
1908	Chicago Cubs (NL)	Detroit Tigers (AL)	4-1
1909	Pittsburgh Pirates (NL)	Detroit Tigers (AL)	4-3
1910	Philadelphia Athletics (AL)	Chicago Cubs (NL)	4-1
1911	Philadelphia Athletics (AL)	New York Giants (NL)	4-2
1912	Boston Red Sox (AL)	New York Giants (NL)	4-3*
1913	Philadelphia Athletics (AL)	New York Giants (NL)	4-1
1914	Boston Braves (NL)	Philadelphia Athletics (AL)	4-0
1915	Boston Red Sox (AL)	Philadelphia Phillies (NL)	4-1
1916	Boston Red Sox (AL)	Brooklyn Dodgers (NL)	4-1
1917	Chicago White Sox (AL)	New York Giants (NL)	4-2
1918	Boston Red Sox (AL)	Chicago Cubs (NL)	4-2
1919	Cincinnati Reds (NL)	Chicago White Sox (AL)	5-3
1920	Cleveland Indians (AL)	Brooklyn Dodgers (NL)	5-2
1921	New York Giants (NL)	New York Yankees (AL)	4-3
1922	New York Giants (NL)	New York Yankees (AL)	4-0*
1923	New York Yankees (AL)	New York Giants (NL)	4-2
1924	Washington Senators (AL)	New York Giants (NL)	4-3
1925	Pittsburgh Pirates (NL)	Washington Senators (AL)	4-3
1926	St Louis Cardinals (NL)	New York Yankees (AL)	4-3
1927	New York Yankees (AL)	Pittsburgh Pirates (NL)	4-0
1928	New York Yankees (AL)	St Louis Cardinals (NL)	4-0
1929	Philadelphia Athletics (AL)	Chicago Cubs (NL)	4-1
1930	Philadelphia Athletics (AL)	St Louis Cardinals (NL)	4-2
1931	St Louis Cardinals (NL)	Philadelphia Athletics (AL)	4-3
1932	New York Yankees (AL)	Chicago Cubs (NL)	4-0
1933	New York Giants (NL)	Washington Senators (AL)	4-1
1934	St Louis Cardinals (NL)	Detroit Tigers (AL)	4-3
1935	Detroit Tigers (AL)	Chicago Cubs (NL)	4-2
1936	New York Yankees (AL)	New York Giants (NL)	4-2
1937	New York Yankees (AL)	New York Giants (NL)	4-1
1938	New York Yankees (AL)	Chicago Cubs (NL)	4-0
1939	New York Yankees (AL)	Cincinnati Reds (NL)	4-0

Major League All-time Top Tens

Batting - Most Runs

Ty Cobb	2245
Babe Ruth	2174
Hank Aaron	2174
Pete Rose	2165
Willie Mays	2062
Stan Musial	1949
Lou Gehrig	1888
Tristram Speaker	1881
Melvin Ott	1859
Frank Robinson	1829

Batting - Most Hits

Pete Rose	4256
Ty Cobb	4191
Hank Aaron	3771
Stan Musial	3630
Tristram Speaker	3515
Carl Yastrzemski	3419
John P 'Honus' Wagner	3418
Eddie Collins	3309
Willie Mays	3283
Napolean Lajoie	3244

Batting - Most Home Runs

Hank Aaron	755
Babe Ruth	714
Willie Mays	660
Frank Robinson	586
Harmon Killibrew	573
Reggie Jackson	563
Michael Schmidt	548
Mickey Mantle	536
James Foxx	534
Ted Williams	521
Willie McCovey	521

Pitching - Most Wins

Cy Young	511

1940	Cincinnati Reds (NL)	Detroit Tigers (AL)	4-3
1941	New York Yankees (AL)	Brooklyn Dodgers (NL)	4-1
1942	St Louis Cardinals (NL)	New York Yankees (AL)	4-1
1943	New York Yankees (AL)	St Louis Cardinals (NL)	4-1
1944	St Louis Cardinals (NL)	St Louis Browns (AL)	4-2
1945	Detroit Tigers (AL)	Chicago Cubs (NL)	4-3
1946	St Louis Cardinals (NL)	Boston Red Sox (AL)	4-3
1947	New York Yankees (AL)	Brooklyn Dodgers (NL)	4-3
1948	Cleveland Indians (AL)	Boston Braves (NL)	4-2
1949	New York Yankees (AL)	Brooklyn Dodgers (NL)	4-1
1950	New York Yankees (AL)	Philadelphia Phillies (NL)	4-0
1951	New York Yankees (AL)	New York Giants (NL)	4-2
1952	New York Yankees (AL)	Brooklyn Dodgers (NL)	4-3
1953	New York Yankees (AL)	Brooklyn Dodgers (NL)	4-2
1954	New York Giants (NL)	Cleveland Indians (AL)	4-0
1955	Brooklyn Dodgers (NL)	New York Yankees (AL)	4-3
1956	New York Yankees (AL)	Brooklyn Dodgers (NL)	4-3
1957	Milwaukee Braves (NL	New York Yankees (AL)	4-3
1958	New York Yankees (AL)	Milwaukee Braves (NL)	4-3
1959	Los Angeles Dodgers (NL)	Chicago White Sox (AL)	4-2
1960	Pittsburgh Pirates (NL)	New York Yankees (AL)	4-3
1961	New York Yankees (AL)	Cincinnati Reds (NL)	4-1
1962	New York Yankees (AL)	San Francisco Giants (NL)	4-3
1963	Los Angeles Dodgers (NL)	New York Yankees (AL)	4-0
1964	St Louis Cardinals (NL)	New York Yankees (AL)	4-3
1965	Los Angeles Dodgers (NL)	Minnesota Twins (AL)	4-3
1966	Baltimore Orioles (AL)	Los Angeles Dodgers (NL)	4-0
1967	St Louis Cardinals (NL)	Boston Red Sox (AL)	4-3
1968	Detroit Tigers (AL)	St Louis Cardinals (NL)	4-3
1969	New York Mets (NL)	Baltimore Orioles (AL)	4-1
1970	Baltimore Orioles (AL)	Cincinnati Reds (NL)	4-1
1971	Pittsburgh Pirates (NL)	Baltimore Orioles (AL)	4-3
1972	Oakland Athletics (AL)	Cincinnati Reds (NL)	4-3
1973	Oakland Athletics (AL)	New York Mets (NL)	4-3
1974	Oakland Athletics (AL)	Los Angeles Dodgers (NL)	4-1
1975	Cincinnati Reds (NL)	Boston Red Sox (AL)	4-3
1976	Cincinnati Reds (NL)	New York Yankees (AL)	4-0
1977	New York Yankees (AL)	Los Angeles Dodgers (NL)	4-3
1978	New York Yankees (AL)	Los Angeles Dodgers (NL)	4-2
1979	Pittsburgh Pirates (NL)	Baltimore Orioles (AL)	4-3
1980	Philadelphia Phillies (NL)	Kansas City Royals (AL)	4-2
1981	Los Angeles Dodgers (NL)	New York Yankees (AL)	4-2
1982	St Louis Cardinals (NL)	Milwaukee Brewers (AL)	4-3
1983	Baltimore Orioles (AL)	Philadelphia Phillies (NL)	4-1
1984	Detroit Tigers (AL)	San Diego Padres (NL)	4-1
1985	Kansas City Royals (AL)	St Louis Cardinals (NL)	4-3
1986	New York Mets (NL)	Boston Red Sox (AL)	4-3
1987	Minnesota Twins (AL)	St Louis Cardinals (NL)	4-3
1988	Los Angeles Dodgers (NL)	Oakland Athletics (AL)	4-1
1989	Oakland Athletics (AL)	San Francisco Giants (NL)	4-0
1990	Cincinnati Reds (NL)	Oakland Athletics (AL)	4-0
1991	Minnesota Twins (AL)	Atlanta Braves (NL)	4-3
1992	Toronto Blue Jays (AL)	Atlanta Braves (NL)	4-2
1993	Toronto Blue Jays (AL)	Philadelphia Phillies (NL)	4-2
1994	Cancelled due to players' strike		

* includes one drawn game

Walter Johnson	416
Chris Matthewson	373
Grover Alexander	373
Warren Spahn	363
Charles 'Kid' Nichols	361
James 'Pud' Galvin	361
Timothy Keefe	342
Steve Carlton	329
Eddie Plank	327

Pitching - Most Strikeouts

Nolan Ryan	5714
Steve Carlton	4136
Bart Blyleven	3701
Tom Seaver	3640
Don Sutton	3574
Gaylord Perry	3534
Walter Johnson	3508
Phil Niekro	3342
Ferguson Jenkins	3192
Robert Gibson	3117

World Series Team Records

Most wins: 22 New York Yankees, 9 St Louis Cardinals, Philadelphia/ Kansas City/ Oakland Athletics/A's, 6 Brooklyn/Los Angeles Dodgers, 5 Boston Red Sox, Pittsburgh Pirates, New York/San Francisco Giants, Cincinnati Reds

Most appearances: 33 New York Yankees, 18 Brooklyn/Los Angeles Dodgers, 16 New York/San Francisco Giants, 15 St Louis Cardinals, 14 Philadelphia/Kansas City/Oakland Athletics/A's, 10 Chicago White Sox; 9 Boston Red Sox, Cincinnati Reds, Detroit Tigers

Most National League titles (from 1876)
21 Brooklyn/Los Angeles Dodgers, 19 New York/San Francisco Giants, 16 Chicago Cubs, 15 St Louis Cardinals, 14 Boston/Milwaukee/ Atlanta Braves, 9 Pittsburgh Pirates

Most American League titles (from 1901)
33 New York Yankees, 15 Philadelphia/Oakland Athletics, 10 Boston Red Sox, 9 Detroit Tigers

Most individual appearances: 14 (75 games) Lawrence 'Yogi' Berra (New York Yankees) 1947, 1949-53, 1955-8, 1960-3 (he was on the winning team 10 times, and also has the records for 259 **at bats** and 71 **base hits**); Mickey Mantle (New York Yankees) 12 (65 games)

World Series Records

Most home runs in one game: 3 'Babe' Ruth (New York Yankees v St Louis Cardinals, 4th game) 6 Oct 1926; Reggie Jackson (New York Yankees v Los Angeles Dodgers, 6th game) 18 Oct 1977 (Jackson hit three consecutive pitches out of the park for his homers)
Most runs in a career: 42 (from 65 games) Mickey Mantle (New York Yankees) 1951-64 (and record 18 home runs and 40 runs batted in)
Most runs and home runs in a series: 10 (5 home runs) Reggie Jackson (New York Yankees) 1977
Most strikeouts in a career: 94 Whitey Ford (New York Yankees) 1950-64 (in 22 games)
Most strikeouts in a series: 35 Bob Gibson (St Louis Cardinals) 1968 (in 22 games)
Perfect pitch (9 innings): Don Larsen (New York Yankees v Brooklyn Dodgers, 5th game) 8 Oct 1956
Record attendance (series): 420,784 Los Angeles Dodgers v Chicago White Sox 1-8 Oct 1959
Record attendance (single game): 92,706 Los Angeles Dodgers v Chicago White Sox (5th game) at Memorial Coliseum, Los Angeles, 6 Oct 1959

Most valuable player award
The only men to have won the coveted award twice are: Sandy Koufax (Los Angeles, NL 1963, 1965), Bob Gibson (St Louis, NL 1964, 1967), Reggie Jackson (Oakland, AL 1973, New York, AL 1977)

Major League Records

Batting
Career
Best batting average: .367 Ty Cobb (Detroit AL, Philadelphia AL) 1905-28
Most runs: 2245 Ty Cobb (Detroit AL, Philadelphia AL) 1905-28
Most home runs: 755 Hank Aaron (Milwaukee NL, Atlanta NL, Milwaukee AL) 1954-76
Most runs batted in: 2297 Hank Aaron (Milwaukee NL, Atlanta NL, Milwaukee AL) 1954-76
Most base hits: 4256 Pete Rose (Cincinnati NL, Philadelphia NL) 1963-86
Total bases: 6856 Hank Aaron (Milwaukee NL, Atlanta NL, Milwaukee AL) 1954-76
Season
Best batting average: .438 Hugh Duffy (Boston NL) 1894
Most runs: 192 William Hamilton (Philadelphia NL) 1894
Most home runs: 61 Roger Maris (New York AL) 1961
Most runs batted in: 190 Hack Wilson (Chicago NL) 1930
Most base hits: 257 George Sisler (St Louis AL) 1920
Total bases: 457 Babe Ruth (New York AL) 1921
Stolen bases: 130 Rickey Henderson (Oakland AL) 1982
General
Consecutive hits: 12 Pinky Higgins (Boston AL) 19-21 Jun 1938; Moose Dropo (Detroit AL) 14-15 Jul 1952
Consecutive games batted safely: 56 Joe DiMaggio (New York AL) 15 May-16 Jul 1941

Consecutive games played: 2130 Lou Gehrig (New York AL) 1 Jun 1925-30 Apr 1939
Pitching
Career
Games won: 511 Cy Young (Cleveland NL, St Louis AL, Boston NL, Boston AL, Cleveland AL) 1890-1911
Shutouts: 113 Walter Johnson (Washington AL) 1907-27
Strikeouts: 5714 Nolan Ryan (New York NL, California AL, Houston NL, Texas AL) 1968-93
No-hit games: 7 Nolan Ryan (4 for California AL 1973-5, 1 Houston NL 1981, 2 Texas AL 1990-1)
Complete games: 751 Cy Young (Cleveland NL, St Louis AL, Boston NL, Boston AL, Cleveland AL) 1890-1911
Season
Games won: 60 Charles Radbourne (Providence NL) 1884
Shutouts: 16 George Bradley (St Louis NL) 1876; Grover Alexander (Philadelphia NL) 1916
Strikeouts: 383 Nolan Ryan (California AL) 1973
General
Consecutive games won 24 Carl Owen Hubbell (New York NL) 1936-7

Base Running - Stolen Bases
Career 1117 Rickey Henderson (Oakland AL, New York AL, Toronto AL) 1979-94
Season 130 Rickey Henderson (Oakland AL) 1982

League leaders

Post-war leaders - taking the best of the AL or NL each year:

Best batting average
1946 Stan Musial (St Louis) NL	.365
1947 Harry Walker (St Louis/Philadelphia) NL	.363
1948 Stan Musial (St Louis) NL	.376
1949 George Kell (Detroit) AL	.343
1950 Billy Goodman (Boston) AL	.354
1951 Stan Musial (St Louis) NL	.355
1952 Stan Musial (St Louis) NL	.336
1953 Carl Furillo (Brooklyn) NL	.344
1954 Willie Mays (New York Giants) NL	.345
1955 Al Kaline (Detroit) AL	.340
1956 Mickey Mantle (New York Yankees) AL	.353
1957 Ted Williams (Boston) AL	.388
1958 Richie Ashburn (Philadelphia) NL	.350
1959 Hank Aaron (Milwaukee) NL	.355
1960 Dick Groat (Pittsburgh) NL	.325
1961 Norm Cash (Detroit) AL	.361
1962 Tommy Davis (Los Angeles) NL	.346
1963 Tommy Davis (Los Angeles) NL	.326
1964 Roberto Clemente (Pittsburgh) NL	.339
1965 Roberto Clemente (Pittsburgh) NL	.329
1966 Maria Alou (Pittsburgh) NL	.342
1967 Roberto Clemente (Pittsburgh) NL	.357
1968 Pete Rose (Cincinnati) NL	.335
1969 Pete Rose (Cincinnati) NL	.348
1970 Rico Carty (Atlanta) NL	.366
1971 Joe Torre (St Louis) NL	.363
1972 Billy Williams (Chicago) NL	.333
1973 Rod Carew (Minnesota) AL	.350
1974 Rod Carew (Minnesota) AL	.364

1975 Rod Carew (Minnesota) AL	.359
1976 Bill Madlock (Chicago) NL	.339
1977 Rod Carew (Minnesota) AL	.388
1978 Dave Parker (Pittsburgh) NL	.334
1979 Keith Hernandez (St Louis) NL	.344
1980 George Brett (Kansas City) AL	.390
1981 Bill Madlock (Pittsburgh) NL	.341
1982 Willie Watson (Kansas City) AL	.332
1983 Wade Boggs (Boston) AL	.361
1984 Tony Gwynn (San Diego) NL	.341
1985 Wade Boggs (Boston) AL	.368
1986 Wade Boggs (Boston AL	.357
1987 Tony Gwynne (San Diego) NL	.370
1988 Wade Boggs (Boston) AL	.366
1989 Kirby Puckett (Minnesota) AL	.339
1990 Willie McGee (St Louis) NL	.335
1991 Julio Franco (Texas) AL	.341
1992 Edgar Martinez (Seattle) AL	.343
1993 Andres Galarraga (Colorado) NL	.370
1994 Tony Gwynn (San Diego) NL	.394

Highest ever average

NL .438 Hugh Duffy (Boston NL) 1894

AL .421 Napolean Lajoie (Philadelphia) 1901

Most seasons with best average

American League

12 Ty Cobb (Detroit) 1907-15, 1917-19

7 Rod Carew (Minnesota) 1969, 1972-5, 1977-8

6 Ted Williams (Boston) 1941-2, 1947-8, 1957-8

National League

8 John P.Wagner (Pittsburgh) 1900, 1903-4, 1906-9, 1911

7 Rogers Hornsby (St Louis) 1920-5, 1928

7 Stan Musial (St Louis) 1943, 1946, 1948, 1950-2, 1957

Most home runs

1946 Hank Greenberg (Detroit) AL	44
1947 Ralph Kiner (Pittsburgh) NL &	
Johnny Mize (New York Giants) NL	51
1948 Ralph Kiner (Pittsburgh) NL &	
Johnny Mize (New York Giants) NL	40
1949 Ralph Kiner (Pittsburgh) NL	54
1950 Ralph Kiner (Pittsburgh) NL	47
1951 Ralph Kiner (Pittsburgh) NL	42
1952 Ralph Kiner (Pittsburgh) NL &	
Hank Sauer (Chicago) NL	37
1953 Eddie Mathews (Milwaukee) NL	47
1954 Ted Kluszewski (Cincinnati) NL	49
1955 Willie Mays (New York Giants) NL	51
1956 Mickey Mantle (New York Yankees) NL	52
1957 Hank Aaron (Milwaukee) NL	44
1958 Ernie Banks (Chicago) NL	47
1959 Eddie Mathews (Milwaukee) NL	46
1960 Ernie Banks (Chicago) NL	41
1961 Orlando Cepeda (San Francisco) NL	46
1962 Willie Mays (San Francisco) NL	49
1963 Harmon Killebrew (Minnesota) AL	45
1964 Harmon Killebrew (Minnesota) AL	49
1965 Willie Mays (San Francisco) NL	52
1966 Frank Robinson (Baltimore) AL	49
1967 Carl Yastrzemski (Boston) AL &	
Harmon Killebrew (Minnesota) AL	44
1968 Frank Howard (Washington) AL	44
1969 Harmon Killebrew (Minnesota) AL	49
1970 Johnny Bench (Cincinnati) NL	45
1971 Willie Stargel (Pittsburgh) NL	48
1972 Johnny Bench (Cincinnati) NL	40
1973 Willie Stargel (Pittsburgh) NL	44
1974 Mike Schmidt (Philadelphia) NL	36
1975 Mike Schmidt (Philadelphia) NL	38
1976 Mike Schmidt (Philadelphia) NL	38
1977 George Foster (Cincinnati) NL	52
1978 Jim Rice (Boston) AL	46
1979 Dave Kingman (Chicago) NL	48
1980 Mike Schmidt (Philadelphia) NL	48
1981 Mike Schmidt (Philadelphia) NL	31
1982 Gorman Thomas (Milwaukee) AL &	
Reggie Jackson (California) AL	39
1983 Mike Schmidt (Philadelphia) NL	40
1984 Tony Armas (Boston) AL	43
1985 Darrell Evans (Detroit) AL	60
1986 Jesse Barfield (Toronto) AL	40
1987 Mark McGwire (Oakland) AL	
& Andre Dawson (Chicago) NL	49
1988 Jose Canseco (Oakland) AL	42
1989 Kevin Mitchell (San Francisco) NL	47
1990 Cecil Fielder (Detroit) AL	51
1991 Cecil Fielder (Detroit) AL	44
& Jose Canseco (Oakland) AL	44
1992 Juan Gonzalez (Texas) AL	43
1993 Juan Gonzalez (Texas) AL	
& Barry Bonds (San Francisco) NL	46
1994 Matt Williams (San Francisco) NL	43

Most seasons leading

American League

12 Babe Ruth (New York) 1918-21, 1923-4, 1926-31

6 Harmon Killebrew 1959, 1962-4, 1967, 1969

National League

8 Mike Schmidt 1974-6, 1980-1, 1983-4, 1986

7 Ralph Kiner (Pittsburgh) 1946-52

6 Gavvy Crovath (Philadelphia) 1913-15, 1917-19

6 Melvin Ott (New York) 1932, 1934, 1936-8, 1942

Earned run average

1946 Hal Newhouser (Detroit) AL	1.94
1947 Warren Spahn (Boston) NL	2.33
1948 Harry Brecheen (St Louis) NL	2.24
1949 Dave Koslo (New York) NL	2.50
1950 Jim Hearn (St Louis/New York) NL	2.49
1951 Saul Rogovin (Detroit/Chicago) AL	2.78
1952 Allie Reynolds (New York) AL	2.07
1953 Warren Spahn (Milwaukee) NL	2.10
1954 John Antonelli (New York) NL	2.29
1955 Billy Pierce (Chicago) AL	1.57
1956 Whitey Ford (New York) AL	2.47
1957 Bobby Schantz (New York) AL	2.45
1958 Whitey Ford (New York) AL	2.01
1959 Hoyt Wilhelm (Baltimore) AL	2.19
1960 Frank Baumann (Chicago) AL	2.68
1961 Richard Donovan (Washington) AL	2.40
1962 Hank Aguirre (Detroit) AL	2.21
1963 Sandy Koufax (Los Angeles) NL	1.88
1964 Dean Chance (Los Angeles) AL	1.64

1965 Sandy Koufax (Los Angeles) NL   2.04
1966 Sandy Koufax (Los Angeles) NL   2.04
1967 Phil Niekro (Atlanta) NL   1.87
1968 Bob Gibson (St Louis) NL   1.12
1969 Juan Marichal (San Francisco) NL   2.10
1970 Diego Segui (Oakland) AL   2.56
1971 Tom Seaver (New York) NL   1.76
1972 Luis Tiant (Boston) AL   1.91
1973 Tom Seaver (New York) NL   2.07
1974 Buzz Capra (Atlanta) NL   2.28
1975 Jim Palmer (Baltimore) AL   2.09
1976 Mark Fidrych (Detroit) AL   2.34
1977 John Candelaria (Pittsburgh) NL   2.34
1978 Ron Guidry (New York) AL   1.74
1979 J R Richard (Houston) NL   2.71
1980 Don Sutton (Los Angeles) NL   2.21
1981 Nolan Ryan (Houston) NL   1.69
1982 Steve Rogers (Montreal) NL   2.40
1983 Atlee Hammaker (San Francisco) NL   2.25
1984 Alejandro Pena (Los Angeles) NL   2.56
1985 Dwight Gooden (New York) NL   1.53
1986 Mike Scott (Houston) AL   2.22
1987 James E Key (Toronto) AL &   2.76
  Nolan Ryan (Houston) NL   2.76
1988 Allan Anderson (Minnesota) AL &
  Teodoro Higuera (Milwaukee) AL   2.45
1989 Scott Garrelts (San Francisco) NL   2.28
1990 Roger Clemens (Boston) AL   1.93
1991 Dennis Martinez (Montreal) NL   2.39
1992 Bill Swift (San Francisco) NL   2.08
1993 Greg Maddux (Atlanta) NL   2.36
1994 Greg Maddux (Atlanta) NL   1.56

Most times leader
American League
9 Lefty Grove (Philadelphia, Boston) 1926, 1929-32, 1935-6, 1938-9
5 Walter Johnson (Washington) 1912-13, 1918-9, 1924
4 Roger Clemens (Boston) 1986, 1990-2
National League
5 Christy Mathewson (New York) 1905, 1908-09, 1911, 1913
5 Pete Alexander (Philadelphia, Chicago) 1915-7, 1919-20
5 Sandy Koufax (Los Angeles) 1962-6
3 Dazzy Vance (Brooklyn) 1924, 1928, 1930
3 Carl Hubbell (New York) 1933-4, 1936
3 Warren Spahn (Boston, Milwaukee) 1947, 1953, 1961
3 Tom Seaver (New York) 1970-1, 1973

Most Valuable Player Awards
Annually since 1931 the Baseball Writers' Association vote for the Most Valuable Player of the Year in both the American and National leagues. *Post-war winners:*

Greg Maddux – voted top pitcher each year 1992-4

	American League	National League
1946	Ted Williams (Boston)	Stan Musial (St Louis)
1947	Joe DiMaggio (New York)	Bob Elliott (Boston)
1948	Louis Boudreau (Cleveland)	Stan Musial (St Louis)
1949	Ted Williams (Boston)	Jack Robinson (Brooklyn)
1950	Philip Rizzuto (New York)	Jim Konstanty (Philadelphia)
1951	'Yogi' Berra (New York)	Roy Campanella (Brooklyn)
1952	Robert Shantz (Philadelphia)	Hank Sauer (Chicago)
1953	Albert Rosen (Cleveland)	Roy Campanella (Brooklyn)
1954	'Yogi' Berra (New York)	Willie Mays (New York)
1955	'Yogi' Berra (New York)	Roy Campanella (Brooklyn)
1956	Mickey Mantle (New York)	Don Newcombe (Brooklyn)
1957	Mickey Mantle New York)	Hank Aaron (Milwaukee)
1958	Jack Jensen (Boston)	Ernest Banks (Chicago)
1959	Nelson Fox (Chicago)	Ernest Banks (Chicago)
1960	Roger Maris (New York)	Dick Groat (Pittsburgh)
1961	Roger Maris (New York)	Frank Robinson (Cincinnati)
1962	Mickey Mantle (New York)	Maurice Wills (Los Angeles)

1963	Elston Howard (New York)	Sandy Koufax (Los Angeles)
1964	Brooks Robinson (Baltimore)	Kenton Boyer (St Louis)
1965	Zoilo Versalles (Minnesota)	Willie Mays (San Francisco)
1966	Frank Robinson (Baltimore)	Roberto Clemente (Pittsburgh)
1967	Carl Yastrzemski (Boston)	Orlando Cepeda (St Louis)
1968	Dennis McLain (Detroit)	Robert Gibson (St Louis)
1969	Harmon Killebrew (Minnesota)	Willie McCovey (San Francisco)
1970	John Powell (Baltimore)	Johnny Bench (Cincinnati)
1971	Vida Blue (Oakland)	Joe Torre (St Louis)
1972	Dick Allen (Chicago)	Johnny Bench (Cincinnati)
1973	Reggie Jackson (Oakland)	Pete Rose (Cincinnati)
1974	Jeffrey Burroughs (Texas)	Steve Garvey (Los Angeles)
1975	Fredric Lynn (Boston)	Joe Morgan (Cincinnati)
1976	Thurman Munson (New York)	Joe Morgan (Cincinnati)
1977	Rod Carew (Minnesota)	George Foster (Cincinnati)
1978	Jim Rice (Boston)	Dave Parker (Pittsburgh)
1979	Donald Baylor (California)	Keith Hernandez (St Louis) & Willie Stargell (Pittsburgh)
1980	George Brett (Kansas City)	Mike Schmidt (Philadelphia)
1981	Rollie Fingers (Milwaukee)	Mike Schmidt (Philadelphia)
1982	Robin Yount (Milwaukee)	Dale Murphy (Atlanta)
1983	Cal Ripken Jr (Baltimore)	Dale Murphy (Atlanta)
1984	Willie Hernandez (Detroit)	Ryne Sandberg (Chicago)
1985	Don Mattingly (New York)	Willie McGee (St Louis)
1986	Roger Clemens (Boston)	Mike Schmidt (Philadelphia)
1987	George Bell (Toronto)	Andre Dawson (Chicago)
1988	Jose Canseco (Oakland)	Kirk Gibson (Los Angeles)
1989	Robin Yount (Milwaukee)	Kevin Mitchell (San Francisco)
1990	Rickey Henderson (Oakland)	Barry Bonds (Pittsburgh)
1991	Cal Ripken Jr (Baltimore)	Terry Pendleton (Atlanta Braves)

Barry Bonds - three years as AL MVP

1992	Dennis Eckersley (Oakland)	Barry Bonds (Pittsburgh)
1993	Frank Thomas (Chicago)	Barry Bonds (Pittsburgh)
1994	Frank Thomas (Chicago)	Jeff Bagwell (Houston)

Most selections

NL: 3 Stan Musial 1943, 1946, 1948; Roy Campanella, Mike Schmidt

AL: 3 James E Foxx (Philadelphia) 1932-3, 1938; Joe Di Maggio 1939, 1941, 1947; Yogi Berra, Mickey Mantle, Barry Bonds

Cy Young Award

Awarded from 1956 to the outstanding pitcher on the major leagues. From 1967 awards have been made for both American and National leagues. *Recent winners:*

	American League	**National League**
1980	Steve Stone (Baltimore)	Steve Carlton (Philadelphia)
1981	Rollie Fingers (Milwaukee)	Fernando Valenzuela (Los Angeles)
1982	Pete Vukovich (Milwaukee)	Steve Carlton (Philadelphia)
1983	LaMarr Hoyt (Chicago)	John Denny (Philadelphia)

1984	Willie Hernandez (Detroit)	Rick Sutcliffe (Chicago)
1985	Bret Saberhagen (Kansas City)	Dwight Gooden (New York)
1986	Roger Clemens (Boston)	Mike Scott (Houston)
1987	Roger Clemens (Boston)	Steve Bedrosian (Philadelphia)
1988	Frank Viola (Minnesota)	Orel Hershiser (Los Angeles)
1989	Bret Saberhagen (Kansas City)	Mark Davis (San Diego)
1990	Bob Welch (Oakland)	Doug Drabek (Pittsburgh)
1991	Roger Clemens (Boston)	Tom Glavine (Atlanta)
1992	Dennis Eckersley (Oakland)	Greg Maddux (Chicago)
1993	Jack McDowell (Chicago)	Greg Maddux (Atlanta)
1994	Dave Cone (Kansas City)	Greg Maddux (Atlanta)

Most wins

4 Steve Carlton (Philadelphia NL) 1972, 1977, 1980, 1982; 3 Sandy Koufax (Los Angeles AL) 1963, 1965-6; James Palmer (Baltimore AL) 1973, 1975-6; Thomas Seaver (New York NL) 1969, 1973, 1975; Roger Clemens (AL) & Greg Maddux (NL) *as above*

NCAA Championship

The College World Series for Division 1 colleges has been held annually from 1947. Since 1950 every championship final has been played at Rosenblatt Stadium, Omaha, Nebraska. *Wins:*

11	Southern California	1948, 1958, 1961, 1963, 1968, 1970-4, 1978
5	Arizona State	1965, 1967, 1969, 1977, 1981
4	Texas	1949-50, 1975, 1983
3	Minnesota	1956, 1960, 1964
3	Arizona	1976, 1980, 1986
2	California	1947, 1957
2	Oklahoma	1951, 1994
2	Michigan	1953, 1962
2	Cal State Fullerton	1979, 1984
2	Miami (Florida)	1982, 1985
2	Stanford	1987-8
2	Louisiana State	1991, 1993
1	Holy Cross 1952, Missouri 1954, Wake Forest 1955, Oklahoma State 1959, Ohio State 1966, Wichita State 1989, Georgia 1990, Pepperdine 1992	

The Arizona State v Ohio State match in 1965 was not resolved until the 15th innings. Arizona won 2-1.

World Amateur Championship

Instituted 1938. Coordinated by the International Baseball Association (IBA), membership of which reached 74 nations in 1992. Held biennially since 1974. *Winners:*

21	Cuba	1939-40, 1942-3, 1950, 1952-3, 1961, 1969-73*, 1976, 1978, 1980, 1984, 1986, 1988, 1990, 1994
3	Venezuela	1941, 1944-5
2	Colombia	1947, 1965, USA 1973*-4
1	United Kingdom 1938, Dominican Republic 1948, Puerto Rico 1951, South Korea 1982	

1973, Cuba and USA shared title

Olympic Games

American baseball has appeared at six Olympic Games as a demonstration sport. In addition, Finnish baseball was included in 1952. Baseball became a medal sport for the first time in 1992. *Winners:*

1912	USA
1936	'World Amateurs'
1956	American Services team
1964	USA
1984	Japan
1988	USA
1992	Cuba

Basketball

The modern game of basketball was invented by Dr James Naismith at the Training School of the International YMCA College at Springfield, Massachussets, USA in December 1891. Games bearing a resemblance to basketball have been played for thousands of years, the earliest being perhaps 'Pok-ta-Pok', played by the Olmecs in Mexico in the 10th century BC.

The early games of basketball had large numbers of players, but five-a-side as standard was agreed in 1895. The AAU organised the first national tournament in the USA in 1897. The first professional league was the National Basketball League (NBL), founded in 1898, but this league only lasted two seasons. The American Basketball League was formed in 1925, but declined and the NBL was refounded in 1937. This organisation merged with the Basketball Association of America in 1949 to form the National Basketball Association (NBA).

The world governing body, the Fédération Internationale de Basketball (FIBA), was founded in 1932 and the sport

Charles Barkley – 'Dream Team' star of 1992

added to the Olympic programme in 1936. FIBA membership reached 198 in 1995.

Olympic Games

First played by men in 1936 and by women in 1976. *Wins:*

Men

10	USA	1936, 1948, 1952, 1956, 1960, 1964, 1968, 1976, 1984, 1992
2	USSR	1972, 1988
1	Yugoslavia	1980

Women

3	USSR/CIS	1976, 1980, 1992
2	USA	1984, 1988

World Championships

First held for men in Buenos Aires in 1950, and for women in 1953. They are each now held quadrennially. *Winners:*

Men

3	USA	1954, 1986, 1994
3	USSR	1967, 1974, 1982
3	Yugoslavia	1970, 1978, 1990
2	Brazil	1959, 1963
1	Argentina	1950

Woen

6	USSR	1959, 1964, 1967, 1971, 1975, 1983
5	USA	1953, 1957, 1979, 1986, 1990
1	Brazil	1994

European Championships

Contested by European nations. Held biennially. *Wins:*

Men

14	USSR	1947, 1951, 1953, 1957, 1959, 1961, 1963, 1965, 1967, 1969, 1971, 1979, 1981, 1985
6	Yugoslavia	1973, 1975, 1977, 1989, 1991, 1995
2	Lithuania	1937, 1939
1	Latvia 1935, Czechoslovakia 1946, Egypt 1949, Hungary 1955, Italy 1983, Greece 1987, Germany 1993	

Women

21	USSR	1950, 1952, 1954, 1956, 1960, 1962, 1964, 1966, 1968, 1970, 1972, 1974, 1976, 1978, 1980, 1981, 1983, 1985, 1987, 1989, 1991
1	Italy 1938, Bulgaria 1958, Spain 1993, Ukraine 1995	

European Championships for Clubs

First held as the European Champions' Cup in 1958 for men and in 1959 for women. *Wins:*

Men

8	Real Madrid (Spa)	1964-5, 1967-8, 1974, 1978, 1980, 1995
5	Varese (Ita)	1970, 1972-3, 1975-6
4	CSKA Moskva (USSR)	1961, 1963, 1969, 1971
3	ASK Riga (USSR)	1958-60
3	Milan (Ita)	1966, 1987-8
3	Split (Yug)	1989-90 Jugoplastika 1991 Pop 84
2	Cantu (Ita)	1982-3

2	Maccabi Tel Aviv (Isr)	1977, 1981
2	Cibona Zagreb (Yug)	1985-6
1	Dynamo Tbilisi (USSR) 1962, Bosna Sarajevo (Yug) 1979, Banco di Roma (Ita) 1984, Partizan Belgrade (Yug) 1992, CSP Limoges (Fra) 1993, Joventut Badalona (Spa) 1994	

Women

18	Daugava Riga (USSR)	1960-2, 1964-75, 1977, 1981-2
5	AS Vicenza (Ita)	1983, 1985-8
2	Slavia Sofia (Bul)	1959, 1963, 1984
2	Dorna Valencia (Spa)	1992-3
1	CKD Praha (Cs) 1976, Sesto San Giovanni (Ita) 1978, Red Star Belgrade (Yug) 1979, Turin (Ita) 1980, Levski Spartak Sofia (Bul) 1984, Jedinstvo Aida Tuzia (Yug) 1989, Enimont Priolo (Ita) 1990, Cesena (Ita) 1991, SFT Como (Ita) 1994	

NBA Champions

The 23 American professional teams are divided into two conferences, the Eastern, subdivided into the Atlantic Division and the Central Division, and the Western, subdivided into the Midwest Division and the Pacific Division. The best teams contest play-offs annually to determine the champions. The American Basketball Association, which had begun in 1967, merged with the NBA in 1976.

National League Champions

1938	Goodyears
1939-40	Firestones
1941-2	Oshkosh
1943-5	Fort Wayne Pistons
1946	Rochester Royals
1947	Chicago Stags
1948	Minneapolis Lakers
1949	Anderson Packers

NBA Champions

1947	Philadelphia Warriors
1948	Baltimore Bullets
1949-50	Minneapolis Lakers
1951	Rochester Royals
1952-4	Minneapolis Lakers
1955	Syracuse Nationals
1956	Philadelphia Warriors
1957	Boston Celtics
1958	St Louis Hawks
1959-66	Boston Celtics
1967	Philadelphia 76ers
1968-9	Boston Celtics
1970	New York Knicks
1971	Milwaukee Bucks
1972	Los Angeles Lakers
1973	New York Knicks
1974	Boston Celtics
1975	Golden State Warriors
1976	Boston Celtics
1977	Portland Trail Blazers
1978	Washington Bullets
1979	Seattle Supersonics
1980	Los Angeles Lakers
1981	Boston Celtics
1982	Los Angeles Lakers

1983	Philadelphia 76ers
1984	Boston Celtics
1985	Los Angeles Lakers
1986	Boston Celtics
1987-8	Los Angeles Lakers
1989-90	Detroit Pistons
1991-3	Chicago Bulls
1994 5	Houston Rockets

Most wins: 16 Boston Celtics

NBA Records

Highest match aggregate: 370 Detroit Pistons beat Denver Nuggets 186-184, Denver, 13 Dec 1983. Extra time was played following a 145-145 tie in regulation time.

Most points in game: 100 Wilt Chamberlain, Philadelphia v New York, 2 Mar 1962.

Most points in play-offs game: 63 Michael Jordan, Chicago v Boston, 20 Apr 1986.

Season's record points: 4029 Wilt Chamberlain for Philadelphia 1962 (at a record average 50.4 points per game).

Career record points: 38,387 Kareem Abdul-Jabbar for Milwaukee Bucks & Los Angeles Lakers 1969-89 (in 1560 games, average 24.61 points per game, with a record 15,837 field goals. He also scored a record 5762 points, including 2396 field goals, in play-off games.

Career record assists: 10,394 John Stockton for Utah Jazz 1984-95 (including eight seasons, 1988-95, leading NBA, a record he shares with Bob Cousy, Boston 1953-60).

Career record rebounds: 23,924 Wilt Chamberlain 1960-73

Leading career scorers (NBA and ABA)

Points	Name	Games	Ave.	Years
38,387	Kareem Abdul-Jabbar	1560	24.6	1970-89
31,419	Wilt Chamberlain	1045	30.1	1960-73
30,026	Julius Erving	1243	24.2	1972-87
29,580	Moses Malone	1455	20.3	1975-95
27,482	Dan Issel	1218	22.6	1971-85
27,313	Elvin Hayes	1303	21.0	1969-84
26,710	Oscar Robertson	1040	25.7	1961-74
26,595	George Gervin	1061	25.1	1973-86
26,395	John Havlicek	1270	20.8	1963-78
25,389	Dominique Wilkins	984	25.8	1982-95
25,466	Alex English	1184	21.5	1977-90
25,279	Rick Barry	1020	24.8	1966-80
25,192	Jerry West	932	27.0	1961-74
24,941	Artis Gilmore	1329	18.8	1972-88
23,177	Adrian Dantley	955	24.3	1977-91
23,149	Elgin Baylor	846	27.4	1959-72

Other averages over 25.0 for more than 10 000 points

22,586	Larry Bird	897	25.1	1980-92
21,998	Michael Jordan	684	32.2	1984-95
21,237	Karl Malone	816	26.0	1985-95
20,880	Bob Pettit	792	26.4	1955-65
12,209	David Robinson	475	25.7	1989-95

Leading career scorers in NBA Playoffs to 1994

Points	Name	Games	Average
5762	Kareem Abdul-Jabbar	237	24.3
4457	Jerry West	153	29.1
4165	Michael Jordan	121	34.4
3897	Larry Bird	164	23.8
3776	John Havlicek	172	22.0
3640	Magic Johnson	186	19.6
3623	Elgin Baylor	134	27.0
3607	Wilt Chamberlain	160	22.5
3182	Kevin McHale	169	18.8
3116	Dennis Johnson	180	17.3
3088	Julius Irving	141	21.9
3023	Hakeem Olajuwon	107	28.3
3022	James Worthy	143	21.1

Other averages over 25.0 for more than 1500 points

2240	Bob Pettit	88	25.5
2169	Karl Malone	79	27.5
1592	George Gervin	59	27.0

NBA Leading Scorers each season

Year	Name (Club)	Games	Points
1950	George Mikan (Minneapolis)	68	1865
1951	George Mikan (Minneapolis)	68	1932
1952	Paul Arizin (Philadelphia)	66	1674

Hakeem Olajuwon – MVP of the 1995 playoffs

1953 Neil Johnston (Philadelphia)	70	1564
1954 Neil Johnston (Philadelphia)	72	1759
1955 Neil Johnston (Philadelphia)	72	1631
1956 Bob Pettit (St Louis)	72	1849
1957 Paul Arizin (Philadelphia)	71	1817
1958 George Yardley (Detroit)	72	2001
1959 Bob Pettit (St Louis)	72	2105
1960 Wilt Chamberlain (Philadelphia)	72	2707
1961 Wilt Chamberlain (Philadelphia)	79	3033
1962 Wilt Chamberlain (Philadelphia)	80	4029
1963 Wilt Chamberlain (San Francisco)	80	3586
1964 Wilt Chamberlain (San Francisco)	80	2948
1965 Wilt Chamberlain (SF/Philadelphia)	80	2534
1966 Wilt Chamberlain (Philadelphia)	79	2649
1967 Rick Barry (San Francisco)	78	2775
1968 Dave Bing (Detroit)	79	2142
1969 Elvin Hayes (San Diego)	82	2327
1970 Jerry West (Los Angeles)	74	2309
1971 Lew Alcindor* (Milwaukee)	82	2596
1972 Kareem Abdul-Jabbar (Milwaukee)	81	2822
1973 Nate Archibald (Kansas City/Omaha)	80	2719
1974 Bob McAdoo (Buffalo)	74	2261
1975 Bob McAdoo (Buffalo)	82	2831
1976 Bob McAdoo (Buffalo)	78	2427
1977 Pete Maravich (New Orleans)	73	2273

Shaquille O'Neal – top scorer in the NBA 1994/5

1978 George Gervin (San Antonio)	82	2232
1979 George Gervin (San Antonio)	80	2365
1980 George Gervin (San Antonio)	78	2585
1981 Adrian Dantley (Utah)	80	2452
1982 George Gervin (San Antonio)	79	2551
1983 Alex English (Denver)	82	2326
1984 Adrian Dantley (Utah)	79	2418
1985 Bernard King (New York)	55	1809
1986 Dominique Wilkins (Atlanta)	78	2366
1987 Michael Jordan (Chicago)	82	3041
1988 Michael Jordan (Chicago)	82	2868
1989 Michael Jordan (Chicago)	81	2633
1990 Michael Jordan (Chicago)	82	2753
1991 Michael Jordan (Chicago)	82	2580
1992 Michael Jordan (Chicago)	80	2404
1993 Michael Jordan (Chicago)	78	2541
1994 David Robinson (San Antonio)	80	2383
1995 Shaquille O'Neal (Orlando)	79	2315

* took name of Kareem Abdul-Jabbar from 1971/2 season

Highest scoring runners-up

1963 Elgin Baylor (Los Angeles)	80	2719
1990 Karl Malone (Utah Jazz)	82	2540
1961 Elgin Baylor (Los Angeles)	73	2538
1982 Moses Malone (Houston)	81	2520

Most seasons leading

7 Wilt Chamberlain, Michael Jordan; 3 Neil Johnston, Bob McAdoo

Most seasons over 2000 points

9	Kareem Abdul-Jabbar	1970-4, 1976-7, 1980-1
8	Alex English	1982-9
8	Michael Jordan	1985, 1987-93
8	Dominique Wilkins	1985-91, 1993
8	Karl Malone	1988-95
7	Wilt Chamberlain	1960-6
7	Oscar Robertson	1961-7
6	George Gervin	1978-83

Years shown are those of second half of the season.

NBA Most Valuable Player

Voted annually by NBA players from 1956 for the Maurice Podoloff Trophy, named after the first commissioner of the NBA, 1946-63:

1956	Bob Pettit (St Louis)
1957	Bob Cousy (Boston)
1958	Bill Russell (Boston)
1959	Bob Pettit (St Louis)
1960	Wilt Chamberlain (Philadelphia)
1961-3	Bill Russell (Boston)
1964	Oscar Robertson (Cincinnati)
1965	Bill Russell (Boston)
1966-8	Wilt Chamberlain (Philadelphia)
1969	Wes Unseld (Baltimore)
1970	Willis Reed (New York)
1971-2	Kareem Abdul-Jabbar* (Milwaukee)
1973	Dave Cowens (Boston)
1974	Kareem Abdul-Jabbar (Milwaukee)
1975	Bob McAdoo (Buffalo)
1976-7	Kareem Abdul-Jabbar (Los Angeles)
1978	Bill Walton (Portland)
1979	Moses Malone (Houston)
1980	Kareem Abdul-Jabbar (Los Angeles)

1981   Julius Erving (Philadelphia)
1982   Moses Malone (Houston)
1983   Moses Malone (Philadelphia)
1984-6 Larry Bird (Boston)
1987   Earvin 'Magic' Johnson (Los Angeles)
1988   Michael Jordan (Chicago)
1989-90 Earvin 'Magic' Johnson (Los Angeles)
1991-2 Michael Jordan (Chicago)
1993   Charles Barkley (Phoenix)
1994   Hakeem Olajuwon (Houston Rockets)
1995   David Robinson (San Antonio)

Most wins: 6 Kareem Abdul-Jabbar, 5 Bill Russell, 4 Wilt Chamberlain, 3 Moses Malone, Larry Bird, 'Magic' Johnson, Michael Jordan
* *still known as Lew Alcindor in 1971*

NCAA Championships

The most important inter-collegiate competition in the USA, first contested in 1939. *Division One Wins:*

11	UCLA	1964-5, 1967-73, 1975, 1995
5	Kentucky	1948-9, 1951, 1958, 1978
5	Indiana	1940, 1953, 1976, 1981, 1987
3	North Carolina	1957, 1982, 1993
2	Oklahoma A&M	1945-6
2	Kansas	1952, 1988
2	San Francisco	1955-6
2	Cincinnati	1961-2
2	North Carolina State	1974, 1983
2	Louisville	1980, 1986
2	Duke	1991-2

1 Oregon 1939, Wisconsin 1941, Stanford 1942, Wyoming 1943, Utah 1944, Holy Cross 1947, City College of New York 1950, LaSalle 1954, California 1959, Ohio State 1960, Loyola (Ill) 1963, Texas Western 1966, Marquette 1977, Michigan State 1979, Georgetown 1984, Villanova 1985, Michigan 1989, Nevada - Las Vegas 1990, Arkansas 1994

One player has been voted the Most Valuable Player in the NCAA final three times: Lew Alcindor of UCLA 1967-9. He subsequently changed his name to Kareem Abdul-Jabbar.

Highest match aggregate: 399 Troy State (258) beat De Vry Institute, Atlanta (141) at Troy 12 Jan 1992

Most points in game: 113 Clarence 'Bevo' Francis for Rio Grande v Hillsdale on 2 Feb 1954 (Div II).

NCAA Division I career scoring average leaders

Points	Name (College)	Games	Ave.	Years
3667	Pete Maravich (LSU)	83	44.2	1968-70
2560	Austin Carr (Notre Dame)	74	34.6	1969-71
2973	Oscar Robertson (Cincinnati)	88	33.8	1958-60
2548	Calvin Murphy (Niagara)	77	33.1	1968-70

Scoring over 3200 points in four years

3249	Freeman Williams (Portland St)	106	30.7	1975-8
3217	Lionel Simmons (La Salle)	131	24.6	1987-90

Maravich averaged over 40 points in each season of his college career: 1968 - 1138 pts av.43.8, 1969- 1148 pts av.44.2, 1970 - 1381 pts av.44.5.
In Division II Travis Grant scored a record 4045 points (av. 33.4) in 121 games for Kentucky State 1969-72.

NCAA Women's championship

First contested 1982. *Division I winners:*

3	Tennessee	1987, 1989, 1991
2	Louisiana Tech	1982, 1988
2	Southern California	1983-4
2	Stanford	1990, 1992

1 Old Dominion 1985, Texas 1986, Texas Tech 1993, North Carolina 1994, Connecticut 1995

Highest match aggregate: 261 St Joseph's (Indiana) beat Northern Kentucky 131-130 on 27 Feb 1988

Biathlon

Combined cross-country skiing and rifle shooting. Competitors ski (freestyle) over prepared courses carrying a 22 calibre rifle weighing 4.54 kg. Men compete individually over 10 km or 20 km distances. During the former they have two shooting competitions and in the latter four, prone and standing, at a target 50 metres away. The relay event is 4 x 7.5 km, each member shooting once prone and once standing. Penalties are imposed for missing the target. The women's equivalent distances are now 7.5 km, 15 km and 3 x 7.5 km relay.

The sport's governing body is L'Union Internationale de Pentathlon Moderne et Biathlon (UIPMB), which took on the administration of biathlon in 1957, and which staged the first world championships the following year.

Olympic games

Men's biathlon has been on the Olympic programme since 1960. Women's events were added in 1992. *Winners:*

Men's 10 kilometres

1980	Frank Ullrich (GDR) 32:10.69
1984	Eirik Kvalfoss (Nor) 30:53.8
1988	Frank-Peter Rötsch (GDR) 25:08.1
1992	Mark Kirchner (Ger) 26:02.3
1994	Sergey Chepikov (Rus) 28:07.0

Men's 20 kilometres

1960	Klas Lestander (Swe) 1:33:21.6
1964	Vladimir Melanin (USSR) 1:20:26.8
1968	Magnar Solberg (Nor) 1:13:45.9
1972	Magnar Solberg (Nor) 1:15:55.5
1976	Nikolay Kruglov (USSR) 1:14:12.26
1980	Anatoliy Alyabyev (USSR) 1:08:16.31
1984	Peter Angerer (FRG) 1:11:52.7
1988	Frank-Peter Rötsch (GDR) 56:33.33
1992	Yevgeniy Redkin (CIS) 57:34.4
1994	Sergey Tarasov (Rus) 57:25.3

Men's 4 x 7.5 kilometres relay

1968	USSR 2:13:02.4
1972	USSR 1:51:44.92

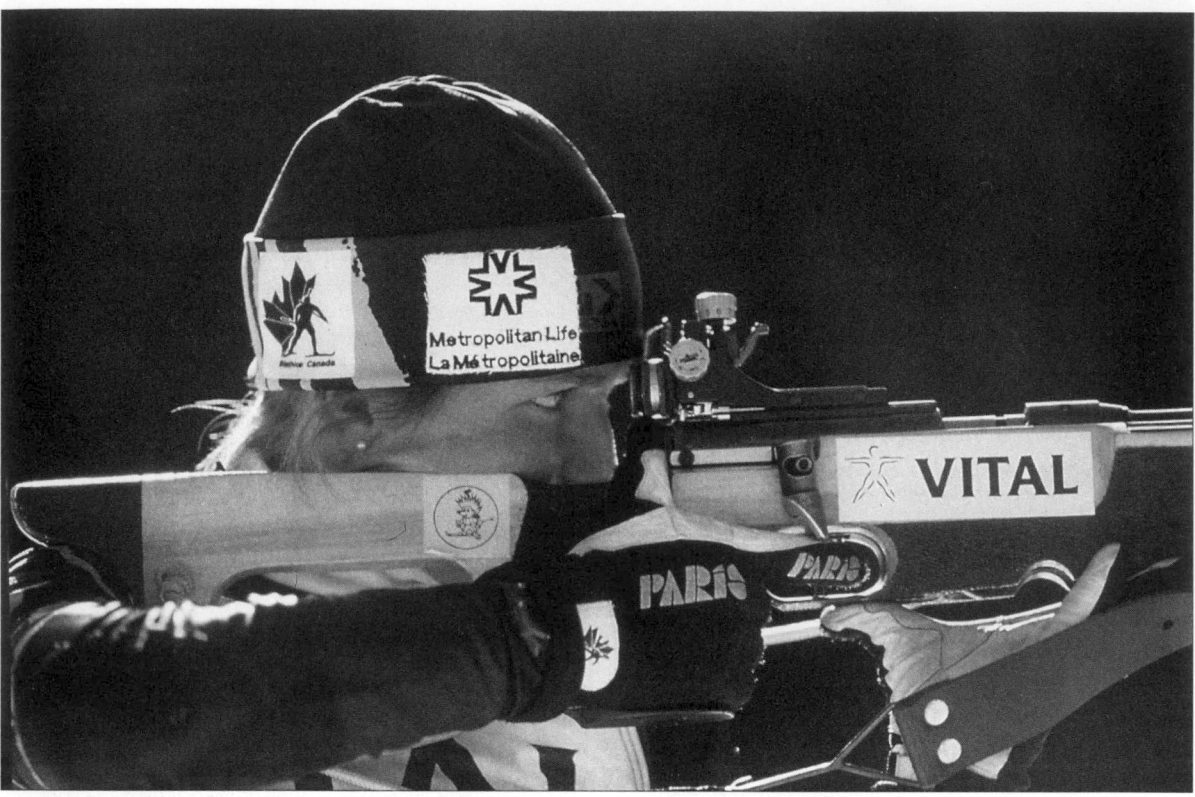

Myriam Bédard has become the most successful woman biathlete at the Olympics

1976	USSR 1:57:55.64
1980	USSR 1:34:03.27
1984	USSR 1:38:51.70
1988	USSR 1:22:30.0
1992	Germany 1:24:43.5
1994	Germany 1:30:22.1

Most gold medals

4   Aleksandr Tikhonov (USSR) relay 1968, 1972, 1976, 1980.

Most medals

5   Aleksandr Tikhonov 4 relay gold, 20km silver 1968

5   Peter Angerer (FRG) gold 20km 1980; silver 10km 1984, relay 1988; bronze relay 1980, 1984

Women's 7.5 kilometres

| 1992 | Anfisa Restzova (CIS) 24:29.2 |
| 1994 | Myriam Bédard (Can) 26:08.8 |

Women's 15 kilometres

| 1992 | Antje Misersky (Ger) 51:47.2 |
| 1994 | Myriam Bédard (Can) 52:06.6 |

Women's 3 x 7.5 kilometres relay

| 1992 | France 1:15:55.6 |

Women's 4 x 7.5 kilometres relay

| 1994 | Russia 1:47:19.5 |

Most gold medals

2   Myriam Bédard (Can) 7.5km & 15km 1994

Most medals

3   Myriam Bédard (Can) two gold 1994, bronze

15km 1992

3   Antje Misersky (Ger) gold 15km 1992, silver 7.5km & relay 1992

3   Anfisa Restzova (Rus) gold 7.5km 1992, relay 1994; bronze relay 1992

World Championships

Held annually from 1958 for men and 1984 for women, with the exception of Olympic years. *Winners:*

Men's 20 kilometres

1958	Adolf Wiklund (Swe)
1959	Vladimir Melanin (USSR)
1961	Kalevi Huuskonen (Fin)
1962	Vladimir Melanin (USSR)
1963	Vladimir Melanin (USSR)
1965	Olav Jordet (Nor)
1966	Jon Istad (Nor)
1967	Viktor Mamatov (USSR)
1969	Aleksandr Tikhonov (USSR)
1970	Aleksandr Tikhonov (USSR)
1971	Dieter Speer (GDR)
1973	Aleksandr Tikhonov (USSR)
1974	Juhani Suutarinen (Fin)
1975	Heikki Ikola (Fin)
1977	Heikki Ikola (Fin)
1978	Odd Lirhus (Nor)
1979	Klaus Siebert (GDR)
1981	Heikki Ikola (Fin)
1982	Frank Ullrich (GDR)
1983	Frank Ullrich (GDR)

1985	Yuriy Kashkarov (USSR)
1986	Valeriy Medvetsev (USSR)
1987	Frank-Peter Rötsch (GDR)
1989	Eirik Kvalfoss (Nor)
1990	Valeriy Medvetsev (USSR)
1991	Mark Kirchner (Ger)
1993	Andreas Zingerle (Ita)
1995	Tomas Sykora (Pol)

Men's team

Sweden	1958
USSR	1959, 1962-3
Finland	1961
Norway	1965

Men's 10 kilometres

1974	Juhani Suutarinen (Fin)
1975	Nikolay Kruglov (USSR)
1977	Aleksandr Tikhonov (USSR)
1978	Frank Ullrich (GDR)
1979	Frank Ullrich (GDR)
1981	Frank Ullrich (GDR)
1982	Eirik Kvalfoss (Nor) 33:03.26
1983	Eirik Kvalfoss (Nor)
1985	Frank-Peter Rötsch (GDR)
1986	Valeriy Medvetsev (USSR)
1987	Frank-Peter Rötsch (GDR)
1989	Frank Luck (GDR)
1990	Mark Kirchner (GDR)
1991	Mark Kirchner (Ger)
1993	Mark Kirchner (Ger)
1995	Patrice Bailly-Salins (Fra)

Men's Relay
(4 x 7.5 km to 1991, 4 x 10 km from 1993)

9	USSR	1969-71, 1973-4, 1977, 1983, 1985-6
6	GDR	1978-9, 1981-2, 1987, 1989
3	Norway	1965-7
2	Italy	1990, 1993
1	Finland	1975
1	Germany	1991
1	Norway	1995

Men's 20 Kilometres Team

2	USSR/CIS	1989, 1992-3
2	Germany	1993, 1995
1	GDR	1990
1	Italy	1991, 1994

Women's 5 kilometres

1984	Venera Chernyshova (USSR)
1985	Sanna Grönlid (Nor)
1986	Kaya Parve (USSR)
1987	Yelena Golovina (USSR)
1988	Petra Schaaf (FRG)

Women's 7.5 kilometres

1989	Anne-Elinor Elvebakk (Nor)
1990	Anne-Elinor Elvebakk (Nor)
1991	Grete Ingeborg Nykkelmo (Nor)
1993	Myriam Bédard (Can)
1995	Anne Briand (Fra)

Women's 10 kilometres

1984	Venera Chernyshova (USSR)

1985	Kaya Parve (USSR)
1986	Eva Korpela (Swe)
1987	Sanna Grönlid (Nor)
1988	Anne-Elinor Elvebakk (Nor)

Women's 15 kilometres

1989	Petra Schaaf (FRG)
1990	Svetlana Davydova (USSR)
1991	Petra Schaaf (Ger)
1993	Petra Schaaf (Ger)
1995	Corinne Niogret (Fra)

Women's relay
(3 x 5km 1984-9, 3 x 7.5km 1990-1, 4 x 7.5km 1993)

7	USSR	1984-91
1	Czech Republic	1993
1	Norway	1995

Women's 15 kilometres team

3	USSR	1989-91
2	Germany	1992, 1995
1	France	1993
1	Belarus	1994

Most World and Olympic titles

Men

14 Aleksandr Tikhonov (USSR) 4 individual, 10 relay 1968-80

10 Frank Ullrich (GDR) 6 individual, 4 relay 1978-83

7 Vladimir Melanin (USSR) 4 individual, 3 team 1959-64

Women

6 Kaya Parve (USSR) 2 individual, 4 relay 1984-6, 1988.

World Cup

Contested at 10km and 20km over a series of five events during each winter. *Winners:*

Men

1978	Frank Ullrich (GDR)
1979	Klaus Siebert (GDR)
1980-2	Frank Ullrich (GDR)
1983	Peter Angerer (FRG)
1984-5	Frank-Peter Rötsch (GDR)
1986	André Sehmisch (GDR)
1987	Frank-Peter Rötsch (GDR)
1988	Fritz Fischer (GDR)
1989	Eirik Kvalfoss (Nor)
1990 1	Sergey Chepikov (USSR)
1992	Jon Åge Tyldum (Nor)
1993	Mikael Löfgren (Swe)
1994	Patrice Bailly-Salins (Fra)
1995	Jon-Age Tyldum (Nor)

Women (7.5km and 15km)

1988	Anne-Elinor Elvebakk (Nor)
1989	Yelena Golovina (USSR)
1990	Jirina Adamicková (Cs)
1991	Svetlana Davydova (USSR)
1992-3	Anfisa Restzova (Rus)
1994	Svetlana Paramygina (Bls)
1995	Anne Briand (Fra)

Billiards

The earliest reference to billiards, which is related to the outdoor game of paille-malle, played on grass, was in the early 15th century. Louis XI, King of France (1461-83), is believed to have had a billiard table. The game became popular in Britain at the turn of the 19th century and the governing body, the Billiards Association (now the Billiards & Snooker Control Council), was formed in 1885.

World Professional Championships

First held in 1870, the championship was organised on a challenge basis until 1909. From 1909 it was run on a knockout basis under Billiard Control Club rules, until becomming dormant in 1934. It was revived on a challenge basis in 1951. In 1980 it was restored to a tournament event and, since 1982, has been held annually. *Winners:*

1870	William Cook (Eng)
1870	John Roberts, Jnr (Eng)
1870	Joseph Bennett (Eng)
1871	John Roberts, Jnr (Eng)
1871	William Cook (Eng)
1875	John Roberts, Jnr (Eng)
1880	Joseph Bennett (Eng)
1885	John Roberts, Jnr (Eng)
1889	Charles Dawson (Eng)
1901	H W Stevenson (Eng)
1901	Charles Dawson (Eng)
1901	H W Stevenson (Eng)
1903	Charles Dawson (Eng)
1908	Melbourne Inman (Eng)
1909-11	H W Stevenson (Eng)
1912-4	Melbourne Inman (Eng)
1919	Melbourne Inman (Eng)
1920	Willie Smith (Eng)
1921-2	Tom Newman (Eng)
1923	Willie Smith (Eng)
1924-7	Tom Newman (Eng)
1928-30	Joe Davis (Eng)
1931	*not held*
1932	Joe Davis (Eng)
1933-4	Walter Lindrum (Aus)
1951	Clark McConachy (NZ)
1968	Rex Williams (Eng)
1971	Leslie Driffield (Eng)
1971	Rex Williams (Eng)
1980	Fred Davis (Eng)
1982	Rex Williams (Eng)
1983	Rex Williams (Eng)
1984	Mark Wildman (Eng)
1985	Ray Edmonds (Eng)
1986	Robbie Foldvari (Aus)
1987-8	Norman Dagley (Eng)
1989	Mike Russell (Eng)
1990	*not held*
1991	Mike Russell (Eng)
1992-3	Geet Sethi (Ind)
1994	Peter Gilchrist (Eng)

Most wins
(pre-1909): John Roberts, Jnr made 8 successful defences of his title 1870-85
(post-1909): 7 Rex Williams 1968-76 (including 5 successful challenges). Tom Newman won a record six titles under knockout conditions, 1921-7

World Amateur Championships

Inaugurated in 1926 it is now scheduled to be held every two years and is organised by the International Billiards & Snooker Federation (IBSF). The 1989 tournament was cancelled. It is a round-robin event with the four leading players then competing in a knock-out tournament. *Winners:*

1926	Joe Earlham (Eng)
1927	Allan Prior (SAf)
1929	Les Hayes (Aus)
1931	Laurie Steeples (Eng)
1933	Sydney Lee (Eng)
1935	Horace Coles (Wal)
1936	Robert Marshall (Aus)
1938	Robert Marshall (Aus)
1951	Robert Marshall (Aus)
1952	Leslie Driffield (Eng)
1954	Tom Cleary (Aus)
1958	Wilson Jones (Ind)
1960	Herbert Beetham (Eng)
1962	Robert Marshall (Aus)
1964	Wilson Jones (Ind)
1967	Leslie Driffield (Eng)
1969	Jack Karnehm (Eng)
1971	Norman Dagley (Eng)
1973	Mohammed Lafir (Sri)
1975	Norman Dagley (Eng)
1977	Michael Ferreira (Ind)
1979	Paul Mifsud (Malta)
1981	Michael Ferreira (Ind)
1983	Michael Ferreira (Ind)
1985	Geet Sethi (Ind)
1987	Geet Sethi (Ind)
1990	Manoj Kothari (Ind)

Most wins: 4 Robert Marshall

United Kingdom Professional Championships

Instituted in 1934, but discontinued in 1951. It was revived from 1979 to 1983, when it was taken off the professional calender. It was revived once more in 1987. *Winners:*

1934-9	Joe Davis
1946	John Barrie
1947	Joe Davis
1948	Sidney Smith
1950	John Barrie
1951	Fred Davis
1979	Rex Williams
1980	Jack Karnehm
1981	Rex Williams
1983	Mark Wildman
1987	Norman Dagley
1988	Ian Williamson
1989-91	Mike Russell
1992-3	Robbie Foldvari (Aus)
1994	Mike Russell
1995	Subhash Agarwal (Ind)

Most wins: 7 Joe Davis

Record breaks

Highest break including the now outlawed cradle cannon 499,135 Tom Reece 3 Jun-6 Jul 1907
Highest certified break using the anchor cannon: 42,746 William Cook 29 May-7 Jun 1907
Official world record break (since introduction of the 25-hazard rule in 1926): 4137 Walter Lindrum 1932
Highest break under the baulk-line rule: 1784 Joe Davis 29 May 1936
Highest official break in amateur competition: 1149 Michael Ferreira 15 Dec 1978
Highest break under current 'two pot' rule: 962 (unfinished) Michael Ferreira 29 Apr 1986

Rex Williams

Three Cushion Billiards

Played on a table without pockets, this variation of billiards dates to 1878. The governing body, the Union Mondiale de Billiard (UMB), was formed in 1928. Popular in the USA and Europe, the lack of pockets makes it a 'cannons-only' game, but there are several variations which demand a high level of skill. In Europe is it known as Carom.

The greatest American exponent, Willie Hoppe, won a total of 51 three-cushion championships throughout the USA.

UMB World Three Cushion Billiards Championships

First held in 1928, annually to 1938, then in 1948, 1952-3, 1958 and annually from 1960. From 1988 the World Cup winner over a series of events has been declared the champion. Raymond Ceulemans (Bel) won a record 20 world titles: 1963-73, 1975-80, 1983, 1985, 1990.

World champions since 1963:

1974	Nobuaki Kobayashi (Jap)
1975-80	Raymond Ceulemans (Bel)
1981	Ludo Dielis (Bel)
1982	Rini van Bracht (Hol)
1983	Raymond Ceulemans (Bel)
1984	Nobuaki Kobayashi (Jap)
1985	Raymond Ceulemans (Bel)
1986	Avelino Rico (Spa)
1987-8	Torbjörn Blomdahl (Swe)
1989	Ludo Dielis (Bel)
1990	Raymond Ceulemans (Bel)
1991-2	Torbjörn Blomdahl (Swe)
1993	Sang Chun Lee (USA)
1994	Koen Ceulemans (Bel)
1995	Rini van Bracht (Hol)

Nine Ball Pool

World Championships were inaugurated in 1990. *Winners:*

Men

1990-1	Earl Strickland (USA)
1992	Johnny Archer (USA)
1993	Chao Feng-Pang (Tai)
1994	Earl Strickland (USA)

Women

1990-1	Robin Bell (USA)
1992	Franziska Stark (Ger)
1993	Lori Jon Jones (USA)
1994	Ewa Mataya-Laurence (Swe)

Bobsleigh and Toboganning

The first known bobsleigh races were run by British enthusiasts in Switzerland in the 1880s, when improvements were made to sleighs to make them go faster. Luge races had been held a few years earlier, and two special luge runs were constructed at Davos, Switzerland in 1879. The earliest known sledge is dated c.6500 BC and was found at Heinola, Finland.

The first purpose-built bobsleigh run was constructed at St Moritz in 1902. There are now Olympic bobsleigh events for two- and four-man teams, who sit in the bob. Skeleton one-man toboggans are used on the Cresta Run, and there was an Olympic event for them in 1924 and 1948. In the skeleton toboggans the riders lie face down, but this form of tobogganing has been superseded in the Olympics by Luge Toboganning, in which the rider sits up or lies back.

International governing bodies: Fédération Internationale de Bobsleigh et de Tobogganing (FIBT), founded in 1923. Luge tobogganing originally came under the auspices of the FIBT, but from 1957 has had its own governing body, the Fédération Internationale de Luge (FIL).

Bobsleigh runs are between 1100m and 1600m in length. The two-man bob has a maximum length of 2.7m and a maximum weight (bob and crew) of 390kg; for a four-man bob the maxima are 3.8m and 630kg; luges are 1.28 - 1.35m in length, and the maximum weight of the luge is 23kg for a single-seater or 27kg for a two-seater. Luge runs are over a minimum of 1000m. Women are not permitted to contest international bobsleigh events but contest single-seater luge races, an Olympic event since 1964.

BOBSLEIGH

Olympic Games

A bob competition for four-man sleds was first held in 1924. The two-man event was introduced in 1932, and both events have been staged at each subsequent Games except for those of 1960, when no run was built at Squaw Valley. *Winners:*

Two-man bob

1932	Hubert Stevens & Curtis Stevens (USA)
1936	Ivan Brown & Alan Washbond (USA)
1948	Felix Endrich & Friedrich Waller (Swi)
1952	Andreas Ostler & Lorenz Nieberl (FRG)
1956	Lamberto Dalla Costa & Giacomo Conti (Ita)
1964	Tony Nash & Robin Dixon (UK)
1968	Eugenio Monti & Luciano de Paolis (Ita)
1972	Wolfgang Zimmerer & Peter Utzschneider (FRG)
1976	Meinhard Nehmer & Bernhard Germeshausen (GDR)
1980	Erich Schärer & Josef Benz (Swi)
1984	Wolfgang Hoppe & Dietmar Schauerhammer (GDR)
1988	Janis Kipurs & Vladimir Kozlov (USSR)
1992	Gustav Weder & Donad Acklin (Swi)
1994	Gustav Weder & Donad Acklin (Swi)

Four-man bob

1924	Switzerland
1928	USA
1932	USA
1936	Switzerland
1948	USA
1952	Germany (FRG)

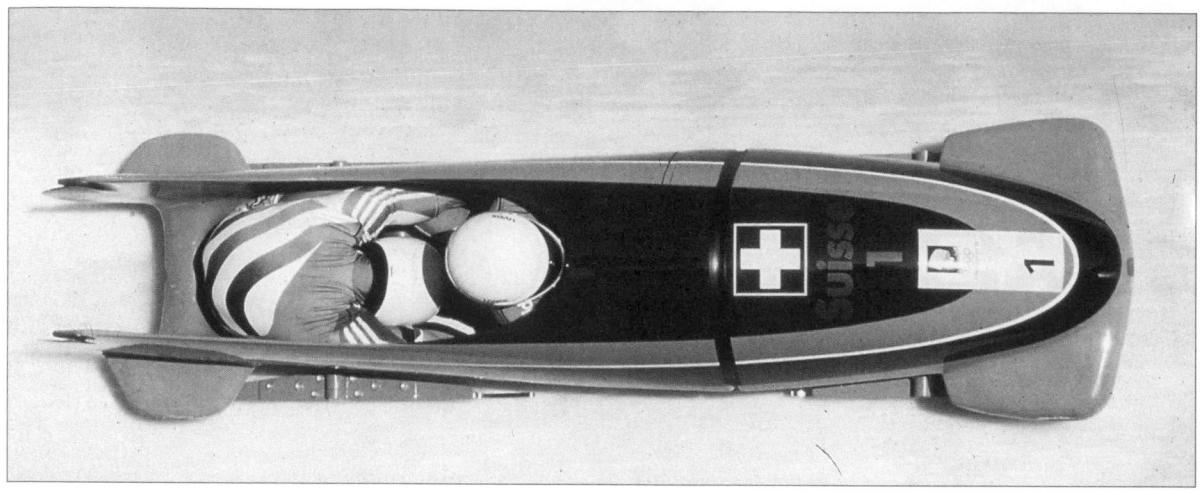

Gustav Weder and Donald Acklin take 2-man gold in Switzerland I at the 1994 Olympic Games

1956	Switzerland
1964	Canada
1968	Italy
1972	Switzerland
1976	GDR
1980	GDR
1984	GDR
1988	Switzerland
1992	Austria
1994	Germany

Skeleton bob

1928	Jennison Heaton (USA)
1948	Nino Bibbia (Ita)

Most gold medals

3 Meinhard Nehmer & Bernhard Germeshausen (GDR) 2-man 1976, 4-man 1976 and 1980.

Most medals

7 Bogdan Musiol (GDR) gold 4-man 1980, five silver 2-man 1984, 1988; 4-man 1984, 1988, 1992; bronze 2-man 1980

6 Eugenio Monti (Ita) two gold 1968, two silver 1956, two bronze 1964.

World Championships

Held annually from 1930 for the four-man bob and 1931 for the two-man bob. The Olympic events (qv) are the world championships in those years. *Winners:*

Two-man bob

1931	Hanns Killian & Sebastian Huber (Ger)
1933	Alexandru Papana & Dumitru Hubert (Rom)
1934	Alexandru Frim & Vasile Dumitrescu (Rom)
1935	Reto Capadrutt & Emil Diener (Swi)
1937	Frederic McEvoy & B H Black (UK)
1938	Bibo Fischer & Rolf Thielacke (Ger)
1939	René Lundnen & J Kuffer (Bel)
1947	Fritz Feierabend & Stephan Waser (Swi)
1949	Felix Endrich & Friedrich Waller (Swi)
1950	Fritz Feierabend & Stephan Waser (Swi)

1951	Andreas Osterl & Lorenz Nieberl (FRG)
1953	Felix Endrich & Fritz Stoeckli (Swi)
1954	Guglielmo Scheibmeier & Andrea Zambelli (Ita)
1955	Fritz Feierabend & Harry Warburton (Swi)
1957-60	Eugenio Monti & Renzo Alverà (Ita)
1961	Eugenio Monti & Sergio Siorpaes (Ita)
1962	Rinaldo Ruatti & Enrico De Lorenzo (Ita)
1963	Eugenio Monti & Sergio Siorpaes (Ita)
1965	Tony Nash & Robin Dixon (UK)
1966	Eugenio Monti & Sergio Siorpaes (Ita)
1967	Erwin Thaler & Reinhold Durnthaler (Aut)
1969	Nevio de Zordo & Adriano Frassinelli (Ita)
1970	Horst Floth & Pepi Bader (FRG)
1971	Gianfranco Gaspari & Mario Armano (Ita)
1973-4	Wolfgang Zimmerer & Peter Utzschneider (FRG)
1975	Giorgio Alverà & Franco Perruquet (Ita)
1977	Hans Hiltebrand & Heinz Meier (Swi)
1978-9	Erich Schärer & Josef Benz (Swi)
1981	Bernhard Germeshausen & Hans-Jürgen Gerhardt (GDR)
1982	Erich Schärer & Josef Benz (Swi)
1983	Ralf Pichler & Urs Leuthold (Swi)
1985-6	Wolfgang Hoppe & Dietmar Schauerhammer (GDR)
1987	Ralf Pichler & Celest Poltera (Swi)
1989	Wolfgang Hoppe & Bogdan Musiol (GDR)
1990	Gustav Weder & Bruno Gerber (Swi)
1991	Rudi Lochner & Markus Zimmermann (Ger)
1993	Christoph Langen & Peer Jöchel (Ger)
1995	Christoph Langen & Olaf Hempel (Ger)

Four-man bob

15	Switzerland	1939, 1947, 1954-5, 1957, 1971, 1973, 1975, 1982-3, 1986-7, 1989-90, 1993
6	FR Germany	1951, 1958, 1962, 1969, 1974, 1979
5	Italy	1930, 1960, 1961, 1963, 1970
4	USA	1949-50, 1953, 1959
4	GDR	1977-8, 1981, 1985

4   Germany   1931, 1934-5, 1991
2   United Kingdom 1937-8
1   Canada   1965

Not decided in 1966 due to a fatal accident and in 1967 because of a thaw.

Most World and Olympic titles: 2-man/4-man

11 Eugenio Monti (Ita) 8/3
7   Erich Schärer (Swi) 4/3
6   Fritz Feierabend (Swi) 3/3
6   Bernhard Germeshausen (GDR) 2/4

World Cup

First held over a series of events in 1984/5 at 2-man and 4-man with an overall title as well.. *Winners:*

Combined

1985   Anton Fischer (FRG)
1986   Ekkehard Fasser (Swi)
1987   Matt Roy (USA)
1988   Ingo Appelt (Aut)
1989   Gustav Weder (Swi)
1990   Maris Poikans (USSR)
1991   Gustav Weder (Swi)
1992   Wolfgang Hoppe (Ger)
1993   Brian Shimer (USA)
1994-5 Pierre Lueders (Can)

2 Man

1985   Anton Fischer (FRG)
1986   Maris Poikans (USSR)
1987   Anton Fischer (FRG)
1988   Janis Kipurs (USSR)
1989   Gustav Weder (Swi)
1990   Christian Schebitz (FRG)
1991   Wolfgang Hoppe (Ger)
1992-3 Günther Huber (Ita)
1994-5 Pierre Lueders (Can)

4 Man

1985   Jeffrey Jost (USA)
1986   Ekkehard Fasser (Swi)
1987   Matt Roy (USA)
1988-9 Ingo Appelt (Aut)
1990   Chris Lori (Can)
1991   Gustav Weder (Swi)
1992   Wolfgang Hoppe (Ger)
1993   Brian Shimer (USA)
1994   Hubert Schösser (Swi)
1994-5 Pierre Lueders (Can)

LUGE TOBOGANNING

Olympic Games

Men's single-seater

1964   Thomas Köhler (GDR)
1968   Manfred Schmid (Aut)
1972   Wolfgang Scheidel (GDR)
1976   Detlef Günther (GDR)
1980   Bernhard Glass (GDR)
1984   Paul Hildgartner (Ita)
1988   Jens Müller (GDR)
1992   Georg Hackl (Ger)
1994   Georg Hackl (Ger)

Women's single-seater

1964   Ortrun Enderlein (GDR)
1968   Erica Lechner (Ita)
1972   Anna-Maria Müller (GDR)
1976   Margit Schumann (GDR)
1980   Vera Sosulya (USSR)
1984   Steffi Martin (GDR)
1988   Steffi Walter (née Martin) (GDR)
1992   Doris Neuner (Aut)
1994   Gerda Weissensteiner (Ita)

Men's two-seater

1964   Josef Feistmantl & Manfred Stengl (Aut)
1968   Thomas Köhler & Klaus Bonsack (GDR)
1972   Paul Hildgartner & Walter Plaikner (Ita)
        and
        Horst Hörnlein & Reinhard Bredow (GDR)
1976   Hans Rinn & Norbert Hahn (GDR)
1980   Hans Rinn & Norbert Hahn (GDR)
1984   Hans Stanggasinger & Franz Wembacher (FRG)
1988   Jörg Hoffmann & Jochen Pietzsch (GDR)
1992   Stefan Krausse & Jan Behrendt (Ger)
1994   Kurt Brugger & Wilfried Huber (Ita)

World Championships

Held in 1955 and annually from 1957 - with the exception of years in which luge events were included in the Olympics, with which they are now merged - to 1981 and now biennially on artificial runs. Separate world championships on natural runs were held in 1979 and biennially from 1980. *Winners:*

Men's single-seater

1955   Anton Salvesen (Nor)
1957   Hans Schaller (FRG)
1958   Jerzy Wojnar (Pol)
1959   Herbert Thaler (Aut)
1960   Helmuth Berndt (FRG)
1961   Jerzy Wojnar (Pol)
1962   Thomas Köhler (GDR)
1963   Fritz Nachmann (FRG)
1965   Hans Plenk (FRG)
1967   Thomas Köhler (GDR)
1969   Josef Feistmantl (Aut)
1970   Josef Fendt (FRG)
1971   Karl Brunner (Ita)
1973   Hans Rinn (GDR)
1974   Josef Fendt (FRG)
1975   Wolfram Fiedler (GDR)
1977   Hans Rinn (GDR)
1978   Paul Hildgartner (Ita)
1979   Detlef Günther (GDR)
1981   Sergey Danilin (USSR)
1983   Miroslav Zajonc (Can)
1985   Michael Walter (GDR)
1987   Markus Prock (Aut)
1989-90 Georg Hackl (FRG)
1991   Arnold Huber (Ita)
1993   Wendel Suckow (USA)
1995   Armin Zoggler (Ita)

Men's two-seater

1955	Hans Krausner & Herbert Thaler (Aut)
1957-8	Josef Strillinger & Fritz Nachmann (FRG)
1960	Reinhold Frosch & Ewald Walch (Aut)
1961	Roman Pichler & Raimondo Prinoth (Ita)
1962	Giovanni Graber & Gianpoulo Ambrosi (Ita)
1963	Ryszard Pedrak & Lucjan Kudzia (Pol)
1965	Wolfgang Scheidel & Michael Köhler (GDR)
1967	Klaus Bonsack & Thomas Köhler (GDR)
1969-70	Manfred Schmid & Ewald Walch (Aut)
1971	Paul Hildgartner & Walter Plaikner (Ita)
1973	Horst Hörnlein & Reinhard Bredow (GDR)
1974-5	Bernd Hann & Ulrich Hann (GDR)
1977	Hans Rinn & Norbert Hahn (GDR)
1978	Dainis Bremse & Aigars Krikis (USSR)
1979	Hans Brandner & Balthasar Schwarm (FRG)
1981	Bernd Hann & Ulrich Hann (GDR)
1983	Jörg Hoffmann & Jochen Pietzsch (GDR)
1985	Jörg Hoffmann & Jochen Pietzsch (GDR)
1987	Jörg Hoffmann & Jochen Pietzsch (GDR)
1989	Stefan Krausse & Jan Behrendt (GDR)
1990	Hansjörg Raffl & Norbert Huber (Ita)
1991	Stefan Krausse & Jan Behrendt (Ger)
1993	Stefan Krausse & Jan Behrendt (Ger)
1995	Stefan Krausse & Jan Behrendt (Ger)

Women's single-seater

1955	Karla Kienzl (Aut)
1956	Maria Isser (Aut)
1957	Maria Semczyszak (Pol)
1959	Elly Lieber (Aut)
1960	Maria Isser (Aut)
1961	Elisabeth Nagele (Swi)
1962-3	Ilse Geisler (GDR)
1965	Ortrun Enderlein (GDR)
1967	Ortrun Enderlein (GDR)
1969	Petra Tierlich (GDR)
1970	Barbara Piecha (Pol)
1971	Elisabeth Demleitner (FRG)
1973-5	Margrit Schumann (GDR)
1977	Margrit Schumann (GDR)
1978	Vera Sosulya (USSR)
1979	Melitta Sollmann (GDR)
1981	Melitta Sollmann (GDR)
1983	Steffi Martin (GDR)
1985	Steffi Martin (GDR)
1987	Cerstin Schmidt (GDR)
1989	Susi Erdmann (GDR)
1990	Gabriele Kohlisch (GDR)
1991	Susi Erdmann (Ger)
1993	Gerda Weissensteiner (Ita)
1995	Gabriele Kohlisch (Ger)

Event cancelled in 1966

Team

1989	Italy
1990	GDR
1991	Germany
1993	Germany
1995	Germany

Cancelled in 1959 and 1966

Most Luge World and Olympic titles

Men: 5 Thomas Köhler (GDR), 5 Hans Rinn (GDR)
Women: 5 Margrit Schumann (GDR).

World Cup

Held over a series of events annually from the 1977/8 season. *Winners:*

Men's single-seater

1978	Anton Winkler (FRG)
1979	Paul Hildgartner (Ita)
1980	Ernst Haspinger (Ita)
1981	Ernst Haspinger (Ita) & Paul Hildgartner (Ita)
1982	Ernst Haspinger (Ita)
1983	Paul Hildgartner (Ita)
1984	Michael Walter (GDR)
1985-7	Norbert Huber (Ita)
1988	Markus Prock (Aut)
1989-90	Georg Hackl (FRG)
1991-5	Markus Prock (Aut)

Men's two-seater

1978-9	Peter Gschnitzer & Karl Brunner (Ita)
1980-2	Günther Lemmerer & Reinhold Sulzbacher (Aut)
1983	Hansjörg Raffl & Norbert Huber (Ita)
1984	Jörg Hoffmann & Jochen Pietzsch (GDR)
1985-6	Hansjörg Raffl & Norbert Huber (Ita)
1987	Thomas Schwab & Wolfgang Staudinger (FRG)
1988	Yevgeniy Belousov & Aleksandr Belyukov (USSR)
1989-93	Hansjörg Raffl & Norbert Huber (Ita)
1994-5	Stefan Krausse & Jan Behrendt (Ger)

Women's single-seater

1978	Regina König (FRG)
1979-81	Angelika Schafferer (Aut)
1982	Vera Sosulya (USSR)
1983	Ute Weiss (GDR)
1984	Steffi Martin (GDR) & Bettina Schmidt (GDR)
1985	Cerstin Schmidt (GDR)
1986	Maria Rainer (Ita)
1987	Cerstin Schmidt (GDR)
1988	Yuliya Antipova (USSR)
1989	Ute Oberhoffner (GDR)
1990	Yuliya Antipova (USSR)
1991-2	Susi Erdmann (Ger)
1993	Gerda Weissensteiner (Ita)
1994	Gabriele Kohlisch (Ger)
1995	Sylke Otto (Ger)

Bowling (Tenpin)

Bowling at 'pins' has existed as a pastime since 5200 BC, but it only started to take shape in its present form in the early 19th century. Dutch or German migrants took the game of ninepins to the United States and the game became immensely popular - so popular that it attracted much gambling and consequently was banned! To get round the law, a tenth pin was added, and they were laid out in a diamond shape. The new game, once again, became very popular. The American Bowling Congress was formed in 1895, and they standardised the rules. The Women's International Bowling Congress (WIBC) was formed in 1916. Prior to the last war the International Bowling Association (IBA) governed the sport, but now the world governing body of the amateur game is the Fédération Internationale des Quilleurs (FIQ). In 1995 there were 83 member nations of the FIQ.

World Championships

The IBA organised four world championships between 1923 and 1936. Since 1954 the championships have been organised by the FIQ, and since 1963 have been held every four years. Women took part for the first time in 1963. *Winners:*

Men

Individual

Year Winner	Score	Games	Ave.
1923 Thure Sandström (Swe)	414	2	207.00
1926 Hugo Lillier (Swe)	829	4	207.25
1929 Mike Schirgio (USA)	836	4	209.00
1936 Karl Goldtammer (Ger)	921	4	230.25
1954 Gösta Algeskog (Swe)	4932	25	197.28
1955 Nils Böckström (Swe)	4838	25	193.52
1958 Kaarlo Asukas (Fin)	5034	25	201.36
1960 Tito Reynolds (Mex)	4963	25	198.52
1963 Les Zikes (USA)	5519	28	197.11
1967 David Pond (UK)	5708	28	203.86
1971 Ed Luther (USA)	5963	28	212.96
1975 Bud Staudt (USA)	5816	28	207.71
1979 Ollie Ongtawco (Phi)	1278	6	213.00
1983 Armando Marino (Col)	1357	6	226.17
1987 Rolland Patrick (Fra)	1332	6	222.00
1991 Ma Ying-chei (Tai)	1327	6	221.17

Doubles

4	Sweden	1923, 1955, 1958, 1987
3	Great Britain	1967, 1975, 1983*
3	United States	1936, 1963, 1991
2	Finland	1926, 1954
2	Australia	1979, 1983*
1	Mexico 1960, Puerto Rico 1971	

* *Shared title*

Best average score: 219.83 Sweden (1987) 2638 pts from 6 games

Trios

2	United States	1987, 1991
1	Malaysia 1979, Sweden 1983	

Best average score: 216.61 Sweden (1983) 3899 pts from 6 games

Teams of five players

4	Finland	1958, 1967, 1975, 1983
4	Sweden	1923, 1926, 1954, 1987
3	United States	1936, 1963, 1971
1	FR Germany 1955, Venezuela 1960, Australia 1979, Taiwan 1991	

Best average score: 211.83 Finland (1983) 6355 pts from 6 games

All-Events

Score from all four events, singles, doubles, trios & team:
1983 Mats Karlsson (Swe) 5242 pts (av. 218.42)
1987 Rick Steelsmith (USA) 5261 (av. 219.21)
1991 Ma Ying-chei (Tai) 5048 (av. 210.33)

Teams of eight players (discontinued 1975)

3	United States	1963, 1967, 1971
2	Sweden	1954, 1958
1	Finland 1955, Mexico 1960, FR Germany 1975	

Best average score: 198.30 United States (1971) 12,691 pts from 8 games

Masters

1979 Gerry Bugden (UK)
1983 Tony Cariello (USA)
1987 Roger Pieters (Bel)
1991 Mika Koivuniemi (Fin)

Women

Individual

Year Winner	Score	Games	Ave.
1963 Helen Shablis (USA)	4535	24	188.96
1967 Helen Weston (USA)	4585	24	191.04
1971 Ashie Gonzales (PR)	4535	24	188.96
1975 Annedore Haefker (FRG)	4615	24	192.29
1979 Lita de la Rosa (Phi)	1220	6	203.33
1983 Lena Sulkanen (Swe)	1293	6	215.50
1987 Edda Piccini (Ita)	1259	6	209.83
1991 Martina Beckel (Ger)	1272	6	212.00

Doubles

2	United States	1963, 1987
2	Japan	1971, 1991
1	Mexico 1960, Sweden 1975, Philippines 1979, Denmark 1983	

Best average score: 213.83 United States (1987) 2566 pts from 6 games

Trios

2	USA	1979, 1987
1	FR Germany 1983, Canada 1991	

Best average score: 200.17 United States (1987) 3603 pts from 6 games

Teams of five players

3	USA	1971, 1979, 1987
1	Finland 1967, Japan 1975, Sweden 1983, S Korea 1991	

Best average score: 200.37 United States (1987) 6011 pts from 6 games

All-Events

1983 Bong Coo (Phi) 4806 pts (av.200.25)
1987 Sandra Jo Shiery (USA) 4894 (av.203.92)
1991 Helle Andersen (Den) 4821 (av. 200.87)

Teams of four players (discontinued 1975)

2	United States	1963*, 1971
1	Mexico 1963*, Finland 1967, Japan 1975	

* There were two titles in 1963

Best average score: 194.00 United States (1971) 4656 pts from 6 games

Masters

1979 Lita de la Rosa (Phi)

1983 Lena Sulkanen (Swe)
1987 Annette Hagre (Swe)
1991 Catherine Willis (Can)
The only perfect game (300) in the world championships was rolled by Rick Steelsmith (USA) during the Trios event at the 1987 championships.

The American Bowling Congress

The most important event run in the USA by the ABC (established in 1895) is the annual Masters Bowling Tournament. *Winners:*

1951	Lee Jouglard
1952	Willard Taylor
1953	Rudy Habetler
1954	Eugene Elkins
1955	Buzz Fazio
1956-7	Dick Hoover
1958	Tom Hennessey
1959	Ray Bluth
1960	Bill Golembiewski
1961	Don Carter
1962	Bill Golembiewski
1963	Harry Smith
1964-5	Billy Welu
1966	Bob Strampe
1967	Lou Scalia
1968	Pete Tountas
1969	Jim Chestney
1970	Don Glover
1971	Jim Godman
1972	Bill Beach
1973	Dave Soutar
1974	Paul Colwell
1975	Ed Ressler Jr.
1976	Nelson Burton Jr.
1977	Earl Anthony
1978	Frank Ellenburg
1979	Doug Meyers
1980	Neil Burton
1981	Randy Lightfoot
1982	Joe Berardi
1983	Mike Lastowski
1984	Earl Anthony
1985	Steve Wunderlich
1986	Mark Fahy
1987	Rick Steelsmith
1988	Del Ballard Jr.
1989	Mike Aulby
1990	Chris Warren
1991	Doug Kent
1992	Ken Johnson
1993	Phil Ware
1994	Hobo Boothe

Most wins: 2 Hoover, Golembiewski, Welu, Anthony

The Professional Bowlers Association

The PBA was formed in the USA in 1958. Its annual Tournament of Champions is held at its home in Akron, Ohio, and is sponsored by Firestone.

Year	Tournament of Champions winners	PBA leading money winners	$
1962	Joe Joseph	Don Carter	22,525
1963	Not held	Dick Weber	26,280
1964	Not held	Don Carter	49,972
1965	Billy Hardwick	Dick Weber	46,333
1966	Wayne Zahn	Bob Strampe	33,592
1967	Jim Stefanich	Dick Weber	47,674
1968	Dave Davis	Jim Stefanich	54,720
1969	Jim Godman	Billy Hardwick	64,160
1970	Don Johnson	Mike McGrath	52,049
1971	Johnny Petraglia	Johnny Petraglia	85,065
1972	Mike Durbin	Don Johnson	56,648
1973	Jim Godman	Don McCune	69,000
1974	Earl Anthony	Earl Anthony	99,585
1975	Dave Davis	Earl Anthony	107,585
1976	Marshall Holman	Earl Anthony	110,833
1977	Mike Berlin	Mark Roth	105,583
1978	Earl Anthony	Mark Roth	134,500
1979	George Pappas	Mark Roth	124,517
1980	Wayne Webb	Wayne Webb	116,700
1981	Steve Cook	Earl Anthony	164,735
1982	Mike Durbin	Earl Anthony	134,760
1983	Joe Berardi	Earl Anthony	135,605
1984	Mike Durbin	Mark Roth	158,712
1985	Mark Williams	Mike Aulby	201,200
1986	Marshall Holman	Walter Williams	145,550
1987	Pete Weber	Pete Weber	179,516
1988	Mark Williams	Brian Voss	225,485
1989	Del Ballard Jr.	Mike Aulby	298,237
1990	Dave Ferraro	Amleto Monacelli	204,775
1991	David Ozio	David Ozio	225,585
1992	Mike McDowell	Mike McDowell	174,215
1993	George Branham	Walter Williams	296,370
1994	Norm Duke	Norm Duke	273,753
1995	Mike Aulby		

Career money leader: Pete Weber $1,706,245 (to May 1995)
Most titles: Earl Anthony 41, Mark Roth 33, Don Johnson, Dick Weber 26; Mike Aulby 22

The Women's International Bowling Congress

The Women's National Bowling Association was founded in 1916, being renamed the Women's International Bowling Congress in 1971. Championships have been held annually from 1916, except for 1943-5. The WIBC tournament attracted a record 75,480 entrants in 1983 for the event held over a three-month period.

WIBC Queens Tournament

WIBC's most prestigious event, first held in 1961. *Winners:*

1961	Janet Harman
1962	Dorothy Wilkinson
1963	Irene Monterosso
1964	D.D.Jacobson
1965	Betty Kuczynski
1966	Judy Lee
1967	Mildred Ignizio
1968	Phyllis Massey
1969	Ann Feigel

1970-1	Mildred Ignizio
1972-3	Dorothy Fothergill
1974	Judy Soutar
1975	Cindy Powell
1976	Pamela Buckner
1977	Dana Stewart
1978	Loa Boxberger
1979-80	Donna Adamek
1981-2	Katsuko Sugimoto (Jap)
1983	Aleta Sill
1984	Kazue Inahashi (Jap)
1985	Aleta Sill
1986	Cora Fiebig
1987	Cathy Almeida
1988	Wendy Macpherson
1989	Carol Gianotti (Aus)
1990	Patty Ann
1991	Dede Davidson
1992	Cindy Coburn-Carroll
1993	Jan Schmidt
1994	Anne Marie Duggan

WIBC career money leader
Aleta Sill $688,681 (to 1 Jun 1995), with season's record $126,325 in 1994
Most titles: 28 Lisa Wagner 1980-95

US Open

First held in 1941 for men and 1949 for women and started by the Bowling Proprietors' Association of America (BPAA). It became the US Open in 1971. *Recent winners:*

Men
1980	Steve Martin
1981	Marshall Holman
1982	Dave Husted

Bowls

The ancient Egyptians are believed to have played a game similar to bowls around 5200 BC but the earliest recorded green is at Southampton in 1299, although one was claimed in Chesterfield in 1294. The modern rules for bowls were drawn up in Scotland in 1848-9 by Glasgow solicitor William Mitchell. The English Bowling Association was founded in 1903 with Test cricketer W G Grace as its first president, although this was preceded by the founding of the International (later Imperial) Bowling Association in 1899, but this lasted only until 1905, when the present world governing body, the International Bowling Board, was formed. The Women's International Bowling Board was formed in 1969.

World Outdoor Championships

Instituted in 1966 for men and 1969 for women the championships are now held every four years. The Leonard Trophy for men is presented to the winning team based on performances in all categories at the world championship. *Winners:*

Men's Singles
1966	David Bryant (Eng)
1972	Malwyn Evans (Wal)
1976	Doug Watson (SAf)

1983	Gary Dickinson
1984	Mark Roth
1985	Marshall Holman
1986	Steve Cook
1987	Del Ballard Jr
1988	Pete Weber
1989	Mike Aulby
1990	Ron Palombi Jr
1991	Pete Weber
1992	Robert Lawrence
1993	Del Ballard Jr
1994	Justin Hromek

Most wins:
4 Don Carter 1952, 1954, 1956, 1958
4 Dick Weber 1962-3, 1965-6

Women
1980	Pat Costello
1981	Donna Adamek
1982	Shinobu Saitoh
1983	Dana Miller
1984	Karen Ellingsworth
1985	Pat Mercatanti
1986	Wendy Macpherson
1987	Carol Norman
1988	Lisa Wagner
1989	Robin Romeo
1990	Dane Miller-Mackie
1991	Anne Marie Dugga
1992	Tish Johnson
1993	Dede Davidson
1994	Aleta Sill

Most wins
8 Marion Ladewig 1949-52, 1954, 1956, 1959, 1963
3 Pat Costello 1974, 1976, 1980

1980	David Bryant (Eng)
1984	Peter Belliss (NZ)
1988	David Bryant (Eng)
1992	Tony Allcock (Eng)

Men's Pairs
1966	Geoff Kelly & Bert Palm (Aus)
1972	Clementi Delgado & Eric Liddell (HK)
1976	Doug Watson & William Moseley (SAf)
1980	Alf Sandercock & Peter Rheuben (Aus)
1984	George Adrain* & Skippy Arculli (USA)
1988	Rowan Brassey & Peter Belliss (NZ)
1992	Richard Corsie & Alex Marshall (Sco)

* Scotsman who substituted for Jim Candelet

Men's Triples
1966	Australia
1972	United States
1976	South Africa
1980	England
1984	Ireland
1988	New Zealand
1992	Israel

Men's Fours
1966	New Zealand
1972	England

1976	South Africa
1980	Hong Kong
1984	England
1988	Ireland
1992	Scotland

Leonard Trophy
1966	Australia
1972	Scotland
1976	South Africa
1980	England
1984	Scotland
1988	England
1992	Scotland

Most wins overall: 5 David Bryant (singles 1966, 1980; 1988 triples and team 1980)

Women's Singles
1969	Gladys Doyle (PNG)
1973	Elsie Wilke (NZ)
1977	Elsie Wilke (NZ)
1981	Norma Shaw (Eng)
1985	Merle Richardson (Aus)
1988	Janet Ackland (Wal)
1992	Margaret Johnston (Ire)

Women's Pairs
1969	Elsie McDonald & May Cridlan (SAf)
1973	Lorna Lucas & Dot Jenkinson (Aus)
1977	Helen Wong & Elvie Chok (HK)
1981	Eileen Bell & Nan Allely (Ire)
1985	Merle Richardson & Fay Craig (Aus)
1988	Margaret Johnston & Phyllis Nolan (Ire)
1992	Margaret Johnston & Phyllis Nolan (Ire)

Women's Triples
1969	South Africa
1973	New Zealand
1977	Wales
1981	Hong Kong
1985	Australia
1988	Australia
1992	Scotland

Women's Fours
1969	South Africa
1973	New Zealand
1977	Australia
1981	England
1985	Scotland
1988	Australia
1992	Scotland

Women's Team
1969	South Africa
1973	New Zealand
1977	Australia
1981	England
1985	Australia
1988	England
1992	Scotland

Most wins overall: 3 Merle Richardson (fours 1977, singles and pairs 1985), Margaret Johnston

World Indoor Championships

Instituted 1979 for singles and 1986 for pairs and sponsored by Embassy. *Winners:*

Singles
1979	David Bryant (Eng)
1980	David Bryant (Eng)
1981	David Bryant (Eng)
1982	John Watson (Sco)
1983	Bob Sutherland (Sco)
1984	Jim Baker (Ire)
1985	Terry Sullivan (Wal)
1986-7	Tony Allcock (Eng)
1988	Hugh Duff (Sco)
1989	Richard Corsie (Sco)
1990	John Price (Wal)
1991	Richard Corsie (Sco)
1992	Ian Schuback (Aus)
1993	Richard Corsie (Sco)
1994	Andy Thomson (Eng)

Most wins: 3 Bryant, Corsie

Pairs
1986-7	David Bryant & Tony Allcock (Eng)
1988	Ian Schuback & Jim Yates (Aus)
1989-92	David Bryant & Tony Allcock (Eng)
1993	Gary Smith & Andy Thomson (Eng)
1994	Cameron Curtis & Ian Schuback (Aus)
1995	Alex Marshall & Richard Corsie (Sco)

Andy Thomson – 1994 World Indoor champion

Women's World Indoor Championships

First held in 1988. *Winners:*

1988-9	Margaret Johnston (Ire)
1990	Fleur Bougourd (UK)
1991	Mary Price (UK)
1992	Sarah Gourlay (Sco)
1993	Kate Adams (Sco)
1994	Jan Woodley (Sco)

International Championships

First held in 1903 and contested by the four Home Countries of the British Isles. There was no championship in 1976. *Wins:*

35	Scotland	1904, 1907-10, 1912-4, 1919, 1921-3, 1928, 1932, 1935-6, 1950, 1952-3, 1963, 1965-75, 1977, 1979-80, 1991
27	England	1903, 1906, 1911, 1924, 1926-7, 1929, 1939, 1947, 1949, 1954-6, 1958-62, 1964, 1983-90, 1993
13	Wales	1920, 1925, 1930-1, 1933-4, 1937-8, 1946, 1948, 1957, 1978, 1982
3	Ireland	1905, 1951, 1981

English Bowling Association Championships

First held in 1903, the year of the formation of the EBA. The most titles won is 16 by David Bryant between 1957 and 1985, with six singles, three pairs, three triples, and four fours titles. *Recent winners:*

Singles

1981	Andy Thomson
1982	Chris Ward
1983	John Bell
1984	Wynne Richards
1985	Roy Keating
1986	Wynne Richards
1987	David Holt
1988	Richard Bray
1989	John Ottaway
1990-1	Tony Allcock
1992	Stephen Farish
1993	John Wickham
1994	Brett Morley

Most wins: 6 David Bryant 1960, 1966, 1971-3, 1975; 4 Percy Baker 1932, 1946, 1952, 1955

Triples

1981	St.Peter's, Hunts.
1982	Lenham, Kent
1983	Marlborough, Suffolk
1984-5	Clevedon, Avon
1986	Poole Park, Dorset
1987	Worcester County
1988	Belgrave, Leicester
1989	Southbourne, Sussex
1990	Cheltenham, Gloucs
1991	Wigton, Cumbria
1992	Chandos Park, Bucks
1993	Preston, Brighton
1994	Torquay, Devon

Fours

1981	Owton Lodge, Durham
1982	Castle, Notts
1983	Bolton, Lancs
1984	Boscombe Cliff, Hants
1985	Aldersbrook, Essex
1986	Stony Stratford, Bucks
1987	Aylesbury Town, Bucks
1988	Summertown, Oxfordshire
1989	Blackheath & Greenwich, Kent
1990	Bath, Avon
1991	Wokingham, Berks
1992	Bournemouth, Hants
1993	Reading, Berks
1994	Cheltenham

Pairs

1981	Burton House, Lincs (Alan Bates & Richard White)
1982	Bedford Borough, Bucks (David Hurst & John McConnell)
1983	Eldon Grove, Durham (George Turley & Mal Hughes)
1984	Lenham, Kent (Ollie Jones & Len Hayes)
1985	Haxby Road, Yorks (Peter Richardson & Frank Maxwell)
1986	Owton Lodge, Durham (Dave Kilner & Cliff Simpson)
1987	Bolton, Lancs (David Holt & Tom Armstrong)
1988	Leicester (John Stephenson & Paul Clarke)
1989	Essex County (Paul Maynard & David McCathie)
1990	Wymondham Dell (John Ottaway & Roger Guy)
1991	Wigton, Cumbria (John Bell & Ronnie Gass)
1992	Blackheath & Greenwich (Gary Smith & Andy Thomson)
1993	Erdington Court (Rob Robinson & Richard Brittan)
1994	Ponteland, Newcastle (Keith Wood & Mike Bennett)

Boxing

From the beginning of time man has fought his fellow man, but the first record of a boxing match was in 1681 when the Duke of Albemarle organised a match between his butler and his butcher. In 1719 James Figg of Oxfordshire, regarded as the first boxing champion, set up his school of arms in London. The earliest prize-ring code of rules was formulated in England in 1743 by the champion pugilist Jack Braughton, and in 1865 the 8th Marquess of Queensberry drew up his famous rules for boxing, directed to fighting with gloves rather than the earlier bare-knuckle fighters.

World Champions

The first world championship fight with gloves and conducted under the Queensberry Rules was on 30 July 1884, when Irish-born Jack Dempsey beat George Fulljames of the

USA in New York for the middleweight title. There has been a proliferation of world champions, with a increase in recent years in the number of weight divisions, and now, the curious and unsatisfactory situation of a proliferation of governing bodies recognising 'world champions'.

The National Boxing Association (NBA) was formed in the USA in 1920. The title was changed to World Boxing Association (WBA) in 1962. In Britain the British Boxing Board of Control (BBBC) was formed in 1929, earlier title fights having been largely under the control of the National Sporting Club.

The WBA recognise world champions, but rather closer to an international governing body is the World Boxing Council (WBC), founded in Mexico City in 1963. Neither body has been able to agree on fight regulations, and the situation has been further complicated by the formation of the International Boxing Federation (IBF) in the USA in 1983, the World Boxing Organisation (WBO) in 1988. All titleholders

recognised by these four bodies are shown in the following lists of champions, but other bodies have also been formed in recent years. For each weight the current weight limits (generally in force from 1970) are indicated. The names for the new intermediate weight categories vary, but the WBC versions have been shown in bold print, with the WBA, IBF and WBO titles beneath.

The following weight limits had been established following discussions in 1910 between boxing authorities in the UK and USA:

Heavyweight - over 175 lb
Light-heavy   175lb
Middleweight   154lb
Welterweight   142lb
Lightweight   133lb
Featherweight   122lb
Bantamweight   116lb
Flyweight   112lb
Paperweight   105lb

Heavyweight
Over 190lb (86.2kg)

Undisputed
1882 John L Sullivan (USA)
1892 James J Corbett (USA)
1897 Bob Fitzsimmons (UK)
1899 James J Jefferies (USA)
1905 Marvin Hart (USA)
1906 Tommy Burns (Can)
1908 Jack Johnson (USA)
1915 Jess Willard (USA)
1919 Jack Dempsey (USA)
1926 Gene Tunney (USA)
1930 Max Schmeling (Ger)
1932 Jack Sharkey (USA)
1933 Primo Carnera (Ita)
1934 Max Baer (USA)
1935 James J Braddock (USA)
1937 Joe Louis (USA)
1949 Ezzard Charles (USA)
1951 Jersey Joe Walcott (USA)
1952 Rocky Marciano (USA)
1956 Floyd Patterson (USA)
1959 Ingemar Johansson (Swe)
1960 Floyd Patterson (USA)
1962 Sonny Liston (USA)
1964 Cassius Clay (USA)
1970 Joe Frazier (USA)
1973 George Foreman (USA)
1974 Muhammad Ali (USA)
1978 Leon Spinks (USA)
1987 Mike Tyson (USA)

WBA
1965 Ernie Terrell (USA)
1968 Jimmy Ellis (USA)
1978 Muhammad Ali (USA)
1979 John Tate (USA)
1980 Mike Weaver (USA)
1982 Mike Dokes (USA)

Joe Louis – 'The Brown Bomber'

1983 Gerrie Coetzee (SAf)
1984 Greg Page (USA)
1985 Tony Tubbs (USA)
1986 Tim Witherspoon (USA)
1986 James Smith (USA)
1987 Mike Tyson (USA)
1990 James 'Buster' Douglas (USA)
1990 Evander Holyfield (USA)
1992 Riddick Bowe (USA)
1993 Evander Holyfield (USA)
1994 Michael Moorer (USA)
1994 George Foreman (USA)
1995 Bruce Seldon (USA)

WBC
1978 Ken Norton (USA)
1978 Larry Holmes (USA)
1984 Tim Witherspoon (USA)
1984 Pinklon Thomas (USA)
1986 Trevor Berbick (Jam)

1989 Mike Tyson (USA)
1990 James 'Buster' Douglas (USA)
1990 Evander Holyfield (USA)
1992 Riddick Bowe (USA)
1992 Lennox Lewis (UK)
1994 Oliver McCall (USA)

IBF
1984 Larry Holmes (USA)
1985 Michael Spinks (USA)
1987 Tony Tucker (USA)
1989 James 'Buster' Douglas (USA)
1990-4 same as WBA
1994 George Foreman (USA)

WBO
1989 Francesco Damiani (Ita)
1991 Ray Mercer (USA)
1992 Michael Mourer (USA)
1993 Tommy Morrison (USA)
1993 Michael Bentt (USA)
1994 Herbie Hide (UK)
1995 Riddick Bowe (USA)

Cruiserweight
or **Junior Heavyweight** *WBO*
Limit 190lb (86.2kg)

Undisputed
1988 Evander Holyfield (USA)

WBA
1982 Ossie Ocasio (PR)
1984 Piet Crous (SAf)
1985 Dwight Muhammad Qawi (USA)
1986 Evander Holyfield (USA)
1989 Taoufik Belbouli (Fra)
1989 Robert Daniels (USA)
1991 Bobby Czyz (USA)
1993 Orlin Norris (USA)

WBC
1979 Marvin Camel (USA)
1980 Carlos de Leon (PR)
1982 S.T.Gordon (USA)
1983 Carlos de Leon (PR)
1985 Alfonso Ratliff (USA)
1985 Bernard Benton (USA)
1986 Carlos de León (PR)
1988 Evander Holyfield (USA)
1989 Carlos de Léon (PR)
1990 Massimiliano Duran (Ita)
1991 Anaclet Wamba (Fra)

IBF
1983 Marvin Camel (USA)
1984 Lee Roy Murphy (USA)
1986 Rickey Parkey (USA)
1987 Evander Holyfield (USA)
1989 Glenn McCrory (UK)
1990 Jeff Lampkin (USA)
1991 James Warring (USA)
1992 Alfred Cole (USA)

WBO
1989 Richard Pultz (USA)
1990 Magne Havnå (Nor)
1992 Tyrone Booze (USA)
1993 Markus Bott (Ger)
1993 Nestor Giovannini (Arg)
1994 Dariusz Michalczewski (Ger)
1995 Ralf Rocchigiani (Ger)

Light Heavyweight
Limit 175lb (79.4kg)

Undisputed
1903 Jack Root (Aut)
1903 George Gardner (Ire)
1903 Bob Fitzsimmons (Eng)
1905 Jack O'Brien (USA)
1912 Jack Dillon (USA)
1916 Battling Levinsky (USA)
1920 Georges Carpentier (Fra)
1922 Battling Siki (Sen)
1923 Mike McTigue (Ire)
1925 Paul Berlenbach (USA)
1926 Jack Delaney (Can)
1927 Jim Slattery (USA)
1927 Tommy Loughran (USA)
1930 Jim Slattery (USA)
1930 Maxie Rosenbloom (USA)
1934 Bob Olin (USA)
1935 John Henry Lewis (USA)
1939 Melio Bettina (USA)
1939 Billy Conn (USA)
1941 Anton Christoforidis (Gre)
1941 Gus Lesnevich (USA)
1948 Freddie Mills (UK)
1950 Joey Maxim (USA)
1952 Archie Moore (USA)
1962 Harold Johnson (USA)
1963 Willie Pastrano (USA)
1965 José Torres (PR)

1966 Dick Tiger (Nig)
1968 Bob Foster (USA)
1983 Michael Spinks (USA)

WBA
1971 Vicente Rondon (Ven)
1974 Victor Galindez (Arg)
1978 Mike Rossman (USA)
1979 Victor Galindez (Arg)
1979 Marvin Johnson (USA)
1980 Eddie Mustafa Muhammad (USA)
1981 Michael Spinks (USA)
1986 Marvin Johnson (USA)
1987 Leslie Stewart (Jam)
1987 Virgil Hill (USA)
1991 Thomas Hearns (USA)
1992 Iran Barkley (USA)
1992 Virgil Hill (USA)

WBC
1974 John Conteh (UK)
1977 Miguel Cuello (Arg)
1978 Mate Parlov (Yug)
1978 Marvin Johnson (USA)
1979 Matthew Saad Muhammad (USA)
1981 Dwight Muhammah Qawi (USA)
1985 J.B.Williamson (USA)
1986 Dennis Andries (UK)
1987 Thomas Hearns (USA)
1988 Donny Lalonde (Can)
1988 Sugar Ray Leonard (USA)
1989 Dennis Andries (UK)
1989 Jeff Harding (Aus)
1990 Dennis Andries (UK)
1991 Jeff Harding (Aus)
1994 Mike McCallum (Jam)
1995 Fabrice Tiozzo (Fra)

IBF
1985 Slobodan Kacar (Yug)

1986 Bobby Czyz (USA)
1987 Prince Charles Williams (USA)
1993 Henry Maske (Ger)

WBO
1988 Michael Moorer (USA)
1991 Leeonzer Barber (USA)
1994 Dariusz Michalczewski (Ger)

Super Middleweight
Limit 168lb (76.2kg).

WBA
1984 Park Chong-pal (SKo)
1988 Fulgencio Obelmejias (Ven)
1989 Baek In-chul (SKo)
1990 Christophe Tiozzo (Fra)
1991 Victor Cordoba (Pan)
1992 Michael Nunn (USA)
1994 Steve Little (USA)
1994 Frank Liles (USA)

WBC
1988 Sugar Ray Leonard (USA)
1990 Mauro Galvano (Ita)
1992 Nigel Benn (UK)

IBF
1984 Murray Sutherland (Can)
1988 Graciano Rocchigiani (FRG)
1990 Lindell Holmes (USA)
1991 Darrin van Horn (USA)
1992 Iran Barkley (USA)
1993 James Toney (USA)
1994 Roy Jones Jr (USA)

WBO
1988 Thomas Hearns (USA)
1991 Chris Eubank (UK)
1995 Steve Collins (UK)

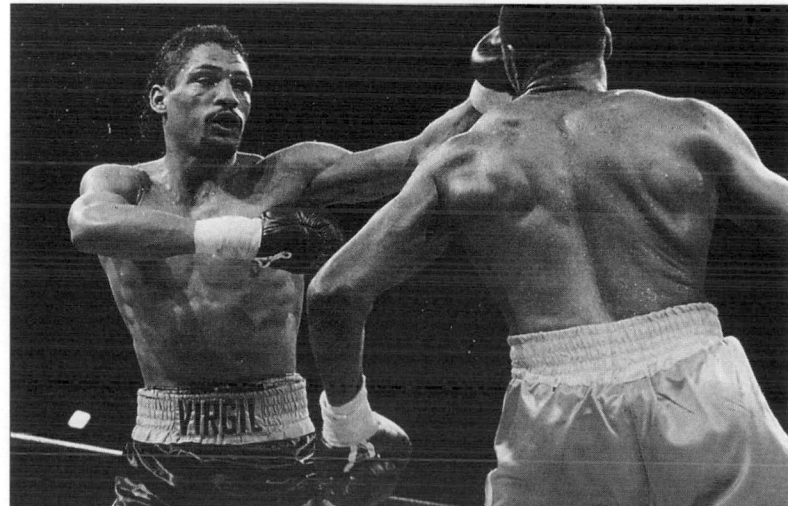

Virgil Hill loses his WBA light-heavy title to Thomas Hearns in 1991

Middleweight
Limit 160lb (72.6kg)

Undisputed
1891 Nonpareil Jack Dempsey (Ire)
1891 Bob Fitzsimmons (UK)
1897 Kid McCoy (USA)
1898 Tommy Ryan (USA)
1908 Stanley Ketchel (USA)
1908 Billy Papke (USA)
1908 Stanley Ketchel (USA)
1910 Billy Papke (USA)
1911 Cyclone Thompson (USA)
1911 Billy Papke (USA)
1912 Frank Mantell (USA)
1912 Billy Papke (USA)
1913 Frank Klaus (USA)
1913 George Chip (USA)
1914 Al McCoy (USA)
1917 Mike O'Dowd (USA)
1920 Johnny Wilson (USA)
1923 Harry Greb (USA)
1926 Tiger Flowers (USA)
1926 Mickey Walker (USA)
1931 Gorilla Jones (USA)
1932 Marcel Thil (Fra)
1937 Fred Apostoli (USA)
1939 Ceferino Garcia (Phi)
1940 Ken Overlin (USA)
1941 Billy Soose (USA)
1941 Tony Zale (USA)
1947 Rocky Graziano (USA)
1948 Tony Zale (USA)
1948 Marcel Cerdan (Alg)
1949 Jake la Motta (USA)
1951 Sugar Ray Robinson (USA)
1951 Randolph Turpin (UK)
1951 Sugar Ray Robinson (USA)
1953 Carl Bobo Olsen (Haw)
1955 Sugar Ray Robinson (USA)
1957 Gene Fullmer (USA)
1957 Sugar Ray Robinson (USA)
1957 Carmen Basilio (USA)
1958 Sugar Ray Robinson (USA)
1960 Paul Pender (USA)
1961 Terry Downes (UK)
1962 Paul Pender (USA)
1962 Dick Tiger (Nig)
1963 Joey Giardello (USA)
1965 Dick Tiger (Nig)
1966 Emile Griffith (USA)
1968 Nino Benvenuti (Ita)
1970 Carlos Monzon (Arg)
1976 Carlos Monzon (Arg)
1977 Rodrigo Valdez (Col)
1978 Hugo Corro (Arg)
1979 Vito Antuofermo (Ita)
1980 Alan Minter (UK)
1980 Marvin Hagler (USA)

WBA
1987 Sambu Kalambay (Zai)
1989 Mike McCallum (Jam)
1992 Reggie Johnson (USA)
1993 John David Jackson (USA)
1994 Jorge Castro (Arg)

WBC
1974 Rodrigo Valdez (Col)
1987 Sugar Ray Leonard (USA)
1987 Thomas Hearns (USA)
1988 Iran Barkley (USA)
1989 Roberto Duran (Pan)
1990 Julian Jackson (USVI)
1993 Gerald McClellan (USA)
1995 Julian Jackson (USVI)

IBF
1987 Frank Tate (USA)
1988 Michael Nunn (USA)
1991 James Toney (USA)
1993 Roy Jones Jr (USA)

WBO
1989 Doug De Witt (USA)
1990 Nigel Benn (UK)
1990 Chris Eubank (UK)
1991 Gerald McClellan (USA)
1993 Chris Pyatt (UK)
1994 Steve Collins (UK)

Super Welterweight
or **Junior Middleweight** *WBA, IBF, WBO*
Limit 154lb (69.9kg)

Undisputed
1962 Denny Moyer (USA)
1963 Ralph Dupas (USA)
1963 Sandro Mazzinghi (Ita)
1965 Nino Benvenuti (Ita)
1966 Kim Ki-soo (SKo)
1968 Sandro Mazzinghi (Ita)
1969 Freddie Little (USA)
1970 Carmelo Bossi (Ita)
1971 Koichi Wajima (Jap)
1974 Oscar Albarado (USA)
1975 Koichi Wajima (Jap)

WBA
1975 Yuh Jae-do (SKo)
1976 Koichi Wajima (Jap)
1976 José Duran (Spa)
1976 Angel Castellini (Arg)
1977 Eddie Gazo (Nic)
1978 Masashi Kudo (Jap)
1979 Ayube Kalule (Uga)
1981 Sugar Ray Leonard (USA)
1981 Tadashi Mihara (Jap)
1982 Davey Moore (USA)
1983 Roberto Duran (Pan)
1984 Mike McCallum (Jam)
1988 Julian Jackson (USVI)
1991 Gilbert Délé (Fra)
1991 Vinny Pazienza (USA)
1992 Julio César Vásquez (Arg)
1995 Pernell Whitaker (USA)

WBC
1975 Miguel de Oliviera (Bra)
1975 Elisha Obed (Bah)
1976 Eckhard Dagge (FRG)
1977 Rocky Mattioli (Ita)
1979 Maurice Hope (UK)
1981 Wilfred Benitez (USA)
1982 Thomas Hearns (USA)
1986 Duane Thomas (USA)
1987 Lupe Aquino (Mex)
1988 Gianfranco Rosi (Ita)
1988 Don Curry (USA)
1989 René Jacquot (Fra)
1989 John Mugabi (Uga)
1990 Terry Norris (USA)
1993 Simon Brown (USA)
1994 Terry Norris (USA)
1994 Luis Santana (Dom)
1995 Carl Daniels (USA)

IBF
1984 Mark Medal (USA)
1984 Carlos Santos (PR)
1986 Buster Drayton (USA)
1987 Matthew Hilton (Can)
1988 Robert Hines (USA)
1989 Darrin Van Horn (USA)
1989 Gianfranco Rosi (Ita)
1994 Vincent Pettway (USA)

WBO
1988 John David Jackson (USA)
1993 Vernon Phillips (USA)

Welterweight
Limit 147lb (66.7kg)

Undisputed
1892 Billy Smith (USA)
1894 Tommy Ryan (USA)
1898 Billy Smith (USA)
1900 Rube Ferns (USA)
1900 Matty Matthews (USA)
1901 Rube Ferns (USA)
1901 Joe Walcott (Bar)
1904 Dixie Kid (USA)
1905 Joe Walcott (Bar)
1906 Honey Mellody (USA)
1907 Mike Sullivan (USA)
1908 Harry Lewis (USA)
1914 Waldemar Holberg (Den)
1914 Tom McCormick (Ire)
1914 Matt Wells (UK)
1915 Mike Glover (USA)
1915 Jack Britton (USA)
1915 Ted Kid Lewis (UK)
1916 Jack Britton (USA)
1917 Ted Kid Lewis (UK)
1919 Jack Britton (USA)
1922 Mickey Walker (USA)
1926 Pete Latzo (USA)
1927 Joe Dundee (Ita)
1928 Jack Thompson (USA)

1929 Jackie Fields (USA)
1930 Jack Thompson (USA)
1930 Tommy Freeman (USA)
1931 Jack Thompson (USA)
1931 Lou Brouillard (Can)
1932 Jackie Fields (USA)
1933 Young Corbett III (Ita)
1933 Jimmy McLarnin (Ire)
1934 Barney Ross (USA)
1934 Jimmy McLarnin (Ire)
1935 Barney Ross (USA)
1938 Henry Armstrong (USA)
1940 Fritzie Zivic (USA)
1941 Red Cochrane (USA)
1946 Marty Servo (USA)
1946 Sugar Ray Robinson (USA)
1951 Johnny Bratton (USA)
1951 Kid Gavilan (Cub)
1954 Johnny Saxton (USA)
1955 Tony de Marco (USA)
1955 Carmen Basilio (USA)
1956 Johnny Saxton (USA)
1956 Carmen Basilio (USA)
1958 Virgil Atkins (USA)
1958 Don Jordon (Dom)
1960 Benny Kid Paret (Cub)
1961 Emile Griffith (USA)
1961 Benny Kid Paret (Cub)
1962 Emile Griffith (USA)
1963 Louis Rodriguez (Cub)
1963 Emile Griffith (USA)
1966 Curtis Cokes (USA)
1969 José Napoles (Cub)
1970 Billy Backus (USA)
1971 José Napoles (Cub)
1981 Sugar Ray Leonard (USA)
1985 Don Curry (USA)
1986 Lloyd Honeyghan (UK)

WBA
1975 Angel Espada (PR)
1976 Pipino Cuevas (Mex)
1980 Thomas Hearns (USA)
1983 Don Curry (USA)
1987 Mark Breland (USA)
1987 Marlon Starling (USA)
1988 Tomas Molinares (Col)
1989 Mark Breland (USA)
1990 Aaron Davis (USA)
1991 Meldrick Taylor (USA)
1992 Crisanto España (Ven)
1994 Ike Quartey (Gha)

WBC
1975 John H.Stracey (UK)
1976 Carlos Palomino (Mex)
1979 Wilfred Benitez (USA)
1979 Sugar Ray Leonard (USA)
1980 Roberto Duran (Pan)
1980 Sugar Ray Leonard (USA)
1983 Milton McCrory (USA)
1987 Lloyd Honeyghan (UK)

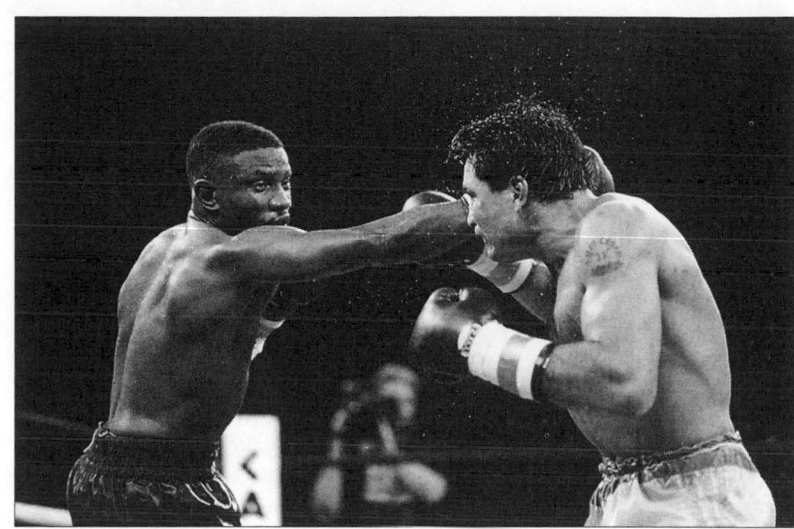

Pernell Whitaker takes the WBA junior-middle title from Vásquez

1987 Jorge Vaca (Mex)
1988 Lloyd Honeyghan (UK)
1989 Marlon Starling (USA)
1990 Maurice Blocker (USA)
1991 Simon Brown (Jam)
1991 James 'Buddy' McGirt (USA)
1993 Pernell Whitaker (USA)

IBF
1984 Don Curry (USA)
1987 Lloyd Honeyghan (UK)
1988 Simon Brown (Jam)
1991 Maurice Blocker (USA)
1993 Félix Trinidad (PR)

WBO
1989 Genaro Leon (Mex)
1989 Manning Galloway (USA)
1993 Gert Bo Jacobsen (Den)
1993 Eamonn Loughran (UK)

Super Lightweight
or **Junior Welterweight** *WBA, IBF, WBO Limit 140lb (63.5kg)*

Undisputed
1922 Pinky Mitchell (USA)
1926 Mushy Callahan (USA)
1930 Jackie Kid Berg (UK)
1931 Tony Canzoneri (USA)
1932 Johnny Jaddick (USA)
1933 Battling Shaw (Mex)
1933 Tony Canzoneri (USA)
1933 Barney Ross (USA)
1946 Tippy Larkin (USA)
1959 Carlos Ortiz (PR)
1960 Duilio Loi (Ita)
1962 Eddie Perkins (USA)
1962 Duilio Loi (Ita)
1963 Roberto Cruz (Phi)
1963 Eddie Perkins (USA)
1965 Carlos Hernández (Ven)

1966 Sandro Lopopolo (Ita)
1967 Paul Fujii (Haw)

WBA
1968 Nicolino Loche (Arg)
1972 Alfonso Frazer (Pan)
1972 Antonio Cervantes (Col)
1976 Wilfred Benitez (USA)
1977 Antonio Cervantes (Col)
1980 Aaron Pryor (USA)
1984 Johnny Bumphus (USA)
1984 Gene Hatcher (USA)
1985 Ubaldo Sacco (Arg)
1986 Patrizio Oliva (Ita)
1987 Juan Martin Coggi (Arg)
1990 Loreto Garza (USA)
1991 Edwin Rosario (PR)
1992 Akinobu Hiranaka (Jap)
1992 Morris East (Phi)
1993 Juan Martin Coggi (Arg)
1994 Frankie Randall (USA)

WBC
1968 Pedro Adigue (Phi)
1970 Bruno Acari (Ita)
1974 Perico Fernandez (Spa)
1975 Saensak Muangsurin (Tha)
1976 Miguel Velasquez (Spa)
1976 Saensak Muangsurin (Tha)
1978 Kim Sang-hyun (SKo)
1980 Saoul Mamby (USA)
1982 Leroy Haley (USA)
1983 Bruce Curry (USA)
1984 Billy Costello (USA)
1985 Lonnie Smith (USA)
1986 Tsuyoshi Hamada (Jap)
1987 René Arredondo (Mex)
1988 Roger Mayweather (USA)
1989 Julio César Chávez (Mex)
1994 Frankie Randall (USA)
1994 Julio César Chávez (Mex)

IBF

1983 Aaron Pryor (USA)
1986 Gary Hinton (USA)
1986 Joe Louis Manley (USA)
1987 Terry Marsh (UK)
1988 James Buddy McGirt (USA)
1988 Meldrick Taylor (USA)
1990 Julio César Chávez (Mex)
1991 Rafael Pineda (Col)
1992 Pernell Whitaker (USA)
1993 Charles Murray (USA)
1994 Jake Rodriguez (USA)
1995 Konstantin Tszyu (Aus)

WBO

1989 Hector Camacho (PR)
1991 Greg Haugen (USA)
1991 Hector Camacho (PR)
1992 Carlos González (Mex)
1993 Zack Padilla (USA)
> *lost title after testing positive for marijuana*

Lightweight
Limit 135lb (61.2kg)

Undisputed
1886 Jack McAuliffe (Ire)
1896 George Lavigne (USA)
1899 Frank Erne (Swi)
1902 Joe Gans (USA)
1908 Battling Nelson (Den)
1910 Ad Wolgast (USA)
1912 Willie Ritchie (USA)
1914 Freddie Welsh (UK)
1917 Benny Leonard (USA)
1925 Jimmy Goodrich (USA)
1925 Rocky Kansas (USA)
1926 Sammy Mandell (USA)
1930 Al Singer (USA)
1930 Tony Canzeroni (USA)
1933 Barney Ross (USA)
1935 Tony Canzeroni (USA)
1936 Lou Ambers (USA)
1938 Henry Armstrong (USA)
1939 Lou Ambers (USA)
1940 Lew Jenkins (USA)
1941 Sammy Angott (USA)
1942 Beau Jack (USA)
1943 Bob Montgomery (USA)
1943 Sammy Angott (USA)
1944 Juan Zurita (Mex)
1945 Ike Williams (USA)
1951 Jimmy Carter (USA)
1952 Lauro Salas (Mex)
1952 Jimmy Carter (USA)
1954 Paddy de Marco (USA)
1954 Jimmy Carter (USA)
1955 Wallace Bud Smith (USA)
1956 Joe Brown (USA)
1962 Carlos Ortiz (PR)
1965 Ismael Laguna (Pan)
1965 Carlos Ortiz (PR)

1968 Carlos Teo Cruz (Dom)
1969 Mando Ramos (USA)
1970 Ismael Laguna (Pan)
1978 Roberto Duran (Pan)

WBA
1970 Ken Buchanan (UK)
1972 Roberto Duran (Pan)
1979 Ernesto Espana (Ven)
1980 Hilmer Kenty (USA)
1981 Sean O'Grady (USA)
1981 Claude Noel (Tri)
1981 Arturo Frias (USA)
1982 Ray Mancini (USA)
1984 Livingstone Bramble (USA)
1986 Edwin Rosario (PR)
1987 Julio César Chávez (Mex)
1989 Edwin Rosario (USA)
1990 Juan Nazario (PR)
1990 Pernell Whitaker (USA)
1992 Joey Gamache (USA)
1992 Tony Lopez (USA)
1993 Dingaan Thobela (SAf)
1993 Olzubek Nazarov (Kgz)

WBC
1971 Pedro Carrasco (Spa)
1972 Mando Ramos (USA)
1972 Chango Carmona (Mex)
1972 Rodolfo Gonzalez (Mex)
1974 Guts Ishimatsu (Jap)
1976 Esteban de Jesús (PR)
1979 Jim Watt (UK)
1981 Alexis Arguello (Nic)
1983 Edwin Rosario (PR)
1984 José Luis Ramirez (Mex)
1985 Hector Camacho (PR)
1987 José Luis Ramirez (Mex)
1988 Julio César Chávez (Mex)
1989 Pernell Whitaker (USA)
1992 Miguel Angel González (Mex)

IBF
1984 Charlie Brown (USA)
1984 Harry Arroyo (USA)
1985 Jimmy Paul (USA)
1986 Greg Haugen (USA)
1987 Vinny Pazienza (USA)
1988 Greg Haugen (USA)
1989 Pernell Whitaker (USA)
1992 Freddie Pendleton (USA)
1994 Rafael Ruelas (USA)
1995 Oscar De La Hoya (USA)

WBO
1989 Amancio Castro (Col)
1989 Mauricio Aceves (Mex)
1990 Dingaan Thobela (SAf)
1992 Giovanni Parisi (Ita)
1994 Oscar De La Hoya (USA)

Super Featherweight
or **Junior Lightweight** WBA, IBF, WBO
Limit 130lb (59kg)

Undisputed
1921 Johnny Dundee (Ita)
1923 Jack Bernstein (USA)
1923 Johnny Dundee (Ita)
1924 Kid Sullivan (USA)
1925 Mike Ballerino (USA)
1925 Tod Morgan (USA)
1929 Benny Bass (USA)
1931 Kid Chocolate (Cub)
1933 Frankie Klick (USA)
1959 Harold Gomes (USA)
1960 Flash Elorde (Phi)
1967 Yoshiaki Numata (Jap)
1967 Hiroshi Kobayashi (Jap)

WBA
1971 Alfredo Marcano (Ven)
1972 Ben Villaflor (Phi)
1973 Kuniaki Shibata (Jap)
1973 Ben Villaflor (Phi)
1976 Sam Serrano (PR)
1980 Yasutsune Uehara (Jap)
1981 Sam Serrano (PR)
1983 Roger Mayweather (USA)
1984 Rocky Lockridge (USA)
1985 Wilfredo Gomez (PR)
1986 Alfredo Layne (Pan)
1986 Brian Mitchell (SAf)
1991 Joey Gamache (USA)
1991 Genaro Hernández (USA)

WBC
1969 René Barrientos (Phi)
1970 Yoshiaki Numata (Jap)
1971 Ricardo Arredondo (Mex)
1974 Kuniaki Shibata (Jap)
1975 Alfredo Escalera (PR)
1978 Alexis Arguello (Nic)
1980 Rafael Limon (Mex)
1981 Cornelius Boza Edwards (Uga)
1981 Rolando Navarette (Phi)
1982 Rafael Limon (Mex)
1982 Bobby Chacon (USA)
1983 Hector Camacho (PR)
1984 Julio César Chávez (Mex)
1988 Azumah Nelson (Gha)
1994 Jesse James Leija (USA)
1994 Gabriel Ruelas (USA)

IBF
1984 Yuh Hwan-kil (SKo)
1985 Lester Ellis (Aus)
1985 Barry Michael (Aus)
1987 Rocky Lockridge (USA)
1988 Tony Lopez (USA)
1989 Juan Molina (PR)
1990 Tony Lopez (USA)
1991 Brian Mitchell (SAf)

1992 John John Molina (PR)
1995 Eddie Hopson (USA)
1995 Tracey Patterson (USA)

WBO
1989 Juan Molina (PR)
1989 Kamel Bou Ali (Tun)
1992 Daniel Londas (Fra)
1992 Jimmy Bredhal (Den)
1994 Oscar De La Hoya (USA)
1994 Regilio Tuur (Hol)

Featherweight
Limit 126lb (57.2kg)

Undisputed
1891 Young Griffo (Aus)
1892 George Dixon (Can)
1897 Solly Smith (USA)
1898 Dave Sullivan (Ire)
1898 George Dixon (Can)
1900 Terry McGovern (USA)
1901 Young Corbett II (USA)
1904 Jimmy Britt (USA)
1904 Tommy Sullivan (USA)
1906 Abe Attell (USA)
1912 Johnny Kilbane (USA)
1923 Eugene Criqui (Fra)
1923 Johnny Dundee (Ita)
1925 Kid Kaplan (USA)
1927 Benny Bass (USA)
1928 Tony Canzoneri (USA)
1928 Andre Routis (Fra)
1929 Battling Battalino (USA)
1932 Kid Chocolate (Cub)
1933 Freddie Miller (USA)
1936 Petey Sarron (USA)
1937 Henry Armstrong (USA)
1938 Joey Archibald (USA)
1940 Harry Jeffra (USA)
1941 Joey Archibald (USA)
1941 Chalky Wright (Mex)
1942 Willie Pep (USA)
1948 Sandy Saddler (USA)
1949 Willie Pep (USA)
1950 Sandy Sadler (USA)
1957 Hogan Kid Bassey (Nig)
1959 Davey Moore (USA)
1963 Sugar Ramos (Cub)
1964 Vicente Saldivar (Mex)

WBA
1968 Raul Rojas (USA)
1968 Shozo Saijyo (Jap)
1971 Antonio Gomez (Ven)
1972 Ernesto Marcel (Pan)
1974 Ruben Olivares (Mex)
1974 Alexis Arguello (Nic)
1977 Rafael Ortega (Pan)
1977 Cecilio Lastra (Spa)
1978 Eusebio Pedroza (Pan)
1985 Barry McGuigan (Ire)
1986 Steve Cruz (USA)

1987 Antonio Esparragoza (Ven)
1991 Park Young-kyun (SKo)
1993 Eloy Rojas (Ven)

WBC
1968 Howard Winstone (UK)
1968 José Legra (Cub)
1969 Johnny Famechon (Fra)
1970 Vicente Saldivar (Mex)
1970 Kuniaki Shibata (Jap)
1972 Clemente Sanchez (Mex)
1972 José Legra (Cub)
1973 Eder Jofre (Bra)
1974 Bobby Chacon (USA)
1975 Ruben Olivares (Mex)
1975 David Kotey (Gha)
1976 Danny Lopez (USA)
1980 Salvador Sanchez (Mex)
1982 Juan Laporte (PR)
1984 Wilfredo Gomez (PR)
1984 Azumah Nelson (Gha)
1988 Jeff Fenech (Aus)
1990 Marcos Villasana (Mex)
1991 Paul Hodkinson (UK)
1993 Gregorio Vargas (Mex)
1993 Kevin Kelley (USA)
1995 Alejandro González (Mex)

IBF
1984 Oh Min-keum (SKo)
1985 Chung Ki-young (SKo)
1986 Antonio Rivera (PR)
1988 Calvin Grove (USA)
1988 Jorge Paez (Mex)
1991 Troy Dorsey (USA)
1991 Manuel Medina (Mex)
1993 Tom Johnson (USA)

WBO
1989 Maurizio Stecca (Ita)
1989 Louie Espinoza (USA)
1990 Jorge Paez (Mex)
1991 Maurizio Stecca (Ita)
1992 Colin McMillan (UK)
1992 Ruben Palacios (Col)
1993 Steve Robinson (UK)

**Super Bantamweight
or Junior Featherweight** *WBA,
IBF, WBO. Limit 122lb (55.3kg)*

Undisputed
1922 Jack Kid Wolfe (USA)
1923 Carl Duane (USA)

WBA
1977 Hong Soo-hwan (SKo)
1978 Ricardo Cardona (Col)
1980 Leo Randolph (USA)
1980 Sergio Palma (Arg)
1982 Leo Cruz (Dom)
1984 Loris Stecca (Ita)
1984 Victor Callejas (PR)
1987 Louis Espinoza (USA)

1987 Julio Gervacio (Dom)
1988 Bernardo Pinango (Ven)
1988 Juan José Estrada (Mex)
1989 Jesús Salud (USA)
1990 Luis Mendoza (Col)
1991 Raúl Pérez (Mex)
1992 Wilfredo Vásquez (PR)

WBC
1976 Rigoberto Riasco (Pan)
1976 Royal Kobayashi (Jap)
1976 Yum Dong-kyun (SKo)
1977 Wilfredo Gomez (PR)
1983 Jaime Garza (USA)
1984 Juan Meza (Mex)
1985 Lupe Pintor (Mex)
1986 Samart Payakarun (Tha)
1987 Jeff Fenech (Aus)
1988 Daniel Zaragoza (Mex)
1990 Paul Banke (USA)
1990 Pedro Decima (Arg)
1991 Kiyoshi Hatanaka (Jap)
1991 Daniel Zaragoza (Mex)
1992 Thierry Jacob (Fra)
1993 Tracy Harris Patterson (USA)
1994 Héctor Acero-Sánchez (Dom)

IBF
1983 Bobby Berna (Phi)
1984 Suh Seung-il (SKo)
1985 Kim Ji-won (SKo)
1987 Lee Seung-hoon (SKo)
1988 José Sanabria (Ven)
1989 Fabrice Benichou (Fra)
1990 Welcome Ncita (SAf)
1992 Kennedy McKinney (USA)
1994 Vuyani Bungu (SAf)

WBO
1989 Kenny Mitchell (USA)
1989 Valerio Nati (Ita)
1990 Orlando Fernandez (PR)
1991 Jesse Benevides (USA)
1992 Duke McKenzie (UK)
1993 Daniel Jiménez (PR)
1995 Marco Antonio Berrera (Mex)

Bantamweight
Limit 118lb (53.5kg)

Undisputed
1891 George Dixon (Can)
1892 Billy Plimmer (UK)
1895 Pedlar Palmer (UK)
1899 Terry McGovern (USA)
1901 Harry Forbes (USA)
1903 Frankie Neil (USA)
1904 Joe Bowker (UK)
1905 Jimmy Walsh (USA)
1907 Owen Moran (UK)
1908 Johnny Coulon (Can)
1914 Kid Williams (Den)
1917 Pete Herman (USA)
1920 Joe Lynch (USA)

1921 Pete Herman (USA)
1921 Johnny Buff (USA)
1922 Joe Lynch (USA)
1924 Abe Goldstein (USA)
1924 Eddie Martin (USA)
1925 Charlie Rosenberg (USA)
1927 Bud Taylor (USA)
1928 Bushy Graham (Ita)
1929 Al Brown (Pan)
1935 Baltazar Sangchilli (Spa)
1936 Tony Marino (USA)
1936 Sixto Escobar (Spa)
1937 Harry Jeffra (USA)
1938 Sixto Escobar (Spa)
1940 Lou Salica (USA)
1942 Manuel Ortiz (USA)
1947 Harold Dade (USA)
1947 Mauel Ortiz (USA)
1950 Vic Toweel (SAf)
1952 Jimmy Carruthers (Aus)
1954 Robert Cohen (Alg)
1956 Mario D'Agata (Ita)
1957 Alphonse Halimi (Alg)
1959 Joe Becerra (Mex)
1960 Eder Jofre (Bra)
1965 Fighting Harada (Jap)
1968 Lionel Rose (Aus)
1969 Ruben Olivares (Mex)
1970 Chucho Castillo (Mex)
1971 Ruben Olivares (Mex)
1972 Rafael Herrera (Mex)
1972 Enrique Pinder (Pan)

WBA
1973 Romeo Anaya (Mex)
1973 Arnold Taylor (SAf)
1974 Hong Soo-hwan (SKo)
1975 Alfonso Zamora (Mex)
1977 Jorge Lujan (Pan)
1980 Julian Solis (PR)
1980 Jeff Chandler (USA)
1984 Richard Sandoval (USA)
1986 Gaby Canizales (USA)
1986 Bernardo Pinango (Ven)
1987 Takuya Muguruma (Jap)
1987 Park Chang-young (SKo)
1987 Wilfredo Vasquez (PR)
1988 Khaokor Galaxy (Tha)
1988 Moon Sung-kil (SKo)
1989 Khaokor Galaxy (Tha)
1989 Luisito Espinosa (Phi)
1991 Israel Contreras (Ven)
1992 Eddie Cook (USA)
1992 Jorge Julio Eliecer (Col)
1993 Junior Jones (USA)
1994 John Michael Johnson (USA)
1994 Daorung Chuvatana (Tha)

WBC
1973 Rafael Herrera (Mex)
1974 Rodolfo Martinez (Mex)
1976 Carlos Zarate (Mex)

1979 Lupe Pintor (Mex)
1983 Alberto Davila (USA)
1985 Daniel Zaragoza (Mex)
1985 Miguel Lora (Col)
1988 Raul Perez (Mex)
1991 Greg Richardson (USA)
1991 Joichiro Tatsuyoshi (Jap)
1992 Victor Rabanales (Mex)
1993 Byun Jong-il (SKo)
1993 Yasuei Yakushiji (Jap)
1995 Wayne McCullough (Ire)

IBF
1984 Satoshi Shingaki (Jap)
1985 Jeff Fenech (Aus)
1987 Kelvin Seabrooks (USA)
1988 Orlando Canizales (USA)

WBO
1989 Israel Contreras (Ven)
1991 Gaby Canizales (USA)
1991 Duke McKenzie (UK)
1992 Rafael Del Valle (PR)
1994 Alfred Kotey (Gha)

Super Flyweight
or **Junior Bantamweight** *WBA, IBF, WBO*
Limit 115lb (52.2kg)

WBA
1981 Gustavo Ballas (Arg)
1981 Rafael Pedroza (Pan)
1982 Jiro Watanabe (Jap)
1984 Khaosai Galaxy (Tha)
1992 Katsuya Onizuka (Jap)
1994 Lee Hyung-chul (SKo)
1995 Alima Goitia (Ven)

WBC
1980 Rafael Orono (Ven)
1981 Kim Chul-ho (SKo)
1982 Rafael Orono (Ven)
1983 Payao Poontarat (Tha)
1984 Jiro Watanabe (Jap)
1986 Gilberto Roman (Mex)
1987 Santos Laciar (Arg)
1987 Jesús Rojas (Col)
1988 Gilberto Román (Mex)
1989 Nana Yaw Konadu (Gha)
1990 Moon Sung-kil (SKo)
1993 José Luis Bueno (Mex)
1994 Hiroshi Kawashima (Jap)

IBF
1983 Chun Joo-do (SKo)
1985 Ellyas Pical (Ina)
1986 Cesar Polanco (Dom)
1986 Chang Tae-il (SKo)
1987 Ellyas Pical (Ina)
1989 Juan Polo Pérez (Col)
1990 Robert Quiroga (USA)
1993 Julio César Borboa (Mex)
1994 Harold Grey (Col)

WBO
1989 José Ruiz (PR)
1992 José Quirino (Mex)
1992 Johnny Bredahl (Den)
1994 Johnny Tapia (USA)

Flyweight
Limit 112lb (50.8kg)

Undisputed
1913 Sid Smith (UK)
1913 Bill Ladbury (UK)
1914 Percy Jones (UK)
1915 Joe Symonds (UK)
1916 Jimmy Wilde (UK)
1923 Pancho Villa (Phi)
1925 Fidel La Barba (USA)
1928 Frankie Genaro (USA)
1929 Emile Pladner (Fra)
1929 Frankie Genaro (USA)
1931 Young Perez (Tun)
1932 Jackie Brown (UK)
1935 Benny Lynch (UK)
1938 Peter Kane (UK)
1943 Jackie Paterson (UK)
1948 Rinty Monaghan (UK)
1950 Terry Allen (UK)
1950 Dado Marino (Haw)
1952 Yoshio Shirai (Jap)
1954 Pascual Pérez (Arg)
1960 Pone Kingpetch (Tha)
1962 Fighting Harada (Jap)
1963 Pone Kingpetch (Tha)
1963 Hiroyuki Ebihara (Jap)
1964 Pone Kingpetch (Tha)
1965 Salvatore Burruni (Ita)

WBA
1966 Horacio Accavallo (Arg)
1969 Hiroyuki Ebihara (Jap)
1969 Bernabe Villacampo (Phi)
1970 Berkrerk Chartvanchai (Tha)
1970 Masao Ohba (Jap)
1973 Chartchai Chionoi (Tha)
1974 Susumu Hanagata (Jap)
1975 Erbito Salavarria (Phi)
1976 Alfonso López (Pan)
1976 Guty Espadas (Mex)
1978 Betulio Gonzalez (Ven)
1979 Luis Ibarra (Pan)
1980 Kim Tae-shik (SKo)
1980 Shoji Oguma (Jap)
1980 Peter Mathebula (SAf)
1981 Santos Laciar (Arg)
1981 Luis Ibarra (Pan)
1981 Juan Herrera (Mex)
1982 Santos Laciar (Arg)
1985 Hilario Zapata (Pan)
1987 Fidel Bassa (Col)
1989 Jesús Rojas (Ven)
1990 Lee Yul-woo (SKo)
1990 Yukihito Tamakama (Jap)
1991 Elvis Alvárez (Col)

1991 Kim Yong-kang (SKo)
1992 Aquiles Guzman (Ven)
1992 David Griman (Ven)
1994 Saen Sor Ploenchit (Tha)

WBC

1966 Walter McGowan (UK)
1966 Chartchai Chionoi (Tha)
1969 Efren Torres (Mex)
1970 Chartchai Chionoi (Tha)
1970 Erbito Salavarria (Phi)
1972 Venice Borkorsor (Tha)
1973 Betulio Gonzalez (Ven)
1974 Shoji Oguma (Jap)
1975 Miguel Canto (Mex)
1979 Park Chan-hee (SKo)
1981 Antonio Avelar (Mex)
1982 Prudencio Cardona (Col)
1982 Freddie Castillo (Mex)
1982 Eleoncio Mercedes (Dom)
1983 Charlie Magri (UK)
1983 Frank Cedeno (Phi)
1984 Koji Kobayashi (Jap)
1984 Gabriel Bernal (Mex)
1984 Sot Chitalada (Tha)
1988 Kim Yong-kang (SKo)
1989 Sot Chitalda (Tha)
1991 Muangchai Kittikasem (Tha)
1993 Yuriy Arbachakov (Rus)

IBF

1983 Kwon Soon-chun (SKo)
1985 Chung Chong-kwan (SKo)
1986 Chung Bi-won (SKo)
1986 Shin Hi-sup (SKo)
1987 Dodie Penalosa (Phi)
1987 Choi Chang-ho (SKo)
1988 Rolando Bohol (Phi)
1988 Duke McKenzie (UK)
1989 Dave McAuley (UK)
1992 Rodolfo Blanco (Col)
1992 Pichit Sitbangprachan (Tha)
1995 Francisco Tejedor (Col)
1995 Danny Romero (USA)

WBO

1989 Elvis Alvarez (Col)
1990 Isidro Pérez (Mex)
1992 Pat Clinton (USA)
1993 Baby Jake Matlala (SAf)
1995 Alberto Jiménez (Mex)

Light Flyweight
or **Junior Flyweight** *WBA, IBF,*
  WBO
Limit 108lb (49kg)

WBA

1975 Jaime Rios (Pan)
1976 Juan José Guzman (Dom)
1976 Yoko Gushiken (Jap)
1981 Pedro Flores (Mex)
1981 Kim Hwan-jin (SKo)
1981 Katsuo Takashiki (Jap)
1983 Lupe Madera (Mex)
1984 Francisco Quiroz (Dom)
1985 Joey Olivo (USA)
1985 Yuh Myung-woo (SKo)
1992 Hiroki Ioka (Jap)
1992 Yuh Myung-woo (SKo)
1993 Leo Gamez (Ven)

WBC

1975 Franco Udella (Ita)
1975 Luis Estaba (Ven)
1978 Freddie Castillo (Mex)
1978 Netrnoi Vorasingh (Tha)
1978 Kim Sung-jun (SKo)
1980 Shigeo Nakajima (Jap)
1980 Hilario Zapata (Pan)
1982 Amado Ursua (Mex)
1982 Tadashi Tomori (Jap)
1982 Hilario Zapata (Pan)
1983 Chang Jung-koo (Kor)
1988 German Torres (Mex)
1989 Lee Yul-woo (SKo)
1989 Humberto González (Mex)
1990 Rolando Pascua (Phi)
1991 Melchor Cob Castro (Mex)
1991 Humberto González (Mex)
1993 Michael Carbajal (USA)

1994 Humberto González (Mex)
1995 Saman Sorjaturong (Tha)

IBF

1983 Dodie Penalosa (Phi)
1986 Choi Chong-hwan (SKo)
1988 Tacy Macalos (Phi)
1989 Muangchai Kittikasem (Tha)
1990 Michael Carbajal (USA)
1994 Humberto González (Mex)
1995 Saman Sorjaturong (Tha)

WBO

1989 José de Jesús (PR)
1992 José Camacho (PR)
1994 Michael Carbajal (USA)

Strawweight
Mini-flyweight *WBA, IBF, WBO*
Limit 105lb (47.6kg)

WBA

1988 Leo Gamez (Dom)
1989 Kim Bong-jun (SKo)
1991 Choi Hi-yong (SKo)
1992 Hideyuki Ohashi (Jap)
1993 Chana Por Pao-in (Tha)

WBC

1987 Lee Kyung-yung (SKo)
1988 Hiroki Ioka (Jap)
1988 Napa Kiatwanchai (Tha)
1989 Choi Jeum-hwan (SKo)
1990 Hideyuki Ohashi (Jap)
1990 Ricardo López (Mex)

IBF

1988 Samuth Sithnaruepol (Tha)
1989 Nico Thomas (Ina)
1989 Eric Chavez (Phi)
1990 Phahlan Lookmingkwan (Tha)
1992 Manuel Melchor (Phi)
1992 Ratanapol Sorvorapin (Tha)

WBO

1989 Rafael Torres (Dom)
1993 Paul Weir (UK(
1993 Alexander Sánchez (PR)

Most World Titles

6 Thomas Hearns
    WBA Welterweight 1980
    WBC Junior middleweight 1982
    WBC Light-heavyweight 1987
    WBC Middleweight 1987
    WBO Super middleweight 1988
    WBA Light-heavyweight 1991
5 Sugar Ray Leonard
    WBC Welterweight 1979
    WBA Junior middleweight 1981
    WBC Middleweight 1987
    WBC Super middleweight 1988
    WBC Light-heavyweight 1988

4 Roberto Duran
    WBA Lightweight 1972
    Welterweight 1980
    WBA Junior middleweight 1983
    WBC Middleweight 1989
3 Bob Fitzsimmons
    Middleweight 1891
    Heavyweight 1897
    Light-heavyweight 1903
3 Tony Canzoneri
    Featherweight 1928
    Lightweight 1930
    Junior welterweight 1931

3 Barney Ross
    Lightweight 1933
    Junior welterweight 1933
    Welterweight 1934
3 Henry Armstrong
    Featherweight 1937
    Welterweight 1938
    Lightweight 1938
3 Wilfredo Benitez
    WBA Junior welterweight 1976
    WBC welterweight 1979
    WBC Super-welterweight 1981
3 Alexis Arguello
    WBA Featherweight 1974
    WBC Junior lightweight 1978
    WBC Lightweight 1981
3 Wilfredo Gomez
    WBC Junior featherweight 1977
    WBC Featherweight 1984
    WBA Junior lightweight 1985
3 Jeff Fenech
    IBF Bantamweight 1985
    WBC Junior featherweight 1987
    WBC Featherweight 1988
3 Julio César Chávez
    WBC Junior lightweight 1984
    WBA Lightweight 1987
    WBC Junior welterweight 1989
3 Hector Camacho
    WBC Junior lightweight 1983
    WBC Lightweight 1985
    WBO Junior welterweight 1989
3 Duke McKenzie
    IBF Featherweight 1988
    WBO Bantamweight 1991
    WBO Super Bantamweight 1992
3 Pernell Whitaker
    IBF/WBC Lightweight 1989 (WBA 1990)
    IBF Junior welterweight 1992
    WBC Welterweight 1993
3 Mike McCallum
    WBA Junior Middle 1984
    WBA Middle 1989
    WBC Light Heavy 1994

Emile Griffith won the welterweight title in 1961 and the middleweight title in 1966. He also claimed to be the first junior-middleweight champion in 1962 but his title was recognised in Austria only.

Most world title fights: 29 Julio César Chávez, 27 Joe Louis

Most world title fight wins: 28 Julio César Chávez, 26 Joe Louis

Louis made a record 25 defences of his heavyweight title, the most in any weight division.

Longest reigning champion: Joe Louis (USA), heavyweight 11 years 252 days

Oldest world champion: 48 years 59 days Archie Moore (USA), light-heavyweight. (Moore may have been only 45 years because of a doubt over his date of birth. In that case George Foreman at 46 (b.22 Jan 1949) would be older.

Youngest world champion: 17 years 176 days Wilfred Benitez (USA), light welterweight
Heaviest world champion: 270lb (122kg) Primo Carnera (Ita)
Tallest world champion: 6ft 6in (1.98m) Ernie Terrell (USA), heavyweight
Jess Willard is often incorrectly quoted as being 6ft 6¹/₂ in tall.

Amateur Boxing

Administered by the International Amateur Boxing Association (AIBA), formed in 1946, whose membership reached 178 nations in 1993. The first national association was the Amateur Boxing Association (ABA) of England, founded in 1880, which staged its first championships in 1881 at four weights: feather, light, middle and heavy.

Olympic Champions

Boxing was included on the Olympic programme in 1904 and 1908 and has been at each Games since 1920. Weight limits shown are those currently in use, followed by previous limits on the following line.

Super-heavyweight - over 91kg
1984 Tyrell Bigg (USA)
1988 Lennox Lewis (Can)
1992 Roberto Balado (Cub)

Heavyweight - 91kg
Over 156lb (71.7kg) 1904-08, over 175lb (79.4kg) 1920-36, over 80kg 1948, over 81kg 1952-80
1904 Samuel Berger (USA)
1908 Albert Leonard Oldham (UK)
1912 Not held
1920 Ronald Rawson (UK)
1924 Otto von Porat (Nor)
1928 Arturo Rodriguez Jurado (Arg)
1932 Santiago Lovell (Arg)
1936 Herbert Runge (Ger)
1948 Rafael Iglesias (Arg)
1952 Edward Sanders (USA)
1956 Peter Rademacher (USA)
1960 Franco de Piccoli (Ita)
1964 Joe Frazier (USA)
1968 George Foreman (USA)
1972 Teofilo Stevenson (Cub)
1976 Teofilo Stevenson (Cub)
1980 Teofilo Stevenson (Cub)
1984 Henry Tillman (USA)
1988 Ray Mercer (USA)
1992 Félix Savon (Cub)

Light-heavyweight - 81 kg
Limit 175lb (79.4kg) 1920-36, 80kg 1948
1920 Eddie Eagan (USA)
1924 Harry Mitchell (UK)
1928 Victor Avendano (Arg)
1932 David Carstens (SAf)
1936 Roger Michelot (Fra)
1948 George Hunter (SAf)
1952 Norvel Lee (USA)
1956 James Boyd (USA)
1960 Cassius Clay (USA)

1964 Cosimo Pinto (Ita)
1968 Dan Poznyak (USSR)
1972 Mate Parlov (Yug)
1976 Leon Spinks (USA)
1980 Slobodan Kacar (Yug)
1984 Anton Jospovic (Yug)
1988 Andrew Maynard (USA)
1992 Torsten May (Ger)

Middleweight - 75kg
Limit 158lb (71.7kg) 1904-08,
160lb (72.6kg) 1920-36, 73kg 1948
1904 Charles Mayer (USA)
1908 John Douglas (UK)
1920 Harry Mallin (UK)
1924 Harry Mallin (UK)
1928 Piero Toscani (Ita)
1932 Carmen Barth (USA)
1936 Jean Despeaux (Fra)
1948 László Papp (Hun)
1952 Floyd Patterson (USA)
1956 Gennadiy Schatkov (USSR)
1960 Edward Crook (USA)
1964 Valeriy Popenchenko (USSR)
1968 Chris Finnegan (UK)
1972 Vyacheslav Lemechev (USSR)
1976 Michael Spinks (USA)
1980 José Gomez (Cub)
1984 Shin Joon-sup (Sko)
1988 Henry Maske (GDR)
1992 Ariel Hernández (Cub)

Light middleweight - 71kg
1952 László Papp (Hun)
1956 László Papp (Hun)
1960 Wilbert McClure (USA)
1964 Boris Lagutin (USSR)
1968 Boris Lagutin (USSR)
1972 Dieter Kottysch (FRG)
1976 Jerzy Rybicki (Pol)
1980 Armando Martinez (Cub)
1984 Frank Tate (USA)
1988 Park Si-hun (Kor)
1992 Juan Carlos Lemus (Cub)

Welterweight - 67kg
Limit 143.75lb (65.3kg) 1904,
147lb (66.7kg) 1920-36
1904 Albert Young (USA)
1908 *not held*
1920 Albert Schneider (Can)
1924 Jean Delarge (Bel)
1928 Edward Morgan (NZ)
1932 Edward Flynn (USA)
1936 Sten Suvio (Fin)
1948 Július Torma (Cs)
1952 Zygmunt Chychla (Pol)
1956 Nicolae Linca (Rom)
1960 Giovanni Benvenuti (Ita)
1964 Marian Kasprzyk (Pol)
1968 Manfred Wolke (GDR)
1972 Emilio Correa (Cub)
1976 Jochen Bachfeld (GDR)

1980 Andrés Aldama (Cub)
1984 Mark Breland (USA)
1988 Robert Wangila (Ken)
1992 Michael Carruth (Ire)

Light-welterweight - 63.5kg
1952 Charles Adkins (USA)
1956 Vladimir Yengibaryan
    (USSR)
1960 Bohumil Nemecek (Cs)
1964 Jerzy Kulej (Pol)
1968 Jerzy Kulej (Pol)
1972 Ray Seales (USA)
1976 Ray Leonard (USA)
1980 Patrizio Oliva (Ita)
1984 Jerry Page (USA)
1988 Vyacheslav Janovskiy (USSR)
1992 Héctor Vincent (Cub)

Lightweight - 60kg
Limit 135lb (61.2kg) 1904, 1920-36,
140lb (63.5kg) 1908, 62kg 1948
1904 Harry Spanger (USA)
1908 Frederick Grace (UK)
1920 Samuel Mosberg (USA)
1924 Hans Neilsen (Den)
1928 Carlo Orlando (Ita)
1932 Lawrence Stevens (SAf)
1936 Imre Harangi (Hun)
1948 Gerald Dreyer (SAf)
1952 Aureliano Bolognesi (Ita)
1956 Dick McTaggart (UK)
1960 Kazimierz Pazdzior (Pol)
1964 Józef Grudzien (Pol)
1968 Ron Harris (USA)
1972 Jan Szczepanski (Pol)
1976 Howard Davis (USA)
1980 Angel Herrera (Cub)
1984 Pernell Whitaker (USA)
1988 Andreas Zuelow (GDR)
1992 Oscar De La Hoya (USA)

Featherweight - 57kg
Limit 125lb (56.7kg) 1904,
126lb (57.1kg) 1908-36, 58kg 1948
1904 Oliver Kirk (USA)
1908 Richard Gunn (UK)
1920 Paul Fritsch (Fra)
1924 John Fields (USA)
1928 Lambertus van Klaveren
(Hol)
1932 Carmelo Robledo (Arg)
1936 Oscar Casanovas (Arg)
1948 Ernesto Formenti (Ita)
1952 Ján Zachara (Cs)
1956 Vladimir Safronov (USSR)
1960 Francesco Musso (Ita)
1964 Stanislav Stepashkin (USSR)
1968 Antonio Roldan (Mex)
1972 Boris Kuznetsov (USSR)
1976 Angel Herrera (Cub)
1980 Rudi Fink (GDR)
1984 Meldrick Taylor (USA)

1988 Giovanni Parisi (Ita)
1992 Andreas Tews (Ger)

Bantamweight - 54kg
Limit 114lb (52.2kg) 1904,
116lb (52.6kg) 1908,
118lb (53.5kg) 1920-36
1904 Oliver Kirk (USA)
1908 Henry Thomas (UK)
1920 Clarence Walker (SAf)
1924 William Smith (SAf)
1928 Vittorio Tamagnini (Ita)
1932 Horace Gwynne (Can)
1936 Ulderico Sergo (Ita)
1948 Tibor Csik (Hun)
1952 Pentti Hämäläinen (Fin)
1956 Wolfgang Behrendt (FRG)
1960 Oleg Grigoryev (USSR)
1964 Takao Sakurai (Jap)
1968 Valeriy Sokolov (USSR)
1972 Orlando Martinez (Cub)
1976 Gu Yung-jo (NKo)
1980 Juan Hernández (Cub)
1984 Maurizio Stecca (Ita)
1988 Kennedy McKinney (USA)
1992 Joel Casamayor (Cub)

Flyweight - 51kg
Limit 105lb (47.6kg) 1904,
112lb (50.8kg) 1920-36
1904 George Finnegan (USA)
1908 *not held*
1920 Frankie Genaro (USA)
1924 Fidel La Barba (USA)
1928 Antal Kocsis (Hun)
1932 István Énekes (Hun)
1936 Willi Kaiser (Ger)
1948 Pascual Perez (Arg)
1952 Nathan Brooks (USA)
1956 Terry Spinks (UK)
1960 Gyula Török (Hun)
1964 Fernando Atzori (Ita)
1968 Ricardo Delgado (Mex)
1972 Georgi Kostadinov (Bul)
1976 Leo Randolph (USA)
1980 Petar Lessov (Bul)
1984 Steve McCrory (USA)
1988 Kim Kwang-sun (SKo)
1992 Choi Chol-su (NKo)

Light-flyweight - 48kg
1968 Francisco Rodriguez (Ven)
1972 György Gedo (Hun)
1976 Jorge Hernández (Cub)
1980 Shamil Sabirov (USSR)
1984 Paul Gonzales (USA)
1988 Ivailo Khristov (Bul)
1992 Rogelio Marcelo (Cub)

Leading medal-winning nations

	Gold	Silver	Bronze	Total
United States	47	20	28	95
USSR/CIS	14	20	18	52
United Kingdom	12	10	21	43
Poland	8	9	26	43
Italy	14	12	13	39
Cuba	19	10	5	34
Germany (inc FRG)	6	11	10	27
Argentina	7	7	9	23

Most individual gold medals:
3 László Papp (Hun) middleweight 1948, light-middleweight 1952, 1956; Teofilo Stevenson (Cub) heavyweight 1972, 1976, 1980
Oldest champion: 37 years 254 days Richard Gunn (UK) featherweight 1908
Youngest champion: 16 years 162 days Jackie Fields (USA) featherweight 1924

Olympic champions who won professional world titles

	Olympic title	First pro title
Fidel LaBarba (USA)	1924 fly	1925 fly
Willie Smith (SAf)	1924 bantam	1927 bantam *
Frankie Genaro (USA)	1920 fly	1928 fly
Jackie Fields (USA)	1924 feather	1929 welter
Pascual Pérez (Arg)	1948 fly	1954 fly
Floyd Patterson (USA)	1952 middle	1956 heavy
Cassius Clay (USA)	1960 light-heavy	1964 heavy
Nino Benvenuti (Ita)	1960 welter	1965 light middle
Joe Frazier (USA)	1964 heavy	1968 heavy
George Foreman (USA)	1968 heavy	1973 heavy
Mate Parlov (Yug)	1972 light-heavy	1978 light-heavy
Leon Spinks (USA)	1976 light-heavy	1978 heavy
Sugar Ray Leonard (USA)	1976 light welter	1979 junior middle
Leo Randolph (USA)	1976 fly	1980 junior fly
Michael Spinks (USA)	1976 middle	1981 light-heavy
Slobodan Kacar (Yug)	1980 light-heavy	1985 middle
Patrizio Oliva (Ita)	1980 light welter	1986 junior welter
Mark Breland (USA)	1984 welter	1987 welter
Frank Tate (USA)	1984 light middle	1987 middle
Meldrick Taylor (USA)	1984 feather	1988 junior welter
Maurizio Stecca (Ita)	1984 bantam	1989 feather
Pernell Whittaker (USA)	1984 light	1989 light
Ray Mercer (USA)	1988 heavy	1991 heavy
Lennox Lewis (UK)	1988 super-heavy	1992 heavy
Giovanni Parisi (Ita)	1988 feather	1992 light
Kennedy McKinney (USA)	1988 bantam	1992 junior feather
Henry Maske (Ger)	1988 middle	1993 light heavy
Oscar De La Hoya (USA)	1992 light	1994 junior light

* Smith won the British version of the world title only

World Amateur Championships

First held in Havana in 1974 these championships have subsequently been staged in between Olympic Games at Belgrade in 1978, Munich 1982, Reno 1986 and Moscow 1989. A challenge series, involving seven of the 1982 champions, was organised in Reno in March 1983, and a second series of challenge bouts for the remaining champions took place in Tokyo two months later - these winners have been included in the tables that follow.

Super-Heavyweight - 91kg +
1982 Tyrell Biggs (USA)
1983 Tyrell Biggs (USA)
1986 Teofilo Stevenson (Cub)
1989 Roberto Balado (Cub)
1991 Roberto Balado (Cub)
1993 Roberto Balado (Cub)
1995 Aleksey Lezin (Rus)

Heavyweight - 91kg
1974 Teofilo Stevenson (Cub)
1978 Teofilo Stevenson (Cub)
1982 Aleksandr Lagubkin (USSR)
1983 Willie DeWitt (Can)
1986 Félix Savón (Cub)
1989 Félix Savón (Cub)
1991 Félix Savón (Cub)
1993 Félix Savón (Cub)
1995 Félix Savón (Cub)

Light-Heavyweight - 81kg
1974 Mate Parlov (Yug)
1978 Sixto Soria (Cub)
1982 Pablo Romero (Cub)
1983 Pablo Romero (Cub)
1986 Pablo Romero (Cub)
1989 Henry Maske (GDR)
1991 Torsten May (Ger)
1993 Ramon Garbey (Cub)
1995 Antonio Tarver (USA)

Middleweight- 75kg
1974 Rufat Riskiyev (USSR)
1978 José Gomez (Cub)
1982 Bernardo Comas (Cub)
1983 Bernardo Comas (Cub)
1986 Darin Allen (USA)
1989 Andrey Kurnyavka (USSR)
1991 Tommaso Russo (Ita)
1993 Ariel Hernández (Cub)
1995 Francisc Vastag (Rom)

Light Middleweight - 71kg
1974 Rolando Garbey (Cub)
1978 Viktor Savchenko (USSR)
1982 Aleksandr Koshkin (USSR)
1983 Shawn O'Sullivan (Can)
1986 Angel Espinosa (Cub)
1989 Israel Akopkokhyan (USSR)
1991 Juan Lemus (Cub)
1993 Francisc Vastag (Rom)
1995 Ariel Hernández (Cub)

Welterweight- 67kg
1974 Emilio Correa (Cub)
1978 Valeriy Rachkov (USSR)
1982 Mark Breland (USA)

1983 Mark Breland (USA)
1986 Kenneth Gould (USA)
1989 Francisc Vastag (Rom)
1991 Juan Hernández (Cub)
1993 Juan Hernández (Cub)
1995 Juan Hernández (Cub)

Light Welterweight - 63.5kg
1974 Ayub Kalule (Uga)
1978 Valeriy Lvov (USSR)
1982 Carlos Garcia (Cub)
1983 Carlos Garcia (Cub)
1986 Vasiliy Shishov (USSR)
1989 Igor Ruzhnikov (USSR)
1991 Konstantin Tszyu (USSR)
1993 Héctor Vincent (Cub)
1995 Héctor Vincent (Cub)

Lightweight- 60kg
1974 Vasiliy Solomin (USSR)
1978 Andeh Davison (Nig)
1982 Angel Herrera (Cub)
1983 Pernell Whitaker (USA)
1986 Adolfo Horta (Cub)
1989 Julio González (Cub)
1991 Marco Rudolph (Ger)
1993 Damian Austin (Cub)

1995 Leonard Doroftei (Rom)

Featherweight - 57kg
1974 Howard Davis (USA)
1978 Angel Herrera (Cub)
1982 Adolfo Horta (Cub)
1983 Adolfo Horta (Cub)
1986 Kelcie Banks (USA)
1989 Airat Khamatov (USSR)
1991 Kirkor Kirkorov (Bul)
1993 Serafim Todorov (Bul)
1995 Serafim Todorov (Bul)

Bantamweight - 54kg
1974 Wilfredo Gomez (PR)
1978 Adolfo Horta (Cub)
1982 Floyd Favors (USA)
1983 Floyd Favors (USA)
1986 Moon Sung-kil (SKo)
1989 Enrique Carrion (Cub)
1991 Serafim Todorov (Bul)
1993 Alexander Khristov (Bul)
1995 Raimkul Malachbekov (Rus)

Flyweight - 51kg
1974 Douglas Rodriguez (Cub)
1978 Henryk Srednicki (Pol)

1982 Yuriy Aleksandrov (USSR)
1983 Steve McCrory (USA)
1986 Pedro Reyes (Cub)
1989 Yuriy Arbachakov (USSR)
1991 István Kovács (Hun)
1993 Waldemar Font (Cub)
1995 Zoltan Lunke (Ger)

Light Flyweight 48kg
1974 Jorge Hernández (Cub)
1978 Stephen Muchoki (Ken)
1982 Ismail Mustafov (Bul)
1983 Rafael Saiz (Cub)
1986 Juan Torres (Cub)
1989 Eric Griffin (USA)
1991 Eric Griffin (USA)
1993 Nshan Muntjian (Arm)
1995 Daniel Petrov (Bul)

Most titles
5 Félix Savón, 3 Teofilo Stevenson, Adolfo Horta (and 1983 world challenge), Roberto Balado, Juan Hernández. Pablo Romero won two and the world challenge in 1983.

Bridge

This card game was developed from whist, with the extra dimension of a competititive auction added. Auction Bridge, in which the highest bidder names trumps, was first played in about 1903. It was superseded by Contract, in which no tricks won in the play are counted towards game unless contracted for in the bidding, a principle used earlier in Plafond. Contract Bridge developed erratically until the present scoring table was devised in 1925 by Harold S Vanderbilt (USA). Highly-publicised matches staged brilliantly by Ely Cuthbertson against Lt-Col. Walter Buller's British team in 1930 and Sydney Lenz's 'official' US team in 1931 attracted worldwide publicity and made Cuthbertson the supreme authority.

The ruling body is the World Bridge Federation, formed in 1958.

World Team Championship

Contested by international teams for the Bermuda Bowl; first held in 1951, at first annually and now biennially. The women's competition for the Venice Cup is now held concurrently. The Cup was presented by the Italian Bridge Federation. *Wins:*

Men - Bermuda Bowl
13 Italy   1957-9, 1961-3, 1965-7, 1969, 1973-5
13 USA*   1950-1, 1953-4, 1970-1, 1976-7, 1979, 1981, 1983, 1985, 1987

   as North America 1970

1   Great Britain 1955, France 1956, Brazil 1989, Iceland 1991, Netherlands 1993

Women - Venice Cup
6   USA   1974, 1976, 1978, 1987, 1989, 1991, 1993
2   Great Britain 1981, 1985

World Team Olympiad

Held every four years from 1960, for a handsome cup, the Vanderbilt Trophy, presented by the inventor of modern bridge scoring. *Winners:*

Year	Open	Women
1960	France	United Arab Republic
1964	Italy	Great Britain
1968	Italy	Sweden
1972	Italy	Italy
1976	Brazil	USA
1980	France	USA
1984	Poland	USA
1988	USA	Denmark
1992	France	Austria

World Championships

Held every four years in between Olympiads, from 1962.

World Pairs (Open)
1962 Pierre Jais & Roger Trézel (Fra)
1966 Cornelius Slavenburg & Hans Kreyns (Hol)
1970 Fritz Babsch & Peter Manhardt (Aut)
1974 Robert Hamman & Robert Wolff (USA)
1978 Marcello Branco & Gabino Cintra (Bra)
1982 Chip Martel & Lew Stansby (USA)
1986 Jeff Meckstroth & Eric Rodwell (USA)
1990 Gabriel Chagas & Marcello Branco (Bra)
1994 Marcin Lesniewski & Marek Szymanowski (Pol)

Women's pairs:

1962 Rixi Markus & Fritzi Gordon (UK)
1966 Joan Durran & Jane Priday (UK)
1970 Mary Jane Farrell & Marilyn Johnson (USA)
1974 Rixi Markus & Fritzi Gordon (UK)
1978 Kathie Wei & Judi Radin (USA)
1982 Carol Sanders & Betty Ann Kennedy (USA)
1986 Jacqui Mitchell & Amalya Kearse (USA)
1990 Kerri Shuman & Karen McCallum (USA)
1994 Bep Vriend & Carla Arnolds (Hol)

Mixed pairs

1990 Peter Weichsel & Juanita Chambers (USA)
1994 Danuta Hocheker & Apolinaire Kowalski (Pol)

World Knock-out Teams (Luis Vuitton Trophy)

1978 Poland, 1982 France, 1986 USA,
1990 FR Germany, 1994 USA

World Women's Team (McConnell Cup)

1994 USA

The most successful individual at world championship play has been Giorgio Belladonna who played on all 13 Italian Bermuda Bowl winning teams and their three Olympiad wins.

Inaugurated in 1986 and based on the use of computer technology. It attracted 66,338 entrants playing exactly the same hands at more than 1000 centres in 76 countries. The 1987 event was contested by 73,256 players at 1537 centres, 1988 by 84,352 players at 1731 centres, 1989 by 85,100 players in 90 countries, 1990 by 88,000 players and 1991 by 90,000 competitors. *Winners:*

1986 Fraisnais & Bouteille (Fra)
1987 Peter Thompson & Robin Stretch (UK)
1988 Jan Horwitz & Barbara Norante (USA)
1989 Wojciech Blegajlo & Dariusz Zembrzuski (Pol)
1990 Sorin Lupan & Søren Godfredsen (Den)
1991 Miroslaw Kopowski & Wieslaw Maczkowski (Pol)
1992 Patrice Baverel & Jean François Hazard (Fra)
1994 Albert Bouwer & John Ruddell (NZ)

Canoeing

International canoe racing is practised in kayaks or Canadian canoes over flat water or, for canoe slalom, on wild water. Kayak is the Inuit word for a canoe made of sealskin, originally stretched over a whalebone frame. Kayak canoeists use a paddle with a blade at each end, but Canadian canoes are propelled by a paddle with a single blade, from a half-kneeling position. Races are designated with K for kayak and C for Canadian canoes followed by the number of canoeists, e.g. K1, K2, K4, C1, C2.

The most important pioneer of canoeing as a sport was John MacGregor, who founded the Canoe Club in Surrey, England in 1866. The sport's governing body is the International Canoe Federation, founded in 1924. From then until 1946 its official title was the 'Champst für Kanusport'. European Championships were first held in 1933, with racing at six categories: K1, C1 and C2 over 1000m; K1, and C1 and C2 for folding crafts, over 10,000m. Olympic recognition followed in 1936. Wild water and slalom canoeing were introduced in the 1930s.

Speed races on still water are contested at 500m and 1000m in a straight line and 10,000m on a circuit. Slalom competitions are contested over a rapid river course of maximum extent 600m, through a series of 25 gates with scoring both for time and as penalty points for faults in negotiating the course. Wild water competitions are contested on a course of at least 3km length.

Olympic Games

The sport has been held at each Olympic Games from 1936, with slalom events also in 1972 and 1992. *Winners:*

Canoe racing - Men

K1 500m

1976 Vasile Diba (Rom) 1:46.41
1980 Vladimir Parfenovich (USSR) 1:43.43
1984 Ian Ferguson (NZ) 1:47.84
1988 Zsolt Gyulay (Hun) 1:44.82
1992 Mikko Kolehmainen (Fin) 1:40.34

K1 1000m

1936 Gregor Hradetzky (Aut) 4:22.9
1948 Gert Fredriksson (Swe) 4:33.2
1952 Gert Fredriksson (Swe) 4:07.9
1956 Gert Fredriksson (Swe) 4:12.8
1960 Erik Hansen (Den) 3:53.00
1964 Rolf Peterson (Swe) 3:57.13
1968 Mihály Hesz (Hun) 4:02.63
1972 Aleksandr Shaparenko (USSR) 3:48.06
1976 Rüdiger Helm (GDR) 3:48.20
1980 Rüdiger Helm (GDR) 3:48.77
1984 Alan Thompson (NZ) 3:45.73
1988 Greg Barton (USA) 3:55.27
1992 Clint Robinson (Aus) 3:37.26

K1 10,000m

1936 Ernst Krebs (Ger) 46:01.6
1948 Gert Fredriksson (Swe) 50:47.7
1952 Thorvald Strömberg (Fin) 47:22.8
1956 Gert Fredriksson (Swe) 47:43.4

K1 4 x 500m relay

1960 Germany 7:39.43

K2 500m

1976 Joachim Mattern & Bernd Olbricht (GDR) 1:35.87
1980 Vladimir Parfenovich & Sergey Chukrai (USSR) 1:32.38
1984 Ian Ferguson & Paul McDonald (NZ) 1:34.21
1988 Ian Ferguson & Paul McDonald (NZ) 1:33.98
1992 Kay Bluhm & Torsten Gütsche (Ger) 1:28.27

K2 1000m

1936 Adolf Kainz & Alfons Dorfner (Aut) 4:03.8
1948 Hans Berglund & Lennart Klingström (Swe) 4:07.3

1952 Kurt Wires & Yrjö Hietanen (Fin) 3:51.1
1956 Michel Scheuer & Meinrad Miltenberger (FRG) 3:49.6
1960 Gert Fredriksson & Sven-Olov Sjödelius (Swe) 3:34.7
1964 Sven-Olov Sjödelius & Nils Utterberg (Swe) 3:38.4
1968 Aleksandr Shaparenko & Vladimir Morozov (USSR) 3:37.54
1972 Nikolay Gorbachev & Viktor Kratassyuk (USSR) 3:31.23
1976 Sergey Nagorny & Vladimir Romanovsky (USSR) 3:29.01
1980 Vladimir Parfenovich & Sergey Chukrai (USSR) 3:26.72
1984 Hugh Fisher & Alwyn Morris (Can) 3:24.22
1988 Greg Barton & Norman Bellingham (USA) 3:32.42
1992 Kay Bluhm & Torsten Gütsche (Ger) 3:16.10

K2 10,000m
1936 Paul Weavers & Ludwig Landen (Ger) 41:45.0
1948 Gunnar Åkerlund & Hans Wetterström (Swe) 46:09.4
1952 Kurt Wires & Yrjö Hietanen (Fin) 44:21.3
1956 János Urányi & László Fábián (Hun) 43:37.0

K4 1000m
1964 USSR 3:14.67
1968 Norway 3:14.38
1972 USSR 3:14.02
1976 USSR 3:08.69
1980 GDR 3:13.76
1984 New Zealand 3:02.28
1988 Hungary 3:00.20
1992 Germany 2:54.18

C1 500m
1976 Aleksandr Rogov (USSR) 1:59.23
1980 Sergey Postrekhin (USSR) 1:53.37
1984 Larry Cain (Can) 1:57.01
1988 Olaf Heukrodt (GDR) 1:56.42
1992 Nikolai Boukhalov (Bul) 1:51.15

C1 1000m
1936 Francis Amyot (Can) 5:32.1
1948 Josef Holecek (Cs) 5:42.0
1952 Josef Holecek (Cs) 4:56.3
1956 Leon Rotman (Rom) 5:05.3
1960 János Parti (Hun) 4:33.93
1964 Jürgen Eschert (GDR) 4:35.14
1968 Tibor Tatai (Hun) 4:36.14
1972 Ivan Patzaichin (Rom) 4:08.94
1976 Matija Ljubek (Yug) 4:09.51
1980 Lubomir Lubenov (Bul) 4:12.38
1984 Ulrich Eicke (FRG) 4:06.32
1988 Ivan Klementyev (USSR) 4:12.78
1992 Nikolai Boukhalov (Bul) 4:05.92

C1 10,000m
1948 Frantisek Capek (Cs) 62:05.2
1952 Frank Havens (USA) 57:41.1
1956 Leon Rotman (Rom) 56:41.0

C2 500m
1976 Sergey Petrenko & Aleksandr Vinogradov (USSR) 1:45.81
1980 Laszlo Foltan & Istvan Vaskuti (Hun) 1:43.39
1984 Matija Ljubek & Mirko Nisovic (Yug) 1:43.67
1988 Viktor Reneyskiy & Nikolay Zhuravskiy (USSR) 1:41.77
1992 Aleksandr Masseikov & Dmitriy Dovgalenok (CIS) 1:41.54

C2 1000m
1936 Vladimir Syrovátka & Jan-Felix Brzák (Cs) 4:50.1
1948 Jan-Felix Brzák & Bohumil Kudrna (Cs) 5:07.1
1952 Bent Peder Rasch & Finn Haunstoft (Den) 4:38.3
1956 Alexe Dumitru & Simion Ismailciuc (Rom) 4:47.4
1960 Leonid Geyshtor & Sergey Makarenko (USSR) 4:17.94
1964 Andrey Khimich & Stepan Oschepkov (USSR) 4:04.64
1968 Ivan Patzaichin & Serghei Covaliov (Rom) 4:07.18
1972 Vladas Chessyunas & Yuriy Lobanov (USSR) 3:52.60
1976 Sergey Petrenko & Aleksandr Vinogradov (USSR) 3:52.76
1980 Ivan Patzaichin & Toma Simionov (Rom) 3:47.65
1984 Ivan Patzaichin & Toma Simionov (Rom) 3:40.60
1988 Viktor Reneyskiy & Nikolay Zhuravskiy (USSR) 3:48.36
1992 Ulrich Papke & Ingo Spelly (Ger) 3:37.42

C2 10,000m
1936 Václav Mottl & Zdenek Skrdlant (Cs) 50:33.5
1948 Stephen Lysack & Stephen Macknowski (USA) 55:55.4
1952 Georges Turlier & Jean Laudet (Fra) 54.08.3
1956 Pavel Kharin & Gratsian Botev (USSR) 54:02.4

Folding kayak
K1: 1936 Gregor Hradetzky (Aut) 50:01.2
K2: 1936 Sven Johansson & Eric Bladström (Swe) 45:48.9

K1 Slalom
1972 Siegbert Horn (GDR)
1992 Pierpaolo Ferrazzi (Ita)

C1 Slalom
1972 Reinhard Eiben (GDR)
1992 Lukas Pollert (Cs)

C2 Slalom
1972 Walter Hofmann & Rolf-Dieter Amend (GDR)
1992 Scott Strausbaugh & Joe Jacobi (USA)

Most gold medals: 6 Gert Fredriksson (Swe) 1948-60; 4 Ivan Patzaichin (Rom) 1968-84, Ian Ferguson (NZ) 1984-8.

Most gold medals at one Games: 3 Vladimir Parfenovich (USSR) 1980, Ian Ferguson (NZ) 1984.

Most medals: 8 Gert Fredriksson 6 gold as above, silver K1 10 000m 1952, bronze K1 1000m 1960; 7 Ivan Patzaichin 4 gold as above, 3 silver C2 500m 1980-84, C2 1000m 1972.

Canoe racing winners - Women

K1 500m
1948 Karen Hoff (Den) 2:31.9
1952 Sylvi Saimo (Fin) 2:18.4
1956 Yelisaveta Dementyeva (USSR) 2:18.9
1960 Antonina Seredina (USSR) 2:08.08
1964 Lyudmila Khvedosyuk (USSR) 2:12.87
1968 Lyudmila Pinayeva (USSR) 2:11.09
1972 Yulia Ryabchinskaya (USSR) 2:03.17
1976 Carola Zirzow (GDR) 2:01.05
1980 Birgit Fischer (GDR) 1:57.96
1984 Agneta Andersson (Swe) 1:58.72
1988 Vania Gecheva (Bul) 1:55.19
1992 Birgit Schmidt (Ger) 1:51.60

K2 500m
1960 Maria Zhubina & Antonina Seredina (USSR)
     1:54.76
1964 Anne-Marie Zimmermann & Roswitha Esser
     (FRG) 1:56.95
1968 Anne-Marie Zimmermann & Roswitha Esser
     (FRG) 1:56.44
1972 Lyudmila Pinayeva & Yekaterina Kuryshko
     (USSR) 1:53.50
1976 Nina Gopova & Galina Kreft (USSR) 1:51.15
1980 Carsta Genäuss & Martina Bischof (GDR) 1:43.88
1984 Agneta Andersson & Anna Olsson (Swe) 1:45.25
1988 Birgit Schmidt & Anke Nothnagel (GDR) 1:43.46
1992 Ramona Portwich & Anke Von Seck (Ger) 1:40.29

K4 500m
1984 Romania 1:38.54
1988 GDR 1:40.78
1992 Hungary 1:58.42

K1 Canoe slalom
1972 Angelika Bahmann (GDR)
1992 Elisabeth Micheler (Ger)

Most gold medals
4 Birgit Schmidt (née Fischer) 1980-92
3 Lyudmila Pinayeva (née Khevedosyuk) 1964-8
3 Anke von Seck (née Nothnagel) 1988-92

Most medals
5 Birgit Schmidt, 4 gold as above and silver K1 500m
   1988
4 Lyudmila Pinayeva, 3 gold as above, bronze K2
   500m 1968
4 Vanya Gecheva gold K1 500m 1988, silver K1
   500m 1980 & K2 500m 1988, bronze K4 500m 1988

Canoe Racing World Championships

First held in 1938, then in 1948, 1950, 1954, 1958, 1963, 1966 and annually from 1970 with the exception of Olympic years. Races at 200 metres were introduced in 1994 when the men's 10,000m and women's 5000m events were abandoned. *Recent winners:*

Men

K1 200m
1994 Sergey Kalesnik (Bls) 36.737

K1 500m
1989 Martin Hunter (Aus) 1:41.65

1990 Sergey Kalesnik (SU) 1:43.58
1991 Renn Crichlow (Can) 1:42.14
1993 Mikko Kolehmainen (Fin) 1:41.96
1994 Zsombor Borhi (Hun) 1:42.236

K1 1000m
1989 Zsolt Gyulay (Hun) 3:38.87
1990 Knut Holmann (Nor) 3:33.18
1991 Knut Holmann (Nor) 3:35.19
1993 Knut Holmann (Nor) 3:42.49
1994 Clint Robinson (Aus) 3:38.714

K1 10 000m
1989 Attila Szabó (Hun) 42:48.94
1990 Philippe Boccara (Fra) 42:24.03
1991 Greg Barton (USA) 41:54.73
1993 Thor Nielsen (Den) 42:12.07

K2 200m
1994 Maciej Freimut & Adam Wysocki (Pol) 36.156

K2 500m
1989 Kay Bluhm & Torsten Gütsche (GDR) 1:31.58
1990 Sergey Kalesnik & Anatoliy Tishchenko (SU)
     1:33.82
1991 Juan José Roman & Juan Manuel Sánchez (Spa)
     1:31.70
1993 Kay Bluhm & Torsten Gütsche (Ger) 1:32.77
1994 Kay Bluhm & Torsten Gütsche (Ger) 1:33.108

K2 1000m
1989 Kay Bluhm & Torsten Gütsche (GDR) 3:11.62
1990 Kay Bluhm & Torsten Gütsche (GDR) 3:15.77
1991 Kay Bluhm & Torsten Gütsche (GDR) 3:15.16
1993 Kay Bluhm & Torsten Gütsche (Ger) 3:21.80
1994 K Møllegård Staal & Thor Nielsen (Den) 3:21.268

K2 10000m
1989 Attila Abrahám & Sándor Hódosi (Hun) 39:24.99
1990 Ivan Lawler & Grayson Bourne (UK) 39:48.21
1991 Philippe Boccara & Pascal Boucherit (Fra)
     38:58.69
1993 Zsombor Borhi & Attila Abrahám (Hun) 38:43.34

K4 200m
1994 Russia 32.180

K4 500m
1989 USSR 1:22.50
1990 USSR 1:25.20
1991 Germany 1:23.25
1993 Russia 1:24.80
1994 Russia 1:21.488

K4 1000m
1989 Hungary 2:55.30
1990 Hungary 2:57.89
1991 Hungary 2:58.15
1993 Germany 3:04.80
1994 Russia 7:01.488

K4 10 000m
1989 USSR 35:58.54
1990 USSR 35:21.86
1991 Germany 35:37.98
1993 Germany 35:23.38

C1 200m
1994 Nikolai Boukhalov (Bul) 41.869

C1 500m
1989 Mikhail Slivinsky (USSR) 1:53.17
1990 Mikhail Slivinsky (USSR) 1:55.95
1991 Mikhail Slivinsky (USSR) 1:52.28
1993 Nikolai Boukhalov (Bul) 1:54.02
1994 Nikolai Boukhalov (Bul) 1:55.264

C1 1000m
1989 Ivan Klementyev (USSR) 4:00.04
1990 Ivan Klementyev (USSR) 4:01.06
1991 Ivan Klementyev (USSR) 4:02.61
1993 Ivan Klementyev (Lat) 4:11.20
1994 Ivan Klementyev (Pol) 4:08.144

C1 10 000m
1989 Ivan Klementyev (USSR) 46:49.96
1990 Zsolt Bohács (Hun) 48:48.24
1991 Zsolt Bohács (Hun) 46:57.58
1993 Zsolt Bohács (Hun) 47:11.29

C2 200m
1994 Aleksandr Maseykov & Dmitriy Dovgalenok
(Bls) 39.792

C2 500m
1989 Nikolay Zhuravsky & Viktor Reneysky (USSR)
1:40.90
1990 Nikolay Zhuravsky & Viktor Reneysky (USSR)
1:46.01
1991 Attila Paliza & Attila Szabó (Hun) 1:42.00
1993 György Kolonics & Csaba Horváth (Hun) 1:46.40
1994 Gheorghe Andriev & Grogore Obreja (Rom)
1:47.780

C2 1000m
1989 Christian Fredriksen & Arne Nielsson (Den)
3:37.08
1990 Ulrich Papke & Ingo Spelly (GDR) 3:38.45
1991 Ulrich Papke & Ingo Spelly (Ger) 3:43.42
1993 Christian Fredriksen & Arne Nielsson (Den)
3:49.52
1994 Andreas Dittmer & Gunar Kirchbach (Ger)
3:50.100

C2 10 000m
1989 Christian Fredriksen & Arne Nielsson (Den)
42:42.59
1990 Christian Fredriksen & Arne Nielsson (Den)
43:04.38
1991 István Gyulai & Pap Petervari (Hun) 42:58.20
1993 Christian Fredriksen & Arne Nielsson (Den)
42:18.58

C4 200m
1994 Russia 3:54.12

C4 500m
1989 USSR 1:31.10
1990 USSR 1.37.00
1991 USSR 1:32.42
1993 Hungary 1:33.95
1994 Hungary 1:30.464

C4 1000m
1989 USSR 3:19.94
1990 USSR 3:24.74
1991 USSR 3:19.50
1993 Hungary 3:30.67
1994 Hungary 3:26.708

Women

K1 200m
1994 Rita Kobán (Hun) 42.904

K1 500m
1989 Katrin Borchert (GDR) 1:53.38
1990 Josefa Idem (Ita) 1:57.58
1991 Katrin Borchert (Ger) 1:53.59
1993 Birgit Schmidt (Ger) 1:53.00
1994 Birgit Schmidt (Ger) 1:53.552

K1 5000m
1989 Katrin Borchert (GDR) 22:15.80
1990 Katrin Borchert (GDR) 22:34.17
1991 Jofefa Idem (Ita) 22:30.70
1993 Susanne Gunnarsson (Swe) 22:39.76

K2 200m
1994 Rita Kobán & Eva Laky (Hun) 40.252

K2 500m
1989 Anke Nothnagel & Heike Singer (GDR) 1:43.17
1990 Ramona Portwich & Anke Von Seck (GDR)
1:46.92
1991 Ramona Portwich & Anke Von Seck (Ger) 1:43.21
1993 Anna Olsson & Agneta Andersson (Swe) 1:48.56
1994 Elzbieta Urbanczyk & Barbara Hajcel (Pol)
1:49.684

K2 5000m
1989 Monike Bünke & Ramona Portwich (GDR)
20:27.05
1990 Ramona Portwich & Anke Von Seck (GDR)
20:46.63
1991 Ramona Portwich & Anke Von Seck (Ger)
20:43.92
1993 Ramona Portwich & Anett Schuck (Ger) 21:33.51

K4 200m
1994 Hungary 37.120

K4 500m
1989 GDR 1:32.90
1990 GDR 1:35.58
1991 Germany 1:36.58
1993 Germany 1:37.99
1994 Germany 1:35.588

Most wins at World Championships and Olympic Games
Men
13 Gert Fredriksson (Swe) K1 500m 1948, 1954; K1
1000m 1948, 1950, 1952, 1954, 1956; K1 10 000m
1948, 1956; K1 4x500m relay 1948, 1950, 1954; K2
1000m 1960
13 Rüdiger Helm (GDR) K1 1000m 1976, 1978-83; K2
500m 1978; K4 500m 1983; K4 10,000m 1978-81
13 Ivan Patzaichin (Rom) C1 1000m 1972-3, 1977; C1

10,000m 1978; C2 500m 1979; C2 1000m 1968, 1970, 1972, 1980-1, 1983-4; C2 10 000m 1982

12 Vladimir Parfenovich (USSR) K1 500m 1979-83; K2 500m 1979-82; K2 1000m 1980-2

11 Yuriy Lobanov (USSR) C2 500m 1974-5, C2 1000m 1972, 1974, 1977, 1979; C2 10,000m 1973-5, 1977, 1979

Women

24 Birgit Schmidt (née Fischer) (GDR) K1 500m 1980-3, 1985, 1987, 1992-4; K2 500m 1981-3, 1985, 1987-8; K4 500m 1979, 1981-3, 1985, 1987-8, 1993-4

Most wins at one individual event

Men

7 Tamas Wichmann (Hun) C1 10,000m 1970-1, 1974, 1977, 1979, 1981-2

6 Rüdiger Helm (GDR) K1 1000m 1976, 1978-83

5 Vladimir Parfenovich (USSR) K1 500m 1979-83

Women

9 Birgit Fischer (GDR) K1 500m as above

5 Lyudmila Pinayeva (USSR) K1 500m 1964, 1966, 1968, 1970-1

Canoe Slalom World Championships

Held biennially since 1949.

Men *Most individual wins:*

5 Jon Lugbill (USA) C1 1979, 1981, 1983, 1987, 1989 (also 7 at C1 team 1979-91)

5 Richard Fox (UK) K1 1981, 1983, 1985, 1989, 1993 (also 5 at K1 team 1981-7, 1993)

3 Manfred Schubert (GDR) C1 1957, 1961, 1963 (also C1 team 1963, C2 team 1959)

Other winners from 1989:

K1: 1991 Shaun Pearce (UK)

C1: 1991 & 1993 Martin Lang (Ger)

C2: 1989 Frank Hemmer & Thomas Loose (FRG)

1991 Franck Adisson & Wilfried Forgues (Fra)

1993 Miroslav Simek & Jirí Rohan (Cze)

Team: C1 - 1989 & 1991 USA, 1993 Slovenia

C2 - 1989 & 1991 France, 1993 Czech Republic

K1 - 1989 Yugoslavia, 1991 France, 1993 UK

Women recent K1 winners:

1985 Margit Messelhäuser (FRG)

1987 Elisabeth Sharman (UK)

1989 Myriam Jérusalmi (Fra)

1991 Elisabeth Micheler (Ger)

1993 Myriam Jérusalmi (Fra)

Women's K1 team - 1989, 1991, 1993 France

Wild Water World Championships

Held biennially since 1959. *Most individual wins:*

Men

4 Jean-Pierre Burny (Bel) K1 1969, 1973, 1975, 1979

4 Gilles Zok (Fra) C1 1981, 1983, 1985, 1987 (also 5 at C1 team 1977-85)

Women

3 Gisela Grothaus (FRG) K1 1973, 1975, 1977 (also 4 K1 team 1973-83)

Shaun Pearce – K1 slalom champion of 1991

Individual winners from 1989

Men K1

1989 Marco Previde-Massara (Ita)

1991 Markus Gickler (Ger)

1993 Markus Gickler (Ger)

Men C1

1989 Andrej Jelenc (Yug)

1991 Tomislav Crnkovic (Yug)

1993 Vladi Panato (Ita)

Men C2

1989 Andrej Grobisa & Srecko Maslé (Yug)

1991 Eric Archambaut & Thierry Carlin (Fra)

1993 Damien Faysse & Pierre Roos (Fra)

Team K1: 1989 France, 1991 Italy, 1993 France

Team C1: 1989 France, 1991 Yugoslavia, 1993 France

Team C2: 1989 FRG, 1991 Germany, 1993 Germany

Women K1

1989 Sabine Kleinhentz (Fra)

1991 Karin Wahl (Ger)

1993 Uschi Profanter (Aut)

Team K1: 1989, 1991, 1993 France

Team C1: 1989 France

Canoe Marathon World Championships

First held at Holme Pierrepont, Nottingham, England in 1988.

Men K1

1988 John Jacoby (Aus)

1990 Kalman Petrovics (Hun)

1992 Ivan Lawler (UK)

1994 Lars Koch (Den)

Men K2

1988 Thor Nielsen & Lars Koch (Den)

1990 Thor Nielsen & Lars Koch (Den)

1992 Ramon Andersson & Steve Wood (Aus)

1994 Ivan Lawler & Steve Harris (UK)

Men C1

1988 Pál Pétervári (Hun)

1990 Stig Jepsen (Den)

1992 Gábor Kolozsvári (Hun)

1994 Arne Nielsson (Den)

Men C2
1988 Steve Train & Andrew Train (UK)
1990 Arne Nielsen & Christian Frederiksen (Den)
1992 Arne Nielsen & Christian Frederiksen (Den)
1994 Zsolt Bohacs & István Gyulai (Hun)

Women K1
1988 Jane Hall (Aus)
1990 Ingeborg Rasmussen (Nor)
1992 Susanne Gunnarsson (Swe)
1994 Susanne Gunnarsson (Swe)

Women K2
1988 Gayle Mayes & Denise Cooper (Aus)
1990 Agnes Erdody & Andrea Baranyai (Hun)
1992 Anett Schuck & Antje Manfroni (Ger)
1994 Denise Cooper & Shelly Jesney (Aus)

Canoe Sailing World Championships
First held in 1938, and then every 3/4 years from 1961. *Recent winners:*
1984 Steve Clark (USA)
1987 Robin Wood (UK)
1990 Lars Guck (USA)
1993 Robin Wood (UK)
Most wins: 3 Alain Emus (UK) 1961, 1965, 1969

Canoe Polo World Championships
First held in 1994, when Australia won both men's and women's events.

Chess

A board game played by two players, each with 16 pieces on a 64-square board. Its origins are uncertain, but it is thought to have originated in the Punjab, India. The earliest definite references are to Chaturanga, the Indian war game imported into Persia. This game evolved into Shatranj, and thence to the modern game of chess. The current pieces have been standard for the past 500 years.

The world governing body is the Fédération Internationale des Échecs (FIDE), formed in 1924. By 1994 it had 150 member nations.

World Champions

The first officially accepted match for the world championship was in 1886 when Wilhelm Steinitz beat Johannes Zukertort. However, champions had been generally accepted since Adolf Anderssen won the world's first international tournament, held in London in 1851. The FIDE took control of the championship in 1948, and there is now a triennial cycle of eliminating contests culminating in a contender to challenge the current champion.

Early champions
1851-8   Adolf Anderssen (Ger)
1858-62   Paul Morphy (USA)
1862-6   Adolf Anderssen (Ger)
1866-94   Wilhelm Steinitz (Aut)

Results of World Championship matches from 1886

Year	Winner	Beat	Score
1886	Wilhelm Steinitz (Aut)	Johannes Zukertort (Prussia)	12.5- 7.5
1889	Wilhelm Steinitz (Aut)	Mikhail Chigorin (Rus)	10.5- 6.5
1890-1	Wilhelm Steinitz (Aut)	Isidor Gunsberg (Hun/UK)	10.5- 8.5
1892	Wilhelm Steinitz (Aut)	Mikhail Chigorin (Rus)	12- 10.5
1894	Emanuel Lasker (Ger)	Wilhelm Steinitz (Aut)	12- 7
1896-7	Emanuel Lasker (Ger)	Wilhelm Steinitz (Aut)	12.5- 4.5
1907	Emanuel Lasker (Ger)	Frank Marshall (USA)	11.5- 3.5
1908	Emanuel Lasker (Ger)	Siegbert Tarrasch (Ger)	10.5- 5.5
1910	Emanuel Lasker (Ger)	Carl Schlechter (Aut)	5- 5
1910	Emanuel Lasker (Ger)	Dawid Janowski (Pol)	9.5-1.5
1921	José Capablanca (Cub)	Emanuel Lasker (Ger)	9- 5
1927	Alexandre Alekhine (Fra)	José Capablanca (Cub)	18.5- 15.5
1929	Alexandre Alekhine (Fra)	Efim Bogolyubov (USSR)	15.5- 9.5
1934	Alexandre Alekhine (Fra)	Efim Bogolyubov (USSR)	15.5- 10.5
1935	Max Euwe (Hol)	Alexandre Alekhine (Fra)	15.5- 14.5
1937	Alexandre Alekhine (Fra)	Max Euwe (Hol)	15.5- 9.5
1948	Mikhail Botvinnik (USSR) won a 5-man tournament to determine successor to Alekhine who died in 1946.		
1951	Mikhail Botvinnik (USSR)	David Bronstein (USSR)	12- 12
1954	Mikhail Botvinnik (USSR)	Vasiliy Smyslov (USSR)	12- 12
1957	Vasiliy Smyslov (USSR)	Mikhail Botvinnik (USSR)	12.5-9.5
1958	Mikhail Botvinnik (USSR)	Vasiliy Smyslov (USSR)	12.5-10.5
1960	Mikhail Tal (USSR)	Mikhail Botvinnik (USSR)	12.5- 8.5
1961	Mikhail Botvinnik (USSR)	Mikhail Tal (USSR)	13- 8
1963	Tigran Petrosyan (USSR)	Mikhail Botvinnik (USSR)	12.5-9.5
1966	Tigran Petrosyan (USSR)	Boris Spassky (USSR)	12.5-11.5
1969	Boris Spassky (USSR)	Tigran Petrosyan (USSR)	12.5-10.5
1972	Robert Fischer (USSR)	Boris Spassky (USSR)	12.5-8.5
1978	Anatoliy Karpov (USSR)	Viktor Korchnoi (USSR)	16.5-15.5
1981	Anatoliy Karpov (USSR)	Viktor Korchnoi (USSR)	11- 7
1984-5	Anatoliy Karpov (USSR)	Gary Kasparov (USSR)	25 - 23*
1985	Gary Kasparov (USSR)	Anatoliy Karpov (USSR)	13-11
1986	Gary Kasparov (USSR)	Anatoliy Karpov (USSR)	12.5-11.5
1987	Gary Kasparov (USSR)	Anatoliy Karpov (USSR)	12-12
1990	Gary Kasparov (USSR)	Anatoliy Karpov (USSR)	12.2-11.5
1993	Gary Kasparov (Aze)	Nigel Short (UK)	12.5- 7.5

* match abandoned

Note that after disputes Kasparov and Short decided to form the Professional Chess Association in 1993 and to play their championship matches outside the auspices of FIDE, who declared that a contest between Anatoliy Karpov and Jan Timman (HOL), who were beaten by Short in the Challengers' Tournament, was to be for the world title. Karpov won 12.5 to 8.5.

Youngest champion: Gary Kasparov at 22 years 210 days in 1985.

Oldest champion: Wilhelm Steinitz was 58 years 10 days when he lost to Lasker in 1894.

Women's World Champions

1927-44	Vera Menchik (UK)
1950-3	Lyudmila Rudenko (USSR)
1953-6	Yelizaveta Bykova (USSR)
1956-8	Olga Rubtsova (USSR)
1958-62	Yelizaveta Bykova (USSR)
1962-78	Nona Gaprindashvili (USSR)
1978-91	Maya Chiburdanidze (USSR)
1991-	Xie Jun (Chn)

Youngest champion: Maya Chiburdanidze was aged 17 when she won the title in 1978.

Chess Olympiads

These world team events, which were first held in 1927, are now held biennially. *Wins:*

18	USSR	1952, 1954, 1956, 1958, 1960, 1962, 1964, 1966, 1968, 1970, 1972, 1974, 1980, 1982, 1984, 1986, 1988, 1990
5	USA	1931, 1933, 1935, 1937, 1976
3	Hungary	1927, 1928, 1978
2	Russia	1992, 1994
1	Poland 1930, Germany 1939, Yugoslavia 1950	

Women

Although women may play in the Olympiads, a separate competition for women only was introduced in 1957, and this event has been held concurrently with the men's from 1972. *Wins:*

11	USSR	1957, 1963, 1966, 1969, 1972, 1974, 1978, 1980, 1982, 1984, 1986
2	Hungary	1988, 1990
2	Georgia	1992, 1994
1	Israel	1976

Teams from the former Soviet Union have dominated the tournaments since they first competed in 1952. The only time that a USSR team placed other than first were second places in 1978 and the women's losses in 1988 and in 1990, on each occasion to Hungary. The USSR did not contest in 1976, when the Olympiad was held in Haifa, Israel. In 1992 the first three places in the men's event were taken by ex-Soviet republics and Georgia won the women's title.

An élite event for Continental champions and other top teams was held in 1985 and 1989; the USSR won on both occasions. World Team 1993 USA

World Cup

The first World Cup was staged over a series of six tournaments between April 1988 and September 1989 and contested by the top 25 grandmasters. The inaugural winner was Gary Kasparov (USSR) with Anatoliy Karpov (USSR) second.

A World Cup tournament was contested by 16 players in Reykjavik, Iceland in Sept-Oct 1991. Vasiliy Ivanchuk (USSR) and Anatoliy Karpov (USSR) were the joint winners.

ELO Ratings

FIDE issues a list of Elo ratings for the world's leading players twice yearly. The system is named after Professor Elo. Grandmaster level is 2500, a rating currently attained by over 100 players. The highest rating ever achieved is 2805 by the world champion Gary Kasparov, reached in December 1992, having in January 1991 surpassed the previous best, 2785 of Robert Fischer. The highest rated woman player is Judit Polgar (Hungary), who reached 2630 at the end of 1993

Polgar had become the youngest ever Grandmaster at 15 years 150 days on 20 December 1991. That record was taken by Peter Leko (Hun) at 14 years 145 days in January 1994.

Cricket

Cricket originated in England in the Middle Ages. Its exact origins are obscure, but bat and ball games were played from the 13th century and games similar to the modern one from around 1550. The earliest major match for which the full score survives was that when England played Kent in London in 1744. In that year the first known Laws of the game were issued. The Marylebone Cricket Club (MCC) was founded in 1787, and until the formation of the Cricket Council in 1968 was accepted as the ruling body of the game from its headquarters at Lord's Cricket Ground, London. The MCC remains responsible for the Laws of Cricket.

The Imperial (International from 1965) Cricket Conference was formed by representatives of England, Australia and South Africa in 1909. India, New Zealand and West Indies were elected members in 1926, Pakistan in 1953 and Sri Lanka in 1981. South Africa ceased to be a member in 1961, but was readmitted to Test cricket in 1992, and later that year Zimbabwe became the ninth Test cricketing nation. The ICC was renamed the International Cricket Council in 1989, and in addition to the nine full members there are 21 associate members and 11 affiliate members.

Test Cricket

The first Test match was played at Melbourne on 15-19 March 1877 between Australia and England, represented by James Lillywhite's touring side. Neither side was truly representative of their countries and indeed such was the case for many matches, now accepted as Test matches, played over the next fifty years or so. The first match in England was against Australia at the Oval on 6-8 September 1880. First Tests by other nations were as follows: South Africa 1889, West Indies 1928, New Zealand 1930, India 1932, Pakistan 1952, Sri Lanka 1982, Zimbabwe 1992.

Summary of Test match results to 1 June 1995

The first figure is number of wins by the team on the left over the team in that column, the second figure is number of draws, Thus in England v Australia Tests, England have won 90, Australia 111, with 84 Tests left drawn.

	A	E	I	NZ	P	SA	SL	WI	Z	Wins	Tests
Australia	-	111/84	24/17*	13/12	12/17	31/15	4/3	32/21*		227	551
England	90/84	-	31/36	34/37	14/31	47/39	3/1	25/38		244	712
India	8/17*	14/36		12/14	4/33	0/3	7/4	7/31	1/1	53	292
New Zealand	7/12	4/37	6/14	-	4/16	3/6	4/7	4/13	1/1	33	236
Pakistan	10/15	7/31	7/33	16/16	-	0/0	10/5	7/11	4/1	61	223
South Africa	13/15	19/39	1/3	11/6	1/0	-	1/2	0/0		46	193
Sri Lanka	0/3	1/1	1/6	2/7	1/5	0/2	-	0/0	0/3	5	62
West Indies	27/21*	46/38	27/31	9/13	12/11	1/0	1/0	-		123	314
Zimbabwe			0/1	0/1	1/1		0/3			1	13

* *plus one tie.* There have been two tied Tests:
9-14 Dec 1960 at Brisbane, Australia v West Indies, 18-22 Sep 1986 at Madras, Australia v India

Team Records

Highest innings totals

903-7 dec	England v A	The Oval	20-23 Aug 1938
849	England v WI	Kingston	3-5 Apr 1930
790-3 dec	West Indies v P	Kingston	27 Feb - 1 Mar 1958
758-8 dec	Australia v WI	Kingston	13-15 Jun 1955
729-6 dec	Australia v E	Lord's	28-30 Jun 1930
708	Pakistan v E	The Oval	6-8 Aug 1987
701	Australia v E	The Oval	18-20 Aug 1934

Highest match aggregates

1981 runs South Africa (530 & 481) v England (316 & 654-5) at Durban 3-14 Mar 1939. This was the 'Timeless Test'. The total playing time was 43 hours 16 minutes, over 10 days, and was left drawn because England had to catch the boat home at the end of their tour.

1815 runs West Indies (286 & 408-5) v England (849 & 272-9 dec) at Kingston 3-12 Apr 1930.

1764 runs Australia (533 & 339-9) v West Indies (276 & 616) at Adelaide 24-29 Jan 1969. This is the record for a five day Test.

All the above three Tests were left drawn.

Highest winning margin

Innings and 579 runs England (903-7 dec) beat Australia (201 & 123) at the Oval 20-24 Aug 1938.

Lowest completed innings totals

26	New Zealand v E	Auckland	28 Mar 1955
30	South Africa v E	Port Elizabeth	14 Feb 1896
30	South Africa v E	Birmingham	16 Jun 1924

Lowest match aggregate

234 runs Australia (153) beat South Africa (36 & 45) 12-15 Feb 1932

Individual Test records

- To 1 Jun 1995

Most Tests

156 Allan Border (Aus) 1978-94
131 Kapil Dev (Ind) 1978-94
125 Sunil Gavaskar (Ind) 1971-87
124 Javed Miandad (Pak) 1976-94
121 Vivian Richards (WI) 1974-91
118 Graham Gooch (Eng) 1975-95
117 David Gower (Eng) 1978-92
116 Desmond Haynes (WI) 1978-94
116 Dilip Vengsarkar (Ind) 1976-92
114 Colin Cowdrey (Eng) 1954-75
110 Clive Lloyd (WI) 1966-85
108 Geoffrey Boycott (Eng) 1964-82
108 Gordon Greenidge (WI) 1974-91
102 Ian Botham (Eng) 1977-92
101 David Boon (Aus) 1984-95
96 Rodney Marsh (Aus) 1970-84
95 Alan Knott (Eng) 1967-81
93 Garfield Sobers (WI) 1954-74
91 Godfrey Evans (Eng) 1946-59
91 Gundappa Viswanath (Ind) 1969-83
90 Bob Willis (Eng) 1971-84
88 Syed Kirmani (Ind) 1976-86
88 Imran Khan (Pak) 1971-92
87 Greg Chappell (Aus) 1970-84
86 Derek Underwood (Eng) 1977-82
86 Richard Hadlee (NZ) 1973-90
85 Walter Hammond (Eng) 1927-47

* *including a record 138 consecutive Tests*

Youngest player: 15 yr 124 days Mushtaq Mohammed (Pak) v WI Lahore 26 Mar 1959.

Oldest player: 52 yr 165 days Wilfred Rhodes (Eng) v WI Kingston 12 Apr 1930.

Longest Test career: 30 yr 314 days Wilfred Rhodes (Eng) 1 Jun 1899 to 12 Apr 1930.

Most Test appearances as captain
(no. matches won in brackets)

93	(32)	Allan Border (Aus)	1984-94
74	(36)	Clive Lloyd (WI)	1974-85
50	(27)	Vivian Richards (WI)	1980-91
48	(21)	Greg Chappell (Aus)	1975-83
48	(14)	Imran Khan (Pak)	1982-92
47	(9)	Sunil Gavaskar (Ind)	1976-85
41	(20)	Peter May (Eng)	1955-61
40	(9)	Nawab of Pataudi Jnr (Ind)	1962-75

39	(12)	Bobby Simpson (Aus)	1963-78
39	(9)	Garfield Sobers (WI)	1965-72

Other captains to have won 15 or more Tests:

31	(18)	Mike Brearley (Eng)	1977-81
30	(15)	Ian Chappell (Aus)	1971-5
24	(15)	Don Bradman (Aus)	1936-48

Test Match Batting

Highest individual innings scores (over 300)

375	Brian Lara v E (WI)	St John's, Antigua	16-18 Apr 1994
365*	Garfield Sobers v P WI	Kingston	27 Feb-1 Mar 1958
364	Leonard Hutton v A (Eng)	The Oval	20-23 Aug 1938
337	Hanif Mohammad v WI (Pak)	Bridgetown	20-23 Jan 1958
336*	Walter Hammond v NZ (Eng)	Auckland	31 Mar-1 Apr 1933
334	Don Bradman (Aus) v E	Leeds	11-12 Jul 1930
333	Graham Gooch (Eng) v I	Lord's	26-27 Jul 1990
325	Andrew Sandham v WI (Eng)	Kingston	3-4 Apr 1930
311	Bobby Simpson v E (Aus)	Manchester	23-25 Jul 1964
310*	John Edrich (Eng) v NZ	Leeds	8-9 Jul 1965
307	Bob Cowper (Aus) v E	Melbourne	12-16 Feb 1966
304	Don Bradman v E (Aus)	Leeds	21-23 Jul 1934
302	Lawrence Rowe (WI) v E	Bridgetown	7-10 Mar 1974

The highest match aggregate in a Test is 456 by Graham Gooch, with 333 and 123 for England v India at Lord's on 26-31 Jul 1990.

Fastest Scoring

100	70 minutes (67 balls) Jack Gregory, Aus v SA, Johannesburg, 12 Nov 1921
	56 balls (81 minutes) Vivian Richards, WI v E, St John's, 15 Apr 1986
200	214 minutes (259 balls) Don Bradman, Aus v E, Leeds, 11 Jul 1930
	220 balls (268 minutes) Ian Botham, Eng v I, The Oval, 8-9 Jul 1982
300	288 minutes Walter Hammond, Eng v NZ, Auckland, 31 Mar - 1 Apr 1933

During his innings of 336 not out in 318 minutes Hammond hit ten sixes, a record for a Test innings. His third hundred took just 47 minutes, the fastest in Test cricket.

Most Test hundreds (double hundreds in brackets)

34 (4)	Sunil Gavaskar (Ind)
29 (12)	Don Bradman (Aus)
27 (2)	Allan Border (Aus)
26 (2)	Garfield Sobers (WI)
24 (4)	Greg Chappell (Aus)
24 (3)	Vivian Richards (WI)
23 (6)	Javed Miandad (Pak)
22 (7)	Walter Hammond (Eng)

Graham Gooch on his way to 210 v NZ 1994

22 (1)	Geoffrey Boycott (Eng)
22 (-)	Colin Cowdrey (Eng)
21 (2)	Neil Harvey (Aus)
20 (2)	Graham Gooch (Eng)
20 (1)	Ken Barrington (Eng)
20 (1)	David Boon (Aus)
19 (4)	Leonard Hutton (Eng)
19 (4)	Gordon Greenidge (WI)
19 (1)	Clive Lloyd (WI)

also scoring 4 double hundreds:

12 (4)	Zaheer Abbas (Pak)

Most runs in a Test career

Runs	Name	Ave.	Tests	Years
11174	Allan Border (Aus)	50.56	156	1978-94
10122	Sunil Gavaskar (Ind)	51.12	125	1971-87
8900	Graham Gooch (Eng)	42.58	118	1975-95
8832	Javed Miandad (Pak)	52.57	124	1976-94
8540	Vivian Richards (WI)	50.23	121	1974-91
8231	David Gower (Eng)	44.25	117	1978-92
8114	Geoffrey Boycott (Eng)	47.72	108	1964-82
8032	Garfield Sobers (WI)	57.78	93	1954-74
7624	Colin Cowdrey (Eng)	44.06	114	1954-75
7558	Gordon Greenidge (WI)	44.72	108	1974-91
7515	Clive Lloyd (WI)	46.67	110	1966-85
7487	Desmond Haynes (WI)	42.29	116	1978-94
7249	Walter Hammond (Eng)	58.45	85	1927-47
7111	David Boon (Aus)	44.16	101	1984-95

7110	Greg Chappell (Aus)	53.86	87	1970-84
6996	Don Bradman (Aus)	99.94	52	1928-48
6971	Leonard Hutton (Eng)	56.67	79	1937-55
6868	Dilip Vengsarkar (Ind)	42.13	116	1976-92
6806	Ken Barrington (Eng)	58.67	82	1955-68
6227	Rohan Kanhai (WI)	47.53	79	1957-74
6149	Neil Harvey (Aus)	48.41	79	1948-63
6080	Gundappa Viswanath (Ind)	41.93	91	1969-83
5807	Denis Compton (Eng)	50.06	78	1937-57
5674	Richie Richardson (WI)	45.03	80	1983-95
5410	Jack Hobbs (Eng)	56.94	61	1908-30
5394	Martin Crowe (NZ)	46.10	74	1982-95
5357	Doug Walters (Aus)	48.26	74	1965-81
5345	Ian Chappell (Aus)	42.42	75	1964-80
5334	John Wright (NZ)	37.83	82	1978-93
5248	Kapil Dev (Ind)	31.05	127	1978-94
5234	Bill Lawry (Aus)	47.15	67	1961-71
5200	Ian Botham (Eng)	33.54	102	1977-92
5138	John Edrich (Eng)	43.54	77	1963-76
5062	Zaheer Abbas (Pak)	44.79	78	1969-85
5005	Mark Taylor (Aus)	45.09	66	1989-95
4882	Tom Graveney (Eng)	44.38	79	1951-69
4869	Bobby Simpson (Aus)	46.81	62	1957-78
4804	Salim Malik (Pak)	45,75	84	1982-95
4737	Ian Redpath (Aus)	43.45	66	1964-76
4656	Allan Lamb (Eng)	36.09	79	1982-92
4555	Herbert Sutcliffe (Eng)	60.73	54	1924-35
4537	Peter May (Eng)	46.77	66	1951-61
4502	Ted Dexter (Eng)	47.89	62	1958-68

Don Bradman at 99.94 has the highest average in Test cricket. In addition to those in the table above, the following have averages of over 55 for more than 10 Tests:

Runs	Name	Ave.	Tests	Years
4455	Everton Weekes (WI)	58.61	48	1948-58
3798	Clyde Walcott (WI)	56.68	44	1948-60
2284	Brian Lara (WI)	55.71	25	1990-5
2256	Graeme Pollock (SAf)	60.97	23	1963-70
2190	George Headley (WI)	60.83	22	1930-54
1540	Edward Paynter (Eng)	59.23	20	1931-39
1072	Sidney Barnes (Aus)	63.05	13	1938-48
995	K S Duleepsinhji (Eng)	58.52	12	1929-31
990	Ernest Tyldesley (Eng)	55.00	14	1921-29
910	Charles Russell (Eng)	56.87	10	1920-23
723	Stewart Dempster (NZ)	65.72	10	1930-33

Fewest innings to reach:
1000 runs: 12 Herbert Sutcliffe, Everton Weekes
2000/3000/4000/5000/6000 runs: 22/33/48/56/68 Don Bradman
7000 runs: 131 Walter Hammond
8000 runs: 157 Garfield Sobers
9000 runs: 192 Sunil Gavaskar
10 000 runs: 212 Sunil Gavaskar

Most runs in a Test series

Runs	average		Tests	Season
974	139.14	Don Bradman (Aus)	5 v E	1930
905	113.12	Walter Hammond (Eng)	5 v A	1928/9
839	83.90	Mark Taylor (Aus)	6 v E	1989

Brian Lara – highest first-class and Test scores

834	92.66	Neil Harvey (Aus)	5 v SA	1952/3
829	118.42	Vivian Richards (WI)	4 v E	1976
827	82.70	Clyde Walcott (WI)	5 v A	1955
824	137.33	Garfield Sobers (WI)	5 v P	1958
810	90.00	Don Bradman (Aus)	5 v E	1936/7
806	201.50	Don Bradman (Aus)	5 v SA	1931/2

The most runs in a series of three Tests or less:

752	125.33	Graham Gooch (Eng)	3 v I	1990*
583	194.33	Zaheer Abbas (Pak)	3 v I	1978
563	563.00	Walter Hammond (Eng)	2 v NZ	1933
558	111.60	Seymour Nurse (WI)	3 v NZ	1969

* Gooch also scored 306 in 3 Tests v NZ in 1990 for a record English summer Test aggregate of 1058 runs av. 96.18.

Most series scoring 500 runs
7 Don Bradman; 6 Sunil Gavaskar, Garfield Sobers

Most centuries in a Test series
5 Clyde Walcott (WI) v A 1955

Test Match Bowling

Nine wickets in an innings

10-53	Jim Laker (Eng)	v A	Manchester	30-31 Jul 1956
9-28	George Lohmann	v SA	Johannesburg	3 Mar 1896
9-37	Jim Laker (Eng)	v A	Manchester	27-30 Jul 1956
9-52	Richard Hadlee (NZ)	v A	Brisbane	8-9 Nov 1985
9-56	Abdul Qadir (Pak)	v E	Lahore	25 Nov 1987
9-57	Devon Malcolm (Eng)	v SA	The Oval	20 Aug 1994
9-69	Jasubhai Patel (Ind)	v A	Kanpur	20 Dec 1959
9-83	Kapil Dev (Ind)	v WI	Ahmedabad	14-16 Nov 1983
9-86	Sarfraz Nawaz (Pak)	v A	Melbourne	14-15 Mar 1979
9-95	John Noreiga (WI)	v I	Port-of-Spain	7-9 Mar 1971
9-102	Subhash Gupte (Ind)	v WI	Kanpur	12 Dec 1958
9-103	Sydney Barnes (Eng)	v SA	Johannesburg	29-30 Dec 1913
9-113	Hugh Tayfield (SAf)	v E	Johannesburg	19-20 Feb 1957
9-121	Arthur Mailey (Aus)	v E	Melbourne	14-16 Feb 1921

Most wickets in a match

19-90	Jim Laker (Eng)	v A	Manchester	26-31 Jul 1956
17-159	Sydney Barnes (Eng)	v SA	Johannesburg	26-30 Dec 1913
16-136	Narendra Hirwani (Ind)	v WI	Madras	11-15 Jan 1988
16-137	Bob Massie (Aus)	v E	Lord's	22-26 Jun 1972

Both Hirwani (8-81 & 8-75) and Massie (8-84 and 8-53) achieved their feats on their Test début.

Devon Malcolm

Five wickets in an innings most times in Tests

(No. of times ten wickets in match shown in brackets)

36 (9)	Richard Hadlee (NZ)
27 (4)	Ian Botham (Eng)
24 (7)	Sydney Barnes (Eng)
23 (7)	Dennis Lillee (Aus)
23 (6)	Imran Khan (Pak)
23 (2)	Kapil Dev (Ind)
22 (4)	Malcolm Marshall (WI)
21 (7)	Clarence Grimmett (Aus)
19 (4)	Waqar Younis (Pak)
18 (3)	Wasim Akram (Pak)
18 (2)	Lance Gibbs (WI)
17 (6)	Derek Underwood (Eng)
17 (3)	Fred Trueman (Eng)
16 (3)	Graham McKenzie (Aus)
16 (2)	Bhagwant Chandrasekhar (I)
16 (1)	Richie Benaud (Aus)
16 (-)	Bob Willis (Eng)

Most wickets in a Test career

Wkts	Name	Ave.	Tests	Years
434	Kapil Dev (Ind)	29.64	131	1978-94
431	Richard Hadlee (NZ)	22.29	86	1973-90
383	Ian Botham (Eng)	28.40	102	1977-92
376	Malcolm Marshall (WI)	20.94	81	1978-91
362	Imran Khan (Pak)	22.81	88	1971-92
355	Dennis Lillee (Aus)	23.92	70	1971-84
325	Bob Willis (Eng)	25.20	90	1971-84
309	Lance Gibbs (WI)	29.09	79	1958-76
307	Fred Trueman (Eng)	21.57	67	1952-65
297	Derek Underwood (Eng)	25.83	86	1966-82
275	Courtney Walsh (WI)	24.54	74	1984-95
270	Craig McDermott (Aus)	28.50	65	1985-95
266	Bishen Bedi (Ind)	28.71	67	1966-79
261	Wasim Akram (Pak)	23.20	61	1985-95
259	Joel Garner (WI)	20.97	58	1977-87
252	Brian Statham (Eng)	24.84	70	1951-65
249	Michael Holding (WI)	23.68	60	1975-87
248	Richie Benaud (Aus)	27.03	63	1952-64
246	Graham McKenzie (Aus)	29.78	60	1961-71
242	Bhagwant Chandrasekhar (Ind)	29.74	58	1964-79
237	Curtley Ambrose (WI)	21.05	54	1988-95
236	Alec Bedser (Eng)	24.89	51	1946-55
236	Abdul Qadir (Pak)	32.80	67	1977-90
235	Garfield Sobers (WI)	34.03	93	1954-74
228	Ray Lindwall (Aus)	23.03	61	1946-60
216	Clarrie Grimmett (Aus)	24.21	37	1925-36
212	Merv Hughes (Aus)	28.38	53	1985-93
202	John Snow (Eng)	26.66	49	1965-76
202	Andy Roberts (WI)	25.61	47	1974-83
200	Jeff Thomson (Aus)	28.00	51	1972-85
193	Jim Laker (Eng)	21.24	46	1948-59
192	Wes Hall (WI)	26.38	48	1958-69
190	Waqar Younis (Pak)	19.15	33	1989-94
189	Sydney Barnes (Eng)	16.43	27	1901-14
189	Erapalli Prasanna (Ind)	30.38	49	1962-78
186	Alan Davidson (Aus)	20.53	44	1953-63
180	Geoff Lawson (Aus)	30.56	46	1980-89
177	Sarfraz Nawaz (Pak)	32.75	55	1969-84
176	Shane Warne (Aus)	24.08	38	1992-5
174	Tony Lock (Eng)	25.58	49	1952-68
171	Iqbal Qasim (Pak)	28.11	50	1976-89
170	Keith Miller (Aus)	22.97	55	1946-56
170	Hugh Tayfield (SAf)	25.91	37	1949-60

Fewest Tests to reach:
100 wickets: 16 George Lohmann (Eng)
200 wickets: 35 Clarrie Grimmett (Aus)
300 wickets: 56 Dennis Lillee (Aus)
In his Test career Lohmann took 112 wickets 1886-96 at 10.75, the lowest average for any bowler taking 25 or more wickets in a Test career. At 34.11 balls per wicket he also has the best striking rate. The next best for both these categories:
John Ferris (Eng/Aus) 61 wickets av.12.70, 36.9 balls/wkt
Michael Proctor (SAf) 41 wickets av.15.02, 37.7 balls/wkt.

Most wickets in a Test series

Wkts		Tests		Season
49	10.93	Sydney Barnes (Eng)	4 v SA	1913/4
46	9.60	Jim Laker (Eng)	5 v A	1956
44	14.59	Clarrie Grimmett (Aus)	5 v SA	1935/6
42	21.26	Terry Alderman (Aus)	6 v E	1981
41	12.85	Rodney Hogg (Aus)	6 v E	1978/9
41	17.36	Terry Alderman (Aus)	6 v E	1989
40	13.95	Imran Khan (Pak)	6 v I	1982/3

The most in a three Test series

35	5.80	George Lohmann (Eng)	3 v SA	1896
34	8.29	Sydney Barnes (Eng)	3 v SA	1912
33	12.15	Richard Hadlee (NZ)	3 v A	1985

Most series taking 20 wickets
9 Fred Trueman, Dennis Lillee, Malcolm Marshall; 7 Lance Gibbs, 6 Clarrie Grimmett, Alan Davidson, Jeff Thomson, Imran Khan, Kapil Dev.

Test Match Wicket Keeping

(ct - caught, st - stumped.)

Most dismissals in an innings
7   (all ct) Wasim Bari, Pak v NZ, Auckland, 23 Feb 1979
7   (all ct) Bob Taylor Eng v I, Bombay, 15 Feb 1980
7   (all ct) Ian Smith, NZ v Sri, Hamilton, 23-24 Feb 1991

Most dismissals in a Test career

Dis		ct	st	Tests	Years
355	Rodney Marsh (Aus)	343	12	96	1970-84
272	Jeffrey Dujon (WI)	267	5	81	1981-91
269	Alan Knott (Eng)	250	19	95	1967-81
248	Ian Healy (Aus)	231	17	73	1988-95
228	Wasim Bari (Pak)	201	27	81	1967-84
219	Godfrey Evans (Eng)	173	46	91	1946-59
198	Syed Kirmani (Ind)	160	38	88	1976-86
189	Deryck Murray (WI)	181	8	62	1963-80
187	Wally Grout (Aus)	163	24	51	1957-66
176	Ian Smith (NZ)	168	8	63	1980-92
174	Bob Taylor (Eng)	167	7	57	1971-84
141	John Waite (SAf)	124	17	50	1951-65
130	Kieran More (Ind)	110	20	49	1986-93
130	Bert Oldfield (Aus)	78	52	54	1920-37

Most dismissals in a Test series

Dis	ct	st	Tests		season
28	28	-	Rodney Marsh (Aus)	5 v E	1982/3
26	23	3	John Waite (SAf)	5 v NZ	1961/2
26	26	-	Rodney Marsh (Aus)	6 v WI	1975/6
26	21	5	Ian Healy (Aus)	6 v E	1993
24	22	2	Deryck Murray (WI)	5 v E	1963
24	24	-	Denis Lindsay (SAf)	5 v A	1966/7
24	21	3	Alan Knott (Eng)	6 v A	1970/1

The most in a three Test series

22	21	1	Amal Silva (Sri)	3 v I	1985

Test Match Catches

(By fielders, not wicket-keepers)

Most catches in an innings
5   Victor Richardson Aus v SA, Durban, 3 Mar 1936
5   Yajurvindra Singh Ind v E, Bangalore, 29-30 Jan 1977
5   Mohammad Azharuddin Ind v Pak, Karachi, 15-16 Nov 1989
5   Krishnamachari Srikkanth Ind v Aus, Perth, 1-2 Feb 1992

Most catches in a Test career

Ct		Tests	Years
156	Allan Border (Aus)	156	1978-94
122	Greg Chappell (Aus)	87	1970-84
122	Vivian Richards (WI)	121	1974-91
120	Colin Cowdrey (Eng)	114	1954-75
120	Ian Botham (Eng)	102	1977-92
110	Bobby Simpson (Aus)	62	1957-78
110	Walter Hammond (Eng)	85	1927-47
109	Garfield Sobers (WI)	93	1954-74
108	Sunil Gavaskar (Ind)	125	1971-87
105	Ian Chappell (Aus)	75	1964-80
103	Graham Gooch (Eng)	118	1975-95
96	Gordon Greenidge (WI)	108	1974-91
94	David Boon (Aus)	101	1984-95
93*	Javed Miandad (Pak)	124	1976-94
93	Mark Taylor	66	1989-95
90	Clive Lloyd (WI)	110	1966-85
87	Tony Greig (Eng)	58	1972-77
87	Richie Richardson (WI)	80	1983-95
83	Ian Redpath (Aus)	66	1964-76
80	Tom Graveney (Eng)	79	1951-69

* and 1 stumping

Most catches in a Test series

Ct		Tests	Season
15	Jack Gregory (Aus)	5 v E	1920-1
14	Greg Chappell (Aus)	6 v E	1974-5
13	Bob Simpson (Aus)	5 v SA	1957-8
13	Bob Simpson (Aus)	5 v WI	1960-1

The most in a three Test series

11	Tony Greig (Eng)	3 v P	1974

All Rounders

Best Test career records - over 2000 runs and 150 wickets:
The final column is the ratio of batting average to bowling average, a good test of ability.

	Tests	Runs	Wkts	Ct	Ratio
Garfield Sobers (WI)	93	8032	235	109	1.70
Imran Khan (Pak)	88	3807	362	28	1.65
Keith Miller (Aus)	55	2958	170	38	1.61
Richard Hadlee (NZ)	83	3124	431	39	1.22
Ian Botham (Eng)	102	5200	383	120	1.18

Name	Tests	Runs	Wkts		Ratio
Kapil Dev (Ind)	131	5248	434	64	1.05
Vinoo Mankad (Ind)	44	2109	162	33	0.97
Richie Benaud (Aus)	63	2201	248	65	0.90
Ravi Shastri (Ind)	80	3830	151	36	0.87

Others with ratios of 1.5 or more, and 1000 runs/50 wickets

Name		Runs		Wkts	Ratio
Walter Hammond (Eng)	85	7249	83	110	1.55
Aubrey Faulkner (SAf)	25	1754	82	20	1.53

Fewest Tests to reach:

1000 runs 100 wickets: 21 Ian Botham, 23 Vinoo Mankad, 25 Kapil Dev

2000 runs 200 wickets: 42 Ian Botham, 50 Kapil Dev, Imran Khan

3000 runs 300 wickets: 71 Ian Botham, 75 Imran Khan, 83 Kapil Dev, Richard Hadlee

300 runs and 20 wickets in a Test series

Runs	Wkts	Name	v.	season
475	34	George Giffen (Aus)	5 v E	1894-5
399	34	Ian Botham (Eng)	6 v A	1981
329	30	Richie Benaud (Aus)	5 v SA	1957-8
545	29	Aubrey Faulkner (SAf)	5 v E	1909-10
430	24	Tony Greig (Eng)	5 v WI	1974
442	23	Jack Gregory (Aus)	5 v E	1920-1
424	23	Garfield Sobers (WI)	5 v I	1962
318	22	Kapil Dev (Ind)	6 v E	1981-2
301	21	Richard Hadlee (NZ)	4 v E	1983
722	20	Garfield Sobers (WI)	5 v E	1966
439	20	Keith Miller (Aus)	5 v WI	1955
362	20	Keith Miller (Aus)	5 v WI	1951-2
322	20	Garfield Sobers (WI)	5 v E	1963

One-Day Internationals

The first ever one-day international match was played at Melbourne on 5 Jan 1971 when Australia beat England by 5 wickets. They have proliferated in recent years, especially in Australia.

World Cup

The first World Cup was held in England in 1975, contested by the six Test playing nations plus Sri Lanka and East Africa at 60-over matches. This tournament was sponsored by the Prudential Assurance Company as were the next World Cup competitions held in England in 1979 and 1983. From 1979 the non-Test playing members of the International Cricket Conference (ICC) have played-off for the ICC Trophy and the right to enter the following World Cup tournament. The 1987 World Cup was held in India and Pakistan, where the matches were contested at 50 overs per innings, as they were in 1992 in Australia and New Zealand.

World Cup Finals

Year	Venue	Result
1975	Lord's	West Indies (291-8) beat Australia (274) by 17 runs
1979	Lord's	West Indies (286-9) beat England (194) by 92 runs
1983	Lord's	India (183) beat West Indies (140) by 43 runs
1987	Calcutta	Australia (253-5) beat England (246-8) by 7 runs
1992	Melbourne	Pakistan (249-6) beat England (227) by 22 runs

World Cup Innings Records

Total: 360-4 West Indies v Sri Lanka at Karachi 13 Oct 1987

Lowest: 45 Canada v England at Manchester 14 Jun 1979

Individual: 181 Vivian Richards, West Indies v Sri Lanka at Karachi 13 Oct 1987

Best bowling: 7-51 Winston Davis, West Indies v Australia at Leeds 11-12 Jun 1983

Dismissals: 5 Syed Kirmani, India v Zimbabwe at Leicester 11 Jun 1983

Economical bowling: 1-6 in 12 overs Bishen Bedi, India v East Africa at Leicester 11 Jun 1975

Hat-trick: Chetan Sharma, India v New Zealand at Nagpur 31 Oct 1987

World Cup Career Records

Most runs:	Runs	Ave.
Javed Miandad (Pak)	1029	44.74
Vivian Richards (WI)	1013	63.31
Graham Gooch (Eng)	897	44.85
Martin Crowe (Nz)	880	55.00
Desmond Haymes (WI)	854	37.13
David Boon (Aus)	815	54.33
Ramiz Raja (Pak)	698	53.69
Kapil Dev (Ind)	669	37.16
Imran Khan (Ind)	666	35.05
Allan Lamb (Eng)	656	50.46
Glenn Turner (NZ)	612	61.20
Zaheer Abbas (Pak)	597	49.75
Arjuna Rantunga (Sri)	594	42.43
Gordon Greenidge (WI)	591	45.46
Dean Jones (Aus)	590	42.14
Geoff Marsh (Aus)	579	48.25

Most wickets:	Wickets	Ave.
Imran Khan (Pak)	34	19.26
Ian Botham (Eng)	30	25.40
Kapil Dev (Ind)	28	31.85
Andy Roberts (WI)	26	21.23
Craig McDermott (Aus)	26	22.57
Wasim Akram (Pak)	25	25.32
Abdul Qadir (Pak)	24	21.08
Phil DeFreitas (Eng)	23	26.17
Richard Hadlee (NZ)	22	19.13
Madan Lal (Ind)	22	19.36
Manoj Prabakhar (Ind)	21	22.85
Michael Holding (WI)	20	17.05

Most dismissals: 22 (18 ct, 4 st) Wasim Bari (Pak)

ICC Trophy winners

1979	Sri Lanka
1982	Zimbabwe
1986	Zimbabwe
1990	Zimbabwe
1994	United Arab Emirates

Highest innings total: 455-9 off 60 overs Papua New Guinea v Gibraltar at Rugeley 18 Jun 1986.

One-Day International Records

Innings Records

Total: 363-7 off 55 overs England v Pakistan at Nottingham 20 Aug 1992

Lowest: 43 Pakistan v West Indies at Cape Town 25 Feb 1993

Individual: 189* Vivian Richards, West Indies v England at Manchester 31 May 1984

Best bowling: 7-37 Aqib Javed, Pakistan v India at Sharjah 25 Oct 1991

Career Records: to July 1995

Most runs

		Ave.	100s	Games
8648	Desmond Haynes (WI)	41.37	17	238
7327	Javed Miandad (Pak)	41.86	8	228
6721	Vivian Richards (WI)	47.00	11	187
6524	Allan Border (Aus)	30.62	3	273
6068	Dean Jones (Aus)	44.61	7	164
5962	David Boon (Aus)	37.03	5	181
5689	Richie Richardson (WI)	33.07	5	205
5288	Mohammad Azharuddin	36.72	3	194
5271	Salim Malik (Pak)	32.33	5	210
5134	Gordon Greenidge (WI)	45.03	11	128
4915	Ramiz Raja (Pak)	33.43	8	159
4536	Arjuna Ranatunga (SL)	35.43	1	164
4517	Martin Crowe (NZ)	37.95	3	139
4389	Aravinda De Silva (SL)	31.80	3	156
4357	Geoff Marsh (Aus)	39.97	9	117
4290	Graham Gooch (Eng)	36.98	8	125

Most dismissals

		Ct	St	Games
204	Jeffrey Dujon (WI)	183	21	169
182	Ian Healy (Aus)	155	27	128
124	Rodney Marsh (Aus)	120	4	92
103	Salim Yousuf (Pak)	81	22	86
95	David Richardson (SAf)	83	12	69
90	Kiran More (Ind)	63	27	94

Most catches by fielder

		Games
127	Allan Border (Aus)	273
101	Vivian Richards (WI)	187
80	Mohammed Azharuddin (Ind)	194
71	Kapil Dev (Ind)	224
70	Richie Richardson (WI)	205

Most wickets

		Average	Games
273	Wasim Akram (Pak)	22.61	189
253	Kapil Dev (Ind)	27.45	224
190	Craig McDermott (Aus)	24.91	129
182	Imran Khan (Pak)	26.62	175
176	Waqar Younis (Pak)	21.59	104
162	Steve Waugh (Aus)	33.41	185
158	Richard Hadlee (NZ)	21.56	115
158	Courtney Walsh (WI)	30.29	142
157	Malcolm Marshall (WI)	26.96	136
154	Curtley Ambrose (WI)	23.18	114
147	Manoj Prabhakar (Ind)	28.50	120
146	Joel Garner (WI)	18.84	98
145	Ian Botham (Eng)	28.54	116
142	Michael Holding (WI)	21.36	102
140	Ewen Chatfield (NZ)	25.86	114
132	Abdul Qadir (Pak)	26.15	104

All-round - over 2000 runs and 100 wickets

	Games	Runs	Wkts	Ct	Ratio
Vivian Richards (WI)	187	6721	118	101	1.31
Imran Khan (Pak)	167	3709	182	37	1.26
Carl Hooper (WI)	133	3071	125	63	1.08
Steve Waugh (Aus)	185	3854	162	62	0.92
Kapil Dev (Ind)	224	3783	253	71	0.87
Ian Botham (Eng)	116	2113	145	36	0.81
Ravi Shastri (Ind)	150	3108	129	40	0.81
Mudassar Nazar (Pak)	122	2653	111	21	0.81

Ratio is batting average to bowling average

Most consecutive matches

131 Richie Richardson for West Indies from 17 Jan 1987 to 1 Nov 1993

First Class Cricket

First-class matches are contested over three or more days. Such matches are now specified by the members of the ICC, but prior to 1947 when the term was first defined, there are doubts about the first-class status of many matches. The Association of Cricket Statisticians (ACS) has done much work in studying the problem and deciding about the status of such matches. They have drawn up lists of matches and, as a consequence, consistency can be achieved in statistical compilations. However there is still some disagreement about the status of various matches, and figures compiled as a result are sometimes at variance with traditional figures. We have respected tradition although incorporating corrections agreed by leading statisticians. First-class cricket is taken as having originated in 1815.

Team Records

Highest innings totals

1107	Victoria v New South Wales at Melbourne 27-28 Dec 1926
1059	Victoria v Tasmania at Melbourne 2-5 Feb 1923
951-7 dec	Sind v Baluchistan at Karachi 18-20 Feb 1974
944-6 dec	Hyderabad v Andhra at Secunderabad 9-11 Jan 1994
918	New South Wales v South Australia at Sydney 5-8 Jan 1901
912-8 dec	Holkar v Mysore at Indore 2-4 Mar 1946
910-6 dec	Railways v Dera Ismail Khan at Lahore 2-4 Dec 1964
903-7 dec	England v Australia at The Oval 20-23 Aug 1938

Highest match aggregate

2376 runs Bombay (651 & 714-8 dec) beat Maharashtra (407 & 604) at Pune over 7 days on 5-11 Mar 1949.

Largest margin of victory

Innings & 851 runs Railways (910-6 dec) beat Dera Ismail Khan (32 & 27) at Lahore on 2-4 Dec 1964.

Lowest completed innings totals

12	Oxford University (batted one short) v MCC and Ground at Oxford 24 May 1877
12	Northamptonshire v Gloucestershire at Gloucester 11 Jun 1907
13	Auckland v Canterbury at Auckland 31 Dec 1877

13   Nottinghamshire v Yorkshire at Nottingham 20-21 Jun 1901

Lowest aggregate in a completed first-class match
105 Australians (41 & 12-1) beat MCC (33 & 19) at Lord's 27 May 1878.

Individual Records - Batting

Highest innings (scores of over 400)
501* Brian Lara Warwickshire v Durham at Edgbaston 3, 6 Jun 1994
499 Hanif Mohammed Karachi v Bahawalpur at Karachi 8-11 Jan 1959
452* Don Bradman New South Wales v Queensland at Sydney 4-6 Jan 1930
443* Bhausahib Nimbalkar Maharashtra v Kathiawar at Pune 16-18 Dec 1948
437 Bill Ponsford Victoria v Queensland at Melbourne 16-17 Dec 1927
429 Bill Ponsford Victoria v Tasmania at Melbourne 3-5 Feb 1923
428 Aftab Baloch Sind v Baluchistan at Karachi 18-20 Feb 1974
424 Archie McLaren Lancashire v Somerset at Taunton 15-16 Jul 1895
405* Graeme Hick Worcestershire v Somerset at Taunton 5-6 May 1988

Fastest scoring
Either minutes or balls received to reach the following scores:

Score	Mins	Balls	
50	8	13	Clive Inman, Leicestershire v Notts at Nottingham 20 Aug 1965
100	26	36	Tom Moody, Warwickshire v Glamorgan at Swansea 27 Jul 1990
	35	40-46	Percy Fender, Surrey v Northants at Northampton 26 Aug 1920
35		54	Steven O'Shaughnessy, Lancashire v Leics at Manchester 13 Sep 1983
43		34	David Hookes, South Australia v Victoria at Adelaide 25 Oct 1982
200	113	123	Ravi Shastri, Bombay v Baroda at Bombay 10 Jan 1985
	120	121	Clive Lloyd, West Indians v Glamorgan at Swansea 9 Aug 1976
	120		Gilbert Jessop, Gloucestershire v Sussex at Hove 1 Jun 1903
300	181		Denis Compton, MCC v N.E. Transvaal at Benoni 3-4 Dec 1948

Edwin Alletson scored 189 runs in 90 mins for Nottinghamshire v Sussex at Hove 20 May 1911, his final 142 runs being hit off 51 balls in 40 minutes. Gilbert Jessop scored 191 in 90 minutes (passing 150 in 63 mins) for the Gentlemen of the South v Players at Hastings 3 Sep 1907.

Six sixes from a six-ball over
Garfield Sobers (Notts) off Malcolm Nash (Glamorgan) at Swansea 31 Aug 1968
Ravi Shastri (Bombay) off Tilak Raj (Baroda) at Bombay on 10 Jan 1985
Playing in a Shell Trophy match for Wellington v Canterbury at Christchurch on 20 Feb 1990, in a deliberate attempt to give away runs Bert Vance bowled an over containing 22 balls, 17 of which were deliberate no-balls (the umpire losing count and declaring over one ball early!). From this over Lee German of Canterbury hit 70 runs, including eight sixes and five fours, Richard Petrie five runs including one four, and with two runs from no-balls off which no runs were hit, a total of 77 runs was conceded.

Most sixes in an innings
15 John Reid in an innings of 296 for Wellington v Northern Districts at Wellington 14-15 Jan 1963.

Most runs in a first-class career and most 100s, 200s, 300s

To the end of the 1994/5 winter season. All English unless stated. The final column shows innings per century

Runs	Name	*Average*	*100s*	*200s*	*300s*	*Inns/100*	*Years*
61237*	Jack Hobbs	50.65	197	16	1	6.7	1905-34
58959	Frank Woolley	40.77	145	9	1	10.6	1906-38
57611	Patsy Hendren	50.80	170	22	1	7.6	1907-38
55061	Philip Mead	47.67	153	13	-	8.8	1905-36
54896*	W G Grace	39.55	126	13	3	11.8	1865-1908
50551	Walter Hammond	56.10	167	36	4	6.0	1920-51
50138*	Herbert Sutcliffe	51.95	149	17	1	7.3	1919-45
48426	Geoffrey Boycott	56.83	151	10	1	6.7	1962-86
47793	Tom Graveney	44.91	122	7	-	10.0	1948-72
43551	Tom Hayward	41.79	104	8	1	10.3	1893-1914
43423	Dennis Amiss	42.86	102	3	-	11.2	1960-87
42719	Colin Cowdrey	42.89	107	3	2	10.6	1950-76
41284	Andrew Sandham	44.82	107	11	1	9.3	1911-38
40859	Graham Gooch	48.93	113	10	1	8.0	1973-95
40140	Len Hutton	55.51	129	11	1	6.3	1934-60
39832	Mike Smith	41.84	66	3	-	16.5	1951-75
39802*	Wilfred Rhodes	30.83	58	3	-	26.3	1896-1930
39790	John Edrich	45.47	103	4	1	9.5	1956-78
39405	Bob Wyatt	40.04	85	2	-	13.4	1923-57

38942	Denis Compton	51.85	123	9	1	6.8	1936-64
38874	Ernest Tyldesley	45.46	102	7	-	9.4	1909-36
37897	Johnny Tyldesley	40.66	86	13	-	11.6	1895-1923
37665	Keith Fletcher	37.77	63	2	-	18.5	1962-88
37354	Gordon Greenidge (WI)	45.88	92	12	-	9.7	1971-92
37252	Jack (J W) Hearne	40.98	96	11	-	10.7	1909-36
37248	Leslie Ames	43.51	102	9	-	9.0	1926-51
37002	Don Kenyon	33.63	74	7	-	15.7	1946-67
36965	Bill Edrich	42.39	86	9	-	11.2	1934-58
36673	Jim Parks	34.76	51	1	-	24.1	1949-76
36479*	David Denton	33.37	69	3	-	16.8	1894-1920
36323	George Hirst	34.13	60	4	1	20.2	1891-1929
36212	Vivian Richards (WI)	49.33	114	10	1	7.0	1971-93
36049	Alan Jones	32.89	56	1	-	20.9	1957-83
36012	Billy Quaife	35.38	72	4	-	16.7	1894-1928
35725	Roy Marshall	35.95	68	3	-	15.5	1945-72
35208	George Gunn	35.96	62	1	-	17.1	1902-32

Others with career averages over 50 and 20000 runs, or 80 100s or 10 200s

34843	Zaheer Abbas (Pak)	51.54	108	10	-	7.1	1965-87
34346	Glenn Turner (NZ)	49.70	103	10	1	7.7	1964-83
33660	Maurice Leyland	40.50	80	5	-	11.6	1920-48
32650	Alvin Kallicharan (WI)	43.64	87	6	-	9.6	1966-90
32317	Mike Gatting	50.57	84	9	-	9.0	1975-95
31847	Joe Hardstaff Jnr	44.35	83	10	-	9.8	1930-55
31131	Allan Lamb	48.64	86	3	-	8.7	1972-94
30886	Charles Fry	50.22	94	16	-	7.0	1892-1921
30574	Percy Holmes	42.11	67	12	?	12.1	1913-35
30546	Reg Simpson	38.32	64	10	-	13.3	1944-63
28774	Rohan Kanhai (WI)	49.01	83	7	-	8.1	1955-82
28647	Javed Miandad (Pak)	53.44	80	11	1	7.9	1973-94
28358	Barry Richards (SAf)	54.74	80	6	1	7.2	1964-83
28315	Garfield Sobers (WI)	54.87	86	6	1	7.1	1953-74
28067	Don Bradman (Aus)	95.14	117	37	6	2.9	1927-49
27592	Peter May	51.00	85	5	-	7.3	1948-63
26439	Arthur Shrewsbury	36.66	59	10	-	13.7	1875-1902
25834	Sunil Gavaskar (Ind)	51.46	81	10	1	7.0	1966-87
25551	Allan Border (Aus)	51.30	68	3	-	8.7	1976-94
24692	K.S.Ranjitsinhji (Ind)	56.37	72	14	-	6.9	1893-1920
24535	Greg Chappell (Aus)	52.20	74	4	-	7.3	1966-84
24001	Graeme Hick	57.41	80	8	1	5.8	1983-95
21699	Neil Harvey (Aus)	50.93	67	7	-	6.9	1946-63
21029	Bobby Simpson (Aus)	56.22	60	12	2	7.3	1952-78
20940	Graeme Pollock (SAf)	54.67	64	5	-	6.8	1960-87
20676	Jimmy Cook (SAf)	50.67	63	5	1	7.3	1972-94

Others with career averages over 55 and 10000 runs, or a century more often than every six innnings

18710	Martin Crowe (NZ)	55.85	67	4	-	5.9	1979-94
18635	Vijay Hazare (Ind)	57.87	60	10	2	6.1	1934-67
16890	Lindsay Hassett (Aus)	58.24	59	8	-	5.5	1932-54
14346	Mark Waugh (Aus)	56.70	48	5	-	6.2	1985-94
13819	Bill Ponsford (Aus)	65.18	47	13	4	5.0	1920-35
13392	Bill Woodfull (Aus)	65.00	49	7	-	5.0	1921-35
13248	Vijay Merchant (Ind)	71.22	44	11	1	5.2	1929-51
12762	Alan Kippax (Aus)	57.22	43	7	1	6.0	1918-36
12614	Arthur Morris (Aus)	53.67	46	4	-	5.4	1940-64
12010	Everton Weekes (WI)	55.34	36	9	1	6.7	1944-64
11820	Clyde Walcott (WI)	56.55	40	4	1	5.9	1941-64
9921	George Headley (WI)	69.80	33	9	1	5.0	1928-54

* ACS figures which are at considerable variance:

Hobbs 61760 runs (av. 50.66), 199 100s; W G Grace 54211 runs (av. 39.45, 124) centuries (11.9 inns per 100); Sutcliffe 50670 runs (av. 52.02), 150 100s; Rhodes 39969 runs (av. 30.81); Denton 36440 runs (av. 33.40).

Graeme Hick - prolific scorer

Least innings to reach 100 centuries
295 Don Bradman, 552 Denis Compton, 619 Len Hutton, 645 Geoffrey Boycott, 658 Zaheer Abbas, 658 Vivian Richards, 680 Walter Hammond, 700 Herbert Sutcliffe.

Most times scoring two centuries in a match
8 Zaheer Abbas (including 200 and 100 four times); 7 Walter Hammond; 6 Jack Hobbs, Glenn Turner; 5 Charles Fry, Graham Gooch.
Uniquely Arthur Fagg scored two double centuries in a match, 244 and 202* Kent v Essex at Colchester 13-15 Jul 1938.

Most centuries in successive innings
6   Charles Fry for Sussex (5) and Rest of England 1901
6   Don Bradman for his XI and for South Australia (5) 1938-9
6   Mike Proctor for Rhodesia 1970-1

Most runs in an English season

Runs	Name	100s	Ave.	Year
3816	Denis Compton	18	90.85	1947
3539	Bill Edrich	12	80.43	1947
3518	Tom Hayward	13	66.37	1906
3429	Len Hutton	12	68.58	1949
3352	Frank Woolley	12	60.94	1928
3336	Herbert Sutcliffe	14	74.13	1932
3323	Walter Hammond	13	67.81	1933
3311	Patsy Hendren	13	70.44	1928
3309	Bobby Abel	7	55.15	1901
also 14 or more centuries				
3024	Jack Hobbs	16	70.32	1925
3011	Walter Hammond	15	75.27	1938
highest average				
2429	Don Bradman	13	115.66	1938
1538	Geoffrey Boycott	6	102.53	1979
2746	Graham Gooch	12	101.70	1990
2503	Geoffrey Boycott	13	100.12	1971

Most seasons scoring 3000 runs
3 Herbert Sutcliffe 1928, 1931, 1932; Patsy Hendren 1923, 1928, 1933; Walter Hammond 1933, 1937, 1938.

Most seasons scoring 2000 runs
17 Jack Hobbs; 15 Patsy Hendren, Herbert Sutcliffe; 13 Frank Woolley; 12 Walter Hammond; 11 James Langridge, Philip Mead; 10 Tom Hayward; 9 Bill Edrich, Len Hutton, Jack Robertson.

Most seasons (English or overseas) scoring 1000 runs
28 W G Grace, Frank Woolley; 27 Colin Cowdrey, Philip Mead; 26 Geoffrey Boycott, Jack Hobbs; 25 Patsy Hendren; 24 Billy Quaife, Herbert Sutcliffe, Dennis Amiss; 23 Alan Jones.

Most sixes in a season: 80 Ian Botham 1985 (in 1530 runs, av. 69.54)

Individual Records - Bowling

Best bowling
The taking of all ten wickets in an innings by a single bowler has been recorded more than 70 times in first-class cricket. Bowlers to have achieved this feat more than once are:
3   Alfred 'Tich' Freeman, Kent 1929, 1930, 1931
2   Vyell Walker, England 1859 and Middlesex 1865
2   W G Grace, MCC 1873, 1886
2   Hedley Verity, Yorkshire 1931, 1932
2   Jim Laker, Surrey and England 1956

The least expensive ten wickets analyses
10-10   Hedley Verity, Yorkshire v Nottinghamshire at Leeds 12 Jul 1932
10-18   George Geary, Leicestershire v Glamorgan at Pontypridd 15 Aug 1929
10-20   Premansu Chatterjee, Bengal v Assam at Jorhat 28 Jan 1957
10-26   Bert Vogler, Eastern Province v Griqualand West at Johannesburg 28 Dec 1906
10-28   A E Moss, Canterbury v Wellington at Christchurch 27-28 Dec 1889 (on his first-class debut)
10-28   William Howell, Australians v Surrey at The Oval 15 May 1899
10-30   Colin Blythe, Kent v Northants at Northampton 1 Jun 1907
10-32   Henry Pickett, Essex v Leicestershire at Leyton 3 Jun 1895

Most wickets in a match
19 (9-37, 10-53) Jim Laker, England v Australia 26-31 Jul 1956

17 wickets in a match has been achieved on 18 occasions; the least expensive being for 48 runs by Colin Blythe, 10-30 and 7-18, Kent v Northants 1 Jun 1907.

Most successive wickets

The feat of taking four wickets with consecutive balls has been achieved on 27 occasions. The only man to do this twice has been Bob Crisp for Western Province in Currie Cup matches in 1931-2 and 1934. The most notable spell was by Pat Pocock for Surrey v Sussex at Eastbourne 15 Aug 1972; his records included five wickets in one over, six wickets in nine balls and seven in eleven.

Most hat-tricks (three wickets with consecutive balls)

7 Douglas Wright (Eng) 1937-49; 6 Charlie Parker (Eng) 1922-30, Tom Goddard (Eng) 1924-47.

Most wickets in a first-class career

All English unless stated. The final two columns show the number of occasions on which the bowler has taken 5 wickets in an innings and 10 wickets in a match.

Mark Waugh – averaging well over 50 in his career

Wkts	Name	Average	5wi	10wm	Years
4187*	Wilfred Rhodes	16.71	287	67	1898-1930
3776	Alfred 'Tich' Freeman	18.42	386	140	1914-36
3278	Charlie Parker	19.46	277	91	1903-35
3061	Jack (J.T.) Hearne	17.75	255	64	1888-1923
2979	Tom Goddard	19.84	251	86	1922-52
2876*	W.G.Grace	17.92	240	64	1865-1908
2874	Alex Kennedy	21.43	225	45	1907-36
2857	Derek Shackleton	18.65	194	38	1948-69
2844	Tony Lock	19.23	196	50	1946-71
2830	Fred Titmus	22.37	168	26	1949-82
2784	Maurice Tate	18.16	195	44	1912-37
2739*	George Hirst	18.72	184	40	1891-1929
2506	Colin Blythe	16.81	218	71	1899-1914
2465	Derek Underwood	20.28	153	47	1963-87
2431	Ewart Astill	23.76	140	22	1906-39
2356	Jack White	18.57	193	58	1909-37
2323	Eric Hollies	20.94	182	40	1932-57
2304	Fred Trueman	18.29	126	25	1949-69
2260	Brian Statham	18.36	123	11	1950-68
2233	Reg Perks	24.07	143	24	1930-55
2221	Johnny Briggs	15.93	200	52	1879-1900
2218	Don Shepherd	21.32	123	28	1950-72
2151	George Dennett	19.82	211	57	1903-26
2105	Tom Richardson	18.42	200	72	1892-1904

Others with career average below 15 and 1500 wickets, or more than 50 times taking 10 wickets in a match

2028	Alfred Shaw	12.12	177	44	1864-97
1956	Hedley Verity	14.90	164	54	1930-39
1841	George Lohmann	13.74	176	57	1884-98
1681	James Southerton	14.46	192	59	1854-79
1673	Arthur Mold	15.54	152	56	1889-1901
1571	Tom Emmett	13.56	121	29	1866-88

The best non-English players

1674	Albert Trott (Aus)	21.09	131	41	1893-1911
1602	Malcolm Marshall (WI)	19.08	85	13	1977-94
1571	Intikhab Alam (Pak)	27.67	85	13	1957-82
1560	Bishen Bedi (Ind)	21.69	106	20	1961-82
1424	Clarrie Grimmett (Aus)	22.28	127	33	1911-41
1417	Mike Proctor (SAf)	19.53	70	15	1965-89

* *ACS figures: Rhodes 4204 wickets (av.16.72), W G Grace 2808 (av 18.15), Hirst 2742 (av.18.73)*

Least matches to reach 1000 wickets

134 Tom Richardson 1892-6, 147 George Dennett 1903-9, 149 Arthur Mold 1899-1905, 156 Jack (J.T.) Hearne 1888-96, 159 George Lohmann 1884-8.

Least matches to reach 2000 wickets

327 Tom Richardson 1892-1903, 347 Jack (J.T.) Hearne 1888-1902, 349 George Dennett 1903-24, 350 Colin Blythe 1899-1912, 350 'Tich' Freeman 1914-29.

Most wickets in an English season

Wickets		Average	Year
304	Alfred 'Tich' Freeman	18.05	1928
298	Alfred 'Tich' Freeman	15.26	1933
290	Tom Richardson	14.37	1895

283	Charlie Turner	11.68	1888
276	Alfred 'Tich' Freeman	15.60	1931
275	Alfred 'Tich' Freeman	16.84	1930
273	Tom Richardson	14.45	1897

200 wickets in a season most often
8 'Tich' Freeman, 5 Charlie Parker, 4 Tom Goddard, 3 Jack (J.T.) Hearne, George Lohmann, Wilfred Rhodes, Tom Richardson, Maurice Tate, Hedley Verity.

100 wickets in a season most often
23 Wilfred Rhodes, 20 Derek Shackleton, 17 'Tich' Freeman, 16 Tom Goddard, Charlie Parker, Reg Perks, Fred Titmus; 15 Jack (J.T.) Hearne, George Hirst, Alex Kennedy.

The best average while taking at least 100 wickets in a season:
8.54 Alfred Shaw, 186 wkts in 1880.

All-Rounders

Best Career Figures
Determined by the best ratios of batting average divided by bowling average (the figure in the first column), for those with at least 10000 runs and 1000 wickets:

	Ratio	Runs	Ave.	Wkts	Ave.	Years
W.G. Grace (Eng)	2.21	54896	39.55	2876	17.92	1865-1908
Frank Tarrant (Aus)	2.06	17857	36.36	1489	17.66	1898-1936
Frank Woolley (Eng)	2.05	58959	40.77	2068	19.85	1906-38
Garfield Sobers (WI)	1.98	28315	54.87	1043	27.74	1953-74
Wilfred Rhodes (Eng)	1.85	39802	30.83	4187	16.71	1895-1930
Mike Proctor (SAf)	1.84	21936	36.01	1417	19.53	1965-89
George Hirst (Eng)	1.82	36272	34.12	2742	18.73	1891-1929
Jack (J.W.) Hearne (Eng)	1.68	37252	40.98	1839	24.43	1909-36
Imran Khan (Pak)	1.65	17771	36.79	1287	22.32	1969-92

Other with 25000 runs and 2000 wickets:

	Ratio	Runs	Ave.	Wkts	Ave.	Years
Trevor Bailey (Eng)	1.44	28642	33.42	2082	23.13	1945-67

Best season's figures in England
2000 runs and 150 wickets in a season

George Hirst	2.78	2385	45.86	208	16.50	1906
Frank Woolley	2.66	2101	42.87	167	16.14	1921
Frank Woolley	2.50	2022	45.95	163	18.37	1922

3000 runs and 100 wickets in a season

James Parks	1.97	3003	50.89	101	25.83	1937

Ratios of over 3.00 for 1000 runs and 100 wickets

W.G. Grace	4.09	1664	52.00	140	12.71	1875
Richard Hadlee (NZ)	3.65	1179	51.26	117	14.05	1981
W.G. Grace	3.30	2622	62.42	130	18.90	1876
Wilfred Rhodes	3.26	1511	39.76	119	12.19	1922
George Hirst	3.16	1844	47.28	128	14.94	1903
W.G. Grace	3.11	1474	39.83	179	12.81	1877
Jack (J.W.) Hearne	3.09	2148	55.07	142	17.83	1920

Best match
George Giffen (Aus) scored 271 and took 9-96 and 7-70, South Australia v Victoria 7-11 Nov 1891.

Individual Records - Wicket-Keeping Dismissals

(ct - caught, st - stumped)

Most dismissals in an innings
9 (8 ct, 1st) Tahir Rashid, Habib Bank v Pakistan Automobile Corporation at Gujranwala 29 Nov 1992

8 (all ct) Wally Grout, Queensland v Western Australia at Brisbane 15 Feb 1960

8 (all ct) David East, Essex v Somerset at Taunton 27 Jul 1985

8 (all ct) Steve Marsh, Kent v Middlesex at Lord's 31 May - 1 Jun 1991

8 (6ct 2 st) Tim Zoehrer, Australians v Surrey at The Oval 27 May 1994

Most stumpings in an innings
6 Hugo Yarnold, Worcestershire v Scotland at Broughty Ferry 2 Jul 1951

Most dismissals in a match
12 (8ct, 4st) Edward Pooley, Surrey v Sussex at The Oval 6-7 Jul 1868

12 (9ct, 3st) Don Tallon, Queensland v New South Wales at Sydney 2-4 Jan 1939

12 (9ct, 3st) Brian Taber, New South Wales v South Australia at Adelaide 13-17 Dec 1968

Most dismissals in a first-class career
All English

Dis	ct	st	Name	Per match	Career
1649	1473	176	Bob Taylor	2.6	1960-88
1527	1270	257	John Murray	2.4	1952-75
1497	1242	255	Herbert Strudwick	2.2	1902-27
1344	1211	133	Alan Knott	2.6	1965-85
1310	933	377	Frederick Huish	2.6	1895-1914
1294	1081	213	Brian Taylor	2.3	1949-73
1253	906	347	David Hunter	2.3	1889-1909
1228	953	275	Harry Butt	2.3	1890-1912
1207	852	355	Jack Board	2.3	1891-1915
1206	904	302	Harry Elliott	2.3	1920-47
1181	1088	93	Jim Parks	1.6	1949-76
1126	949	177	Roy Booth	2.4	1951-70
1121	703	418	Les Ames	1.9	1926-51
1099	961	138	David Bairstow	2.4	1970-90
1095	754	341	George Duckworth	2.2	1923-47
1082	748	334	Harold Stephenson	2.3	1948-64
1071	895	176	Jimmy Binks	2.1	1955-69
1066	816	250	Godfrey Evans	2.3	1939-69

Best non-English

Dis	ct	st	Name	Per match	Career
869	804	65	Rodney Marsh (Aus)	3.4	1968-84
849	741	108	Deryck Murray (WI)	2.3	1961-80
824	703	121	Farokh Engineer (Ind)	2.5	1958-76
812	667	145	Wasim Bari (Pak)	2.9	1964-83

Over 380 dismissals and 3 per match

Dis	ct	st	Name	Per match	Career
621	567	54	Ray Jennings (SAf)	3.9	1973-93
587	473	114	Wally Grout (Aus)	3.2	1946-66
470	438	32	David Richardson (SA)	3.0	1977-94
461	423	38	Tim Zoehrer (Aus)	3.1	1980-94
430	394	36	Ian Healy (Aus)	3.3	1986-94
395	345	50	Brian Taber (Aus)	3.1	1964-74
394	358	36	Richard Ryall (SAf)	3.5	1980-94
385	354	31	John Maclean (Aus)	3.6	1968-79

Most dismissals in an English season

Dis	ct	st	Name	Year
127	79	48	Leslie Ames	1929
122	70	52	Leslie Ames	1928
110	62	48	Hugo Yarnold	1949
107	77	30	George Duckworth	1928
107	96	11	Jimmy Binks	1960
104	40	64	Leslie Ames	1932
104	82	22	John Murray	1957
102	70	32	Frederick Huish	1913
102	95	7	John Murray	1960

Catches By Fielders
Most catches in an innings
7   Micky Stewart, Surrey v Northants at Northampton 7 Jun 1957

7   Tony Brown, Gloucestershire v Notts at Nottingham 26 Jul 1966

Most catches in a match
10   (4 & 6) Walter Hammond, Gloucestershire v Surrey at Cheltenham 16-17 Aug 1928

Most catches in a first-class career
(All English unless stated)

Catches	Name	Per match	Career
1018	Frank Woolley	1.04	1906-38
887	W.G. Grace (874 ACS)	1.00	1865-1908
830	Tony Lock	1.27	1946-71
819	Walter Hammond	1.29	1920-51
813	Brian Close	1.04	1949-86
784	John Langridge	1.37	1928-55
764	Wilfred Rhodes	0.61	1896-1930
758	Arthur Milton	1.22	1948-74
754	Patsy Hendren	0.91	1907-38
697	Peter Walker	1.49	1956-72
695	John Tunnicliffe	1.40	1891-1907
675	James Seymour	1.22	1900-26
671	Philip Mead	0.82	1905-36
644	Keith Fletcher	0.88	1962-88
638	Colin Cowdrey	0.92	1950-76
634	Micky Stewart	1.19	1954-72

Highest averages per match of those taking 300 or more

602	Graham Roope	1.50	1964-86
383	Bobby Simpson (Aus)	1.49	1952-78
328	Hugh Trumble (Aus)	1.54	1887-1904

Most catches in an English season

78	Walter Hammond	1928
77	Micky Stewart	1957
73	Peter Walker	1961
71	Philip Sharpe	1962
70	John Tunnicliffe	1901

County Championships

The first recorded inter-county match was contested in 1709 between Kent and Surrey, and the first county to be acclaimed as champions were Sussex in 1827. Such references became more frequent from 1864, the year in which overarm bowling was legalised, but it was not until the 1890 season that the County Championship was officially recognised and a points system introduced.

From 1827 to 1862 the Southern counties of Kent, Surrey and Sussex generally proved the best, with an occasional challenge from Nottinghamshire. From 1864, when eight counties took part in inter-county matches, to 1889 the following champion counties were proclaimed, principally on the basis of fewest matches lost (* shared):

Surrey   1864, 1887-8, 1889*

Gloucestershire   1873*, 1874, 1876-7

Nottinghamshire   1865, 1868, 1869*, 1871-2, 1873*, 1875, 1879*, 1880, 1882*, 1883-6, 1889*

Middlesex   1866

Yorkshire   1867, 1869*, 1870

Lancashire   1879*, 1881, 1882*, 1889*

Undecided in 1878

County Champions from 1890
The Championship was sponsored by Schweppes in 1977-83 and by Britannic Assurance from 1984. *Wins:*

30* Yorkshire   1893, 1896, 1898, 1900-2, 1905, 1908, 1912, 1919, 1922-5, 1931-3, 1935, 1937-9, 1946, 1949*, 1959-60, 1962-3, 1966-8

16*	Surrey	1890-2, 1894-5, 1899, 1914, 1950*, 1952-8, 1971
12#	Middlesex	1903, 1920-1, 1947, 1949*, 1976, 1977*, 1980, 1982, 1985, 1990, 1993
8*	Lancashire	1897, 1904, 1926-8, 1930, 1934, 1950*
7*	Kent	1906, 1909-10, 1913, 1970, 1977*, 1978
6	Essex	1979, 1983-4, 1986, 1991-2
5	Worcestershire	1964-5, 1974, 1988-9
4	Nottinghamshire	1907, 1929, 1981, 1987
4	Warwickshire	1911, 1951, 1972, 1994
2	Glamorgan	1948, 1969
2	Hampshire	1961, 1973
1	Derbyshire	1936
1	Leicestershire	1975

* *including 1 tie, # including two ties*

Most appearances: 763 Wilfred Rhodes (Yorkshire) 1898-1930, 707 Frank Woolley (Kent) 1906-38.

Gillette Cup/NatWest Bank Trophy

Introduced as the Gillette Cup in 1963 as a one-day knock-out event contested by the first-class counties over one innings per side of 65 overs (60 overs from 1964). From 1981 it has been contested for the NatWest Bank Trophy, and Ireland, Scotland and the leading minor counties also take part. *Wins:*

5	Lancashire	1970-2, 1975, 1990
4	Sussex	1963-4, 1978, 1986
4	Middlesex	1977, 1980, 1984, 1988
4	Warwickshire	1966, 1968, 1989, 1993
2	Yorkshire	1965, 1969
2	Kent	1967, 1974
2	Somerset	1979, 1983
2	Northamptonshire	1976, 1992
1	Gloucestershire 1973, Derbyshire 1981
1	Surrey 1982, Essex 1985, Nottinghamshire 1987
1	Hampshire 1991, Worcestershire 1994

Team Records (all 60 overs per innings)
Highest innings: 413-4 Somerset v Devon at Torquay 27 Jun 1990
Highest in final: 322-5 Warwickshire v Sussex at Lord's 4 Sep 1993
Lowest completed innings: 39 Ireland v Sussex at Hove 3 Jul 1985
Largest runs margin: 346 Somerset beat Devon (67) at Torquay 27 Jun 1990

Individual Innings Records
Highest innings: 206 Alvin Kallicharan, Warwickshire v Oxfordshire at Birmingham 4 Jul 1984
Best bowling: 8-21 Michael Holding, Derbyshire v Sussex at Hove 22 June 1988
Most economical bowling: 1-3 in 12 overs Jack Simmons, Lancashire v Suffolk at Bury St Edmunds 3 Jul 1985
Most dismissals: 7 (all ct) Alec Stewart, Surrey v Glamorgan at Swansea 27 Jul 1994

Individual Career Records 1963-94
Most runs: 2383 Graham Gooch (Essex) 1973-94
1964 Mike Gatting (Middlesex) 1975-94
1950 Dennis Amiss (Warwicks) 1963-87
1920 Clive Lloyd (Lancs) 1969-86

Most wickets: 81 Geoff Arnold (Surrey/Sussex) 1963-80, 79 Jack Simmons (Lancs) 1970-89
78 Peter Lever (Lancs) 1963-76
77 Derek Underwood (Kent) 1963-87
Most dismissals: 66 Bob Taylor (Derby) 1963-84
65 Alan Knott (Kent) 1965-85
61 Paul Downton (Kent, Middlesex) 1978-90
Most catches by fielder: 26 Jack Simmons (Lancs) 1970-89

Benson & Hedges Cup

A one-day competition played at 55 overs per innings, and contested by 22 teams, the 18 first-class counties and teams representing the Minor Counties, Ireland, Scotland and the Combined Universities. Played on a zonal basis of four groups of five and then by knock-out, except for 1993-4 when it was all by knock-out. *Wins:*

3	Kent	1973, 1976, 1978
3	Leicestershire	1972, 1975, 1985
3	Lancashire	1984, 1990, 1995
2	Somerset	1981-2
2	Middlesex	1983, 1986
2	Hampshire	1988, 1992
1	Surrey 1974, Gloucestershire 1977, Essex 1979
1	Northamptonshire 1980, Yorkshire 1987
1	Nottinghamshire 1989, Worcestershire 1991
1	Derbyshire 1993, Warwickshire 1994

Team Records
Highest innings: 388-7 Essex v Scotland at Chelmsford 30 Apr 1992
Lowest completed innings: 50 Hampshire v Yorkshire at Leeds 4 May 1991

Individual Innings Records
Highest innings: 198* Graham Gooch, Essex v Sussex at Hove 25 May 1982
Best bowling: 7-12 Wayne Daniel, Middlesex v Minor Counties (East) at Ipswich 22 Apr 1978
Most economical bowling: 1-3 in 11 overs Chris Old, Yorkshire v Middlesex at Lord's 6 Jun 1979
Most dismissals: 8 (all ct) Derek Taylor, Somerset v Combined Universities at Taunton 8 May 1982

Individual Career Records 1972-94
Most runs: 4934 Graham Gooch (Essex) 1973-95
2761 Chris Tavare (Universities, Kent, Somerset) 1975-93
2663 Derek Randall (Notts) 1972-93
2578 Mike Gatting (Middlesex) 1976-94
2557 Allan Lamb (Northants) 1978-94
Most wickets: 149 John Lever (Essex) 1972-89
132 Ian Botham (Somerset, Worcs, Durham) 1974-93
107 Stuart Turner (Essex, Minor Counties) 1972-88
107 Derek Underwood (Kent) 1972-87
Most dismissals: 122 David Bairstow (Yorks) 1972-90
88 Alan Knott (Kent) 1972-85
83 Geoff Humpage (Warwicks) 1976-9
Most catches by fielder: 62 Graham Gooch (Essex) 1973-94

Sunday League

Introduced in 1969 and played on Sundays by the first-class counties in matches of 40 overs per innings (except 50 in 1993). John Player League 1969-86, Refuge Assurance League 1987-91, no sponsor 1992, Axa Equity and Law from 1993. *Wins:*

3	Kent	1972-3, 1976
3	Essex	1981, 1984-5
3	Hampshire	1975, 1978, 1986
3	Worcestershire	1971, 1987-8
3	Lancashire	1969-70, 1989
2	Leicestershire	1974, 1977
2	Warwickshire	1980, 1994
1	Somerset 1979, Sussex 1982, Yorkshire 1983	
1	Derbyshire 1990, Nottinghamshire 1991	
1	Middlesex 1992, Glamorgan 1993	

Refuge Assurance Cup

In 1988-91 the first four teams in the Refuge Assurance League met in semi-finals, and then a final. *Winners:* 1988 Lancashire, 1989 Essex, 1990 Middlesex, 1991 Worcestershire

Sunday League Team Records

Highest innings: 375-4 Surrey v Yorkshire at Scarborough 11 Sep 1994
Lowest completed innings: 23 Middlesex v Yorkshire at Leeds 23 Jun 1974
Largest runs margin: 220 runs Somerset (360-3) beat Glamorgan (140) at Neath 22 Jul 1990

Individual Innings Records

Highest innings: 176 Graham Gooch, Essex v Glamorgan at Southend 17 Jul 1983
Best bowling: 8-26 Keith Boyce, Essex v Lancashire at Manchester 30 May 1971; 4 wickets in 4 balls Alan Ward, Derbyshire v Sussex, Derby 7 Jun 1970

Most economical bowling: 0-0 in 8 overs Brian Langford, Somerset v Essex at Yeovil 27 Jul 1969
Most dismissals: 7 (6 ct, 1 st) Bob Taylor, Derbyshire v Lancashire at Manchester 4 May 1975

Season's Records

Most runs: 917 (av. 70.53) Tom Moody (Worcestershire) 1991
Most wickets: 34 (av. 13.17) Bob Clapp (Somerset) 1974, Clive Rice (Notts) 1986
Most dismissals: 29 (26 ct 3 st) Steven Rhodes (Worcs) 1987

Individual Career Records 1969-94

Most runs: 7906 Graham Gooch (Essex) 1973-94, 7378 Wayne Larkins (Northants, Durham) 1972-94, 7062 Derek Randall (Notts) 1971-93, 7040 Dennis Amiss (Warwicks) 1969-87, 6935 Bill Athey (Yorks, Gloucs) 1976-94, 6650 Clive Radley (Middlesex) 1969-87, 6639 David Turner (Hants) 1969-89, 6506 Peter Willey (Northants, Leics) 1969-91
Most wickets: 386 John Lever (Essex) 1969-89, 346 Derek Underwood (Kent) 1969-87, 333 John Emburey (Middlesex) 1975-94, 307 Jack Simmons (Lancs) 1969-89, 303 Stuart Turner (Essex) 1969-86, 284 Norman Gifford (Worcs/Warwicks) 1969-88, 281 Eddie Hemmings (Warwicks, Notts, Sussex) 1969-94, 267 John Shepherd (Kent/Glos) 1969-87
Most dismissals: 257 David Bairstow (Yorkshire) 1970-90, 236 Bob Taylor (Derby) 1969-84, 223 Eifion Jones (Glamorgan) 1969-83, 218 Alan Knott (Kent) 1969-85
Most catches by fielder: 101 John Steele (Leics, Glamorgan) 1970-86, 100 Paul Terry (Hants) 1978-94

First Class Counties

Placings in the first three in the County Championship 1890-1994 and Sunday League (SL) 1969-94, and wins (W), runners-up (RU) or losing semi-finalists (SF) in the Gillette Cup/Nat West Bank Trophy (GC/NW) 1963-94 and Benson & Hedges Cup (B&H) 1972-94. The final column shows the year in which the counties first took part in the Championship or in its preceding inter-county matches from 1864.

County	County Champs			GC/NW			B&H			SL			First Year
	1st	2nd	3rd	W	RU	SF	W	RU	SF	1st	2nd	3rd	
Derbyshire	1	1	4	1	1	1	1	2	1	1	-	1	1871
Durham	-	-	-	-	-	-	-	-	-	-	-	-	1992
Essex	6	3	2	1	-	3	1	4	3	3	5'	3	1895
Glamorgan	2	2	3	-	1	1	-	-	1	1	-	-	1921
Gloucestershire	-	6	7	1	-	3	1	-	1	-	1	1	1870
Hampshire	2	3	5	1	-	8	2	-	3	3	1	3	1864
Kent	7'	9	9"	2	3	2	3	3	5	3	3	4	1864
Lancashire	8'	13'	10'	5	3	5	2	2	4	3	2	2	1865
Leicestershire	1	2	3'	-	1	2	3	1	2	2	1	2	1895
Middlesex	12"	11	13	4	2	7	2	1	2	1	1	3	1864
Northamptonshire	-	4	4	2	4	3	1	1	2	-	-	1	1905
Nottinghamshire	4	5	5	1	1	1	1	1	3	1	2	1	1864
Somerset	-	-	5	2	2	5	2	-	5	1	6'	-	1882
Surrey	16'	7	11	1	3	5	1	2	4	-	-	1	1864
Sussex	-	7	2'	4	4	4	-	-	1	1	1	1	1864
Warwickshire	4	3	1	4	4	6	1	1	4	2	-	1	1895
Worcestershire	5	5'	1	1	3	6	1	4	2	3	3	1	1899
Yorkshire	30'	13"	11'	2	-	2	1	1	3	1	1	-	1864

' Including one tie for place, " including two ties for place

Cricket in Australia

Most Runs in an Australian Season

Runs	Av.	Player	Season
1690	93.88	Don Bradman (NSW)	1928/9
1659	63.80	Neil Harvey (Vic)	1952/3
1586	113.28	Don Bradman (NSW)	1929/30
1553	91.35	Walter Hammond (Eng)	1928/9
1552	86.22	Don Bradman (SA)	1936/7

Don Bradman exceeded 1000 runs in a record 12 Australian seasons

Most Wickets in an Australian Season

Wkts	Ave.	Player	Season
106	13.59	Charlie Turner (NSA)	1887/8
93	22.54	George Giffen (SA) *	1894/5
82	23.69	Clarrie Grimmett (SA)	1929/30
82	19.25	Richie Benaud (NSW)	1958/9
81	22.53	Arthur Mailey (NSW)	1920/1

* George Giffen also scored 902 runs (av. 50.11) in 1894/5 for the best ever all-round figures

Most Dismissals in an Australian Season

67 (63 ct 4 st)   Rodney Marsh (WA)   1975/6

Sheffield Shield

The annual first-class inter-state competition has been contested for the shield, purchased with money donated by the 3rd Earl of Sheffield, from 1891/2. The original three states were joined by Queensland in 1926/7, Western Australia 1947/8 and Tasmania 1977/8. From 1983 the Shield winner has been determined by a final between the top two teams. *Winners: year shown is that of second half of the season:*

42 New South Wales 1896-7, 1900, 1902-7, 1909, 1911-2, 1914, 1920-1, 1923, 1926, 1929, 1932-3, 1938, 1940, 1949-50, 1952, 1954-62, 1965-6, 1983, 1985-6, 1990, 1993-4
25 Victoria 1893, 1895, 1898-9, 1901, 1908, 1915, 1922, 1924-5, 1928, 1930-1, 1934-5, 1937, 1947, 1951, 1963, 1967, 1970, 1974, 1979-80, 1991
12 South Australia 1894, 1910, 1913, 1927, 1936, 1939, 1953, 1964, 1969, 1971, 1976, 1982
11 Western Australia 1948, 1968, 1972-3, 1975, 1977-8, 1981, 1984, 1987-9, 1992
1 Queensland 1995

Limited Overs Competitions

The Australian states currently contest a knock-out competition for the Mercantile Mutual Cup at matches of 50 overs per innings. Sponsors have been V&G two years from 1969/70, Coca-Cola two years from 1971/2, Gillette six years from 1973/4, McDonald's nine years from 1978/9, FAI Insurance four years from 1988/9 and Mercantile Mutual 1992/3. New Zealand also took part in the first six years. *Winners: (year shown is for second half of the season):*

8 Western Australia 1971, 1974, 1977-8, 1983, 1986, 1990-1
5 New South Wales 1985, 1988, 1992-4
4 Queensland 1976, 1981-2, 1989
3 New Zealand 1970, 1973, 1975
2 Victoria 1972, 1980, 1995
2 South Australia 1984, 1987
1 Tasmania 1979

Innings records

Highest team score: 325-6 S.Australia v Tasmania in final at Hobart 15 Mar 1987
Highest individual innings: 164 Rick McCosker, NSW v S.Australia at Sydney 3 Dec 1981
Best bowling: 7-34 Carl Rackemann, Queensland v S.Australia, 19 Feb 1989
Most economical bowling: 1-8 in 10 overs Graham Porter, W.Australia v Victoria at Perth 10 Oct 1986
Most dismissals: 6 (6 ct) Ken Wadsworth, New Zealand v NSW at Sydney 30 Dec 1969

India

Most runs in a season: 1604 (av. 64.16) Chandu Borde 1964/5. Vijay Hazare scored 1423 runs in 1943/4 at an average of 177.87, the highest ever recorded for 1000 runs in a season.
Most wickets in a season: 88 Bishen Bedi 1974/5 (av. 15.02) and 1976/7 (av. 19.30).
Most dismissals in a season: 43 (32ct 11st) Farokh Engineer 1964/5, 43 (37ct 6st) Vijay Yadav 1991/2

In the Indian sub-continent (India, Pakistan, Sri Lanka and Burma)

Most runs in a season: 2121 (av. 88.37), including a record 10 centuries, Sunil Gavaskar (Ind) 1978/9
Most wickets in a season: 116 (av. 13.78) Maurice Tate (Eng) 1926/7

Ranji Trophy

The annual Indian first-class inter-state competition was instituted in 1934 in memory of K S Ranjitsinhji. It is contested on a zonal basis, culminating in a knock-out competition. *Winners: year given is that of the second half of the season*

32 Bombay 1935-6, 1942, 1945, 1949, 1952, 1954, 1956-7, 1959-73, 1975-7, 1981, 1984-5, 1994-5
6 Delhi 1979-80, 1982, 1986, 1989, 1992
4 Baroda 1943, 1947, 1950, 1958
4 Holkar 1946, 1948, 1951, 1953
3 Karnataka 1974, 1978, 1983
2 Maharashtra 1940-1
2 Hyderabad 1938, 1987
2 Bengal 1939, 1990
1 Nawanagar 1937, Western India 1944,
1 Madras 1955, Tamil Nadu 1988
1 Haryana 1991, Punjab 1993

New Zealand

Most runs in season: 1676 (av. 93.11) Martin Crowe 1986/7
Most wickets in season: 66 (av. 16.48) Stephen Boock 1977/8
Most dismissals in season: 41 Ervin McSweeney 1984/5 (31 ct 10 st) and 1989/90 (35ct 6st)

Plunket Shield

First-class competition run on a challenge basis 1906-21, and on a league basis 1921/2 to 1974/5. The Shield was presented by Lord Plunket, Governor-General of New Zealand. Challenge holders: 1906-7 Canterbury, 1907-11 Auckland, 1911-2 Canterbury, 1912-3 Auckland, 1913-8 Canterbury, 1918-9 Wellington, 1919-20 Canterbury, 1920-1 Auckland, 1921 Wellington.

League wins: year given is that of second half of the season:

14	Wellington	1924, 1926, 1928, 1930, 1932, 1936, 1950, 1955, 1957, 1961-2, 1966, 1973-4
12	Auckland	1922, 1927, 1929, 1934, 1937-40, 1947, 1959, 1964, 1969
9	Canterbury	1923, 1931, 1935, 1946, 1949, 1952, 1956, 1960, 1965,
9	Otago	1925, 1933, 1948, 1951, 1953, 1958, 1970, 1972, 1975
4	Central Districts	1954, 1967-8, 1971
1	Northern Districts	1963

Shell Series

From 1975-6 the first-class provincial competition has been sponsored by Shell. In the first four years the Shell Cup was awarded to the League winners and the Shell Trophy to winners of a knock-out competition. From 1979/80 the Shell Trophy has been won by the league winners, and the Shell Cup by the winners of the limited-overs competition.

Cup winners 1976-9: 1976 Canterbury, 1977 Northern Districts, 1978 Canterbury, 1979 Otago.

Trophy winners *(* shared)*

5	Auckland	1978, 1981, 1989, 1991, 1995
4	Otago	1977, 1979, 1986, 1988
4	Wellington	1982, 1983, 1985, 1990
3	Northern Districts	1980, 1992*, 1993
3	Canterbury	1976, 1984, 1994
2	Central Districts	1987, 1992*

Limited Overs Competition

Now contested for the Shell Cup, but previously sponsored by the NZ Motor Corporation, 1971-7 and Gillette 1977-9.

8	Canterbury	1972, 1976-8, 1986, 1992-4
7	Auckland	1973, 1979, 1981, 1983-4, 1987, 1990
5	Wellington	1974-5, 1982, 1989, 1991
2	Northern Districts	1980, 1995
1	Central Districts	1985, Otago 1988

Most runs in season: 1649 (av. 63.42) Saadat Ali 1983/4
Most wickets in season: 107 (av. 16.06) Ijaz Faqih 1985/6
Most dismissals in season: 70 (62ct 8st) Ashraf Ali 1986/7

Quaid-e-Azam Trophy

Pakistan's major national first-class championship is named after Mohammad Ali Jinnah, who was known as Quaid-e-Azam, or 'Great Leader'. *Winners: year given is that of second half of the season:*

9	Karachi	1955, 1959-60, 1963 (Karachi A), 1968, 1986, 1991-3 (Whites)
5	National Bank	1976, 1979, 1982, 1984, 1987
5	Karachi Blues	1962, 1964, 1966, 1971, 1995
4	United Bank	1977, 1981, 1983, 1985
3	PIA	1970, 1980, 1990
2	Bahawalpur	1954, 1958
2	Punjab	1957, 1975 (Punjab A)
2	Railways	1973-4
2	Habib Bank	1978, 1988
2	Lahore	1969, 1994 (Lahore City)
1	ADBP	1989

Most runs in a season: 1915 (av. 68.39) John Reid (NZ) 1961/2
Most wickets in a season: 106 (av. 19.39) Richie Benaud (Aus) 1957/8
Most dismissals in a season: 65 (57ct 8st) Ray Jennings 1982/3

Currie Cup - Castle Cup

The annual first-class competition for the South African provinces. The Cup was presented by Sir Donald Currie and first contested in the 1889/90 season. Until 1966 it was not normally contested in the seasons when a touring team visited South Africa. From 1991/2 the competition has been for the Castle Cup. *Winners (* shared wins): year given is that of second half of the season:*

28 (4*)	Transvaal	1890, 1895, 1903-5, 1907, 1922*, 1924, 1926-7, 1930, 1935, 1938*, 1951, 1959, 1966*, 1969, 1970*, 1971-3, 1979-80, 1983-5, 1987-8
22 (3*)	Natal	1911, 1913, 1922*, 1934, 1937, 1938*, 1947-8, 1952, 1955, 1960-1, 1963-4, 1966*, 1967-8, 1974, 1976-7, 1981, 1995
17 (3*)	Western Province	1893-4, 1897-8, 1909, 1921, 1922*, 1932, 1953, 1956, 1970*, 1975, 1978, 1982, 1986, 1990*, 1991
3 (1*)	Eastern Province	1989, 1990*, 1992
2	Orange Free State	1993-4
1	Kimberley (now Griqualand West)	1891

Limited Overs Competition

The South African limited overs competition was contested for the Gillette Cup from 1969/70 to 1976/7, for the Datsun Shield 1977/8 to 1982/3, the Nissan Shield 1983/4 to 1991/2 and the Total Power Shield 1992/3. Not held 1993/4. *Winners:*

9	Transvaal	1974, 1979-81, 1983-6, 1991
5	Western Province	1970-1, 1973, 1982, 1989
4	Eastern Province	1972, 1976, 1988, 1990
3	Natal	1975, 1977, 1987
2	Orange Free State	1992-3
1	Rhodesia	1978

Night Trophy

A limited overs competition played at night under floodlights was introduced in 1981/2 and sponsored from then by Benson & Hedges. *Winners:*

5	Transvaal	1982-3, 1985, 1991, 1993
3	Western Province	1986-8
3	Orange Free State	1989, 1994-5
2	Eastern Province	1990, 1992
1	Natal	1984

Most runs in a season: 1765 (av. 135.76) Patsy Hendren (Eng) 1929/30
Most wickets in a season: 80 (av. 12.46) Edward Dowson (Eng) 1901/02
Most dismissals in a season: 33 Jeffrey Dujon 1983 (31ct 2 st) and 1986 (33ct)

Red Stripe Cup (Shell Shield from 1966 to 1987)

This annual first-class competition for the West Indian teams has been contested annually from 1966, except in 1968. *Winners (* shared):*

14	Barbados	1966-7, 1972, 1974, 1976*, 1977-80, 1982, 1984, 1986, 1991, 1995
5	Guyana	1973, 1975, 1983, 1987, 1993
4	Trinidad & Tobago	1970-1, 1976*, 1985
4	Jamaica	1969, 1988-9, 1992
2	Leeward Islands	1990, 1994
1	Combined Islands	1981

There was a triangular Inter-Colonial tournament first held in 1893, up to 1939, but not resumed after the war. Wins: Trinidad 11, Barbados 10, Demerara/British Guiana 5.

Other post-war tournaments prior to the Shell Shield were won by British Guiana in 1957, 1962 and 1964.

Women's Cricket

The first women's cricket match recorded was at Gosden Common in Surrey, England in 1745. The first women's club was the White Heather Club, founded at Nun Appleton, Yorkshire in 1887 and the first women's Test match was played between England and Australia at Brisbane on 28-31 December 1934.

The Women's Cricket Association (WCA) was formed in England in 1926 and the International Women's Cricket Council (IWCC) in 1958.

World Cup

First held in 1973. *Winners:*

1973 England
1978 Australia
1982 Australia
1988 Australia
1993 England

Highest team score
297 New Zealand v Netherlands 1988

Highest individual scores
143* Lindsay Reeler (Australia) v Netherlands 29 Nov 1988
138* Jeanette Brittin, England v International XI, Hamilton (NZ) 14 Jan 1982
134* Lynne Thomas (England) v International XI 23 Jun 1973

Best bowling
6-10 Jackie Lord (New Zealand) v India 14 Jan 1982
6-20 Glenys Page (New Zealand) v Trinidad & Tobago 23 Jun 1973

Test records

Highest innings: 503-5 dec. England v New Zealand, Christchurch, 16-18 Feb 1935
Lowest innings: 35 England v Australia, St.Kilda, Melbourne, 22 Feb 1958

Individual Records
Highest innings
193 Denise Annetts, Australia v England, Collingham, 23-24 Aug 1987 (381 min)
190 Sandiya Aggarwal, India v England, Worcester, 14 July 1986 (563 min)

189 Betty Snowball, England v New Zealand, Christchurch, 16 Feb 1935 (222 min)

Best bowling
7-6 Mary Duggan, England v Australia, St.Kilda, Melbourne, 22 Feb 1958
7-7 Betty Wilson, Australia v England, St.Kilda, Melbourne, 22 Feb 1958 (including the only hat trick in women's Test cricket)

Best match analysis:
11-16 Betty Wilson, 7-7 and 4-9, as above 22 Feb 1958
11-63 Julia Greenwood, 6-46 and 5-17, England v West Indies, Canterbury, 16-18 June 1979

Most dismissals
8 in an innings: Lisa Nye (6c, 2 st) for England v New Zealand, New Plymouth, 12-15 Feb 1992

Career records
Most Tests: 25 Rachael Heyhoe-Flint, England 1960-79
Most runs: 1814 Rachael Heyhoe-Flint (Eng) in 25 Tests, av. 49.02 1960-79
Highest average: 59.88 Enid Bakewell (Eng), 1078 runs in 12 Tests 1968-79
Most centuries: 4 Enid Bakewell (Eng) and Rachel Heyhoe-Flint (Eng)
Most wickets: 77 Mary Duggan (Eng) in 17 Tests, av 13.49 1949-63
Most dismissals: 53 Christina Matthews (Aus) in 19 Tests

England have played Australia in 33 Tests from 1934 to 1987, England have won 6, Australia 6, one match was abandoned and 20 have been drawn.

European Cup
First held in 1989, and won by England then and in 1990, 1991. and 1995

National Club League Competition
Run annually by the WCA from 1988, with English clubs playing in area competitions leading to national semi-finals and final. The 1988 Finals were abandoned due to bad weather, with Somerset Wanderers, Wakefield, Redoubtables and Vagabonds reaching semi-finals. *Subsequent winners:*

1989-90	Wakefield
1991	Wolverhampton
1992-3	Wakefield
1994	Redoutables

Club Knockout Competition
Organised annually by the WCA.*Winners:*

1974	Edgbaston
1975	Wallington
1977	Wallington
1978	Riverside
1979-82	Gunnersbury
1983	Vagabonds
1984	Invicta
1985	Somerset Wanderers
1987	Vagabonds
1988	Wolverhampton
1989-90	Wakefield
1991	North Riding

1993   Wakefield
1994   Sherwood & Newark
Not held in 1976, 1986, 1992

Area Championships
Organised annually since 1980 (except for 1983-4,

1987) by the WCA. *Wins:*

Middlesex   1980-1, 1985, 1986 (tied with Kent)
East Midlands   1988-91
West Midlands   1982
Yorkshire   1992-4

Croquet

Croquet is played with ball and mallet and six hoops with a peg laid out on a grass lawn 35 yd (31.9m) long by 28 yd (25.6m) wide. While its exact origins are obscure, it was probably derived from the French game Jeu de Mail, played from the 12th century. A game resembling croquet, probably of foreign origin, was played in Ireland in the 1830s. Jean Jaques, the sports goods manufacturers, made the first croquet sets in England in the 1850s and published a book on the game in 1857. Ten years later the first championships were held at Evesham, Worcestershire.

The All-England Croquet Club was founded at Wimbledon in 1869 and the current governing body, the Croquet Association was formed in 1896. The game was played at the 1900 Olympic Games, when all the contestants were French.

World Championships
First held at Hurlingham in 1989. Cancelled in 1993.
1989   Joe Hogan (NZ)
1990   Robert Fulford (UK)
1991   John Walters (UK)
1992   Robert Fulford (UK)
1994   Robert Fulford (UK)
1995   Chris Clarke (UK)

MacRobertson International Shield
Contested by Australia, Great Britain and New Zealand, first in 1925. *Wins:*
9   Great Britain   1925, 1937, 1956, 1963, 1969, 1974, 1982, 1990, 1993
3   Australia   1928, 1930, 1935
3   New Zealand   1950, 1979, 1986

The Croquet Championship
First held in 1867. Recent champions and most wins:

Open Championship
1977   Michael Heap
1978   Nigel Aspinall
1979   David Openshaw
1980   William de R Prichard
1981   David Openshaw
1982-4 Nigel Aspinall
1985   David Openshaw
1986   Joe Hogan (NZ)
1987   Mark Avery
1988   Stephen Mulliner
1989   Joe Hogan (NZ)
1990   Stephen Mulliner
1991-2 Robert Fulford
1993-5 Reg Bamford (SAf)
Most wins
10 John W Solomon 1953, 1956, 1959, 1961, 1963-8

8   Nigel Aspinall 1969, 1974-6, 1978, 1982-4
7   Humphrey Hicks 1932, 1939, 1947-50, 1952
5   Cyril Corbally 1902-3, 1906, 1908, 1913
Most wins by a woman
4   Dorothy Steel 1925, 1933, 1935-6

Open Doubles
First played in 1924.
1977-8 Nigel Aspinall & William Ormerod
1979   Bernard Neal & S R Hemsted
1980   William de B Prichard & Stephen Mulliner
1981   Stephen Mulliner & Mark Ormerod
1982   Martin Murray & Andrew Hope
1983   John McCullough & Phil Cordingley
1984   Nigel Aspinall & Stephen Mulliner
1985   David Openshaw & Mark Avery
1986   Nigel Aspinall & Stephen Mulliner
1987   David Openshaw & Mark Avery
1988   Nigel Aspinall & Stephen Mulliner
1989   Joe Hogan & Bob Jackson (NZ)
1990-3 Robert Fulford & Chris Clarke
1994   Reg Bamford(SAf) & Stephen Mulliner
1995   S Cornish & David Maugham
Most wins
10 John W Solomon & Edmond Cotter 1954-5, 1958-9, 1961-5, 1969
10 Nigel Aspinall with William Ormerod 1971-2, 1975-6, 1977-8, with J W Simon 1966, 1968, 1970, with Stephen Mulliner 1984, 1986, 1988

Men's Championship
First played in 1925.
1977   Edgar Jackson
1978   Paul Hands
1979   George Noble
1980   Martin Murray
1981   David Openshaw
1982   Martin Murray
1983   Nigel Aspinall
1984-5 Stephen Mulliner
1986   David Foulser
1987   Keith Aiton
1988   Mark Saurin
1989   Keith Aiton
1990   Robert Fulford
1991   David Openshaw
1992   Colin Irwin
1993   Reg Bamford (SAf)
1994   Michael Taylor (Aus)
Most wins
10 John W Solomon 1951, 1953, 1958-60, 1962, 1964-5, 1971-2
9   Humphrey Hicks 1930, 1932, 1948-50, 1955-6, 1961, 1966

Women's Championship

First played in 1869.

1980	Barbara Meachem
1981	Veronica Carlisle
1982-3	Susan Wiggins (NZ)
1984	Veronica Carlisle
1985	Mary Collin
1986	Susan Wiggins (NZ)
1987	Mary Collin
1988	Debbie Cornelius
1989	Bo Harris
1990	Frances Ransom
1991-3	Gail Curry

Note she won in 1993 under the name of 'D Root'

1994	Debbie Cornelius

Most wins:

15 Dorothy Steel 1919, 1922, 1925-7, 1929-30, 1932-9
6 Miss Walsh 1871-3, 1878-80
6 Joan Warwick 1960, 1962, 1965-6, 1968-9
6 Hope Rotherham 1952-3, 1955, 1959, 1963-4

Mixed Doubles

First played in 1899.

1980	Brian Sykes & Susan Sykes (née Foden)
1981	Martin Murray & Barbara Meacham
1982	Nigel Aspinall & Carol Knox
1983	Martin Murray & KayYeoman
1984	Ian Bond & Veronica Carlisle
1985	Keith Aiton & Mary Collin
1986	Tom Griffith & Jan Macleod
1987	Nigel Aspinall & Debbie Cornelius
1988	Paul Smith & Lady Carmen Bazley
1989	Ian Maugham & Bo Harris
1990	Mark Saurin & Fiona McCoig
1991	Ray Ransom & Frances Ransome
1992	John Haslam & Gail Curry
1993	David Goacher & Frances Ransome
1994	Lewis Palmer & Annabel McDiarmid

Most titles at all events:

31 John W Solomon 10 open, 10 men 's, 10 doubles, 1 mixed doubles
31 Dorothy Steel 4 open, 15 women 's, 5 doubles, 7 mixed doubles
27 Humphrey Hicks 7 open, 9 men 's, 7 doubles, 4 mixed doubles

President's Cup - British Masters

An annual invitation event for the best eight players, first held in 1934, renamed the British Masters from 1992.

Most wins:

11 Nigel Aspinall 1969-70, 1973-6, 1978, 1980, 1982, 1984-5
9 John W Solomon 1955, 1957-9, 1962-4, 1968, 1971
6 Edmond Cotter 1949-50, 1952-3, 1956, 1960
5 Humphrey Hicks 1947-8, 1951, 1954, 1961
5 Stephen Mulliner 1981, 1983, 1986-7, 1992

Other recent winners

1988	Chris Clarke
1989	Robert Fulford
1990	David Maugham
1991	Chris Clarke
1993-4	David Maugham

The lowest ever handicap was minus 5.5 by Humphrey Hicks. The limit is now fixed at minus 5.

Curling

Curling resembles bowls on ice and is known as the 'roaring game', due to the noise made by the curling stone (which weighs about 40lb/18kg) as it runs over the ice rink. The curlers use brooms to sweep the rink ahead of their stone to remove impediments and smooth the ice. The game became popular in Scotland, but it may have originated in the Netherlands more than 400 years ago. The Grand Caledonian Curling Club was formed in Edinburgh in 1838. Five years later it added Royal to its title and eventually became the international governing body of the sport.

Scots introduced curling to Canada, where the first club was the Royal Montreal Curling Club, founded in 1807. The first club in the USA was the Orchard Lake Club, formed in Michigan in 1832.

The first international match was between Canada and the USA in 1884, the start of the Gordon International Medal series, now contested annually by clubs representing the Canadian branch of the Royal Caledonian Curling Club and the Grand National Curling Club of America. The Strathcona Cup series between Canada and Scotland started in 1903. The International Curling Federation was founded in 1966 and had 30 member nations affiliated in 1992.

World Championships

Men

Played annually for the Scotch Whisky Cup 1959-67 and for the Air Canada Silver Broom 1968-86. *Winners:*

Year	Nation	Skip
1959-60	Canada	Ernie Richardson
1961	Canada	Hec Gervais
1962-3	Canada	Ernie Richardson
1964	Canada	Lyall Dagg
1965	USA	Bud Somerville
1966	Canada	Ron Northcott
1967	Scotland	Chuck Hay
1968-9	Canada	Ron Northcott
1970-1	Canada	Don Duguid
1972	Canada	Orest Meleschuk
1973	Sweden	Kjell Oscarius
1974	USA	Bud Somerville
1975	Switzerland	Otto Danielli
1976	USA	Bruce Roberts
1977	Sweden	Ragnar Kamp
1978	USA	Bob Nichols
1979	Norway	Kristian Sørum
1980	Canada	Rick Falk
1981	Switzerland	Jürg Tanner
1982	Canada	Al Hackner
1983	Canada	Ed Werenich

1984	Norway	Eigel Ramsfjell
1985	Canada	Al Hackner
1986	Canada	Ed Lukovich
1987	Canada	Russ Howard
1988	Norway	Eigel Ramsfjell
1989	Canada	Pat Ryan
1990	Canada	Ed Werenich
1991	Scotland	David Smith
1992	Switzerland	Markus Eggler
1993	Canada	Russ Howard
1994	Canada	Rick Folk
1995	Canada	Kerry Burtnyk

Most wins: 23 Canada, 4 USA
Most times as winning skip: 4 Ernie Richardson, 3 Ron Northcott

Women

Played annually from 1979. *Winners:*

1979	Switzerland	Gaby Casanova
1980	Canada	Mary Mitchell
1981	Sweden	Elisabeth Högström
1982	Denmark	Marianne Jørgensen
1983	Switzerland	Erika Müller
1984	Canada	Connie Laliberte

1985	Canada	Linda Moore
1986	Canada	Marilyn Darte
1987	Canada	Pat Saunders
1988	FR Germany	Andrea Schöpp
1989	Canada	Heather Euston
1990-1	Norway	Djordy Nordby
1992	Sweden	Elisabet Johansson
1993-4	Canada	Sandra Peterson
1995	Sweden	Elisabet Gustafson

Most wins: 8 Canada

Olympic Games

Curling was included as a demonstration sport at the Games of 1924, 1932 and 1964, and again in 1988 and 1992. A specialised German version of the game was demonstrated in 1936. *Recent winners:*

Men

1988	Norway	Eigil Ramsfjell
1992	Switzerland	Urs Dick

Women

1988	Canada	Linda Moore
1992	Germany	Andrea Schöpp

Cycling

The forerunner of the bicycle, the célerifère was demonstrated in the garden of the Palais Royale, Paris in 1791. The first treadle-propelled bicycle was designed by Scottish blacksmith Kirkpatrick Macmillan in 1839, but the first practical bicycle was the vélocipède built in March 1861 by Pierre and his son Ernest Michaux of Paris. The first cycling club, the Liverpool Velocipede Club, was formed in 1867 and the first race took place the following year, over 1200 metres at the Parc St Cloud, Paris, and won by Englishman James Moore. The first international organisation was the International Cyclist Association (ICA), founded in 1892, which promoted the first world championships the following year. The current governing body, the Union Cycliste International (UCI) was founded in 1900. In 1965 two federations were formed within the UCI - the Fédération de Cyclisme Amateur (FIAC) and the Fédération Internationale de Cyclisme Professional (FICP). The UCI had 162 member nations by 1994.

Olympic Games

Cycling was included in the first Olympics of 1896 and at every Games since except 1904 when there were no official events. A women's road race was introduced in 1984, and the sprint added in 1988 *Winners:*

Men

Sprint

1896 and 1900 over 2000 metres, since then at 1000 metres. Now raced over the best of three races.

1896	Paul Masson (Fra) 4:56.0
1900	Georges Taillandier (Fra) 2:52.0 *2000m* (13.0)
1906	Francesco Verri (Ita) 1:42.2
1908	*declared void as riders exceeded time limit*
1920	Maurice Peeters (Hol) 1:38.3
1924	Lucien Michard (Fra)
1928	Roger Beaufrand (Fra)
1932	Jacobus van Egmond (Hol)
1936	Toni Merkens (Ger)
1948	Mario Ghella (Ita)
1952	Enzo Sacchi (Ita)
1956	Michel Rousseau (Fra)
1960	Sante Gaiardoni (Ita)
1964	Giovanni Pettenella (Ita)
1968	Daniel Morelon (Fra)
1972	Daniel Morelon (Fra)
1976	Anton Tkac (Cs)
1980	Lutz Hesslich (GDR)
1984	Mark Gorski (USA)
1988	Lutz Hesslich (GDR)
1992	Jens Fiedler (Ger)

1000 metres time trial

1896 and 1906 raced over 333.33 metres.

1896	Paul Masson (Fra) 24.0
1906	Francesco Verri (Ita) 22.8
1928	Willy Falck-Hansen (Den) 1:14.4
1932	Edgar Gray (Aus) 1.13.0
1936	Arie van Vliet (Hol) 1:12.0
1948	Jacques Dupont (Fra) 1:13.5
1952	Russell Mockridge (Aus) 1:11.1
1956	Leandro Faggin (Ita) 1:09.8
1960	Sante Gaiardoni (Ita) 1:07.27
1964	Patrick Sercu (Bel) 1:09.59
1968	Pierre Trentin (Fra) 1:03.91
1972	Niels-Christian Fredborg (Den) 1:06.44
1976	Klaus-Jürgen Grünke (GDR) 1:05.93
1980	Lothar Thoms (GDR) 1:02.955
1984	Freddy Schmidtke (FRG) 1:06.10
1988	Aleksandr Kirichenko (USSR) 1:04.499
1992	José Manuel Moreno (Spa) 1:03.342

4000 metres individual pursuit
1964 Jirí Daler (Cs) 5:04.75
1968 Daniel Rebillard (Fra) 4:41.71
1972 Knut Knudsen (Nor) 4:45.74
1976 Gregor Braun (GDR) 4:47.61
1980 Robert Dill-Bundi (Swi) 4:35.66

1984 Steve Hegg (USA) 4:39.55
1988 Gintautas Umaras (USSR) 4:32.00
1992 Chris Boardman (UK)
Boardman caught his opponent Jens Lehmann a lap from the finish; he recorded a record time of 4:24.496 in a preliminary round.

50 kilometres points race
Introduced 1984
1984 Roger Ilegems (Bel) 37 pts
1988 Dan Frost (Den) 38 pts
1992 Giovanni Lombardi (Ita) 44

4000 metres team pursuit
Held over 1810.5 metres in 1908.
1908 Great Britain 2:18.6
1920 Italy 5:20.0
1924 Italy 5:15.0
1928 Italy 5:01.8
1932 Italy 4:53.0
1936 France 4:45.0
1948 France 4:57.8
1952 Italy 4:46.1
1956 Italy 4:37.4
1960 Italy 4:30.90

1964 FR Germany 4:35.67
1968 Denmark 4:22.44
1972 FR Germany 4:22.14
1976 FR Germany 4:21.06
1980 USSR 4:15.70
1984 Australia 4:25.99
1988 USSR 4:13.31
1992 Germany 4:08.791

Team road race
1912-20 combined times of best four riders in the individual race. 1924-52 combined times of best three. 1956 based on placings.
1912 Sweden 44:35:33.6
1920 France 19:16:43.2
1924 France 19:13:14.0

1928 Denmark 15:09:14.0
1932 Italy 7:27:15.2
1936 France 7:39:16.2
1948 Belgium 15:58:17.4
1952 Belgium 15:20:46.6
1956 France 22 points

100 km team time trial
1960 Italy 2:14:33.53
1964 Netherlands 2:26:31.19
1968 Netherlands 2:07:49.06
1972 USSR 2:11:17.8
1976 USSR 2:08:53.0
1980 USSR 2:01:21.7
1984 Italy 1:58:28.0
1988 GDR 1:57:47.7
1992 Germany 2:01:39

Individual road race
Distance in kilometres shown for each year.
1896 87km Aristidis Konstantinidis (Gre) 3:22:31.0
1906 84 Fernand Vast (Fra) 2:41:28.0
1912 320 Rudolph Lewis (SAf) 10:42:39.0
1920 175 Harry Stenqvist (Swe) 4:40:01.8
1924 188 Armand Blanchonnet (Fra) 6:20:48.0
1928 168 Henry Hansen (Den) 4:47:18.0
1932 100 Attilio Pavesi (Ita) 2:28:05.6
1936 100 Robert Charpentier (Fra) 2:33:05.0
1948 194.63 José Beyaert (Fra) 5:18:12.6
1952 190.4 André Noyelle (Bel) 5:06:03.4
1956 187.73 Ercole Baldini (Ita) 5:21:17.0
1960 175.38 Viktor Kapitonov (USSR) 4:20:37.0
1964 194.83 Mario Zanin (Ita) 4:39:51.63
1968 196.2 Pierfranco Vianelli (Ita) 4:41:25.24
1972 182.4 Hennie Kuiper (Hol) 4:14:37.0
1976 175 Bernt Johansson (Swe) 4:46:52.0
1980 189 Sergey Sukhoruchenkov (USSR) 4:48:28.9
1984 196 Alexi Grewal (USA) 4:59:57.0
1988 196.8 Olaf Ludwig (GDR) 4:32:22.0
1992 195 Fabio Casartelli (Ita) 4:35:21.00

Women

Road race
1984 79 Connie Carpenter-Phinney (USA) 2:11:11.0
1988 82 Monique Knol (Hol) 2:00:52.0
1992 81 Kathryn Watt (Aus) 2:04:42

Sprint (1000m)
1988 Erika Salumyae (USSR)
1992 Erika Salumyae (Est)

3000 metres individual pursuit
1992 Petra Rossner (Ger)

Superseded men's track events
660yd 1908 Victor Johnson (UK) 51.2

5km	1906	Francesco Verri (Ita) 8:35.0
	1908	Benjamin Jones (UK) 8:36.2
10 km	1896	Paul Masson (Fra) 17:54.2
20 km	1906	William Pett (UK) 29:00.0
	1908	Charles Kingsbury (UK) 34:13.6
50 km	1920	Henry George (Bel) 1:16:43.2
	1924	Jacobus Willems (Hol) 1:18:24.0
100 km	1896	Léon Flameng (Fra) 3:08:19.2
	1908	Charles Bartlett (UK) 2:41:48.6
12hrs	1896	Adolf Schmal (Aut) 314.997km

In 1904 track races were won by:
Marcus Hurley (USA) at $1/4$, $1/3$, $1/2$ and 1 mile;
Burton Downing (USA) at 2 and 25 miles
Charles Schlee (USA) at 5 miles.

Men's 2000 metres tandem
From 1924-72 times recorded only over last 200m.
1906 John Matthews & Arthur Rushen (UK) 2:57.0
1908 Maurice Schilles & André Auffray (Fra) 3:07.8
1920 Harry Ryan & Thomas Lance (UK) 2:49.4
1924 Lucien Choury & Jean Cugnot (Fra) 12.6
1928 Bernhard Leene & Daan van Dijk (Hol) 11.8
1932 Maurice Perrin & Louis Chaillot (Fra) 12.0
1936 Ernst Ihbe & Carl Lorenz (Ger) 11.8
1948 Renato Perona & Ferdinando Terruzzi (Ita) 11.3
1952 Lionel Cox & Russell Mockridge (Aus) 11.0
1956 Ian Browne & Anthony Marchant (Aus) 10.8
1960 Giuseppe Beghetto & Sergio Bianchetto (Ita) 10.7
1964 Sergio Bianchetto & Angelo Damiano (Ita) 10.75
1968 Daniel Morelon & Pierre Trentin (Fra) 9.83
1972 Vladimir Semenets & Igor Tselovalnikov (USSR) 10.52

Most Olympic gold medals: 3 Paul Masson (Fra) 1896, Francisco Verri (Ita) 1906, Robert Charpentier (Fra) 1936, Daniel Morelon (Fra) 1968-72.

Most Olympic medals: 5 Morelon, who also won a silver in 1976 and bronze in 1964, both in the sprint.

World Championships

World Championships were first held in 1893 in Chicago, with two events: the sprint and the motor-paced race over 100 km. A road race was first held in 1921 and women's events were introduced in 1959. Separate world championships are not contested in Olympic years for events on the Olympic programme (qv).

Events currently contested, with those to have won most often, and winners from 1970 are as follows. The distinction between amateurs and professionals for track races was abolished in 1993.

Sprint (Amateur)
First held 1893.

1969-71	Daniel Morelon (Fra)
1973	Daniel Morelon (Fra)
1974	Anton Tkác (Cs)
1975	Daniel Morelon (Fra)
1977	Hans-Jürgen Geschke (GDR)
1978	Anton Tkác (Cs)
1979	Lutz Hesslich (GDR)
1981-2	Sergey Kopylov (USSR)
1983	Lutz Hesslich (GDR)
1985	Lutz Hesslich (GDR)
1986	Michael Hübner (GDR)
1987	Lutz Hesslich (GDR)
1989-90	Bill Huck (GDR)
1991	Jens Fiedler (Ger)

Most wins: 7 Morelon 1966-7, 1969-71, 1973, 1975; 4 William Bailey (UK) 1909-11, 1913; 4 Hesslich

Sprint
(Professional to 1992, then Open)

1970	Gordon Johnson (Aus)
1971	Leijin Loevesijn (Hol)
1972-3	Robert van Lancker (Bel)
1974	Peder Pedersen (Den)
1975-6	John Nicholson (Aus)
1977-86	Koichi Nakano (Jap)
1987	Noboyuki Tawara (Jap)
1988	Stephen Pate (Aus)
1989	Claudio Golinelli (Ita)
1990	Michael Hübner (GDR)
1991	left vacant after winner Carey Hall (Aus) failed a drugs test
1992	Michael Hübner (Ger)
1993	Gary Niewand (Aus)
1994	Martin Nothstein (USA

Most wins: 10 Nakano, 7 Jeff Scherens (Bel) 1932-7, 1947; Antonio Maspes (Ita) 1955-6, 1959-62, 1964; 6 Thorvald Ellegaard (Den) 1901-3, 1906, 1908, 1911; 5 Piet Moeskops (Hol) 1921-4, 1926; 4 Lucien Michard (Fra) 1927-30; Reg Harris (UK) 1949-51, 1954

1km time trial
(Amateur to 1991, now Open)
First held 1966.

1970	Niels Fredborg (Den)
1971	Eduard Rapp (USSR)
1973	Janusz Kierzkowski (Pol)
1974	Eduard Rapp (USSR)
1975	Klaus Grünke (GDR)
1977-9	Lothar Thoms (GDR)
1981	Lothar Thoms (GDR)
1982	Fredy Schmidtke (FRG)
1983	Sergey Kopylov (USSR)
1985	Jens Glücklich (GDR)
1986	Maik Malchow (GDR)
1987	Martin Vinnicombe (Aus)
1989	Jens Glücklich (GDR)
1990	Aleksandr Kirichenko (USSR)
1991	José Manuel Moreno (Spa)
1993-4	Florian Rousseau (Fra)

Most wins: 4 Thoms, 3 Niels Fredborg (Den) 1967-8, 1970

4 km pursuit
(Amateur to 1991, now Open)
First held 1946.

1970	Xavier Kurmann (Swi)
1971	Martin-Emilio Rodriguez (Col)
1973	Knut Knudsen (Nor)
1974	Hans Lutz (FRG)
1975	Thomas Huschke (GDR)
1977	Norbert Durpisch (GDR)
1978	Detlef Macha (GDR)
1979	Nikolay Makarov (USSR)
1981-2	Detlef Macha (GDR)
1983	Viktor Kupovets (USSR)
1985-6	Vyacheslav Yekimov (USSR)
1987	Gintautas Umaras (USSR)
1989	Vyacheslav Yekimov (USSR)
1990	Yevgeniy Berzin (USSR)
1991	Jens Lehmann (Ger)
1993	Graeme Obree (UK)
1994	Chris Boardman (UK)

Most wins: 3 Tiemen Groen (Hol) 1964-6; Macha, Yekimov

Professional 5km pursuit
First held in 1939, when it was left unfinished, and then 1946.

1970	Hugh Porter (UK)
1971	Dirk Baert (Bel)
1972-3	Hugh Porter (UK)
1974-5	Roy Schuiten (Hol)
1976	Francesco Moser (Ita)
1977-8	Gregor Braun (FRG)
1979	Bert Osterbosch (Hol)
1980	Tony Doyle (UK)
1981-2	Alain Bondue (Fra)
1983	Steele Bishop (Aus)

1984-5	Hans-Henrik Oersted (Den)
1986	Tony Doyle (UK)
1987	Hans-Henrik Oersted (Den)
1988	Lech Piasecki (Pol)
1989	Colin Sturgess (UK)
1990	Vyacheslav Yekimov (USSR)
1991	Francis Moreau (Fra)
1992	Mike McCarthy (USA)

Most wins: 4 Hugh Porter (UK) 1968, 1970, 1972-3; 3 Guido Messina (Ita) 1954-6; 3 Roger Rivière (Fra) 1957-9; 3 Leandro Faggin (Ita) 1963, 1965-6, 3 Oersted

Team pursuit
(Amateur to 1991, now Open)
First held 1962. *Wins:*

8	Germany	FRG 1962, 1964, 1970, 1973-5, 1983, GER 1991
7	USSR	1963, 1965, 1967, 1969, 1982, 1987, 1990
5	GDR	1977-9, 1981, 1989
4	Italy	1966, 1968, 1971, 1985
1	Czechoslovakia	1986
1	Australia	1993
1	Germany	1994

Keirin (Professional to 1992, now Open). First held 1980.

1980-1	Danny Clark (Aus)
1982	Gordon Singleton (Can)
1983	Urs Freuler (Swi)
1984	Robert Dill-Bundi (Swi)
1985	Urs Freuler (Swi)
1986	Michel Vaarten (Bel)
1987	Harumi Honda (Jap)
1988	vacant, winner Claudio Golinelli (Ita) failed drugs test
1989	Claudio Golinelli (Ita)
1990-2	Michael Hübner (GDR/Ger)
1993	Gary Niewand (Aus)
1994	Martin Nothstein (USA)

Most wins: 3 Hübner

50 km points race (Amateur)
First held 1976

1976	Walter Baumgartner (Swi)
1977	Constant Tourne (Bel)
1978	Noel de Jonckheere (Bel)
1979	Jirí Slama (Cs)
1980	Gary Sutton (Aus)
1981	Lutz Haueisen (GDR)
1982	Hans-Joachim Pohl (GDR)
1983	Michael Marcussen (Den)
1985	Martin Penc (Cs)
1986	Dan Frost (Den)
1987	Marat Ganeyev (USSR)

1989 Marat Satybyldiev (USSR)
1990 Stephen McGlede (Aus)
1991 Bruno Risi (Swz)

Points
(Professional to 1992, now Open)
First held 1980.
1980 Stan Tourne (Bel)
1981-7 Urs Freuler (Swi)
1988 Daniel Wyder (Swi)
1989 Urs Freuler (Swi)
1990 Laurent Biondi (Fra)
1991 Vyacheslav Yekimov (USSR)
1992 Bruno Risi (Swz)
1993 Etienne De Wilde (Bel)
1994 Bruno Risi (Swz)
Most wins: 8 Freuler

Motor-paced (Amateur)
Held at 100 km 1893-1914, for 1
hour 1958-71, at 50 km from 1972.
1970 Cees Stam (Hol)
1971-3 Horst Gnas (FRG)
1974 Jean Breuer (FRG)
1975-7 Gaby Minneboo (Hol)
1978 Rainer Podlesch (GDR)
1979 Matthe Pronk (Hol)
1980 Gaby Minneboo (Hol)
1981 Matthe Pronk (Hol)
1982 Gaby Minneboo (Hol)
1983 Rainer Podlesch (GDR)
1984 Jan de Nijs (Hol)
1985 Roberto Dotti (Ita)
1986-7 Mario Gentili (Ita)
1988 Vacant; original winner,
 Vincenzo Colamartino (Ita)
 failed drugs test
1989-91 Roland Königshofer (Aut)
1992 Carsten Podlesch (Ger)
Most wins: 7 Leon Meredith (UK)
1904-5, 1907-9, 1911, 1913; 5
Minneboo; 3 Gnas, Königshofer

Motor-paced
(Professional to 1992, now Open)
First held 1895. Held at 100 km
1895-1971, over 1 hour from 1972.
1970 Ehrenfried Rudolph (FRG)
1971-2 Theo Verschueren (Bel)
1973-4 Cees Stam (Hol)
1975 Dieter Kemper (FRG)
1976 Wilfried Peffgen (FRG)
1977 Cees Stam (Hol)
1978 Wilfried Peffgen (FRG)
1979 Martin Venix (Hol)
1980 Wilfried Peffgen (FRG)
1981 René Kos (Hol)
1982 Martin Venix (Hol)
1983 Bruno Vicini (Ita)
1984 Horst Schütz (FRG)
1985-6 Bruno Vicini (Ita)
1987 Max Hürtzler (Swi)

1988 Danny Clark (Aus)
1989 Giovanni Renosto (Ita)
1990 Walter Brugna (Ita)
1991 Danny Clark (Aus)
1992 Peter Steiger (Swi)
1993 Jens Veggerby (Den)
1994 Carsten Podlesch (Ger)
Most wins: 6 Guillermo Timoner
(Spa) 1955, 1959-60, 1962, 1964-5; 4
Victor Linart (Bel) 1921, 1924, 1926-7

Tandem sprint
(Amateur to 1991, now Open)
First held 1966.
1970 Jürgen Barth & Rainer
 Müller (FRG)
1971 Jürgen Geschke & Werner
 Otto (GDR)
1973-4 Vladimir Vackár &
 Miroslav Vymazal (Cs)
1976 Benedykt Kocot & Janusz
 Kotlinski (Pol)
1977-8 Vladimir Vackár &
 Miroslav Vymazal (Cs)
1979 Yave Cahard & Frank
 Depine (Fra)
1980-2 Ivan Kucirek & Pavel
 Martinek (Cs)
1983 Philippe Vernet & Frank
 Depine (Fra)
1984 Jürgen Greil & Frank
 Weber (FRG)
1985-6 Vitezlav Voboril & Roman
 Rehousek (Cs)
1987-9 Fabrice Colas & Frédéric
 Magné (Fra)
1990 Gianluca Capitano &
 Federico Paris (Ita)
1991 Eyk Pokorny & Emanuel
 Raasch (Ger)
1992 Gianluca Capitano &
 Federico Paris (Ita)
1993 Federico Paris & Roberto
 Chiappa (Ita)
1994 Fabrice Colas & Frédéric
 Magné (Fra)
Most wins: 4 Vackár & Vymazal,
Colas & Magné

Amateur road race
1970 Jørgen Schmidt (Den)
1971 Regis Ovion (Fra)
1973 Ryszard Szurkowski (Pol)
1974 Janusz Kowalski (Pol)
1975 André Gevers (Hol)
1977 Claudio Corti (Ita)
1978 Gilbert Glaus (Swi)
1979 Gianni Giacomini (Ita)
1981 Andrey Vedernikov (USSR)
1982 Bernd Drogan (GDR)
1983 Uwe Raab (GDR)
1985 Lech Piasecki (Pol)

1986 Uwe Ampler (GDR)
1987 Richard Vivien (Fra)
1989 Joachim Halupczok (Pol)
1990 Mirko Gualdi (Ita)
1991 Viktor Ryaksinskiy (USSR)
1993 Jan Ullrich (Ger)
1994 Alex Pedersen (Den)
Most wins: 2 Giuseppe Martano
(Ita) 1930, 1932; Gustav Adolf
Schur (GDR) 1958-9.

Team time trial (Amateur)
First held 1962. Contested on the
roads at approximately 100 km.
Wins:

7	Italy	1962, 1964-5, 1987, 1991, 1993, 1994
5	USSR	1970, 1977, 1983, 1985, 1990
3	Sweden	1967-9, 1974
3	Netherlands	1978, 1982, 1986
3	GDR	1979, 1981, 1989
2	Poland	1973, 1975
1	France	1963
1	Denmark	1966
1	Belgium	1971

Professional road race
First held 1927.
1927 Alfredo Binda (Ita)
1928-9 Georges Ronsse (Bel)
1930 Alfredo Binda (Ita)
1931 Learco Guerra (Ita)
1932 Alfredo Binda (Ita)
1933 Georges Speicher (Fra)
1934 Karel Kaers (Bel)
1935 Jean Aerts (Bel)
1936 Antonin Magne (Fra)
1937 Eloi Meulenberg (Bel)
1938 Marcel Kint (Bel)
1946 Hans Knecht (Swi)
1947 Theo Middelkamp (Hol)
1948 Alberic Schotte (Bel)
1949 Rik van Steenbergen (Bel)
1950 Alberic Schotte (Bel)
1951 Ferdinand Kübler (Swi)
1952 Heinz Müller (Ger)
1953 Fausto Coppi (Ita)
1954 Louison Bobet(Fra)
1955 Stan Ockers (Bel)
1956-7 Rik van Steenbergen (Bel)
1958 Ercole Baldini (Ita)
1959 André Darrigade (Fra)
1960-1 Rik van Looy (Bel)
1962 Jean Stablinski (Fra)
1963 Benoni Beheyt (Bel)
1964 Jan Janssen (Hol)
1965 Tom Simpson (UK)
1966 Rudi Altig (Ger)
1967 Eddy Merckx (Bel)
1968 Vittorio Adorni (Ita)
1969 Harm Ottenbros (Hol)

1970	Jean-Pierre Monseré (Bel)	
1971	Eddy Merckx (Bel)	
1972	Marino Basso (Ita)	
1973	Felice Gimondi (Ita)	
1974	Eddy Merckx (Bel)	
1975	Hennie Kuiper (Hol)	
1976	Freddy Maertens (Bel)	
1977	Francesco Moser (Ita)	
1978	Gerrie Knetemann (Hol)	
1979	Jan Raas (Hol)	
1980	Bernard Hinault (Fra)	
1981	Freddy Maertens (Bel)	
1982	Giuseppe Saronni (Ita)	
1983	Greg LeMond (USA)	
1984	Claude Criquielion (Bel)	
1985	Joop Zoetemelk (Hol)	
1986	Moreno Argentin (Ita)	
1987	Stephen Roche (Ire)	
1988	Maurizio Fondriest (Ita)	
1989	Greg LeMond (USA)	
1990	Rudy Dhaenens (Bel)	
1991-2	Gianni Bugno (Ita)	
1993	Lance Armstrong (USA)	
1994	Luc Leblanc (Fra)	

Most wins: 3 Binda, van Steenbergen, Merckx.

Individual road time trial
First held in 1994 over 42km
1994   Chris Boardman (UK)

Women's sprint
First held 1958.

1969-71	Galina Tsareva (USSR)
1972	Galina Yermolayeva (USSR)
1973	Sheila Young (USA)
1974	Tamara Piltsikova (USSR)
1975	Sue Novarra (USA)
1976	Sheila Young (USA)
1977-9	Galina Tsareva (USSR)
1980	Sue Reber (Novarra) (USA)
1981	Sheila Ochowitz (née Young) (USA)

1982-4	Connee Paraskevin (USA)
1985	Iasabelle Nicoloso (Fra)
1986	Christa Rothenburger (GDR)
1987	Erika Salumyae (USSR)
1989	Erika Salumyae (USSR)
1990	Connie Young-Paraskevin (USA)
1991	Ingrid Haringa (Hol)
1993	Tatyana Dubnicoff (Can)
1994	Galina Yenyukhina (Rus)

Most wins: 6 Galina Yermolayeva (USSR) 1958-61, 1963, 1972; Tsareva

Women's 3km pursuit

1970-4	Tamara Garkushina (USSR)
1975-6	Keetie van Oosten-Hage (Hol)
1977	Vera Kuznetsova (USSR)
1978-9	Keetie van Oosten-Hage (Hol)
1980-1	Nadezhda Kibardina (USSR)
1982	Rebecca Twigg (USA)
1983	Connie Carpenter (USA)
1984-5	Rebecca Twigg (USA)
1986	Jeannie Longo (Fra)
1987	Rebecca Twigg (USA)
1988-9	Jeannie Longo (Fra)
1990	Leontien van Moorsel (Hol)
1991	Petra Rossner (Ger)
1993	Rebecca Twigg (USA)
1994	Marion Clignet (Fra)

Most wins: 6 Tamara Garkushina (USSR) 1967, 1970-4; 5 Beryl Burton (UK) 1959-60, 1962-3, 1966; 4 van Oosten-Hage, Twigg

Women's 30 km points

1987	(demonstration event) Sally Hodge (UK)
1989	Jeannie Longo (Fra)
1990	Karen Holliday (NZ)
1991-4	Ingrid Haringa (Hol)

Most wins: 4 Haringa

Women's road race
First held 1958.

1970-1	Anna Konkina (USSR)
1972	Geneviève Gambillon (Fra)
1973	Nicole Vandenbroeck (Bel)
1974	Geneviève Gambillon (Fra)
1975	Trijntje Fopma (Hol)
1976	Keetie van Oosten-Hage (Hol)
1977	Josiane Bost (Fra)
1978	Beate Habetz (FRG)
1979	Petra de Bruin (Hol)
1980	Beth Heiden (USA)
1981	Ute Enzenauer (FRG)
1982	Mandy Jones (UK)
1983	Marianne Berglund (Swe)
1985-7	Jeannie Longo (Fra)
1989	Jeannie Longo (Fra)
1990	Catherine Marsal (Fra)
1991	Leontien van Moorsel (Hol)
1993	Leontien van Moorsel (Hol)
1994	Monica Valvik (Nor)

Most wins: 4 Yvonne Reynders (Bel) 1959, 1961, 1963, 1966

Women's 50 km team trial
First held 1987

1987	USSR
1988	Italy
1989	USSR
1990	Netherlands
1991	France
1992	USA
1993-4	Russia

Individual road time trial
First held in 1994 over 29.6km.
1994   Karen Kurreck (USA) 38:22

Three women's cycling world champions, Beth Heiden, Sheila Young and Christa Rothenburger, have also been world champions at speed skating.

Tour de France

The Tour de France is the greatest cycle race in the world and its popularity attracts the largest audience of any sporting event with more than 10 million people watching the annual race. It was first held in 1903 and the riders cover a course which varies each year, always including several mountain stages as well as time trials, over a three week period. The distance in recent years has been around 4000 km (3635km in 1995), but from 1911 to 1929 it was always over 5000 km. *Winners:*

1903	Maurice Garin (Fra)	1921	Léon Scieur (Bel)	1935	Romain Maës (Bel)
1904	Henri Cornet (Fra)	1922	Firmin Lambot (Bel)	1936	Sylvère Maës (Bel)
1905	Louis Trousselier (Fra)	1923	Henri Pélissier (Fra)	1937	Roger Lapébie (Fra)
1906	René Pottier (Fra)	1924-5	Ottavio Bottecchia (Ita)	1938	Gino Bartali (Ita)
1907-8	Lucien Petit-Breton (Fra)	1926	Lucien Buysse (Bel)	1939	Sylvère Maës (Bel)
1909	François Faber (Lux)	1927-8	Nicholas Frantz (Lux)	1947	Jean Robic (Fra)
1910	Octave Lapize (Fra)	1929	Maurice De Waele (Bel)	1948	Gino Bartali (Ita)
1911	Gustave Garrigou (Fra)	1930	André Leducq (Fra)	1949	Fausto Coppi (Ita)
1912	Odile Defraye (Bel)	1931	Antonin Magne (Fra)	1950	Ferdinand Kübler (Swi)
1913-4	Philippe Thys (Bel)	1932	André Leducq (Fra)	1951	Hugo Koblet (Swi)
1919	Firmin Lambot (Bel)	1933	Georges Speicher (Fra)	1952	Fausto Coppi (Ita)
1920	Philippe Thys (Bel)	1934	Antonin Magne (Fra)	1953-5	Louison Bobet (Fra)

1956	Roger Walkowiak (Fra)	1968	Jan Janssen (Hol)	1981-2 Bernard Hinault (Fra)
1957	Jacques Anquetil (Fra)	1969-72 Eddy Merckx (Bel)	1983-4 Laurent Fignon (Fra)
1958	Charly Gaul (Lux)	1973	Luis Ocaña (Spa)	1985 Bernard Hinault (Fra)
1959	Federico Bahamontès (Spa)	1974	Eddy Merckx (Bel)	1986 Greg LeMond (USA)
1960	Gastone Nencini (Ita)	1975	Bernard Thévenet (Fra)	1987 Stephen Roche (Ire)
1961-4	Jacques Anquetil (Fra)	1976	Lucien van Impe (Bel)	1988 Pedro Delgado (Spa)
1965	Felice Gimondi (Ita)	1977	Bernard Thévenet (Fra)	1989-90 Greg LeMond (USA)
1966	Lucien Aimar (Fra)	1978-9 Bernard Hinault (Fra)	1991-5 Miguel Induráin (Spa)
1967	Roger Pingeon (Fra)	1980	Joop Zoetemelk (Hol)	

Fastest average speed: 39.504 km/h Miguel Induráin over 3983km in 1992

Longest race: 5745 km (3569 miles) 1926

Most starters: 210 in 1986

Most finishers: 158 in 1991

Most races: 16 Joop Zoetemelk 1970-86

Greatest victory margin: 2 hr 49 mins Maurice Garin in 1903

Narrowest victory margin: 8 secs Greg LeMond over Laurent Fignon in 1989

Most stage wins:

35 Eddy Merckx, 28 Bernard Hinault, 25 André Leducq, 22 André Darrigade, 20 Nicolas Frantz

Most stage wins in one year: 8 Charles Pelissier

1930, Eddy Merckx 1970 & 1974, Freddy Maertens 1976

Most successful Tour de France riders: six points for a win, 4-3-2-1 for 2nd to 5th places

Name	Years	1st	2nd	3rd	4th	5th	Pts
Bernard Hinault	1978-86	5	2	-	-	-	38
Joop Zoetemelk	1970-82	1	6	-	3	1	37
Eddy Merckx	1969-75	5	1	-	-	-	34
Jacques Anquetil	1957-64	5	-	1	-	-	33
Lucien van Impe	1971-83	1	3	3	2	1	32
Miguel Induráin	1991-5	5	-	-	-	-	30
Raymond Poulidor	1962-76	-	3	5	-	-	27
Greg LeMond	1984-90	3	1	1	-	-	25
Louison Bobet	1948-55	3	-	1	1	-	23
Bernard Thévenet	1971-7	2	1	-	1	-	18

Giro d'Italia

After the Tour de France, the Tour of Italy (Giro d'Italia) is the second most presitigous of the continental tours. It was first held in 1909 and until 1950 when Switzerland's Hugo Koblet won, all winners had been Italian. *Winners:*

1909	Luigi Ganna (Ita)
1910-11	Carlo Galleti (Ita)
1912	*Team Atala (team race only)*
1913	Carlo Oriani (Ita)
1914	Alfonso Calzolari (Ita)
1915-18	*not held*
1919	Constante Girardengo (Ita)
1920	Gaetano Belloni (Ita)
1921-2	Giovanni Brunero (Ita)
1923	Constante Girardengo (Ita)
1924	Giuseppe Enrici (Ita)
1925	Alfredo Binda (Ita)
1926	Giovanni Brunero (Ita)
1927-9	Alfredo Binda (Ita)
1930	Luigi Marchisio (Ita)
1931	Francesco Camusso (Ita)
1932	Antonio Pesenti (Ita)
1933	Alfredo Binda (Ita)
1934	Learco Guerra (Ita)
1935	Vasco Bergamaschi (Ita)
1936-7	Gino Bartali (Ita)
1938-9	Giovanni Valetti (Ita)
1940	Fausto Coppi (Ita)
1941-5	*not held*
1946	Gino Bartali (Ita)
1947	Fausto Coppi (Ita)
1948	Fiorenzo Magni (Ita)
1949	Fausto Coppi (Ita)

1950	Hugo Koblet (Swi)
1951	Fiorenzo Magni (Ita)
1952-3	Fausto Coppi (Ita)
1954	Carlo Clerici (Swi)
1955	Fiorenzo Magni (Ita)
1956	Charly Gaul (Lux)
1957	Gastone Nencini (Ita)
1958	Ercole Baldini (Ita)
1959	Charly Gaul (Lux)
1960	Jacques Anquetil (Fra)
1961	Arnaldo Pambianco (Ita)
1962-3	Franco Balmanion (Ita)
1964	Jacques Anquetil (Fra)
1965	Vittorio Adorni (Ita)
1966	Gianni Motta (Ita)
1967	Felice Gimondi (Ita)
1968	Eddy Merckx (Bel)
1969	Felice Gimondi (Ita)
1970	Eddy Merckx (Bel)
1971	Gosta Petterson (Swe)
1972-4	Eddy Merckx (Bel)
1975	Fausto Bertoglio (Ita)
1976	Felice Gimondi (Ita)
1977	Michel Pollentier (Bel)
1978	Johan De Muynck (Bel)
1979	Giuseppe Saronni (Ita)
1980	Bernard Hinault (Fra)
1981	Giovani Battaglin (Ita)
1982	Bernard Hinault (Fra)
1983	Giuseppe Saronni (Ita)
1984	Francesco Moser (Ita)
1985	Bernard Hinault (Fra)
1986	Roberto Visentini (Ita)
1987	Stephen Roche (Ire)
1988	Andy Hampsten (USA)
1989	Laurent Fignon (Fra)

1990	Gianni Bugno (Ita)
1991	Franco Chioccioli (Ita)
1992-3	Miguel Induráin (Spa)
1994	Yevgeniy Berzin (Rus)
1995	Tony Rominger (Swz)

Most wins:

5 Binda, Coppi, Merckx

Six cyclists have won the Giro and the Tour de France in the same year:
Fausto Coppi 1952
Jacques Anquetil 1964
Eddy Merckx 1970, 1972, 1974;
Bernard Hinault 1982, 1985;
Stephen Roche 1987
Miguel Induráin 1992

Vuelta a España

The Tour of Spain is the third major tour of the continental season. It was first held in 1935, and annually from 1955. *Winners:*

1935-6	Gustave Deloor (Bel)
1941-2	Julian Berrendero (Spa)
1945	Delio Rodriguez (Spa)
1946	Dalmacio Langarica (Spa)
1947	Edward Van Dyck (Bel)
1948	Bernardo Ruiz (Spa)
1950	Emilio Rodriguez (Spa)
1955	Jean Dotto (Fra)
1956	Angelo Conterno (Ita)
1957	Jesus Loreno (Spa)
1958	Jean Stablisnki (Fra)
1959	Antonio Suarez (Spa)
1960	Frans De Mulder (Bel)
1961	Angelo Soler (Spa)
1962	Rudi Altig (Ger)

1963	Jacques Anquetil (Fra)
1964	Raymond Poulidor (Fra)
1965	Rolf Wolfshohl (FRG)
1966	Francesco Gabica (Spa)
1967	Jan Janssen (Hol)
1968	Felice Gimondi (Ita)
1969	Roger Pingeon (Fra)
1970	Luis Ocaña (Spa)
1971	Ferdinand Bracke (Bel)
1972	José Manuel Fuente (Spa)
1973	Eddy Merckx (Bel)
1974	José Manuel Fuente (Spa)
1975	Agust. Tamames (Spa)
1976	José Pesarrodona (Spa)
1977	Freddie Maertens (Bel)
1978	Bernard Hinault (Fra)
1979	Joop Zoetemelk (Hol)
1980	Faustino Ruperez (Spa)
1981	Giovani Battaglin (Ita)
1982	Marino Lejaretta (Spa)
1983	Bernard Hinault (Fra)
1984	Eric Caritoux (Fra)
1985	Pedro Delgado (Spa)
1986	Alvaro Pino (Spa)
1987	Luis Herrera (Col)
1988	Sean Kelly (Ire)
1989	Pedro Delgado (Spa)
1990	Marco Giovannetti (Ita)
1991	Melchior Mauri (Spa)
1992-4	Tony Rominger (Swi)

Most wins: 3 Rominger; 2 Gustave Deloor (Bel) 1935-6, Julio Berrendero (Spa) 1941-2, José Manuel Fuente (Spa) 1972, 1974, Bernard Hinault (Fra) 1978, 1983, Delgado as above
Most stage wins in one tour: 7 Laurent Jalabert (Fra) 1994

Tour DuPont

Held annually in the USA from 1989.
Winners:

1989	Dag Otto Lauritzen (Nor)
1990	Raul Alcala (Mex)
1991	Erik Breukink (Hol)
1992	Greg LeMond (USA)
1993	Raul Alcala (Mex)
1994	Vyacheslav Yekimov (Rus)
1995	Lance Armstrong (USA)

The Classics

Winners from 1970 of the races that make up the major classic races on the continent.

Milan - San Remo

The first major classic of the season, it is the longest unpaced race of all the classics (initially at 281 km, and now about 290 km). First held in 1907 it is known as the Primavera in Italy.

1970	Michele Dancelli (Ita)
1971-2	Eddy Merckx (Bel)
1973	Roger De Vlaeminck (Bel)
1974	Felice Gimondi (Ita)
1975-6	Eddy Merckx (Bel)
1977	Jan Raas (Bel)
1978-9	Roger De Vlaeminck (Bel)
1980	Pierino Gavazzi (Ita)
1981	Alfons De Wolf (Bel)
1982	Marc Gomez (Fra)
1983	Giuseppe Saronni (Ita)
1984	Francesco Moser (Ita)
1985	Hennie Kuiper (Hol)
1986	Sean Kelly (Ire)
1987	Erich Mächler (Swi)
1988-9	Laurent Fignon (Fra)
1990	Gianni Bugno (Ita)
1991	Claudio Chiappucci (Ita)
1992	Sean Kelly (Ire)
1993	Maurizio Fondriest (Ita)
1994	Giorgio Furlan (Ita)
1995	Laurent Jalabert (Fra)

Most wins: 7 Merckx 1966-7, 1969, 1971-2, 1975-6; 6 Girardengo (Ita) 1918, 1921, 1923, 1925-6, 1928

Tour of Flanders

First held in 1913 the race takes place around Ghent, Belgium. One of the major features of the race are the steep cobbled climbs, notably the Koppenberg from 1975 to 1987.

1970	Erik Leman (Bel)
1971	Evert Dolman (Hol)
1972-3	Erik Leman (Bel)
1974	Cees Bal (Hol)
1975	Eddy Merckx (Bel)
1976	Walter Planckaert (Bel)
1977	Roger De Vlaeminck (Bel)
1978	Walter Godefroot (Bel)
1979	Jan Raas (Hol)
1980	Michel Pollentier (Bel)
1981	Hennie Kuiper (Hol)
1982	René Martens (Bel)
1983	Jan Raas (Hol)
1984	Johan Lammerts (Hol)
1985	Eric Vanderaerden (Bel)
1986	Adri Van der Poel (Bel)
1987	Claude Criquielion (Bel)
1988	Eddy Planckaert (Bel)
1989	Edwig Van Hooydonck (Bel)
1990	Moreno Argentin (Ita)
1991	Edwig Van Hooydonck (Bel)
1992	Jacky Durand (Fra)
1993	Johan Museeuw (Bel)
1994	Giovanni Bugno (Ita)
1995	Johan Museeuw (Bel)

Most wins: 3 Achiel Buysse (Bel) 1940-1, 1943; Fiorenzo Magni (Ita) 1949-51, Leman

Paris-Roubaix

Regarded as the toughest one-day race in the world, hence its nickname, 'The Hell of the North'. The latter stages of the race are over farm tracks and cobbled roads. c.260 km. First held in 1896.

1970	Eddy Merckx (Bel)
1971	Roger Rosiers (Bel)
1972	Roger De Vlaeminck (Bel)
1973	Eddy Merckx (Bel)
1974-5	Roger De Vlaeminck (Bel)
1976	Marc De Meyer (Bel)
1977	Roger De Vlaeminck (Bel)
1978-80	Francesco Moser (Ita)
1981	Bernard Hinault (Fra)
1982	Jan Raas (Bel)
1983	Hennie Kuiper (Hol)
1984	Sean Kelly (Ire)
1985	Marc Madiot (Fra)
1986	Sean Kelly (Ire)
1987	Eric Vanderaerden (Bel)
1988	Dirk De Mol (Bel)
1989	Jean-Marie Wampers (Bel)
1990	Eddy Planckaert (Bel)
1991	Marc Madiot (Fra)
1992-3	Gilbert Duclos-Lassalle (Fra)
1994	Andrey Tchmil (Mol)
1995	Franco Ballerini (Ita)

Most wins: 4 De Vlaeminck, 3 Octave Lapize (Fra) 1909-11, Gaston Rebry (Bel) 1931, 1934-5; Rik Van Looy (Bel) 1961-2, 1965; Merckx 1968, 1970, 1973; Moser

Flèche Wallonne

The Flèche Wallonne is staged around the hilly Ardennes district of Belgium, recently a little over 200km around Huy after many years of different routes. It was first held in 1936.

1970	Eddy Merckx (Bel)
1971	Roger De Vlaeminck (Bel)
1972	Eddy Merckx (Bel)
1973	André Derrickx (Bel)
1974	Frans Verbeeck (Bel)
1975	André Derrickx (Bel)
1976	Joop Zoetemelk (Hol)
1977	Freddie Maertens (Bel)
1978	Michel Laurent (Fra)
1979	Bernard Hinault (Fra)
1980	Giuseppe Saronni (Ita)
1981	Daniël Willems (Bel)
1982	Mario Beccia (Bel)
1983	Bernard Hinault (Fra)
1984	Kim Andersen (Den)
1985	Claude Criquielion (Bel)
1986	Laurent Fignon (Fra)
1987	Jean Claude Leclercq (Fra)
1988	Rolf Golz (FRG)
1989	Claude Criquielion (Bel)
1990-1	Moreno Argentin (Ita)

1992	Giorgio Furlan (Ita)
1993	Maurizio Fondriest (Ita)
1994	Moreno Argentin (Ita)
1995	Laurent Jalabert (Fra)

Most wins: 3 Marcel Kint (Bel) 1943-5, Merckx 1967, 1970, 1972; Argentin

Liège-Bastogne-Liège

First held in 1892 it is the oldest of the Belgian classics and recognised as the toughest of the classics, although shorter than some at about 250 km. Until 1912 it was for amateurs only. Like the Flèche Wallonne it takes place around the Ardennes district.

1970	Roger De Valeminck (Bel)
1971-3	Eddy Merckx (Bel)
1974	Georges Pintens (Bel)

original winner Ronald Dewitte disqualified

1975	Eddy Merckx (Bel)
1976	Jos Bruyère (Bel)
1977	Bernard Hinault (Fra)
1978	Jos Bruyère (Bel)
1979	Dietrich Thurau (FRG)
1980	Bernard Hinault (Fra)
1981	Josef Fuchs (Swi)

original winner J Van de Velde (Hol) disqualified on a positive drugs test

1982	Silvano Contini (Ita)
1983	Steven Rooks (Hol)
1984	Sean Kelly (Ire)
1985-7	Moreno Argentin (Ita)
1988	Adri Van der Poel (Bel)
1989	Sean Kelly (Ire)
1990	Eric Van Lancker (Bel)
1991	Moreno Argentin (Ita)
1992	Dirk De Wolf (Bel)
1993	Rolf Sorensen (Den)
1994	Yevgeniy Berzin (Rus)
1995	Mauro Gianetti (Swi)

Most wins: 5 Merckx 1969, 1971-3, 1975; 4 Argentin, 3 Léon Houa (Bel) 1892-4, Alphonse Scheppers (Bel) 1929, 1931, 1935; 3 Alfred Debruyne (Bel) 1956, 1958-9

Paris-Brussels

First held in 1893, but not again until 1906 when professionals were allowed to compete. The race was discontinued in 1966 and replaced on the 'Classics' list by the Frankfurt Grand Prix, but it returned in 1973.

1973	Eddy Merckx (Bel)
1974	Marc De Meyer (Bel)
1975	Freddie Maertens (Bel)
1976	Felice Gimondi (Ita)
1977	Ludo Peeters (Bel)
1978	Jan Raas (Hol)
1979	Ludo Peeters (Bel)

1980	Pierino Gavazzi (Ita)
1981	Roger De Vlaeminck (Bel)
1982	Jaak Hanegraaf (Hol)
1983	Tommy Primm (Swe)
1984	Eric Vanderaerden (Bel)
1985	Adri Van der Poel (Bel)
1986	Guido Bontempi (Ita)
1987	Wim Arras (Bel)
1988	Rolf Golz (Ger)
1989	Jelle Nijdam (Hol)
1990	Franco Ballerini (Ita)
1991	Brian Holm (Den)
1992	Rolf Sorensen (Den)
1993	Francis Moreau (Fra)
1994	Rolf Sorensen (Den)

Most wins: 3 Octave Lapize (Fra) 1911-3, Felix Sellier (Bel) 1922-4

Tour of Lombardy

The Tour of Lombardy is one of the Autumn Classics and traditionally marks the end of the road-racing season on the continent. It was first held in 1905 and is often referred to as 'The Race of the Falling Leaves'.

1970	Franco Bitossi (Ita)
1971-2	Eddy Merckx (Bel)
1973	Felice Gimondi (Ita)
1974	Roger De Vlaeminck (Bel)
1975	Francesco Moser (Ita)
1976	Roger De Vlaeminck (Bel)
1977	Gianbattista Baroncelli (Ita)
1978	Francesco Moser (Ita)
1979	Bernard Hinault (Fra)
1980	Alfons De Wolf (Bel)
1981	Hennie Kuiper (Hol)
1982	Giuseppe Saronni (Ita)
1983	Sean Kelly (Ire)
1984	Bernard Hinault (Fra)
1985	Sean Kelly (Ire)
1986	Gianbattista Baroncelli (Ita)
1987	Moreno Argentin (Ita)
1988	Charly Mottet (Fra)
1989	Tony Rominger (Swi)
1990	Gilles Delion (Fra)
1991	Sean Kelly (Ire)
1992	Tony Rominger (Swi)
1993	Pascal Richard (Swi)
1994	Vladislav Bobrik (Rus)

Most wins*:* 5 Fausto Coppi (Ita) 1946-9, 1954; 4 Alfredo Binda (Ita) 1925-7, 1931; 3 Costante Girardengo (Ita) 1919, 1921-2; 3 Gino Bartali (Ita) 1936, 1939-40

Grand Prix des Nations

Regarded as the time-trialists unofficial world championship and the only time trial in the World Cup. The venue for the race has varied over the years but was always held in France from the

first in 1932 until a move to Pisa in Italy in 1991. *Winners from 1969:*

1969-70	Herman Van Springel (Bel)
1971	Luis Ocaña (Spa)
1972	Roger Swerts (Bel)
1973	Eddy Merckx (Bel)
1974-5	Roy Schuiten (Hol)
1976	Freddy Maertens (Bel)
1977-9	Bernard Hinault (Fra)
1980	Jean-Luc Vandenbroucke (Bel)
1981	Daniël Gisiger (Swi)
1982	Bernard Hinault (Fra)
1983	Daniël Gisiger (Swi)
1984	Bernard Hinault (Fra)
1985	Charly Mottet (Fra)
1986	Sean Kelly (Ire)
1987-8	Charly Mottet (Fra)
1989	Laurent Fignon (Fra)
1990	Thomas Wegmüller (Swi)
1991	Tony Rominger (Swi)
1992	Johan Bruyneel (Bel)
1993	Armand de las Cuevas (Fra)
1994	Tony Rominger (Swi)

Most wins: 9 Jacques Anquetil (Fra) 1953-8, 1961, 1965-6; 5 Hinault (Fra), 3 Antonin Magne (Fra) 1934-6

Paris-Nice

An gruelling early-season stage race, the riders cover more than 1100 km in six days.

Most wins: 7 Sean Kelly (Ire) 1982-8; 5 Jacques Anquetil (Fra) 1957, 1961, 1963, 1965-6; 3 Eddy Merckcx (Bel) 1969-71; Joop Zoetemelk (Hol) 1974-5, 1979

Most wins in a season

54	Eddy Merckx (Bel) 1971
53	Freddy Maertens (Bel) 1977
52	Freddy Maertens 1976
52	Eddy Merckx 1970
51	Eddy Merckx 1973
50	Eddy Merckx 1972
42	Rik Van Looy (Bel) 1965

World Cup

The first World Cup, sponsored by Perrier, was introduced in 1989. Riders amassed points in 12 major races, including six classics, throughout the year. *Winners:*

1989	Sean Kelly (Ire)
1990	Gianni Bugno (Ita)
1991	Maurizio Fondriest (Ita)
1992	Olaf Ludwig (Ger)
1993	Maurizio Fondriest (Ita)
1994	Gianluca Bortolani (Ita)

The Classic riders

The riders to have had most wins in the Classic races: Milan - San Remo (MR), Tour of Flanders (Fl), Paris-Roubaix (PR), Flèche Wallonne (FW), Liège-Bastogne-Liège (LB), Paris-Brussels (PB), Tour of Lombardy (TL) and Bordeaux-Paris (BP), the Grand Prix des Nations (GN), the World Road Race Championship (WC) and the three prestigious Continental tours: Tour de France (Fr), Tour of Italy (It), Tour of Spain (Sp).

Name	MR	Fl	PR	FW	LB	PB	TL	BP	GN	WC	Fr	It	Sp	Total
Eddy Merckx	7	2	3	3	5	1	2	-	1	3	5	5	1	38
Bernard Hinault	-	-	1	2	2	-	2	-	5	1	5	3	2	23
Fausto Coppi	3	-	1	1	-	-	5	-	2	1	2	5	-	20
Jacques Anquetil	-	-	-	-	1	-	-	1	9	-	5	2	1	19
Alfredo Binda	2	-	-	-	-	-	4	-	-	3	-	5	-	14
Roger De Vlaeminck	3	1	4	1	1	1	3	-	-	-	-	-	-	14
Rik van Looy	1	2	3	1	1	2	1	-	-	2	-	-	-	13
Gino Bartali	4	-	-	-	-	-	3	-	-	-	2	3	-	12
Felice Gimondi	1	-	1	-	-	1	2	-	2	1	1	2	1	12
Rik van Steenbergen	1	2	2	2	-	1	-	-	-	3	-	-	-	11
Sean Kelly	2	-	2	-	2	-	3	-	1	-	-	-	1	11
Herman van Springel	-	-	-	-	-	-	1	7	2	-	-	-	-	10
Louison Bobet	1	1	1	-	-	-	1	1	1	1	3	-	-	10
Moreno Argentin	-	1	-	3	4	-	1	-	-	1	-	-	-	10

Super Prestige Pernod Competition

Various European races were designated as counting towards a season-long competition with varying points depending upon status of the race, and the rider's finishing position. The rider with the most points at the end of the season won the Super Prestige Pernod Trophy. The first award was made in 1959, and won by Henri Anglade(Fra). Winners from 1977.

1977 Freddie Maertens (Bel)
1978 Francesco Moser (Ita)
1979-82 Bernard Hinault (Fra)
1983 Greg LeMond (USA)
1984-6 Sean Kelly (Ire)
1987 Stephen Roche (Ire)

Tour of Britain (Milk Race)

Until 1983 the Milk Race was an amateur-only event but it has since gone open. First held in 1951 it was originally sponsored by the Daily Express, but then by the Milk Marketing Board from 1958 when the race resumed after a two year lay-off. *Winners:*

1951 Ian Steel (UK)
1952 Ken Russell (UK)
1953 Gordon Thomas (UK)
1954 Eugene Tamburlini (Fra)
1955 Anthony Hewson (UK)
1958 Richard Durlacher (Aut)
1959-60 Bill Bradley (UK)
1961 Billy Holmes (UK)
1962 Eugen Pokorny (Pol)
1963 Peter Chisman (UK)
1964 Arthur Metcalfe (UK)
1965 Les West (UK)
1966 Josef Gawliczek (Pol)
1967 Les West (UK)
1968 Gösta Pettersson (Swe)
1969 Fedor Den Hertog (Hol)
1970 Jirí Mainus (Cs)
1971 Fedor Den Hertog (Hol)
1972 Hennie Kuiper (Hol)
1973 Piet van Katwijk (Hol)
1974 Roy Schuiten (Hol)
1975 Bernt Johansson (Swe)
1976 Bill Nickson (UK)
1977 Said Gusseinov (USSR)
1978 Jan Brzezny (Pol)
1979 Yuriy Kashirin (USSR)
1980 Ivan Mitchtenko (USSR)
1981 Sergey Krivocheyev (USSR)
1982 Yuriy Kashirin (USSR)
1983 Matt Eaton (USA)
1984 Oleg Czougeda (USSR)
1985 Eric van Lancker (Bel)
1986 Joey McLoughlin (UK)
1987 Malcolm Elliott (UK)
1988 Vasiliy Zhdanov (USSR)
1989 Brian Walton (Can)
1990 Shane Sutton (Aus)
1991 Chris Walker (UK)
1992 Conor Henry (Ire)
1993 Chris Lillywhite (UK)
1994 Maurizio Fondriest (Ita)

Most wins: 2 Bill Bradley, Les West, Fedor Den Hertog, Yuriy Kashirin

Tony Rominger - World Cup winner 1994

World Speed Records

From 1 Jan 1993 the list of records accepted by the UCI was drastically reduced, with no distinction as previously for professionals and amateurs and for open air or indoor tracks or for low or high altitude. The records now accepted by the UCI are as follows:

Men - Unpaced Standing Start

Distance	min:sec			
1km	1:02.091	Maic Malchow (GDR)	Colorado Springs	28 Aug 1986
4km	4:20.894	Graeme Obree (UK)	Hamar, Norway	19 Aug 1993
4km team	4:03.840	Australia	Hamar, Norway	20 Aug 1993
		(Brett Aitken, Stuart O'Grady, Tim O'Shannessy, Bill Joe Shearsby)		

Men - Unpaced Flying Start

200m	10.099	Vladimir Adamashvili (USSR)	Moscow	6 Aug 1990
500m	26.649	Aleksandr Kirichenko (USSR	Moscow	29 Oct 1988

Women - Unpaced Standing Start

500m	33.438	Galina Yenyukhina (Rus)	Moscow	29 Apr 1993
3km	3:37.347	Rebecca Twigg (USA)	Hamar, Norway	20 Aug 1993

Women - Unpaced Flying Start

200m	10.831	Olga Slyusareva (Rus)	Moscow	25 Apr 1993
500m	29.655	Erika Salumyae (USSR/Est)	Moscow	6 Aug 1987

The classic speed record is that for 1 hour. The **men's record** – in kilometres – has progressed:

38.220	Jules Dubois (Fra)	Paris	31 Oct 1894
39.240	Oscar van den Eynde (Bel)	Paris	30 Jul 1897
40.781	Willie Hamilton (USA)	Denver	9 Jul 1898
41.110	Lucien Petot-Bretor (Fra)	Paris	24 Aug 1905
41.520	Marcel Berthet (Fra)	Paris	20 Jun 1907
42.360	Oscar Egg (Swi)	Paris	22 Aug 1912
42.741	Marcel Berthet (Fra)	Paris	7 Aug 1913
43.525	Oscar Egg (Swi)	Paris	21 Aug 1913
43.775	Marcel Berthet (Fra)	Paris	20 Sep 1913
44.247	Oscar Egg (Swi)	Paris	18 Jun 1914
44.588	Jan Van Hout (Hol)	Roermond	25 Aug 1933
44.777	Maurice Richard (Fra)	Milan	14 Oct 1935
45.090	Giuseppe Olmo (Ita)	Milan	31 Oct 1935
45.398	Maurice Richard (Fra)	Milan	14 Oct 1936
45.558	Frans Slaats (Hol)	Milan	29 Sep 1937
45.767	Maurice Archambaud (Fra)	Milan	3 Nov 1937
45.871	Fausto Coppi (Ita)	Milan	7 Nov 1942
46.159	Jacques Anquetil (Fra)	Milan	29 Jun 1956
46.393	Ercole Baldini (Ita)	Milan	19 Sep 1956
46.923	Roger Rivière (Fra)	Milan	18 Sep 1957
47.346	Roger Rivière (Fra)	Milan	23 Sep 1958
47.493u	Jacques Anquetil (Fra)	Milan	27 Sep 1967
48.093	Ferdi Bracke (Bel)	Rome	30 Oct 1967
48.653	Ole Ritter (Den)	Mexico City	6 Dec 1968
49.431	Eddy Merckx (Bel)	Mexico City	25 Oct 1972
50.808	Francesco Moser (Ita)	Mexico City	19 Jan 1984
51.151	Francesco Moser (Ita)	Mexico City	23 Jan 1984
51.596	Graeme Obree (UK)	Hamar	17 Jul 1993
52.270	Chris Boardman (UK)	Bordeaux	28 Jul 1993
52.713	Graeme Obree (UK)	Bordeaux	27 Apr 1994
53.040	Miguel Induráin (Spa)	Bordeaux	2 Sep 1994
53.832	Tony Rominger (Swz)	Bordeaux	22 Oct 1994
55.291	Tony Rominger (Swz)	Bordeaux	6 Nov 1994

The **women's record** has progressed:

41.347	Elsy Jacobs (Lux)	Milan	9 Nov 1958
41.471	Maria Cressari (Ita)	Mexico City	25 Nov 1972
43.082	Cornelia Van Oosten (Hol)	Munich	16 Sep 1978
46.352	Jeannie Longo (Fra)	Mexico City	1 Oct 1989
47.112	Catherine Marsal (Fra)	Bordeaux	29 Apr 1995
47.411	Yvonne McGregor (UK)	Manchester	17 Jun 1995

Catherine Marsal – upheld the French tradition for the 1 hour by setting a new women's record in 1995

Cyclo-Cross

World Championships

First held in 1950. From 1967 to 1993 they were split into amateur and professional categories.

Open and Professional champions

1950	Jean Robic (Fra)
1951-3	Roger Rondeaux (Fra)
1954-8	André Dufraisse (Fra)
1959	Renato Longo (Ita)
1960-1	Rolf Wolfshohl (FRG)
1962	Renato Longo (Ita)
1963	Rolf Wolfshohl (FRG)
1964-5	Renato Longo (Ita)
1966	Eric De Vlaeminck (Bel)
1967	Renato Longo (Ita)
1968-73	Eric De Vlaeminck (Bel)
1974	Albert van Damme (Bel)
1975	Roger De Vlaeminck (Bel)
1976-9	Albert Zweifel (Swi)
1980	Roland Liboton (Bel)
1981	Johannes Stamsnijder (Hol)
1982-4	Roland Liboton (Bel)
1985	Klaus-Peter Thaler (FRG)
1986	Albert Zweifel (Swi)
1987	Klaus-Peter Thaler (FRG)
1988	Pascal Richard (Swi)
1989	Danny De Bie (Bel)
1990	Henk Baars (Hol)
1991	Radomir Simunek (Cs)
1992	Mike Kluge (Ger)
1993	Dominique Arnould (Fra)
1994	Paul Herijgers (Bel)
1995	Dieter Runkel (Swi)

Most wins: 7 Eric De Vlaeminck; 5 André Dufraisse, Renato Longo

Amateur champions

1967	Michel Pelchat (Fra)
1968	Roger De Vlaeminck (Bel)
1969	René Declercq (Bel)
1970-1	Robert Vermeire (Bel)
1972	Norbert De Deckere (Bel)
1973	Klaus-Peter Thaler (FRG)
1974-5	Robert Vermeire (Bel)
1976	Klaus-Peter Thaler (FRG)
1977	Robert Vermeire (Bel)
1978	Roland Liboton (Bel)
1979	Vito Di Tano (Ita)
1980	Fritz Saladin (Swi)
1981-2	Milos Fisera (Cs)
1983-4	Radomir Simunek (Cs)
1985	Mike Kluge (FRG)
1986	Vito Di Tano (Ita)
1987	Mike Kluge (FRG)
1988	Karel Camrda (Cs)
1989	Ondrej Glajza (Cs)
1990	Andreas Brüsser (Swz)
1991	Thomas Frischknecht (Swz)
1992	Daniele Pontoni (Ita)
1993	Henrik Djernis (Den)

Most wins: 5 Robert Vermeire

Amateur Team(1979 to 1993), now Open Team

1979	Poland
1980	Switzerland
1981	Italy
1982-4	Czechoslovakia
1985	Switzerland
1986	Belgium
1987	Czechoslovakia
1988	Switzerland
1989	Czechoslovakia
1990-2	Switzerland
1993	France
1994	Belgium

Mountain-Bike World Championships

Men Cross-country

1990	Ted Overend (USA)
1991	John Tomac (USA)
1992-4	Henrik Djemis (Den)

Men Downhill

1990	Greg Herbold (USA)
1991	Albert Iten (Swi)
1992	Dave Cullinan (USA)
1993	Mike King (USA)
1994	François Gachet (Fra)

Women Cross-country

1990	Julie Furtado (USA)
1991	Ruthie Matthes (USA)
1992	Silvia Fürst (Swi)
1993	Paula Pezzo (Ita)
1994	Alison Sydor (Can)

Women Downhill

1990	Cindy Devine (Can)
1991	Giovanna Bonazzi (Ita)
1992	Julie Furtado (USA)
1993	Giovanna Bonazzi (Ita)
1994	Missy Glove (USA)

Darts

Darts, or Dartes, were first used as a means of self defence during battles in Ireland in the 16th century. The Pilgrim Fathers played darts aboard the Mayflower on their way to discovering the New World in 1620. The modern game, however, dates to 1896 when Brian Gamlin of Bury, Lancashire, devised the present numbering system. The National Darts Association was formed in 1924 and the British Darts Organisation (BDO) was established in 1973. Darts developed into a popular television sport, with more than 6 million people playing in Britain alone.

In 1992, dissatisfied with the WBO's organisation of the game, many of the world's top players formed the World Darts Council (WDC), and that organisation introduced its own World Championship at the end of 1993.

BDO World Professional Championship

The world professional championship, sponsored by Embassy, is the professional players' leading tournament. It was instituted by the BDO at the Heart of the Midlands Night Club, Nottingham in 1978. Between 1979 and 1985 the tournaments were held at Jollees Night Club, Stoke-on-Trent and from 1986 at the Lakeside Country Club, Frimley Green, Surrey.

Year	Winner	Runner-up	Score
1978	Leighton Rees (Wal)	John Lowe (Eng)	11-7
1979	John Lowe (Eng)	Leighton Rees (Wal)	5-0
1980	Eric Bristow (Eng)	Bobby George (Eng)	5-3
1981	Eric Bristow (Eng)	John Lowe (Eng)	5-3
1982	Jocky Wilson (Sco)	John Lowe (Eng)	5-3
1983	Keith Deller (Eng)	Eric Bristow (Eng)	6-5
1984	Eric Bristow (Eng)	Dave Whitcombe (Eng)	7-1
1985	Eric Bristow (Eng)	John Lowe (Eng)	6-2
1986	Eric Bristow (Eng)	Dave Whitcombe (Eng)	6-0
1987	John Lowe (Eng)	Eric Bristow (Eng)	6-4
1988	Bob Anderson (Eng)	John Lowe (Eng)	6-4
1989	Jocky Wilson (Sco)	Eric Bristow (Eng)	6-4
1990	Phil Taylor (Eng)	Eric Bristow (Eng)	6-1
1991	Dennis Priestley (Eng)	Eric Bristow (Eng)	6-0
1992	Phil Taylor (Eng)	Mike Gregory (Eng)	6-5
1993	John Lowe (Eng)	Alan Warriner (Eng)	6-3
1994	John Part (Can)	Bobby George (Eng)	6-0
1995	Richie Burnett (Wal)	Raymond Barneveld (Hol)	6-3

1977 played over the best of 21 legs, 1978-82 best of 9 sets, 1983 best of 11 sets, 1984 best of 13 sets, 1985-95 best of 11 sets

WDC World Championships

The first championships, sponsored by Skol and organised by the breakaway group of top players was played at Purfleet, Surrey, ending on 1 Jan 1994.

Year	Winner	Runner-up	Score
1993/4	Dennis Priestley (Eng)	Phil Taylor (Eng)	6-1
1994/5	Phil Taylor (Eng) bt	Rod Harrington (Eng)	6-2

World Masters

The first World Masters took place at the West Centre Hotel, Fulham in 1974. Now sponsored by Winmau. *Winners:*

1974	Cliff Inglis (Eng)
1975	Alan Evans (Wal)
1976	John Lowe (Eng)
1977	Eric Bristow (Eng)
1978	Ronnie Davis (Eng)
1979	Eric Bristow (Eng)
1980	John Lowe (Eng)
1981	Eric Bristow (Eng)
1982	Dave Whitcombe (Eng)
1983-4	Eric Bristow (Eng)
1985	Dave Whitcombe (Eng)
1986-8	Bob Anderson (Eng)
1989	Peter Evison (Eng)
1990	Phil Taylor (Eng)
1991	Rod Harrington (Eng)
1992	Dennis Priestley (Eng)
1993	Steve Beaton (Eng)
1994	Richie Burnett (Wal) (held Jan 1995)

World Cup

A biennial event, the first World Cup was at Wembley in 1977. The winning nation is the team with the most points after a singles, pairs and fours competition. The women's competition was introduced in 1983.

Team winners

Wales	1977
England	1979, 1981, 1983, 1985, 1987, 1989, 1991, 1993

Individual title

1977	Leighton Rees (Wal)
1979	Nicky Virachkul (USA)
1981	John Lowe (Eng)
1983	Eric Bristow (Eng)
1985	Eric Bristow (Eng)
1987	Eric Bristow (Eng)
1989	Eric Bristow (Eng)
1991	John Lowe (Eng)
1993	Roland Scholten (Hol)

Most winning teams: 7 John Lowe, Eric Bristow (both England)

World Match Play

Held annually 1984-8 and reintroduced by the WDC in 1994. *Winners:*

1984	John Lowe (Eng)
1985	Eric Bristow (Eng)
1986	Mike Gregory (Eng)
1987	Bob Anderson (Eng)
1988	Eric Bristow (Eng)
1994	Larry Butler (USA)

Women's darts

World Cup

Instituted in 1983 and played at the same time as the men's competition.

Team winners

England	1983, 1985, 1989
USA	1987, 1993
New Zealand	1991

Individual title

1983	Sandy Reitan (USA)
1985	Linda Batten (UK)
1987	Valerie Maycum (Hol)
1989	Eva Grisby (USA)
1991	Jill MacDonald (NZ)
1993	Stacy Bromberg (USA)

World Masters

1982	Ann-Marie Davies (Wal)
1983	Sonja Ralphs (Eng)
1984	Kathy Wones (Eng)
1985	Lilian Barnett (NZ)
1986	Kathy Wones (Eng)
1987	Ann Thomas (Wal)
1988-9	Mandy Solomons (Eng)
1990	Rhian Speed (UK)
1991	Sandy Reitan (USA)
1992	Leanne Maddock (Wal)
1993	Mandy Solomons (Eng)
1994	Deta Hedman (Eng)

Equestrian Sports

The earliest known show jumping competition was in Ireland when the Royal Dublin Society held its first 'Horse Show' on 15 Apr 1864. The Societé Hippique Française was founded in 1865 and held its first Concours Hippique in Paris in 1866. The first event in England was at the Agricultural Hall, London in 1869.

Dressage competition derived from the exercises taught at 16th century Italian and French horsemanship academies, while the three-day event developed from cavalry endurance rides. One of the earliest known three-day event competitions was from Vienna to Berlin in 1892. The international governing body, the Fédération Equestre Internationale (FEI), was founded in Brussels in 1921, initially with eight member nations. The current president is HRH Princess Anne, who succeeded her father, HRH Prince Philip in 1986, and membership reached 96 nations in 1992.

World championships at six different equestrian disciplines - show jumping, three-day eventing, dressage, carriage driving, endurance riding and vaulting - were first combined at the first World Equestrian Games held in Stockholm in 1990; the second was held at The Hague in 1994.

Show Jumping

Olympic Games

Although not connected with events staged with the World Fair, what is regarded now as the first Olympic show jumping were the three days of international competition staged by the Societé Hippique Française in Paris in 1900, with jumping, high jump and long jump events. Two equestrian events were planned for 1908, but not held due to the paucity of entries, so show jumping was officially introduced in 1912. The 1956 competition took place in Stockholm, Sweden, because of quarantine restrictions in force in Australia at the time. *Winners:*

Individual

	Rider	Horse
1900	Aimé Haegeman (Bel)	Benton II
1912	Jean Cariou (Fra)	Mignon
1920	Tommaso Lequio (Ita)	Trebecco
1924	Alphonse Gemuseus (Swi)	Lucette
1928	Frantisek Ventura (Cs)	Eliot
1932	Takeichi Nishi (Jap)	Uranus
1936	Kürt Hasse (Ger)	Tora
1948	Humberto Mariles Cortés (Mex)	Arete

1952	Pierre Jonquères d'Oriola (Fra)	Ali Baba
1956	Hans Günter Winkler (Ger)	Halla
1960	Raimondo d'Inzeo (Ita)	Posillipo
1964	Pierre Jonquères d'Oriola (Fra)	Lutteur B
1968	William Steinkraus (USA)	Snowbound
1972	Graziano Mancinelli (Ita)	Ambassador
1976	Alwin Schockemöhle (FRG)	Warwick Rex
1980	Jan Kowalczyk (Pol)	Artemor
1984	Joe Fargis (USA)	Touch of Class
1988	Pierre Durand (Fra)	Jappeloup
1992	Ludger Beerbaum (Ger)	Classic Touch

Team

6	FR Germany	1936 (as Germany), 1956, 1960, 1964, 1972, 1988
3	Sweden	1912, 1920, 1924
1	Spain 1928, Mexico 1948	
1	Great Britain 1952, Canada 1968	
1	France 1976, USSR 1980	
1	USA 1984, Netherlands 1992	

No medals awarded 1932, when event not completed as no nation completed the course with three riders.

Most gold medals

5 Hans Günter Winkler (FRG) team 1956, 1960, 1964, 1972; individual 1956

Most medals

7 Hans Günter Winkler 5 gold, team silver 1976, team bronze 1968

6 Raimondo d'Inzeo (Ita) 1 gold (ind. 1960), 2 silver (team and ind. 1956), 3 bronze team 1960, 1964, 1972)

6 Piero d'Inzeo (Ita) 2 silver, 4 bronze (ind. silver 1960, bronze 1960, 1 team silver and 3 team bronze as for his younger brother Raimondo).

World Championships

Instituted in 1953, the championships are now held every four years. In the individual final each rider has to ride not only his own horse but also those of the other finallists. In 1965, 1970 and 1974, women had a separate competition on their own horses only, but now compete equally with their male counterparts. A team competition was introduced in 1978. *Winners:*

Individual

	Horse	Rider
1953	Francisco Goyoago (Spa)	Quorum
1954	Hans Günter Winkler (FRG)	Halla
1955	Hans Günter Winkler (FRG)	Halla
1956	Raimondo d'Inzeo (Ita)	Merano
1960	Raimondo d'Inzeo (Ita)	Gowran Girl
1966	Pierre Jonquères d'Oriola (Fra)	Pomone B
1970	David Broome (UK)	Beethoven
1974	Hartwig Steenken (FRG)	Simona
1978	Gerd Wiltfang (FRG)	Roman
1982	Norbert Koof (FRG)	Fire II
1986	Gail Greenhough (Can)	Mr. T
1990	Eric Navet (Fra)	Quito de Baussy
1994	Franke Sloothaak (Ger)	San Patrignano Weihaiwej

Nick Skelton – World Cup winner 1995

Women

1965	Marion Coakes (UK)	Stroller
1970	Janou Lefèbvre (Fra)	Rocket
1974	Janou Tissot (née Lefèbvre) (Fra)	Rocket

Team

3	France	1982, 1986, 1990
1	Great Britain 1978, USA 1986, Germany 1994	

Most titles

2 Hans Günter Winkler, Raimondo d'Inzeo, Janou Tissot (née Lefèbvre)

Volvo World Cup

Instituted by the FEI in 1979 and contested over a series of primarily indoor competitions held between October and April with an annual final. *Winners:*

1979	Hugo Simon (Aut)	Gladstone
1980	Conrad Homfeld (USA)	Balbuco
1981	Michael Matz (USA)	Jet Run
1982	Melanie Smith (USA)	Calypso
1983	Norman Dello Joio (USA)	I Love You
1984	Mario Deslauriers (Can)	Aramis
1985	Conrad Homfeld (USA)	Abdullah
1986	Leslie Burr-Lenehan (USA)	McLain
1987	Katharine Burdsall (USA)	The Natural
1988-9	Ian Millar (Can)	Big Ben

1990-1	John Whitaker (UK)	Milton
1992	Thomas Fruhmann (Aut)	Bockmann's Genius
1993	Ludger Beerbaum (Ger)	Ratinoz
1994	Jos Lansink (Hol)	Bollvorm's Libero
1995	Nick Skelton (UK)	Everest Dollar Girl

Nation's Cup

The President's Cup was introduced by the FEI in 1965 for Nations Cup teams. The performances by national teams of four at selected meetings count towards the Cup, with different countries staging just one Nations Cup meeting, which must be at its official International Horse Show. Renamed the Prince Philip Trophy in 1985, to mark his 21st year in office as FEI President, and the Gucci Trophy from 1987.

Winning nations:

14	Great Britain	1965, 1967, 1970, 1972-4, 1977-9, 1983, 1985-6, 1989, 1991
8	Germany/FRG	1969, 1971, 1975-6, 1981-2, 1984, 1994
4	France	1980, 1987-8, 1990, 1992
2	USA	1966, 1968

European Championships

Inaugurated in 1957, and staged biennially from 1963, men and women had separate competitions (and were allowed to ride two horses) until 1975, when the FEI introduced a team event as well as an individual competition open to both men and women. In 1957 and 1959 they were conducted with a change-horse final, as per the World Championships, but that was then abandoned. *Winners (with first horses prior to 1975):*

Men

	Rider	Horse
1957	Hans Günter Winkler (FRG)	Sonnenglanz
1958	Fritz Thiedemann (FRG)	Meteor
1959	Piero d'Inzeo (Ita)	Uruguay
1961	David Broome (UK)	Sunsalve
1962	David Barker (UK)	Mister Softee
1963	Graziano Mancinelli (Ita)	Rockette
1965	Hermann Schridde (FRG)	Dozent
1966	Nelson Pessoa (Bra)	Gran Geste
1967	David Broome (UK)	Mister Softee
1969	David Broome (UK)	Mister Softee
1971	Hartwig Steenken (FRG)	Simona
1973	Paddy McMahon (UK)	Pennwood Forge Mill
1975	Alwin Schockemöhle (FRG)	Warwick
1977	Johan Heins (Hol)	Seven Valleys
1979	Gerhard Wiltfang (FRG)	Roman
1981	Paul Schockemöhle (FRG)	Deister
1983	Paul Schockemöhle (FRG)	Deister
1985	Paul Schockemöhle (FRG)	Deister
1987	Pierre Durand (Fra)	Jappeloup
1989	John Whitaker (UK)	Next Milton
1991	Eric Navet (Fra)	Quito de Baussy
	(horse later failed drugs test)	
1993	Willi Melliger (Swi)	Quinta C

Team

4	Great Britain	1979, 1985, 1987, 1989
2	FR Germany	1975, 1981
2	Netherlands	1977, 1991
2	Switzerland	1983, 1993

Women

1957	Pat Smythe (UK)	Flanagan
1958	Guilia Serventi (Ita)	Doly
1959	Ann Townsend (UK)	Bandit IV
1960	Susan Cohen (UK)	Clare Castle
1961	Pat Smythe (UK)	Scorchin
1962	Pat Smythe (UK)	Flanagan
1963	Pat Smythe (UK)	Flanagan
1966	Janou Lefèbvre (Fra)	Kenavo
1967	Kathy Kusner (USA)	Untouchable
1968	Anneli Drummond-Hay (UK)	Merely-a-Monarch
1969	Iris Kellett (Ire)	Morning Light
1971	Ann Moore (UK)	Psalm
1973	Ann Moore (UK)	Psalm

Flanagan is the only horse to have won four European Championships, the three above and in 1961 when he was Pat Smythe's second horse.

Royal International Horse Show

First staged as the International Horse Show in the Grand Hall at Olympia in 1907. The world's first Nations Cup for teams was staged in 1909. The Show has been held annually at Wembley, but at Hickstead in 1993. The two most famous events are the:

King George V Gold Cup

King George V presented a gold international perpetual challenge trophy. It was first contested in 1911, and the competition is regarded as the principle annual show jumping event for male riders. Any rider winning the event three times keeps the trophy. *Post war winners:*

1947	Pierre Jonquères d'Oriola (Fra)	Marquis III
1948	Harry Llewellyn (UK)	Foxhunter
1949	Brian Butler (UK)	Tankard
1950	Harry Llewellyn (UK)	Foxhunter
1951	Kevin Barry (Ire)	Ballyneety
1952	Carlos Figueroa (Spa)	Gracieux
1953	Harry Llewellyn (UK)	Foxhunter
1954	Fritz Thiedemann (FRG)	Meteor
1955	Luigi Cartesegna (Ita)	Brando
1956	William Steinkraus (USA)	First Boy
1957	Piero d'Inzeo (Ita)	Uruguay
1958	Hugh Wiley (USA)	Master William
1959	Hugh Wiley (USA)	Nautical
1960	David Broome (UK)	Sunsalve
1961-2	Piero d'Inzeo (Ita)	The Rock
1963	Thomas Wade (Ire)	Dundrum
1964	William Steinkraus (USA)	Sinjon
1965	Hans Günter Winkler (FRG)	Fortun
1966	David Broome (UK)	Mister Softee
1967	Peter Robeson (UK)	Firecrest
1968	Hans Günter Winkler (FRG)	Enigk
1969	Ted Edgar (UK)	Uncle Max

1970	Harvey Smith (UK)	Mattie Brown
1971	Gerd Wiltfang (FRG)	Askan
1972	David Broome (UK)	Sportsman
1973	Paddy McMahon (UK)	Pennwood Forge Mill
1974	Frank Chapot (USA)	Main Spring
1975	Alwin Schockemöhle (FRG)	Rex the Robber
1976	Michael Saywell (UK)	Chain Bridge
1977	David Broome (UK)	Philco
1978	Jeff McVean (Aus)	Claret
1979	Robert Smith (UK)	Video
1980	David Bowen (UK)	Scorton
1981	David Broome (UK)	Mr. Ross
1982	Michael Whitaker (UK)	Disney Way
1983	Paul Schockemöhle (FRG)	Deister
1984	Nick Skelton (UK)	St. James
1985	Malcolm Pyrah (UK)	Towerlands Anglezark
1986	John Whitaker (UK)	Next Ryan's Son
1987	Malcolm Pyrah (UK)	Towerlands Anglezark
1988	Robert Smith (UK)	Brook Street Boysie
1989	Michael Whitaker (UK)	Next Didi
1990	John Whitaker (UK)	Milton
1991	David Broome (UK)	Lannegan
1992	Michael Whitaker (UK)	Midnight Madness
1993	Nick Skelton (UK)	Limited Edition
1994	Michael Whitaker (UK)	Midnight Madness
1995	Robert Splaine (Ire)	Heather Blaze

Most wins
Rider: 6 David Broome, 4 Michael Whitaker, 3 Jack Talbot-Ponsonby 1930, 1932, 1934; Harry Llewellyn, Piero d'Inzeo
Horse: 3 Foxhunter 1948, 1950, 1953

Queen Elizabeth II Cup

The Queen Elizabeth II Cup is the women's equivalent of the King George V Gold Cup. It was inaugurated in 1949. *Winners:*

1949	Iris Kellett (Ire)	Rusty
1950	Gill Palethorpe (UK)	Silver Cloud
1951	Iris Kellett (Ire)	Rusty
1952	Gill Rich (UK)	Quicksilver III
1953	Marie Delfosse (UK)	Fanny Rosa
1954	Josée Bonnaud (Fra)	Charleston
1955-6	Dawn Palethorpe (UK)	Earlsrath Rambler
1957	Elizabeth Anderson (UK)	Sunsalve
1958	Pat Smythe (UK)	Mr. Pollard
1959	Anna Clement (FRG)	Nico
1960	Susan Cohen (UK)	Clare Castle
1961	Lady Sarah FitzAlan Howard (UK)	Oorskiet
1962	Judy Crago (UK)	Spring Fever
1963	Julie Nash (UK)	Trigger Hill
1964	Gillian Makin (UK)	Jubilant
1965	Marion Coakes (UK)	Stroller
1966	Althea Roger Smith (UK)	Havana Royal
1967	Betty Jennaway (UK)	Grey Leg
1968	Mary Chapot (USA)	White Lightning
1969	Alison Westwood (UK)	The Maverick VII
1968	Anneli Drummond-Hay (UK)	Merely-a-Monarch
1971	Marion Mould (née Coakes) (UK)	Stroller
1972	Ann Moore (UK)	Psalm
1973	Ann Moore (UK) &	Psalm
	Alison Dawes (née Westwood)	Mr. Banbury
1974	Jean Davenport (UK)	All Trumps
1975	Jean Davenport (UK)	Hang On
1976	Marion Mould (UK)	Elizabeth Ann
1977	Liz Edgar (UK)	Everest Wallaby
1978	Caroline Bradley (UK)	Marius
1979	Liz Edgar (UK)	Forever
1980	Caroline Bradley (UK)	Tigre
1981-2	Liz Edgar (UK)	Everest Forever
1983	Jean Germany (UK)	Mandingo
1984	Véronique Whitaker (UK)	Next's Jingo
1985	Sue Pountain (UK)	Ned Kelly VI
1986	Liz Edgar (UK)	Everest Rapier
1987	Gillian Greenwood (UK)	Monsanta
1988-9	Janet Hunter (UK)	Everest Lisnamarrow
1990	Emma-Jane Mac (UK)	Everest Oyster
1991	Janet Hunter (UK)	Everest Lisnamarrow
1992	Tina Cassan (UK)	Genesis
1993	Tina Cassan (UK)	Bond Xtra
1994	Di Lampard (UK)	Abbervail Dream
1995	Marion Hughes (Ire)	Flo Jo

Most wins
5 Liz Edgar, 3 Marion Mould (née Coakes)
The only horse to win the King George V Gold Cup and Queen Elizabeth II Cup is Sunsalve, 1957, 1960.

British Show Jumping Derby

Held annually at the All-England Jumping Centre Hickstead in Sussex, the first Derby was in 1961. A Derby is contested over a course of c.1300m, about 500m longer than an Olympic Nations Cup course.

1961	Seamus Hayes (Ire)	Goodbye III
1962	Pat Smythe (UK)	Flanagan
1963	Nelson Pessoa (Bra)	Gran Geste
1964	Seamus Hayes (Ire)	Goodbye III
1965	Nelson Pessoa (Bra)	Gran Geste
1966	David Broome (UK)	Mister Softee
1967	Marion Coakes (UK)	Stroller
1968	Alison Westwood (UK)	The Maverick VII
1969	Anneli Drummond-Hay (UK)	Xanthos II
1970	Harvey Smith (UK)	Mattie Brown
1971	Harvey Smith (UK)	Mattie Brown
1972	Hendrick Snoek (FRG)	Shirokko
1973	Alison Dawes (née Westwood)	Mr. Banbury
1974	Harvey Smith (UK)	Salvador
1975	Paul Darragh (Ire)	Pele
1976-9	Eddie Macken (Ire)	Boomerang
1980	Michael Whitaker (UK)	Owen Gregory
1981	Harvey Smith (UK)	Sanyo Video
1982	Paul Schockemöhle (FRG)	Deister
1983	John Whitaker (UK)	Ryan's Son

1984	John Ledingham (Ire)	Gabhran
1985	Paul Schockemöhle (FRG)	Lorenzo
1986	Paul Schockemöhle (FRG)	Deister
1987	Nick Skelton (UK)	Raffles
1988-9	Nick Skelton (UK)	Apollo
1990	Joe Turi (UK)	Vital
1991-2	Michael Whittaker	Monsanta
1993	Michael Whittaker	My Messieur
1994	John Ledingham	Kilbaha

Most wins: 4 Eddie Macken, Harvey Smith, Michael Whitaker; 3 Paul Schockemöhle, Nick Skelton

Jumping Records

The official high jump world record is 2.47m (8 ft 1 1/4 in) by Huasó, ridden by Capt.Alberto Larraguibel (Chl) on 5 Feb 1949; the indoor record is 2.40m by Franke Sloothaak (Ger) on Optibeurs Leonardi on 9 Jun 1991. The world long jump record is 8.40m (27 ft 6 3/4in) by Something, ridden by André Ferreira (SAf) on 26 Apr 1975.

Three-day Eventing

Competitors ride the same horse in a) a dressage test, b) an endurance competition of four phases: roads and track 16-20 km in Games and championships, steeplechase of 3105-3450m, roads and track again, cross country of 7410-7980m, c) a jumping test.

Olympic Games

Both individual and team competitions were first held at the 1912 Games, when it was known as 'the military' and restricted to army officers. The current three event pattern was established at Paris in 1924. *Winners:*

Individual

1912	Axel Nordlander (Swe)	Lady Artist
1920	Helmer Mörner (Swe)	Germania
1924	Adolph v d Voort van Zijp (Hol)	Silver Piece
1928	Charles Pahud de Mortanges (Hol)	Marcroix
1932	Charles Pahud de Mortanges (Hol)	Marcroix
1936	Ludwig Stubbendorff (Ger)	Nurmi
1948	Bernard Chevallier (Fra)	Aiglonne
1952	Hans von Blixen-Finecke Jr (Swe)	Jubal
1956	Petrus Kastenman (Swe)	Iluster
1960	Lawrence Morgan (Aus)	Salad Days
1964	Mauro Checcoli (Ita)	Surbean
1968	Jean-Jacques Gùyon (Fra)	Pitou
1972	Richard Meade (UK)	Laurieston
1976	Edmund Coffin (USA)	Bally-Cor
1980	Federico Roman (Ita)	Rossinan
1984	Mark Todd (NZ)	Charisma
1988	Mark Todd (NZ)	Charisma
1992	Matthew Ryan (Aus)	Kibah Tic Toc

Team

4	USA	1932, 1948, 1976, 1984
3	Sweden	1912, 1920, 1952
3	Great Britain	1956, 1968, 1972
3	Germany	1936, 1938, F R Germany 1988

2	Netherlands	1924, 1928
2	Australia	1960, 1992
1	Italy 1964, USSR 1980	

Most gold medals: 4 Charles Pahud de Mortanges (Hol) team 1924, 1928; individual 1928, 1932 (also won team silver 1932 for a record five medals)

World Championships

Instituted in 1966, men and women have competed together at all championships.

Individual

1966	Carlos Moratorio (Arg)	Chalon
1970	Mary Gordon-Watson (UK)	Cornishman V
1974	Bruce Davidson (USA)	Irish Cap
1978	Bruce Davidson (USA)	Might Tango
1982	Lucinda Green (UK	Regal Realm
1986	Virginia Leng (UK)	Priceless
1990	Blyth Tait (NZ)	Messiah
1994	Vaughan Jefferis (NZ)	Bounce

Team wins

4	Great Britain	1970, 1982, 1986, 1994
1	Ireland 1966, USA 1974	
1	Canada 1978, New Zealand 1990	

Most gold medals

3 Bruce Davidson ind. 1974, 1978, team 1974
3 Virginia Leng ind. 1986, team 1982, 1986

European Championships

Individual

1953	Lawrence Rook (UK)	Starlight
1954	Albert Hill (UK)	Crispin
1955	Frank Weldon (UK)	Kilbarry
1957	Sheila Willcox (UK)	High and Mighty
1959	Hans Schwarzenbach (Swi)	Burn Trout
1962	James Templar (UK)	M'Lord Connolly
1965	Marian Babirecki (Pol)	Volt
1967	Eddie Boylan (Ire)	Durlas Eile
1969	Mary Gordon-Watson (UK)	Cornishman V
1971	HRH Princess Anne (UK)	Doublet
1973	Aleksandr Yevdokimov (USSR)	Jeger
1975	Lucinda Prior-Palmer (UK)	Be Fair
1977	Lucinda Prior-Palmer (UK)	George
1979	Nils Haagensen (Den)	Monaco
1981	Hansueli Schmutz (Swi)	Oran
1983	Rachel Bayliss (UK)	Mystic Minstrel
1985	Virginia Holgate (UK)	Priceless
1987	Virginia Leng (née Holgate) (UK)	Night Cap
1989	Virginia Leng (UK)	Master Craftsman
1991	Ian Stark (UK)	Glenburnie
1993	Jean-Louis Bigot (Fra)	Twist la Beige

Team wins

12	Great Britain	1953-5, 1957, 1967, 1969, 1971, 1977, 1981, 1985, 1987, 1989
3	USSR	1962, 1965, 1975
2	FR Germany	1959, 1973
2	Sweden	1983, 1993
1	Ireland	1979

Badminton

The Badminton Horse Trials take place in the grounds of Badminton House in Gloucestershire, home of the Beaufort family. The first event was in 1949, and the annual attendance is around 200,000. *Winners:*

1949	John Shedden (UK)	Golden Willow
1950	Tony Collings (UK)	Remus
1951	Hans Schwarzenbach (Swi)	Vae Victus
1952	Mark Darley (Ire)	Emily Little
1953	Lawrence Rook (UK)	Starlight
1954	Margaret Hough (UK)	Bambi
1955-6	Frank Weldon (UK) #	Kilbarry
1957-8	Sheila Willcox (UK)	High and Mighty
1959	Sheila Waddington (UK) (née Wilcox)	Airs and Graces
1960	Bill Roycroft (Aus)	Our Solo
1961	Lawrence Morgan (Aus)	Salad Days
1962	Anneli Drummond-Hay (UK)	Merely-a-Monarch
1963	Susan Fleet (UK) *	Gladiator
1964	James Templer (UK)	M'Lord Connolly
1965	Eddie Boylan (Ire)	Durlas File
1966	*Not held*	
1967	Celia Ross-Taylor (UK)	Jonathan
1968	Jane Bullen (UK)	Our Nobby
1969	Richard Walker (UK)	Pasha
1970	Richard Meade (UK)	The Poacher
1971-2	Mark Phillips (UK)	Great Ovation
1973	Lucinda Prior-Palmer (UK)	Be Fair
1974	Mark Phillips (UK)	Columbus
1975	*Cancelled after dressage*	
1976	Lucinda Prior-Palmer (UK)	Wideawake
1977	Lucinda Prior-Palmer (UK)	George
1978	Jane Holderness-Roddam (née Bullen) (UK)	Warrior
1979	Lucinda Prior-Palmer (UK)	Killaire
1980	Mark Todd (NZ)	Southern Comfort
1981	Mark Phillips (UK)	Lincoln
1982	Richard Meade (UK)	Speculator III
1983	Lucinda Green (née Prior-Palmer)	Regal Realm
1984	Lucinda Green (UK)	Beagle Bay
1985	Virginia Holgate (UK)	Priceless
1986	Ian Stark (UK)	Sir Wattie
1987	*Not held*	
1988	Ian Stark (UK)	Sir Wattie
1989	Virginia Leng (née Holgate) (UK)	Master Craftsman
1990	Nicola McIrvine (UK)	Middle Road
1991	Rodney Powell (UK)	The Irishman
1992	Mary Thomson (UK)	King William
1993	Virginia Leng (UK)	Houdini
1994	Mark Todd (NZ)	Horton Point
1995	Bruce Davidson (USA)	Eagle Lion

Most wins: 6 Lucinda Green (née Prior-Palmer), 4 Mark Phillips, 3 Sheila Waddington (née Willcox), Virginia Leng (née Holgate)

*# Held at Windsor 1955, * reduced to a one day event because of the weather*

Bruce Davidson – the only double world champion at three-day eventing

Burghley Horse Trials

Held each September on the estate surrounding Burghley House in Lincolnshire, this is the major event of the autumn trials season. Burghley House was the home of the former Olympic athletics gold medallist, David Burghley, the Marquess of Exeter. *Winners:*

1968	Anneli Drummond-Hay (UK)	Merely-a-Monarch
1963	Harry Freeman-Jackson (Ire)	St. Finbar
1964	Richard Meade (UK)	Barberry
1965	Jeremy Beale (UK)	Victoria Bridge
1967	Lorna Sutherland (UK)	Popadom
1968	Sheila Willcox (UK)	Fair and Square
1969	Gillian Watson (UK)	Shaitan
1970	Judy Bradwell (UK)	Don Camillo
1972	Janet Hodgson (UK)	Larkspur
1973	Mark Phillips (UK)	Maid Marion
1975	Aly Pattinson (UK)	Carawich
1976	Jane Holderness-Roddam (UK)	Warrior
1977	Lucinda Prior-Palmer (UK)	George
1978	Lorna Clarke (UK	Greco
1979	Andrew Hoy (Aus)	Davy
1980	Richard Walker (UK)	John of Gaunt
1981	Lucinda Prior-Palmer (UK)	Beagle Bay
1982	Richard Walker (UK)	Ryan's Cross
1983	Virginia Holgate (UK)	Priceless
1984	Virginia Holgate (UK)	Night Cap
1986	Virginia Leng (née Holgate) (UK)	Murphy Himself
1987	Mark Todd (NZ)	Wilson Fair
1988	Jane Thelwall (UK)	King's Jester
1990	Mark Todd (NZ)	Face The Music
1991	Mark Todd (NZ)	Welton Greylag
1992	Charlotte Hollingsworth (UK)	The Cool Customer
1993	Stephen Bradley (USA)	Sassy Reason
1994	Willim Fox-Pitt (UK)	Chaka

1962, 1971, 1985, 1989 see European Championship
1966, 1974 see World Championship

Most wins
3 Virginia Leng (née Holgate), Mark Todd
2 Lorna Clarke (née Sutherland), Lucinda Prior-Palmer, Richard Walker

Dressage

Olympic Games

The individual competition was included in the 1912 Games, but the team competition was not introduced until 1928.

Individual

1912	Carl Bonde (Swe)	Emperor
1920	Janne Lundblad (Swe)	Uno
1924	Ernst Linder (Swe)	Piccolomini
1928	Carl von Langen (Ger)	Draufgänger
1932	Xavier Lesage (Fra)	Taine
1936	Heinz Pollay (Ger)	Kronos
1948	Hans Moser (Swi)	Hummer
1952	Henri St Cyr (Swe)	Master Rufus
1956	Henri St Cyr (Swe)	Juli
1960	Sergey Filatov (USSR)	Absent
1964	Henri Chammartin (Swi)	Woermann
1968	Ivan Kizimov (USSR)	Ichor
1972	Liselott Linsenhoff (FRG)	Piaff
1976	Christine Stückelberger (Swi)	Granat
1980	Elisabeth Theurer (Aut)	Mon Cherie
1984	Reiner Klimke (FRG)	Ahlerich
1988	Nicole Uphoff (FRG)	Rembrandt
1992	Nicole Uphoff (Ger)	Rembrandt

Team
8	Germany/FRG	1928, 1936, 1964, 1992 FRG: 1968, 1976, 1984, 1988
2	France	1932, 1948
2	Sweden	1952, 1956
2	USSR	1972, 1980

Not held in 1960

Most gold medals
6 Reiner Klimke (FRG) team gold 1964, 1968, 1976, 1984, 1988, individual 1984; 4 Henri St Cyr (Swe) team 1952, 1956; individual 1952, 1956

Most medals
8 Klimke, six gold, individual bronze 1968, 1976

World Championships

Inaugurated 1966. *Winners:*

Individual
1966	Josef Neckermann (FRG)	Mariano
1970	Yelena Petuchkova (USSR)	Pepel
1974	Reiner Klimke (FRG)	Mehmed
1978	Christine Stückelberger (Swi)	Granat
1982	Reiner Klimke (FRG)	Ahlerich
1986	Anne Grethe Jensen (Den)	Marzog
1990	Nicole Uphoff (FRG)	Rembrandt
1994	Isabell Werth (Ger)	Gigolo

Freestyle Dressage World Champions
1994	Anky van Grunsven (Hol)	Olympic Bonfire

Team
7	Germany	FRG 1966, 1974, 1978, 1982, 1986, 1990; GER 1994
1	USSR	1970

Most gold medals
6 Reiner Klimke, 2 individual, 4 team 1966, 1974, 1982, 1986

FEI World Cup

First held in 1986. *Winners:*

1986	Anne Grethe Jensen (Den)	Marzog
1987-8	Christine Stückelberger (Swi)	Gauguin de Lully
1989	Margrit Otto-Crepin (Fra)	Corlandus
1990	Sven Rothenberger (FRG)	Andiamo
1991	Kyra Kyrklund (Fin)	Matador
1992	Isabell Werth (Ger)	Fabienne
1993-4	Monica Theodorescu (Ger)	Ganimedes Tecrent

European Championships

Inaugurated 1963. *Winners:*

Individual

1963	Henri Chammartin (Swi)	Wolfdietrich
1965	Henri Chammartin (Swi)	Wolfdietrich
1967	Reiner Klimke (FRG)	Dux
1969	Liselott Linsenhoff (FRG)	Piaff
1971	Liselott Linsenhoff (FRG)	Piaff
1973	Reiner Klimke (FRG)	Mehmed
1975	Christine Stückelberger (Swi)	Granat
1977	Christine Stückelberger (Swi)	Granat
1979	Elisabeth Theurer (Aut)	Mon Cherie
1981	Uwe Schulten-Baumer (FRG)	Madras
1983	Anne Grethe Jensen (Den)	Marzog
1985	Reiner Klimke (FRG)	Ahlerich
1987	Margrit Otto-Crepin (Fra)	Corlandus
1989	Nicole Uphoff (FRG)	Rembrandt
1991	Isabelle Werth (Ger)	Gigolo II
1993	Isabelle Werth (Ger)	Gigolo II

Team

15	FRG/Germany	1965, 1967, 1969, 1971, 1973, 1975, 1977, 1979, 1981, 1983, 1985, 1987, 1989, 1991, 1993
1	Great Britain	1963

Carriage Driving

Rules for driving events were established by the FEI in 1970. Combined driving for teams of four horses or for pairs consists of a) presentation and dressage, b) endurance marathon of 23-27 km, c) obstacle driving.

World Championships

Instituted in 1972 and subsequently held every two years.

Individual

1972	Auguste Dubey (Swi)
1974	Sándor Fülöp (Hun)
1976	Imre Abonyi (Hun)
1978	György Bárdos (Hun)
1980	György Bárdos (Hun)
1982	Tjeerd Velstra (Hol)
1984	László Juhász (Hun)
1986	Tjeerd Velstra (Hol)
1988	Ijsbrand Chardon (Hol)
1990	Tómas Eriksson (Swe)*
1992	Ijsbrand Chardon (Hol)
1994	Michael Freund (Ger)

Team

3	Netherlands	1982, 1986, 1988
3	Great Britain	1972, 1974, 1980
3	Hungary	1976, 1978, 1984
2	Germany	1992, 1994
1	Sweden	1990*

Members of three winning teams: György Bárdos and Sándor Fülöp (Hun), Ijsbrand Chardon (Hol)

* *The original winner Ad Aarts (Hol) lost his title after his horse Pablo failed a dope test. The Netherlands also lost their team title.*

World Pairs

An open FEI Pairs Championship was held in Paris in 1983. Its success led to the introduction of the World Pair Driving

Championship, first held in 1985 at Sandringham, England. This site was offered by HRH Prince Philip, then the FEI president and himself a successful Four-in-Hand driver. *Winners:*

	Team	Individual
1983	Netherlands	Paul Gregory (UK)
1985	Switzerland	Ekkert Meinecke (FRG)
1987	FR Germany	László Kecskerneti (Hun)
1989	Hungary	Udo Hochgeschorz (Can)
1991	USA	Werner Ullrich (Swz)
1993	Austria	Georg Moser (Aut)

Endurance Riding

World Championships

Instituted in 1986 and subsequently held every two years.

Individual

1986	Casandra Schuler (US)	Skiko's Omar
1988	Becky Hart (USA)	Grand Sultan
1990	Becky Hart (USA)	Grand Sultan
1992	Becky Hart (USA)	Grand Sultan
1994	Valerie Kanavy (USA)	Pieraz

Team

2	Great Britain	1986, 1990
2	France	1992, 1994
1	USA	1988

Vaulting

World Championships

Instituted in 1986, and subsequently held every two years.

Individual - Men

1986	Dietmar Ott (FRG)
1988	Christoph Pensing (FRG)
1990	Michael Lehner (FRG)
1992	Christoph Lensing (Ger)
1994	Thomas Fiskbaek (Den)

Individual - Women

1986	Silke Bernhard (FRG)
1988	Silke Bernhard (FRG)
1990	Silke Bernhard (FRG)
1992	Barbara Strobel (Ger)
1994	Tanja Benedetto (Ger)

Team

3	FRG/GER	1986, 1988, 1992
2	Switzerland	1990, 1994

Equestrian sports - women's name changes

First name	*Single*	*Married*
Jane	Bullen	Holderness-Roddam
Marion	Coakes	Mould
Jean	Goodwin	Davenport
Virginia	Holgate	Leng
Janou	Lefèbvre	Tissou
Lucinda	Prior-Palmer	Green
Lorna	Sutherland	Clarke
Sheila	Willcox	Waddington
Alison	Westwood	Dawes

Fencing

Fencing, the sport of fighting with a sword, is one of man's oldest pastimes, obviously related to the use of swords in war or single combat. There is evidence of swordsmanship in Egypt as early as 1360 BC. Fencing was widespread in the Middle Ages, and the rapier had been developed as the principal weapon by the end of the 16th century.

Modern weapons are the épée, foil and sabre. With the épée (weighing 770 grams) the conditions closely follow those that once appertained to duelling and the whole body is a target area. With the lighter weapons, for the foil (maximum weight 500 grams) the target area is the metallic jacket covering the top half of the body, and for the sabre (500 grams) above the waist, including the head. For the two latter weapons a hit must follow prescribed movements - the 'phrase'.

The world governing body, the Fédération Internationale d'Escrime (FIE), was founded in Paris in 1913.

Olympic Games

Fencing has been included at all Olympic Games, and these tournaments count as world championships in Olympic years. At the Games between 1896 and 1906, in addition to the competitions, of which the winners are shown below, there were also events for Fencing Masters, at which these professionals competed against the other contestants. Women first competed in 1924 (with the foil); electronic scoring was introduced for the épée in 1936 and for the foil in 1956. *Winners:*

Men	Foil	Epée	Sabre
1896	Emile Gravelotte (Fra)	Not held	Jean Georgiadis (Gre)
1900	Emile Coste (Fra)	Ramón Fonst (Cub)	Georges de la Falaise (Fra)
1904	Ramón Fonst (Cub)	Ramón Fonst (Cub)	Manuel Diaz (Cub)
1906	Georges Dillon-Kavanagh (Fra)	Georges de la Falaise (Fra)	Jean Georgiadis (Gre)
1908	Not held	Gaston Alibert (Fra)	Jenö Fuchs (Hun)
1912	Nedo Nadi (Ita)	Paul Anspach (Bel)	Jenö Fuchs (Hun)
1920	Nedo Nadi (Ita)	Armand Massard (Fra)	Nedo Nadi (Ita)
1924	Roger Ducret (Fra)	Charles Delporte (Bel)	Sándor Posta (Hun)
1928	Lucien Gaudin (Fra)	Lucien Gaudin (Fra)	Odön Tersztyanszky (Hun)
1932	Gustavo Marzi (Ita)	Giancarlo Cornaggia-Medici (Ita)	György Piller (Hun)
1936	Giulio Gaudini (Ita)	Franco Riccardi (Ita)	Endre Kabos (Hun)
1948	Jean Buhan (Fra)	Luigi Cantone (Ita)	Aladár Gerevich (Hun)
1952	Christian d'Oriola (Fra)	Edoardo Mangiarotti (Ita)	Pál Kovács (Hun)
1956	Christian d'Oriola (Fra)	Carlo Pavesi (Ita)	Rudolf Kárpáti (Hun)
1960	Viktor Zhdanovich (USSR)	Giuseppe Delfino (Ita)	Rudolf Kárpáti (Hun)
1964	Egon Franke (Pol)	Grigoriy Kriss (USSR)	Tibor Pézsa (Hun)
1968	Ion Drimba (Rom)	Gyözö Kulcsár (Hun)	Jerzy Pawlowski (Pol)
1972	Witold Woyda (Pol)	Csaba Fenyvesi (Hun)	Viktor Sidiak (USSR)
1976	Fabio Dal Zotto (Ita)	Alexander Pusch (FRG)	Viktor Krovopuskov (USSR)
1980	Vladimir Smirnov (USSR)	Johan Harmenberg (Swe)	Viktor Krovopuskov (USSR)
1984	Mauro Numa (Ita)	Philippe Boisse (Fra)	Jean François Lamour (Fra)
1988	Stefano Cerioni (Ita)	Arnd Schmitt (FRG)	Jean François Lamour (Fra)
1992	Philippe Omnès (Fra)	Eric Srecki (Fra)	Bence Szabó (Hun)

Men's team *Wins:*

Foil

6	France	1924, 1932, 1948, 1952, 1968, 1980
5	Italy	1920, 1928, 1936, 1956, 1984
3	USSR	1960, 1964, 1988
2	Germany	1976 (FRG), 1992
1	Cuba 1904, Poland 1972	

Epée

7	France	1906, 1908, 1924, 1932, 1948, 1980, 1988
6	Italy	1920, 1928, 1936, 1952, 1956, 1960
3	Hungary	1964, 1968, 1972
2	Germany	1984 (FRG), 1992
1	Belgium 1912, Sweden 1976	

Sabre

10	Hungary	1908, 1912, 1928, 1932, 1936, 1948, 1952, 1956, 1960, 1988
5	USSR/CIS	1964, 1968, 1976, 1980, 1992 (CIS)
4	Italy	1920, 1924, 1972, 1984
1	Germany	1906

Women's foil

1924 Ellen Osiier (Den)
1928 Helene Mayer (Ger)
1932 Ellen Preis (Aut)
1936 Ilona Elek (Hun)
1948 Ilona Elek (Hun)
1952 Irene Camber (Ita)
1956 Gillian Sheen (UK)
1960 Heidi Schmid (FRG)
1964 Ildikó Ujlaki-Rejtö (Hun)
1968 Yelena Novikova (USSR)
1972 Antonella Ragno-Lonzi (Ita)
1976 Ildikó Schwarczenberger (Hun)
1980 Pascale Trinquet (Fra)
1984 Luan Jujie (Chn)

1988 Anja Fichtel (FRG)
1992 Giovanna Trillini (Ita)

Women's foil team wins
4   USSR   1960, 1968, 1972, 1976
2   FR Germany   1984, 1988
1   Hungary 1964, France 1980, Italy 1992

Most Olympic medals - individual (I) and team (T)
Men

Name	G I/T	S I/T	B I/T	Years
13 Edoardo Mangiarotti (Ita)	1/5	1/4	2/-	1936-60
10 Aladár Gerevich (Hun)	1/6	1/-	1/1	1932-60
9 Giulio Gaudini (Ita)	1/2	1/3	2/-	1928-36
8 Roger Ducret (Fra)	1/2	2/2	1/-	1920-28
8 Philippe Cattiau (Fra)	-/3	2/2	-/1	1920-36
7 Pál Kovács (Hun)	1/5	-/-	1/-	1936-60

Others with five or more including four gold medals:

6	Nedo Nadi (Ita)	3/3	-/-	-/-	1912-20
6	Christian d'Oriola (Fra)	2/2	1/1	-/-	1948-56
6	Rudolf Kárpáti (Hun)	2/4	-/-	-/-	1948-60
6	Lucien Gaudin (Fra)	2/2	-/2	-/-	1920-28
6	Giuseppe Delfino (Ita)	1/3	1/1	-/-	1952-64
6	Gyözö Kulcsár (Hun)	1/3	-/-	2/-	1964-76
6	Viktor Sidiak (USSR)	1/3	-/1	1/-	1968-80
5	Ramón Fonst (Cub)	3/1	1/-	-/-	1900-04

Nadi won a record five gold medals at one Games in 1920.

Women

7	Ildikó Sagi-Ujlaki-Rejtö (Hun)	1/1	-/3	1/1	1960-76
6	Yelena Byclova (USSR) (née Novikova)	1/3	-/1	1/-	1968-80

World Championships

Held annually except in Olympic years (see above). From 1921 to 1935 they were styled as European Championships. *Winners:*

Men	Foil	Epée	Sabre
1921	-	Lucien Gaudin (Fra)	-
1922	-	Raoul Herde (Nor)	Adrianus de Jong (Hol)
1923	-	Wouter Brouwer (Hol)	Adrianus de Jong (Hol)
1925	-	-	János Garay (Hun)
1926	Giorgio Chiavacci (Ita)	Georges Tainturier (Fra)	Sándor Gambos (Hun)
1927	Oreste Puliti (Ita)	Georges Buchard (Fra)	Sándor Gambos (Hun)
1929	Oreste Puliti (Ita)	Philippe Cattiau (Fra)	Gyula Glykais (Hun)
1930	Giulio Gaudini (Ita)	Philippe Cattiau (Fra)	György Piller (Hun)
1931	René Lemoine (Fra)	Georges Buchard (Fra)	György Piller (Hun)
1933	Gioacchino Guaragna (Ita)	Georges Buchard (Fra)	Endre Kabos (Hun)
1934	Giulio Gaudini (Ita)	Pál Dunay (Hun)	Endre Kabos (Hun)
1935	shared by four men	Hans Drakenberg (Swe)	Aladár Gerevich (Hun)
1937	Gustavo Marzi (Ita)	Bernard Schmetz (Fra)	Pál Kovács (Hun)
1938	Gioacchino Guaragna (Ita)	Michel Pécheux (Fra)	Aldo Montano (Ita)
1947	Christian d'Oriola (Fra)	Edouard Artigas (Fra)	Aldo Montano (Ita)
1949	Christian d'Oriola (Fra)	Dario Mangiarotti (Ita)	Gastone Daré (Fra)
1950	Renzo Nostino (Ita)	Mogens Luchow (Den)	Jean Levavasseur (Fra)
1951	Manlio Di Rosa (Ita)	Edoardo Mangiarotti (Ita)	Aladár Gerevich (Hun)
1953	Christian d'Oriola (Fra)	Jozsef Sakovics (Hun)	Pál Kovács (Hun)
1954	Christian d'Oriola (Fra)	Edoardo Mangiarotti (Ita)	Rudolf Kárpáti (Hun)
1955	Jozsef Gyuricza (Hun)	Giorgio Anglesio (Ita)	Aladár Gerevich (Hun)
1957	Mihaly Fülöp (Hun)	Armand Mouyal (Fra)	Jerzy Pawlowski (Pol)
1958	Giancarlo Bergamini (Ita)	Bill Hoskyns (UK)	Yakov Rylsky (USSR)
1959	Allan Jay (UK)	Bruno Khabarov (USSR)	Rudolf Kárpáti (Hun)
1961	Ryszard Parulski (Pol)	Jack Guittet (Fra)	Yakov Rylsky (USSR)
1962	German Sveshnikov (USSR)	Istvan Kausz (Hun)	Zoltan Horvath (Hun)
1963	Jean-Claude Magnan (Fra)	Roland Losert (Aut)	Yakov Rylsky (USSR)
1965	Jean-Claude Magnan (Fra)	Zoltan Nemere (Hun)	Jerzy Pawlowski (Pol)
1966	German Sveshnikov (USSR)	Aleksey Nikanchikov (USSR)	Jerzy Pawlowski (Pol)
1967	Viktor Putyatin (USSR)	Aleksey Nikanchikov (USSR)	Mark Rakita (USSR)
1969	Friedrich Wessel (FRG)	Bogdan Andrzejewski (Pol)	Viktor Sidiak (USSR)
1970	Friedrich Wessel (FRG)	Aleksey Nikanchikov (USSR)	Tibor Pézsa (Hun)
1971	Vasiliy Stankovich (USSR)	Grigoriy Kriss (USSR)	Michele Maffei (Ita)
1973	Christian Noël (Fra)	Rolf Edling (Swe)	Mario Aldo Monttano (Ita)
1974	Aleksandr Romankov (USSR)	Rolf Edling (Swe)	Mario Aldo Monttano (Ita)
1975	Christian Noël (Fra)	Alexander Pusch (FRG)	Vladimir Nazlimov (USSR)
1977	Aleksandr Romankov (USSR)	Johan Harmenberg (Swe)	Pál Gerevich (Hun)

1978	Didier Flament (Fra)	Alexander Pusch (FRG)	Viktor Krovopuskov (USSR)
1979	Aleksandr Romankov (USSR)	Philippe Riboud (Fra)	Vladimir Nazlimov (USSR)
1981	Vladimir Smirnov (USSR)	Zoltan Szekely (Hun)	Mariusz Wodke (Pol)
1982	Aleksandr Romankov (USSR)	Jenö Pap (Hun)	Viktor Krovopuskov (USSR)
1983	Aleksandr Romankov (USSR)	Ellmar Bormann (FRG)	Vasiliy Etropolski (Bul)
1985	Mauro Numa (Ita)	Philippe Boisse (Fra)	György Nébald (Hun)
1986	Andrea Borella (Ita)	Philippe Riboud (Fra)	Sergey Mindirgassov (USSR)
1987	Mathias Gey (FRG)	Volker Fischer (FRG)	Jean François Lamour (Fra)
1989	Alexander Koch (FRG)	Manuel Pereira (Spa)	Grigoriy Kirienko (USSR)
1990	Philippe Omnès (Fra)	Thomas Gerull (FRG)	György Nébald (Hun)
1991	Ingo Weissenborn (Ger)	Andrey Shuvalov (USSR)	Grigoriy Kirienko (USSR)
1993	Alexander Koch (Ger)	Pavel Kolobkov (Rus)	Grigoriy Kirienko (Rus)
1994	Rolando Tucker (Cub)	Pavel Kolobkov (Rus)	Felix Becker (Ger)
1995	Dmitriy Shevchenko (Rus)	Eric Srecki (Fra)	Grigoriy Kirienko (Rus)
Most wins:	5 Aleksandr Romankov (USSR)	3 Georges Buchard (Fra)	4 Grigoriy Kirienko (Rus)
	4 Christian d'Oriola (Fra)	3 Aleksey Nikanchikov (USSR)	

Men's team foil *wins:*

16	Italy	1929-31, 1933-5, 1937-8, 1949-50, 1954-5, 1985-6, 1990, 1994
14	USSR	1959, 1961-3, 1965-6, 1969-70, 1973-4, 1979, 1981-2, 1989
6	France	1947, 1951, 1953, 1958, 1971, 1975
4	FRG/Germany	1977, 1983, 1987, 1993
2	Cuba	1991, 1995
1	Hungary 1957, Romania 1967, Poland 1978	

Men's team epée *wins:*

13	Italy	1931, 1933, 1937, 1949-50, 1953-5, 1957-8, 1989-90, 1993
11	France	1934-5, 1938, 1947, 1951, 1962, 1965-6, 1982-3, 1994
7	USSR	1961, 1967, 1969, 1979, 1981, 1987, 1991
4	Hungary	1959, 1970-1, 1978
4	Germany	FRG 1973, 1985-6; GER 1995
3	Sweden	1974-5, 1977
1	Belgium 1930, Poland 1963	

Men's team sabre *wins:*

19	Hungary	1930-1, 1933-5, 1937, 1951, 1953-5, 1957-8, 1966, 1973, 1978, 1981-2, 1991, 1993
15	USSR	1965, 1967, 1969-71, 1974-5, 1977, 1979, 1983, 1985-7, 1989-90
5	Italy	1938, 1947, 1949-50, 1995
4	Poland	1959, 1961-3
1	Russia	1994

Women's foil

1929	Helene Mayer (Ger)
1930	Jenny Addams (Bel)
1931	Helene Mayer (Ger)
1933	Gwen Neligan (UK)
1934	Ilona Elek (Hun)
1935	Ilona Elek (Hun)
1937	Helene Mayer (Ger)
1938	Marie Sediva (Cs)
1947	Ellen Müller-Preiss (Aut)
1949	Ellen Müller-Preiss (Aut)
1950	Ellen Müller-Preiss (Aut) & Renée Garilhe (Fra)
1951	Ilona Elek (Hun)
1953	Irene Camber (Ita)
1954	Karen Lachman (Den)
1955	Lidia Dömölki (Hun)
1957	Aleksandra Zabelina (USSR)
1958	Valentina Kiselyeva (USSR)
1959	Yelina Yefimova (USSR)
1961	Heidi Schmid (FRG)
1962	Olga Szabo-Orban (Rom)
1963	Ildikó Rejtö (Hun)
1965	Galina Gorokhova (USSR)
1966	Tatyana Samusenko (USSR)
1967	Aleksandra Zabelina (USSR)
1969	Yelena Novikova (USSR)
1970	Galina Gorokhova (USSR)
1971	Marie-Chantal Demaille (Fra)
1973	Valentina Nikonova (USSR)
1974	Ildikó Bóbis (Hun)
1975	Ecaterina Stahl (Rom)
1977	Valentina Sidorova (USSR)
1978	Valentina Sidorova (USSR)
1979	Cornelia Hanisch (FRG)
1981	Cornelia Hanisch (FRG)
1982	Naila Giliazova (USSR)
1983	Dorina Vaccaroni (Ita)
1985	Cornelia Hanisch (FRG)
1986	Anja Fichtel (FRG)
1987	Elisabeta Tufan (Rom)
1989	Olga Velichko (USSR)
1990	Anja Fichtel (FRG)
1991	Giovanna Trillini (Ita)
1993	Francesca Bortolozzi (Ita)
1994	Reka Szabo-Lazar (Rom)
1995	Laura Badea (Rom)

Most wins: 3 Helène Mayer, Ilona Elek, Ellen Müller-Preiss, Cornelia Hanisch

Women's team foil *wins:*

15	USSR	1956, 1958, 1961, 1963, 1965-6, 1970-1, 1974-5, 1977-9, 1981, 1986
13	Hungary	1933-5, 1937, 1952-5, 1959, 1962, 1967, 1973, 1987
6	Italy	1957, 1982-3, 1990-1, 1995
4	FRG/Germany 1936, 1985, 1989, 1993	

3	Denmark	1932, 1947-8
2	France	1950-1
2	Romania	1969, 1994

Women's epée

1989	Anja Straub (Swi)
1990	Taime Chappe (Cub)
1991	Marianne Horváth (Hun)
1993	Oksana Yermakova (Est)
1994	Laura Chiesa (Ita)
1995	Joanna Jakimiuk (Pol)

Women's Team epée

4	Hungary	1989, 1991, 1993, 1995
1	FR Germany	1990
1	Spain	1994

Fives (Eton)

The game of Eton Fives as now known originated at Eton College in 1840, when courts were built which incorporated features of the area where a handball game had been played before (first recorded in 1825). The courts had a distinctive built-in buttress, which had been used by boys playing against the outside of the chapel.

The Amateur Championship

Played, as doubles, annually for the Kinnaird Cup. First held in 1928. *Most wins by one pair:*

- 10 Brian Matthews & John Reynolds 1981-90
- 8 Anthony Hughes and Arthur Campbell 1958, 1965-8, 1971, 1973, 1975
- 3 Howard Fabian & John Webb 1937, 1939, 1948
- 3 Peter May & John May 1951-3
- 3 Jimmy Biggs & Jim Wallis 1961-2, 1964

Reynolds also won with Manuel de Souza-Girao in 1991, Hughes also won in 1963 with David Guilford.

Recent winners:

1992	Mark Moore & Gary Baker
1993-4	Robin Mason & Andrew Mole

Fives (Rugby)

This court game was first played around 1850. The court differs from that used for Eton Fives in that there is no buttress. The Rugby Fives Association was formed in 1927. It drew up a standard set of rules in 1930 and in the following year established the standard court dimensions, 28ft (8.54m) long and 18ft (5.49m wide).

National Singles Championship

Contested annually for the Jesters' Club Cup from 1932, except for the war years 1940-7. *Most wins:*

- 21 Wayne Enstone 1973-8, 1980-94
- 4 John Pretlove 1953, 1955-6, 1958
- 4 Eric Marsh 1960-3
- 3 Philip Malt 1933-5

The winner in 1979 was David Hebden.

National Doubles Championship

Contested annually for the Cyriax Cup, first in 1926, then annually 1930-9 and from 1947. *Most wins:*

- 11 Wayne Enstone 1975-9 (with John East), 1986 (with Steve Ashton), 1991-5 (with Neil Roberts)
- 10 Ian Fuller & David Hebden 1980-5, 1987-90
- 7 John Pretlove 1952, 1954, 1956-9, 1961 (4 with Dennis Silk 1956-9)
- 7 David Gardner 1960, 1965-6, 1970-2, 1974
- 5 John East 1975-9

Invitation World Championships

Held each year from 1983 to 1985, winners each time: singles: Wayne Enstone, doubles: Wayne Enstone & Steve Ashton.

Football

The Chinese played a form of football, Tsu chu (meaning 'to kick a ball of stuffed leather'), over 2500 years ago. Other versions may have been played in various parts of the world, but much of the game's development came in England. An early reference to the sport came in 1314 when Edward II issued a prohibition on the game due to the exces-

Brazil's Romario – star of the 1994 World Cup

sive noise people were making hustling over footballs in the streets of London. Three subsequent British monarchs also banned the sport, for one reason or another, until it became organised in the 19th century. The first rules were drawn up at Cambridge University in 1848 and there were various modifications over the next decades. The Sheffield club, the oldest club still in existence, was formed in 1855, and the Football Association was founded in London in 1863. The sport grew rapidly in popularity world-wide, and the Fédération Internationale de Football Association (FIFA), the world governing body, was formed in Paris in 1904. On its 90th anniversary in 1994 it had 191 members.

World Cup

The first World Cup for the Jules Rimet Trophy was held in Uruguay in 1930, contested by 13 nations. Jules Rimet was the president of FIFA. A qualifying tournament was introduced in 1934, and the competition has been staged every four years since, with the exception of the war years. Brazil won the trophy outright in 1970 following their third win and teams now compete for the FIFA World Cup. A record 157 nations contested the 1994 event, with 24 qualifying for the finals tournament in the USA. For the 1998 tournament the number of teams contesting the final stage has been raised to 32: the hosts France, holders Brazil and places allocated as follows: Europe 14, Africa 5, South America 4, Asia/Oceania 4, Concacaf 3.

Finals

(Goalscorers are shown beneath each team)

Year	Winners		Runners-up		Venue	Attendance
1930	**Uruguay** Dorado, Cea, Iriarte, Castro	4	**Argentina** Peucelle, Stabile	2	Montevideo, URU	90,000
1934	**Italy** Orsi, Schiavio	2	**Czechoslovakia** Puc	1 *	Rome, ITA	55,000
1938	**Italy** Colaussi 2, Piola 2	4	**Hungary** Titkos, Sarosi	2	Paris, FRA	50,000
1950	**Uruguay** Schiaffino, Ghiggia	2	**Brazil** Friaca	1 **	Rio de Janeiro, BRA	199,854
1954	**F R Germany** Rahn 2, Morlock	3	**Hungary** Puskas, Czibor	2	Berne, SWI	55,000
1958	**Brazil** Vava 2, Pele 2, Zagalo	5	**Sweden** Liedholm, Simonsson	2	Stockholm, SWE	49,737
1962	**Brazil** Amarildo, Zito, Vava	3	**Czechoslovakia** Masopust	1	Santiago, CHI	69,068
1966	**England** Hurst 3, Peters	4	**F R Germany** Haller, Weber	2 *	Wembley, ENG	93,000
1970	**Brazil** Pele, Gerson, Jairzinho, C. Alberto	4	**Italy** Boninsegna	1	Mexico City, MEX	110,000
1974	**F R Germany** Breitner (pen), Muller	2	**Netherlands** Neeskens (pen)	1	Munich, FRG	77,833
1978	**Argentina** Kempes 2, Bertoni	3	**Netherlands** Nanninga	1 *	Buenos Aires, ARG	77,000
1982	**Italy** Rossi, Tardelli, Altobelli	3	**F R Germany** Breitner	1	Madrid, SPA	92,000
1986	**Argentina** Brown, Valdano, Burruchaga	3	**F R Germany** Rummenigge, Völler	2	Mexico City, MEX	114,580
1990	**F R Germany** Brehme (pen)	1	**Argentina**	0	Rome, ITA	73,603
1994	**Brazil** Won by Brazil 3-2 on penalties	0	**Italy**	0 *	Pasadena, USA	90,000

* *after extra time,* ** *deciding match of final pool*

Leading nations

A summary of the leading nations' records in the final stages of the World Cup, including those nations to have appeared in nine or more finals tournaments (Apps.) or to have won 15 or more matches.

	Wins	2nd	SF	Apps.	Games Played	Won	Drawn	Lost	Goals For	Against
Brazil	4	1	3	15	73	50	12	11	159	68
Germany (FRG)	3	3	3	13	73	42	16	15	154	97
Italy	3	2	2	13	61	35	13	13	97	59

Argentina	2	2	-	11	52	26	9	17	90	65
Uruguay	2	-	2	9	37	15	8	14	61	52
England	1	-	1	9	41	18	12	11	55	38
Hungary	-	2	-	9	32	15	3	14	87	57
Sweden	-	1	3	9	37	13	7	13	62	60
France	-	-	3	9	34	15	5	14	71	56
USSR/Russia 94	-	-	1	8	34	16	6	12	60	40
Yugoslavia	-	-	1	8	33	15	5	13	55	42
Spain	-	-	1	9	37	15	9	13	53	44
Belgium	-	-	1	9	29	9	4	16	37	53

Note: Germany includes FRG 1950-90, Russia includes USSR 1958-90.

Highest score (final rounds): 10-1 Hungary v El Salvador, 15 Jun 1982
Highest score (qualifying rounds): 13-0 New Zealand v Fiji, 15 Aug 1981

Finals tournament records
Most appearances: 21 Uwe Seeler (FRG) 1958-70, Wladyslaw Szmuda (Pol) 1974-86, Diego Maradona (Arg) 1982-94, Lothar Matthäus (FRG/Ger) 1982-94; 20 Grzegorz Lato (Pol) 1974-82
Most final tournaments: 5 Antonio Carbajal (Mex) 1950-66

Most goals in each tournament
1930	Guillermo Stabile (Arg)	8
1934	three men	4
1938	Leonidas da Silva (Bra)	8
1950	Ademir de Menenzes (Bra)	9
1954	Sándor Kocsis (Hun)	11
1958	Just Fontaine (Fra)	13
1962	six men	4
1966	Eusebio (Por)	9
1970	Gerd Müller (FRG)	10
1974	Gregorz Lato (Pol)	7
1978	Mario Kempes (Arg)	6
1982	Paolo Rossi (Ita)	6
1986	Gary Lineker (Eng)	6
1990	Salvatore Schillaci (Ita)	6
1994	Hristo Stoichkov (Bul)	6
	Oleg Salenko (Rus)	6

Most goals in career
14 Gerd Müller (FRG) 1970-74, 13 Just Fontaine (Fra) 1958, 12 Pele (Bra) 1958-70

Most goals in one game
5 Oleg Salenko (Rus) v Cameroon 1994
4 Leonidas (Bra) v Poland 1938
4 Ernst Willimowski (Pol) v Brazil 1938,
4 Gustav Wetterström (Swe) v Cuba 1938
4 Juan Schiaffino (Uru) v Bolivia 1950
4 Ademir (Bra) v Sweden 1950
4 Sándor Kocsis (Hun) v F R Germany 1954
4 Just Fontaine (Fra) v F R Germany 1958
4 Eusebio (Por) v North Korea 1966
4 Emilio Butragueño (Spa) v Denmark 1986

Golden Ball Award
Selected at each World Cup from 1982 by a panel of international journalists.
1982   Paolo Rossi (Ita)
1986   Diego Maradona (Arg)
1990   Toto Schillaci (Ita)
1994   Romario (Bra)

Olympic Games
Soccer was unofficially played in the first modern Olympics in 1896. It was included in the Paris Games four years later but some sources still regard it as an unofficial competition, as with those of 1904 and 1906. It has been an official sport at all Olympics from 1908, except for 1932 when it was not staged at Los Angeles. Because of the strength of the so called 'non-professional' Eastern-bloc nations, FIFA ruled that all players who had competed in the 1982 World Cup could not compete in the Los Angeles Olympics two years later. As it transpired, the ban had no effect on the eastern

Hristo Stoichkov – joint World Cup top scorer in 1994

European nations because of their boycott of the Games. A record 126 nations took part in the qualifying tournament for the 1992 Games, when the competition was restricted to players under the age of 23.

Finals

Year	Winner	Runner-up
1900	Upton Park FC (UK) 4	UFSA (Fra) 0
1904	Galt FC, Ontario (Can) 7	Christian Brothers College (USA) 2
1906	Denmark 5	Smyrna (Gre) 2
1908	Great Britain 2	Denmark 0
1912	Great Britain 4	Denmark 2
1920	Belgium 2	Czechoslovakia 0

(Czechoslovakia disqualified after walking off the pitch as a protest against refereeing decisions. Spain were awarded the silver medal)

Year	Winner	Runner-up
1924	Uruguay 3	Switzerland 0
1928	Uruguay 2 (after 1-1 draw)	Argentina 1
1936	Italy 2	Austria 1*
1948	Sweden 3	Yugoslavia 1
1952	Hungary 2	Yugoslavia 0
1956	USSR 2	Yugoslavia 0
1960	Yugoslavia 3	Denmark 1
1964	Hungary 2	Czechoslovakia 1
1968	Hungary 4	Bulgaria 1
1972	Poland 2	Hungary 1
1976	GDR 3	Poland 1
1980	Czechoslovakia 2	GDR 0
1984	France 2	Brazil 0
1988	USSR 2	Brazil 1*
1992	Spain 3	Poland 2

* *after extra time*

Leading medal winning nations

Total		Gold	Silver	Bronze
5	Hungary	3	1	1
5	USSR	2	-	3
5	Denmark	1	3	1
5	Yugoslavia	1	3	1
3	Great Britain	3	-	-
3	Poland	1	2	-
3	GDR	1	1	1
3	Sweden	1	-	2
3	Netherlands	-	-	3

Biggest win: 17-1 Denmark v France 'A' 1908
Most goals in an Olympic tournament: 12 Ferenc Bene (Hun) 1964
Olympic champions/World Cup holders simultaneously:
Uruguay 1928 Olympics, 1930 World Cup; Italy 1934 World Cup, 1936 Olympics, 1938 World Cup

European Championship

Held every four years, the championship is played over a two-year period. Originally called the European Nations Cup, it took its present name in 1968. Competing nations contest the Henri Delaunay Cup, named after the former General Secretary of the Union of European Football Associations (UEFA).

Finals

Year	Winners		Runners-up		Venue	Attendance
1960	**USSR** Metreveli, Ponedelnik	2	**Yugoslavia** Galic	1 *	Paris	17,966
1964	**Spain** Pereda, Marcellino	2	**USSR** Khusainov	1	Madrid	105,000
1968	**Italy** Domenghini	1	**Yugoslavia** Dzajic	1 *	Rome	85,000
Replay	**Italy** Riva, Anastasi	2	**Yugoslavia**	0	Rome	50,000
1972	**F R Germany** G Müller 2, Wimmer	3	**USSR**	0	Brussels	43,437
1976	**Czechoslovakia** Svehlik, Dobiás	2	**F R Germany** D Müller, Hölzenbein	2 *	Belgrade	45,000
	(Czechoslovakia won 5-4 on penalties)					
1980	**F R Germany** Hrubesch 2	2	**Belgium** Van der Eycken	1	Rome	47,864
1984	**France** Platini, Bellone	2	**Spain**	0	Paris	47,000
1988	**Netherlands** Gullit, Van Basten	2	**USSR**	0	Munich	72,308
1992	**Denmark** Jensen, Vilfort	2	**Germany**	0	Göteborg	37,800

* *after extra time*
Most wins: 2 F R Germany
Most finals: 4 USSR, Germany/FRG

European Champion Clubs' Cup

Popularly known as the European Cup it is an annual knockout competition for the league champions of all UEFA affiliated countries. It was first held in 1955/6, shortly after the formation of UEFA, and was the idea of Gabriel Hanot, the soccer editor of the French daily newspaper L'Equipe. From the 1991/2 season the competition structure was modified so that the top eight teams take part in the Champions League, with home and away matches between teams in two groups of four. the winners of each group meeting in the final.

Finals

Year	Winners		Runners-up		Venue	Attendance
1956	**Real Madrid** Rial 2, Di Stéfano, Marquitos	4	**Stade de Reims** Leblond, Templin, Hidalgo	3	Paris	38,000
1957	**Real Madrid** Di Stéfano (pen), Gento	2	**Fiorentina**	0	Madrid	124,000
1958	**Real Madrid** Di Stéfano, Rial, Gento	3	**AC Milan** Schiaffino, Grillo	2 *	Brussels	67,000
1959	**Real Madrid** Mateos, Di Stéfano	2	**Stade de Reims**	0	Stuttgart	80,000
1960	**Real Madrid** Puskas 4, Di Stéfano 3	7	**Eintracht Frankfurt** Stein 2, Kress	3	Glasgow	127,621
1961	**Benfica** Aguas, Coluna, Ramallets (og)	3	**Barcelona** Kocsis, Czibor	2	Berne	27,000
1962	**Benfica** Eusebio 2 (1 pen), Aguas, Cavem, Coluna	5	**Real Madrid** Puskas 3	3	Amsterdam	65,000
1963	**AC Milan** Altafini 2	2	**Benfica** Eusebio	1	London	45,000
1964	**Internazionale Milan** Mazzola 2, Milani	3	**Real Madrid** Felo	1	Vienna	72,000
1965	**Internazionale Milan** Jair	1	**Benfica**	0	Milan	80,000
1966	**Real Madrid** Amancio, Serena	2	**Partizan Belgrade** Vasovic	1	Brussels	55,000
1967	**Glasgow Celtic** Gemmell, Chalmers	2	**Internazionale Milan** Mazzola (pen)	1	Lisbon	54,000
1968	**Manchester United** Charlton 2, Best, Kidd	4	**Benfica** Graca	1 *	London	100,000
1969	**AC Milan** Prati 3, Sormani	4	**Ajax** Vasovic (pen)	1	Madrid	31,000
1970	**Feyenoord** Israel, Kindvall	2	**Glasgow Celtic** Gemmell	1 *	Milan	53,000
1971	**Ajax** van Dijk, Haan	2	**Panathinaikos**	0	London	83,000
1972	**Ajax** Cruyff 2	2	**Internazionale Milan**	0	Rotterdam	61,000
1973	**Ajax** Rep	1	**Juventus**	0	Belgrade	89,000
1974	**Bayern München** Schwarzenbeck	1	**Athlético Madrid** Luis	1 *	Brussels	65,000
Replay	**Bayern München** Hoeness 2, Müller 2	4	**Athlético Madrid**	0	Brussels	23,000
1975	**Bayern München** Roth, Müller	2	**Leeds United**	0	Paris	48,000
1976	**Bayern München** Roth	1	**St Etienne**	0	Glasgow	54,864
1977	**Liverpool** McDermott, Smith, Neal (pen)	3	**Borussia Mönchengladbach** Simonsen	1	Rome	52,000
1978	**Liverpool** Dalglish	1	**FC Bruges**	0	London	92,000
1979	**Nottingham Forest** Francis	1	**Malmö FF**	0	München	57,000

Year	Winners		Runners-up		Venue	Attendance
1980	**Nottingham Forest** Robertson	1	**Hamburger SV**	0	Madrid	50,000
1981	**Liverpool** A Kennedy	1	**Real Madrid**	0	Paris	48,360
1982	**Aston Villa** Withe	1	**Bayern München**	0	Rotterdam	46,000
1983	**Hamburger SV** Magath	1	**Juventus**	0	Athens	75,000
1984	**Liverpool** Neal (Liverpool won 4-2 on penalties)	1	**AS Roma** Pruzzo	1 *	Rome	69,693
1985	**Juventus** Platini (pen)	1	**Liverpool**	0	Brussels	58,000
1986	**Steaua Bucuresti** (Steaua won 2-0 on penalties)	0	**Barcelona**	0 *	Seville	70,000
1987	**FC Porto** Madjer, Juary	2	**Bayern München** Kögl	1	Vienna	56,000
1988	**PSV Eindhoven** (Eindhoven won 6-5 on penalties)	0	**Benfica**	0 *	Stuttgart	55,000
1989	**AC Milan** Gullit 2, Van Basten 2	4	**Steaua Bucuresti**	0	Barcelona	97,000
1990	**AC Milan** Rijkaard	1	**Benfica**	0	Vienna	57.500
1991	**Crvena Zvezda Beograd** (Beograd won 5-3 on penalties)	0	**Marseille**	0 *	Bari	50,000
1992	**Barcelona** R Koeman	1	**Sampdoria**	0 *	Wembley	70,827
1993	**Marseille** Boli	1	**AC Milan**	0	Munich	64,400
1994	**AC Milan** Massaro 2, Savicevic, Desailly	4	**Barcelona**	0	Athens	75.000
1995	**Ajax** Kluivert	1	**AC Milan**	0	Vienna	49,730

* *after extra time*

Biggest win: 12-2 Feyenoord v Reykjavik (1st round) 17 Sep 1969

Biggest win (final): 7-3 Real Madrid v Eintracht 18 May 1960

Biggest win (aggregate): 18-0 (8-0 & 10-0) Benfica v Stade Dudelange (preliminary round) Sep & Oct 1965

European Cup Winners Cup

The Cup Winners' Cup is open to winners of domestic senior cup competitions in UEFA-affiliated countries. The first final in 1961 was over two legs, but all subsequent finals have been played as a single game.

Finals

Year	Winners		Runners-up		Venue	Attendance
1961	**Fiorentina** Milani 2	2	**Glasgow Rangers**	0	Glasgow	80,000
	Fiorentina Milani, Hamrin (Fiorentina won 4-1 on aggregate)	2	**Glasgow Rangers** Scott	1	Florence	50,000
1962	**Athlético Madrid** Peiro	1	**Fiorentina** Hamrin	1	Glasgow	27,289
Replay	**Athlético Madrid** Jones, Mendonca, Peiro	3	**Fiorentina**	0	Stuttgart	38,120
1963	**Tottenham Hotspur** Greaves 2, Dyson 2, White	5	**Athlético Madrid** Collar (pen)	1	Rotterdam	49,143
1964	**Sporting Lisbon** Figueiredo 2, Dansky (og)	3	**MTK Budapest** Sándor 2, Kuti	3 *	Brussels	3,208
Replay	**Sporting Lisbon** Morais	1	**MTK Budapest**	0	Antwerp	19,924
1965	**West Ham United** Sealey	2 2	**München 1860**	0	London	97,974

European Cup Final action – Marco Simone of AC Milan with Ajax defenders in 1995

Year	Winners		Runners-up		Venue	Attendance
1966	**Borussia Dortmund** Held, Libuda	2	**Liverpool** Hunt	1 *	Glasgow	41,657
1967	**Bayern München** Roth	1	**Glasgow Rangers**	0 *	Nürnberg	69,480
1968	**AC Milan** Hamrin 2	2	**Hamburger SV**	0	Rotterdam	53,276
1969	**Slovan Bratislava** Cvetler, Hrivnak, Jan Capkovich	3	**Barcelona** Zaldua, Rexach	2	Basle	19,478
1970	**Manchester City** Young, Lee (pen)	2	**Gornik Zabrze** Oslizlo	1	Vienna	7,968
1971	**Chelsea** Osgood	1	**Real Madrid** Zoco	1 *	Athens	42,000
Replay	**Chelsea** Dempsey, Osgood	2	**Real Madrid** Fleitas	1	Athens	35,000
1972	**Glasgow Rangers** Johnston 2, Stein	3	**Dynamo Moscow** Yestrekov, Makovikov	2	Barcelona	24,701
1973	**AC Milan** Chiarugi	1	**Leeds United**	0	Salonica	45,000
1974	**FC Magdeburg** Lanzi (og), Seguin	2	**AC Milan**	0	Rotterdam	4,641
1975	**Dynamo Kiev** Onischenko 2, Blokhin	3	**Ferencvaros**	0	Basle	10,897
1976	**Anderlecht** Rensenbrink 2 (1 pen) Van der Elst 2	4	**West Ham United** Holland, Robson	2	Brussels	58,000
1977	**Hamburger SV** Volkert (pen), Magath	2	**Anderlecht**	0	Amsterdam	66,000
1978	**Anderlecht** Rensenbrink 2, Van Binst 2	4	**FK Austria**	0	Paris	48,679

Year	Winners		Runners-up		Venue	Attendance
1979	**Barcelona** Sánchez, Asensi, Rexach, Krankl	4	**Fortuna Düsseldorf** Seel 2, K.Allofs	3 *	Basle	58,000
1980	**Valencia** (Valencia won 5-4 on penalties)	0	**Arsenal**	0 *	Brussels	35,000
1981	**Dynamo Tbilisi** Gutsayev, Daraselia	2	**Carl Zeiss Jena** Hoppe	1	Düsseldorf	9,000
1982	**Barcelona** Simonsen, Quini	2	**Standard Liège** Vandermissen	1	Barcelona	100,000
1983	**Aberdeen** Black, Hewitt	2	**Real Madrid** Juanito (pen)	1 *	Göteborg	17,804
1984	**Juventus** Vignola, Boniek	2	**FC Porto** Sousa	1	Basle	60,000
1985	**Everton** Gray, Steven, Sheedy	3	**SK Rapid Wien** Krankl	1	Rotterdam	50,000
1986	**Dynamo Kiev** Zavarov, Blokhin, Yevtushenko	3	**Athlético Madrid**	0	Lyon	39,300
1987	**Ajax Amsterdam** Van Basten	1	**Lokomotiv Leipzig**	0	Athens	35,000
1988	**KV Mechelen** Den Boer	1	**Ajax Amsterdam**	0	Strasbourg	39,446
1989	**Barcelona** Salinas, Recarte	2	**Sampdoria**	0	Berne	45,000
1990	**Sampdoria** Vialli 2	2	**RSC Anderlecht**	0 *	Göteborg	20,103
1991	**Manchester United** Hughes 2	2	**Barcelona** R Koeman	1	Rotterdam	45,000
1992	**Werder Bremen** Allofs, Rufer	2	**Monaco**	0	Lisbon	16,000
1993	**Parma** Minotti, Melli, Cuoghi	3	**Antwerp** Seveneyns	1	Wembley	37,393
1994	**Arsenal** Smith	1	**Parma**	0	Copenhagen	33,765
1995	**Real Zaragoza** Esnaider, Nayim	2	**Arsenal** Hartson	1 *	Paris	42,224

* *after extra time*

Biggest win: 16-1 Sporting Lisbon v Apoel Nicosia (1st round) 13 Nov 1963
Biggest win (final): 5-1 Tottenham Hotspur v Atlético Madrid 15 May 1963
Biggest win (aggregate): 21-0 (8-0 & 13-0) Chelsea v Jeunesse Hautcharage (1st round) 15 & 29 Sep 1971

UEFA Cup

Initially intended, when established in 1955, as a tournament for European cities that sponsored international trade fairs, hence the competition's original name, the International Industries Fairs Inter- Cities Cup, commonly known as the Fairs Cup. The first tournament took three years to complete. The second Fairs Cup predominantly involved club sides and from 1960/1 the competition became an annual event. It became known as the European Fairs Cup in 1966 and in 1971 the UEFA Cup. The competition is open to leading sides not eligible for the other two main European competitions. The final is played over two legs on a home and away basis. The matches are shown in the order in which they were played:

Finals

Year	Home team		Away team		Attendance
1958	**London** Greaves, Langley (pen)	2	**Barcelona** Tejada, Martinez	2	45,466
	Barcelona Suárez 2, Evaristo 2, Martinez, Verges (Barcelona won 8-2 on aggregate)	6	**London**	0	62,000
1960	**Birmingham City**	0	**Barcelona**	0	40,500
	Barcelona Czibor 2, Martinez, Coll (Barcelona won 4-1 on aggregate)	4	**Birmingham City** Hooper	1	70,000
1961	**Birmingham City** Hellawell, Orritt	2	**AS Roma** Manfredini 2	2	21,005

Year	*Home team*		*Away team*		*Attendance*
	AS Roma	2	**Birmingham City**	0	60,000
	Farmer (og), Pestrin				
	(AS Roma won 4-2 on aggregate)				
1962	**Valencia**	6	**Barcelona**	2	65,000
	Guillot 3, Yosu 2, H Nunez		Kocsis 2		
	Barcelona	1	**Valencia**	1	60,000
	Kocsis		Guillot		
	(Valencia won 7-3 on aggregate)				
1963	**Dinamo Zagreb**	1	**Valencia**	2	40,000
	Zambata		Waldo, Urtiaga		
	Valencia	2	**Dinamo Zagreb**	0	55,000
	Mano, Nunez				
	(Valencia won 4-1 on aggregate)				
1964	**Real Zaragoza**	2	**Valencia**	1	50,000
	Villa, Marcelino		Urtiaga		
	(Played over one leg at Barcelona)				
1965	**Ferencvaros**	1	**Juventus**	0	25,000
	Fenyvesi		(Played over one leg, at Turin)		
1966	**Barcelona**	0	**Real Zaragoza**	1	70,000
			Canario		
	Real Zaragoza	2	**Barcelona**	4 *	70,000
	Marcelino 2		Pujol 3, Zaballa		
	(Barcelona won 4-3 on aggregate)				
1967	**Dinamo Zagreb**	2	**Leeds United**	0	40,000
	Cercek 2				
	Leeds United	0	**Dinamo Zagreb**	0	35,604
	(Dinamo Zagreb won 2-0 on aggregate)				
1968	**Leeds United**	1	**Ferencvaros**	0	25,368
	Jones				
	Ferencvaros	0	**Leeds United**	0	76,000
	(Leeds United won 1-0 on aggregate)				
1969	**Newcastle United**	3	**Ujpest Dozsa**	0	60,000
	Moncur 2, Scott				
	Ujpest Dozsa	2	**Newcastle United**	3	37,000
	Bene, Gorocs		Moncur, Arentoft, Foggon		
	(Newcastle United won 6-2 on aggregate)				
1970	**RSC Anderlecht**	3	**Arsenal**	1	37,000
	Mulder 2, Devrindt		Kennedy		
	Arsenal	3	**RSC Anderlecht**	0	51,612
	Kelly, Radford, Sammels				
	(Arsenal won 4-3 on aggregate)				
1971	**Juventus**	0	**Leeds United**	0	40,000
	(abandoned after 51 minutes, waterlogged pitch)				
Replay	**Juventus**	2	**Leeds United**	2	42,000
	Bettega, Capello		Madeley, Bates		
	Leeds United	1	**Juventus**	1	42,483
	Clarke		Anastasi		
	(Leeds United won on the away goals rule)				
1972	**Wolverhampton W.**	1	**Tottenham Hotspur**	2	38,362
	McCalliog		Chivers 2		
	Tottenham Hotspur	1	**Wolverhampton W.**	1	54,303
	Mullery		Wagstaffe		
	(Tottenham Hotspur won 3-2 on aggregate)				
1973	**Liverpool**	0	**Borussia Mönchengladbach**	0	44,967
	(abandoned after 27 minutes waterlogged pitch)				
Replay	**Liverpool**	3	**Borussia Mönchengladbach**	0	41,169
	Keegan 2, Lloyd				
	Borussia Mönchengladbach	2	**Liverpool**	0	35,000
	Heynckes 2				
	(Liverpool won 3-2 on aggregate)				

Year	Home team		Away team		Attendance
1974	**Tottenham Hotspur**	2	**Feyenoord**	2	46,281
	England, van Daele (og)		van Hanegem, De Jong		
	Feyenoord	2	**Tottenham Hotspur**	0	59,317
	Rijsbergen, Ressel				
	(Feyenoord won 4-2 on aggregate)				
1975	**Borussia Mönchengladbach**	0	**Twente Enschede**	0	42,368
	Twente Enschede	1	**Borussia Mönchengladbach**	5	21,767
	Drost		Heynckes 3, Simonsen 2 (1 pen)		
	(Borussia Mönchengladbach won 5-1 on aggregate)				
1976	**Liverpool**	3	**FC Bruges**	2	49,981
	Kennedy, Case, Keegan (pen)		Lambert, Cools		
	FC Bruges	1	**Liverpool**	1	32,000
	Lambert (pen)		Keegan		
	(Liverpool won 4-3 on aggregate)				
1977	**Juventus**	1	**Athletic Bilbao**	0	75,000
	Tardelli				
	Athletic Bilbao	2	**Juventus**	1	43,000
	Irureta, Carlos		Bettega		
	(Juventus won on the away-goals rule)				
1978	**SEC Bastia**	0	**PSV Eindhoven**	0	15,000
	PSV Eindhoven	3	**SEC Bastia**	0	27,000
	W van der Kerkhof, Deykers, van der Kuijlen				
	(Eindhoven won 3-0 on aggregate)				
1979	**Crvena Zvezda Beograd**	1	**Borussia Mönchengladbach**	1	87.500
	Sestic		Juristic (og)		
	Borussia Mönchengladbach	1	**Crvena Zvezda Beograd**	0	45,000
	Simonsen (pen)				
	(Borussia Mönchengladbach won 2-1 on aggregate)				
1980	**Borussia Mönchengladbach**	3	**Eintracht Frankfurt**	2	25,000
	Kulik 2, Matthäus		Karger, Holzenbein		
	Eintracht Frankfurt	1	**Borussia Mönchengladbach**	0	60,000
	Schaub				
	(Eintracht won on the away-goals rule)				
1981	**Ipswich Town**	3	**AZ 67 Alkmaar**	0	27,532
	Wark (pen), Thijssen, Mariner				
	AZ 67 Alkmaar	4	**Ipswich Town**	2	28,500
	Welzl, Metgod, Tol, Jonker		Thijssen, Wark		
	(Ipswich Town won 5-4 on aggregate)				
1982	**IFK Göteborg**	1	**Hamburger SV**	0	42,548
	Tord Holmgren				
	Hamburger SV	0	**IFK Göteborg**	3	60,000
			Corneliusson, Nilsson, Fredriksson (pen)		
	(Göteborg won 4-0 on aggregate)				
1983	**RSC Anderlecht**	1	**Benfica**	0	60,000
	Brylle				
	Benfica	1	**RSC Anderlecht**	1	80,000
	Sheu		Lozano		
	(Anderlecht won 2-1 on aggregate)				
1984	**RSC Anderlecht**	1	**Tottenham Hotspur**	1	40,000
	Olsen		Miller		
	Tottenham Hotspur	1	**RSC Anderlecht**	1 *	46,205
	Roberts		Czerniatynski		
	(Tottenham H won 4-3 on penalties)				
1985	**Videoton SC**	0	**Real Madrid**	3	30,000
			Michel, Santillana, Juanito		
	Real Madrid	0	**Videoton SC**	1	90,000
	(Real Madrid won 3-1 on aggregate)		Majer		

Year	Home team		Away team		Attendance
1986	**Real Madrid**	5	**FC Köln**	1	80,000
	Valdano 2, Sánchez,		K Allofs		
	Gordillo, Santillana				
	FC Köln	2	**Real Madrid**	0	15,000
	Bein, Geilenkirchen				
	(Real Madrid won 5-3 on aggregate)				
1987	**IFK Göteborg**	1	**Dundee United**	0	50,023
	Pettersson				
	Dundee United	1	**IFK Göteborg**	1	20,911
	Clark		Nilsson		
	(Göteborg won 2-1 on aggregate)				
1988	**Español**	3	**Bayer Leverkusen**	0	42,000
	Losada 2, Soler				
	Bayer Leverkusen	3	**Español**	0 *	22,000
	Tita, Goetz, Cha-Bum Kun				
	(Leverkusen won 3-2 on penalties)				
1989	**Napoli**	2	**Stuttgart**	1	83,000
	Maradona (pen), Careca		Gaudino		
	Stuttgart	3	**Napoli**	3	67,000
	Klinsmann, O Schmaler,		Alemao, Ferrara, Careca		
	Gaudino				
	(Napoli won 5-4 on aggregate)				
1990	**Juventus**	3	**Fiorentina**	1	45.000
	Galia, Casiraghi		Buso		
	De Agostini				
	Fiorentina	0	**Juventus**	0	32,000
	(Juventus won 3-1 on aggregate)				
1991	**Internazionale Milan**	2	**AS Roma**	0	68,887
	Matthäus (pen), Berti				
	AS Roma	1	**Internazionale Milan**	0	70,901
	Rizzitelli				
	(Inter won 2-1 on aggregate)				
1992	**Torino**	2	**Ajax**	2	65,377
	Casagrande 2		W Jonk, Pettersson		
	Ajax	0	**Torino**	0	40,000
	(Ajax won on away goals)				
1993	**Borussia Dortmund**	1	**Juventus**	3	37,000
	Rummenigge		D Baggio, R Baggio 2		
	Juventus	3	**Borussia Dortmund**	0	70,000
	D Baggio 2, Möller				
	(Juventus won 6-1 on aggregate)				
1994	**Salzburg**	0	**Internazionale Milan**	1	40,000
			Berti		
	Internazionale Milan	1	**Salzburg**	0	80,000
	Jonk				
	(Inter won 2-0 on aggregate)				
1995	**Parma**	1	**Juventus**	0	26,350
	D Baggio				
	Juventus	1	**Parma**	1	80.750
	Vialli		D Baggio		
	(Parma won 2-1 on aggregate)				

* after extra time

Biggest win: 13-0 Cologne v Union Luxembourg (1st round) 5 Oct 1965
Biggest win (final/aggregate): 8-2 (2-2 & 6-0) Barcelona v London 5 Mar & 1 May 1958
Biggest win (aggregate): 21-0 (9-0 & 12-0) Feyenoord v US Rumelange (1st round) 13 & 27 Sep 1972

Europe's Leading teams

Teams that have won four or more major European tournaments:

Ch = Champion's Cup, CW = Cup Winners Cup, UEFA = Fairs/UEFA Cup

Total		Ch	CW	UEFA
8	Real Madrid	6	-	2
7	AC Milan	5	2	-
7	Barcelona	1	3	3
6	Liverpool	4	-	2
6	Ajax	4	1	1
5	Juventus	1	1	3
4	Bayern München	3	1	-
4	Internazionale Milan	2	-	2

European Super Cup

After Ajax won the European Cup for the second successive year in 1972 the Dutch newspaper De Telegraaf suggested they play the winners of the Cup Winners' Cup for a Super Cup. They played, and beat, Glasgow Rangers over two legs and became the first winners. UEFA did not officially recognise the event until 1974. There was no competition in 1981 and 1985. In 1984, 1986 and 1991 the cup was decided on one match.

Year	Winners	Runners-up	Result(s)
1972	Ajax *	Glasgow Rangers	3-1, 3-2
1973	Ajax *	AC Milan	0-1, 6-0
1974#	Bayern München *	FC Magdeburg	3-2, 2-1
1975	Dynamo Kiev	Bayern München *	1-0, 2-0
1976	Anderlecht	Bayern München *	1-2, 4-1
1977	Liverpool *	Hamburger SV	1-1, 6-0
1978	RSC Anderlecht	Liverpool *	3-1, 1-2
1979	Nottingham Forest*	Barcelona	1-0, 1-1
1980	Valencia	Nottingham Forest*	1-2, 1-0
	(Valencia won on the away goals rule)		
1982	Aston Villa *	Barcelona	0-1, 3-0
1983	Aberdeen	Hamburger SV *	0-0, 2-0
1984	Juventus	Liverpool *	2-0
1986	Steaua Bucuresti *	Dynamo Kiev	1-0
1987	FC Porto *	Ajax	1-0, 1-0
1988	KV Mechelen	PSV Eindhoven *	3-0, 0-1
1989	AC Milan *	Barcelona	1-1, 1-0
1990	AC Milan *	Sampdoria	1-1, 2-0
1991	Manchester United	Crvena Zvezda Beograd *	1-0
1992	Barcelona *	Werder Bremen	1-1, 2-1
1994	Parma	AC Milan	0-1, 2-0
1995	AC Milan *	Arsenal	0-0, 2-0

* indicates European Cup holders
 # The two scheduled clubs, Bayern München and Magdeburg, were drawn together in the second round of the 1974/5 European Champions Cup. They decided the results of that match would decide that season's Super Cup winners.

Copa America

In 1910 an Argentine national side, composed mainly of British exiles, suggested a tournament against Uruguay and Chile. This was the forerunner of the South American Cham-

pionship which was inaugurated in 1916, the year of the formation of the South American Football Confederation. Organisation has left a lot to be desired over the years and the popularity of the event dropped considerably in the 1960s, particularly after the introduction of the Copa Libertadores, when club soccer was regarded as more important than the international game in some countries. The championship was revived in 1975, after a gap of eight years, and is now played as the Copa América, with the ten competing nations split into two groups, and then the top two from each group playing off. Held every four years 1975-87 and now every two years. *Winners:*

14	Argentina	1921, 1925, 1927, 1929, 1937, 1941*, 1945*, 1946*, 1947, 1955, 1957, 1959, 1991, 1993
14	Uruguay	1916-7, 1920, 1923-4, 1926, 1935*, 1942, 1956*, 1959*,1967, 1983, 1987, 1995
4	Brazil	1919, 1922, 1949, 1989
2	Peru	1939, 1975
2	Paraguay	1953, 1979
1	Bolivia	1963

South American Cup

First contested in 1960 as the South American Champion's Club Cup. Like the European Cup it was open to national league champions of countries affiliated to the South American Confederation. In 1965 league runners-up were also allowed to enter the competition and, that year, its name was changed to the Copa Libertadores de América. *Winners:*

1960-1	Peñarol (Uru)
1962-3	Santos (Bra)
1964-5	Independiente (Arg)
1966	Peñarol (Uru)
1967	Racing Club (Arg)
1968-70	Estudiantes (Arg)
1971	Nacional Montevideo (Uru)
1972-5	Independiente (Arg)
1976	Cruzeiro (Bra)
1977-8	Boca Juniors (Arg)
1979	Olimpia (Par)
1980	Nacional Montevideo (Uru)
1981	Flamengo (Bra)
1982	Peñarol (Uru)
1983	Gremio (Bra)
1984	Independiente (Arg)
1985	Argentinos Juniors (Arg)
1986	River Plate (Arg)
1987	Peñarol (Uru)
1988	Nacional Montevideo (Uru)
1989	Nacional Medellin (Col)
1990	Olimpia (Par)
1991	Colo Colo (Chl)
1992-3	São Paulo (Bra)
1994	Vélez Sársfield (Arg)

Most wins: 7 Independiente, 5 Peñarol, 3 Estudiantes, Nacional (Uru)

World Club Championship

The World Club Championship was first held in 1960 as a meeting between the winners of the European Champion Club's Cup and the Copa Libertadores. The two competing teams played each other on a home and away basis (with the exception of 1973) but since 1980 the winners have been decided by one match (for the Intercontinental Cup) played in Tokyo. There were no championship matches in 1975 and 1978. During the 1970s many of the matches became very physical affairs and on five occasions the European Cup holders refused to take part; their places were taken by the runners-up. Prior to 1969, if both sides won a match each, a third match was played to decide the winner. *Results:*

Year	Winners	Runners-up	Result(s)	Play-off
1960	Real Madrid (Spa)	Peñarol (Uru)	0-0, 5-1	
1961	Peñarol (Uru)	Benfica (Por)	0-1, 5-0	2-1
1962	Santos (Bra)	Benfica (Por)	3-2, 5-2	
1963	Santos (Bra)	AC Milan (Ita)	2-4, 4-2	1-0
1964	Internazionale Milan (Ita)	Independiente (Arg)	0-1, 2-0	1-0
1965	Internazionale Milan (Ita)	Independiente (Arg)	3-0, 0-0	
1966	Peñarol (Uru)	Real Madrid (Spa)	2-0, 2-0	
1967	Racing Club (Arg)	Celtic (Sco)	0-1, 2-1	1-0
1968	Estudiantes (Arg)	Manchester United (Eng)	1-0, 1-1	
1969	AC Milan (Ita)	Estudiantes (Arg)	3-0, 1-2	
1970	Feyenoord (Hol)	Estudiantes (Arg)	2-2, 1-0	
1971	Nacional Montevideo (Uru)	Panathinaikos (Gre)	1-1, 2-1	
1972	Ajax (Hol)	Independiente (Arg)	1-1, 3-0	
1973	Independiente (Arg)	Juventus (Ita)	1-0	
1974	Atlético Madrid (Spa)	Independiente (Arg)	0-1, 2-0	
1976	Bayern München (FRG)	Cruzeiro (Bra)	2-0, 0-0	
1977	Boca Juniors (Arg)	Borussia Mönchengladbach (FRG)	2-2, 3-0	
1979	Olimpia (Par)	Malmö (Swe)	1-0, 2-1	
1980	Nacional Montevideo (Uru)	Nottingham Forest (Eng)	1-0	
1981	Flamengo (Bra)	Liverpool (Eng)	3-0	
1982	Peñarol (Uru)	Aston Villa (Eng)	2-0	
1983	Gremio (Bra)	Hamburger SV (FRG)	2-1	
1984	Independiente (Arg)	Liverpool (Eng)	1-0	
1985	Juventus (Ita)	Argentinos Juniors (Arg)	2-2	

(Juventus won 4-2 on penalties)

1986	River Plate (Arg)	Steaua Bucuresti (Rom)	1-0	
1987	FC Porto (Por)	Peñarol (Uru)	2-1	
1988	Nacional (Uru)	PSV Eindhoven (Hol)	2-2	

(Nacional won 7-6 on penalties)

1989	AC Milan (Ita)	Atletico Medellin (Col)	1-0	
1990	AC Milan (Ita)	Olimpia Asuncion (Par)	3-0	
1991	Crvena Zvezda Beograd (Yug)	Colo Colo (Chl)	3-0	
1992	São Paulo (Bra)	Barcelona (Spa)	2-1	
1993	São Paulo (Bra)	AC Milan (Ita)	3-2	
1994	Vélez Sársfield (Arg)	AC Milan (Ita)	2-0	

Most wins: 3 Peñarol, Nacional, AC Milan.

European wins: 12, South American wins: 17

No European team has won a match in South America. Real Madrid (1960), Internazionale Milan (1965), Feyenoord (1970), Ajax (1972) and Bayern München (1976) all managed to draw.

Biggest attendance: 150,000 Santos v AC Milan (2nd leg 1963) at Rio de Janeiro

First contested in the Sudan in 1957, and now held biennially. *Winners:*

1957 Egypt
1959 Egypt
1962 Ethiopia
1963 Ghana
1965 Ghana
1968 Zaïre
1970 Sudan
1972 Congo
1974 Zaïre
1976 Morocco
1978 Ghana
1980 Nigeria
1982 Ghana
1984 Cameroon
1986 Egypt
1988 Cameroon
1990 Algeria
1992 Ivory Coast
1994 Nigeria

International Caps

England's Billy Wright was the first player to reach the milestone of making 100 senior international appearances. His 100th match was against Scotland at Wembley on 11 April 1959. Since then many players have passed the 100 mark. The most capped players have been:

147 Majed Abdullah (Saudi Arabia) 1978-94
127 Thomas Ravelli (Swe) 1981-95
125 Peter Shilton (Eng) 1970-90
122 Lothar Matthäeus (FRG/Ger) 1980-94
120 * Rivelino (Bra) 1968-79
119 Pat Jennings (NI) 1964-86
117 Heinz Hermann (Swi) 1978-92
115 Björn Nordqvist (Swe) 1963-78
112 Dino Zoff (Ita) 1968-83
111 * Pele (Bra) 1957-71
111 * Hector Chumpitaz (Per) 1963-82

In addition to Shilton and Jennings, the following British players have won 100 caps:

108 Bobby Moore (Eng) 1962-73
106 Bobby Charlton (Eng) 1958-70
105 Billy Wright (Eng) 1946-59
102 Kenny Dalglish (Sco) 1971-86

* *Revised figures excluding matches against club sides and other representative selections. Including these Chumpitaz had 150 appearances.*

Most Expensive Transfers

£13 million   Gianluigi Lentini, Torino to AC Milan, July 1992

£12.5 million Gianluca Vialli, Sampdoria to Juventus, June 1992

£12 million   Dennis Bergkamp, Ajax to Inter Milan, June 1993

£10 million   Jean-Pierre Papin, Marseille to AC Milan, June 1992

Most expensive transfers involving British players

£8.5 million   Stan Collymore, Nottingham Forest to Liverpool, June 1995

£7 million   Andy Cole, Newcastle United to Manchester United, Jan 1995

£7 million   Paul Ince, Manchester United to Internazionale Milano, June 1995

£6.5 million   David Platt, Bari to Juventus, May 1992

£6 million   Les Ferdinand, Queens Park Rangers to Newcastle United, June 1995

Individual Goalscoring Records for First Class Matches

Most goals in one game

World record: 16 Stephan Stanis (Racing Club Lens v Aubry-Asturies) 13 Dec 1942

International: 10 Sofus Nielsen (Denmark v France) 1908 Olympics, 10 Gottfried Fuchs (Germany v Russia) 1912 Olympics

British international record: 6 Joe Bambrick (Northern Ireland v Wales) 1 Feb 1930

World Cup: 5 Oleg Salenko (Russia v Cameroon) 28 June 1994

Major European competition: 6 Lothar Emmerich (Borussia Dortmund v Floriana) Cup Winners' Cup 1st round 13 Oct 1965

FA Cup (proper): 9 Ted MacDougall (Bournemouth v Margate) 1st round 20 Nov 1971

FA Cup (preliminary round): 10 Chris Marron (South Shields v Radcliffe) 20 Sep 1947

Football League Cup: 6 Frankie Bunn (Oldham Athletic v. Scarborough) 25 Oct 1989

Football League: 10 Joe Payne (Luton Town v Bristol Rovers) Div 3S 13 Apr 1936

Scottish Cup: 13 John Petrie (Arbroath v Bon Accord) Cup 5 Sep 1885

Scottish League: 8 Jimmy McGrory (Celtic v Dunfermline Athletic) Div 1 14 Jan 1928

Most goals in a career

World record: 1329 Artur Friedenreich (Germania, CA Ipiranga, Americano, CA Paulistano, São Paulo, Flamengo) 1909-35

Full internationals: 97 Pele (Bra) 1957-70

British record in full internationals: 49 Bobby Charlton (Eng) 1958-70

World Cup: 14 Gerd Müller (FRG) 1970-74

European Cup: 49 Alfredo di Stéfano (Real Madrid) 1955-64

Football League: 434 Arthur Rowley (West Bromwich Albion, Fulham, Leicester, Shrewsbury Town) 1946-65

Scottish League: 410 Jimmy McGrory (Celtic, Clydebank) 1922-38

Hat tricks in major finals

World Cup: Geoff Hurst (England v F R Germany) 30 Jul 1966

European Championship and European Cup Winners' Cup: none

European Cup: Ferenc Puskas (4 goals) (Real Madrid v Eintracht) 18 May 1960, Alfredo di Stéfano (Real Madrid v Eintracht) 18 May 1960, Ferenc Puskas (Real Madrid v Benfica) 2 May 1962, Pierino Prati (AC Milan v Ajax) 28 May 1969

UEFA/Fairs Cup: Vicente Guillot (Valencia v Barcelona) 8 Sep 1962, Luis Pujol (Barcelona v Real Zaragoza) 21 Sep 1966, Jupp Heynckes (Borussia Mönchengladbach v Twente Enschede) 21 May 1975

FA Cup: William Townley (Blackburn Rovers v Sheffield Wednesday) 29 Mar 1890, Jimmy Logan (Notts County v Bolton Wanderers) 31 Mar 1894, Stan Mortensen (Blackpool v Bolton Wanderers) 2 May 1953

Football League/Milk/Littlewoods Cup: none

Scottish FA Cup

Jimmy Quinn (Celtic v Rangers) 16 Apr 1904
Dixie Deans (Celtic v Hibernian) 6 May 1972

Scottish League Cup

Davie Duncan (East Fife v Falkirk) 1 Nov 1948
Willie Bauld (Hearts v Motherwell) 23 Oct 1954
John McPhail (Celtic v Rangers) 19 Oct 1957
Jim Forrest (4 g) (Rangers v Morton) 26 Oct 1963
Bobby Lennox (Celtic v Hibernian) 5 Apr 1969
Dixie Deans (Celtic v Hibernian) 26 Oct 1974
Joe Harper (Hibernian v Celtic) 26 Oct 1974
Ally McCoist (Rangers v Celtic) 25 Mar 1984

Most hat tricks in a career: 92 Pele 1956-77. British record: 37 Dixie Dean 1924-39

British International Championship

The oldest international championship in the world, contested annually from 1883/4 until 1983/4 by the four home countries of England, Scotland, Wales and Northern Ireland (formerly Ireland). Each country played each other once with two points for a win and one for a draw. The title was shared if points were equal until 1979/80 when goal difference was used in case of a tie. With a decline in interest this Home International Championship ended after the 1983/4 season. In 1955/6 all four nations shared the title with three points each and the championship was not completed in 1980/1. *Outright wins:*

34	England	1888, 1891-3, 1895, 1898-9, 1901, 1904-5, 1909, 1911, 1913, 1930, 1932, 1938, 1947-8, 1950, 1954-5, 1957, 1961, 1965-6, 1968-9, 1971, 1973, 1975, 1978-9, 1982-3
24	Scotland	1884-5, 1887, 1889, 1894, 1896-7, 1900, 1902, 1910, 1921-3, 1925-6, 1929, 1936, 1949, 1951, 1962-3, 1967, 1976-7
7	Wales	1907, 1920, 1924, 1928, 1933-4, 1937
3	N Ireland	1914 (Ireland), 1980, 1984

Football League

The Football League was the brainchild of William McGregor of Aston Villa who called the first meeting of interested clubs to the Anderton's Hotel, Fleet Street, London on 22 March 1888. The first formal meeting took place less than a month later on 17 April at the Royal Hotel, Manchester, when 12 members, all from the Midlands or North of England, agreed to form the Football League. The first matches were played the following September. A Second Division was formed in 1892 when most members of the old Football Alliance joined the League. A Third Division was added in 1920 and when 20 Northern clubs joined the League in 1921 the Third Division was split into two sections, Northern and Southern. The complement of 92 clubs was reached in 1950 and in 1958 the geographically divided Third Divisions were split into Third and Fourth Divisions. In 1991 the number of members rose to 93 before Aldershot and Maidstone left the League in 1992.

First Division champions

Season	Champions	Pts
1888/9	Preston North End	40
1889/90	Preston North End	33
1890/1	Everton	29
1891/2	Sunderland	42
1892/3	Sunderland	48
1893/4	Aston Villa	44
1894/5	Sunderland	47
1895/6	Aston Villa	45
1896/7	Aston Villa	47
1897/8	Sheffield United	42
1898/9	Aston Villa	45
1899/00	Aston Villa	50
1900/1	Liverpool	45
1901/2	Sunderland	44
1902/3	Sheffield Wednesday	42
1903/4	Sheffield Wednesday	47
1904/5	Newcastle United	48
1905/6	Liverpool	51
1906/7	Newcastle United	51
1907/8	Manchester United	52
1908/9	Newcastle United	53
1909/10	Aston Villa	53
1910/1	Manchester United	52
1911/2	Blackburn Rovers	49
1912/3	Sunderland	54
1913/4	Blackburn Rovers	51
1914/5	Everton	46
1919/20	West Bromwich Albion	60
1920/1	Burnley	59
1921/2	Liverpool	57
1922/3	Liverpool	60
1923/4	Huddersfield Town	57
1924/5	Huddersfield Town	58
1925/6	Huddersfield Town	57
1926/7	Newcastle United	56
1927/8	Everton	53
1928/9	Sheffield Wednesday	52
1929/30	Sheffield Wednesday	60
1930/1	Arsenal	66
1931/2	Everton	56
1932/3	Arsenal	58
1933/4	Arsenal	59
1934/5	Arsenal	58
1935/6	Sunderland	56
1936/7	Manchester City	57
1937/8	Arsenal	52
1938/9	Everton	59
1946/7	Liverpool	57
1947/8	Arsenal	59
1948/9	Portsmouth	58
1949/50	Portsmouth	56
1950/1	Tottenham Hotspur	60
1951/2	Manchester United	57
1952/3	Arsenal	54
1953/4	Wolverhampton Wanderers	57
1954/5	Chelsea	52
1955/6	Manchester United	60
1956/7	Manchester United	64
1957/8	Wolverhampton Wanderers	64
1958/9	Wolverhampton Wanderers	61
1959/60	Burnley	55
1960/1	Tottenham Hotspur	66
1961/2	Ipswich Town	56
1962/3	Everton	61
1963/4	Liverpool	57
1964/5	Manchester United	61
1965/6	Liverpool	61
1966/7	Manchester United	60
1967/8	Manchester City	58
1968/9	Leeds United	67
1969/70	Everton	66
1970/1	Arsenal	65
1971/2	Derby County	58
1972/3	Liverpool	60
1973/4	Leeds United	62
1974/5	Derby County	53
1975/6	Liverpool	60
1976/7	Liverpool	57
1977/8	Nottingham Forest	64
1978/9	Liverpool	68
1979/80	Liverpool	60
1980/1	Aston Villa	60
1981/2	Liverpool	87
1982/3	Liverpool	82
1983/4	Liverpool	80
1984/5	Everton	90
1985/6	Liverpool	88
1986/7	Everton	86
1987/8	Liverpool	90
1988/9	Arsenal	76
1989/90	Liverpool	79
1990/1	Arsenal	83
1991/2	Leeds United	82

Maximum points available: 44 1888/9 to 1890/1, 52 1891/2, 60 1892/3 to 1897/8, 68 1898/9 to 1904/5, 76 1905/6 to 1914/5, 84 1919/20 to 1980/1, 126 1981/2 to 1986/7, 120 1987/8, 114 1988/9 to 1990/1, 126 1991/2

FA Premier League

The top 22 clubs from the Football League Division One formed the FA Premier League from 1992/3, with the Football League of three divisions succeeding the previous

Divisions 2-4. From 1995/6 the Premier League is reduced to 20 clubs. *Winners:*

1992/3	Manchester United	84
1993/4	Manchester United	92
1994/5	Blackburn Rovers	89

Most titles

Division 1	18 Liverpool, 10 Arsenal, 9 Everton, 9 Manchester United (inc Premier 1993-4), 7 Aston Villa
Division 2	6 Leicester City, Manchester City
Division 3	2 Portsmouth, Oxford United
Division 3(S)	3 Bristol City
Division 3(N)	3 Barnsley, Doncaster Rovers, Lincoln City
Division 4	2 Chesterfield, Doncaster Rovers, Peterborough United

Champions of most divisions

Wolverhampton Wanderers have uniquely been champions of Divisions 1, 2, 3, 4 and 3N (one win at each of the last three). Burnley have been champions of Divisions 1, 2, 3 and 4.

Clubs that have been champions of Divisions 1, 2 and 3 (including 3N or 3S):

Aston Villa, Blackburn R, Wolverhampton W, Preston North End, Derby County, Ipswich Town, Nottingham Forest, Sunderland

Grimsby Town have been champions of Divisions 2, 3, 4 and 3N

Huddersfield Town and Sheffield United have also been champions of Divisions 1 and 4

Most points in a season

	Old system - 2 points for win	System from 1981 - 3 points for win
Premier	92 Manchester United 1993/4	
Div 1	68 Liverpool 1978/9	90 Everton 1984/5 Liverpool 1987/8
Div 2	70 Tottenham Hotspur 1919/20	99 Chelsea 1988/9
Div 3	70 Aston Villa 1971/2	97 Bournemouth 1986/7
Div 4	74 Lincoln City 1975/6	102 Swindon Town 1985/6

Most goals scored in a season (42 games except for * 46 games)

Division 1	128 Aston Villa 1930/1
Division 2	122 Middlesbrough 1926/7
Division 3	111* Queen's Park Rangers 1961/2
Division 4	134* Peterborough United 1960/1
Division 3(S)	127 Millwall 1927/8
Division 3(N)	128 Bradford City 1928/9

Highest scores

13-0	Stockport County v Halifax Town 6 Jan 1934 Div 3N
13-0	Newcastle United v Newport County 5 Oct 1946 Div 2
13-4	Tranmere Rovers v Oldham Athletic 26 Dec 1935 Div 3N
12-0	West Bromwich Albion v Darwen 4 Apr 1892 Div 1
12-0	Small Heath (later Birmingham City) v Walsall Town Swifts 17 Dec 1892 Div 2
12-0	Darwen v Walsall 26 Dec 1896 Div 2
12-0	Arsenal v Loughborough Town 12 Mar 1900 Div 2
12-0	Small Heath (later Birmingham City) v Doncaster Rovers 11 Apr 1903 Div 2
12-0	Nottingham Forest v Leicester Fosse 21 Apr 1909 Div 1
12-0	Chester v York City 1 Feb 1936 Div 3N
12-0	Luton Town v Bristol Rovers 13 Apr 1936 Div 3S

Other divisional records

11-0	Oldham Athletic v Southport 26 Dec 1962 Div 4
10-0	Gillingham v Chesterfield 5 Sep 1987 Div 3

Most individual goals in a game

10	Joe Payne, Luton Town v Bristol Rovers 13 Apr 1936 Div 3S
9	Robert Bell, Tranmere Rovers v Oldham Athletic 26 Dec 1935 Div 3N
7	Arthur Whitehurst, Bradford City v Tranmere Rovers 6 Mar 1929 Div 3N
7	Ted Drake, Arsenal v Aston Villa 14 Dec 1935 Div 1
7	Ted Harston, Mansfield Town v Hartlepool United 23 Jan 1937 Div 3N
7	Eric Gemmell, Oldham Athletic v Chester 19 Jan 1952 Div 3N
7	Tommy Briggs, Blackburn Rovers v Bristol Rovers 5 Feb 1955 Div 2
7	Neville Coleman, Stoke City v Lincoln City 23 Feb 1957 Div 2

Most individual goals in a season

Div 1	60 Dixie Dean, Everton 1927-8
Div 2	59 George Camsell, Middlesbrough 1926-7
Div 3S	55 Joe Payne, Luton Town 1936-7
Div 3N	55 Ted Harston, Mansfield Town 1936-7
Div 4	52 Terry Bly, Peterborough United 1960-1

Jürgen Klinsmann – starred for Spurs in 1994/5

FA Cup

The idea for the Football Association Challenge Cup came from the secretary of the Football Association, Charles Alcock, who put forward his plans at a meeting attended by 12 clubs on 18 October 1871. The following 15 teams entered the first competition: Wanderers, Harrow Chequers, Clapham Rovers, Upton Park, Crystal Palace, Hitchin, Maidenhead, Great Marlow, Barnes, Civil Service, Royal Engineers, Reigate Priory, Donington School, Hampstead Heathens, Queen's Park (Glasgow). Contested annually on a knock-out basis. Sponsored by Littlewoods Pools from 1994/5. *Finals:*

Year	*Winners*		*Runners-up*		*Venue*	*Attendance*
1872	**Wanderers** Betts	1	**Royal Engineers**	0	Kennington Oval	2,000
1873	**Wanderers** Kinnaird, Wollaston	2	**Oxford University**	0	Lillie Bridge	3,000
1874	**Oxford University** Mackarness, Patton	2	**Royal Engineers**	0	Kennington Oval	2,000
1875	**Royal Engineers** Renny-Tailyour	1	**Old Etonians** Bonsor	1 *	Kennington Oval	3,000
Replay	**Royal Engineers** Renny-Tailyour, Stafford	2	**Old Etonians**	0	Kennington Oval	3,000
1876	**Wanderers** Edwards	1	**Old Etonians** Bonsor	1	Kennington Oval	3,000
Replay	**Wanderers** Hughes 2, Wollaston	3	**Old Etonians**	0	Kennington Oval	3,500
1877	**Wanderers** Lindsay, Kenrick	2	**Oxford University** Kinnaird (og)	1 *	Kennington Oval	3,000
1878	**Wanderers** Kenrick 2, Kinnaird	3	**Royal Engineers** unknown	1	Kennington Oval	4,500
1879	**Old Etonians** Clerke	1	**Clapham Rovers**	0	Kennington Oval	5,000
1880	**Clapham Rovers** Lloyd-Jones	1	**Oxford University**	0	Kennington Oval	6,000
1881	**Old Carthusians** Wyngard, Parry, Todd	3	**Old Etonians**	0	Kennington Oval	4,500
1882	**Old Etonians** Macauley	1	**Blackburn Rovers**	0	Kennington Oval	6,500
1883	**Blackburn Olympic** Matthews, Crossley	2	**Old Etonians** Goodhart	1 *	Kennington Oval	8,000
1884	**Blackburn Rovers** Sowerbutts, Forrest	2	**Queen's Park** Christie	1	Kennington Oval	4,000
1885	**Blackburn Rovers** Forrest, Brown	2	**Queen's Park**	0	Kennington Oval	12,500
1886	**Blackburn Rovers**	0	**West Bromwich Albion**	0	Kennington Oval	15,000
Replay	**Blackburn Rovers** Brown, Sowerbutts	2	**West Bromwich Albion**	0	Racecourse Ground, Derby	12,000
1887	**Aston Villa** Hunter, Hodgetts	2	**West Bromwich Albion**	0	Kennington Oval	15,500
1888	**West Bromwich Albion** Woodhall, Bayliss	2	**Preston North End** Dewhurst	1	Kennington Oval	19,000
1889	**Preston North End** Dewhurst, Ross, Thomson	3	**Wolverhampton W**	0	Kennington Oval	22,000
1890	**Blackburn Rovers** Townley 3, Walton John Southworth, Lofthouse	6	**Sheffield Wednesday** Bennett	1	Kennington Oval	20,000
1891	**Blackburn Rovers** Southworth, Dewar, Townley	3	**Notts County** Oswald	1	Kennington Oval	23,000
1892	**West Bromwich Albion** Nicholls, Geddes, Reynolds	3	**Aston Villa**	0	Kennington Oval	32,810

Year	Winners		Runners-up		Venue	Attendance
1893	**Wolverhampton W.** Allen	1	**Everton**	0	Fallowfield	45,000
1894	**Notts County** Logan 3, Watson	4	**Bolton Wanderers** Cassidy	1	Goodison Park	37,000
1895	**Aston Villa** Devey	1	**West Bromwich Albion**	0	Crystal Palace	42,560
1896	**Sheffield Wednesday** Spiksley 2	2	**Wolverhampton W** Black	1	Crystal Palace	48,836
1897	**Aston Villa** Devey, Campbell, Crabtree	3	**Everton** Bell, Hartley	2	Crystal Palace	65,891
1898	**Nottingham Forest** Capes 2, McPherson	3	**Derby County** Bloomer	1	Crystal Palace	62,017
1899	**Sheffield United** Bennett, Priest, Beers, Almond	4	**Derby County** Boag	1	Crystal Palace	73,833
1900	**Bury** McLuckie 2, Wood, Plant	4	**Southampton**	0	Crystal Palace	68,945
1901	**Tottenham Hotspur** Brown 2	2	**Sheffield United** Bennett, Priest	2	Crystal Palace	110,820
Replay	**Tottenham Hotspur** Cameron, Smith, Brown	3	**Sheffield United** Priest	1	Burnden Park	20,470
1902	**Sheffield United** Common	1	**Southampton** Wood	1	Crystal Palace	76,914
Replay	**Sheffield United** Hedley, Barnes	2	**Southampton** Brown	1	Crystal Palace	33,068
1903	**Bury** Leeming 2, Ross, Sagar, Plant, Wood	6	**Derby County**	0	Crystal Palace	63,102
1904	**Manchester City** Meredith	1	**Bolton Wanderers**	0	Crystal Palace	61,374
1905	**Aston Villa** Hampton 2	2	**Newcastle United**	0	Crystal Palace	101,117
1906	**Everton** Young	1	**Newcastle United**	0	Crystal Palace	75,609
1907	**Sheffield Wednesday** Stewart, Simpson	2	**Everton** Sharp	1	Crystal Palace	84,584
1908	**Wolverhampton W** Hunt, Hedley, Harrison	3	**Newcastle United** Howie	1	Crystal Palace	74,967
1909	**Manchester United** A Turnbull	1	**Bristol City**	0	Crystal Palace	71,401
1910	**Newcastle United** Rutherford	1	**Barnsley** Tuffnell	1	Crystal Palace	77,747
Replay	**Newcastle United** Shepherd 2 (1 pen)	2	**Barnsley**	0	Goodison Park	69,000
1911	**Bradford City**	0	**Newcastle United**	0	Crystal Palace	69,098
Replay	**Bradford City** Spiers	1	**Newcastle United**	0	Old Trafford	58,000
1912	**Barnsley**	0	**West Bromwich Albion**	0	Crystal Palace	54,556
Replay	**Barnsley** Tuffnell	1	**West Bromwich Albion**	0 *	Bramall Lane	38,555
1913	**Aston Villa** Barber	1	**Sunderland**	0	Crystal Palace	120,081
1914	**Burnley** Freeman	1	**Liverpool**	0	Crystal Palace	72,778
1915	**Sheffield United** Simmons, Kitchen, Fazackerley	3	**Chelsea**	0	Old Trafford	49,557
1920	**Aston Villa** Kirton	1	**Huddersfield Town**	0 *	Stamford Bridge	50,018
1921	**Tottenham Hotspur** Dimmock	1	**Wolverhampton W**	0	Stamford Bridge	72,805

Year	Winners		Runners-up		Venue	Attendance
1922	**Huddersfield Town**	1	**Preston North End**	0	Stamford Bridge	53,000
	Smith (pen)					
1923	**Bolton Wanderers**	2	**West Ham United**	0	Wembley	126,047
	Jack, J R Smith					
1924	**Newcastle United**	2	**Aston Villa**	0	Wembley	91,695
	Harris, Seymour					
1925	**Sheffield United**	1	**Cardiff City**	0	Wembley	91,763
	Tunstall					
1926	**Bolton Wanderers**	1	**Manchester City**	0	Wembley	91,447
	Jack					
1927	**Cardiff City**	1	**Arsenal**	0	Wembley	91,206
	Ferguson					
1928	**Blackburn Rovers**	3	**Huddersfield Town**	1	Wembley	92,041
	Roscamp 2, McLean		Jackson			
1929	**Bolton Wanderers**	2	**Portsmouth**	0	Wembley	92,576
	Butler, Blackmore					
1930	**Arsenal**	2	**Huddersfield Town**	0	Wembley	92,488
	James, Lambert					
1931	**West Bromwich Albion**	2	**Birmingham**	1	Wembley	92,406
	W G Richardson 2		Bradford			
1932	**Newcastle United**	2	**Arsenal**	1	Wembley	92,298
	Allen 2		John			
1933	**Everton**	3	**Manchester City**	0	Wembley	92,950
	Stein, Dean, Dunn					
1934	**Manchester City**	2	**Portsmouth**	1	Wembley	93,258
	Tilson 2		Rutherford			
1935	**Sheffield Wednesday**	4	**West Bromwich Albion**	2	Wembley	93,204
	Rimmer 2, Hooper, Palethorpe		Boyes, Sandford			
1936	**Arsenal**	1	**Sheffield United**	0	Wembley	93,384
	Drake					
1937	**Sunderland**	3	**Preston North End**	1	Wembley	93,495
	Gurney, Carter, Burbanks		F O'Donnell			
1938	**Preston North End**	1	**Huddersfield Town**	0 *	Wembley	93,497
	Mutch (pen)					
1939	**Portsmouth**	4	**Wolverhampton W**	1	Wembley	99,370
	Parker 2, Barlow, Anderson		Dorsett			
1946	**Derby County**	4	**Charlton Athletic**	1 *	Wembley	98,215
	Stamps 2, Doherty, H Turner (og)		H Turner			
1947	**Charlton Athletic**	1	**Burnley**	0 *	Wembley	99,000
	Duffy					
1948	**Manchester United**	4	**Blackpool**	2	Wembley	99,000
	Rowley 2, Pearson, Anderson		Shimwell (pen), Mortensen			
1949	**Wolverhampton W**	3	**Leicester City**	1	Wembley	99,500
	Pye 2, Smyth		Griffiths			
1950	**Arsenal**	2	**Liverpool**	0	Wembley	100,000
	Lewis 2					
1951	**Newcastle United**	2	**Blackpool**	0	Wembley	100,000
	Milburn 2					
1952	**Newcastle United**	1	**Arsenal**	0	Wembley	100,000
	G Robledo					
1953	**Blackpool**	4	**Bolton Wanderers**	3	Wembley	100,000
	Mortensen 3, Perry		Lofthouse, Moir, Bell			
1954	**West Bromwich Albion**	3	**Preston North End**	2	Wembley	100,000
	Allen 2 (1 pen), Griffin		Morrison, Wayman			
1955	**Newcastle United**	3	**Manchester City**	1	Wembley	100,000
	Milburn, Mitchell, Hannah		Johnstone			
1956	**Manchester City**	3	**Birmingham City**	1	Wembley	100,000
	Hayes, Dyson, Johnstone		Kinsey			

Year	Winners		Runners-up		Venue	Attendance
1957	**Aston Villa** McParland 2	2	**Manchester United** Taylor	1	Wembley	100,000
1958	**Bolton Wanderers** Lofthouse 2	2	**Manchester United**	0	Wembley	100,000
1959	**Nottingham Forest** Dwight, Wilson	2	**Luton Town** Pacey	1	Wembley	100,000
1960	**Wolverhampton W** McGrath (og), Deeley 2	3	**Blackburn Rovers**	0	Wembley	100,000
1961	**Tottenham Hotspur** Smith, Dyson	2	**Leicester City**	0	Wembley	100,000
1962	**Tottenham Hotspur** Greaves, Smith, Blanchflower (pen)	3	**Burnley** Robson	1	Wembley	100,000
1963	**Manchester United** Herd 2, Law	3	**Leicester City** Keyworth	1	Wembley	100,000
1964	**West Ham United** Sissons, Hurst, Boyce	3	**Preston North End** Holden, Dawson	2	Wembley	100,000
1965	**Liverpool** Hunt, St John	2	**Leeds United** Bremner	1 *	Wembley	100,000
1966	**Everton** Trebilcock 2, Temple	3	**Sheffield Wednesday** McCalliog, Ford	2	Wembley	100,000
1967	**Tottenham Hotspur** Robertson, Saul	2	**Chelsea** Tambling	1	Wembley	100,000
1968	**West Bromwich Albion** Astle	1	**Everton**	0 *	Wembley	100,000
1969	**Manchester City** Young	1	**Leicester City**	0	Wembley	100,000
1970	**Chelsea** Houseman, Hutchinson	2	**Leeds United** Charlton, Jones	2 *	Wembley	100,000
Replay	**Chelsea** Osgood, Webb	2	**Leeds United** Jones	1 *	Old Trafford	62,078
1971	**Arsenal** Kelly, George	2	**Liverpool** Heighway	1 *	Wembley	100,000
1972	**Leeds United** Clarke	1	**Arsenal**	0	Wembley	100,000
1973	**Sunderland** Porterfield	1	**Leeds United**	0	Wembley	100,000
1974	**Liverpool** Keegan 2, Heighway	3	**Newcastle United**	0	Wembley	100,000
1975	**West Ham United** A Taylor 2	2	**Fulham**	0	Wembley	100,000
1976	**Southampton** Stokes	1	**Manchester United**	0	Wembley	100,000
1977	**Manchester United** Pearson, J Greenhoff	2	**Liverpool** Case	1	Wembley	100,000
1978	**Ipswich Town** Osborne	1	**Arsenal**	0	Wembley	100,000
1979	**Arsenal** Talbot, Stapleton, Sunderland	3	**Manchester United** McQueen, McIlroy	2	Wembley	100,000
1980	**West Ham United** Brooking	1	**Arsenal**	0	Wembley	100,000
1981	**Tottenham Hotspur** Hutchison (og)	1	**Manchester City** Hutchison	1 *	Wembley	100,000
Replay	**Tottenham Hotspur** Villa 2, Crooks	3	**Manchester City** Mackenzie, Reeves (pen)	2	Wembley	92,000
1982	**Tottenham Hotspur** Hoddle	1	**Queen's Park Rangers** Fenwick	1 *	Wembley	100,000

Year	Winners		Runners-up		Venue	Attendance
Replay	**Tottenham Hotspur**	1	**Queen's Park Rangers**	0	Wembley	90,000
	Hoddle (pen)					
1983	**Manchester United**	2	**Brighton & Hove Albion**	2 *	Wembley	100,000
	Stapleton, Wilkins		Smith, Stevens			
Replay	**Manchester United**	4	**Brighton & Hove Albion**	0	Wembley	92,000
	Robson 2, Whiteside, Muhren (pen)					
1984	**Everton**	2	**Watford**	0	Wembley	100,000
	Sharp, Gray					
1985	**Manchester United**	1	**Everton**	0 *	Wembley	100,000
	Whiteside					
1986	**Liverpool**	3	**Everton**	1	Wembley	98,000
	Rush 2, Johnston		Lineker			
1987	**Coventry City**	3	**Tottenham Hotspur**	2 *	Wembley	98,000
	Bennett, Houchen, Mabbutt (og)		C Allen, Mabbutt			
1988	**Wimbledon**	1	**Liverpool**	0	Wembley	98,203
	Sanchez					
1989	**Liverpool**	3	**Everton**	2 *	Wembley	82,800
	Rush 2, Aldridge		McCall 2			
1990	**Manchester United**	3	**Crystal Palace**	3 *	Wembley	80,000
	Hughes 2, Pemberton (og)		I Wright 2, O'Reilly			
Replay	**Manchester United**	1	**Crystal Palace**	0	Wembley	80,000
	Martin					
1991	**Tottenham Hotspur**	2	**Nottingham Forest**	1 *	Wembley	80,000
	Stewart, Walker (og)		Pearce			
1992	**Liverpool**	2	**Sunderland**	0	Wembley	79,544
	Thomas, I Rush					
1993	**Arsenal**	1	**Sheffield Wednesday**	1 *	Wembley	79,347
	Wright		Hirst			
Replay	**Arsenal**	2	**Sheffield Wednesday**	1 *	Wembley	62,267
	Wright, Linighan		Waddle			
1994	**Manchester United**	4	**Chelsea**	0	Wembley	79,634
	Cantona (2 pen), Hughes, McClair					
1995	**Everton**	1	**Manchester United**	0	Wembley	79,592
	Rideout					

* after extra time

Most wins: 8 Tottenham Hotspur, Manchester United; 7 Aston Villa, 6 Blackburn Rovers, Newcastle United
Most winners' medals: 5 James Forrest (Blackburn Rovers) 1884-86, 1890-1, Hon. Arthur Kinnaird (Wanderers) 1873, 1877-8 (Old Etonians) 1879, 1882, Charles Wollaston (Wanderers) 1872-3, 1876-8
Biggest win: 26-0 Preston North End v Hyde United (1st round) 15 Oct 1887
Biggest win (final): 6-0 Bury v Derby County 18 Apr 1903

Second Division finalists

The following clubs from the second division (formed 1892/3) of the Football League have reached the FA Cup final (* winners):

1894 Notts County *
1904 Bolton Wanderers
1908 Wolverhampton Wanderers *
1910 Barnsley
1912 Barnsley *
1920 Huddersfield Town
1921 Wolverhampton Wanderers
1923 West Ham United
1931 West Bromwich Albion *
1936 Sheffield United
1947 Burnley
1949 Leicester City
1964 Preston North End
1973 Sunderland *
1975 Fulham
1976 Southampton *
1980 West Ham United *
1982 Queen's Park Rangers
1992 Sunderland

No clubs from the 3rd or 4th divisions have reached the FA Cup final but non-league clubs, since the formation of the League, to have reached the final have been Southampton 1900 and 1902, Tottenham Hotspur 1901*

English League Cup

Insitituted as the Football League Cup in 1960/1, but it was not until the 1969/70 season that all 92 Football League teams took part. All finals up to 1966 were played on a two-leg basis but since then they have been played at Wembley Stadium. With sponsorship from the Milk Marketing Board in 1982 the Cup's name was changed to the Milk Cup, from 1986 to 1990 it was the Littlewoods Cup, in 1991-2 the Rumbelows Cup and from 1993 the Coca-Cola Cup.

Year	*Winners*		*Runners-up*		*Venue*	*Attendance*
1961	**Rotherham United**	2	**Aston Villa**	0		12,226
	Webster, Kirkman					
	Aston Villa	3	**Rotherham United**	0 *		31,202
	O'Neill, Burrows, McParland					
	(Aston Villa won 3-2 on aggregate)					
1962	**Rochdale**	0	**Norwich City**	3		11,123
			Lythgoe 2, Punton			
	Norwich City	1	**Rochdale**	0		19,708
	Hill					
	(Norwich City won 4-0 on aggregate)					
1963	**Birmingham City**	3	**Aston Villa**	1		31,850
	Leek 2, Bloomfield		Thomson			
	Aston Villa	0	**Birmingham City**	0		37,920
	(Birmingham City won 3-1 on aggregate)					
1964	**Stoke City**	1	**Leicester City**	1		22,309
	Bebbington		Gibson			
	Leicester City	3	**Stoke City**	2		25,372
	Stringfellow, Gibson, Riley		Viollet, Kinnell			
	(Leicester City won 4-3 on aggregate)					
1965	**Chelsea**	3	**Leicester City**	2		20,690
	Tambling, McCreadie, Venables (pen)		Appleton, Goodfellow			
	Leicester City	0	**Chelsea**	0		26,958
	(Chelsea won 3-2 on aggregate)					
1966	**West Ham United**	2	**West Bromwich Albion**	1		28,341
	Moore, Byrne		Astle			
	West Bromwich Albion	4	**West Ham United**	1		31,925
	Kaye, Brown, Clark, Williams		Peters			
	(West Bromwich Albion won 5-3 on aggregate)					
1967	**Queen's Park Rangers**	3	**West Bromwich Albion**	2	Wembley	97,952
	R Morgan, Marsh, Lazarus		Clark 2			
1968	**Leeds United**	1	**Arsenal**	0	Wembley	97,887
	Cooper					
1969	**Swindon Town**	3	**Arsenal**	1	Wembley	98,189
	Rogers 2, Smart		Gould			
1970	**Manchester City**	2	**West Bromwich Albion**	1	Wembley	97,963
	Doyle, Pardoe		Astle			
1971	**Tottenham Hotspur**	2	**Aston Villa**	0	Wembley	100,000
	Chivers 2					
1972	**Stoke City**	2	**Chelsea**	1	Wembley	100,000
	Conroy, Eastham		Osgood			
1973	**Tottenham Hotspur**	1	**Norwich City**	0	Wembley	100,000
	Coates					
1974	**Wolverhampton W**	2	**Manchester City**	1	Wembley	100,000
	Hibbitt, Richards		Bell			
1975	**Aston Villa**	1	**Norwich City**	0	Wembley	100,000
	Graydon					
1976	**Manchester City**	2	**Newcastle United**	1	Wembley	100,000
	Barnes, Tueart		Gowling			
1977	**Aston Villa**	0	**Everton**	0	Wembley	100,000

Year	Winners		Runners-up		Venue	Attendance
Replay	**Aston Villa**	1	**Everton**	1 *	Hillsborough	55,000
	Kenyon (og)		Latchford			
Replay	**Aston Villa**	3	**Everton**	2 *	Old Trafford	54,749
	Little 2, Nicholl		Latchford, Lyons			
1978	**Nottingham Forest**	0	**Liverpool**	0 *	Wembley	100,000
Replay	**Nottingham Forest**	1	**Liverpool**	0	Old Trafford	54,375
	Robertson (pen)					
1979	**Nottingham Forest**	3	**Southampton**	2	Wembley	100,000
	Birtles 2, Woodcock		Peach, Holmes			
1980	**Wolverhampton W**	1	**Nottingham Forest**	0	Wembley	100,000
	Gray					
1981	**Liverpool**	1	**West Ham United**	1 *	Wembley	100,000
	A Kennedy		Stewart (pen)			
Replay	**Liverpool**	2	**West Ham United**	1	Villa Park	36,693
	Dalglish, Hansen		Goddard			
1982	**Liverpool**	3	**Tottenham Hotspur**	1 *	Wembley	100,000
	Whelan 2, Rush		Archibald			
1983	**Liverpool**	2	**Manchester United**	1 *	Wembley	100,000
	Kennedy, Whelan		Whiteside			
1984	**Liverpool**	0	**Everton**	0 *	Wembley	100,000
Replay	**Liverpool**	1	**Everton**	0	Maine Road	52,089
	Souness					
1985	**Norwich City**	1	**Sunderland**	0	Wembley	100,000
	Chisholm (og)					
1986	**Oxford United**	3	**Queen's Park Rangers**	0	Wembley	90,396
	Hebberd, Houghton, Charles					
1987	**Arsenal**	2	**Liverpool**	1	Wembley	96,000
	Nicholas 2		Rush			
1988	**Luton Town**	3	**Arsenal**	2	Wembley	95,732
	B Stein 2, Wilson		Hayes, Smith			
1989	**Nottingham Forest**	3	**Luton Town**	1	Wembley	76,130
	Clough 2 (1 pen), Webb		Harford			
1990	**Nottingham Forest**	1	**Oldham**	0	Wembley	74,343
	Jemson					
1991	**Sheffield Wednesday**	1	**Manchester United**	0	Wembley	80,000
	Sheridan					
1992	**Manchester United**	1	**Nottingham Forest**	0	Wembley	76,810
	McClair					
1993	**Arsenal**	2	**Sheffield Wednesday**	1	Wembley	74,007
	Merson, Morrow		Harkes			
1994	**Aston Villa**	3	**Manchester United**	1	Wembley	77,231
	Atkinson, Saunders 2 (1 pen)		Hughes			
1995	**Liverpool**	2	**Bolton Wanderers**	1	Wembley	75,595
	McManaman 2		Thompson			

* *after extra time*

Most wins: 5 Liverpool, 4 Nottingham Forest, Aston Villa

Most winners' medals: 5 Ian Rush, 4 Phil Neal, Alan Kennedy, Kenny Dalglish, Sammy Lee, Graeme Souness (all Liverpool)

Biggest win: 10-0 West Ham United v Bury (2nd round, 2nd leg) 25 Oct 1983, 10-0 Liverpool v Fulham (2nd round, 1st leg) 23 Sep 1986

Biggest win (final): 4-1 West Bromwich Albion v West Ham United (2nd leg) 23 Mar 1966

The following non-first division sides have reached the final: (* winners)

Div.2: 1961 Rotherham United, 1962 Norwich City *, 1975 Aston Villa * and Norwich City, 1981 West Ham United, 1990 Oldham Athletic, 1991 Sheffield Wednesday*

Div.3: 1967 Queen's Park Rangers *, 1969 Swindon Town *, 1971 Aston Villa

Div.4: 1962 Rochdale

The Leading English Football League Clubs *at end 1994/95*

This table shows the leading English clubs, detailing their honours and (for fun) awarding points as follows:
Football League Division 1 (now Prenier League) 1st - 12, 2nd - 10, 3rd - 8; Division 2 champions (Div. 1 from 1993) - 1 point
FA Cup: W - winners 10, RU - runners-up - 8, SF - losing semi-finalists 4
Football League Cup: W - winners 8, RU - runners-up 4, SF - losing semi-finalists 2

Name	*FL Div 1/P*			*Div 2/1*	*FA Cup*			*FL Cup*			*Points*
	1st	2nd	3rd	1st	W	RU	SF	W	RU	SF	
Liverpool	18	10	2	4	4	5	10	5	2	2	508
Manchester United	9	11	3	2	8	5	7	1	3	3	418
Everton	9	7	7	1	5	7	11	-	2	1	395
Aston Villa	7	10	2	2	7	2	8	4	2	3	366
Arsenal	10	3	4	-	6	6	6	2	3	2	346
Tottenham Hotspur	2	4	8	2	8	1	6	2	1	5	272
Sunderland	6	5	8	1	2	2	7	-	1	1	257
Wolverhampton Wanderers	3	5	6	2	4	4	5	2	-	1	242
Sheffield Wednesday	4	1	7	5	3	3	10	1	1	1	222
Manchester City	2	3	3	6	4	4	2	2	1	2	188
Newcastle United	4	-	3	2	6	5	2	-	1	-	186
West Bromwich Albion	1	2	1	2	5	5	9	1	2	1	186
Blackburn Rovers	3	1	3	1	6	2	8	-	-	2	183
Preston North End	2	6	2	3	2	5	3	-	-	-	175
Nottingham Forest	1	2	4	2	2	1	9	4	2	-	170
Derby County	2	3	4	4	1	3	9	-	-	1	162
Leeds United	3	5	1	3	1	3	4	1	-	3	161
Huddersfield Town	3	3	3	1	1	4	2	-	-	1	143
Burnley	2	2	5	2	1	2	5	-	-	-	132
Chelsea	1	-	3	2	1	3	7	1	1	3	118
Bolton Wanderers	-	-	3	2	4	3	5	-	1	1	116
Sheffield United	1	2	-	1	4	2	5	-	-	-	109
Ipswich Town	1	2	3	3	1	-	2	-	-	2	81
Leicester City	-	1	1	6	-	4	3	1	1	-	80
West Ham United	-	-	1	2	3	1	2	-	2	5	74
Southampton	-	1	-	-	1	2	7	-	1	1	70
Portsmouth	2	-	1	-	1	2	2	-	-	-	66

Scottish Football League

The Scottish League was formed in 1890, two years after the Football League. A second division was added in 1893 and the biggest re-organisation in the League since its formation came in 1975/6 when it was completely re-structured. The leading ten teams formed a new Premier Division while the remaining teams were divided into Divisions 1 and 2. The number of teams in the Premier Division was extended to twelve in 1986/7, but reduced back to ten from 1988/9, then twelve 1991/2 and ten again in 1994/5. when there were also ten clubs in each of Divisions 1, 2 and 3.

First Division/Premier Division champions

Season	Champions	Pts	Max	Season	Champions	Pts	Max	Season	Champions	Pts	Max
				1903/4	Third Lanark	43	52	1919/20	Rangers	71	84
				1904/5	Celtic	41	52	1920/1	Rangers	76	84
1890/1	Dumbarton	29	36	1905/6	Celtic	49	60	1921/2	Celtic	67	84
	& Rangers	29	36	1906/7	Celtic	55	68	1922/3	Rangers	55	76
1891/2	Dumbarton	37	44	1907/8	Celtic	55	68	1923/4	Rangers	59	76
1892/3	Celtic	29	36	1908/9	Celtic	51	68	1924/5	Rangers	60	76
1893/4	Celtic	29	36	1909/10	Celtic	54	68	1925/6	Celtic	58	76
1894/5	Hearts	31	36	1910/1	Rangers	52	68	1926/7	Rangers	56	76
1895/6	Celtic	30	36	1911/2	Rangers	51	68	1927/8	Rangers	60	76
1896/7	Hearts	28	36	1912/3	Rangers	53	68	1928/9	Rangers	67	76
1897/8	Celtic	33	36	1913/4	Celtic	65	76	1929/30	Rangers	60	76
1898/9	Rangers	36	36	1914/5	Celtic	65	76	1930/1	Rangers	60	76
1899/00	Rangers	32	36	1915/6	Celtic	67	76	1931/2	Motherwell	66	76
1900/1	Rangers	35	40	1916/7	Celtic	64	76	1932/3	Rangers	62	76
1901/2	Rangers	28	36	1917/8	Rangers	56	68	1933/4	Rangers	66	76
1902/3	Hibernian	37	44	1918/9	Celtic	58	68	1934/5	Rangers	55	76

Season	Champions	Pts	Max	Season	Champions	Pts	Max	Season	Champions	Pts	Max
1935/6	Celtic	66	76	1963/4	Rangers	55	68	1983/4	Aberdeen	57	72
1936/7	Rangers	61	76	1964/5	Kilmarnock	50	68	1984/5	Aberdeen	59	72
1937/8	Celtic	61	76	1965/6	Celtic	57	68	1985/6	Celtic	50	72
1938/9	Rangers	59	76	1966/7	Celtic	58	68	1986/7	Rangers	69	88
1946/7	Rangers	46	68	1967/8	Celtic	63	68	1987/8	Celtic	72	88
1947/8	Hibernian	48	68	1968/9	Celtic	54	68	1988/9	Rangers	56	72
1948/9	Rangers	46	68	1969/70	Celtic	57	68	1989/90	Rangers	51	72
1949/50	Rangers	50	68	1970/1	Celtic	56	68	1990/1	Rangers	55	72
1950/1	Hibernian	48	68	1971/2	Celtic	60	68	1991/2	Rangers	72	88
1951/2	Hibernian	45	68	1972/3	Celtic	57	68	1992/3	Rangers	73	88
1952/3	Rangers	43	68	1973/4	Celtic	53	68	1993/4	Rangers	58	88
1953/4	Celtic	43	68	1974/5	Rangers	56	68	1994/5	Rangers	69	108
1954/5	Aberdeen	49	68	**Premier Division**							
1955/6	Rangers	52	68	1975/6	Rangers	54	72				
1956/7	Rangers	55	68	1976/7	Celtic	55	72				
1957/8	Hearts	62	68	1977/8	Rangers	55	72				
1958/9	Rangers	50	68	1978/9	Celtic	48	72				
1959/60	Hearts	54	68	1979/80	Aberdeen	48	72				
1960/1	Rangers	51	68	1980/1	Celtic	56	72				
1961/2	Dundee	54	68	1981/2	Celtic	55	72				
1962/3	Rangers	57	68	1982/3	Dundee Utd	56	72				

Most wins: 45 Rangers, 35 Celtic, 4 Aberdeen, Hearts, Hibernian
Biggest win: 13-2 East Fife v Edinburgh City 11 Dec 1937 Div 2
Biggest win (Division 1 or Premier Division): 11-0 Celtic v Dundee 26 Oct 1895

Most individual goals in a match

8 Owen McNally (Arthurlie v Armadale) 1 Oct 1927 Div 2

8 Jimmy McGrory (Celtic v Dunfermline Athletic) 14 Jan 1928 Div 1

8 Jim Dyet (King's Park v Forfar Athletic) 2 Jan 1930 Div 2

8 John Calder (Morton v Raith Rovers) 18 Mar 1936 Div 2

Most individual goals in a season

66 Jim Smith (Ayr United) 1927/8 Div 2

53 Robert Skinner (Dunfermline Athletic) 1925/6 Div 2

52 Bill McFadyen (Motherwell) 1931/2 Div 1

50 Jimmy McGrory (Celtic) 1935/6 Div 1

Scottish FA Cup

When Queen's Park called a meeting of clubs on 13 March 1873 it was with the intention of organising a cup competition, similar to the FA Cup. Eight clubs attended that first meeting and Queen's Park's wishes were granted but, at the same meeting, it was decided to form the Scottish Football Association and so the new cup competition was called the Scottish Football Association Cup.

The venue of the Final has been Hampden Park, except for: Hamilton Crescent 1876-7, Cathkin Park 1880, 1882, 1886; Kinning Park 1881, Ibrox Park 1890, 1892-3, 1895, 1900-1, 1906, 1910-12, 1914, 1924; Logie Green 1896, Celtic Park 1902-3, 1913, 1921. Now sponsored by Tennents.

Year	Winners		Runners-up		Attendance
1874	Queen's Park	2	Clydesdale	0	3,500
1875	Queen's Park	3	Renton	0	7,000
1876	Queen's Park	1	Third Lanark	1	10,000
Replay	Queen's Park	2	Third Lanark	0	6,000
1877	Vale of Leven	0	Rangers	0	10,000
Replay	Vale of Leven	1	Rangers	1	15,000
Replay	Vale of Leven	3	Rangers	2	12,000
1878	Vale of Leven	1	Third Lanark	0	5,000
1879	Vale of Leven	1	Rangers	1	9,000
	Awarded trophy as Rangers refused to appear for the *Replay*				
1880	Queen's Park	3	Thornlibank	0	4,000
1881	Queen's Park	2	Dumbarton	1	15,000
	Replayed due to spectator invasion of pitch				
Replay	Queen's Park	3	Dumbarton	1	7,000
1882	Queen's Park	2	Dumbarton	2	12,500
Replay	Queen's Park	4	Dumbarton	1	14,000
1883	Dumbarton	2	Vale of Leven	2	9,000
Replay	Dumbarton	2	Vale of Leven	1	12,000
1884	Queen's Park awarded cup as Vale of Leven failed to appear				
1885	Renton	0	Vale of Leven	0	2,500
Replay	Renton	3	Vale of Leven	1	3,500
1886	Queen's Park	3	Renton	1	7,000
1887	Hibernian	2	Dumbarton	1	12,000
1888	Renton	6	Cambuslang	1	11,000
1889	Third Lanark	3	Celtic	1	18,000
	Game declared void due to snowstorm				
Replay	Third Lanark	2	Celtic	1	13,000
1890	Queen's Park	1	Vale of Leven	1	11,000
Replay	Queen's Park	2	Vale of Leven	1	14,000
1891	Hearts	1	Dumbarton	0	10,836
1892	Celtic	1	Queen's Park	0	40,000
	*Replay*ed due to spectator disruption				
Replay	Celtic	5	Queen's Park	1	26,000
1893	Queen's Park	0	Celtic	1	18,771
	*Replay*ed due to frosty pitch				
Replay	Queen's Park	2	Celtic	1	13,239
1894	Rangers	3	Celtic	1	17,000
1895	St.Bernard's	2	Renton	1	15,000
1896	Hearts	3	Hibernian	1	17,034
1897	Rangers	5	Dumbarton	1	14,000
1898	Rangers	2	Kilmarnock	0	13,000

Year	Winners	Runners-up	Attendance
1899	Celtic 2	Rangers 0	25,000
1900	Celtic 4	Queen's Park 3	15,000
1901	Hearts 4	Celtic 3	12,000
1902	Hibernian 1	Celtic 0	16,000
1903	Rangers 1	Hearts 1	40,000
Replay	Rangers 0	Hearts 0	35,000
Replay	Rangers 2	Hearts 0	32,000
1904	Celtic 3	Rangers 2	65,000
1905	Third Lanark 0	Rangers 0	54,000
Replay	Third Lanark 3	Rangers 1	55,000
1906	Hearts 1	Third Lanark 0	25,000
1907	Celtic 3	Hearts 0	50,000
1908	Celtic 5	St Mirren 1	55,000
1909	Celtic 2	Rangers 2	70,000
Replay	Celtic 1	Rangers 1	61,000
	Owing to a riot, cup withheld after two drawn games		
1910	Dundee 2	Clyde 2	62,300
Replay	Dundee 0	Clyde 0	24,500
Replay	Dundee 2	Clyde 1	25,400
1911	Celtic 0	Hamilton A 0	45,000
Replay	Celtic 2	Hamilton A 0	24,700
1912	Celtic 2	Clyde 0	46,000
1913	Falkirk 2	Raith Rovers 0	45,000
1914	Celtic 0	Hibernian 0	56,000
Replay	Celtic 4	Hibernian 1	40,000
1920	Kilmarnock 3	Albion Rovers 2	95,000
1921	Partick Thistle 1	Rangers 0	28,300
1922	Morton 1	Rangers 0	75,000
1923	Celtic 1	Hibernian 0	80,100
1924	Airdrieonians 2	Hibernian 0	59,218
1925	Celtic 2	Dundee 1	75,137
1926	St Mirren 2	Celtic 0	98,620
1927	Celtic 3	East Fife 1	80,070
1928	Rangers 4	Celtic 0	118,115
1929	Kilmarnock 2	Rangers 0	114,708
1930	Rangers 0	Partick Thistle 0	107,475
Replay	Rangers 2	Partick Thistle 1	103,686
1931	Celtic 2	Motherwell 2	105,000
Replay	Celtic 4	Motherwell 2	98,579
1932	Rangers 1	Kilmarnock 1	111,982
Replay	Rangers 3	Kilmarnock 0	104,965
1933	Celtic 1	Motherwell 0	102,339
1934	Rangers 5	St Mirren 0	113,403
1935	Rangers 2	Hamilton A 1	87,286
1936	Rangers 1	Third Lanark 0	88,859
1937	Celtic 2	Aberdeen 1	147,365
1938	East Fife 1	Kilmarnock 1	80,091
Replay	East Fife 4	Kilmarnock 2	92,716
1939	Clyde 4	Motherwell 0	94,799
1947	Aberdeen 2	Hibernian 1	82,140
1948	Rangers 1	Morton 1	129,176
Replay	Rangers 1	Morton 0	133,570
1949	Rangers 4	Clyde 1	108,435
1950	Rangers 3	East Fife 0	118,262
1951	Celtic 1	Motherwell 0	131,943
1952	Motherwell 4	Dundee 0	136,274
1953	Rangers 1	Aberdeen 1	129,681
Replay	Rangers 1	Aberdeen 0	112,619
1954	Celtic 2	Aberdeen 1	129,926
1955	Clyde 1	Celtic 1	106,111
Replay	Clyde 1	Celtic 0	68,735
1956	Hearts 3	Celtic 1	133,339
1957	Falkirk 1	Kilmarnock 1	83,000
Replay	Falkirk 2	Kilmarnock 1	79,785
1958	Clyde 1	Hibernian 0	95,124
1959	St Mirren 3	Aberdeen 1	108,591
1960	Rangers 2	Kilmarnock 0	108,017
1961	Dunfermline A 0	Celtic 0	113,618
Replay	Dunfermline A 2	Celtic 0	87,866
1962	Rangers 2	St Mirren 0	126,930
1963	Rangers 1	Celtic 1	129,527
Replay	Rangers 3	Celtic 0	120,263
1964	Rangers 3	Dundee 1	120,982
1965	Celtic 3	Dunfermline A 2	108,800
1966	Rangers 0	Celtic 0	126,552
Replay	Rangers 1	Celtic 0	98,202
1967	Celtic 2	Aberdeen 0	127,117
1968	Dunfermline A 3	Hearts 1	56,366
1969	Celtic 4	Rangers 0	132,874
1970	Aberdeen 3	Celtic 1	108,434
1971	Celtic 1	Rangers 1	120,092
Replay	Celtic 2	Rangers 1	103,332
1972	Celtic 6	Hibernian 1	106,102
1973	Rangers 3	Celtic 2	122,714
1974	Celtic 3	Dundee United 0	75,959
1975	Celtic 3	Airdrieonians 1	75,457
1976	Rangers 3	Hearts 1	85,354
1977	Celtic 1	Rangers 0	54,252
1978	Rangers 2	Aberdeen 1	61,563
1979	Rangers 0	Hibernian 0	50,610
Replay	Rangers 0	Hibernian 0	33,506
Replay	Rangers 3	Hibernian 2	30,602
1980	Celtic 1	Rangers 0 *	70,303
1981	Rangers 0	Dundee United 0	55,000
Replay	Rangers 4	Dundee United 1	43,009
1982	Aberdeen 4	Rangers 1 *	53,788
1983	Aberdeen 1	Rangers 0 *	62,979
1984	Aberdeen 2	Celtic 1 *	58,900
1985	Celtic 2	Dundee United 1	60,346
1986	Aberdeen 3	Hearts 0	62,841
1987	St Mirren 1	Dundee United 0 *	51,792
1988	Celtic 2	Dundee United 1	74,000
1989	Celtic 1	Rangers 0	72,069
1990	Aberdeen 0	Celtic 0 *	60,493
	Aberdeen won 9-8 on penalties		
1991	Motherwell 4	Dundee United 3 *	57,319
1992	Rangers 2	Airdrieonians 1	44,045
1993	Rangers 2	Aberdeen 1	50,715
1994	Dundee United 1	Rangers 0	38,000
1995	Celtic 1	Airdrie 0	36,915

* after extra time

Most wins: 30 Celtic, 26 Rangers, 10 Queen's Park

Biggest win: 36-0 Arbroath v Bon Accord (1st round) 5 Sep 1885

Biggest win (final): 6-1 Renton v Cambuslang 4 Feb 1888, 6-1 Celtic v Hibernian 6 May 1972

Most individual goals in one match: 13 John Petrie (Arbroath v Bon Accord) 1st round 12 Sep 1885

Most winner's medals: 8 Charles Campbell (Queen's Park) 1874-6, 1880-2, 1884, 1886

Scottish League Cup

The Scottish League Cup was first contested in 1946/7, replacing the Southern League Cup that had been played during the war. Prior to 1977/8 the teams were split into eight or nine groups, with the winners going through to a knockout competition. The Cup became known as the Skol Cup in 1984/5 and as the Coca-Cola Cup from 1994/5. All finals have been at Hampden Park, unless otherwise stated.

Year	Winners	Runners-up
1946/7	Rangers 4	Aberdeen 0
1947/8	East Fife 1	Falkirk 1 *
Replay	East Fife 4	Falkirk 1
1948/9	Rangers 2	Raith Rovers 0
1949/50	East Fife 3	Dunfermline A 0
1950/1	Motherwell 3	Hibernian 0
1951/2	Dundee 3	Rangers 2
1952/3	Dundee 2	Kilmarnock 0
1953/4	East Fife 3	Partick Thistle 2
1954/5	Hearts 4	Motherwell 2
1955/6	Aberdeen 2	St Mirren 1
1956/7	Celtic 0	Partick Thistle 0 *
Replay	Celtic 3	Partick Thistle 0
1957/8	Celtic 7	Rangers 1
1958/9	Hearts 5	Partick Thistle 1
1959/60	Hearts 2	Third Lanark 1
1960/1	Rangers 2	Kilmarnock 0
1961/2	Rangers 1	Hearts 1 *
Replay	Rangers 3	Hearts 1
1962/3	Hearts 1	Kilmarnock 0
1963/4	Rangers 5	Morton 0
1964/5	Rangers 2	Celtic 1
1965/6	Celtic 2	Rangers 1
1966/7	Celtic 1	Rangers 0
1967/8	Celtic 5	Dundee 3
1968/9	Celtic 6	Hibernian 2
1969/70	Celtic 1	St.Johnstone 0
1970/1	Rangers 1	Celtic 0
1971/2	Partick Thistle 4	Celtic 1
1972/3	Hibernian 2	Celtic 1
1973/4	Dundee 1	Celtic 0
1974/5	Celtic 6	Hibernian 3
1975/6	Rangers 1	Celtic 0
1976/7	Aberdeen 2	Celtic 1
1977/8	Rangers 2	Celtic 1
1978/9	Rangers 2	Aberdeen 1
1979/80	Dundee United 0	Aberdeen 0
Replay	Dundee United 3	Aberdeen 0 **
1980/1	Dundee United 3	Dundee 0 **
1981/2	Rangers 2	Dundee United 1
1982/3	Celtic 2	Rangers 1
1983/4	Rangers 3	Celtic 2 *
1984/5	Rangers 1	Dundee United 0
1985/6	Aberdeen 3	Hibernian 0
1986/7	Rangers 2	Celtic 1
1987/8	Rangers 3	Aberdeen 3 *
	(Rangers won 5-3 on penalties)	
1988/9	Rangers 3	Aberdeen 2
1989/90	Aberdeen 2	Rangers 1 *
1990/1	Rangers 2	Celtic 1 *
1991/2	Hibernian 2	Dunfermline 0
1992/3	Rangers 2	Aberdeen 1
1993/4	Rangers 2	Hibernian 1
1994/5	Raith Rovers 2	Celtic 2 *
	(Raith Rovers won 6-5 on penalties)	

*after extra time, ** played at Dens Park, Dundee

Most wins: 19 Rangers, 9 Celtic

Biggest win (final): 7-1 Celtic v Rangers 19 Oct 1957

Most successful Scottish clubs

Wins		League	Cup	Lg.Cup
89	Rangers	45	26	19
73	Celtic	35	30	9
15	Aberdeen	4	7	4
13	Hearts	4	5	4
10	Queen's Park	-	10	

Awards

World Footballer of the Year

Elected annually by *World Soccer* from 1982. *Winners:*
1982 Paolo Rossi (Ita, Juventus)
1983 Zico (Bra, Udinese)
1984 Michel Platini (Fra, Juventus)
1985 Michel Platini (Fra, Juventus)
1986 Diego Maradona (Arg, Napoli)
1987 Ruud Gullit (Hol, AC Milan)
1988 Marco Van Basten (Hol, AC Milan)
1989 Ruud Gullit (Hol, AC Milan)
1990 Lothar Matthäus (FRG, Internazionale Milan)
1991 Jean-Pierre Papin (Fra, Marseille)
1992 Marco Van Basten (Hol, AC Milan)
1993 Roberto Baggio (Ita, Juventus)
1994 Paulo Maldini (Ita, AC Milan)

FIFA World Footballer of the Year

Presented by FIFA, the European Sports Management Association and Adidas, and selected annually by national team coaches from around the world.
1991 Lothar Matthäus (Ger, Internazionale Milan)
1992 Marco Van Basten (Hol, AC Milan)
1993 Roberto Baggio (Ita, Juventus)
1994 Romario (Bra, Barcelona)

European Footballer of the Year

Le Ballon D'Or (Golden Ball) is awarded each year by the French newspaper *France Football* who ask journalists in UEFA affiliated countries to draw up a list of their five nominees. *Winners:*
1956 Stanley Matthews (UK, Blackpool)
1957 Alfredo di Stéfano (Spa, Real Madrid)
1958 Raymond Kopa (Fra, Real Madrid)
1959 Alfredo di Stéfano (Spa, Real Madrid)
1960 Luis Suárez (Spa, Barcelona)
1961 Omar Sivori (Ita, Juventus)
1962 Josef Masopust (Cs, Dukla Praha)
1963 Lev Yashin (USSR, Dynamo Moscow)
1964 Denis Law (UK, Manchester United)
1965 Eusébio (Por, Benfica)
1966 Bobby Charlton (UK, Manchester United)
1967 Florian Albert (Hun, Ferencváros)
1968 George Best (UK, Manchester United)

1969 Gianni Rivera (Ita, AC Milan)
1970 Gerd Müller (FRG, Bayern München)
1971 Johan Cruyff (Hol, Ajax)
1972 Franz Beckenbauer (FRG, Bayern München)
1973 Johan Cruyff (Hol, Barcelona)
1974 Johan Cruyff (Hol, Barcelona)
1975 Oleg Blokhin (USSR, Dynamo Kiev)
1976 Franz Beckenbauer (FRG, Bayern München)
1977 Allan Simonsen (Den, Borussia Mönchengladbach)
1978 Kevin Keegan (UK, Hamburger SV)
1979 Kevin Keegan (UK, Hamburger SV)
1980 Karl-Heinz Rummenigge (FRG, Bayern München)
1981 Karl-Heinz Rummenigge (FRG, Bayern München)
1982 Paolo Rossi (Ita, Juventus)
1983 Michel Platini (Fra, Juventus)
1984 Michel Platini (Fra, Juventus)
1985 Michel Platini (Fra, Juventus)
1986 Igor Belanov (USSR, Dynamo Kiev)
1987 Ruud Gullit (Hol, AC Milan)
1988 Marco Van Basten (Hol, AC Milan)
1989 Marco Van Basten (Hol, AC Milan)
1990 Lothar Matthäus (FRG, Internazionale Milan)
1991 Jean-Pierre Papin (Fra, Marseille)
1992 Marco Van Basten (Hol, AC Milan)
1993 Roberto Baggio (Ita, Juventus)
1994 Hristo Stoichkov (Bul, Barcelona)
Most wins: 3 Cruyff, Platini, Van Basten

Football Writers' Player of the Year
The Football Writers' Association was founded in 1947 and since 1947/8 its members have voted for their Player of the Year. *Winners:*
1948 Stanley Matthews (Blackpool)
1949 Johnny Carey (Manchester United)
1950 Joe Mercer (Arsenal)
1951 Harry Johnston (Blackpool)
1952 Billy Wright (Wolverhampton Wanderers)
1953 Nat Lofthouse (Bolton Wanderers)
1954 Tom Finney (Preston North End)
1955 Don Revie (Manchester City)
1956 Bert Trautmann (Manchester City)
1957 Tom Finney (Preston North End)
1958 Danny Blanchflower (Tottenham Hotspur)
1959 Syd Owen (Luton Town)
1960 Bill Slater (Wolverhampton Wanderers)
1961 Danny Blanchflower (Tottenham Hotspur)
1962 Jimmy Adamson (Burnley)
1963 Stanley Matthews (Stoke City)
1964 Bobby Moore (West Ham United)
1965 Bobby Collins (Leeds United)
1966 Bobby Charlton (Manchester United)
1967 Jackie Charlton (Leeds United)
1968 George Best (Manchester United)
1969 Tony Book (Manchester City) &
    Dave Mackay (Derby County)
1970 Billy Bremner (Leeds United)
1971 Frank McLintock (Arsenal)
1972 Gordon Banks (Stoke City)
1973 Pat Jennings (Tottenham Hotspur)
1974 Ian Callaghan (Liverpool)
1975 Alan Mullery (Fulham)

1976 Kevin Keegan (Liverpool)
1977 Emlyn Hughes (Liverpool)
1978 Kenny Burns (Nottingham Forest)
1979 Kenny Dalglish (Liverpool)
1980 Terry McDermott (Liverpool)
1981 Frans Thijssen (Ipswich Town)
1982 Steve Perryman (Tottenham Hotspur)
1983 Kenny Dalglish (Liverpool)
1984 Ian Rush (Liverpool)
1985 Neville Southall (Everton)
1986 Gary Lineker (Everton)
1987 Clive Allen (Tottenham Hotspur)
1988 John Barnes (Liverpool)
1989 Steve Nicol (Liverpool)
1990 John Barnes (Liverpool)
1991 Gordon Strachan (Leeds United)
1992 Gary Lineker (Tottenham Hotspur)
1993 Chris Waddle (Sheffield Wednesday)
1994 Alan Shearer (Blackburn Rovers)
1995 Jürgen Klinsmann (Tottenham Hotspur)
Most wins: 2 Finney, Blanchflower, Matthews, Dalglish, Barnes, Lineker
Most wins (clubs): 10 Liverpool, 7 Tottenham Hotspur
Winners never to win a full international cap:
Bert Trautmann (1956), Jimmy Adamson (1962), Tony Book (1969)
Winners while with a second division club:
Stanley Matthews (1963), Dave Mackay (1969), Alan Mullery (1975)

Professional Footballers' Association Player of the Year
At the end of each season the professional players vote for their Player of the Year, a trophy much cherished by its winners. The first such award was made in 1974. A Young Player award is also presented annually, as well as a Merit Award. *Winners:*
Player of the Year
1974 Norman Hunter (Leeds United)
1975 Colin Todd (Derby County)
1976 Pat Jennings (Tottenham Hotspur)
1977 Andy Gray (Aston Villa)
1978 Peter Shilton (Nottingham Forest)
1979 Liam Brady (Arsenal)
1980 Terry McDermott (Liverpool)
1981 John Wark (Ipswich Town)
1982 Kevin Keegan (Southampton)
1983 Kenny Dalglish (Liverpool)
1984 Ian Rush (Liverpool)
1985 Peter Reid (Everton)
1986 Gary Lineker (Everton)
1987 Clive Allen (Tottenham Hotspur)
1988 John Barnes (Liverpool)
1989 Mark Hughes (Manchester United)
1990 David Platt (Aston Villa)
1991 Mark Hughes (Manchester United)
1992 Gary Pallister (Manchester United)
1993 Paul McGrath (Aston Villa)
1994 Eric Cantona (Fra, Manchester United)
1995 Alan Shearer (Blackburn Rovers)

Scottish Footballer Player of the Year
Awarded annually by the Scottish PFA
1965 Billy McNeill (Celtic)
1966 John Greig (Rangers)
1967 Ronnie Simpson (Celtic)
1968 Gordon Wallace (Raith Rovers)
1969 Bobby Murdoch (Celtic)
1970 Pat Stanton (Hibernian)
1971 Martin Buchan (Aberdeen)
1972 Dave Smith (Rangers)
1973 George Connelly (Celtic)
1974 Scotland World Cup squad
1975 Sandy Jardine (Rangers)
1976 John Greig (Rangers)
1977 Danny McGrain (Celtic)
1978 Derek Johnstone (Rangers)
1979 Andy Ritchie (Morton)
1980 Gordon Strachan (Aberdeen)
1981 Alan Rough (Partick Thistle)
1982 Paul Sturrock (Dundee United)
1983 Charlie Nicholas (Celtic)
1984 Willie Miller (Aberdeen)
1985 Hamish McAlpine (Dundee United)
1986 Sandy Jardine (Hearts)
1987 Brian McClair (Celtic)
1988 Paul McStay (Celtic)
1989 Richard Gough (Rangers)
1990 Alex McLeish (Aberdeen)
1991 Maurice Malpas (Dundee United)
1992 Ally McCoist (Rangers)
1993 Andy Goram (Rangers)
1994 Mark Hateley (Rangers)
1995 Brian Laudrup (Rangers, Den)

Ian Rush – Footballer of the Year in 1984

Women's Soccer

World Championship
After a qualifying tournament the first ever women's World Championships were contested by teams from 12 nations in China in 1991. Results of finals:

1991	USA 2		Norway 1	
1995	Norway 2		Germany 0	

European Championship
First held in 1983/4. *Winners*:
1984 Sweden
1987 Norway
1989 F R Germany
1991 F R Germany
1993 Norway

Gaelic Football

A 15-a-side game, Gaelic football, the most popular sport in Ireland with about 250,000 players, has common features with soccer, rugby and Australian Rules football. The first reference of a game resembling Gaelic football was in 1712 when a match between Meath and Louth took place at Slane. The rules were standardized following the formation of the Gaelic Athletic Association, the governing body in Ireland for handball, hurling and rounders as well as for Gaelic football, in 1884. The number of players per team was fixed at 21 in 1884, but reduced to 17 in 1892 and to 15 in 1913.

All Ireland Championships

The sport's principal championship; the final is played at Dublin's Croke Park on the third Sunday in September each year for the Sam Maguire Trophy. Held annually from 1887, except for 1888 when this inter-county event was unfinished. *Most wins*:

30	Kerry	1903-4, 1909, 1913-4, 1924, 1926, 1929-32, 1937, 1939-41, 1946, 1953, 1955, 1959, 1962, 1969-70, 1975, 1978-81, 1984-6
21	Dublin	1891-2, 1894, 1897-9, 1901-2, 1906-8, 1921-3, 1942, 1958, 1963, 1974, 1976-7, 1983
7	Galway	1925, 1934, 1938, 1956, 1964-6
6	Cork	1890, 1911, 1945, 1973, 1989-90
5	Wexford	1893, 1915-8
5	Cavan	1933, 1935, 1947-8, 1952
5	Meath	1949, 1954, 1967, 1987-8
5	Down	1960-1, 1968, 1991, 1994
4	Tipperary	1889, 1895, 1900, 1920
4	Kildare	1905, 1919, 1927-8
3	Louth	1910, 1912, 1957
3	Mayo	1936, 1950-1
3	Offaly	1971-2, 1982
2	Limerick	1887, 1896
2	Roscommon	1943-4
1	Donegal	1992
1	Derry	1993

Most appearances in final: 46 Kerry, 34 Dublin
Highest team score in a final: 27 Dublin (5 goals, 12 points) beat Armagh 15 (3, 6) in 1977
Highest aggregate score in a final: 45 Cork (26) beat Galway (19) in 1973.
Most individual appearances: 10, including a record 8 wins by the Kerry players Pat Spillane, Paudie O'Shea, Denis 'Ogie' Moran, Ger Power and Mike Sheehy 1975-86.
Highest attendance: 90,556 in 1961.

Gliding

There is some evidence of the use of gliders in Ancient Egypt about four thousand years ago, and the ability to float in the air like a bird has long been of fascination for man. Gliding (or soaring) as a sport began to gain popular appeal in the 1930s in Europe and the USA.

Records

A wide variety of world records are maintained for single-seater and for multi-seater gliders, for both men and women pilots. There are also records for motor gliders.

Single Seaters

(Category: Record, Pilot, Glider, Venue, Date)

Straight distance: 1460.8km Hans-Werner Grosse (FRG), ASW-12, Lübeck (FRG) to Biarritz (Fra), 25 Apr 1972

Declared goal distance: 1254.26km Bruce Drake, David Speight, Dick Georgeson (NZ), all in Nimbus 2s, Te Anau to Te Araroa, New Zealand, 14 Jan 1978

Goal and return distance: 1646.68km Tom Knauff (USA), Nimbus 3, Williamsport, Pa. to Knoxville, Tn. USA, 25 Apr 1983

Triangular distance: 1362.68km Tom Knauff (USA), Nimbus 3; Leonard McMaster, John Seymour, Karl Striedieck (USA), ASW-20B; Robert Robertson (UK), Ventus A, all at Julian, PA, USA on 2 May 1986

Height gain 12849m Paul Bikle (USA), Schweizer SGS 1-23E, Mojave, Cal., USA, 25 Feb 1961

Absolute altitude 14938m Robert Harris (USA), Grob G102, California, 17 Feb 1986

Speed over triangular course:

100km   195.30 km/h Ingo Renner (Aus), Nimbus 3, 14 Dec 1982

300km   169.50 km/h Jean-Paul Castel (Fra), Nimbus 3, 15 Nov 1986

500km   164.11 km/h Jean-Paul Castel (Fra), Nimbus 3, 10 Dec 1986

750km   170.06 km/h Beat Bünzli (Swz), Glaser-Dirks DG-400, 9 Jan 1988

1000km 145.33 km/h Hans-Werner Grosse (FRG), ASW-17, 3 Jan 1979

1250km 133.24 km/h Hans-Werner Grosse (FRG), ASW-17, 9 Dec 1980

Women's Single Seaters

Straight distance 949.7 km Karla Karel (UK), LS-3, Tocumwal, NSW, Australia, 20 Jan 1980

Goal distance 951.43 km Joann Shaw (USA), Nimbus 2, Hobbs, NM, USA, 2 Jul 1990

Goal and return distance 1127.68 km Doris Grove (USA), Nimbus 2, Lockhaven, PA, USA, 28 Sep 1981

Triangular distance 847.27 km Joanne Shaw (USA), Nimbus 2, Snyder, Tx, USA, 5 Aug 1984

Height gain 10,212m Yvonne Loader (NZ), Nimbus 2, Omarama, NZ, 12 Jan 1988

Absolute altitude 12,637m Sabrina Jackintell (USA), Astir GS, Colorado Springs, USA, 14 Feb 1979

Speed over triangular course:

100km   145.49 km/h Susan Beatty (SAf), ASW 20 B, 24 Dec 1990

300km   143.90 km/h Susan Beatty (SAf), ASW 20 B, 26 Dec 1990

500km   133.14 km/h Susan Martin (Aus), LS-3, 29 Jan 1979

750km   127.29 km/h Susan Beatty (SAf), ASW 20 B, 21 Dec 1990

World Championships

First held in 1937 and now staged biennially. *Winners:*

Open Category

1937 Heini Dittmar (Ger)
1948 Per Persson (Swe)
1950 Billy Nilsson (Swe)
1952 Philip Wills (UK)
1954 Gérard Pierre (Fra)
1956 Paul MacCready (USA)
1958 Ernst Haase (FRG)
1960 Rudolf Hossinger (Arg)
1963 Eduard Makula (Pol)
1965 Jan Wroblewski (Pol)
1968 Harro Wödl (Aut)
1970 George Moffat (USA)
1972 Göran Ax (Swe)
1974 George Moffat (USA)
1976 George Lee (UK)
1978 George Lee (UK)
1981 George Lee (UK)
1983 Ingo Renner (Aus)
1985 Ingo Renner (Aus)
1987 Ingo Renner (Aus)
1989 Claude Lopitaux (Fra)
1991 Janusz Centka (Pol)
1993 Janusz Centka (Pol)
1995 Ray Lynskey (NZ)

Two-seater

1952 Luis Juez & J Ara (Spa)
1954 Z Rain & P Komac (Yug)
1956 Nick Goodhart & Frank Foster (UK)

Standard Class

1958 Adam Witek (Pol)
1960 Heinz Huth (FRG)
1963 Heinz Huth (FRG)
1965 Francois Henry (Fra)
1968 A J Smith (USA)
1970 Helmut Reichmann (FRG)
1972 Jan Wroblewski (Pol)
1974 Helmut Reichmann (FRG)
1976 Ingo Renner (Aus)
1978 Baer Selen (Hol)
1981 Marc Schroeder (Fra)
1983 Stig Oye (Den)

1985 Leonardo Brigliadori (Ita)
1987 Markku Kuittinen (Fin)
1989 Jacques Aboulin (Fra)
1991 Baer Selen (Hol)
1993 Andy Davis (UK)
1995 Markku Kuittinen (Fin)

15 Metres Class
1978 Helmut Reichmann (FRG)
1981 Göran Ax (Swe)
1983 Kees Musters (Hol)
1985 Doug Jacobs (USA)
1987 Brian Speckley (UK)
1989 Bruno Gartenbrink (FRG)
1991 Bradley Edwards (Aus)
1993 Gilbert Gerbaud & Éric Napoleon (Fra)
1995 Éric Napoleon (Fra)
Most titles: 4 Renner, 3 Reichmann, Lee

Golf

The exact origins of golf are uncertain, as with so many sports. The Chinese played a form of golf 1800 years ago, and the French, Dutch and Belgians played something resembling the sport in the middle ages. Scotland, must however be regarded as the home of golf. The game was banned in 1457 but golf was later played by Scottish royalty such as James IV and Mary. The world's first golf club, the Honourable Company of Edinburgh golfers, was founded in 1744. The ruling body of the sport, in the eyes of most countries, is the Royal & Ancient situated at St Andrews. The Society of St Andrews Golfers, the forerunner of the R&A, played its first game of golf over the famous St Andrews links on 14 May 1754. The United States Golf Association (USGA) was founded in 1894. The first international federation was founded in 1989 when the World Golf Association was formed with the purpose of gaining Olympic status for the sport.

British Open

The Open first took place at Prestwick on 17 October 1860 with eight competitors playing over three 12-hole rounds. Prestwick hosted the first twelve Opens and all subsequent championships have been played over seaside links. The original prize was a Championship Belt but this was won outright by Tom Morris junior in 1870 and there was no event the following year. When it resumed in 1872 the prize was the silver claret jug, still awarded to the champion today. Played over 36 holes 1860-91 and thereafter at 72 holes. Prize money (totalling £10) was introduced in 1863. The total grew at first steadily and in recent years rapidly: some landmarks being £110 in 1892, £500 1931, £1000 1946, £5000 1959, £10,000 1965, £50,000 1972, £200,000 1980, £651,000 1987, £900,000 1991, 1,250,000 1995. *Winners, with scores and venue:*

	Score	Venue
1860 Willie Park, Snr (UK)	174	Prestwick
1861 Tom Morris, Snr (UK)	163	Prestwick
1862 Tom Morris, Snr (UK)	163	Prestwick
1863 Willie Park, Snr (UK)	168	Prestwick
1864 Tom Morris, Snr (UK)	167	Prestwick
1865 Andrew Strath (UK)	162	Prestwick
1866 Willie Park, Snr (UK)	169	Prestwick
1867 Tom Morris, Snr (UK)	170	Prestwick
1868 Tom Morris, Jnr (UK)	157	Prestwick
1869 Tom Morris, Jnr (UK)	154	Prestwick
1870 Tom Morris, Jnr (UK)	149	Prestwick
1872 Tom Morris, Jnr (UK)	166	Prestwick
1873 Tom Kidd (UK)	179	St Andrews
1874 Mungo Park (UK)	159	Musselburgh
1875 Willie Park, Snr (UK)	166	Prestwick
1876 Bob Martin (UK)	176	St Andrews
1877 Jamie Anderson (UK)	160	Musselburgh
1878 Jamie Anderson (UK)	157	Prestwick
1879 Jamie Anderson (UK)	169	St Andrews
1880 Robert Ferguson (UK)	162	Musselburgh
1881 Robert Ferguson (UK)	170	Prestwick
1882 Robert Ferguson (UK)	171	St Andrews
1883 Willie Fernie (UK)	158*	Musselburgh
1884 Jack Simpson (UK)	160	Prestwick
1885 Bob Martin (UK)	171	St Andrews
1886 David Brown (UK)	157	Musselburgh
1887 Willie Park, Jnr (UK)	161	Prestwick
1888 Jack Burns (UK)	171	St Andrews
1889 Willie Park, Jnr (UK)	155*	Musselburgh
1890 John Ball (UK) #	164	Prestwick
1891 Hugh Kirkaldy (UK)	166	St Andrews
1892 Harold H Hilton (UK) #	305	Muirfield
1893 William Auchterlonie (UK)	322	Prestwick
1894 John H Taylor (UK)	326	Sandwich
1895 John H Taylor (UK)	322	St Andrews
1896 Harry Vardon (UK)	316*	Muirfield
1897 Harold H Hilton (UK) #	314	Hoylake
1898 Harry Vardon (UK)	307	Prestwick
1899 Harry Vardon (UK)	310	Sandwich
1900 John H Taylor (UK)	309	St Andrews
1901 James Braid (UK)	309	Muirfield
1902 Sandy Herd (UK)	307	Hoylake
1903 Harry Vardon (UK)	300	Prestwick
1904 Jack White (UK)	296	Sandwich
1905 James Braid (UK)	318	St Andrews
1906 James Braid (UK)	300	Muirfield
1907 Arnaud Massy (Fra)	312	Hoylake
1908 James Braid (UK)	291	Prestwick
1909 John H Taylor (UK)	295	Deal
1910 James Braid (UK)	299	St Andrews
1911 Harry Vardon (UK)	303	Sandwich
1912 Edward Ray (UK)	295	Muirfield
1913 John H Taylor (UK)	304	Hoylake
1914 Harry Vardon (UK)	306	Prestwick
1920 George Duncan (UK)	303	Deal
1921 Jock Hutchinson (USA)	296*	St Andrews
1922 Walter Hagen (USA)	300	Sandwich
1923 Arthur Havers (UK)	295	Troon
1924 Walter Hagen (USA)	301	Hoylake
1925 Jim Barnes (USA)	300	Prestwick
1926 Bobby Jones (USA) #	291	Royal Lytham

1927 Bobby Jones (USA) #	285	St Andrews
1928 Walter Hagen (USA)	292	Sandwich
1929 Walter Hagen (USA)	292	Muirfield
1930 Bobby Jones (USA) #	291	Hoylake
1931 Tommy Armour (USA)	296	Carnoustie
1932 Gene Sarazen (USA)	283	Prince's
1933 Densmore Shute (USA)	292*	St Andrews
1934 Henry Cotton (UK)	283	Sandwich
1935 Alfred Perry (UK)	283	Muirfield
1936 Alfred Padgham (UK)	287	Hoylake
1937 Henry Cotton (UK)	290	Carnoustie
1938 Reg Whitcombe (UK)	295	Sandwich
1939 Dick Burton (UK)	290	St Andrews
1946 Sam Snead (USA)	290	St Andrews
1947 Fred Daly (UK)	293	Hoylake
1948 Henry Cotton (UK)	284	Muirfield
1949 Bobby Locke (SAf)	283*	Sandwich
1950 Bobby Locke (SAf)	279	Troon
1951 Max Faulkner (UK)	285	Portrush
1952 Bobby Locke (SAf)	287	Royal Lytham
1953 Ben Hogan (USA)	282	Carnoustie
1954 Peter Thomson (Aus)	283	Royal Birkdale
1955 Peter Thomson (Aus)	281	St Andrews
1956 Peter Thomson (Aus)	286	Hoylake
1957 Bobby Locke (SAf)	279	St Andrews
1958 Peter Thomson (Aus)	278*	Royal Lytham
1959 Gary Player (SAf)	284	Muirfield
1960 Kel Nagle (Aus)	278	St Andrews
1961 Arnold Palmer (USA)	284	Royal Birkdale
1962 Arnold Palmer (USA)	276	Troon
1963 Bob Charles (NZ)	277*	Royal Lytham
1964 Tony Lema (USA)	279	St Andrews
1965 Peter Thomson (Aus)	285	Royal Birkdale
1966 Jack Nicklaus (USA)	282	Muirfield
1967 Roberto de Vicenzo (Arg)	278	Hoylake
1968 Gary Player (SAf)	289	Carnoustie
1969 Tony Jacklin (UK)	280	Royal Lytham
1970 Jack Nicklaus (USA)	283*	St Andrews
1971 Lee Trevino (USA)	278	Royal Birkdale
1972 Lee Trevino (USA)	278	Muirfield
1973 Tom Weiskopf (USA)	276	Troon
1974 Gary Player (SAf)	282	Royal Lytham
1975 Tom Watson (USA)	279*	Carnoustie
1976 Johnny Miller (USA)	279	Royal Birkdale
1977 Tom Watson (USA)	268	Turnberry
1978 Jack Nicklaus (USA)	281	St Andrews
1979 Seve Ballesteros (Spa)	283	Royal Lytham
1980 Tom Watson (USA)	271	Muirfield
1981 Bill Rogers (USA)	276	Sandwich
1982 Tom Watson (USA)	284	Troon
1983 Tom Watson (USA)	275	Royal Birkdale
1984 Seve Ballesteros (Spa)	276	St Andrews
1985 Sandy Lyle (UK)	282	Sandwich
1986 Greg Norman (Aus)	280	Turnberry
1987 Nick Faldo (UK)	279	Muirfield
1988 Seve Ballesteros (Spa)	273	Royal Lytham
1989 Mark Calcavecchia (USA)	275*	Troon
1990 Nick Faldo (UK)	270	St Andrews
1991 Ian Baker-Finch (Aus)	272	Royal Birkdale
1992 Nick Faldo (UK)	272	Muirfield
1993 Greg Norman (Aus)	267	Sandwich
1994 Nick Price (Zim)	268	Turnberry
1995 John Daly (USA)	282*	St Andrews

* after play-off, # amateur champions

Most wins: 6 Vardon; 5 Braid, Taylor, Thomson, Watson

Most top 3 placings: 13 Nicklaus (record 7 times runner-up), 12 Vardon, Taylor; 11 Braid

Most top 6 placings: 18 Taylor, 17 Nicklaus, 16 Vardon, Braid; 12 Thomson

United States Open

First played on a 9-hole course at Newport, Rhode Island on 4 October 1895, when English-born Horace Rawlins won and collected a cheque for $150 (from a total of $335). Played over 72 holes (36 in 1895-7). Prize money reached $1200 in 1916, $5000 1929, $15,000 1950, $131,690 1965, $506,184 1983, $1 milion 1990, $2 million 1995. *Winners (all USA unless otherwise stated):*

	Score	Venue
1895 Horace Rawlins	173	Newport
1896 James Foulis	152	Shinnecock Hills
1897 Joe Lloyd	162	Chicago
1898 Fred Herd	328	Myopia Hunt
1899 Willie Smith	315	Baltimore
1900 Harry Vardon (UK)	313	Chicago
1901 Willie Anderson	331*	Myopia Hunt
1902 Laurie Auchterlonie	307	Garden City
1903 Willie Anderson	307*	Baltusrol
1904 Willie Anderson	303	Glen View
1905 Willie Anderson	314	Myopia Hunt
1906 Alex Smith	295	Onwentsia
1907 Alex Ross	302	Philadelphia
1908 Fred McLeod	322*	Myopia Hunt
1909 George Sargent	290	Englewood
1910 Alex Smith	298*	Philadelphia
1911 John McDermott	307*	Chicago
1912 John McDermott	294	Buffalo
1913 Francis Ouimet #	304*	Brookline
1914 Walter Hagen	290	Midlothian
1915 Jerome Travers #	297	Baltusrol
1916 Charles Evans, Jnr #	286	Minikahda
1919 Walter Hagen	301*	Brae Burn
1920 Edward Ray (UK)	295	Inverness
1921 Jim Barnes	289	Columbia
1922 Gene Sarazen	288	Skokie
1923 Bobby Jones #	296*	Inwood
1924 Cyril Walker	297	Oakland Hills
1925 Willie Macfarlane	291*	Worcester
1926 Bobby Jones #	293	Scioto
1927 Tommy Armour	301*	Oakmont
1928 Johnny Farrell	294*	Olympia Fields
1929 Bobby Jones #	294*	Winged Foot
1930 Bobby Jones #	287	Interlachen
1931 Billy Burke	292*	Inverness
1932 Gene Sarazen	286	Fresh Meadow
1933 Johnny Goodman #	287	North Shore

1934 Olin Dutra	293	Merion
1935 Sam Parks, Jnr	299	Oakmont
1936 Tony Manero	282	Baltusrol
1937 Ralph Guldahl	281	Oakland Hills
1938 Ralph Guldahl	284	Cherry Hills
1939 Byron Nelson	284*	Philadelphia
1940 Lawson Little	287*	Canterbury
1941 Craig Wood	284	Colonial
1946 Lloyd Mangrum	284*	Canterbury
1947 Lew Worsham	282*	St Louis
1948 Ben Hogan	276	Riviera
1949 Cary Middlecoff	286	Medinah
1950 Ben Hogan	287*	Merion
1951 Ben Hogan	287	Oakland Hills
1952 Julius Boros	281	Northwood
1953 Ben Hogan	283	Oakmont
1954 Ed Furgol	284	Baltusrol
1955 Jack Fleck	287*	Olympic
1956 Cary Middlecoff	281	Oak Hill
1957 Dick Mayer	282*	Inverness
1958 Tommy Bolt	283	Southern Hills
1959 Billy Casper	282	Winged Foot
1960 Arnold Palmer	280	Cherry Hills
1961 Gene Littler	281	Oakland Hills
1962 Jack Nicklaus	283*	Oakmont
1963 Julius Boros	293*	Brookline
1964 Ken Venturi	278	Congressional
1965 Gary Player (SAf)	282*	Bellerive
1966 Billy Casper	278*	Olympic
1967 Jack Nicklaus	275	Baltusrol
1968 Lee Trevino	275	Oak Hill
1969 Orville Moody	281	Champions
1970 Tony Jacklin (UK)	281	Hazeltine
1971 Lee Trevino	280*	Merion
1972 Jack Nicklaus	290	Pebble Beach
1973 Johnny Miller	279	Oakmont
1974 Hale Irwin	287*	Winged Foot
1975 Lou Graham	287	Medinah
1976 Jerry Pate	277	Atlanta
1977 Hubert Green	278	Southern Hills
1978 Andy North	285	Cherry Hills
1979 Hale Irwin	284	Inverness
1980 Jack Nicklaus	272	Baltusrol
1981 David Graham (Aus)	273	Merion
1982 Tom Watson	282	Pebble Beach
1983 Larry Nelson	280	Oakmont
1984 Fuzzy Zoeller	276*	Winged Foot
1985 Andy North	279	Oakland Hills

Ernie Els – a marvellous year in 1994

1986 Raymond Floyd	279	Shinnecock Hills
1987 Scott Simpson	277	Olympic Club
1988 Curtis Strange	278	Brookline
1989 Curtis Strange	278	Oak Hill
1990 Hale Irwin	280*	Medinah
1991 Payne Stewart	282*	Hazeltine
1992 Tom Kite	285	Monterey
1993 Lee Janzen	272	Ballustrol
1994 Ernie Els (SAf)	279*	Oakmont
1995 Corey Pavin	280	Shinnecock Hills

* *after play-off, # amateur champions*

Most wins: 4 Anderson, Jones, Hogan, Nicklaus

Most top 3 placings: 9 Nicklaus, 7 Hogan, Sarazen; 6 Anderson, Palmer

Most top 6 placings: 12 Hogan, 11 Anderson, Hagan, Sarazen, Palmer, Nicklaus

US Masters

Held annually at the Augusta National course in Georgia from 1934. Both the course and the tournament were the idea of the legendary golfer Bobby Jones. Entry to the Masters is by invitation only and the eventual winner is presented with the coveted green jacket. Contested over 72 holes of strokeplay. *Winners (all USA unless otherwise stated):*

1934 Horton Smith	284		1939 Ralph Guldahl	279
1935 Gene Sarazen	282*		1940 Jimmy Demaret	280
1936 Horton Smith	285		1941 Craig Wood	280
1937 Byron Nelson	283		1942 Byron Nelson	280*
1938 Henry Picard	285		1946 Herman Keiser	282
			1947 Jimmy Demaret	281
			1948 Claude Harmon	279
			1949 Sam Snead	282

Year	Winner	Score
1950	Jimmy Demaret	283
1951	Ben Hogan	280
1952	Sam Snead	286
1953	Ben Hogan	274
1954	Sam Snead	289*
1955	Cary Middlecoff	279
1956	Jack Burke, Jnr	289
1957	Doug Ford	282
1958	Arnold Palmer	284
1959	Art Wall, Jnr	284
1960	Arnold Palmer	282*
1961	Gary Player (SAf)	280
1962	Arnold Palmer	280*
1963	Jack Nicklaus	286
1964	Arnold Palmer	276
1965	Jack Nicklaus	271
1966	Jack Nicklaus	288*
1967	Gay Brewer	280
1968	Bob Goalby	277
1969	George Archer	281
1970	Billy Casper	279*
1971	Charles Coody	279
1972	Jack Nicklaus	286
1973	Tommy Aaron	283
1974	Gary Player (SAf)	278
1975	Jack Nicklaus	276
1976	Raymond Floyd	271
1977	Tom Watson	276
1978	Gary Player (SAf)	277
1979	Fuzzy Zoeller	280*
1980	Seve Ballesteros (Spa)	275
1981	Tom Watson	280
1982	Craig Stadler	284*
1983	Seve Ballesteros (Spa)	280
1984	Ben Crenshaw	277
1985	Bernhard Langer (FRG)	282
1986	Jack Nicklaus	279
1987	Larry Mize	285*
1988	Sandy Lyle (UK)	281
1989	Nick Faldo (UK)	283*
1990	Nick Faldo (UK)	278*
1991	Ian Woosnam (UK)	277
1992	Fred Couples	275
1993	Bernhard Langer (Ger)	277
1994	José Maria Olazábal (Spa)	279
1995	Ben Crenshaw	274

* *after play-off*

Most wins: 6 Nicklaus, 4 Palmer

Most top 5 placings: 16 Nicklaus, 9 Snead, Hogan, Palmer

United States PGA Championship

First held in 1916, the championship was a match-play event until 1958, when it became a stroke-play competition over four rounds. Entry is based on qualification from the PGA (Professional Golfers Association) tour; it is the least publicised of the four majors. *Winners (all USA unless otherwise stated):*

Year	Winner	Score	Venue
1916	Jim Barnes	1 up	Siwanoy
1919	Jim Barnes	6 & 5	Engineers
1920	Jock Hutchison	1 up	Flossmoor
1921	Walter Hagen	3 & 2	Inwood
1922	Gene Sarazen	4 & 3	Oakmont
1923	Gene Sarazen	at 38th	Pelham
1924	Walter Hagen	2 up	French Lick
1925	Walter Hagen	6 & 5	Olympia Fields
1926	Walter Hagen	5 & 3	Salisbury
1927	Walter Hagen	1 up	Cedar Crest
1928	Leo Diegel	6 & 5	Five Farms
1929	Leo Diegel	6 & 4	Hill Crest
1930	Tommy Armour	1 up	Fresh Meadow
1931	Tom Creavy	2 & 1	Wannamoisett
1932	Olin Dutra	4 & 3	Keller
1933	Gene Sarazen	5 & 4	Blue Mound
1934	Paul Runyan	at 38th	Park
1935	Johnny Revolta	5 & 4	Twin Hills
1936	Densmore Shute	3 & 2	Pinehurst
1937	Densmore Shute	at 37th	Pittsburgh
1938	Paul Runyan	8 & 7	Shawnee
1939	Henry Picard	at 37th	Pomonok
1940	Byron Nelson	1 up	Hershey
1941	Vic Ghezzi	at 38th	Cherry Hills
1942	Sam Snead	2 & 1	Sea View
1944	Bob Hamilton	1 up	Manito
1945	Byron Nelson	4 & 3	Morraine
1946	Ben Hogan	6 & 4	Portland
1947	Jim Ferrier	2 & 1	Plum Hollow
1948	Ben Hogan	7 & 6	Norwood Hills
1949	Sam Snead	3 & 2	Hermitage
1950	Chandler Harper	4 & 3	Scioto
1951	Sam Snead	7 & 6	Oakmont
1952	Jim Turnesa	1 up	Big Spring
1953	Walter Burkemo	2 & 1	Birmingham
1954	Chick Harbert	4 & 3	Keller
1955	Doug Ford	4 & 3	Meadowbrook
1956	Jack Burke	3 & 2	Blue Hill
1957	Lionel Hebert	2 & 1	Miami Valley
1958	Dow Finsterwald	276	Llanerch
1959	Bob Rosburg	277	Minneapolis
1960	Jay Hebert	281	Firestone
1961	Jerry Barber	277*	Olympia Fields
1962	Gary Player (SAf)	278	Aronomink
1963	Jack Nicklaus	279	Dallas
1964	Bobby Nichols	271	Columbus
1965	Dave Marr	280	Laurel Valley
1966	Al Geiberger	280	Firestone
1967	Don January	281*	Columbine
1968	Julius Boros	281	Pecan Valley
1969	Raymond Floyd	276	NCR, Dayton
1970	Dave Stockton	279	Southern Hills
1971	Jack Nicklaus	281	PGA National
1972	Gary Player (SAf)	281	Oakland Hills
1973	Jack Nicklaus	277	Canterbury
1974	Lee Trevino	276	Tanglewood
1975	Jack Nicklaus	276	Firestone
1976	Dave Stockton	281	Congressional
1977	Lanny Wadkins	282*	Pebble Beach
1978	John Mahaffey	276*	Oakmont
1979	David Graham (Aus)	272*	Oakland Hills
1980	Jack Nicklaus	274	Oak Hill
1981	Larry Nelson	273	Atlanta
1982	Raymond Floyd	272	Southern Hills
1983	Hal Sutton	274	Riviera
1984	Lee Trevino	273	Shoal Creek
1985	Hubert Green	278	Cherry Hills
1986	Bob Tway	276	Toledo
1987	Larry Nelson	287*	Palm Beach
1988	Jeff Sluman	272	Oak Tree
1989	Payne Stewart	276	Kemper Lakes
1990	Wayne Grady (Aus)	282	Shoal Creek
1991	John Daly	276	Crooked Stick
1992	Nick Price (Zim)	278	St Louis
1993	Paul Azinger	272*	Toledo
1994	Nick Price (Zim)	269	Southern Hills

* *after play-off*

Most wins: 5 Hagen, Nicklaus; 3 Sarazen, Snead

The Majors - Records

Lowest four round total
The Open	267 Greg Norman 1993	
US Open	272 Jack Nicklaus 1980	
	272 Lee Janzen 1993	
US PGA	271 Bobby Nichols 1964	
US Masters	271 Jack Nicklaus 1965	
	271 Raymond Floyd 1976	

Lowest single round
The Open	63 Mark Hayes (USA) 2nd Rd 1977
	63 Isao Aoki (Jap) 3rd Rd 1980
	63 Greg Norman (Aus) 2nd Rd 1986
	63 Paul Broadhurst (UK) 3rd Rd 1990
	63 Jodie Mudd (USA) 4th Rd 1991
	63 Nick Faldo (UK) 2nd Rd 1993
	63 Payne Stewart (USA) 4th Rd 1993
US Open	63 Johnny Miller (USA) 4th Rd 1973
	63 Tom Weiskopf (USA) 1st Rd 1980
	63 Jack Nicklaus (USA) 1st Rd 1980
US PGA	63 Bruce Crampton (Aus) 2nd Rd 1975
	63 Raymond Floyd (USA) 1st Rd 1982
	63 Gary Player (SAf) 2nd Rd 1984
	63 Vijay Singh (Fiji) 3rd Rd 1993
US Masters	63 Nick Price (SAf) 3rd Rd 1986

Oldest winners
The Open	46y 99d Tom Morris, Snr. 1867
US Open	43y 284d Raymond Floyd 1986
US PGA	48y 140d Julius Boros 1968
US Masters	46y 82d Jack Nicklaus 1986

Youngest winners
The Open	17y 249d Tom Morris, Jnr. 1868
US Open	19y 318d John McDermott 1911
US PGA	20y 173d Gene Sarazen 1922
US Masters	23y 4d Severiano Ballesteros 1980

Most wins in majors
A British Open, B US Open, C US PGA, D US Masters

		A	B	C	D
18	Jack Nicklaus	3	4	5	6
11	Walter Hagen	4	2	5	-
9	Ben Hogan	1	4	2	2
9	Gary Player	3	1	2	3
8	Tom Watson	5	1	-	2
7	Harry Vardon	6	1	-	-
7	Bobby Jones	3	4	-	-
7	Gene Sarazen	1	2	3	1
7	Sam Snead	1		3	3
7	Arnold Palmer	2	1	-	4

When he won the Masters in 1935 Gene Sarazen became the first man to have won all four majors. No man has won all four in one year, but in 1953 Ben Hogan won three (British Open, US Open and Masters); he did not contest the PGA. In 1986 Greg Norman led going into the final round of all four, but won only one, the British Open.
Jack Nicklaus also won two US Amateur titles and Bobby Jones won five US Amateur and one British Amateur. Jones uniquely won the Open and Amateur Championships of the USA and Britain in one year, 1930.

World Match Play Championship

An annual end-of-season knockout competition held at Wentworth, Surrey. The number of entrants was originally eight but has since been increased to 12 (16 in 1977-8). Each match consists of two rounds, one in the morning and one in the afternoon. Sponsored by Piccadilly 1964-76, Colgate 1977-8, Suntory 1979-91, Toyota from 1992.

Year	Winner	Runner-up	Score
1964	Arnold Palmer (USA)	Neil Coles (UK)	2 & 1
1965	Gary Player (SAf)	Peter Thomson (Aus)	3 & 2
1966	Gary Player (SAf)	Jack Nicklaus (USA)	6 & 4
1967	Arnold Palmer (USA)	Peter Thomson (Aus)	1 up
1968	Gary Player (SAf)	Bob Charles (NZ)	1 up
1969	Bob Charles (NZ)	Gene Littler (USA)	at 37th
1970	Jack Nicklaus (USA)	Lee Trevino (USA)	2 & 1
1971	Gary Player (SAf)	Jack Nicklaus (USA)	5 & 4
1972	Tom Weiskopf (USA)	Lee Trevino (USA)	4 & 3
1973	Gary Player (SAf)	Graham Marsh (Aus)	at 40th
1974	Hale Irwin (USA)	Gary Player (SAf)	3 & 1
1975	Hale Irwin (USA)	Al Geiberger (USA)	4 & 2
1976	David Graham (Aus)	Hale Irwin (USA)	at 38th
1977	Graham Marsh (Aus)	Raymond Floyd (USA)	5 & 3
1978	Isao Aoki (Jap)	Simon Owen (NZ)	3 & 2
1979	Bill Rogers (USA)	Isao Aoki (Jap)	1 up
1980	Greg Norman (Aus)	Sandy Lyle (UK)	1 up
1981	Seve Ballesteros (Spa)	Ben Crenshaw (USA)	1 up

Ben Crenshaw – Masters champion of 1984 and 1995

1982	Seve Ballesteros (Spa)	Sandy Lyle (UK)	at 37th
1983	Greg Norman (Aus)	Nick Faldo (UK)	3 & 2
1984	Seve Ballesteros (Spa)	Bernhard Langer (FRG)	2 & 1
1985	Seve Ballesteros (Spa)	Bernhard Langer (FRG)	6 & 5
1986	Greg Norman (Aus)	Sandy Lyle (UK)	2 & 1
1987	Ian Woosnam (UK)	Sandy Lyle (UK)	1 up
1988	Sandy Lyle (UK)	Nick Faldo (UK)	2 & 1
1989	Nick Faldo (UK)	Ian Woosnam (UK)	1 up
1990	Ian Woosnam (UK)	Mark McNulty (Zim)	4 & 2
1991	Seve Ballesteros (Spa)	Nick Price (Zim)	3 & 2
1992	Nick Faldo (UK)	Jeff Sluman (USA)	8 & 7
1993	Corey Pavin (USA	Nick Faldo (UK)	1 up
1994	Ernie Els (SAf)	Colin Montgomery (UK)	4 & 2

Most wins: 5 Player, Ballesteros; 3 Norman
Biggest winning margin: 11 & 9 Tom Watson
(USA) v Dale Hayes (SAf), 1st round 1979

Volvo PGA Championship

The PGA Close Championships, restricted to British and Irish golfers was instituted in 1955. Both 'closed' and 'open' championships were held in 1968, but from 1969 it has been an open championship on the PGA tour. Not played 1970-1, it is now sponsored by Volvo and has been played at Wentworth each year from 1984. *Winners from 1972:*

1972	Tony Jacklin (UK)	279
1973	Peter Oosterhuis (UK)	280
1974	Maurice Bembridge (UK)	278
1975	Arnold Palmer (USA)	285
1976	Neil Coles (UK)	280
1977	Manuel Pinero (Spa)	283
1978	Nick Faldo (UK)	278
1979	Vicente Fernández (Arg)	288
1980	Nick Faldo (UK)	283
1981	Nick Faldo (UK)	274
1982	Tony Jacklin (UK)	284
1983	Seve Ballesteros (Spa)	278
1984	Howard Clark (UK) (3 rounds)	204
1985	Paul Way (UK)	282
1986	Rodger Davis (Aus)	281
1987	Bernard Langer (Ger)	270
1988	Ia Woosnam (UK)	274
1989	Nick Faldo (UK)	272
1990	Mike Harwood (Aus)	271
1991	Seve Ballesteros (Spa)	271
1992	Tony Johnstone (Zim)	272
1993	Bernard Langer (Ger)	274
1994	José Maria Olazábal (Spa)	271
1995	Bernard Langer (Ger)	279

Tournament Players Championship

Introduced into the US tour at Atlanta in 1974, with the intention of being a fifth 'major', a status it has not really achieved, although its prize money has been amongst the highest on the PGA tour. Open only to players who have won official PGA Tour events in the previous year. From 1977 it has been played on the TPC's own course at Sawgrass, Ponte Vedra, Florida. *Winners (all USA unless stated):*

1974	Jack Nicklaus	272
1975	Al Geiberger	270
1976	Jack Nicklaus	269
1977	Mark Hayes	289
1978	Jack Nicklaus	289
1979	Lanny Wadkins	283
1980	Lee Trevino	278
1981	Raymond Floyd	285
1982	Jerrry Pate	280
1983	Hal Sutton	283
1984	Fred Couples	277
1985	Calvin Peete	274
1986	John Mahaffey	275
1987	Sandy Lyle (UK)	274
1988	Mark McCumber	273
1989	Tom Kite	279
1990	Jodie Mudd	278
1991	Steve Elkington (Aus)	276
1992	Davis Love III	273
1993	Nick Price (Zim)	270
1994	Greg Norman (Aus)	264
1995	Lee Janzen	283

PGA Tour Championship

In 1993 and 1994 the top 30 money-winners on the tour played for a $3 million purse at the Olympic Club, San Francisco. The winner took $540,000. *Winners:*

1993	Jim Gallagher Jr (USA)	277
1994	Mark McCumber (USA)	274

Johnny Walker World Championship

First held at the Tryall Golf Club, Montego Bay, Jamaica in 1991, when total prize money was a world record $2,550,000, including $525,000 for first place. Those figures were increased to $2.7 million and $550,000 from 1992.

1991	Fred Couples (USA)	281
1992	Nick Faldo (UK)	274*
1993	Larry Mize (USA)	266
1994	Ernie Els (SAf)	268

World Cup

The World Cup was the idea of American industrialist Jay Hopkins, who saw the need for an international team competition for male professionals, other than for those of Great Britain and the United States. Contested annually over 72 holes of stroke-play by two-man teams. Interest in the competition fell in the 1980s and it was not played in 1981 or 1986.

Year	Winning Team		Leading Individual	
1953	Argentina (Roberto de Vicenzo & Antonio Cerda)	287*	Antonio Cerda (Arg)	140*
1954	Australia (Peter Thomson & Kel Nagle)	556	Stan Leonard (Can)	275
1955	USA (Ed Furgol & Chick Harbert)	560	Ed Furgol (USA)	279

Year	Winning Team		Leading Individual	
1956	USA (Ben Hogan & Sam Snead)	567	Ben Hogan (USA)	277
1957	Japan (Torakichi Nakamura & Koichi Ono)	557	Torakichi Nakamura (Jap)	274
1958	Ireland (Harry Bradshaw & Christy O'Connor)	579	Angel Miguel (Spa)	286
	Migeul beat Harry Bradshaw (Ire) in a play-off for leading individual.			
1959	Australia (Kel Nagle & Peter Thomson)	563	Stan Leonard (Can)	275
1960	USA (Arnold Palmer & Sam Snead)	565	Flory van Donck (Bel)	279
1961	USA (Jimmy Demaret & Sam Snead)	560	Sam Snead (USA)	272
1962	USA (Arnold Palmer & Sam Snead)	557	Roberto de Vicenzo (Arg)	276
1963	USA (Jack Nicklaus & Arnold Palmer)	482*	Jack Nicklaus (USA)	237*
1964	USA (Jack Nicklaus & Arnold Palmer)	554	Jack Nicklaus (USA)	276
1965	South Africa (Harold Henning & Gary Player)	571	Gary Player (SAf)	281
1966	USA (Jack Nicklaus & Arnold Palmer)	548	George Knudson (Can)	272
1967	USA (Jack Nicklaus & Arnold Palmer)	557	Arnold Palmer (USA)	276
1968	Canada (Al Balding & George Knudson)	569	Al Balding (Can)	274
1969	USA (Orville Moody & Lee Trevino)	552	Lee Trevino (USA)	275
1970	Australia (Bruce Devlin & David Graham)	544	Roberto de Vicenzo (Arg)	269
1971	USA (Jack Nicklaus & Lee Trevino)	555	Jack Nicklaus (USA)	271
1972	Taiwan (Hsieh Min-nan & Lu Liang-huan)	438*	Hsieh Min-nan (Tai)	217*
1973	USA (Johnny Miller & Jack Nicklaus)	558	Johnny Miller (USA)	277
1974	South Africa (Bobby Cole & Dale Hayes)	554	Bobby Cole (SAf)	271
1975	USA (Lou Graham & Johnny Miller)	554	Johnny Miller (USA)	275
1976	Spain (Severiano Ballesteros & Manuel Pinero)	574	Ernesto Pérez Acosta (Mex)	282
1977	Spain (Severiano Ballesteros & Antonio Garrido)	591	Gary Player (SAf)	289
1978	USA (John Mahaffey & Andy North)	564	John Mahaffey (USA)	281
1979	USA (John Mahaffey & Hale Irwin)	575	Hale Irwin (USA)	285
1980	Canada (Dan Halldorson & Jim Nelford)	572	Sandy Lyle (Sco)	282
1982	Spain (José-Maria Canizares & Manuel Pinero)	563	Manuel Pinero (Spa)	281
1983	USA (Rex Caldwell & John Cook)	565	Dave Barr (Can)	276
1984	Spain (José-Maria Canizares & José Rivero)	414*	José-Maria Canizares (Spa)	205*
1985	Canada (Dan Halldorson & Dave Barr)	559	Howard Clark (Eng)	272
1987	Wales (Ian Woosnam & David Llewellyn)	574	Ian Woosnam (Wal)	274
1988	USA (Ben Crenshaw & Mark McCumber)	560	Ben Crenshaw (USA)	275
1989	Australia (Peter Fowler & Wayne Grady)	278*	Peter Fowler (Aus)	137*
1990	Germany (Bernhard Langer & Torsten Giedeon)	556	Payne Stewart (USA)	271
1991	Sweden (Anders Forsbrand & Per-Ulrik Johansson)	563	Ian Woosnam (Wal)	273
1992	USA (Fred Couples, Davis Love III)	548	Brett Ogle (Aus)	270"
1993	USA (Fred Couples, Davis Love III)	556	Bernhard Langer (Ger)	272
1994	USA (Fred Couples, Davis Love III)	536	Fred Couples (USA)	265

Most team wins: 20 USA. Team wins by individuals: 6 Nicklaus, Palmer
Most Individual titles: 3 Nicklaus, Couples, Love
* *played over 36 holes in 1953, 63 holes in 1963, 54 holes in 1972 and 1984. Rain reduced play to 36 holes in 1989.*

Ryder Cup

The Ryder Cup started as a result of the efforts of wealthy businessman Samuel Ryder. It was launched in 1927, the year after a successful match between Great Britain and the United States at Wentworth. Held every two years the countries take it in turn to play host. Opposing the USA were Great Britain 1927-71, Great Britain and Ireland 1973-77, Europe from 1979. The current format is for four foursomes and four fourball matches on each of the first two days, and 12 singles on the third and final day.

Year	Venue	Winners	Score
1927	Worcester, Massachusetts	USA	9.5-2.5
1929	Moortown, Yorkshire	GB	7-5
1931	Scioto, Ohio	USA	9-3
1933	Southport & Ainsdale, Lancs.	GB	6.5-5.5
1935	Ridgewood, New Jersey	USA	9-3
1937	Southport & Ainsdale, Lancs.	USA	8-4
1947	Portland, Oregan	USA	11-1
1949	Ganton, Yorkshire	USA	7-5
1951	Pinehurst, North Carolina	USA	9.5-2.5
1953	Wentworth, Surrey	USA	6.5-5.5
1955	Thunderbird G&CC, California	USA	8-4
1957	Lindrick, Yorkshire	GB	7.5-4.5
1959	Eldorado CC, California	USA	8.5-3.5
1961	Royal Lytham, Lancs.	USA	14.5 -9.5
1963	Atlanta, Georgia	USA	23-9
1965	Royal Birkdale, Lancs.	USA	19.5-12.5
1967	Houston, Texas	USA	23.5-8.5
1969	Royal Birkdale, Lancs.	Drawn	16-16

1971	St Louis, Missouri	USA	18.5-13.5
1973	Muirfield, Scotland	USA	19-13
1975	Laurel Valley, Pennsylvania	USA	21-11
1977	Royal Lytham, Lancs.	USA	12.5-7.5
1979	Greenbrier, West Virginia	USA	17-11
1981	Walton Heath, Surrey	USA	18.5-9.5
1983	PGA National, Florida	USA	14.5-13.5
1985	The Belfry, Sutton Coldfield	Europe	16.5-11.5
1987	Muirfield Village, Ohio	Europe	15-13
1989	The Belfry, Sutton Coldfield	Drawn	14-14
1991	Kiawah Island, SouthCarolina	USA	14.5-13.5
1993	The Belfry, Sutton Coldfield	USA	15-13

Most wins: 23 United States

Most selections: 10 Christy O'Connor (Ire) 1955-73

Oldest players: 51y 22d Ray Floyd (USA) 1993, 50y 66d Edward Ray (GB) 1927

Youngest player: 20y 59d Nick Faldo (GB&I) 1977

Leading players records

Golfers who have played 20 or more matches. pts = points as 1 for win, 1/2 for halved match

Name	Years	Cups	pl	w	l	h	pts
GB/GB & Ireland/Europe							
Severiano Ballesteros	1979-93	7	34	19	10	5	21.5
Nick Faldo	1977-93	9	36	19	13	4	21
Tony Jacklin	1967-79	7	35	13	14	8	17
Neil Coles	1961-77	8	40	12	21	7	15.5
Bernard Gallacher	1969-83	8	31	13	13	5	15.5
Peter Oosterhuis	1971-81	6	28	14	11	3	15.5
Bernhard Langer	1981-93	7	29	13	11	5	15.5
Ian Woosnam	1983-93	6	26	12	10	4	14
José-Maria Olazábal	1987-93	4	20	12	6	3	13.5
Christy O'Connor	1955-73	10	35	11	20	4	13
Peter Alliss	1953-69	8	30	10	15	5	12.5
Brian Barnes	1969-79	6	26	11	14	1	11.5
Brian Huggett	1963-75	6	24	8	10	6	11
Bernard Hunt	1953-69	8	28	6	16	6	9
Mark James	1977-93	6	22	7	14	1	7.5
Sam Torrance	1981-93	7	22	4	13	5	6.5
United States							
Billy Casper	1961-75	8	37	20	10	7	23.5
Arnold Palmer	1961-73	6	32	22	8	2	23
Lanny Wadkins	1977-93	8	33	20	11	2	21
Lee Trevino	1969-81	6	30	17	7	6	20
Jack Nicklaus	1969-81	6	28	17	8	3	18.5
Gene Littler	1961-75	7	27	14	5	8	18
Tom Kite	1979-93	7	28	15	9	4	17
Hale Irwin	1975-91	5	20	13	5	2	14
Raymond Floyd	1969-93	8	31	12	16	3	13.5
Also with 10 or more wins							
Sam Snead *	1937-59	7	13	10	2	1	10.5
Tom Watson	1977-89	4	15	10	4	1	10.5

* Snead was also selected for 1939 and 1941 teams when the match was not contested.

Spanish pair Seve Ballesteros and José-Maria Olazábal working well together in the Ryder Cup

Lanny Wadkins

Alfred Dunhill Cup

International knockout team tournament for teams of three professionals. Inaugurated in 1985 and played at St Andrews, Scotland. *Finals:*

1985	Australia 3	USA 0
1986	Australia 3	Japan 0
1987	England 2	Scotland 1
1988	Ireland 2	Australia 1
1989	USA 3	Japan 2
1990	Ireland 3.5	England 2.5
1991	Sweden 2	South Africa 1
1992	England 2.5	Scotland 0.5
1993	USA 2	England 1
1994	Canada 2	USA 1

President's Cup

Inaugurated in 1994 and contested by teams from the USA and from non-European international players. All 12 in each team contest singles with two sets of five four-balls and foursomes. The USA won the first match 20-12.

Leading Annual Money Winners

European Tour	£
1961 Bernard Hunt (UK)	4,492
1962 Peter Thomson (Aus)	5,764
1963 Bernard Hunt (UK)	7,209
1964 Neil Coles (UK)	7,890
1965 Peter Thomson (Aus)	7,011
1966 Bruce Devlin (Aus)	13,205

1967 Gay Brewer (USA)	20,235	
1968 Gay Brewer (USA)	23,107	
1969 Billy Casper (USA)	23,483	
1970 Christy O'Connor (Ire)	31,532	
1971 Gary Player (SAf)	11,281	
1972 Bob Charles (NZ)	18,538	
1973 Tony Jacklin (UK)	24,839	
1974 Peter Oosterhuis (UK)	32,127	
1975 Dale Hayes (SAf)	20,507	
1976 Seve Ballesteros (Spa)	39,504	
1977 Seve Ballesteros (Spa)	46,436	
1978 Seve Ballesteros (Spa)	54,348	
1979 Sandy Lyle (UK)	49,233	
1980 Greg Norman (Aus)	74,829	
1981 Bernhard Langer (FRG)	95,991	
1982 Sandy Lyle (UK)	86,141	
1983 Nick Faldo (UK)	140,761	
1984 Bernhard Langer (FRG)	160,883	
1985 Sandy Lyle (UK)	199,020	
1986 Seve Ballesteros (Spa)	259,275	
1987 Ian Woosnam (UK)	439,075	
1988 Seve Ballesteros (Spa)	502,000	
1989 Ronan Rafferty (Ire)	465,981	
1990 Ian Woosnam (UK)	574,166	
1991 Seve Ballesteros (Spa)	545,353	
1992 Nick Faldo (UK)	708,522	
1993 Colin Montgomerie (UK)	613,682	
1994 Colin Montgomerie (UK)	762,719	

Most times leading: 5 Ballesteros

Woosnam's total worldwide earnings in 1987 were a record £1,042,662, Bernard Langer (Ger) won a world-wide $2,185,358 in 1991 and Faldo £1,558,978 in 1992.

USA

All winners from USA unless otherwise stated.

Total winnings shown in dollars:

1934 Paul Runyan	6,767
1935 Johnny Revolta	9,543
1936 Horton Smith	7,682
1937 Harry Cooper	14,138
1938 Sam Snead	19,534
1939 Henry Picard	10,303
1940 Ben Hogan	10,655
1941 Ben Hogan	18,358
1942 Ben Hogan	13,143
1943 *statistics not compiled*	
1944 Byron Nelson	37,967*
1945 Byron Nelson	63,335*
1946 Ben Hogan	42,556
1947 Jimmy Demaret	27,936
1948 Ben Hogan	32,112
1949 Sam Snead	31,593
1950 Sam Snead	35,758
1951 Lloyd Mangrum	26,088
1952 Julius Boros	37,032
1953 Lew Worsham	34,002
1954 Bob Toski	65,819
1955 Julius Boros	63,121
1956 Ted Kroll	72,835
1957 Dick Mayer	65,835
1958 Arnold Palmer	42,607
1959 Art Wall, Jnr	53,167

1960 Arnold Palmer	75,262
1961 Gary Player (SAf)	64,450
1962 Arnold Palmer	81,448
1963 Arnold Palmer	128,230
1964 Jack Nicklaus	113,284
1965 Jack Nicklaus	140,752
1966 Billy Casper	121,944
1967 Jack Nicklaus	188,998
1968 Billy Casper	205,168
1969 Frank Beard	164,707
1970 Lee Trevino	157,037
1971 Jack Nicklaus	244,490
1972 Jack Nicklaus	320,542
1973 Jack Nicklaus	308,362
1974 Johnny Miller	353,021
1975 Jack Nicklaus	298,149
1976 Jack Nicklaus	266,438
1977 Tom Watson	310,653
1978 Tom Watson	362,428
1979 Tom Watson	462,636
1980 Tom Watson	530,808
1981 Tom Kite	375,698
1982 Craig Stadler	446,462
1983 Hal Sutton	426,668
1984 Tom Watson	476,260
1985 Curtis Strange	542,321
1986 Greg Norman (Aus)	653,296
1987 Curtis Strange	925,941
1988 Curtis Strange	1,147,644
1989 Tom Kite	1,395,278
1990 Greg Norman (Aus)	1,165,477
1991 Corey Pavin	979,430
1992 Fred Couples	1,344,188
1993 Nick Price (Zim)	1,478,557
1994 Nick Price (Zim)	1,499,927

* Nelson received War Bonds

Most times leading: 8 Nicklaus

Harry Vardon Trophy

European Tour

Awarded annually from 1937, when the first winner was Charles Whitcombe, to the leading player in the Order of Merit. *Most wins:*

5 Severiano Ballesteros (Spa) 1976-8, 1986, 1988
4 Peter Oosterhuis (UK) 1971-4
3 Bobby Locke (SAf) 1946, 1950, 1954
3 Bernard Hunt (UK) 1958, 1960, 1965
3 Sandy Lyle (UK) 1979-80, 1985

USA

Awarded annually by the USPGA to the player who has the lowest stroke average in PGA Tournaments in that year. *Most wins:*

5 Billy Casper 1960, 1963, 1965-6, 1968
5 Lee Trevino 1970-2, 1974, 1980
4 Sam Snead 1938, 1949-50, 1955
4 Arnold Palmer 1961-2, 1964, 1967

All-time Earnings

European Tour

	Amount	Wins	Years
Nick Faldo (UK)	£3,988,568	28	1976-94
Bernhard Langer (FRG)	£3,901,056	31	1976-94
Severiano Ballesteros (Spa)	£3,892,774	53	1974-94
Ian Woosnam (UK)	£3,805,781	28	1978-94
José Maria Olazábal (Spa)	£2,953,697	15	1986-94
Sam Torrance (UK)	£2,520,973	18	1971-94
Mark McNulty (Zim)	£2,445,813	12	1978-94
Ronan Rafferty (UK)	£2,255,558	8	1981-94
Sandy Lyle (UK)	£2,252,867	18	1977-94
Mark James (UK)	£2,252,769	16	1976-94

United States Tour to 4 June 1995

	Amount	Wins	Years
Tom Kite (USA)	$9,261,125	19	1972-95
Greg Norman (Aus)	$8,564,270	13	1983-95
Payne Stewart (USA)	$7,098,151	9	1981-95
Fred Couples (USA)	$7,038,439	11	1980-95
Tom Watson (USA)	$6,961,715	32	1971-95
Nick Price (Zim)	$6,891,801	14	1983-95
Paul Azinger (USA)	$6,886,370	11	1981-95
Ben Crenshaw (USA)	$6,735,999	19	1973-95
Curtis Strange (USA)	$6,689,530	17	1977-95
Corey Pavin (USA)	$6,299,611	12	1984-95
Lanny Wadkins (USA)	$6,025,455	21	1971-95
Craig Stadler (USA)	$5,862,631	11	1976-95
Hale Irwin (USA)	$5,840,974	20	1968-95
Mark Calcavecchia	$5,740,790	7	1981-95
Chip Beck (USA	$5,692,033	4	1979-95
Bruce Lietzke (USA)	$5,667,122	13	1974-95
Mark O'Meara (USA)	$5,574,851	9	1981-95
Jack Nicklaus (USA)	$5,429,917	71	1962-95
David Frost (SAf)	$5,403,376	9	1985-95
Davis Love III (USA	$5,303,367	9	1986-95
Ray Floyd (USA)	$5,175,499	22	1963-95

Most tournament wins: 81 Sam Snead (1937-65), 71 Jack Nicklaus, 63 Ben Hogan, 60 Arnold Palmer, 52 Byron Nelson, 51 Billy Casper, 40 Walter Hagen, Cary Middlecoff; 38 Gene Sarazen

Records

European Tour
Most wins in a season: 7 Norman Von Nida (Aus) 1947, Flory Van Donck (Bel) 1953
Most consecutive wins: 4 Alf Padgham (UK) 1935-6, Severiano Ballesteros (Spa) 1986
Lowest score (72 holes): 258 David Llewellyn (UK) 1988 Biarritz Open, Ian Woosnam (UK) Monte Carlo Open 1990
Lowest score (18 holes): 60 Baldovino Dassu (Ita) 1971 Swiss Open, David Llewellyn (UK) 1988 Biarritz Open, Paul Curry (UK) 1992 Scottish Open, Jamie Spence 1992 European Masters, Johan Ryström (Swe) and Darren Clarke (UK) Monte Carlo Open 1992
Oldest winner: 58y Sandy Herd (UK) 1926 News of the World
Youngest winner: 19y 121d Severiano Ballesteros (Spa) 1976 Dutch Open

US PGA Tour
Most wins in a season: 18 Byron Nelson (USA) 1945
Most consecutive wins: 11 Byron Nelson 1945
Lowest score (72 holes): 257 Mike Souchak (USA) 1955 Texas Open
Lowest score (18 holes): 59 Al Geiberger (USA) 1977 Memphis Classic; 59 Chip Beck (USA) 1991 Las Vegas Invitational
Oldest winner: 52y 312d Sam Snead 1965 Greater Greensboro Open
Youngest winner: 19y 10m John McDermott (USA) 1911 US Open

US Senior PGA Tour
Most career wins: 24 Miller Barber (USA) 1981-92
Highest earnings: Career: $5,201,105 Bob Charles (NZ) to January 1995. Season: $1,190,518 Lee Trevino (USA) 1990

Sony World Rankings

Introduced in 1986 in an attempt to rank players on their achievements worldwide. Top-ranked players have been:

Name	Years
Greg Norman (Aus)	1986-9, 1990, 1994-5
Nick Faldo (UK)	1990-1, 1992-4
Seve Ballesteros (Spa)	1986, 1989
Ian Woosnam (UK)	1991-2
Fred Couples (USA)	1992
Bernhard Langer (Ger)	1992
Nick Price (Zim)	1994-5

US Amateur Championship

Although unofficial US Amateur championships had been held previously, the first official championship was at Newport, Rhode Island in 1895. They were held during the same week, and at the same venue, as the inaugural US Open. Originally a match-play competition, it changed to being stroke-play in 1965, but reverted to match-play in 1973
Recent winners (all USA):

1977	John Fought
1978	John Cook
1979	Mark O'Meara
1980	Hal Sutton
1981	Nathaniel Crosby
1982-3	Jay Sigel
1984	Scott Verplank
1985	Sam Randolph
1986	Buddy Alexander
1987	Bill Mayfair
1988	Eric Meeks
1989	Chris Patton
1990	Phil Mickelson
1991	Mitch Voges
1992	Justin Leonard
1993	John Harris
1994	Tiger Woods

Most wins: 5 Bobby Jones 1924-5, 1927-8, 1930; 4 Jerome Travers 1907-8, 1912-3; Walter Travis 1900-01, 1903
Lowest score (stroke-play): 279 Lanny Wadkins 1970
Biggest winning margin - final (match-play): 12 & 11 Charles Blair Macdonald 1895

The Amateur Championship

In 1885 Thomas Owen Potter of Hoylake organised the first British Amateur Championship at his home course - eight years after the Royal & Ancient showed little interest in running such a competition. Since 1886, however, the championships have been run by the R&A. It has always been a knockout match-play competition and since 1983 all competitors have to play two medal rounds to reduce the field to 64. _Recent winners:_

1977-8	Peter McEvoy (UK)
1979	Jay Sigel (USA)
1980	Duncan Evans (UK)
1981	Phillipe Ploujoux (Fra)
1982	Martin Thompson (UK)
1983	Andrew Parkin (UK)
1984	José-Maria Olazabal (Spa)
1985	Garth McGimpsey (UK)
1986	David Curry (UK)
1987	Paul Mayo (UK)
1988	Christian Hardin (Swe)
1989	Stephen Dodd (UK)
1990	Rolf Muntz (Hol)
1991	Gary Wolstenholme (UK)
1992	Stephen Dundas (UK)
1993	Iain Pyman (UK)
1994	Lee James (UK)
1995	Gordon Sherry (UK)

Most wins: 8 John Ball (UK) 1888, 1890, 1892, 1894, 1899, 1907, 1910, 1912; 5 Michael Bonallack (UK) 1961, 1965, 1968-70; 4 Harold Hilton (UK) 1900-1, 1911, 1913; 3 Joe Carr (Ire) 1953, 1958, 1960
Biggest winning margin (final): 14 & 13 W Lawson Little (USA) beat Jack Wallace (UK), 1934

Walker Cup

Following the success of an international match between amateur teams from the USA and Great Britain at Hoylake in 1921 the first official series of Walker Cup matches took place the following year. The trophy was donated by George Herbert Walker, a former president of the USA Golf Association. It is a biennial event, held alternately in the British Isles (Great Britain and Ireland playing from 1981) and the USA.

Year	Venue	Winners	Score
1922	Long Island, New York	USA	8 - 4
1923	St Andrews, Scotland	USA	6.5- 5.5
1924	Garden City, New York	USA	9 - 3
1926	St Andrews, Scotland	USA	6.5- 5.5
1928	Chicago GC, Illinois	USA	11 - 1
1930	Royal St George's, Sandwich	USA	10 - 2
1932	Brookline, Massachusetts	USA	9.5- 2.5
1934	St Andrews, Scotland	USA	9.5- 2.5
1936	Pine Valley, New Jersey	USA	10.5- 1.5
1938	St Andrews, Scotland	GB	7.5- 4.5
1947	St Andrews, Scotland	USA	8 - 4
1949	Winged Foot, New York	USA	10 - 2
1951	Royal Birkdale, Southport	USA	7.5- 4.5
1953	Kittansett, Massachusetts	USA	9 - 3
1955	St Andrews, Scotland	USA	10 - 2
1957	Minikhada, Minnesota	USA	8.5- 3.5
1959	Muirfield, Scotland	USA	9 - 3
1961	Seattle, Washington	USA	11 - 1
1963	Turnberry, Scotland	USA	14 -10
1965	Baltimore, Maryland	Drawn	12 -12
1967	Royal St George's, Sandwich	USA	15 - 9
1969	Milwaukee, Wisconsin	USA	13 -11
1971	St Andrews, Scotland	GB	13 -11
1973	Brookline, Massachusetts	USA	14- 10
1975	St Andrews, Scotland	USA	15.5- 8.5
1977	Shinnecock Hills, New York	USA	16 - 8
1979	Muirfield, Scotland	USA	15.5- 8.5
1981	Cypress Point, California	USA	15 - 9
1983	Royal Liverpool, Hoylake	USA	13.5-10.5
1985	Pine Valley, Philadelphia	USA	13 -11
1987	Sunningdale, Berkshire	USA	16.5-7.5
1989	Peachtree, Georgia	GB & I	12.5-11.5
1991	Portmarnock, Ireland	USA	14-10
1993	Interlachen, Minneapolis	USA	19-5

Most wins: 30 USA
Most appearances: 10 Joe Carr (GB) 1947-67

Leading players records

Golfers who have played 15 or more matches or who have won 10 or more matches. Note that some men were also selected on other occasions, but these records include only those Cups in which they actually played. Pts = points as 1 for win, 0.5 for halved match.

Name	Years	Cups	pl	w	l	h	pts
GB/GB & Ireland							
Michael Bonnallack	1959-73	8	25	8	14	3	9.5
Peter McEvoy	1977-89	5	18	5	11	2	6
Joe Carr	1947-67	10	20	5	14	1	5.5
United States							
Jay Sigel	1977-93	9	33	18	10	5	20.5
William Campbell	1951-75	7	18	11	4	3	12.5
William Patton	1955-65	5	14	11	3	0	11
Francis Ouimet	1922-34	7	16	9	5	2	10
Bob Lewis Jr	1981-7	4	14	10	4	0	10

World Amateur Team Championship

An international team competiition for four-man teams. It has been held biennially from 1958. The winning team receives the Eisenhower Trophy, named after the former USA President Dwight D Eisenhower, a great golfing enthusiast. The best three scores by members of the four-man teams, each playing four rounds of strokeplay determines the result.

Year	Winning Team	Score	Leading Individual	Score
1958	Australia	918	Bruce Devlin (Aus)	301
			Reid Jack (Sco)	301
			Bill Hyndman (USA)	301
1960	USA	834	Jack Nicklaus (USA)	269
1962	USA	854	Gary Cowan (Can)	280
1964	GB & Ireland	895	Hsieh Min-nan (Tai)	294
1966	Australia	877	Ronnie Shade (UK)	281
1968	USA	868	Michael Bonallack (UK)	286
			Vinnie Giles (USA)	286
1970	USA	854	Victor Regalado (Mex)	280
1972	USA	865	Tony Gresham (Aus)	285
1974	USA	888	Jerry Pate (USA)	294
			Jaime Gonzalez (Bra)	294
1976	GB & Ireland	892	Ian Hutcheon (UK)	293
			Chen Tze-ming (Tai)	293
1978	USA	873	Bob Clampett (USA)	287
1980	USA	848	Hal Sutton (USA)	276
1982	USA	859	Luis Carbonetti (Arg)	284
1984	Japan	870	Luis Carbonetti (Arg)	286
1986	Canada	838	Eduardo Herrera (Col)	275
1988	GB & Ireland	882	Peter McEvoy (GB)	284
1990	Sweden	879	Mathias Grönberg (Swe)	286
1992	New Zealand	823	Philip Tataurangi (NZ)	271
1994	USA	838	Allen Doyle (USA)	277

Most wins: 10 USA

Women's Golf

The Women's Professional Golf Association (WPGA) was formed in the USA in 1944 and reformed in 1948 as the LPGA (Ladies for Women's).

US Women's Open

First held in 1946 at Spokane, Washington at match-play, but at 72 holes of stroke-play annually on different courses from 1947. *Winners (all USA, unless stated) :*

		Score
1946	Patty Berg	5 & 4
1947	Betty Jameson	295
1948	Mildred Zaharias	300
1949	Louise Suggs	291
1950	Mildred Zaharias	291
1951	Betsy Rawls	293
1952	Louise Suggs	284
1953	Betsy Rawls	302
1954	Mildred Zaharias	291
1955	Fay Crocker	299
1956	Kathy Cornelius	302
1957	Betsy Rawls	299
1958	Mickey Wright	290
1959	Mickey Wright	287
1960	Betsy Rawls	292
1961	Mickey Wright	293
1962	Murle Lindstrom	301
1963	Mary Mills	289
1964	Mickey Wright	290
1965	Carol Mann	290
1966	Sandra Spuzich	297
1967	Catherine Lacoste (Fra)	294
1968	Susie Berning	289
1969	Donna Caponi	294
1970	Donna Caponi	287
1971	JoAnne Carner	288
1972	Susie Berning	299
1973	Susie Berning	290
1974	Sandra Haynie	295
1975	Sandra Palmer	295
1976	JoAnne Carner	292
1977	Hollis Stacy	292
1978	Hollis Stacy	289
1979	Jerilyn Britz	284
1980	Amy Alcott	280
1981	Pat Bradley	279
1982	Janet Alex	283
1983	Jan Stephenson	290
1985	Kathy Baker	280
1986	Jane Geddes	287
1987	Laura Davies (UK)	285
1988	Liselotte Neumann (Swi)	277
1989	Betsy King	278
1990	Betsy King	284
1991	Meg Mallon	283
1992	Patty Sheehan	280*
1993	Lauri Merten	280
1994	Patty Sheehan	277
1995	Annika Sorenstam (Swe)	278

Most wins: 4 Wright, Rawls
Lowest aggregate: 277 Neumann 1988, Sheehan 1994
Lowest round: 65 Sally Little 4th 1978, Judy Dickinson 3rd 1985, Ayako Okamoto (Jap) 4th 1989
Biggest margin of victory: 14 strokes Louise Suggs 1949
Oldest winner: Fay Crocker 40yr 11 months 1955
Youngest winner: Catherine Lacoste 22 yr 5 days 1967

US LPGA Championship

First held in 1955 at match-play, and subsequntly over 72 holes of stroke-play. Sponsored by Mazda from 1987, McDonalds 1994. *Winners (all USA):*

1955	Beverly Hanson	4 & 3
1956	Marlene Hagge	291
1957	Louise Suggs	285
1958	Mickey Wright	288
1959	Betsy Rawls	288
1960	Mickey Wright	292
1961	Mickey Wright	287
1962	Judy Kimball	282
1963	Mickey Wright	294
1964	Mary Mills	278

1965 Sandra Haynie	279
1966 Gloria Ehret	282
1967 Kathy Whitworth	284
1968 Sandra Post	294
1969 Betsy Rawls	293
1970 Shirley Englehorn	285
1971 Kathy Whitworth	288
1972 Kathy Ahern	293
1973 Mary Mills	288
1974 Sandra Haynie	288
1975 Kathy Whitworth	288
1976 Betty Burfeindt	287
1977 Chako Higuchi	279
1978 Nancy Lopez	275
1979 Donna Caponi	279
1980 Sally Little	285
1981 Donna Caponi	280
1982 Jan Stephenson	279
1983 Patty Sheehan	279
1984 Patty Sheehan	272
1985 Nancy Lopez	273
1986 Pat Bradley	277
1987 Jane Geddes	275
1988 Sherri Turner	281
1989 Nancy Lopez	274
1990 Beth Daniel	280
1991 Meg Mallon	274
1992 Betsy King	267
1993 Patty Sheehan	276
1994 Laura Davies (UK)	279
1995 Kelley Robbins	274

Most wins: 4 Wright
Lowest round: 63 Patty Sheahan 1984 at King's Island, Ohio
In 1992 at Bethesda, Maryland Betsy King set records for: **Biggest margin of victory**, 11 strokes, and **Lowest aggregate** 267 (68, 66, 67, 66), 17-under par, the first time in a major US tournament that a woman has had four rounds in the 60s.

Nabisco Dinah Shore

Inaugurated 1972 as the Colgate-Dinah Shore, with Nabisco taking over as sponsors in 1983, when it was designated major status. *Winners:*

1972 Jane Blalock	213
1973 Mickey Wright	284
1974 Jo Ann Prentice	289*
1975 Sandra Palmer	283
1976 Judy Rankin	285
1977 Kathy Whitworth	289
1978 Sandra Post	283*
1979 Sandra Post	276
1980 Donna Caponi	275
1981 Nancy Lopez	277
1982 Sally Little	278
1983 Amy Alcott	282
1984 Juli Inkster	280*
1985 Alice Miller	275
1986 Pat Bradley	280
1987 Betsy King	283*
1988 Amy Alcott	274

Laura Davies – world no. 1

1989 Juli Inkster	279
1990 Betsy King	283
1991 Amy Alcott	273
1992 Dottie Mochrie	279*
1993 Helen Alfredsson (Swe)	284
1994 Donna Andrews	276
1995 Nanci Bowen	285

Du Maurier Classic

First held in 1973 as the La Canadienne, and known as the Peter Jackson Classic 1974-82. Granted Major status in 1979. *Winners from 1979:*

1979 Amy Alcott	285
1980 Pat Bradley	277
1981 Jan Stephenson	278
1982 Sandra Haynie	280
1983 Hollis Stacy	277
1984 Juli Inkster	279
1985 Pat Bradley	278
1986 Pat Bradley	276*
1987 Jody Rosenthal	272
1988 Sally Little	279
1989 Tammie Green	279
1990 Cathy Johnston	276
1991 Nancy Scranton	279
1992 Sherri Steinhauer	277
1993 Brandie Burton	277*
1994 Martha Nause	279

Liselotte Neumann

The Women's 'Majors'

The four majors in US women's golf are:

A US Women's Open, first held 1946

B LPGA Championship, inaugurated 1955

C Nabisco Dinah Shore - major status from 1983

D Du Maurier Classic - major status from 1979

The Western Open (E) and Titleholders Championship (F) both used to be Majors.

Most wins (since formation of the US LPGA in 1950):

	A	B	C	D	E	F
12 Mickey Wright	4	4	-	-	2	2
8 Betsy Rawls	4	2	-	-	-	2
7 Patty Berg	-	-	-	-	3	4
6 Louise Suggs	1	1	-	-	3	1
6 Kathy Whitworth	-	3	-	-	2	1
6 Pat Bradley	1	1	1	3	-	-
5 Mildred Zaharias	2	-	-	-	2	1
5 Amy Alcott	1	-	3	1	-	-
5 Betsy King	2	1	2	-	-	-
5 Patty Sheehan	2	3	-	-	-	-
4 Susie Berning	3	-	-	-	-	1
4 Donna Caponi	2	2	-	-	-	-
4 Sandra Haynie	1	2	-	1	-	-
4 Nancy Lopez	-	3	1	-	-	-
4 Hollis Stacey	3	-	-	1	-	-

British Women's Open Championship

Contested annually at stroke-play from 1976, except for 1983. *Winners:*

1976 Jennifer Lee Smith (UK)		299
1977 Vivien Saunders (UK)		306
1978 Janet Melville (UK)		310
1979 Alison Sheard (SAf)		301
1980 Debbie Massey (USA)		294
1981 Debbie Massey (USA)		295
1982 Marta Figeuras-Dotti (Spa)		296
1984 Ayako Okamoto (Jap)		289
1985 Betsy King (USA)		300
1986 Laura Davies (UK)		283
1987 Alison Nicholas (UK)		296
1988 Corinne Dibnah (Aus)		295
1989 Jane Geddes (USA)		274
1990 Helen Alfredsson (Swe)		288
1991 Penny Grice-Whittaker		284
1992 Patty Sheehan (USA)		207

Match restricted to 54 holes due to weather; Sheehan first to win US and British Opens in the same year

1993 Karen Lunn (Aus)		275
1994 Liselotte Neumann (Swe)		280

British Women's Open Amateur Championship

First held in 1893 and contested annually at match-play. *Recent winners:*

1977 Angela Uzielli (UK)
1978 Edwina Kennedy (Aus)
1979 Maureen Madill (Ire)
1980 Anne Sander (USA)
1981 Belle Robertson (UK)
1982 Katrina Douglas (UK)
1983 Jill Thornhill (UK)
1984 Jody Rosenthal (USA)
1985 Lilian Behan (Ire)
1986 Marnie McGuire (NZ)
1987 Janet Collingham (UK)
1988 Joanne Furby (UK)
1989 Helen Dobson (UK)
1990 Julie Hall (UK)
1991 Valérie Michaud (Fra)
1992 Pernille Pedersen (Den)
1993 Catriona Lambert (UK)
1994 Emma Duggleby (UK)

Most wins: 4 Cecil Leitch 1914, 1920-1, 1926; 4 Joyce Wethered 1922, 1924-5, 1929; 3 Lady Margaret Scott 1893-5, 3 May Hezlet 1899, 1902, 1907; 3 Enid Wilson 1931-3, Jesse Valentine (née Anderson) 1937, 1955, 1958

Most finals: 6 Leitch, also runner-up 1922, 1925

Biggest winning margin in final: 9 & 7 Joyce Wethered beat Cecil Leitch 1922

Oldest winner: Belle Robertson 45y 56d 1981.

Youngest winner: May Hezlet 17y 7 days 1899.

US Women's Amateur Championship

Held at stroke-play in 1895, and annually at match-play from 1896, except for the war years of 1917-8, 1942-5.

Most wins: 6 Glenna Vare (née Collett) 1922, 1925, 1928-30, 1935: 5 JoAnne Carner (née Gunderson) 1957,

1960, 1962, 1966, 1968; 3 Beatrix Hoyt 1896-8; Margaret Curtis 1907, 1911-12; 3 Alexa Stirling 1916, 1919-20; 3 Dorothy Campbell Hurd 1909-10, 1924; 3 Virginia van Wie 1932-4; 3 Anne Quast (later Decker, Welts, Sander) 1958, 1961, 1963; 3 Juli Inkster 1980-2
Biggest winning margin in final: 14 & 13 Anne Quast beat Phyllis Preuss 1961
Oldest winner: Dorothy Campbell Hurd, 41 years 4 months 1924
Youngest winner: Laura Baugh 16 years 82 days 1971

Women's World Amateur Team Championship

Contested biennially from 1964 by teams of three for the Espirito Santo Trophy. *Wins:*

12	USA	1966, 1968, 1970, 1972, 1974, 1976, 1980, 1982, 1984, 1988, 1990, 1994
2	Spain	1986, 1992
1	France 1964, Australia 1978	

Lowest aggregate total (72 holes): 569 USA 1994
Lowest individual aggregate: 278 Wendy Ward (USA) 1994
Lowest individual round: 65 Pak Se-ri (SKo) 1994

US LPGA Tournament Records

Lowest score - 72 holes: 268 Nancy Lopez 1985 Henredon Classic, Willow Creek GC, NC
Lowest score - 18 holes: 62 Mickey Wright 1964 Tall City Open, Hogan Park CC, Texas; 62 Vicki Fergon 1984 San Jose Classic, Almaden G&CC; Laura Davies (UK) 1991 Rail Charity Golf Classic, Springfield, Illinois; 62 Hollis Stacy 1992 Safeco Classic, Meridian Valley CC, Seattle
Most consecutive wins: 4 Mickey Wright 1962 and in 1963, Kathy Whitworth 1969. Nancy Lopez won five successive tournaments that she contested 1978
Most wins in a season: 13 Mickey Wright 1963
Oldest winner: 46yr 163d JoAnne Carner 1985 Safeco Classic
Youngest winner: 18yr 14d Marlene Hagge 1952 Sarasota Open

All-time Career Money Leaders - US LPGA Circuit

On US LPGA circuit as at 19 Jun 1995

	Amount	Wins	Years
Betsy King	$5,050,411	29	1977-95
Pat Bradley	$4,997,634	31	1974-95
Beth Daniel	$4,750,805	31	1979-95
Patty Sheehan	$4,649,963	33	1980-95
Nancy Lopez	$4,181,778	47	1977-95
Amy Alcott	$3,094,347	29	1975-95
Dottie Mochrie	$2,893,102	9	1988-95
JoAnne Carner	$2,874,795	42	1970-95
Ayoko Okamoto (Jap)	$2,724,475	17	1981-95
Jane Geddes	$2,417.458	11	1983-95
Rosie Jones	$2,408,076	6	1982-95
Jan Stephenson (Aus)	$2,280,519	16	1974-95
Juli Inkster	$2,157,836	15	1983-95
Colleen Walker	$2,143,097	7	1982-95
Laura Davies	$2,116,833	10	1988-95
Meg Mallon	$2,059,380	6	1987-95
Hollis Stacey	$2,037,295	18	1974-95
Also			
Kathy Whitworth	$1,731,770	88	1959-95

Progressive record for the amount won in a season from $20,000 to over $200,000

1956	Marlene Hagge	$20,235
1959	Betsy Rawls	26,774
1963	Mickey Wright	31,269
1966	Kathy Whitworth	33,517
1968	Kathy Whitworth	48,379
1972	Kathy Whitworth	65,063
1973	Kathy Whitworth	82,854
1974	JoAnne Carner	87,094
1975	Sandra Palmer	94,805
1976	Judy Rankin	150,734
1978	Nancy Lopez	189,813
1979	Nancy Lopez	215,987

Yearly leaders from 1980

1980	Beth Daniel	231,000
1981	Beth Daniel	206,978
1982	JoAnne Carner	310,399
1983	JoAnne Carner	291,404
1984	Betsy King	266,771
1985	Nancy Lopez	416,472
1986	Pat Bradley	492,021
1987	Ayoko Okomoto (Jap)	466,034
1988	Sherru Turner	350,851
1989	Betsy King	654,132
1990	Beth Daniel	863,578
1991	Pat Bradley	763,118
1992	Dottie Mochrie	693,355
1993	Betsy King	595,992
1994	Laura Davies (UK)	687,201

Most seasons as leading money winner
8 Kathy Whitworth 1965-8, 1970-3; 4 Mildred 'Babe' Zaharias 1948-51; 4 Mickey Wright 1961-4
Most LPGA tournament wins
88 Kathy Whitworth, 82 Mickey Wright, 57 Patty Berg (inc.13 pre LPGA), 55 Betsy Rawls, 50 Louise Suggs, 47 Nancy Lopez, 42 Sandra Haynie, JoAnne Carner; 38 Carol Mann, 33 Patty Sheehan, 31 Mildred 'Babe' Zaharias, Beth Daniel; 30 Pat Bradley

Women's PGA European Tour

Money leaders from the formalisation of the WPGA tour in 1979:

Year	Top money winner	£
1979	Alison Sheard (UK)	4,965
1980	Muriel Thomson (UK)	8,008
1981	Jenny Lee Smith (UK)	13,519
1982	Jenny Lee Smith (UK)	12,551
1983	Beverly Huke (UK)	9,226
1984	Dale Reid (UK)	28,239
1985	Laura Davies (UK)	21,736
1986	Laura Davies (UK)	37,500
1987	Dale Reid (UK)	53,815
1988	Marie-Laure de Lorenzi (Fra)	99,360
1989	Marie-Laure de Lorenzi (Fra)	77,534
1990	Trish Johnson (UK)	83,403
1991	Corinne Dibnah (Aus)	89,058

1992	Laura Davies (UK)	66,333
1993	Karen Lunn (Aus)	66,266
1994	Liselotte Neumann (Swe)	102,750

The Order of Merit winners have been the same as the leading money winner except for: 1979 Catherine Panton (UK), 1983 Muriel Thomson (UK)

Curtis Cup

A biennial team competition involving women's team from the United States and Great Britain and Ireland. It was first held at Wentworth in 1932 and is named after American sisters Margaret and Harriot Curtis.

Year	Venue	Winners	Score
1932	Wentworth, Surrey	USA	5.5-3.5
1934	Chevy Chase, Maryland	USA	6.5-2.5
1936	Gleneagles, Scotland	Drawn	4.5-4.5
1938	Essex, Massachusetts	USA	5.5-3.5
1948	Royal Birkdale, Southport	USA	6.5-2.5
1950	Buffalo CC, New York	USA	7.5-1.5
1952	Muirfield, Scotland	GB&I	5-4
1954	Merion, Pennsylvania	USA	6-3
1956	Prince's, Sandwich	GB&I	5-4
1958	Brae Burn, Massachusetts	Drawn	4.5-4.5
1960	Lindrick, Sheffield	USA	6.5-2.5
1962	Broadmoor, Colorado Springs	USA	8-1
1964	Royal Porthcawl, Wales	USA	10.5-7.5
1966	Hot Springs, Virginia	USA	13-5
1968	Royal County Down, Ireland	USA	10.5-7.5
1970	Brae Burn, Massachusetts	USA	11.5 -6.5
1972	Western Gailes, Scotland	USA	10-8
1974	San Francisco, California	USA	13-5
1976	Royal Lytham, Lancashire	USA	11.5 -6.5
1978	Apawamis, New York	USA	12-6
1980	St Pierre, Chepstow	USA	13-5
1982	Denver, Colorado	USA	14.5-3.5
1984	Muirfield, Scotland	USA	9.5-8.5
1986	Prairie Dunes, Kansas	GB&I	13 -5
1988	Royal St George's, Sandwich	GB&I	11-7
1990	Somerset Hills, New Jersey	USA	14-4

Solheim Cup

| 1992 | Royal Liverpool, Hoylake | GB&I | 10-8 |
| 1994 | Chattanooga, Tennessee | Drawn | 9-9 |

Most wins: 20 USA

Most appearances: 9 Mary McKenna (GB&I) 1970-86, 8 Anne Sander (USA), Carol Semple Thompson (USA)

Leading players records

Golfers who have played 20 or more matches or won 10 or more. pts = points as 1 for win, 1/2 for halved match

Name	Years	Cups	pl	w	l	h	pts
GB/GB & Ireland							
Mary McKenna	1970-86	9	30	10	16	4	12
Belle Robertson	1960-86	7	24	5	12	7	8.5
United States							
Carol Semple Thompson	1974-94	8	24	15	7	2	16
Anne Quast Sander	1958-90	8	22	11	7	4	13
Phyllis Preuss	1962-70	5	15	10	4	1	10.5

The first team competition between women's teams from the United States and Europe, along the lines of the Ryder Cup for men, was staged in 1990. *Winners:*

Year	Venue	Winners	Score
1990	Orlando, Florida	USA	11.5-4.5
1992	Dalmahoy, Scotland	Europe	11.5-6.5
1994	The Greenbrier, West Virginia	USA	13-7

Sunrise Cup

The first women's professional team championship was staged at the Sunrise golf and country club near Taipeh, Taiwan in 1992. Contested by teams of two over 54 holes. *Winners:*

1992 Sweden (Helen Alfredsson, Liselotte Neumann) 445
Best individual: Neumann and Trish Johnson (Eng) 219

Greyhound Racing

The first greyhound meeting was staged at Hendon, North London in September 1876, with a railed hare operated by a windlass. The sport became popular with the perfecting of a mechanical hare by Owen Patrick Smith in the USA in 1919. Smith and George Sawyer formed the International Greyhound Racing Association at Tulsa in 1920.

The oldest greyhound track in the world, still in operation, is the St Petersburg, Florida, Kennel Club, opened on 3 Jan 1925. The first meeting with a mechanical hare in Great Britain was run at Belle Vue, Manchester on 24 Jul 1926, in which year the Greyhound Racing Association was formed.

Greyhound Derby

The most prestigious race in British greyhound racing, the Derby was instituted in 1927, run over 500 yards at the White City, London. From 1928 to 1974 it was run over 525 yards, at 500m 1975-84 and subsequently at 480m and now 460m. The 1940 race was at Harringay, and since 1985, following the closure of the White City, the races have been held at Wimbledon. *Winners:*

1927	Entry Badge
1928	Bother Ash
1929-30	Mick The Miller
1931	Seldom Led
1932	Wild Woolley
1933	Future Cutlet
1934	Davesland
1935	Greta Ranee
1936	Fine Jubilee
1937	Wattle Bark
1938	Lone Keel
1939	Highland Rum
1940	G.R.Archduke
1945	Ballyhennessy Seal
1946	Mondays News

1947	Trevs Perfection	1991	Ballinderry Ash	1956	Blue Sand
1948	Priceless Border	1992	Farloe Melody	1957	Tanyard Tulip
1949	Narogar Ann	1993	Ringa Hustle	1958	Fodda Champion
1950	Ballymac Ball	1994	Moral Standards	1959	Prince Poppit
1951	Ballylanigan Tanist	1995	Moaning Lad	1960	Bruff Chariot
1952	Endless Gossip			1961	Ballintona Special
1953	Daw's Dancer			1962	Corsica Reward
1954	Paul's Fun			1963	Indoor Sport
1955	Rushton Mack			1964	Two Aces
1956	Dunmore King			1965	I'm Crazy
1957	Ford Spartan			1966	Halfpenny King
1958	Pigalle Wonder			1967	The Grange Santa
1959	Mile Bush Pride			1968	Ballintore Santa
1960	Duleek Dandy			1969	Tony's Friend
1961	Palm's Printer			1970-2	Sherry's Prince
1962	The Grand Canal			1973	Killone Flash
1963	Lucky Boy Boy			1974	Shanney's Darkie
1964	Hack Up Chieftain			1975	Pier Hero
1965	Chittering Clapton			1976	Weston Pete
1966	Faithful Hope			1977	Salerno
1967	Tric-Trac			1978-9	Top O' The Tide
1968	Camira Flash			1980	Gilt Edge Flyer
1969	Sand Star			1981	Bobcol
1970	John Silver			1982	Face The Nutt
1971	Dolores Rocket			1983	Sir Winston
1972-3	Patricia's Hope			1984	Kilcoe Foxy
1974	Jimsum			1985	Seaman's Star
1975	Tartan Khan			1986	Castelyons Cash
1976	Mutts Silver			1987	Cavan Town
1977	Balliniska Band			1988	Breek's Rocket
1978	Lacca Champion			1989	Lemon Chip
1979	Sarah's Bunny			1990	Gizmo Pasha
1980	Indian Joe			1991	Ideal Man & Ballycarney Dell
1981	Parkdown Jet			1992	Kildare Slippy
1982	Laurie's Panther			1993	Arfur Daley
1983	I'm Slippy			1994	Randy Savage
1984	Whisper Wishes				
1985	Pagan Swallow				
1986	Tico				
1987	Signal Spark				
1988	Hit the Lid				
1989	Lartigue Note				
1990	Slippy Blue				

Most wins: 2 Mick The Miller, Patricia's Hope
Shortest priced winner: 1-4 Entry Badge, the first in 1927
Longest priced winner: 25-1 Dullek Dandy 1960, Tartan Khan 1975

Greyhound Grand National

The first of the year's classics, for hurdlers, the race was first run in 1927 at the White City. Since 1985 it has been run at Hall Green, Birmingham. 1927-74 run over 500 yards, from 1975 over 474 metres and five flights of hurdles.

1927	Bonzo
1928	Cormorant
1929	Lavator
1930	Stylish Cutlet
1931	Rule The Roost
1932	Long Hop
1933	Scapegoat
1934	Lemonition
1935	Quarter Day
1936	Kilganny Bridge
1937	Flying Wedge
1938	Juvenile Classic
1939	Valiant Bob
1940	Juvenile Classic
1946	Barry From Limerick
1947	Baytown Pigeon
1948	Joves Reason
1949-50	Blossom of Anagura
1951	XPDNC
1952	Whistling Laddie
1953	Denver Berwick
1954	Prince Lawrence
1955	Barrowside

Most wins: 3 Sherry's Prince

Career Records

Most wins: 143 JR's Ripper (USA) 1982-6
Most consecutive wins: 37 J.J.Doc Richard (USA) 1994-5

Gymnastics

The ancient Greeks and Romans were exponents of gymnastics and excelled at the Ancient Olympic Games over 2000 years ago. Modern techniques, however, were developed in Germany towards the latter part of the 18th-century and the first teacher of modern gymnastics was Johann Friedrich Simon at Basedow's School, Dessau, in 1776. Regarded as the father figure of modern gymnastics was Friedrich Jahn, who founded the Turnverein in Berlin in 1811. In Britain the Amateur Gymnastics Association was formed in 1888. The International Gymnastics Federation (IGF) was formed in 1891.

Apparatus

Men

Parallel bars - two bars of round cross section, 350 cm long, set 42 cm apart, and supported 175 cm above the floor on uprights fixed to a broad stable base.
Horizontal bar - bar 240 cm long supported 255 cm above the ground by an upright at each end and braced with wires.
Pommel horse - similar to vaulting horse; 110 cm high, 163 cm long, but with two raised handles at the centre.
Rings - two rigid rings 18 cm in diameter suspended 250 cm from the floor by two wires 50 cm apart

attached to a frame, braced with wires, 550 cm high.

Horse vault - Horse is 163 cm long, 135 cm high. Springboard is 120 cm long, placed in line with the long side of the horse.

Men & Women

Floor exercises - on a 12m square area.

Women

Asymmetrical bars - two horizontal bars 350 cm long, arranged parallel to one another but at different heights. Lower is 150 cm and upper 230 cm above the floor. Each is supported by an upright at each end, and these two frames are placed 43 cm apart.

Beam - rigid beam of wood 5m long mounted horizontally, 10 cm wide at 120 cm above the floor.

Horse vault - Horse is 163 cm long 120 cm high. Springboard as for men's.

Modern Rhythmic Gymnastics

In this women's sport the disciplines are characterized by the handling of light portable objects, skipping ropes, hoops, clubs, ribbons and balls, to musical accompaniment. The IGF recognised rhythmic gymnastics in 1962, world championships were first held in 1963 and the sport was added to the Olympics in 1984.

Olympic Games

Gymnastics was included in the first Modern Olympics of 1896. A women's competition was first included in 1928. *Winners:*

Men's Team

5	Japan	1960, 1964, 1968, 1972, 1976
5	USSR/CIS	1952, 1956, 1980, 1988, 1992
4	Italy	1912, 1920, 1924, 1932,
2	USA	1904 (TG Philadelphia), 1984
1	Norway 1906, Sweden 1908, Switzerland 1928, Germany 1936, Finland 1948	

Men - combined exercises

1900 Gustave Sandras (Fra)
1904 Julius Lenhart (Aut) #
1906 Pierre Payssé (Fra) *
1908 Alberto Braglia (Ita)
1912 Alberto Braglia (Ita)
1920 Giorgio Zampori (Ita)
1924 Leon Stukelj (Yug)
1928 Georges Miez (Sui)
1932 Romeo Neri (Ita)
1936 Alfred Schwarzmann (Ger)
1948 Veikko Huhtanen (Fin)
1952 Viktor Chukarin (USSR)
1956 Viktor Chukarin (USSR)
1960 Boris Shakhlin (USSR)
1964 Yukio Endo (Jap)
1968 Sawao Kato (Jap)
1972 Sawao Kato (Jap)
1976 Nikolay Andrianov (USSR)
1980 Aleksandr Ditiatin (USSR)

Vitaliy Scherbo – winner of a record 11 gold medals at the Olympics and World Championships

1984 Koji Gushiken (Jap)
1988 Vladimir Artemov (USSR)
1992 Vitaliy Scherbo (CIS/Bls)
* *won two competitions in 1906 - 5 events and 6 events*
# *member of USA Philadelphia Club who won team event*

Men - floor exercises
1932 István Pelle (Hun)
1936 Georges Miez (Swi)
1948 Ferenc Pataki (Hun)
1952 William Thoresson (Swe)
1956 Valentin Muratov (USSR)
1960 Nobuyuki Aihara (Jap)
1964 Franco Menichelli (Ita)
1968 Sawao Kato (Jap)
1972 Nikolay Andrianov (USSR)
1976 Nikolay Andrianov (USSR)
1980 Roland Brückner (GDR)
1984 Li Ning (Chn)
1988 Sergey Kharikov (USSR)
1992 Li Xiaoshuang (Chn)

Men - parallel bars
1896 Alfred Flatow (Ger)
1904 George Eyser (USA)
1924 August Güttinger (Swi)
1928 Ladislav Vácha (Cs)
1932 Romeo Neri (Ita)
1936 Konrad Frey (Ger)
1948 Michael Reusch (Swi)
1952 Hans Eugster (Swi)
1956 Viktor Chukarin (USSR)
1960 Boris Shakhlin (USSR)
1964 Yukio Endo (Jap)
1968 Akinori Nakayama (Jap)
1972 Sawao Kato (Jap)
1976 Sawao Kato (Jap)
1980 Aleksandr Tkachev (USSR)
1984 Bart Conner (USA)
1988 Vladimir Artemov (USSR)
1992 Vitaliy Scherbo (CIS/Bls)

Men - pommel horse
1896 Louis Zutter (Swi)
1904 Anton Heida (USA)
1924 Josef Wilhelm (Swi)
1928 Hermann Hänggi (Swi)
1932 István Pelle (Hun)
1936 Konrad Frey (Ger)
1948 Paavo Aaltonen (Fin), Veikko Huhtanen (Fin) & Ilmari Savolainen (Fin)
1952 Viktor Chukarin (USSR)
1956 Boris Shakhlin (USSR)
1960 Eugen Ekman (Fin) & Boris Shakhlin (USSR)
1964 Miroslav Cerar (Yug)
1968 Miroslav Cerar (Yug)
1972 Viktor Klimenko (USSR)
1976 Zoltán Magyar (Hun)
1980 Zoltán Magyar (Hun)

1984 Li Ning (Chn) & Peter Vidmar (USA)
1988 Dmitriy Bilozerchev (USSR), Zsolt Borkai (Hun) & Lyubomir Gueraskov (Bul)
1992 Vitaliy Scherbo (CIS/Bls) & Pae Gil-su (NKo)

Men - rings
1896 Ioannis Mitropoulos (Gre)
1904 Hermann Glass (USA)
1924 Francesco Martino (Ita)
1928 Leon Skutelj (Yug)
1932 George Gulack (USA)
1936 Alois Hudec (Cs)
1948 Karl Frei (Swi)
1952 Grant Shaginyan (USSR)
1956 Albert Azaryan (USSR)
1960 Albert Azaryan (USSR)
1964 Takuji Hayata (Jap)
1968 Akinori Nakayama (Jap)
1972 Akinori Nakayama (Jap)
1976 Nikolay Andrianov (USSR)
1980 Aleksandr Ditiatin (USSR)
1984 Koji Gushiken (Jap) & Li Ning (Chn)
1988 Holger Behrendt (GDR) & Dmitriy Bilozerchev (USSR)
1992 Vitaliy Scherbo (CIS/Bls)

Men - horizontal Bar
1896 Hermann Weingärtner (Ger)
1904 Anton Heida (USA) & Edward Hennig (USA)
1924 Leon Stukelj (Yug)
1928 Georges Miez (Swi)
1932 Dallas Bixler (USA)
1936 Aleksanteri Saarvala (Fin)
1948 Josef Stadler (Swi)
1952 Jack Günthard (Swi)
1956 Takashi Ono (Jap)
1960 Takashi Ono (Jap)
1964 Boris Shakhlin (USSR)
1968 Mikhail Voronin (USSR) & Akinori Nakayama (Jap)
1972 Mitsuo Tsukahara (Jap)
1976 Mitsuo Tsukahara (Jap)
1980 Stoyan Deltchev (Bul)
1984 Shinji Morisue (Jap)
1988 Vladimir Artemov (USSR) & Valeriy Lyukin (USSR)
1992 Trent Dimas (USA)

Men - horse vault
1896 Carl Schuhmann (Ger)
1904 Anton Heida (USA) & George Eyser (USA)
1924 Frank Kriz (USA)
1928 Eugen Mack (Swi)
1932 Savino Guglielmetti (Ita)
1936 Alfred Schwarzmann (Ger)
1948 Paavo Aaltonen (Fin)
1952 Viktor Chukarin (USSR)

1956 Helmuth Bantz (Ger) & Valentin Muratov (USSR)
1960 Takashi Ono (Jap) & Boris Shakhlin (USSR)
1964 Haruhiro Yamashita (Jap)
1968 Mikhail Voronin (USSR)
1972 Klaus Köste (GDR)
1976 Nikolay Andrianov (USSR)
1980 Nikolay Andrianov (USSR)
1984 Lou Yun (Chn)
1988 Lou Yun (Chn)
1992 Vitaliy Scherbo (CIS/Bls)

Women's team
10   USSR/CIS 1952, 1956, 1960, 1964, 1968, 1972, 1976, 1980, 1988, 1992
1   Netherlands 1928, Germany 1936, Czechoslovakia 1948, Romania 1984

Women - combined exercises
1952 Maria Gorokhovskaya (USSR)
1956 Larisa Latynina (USSR)
1960 Larisa Latynina (USSR)
1964 Vera Cáslavská (Cs)
1968 Vera Cáslavská (Cs)
1972 Lyudmila Tourischeva (USSR)
1976 Nadia Comaneci (Rom)
1980 Yelena Davydova (USSR)
1984 Mary Lou Retton (USA)
1988 Yelena Shushunova (USSR)
1992 Tatyana Gutsu (CIS/Ukr)

Women - asymmetrical bars
1952 Margit Korondi (Hun)
1956 Agnes Keleti (Hun)
1960 Polina Astakhova (USSR)
1964 Polina Astakhova (USSR)
1968 Vera Cáslavská (Cs)
1972 Karin Janz (GDR)
1976 Nadia Comaneci (Rom)
1980 Maxi Gnauck (GDR)
1984 Ma Yanhong (Chn) & Julianne McNamara (USA)
1988 Daniela Silivas (Rom)
1992 Li Lu (Chn)

Women - balance beam
1952 Nina Bocharova (USSR)
1956 Agnes Keleti (Hun)
1960 Eva Bosáková (Cs)
1964 Vera Cáslavská (Cs)
1968 Natalya Kuchinskaya (USSR)
1972 Olga Korbut (USSR)
1976 Nadia Comaneci (Rom)
1980 Nadia Comaneci (Rom)
1984 Simona Pauca (Rom) & Ecaterina Szabo (Rom)
1988 Daniela Silivas (Rom)
1992 Tatyana Lysenko (CIS/Ukr)

Women - floor exercises

1952 Agnes Keleti (Hun)
1956 Larisa Latynina (USSR) &
    Agnes Keleti (Hun)
1960 Larisa Latynina (USSR)
1964 Larisa Latynina (USSR)
1968 Larisa Petrik (USSR) &
    Vera Cáslavská (Cs)
1972 Olga Korbut (USSR)
1976 Nelli Kim (USSR)
1980 Nelli Kim (USSR) &
    Nadia Comaneci (Rom)
1984 Ecaterina Szabo (Rom)
1988 Daniela Silivas (Rom)
1992 Lavinia Milosovici (Rom)

Women - horse vault

1952 Yekaterina Kalinchuk (USSR)
1956 Larisa Latynina (USSR)
1960 Margarita Nikolayeva (USSR)
1964 Vera Cáslavská (Cs)
1968 Vera Cáslavská (Cs)
1972 Karin Janz (GDR)
1976 Nelli Kim (USSR)
1980 Natalya Shaposhnikova
    (USSR)

1984 Ecaterina Szabo (Rom)
1988 Svetlana Boginskaya (USSR)
1992 Lavinia Milosovici (Rom) &
    Henrietta Ónodi (Hun)

Women -Rhythmic Gymnastics

1984 Lori Fung (Can)
1988 Marina Lobach (USSR)
1992 Aleksandra Timoschenko
    (CIS/Ukr)

Discontinued events

Men - parallel bars (Team)
1896 Germany

Men - horizontal bars (Team)
1896 Germany

Men - rope climbing
1896 Nicolaos Andriakopoulos (Gre)
1904 George Eyser (USA)
1906 Georgios Aliprantis (Gre)
1924 Bedrich Supcik (Cs)
1932 Raymond Bass (USA)

Men - club swinging
1904 Edward Hennig (USA)
1932 George Roth (USA)

Men - seven event competition
1904 Anton Heida (USA)

Men - nine event competition
1904 Adolf Spinnler (Swi)

Men - triathlon (100 yards, long jump, shot)
1904 Max Emmerich (USA)

Men - sidehorse vault
1924 Albert Séguin (Fra)

Men - tumbling
1932 Rowland Wolfe (USA)

Men - Swedish event (team)
1912 Sweden
1920 Sweden

Men - free system (team)
1912 Norway
1920 Denmark

Women - portable apparatus (team)
1952 Sweden
1956 Hungary

Most Olympic medals (G gold, S silver, B bronze)

Total	Gymnast	G	S	B	Years
Men					
15	Nikolay Andrianov (USSR)	7	5	3	1972-80
13	Boris Shakhlin (USSR)	7	4	2	1956-64
13	Takashi Ono (Jap)	5	4	4	1956-64
12	Sawao Kato (Jap)	8	3	1	1968-76
11	Viktor Chukarin (USSR)	7	3	1	1952-6
10	Akinori Nakayama (Jap)	6	2	2	1968-72
10	Aleksandr Ditiatin (USSR)	3	6	1	1976-80
9	Mitsuo Tsukahara (Jap)	5	1	3	1968-76
9	Elizo Kenmotsu (Jap)	3	3	3	1968-76
9	Mikhail Voronin (USSR)	2	6	1	1968-72
9	Yuriy Titov (USSR)	1	5	3	1956-64

Vitaliy Shcherbo won a record 6 gold medals at one Games in 1992

Also 4 gold medals: Georges Miesz (Swi), Anton Heida (USA), Yukio Endo (Jap), Giorgio Zampori (Ita), Valentin Muratov (USSR), Vladimir Artemov (USSR)

Total	Gymnast	G	S	B	Years
Women					
18	Larisa Latynina (USSR)	9	5	4	1956-64
11	Vera Cáslavská (Cs)	7	4	0	1964-8
10	Agnes Kaleti (Hun)	5	3	2	1952-6
10	Polina Astakhova (USSR)	5	2	3	1956-64
9	Nadia Comaneci (Rom)	5	3	1	1976-80
9	Lyudmila Tourischeva (USSR)	4	3	2	1968-76

Also 4 gold medals: Olga Korbut (USSR), Nelli Kim (USSR)

World Championships

First held for men at Antwerp in 1903 and every two years until 1913. They were re-introduced in 1922 and held every four years with the Olympic champions also being the world champions. Since 1979 they have reverted to being held biennially.

The first women's championships were held in 1934. Team championships, separate from the individual events were held in 1994. *Winners:*

Men's team

8	USSR	1954, 1958, 1979, 1981, 1985, 1987, 1989, 1991
7	Czechoslovakia	1907, 1911, 1913, 1922, 1926, 1930, 1938
5	Japan	1962, 1966, 1970, 1974, 1978
3	France	1903, 1905, 1909
2	China	1983, 1994
1	Switzerland	1950

There was no team competition in 1934.

Men - combined exercises

1903 Joseph Martinez (Fra/Alg)
1905 Marcel Lalu (Fra)
1907 Josef Cada (Cs)
1909 Marco Torrès (Fra)
1911 Ferdinand Steiner (Cs)
1913 Marco Torrès (Fra)
1922 Peter Sumi (Yug) &
    Frantisek Pechacek (Cs)
1926 Peter Sumi (Yug)

1930 Josip Primozic (Yug)
1934 Eugen Mack (Swi)
1938 Jan Gajdos (Cs)
1950 Walter Lehmann (Swi)
1954 Viktor Chukarin (USSR)
1958 Boris Shakhlin (USSR)
1962 Yuriy Titov (USSR)
1966 Mikhail Voronin (USSR)
1970 Eizo Kenmotsu (Jap)
1974 Shigeru Kasamatsu (Jap)
1978 Nikolay Andrianov (USSR)
1979 Aleksandr Ditiatin (USSR)
1981 Yuriy Korolev (USSR)
1983 Dmitriy Bilozerchev (USSR)
1985 Yuriy Korolev (USSR)
1987 Dmitriy Bilozerchev (USSR)
1989 Igor Korobchinskiy (USSR)
1991 Grigoriy Misutin (USSR)
1993 Vitaliy Scherbo (Bls)
1994 Ivan Ivankov (Bls)

Men - floor exercises
1913 Giorgio Zampori (Ita) &
    V Rabic (Cs)
1930 Josip Primozic (Yug)
1934 Georges Miesz (Swi)
1938 Jan Gajdos (Cs)
1950 Josef Stadler (Swi)
1954 Valentin Muratov (USSR)
    & Masao Takemoto (Jap)
1958 Masao Takemoto (Jap)
1962 Nobuyuki Aihara (Jap)
    & Yukio Endo (Jap)
1966 Akinori Nakayama (Jap)
1970 Akinori Nakayama (Jap)
1974 Shigeru Kasamatsu (Jap)
1978 Kurt Thomas (USA)
1979 Kurt Thomas (USA) &
    Roland Brückner (GDR)
1981 Yuriy Korolev (USSR) &
    Li Yuejiu (Chn)
1983 Tong Fei (Chn)
1985 Tong Fei (Chn)
1987 Lou Yun (Chn)
1991 Igor Korobchinskiy (USSR)
1993 Grigoriy Misutin (Ukr)
1994 Vitaliy Scherbo (Bls)

Men - horizontal bar
1903 Joseph Martinez (Fra/Alg)
    & Pierre Payssé (Fra)
1905 Marcel Lalu (Fra)
1907 Georges Charmoille (Fra)
    & Frantisek Erben (Cs)
1909 Joseph Martinez (Fra),
    Josef Cada (Cs) &
    Frantisek Erben (Fra)
1911 Josef Cada (Cs)
1913 Josef Cada (Cs)
1922 Miroslav Klinger (Cs)
1926 Leon Stukelj (Yug)
1930 István Pelle (Hun)

1934 Ernst Winter (Ger)
1950 Paavo Aaltonen (Fin)
1954 Valentin Muratov (USSR)
1958 Boris Shakhlin (USSR)
1962 Takashi Ono (Jap)
1966 Akinori Nakayama (Jap)
1970 Eizo Kenmotsu (Jap)
1974 Eberhard Gienger (FRG)
1978 Shigeru Kasamatsu (Jap)
1979 Kurt Thomas (USA)
1981 Aleksandr Tkachev (USSR)
1983 Dmitriy Bilozerchev (USSR)
1985 Tong Fei (Chn)
1987 Dmitriy Bilozerchev (USSR)
1989 Li Chunyang (Chn)
1991 Li Chunyang (Chn) &
    Ralf Büchner (Ger)
1993 Sergey Kharkov (Rus)
1994 Vitaliy Scherbo (Bls)

Men - parallel bars
1903 Joseph Martinez (Fra) &
    Francois Hentges (Lux)
1905 Joseph Martinez (Fra/Alg)
1907 Jos Lux (Fra)
1909 Joseph Martinez (Fra/Alg)
1911 Giorgio Zampori (Ita)
1913 Giorgio Zampori (Ita) &
    Guido Boni (Ita)
1922 Leon Stukelj (Yug),
    Stane Derganc (Yug),
    N Jindrich (Cs),
    Miroslav Klinger (Cs) &
    Vlado Simoncic (Yug)
1926 Ladislav Vácha (Cs)
1930 Josip Primozic (Yug)
1934 Eugen Mack (Swi)
1938 Michael Reusch (Swi)
1950 Hans Eugster (Swi)
1954 Viktor Chukarin (USSR)
1958 Boris Shakhlin (USSR)
1962 Miroslav Cerar (Yug)
1966 Sergey Diomidov (USSR)
1970 Akinori Nakayama (Jap)
1974 Eizo Kenmotsu (Jap)
1978 Eizo Kenmotsu (Jap)
1979 Bart Conner (USA)
1981 Aleksandr Ditiatin (USSR) &
    Koji Gushiken (Jap)
1983 Vladimir Artemov (USSR) &
    Lou Yun (Chn)
1985 Silvio Kroll (GDR) &
    Valentin Mogilnyi (USSR)
1987 Vladimir Artemov (USSR)
1989 Li Jing (Chn) &
    Vladimir Artemov (USSR)
1991 Li Jing (Chn)
1993 Vitaliy Scherbo (Bls)
1994 Huang Liping (Chn)

Men - horse vault
1903 G De Jaeghere (Fra), Jos Lux

(Fra) & N Thysen (Hol)
1905 G De Jaeghere (Fra)
1907 Frantisek Erben (Cs)
1913 Karel Stary (Cs),
    Ben Sadoun (Fra),
    Osvaldo Palazzi (Ita) &
    Stane Vidmar (Yug)
1934 Eugen Mack (Swi)
1938 Eugen Mack (Swi)
1950 Ernst Gebendinger (Swi)
1954 Leo Sotornik (Cs)
1958 Yuriy Titov (USSR)
1962 Premysel Krbec (Cs)
1966 Haruhiro Matsuda (Jap)
1970 Mitsuo Tsukahara (Jap)
1974 Shigeru Kasamatsu (Jap)
1978 Junichi Shimizu (Jap)
1979 Aleksandr Ditiatin (USSR)
1981 Ralf-Peter Hemmann (GDR)
1983 Artur Akopian (USSR)
1985 Yuriy Korolev (USSR)
1987 Silvio Kroll (GDR) &
    Lou Yun (Chn)
1989 Jörg Behrendt (GDR)
1991 Yu Ok-yul (SKo)
1993-4 Vitaliy Scherbo (Bls)

Men - rings
1903 Joseph Martinez (Fra/Alg) &
    Jos Lux (Lux)
1909 Guido Romano (Ita) &
    Marco Torres (Fra)
1911 Ferdinand Steiner (Cs),
    Dominique Follacci (Fra) &
    Pietro Bianchi (Ita)
1913 Laurent Grech (Fra),
    Marco Torres (Fra),
    Giorgio Zampori (Ita) &
    Guido Boni (Ita)
1922 Laurent Karasek (Cs),
    Josef Maly (Cs),
    Leon Stukelj (Yug) &
    Peter Sumi (Yug)
1926 Leon Stukelj (Yug)
1930 Emanuel Löffler (Cs)
1934 Alois Hudec (Cs)
1938 Alois Hudec (Cs)
1950 Walter Lehmann (Swi)
1954 Albert Azarian (USSR)
1958 Albert Azarian (USSR)
1962 Yuriy Titov (USSR)
1966 Mikhail Voronin (USSR)
1970 Akinori Nakayama (Jap)
1974 Nikolay Andrianov (USSR)
    & Dan Grecu (Rom)
1978 Nikolay Andrianov (USSR)
1979 Aleksandr Ditiatin (USSR)
1981 Aleksandr Ditiatin (USSR)
1983 Dmitriy Bilozerchev (USSR)
    & Koji Gushiken (Jap)
1985 Li Ning (Chn) &
    Yuriy Korolev (USSR)

1987 Yuriy Korolev (USSR)
1989 Andreas Aguilar (FRG)
1991 Grigoriy Misutin (USSR)
1993-4 Yuri Chechi (Ita)

Men - pommel horse
1911 Osvaldo Palazzi (Ita)
1913 Giorgio Zampori (Ita),
      N Aubrey (Fra) &
      Osvaldo Palazzi (Ita)
1922 Miroslav Klinger (Cs),
      N Jindrich (Cs) &
      Leon Stukelj (Yug)
1926 Jan Karafiát (Cs)
1930 Josip Primozic (Yug)
1934 Eugène Mack (Swi)
1938 Michael Reusch (Swi) &
      Vratislav Petracek (Cs)
1950 Josef Stalder (Swi)
1954 Grant Chaginyan (USSR)
1958 Boris Shakhlin (USSR)
1962 Miroslav Cerar (Yug)
1966 Miroslav Cerar (Yug)
1970 Miroslav Cerar (Yug)
1974 Zoltán Magyar (Hun)
1978 Zoltán Magyar (Hun)
1979 Zoltán Magyar (Hun)
1981 Michael Nikolay (GDR) &
      Li Xiaoping (Chn)
1983 Dmitriy Bilozerchev (USSR)
1985 Valentin Mogilnyi (USSR)
1987 Dmitriy Bilozerchev (USSR)
      & Zsolt Borkai (Hun)
1989 Valentin Mogilnyi (USSR)
1991 Valeriy Belenkiy (USSR)
1993 Gil Su-pae (NKo)
1994 Marius Urzica (Rom)

Women's team
11 USSR   1954, 1958, 1962,
                1970, 1974, 1978,
                1981, 1983, 1985,
                1989, 1991
3   Czechoslovakia 1934, 1938,
                1966
3   Romania   1979, 1987, 1994
1   Sweden   1950

Women - combined exercises
1934 Vlasta Dekanová (Cs)
1938 Vlasta Dekanová (Cs)
1950 Helena Rakoczy (Pol)
1954 Galina Roudiko (USSR)
1958 Larisa Latynina (USSR)
1962 Larisa Latynina (USSR)
1966 Vera Cáslavská (Cs)
1970 Lyudmila Tourischeva
      (USSR)
1974 Lyudmila Tourischeva
      (USSR)
1978 Yelena Mukhina (USSR)
1979 Nelli Kim (USSR)
1981 Olga Bicherova (USSR)

1983 Natalya Yurchenko (USSR)
1985 Oksana Omelianchik (USSR)
      & Yelena Shushunova (USSR)
1987 Aurelia Dobre (Rom)
1989 Svetlana Boginskaya (USSR)
1991 Kim Zmeskal (USA)
1993-4 Shannon Miller (USA)

Women - parallel bars
1938 Vlasta Dekanová (Cs)

Women - horse vault
1938 Matylda Pálfyová (Cs) &
      Marta Majowska (Pol)
1950 Helena Rakoczy (Pol)
1954 Tamara Manina (USSR) &
      Anna Petersson (Swe)

1958 Larisa Latynina (USSR)
1962 Vera Cáslavská (Cs)
1966 Vera Cáslavská (Cs)
1970 Erika Zuchold (GDR)
1974 Olga Korbut (USSR)
1978 Nelli Kim (USSR)
1979 Dumitrata Turner (Rom)
1981 Maxi Gnauck (GDR)
1983 Boriana Stoyanova (Bul)
1985 Yelena Shushunova (USSR)
1987 Yelena Shushunova (USSR)
1989 Olessia Dudnik (USSR)
1991 Lavinia Milosovici (Rom)
1993 Yelena Piskun (Bls)
1994 Gina Gogean (Rom)

Shannon Miller – America's most successful gymnast

Women - balance beam

1938	Vlasta Dekanová (Cs)
1950	Helena Rakoczy (Pol)
1954	Keiko Tanaka (Jap)
1958	Larisa Latynina (USSR)
1962	Eva Bosáková (Cs)
1966	Natalya Kuchinskaya (USSR)
1970	Erika Zuchold (GDR)
1974	Lyudmila Tourischeva (USSR)
1978	Nadia Comaneci (Rom)
1979	Vera Cerna (Cs)
1981	Maxi Gnauck (GDR)
1983	Olga Mostepanova (USSR)
1985	Daniela Silivas (Rom)
1987	Aurelia Dobre (Rom)
1989	Daniela Silivas (Rom)
1991	Svetlana Boginskaya (USSR)
1993	Lavinia Milosovici (Rom)
1994	Shannon Miller (USA)

Women - floor exercises

1938	Matylda Pálfyová (Cs)
1950	Helena Rakoczy (Pol)
1954	Tamara Manina (USSR)
1958	Eva Bosáková (Cs)
1962	Larisa Latynina (USSR)
1966	Natalya Kuchinskaya (USSR)
1970	Lyudmila Tourischeva (USSR)
1974	Lyudmila Tourischeva (USSR)
1978	Nelli Kim (USSR) & Yelena Mukhina (USSR)
1979	Emilia Eberle (Rom)
1981	Natalya Ilyenko (USSR)
1983	Ecaterina Szabo (Rom)
1985	Oksana Omelianchik (USSR)
1987	Yelena Shushunova (USSR) & Daniela Silivas (Rom)
1989	Daniela Silivas (Rom) & Svetlana Boginskaya (USSR)
1991	Cristina Bontas (Rom) & Oksana Chusovitina (USSR)
1993	Shannon Miller (USA)
1994	Dina Kochetkova (Rus)

Women - asymmetrical bars

1950	Helena Rakoczy (Pol)
1954	Agnes Kaleti (Hun)
1958	Larisa Latynina (USSR)
1962	Irina Pervuschina (USSR)
1966	Natalya Kuchinskaya (USSR)
1970	Karin Janz (GDR)
1974	Annelore Zinke (GDR)
1978	Marcia Frederick (USA)
1979	Ma Yanhong (Chn) & Maxi Gnauck (GDR)
1981	Maxi Gnauck (GDR)
1983	Maxi Gnauck (GDR)
1985	Gabriela Fahnrich (GDR)
1987	Daniela Silivas (Rom) &

	Dörte Thümmler (GDR)
1989	Fan Di (Chn) & Daniela Silivas (Rom)
1991	Kim Gwang-suk (NKo)
1993	Shannon Miller (USA)
1994	Li Luo (Chn)

Most Individual Gold Medals, Olympics and World Championships

Men

11	Vitaliy Scherbo (Bls) 1992-4
10	Boris Shakhlin (USSR) 1956-64
9	Leon Stukelj (Yug) 1922-8
9	Akinori Nakayama (Jap) 1966-72
9	Nikolay Andrianov (USSR) 1972-80
9	Dmitriy Bilozerchev (USSR) 1983-8
7	Joseph Martinez (Fra) 1903-9
6	Eugen Mack (Swi) 1928-38
6	Yuriy Korolev (USSR) 1981-7
6	Vladimir Artemov (USSR) 1983-9

Women

12	Larisa Latynina (USSR) 1956-64
10	Vera Cáslavská (Cs) 1962-8
9	Daniela Silivas (Rom) 1985-9
6	Lyudmila Tourischeva (USSR) 1968-76
6	Nadia Comaneci (Rom) 1976-80
6	Nelli Kim (USSR) 1976-80
6	Maxi Gnauck (GDR) 1979-83

World Championships only

Most gold medals - individual

Men: 7 Dmitriy Bilozerchev; 6 Yuriy Korolev, Vitaliy Scherbo; 5 Eugen Mack, Akinori Nakayama, Aleksandr Ditiatin (USSR)
Women: 6 Daniela Silivas; 5 Larisa Latynina, Lyudmila Tourischeva, Shannon Miller (USA)

Most medals

Men: 12 Eizo Kenmotsu (Jap); 10 Akinori Nakayama, Boris Shakhlin, Nikolay Andrianov
Women: 9 Larisa Latynina, Lyudmila Tourischeva, Eva Bosáková (Cs)

World Individual Event Championships

Held for the first time in Paris in 1992.

Men's Winners

Floor exercises: Igor Korobchinskiy (Rus)
Horizontal Bar: Grigoriy Misutin (CIS)

Parallel bars: Li Jing (Chn) & Aleksey Voropayev (CIS)
Horse vault: Yu Ok-yul (SKo)
Rings: Vitaliy Scherbo (Bls)
Pommel horse: Gil Su-pae (NKo) & Vitaliy Shcherbo (Bls)

Women's winners

Horse vault: Henrietta Ónodi (Hun)
Balance beam: Kim Zmeskal (USA)
Floor exercises: Kim Zmeskal (USA)
Asymmetrical bars: Lavinia Milosevici (Rom)

World Cup

First held 1975.

Overall Champions

Men

1975	Nikolay Andrianov (USSR)
1977	Nikolay Andrianov (USSR) & Vladimir Markelov (USSR)
1978	Aleksandr Ditiatin (USSR)
1979	Aleksandr Ditiatin (USSR)
1982	Li Ning (Chn)
1986	Yuriy Korolev (USSR) & Li Ning (Chn)
1990	Valeriy Belenky (SU)

Women

1975	Lyudmila Tourischeva (USSR)
1977	Maria Filatova (USSR
1978	Maria Filatova (USSR)
1979	Stella Zakharova (USSR)
1982	Olga Bicherova (USSR) & Natalya Yurchenko (USSR)
1986	Yelena Shushunova (USSR)
1990	Tatyana Lisenko (USSR)

European Championships

First held 1955.

Men - overall champions

1955	Boris Shakhlin (USSR)
1957	Joachim Blume (Spa)
1959	Yuriy Titov (USSR)
1961	Miroslav Cerar (Yug)
1963	Miroslav Cerar (Yug)
1965	Franco Menichelli (Ita)
1967	Mikhail Voronin (USSR)
1969	Mikhail Voronin (USSR)
1971	Viktor Klimenko (USSR)
1973	Viktor Klimenko (USSR)
1975	Nikolay Andrianov (USSR)
1977	Vladimir Markelov (USSR)
1979	Stoyan Deltchev (Bul)
1981	Aleksandr Tkachev (USSR)
1983	Dmitriy Bilozerchev (USSR)
1985	Valeriy Lyukin (USSR)

1987 Valeriy Lyukin (USSR)
1989 Igor Korobchinskiy (USSR)
1990 Valentin Mogilnyi (USSR)
1992 Igor Korobchinskiy (Rus)
1994 Ivan Ivankov (Bul)

Women - overall champions
1957 Larisa Latynina (USSR)
1959 Natalie Kot (Pol)
1961 Larisa Latynina (USSR)
1963 Mirjana Bilic (Yug)
1965 Vera Cáslavská (Cs)
1967 Vera Cáslavská (Cs)
1969 Karin Janz (GDR)
1971 Lyudmila Tourischeva USSR) & Tamara Lazakovich (USSR)
1973 Lyudmila Tourischeva (USSR)
1975 Nadia Comaneci (Rom)
1977 Nadia Comaneci (Rom)
1979 Nadia Comaneci (Rom)
1981 Maxi Gnauck (GDR)
1983 Olga Bicherova (USSR)
1985 Yelena Shushunova (USSR)
1987 Daniela Silivas (Rom)

1989-90 Svetlana Boginskaya (USSR)
1992 Tatyana Gutsu (Ukr)
1994 Gina Gogean (Rom)

Rhythmic Gymnastics World Champions

Team winners:

8	Bulgaria	1969, 1971, 1981, 1983, 1985, 1987, 1989 (tie), 1993
6	USSR	1967, 1973, 1977, 1979, 1989 (tie), 1991
2	Russia	1992, 1994
1	Italy	1975

Individual overall winners
1963 Lyudmila Savinkova (USSR)
1965 Hana Micechová (Cs)
1967 Yelena Karpukhina (USSR)
1969 Maria Gigova (Bul)
1971 Maria Gigova (Bul)
1973 Maria Gigova (Bul) & Galina Shugarova (USSR)
1975 Carmen Rischer (FRG)
1977 Irina Deryugina (USSR)
1979 Irina Deryugina (USSR)

1981 Anelia Ralenkova (Bul)
1983 Diliana Georgieva (Bul)
1985 Diliana Georgieva (Bul)
1987 Bianka Panova (Bul) *
1989 Aleksandra Timoschenko (USSR)
1991 Oksana Skaldina (USSR)
1992 Oksana Kostina (Rus)
1993-4 Maria Petrova (Bul)

* *In 1987 Bianka Panova won all four disciplines, all with maximum scores, a unprecedented achievement.*
In 1991 Aleksandra Timoshenko also won all four individual titles, although she had been second to Skaldina in the preceding overall event.

Rhythmic Gymnastics World Cup

Individual overall winners
1983 Lilia Ignatova (Bul)
1986 Lilia Ignatova (Bul)
1990 Oksana Skaldina (USSR)

Team
1983 USSR
1986 Bulgaria
1990 USSR

Handball

The modern game, similar to association football, with hands substituted for feet, was first played in Germany around 1895. The first international match was played at Halle/Salle on 3 Sep 1925 when Austria beat Germany 6-3. Germany has long been a stronghold of the game, and it was introduced to the Olympic Games at Berlin in 1936 as an 11-a-side outdoor game. When reintroduced in 1972, again in Germany, at Munich, it was as an indoor 7-a-side game, and this version of the game has been predominant since 1952. The indoor court is 40m long by 20m wide; the goals are 2m high and 3m wide.

Prior to 1928 the International Amateur Athletic Federation looked after the interests of handball, but in that year the International Amateur Handball Federation (FIHA) was founded with Avery Brundage (USA), later the President of the IOC, as its first president. The current governing body, the International Handball Federation (IHF) was founded in 1946, replacing the FIHA. The growth of the game is demonstrated by the fact that the IHF comprised 133 member federations by 1994.

Olympic Games

Played outdoors at 11-a-side in 1936, indoors at 7-a-side from 1972 (men) and 1976 (women). *Winners:*

Men
1936 Germany
1972 Yugoslavia
1976 USSR
1980 GDR
1984 Yugoslavia
1988 USSR
1992 CIS

Women
1976 USSR
1980 USSR
1984 Yugoslavia
1988 South Korea
1992 South Korea

World Championships

First held outdoors in 1938 for men and 1949 for women. Men's nations are now divided into three groups A, B and C; and the women into A and B groups. *Winners:*

Men Outdoors
1938 Germany
1948 Sweden
1952 FR Germany
1955 FR Germany
1959 FR Germany/GDR
1963 GDR
1966 FR Germany

Men Indoors (A group)
1938 Germany
1954 Sweden
1958 Sweden
1961 Romania
1964 Romania

1967	Czechoslovakia
1970	Romania
1974	Romania
1978	FR Germany
1982	USSR
1986	Yugoslavia
1990	Sweden
1993	Russia
1995	France

Women Outdoors
1949	Hungary
1956	Romania
1960	Romania

Women Indoors (A)
1957	Czechoslovakia
1962	Romania
1965	Hungary
1971	GDR
1973	Yugoslavia
1975	GDR
1979	GDR
1982	USSR
1986	USSR
1990	USSR
1993	Germany

Oh Sung-ok of Olympic champions South Korea

European Cup

Contested by national champions. First held in 1957 (men), 1961 (women). *Winners:*

Men
1957	Stadtmannschaft Prague (Cs)
1959	RIK Göteborg (Swe)
1961-2	Frischauf Göppongen (FRG)
1963	Dukla Prague (Cs)
1965	Dinamo Bucharest (Rom)
1966	DHfK Leipzig (GDR)
1967	Vfl Gummersbach (FRG)
1968	Steaua Bucharest (Rom)
1970-1	Vfl Gummersbach (FRG)
1972	Partizan Bjelovar (Yug)
1973	MAI Moscow (USSR)
1974	Vfl Gummersbach (FRG)
1975	ASK Vorwärts Frankfurt/Oder (GDR)
1976	Borac Banjalukar (Yug)
1977	Steaua Bucharest (Rom)
1978	SC Magdeburg (GDR)
1979-80	TV Grosswallstadt (FRG)
1981	SC Magdeburg (GDR)
1982	Honved SE, Budapest (Hun)
1983	VfL Gummersbach (FRG)
1984	Dukla Prague (Cs)
1985-6	Metaloplastika Sabac (Yug)
1987	SKA Minsk (USSR)
1988	CSKA Moscow (USSR)
1989-90	SKA Minsk (USSR)
1991	FC Barcelona (Spa)
1992-3	RK/Badel Zagreb (Cro)
1994	TEKA Santander (Spa)
1995	Irun (Spa)

Most wins: 5 Vfl Gummersbach

Women
1961	Stiinta Bucharest (Rom)
1962	Spartak Prague (Cs)
1963	Trud Moscow (USSR)
1964	Rapid Bucharest (Rom)
1965	HG København (Den)
1966	SC Leipzig (GDR)
1967-8	Zalgiris Kaunas (USSR)
1970-3	Spartak Kiev (USSR)
1974	SC Leipzig (GDR)
1975	Spartak Kiev (USSR)
1976	Radnicki Belgrad (Yug)
1977	Spartak Kiev (USSR)
1978	TSC Berlin (GDR)
1979	Spartak Kiev (USSR)
1980	RK Radnicki Belgrad (Yug)
1981	Spartak Kiev (USSR)
1982	Vasas SC, Budapest (Hun)
1983	Spartak Kiev (USSR)
1984	Radnicki Belgrad (Yug)
1985-8	Spartak Kiev (USSR)
1989-90	Hypobank Sudstadt (Aut)
1991	TV Lützellinden (Ger)
1992-5	Hypobank Südstadt Wien (Aut) (Hypo Niederösterreich)

Most wins: 13 Spartak Kiev

European Cup Winners Cup

First held 1976 (men), 1977 (women). *Winners:*

Men
1976	Balonmano Granollers (Spa)
1977	MAI Moskva (USSR)
1978-9	VfL Gummersbach (FRG)
1980	Calpisa Alicante (Spa)
1981	TuS Nettelstedt (FRG)
1982	SC Empor Rostock (GDR)
1983	SKA Minsk (USSR)
1984-6	FC Barcelona (Spa)
1987	CSKA Moscow (USSR)

1988	SKA Minsk (USSR)
1989	Tusam Essen (FRG)
1990	Teka Santander (Spa)
1991	Bidasoa Irun (Spa)
1992	Bramac Veszpram (Hun)
1993	Olympique Marselle Vitrolles (Fra)
1994-5	FC Barcelona (Sap)

Most wins: 4 FC Barcelona

Women

1977	TSC Berlin (GDR)
1978	Ferencvarosi Budapest (Hun)
1979	TSC Berlin (GDR)
1980	Iskra Partizanske (Cs)
1981	Spartacus Budapest (Hun)
1982-3	RK Osiejek (Yug)
1984	Dalma Split (Yug)
1985	Budocnost Titograd (Yug)
1986	Radnicki Belgrad (Yug)
1987-8	Kuban Krasnodar (USSR)
1989	Stiinta Bacau (Rom)
1990	Rostelmach Rostov (USSR)
1991-2	Radnicki Belgrad (Yug)
1993	TV Lützellinden (Ger)
1994	TUS Walle Bremen (Ger)
1995	Dunsferr (Hun)

Most wins: 3 Kuban Krasnodar

IHF Cup

First held in the 1982. *Winners:*

Men

1982	Vfl Gummersbach (FRG)
1983	IL Saporozhye (USSR)
1984	TV Grosswallstadt (FRG)
1985	Minaur Baia Mare (Rom)
1986	Raba Vasas Etö Györ (Hun)
1987	Granitas Kaunas (USSR)
1988	Minaur Baia Mare (Rom)
1989	Türu Düsseldorf (FRG)
1990	Kuban Krasnodar (USSR)
1991	Borac Banja-Luka (Yug)
1992	SG Wallau-Massenheim (Ger)
1993	Teka Santander (Spa)
1994	Alzira Avidesa (Spa)
1995	Granollers (Spa)

Women

1982	IHK Tresnjevka, Zagreb (Yug)
1983	Automobilist Baku (USSR)
1984	Chimistul Vilcea (Rom)
1985	ASK Vorwärts Frankfurt/Oder (GDR)
1986	SC Leipzig (GDR)
1987	Budocnost Titograd (Yug)
1988	Egle Vilnius (USSR)
1989	Chimistul Vilcea (Rom)
1990	ASK Vorwärts Frankfurt (GDR)
1991	Lokomotive Zagreb (Yug)
1992	SC Leipzig (Ger)
1993	Rapid Bucuresti (Rom)
1994	HK Viborg (Den)
1995	Debrecen (Hun)

A unique achievement in winning all possible competitions in one year was when Vfl Gummersbach (FRG) in 1983 won the FRG national championship and cup, the European Champions Cup and the IHF Super Cup, contested by the winners of the two European Cup competitions.

Scoring record

Highest score in an international match: USSR beat Afghanistan 86-2 in the 'Friendly Army Tournament' at Miskolc, Hungary, August 1981.

Court Handball

Handball played against walls or in a court is a game of ancient Celtic origin. The game has been particularly prominent in Ireland and the USA, and the first ever international match was between the champions of these nations in 1887, when Phil Casey (USA) beat Bernard McQuade (Ire). In Ireland and Australia the court is 60 ft (18.3m) long and 30 ft (9.1m) wide, but a smaller court of 40 ft (12m) long and 20ft (6.1m) wide is used in North America.

The first US Championships under the suspices of the AAU were held in 1919 at four-wall singles and doubles. The United States Handball Association (USHA) was founded in 1951.

USHA Professional Championships

First held in 1951. *Recent four-wall winners:*

Pro singles

1989	Alfonso 'Poncho' Monreal
1990	Naty Alvarado
1991	John Bike
1992	Octavio Silveyra
1993	David Chapman
1994	Octavio Silveyra

Most wins: 11 Naty Alvarado 1977, 1979-80, 1982-7, 1990; 6 Jim Jacobs 1955-7, 1960, 1964-5; 6 Fred Lewis 1972, 1974-6, 1978, 1981

Open doubles

1989	Danny Bell and Charlie Kalil
1990	Doug Glatt and Rod Prince
1991	John Bike and Octavio Silveyra
1992-3	Naty Alvarado Jr & David Chapman
1994	John Bike and Octavio Silveyra

Most wins: 8 Marty Decatur 1962-3, 1965, 1967-8, 1975, 1978-9 (the first five with Jim Jacobs); 6 Jim Jacobs 1960, 1962-3, 1965, 1967-8; 5 John Sloan 1957-9, 1961, 1964

Hang Gliding

An elementary form of hang glider is reputed to have been used by the monk, Eilmer, to fly from the top of Malmesbury Abbey, Wiltshire. The first modern pioneer of hang gliding was Otto Lilienthal in Germany in the 1890s. Duration and distance records have increased substantially in recent years as pilots have utilised optimum conditions and improved designs.

World Championships

An unofficial world championship was held in 1975, won by David Cronk (USA),, and the first official championships the following year at Kössen in Austria. *Winners have been:*

Team Champions

1976	Austria
1979	France
1981	Great Britain
1983	Australia
1985	Great Britain
1988	Australia
1989	Great Britain
1991	Great Britain
1993	USA

Individual Champions

1976   Class I - Standard: Christian Steinbach (Aut)
        Class II - High Aspect Ratio: Terry Dolore (NZ)
        Class III - Open: Ken Battle (Aus)
1979   Class I - Weight Shift: Josef Guggenmos (FRG)
        Class II - Movable Surfaces: Rex Miller (USA)
1981   Class I - Weight Shift: Pepe Lopes (Bra)
        Class II - Movable Surfaces: Graeme Bird (NZ)
1983   Steve Moyes (Aus)
1985   John Pendry (UK)
1988   Rick Duncan (Aus)
1989   Robbie Whittall (UK)
1991   Tomás Schanek (Cs)
1993   Tomás Schanek (Cs)

Women's World Championships

Held separately, first in 1987. *Winners:*

Individual

1987	Judy Leden (UK)
1991	Judy Leden (UK)
1993	Françoise Dieuzeide (Fra)
1994	Annelise Müller (Swi)

Team

1987	UK
1991	France
1993-4	Switzerland

Records officially recognised by the FAI

(Category: Record, Pilot, Glider, Venue, Date)

Men - FAI Class1 - hang gliders with a rigid primary structure, controlled by weight shift

Straight line distance: 488.2 km Larry Tudor (USA), Hobbs, New Mexico to Elkart, Kansas, USA, 3 Jul 1990

Height gain 4340m Larry Tudor (USA), Horseshoe Meadows, USA, 4 Aug 1985

Distance via a single turn point: 412.6 km Mark Gibson (USA), Horseshoe Meadows, USA, 31 Jul 1992

Declared goal distance: 488.2 km Larry Tudor (USA), Hobbs, New Mexico to Elkart, Kansas, USA, 3 Jul 1990

Out and return distance: 310.3 km Geoffrey Loyns (UK) & Larry Tudor (USA), Horseshoe Meadows, USA, 26 Jun 1988

Distance over triangular course: 196.1 km James Lee (USA), Wild Horse Mesa, USA, 4 Jul 1991

Men - FAI Class 2 - hang gliders with a rigid primary structure, movable control surface

Straight line distance: 230.2 km William Woodruff (USA), Lone Pine, CA, USA 26 Jun 1993

Height gain: 3820m Rainer Scholl (FRG), Horseshoe Meadows, USA 5 Aug 1985

Women - FAI CLASS 1 - hang gliders with a rigid primary structure, controlled by weight shift

Straight line distance: 335.8 km Kari Castle (USA), Horseshoe Meadows, USA, 22 Jul 1991

Height gain: 3970m Judy Leden (UK), Karuman, South Africa, 1 Dec 1992

Distance via a single turn point: 292.1 km Kari Castle (USA), Hobbs, New Mexico, USA, 1 Jul 1990

Declared goal distance 212.5 km Liavan Mallin (Ire), Horseshoe Meadows, USA, 13 Jul 1989

Out and return distance: 132.0 km Tove Buas-Hansen (Nor), Gunter, USA, 6 Jul 1989

Distance over triangular course: 114.1 km Judy Leden (UK), Kössen, Austria, 22 Jun 1991

Paragliding Records FAI Class 3

Men

Straight line distance: 283.9 km Alex Louw (SAf), Kuruman, South Africa, 31 Dec 1993

Height gain: 4530m Rob Whittal (UK), Brandvlei, South Africa, 6 Jan 1993

Distance via a single turn point: 252.0 km Rob Whittal (UK), Kuruman, South Africa, 22 Jan 1993

Declared goal distance: 182.5 km Etsushi Matsuo & Masahiso Minegishi (Jap), Kuruman, South Africa, 28 Dec 1992

Distance over triangular course: 153.5 km Pierre Bouilloux (Fra), Chamonix, France, 30 Jun 1994

Women

Straight line distance: 128.5 km Judy Leden (UK), Vryburgn, South Africa, 9 Dec 1992

Height gain: 2970m Vrena Muhr (Ger), Bitterwasser Fram, Namibia, 13 Dec 1991

Distance via a single turn point: 129.1 km Judy Leden (UK), Vryburgn, South Africa, 9 Dec 1992.

Declared goal distance: 100.7 km Sarah Fenwick (UK), Piedrahita, Spain, 18 Jul 1994

Distance over triangular course: 50.3 km Judy Leden & Sarah Fenwick (UK), Piedrahita, Spain, 20 Jul 1994

Microlight Records

The Fédération Aéronautique Internationale recognise records for microlights in their class R (sub-divisions R1 landplanes, R2 seaplanes and R4 foot launched powered hang gliders), The following are the overall bests:

Altitude: R1 solo - 9720m Serge Zin (Fra), Saint Auban, France 18 Sep 1994

Distance in a straight line without landing: R1 solo - 1369.0 km Bernard d'Otreppe (Bel), Fréjus La Palud, France 6 Sep 1988

Distance over a closed circuit without landing: R1 solo - 1071.2 km Michel Serane (Fra), Besançon-Thise, France 5 Aug 1991

Speed over a straight 15/25 km course: R1 multiplace - 194.50 km/h Philippe Zen & Rodolphe de

Frayssinet (Fra), Belley-Peyrieu, France 1 Jun 1994
Speed over 50 km closed circuit without landing: R1 multiplace - 163.02 km/h Philippe Zen & Patrick Durand (Fra), Belley-Peyrieu, France 4 Jun 1994

Speed over 100km closed circuit without landing: R1 multiplace - 131.83 km/h Philippe Zen & Gilbert Huguet (Fra), Yenne, France 2 Jun 1994

Harness Racing

A form of racing in which the horses trot or pace while being driven in a light two-wheeled cart, the sulky. Pacers have a lateral gait, as they move their fore and hind legs in unison on one side and then the other, whereas trotters have a diagonal gait, in that their off fore and near hind legs are brought together in unison, followed by their near fore and off hind legs. Standardbred horses (which race up to a certain standard of speed) are raced as opposed to thoroughbreds in horse racing. Race tracks are of dirt surface, oval in shape, of a half-a-mile to a mile in circumference.

Trotting races were first held in the Netherlands in 1554, and the sulky first appeared in harness racing in 1829. The sport became very popular in the USA in the 19th century, and the National Trotting Association was founded, originally as the National Association for the Promotion of the Interests of the Trotting Turf in 1870. It brought needed controls to a sport that had been threatened by gambling corruption.

1 mile records

Trotting record: 1:51.0 *Pine Chip* (driver, John Campbell) at Lexington, Kentucky 1 Oct 1994
Trotting race record: 1:51.8 *Beat The Wheel* (driver, Cat Manzi) at Meadowlands, East Rutherford, NJ 7 Jul 1994
Pacing record: 1:48.4 *Matt's Scooter* (driver, Michel Lachance) at Lexington, Kentucky 23 Sep 1988
Pacing race record: 1:49.4 *Artsplace* (driver, Catello Manzi) at Meadowlands, East Rutherford, NJ 20 Aug 1992

The Hambletonian

The most famous race in North America is the Hambletonian Stakes, run annually for three-year-olds. It was first staged at Syracuse, New York in 1926; then at Syracuse, Lexington, and the New York tracks of Yonkers and Goshen, Du Quoin, Illinois 1956-80 and at Meadowlands, East Rutherford, NJ from 1981. Hambletonian, born in 1849, although only an ordinary racer, had a most notable influence on the breeding of American trotters. *Winners since 1970:*

Year	Horse	Driver
1970	Timothy T	John Simpson Jr.
1971	Speedy Crown	Howard Beissinger
1972	Super Bowl	Stanley Dancer
1973	Flirth	Ralph Baldwin
1974	Christopher T	Bill Haughton
1975	Bonefish	Stanley Dancer
1976	Steve Lobell	Bill Haughton
1977	Green Speed	Bill Haughton
1978	Speedy Somolli	Howard Beissinger
1979	Legend Hanover	George Sholty
1980	Burgomeister	Bill Haughton
1981	Shiaway St.Pat	Ray Remmen
1982	Speed Bowl	Tommy Haughton
1983	Duenna	Stanley Dancer
1984	Historic Freight	Ben Webster
1985	Prakas	Bill O'Donnell
1986	Nuclear Kosmos	Ulf Thoresen
1987	Mack Lobell	John Campbell
1988	Armbro Goal	John Campbell
1989	Park Avenue Joe Probe *(tied)*	Ron Wables Bill Fahy
1990	Harmonious	John Campbell
1991	Giant Victory	Jack Moiseyev
1992	Alf Palema	Mickey McNichol
1993	American Winner	Ron Pierce
1994	Victory Dream	Mike LaChance

Race record: 1:53 $^1/_5$ American Winner 1993
The prize purse first passed $100,000 with $117,118 in 1953, when the winner was Helicopter; $200,000 in 1975 when it was $232,192; $500,000 in 1981 when it was $838,000 and the million dollars in 1983 at $1,080,000. A record $1,380,000 was paid in 1992.

The Little Brown Jug

Pacing's three-year-old classic has been held annually at Delaware, Ohio from 1946. The name honours a great 19th century pacer. *Winners from 1970:*

Year	Horse	Driver
1970	Most Happy Fella	Stanley Dancer
1971	Nansemond	Herve Filion
1972	Strike Out	Keith Waples
1973	Melvin's Woe	Joe O'Brien
1974	Ambro Omaha	Bill Haughton
1975	Seatrain	Ben Webster
1976	Keystone Ore	Stanley Dancer
1977	Governor Skipper	John Chapman
1978	Happy Escort	Bill Popfinger
1979	Hot Hitter	Herve Filion
1980	Niatross	Clint Galbraith
1981	Fan Hanover (filly)	Glen Garnsey
1982	Merger	John Campbell
1983	Ralph Hanover	Ron Waples
1984	Colt Forty Six	Chris Boring
1985	Nihilator	Bill O'Donnell
1986	Barbery Spur	Bill O'Donnell
1987	Jaguar Spur	Dick Stillings
1988	B.J.Scoot	Bill Fahey
1989	Goalie Jeff	Michel Lachance
1990	Beach Towel	Ray Remmen
1991	Precious Bunny	Jack Moiseyev
1992	Fake Left	Ron Waples
1993	Life Sign	John Campbell
1994	Magical Mike	Michel Lachance

Race record: 1:52 Life Sign 1993

Leading Drivers

Most wins in a year
Progressive record
210 Robert G Farrington 1961
312 Robert G Farrington 1964

407 Herve Filion 1968
486 Herve Filion 1970
543 Herve Filion 1971
605 Herve Filion 1972
637 Herve Filion 1974
770 Michel Lachance 1986
798 Herve Filion 1988
814 Herve Filion 1989
843 Walter Case Jr 1992

The all-time money-winning drivers to 17 May 1995

Driver	Winnings	Races (with position on all-time list)
John Campbell	$130,945,655	6853 (4)
Herve Filion	$84,503,370	14,685 (1)
Bill O'Donnell	$82,408,600	5031 (20)
Michel Lachance	$78,071,314	7175 (2)
Ron Waples	$60,475,351	6046 (9)
Jack Moiseyev	$53,166,052	6222 (8)
Catello Manzi	$52,431,265	6453 (7)
Douglas Brown	$51,956,987	6003 (10)
Carmine Abbatiello	£49,817,572	7137 (3)
Dave Magee	$46,131,042	6750 (5)

In top ten by races won
Walter Case Jr $24,765,382   6481 (6)

The first driver to win $1 million in a year was Stanley Dancer, $1,051,538 in 1964; $2 million was passed by Herve Filion with $2,473,265 in 1972 and $10 million in 1985.

Top money-winning drivers from 1980

1980	John Campbell	$3,732,306
1981	Bill O'Donnell	$4,065,608
1982	Bill O'Donnell	$5,755,067
1983	John Campbell	$6,104,082
1984	Bill O'Donnell	$9,059,184
1985	Bill O'Donnell	$10,207,372
1986	John Campbell	$9,515,055
1987	John Campbell	$10,186,495
1988	John Campbell	$11,148,565
1989	John Campbell	$9,738,450
1990	John Campbell	$11,620,878
1991	Jack Moiseyev	$9,568,468
1992	John Campbell	$8,202,108
1993	John Campbell	$9,926,482
1994	John Campbell	$9,834,139

Most years as leading money-winning driver from 1948

12 Bill Haughton 1952-9, 1963, 1965, 1967-8
11 John Campbell 1979-80, 1983, 1986-90, 1992-4
7 Herve Filion 1970-4, 1976-7

Top money-winning horses
Top money winning trotter in the USA:
$4,907,307 Peace Corps 1988-93 (over $5.7 million in all)
Top money winning pacers in the USA:
$3,225,653 Nihilator 1984-5
The first to win $1 million in a year and current record:
Pacer: Niatross $1,414,313 in 1980, first over $2m:

Beach Towel $2,091,860 in 1990; record: $2,264,714 Cam's Card Shark 1994
Trotter: Joie De Vie $1,007,705 in 1983, record $1,878,798 Mack Lobell in 1987
The largest ever purse was $2,161,000 for the Woodrow Wilson two-year-old race for pacers at Meadowlands, New Jersey on 16 Aug 1984. The winner, Nihilator, driven by Bill O'Donnell, earned a record $1,080,500.

Harness Horse of the Year

Chosen annually by the US Trotting Association and the US Harness Writers Association: *Most wins:*
3 Bret Hanover 1964-6, Nevele Pride 1967-9; 2 Scott Frost 1955-6, Adios Butler 1960-1, Albatross 1971-2, Niatross 1980-1, Cam Fella 1982-3, Mack Lobell 1987-8.
Recent winners: 1989 Matt's Scooter, 1990 Beach Towel, 1991 Precious Bunny, 1992 Artsplace, 1993, Staying Together, 1994 Cam's Card Shark

Australian Harness Racing

The Inter-Dominion Championship
The first trotting race in Australia was at Parramatta in 1810. The most important race in the Southern Hemisphere is the Inter-Dominion Championship, first held in 1936. Held annually at various venues in Australia and New Zealand. Run at varying distances between 1.5 and 2 miles (2414-3218m).
Winners from 1970 (shown in brackets is the Australian state or New Zealand ownership):

Year	Horse	Driver
1970	Bold David (Vic)	Alf Simons
1971	Stella Frost (NZ)	Dinny Townley
1972	Welcome Advice (NSW)	Alan Harpley
1973	Hondo Grattan (NSW)	Tony Turnbull
1974	Hondo Grattan (NSW)	Tony Turnbull
1975	Young Quinn (NZ)	John Langdon
1976	Carclew (SA)	Chris Lewis
1977	Stanley Rio (NZ)	John Noble
1978	Markovina (SA)	Bruce Gath
1979	Rondel (NZ)	Peter Wolfenden
1980	Koala King (NSW)	Brian Hancock
1981	San Simeon (WA)	Lyle Austin
1982	Rhett's Law (WA)	Colin Warwick
1983	Gammalite (Vic)	Bill Clarke
1984	Gammalite (Vic)	Bill Clarke
1985	Preux Chevalier (WA)	Barry Perkins
1986	Village Kid (WA)	Chris Lewis
1987	Lightning Blue (Vic)	Jim O'Sullivan
1988	Our Maestro (Qld)	Brian Hancock
1989	Jodie's Babe (Vic)	Scott Stewart
1990	Thorate (Tas)	Howard Wilson
1991	Mark Hanover (NZ)	Mark Purdon
1992	Westburn Grant (NSW)	Vic Frost
1993	Jack Morris (Vic)	Rod Chambers
1994	Weona Warrior (NSW)	Brian Hancock

Most wins: 2 Captain Sandy (NZ) 1950, 1953; Hondo Grattan 1973-4; Gammalite 1983-4
Race record: 1:55.6 mile rate for 2100m by Village Kid in 1986.

Records
Drivers - most wins in a season: 203 Andrew Peace 1988/9
Top money-winning horse: Village Kid (WA) $2,117,870 in 1984-94
Highest stakewinner in a season: Westburn Grant (NSW) $631,355 1991/2
Most wins in a season: 34 Cane Smoke (Qld) 1985/6
Most wins in a career: 119 Cane Smoke (Qld) 1981-90

Hockey

Stick and ball games date back some 4000 years, with modern hockey, which is played by teams of 11-a-side, becoming established in the 19th century. The sport's first governing body was an English Hockey Association, formed in London in 1875. The current English men's governing body, the Hockey Association was founded in 1886 and the All-England Women's Hockey Association in 1895, a year after the Irish Ladies' Hockey Union.

The current international governing body, the Fédération Internationale de Hockey (FIH) was formed in 1924. A separate body governed women's hockey until both men's and women's games were united under the auspices of the FIH in 1982. In 1994 there were 120 member federations of the FIH

The sport was long dominated by India and Pakistan, who won every Olympic tournament from 1928 to 1968. From then, however, success has been more widespread, with the amazing result at the 1986 World Cup of India and Pakistan in 11th and 12th places.

Olympic Games

Men's winners

England	1908, 1920
India	1928, 1932, 1936, 1948, 1952, 1956, 1964, 1980
Pakistan	1960, 1968, 1984
Germany	1972 (FRG), 1992
New Zealand	1976
Great Britain	1988

Highest score: India beat USA 24-1 at Los Angeles 1932
Most gold medals: six Indian players have won three gold medals: Richard Allen 1928-36, Dhyan Chand 1928-36, Randhir Singh Gentle 1948-56, Leslie Claudius 1948-56, Ranganandan Francis 1948-56, Udham Singh 1952-64. Claudius and Udham Singh also won silver medals in 1960.

Women's winners

1980 Zimbabwe	1988 Australia
1984 Netherlands	1992 Spain

FIH World Cup

First contested in 1971 for men, 1974 for women. Now held every four years. *Winners:*

Men

Pakistan	1971, 1978, 1982, 1994
Netherlands	1973, 1990
India	1975
Australia	1986

Women

Netherlands	1974, 1978, 1983, 1986, 1990
FR Germany	1976, 1981
Australia	1994

World Championships

Twice organised by the International Federation of Women's Hockey Association (IFWHA). The IFWHA merged with the FIH in 1983. *Winners:*

1975 England	1979 Netherlands

Champions' Trophy

First held in Lahore, Pakistan in 1978, the leading six men's teams contest this trophy annually. *Winners:*

1978	Pakistan
1980	Pakistan
1981-2	Netherlands
1983-5	Australia
1986-8	FR Germany
1989-90	Australia
1991	Germany
1993	Australia
1994	Pakistan

Women's Champions' Trophy

First contested in 1987. *Winners:*

1987	Netherlands
1989	South Korea
1991	Australia
1993	Australia

European Championships

Contested by national teams at four-yearly intervals. First contested for men in 1970, and for women in 1984. *Winners:*

Men

1970	FR Germany
1974	Spain
1978	FR Germany
1983	Netherlands
1987	Netherlands
1991	Germany

Women

1984	Netherlands
1987	Netherlands
1991	England
1995	Netherlands

European Cup for Club Champions

First held unofficially in 1969 and 1970 and officially from 1971. *Winners:*

Men

1969-70	Club Egara de Tarrasa (Spa)
1971-5	SC Frankfurt 1880 (FRG)
1976-8	Southgate (Eng)
1979	Klein Zwitserland (Hol)
1980	Slough (Eng)
1981	Klein Zwitserland (Hol)

1982-3	Dynamo Alma-Ata (USSR)
1984	TG 1846 Frankenthal (FRG)
1985	Atletico Tarrasa (Spa)
1986	Kampong, Utrecht (Hol)
1987	Bloemendaal (Hol)
1988-95	Uhlenhorst Mülheim (FRG/Ger)

Women

1974	Harvestehuder Hamburg (FRG)
1976-82	Amsterdam (Hol)
1983-7	HGC Wassenaar (Hol)
1988-90	Amsterdam (Hol)
1991	HGC Wassenaar (Hol)
1992	Amsterdam (Hol)
1993	Rüsselsheimer RK (Ger)
1994	HGC Wassenaar (Hol)
1995	SV Kampong (Hol)

European Cup Winners Cup

Men's event first held in 1990. Contested by winners of national cup competitions, or, if none held, league runners-up. Women's event first held in 1991. *Winners*

Men

1990	Hounslow (UK)
1991	Kampong (Hol)
1992-3	HGC Wassenaar (Hol)
1994	Atletico Tarrasa (Spa)
1995	Harvestehuder Hamburg (Ger)

Women

1991	Rhythm Grodno (SU)
1992	Sutton Coldfield (UK)
1993	HGC Wassenaar (Hol)
1994	Bayer Leverkusen (Ger)
1995	Rüsselsheimer RK (Ger)

European Indoor Cup

First contested in 1974, the men's event has been won every time contested by Germany (FRG) 1974, 1976, 1980, 1984, 1988, 1991, 1994.

Similarly the women's cup has also only been won by Germany: 1974, 1977, 1981, 1985, 1987, 1990 and 1993.

English National Club Champions

Winners of the knock-out competition for the Hockey Association Cup. From 1993 sponsored by the Royal Bank of Scotland. *Winners:*

1972-3	Hounslow
1974-5	Southgate
1976	Nottingham
1977	Slough
1978	Guildford
1979-81	Slough
1982	Southgate
1983	Neston
1984	East Grinstead
1985-8	Southgate
1989	Hounslow
1990	Havant
1991-3	Hounslow
1994	Teddington
1995	Guildford

English National Inter-League

First held in 1975, and contested by the winners of all the major English leagues. For the Poundstretcher League Cup from 1989. *Winners:*

1975	Bedfordshire Eagles
1976	Slough
1977-8	Southgate
1979	Isca
1980-3	Slough
1984	Neston
1985-6	East Grinstead
1987	Slough
1988	Southgate
1989	Hounslow
1990	Havant
1991	Hounslow
1992	Harleston

National League

1993	Hounslow
1994	Havant
1995	Teddington

National Women's Club Champions

From 1992 for the AEWHA Cup.

1977-8	Chelsea CPE
1979	Chelmsford
1980	Norton
1981	Sutton Coldfield
1982-3	Slough
1984	Sheffield
1985	Ipswich
1986	Slough
1987-9	Ealing
1990-1	Sutton Coldfield
1992	Hightown
1993	Leicester
1994	Slough
1995	Hightown

National Women's League

Sponsored by Typhoo, and inaugurated in 1989/90. *Winners:*

1990-2	Slough
1993	Ipswich
1994	Leicester

County Championships

Men

First held in 1957/8 season. Moved to December in 1985 and 1986, so those winners are shown as the following year (i.e. second half of the season). *Wins:*

8	Middlesex	1959, 1961, 1977, 1981, 1988-91
4	Kent	1964-5, 1975, 1979
4	Wiltshire	1967-8, 1970, 1972
3	Hertfordshire	1960, 1974, 1976
3	Surrey	1963, 1973, 1986
3	Lancashire	1969, 1978, 1983
3	Staffordshire	1971, 1993-4
3	Yorkshire	1984, 1992, 1995
2	Worcestershire	1985, 1987

2　Buckinghamshire　1980, 1982
1　Lincolnshire 1958, Durham 1962, Cheshire 1966

Women

First held in 1968/9 season (*tied*). Moved from December to the end of season in May from 1992, so no 1991 winner. *Wins:*

13　Lancashire　1969*, 1970, 1971*, 1973-4, 1976-7, 1979, 1985, 1989-90, 1992-3
3　Hertfordshire　1969*, 1971*, 1978
3　Leicestershire　1975*, 1980*, 1983
2　Suffolk　1980*, 1982
2　Staffordshire　1981, 1987
2　Middlesex　1984, 1986
2　Kent　1987-8
1　Essex 1972, Surrey 1975*, Yorkshire 1994

Horse Racing

The Ancient Egyptians are believed to have participated in horse racing more than 3000 years ago, and the sport certainly formed part of the ancient Olympic Games. Smithfield, in London, staged the first regular race meetings in the 12th century and Britain's oldest race course, on the Roodee at Chester, staged its first meeting on 9 February 1540. The Jockey Club was formed in 1750, and in 1752 the earliest recorded steeplechase took place in Co. Cork, Ireland.

The English Classics

Five races run from April to September each year for three-year-olds.

1000 Guineas

The first classic of the English season, for fillies only, carrying 9 stone. Raced over 1 mile at Newmarket and was first run in 1814. Sponsored by General Accident 1984-92, Madagans 1993-4. *Post-war winners:*

Year	Winnner	Jockey
1946	Hypericum	Doug Smith
1947	Imprudence	Rae Johnstone
1948	Queenpot	Gordon Richards
1949	Musidora	Edgar Britt
1950	Camaree	Rae Johnstone
1951	Belle of All	Gordon Richards
1952	Zabara	Ken Gethin
1953	Happy Laughter	Manny Mercer
1954	Festoon	Scobie Breasley
1955	Meld	Harry Carr
1956	Honeylight	Edgar Britt
1957	Rose Royal II	Charlie Smirke
1958	Bella Paola	Serge Boullenger
1959	Petite Etoile	Doug Smith
1960	Never Too Late	Roger Poincelet
1961	Sweet Solera	Bill Rickaby
1962	Abermaid	Bill Williamson
1963	Hula Dancer	Roger Poincelet
1964	Pourparler	Garnie Bougoure
1965	Night Off	Bill Williamson
1966	Glad Rags	Paul Cook

1967	Fleet	George Moore
1968	Caergwrle	Sandy Barclay
1969	Full Dress II	Ron Hutchinson
1970	Humble Duty	Lester Piggott
1971	Altesse Royale	Yves Saint-Martin
1972	Waterloo	Eddie Hide
1973	Mysterious	Geoff Lewis
1974	Highclere	Joe Mercer
1975	Nocturnal Spree	Johnny Roe
1976	Flying Water	Yves Saint-Martin
1977	Mrs McArdy	Eddie Hide
1978	Enstone Spark	Ernie Johnson
1979	One in a Million	Joe Mercer
1980	Quick As Lightning	Brian Rouse
1981	Fairy Footsteps	Lester Piggott
1982	On The House	John Reid
1983	Ma Biche	Freddie Head
1984	Pebbles	Philip Robinson
1985	Oh So Sharp	Steve Cauthen
1986	Midway Lady	Ray Cochrane
1987	Miesque	Freddie Head
1988	Ravinella	Gary Moore
1989	Musical Bliss	Walter Swinburn
1990	Salsabil	Willie Carson
1991	Shadayid	Willie Carson
1992	Hatoof	Walter Swinburn
1993	Sayyedati	Walter Swinburn
1994	Las Meninas	Jimmy Reid
1995	Harayir	Richard Hills

Most wins - Jockey:
7 George Fordham - 1859 Mayonaise, 1861 Nemesis, 1865 Siberia, 1868 Formosa, 1869 Scottish Queen, 1881 Thebais, 1883 Hauteur
6 Frank Buckle - 1818 Corinne, 1820 Rowena, 1821 Zeal, 1822 Whizgig, 1823 Zinc, 1827 Arab
5 Jem Robinson - 1824 Cobweb, 1828 Zoe, 1830 Charlotte West, 1841 Potentia, 1844 Sorella
5 John Barnham Day - 1826 Problem, 1834 May-day, 1836 Destiny, 1837 Chapeau d'Espagne, 1840 Crucifix

Most wins - Trainer: 9 Robert Robson - 1818 Corinne, 1819 Catgut, 1820 Rowena, 1821 Zeal, 1822 Whizgig, 1823 Zinc, 1825 Tontine, 1826 Problem, 1827 Arab

Most wins - Owner: 8 4th Duke of Grafton - 1819 Catgut, 1820 Rowena, 1821 Zeal, 1822 Whizgig, 1823 Zinc, 1825 Tontine, 1826 Problem, 1827 Arab

Fastest time: 1min 36.85sec Oh So Sharp 1985

Biggest winning margin: 20 lengths Mayonaise 1859

2000 Guineas

First run at Newmarket in 1809, it is the other early-season classic. Run over 1 mile; colts carry 9st, and fillies (rarely entered) 8st 9lb. Seven fillies have won the race, the last Garden Path in 1944. Sponsored by General Accident 1984-92, Madagans 1993-4. *Post-war winners:*

Year	Winnner	Jockey
1946	Happy Knight	Tommy Weston
1947	Tudor Minstrel	Gordon Richards
1948	My Babu	Charlie Smirke

A great battle between Pennekamp (left) and Celtic Swing in the 2000 Guineas at Newmarket in 1995

Year	Horse	Jockey
1949	Nimbus	Charlie Elliott
1950	Palestine	Charlie Smirke
1951	Ki Ming	Scobie Breasley
1952	Thunderhead II	Roger Poincelet
1953	Nearula	Edgar Britt
1954	Darius	Manny Mercer
1955	Our Babu	Doug Smith
1956	Gilles de Retz	Frank Barlow
1957	Crepello	Lester Piggott
1958	Pall Mall	Doug Smith
1959	Taboun	George Moore
1960	Martial	Ron Hutchinson
1961	Rockavon	Norman Stirk
1962	Privy Councillor	Bill Rickaby
1963	Only For Life	Jimmy Lindley
1964	Baldric II	Bill Pyers
1965	Niksar	Duncan Keith
1966	Kashmir II	Jimmy Lindley
1967	Royal Palace	George Moore
1968	Sir Ivor	Lester Piggott
1969	Right Tack	Geoff Lewis
1970	Nijinsky	Lester Piggott
1971	Brigadier Gerard	Joe Mercer
1972	High Top	Willie Carson
1973	Mon Fils	Frankie Durr
1974	Nonoalco	Yves Saint-Martin
1975	Bolkonski	Gianfranco Dettori
1976	Wollow	Gianfranco Dettori
1977	Nebbiolo	Gabriel Curran
1978	Roland Gardens	Frankie Durr
1979	Tap On Wood	Steve Cauthen
1980	Known Fact	Willie Carson
1981	To-Agori-Mou	Greville Starkey
1982	Zino	Freddie Head
1983	Lomond	Pat Eddery
1984	El Gran Senor	Pat Eddery
1985	Shadeed	Lester Piggott
1986	Dancing Brave	Greville Starkey
1987	Don't Forget Me	Willie Carson
1988	Doyoun	Walter Swinburn
1989	Nashwan	Willie Carson
1990	Tirol	Michael Kinane
1991	Mystiko	Michael Roberts
1992	Rodrigo de Triano	Lester Piggott
1993	Zafonic	Pat Eddery
1994	Mister Baileys	Jason Weaver
1995	Pennekamp	Thierry Jarnet

Most wins - Jockey:

9 Jem Robinson - 1825 Enamel, 1828 Cadland, 1831 Riddlesworth, 1833 Clearwell, 1834 Glencoe, 1835 Ibrahim, 1836 Bay Middleton, 1847 Conyngham, 1848 Flatchatcher

6 John Osborne 1857 Vedette, 1869 Pretender, 1871 Bothwell, 1872 Prince Charlie, 1875 Camballo, 1888 Ayrshire

5 Frank Buckle - 1810 Hephestion, 1820 Pindarrie, 1821 Reginald, 1822 Pastille, 1827 Turcoman

5 Charlie Elliott - 1923 Ellangowan, 1928 Flamingo, 1940 Djebel, 1941 Lambert Simnel, 1949 Nimbus

5 Lester Piggott - 1957, 1968, 1970, 1985, 1992
Most wins - Trainer: 7 John Scott 1842 Meteor, 1843 Cotherstone, 1849 Nunnykirk, 1853 West Australian, 1856 Fazzoletto, 1860 The Wizard, 1862 The Marquis
Most wins - Owner:
5 4th Duke of Grafton - 1820 Pindarrie, 1821 Reginald, 1822 Pastille, 1826 Dervise, 1827 Turcoman;
5 5th Earl of Jersey 1831 Riddlesworth, 1834 Glencoe, 1835 Ibrahim, 1836 Bay Middleton, 1837 Achmet
Fastest time: 1min 35.08sec Mister Baileys 1994
Biggest winning margin: 8 lengths Tudor Minstrel 1947

The Derby

The greatest of the Classics is raced each June over 1 mile 4 furlongs at Epsom Downs, except for 1915-8 and 1940-5, when the race was run at Newmarket. Since 1984 it has been sponsored by Ever Ready. Colts carry 9st, and fillies, if entered 8st 9lb. *Winners - fillies shown by #:*

Year	Winner	Jockey
1780	Diomed	Sam Arnull
1781	Young Eclipse	Charles Hindley
1782	Assassin	Sam Arnull
1783	Saltram	Charles Hindley
1784	Sergeant	John Arnull
1785	Aimwell	Charles Hindley
1786	Noble	J White
1787	Sir Peter Teazle	Sam Arnull
1788	Sir Thomas	William South
1789	Skyscraper	Sam Chifney, snr
1790	Rhadamanthus	John Arnull
1791	Eager	Matt Stephenson
1792	John Bull	Frank Buckle
1793	Waxy	Bill Clift
1794	Daedalus	Frank Buckle
1795	Spread Eagle	Anthony Wheatley
1796	Didelot	John Arnull
1797	(unamed colt)	John Singleton
1798	Sir Harry	Sam Arnull
1799	Archduke	John Arnull
1800	Champion	Bill Clift
1801	Eleanor #	John Saunders
1802	Tyrant	Frank Buckle
1803	Ditto	Bill Clift
1804	Hannibal	Bill Arnull
1805	Cardinal Beaufort	Denni Fitzpatrick
1806	Paris	John Shepherd
1807	Election	John Arnull
1808	Pan	Frank Collinson
1809	Pope	Tom Goodison
1810	Whalebone	Bill Clift
1811	Phantom	Frank Buckle
1812	Octavius	Bill Arnull
1813	Smolensko	Tom Goodison
1814	Blucher	Bill Arnull
1815	Whisker	Tom Goodison
1816	Prince Leopold	Will Wheatley
1817	Azor	Jem Robinson
1818	Sam	Sam Chifney, jnr
1819	Tiresias	Bill Clift
1820	Sailor	Sam Chifney, jnr
1821	Gustavus	Sam Day
1822	Moses	Tom Goodison
1823	Emilius	Frank Buckle
1824	Cedric	Jem Robinson
1825	Middleton	Jem Robinson
1826	Lapdog	George Dockeray
1827	Mameluke	Jem Robinson
1828	Cadland	Jem Robinson
1829	Frederick	John Forth
1830	Priam	Sam Day
1831	Spaniel	Will Wheatley
1832	St.Giles	Bill Scott
1833	Dangerous	Jem Chapple
1834	Plenipotentiary	Patrick Conolly
1835	Mundig	Bill Scott
1836	Bay Middleton	Jem Robinson
1837	Phosphorus	George Edwards
1838	Amato	Jim Chapple
1839	Bloomsbury	Sim Templeman
1840	Little Wonder	William MacDonald
1841	Coronation	Patrick Conolly
1842	Attila	Bill Scott
1843	Cotherstone	Bill Scott
1844	Orlando	Nat Flatman
1845	The Merry Monarch	Foster Bell
1846	Pyrrhus the First	Sam Day
1847	Cossack	Sim Templeman
1848	Surplice	Sim Templeman
1849	The Flying Dutchman	Charlie Marlow
1850	Voltigeur	Job Marson
1851	Teddington	Job Marson
1852	Daniel O'Rourke	Frank Butler
1853	West Australian	Frank Butler
1854	Andover	Alfred Day
1855	Wild Dayrell	Robert Sherwood
1856	Ellington	Tom Aldcroft
1857	Blink Bonny #	Jack Charlton
1858	Beadsman	John Wells
1859	Musjid	John Wells
1860	Thormanby	Harry Custance
1861	Kettledrum	Ralph Bullock
1862	Caractacus	John Parsons
1863	Macaroni	Tom Challoner
1864	Blair Athol	Jim Snowden
1865	Gladiateur	Harry Grimshaw
1866	Lord Lyon	Harry Custance
1867	Hermit	John Daley
1868	Blue Gown	John Wells
1869	Pretender	John Osborne
1870	Kingcraft	Tom French
1871	Favonius	Tom French
1872	Cremorne	Charlie Maidment
1873	Doncaster	Fred Webb
1874	Gearge Frederick	Harry Custance
1875	Galopin	Jack Morris
1876	Kisber	Charlie Maidment
1877	Silvio	Fred Archer
1878	Sefton	Harry Constable
1879	Sir Bevys	George Fordham

Year	Horse	Jockey
1880	Bend Or	Fred Archer
1881	Iroquois	Fred Archer
1882	Shotover #	Tom Cannon
1883	St.Blaise	Charlie Wood
1884	St.Gatien	Charlie Wood
	Harvester (dead-heat)	Sam Loates
1885	Melton	Fred Archer
1886	Ormonde	Fred Archer
1887	Merry Hampton	Jack Watts
1888	Ayrshire	Fred Barrett
1889	Donovan	Tommy Loates
1890	Sainfoin	Jack Watts
1891	Common	George Barrett
1892	Sir Hugo	Fred Allsopp
1893	Isinglass	Tommy Loates
1894	Ladas	Jack Watts
1895	Sir Visto	Sam Loates
1896	Persimmon	Jack Watts
1897	Galtee More	Charlie Wood
1898	Jeddah	Otto Madden
1899	Flying Fox	Morny Cannon
1900	Diamond Jubilee	Herbert Jones
1901	Volodyovski	Lester Reiff
1902	Ard Patrick	Skeets Martin
1903	Rock Sand	Danny Maher
1904	St.Amant	Kempton Cannon
1905	Cicero	Danny Maher
1906	Spearmint	Danny Maher
1907	Orby	Johnny Reiff
1908	Signorinetta #	Billy Bullock
1909	Minoru	Herbert Jones
1910	Lemberg	Bernard Dillon
1911	Sunstar	George Stern
1912	Tagalie #	Johnny Reiff
1913	Aboyeur	Edwin Piper
1914	Durbar II	Matt MacGee
1915	Pommern	Steve Donoghue
1916	Fifinella #	Joe Childs
1917	Gay Crusader	Steve Donaghue
1918	Gainsborough	Joe Childs
1919	Grand Parade	Fred Templeman
1920	Spion Kop	Frank O'Neill
1921	Humorist	Steve Donoghue
1922	Captain Cuttle	Steve Donoghue
1923	Papyrus	Steve Donoghue
1924	Sansovino	Tommy Weston
1925	Manna	Steve Donoghue
1926	Coronach	Joe Childs
1927	Call Boy	Charlie Elliott
1928	Fellstead	Harry Wragg
1929	Trigo	Joe Marshall
1930	Blenheim	Harry Wragg
1931	Cameronian	Freddie Fox
1932	April the Fifth	Fred Lane
1933	Hyperion	Tommy Weston
1934	Windsor Lad	Charlie Smirke
1935	Bahram	Freddie Fox
1936	Mahmoud	Charlie Smirke
1937	Mid-day Sun	Michael Beary
1938	Bois Roussel	Charlie Elliott
1939	Blue Peter	Eph Smith
1940	Pont l'Eveque	Sam Wragg
1941	Owen Tudor	Billy Nevett
1942	Watling Street	Harry Wragg
1943	Straight Deal	Tommy Carey
1944	Ocean Swell	Billy Nevett
1945	Dante	Billy Nevett
1946	Airborne	Tommy Lowrey
1947	Pearl Diver	George Bridgland
1948	My Love	Rae Johnstone
1949	Nimbus	Charlie Elliott
1950	Galcador	Rae Johnstone
1951	Arctic Prince	Charlie Spares
1952	Tulyar	Charlie Smirke
1953	Pinza	Gordon Richards
1954	Never Say Die	Lester Piggott
1955	Phil Drake	Freddie Palmer
1956	Lavandin	Rae Johnstone
1957	Crepello	Lester Piggott
1958	Hard Ridden	Charlie Smirke
1959	Parthia	Harry Carr
1960	St.Paddy	Lester Piggott
1961	Psidium	Roger Poincelet
1962	Larkspur	Neville Sellwood
1963	Relko	Yves Saint-Martin
1964	Santa Claus	Scobie Breasley
1965	Sea Bird II	Pat Glennon
1966	Charlottown	Scobie Breasley
1967	Royal Palace	George Moore
1968	Sir Ivor	Lester Piggott
1969	Blakeney	Ernie Johnson
1970	Nijinsky	Lester Piggott
1971	Mill Reef	Geoff Lewis
1972	Roberto	Lester Piggott
1973	Morston	Eddie Hide
1974	Snow Knight	Brian Taylor
1975	Grundy	Pat Eddery
1976	Empery	Lester Piggott
1977	The Minstrel	Lester Piggott
1978	Shirley Heights	Greville Starkey
1979	Troy	Willie Carson
1980	Henbit	Willie Carson
1981	Shergar	Walter Swinburn
1982	Golden Fleece	Pat Eddery
1983	Teenoso	Lester Piggott
1984	Secreto	Christy Roche
1985	Slip Anchor	Steve Cauthen
1986	Shahrastani	Walter Swinburn
1987	Reference Point	Steve Cauthen
1988	Kahyasi	Ray Cochrane
1989	Nashwan	Willie Carson
1990	Quest For Fame	Pat Eddery
1991	Generous	Alan Munro
1992	Dr Devious	John Reid
1993	Commander In Chief	Michael Kinane
1994	Erhaab	Willie Carson
1995	Lammtarra	Walter Swinburn

Most wins - Jockey:
9 Lester Piggott; 6 Jem Robinson, Steve Donoghue; 5 John Arnull, Bill Clift, Frank Buckle, Fred Archer; 4 Sam Arnull, Tom Goodison, Bill Scott, Jack Watts, Charlie Smirke, Willie Carson

Most wins - Trainer: 7 Robert Robson 1793, 1802, 1809-10, 1815, 1817, 1823; John Porter 1868, 1882-3, 1886, 1890-1, 1899; Fred Darling 1922, 1925-6, 1931, 1938, 1940-1

Most wins - Owner:

5 3rd Earl of Egremont 1782, 1804, 1806-7, 1826

5 HH Aga Khan III 1930, 1935-6, 1948 (half-share), 1952

4 John Bowes 1835, 1843, 1852-3; Sir Joseph Hawley 1851, 1858-9, 1868

4 1st Duke of Westminster 1880, 1882, 1886, 1899

4 Sir Victor Sassoon 1953, 1957-8, 1960

Fastest time: 2min 32.31 Lammtarra 1995

Biggest winning margin: 10 lengths Shergar 1981

The Oaks

Raced at Epsom, over 1 mile 4 furlongs for fillies only, all of whom carry 9st. It was raced at Newmarket during both World Wars. From 1984-92 the race was sponsored by Gold Seal, from 1993 by Energizer. Named after the Epsom home of the 12th Earl of Derby, the first race was in 1779. *Post-war winners:*

Year	Winnner	Jockey
1946	Steady Aim	Harry Wragg
1947	Imprudence	Rae Johnstone
1948	Masaka	Billy Nevett
1949	Musidora	Edgar Britt
1950	Asmena	Rae Johnstone
1951	Neasham Belle	Stan Clayton
1952	Frieze	Edgar Britt
1953	Ambiguity	Joe Mercer
1954	Sun Cap	Rae Johnstone
1955	Meld	Harry Carr
1956	Sicarelle	Freddie Palmer
1957	Carrozza	Lester Piggott
1958	Bella Paola	Max Garcia
1959	Petite Etoile	Lester Piggott
1960	Never Too Late	Roger Poincelet
1961	Sweet Solera	Bill Rickaby
1962	Monade	Yves Saint-Martin
1963	Noblesse	Garnie Bougoure
1964	Homeward Bound	Greville Starkey
1965	Long Look	Jack Purtell
1966	Valoris	Lester Piggott
1967	Pia	Eddie Hide
1968	La Lagune	Gérard Thiboeuf
1969	Sleeping Partner	John Gorton
1970	Lupe	Sandy Barclay
1971	Altesse Royale	Geoff Lewis
1972	Ginevra	Tony Murray
1973	Mysterious	Geoff Lewis
1974	Polygamy	Pat Eddery
1975	Juliette Marny	Lester Piggott
1976	Pawneese	Yves Saint-Martin
1977	Dunfermline	Willie Carson
1978	Fair Salinia	Greville Starkey
1979	Scintillate	Pat Eddery
1980	Bireme	Willie Carson
1981	Blue Wind	Lester Piggott
1982	Time Charter	Billy Newnes
1983	Sun Princess	Willie Carson
1984	Circus Plume	Lester Piggott
1985	Oh So Sharp	Steve Cauthen
1986	Midway Lady	Ray Cochrane
1987	Unite	Walter Swinburn
1988	Diminuendo	Steve Cauthen
1989*	Snow Bride	Steve Cauthen
1990	Salsabil	Willie Carson
1991	Jet Ski Lady	Christy Roche
1992	User Friendly	George Duffield
1993	Intrepidity	Michael Roberts
1994	Ballanchine	Frankie Dettori
1995	Moonshell	Frankie Dettori

* *Aliysa ridden by Walter Swinburn won the race, but on 20 Nov 1990 it was announced that he had been disqualified due to the presence of camphor in a post-race urine test.*

Most wins - Jockey:

9 Frank Buckle - 1797 Niké, 1798 Bellisimma, 1799 Bellina, 1802 Scotia, 1803 Theophania, 1805 Meteora, 1817 Neva, 1818 Corinne, 1823 Zinc

6 Frank Butler - 1843 Poison, 1844 The Princess, 1849 Lady Evelyn, 1850 Rhedycina, 1851 Irish, 1852 Songstress

6 Lester Piggott - as above

Most wins - Trainer: 12 Robert Robson - 1802 Scotia, 1804 Pelisse, 1805 Meteora, 1807 Briseïis, 1808 Morel, 1809 Maid of Orleans, 1813 Music, 1815 Minuet, 1818 Corinne, 1822 Pastille, 1823 Zinc, 1825 Wings

Most wins - Owner: 6 4th Duke of Grafton 1813 Music, 1815 Minuet, 1822 Pastille, 1823 Zinc, 1828 Turquoise, 1831 Oxygen

Fastest time: 2min 34.19sec Intrepidity 1993

Biggest winning margin: 12 lengths Sun Princess 1983

St Leger

The oldest of the five Classics it was first held in 1776. It is run over a distance of 1 mile 6 furlongs 132 yards at Doncaster. Both colts and fillies enter; colts carry 9st, filles 8st 11lb. During the First World War the race was held at Newmarket (1915-8) and during the Second World War at Thirsk (1940), Manchester (1941), Newmarket (1942- 4), and York (1945). Sponsored by Holsten Pils 1984-8, Coalite 1991-3, Teleconnection 1994. Because of damage to the Doncaster track the 1989 race was moved to Ayr, the first time an English classic had been held in Scotland. *Post-war winners:*

Year	Winner	Jockey
1946	Airborne	Tommy Lowrey
1947	Sayajirao	Edgar Britt
1948	Black Tarquin	Edgar Britt
1949	Ridge Wood	Michael Beary
1950	Scratch II	Rae Johnstone
1951	Talma II	Rae Johnstone
1952	Tulyar	Charlie Smirke
1953	Premonition	Eph Smith
1954	Never Say Die	Charlie Smirke
1955	Meld *	Harry Carr
1956	Cambremer	Freddie Palmer
1957	Ballymoss	Tommy Burns
1958	Alcide	Harry Carr
1959	Cantelo *	Eddie Hide
1960	St.Paddy	Lester Piggott
1961	Aurelius	Lester Piggott

1962	Hethersett	Harry Carr
1963	Ragusa	Garnie Bougoure
1964	Indiana	Jimmy Lindley
1965	Provoke	Joe Mercer
1966	Sodium	Frankie Durr
1967	Ribocco	Lester Piggott
1968	Ribero	Lester Piggott
1969	Intermezzo	Ron Hutchinson
1970	Nijinsky	Lester Piggott
1971	Athens Wood	Lester Piggott
1972	Boucher	Lester Piggott
1973	Peleid	Frankie Durr
1974	Bustino	Joe Mercer
1975	Bruni	Tony Murray
1976	Crow	Yves Saint-Martin
1977	Dunfermline *	Willie Carson
1978	Julio Mariner	Eddie Hide
1979	Son of Love	Alain Lequeux
1980	Light Cavalry	Joe Mercer
1981	Cut Above	Joe Mercer
1982	Touching Wood	Paul Cook
1983	Sun Princess *	Willie Carson
1984	Commanche Run	Lester Piggott
1985	Oh So Sharp *	Steve Cauthen
1986	Moon Madness	Pat Eddery
1987	Reference Point	Steve Cauthen
1988	Minster Son	Willie Carson
1989	Michelozzo	Steve Cauthen
1990	Snurge	Richard Quinn
1991	Toulon	Pat Eddery
1992	User Friendly *	George Duffield
1993	Bob's Return	Philip Robinson
1994	Moonax	Pat Eddery

* fillies

Most wins - Jockey:
9 Bill Scott - 1821 Jack Spigot, 1825 Memnon, 1828 The Colonel, 1829 Rowton, 1838 Don John, 1839 Charles the Twelfth, 1840 Launcelot, 1841 Satirist, 1846 Sir Tatton Sykes

8 John Jackson -1791 Young Traveller, 1794 Beningbrough, 1796 Ambrosia, 1798 Symmetry, 1805 Staveley, 1813 Altisidora, 1815 Filho da Puta, 1822 Theodore

8 Lester Piggott, as above

Most wins - Trainer: 16 John Scott 1827 Matilda, 1828 The Colonel, 1829 Rowton, 1832 Margrave, 1834 Touchstone, 1838 Don John, 1839 Charles the Twelfth, 1840 Launcelot, 1841 Satirist, 1845 The Baron, 1851 Newminster, 1853 West Australian, 1856 Warlock, 1857 Imperieuse, 1859 Gamester, 1862 The Marquis

Most wins - Owner: 7 9th Duke of Hamilton 1786 Paragon, 1787 Spadille, 1788 Young Flora, 1792 Tartar, 1808 Petronius, 1809 Ashton, 1814 William

Fastest time: 3min 1.6sec Coronach 1926, Windsor Lad 1934

Biggest winning margin: 12 lengths Never Say Die 1954

Leading Jockeys at the five Classics

	Total	Derby	Oaks	2000	1000	Leger	Years
Lester Piggott	30	9	6	5	2	8	1954-92
Frank Buckle	27	5	9	5	6	2	1792-1827
Jem Robinson	24	6	2	9	5	2	1817-48
Fred Archer	21	5	4	4	2	6	1874-86
Bill Scott	19	4	3	3	-	9	1821-46
Jack Watts	19	4	4	2	4	5	1883-97
Willie Carson	17	4	4	4	2	3	1972-94
John Barham Day	16	-	5	4	5	2	1826-41
George Fordham	16	1	5	3	7	-	1859-83
Joe Childs	15	3	4	2	2	4	1912-33
Frank Butler	14	2	6	2	2	2	1843-53
Steve Donoghue	14	6	2	3	1	2	1915-37
Charlie Elliott	14	3	2	5	4	-	1923-49
Gordon Richards	14	1	2	3	3	5	1930-53

Leading Trainers at the five Classics

John Scott	40	5	8	7	4	16	1827-63
Robert Robson	34	7	12	6	9	-	1793-1827
Mat Dawson	28	6	5	5	6	6	1853-95
John Porter	23	7	3	5	2	6	1868-1900
Alec Taylor	21	3	8	4	1	5	1905-27
Fred Darling	19	7	2	5	2	3	1916-47
Noel Murless	19	3	5	2	6	3	1948-73

Leading Owners at the five Classics

4th Duke of Grafton	20	1	6	5	8	-	1813-31
17th Earl of Derby	20	3	2	2	7	6	1910-45
HH Aga Khan III	17	5	2	3	1	6	1924-57
6th Viscount Falmouth	16	2	4	3	4	3	1862-83

Triple Crown

The English Triple Crown of 2000 Guineas, Derby and St.Leger has been won by:

West Australian 1853, Gladiateur 1865, Lord Lyon 1866, Ormonde 1866, Common 1891, Isinglass 1893, Galtee More 1897, Flying Fox 1899, Diamond Jubilee 1900, Rock Sand 1903, Pommern 1915, Gay Crusader 1917, Gainsborough 1918, Bahram 1935, Nijinsky 1970.

The following horses have won the Fillies Triple Crown - 1000 Guineas, Oaks and St.Leger: Hannah 1871, Apology 1874, La Fléche 1892, Pretty Polly 1904, Sun Chariot 1942, Meld 1955, Oh So Sharp 1985

Four classics, all except the Derby, were won by: Formosa 1868 and Sceptre 1902.

Group One Races in England

Pattern racing was introduced into Europe in 1971, with the major races classified into Groups 1, 2 and 3. The following are the leading Group One races, with winners - horses and jockeys (mostly from 1970).

Top Irish jockey Michael Kinane

Coronation Cup

Raced at Epsom each year, the day after the Derby. It is run over 1 mile 4 furlongs. First run 1902 to cleverate the Cornation of King Edward VII. Raced at Newbury 1915-6, Newmarket 1941, 1943-5. Now sponsored by Hanson Trust, using their Ever Ready brand name from 1993.

1970	Caliban	Sandy Barclay
1971	Lupe	Geoff Lewis
1972	Mill Reef	Geoff Lewis
1973	Roberto	Lester Piggott
1974	Buoy	Joe Mercer
1975	Bustino	Joe Mercer
1976	Quiet Fling	Lester Piggott
1977	Exceller	Gérard Dubroeucq
1978	Crow	Pat Eddery
1979	Ile de Bourbon	John Reid
1980	Sea Chimes	Lester Piggott
1981	Master Willie	Phillip Waldron
1982	Easter Sun	Bruce Raymond
1983	Be My Native	Lester Piggott
1984	Time Charter	Steve Cauthen
1985	Rainbow Quest	Pat Eddery
1986	Saint Estephe	Pat Eddery
1987	Triptych	Tony Cruz
1988	Triptych	Steve Cauthen
1989	Sherriff's Star	Ray Cochrane
1990	In The Wings	Cash Asmussen
1991	In The Groove	Steve Cauthen
1992	Saddler's Hall	Walter Swinburn
1993	Opera House	Michael Roberts
1994	Apple Tree	Thierry Jarnet
1995	Sunshack	Pat Eddery

Most wins: 2 Pretty Polly 1905-6, The White Knight 1907-8, Petite Etoile 1960-1, Triptych 1987-8

St James's Palace Stakes

For 3-year-olds at the Royal Ascot meeting over 1 mile; first run in 1834.

1970	Saintly Song	Sandy Barclay
1971	Brigadier Gerard	Joe Mercer
1972	Sun Prince	Jimmy Lindley
1973	Thatch	Lester Piggott
1974	Averof	Brian Taylor
1975	Bolkonski	Gianfranco Dettori
1976	Radetzky	Pat Eddery
1977	Don	Eddie Hide
1978	Jaazeiro	Lester Piggott
1979	Kris	Joe Mercer
1980	Posse	Pat Eddery
1981	To-Agori-Mou	Greville Starkey
1982	Dara Monarch	Michael Kinane
1983	Horage	Steve Cauthen
1984	Chief Singer	Ray Cochrane
1985	Bairn	Lester Piggott
1986	Sure Blade	Brent Thomson
1987	Half A Year	Ray Cochrane
1988	Persian Heights	Pat Eddery
1989	Shaadi	Walter Swinburn
1990	Shavian	Steve Cauthen
1991	Marju	Willie Carson
1992	Brief Truce	Michael Kinane
1993	Kingmambo	Cash Asmussen
1994	Grand Lodge	Michael Kinane
1995	Bahri	Willie Carson

Coronation Stakes

For 3-year-old fillies at the Royal Ascot meeting over 1 mile; first run in 1840, celebrating, a little belatedly, the coronation of Queen Victoria in 1837.

1970	Humble Duty	Duncan Keith
1971	Magic Flute	Geoff Lewis
1972	Calve	Lester Piggott
1973	Jacinth	John Gorton
1974	Lisadell	Lester Piggott
1975	Roussalka	Lester Piggott
1976	Kesar Queen	Yves Saint-Martin
1977	Orchestration	Pat Eddery
1978	Sutton Place	Walter Swinburn

1979	One in a Million	Joe Mercer
1980	Cairn Rouge	Tony Murray
1981	Tolmi	Eddie Hide
1982	Chalon	Lester Piggott
1983	Flame of Tara	Declan Gillespie
1984	Katies	Philip Robinson
1985	Al Bahathri	Tony Murray
1986	Sonic Lady	Walter Swinburn
1987	Milligram	Walter Swinburn
1988	Magic of Life	Pat Eddery
1989	Golden Opinion	Cash Asmussen
1990	Chimes of Freedom	Steve Cauthen
1991	Kooyonga	Warren O'Connor
1992	Marling	Walter Swinburn
1993	Gold Splash	Gerald Mosse
1994	Kissing Cousin	Michael Kinane
1995	Ridgewood Pearl	John Murtagh

Ascot Gold Cup

The highlight of the Royal Ascot meeting, the Gold Cup has been contested since 1807. It is the premier long distance race on the flat, run over 2 miles 4 furlongs. Between 1845-53 it was run as the Emperor's Plate in honour of the Tsar of Russia. Held at Newmarket in 1917-8 (as the Newmarket Gold Cup), and in 1941-4.

1970	Precipice Wood	Jimmy Lindley
1971	Random Shot	Geoff Lewis
1972	Erimo Hawk	Pat Eddery
1973	Lassalle	Jimmy Lindley
1974	Ragstone	Ron Hutchinson
1975	Sagaro	Lester Piggott
1976	Sagaro	Lester Piggott
1977	Sagaro	Lester Piggott
1978	Shangamuzo	Greville Starkey
1979	Le Moss	Lester Piggott
1980	Le Moss	Joe Mercer
1981	Ardross	Lester Piggott
1982	Ardross	Lester Piggott
1983	Little Wolf	Willie Carson
1984	Gildoran	Steve Cauthen
1985	Gildoran	Brent Thomson
1986	Longboat	Willie Carson
1987	Paean	Steve Cauthen
1988	Sadeem	Greville Starkey
1989	Sadeem	Willie Carson
1990	Ashal	Richard Hills
1991	Indian Queen	Walter Swinburn
1992	Drum Taps	Frankie Dettori
1993	Drum Taps	Frankie Dettori
1994	Arcadian Heights	Michael Hills
1995	Double Trigger	Jason Weaver

Most wins: 3 Sagaro

Eclipse Stakes

Named after the great horse Eclipse and first run in 1886. Raced over 1 mile 2 furlongs at Sandown Park each July. Run at Ascot 1946, Kempton Park 1973. Sponsored by Benson & Hedges 1974-5, Coral since then.

1970	Connaught	Sandy Barclay
1971	Mill Reef	Geoff Lewis
1972	Brigadier Gerard	Joe Mercer

1973	Scottish Rifle	Ron Hutchinson
1974	Coup de Feu	Pat Eddery
1975	Star Appeal	Greville Starkey
1976	Wollow	Franco Dettori
1977	Artaius	Lester Piggott
1978	Gunner B	Joe Mercer
1979	Dickens Hill	Tony Murray
1980	Ela-Mana-Mou	Willie Carson
1981	Master Willie	Phillip Waldron
1982	Kalaglow	Greville Starkey
1983	Solford	Pat Eddery
1984	Sadlers Wells	Pat Eddery
1985	Pebbles	Steve Cauthen
1986	Dancing Brave	Greville Starkey
1987-8	Mtoto	Michael Roberts
1989	Nashwan	Willie Carson
1990	Elmaamul	Willie Carson
1991	Environment Friend	George Duffield
1992	Kooyonga	Warren O'Connor
1993	Opera House	Michael Kinane
1994	Ezzoud	Walter Swinburn
1995	Halling	Walter Swinburn

Most wins: 2 Buchan 1919-20, Polyphontes 1924-5, Mtoto, as above

July Cup

Run at Newmarket over 6 furlongs. First run 1876. Sponsored by William Hill 1978-86, Norcros 1987-8, Carroll Foundation 1989-94.

1970	Huntercombe	Sandy Barclay
1971	Realm	Brian Taylor
1972	Parsimony	Ron Hutchinson
1973	Thatch	Lester Piggott
1974	Saritamer	Lester Piggott
1975	Lianger	Yves Saint-Martin
1976	Lochnager	Eddie Hide
1977	Gentilhombre	Paul Cook
1978	Solinus	Lester Piggott
1979	Thatching	Lester Piggott
1980	Moorestyle	Lester Piggott
1981	Marwell	Walter Swinburn
1982	Sharpo	Pat Eddery
1983	Habibti	Willie Carson
1984	Chief Singer	Ray Cochrane
1985	Never So Bold	Steve Cauthen
1986	Green Desert	Walter Swinburn
1987	Ajdal	Walter Swinburn
1988	Soviet Star	Cash Asmussen
1989	Cadeaux Genereux	Paul Eddery
1990	Royal Academy	John Reid
1991	Polish Patriot	Ray Cochrane
1992	Mr Brooks	Lester Piggott
1993	Hamas	Willie Carson
1994	Owington	Paul Eddery
1995	Lake Coniston	Pat Eddery

Most wins: 3 Sundridge 1902-4

King George VI & Queen Elizabeth II Diamond Stakes

First run in 1951 as the King George VI & Queen Elizabeth Festival of Britain Stakes. It became the King George VI & Queen Elizabeth Stakes in 1952 and the word 'Diamond' was added in 1975. Raced over 1 mile 4 furlongs at Ascot, it is one of the leading weight-for-age races in Europe.

1951	Supreme Court	Charlie Elliott
1952	Tulyar	Charlie Smirke
1953	Pinza	Gordon Richards
1954	Aureole	Eph Smith
1955	Vimy	Roger Poincelet
1956	Ribot	Enrico Camici
1957	Montaval	Freddie Palmer
1958	Ballymoss	Scobie Breasley
1959	Alcide	Willie Carr
1960	Aggressor	Jimmy Lindley
1961	Right Royal V	Roger Poincelet
1962	Match III	Yves Saint-Martin
1963	Ragusa	Georges Bougoure
1964	Nasram II	Bill Pyers
1965	Meadow Court	Lester Piggott
1966	Aunt Edith	Lester Piggott
1967	Busted	George Moore
1968	Royal Palace	Sandy Barclay
1969	Park Top	Lester Piggott
1970	Nijinsky	Lester Piggott
1971	Mill Reef	Geoff Lewis
1972	Brigadier Gerard	Joe Mercer
1973	Dahlia	Bill Pyers
1974	Dahlia	Lester Piggott
1975	Grundy	Pat Eddery
1976	Pawneese	Yves Saint-Martin
1977	The Minstrel	Lester Piggott
1978	Ile de Bourbon	John Reid
1979	Troy	Willie Carson
1980	Ela-Mana-Mou	Willie Carson
1981	Shergar	Walter Swinburn
1982	Kalaglow	Greville Starkey
1983	Time Charter	Joe Mercer
1984	Teenoso	Lester Piggott
1985	Petoski	Willie Carson
1986	Dancing Brave	Pat Eddery
1987	Reference Point	Steve Cauthen
1988	Mtoto	Michael Roberts
1989	Nashwan	Willie Carson
1990	Belmez	Michael Kinane
1991	Generous	Alan Munro
1992	St Jovite	Stephen Craine
1993	Opera House	Michael Roberts
1994	King's Theatre	Michael Kinane
1995	Lammtarra	Frankie Dettori

Most wins: 2 Dahlia

Sussex Stakes

Raced over 1 mile at Goodwood. Sponsored from 1985 by the Swettenham Stud (headed by Robert Sangster). First run in 1841 as a race for 2-year-olds over 6 furlongs. For 3-year-olds 1878-59, 3 & 4-year-olds 1960-74, 3-year-old upwards since 1975.

1970	Humble Duty	Duncan Keith
1971	Brigadier Gerard	Joe Mercer
1972	Sallust	Joe Mercer
1973	Thatch	Lester Piggott
1974	Aces of Aces	Jimmy Lindley
1975	Bolkonski	Franco Dettori
1976	Wollow	Franco Dettori
1977	Artaius	Lester Piggott
1978	Jaazeiro	Lester Piggott
1979	Kris	Joe Mercer
1980	Posse	Pat Eddery
1981	King's Lake	Pat Eddery
1982	On The House	John Reid
1983	Noalcoholic	George Duffield
1984	Chief Singer	Ray Cochrane
1985	Rousillon	Greville Starkey
1986	Sonic Lady	Walter Swinburn
1987	Soviet Star	Greville Starkey
1988	Warning	Pat Eddery
1989	Zilzal	Walter Swinburn
1990	Distant Relative	Willie Carson
1991	Second Set	Frankie Dettori
1992	Marling	Pat Eddery
1993	Bigstone	Dominic Boeuf
1994	Distant View	Pat Eddery
1995	Sayyedati	Brett Doyle

Juddmonte International Stakes

Inaugurated in 1972, known as the Benson & Hedges Gold Cup until 1985, the Matchmaker International 1986-7, and International Stakes in 1988. The principal race of the three-day August meeting at York, it is run over 1 mile 2 furlongs.

1972	Roberto	Braulio Baeza
1973	Moulton	Geoff Lewis
1974	Dahlia	Lester Piggott
1975	Dahlia	Lester Piggott
1976	Wollow	Franco Dettori
1977	Relkino	Willie Carson
1978	Hawaiian Sound	Lester Piggott
1979	Troy	Willie Carson
1980	Master Willie	Phillip Waldron
1981	Beldale Flutter	Pat Eddery
1982	Assert	Pat Eddery
1983	Caerleon	Pat Eddery
1984	Cormorant Wood	Steve Cauthen
1985	Commanche Run	Lester Piggott
1986	Shardari	Walter Swinburn
1987	Triptych	Steve Cauthen
1988	Persian Heights	Pat Eddery
1989	Ile de Chypre	Tony Clark
1990	In The Groove	Steve Cauthen
1991	Terimon	Michael Roberts
1992	Rodrigo de Triano	Lester Piggott
1993-4	Ezzoud	Walter Swinburn

Yorkshire Oaks

Held at York over 1 mile 4 furlongs. First run in 1849. For 3-year-old fillies, but from 1994 also older horses. Now sponsored by Aston Upthorpe.

1970	Lupe	Sandy Barclay
1971	Fleet Wahine	Geoff Lewis

1972	Attica Meli	Geoff Lewis
1973	Mysterious	Geoff Lewis
1974	Dibidale	Willie Carson
1975	May Hill	Pat Eddery
1976	Sarah Siddons	Christy Roche
1977	Busaca	Pat Eddery
1978	Fair Salinia	Greville Starkey
1979	Connaught Bridge	Joe Mercer
1980	Shoot A Line	Lester Piggott
1981	Condessa	Declan Gillespie
1982	Awaasif	Lester Piggott
1983	Sun Princess	Willie Carson
1984	Circus Plume	Willie Carson
1985	Sally Brown	Walter Swinburn
1986	Untold	Greville Starkey
1987	Bint Pasha	Richard Quinn
1988	Diminuendo	Steve Cauthen
1989	Roseate Tern	Willie Carson
1990	Hellenic	Willie Carson
1991	Magnificent Star	Tony Cruz
1992	User Friendly	George Duffield
1993	Only Royale	Ray Cochrane
1994	Only Royale	Frankie Dettori

Nunthorpe Stakes

Run over 5 furlongs at York for 2-year-olds and up. First run 1903, run at Newmarket 1942-4, and as the William Hill Sprint Championship 1976-89. Now the Keeneland Nunthorpe Stakes.

1970	Huntercombe	Sandy Barclay
1971	Swing Easy	Lester Piggott
1972	Deep Diver	Bill Williamson
1973	Sandford Lad	Tony Murray
1974	Blue Cashmere	Eddie Hide
1975	Bay Express	Willie Carson
1976	Lochnager	Eddie Hide
1977	Haveroid	Eddie Hide
1978	Solinus	Lester Piggott
1979	Ahonoora	Greville Starkey
1980-2	Sharpo	Pat Eddery
1983	Habibti	Willie Carson
1984	Committed	Brent Thomson
1985	Never So Bold	Steve Cauthen
1986	Last Tycoon	Yves Saint-Martin
1987	Ajdal	Walter Swinburn
1988	Handsome Sailor	Michael Hills
1989	Cadeaux Genereaux	Pat Eddery
1990	Dayjur	Willie Carson
1991	Sheikh Albadou	Pat Eddery
1992	Lyric Fantasy	Michael Roberts
1993	Lochsong	Frankie Dettori
1994	Piccolo	Jimmy Reid

Haydock Park Sprint Cup

Run over 6 furlongs at Haydock Park for 2-year-olds and up. First run 1966 as the Vernons November Sprint Cup. Vernons Sprint Cup 1968-88, Ladbroke Sprint Cup 1989-91. Sponsored by Hazlewood Foods 1993. Group One since 1988.

1988	Dowsing	Pat Eddery
1989	Danehill	Pat Eddery
1990	Dayjur	Willie Carson
1991	Polar Falcon	Cash Asmussen

1992	Sheikh Albadou	Bruce Raymond
1993	Wolfhound	Michael Roberts
1994	Lavinia Fontana	Jason Weaver

Fillies Mile

Run over 1 mile by fillies at Ascot in September. First run 1973 as the Green Shield Stakes, with various sponsors since.

1990	Shamshir	Frankie Dettori
1991	Culture Vulture	Tommy Quinn
1992	Ivanka	Michael Roberts
1993	Fairy Heights	Cash Asmussen
1994	Aqaarid	Willie Carson

Queen Elizabeth II Stakes

Raced over 1 mile at Ascot. First run 1955, Group 2 pre1987.

1987	Milligram	Pat Eddery
1988	Warning	Pat Eddery
1989	Zilzal	Walter Swinburn
1990	Markofdistinction	Frankie Dettori
1991	Selkirk	Ray Cochrane
1992	Lahib	Willie Carson
1993	Bigstone	Pat Eddery
1994	Maroof	Richard Hills

Cheveley Park Stakes

Run over the last 6 furlongs of the Bunbury Mile at Newmarket by 2-year-old fillies. First run in 1870. Sponsored by William Hill 1973-83, Tattersalls from 1985, Shadwell Stud from 1993.

1970	Magic Flute	Sandy Barclay
1971	Waterloo	Eddie Hide
1972	Jacinth	John Gorton
1973	Gentle Thoughts	Bill Pyers
1974	Cry Of Truth	John Gorton
1975	Pasty	Pat Eddery
1976	Durtal	Lester Piggott
1977	Sookera	Walter Swinburn
1978	Devon Ditty	Greville Starkey
1979	Mrs Penny	John Matthias
1980	Marwell	Lester Piggott
1981	Woodstream	Pat Eddery
1982	Ma Biche	Freddie Head
1983	Desirable	Steve Cauthen
1984	Park Appeal	Declan Gillespie
1985	Embla	Angel Cordero
1986	Minstrella	John Reid
1987	Ravinella	Gary Moore
1988	Pass the Peace	Richard Quinn
1989	Dead Certain	Cash Asmussen
1990	Capricciosa	John Reid
1991	Marling	Walter Swinburn
1992	Sayyedati	Walter Swinburn
1993	Prophecy	Pat Eddery
1994	Gay Gallanta	Pat Eddery

Middle Park Stakes

A 6-furlong sprint for 2-year-olds run at Newmarket. First run in 1866 as the Middle Park Plate. Became Middle Park Stakes 1922. 1940 race at Nottingham. Tattersalls sponsors 1986-9, Newgate Stud from 1990.

1970	Brigadier Gerard	Joe Mercer
1971	Sharpen Up	Willie Carson

1972	Tudenham	Jimmy Lindley
1973	Habat	Pat Eddery
1974	Steel Heart	Lester Piggott
1975	Hittite Glory	Frankie Durr
1976	Tachypous	Geoff Lewis
1977	Formidable	Pat Eddery
1978	Junius	Lester Piggott
1979	Known Fact	Willie Carson
1980	Mattaboy	Lester Piggott
1981	Cajun	Lester Piggott
1982	Diesis	Lester Piggott
1983	Creag-an-Sgor	Steve Cauthen
1984	Bassenthwaite	Pat Eddery
1985	Stalker	Joe Mercer
1986	Mister Majestic	Ray Cochrane
1987	Gallic League	Steve Cauthen
1988	Mon Tresor	Michael Roberts
1989	Balla Cove	Steve Cauthen
1990	Lycius	Cash Asmussen
1991	Rodrigo de Triano	Willie Carson
1992	Zieten	Steve Cauthen
1993	First Trump	Michael Hills
1994	Fard	Willie Carson

Champion Stakes

Run at Newmarket over 1 mile 2 furlongs. First run in 1877. Dubai Champion Stakes from 1982.

1970	Lorenzaccio	Geoff Lewis
1971	Brigadier Gerard	Joe Mercer
1972	Brigadier Gerard	Joe Mercer
1973	Hurry Harriet	Jean Cruguet
1974	Giacometti	Lester Piggott
1975	Rose Bowl	Willie Carson
1976	Vitiges	Pat Eddery
1977	Flying Water	Yves Saint-Martin
1978	Swiss Maid	Greville Starkey
1979	Northern Baby	Philippe Paquet
1980	Cairn Rouge	Tony Murray
1981	Vayrann	Yves Saint-Martin
1982	Time Charter	Billy Newnes
1983	Cormorant Wood	Steve Cauthen
1984	Palace Music	Yves Saint-Martin
1985	Pebbles	Pat Eddery
1986	Triptych	Tony Cruz
1987	Triptych	Tony Cruz
1988	Indian Skimmer	Michael Roberts
1989	Legal Case	Ray Cochrane
1990	In The Groove	Steve Cauthen
1991	Tel Quel	Thierry Jarnet
1992	Rodrigo de Triano	Lester Piggott
1993	Hatoof	Walter Swinburn
1994	Dernier Empereur	Sylvain Guillot

Most wins: 2 Lemberg 1910-1, Orpheus 1920-1, Fairway 1928-9, Wychwood Abbot 1935-6, Hippius 1940-1, Dynamite 1951-2, Brigadier Gerard, Triptych.

Dewhurst Stakes

An end-of-season race for 2-year-olds at Newmarket, over 7 furlongs. It was first run in 1875 and was sponsored by William Hill 1973-86, then by Three Chimneys.

Year	Winners since 1970	Jockey
1970	Mill Reef	Geoff Lewis
1971	Crowned Prince	Lester Piggott
1972	Lunchtime	Pat Eddery
1973	Cellini	Lester Piggott
1974	Grundy	Pat Eddery
1975	Wollow	Franco Dettori
1976	The Minstrel	Lester Piggott
1977	Try My Best	Lester Piggott
1978	Tromos	John Lynch
1979	Monteverdi	Lester Piggott
1980	Storm Bird	Pat Eddery
1981	Wind and Wuthering	Philip Waldron
1982	Diesis	Lester Piggott
1983	El Gran Senor	Pat Eddery
1984	Kala Dancer	Geoff Baxter
1985	Huntingdale	Michael Hills
1986	Ajdal	Walter Swinburn
1987	*Cancelled*	
1988	Prince of Dance	Willie Carson
dead heat: Scenic		Michael Hills
1989	Dashing Blade	John Matthias
1990	Generous	Richard Quinn
1991	Dr Devious	Willie Carson
1992	Zafonic	Pat Eddery
1993	Grand Lodge	Pat Eddery
1994	Pennekamp	Thierry Jarnet

Racing Post Trophy

Run over 1 mile at Doncaster for 2-year-olds. Run as the Tiemform Gold Cup 1961-4, Observer Gold Cup 1965-75, William Hill Futurity 1976-88.

1970	Linden Tree	Duncan Keith
1971	High Top	Willie Carson
1972	Noble Decree	Lester Piggott
1973	Apalachee	Lester Piggott
1974	Green Dancer	Frankie Head
1975	Take Your Place	Gianfranco Dettori
1976	Sporting Yankee	Pat Eddery
1977	Dactylographer	Pat Eddery
1978	Sandy Creek	Christy Roche
1979	Hello Gorgeous	Joe Mercer
1980	Beldale Flutter	Pat Eddery
1981	Count Pahlen	Geoff Baxter
1982	Dunbeath	Lester Piggott
1983	Alphabatim	Greville Starkey
1984	Lanfranco	Lester Piggott
1985	Bakharoff	Greville Starkey
1986	Reference Point	Pat Eddery
1987	Emmson	Willie Carson
1988	Al Hareb	Willie Carson
1989	Be My Chief	Steve Cauthen
1990	Peter Davies	Steve Cauthen
1991	Seattle Rhyme	Cash Asmussen
1992	Armiger	Pat Eddery
1993	King's Theatre	Willie Ryan
1994	Celtic Swing	Kevin Darley

Irish Classics

All Irish Classics are run at the Curragh, situated in County Kildare. The distances of all five races are the same as their English counterparts. *Winners since 1970:*

2000 Guineas

First run 1921. Sponsored by Airlie/Coolmore, now First National Building Society.

1970	Decies	Lester Piggott
1971	King's Company	Freddie Head
1972	Ballymore	Christy Roche
1973	Sharp Edge	Joe Mercer
1974	Furry Glen	George McGrath
1975	Grundy	Pat Eddery
1976	Northern Treasure	Gabriel Curran
1977	Pampapaul	Franco Dettori
1978	Jaazeiro	Lester Piggott
1979	Dickens Hill	Tony Murray
1980	Nikoli	Christy Roche
1981	King's Lake	Pat Eddery
1982	Dara Monarch	Michael Kinane
1983	Wassl	Tony Murray
1984	Sadlers Wells	George McGrath
1985	Triptych	Christy Roche
1986	Flash of Steel	Michael Kinane
1987	Don't Forget Me	Willie Carson
1988	Prince of Birds	Declan Gillespie
1989	Shaadi	Walter Swinburn
1990	Tirol	Pat Eddery
1991	Fourstars Allstar	Mike Smith
1992	Rodrigo de Triano	Lester Piggott
1993	Barathea	Michael Roberts
1994	Turtle Island	John Reid
1995	Spectrum	John Reid

1000 Guineas

First run 1922. Now sponsored by Airlie/Coolmore.

1970	Black Satin	Ron Hutchinson
1971	Favoletta	Lester Piggott
1972	Pidget	Walter Swinburn, Snr.
1973	Cloonagh	Greville Starkey
1974	Gaily	Ron Hutchinson
1975	Miralla	Ryan Parnell
1976	Sarah Siddons	Christy Roche
1977	Lady Capulet	Tom Murphy
1978	More So	Christy Roche
1979	Godetia	Lester Piggott
1980	Cairn Rouge	Tony Murray
1981	Arctique Royale	Gabriel Curran
1982	Prince's Polly	Walter Swinburn
1983	L'Attrayante	Alain Badel
1984	Katies	Philip Robinson
1985	Al Bahathri	Tony Murray
1986	Sonic Lady	Walter Swinburn
1987	Forest Flower	Tony Ives
1988	Trusted Partner	Michael Kinane
1989	Ensconce	Ray Cochrane
1990	In The Groove	Steve Cauthen
1991	Kooyonga	Willie Carson
1992	Marling	Walter Swinburn
1993	Nicer	Michael Hills
1994	Mehthaaf	Willie Carson
1995	Ridgewood Pearl	Christy Roche

Derby

First run 1866 at 1 mile 6 furlongs, reduced to 1 mile 4 furlongs in 1872. Now sponsored by Budweiser.

1970	Nijinsky	Liam Ward
1971	Irish Ball	Fredo Gilbert
1972	Steel Pulse	Bill Williamson
1973	Weaver's Hall	George McGrath
1974	English Prince	Yves Saint-Martin
1975	Grundy	Pat Eddery
1976	Malacate	Philippe Paquet
1977	The Minstrel	Lester Piggott
1978	Shirley Heights	Greville Starkey
1979	Troy	Willie Carson
1980	Tyrnavos	Tony Murray
1981	Shergar	Lester Piggott
1982	Assert	Christy Roche
1983	Shareef Dancer	Walter Swinburn
1984	El Gran Senor	Pat Eddery
1985	Law Society	Pat Eddery
1986	Shahrastani	Walter Swinburn
1987	Sir Harry Lewis	Steve Cauthen
1988	Kahyasi	Ray Cochrane
1989	Old Vic	Steve Cauthen
1990	Salsabil	Willie Carson
1991	Generous	Alan Munro
1992	St Jovite	Christy Roche
1993	Commander In Chief	Pat Eddery
1994	Balanchine	Frankie Dettori
1995	Winged Love	Olivier Peslier

Note : Salsabil and Balanchine have been the first fillies to win the race since 1900.

Oaks

First run in 1895. Now sponsored by Kildangan Stud.

1970	Santa Tina	Lester Piggott
1971	Altesse Royale	Geoff Lewis
1972	Regal Exception	Maurice Philipperon
1973	Dahlia	Bill Pyers
1974	Dibidale	Willie Carson
1975	Juliette Marny	Lester Piggott
1976	Lagunette	Philippe Paquet
1977	Olwyn	John Lynch
1978	Fair Salinia	Greville Starkey
1979	Godetia	Lester Piggott
1980	Shoot A Line	Willie Carson
1981	Blue Wind	Walter Swinburn
1982	Swiftfoot	Willie Carson
1983	Give Thanks	Declan Gillespie
1984	Princess Pati	Pat Shanahan
1985	Helen Street	Willie Carson
1986	Colorspin	Pat Eddery
1987	Unite	Walter Swinburn
1988	Diminuendo	Steve Cauthen
dead heat: Melodist		Walter Swinburn

1989	Alydaress	Michael Kinane
1990	Knight's Baroness	Richard Quinn
1991	Possessive Dancer	Steve Cauthen
1992	User Friendly	George Duffield
1993	Wemyss Bight	Pat Eddery
1994	Bolas	Pat Eddery
1995	Pure Grain	John Reid

St Leger

First run in 1915. Now sponsored by Jefferson Smurfit and from 1983 open to older horses as weight for age.

1970	Allangrange	George McGrath
1971	Parnell	Alan Simpson
1972	Pidget	Thomas Burns
1973	Conor Pass	Peter Jarman
1974	Mistigri	Christy Roche
1975	Caucasus	Lester Piggott
1976	Meneval	Lester Piggott
1977	Transworld	Thomas Murphy
1978	M-Lolshan	Brian Taylor
1979	Niniski	Willie Carson
1980	Gonzales	Raymond Carroll
1981	Protection Racket	Brian Taylor
1982	Touching Wood	Paul Cook
1983	Mountain Lodge	Declan Gillespie
1984	Opale	Darrell McHargue
1985	Leading Counsel	Pat Eddery
1986	Authaal	Christy Roche
1987	Eurobird	Cash Asmussen
1988	Dark Lomond	Declan Gillespie
1989	Petite Ile	Ron Quinton
1990	Ibn Bey	Richard Quinn
1991	Turgeon	Tony Cruz
1992	Mashaallah	Steve Cauthen
1993	Vintage Crop	Michael Kinane
1994	Vintage Crop	Michael Kinane

The French Classics

Poule d'Essai des Pouliches

The equivalent of the 1000 Guineas it is run at Longchamp over 1600 metres (1 mile). First run 1883. Held at Le Tremblay 1943, Maisons-Laffitte 1944-5. *Winners since 1970:*

1970	Pampered Miss	Maurice Philipperon
1971	Bold Fascinator	Bill Williamson
1972	Mata Hari	Jean Cruguet
1973	Allez France	Yves Saint-Martin
1974	Dumka	Alain Lequeux
1975	Ivanjica	Freddie Head
1976	Riverqueen	Freddie Head
1977	Madelia	Yves Saint-Martin
1978	Dancing Maid	Freddie Head
1979	Three Troikas	Freddie Head
1980	Aryenne	Maurice Philipperon
1981	Ukraine Girl	Pat Eddery
1982	River Lady	Lester Piggott
1983	L'Attrayante	Alain Badel
1984	Masarika	Yves Saint-Martin
1985	Silvermine	Freddie Head

1986	Baiser Volé	Guy Guignard
1987	Miesque	Freddie Head
1988	Ravinella	Gary Moore
1989	Pearl Bracelet	Alfred Gilbert
1990	Houseproud	Pat Eddery
1991	Danseuse Du Soir	Dominic Boeuf
1992	Culture Vulture	Richard Quinn
1993	Madeleins's Dream	Cash Asmussen
1994	East Of The Moon	Cash Asmussen
1995	Matiara	Freddie Head

Poule d'Essai des Poulains

Also run at Longchamp over 1600 metres, it is the equivalent of the 2000 Guineas. First run 1883. Run at Auteuil 1940, Le Tremblay 1943, Maisons-Laffitte 1944-5. *Winners since 1970:*

1970	Caro	Bill Williamson
1971	Zug	Jean-Claude Desaint
1972	Riverman	Jean-Claude Desaint
1973	Kalamoun	Henri Samani
1974	Moulines	Maurice Philipperon
1975	Green Dancer	Freddie Head
1976	Red Lord	Freddie Head
1977	Blushing Groom	Henri Samani
1978	Nishapour	Henri Samani
1979	Irish River	Maurice Philipperon
1980	In Fijar	Georges Doleuze
1981	Recitation	Greville Starkey
1982	Melyno	Yves Saint-Martin
1983	L'Emigrant	Cash Asmussen
1984	Siberian Express	Fredo Gibert
1985	No Pass No Sale	Yves Saint-Martin
1986	Fast Topaze	Cash Asmussen
1987	Soviet Star	Greville Starkey
1988	Blushing John	Freddie Head
1989	Kendor	Maurice Phillipron
1990	Linamix	Freddie Head
1991	Hector Protector	Freddie Head
1992	Shanghai	Freddie Head
1993	Kingmambo	Cash Asmussen
1994	Green Tune	Olivier Doleuze
1995	Vettori	Frankie Dettori

Prix du Jockey Club

The French Derby, it was first run in 1836 Raced over 2400 metres (1miles 4 furlongs) at Chantilly. Raced at Longchamp 1919-20, 1941-2, 1945-7, Auteuil 1940, Le Trembay 1943-4. *Winners since 1970:*

1970	Sassafras	Yves Saint-Martin
1971	Rheffic	Bill Pyers
1972	Hard To Beat	Lester Piggott
1973	Roi Lear	Freddie Head
1974	Caracolero	Philippe Paquet
1975	Val de L'Orme	Freddie Head
1976	Youth	Freddie Head
1977	Crystal Palace	Gérard Dubroeucq

1978	Acamas	Yves Saint-Martin
1979	Top Ville	Yves Saint-Martin
1980	Policeman	Willie Carson
1981	Bikala	Serge Gorli
1982	Assert	Christy Roche
1983	Caerleon	Pat Eddery
1984	Darshaan	Yves Saint-Martin
1985	Mouktar	Yves Saint-Martin
1986	Bering	Gary Moore
1987	Natroun	Yves Saint-Martin
1988	Hours After	Pat Eddery
1989	Old Vic	Steve Cauthen
1990	Sanglamore	Pat Eddery
1991	Suave Dancer	Cash Asmussen
1992	Polytain	Frankie Dettori
1993	Hernando	Cash Asmussen
1994	Celtic Arms	Gerald Mosse
1995	Celtic Swing	Kevin Darley

Prix de Diane Hermes

The equivalent of the Oaks. It is run over 2100 metres (c.1 mile 2 furlongs) at Chantilly. Prix de Diane 1843-1976, Prix de Diane Revlon 1977-81, Prix de Diane Hermes since then. Raced at Longchamp 1919-20, 1941-2, 1945-7, Le Trembay 1943-4. *Winners since 1970:*

1970	Sweet Mimosa	Bill Williamson
1971	Pistol Packer	Freddie Head
1972	Rescousse	Yves Saint-Martin
1973	Allez France	Yves Saint-Martin
1974	Highclere	Joe Mercer
1975	*No race*	
1976	Pawneese	Yves Saint-Martin
1977	Madelia	Yves Saint-Martin
1978	Reine de Saba	Freddie Head
1979	Dunette	Georges Doleuze
1980	Mrs.Penny	Lester Piggott
1981	Madam Gay	Lester Piggott
1982	Harbour	Freddie Head
1983	Escaline	Gary Moore
1984	Northern Trick	Cash Asmussen
1985	Lypharita	Lester Piggott
1986	Lacovia	Freddie Head
1987	Indian Skimmer	Steve Cauthen
1988	Restless Kara	Gérard Mossé
1989	Lady In Silver	Tony Cruz
1990	Rafha	Willie Carson
1991	Caerlina	Eric Legrix
1992	Jolypha	Pat Eddery
1993	Shemaka	Gerald Mosse
1994	East Of The Moon	Cash Asmussen
1995	Carling	Thierry Thulliez

Prix Royal Oak

Run over 3100 metres (c.1 mile 7 furlongs) at Longchamp. Roughly the equivalent of the St.Leger, it was open only to 3-year-olds until 1978 but since then it has been open to 3-year-olds and upwards. First run 1869. Run at Le Tremblay 1943-4. *Winners since 1970:*

1970	Sassafras	Yves Saint-Martin
1971	Bourbon	Freddie Head

1972	Pleben	Marcel Depalmas
1973	Lady Berry	Marcel Depalmas
1974	Busiris	Freddie Head
1975	Henri Le Balafre	Henri Samani
1976	Exceller	Georges Dubroecq
1977	Rex Magan	Philippe Paquet
1978	Brave Johnny	Henri Samani
1979	Niniski	Willie Carson
1980	Gold River	Freddie Head
1981	Ardross	Lester Piggott
1982	Denel	Yves Saint-Martin
1983	Old Country	Pat Eddery
1984	Agent Double	Freddie Head
1985	Mersey	Jean-Luc Kessas
1986	El Cuite	Steve Cauthen
1987	Royal Gait	Alfred Gilbert
1988	Star Lift	Cash Asmussen
1989	Top Sunrise	Freddie Head
1990	Braashee	Michael Roberts
deadheat:	Indian Queen	Walter Swinburn
1991	Turgeon	Tony Cruz
1992	Assessor	Richard Quinn
1993	Mashaallah	Frankie Dettori
1994	Moonax	Pat Eddery

Prix de l'Arc de Triomphe

Europe's most prestigious race. It is run over 2400 metres (c. 1 mile 4 furlongs) at Longchamp on the first Sunday in October. It was first run in 1920. The 1943-4 races were at Le Tremblay over 2300m (c.1 mile 3 furlongs).

1920	Comrade	Frank Bullock
1921	Ksar	George Stern
1922	Ksar	Frank Bullock
1923	Parth	Frank O'Neill
1924	Massine	Fred Sharpe
1925	Priori	Marcel Allemand
1926	Biribi	Domingo Torterolo
1927	Mon Talisman	Charles Semblat
1928	Kantar	Arthur Esling
1929	Ortello	Paolo Caprioli
1930	Motrico	Marcel Fruhinsholtz
1931	Pearl Cap	Charles Semblat
1932	Motrico	Charles Semblat
1933	Crapom	Paolo Caprioli
1934	Brantôme	Charles Bouillon
1935	Samos	Wally Sibbritt
1936	Corrida	Charlie Elliott
1937	Corrida	Charlie Elliott
1938	Eclair au Chocolat	Charles Bouillon
1941	La Pacha	Paul Francolon
1942	Djebel	Jacko Doyasbère
1943	Verso II	Guy Duforez
1944	Ardan	Jacko Doyasbère
1945	Nikellora	Rae Johnstone
1946	Caracalla	Charlie Elliott
1947	Le Paillon	Fernand Rochetti
1948	Migoli	Charlie Smirke
1949	Coronation	Roger Poincelet
1950	Tantième	Jacko Doyasbère

Year	Horse	Jockey	Year	Horse	Jockey
1951	Tantième	Jacko Doyasbère	1978	Alleged	Lester Piggott
1952	Nuccio	Roger Poincelet	1979	Three Troikas	Freddie Head
1953	La Sorellina	Maurice Larraun	1980	Detroit	Pat Eddery
1954	Sica Boy	Rae Johnstone	1981	Gold River	Gary Moore
1955	Ribot	Enrico Camici	1982	Akiyda	Yves Saint-Martin
1956	Ribot	Enrico Camici	1983	All Along	Walter Swinburn
1957	Oroso	Serge Boullenger	1984	Sagace	Yves Saint-Martin
1958	Ballymoss	Scobie Breasley	1985	Rainbow Quest	Pat Eddery
1959	Saint Crespin	George Moore	1986	Dancing Brave	Pat Eddery
1960	Puissant Chef	Max Garcia	1987	Trempolino	Pat Eddery
1961	Molvedo	Enrico Camici	1988	Tony Bin	John Reid
1962	Soltikoff	Marcel Depalmas	1989	Carroll House	Michael Kinane
1963	Exbury	Jean Deforge	1990	Saumarez	Gerald Mossé
1964	Prince Royal II	Roger Poincelet	1991	Suave Dancer	Cash Asmussen
1965	Sea Bird II	Pat Glennon	1992	Subotica	Thierry Jarnet
1966	Bon Mot	Freddie Head	1993	Urban Sea	Eric Saint-Martin
1967	Topyo	Bill Pyers	1994	Carnegie	Thierry Jarnet
1968	Vaguely Noble	Bill Williamson			
1969	Levmoss	Bill Williamson			
1970	Sassafras	Yves Saint-Martin			
1971	Mill Reef	Geoff Lewis			
1972	San San	Freddie Head			
1973	Rheingold	Lester Piggott			
1974	Allez France	Yves Saint-Martin			
1975	Star Appeal	Greville Starkey			
1976	Ivanjica	Freddie Head			
1977	Alleged	Lester Piggott			

Most wins - Horse: 2 Ksar, Motrico, Corrida, Tantième, Ribot, Alleged

Most wins - Jockey: 4 Jacko Doyasbère, Freddie Head, Yves Saint-Martin, Pat Eddery

Most wins - Trainer: 4 Charles Semblat 1942, 1944, 1946, 1949; Alec Head 1952, 1959, 1976, 1981; François Mathet 1950-1, 1970, 1982

Most wins - Owner: 6 Marcel Boussac 1936-7, 1942, 1944, 1946, 1949

Fastest winning time: 2:26.3 Trempolino, 1987

Champion Jockeys (Flat)

The champion jockeys on the flat in Britain since 1900, determined on most winners each year, have been:

Year	Champion	Winners	Year	Champion	Winners	Year	Champion	Winners
1900	Lester Reiff	143	1925	Gordon Richards	118	1957	Scobie Breasley	173
1901	Otto Madden	130	1926	Tommy Weston	95	1958	Doug Smith	165
1902	Willie Lane	170	1927	Gordon Richards	164	1959	Doug Smith	157
1903	Otto Madden	154	1928	Gordon Richards	148	1960	Lester Piggott	170
1904	Otto Madden	161	1929	Gordon Richards	135	1961	Scobie Breasley	171
1905	Elijah Wheatley	124	1930	Freddy Fox	129	1962	Scobie Breasley	179
1906	Billy Higgs	149	1931	Gordon Richards	145	1963	Scobie Breasley	176
1907	Billy Higgs	146	1932	Gordon Richards	190	1964	Lester Piggott	140
1908	Danny Maher	139	1933	Gordon Richards	259	1965	Lester Piggott	166
1909	Frank Wootton	165	1934	Gordon Richards	212	1966	Lester Piggott	191
1910	Frank Wootton	137	1935	Gordon Richards	217	1967	Lester Piggott	117
1911	Frank Wootton	187	1936	Gordon Richards	174	1968	Lester Piggott	139
1912	Frank Wootton	118	1937	Gordon Richards	216	1969	Lester Piggott	163
1913	Danny Maher	115	1938	Gordon Richards	200	1970	Lester Piggott	162
1914	Steve Donoghue	129	1939	Gordon Richards	155	1971	Lester Piggott	162
1915	Steve Donoghue	62	1940	Gordon Richards	68	1972	Willie Carson	132
1916	Steve Donoghue	43	1941	Harry Wragg	71	1973	Willie Carson	163
1917	Steve Donoghue	42	1942	Gordon Richards	67	1974	Pat Eddery	148
1918	Steve Donoghue	66	1943	Gordon Richards	65	1975	Pat Eddery	164
1919	Steve Donoghue	129	1944	Gordon Richards	88	1976	Pat Eddery	162
1920	Steve Donoghue	143	1945	Gordon Richards	104	1977	Pat Eddery	176
1921	Steve Donoghue	141	1946	Gordon Richards	212	1978	Willie Carson	182
1922	Steve Donoghue	102	1947	Gordon Richards	269	1979	Joe Mercer	164
1923	Steve Donoghue	89	1948	Gordon Richards	224	1980	Willie Carson	165
	Charlie Elliott	89	1949	Gordon Richards	261	1981	Lester Piggott	179
1924	Charlie Elliott	106	1950	Gordon Richards	201	1982	Lester Piggott	188
			1951	Gordon Richards	227	1983	Willie Carson	159
			1952	Gordon Richards	231	1984	Steve Cauthen	130
			1953	Gordon Richards	191	1985	Steve Cauthen	195
			1954	Doug Smith	129	1986	Pat Eddery	177
			1955	Doug Smith	168	1987	Steve Cauthen	197
			1956	Doug Smith	155	1988	Pat Eddery	183

Year	Jockey	Wins
1989	Pat Eddery	171
1990	Pat Eddery	209
1991	Pat Eddery	165
1992	Michael Roberts	206
1993	Pat Eddery	169
1994	Frankie Dettori	233

Most times champion

26	Gordon Richards	as above
14	George Fordham 1855-63, 1865, 1867-9, 1871*	
13	Fred Archer	1874-86
13	Elnathan Flatman	1840-52
11	Lester Piggott	as above
10	Steve Donoghue	as above

* shared title

Progressive records of most wins in a season since 1840

1840	Elnathan Flatman	50
1841	Elnathan Flatman	68
1845	Elnathan Flatman	81
1846	Elnathan Flatman	81
1847	Elnathan Flatman	89
1848	Elnathan Flatman	104
1856	George Fordham	108
1859	George Fordham	118
1860	George Fordham	146
1862	George Fordham	166
1875	Fred Archer	172
1876	Fred Archer	207
1877	Fred Archer	218
1878	Fred Archer	229
1883	Fred Archer	232
1884	Fred Archer	241
1885	Fred Archer	246
1933	Gordon Richards	259
1947	Gordon Richards	269

Michael Roberts had a record 1068 rides in a season in 1992.

Most career wins in Britain

Wins	Jockey	Years
4870	Gordon Richards	1921-54
4493	Lester Piggott	1948-94
3637	Willie Carson	1962-94
3574	Pat Eddery	1969-94
3111	Doug Smith	1931-67
2810	Joe Mercer	1950-85
2748	Fred Archer	1870-86
2591	Edward Hide	1951-85
2587	George Fordham	1850-84
2313	Eph Smith	1930-65
2161	Scobie Breasley	1950-68
2067	Bill Nevett	1924-56

Leading Trainers since 1945

1945	Walter Earl	£29,557
1946	Frank Butters	56,140
1947	Fred Darling	65,313
1948	Noel Murless	66,542
1949	Frank Butters	71,721
1950	Charles Semblat (Fra)	57,044
1951	Jack Jarvis	56,397
1952	Marcus Marsh	92,093
1953	Jack Jarvis	71,546
1954	Cecil Boyd-Rochfort	65,326
1955	Cecil Boyd-Rochfort	74,424
1956	Charles Elsey	61,621
1957	Noel Murless	116,898
1958	Cecil Boyd-Rochfort	84,186
1959	Noel Murless	145,727
1960	Noel Murless	118,327
1961	Noel Murless	95,972
1962	Dick Hern	70,206
1963	Paddy Prendergast (Ire)	125,294
1964	Paddy Prendergast (Ire)	128,102
1965	Paddy Prendergast (Ire)	75,323
1966	Vincent O'Brien (Ire)	123,848
1967	Noel Murless	256,899
1968	Noel Murless	141,508
1969	Arthur Budgett	105,349
1970	Noel Murless	199,524
1971	Ian Balding	157,488
1972	Dick Hern	206,767
1973	Noel Murless	132,984
1974	Peter Walwyn	206,445
1975	Peter Walwyn	382,527
1976	Henry Cecil	261,301
1977	Vincent O'Brien (Ire)	439,124
1978	Henry Cecil	382,812
1979	Henry Cecil	683,971
1980	Dick Hern	831,964
1981	Michael Stoute	723,786
1982	Henry Cecil	872,614
1983	Dick Hern	549,598
1984	Henry Cecil	551,939
1985	Henry Cecil	1,148,206
1986	Michael Stoute	1,269,933
1987	Henry Cecil	1,896,689
1988	Henry Cecil	1,186,122
1989	Michael Stoute	2,000,330
1990	Henry Cecil	1,927,735
1991	Paul Cole	1,264,071
1992	Richard Hannon	1,154,210
1993	Henry Cecil	1,248,395
1994	Michael Stoute	1,914,609

Most times leading trainer (since 1896): 12 Alec Taylor 1907, 1909-10, 1914, 1917-23, 1925; 10 Henry Cecil, as above; 9 Noel Murless, as above; 8 Frank Butters 1927-8, 1932, 1934-5, 1944, 1946, 1949; 6 Fred Darling 1926, 1933, 1940-2, 1947

Leading Owners since 1945

1945	17th Earl of Derby	£25,067
1946	HH Aga Khan III	24,118
1947	HH Aga Khan III	44,020
1948	HH Aga Khan III	46,393
1949	HH Aga Khan III	68,916
1950	Marcel Boussac	57,044
1951	Marcel Boussac	39,339
1952	HH Aga Khan III	92,518
1953	Sir Victor Sassoon	58,579
1954	HM The Queen	40,993
1955	Lady Zia Wernher	46,345
1956	Major Lionel Holliday	39,327
1957	HM The Queen	62,211
1958	John McShain	63,264
1959	Prince Aly Khan	100,668
1960	Sir Victor Sassoon	90,069
1961	Major Lionel Holliday	39,227
1962	Major Lionel Holliday	70,206
1963	Jim Mullion	68,882
1964	Mrs Howell Jackson	98,270
1965	Jean Ternynck	65,301
1966	Lady Zia Wernher	78,075
1967	Jim Joel	120,925
1968	Raymond Guest	97,075
1969	David Robinson	92,553
1970	Charles Engelhard	182,059
1971	Paul Mellon	138,786
1972	Mrs Jean Hislop	155,190
1973	Nelson Bunker Hunt	124,771
1974	Nelson Bunker Hunt	147,244
1975	Dr Carlo Vittadini	209,492
1976	Daniel Wildenstein	244,500
1977	Robert Sangster	348,023
1978	Robert Sangster	160,405
1979	Sir Michael Sobell	339,751
1980	Simon Weinstock	236,332
1981	HH Aga Khan IV	441,654
1982	Robert Sangster	397,749
1983	Robert Sangster	461,488
1984	Robert Sangster	395,901
1985	Sheikh Mohammad	1,082,502
1986	Sheikh Mohammad	830,121
1987	Sheikh Mohammad	1,232,240
1988	Sheikh Mohammad	1,143,343
1989	Sheikh Mohammad	1,296,148
1990	Hamdam Al-Maktoum	1,536,821
1991	Sheikh Mohammad	1,077,271
1992	Sheikh Mohammad	1,194,380
1993	Sheikh Mohammad	1,704,751
1994	Sheikh Mohammad	2,666,730

Most times leading owner (since 1882): 13 HH Aga Khan III 1924, 1929-30, 1932, 1934-5, 1937, 1944, 1946-9, 1952; 9 Sheikh Mohammad, as above; 6 17th Earl of Derby 1923, 1927-8, 1933, 1938, 1945; 5 Robert Sangster, as above

Leading Money Winners - Season by Season

The leading horses in terms of first prizemoney won each season in Britain since 1945 have been:

Year	Horse	
1945	Sun Stream	£13,685
1946	Airborne	20,345
1947	Migoli	17,215
1948	Black Tarquin	21,423
1949	Nimbus	30,236
1950	Palestine	21,583
1951	Supreme Court	36,016
1952	Tulyar	75,173
1953	Pinza	44,101
1954	Never Say Die	30,332
1955	Meld	42,562
1956	Ribot	23,727
1957	Crepello	32,257
1958	Ballymoss	38,686
1959	Petite Etoile	55,487
1960	St Paddy	71,256
1961	Sweet Solera	36,988
1962	Hethersett	38,497
1963	Ragusa	66,011
1964	Santa Claus	72,067
1965	Sea Bird II	65,301
1966	Charlottown	78,075
1967	Royal Palace	92,998
1968	Sir Ivor	97,075
1969	Blakeney	63,108
1970	Nijinsky	159,681
1971	Mill Reef	121,913
1972	Brigadier Gerard	151,213
1973	Dahlia	79,230
1974	Dahlia	120,771
1975	Grundy	188,375
1976	Wollow	166,389
1977	The Minstrel	201,184
1978	Ile de Bourbon	136,012
1979	Troy	310,359
1980	Ela-Mana-Mou	236,332
1981	Shergar	295,654
1982	Kalaglow	242,304
1983	Sun Princess	221,356
1984	Secreto (USA)	227,680
1985	Oh So Sharp	311,576
1986	Dancing Brave	423,601
1987	Reference Point	683,029
1988	Mtoto	412,002
1989	Nashwan	772,045
1990	In The Groove	475,524
1991	Generous	631,945
1992	Rodrigo de Triano	494,764
1993	Commander In Chief	877,391
1994	Erhaab	582,588

All winners 3-year olds except the following: Ribot, Ballymoss, Brigadier Gerard, Dahlia (1974), Kalaglow.

International Classification

The official Handicappers in Great Britain, Ireland and France have jointly compiled International Classifications each year from 1977. Racing in Italy and West Germany was added from 1985. These ratings are now produced for six categories: colts and filles each at 2-y-o and 3-y-o, older male and older female. The highest rating overall has been achieved by the following horses each year:

1977 Alleged (Ire) 3-y-o 138
1978 Alleged (Ire) 4-y-o 140
1979 Three Troikas # (Fra) 3-y-o 137
1980 Moorestyle (UK) 3-y-o 131
1981 Shergar (UK) 3-y-o 140
1982 Golden Fleece (Ire) 3-y-o 134
1983 Shareef Dancer (UK) 3-y-o 133
1984 El Gran Senor (Ire) 3-y-o 138
1985 Slip Anchor (UK) 3-y-o 135
1986 Dancing Brave (UK) 3-y-o 141
1987 Reference Point (UK) 3-y-o 135
1988 Warning (UK) 3-y-o 133
1989 Old Vic (Ire) 3-y-o 134
    Zilzal (Fra) 3-y-o 134
1990 Dayjur (UK) 3-y-o 133
1991 Generous (UK) 3-y-o 137
1992 St Jovite (Ire) 3-y-o 135
1993 Zafonic (UK) 3-y-o 130
1994 Celtic Swing (UK) 2-y-o 130
    Ballanchine # (Fra) 3-y-o 130
fillies

Racegoers Club 'Racehorse of the Year'

Introduced by the Racecourse Association in 1965, the Racegoers Club took over reponsibility for the award in 1978. Their members take part in a poll each year to decide their 'Horse of the Year'. *Winners:*

1965	Sea Bird II
1966	Charlottown
1967	Busted
1968	Sir Ivor
1969	Park Top
1970	Nijinsky
1971	Mill Reef
1972	Brigadier Gerard
1973-4	Dahlia
1975	Grundy
1976	Pawneese
1977	The Minstrel
1978	Shirley Heights
1979	Troy
1980	Moorestyle
1981	Shergar
1982	Ardross
1983	Habibti
1984	Provideo
1985	Pebbles
1986	Dancing Brave
1987	Reference Point
1988	Mtoto
1989	Nashwan
1990	Dayjur
1991	Generous
1992	User Friendly
1993	Lochsong
1994	Barathea

National Hunt Racing
Steeplechasing and hurdling in Britain

Grand National

The most famous steeplechase in the world has been run annually at Aintree, Liverpool since 1847 with the exception of the war years. It was held at Gatwick in 1916-8. It was run at Aintree as the Grand Liverpool Steeple Chase 1839-42 and as the Liverpool and national Steeple Chase 1843-6. Also shown below are the winners of a preceding steeplechase run at a course in Maghull, some four miles from the present site at Aintree, in 1836-8. The current course takes in 30 fences over two circuits and is 4 miles 4 furlongs long. Now sponsored by Martell. *Winners (Amateur riders have their titles, e.g. Mr, Capt.). Weights are shown in stones and pounds.):*

Year	Winner	Jockey	Weight
1836	The Duke	-	-
1837	The Duke	Mr Potts	12-0
1838	Sir William	Tom Oliver	12-0
1839	Lottery	Jem Mason	12-0
1840	Jerry	Mr B Bretherton	12-0
1841	Charity	H N Powell	12-0
1842	Gay Lad	Tom Oliver	12-0
1843	Vanguard	Tom Oliver	11-10
1844	Discount	H Crickmere	10-12
1845	Cureall	Bill Loft	11-5
1846	Pioneer	W Taylor	11-12
1847	Matthew	Denny Wynne	10-6
1848	Chandler	Capt. Josey Little	11-12

Year	Winner	Jockey	Weight	Year	Winner	Jockey	Weight
1849	Peter Simple	Tom Cunningham	11-0	1908	Rubio	Henry Bletsoe	10-5
1850	Abd-el-Kader	Chris Green	9-12	1909	Lutteur III	George Parfrement	10-11
1851	Abd-el-Kader	T Abbott	10-4	1910	Jenkinstown	Bob Chadwick	10-5
1852	Miss Mowbray	Mr Alec Goodman	10-4	1911	Glenside	Mr Jack Anthony	10-3
1853	Peter Simple	Tom Oliver	10-10	1912	Jerry M	Ernie Piggott	12-7
1854	Bourton	J Tasker	11-12	1913	Covertcoat	Percy Woodland	11-6
1855	Wanderer	J Hanlon	9-8	1914	Sunloch	William Smith	9-7
1856	Freetrader	George Stevens	9-6	1915	Ally Sloper	Mr Jack Anthony	10-6
1857	Emigrant	Charlie Boyce	9-10	1916	Vermouth	John Reardon	11-10
1858	Little Charley	William Archer	10-7	1917	Ballymacad	Ted Driscoll	9-12
1859	Half Caste	Chris Green	9-7	1918	Poethlyn	Ernie Piggott	11-6
1860	Anatis	Mr Tommy Pickernell	9-10	1919	Poethlyn	Ernie Piggott	12-7
1861	Jealousy	Joe Kendall	9-12	1920	Troytown	Mr Jack Anthony	11-9
1862	Huntsman	Harry Lamplugh	11-0	1921	Shaun Spadah	Dick Rees	11-7
1863	Emblem	George Stevens	10-10	1922	Music Hall	Bilbie Rees	11-8
1864	Emblematic	George Stevens	10-6	1923	Sergeant		
1865	Alcibiade	Capt. Bee Coventry	11-4		Murphy	Capt. Tuppy Bennett	11-3
1866	Salamnader	Mr Alec Goodman	10-7	1924	Master Robert	Bob Trudgill	10-5
1867	Cortolvin	John Page	11-13	1925	Double Chance	Major Jack Wilson	10-9
1868	The Lamb	Mr George Ede	10-7	1926	Jack Horner	Billy Watkinson	10-5
1869	The Colonel	George Stevens	10-7	1927	Sprig	Ted Leader	12-4
1870	The Colonel	George Stevens	11-12	1928	Tipperary Tim	Mr Bill Dutton	10-0
1871	The Lamb	Mr Tommy Pickernell	11-4	1929	Gregalach	Bob Everett	11-4
1872	Casse Tête	John Page	10-0	1930	Shaun Goilin	Tommy Cullinan	11-0
1873	Disturbance	Mr Maunsell Richardson	11-11	1931	Grakle	Bob Lyall	11-7
1874	Reugny	Mr Maunsell Richardson	10-12	1932	Forbra	Jim Hamey	10-7
1875	Pathfinder	Mr Tommy Pickernell	10-11	1933	Kellsboro' Jack	Dudley Williams	11-9
1876	Regal	Joe Cannon	11-3	1934	Golden Miller	Gerry Wilson	12-2
1877	Austerlitz	Mr Fred Hobson	10-8	1935	Reynoldstown	Mr Frank Furlong	11-4
1878	Shifnal	Jack Jones	10-12	1936	Reynoldstown	Mr Fulke Walwyn	12-2
1879	The Liberator	Mr Garrett Moore	11-4	1937	Royal Mail	Evan Williams	11-13
1880	Empress	Mr Tommy Beasley	10-7	1938	Battleship	Bruce Hobbs	11-6
1881	Woodbrook	Mr Tommy Beasley	11-3	1939	Workman	Tim Hyde	10-6
1882	Seaman	Lord Manners	11-6	1940	Bogskar	Mervyn Jones	10-4
1883	Zoëdone	Count Graf Karl Kinsky	11-0	1946	Lovely Cottage	Capt. Bobby Petre	10-8
1884	Voluptuary	Mr Ted Wilson	10-5	1947	Caughoo	Eddie Dempsey	10-0
1885	Roquefort	Mr Ted Wilson	11-0	1948	Sheila's Cottage	Arthur Thompson	10-7
1886	Old Joe	Tom Skelton	10-9	1949	Russian Hero	Leo McMorrow	10-8
1887	Gamecock	Bill Daniels	11-0	1950	Freebooter	Jimmy Power	11-11
1888	Playfair	George Mawson	10-7	1951	Nickel Coin	Johnny Bullock	10-1
1889	Frigate	Mr Tommy Beasley	11-5	1952	Teal	Arthur Thompson	10-12
1890	Ilex	Arthur Nightingall	10-5	1953	Early Mist	Bryan Marshall	11-2
1891	Come Away	Mr Harry Beasley	11-12	1954	Royal Tan	Bryan Marshall	11-7
1892	Father O'Flynn	Capt. Roddy Owen	10-5	1955	Quare Times	Pat Taaffe	11-0
1893	Cloister	Bill Dollery	12-7	1956	E.S.B.	Dave Dick	11-3
1894	Why Not	Arthur Nightingall	11-3	1957	Sundew	Fred Winter	11-7
1895	Wild Man from			1958	Mr What	Arthur Freeman	10-6
	Borneo	Mr Joe Widger	10-1	1959	Oxo	Michael Scudamore	10-13
1896	The Soarer	Mr David Campbell	9-13	1960	Merryman II	Gerry Scott	10-12
1897	Manifesto	Terry Kavanagh	11-3	1961	Nicolaus Silver	Bobby Beasley	10-1
1898	Drogheda	John Gourley	10-12	1962	Kilmore	Fred Winter	10-4
1899	Manifesto	George Williamson	12-7	1963	Ayala	Pat Buckley	10-0
1900	Ambush II	Algy Anthony	11-3	1964	Team Spirit	Willie Robinson	10-3
1901	Grudon	Arthur Nightingall	10-0	1965	Jay Trump	Mr Tommy Smith	11-5
1902	Shannon Lass	David Read	10-1	1966	Anglo	Tim Norman	10-0
1903	Drumcree	Percy Woodland	11-3	1967	Foinavon	John Buckingham	10-0
1904	Moifaa	Arthur Birch	10-7	1968	Red Alligator	Brian Fletcher	10-0
1905	Kirkland	Tich Mason	11-5	1969	Highland		
1906	Ascetic's Silver	Hon. Aubrey Hastings	10-9		Wedding	Eddie Harty	10-4
1907	Eremon	Alf Newey	10-1	1970	Gay Trip	Pat Taaffe	11-5

1971	Specify	John Cook	10-13
1972	Well To Do	Graham Thorner	10-1
1973	Red Rum	Brian Fletcher	10-5
1974	Red Rum	Brian Fletcher	12-0
1975	L'Escargot	Tommy Carberry	11-3
1976	Rag Trade	John Burke	10-12
1977	Red Rum	Tommy Stack	11-8
1978	Lucius	Bob Davies	10-9
1979	Rubstic	Maurice Barnes	10-0
1980	Ben Nevis	Mr Charlie Fenwick	10-12
1981	Aldaniti	Bob Champion	10-13
1982	Grittar	Mr Dick Saunders	11-5
1983	Corbière	Ben De Haan	11-4
1984	Hallo Dandy	Neale Doughty	10-2
1985	Last Suspect	Hywel Davies	10-5
1986	West Tip	Richard Dunwoody	10-11
1987	Maori Venture	Steve Knight	10-13
1988	Rhyme'N Reason	Brendan Powell	10-11
1989	Little Polveir	Jimmy Frost	10-3
1990	Mr Frisk	Mr Marcus Armytage	10-6
1991	Seagram	Nigel Hawke	10-6
1992	Party Politics	Carl Llewellyn	10-7

1993 *race void after false start*

1994	Miinnehoma	Richard Dunwoody	10-8
1995	Royal Athlete	Jason Titley	10-6

Most wins - Horse: 3 Red Rum, 2 Abd-el-Kader, Peter Simple, The Colonel, The Lamb, Manifesto, Reynoldstown, Poethlyn

Most wins - Jockey: 5 George Stevens, 4 Tom Oliver, 3 Mr Tommy Pickernell, Mr Tommy Beasley, Arthur Nightingall, Ernie Piggott, Mr Jack Anthony, Brian Fletcher

Most wins - Trainer: 4 Fred Rimell 1956, 1961, 1970, 1976
4 Aubrey Hastings 1906, 1915, 1917*, 1924
3 William Holman 1856, 1858, 1860
3 William Moore 1894, 1896, 1899
3 Tom Coulthwaite 1907, 1910, 1931
3 Vincent O'Brien 1953-5
3 Neville Crump 1948, 1952, 1960
3 Donald McCain 1973-4, 1977
3 Tim Forster 1972, 1980, 1985
* Gatwick race

Most wins - Owner: 3 James Machell 1873-4, 1876; Sir Charles Assheton-Smith 1893, 1912-3; Noel Le Mare 1973-4, 1977

Fastest winning time: 8:47.8 Mr Frisk 1990

Record field: 66 in 1929

Richest prize: £99,943 by Party Politics in 1992

Cheltenham Gold Cup

The Cheltenham Gold Cup is the most prestigious race on the National Hunt calendar in Britain. It was first held in 1924; the course has varied over the years but is now 3 miles 2 furlongs 110 yards over 22 fences. Since 1980 the race has been sponsored by the Horserace Totalisator Board. There was no race in 1931, 1937, 1943-4. All horses now carry 12 stone. The £122,540 for the 1995 winner Master Oats is the richest prize won over jumps in Britain.

Richard Dunwoody

Year	Winner	Jockey
1924	Red Splash	Dick Rees
1925	Ballinode	Ted Leader
1926	Koko	Tim Hamey
1927	Thrown In	Mr Hugh Grosvenor
1928	Patron Saint	Dick Rees
1929	Easter Hero	Dick Rees
1930	Easter Hero	Tommy Cullinan
1932	Golden Miller	Ted Leader
1933	Golden Miller	Billy Stott
1934	Golden Miller	Gerry Wilson
1935	Golden Miller	Gerry Wilson
1936	Golden Miller	Evan Williams
1938	Morse Code	Danny Morgan
1939	Brendan's Cottage	George Owen
1940	Roman Hackle	Evan Williams
1941	Poet Prince	Roger Burford
1942	Médoc II	Frenchie Nicholson
1945	Red Rower	Davy Jones
1946	Prince Regent	Tim Hyde
1947	Fortina	Mr Dick Black
1948	Cottage Rake	Aubrey Brabazon
1949	Cottage Rake	Aubrey Brabazon
1950	Cottage Rake	Aubrey Brabazon
1951	Silver Fame	Martin Molony
1952	Mont Tremblant	Dave Dick
1953	Knock Hard	Tim Molony
1954	Four Ten	Tommy Cusack

1955	Gay Donald	Tony Grantham
1956	Limber Hill	Jimmy Power
1957	Linwell	Michael Scudamore
1958	Kerstin	Stan Hayhurst
1959	Roddy Owen	Bobby Beasley
1960	Pas Seul	Bill Rees
1961	Saffron Tartan	Fred Winter
1962	Mandarin	Fred Winter
1963	Mill House	Willie Robinson
1964	Arkle	Pat Taaffe
1965	Arkle	Pat Taaffe
1966	Arkle	Pat Taaffe
1967	Woodland Venture	Terry Biddlecombe
1968	Fort Leney	Pat Taaffe
1969	What a Myth	Paul Kelleway
1970	L'Escargot	Tommy Carberry
1971	L'Escargot	Tommy Carberry
1972	Glencaraig Lady	Frank Berry
1973	The Dikler	Ron Barry
1974	Captain Christy	Bobby Beasley
1975	Ten Up	Tommy Carberry
1976	Royal Frolic	John Burke
1977	Davy Lad	Dessie Hughes
1978	Midnight Court	John Francome
1979	Alverton	Jonjo O'Neill
1980	Master Smudge	Richard Hoare
1981	Little Owl	Mr Jim Wilson
1982	Silver Buck	Robert Earnshaw
1983	Bregawn	Graham Bradley
1984	Burrough Hill Lad	Phil Tuck
1985	Forgive 'N' Forget	Martin Dwyer
1986	Dawn Run	Jonjo O'Neill
1987	The Thinker	Ridley Lamb
1988	Charter Party	Richard Dunwoody
1989	Desert Orchid	Simon Sherwood
1990	Norton's Coin	Graham McCourt
1991	Garrison Savannah	Mark Pitman
1992	Cool Ground	Adrian Maguire
1993	Jodami	Mark Dwyer
1994	The Fellow	Adam Kondrat
1995	Master Oats	Norman Williamson

Most wins - Horse: 5 Golden Miller, 3 Cottage Rake, Arkle; 2 Easter Hero, L'Escargot
Most wins - Jockey: 4 Pat Taafe, 3 Dick Rees, Aubrey Brabazon, Tommy Carberry
Most wins - Trainer: 5 Tom Dreaper 1946, 1964-6, 1968; 4 Basil Briscoe 1932-5; Vincent O'Brien 1948-50, 1953; Fulke Walwyn 1952, 1962-3, 1973
Most wins - Owner: 7 Miss Dorothy Paget 1932-6, 1940, 1952; 4 Anne, Duchess of Westminster 1964-6, 1975; 3 Frank Vickerman 1948-50
Fastest winning time: 6:23.4 Silver Fame 1951
Most placings by a horse: 6 Golden Miller (5 wins, 2nd 1938); 4 The Dikler (won 1972, 2nd 1973, 3rd 1971-2)

Champion Hurdle

The leading race in England for hurdlers, the Champion Hurdle was inaugurated in 1927. It is raced at Cheltenham during the Spring Festival meeting and is now over two miles 110 yards. The race was sponsored by Waterford Crystal 1978-92 and by Smurfit from 1993. There was no race in 1931, 1943-4. The current weights are 11st 6lb for 4-year olds, 12st for older horses with a 5lb allowance for mares.

Year	Winner	Jockey
1927	Blaris	George Duller
1928	Brown Jack	Bilbie Rees
1929	Royal Falcon	Dick Rees
1930	Brown Tony	Tommy Cullinan
1932	Insurance	Ted Leader
1933	Insurance	Billy Stott
1934	Chenango	Danny Morgan
1935	Lion Courage	Gerry Wilson
1936	Victor Norman	Frenchie Nicholson
1937	Free Fare	Georges Pellerin
1938	Our Hope	Capt. Perry Harding
1939	African Sister	Keith Piggott
1940	Solford	Sean Magee
1941	Seneca	Ron Smyth
1942	Forestation	Ron Smyth
1945	Brains Trust	Fred Rimell

Adrian Maguire

Year	Horse	Jockey
1946	Distel	Bobby O'Ryan
1947	National Spirit	Danny Morgan
1948	National Spirit	Ron Smyth
1949	Hatton's Grace	Aubrey Brabazon
1950	Hatton's Grace	Aubrey Brabazon
1951	Hatton's Grace	Tim Molony
1952	Sir Ken	Tim Molony
1953	Sir Ken	Tim Molony
1954	Sir Ken	Tim Molony
1955	Clair Soliel	Fred Winter
1956	Doorknocker	Harry Sprague
1957	Merry Deal	Grenville Underwood
1958	Bandalore	George Slack
1959	Fare Time	Fred Winter
1960	Another Flash	Bobby Beasley
1961	Eborneezer	Fred Winter
1962	Anzio	Willie Robinson
1963	Winning Fair	Mr Alan Lillingston
1964	Magic Court	Pat McCarron
1965	Kirriemuir	Willie Robinson
1966	Salmon Spray	Johnny Haine
1967	Saucy Kit	Roy Edwards
1968	Persian War	Jimmy Uttley
1969	Persian War	Jimmy Uttley
1970	Persian War	Jimmy Uttley
1971	Bula	Paul Kelleway
1972	Bula	Paul Kelleway
1973	Comedy of Errors	Bill Smith
1974	Lanzarote	Richard Pitman
1975	Comedy of Errors	Ken White
1976	Night Nurse	Paddy Broderick
1977	Night Nurse	Paddy Broderick
1978	Monksfield	Tommy Kinane
1979	Monksfield	Dessie Hughes
1980	Sea Pigeon	Jonjo O'Neill
1981	Sea Pigeon	John Francome
1982	For Auction	Mr Colin Magnier
1983	Gaye Brief	Richard Linley
1984	Dawn Run	Jonjo O'Neill
1985	See You Then	Steve Smith-Eccles
1986	See You Then	Steve Smith-Eccles
1987	See You Then	Steve Smith-Eccles
1988	Celtic Shot	Peter Scudamore
1989	Beech Road	Richard Guest
1990	Kribensis	Richard Dunwoody
1991	Morley Street	Jimmy Frost
1992	Royal Gait	Graham McCourt
1993	Granville Again	Peter Scudamore
1994	Flakey Dove	Mark Dwyer
1995	Alderbrook	Norman Williamson

Most wins - Horse: 3 Hatton's Grace, Sir Ken, Persian War, See You Then; 2 Insurance, National Spirit, Bula, Comedy of Errors, Night Nurse, Monksfield, Sea Pigeon

Most wins - Jockey: 4 Tim Moloney, 3 Ron Smyth, Fred Winter, Jimmy Uttley, Steve Smith-Eccles

Most wins - Trainer: 5 Peter Easterby 1967, 1976-7, 1980-1; 4 Vic Smyth 1941-2, 1947-8; Fred Winter 1971-2, 1974, 1988; 3 Vincent O'Brien 1949-51; Willie Stephenson 1952-4; Ryan Price 1955, 1959, 1961; Colin Davies 1968-70; Nicky Henderson 1985-7

Most wins - Owner: 4 Miss Dorothy Paget 1932-3, 1940, 1946; 3 Mrs.Moya Keogh 1949-51; Maurice Kingsley 1952-4; Henry Alper 1968-70; Stype Wood Stud Ltd. 1985-7

Fastest winning time: 3:50.7 Kribensis 1990

Other Principal National Hunt Races

Whitbread Gold Cup

The Whitbread Gold Cup has a special place in British National Hunt racing, as when inaugurated in 1957 it was the first race to attract major commercial sponsorship. Run at Sandown Park over 3 miles 5 furlongs 18 yards. The 1973 race was at Newcastle.

Year	Winner	Jockey	Weight
1957	Much Obliged	Henry East	10-12
1958	Taxidermist	Hon. John Lawrence	10-8
1959	Done Up	Harry Sprague	10-13
1960	Plummers Plain	Ron Harrison	10-0
1961	Pas Seul	Dave Dick	12-0
1962	Frenchman's Cove	Stan Mellor	11-3
1963	Hoodwinked	Paddy Buckley	10-9
1964	Dormant	Paddy Buckley	9-7
1965	Arkle	Pat Taaffe	12-7
1966	What a Myth	Paul Kelleway	9-8
1967	Mill House	David Nicholson	11-11
1968	Larbawn	Macer Gifford	10-9
1969	Larbawn	Josh Gifford	11-4
1970	Royal Toss	Richard Pitman	10-0
1971	Titus Oates	Ron Barry	11-13
1972	Grey Sombrero	Willie Shoemark	9-10
1973	Charlie Potheen	Ron Barry	12-0
1974	The Dikler	Ron Barry	11-13
1975	April Seventh	Stephen Knight	9-13
1976	Otter Way	John King	10-10
1977	Andy Pandy	John Burke	10-12
1978	Strombolus	Tommy Stack	10-0
1979	Diamond Edge	Bill Smith	11-11
1980	Royal Mail	Phillip Blacker	11-5
1981	Diamond Edge	Bill Smith	11-7
1982	Shady Deal	Richard Rowe	10-0
1983	Drumlargan	Mr Frank Codd	10-10
1984	Special Cargo	Kevin Mooney	11-2
1985	By The Way	Robert Earnshaw	10-0
1986	Plundering	Simon Sherwood	10-6
1987	Lean Ar Aghaidh	Guy Landau	9-10
1988	Desert Orchid	Simon Sherwood	11-11
1989	Brown Windsor	Mark Bowlby	10-0
1990	Mr Frisk	Mr Marcus Armytage	10-5
1991	Docklands Express	Anthony Tory	10-3
1992	Topsham Bay	Hywel Davies	10-0
1993	Topsham Bay	Richard Dunwoody	10-0
1994	Ushers Island	Charlie Swan	10-0
1995	Cache Fleur	Richard Dunwoody	9-10

Mackeson Gold Cup

Held annually over 2 miles 4 furlongs at Cheltenham since 1960, with the exception of 1976 when it was run at Haydock Park.

Year	Winner	Jockey	Weight
1960	Fortria	Pat Taaffe	12-8
1961	Scottish Memories	Chris Finnegan	10-7
1962	Fortria	Pat Taaffe	12-0
1963	Richard of Bordeaux	Bobby Beasley	10-5
1964	Super Flash	Stan Mellor	10-5
1965	Dunkirk	Bill Rees	12-7
1966	Pawnbroker	Paddy Broderick	11-9
1967	Charlie Worcester	Josh Gifford	10-11
1968	Jupiter Boy	Eddie Harty	10-3
1969	Gay Trip	Terry Biddlecombe	11-5
1970	Chatham	Ken White	10-3
1971	Gay Trip	Terry Biddlecombe	11-3
1972	Red Candle	Jim Fox	10-0
1973	Skymas	Tommy Murphy	10-5
1974	Bruslie	Andy Turnell	10-7
1975	Clear Cut	Dennis Greaves	10-9
1976	Cancello	Dennis Atkins	11-1
1977	Bachelor's Hall	Martin O'Halloran	10-6
1978	Bawnogues	Craig Smith	10-7
1979	Man Alive	Ron Barry	10-9
1980	Bright Highway	Gerry Newman	11-1
1981	Henry Kissinger	Paul Barton	10-13
1982	Fifty Dollars More	Richard Linley	11-0
1983	Pounentes	Neale Doughty	10-6
1984	Half Free	Richard Linley	11-10
1985	Half Free	Richard Linley	11-10
1986	Very Promising	Richard Dunwoody	11-13
1987	Beau Ranger	Mark Perrett	10-2
1988	Pegwell Bay	Peter Scudamore	11-2
1989	Joint Sovereignty	Graham McCourt	10-4
1990	Multum In Parvo	Norman Williamson	10-2
1991	Another Coral	Richard Dunwoody	10-0
1992	Tipping Tim	Carl Llewellyn	10-10
1993	Bradbury Star	Declan Murphy	11-8
1994	Bradbury Star	Philip Hide	12-0

Hennessy Cognac Gold Cup

Run at Newbury over 3 miles 2 furlongs 82 yards. Inaugurated in 1957, and run at Cheltenham 1957-9.

Year	Winner	Jockey	Weight
1957	Mandarin	Gerry Madden	11-0
1958	Taxidermist	John Lawrence	11-1
1959	Kerstin	Stan Hayhurst	11-10
1960	Knucklecracker	Derek Ancil	11-1
1961	Mandarin	Willie Robinson	11-5
1962	Springbok	Gerry Scott	10-8
1963	Mill House	Willie Robinson	12-0
1964	Arkle	Pat Taaffe	12-7
1965	Arkle	Pat Taaffe	12-7
1966	Stalbridge Colonist	Stan Mellor	10-2
1967	Rondetto	Jeff King	10-1

Year	Winner	Jockey	Weight
1968	Man Of The West	Willie Robinson	10-0
1969	Spanish Steps	John Cooke	11-6
1970	Border Mask	David Mould	11-1
1971	Bighorn	David Cartwright	10-11
1972	Charlie Potheen	Richard Pitman	11-4
1973	Red Candle	Jim Fox	10-4
1974	Royal Marshall II	Graham Thorner	10-0
1975	April Seventh	Andy Turnell	11-2
1976	Zeta's Son	Ian Watkinson	10-9
1977	Bachelor's Hall	Martin O'Halloran	10-10
1978	Approaching	Bob Champion	10-6
1979	Fighting Fit	Richard Linley	11-7
1980	Bright Highway	Gerry Newman	11-6
1981	Diamond Edge	Bill Smith	11-10
1982	Bregawn	Graham Bradley	11-10
1983	Brown Chamberlin	John Francome	11-8
1984	Burrough Hill Lad	John Francome	12-0
1985	Galway Blaze	Mark Dwyer	10-0
1986	Broadheath	Paul Nicholls	10-5
1987	Playschool	Paul Nicholls	10-8
1988	Strands of Gold	Peter Scudamore	10-0
1989	Ghofar	Hywel Davies	10-0
1990	Arctic Call	Jamie Osborne	11-0
1991	Chatam	Peter Scudamore	10-6
1992	Sibton Abbey	Adrian Maguire	10-0
1993	Cogent	Dan Fortt	10-8
1994	One Man	Tony Dobbin	10-0

King George VI Rank Chase

The traditional Boxing Day fixture over 3 miles at Kempton Park, first run in 1947, brings together a small, but quality field of steeplechasers. Not held due to bad weather in 1961-2, 1967-8, 1970, 1981.

Year	Winner	Jockey	Weight
1947	Rowland Roy	Bryan Marshall	11-13
1948	Cottage Rake	Aubrey Brabazon	12-6
1949	Finnure	Dick Francis	11-10
1950	Manicou	Bryan Marshall	11-8
1951	Statecraft	Anthony Grantham	11-11
1952	Halloween	Fred Winter	11-13
1953	Galloway Braes	Robert Morrow	12-6
1954	Halloween	Fred Winter	12-10
1955	Limber Hill	James Power	11-13
1956	Rose Park	Michael Scudamore	11-7
1957	Mandarin	Gerry Madden	12-0
1958	Lochroe	Arthur Freeman	11-7
1959	Mandarin	Gerry Madden	11-5
1960	Saffron Tartan	Fred Winter	11-7
1963	Mill House	Willie Robinson	12-0
1964	Frenchman's Cove	Stan Mellor	11-7
1965	Arkle	Pat Taaffe	12-0
1966	Dormant	John King	11-0
1969	Titus Oates	Stan Mellor	11-10
1971	The Dikler	Barry Brogan	11-7
1972	Pendil	Richard Pitman	12-0
1972	Pendil	Richard Pitman	12-0
1974	Captain Christy	Bobby Coonan	12-0

1975	Captain Christy	Gerry Newman	12-0
1976	Royal Marshall	Graham Thorner	11-7
1977	Bachelor's Hall	Martin O'Halloran	11-7
1978	Gay Spartan	Tommy Carmody	11-10
1979	Silver Buck	Tommy Carmody	11-10
1980	Silver Buck	Tommy Carmody	11-10
1982	Wayward Lad	John Francome	11-10
1983	Wayward Lad	Robert Earnshaw	11-10
1984	Burrough Hill Lad	John Francome	11-10
1985	Wayward Lad	Graham Bradley	11-10
1986	Desert Orchid	Colin Brown	11-10
1987	Nupsala	Andre Pommier	11-10
1988	Desert Orchid	Simon Sherwood	11-10
1989	Desert Orchid	Richard Dunwoody	11-10
1990	Desert Orchid	Richard Dunwoody	11-10
1991	The Fellow	Adam Kondrat	11-10
1992	The Fellow	Adam Kondrat	11-10
1993	Barton Bank	Adrian Maguire	11-10
1994	Algan	Philippe Chevalier	11-10

Champion Jockeys (National Hunt)

Prior to the 1925/6 season the championship was decided by winners in a calendar year. Since then it has been taken over the season on most winners. *Leading jockeys since 1944/5:*

Year	Champion	Winners
1944/5	Frenchie Nicholson	15
	Fred Rimell	15
1945/6	Fred Rimell	54
1946/7	Jack Dowdeswell	58
1947/8	Bryan Marshall	66
1948/9	Tim Molony	60
1949/50	Tim Molony	95
1950/1	Tim Molony	83
1951/2	Tim Molony	99
1952/3	Fred Winter	121
1953/4	Dick Francis	76
1954/5	Tim Molony	67
1955/6	Fred Winter	74
1956/7	Fred Winter	80
1957/8	Fred Winter	82
1958/9	Tim Brookshaw	83
1959/60	Stan Mellor	68
1960/1	Stan Mellor	118
1961/2	Stan Mellor	80
1962/3	Josh Gifford	70
1963/4	Josh Gifford	94
1964/5	Terry Biddlecombe	114
1965/6	Terry Biddlecombe	102
1966/7	Josh Gifford	122
1967/8	Josh Gifford	82
1968/9	Bob Davies	77
	Terry Biddlecombe	77
1969/70	Bob Davies	91
1970/1	Graham Thorner	74
1971/2	Bob Davies	89
1972/3	Ron Barry	125
1973/4	Ron Barry	94
1974/5	Tommy Stack	82
1975/6	John Francome	96
1976/7	Tommy Stack	97

1977/8	Jonjo O'Neill	149
1978/9	John Francome	95
1979/80	Jonjo O'Neill	115
1980/1	John Francome	105
1981/2	John Francome	120
	Peter Scudamore	120
1982/3	John Francome	106
1983/4	John Francome	131
1984/5	John Francome	101
1985/6	Peter Scudamore	91
1986/7	Peter Scudamore	123
1987/8	Peter Scudamore	132
1988/9	Peter Scudamore	221
1989/90	Peter Scudamore	170
1990/1	Peter Scudamore	141
1991/2	Peter Scudamore	175
1992/3	Richard Dunwoody	173
1993/4	Richard Dunwoody	198

Most times champion (since 1900): 8 Peter Scudamore (including one shared) as above; 7 Gerry Wilson 1932/3-1937/8, 1940/1; John Francome, as above; 6 Tich Mason 1901-2, 1904-7; 5 Bilbie Rees 1920-1, 1924-5, 1926/7; Billy Stott 1927/8-1931/2; Tim Moloney, as above

Progressive record of most wins in a season/year (since 1900)

1900	Mr H S Sidney	53
1901	Tich Mason	58
1902	Tich Mason	67
1905	Tich Mason	73
1911	Bill Payne	76
1912	Ivor Anthony	78
1922	Jack Anthony	78
1924	Bilbie Rees	108
1952/3	Fred Winter	121
1966/7	Josh Gifford	122
1972/3	Ron Barry	125
1977/8	Jonjo O'Neill	149
1988/9	Peter Scudamore	221

Most wins in a National Hunt career

Jockey	Wins	Years
Peter Scudamore	1677	1978-93
John Francome	1138	1970-85
Richard Dunwoody	1107	1983-94
Stan Mellor	1035	1952-72
Fred Winter	923	1939-64
Bob Davies	911	1966-82
Terry Biddlecombe	908	1958-74
Jonjo O'Neill	885	1972-86
Steve Smith Eccles	861	1974-94
Ron Barry	823	1964-83

Hennessy Cognac Gold Cup

Ireland's richest steeplechase, first run at Leopardstown in 1987 over 3 miles. Originally the Vincent O'Brien Irish Gold Cup.

1987	Forgive 'N' Forget	Mark Dwyer
1988	Playschool	Paul Nicholls
1989	Carvill's Hill	Ken Morgan

1990	Nick the Brief	Michael Lynch
1991	Nick The Brief	Robert Supple
1992	Carvill's Hill	Peter Scudamore
1993-4	Jodami	Mark Dwyer

National Hunt Champion Horse of the Year

Awarded to the champion jumper annually, the voting is along similar lines to that for the flat racehorse of the year. *Winners:*

1965/6	Arkle
1966/7	Mill House
1967/8	Persian War
1968/9	Persian War
1969/70	Persian War
1970/1	Bula
1971/2	Bula
1972/3	Pendil
1973/4	Red Rum
1974/5	Comedy of Errors
1975/6	Night Nurse
1976/7	Night Nurse
1977/8	Midnight Court
1978/9	Monksfield
1979/80	Sea Pigeon
1980/1	Sea Pigeon
1981/2	Silver Buck
1982/3	Gaye Brief
1983/4	Dawn Run
1984/5	Borough Hill Lad
1985/6	Dawn Run
1986/7	Desert Orchid
1987/8	Desert Orchid
1988/9	Desert Orchid
1989/90	Desert Orchid
1990/1	Morley Street
1991/2	Remittance Man
1992/3	Jodami
1993/4	The Fellow

Horse Racing in the USA

The Triple Crown

Like the English Classics, the three races that make up the American Triple Crown are for 3-year-olds only.

Kentucky Derby

Raced annually on the first Saturday in May at Churchill Downs, Louisville over 1 mile 2 furlongs. First run in 1875, and at a distance of 1 mile 4 furlongs 1879-95. *Winners since 1970:*

Year	Winner	Jockey
1970	Dust Commander	Mike Manganello
1971	Canonero	Gustavo Avila
1972	Riva Ridge	Ron Turcotte
1973	Secretariat	Ron Turcotte
1974	Cannonade	Angel Cordero, Jr
1975	Foolish Pleasure	Jacinto Vasquez
1976	Bold Forbes	Angel Cordero, Jr
1977	Seattle Slew	Jean Cruguet
1978	Affirmed	Steve Cauthen
1979	Spectacular Bid	Ron Franklin
1980	Genuine Risk *	Jacinto Vasquez

1981	Pleasant Colony	Jorge Velasquez
1982	Gato Del Sol	Eddie Delahoussaye
1983	Sunny's Halo	Eddie Delahoussaye
1984	Swale	Laffit Pincay, Jr
1985	Spend A Buck	Angel Cordero, Jr
1986	Ferdinand	Billie Shoemaker
1987	Alysheba	Chris McCarron
1988	Winning Colors *	Gary Stevens
1989	Sunday Silence	Pat Valenzuela
1990	Unbridled	Craig Perret
1991	Strike The Gold	Chris Antley
1992	Lil E Tee	Pat Day
1993	Sea Hero	Jerry Bailey
1994	Go For Gin	Chris McCarron
1995	Thunder Gulch	Gary Stevens

* *fillies*

Most wins - Jockey:
5 Eddie Arcaro 1938, 1941, 1945, 1948, 1952
5 Bill Hartack 1957, 1960, 1962, 1964, 1969
Most wins - Trainer: 6 Ben Jones 1938, 1941, 1944, 1948-9, 1952
Most wins - Owner: 8 Calumet Farm 1941, 1944, 1948-9, 1952, 1957-8, 1968
Fastest time: 1 min 59.4 sec Secretariat 1973

Preakness Stakes

Raced at Pimlico, Baltimore, Maryland over 1 mile 1.5 furlongs (1 mile 4 furlongs 1873-88, and at distances between 1m 70y and 1 mile 2 furlongs 1889-1925) *Winners since 1970:*

1970	Personality	Eddie Belmonte
1971	Canonero	Gustavo Avila
1972	Bee Bee Bee	Eddie Nelson
1973	Secretariat	Ron Turcotte
1974	Little Current	Miguel Rivera
1975	Master Derby	Darrell McHargue
1976	Elocutionist	John Lively
1977	Seattle Slew	Jean Cruguet
1978	Affirmed	Steve Cauthen
1979	Spectacular Bid	Ron Franklin
1980	Codex	Angel Cordero, Jr
1981	Pleasant Colony	Jorge Velasquez
1982	Aloma's Ruler	Jack Kaenel
1983	Deputed Testamony	Don Miller jr
1984	Gate Dancer	Angel Cordero, Jr
1985	Tank's Prospect	Pat Day
1986	Snow Chief	Alex Solis
1987	Alysheba	Chris McCarron
1988	Risen Star	Eddie Delahoussaye
1989	Sunday Silence	Pat Valenzuela
1990	Summer Squall	Pat Day
1991	Hansel	Jerry Bailey
1992	Pine Bluff	Chris McCarron
1993	Prairie Bayou	Mike Smith
1994	Tabasco Cat	Pat Day
1995	Timber Country	Pat Day

Most wins - Jockey: 6 Eddie Arcaro 1941, 1948, 1950-1, 1955, 1957
Most wins - Trainer: 7 Robert Wyndham Walden 1875, 1878-82, 1888

Most wins - Owner: 5 George Lorillard 1878-82
Fastest time: 1 min 53.2 sec Tank's Prospect 1985

Belmont Stakes

The oldest of the three Triple Crown races, it was first run in 1867 at Jerome Park. The race moved to Morris Park in 1889 and to Belmont Park. New York in 1890. Raced at 1 mile 5 furlongs 1867-73, at shorter distances 1890-25, and the current distance of 1 mile 4 furlongs in 1874-89 and from 1926
Winners since 1970:

1970	Echelon	John Rotz
1971	Pass Catcher	Walter Blum
1972	Riva Ridge	Ron Turcotte
1973	Secretariat	Ron Turcotte
1974	Little Current	Miguel Rivera
1975	Avatar	Billie Shoemaker
1976	Bold Forbes	Angel Cordero, Jr
1977	Seattle Slew	Jean Cruguet
1978	Affirmed	Steve Cauthen
1979	Coastal	Ruben Hernandez
1980	Temperence Hill	Eddie Maple
1981	Summing	George Martens
1982	Conquistador Cielo	Laffit Pincay, Jr
1983	Caveat	Laffit Pincay, Jr
1984	Swale	Laffit Pincay, Jr
1985	Creme Fraiche	Eddie Maple
1986	Danzig Connection	Chris McCarron
1987	Bet Twice	Craig Perrett
1988	Risen Star	Eddie Delahoussaye
1989	Easy Goer	Pat Day
1990	Go And Go	Michael Kinane
1991	Hansel	Jenny Bailey
1992	A.P.Indy	Eddie Delahoussaye
1993	Colonial Affair	Julie Krone*
1994	Tabasco Cat	Pat Day
1995	Thunder Gulch	Gary Stevens

* *Krone became the first woman jockey to ride the winner of a Triple Crown race.*

Most wins - Jockey: 6 Jimmy McLaughlin 1882-4, 1886-8; 6 Eddie Arcaro 1941-2, 1945, 1948, 1952, 1955
Most wins - Trainer: 8 James Rowe Sr 1883-4, 1901, 1904, 1907-8, 1910, 1913
Most wins - Owner: 5 Dwyer Bros 1883-4, 1886-8; 5 James R Keene 1901, 1904, 1907-8, 1910; 5 William Woodward Sr (Belair Stud) 1930, 1932, 1935-6, 1939
Fastest time: 2 min 24.0 sec Secretariat 1973 (won by a record 31 lengths)
In 1993 Julie Krone became the first woman to ride the winner of a triple crown race.
The following 11 horses have successfully won all legs of the Triple Crown:
1919 Sir Barton 1930 Gallant Fox, 1935 Omaha, 1937 War Admiral, 1941 Whirlaway, 1943 Count Fleet 1946 Assault, 1948 Citation, 1973 Secretariat, 1977 Seattle Slew, 1978 Affirmed
Jockeys to have ridden most winners in Triple Crown races: 17 Eddie Arcaro, 11 Billie Shoemaker, 9 Bill Hartack, Earle Sande; 8 Jimmy McLaughlin

The Breeders' Cup

The Breeders' Cup programme was founded in 1984 and administered by breeders with the aim of stimulating throughbred racing in the USA. The series offers more than $20 million annually, $10 million in the seven races run on the Breeders' Cup Event Day each November. The top purse, $3 million, is for the Breeders' Cup Classic ($1.35m to the winning owner). The purse for the Breeders' Cup Turf is $2 million, and the other races are each for $1 million. Various venues have been used, from the first meeting at Hollywood Park in 1984. Distances shown are those run currently
Winners:

Breeders' Cup Sprint (6 furlongs)

1984	Ellio	Craig Perret
1985	Precisionist	Chris McCarron
1986	Smile	Jacinto Vasquez
1987	Very Subtle	Pat Valenzuela
1988	Gulch	Angel Cordero
1989	Dancing Spree	Angel Cordero
1990	Safely Kept	Craig Perret
1991	Skeikh Albadou	Pat Eddery
1992	Thirty Slews	Eddie Delahoussaye
1993	Cardmania	Eddie Delahoussaye
1994	Cherokee Run	Mike Smith

Breeders' Cup Juvenile Fillies (1 mile 110y)

1984	Outstandingly	Walter Guerra
1985	Twilight Ridge	Jorge Velasquez
1986	Brave Raj	Pat Valenzuela
1987	Epitome	Pat Day
1988	Open Mind	Angel Cordero
1989	Go For Wand	Randy Romero
1990	Meadow Star	José Santos
1991	Pleasant Stage	Eddie Delahoussaye
1992	Eliza	Pat Valenzuela
1993	Phone Chatter	Laffit Pincay, Jr
1994	Flanders	Pat Day

Breeders' Cup Distaff (1 mile 1 furlong)

1984	Princess Rooney	Eddie Delahoussaye
1985	Life's Magic	Angel Cordero, Jr
1986	Lady's Secret	Pat Day
1987	Sacahuista	Randy Romero
1988	Personal Ensign	Randy Romero
1989	Bayakoa	Laffit Pincay, Jr
1990	Bayakoa	Laffit Pincay, Jr
1991	Dance Smartly	Pat Day
1992	Paseana	Chris McCarron
1993	Hollywood Wildcat	Eddie Delahoussaye
1994	One Dreamer	Gary Stevens

Breeders' Cup Mile

1984	Royal Heroine	Fernando Toro
1985	Cozzene	Walter Guerra

1986	Last Tycoon	Yves Saint-Martin
1987	Miesque	Freddy Head
1988	Miesque	Freddy Head
1989	Steinlen	José Santos
1990	Royal Academy	Lester Piggott
1991	Opening Verse	Pat Valenzuela
1992	Lure	Mike Smith
1993	Lure	Mike Smith
1994	Barathea	Frankie Dettori

Breeders' Cup Juvenile (1 mile 110y)

1984	Chief's Crown	Don MacBeth
1985	Tasso	Laffit Pincay, Jr
1986	Capote	Laffit Pincay, Jr
1987	Success Express	José Santos
1988	Is It True?	Laffit Pincay, Jr
1989	Rhythm	Craig Perret
1990	Fly So Free	José Santos
1991	Arazi	Pat Valenzuela
1992	Gilded Time	Chris McCarron
1993	Brocco	Gary Stevens
1994	Timber Country	Pat Day

Breeders' Cup Turf (1 mile 4 furlongs)

1984	Lashkari	Yves Saint-Martin
1985	Pebbles	Pat Eddery
1986	Manila	José Santos
1987	Theatrical	Pat Day
1988	Great Communicator	Ray Sibille
1989	Prized	Eddie Delahoussaye
1990	In The Wings	Gary Stevens
1991	Miss Alleged	Eric Legrix
1992	Fraise	Pat Valenzuela
1993	Kotashaan	Kent Desormeaux
1994	Tikkanen	Mike Smith

Breeders' Cup Classic (1 mile 2 furlongs)

1984	Wild Again	Pat Day
1985	Proud Truth	Jorge Velasquez
1986	Skywalker	Laffit Pincay, Jr
1987	Ferdinand	Billie Shoemaker
1988	Alysheba	Chris McCarron
1989	Sunday Silence	Chris McCarron
1990	Unbridled	Pat Day
1991	Black Tie Affair	Jenny Bailey
1992	A.P.Indy	Eddie Delahoussaye
1993	Arcangues	Jerry Bailey
1994	Concern	Jerry Bailey

Most wins - Jockeys: 8 Day, 7 Pincay, Delahoussaye; 5 Santos, McCarron, Valenzuela; 4 Cordero, Smith
Most wins - Trainer: 12 D.Wayne Lukas

Arlington Million

A weight-for-age race at 1m 2f for 3-year-olds and upwards run annually from 1981 at Arlington Park, Chicago.

1981	John Henry	Billie Shoemaker
1982	Perrault	Laffit Pincay, Jr
1983	Tolomeo	Pat Eddery

Pat Valenzuela won the Juvenile on Arazi in 1991

1984	John Henry	Chris McCarron
1985	Teleprompter	Tony Ives
1986	Estrapade	Fernandez Toro
1987	Manila	Angel Cordero
1988	Mill Native	Cash Asmussen
1989	Steinlen	José Santos
1990	Golden Pheasant	Gary Stevens
1991	Tight Spot	Laffit Pincay, Jr
1992	Dear Doctor	Cash Asmussen
1993	Star of Cozzene	José Santos
1994	Paradise Creek	Pat Day

Washington DC International

The Washington International was the idea of John D Schapiro, the president of Laurel Racecourse in Maryland. The first International was at Laurel Park in October 1952 and was run over 1 mile 2 furlongs. The race showed a steady decline in international status, and Schapiro sold his interest in the track in 1984.

Most wins
Horse: 2 Bald Eagle (1959-60), Fort Marcy (1967, 1970)
Jockey: 3 Lester Piggott (Sir Ivor 1968, Karabas 1969, Argument 1980); Manuel Ycaza (Bald Eagle 1959-60, Fort Marcy 1967)

Annual US Leading Money-winning horses from 1946

Year	Leading horse	
1946	Assault	$424,195
1947	Armed	376,325
1948	Citation	709,470
1949	Ponder	321,825
1950	Noor	346,940
1951	Counterpoint	250,525
1952	Crafty Admiral	277,255
1953	Native Dancer	513,425
1954	Determine	328,700
1955	Nashua	752,550
1956	Needles	440,850
1957	Round Table	600,383
1958	Round Table	662,780
1959	Sword Dancer	537,004
1960	Bally Ache	455,045
1961	Carry Back	565,349
1962	Never Bend	402,969

Year	Leading horse	
1963	Candy Spots	604,481
1964	Gun Bow	580,100
1965	Buckpasser	568,096
1966	Buckpasser	669,078
1967	Damascus	817,941
1968	Forward Pass	546,674
1969	Arts and Letters	555,604
1970	Personality	444,049
1971	Riva Ridge	503,263
1972	Droll Roll	471,633
1973	Secretariat	860,404
1974	Chris Evert	551,063
1975	Foolish Pleasure	716,278
1976	Forego	491,701
1977	Seattle Slew	641,370
1978	Affirmed	901,541
1979	Spectacular Bid	1,279,334
1980	Temperance Hill	1,130,452
1981	John Henry	1,148,800
1982	Perrault	1,197,400
1983	All Along	2,138,963
1984	Slew O'Gold	2,627,944
1985	Spend A Buck	3,552,704
1986	Snow Chief	1,875,200
1987	Alysheba	2,511,156
1988	Alysheba	3,808,600
1989	Sunday Silence	4,578,454
1990	Unbridled	3,718,149
1991	Dance Smartly	2,876,821
1992	A.P.Indy	2,622,560
1993	Kotashaan	2,810,528
1994	Concern	2,541,670

Annual US Leading Money-winning jockeys

1946	Ted Atkinson	$1,036,825
1947	Doug Dodson	1,429,949
1948	Eddie Arcaro	1,686,230
1949	Steve Brooks	1,316,817
1950	Eddie Arcaro	1,410,160
1951	Billie Shoemaker	1,329,890
1952	Eddie Arcaro	1,859,591
1953	Billie Shoemaker	1,784,187
1954	Billie Shoemaker	1,876,760
1955	Eddie Arcaro	1,864,796
1956	Bill Hartack	2,343,955
1957	Bill Hartack	3,060,501
1958	Billie Shoemaker	2,961,693
1959	Billie Shoemaker	2,843,133
1960	Billie Shoemaker	2,123,961
1961	Billie Shoemaker	2,690,819
1962	Billie Shoemaker	2,916,844
1963	Billie Shoemaker	2,526,925
1964	Billie Shoemaker	2,649,553
1965	Braulio Baeza	2,582,702
1966	Braulio Baeza	2,951,022
1967	Braulio Baeza	3,088,888
1968	Braulio Baeza	2,835,108
1969	Jorge Velasquez	2,542,315
1970	Laffit Pincay Jr	2,626,526
1971	Laffit Pincay Jr	3,784,377
1972	Laffit Pincay Jr	3,225,827
1973	Laffit Pincay Jr	4,093,492
1974	Laffit Pincay Jr	4,251,060
1975	Braulio Baeza	3,695,198
1976	Angel Cordero Jr	4,709,500
1977	Steve Cauthen	6,151,750
1978	Darrel McHargue	6,029,885
1979	Laffit Pincay Jr	8,913,535
1980	Chris McCarron	7,663,300
1981	Chris McCarron	8,397,604
1982	Angel Cordero Jr	9,483,590
1983	Angel Cordero Jr	10,116,697
1984	Chris McCarron	12,045,813
1985	Laffit Pincay	13,353,299
1986	José Santos	11,329,297
1987	José Santos	12,375,433
1988	José Santos	14,877,298
1989	José Santos	13,838,389
1990	Gary Stevens	13,881,198
1991	Chris McCarron	14,441,083
1992	Kent Desormeaux	14,193,006
1993	Mike Smith	14,008,148
1994	Mike Smith	15,979,820

Total Career Earnings (US Dollars)

Horses

Alysheba	6,679,242	1986-8
John Henry	6,597,947	1977-84
Sunday Silence	4,968,554	1988-90
Easy Goer	4,873,770	1988-90

Most won in a year: $4,578,454 by Sunday Silence in 1989

Jockeys

Jockeys	Dollars	Wins	Years
Laffit Pincay	183,910,301	8213	1966-94
Chris McCarron	177,686,860	6074	1974-94
Angel Cordero Jr	164,528,217	7057	1960-92
Pat Day	149,339,825	6308	1972-94
Eddie Delahoussaye	138,120,927	5375	1970-94
Billie Shoemaker	123,375,524	8833	1949-90
Jorge Velasquez	123,252,413	6682	1965-94

Also over 6000 winners

David Gall	20,837,406	6611	1957-94
Larry Snyder	47,207,289	6388	1953-94
Carl Gambardella	29,389,041	6349	1956-94
Sandy Hawley	81,863,406	6205	1968-94
Johnny Longden	24,665,800	6032	1926-66

Most wins in a year

No	Jockey	Year	Rides
598	Kent Desormeaux	1989	2312
546	Chris McCarron	1974	2199
515	Sandy Hawley	1973	1925
487	Steve Cauthen	1977	2075
485	Billie Shoemaker	1953	1683

Trainers

Greatest season's earnings: $17,842,358 D Wayne Lukas in 1988 from 318 winners.

Greatest career earnings: $149,272,207 D Wayne Lukas 1977-94

Most wins in a year: 496 Jack Van Berg 1976

Most wins in a career: 6609 Dale Baird 1962-94

Most wins in stakes races: 746 D Wayne Lukas

Eclipse Awards

From 1971 the annual polls conducted by the Throughbred Racing Associations, the Daily Racing Form and the National Turf Writers' Association have been combined to determine the recipients of the Eclipse Awards.

Overall Horse of the Year:

1971	Ack Ack
1972-3	Secretariat
1974-6	Forego
1977	Seattle Slew
1978-9	Affirmed
1980	Spectacular Bid
1981	John Henry
1982	Conquistador Cielo
1983	All Along
1984	John Henry
1985	Spend A Buck
1986	Lady's Secret
1987	Ferdinand
1988	Alysheba
1989	Sunday Silence
1990	Criminal Type

Year	Winner	Jockey
1991	Black Tie Affair	
1992	A.P.Indy	
1993	Kotashaan	
1994	Holy Bull	

Most wins in the Throughbred Racing Association Poll prior to 1971: 5 Kelso 1960-4, 2 Challedon 1940-1, Whirlaway 1941-2, Native Dancer 1952 (tie), 1954.

Australia - Melbourne Cup

The highlight of the racing season in Australia is the Melbourne Cup. Like Royal Ascot it is as much a social occasion as a race-day. Always held on the first Tuesday in November, it was inaugurated in 1861. The race is for 3-year-olds and upwards, and, since 1972 has been over 3200 metres of the Flemington racecourse in Victoria. Prior to then it was over the Imperial equivalent of two miles. Now sponsored by Fosters. *Post-war winners:*

Year	Winner	Jockey
1945	Rainbird	Billy Cook
1946	Russia	Darby Munro
1947	Hiraji	Jack Purtell
1948	Rimfire	Ray Neville
1949	Foxzami	Bill Fellows
1950	Comic Court	Pat Glennon
1951	Delta	Neville Sellwood
1952	Dalray	Bill Williamson
1953	Wodalla	Jack Purtell
1954	Rising Fast	Jack Purtell
1955	Toparoa	Neville Sellwood
1956	Evening Peal	George Podmore
1957	Straight Draw	Noel McGrowdie
1958	Baystone	Mel Schumacher
1959	Macdougal	Pat Glennon
1960	Hi Jinx	Bill Smith
1961	Lord Fury	Roy Selkrig
1962	Even Stevens	Les Coles
1963	Gatum Gatum	Jim Johnson
1964	Polo Prince	Ron Taylor
1965	Light Fingers	Roy Higgins
1966	Galilee	John Miller
1967	Red Handed	Roy Higgins
1968	Rain Lover	Jim Johnson
1969	Rain Lover	Jim Johnson
1970	Baghdad Note	Midge Didham
1971	Silver Knight	Bruce Marshall
1972	Piping Lane	John Letts
1973	Gala Supreme	Frank Reys
1974	Think Big	Harry White
1975	Think Big	Harry White
1976	Van der Hum	Bobby Skelton
1977	Gold and Black	John Duggan
1978	Arwon	Harry White
1979	Hyperno	Harry White
1980	Beldale Ball	John Letts
1981	Just a Dash	Peter Cook
1982	Gurner's Lane	Mick Dittman
1983	Kiwi	Jimmy Cassidi
1984	Black Knight	Peter Cook
1985	What A Nuisance	Pat Hyland
1986	At Talaq	Michael Clarke
1987	Kensei	Larry Olsen
1988	Empire Rose	Tony Allan
1989	Tawrrific	Shane Dye
1990	Kingston Rule	Darren Beadman
1991	Let's Elope	Stephen King
1992	Subzero	Greg Hall
1993	Vintage Crop (Ire)	Michael Kinane
1994	Jeune	Wayne Harris

Most wins - Jockey: 4 Bobby Lewis (The Victory 1902, Patrobas 1915, Artilleryman 1919, Trivalve 1927); Harry White, as above
Most wins - Trainer: 9 Bart Cummings 1965-7, 1974-5, 1977, 1979, 1990-1
Most wins - Horse: 2 Archer 1861-2, Peter Pan 1932, 1934, Rain Lover 1968-9, Think Big 1974-5
Fastest winning time: 3:16.3 Kingston Rule 1990

Japan Cup

The world's richest turf race is now the Japan Cup, run each November in Tokyo over 1m 4f. The 1993 race was worth £914,480. *Winners:*

Year	Winner	Jockey
1981	Mairzy Doates	Cash Asmussen
1982	Half Ired	Don Macbeth
1983	Stanerra	Brian Rouse
1984	Katsuragi Ace	Katsuti Nishiura
1985	Symboli Rudolf	Yukio Okabe
1986	Jupiter Island (UK)	Pat Eddery
1987	Le Glorieux	Alain Lequeux
1988	Pay The Butler (US)	Chris McCarron
1989	Horlicks	Lance O'Sullivan
1990	Better Loosen Up (Aus)	Michael Clarke
1991	Golden Pheasant (US)	Gary Stevens
1992	Tokai Teio	Yukio Okabe
1993	Legacy World	Hiroshi Kawachi
1994	Marvellous Crown	Katsumi Minai

Hurling

Played at 15-a-side with stick and ball, hurling, the second most popular traditional sport in Ireland, is of great antiquity. It was included in the Tailteann Games (instituted 1829 BC). It was outlawed in Ireland in 1367 by the statute of Kilkenny. The Irish Hurling Union was founded in 1879 and the rules standardised following the formation of the Gaelic Athletic Association in 1884.

All Ireland Championships

Played on the first Sunday in September each year the All-Ireland Final is the highlight of the hurling season. The final of this inter-county event takes place at Dublin's Croke Park and the winning team receives the McCarthy Cup. Contested annually from 1887, with the exception of the unfinished championship of 1888. *Wins:*

27 Cork	1890, 1892-4, 1902-3, 1919, 1926, 1928-9, 1931,1941-4, 1946, 1952-4, 1966, 1970, 1976-8, 1984, 1986, 1990	

25	Kilkenny	1904-5, 1907, 1909, 1911-3, 1922, 1932-3, 1935, 1939, 1947, 1957, 1963, 1967, 1969, 1972, 1974-5, 1979, 1982-3, 1992-3
24	Tipperary	1887, 1895-6, 1898-1900, 1906, 1908, 1916, 1925, 1930, 1937, 1945, 1949-51, 1958, 1961-2, 1964-5, 1971, 1989, 1991
7	Limerick	1897, 1918, 1921, 1934, 1936, 1940, 1973
6	Dublin	1889, 1917, 1920, 1924, 1927, 1938
5	Wexford	1910, 1955-6, 1960, 1968
4	Galway	1923, 1980, 1987-8
3	Offaly	1981, 1985, 1994
2	Waterford	1948, 1959
1	Kerry	1891
1	London Irish	1901
1	Clare	1914
1	Laois	1915

Highest team score in a final: Tipperary 41 (4 goals, 29 points) Antrim 18 (3, 9) in 1989

Highest aggregate score in a final: 64 Cork 39 (6, 21) beat Wexford 25 (5, 10) in 1970
Most individual appearances: 10 Christy Ring (Cork and Munster) 1941-54, John Doyle (Tipperary) 1949-65, each with eight wins; 10 (with 7 wins) Frank Cummins (Kilkenny) 1969-83
Highest individual score: 19 (5 goals, 4 points) Michael Ahearne (Cork) 1928, 18 (2 goals, 12 points) Nicholas English (Tipperary) 1989
Highest attendance: 84,856 in 1954.

Players to have won all-Ireland medals in both Gaelic Football and Hurling

Jack Lynch (Cork) Hurling 1941-4, 1946; Football 1945
Ray Cummins (Cork) Hurling 1971-2, 1977; Football 1971, 1973
Jimmy Barry Murphy (Cork) Hurling 1976-8, 1983, 1986; Football 1973-4
Brian Murphy (Cork) Hurling 1978, 1981; Football 1973, 1976
Liam Currans (Offaly) Hurling 1981; Football 1982
Teddy McCarthy (Cork) Hurling & Football 1990 (first to do so in same year)

Ice Hockey

Played by teams of 6-a-side with stick and puck. It probably derives from bandy, played on ice-covered pitches, and the 1850s are usually cited for the advent of the puck in Canada, where the game has for long been the major sport. The first rules for Ice Hockey were drawn up by W F Robertson and R F Smith, students at McGill University, Montreal. The Ontario Hockey Association was formed in 1887.

The sport's governing body is the International Ice Hockey Federation (IIHF), founded in 1908 by Belgium, Bohemia, England, France and Switzerland.

Olympic Games

An Olympic sport from 1920, ice hockey was contested at the summer Games of 1920, but thereafter at the Winter Olympics. *Wins:*

8	USSR/CIS	1956, 1964, 1968, 1972, 1976, 1984, 1988, 1992 (CIS)
6	Canada	1920, 1924, 1928, 1932, 1948, 1952
2	USA	1960, 1980
1	Great Britain	1936
1	Sweden	1994

Most gold medals by an individual: 3 by the USSR players Vitaliy Davidov, Anatoliy Firssov, Viktor Kuzkin and Aleksandr Ragulin 1964-72; Vladislav Tretyak 1972-84, Andrey Khomutov 1984-92.

World Championships

Held annually from 1930, except for the war years and in 1980. In Olympic years up to 1968 those championships were also recognised as the world championships. *Most wins:*

22	USSR	1954, 1956, 1963-71, 1973-5, 1978-9, 1981-3, 1986, 1989-90
20	Canada	1920, 1924, 1928, 1930-2, 1934-5, 1937-9, 1948, 1950-2, 1955, 1958-9, 1961, 1994
6	Czechoslovakia	1947, 1949, 1972, 1976-7, 1985
5	Sweden	1953, 1957, 1962, 1987, 1991-2
2	USA	1933, 1960
1	Great Britain	1936
1	Russia	1993
1	Finland	1995

Highest score in a world championship match: Australia beat New Zealand 58-0 at Perth, 14 Mar 1987.

Women's World Championships

First held in 1990. *Winners:*

3	Canada	1990, 1992, 1994

European Championships

Held annually, first in 1910. In recent years held concurrently with World Championships, but not from 1980 in Olympic years, until abandoned after 1991. *Champions:*

29	USSR	1954-6, 1958-60, 1963-70, 1973-5, 1978-83, 1985-7, 1989-91
15	Czechoslovakia	Bohemia: 1911-2, 1914; Cs: 1922, 1925, 1929, 1933, 1947-9, 1961, 1971-2, 1976-7
9	Sweden	1921, 1923, 1928, 1932, 1951-3, 1957, 1962
4	Great Britain	1910, 1936-8
4	Switzerland	1926, 1935, 1939, 1950
2	Austria	1927, 1931
2	Germany	1930, 1934
1	Belgium	1913
1	France	1924

Women's European Championships

Won by Finland on each occasion staged: 1989, 1991, 1993, 1995

The IIHF Canada Cup

First held in 1979, this tournament is contested by the world's six best teams. *Winners:*
1979 Canada, 1981 USSR, 1984 Canada, 1987 Canada, 1991 Canada.

National Hockey League

Hockey Association. It is now contested by 24 teams, 8 from Canada and 16 from the USA, divided into two divisions within two conferences: Adams and Patrick Divisions in the Wales Conference; Norris and Smythe Divisions in the Campbell Conference. The top teams play-off annually for the Stanley Cup, which was first presented in 1893 by Lord Stanley of Preston, then Governor-General of Canada. From 1894 it was contested by amateur teams for the Canadian Championship. From 1910 it became the award for the winners of the professional league play-offs.

Year given is that of second half of season. There were two contests in 1896 and 1907, and in 1919 the series was unfinished due to an influenza outbreak.

Stanley Cup *wins:*
24 Montreal Canadiens 1916, 1924, 1930-1, 1944, 1946, 1953, 1956-60, 1965-6, 1968-9, 1971, 1973, 1976-9, 1986, 1993
11 Toronto Maple Leafs 1932, 1942, 1945, 1947-9, 1951, 1962-4, 1967
7 Detroit Red Wings 1936-7, 1943, 1950, 1952, 1954-5
6 Ottawa Senators 1909, 1911, 1920-1, 1923, 1927
5 Boston Bruins 1929, 1939, 1941, 1970, 1972
5 Edmonton Oilers 1984-5, 1987-8, 1990
4 Montreal Victorias 1895, 1896 (Dec), 1897-8
4 Montreal Wanderers 1906-8, 1910
4 New York Islanders 1980-3
4 New York Rangers 1928, 1933, 1940, 1994
3 Montreal AAA 1893-4, 1902
3 Ottawa Silver Seven 1903-5
3 Chicago Black Hawks 1934, 1938, 1961
2 Winnipeg Victorias 1896 (Feb), 1901
2 Québec Bulldogs 1912-3
2 Montreal Maroons 1926, 1935
2 Philadelphia Flyers 1974-5

A missed penalty by Canada, who lose 2-3 to Sweden at the 1994 Olympics

2 Montreal Shamrocks 1899, 1900
2 Pittsburgh Penguins 1991-2
1 Kenora Thistles 1907 (Jan), Toronto Ontarios 1914, Vancouver Millionaires 1915, Seattle Metropolitans 1917, Toronto Arenas 1918, Toronto St Patricks 1922, Victoria Cougars 1925, Calgary Flames 1989, New Jersey Devils 1995.
Most finals: 31 Montreal Canadiens, 21 Toronto Maple Leafs, 18 Detroit Red Wings

Conn Smythe Trophy

For the most valuable player in the play-offs has been awarded annually from 1965. *Winners from 1980:*

1980 Bryan Trottier (NY Islanders)
1981 Butch Goring (NY Islanders)
1982 Mike Bossy (NY Islanders)
1983 Billy Smith (NY Islanders)
1984 Mark Messier (Edmonton)
1985 Wayne Gretzky (Edmonton)
1986 Patrick Roy (Montreal)
1987 Ron Hextall (Philadelphia)
1988 Wayne Gretzky (Edmonton)
1989 Al MacInnis (Calgary)
1990 Bill Ranford (Edmonton)
1991-2 Mario Lemieux (Pittsburgh)
1993 Patrick Roy (Montreal)
1994 Brian Leetch (New York)
1995 Claude Lemieux (New Jersey)
The only players to win it twice: Bobby Orr (Boston) 1970, 1972; Bernie Parent (Philadelphia) 1974-5, Wayne Gretzky and Mario Lemieux.

NHL Career Scoring Leaders

For regular season games, not including playoffs.

Name	Goals	Assists	Pts	Games	Years
Wayne Gretzky	814	1692	2506	1173	1979-95
Gordie Howe	801	1049	1850	1767	1946-71
Marcel Dionne	731	1040	1771	1348	1971-89
Phil Esposito	717	873	1590	1282	1963-81
Stan Mikita	541	926	1467	1394	1958-80
Bryan Trottier	524	901	1425	1279	1975-94
John Bucyk	556	813	1369	1540	1955-78
Mark Messier	492	877	1369	1127	1979-95
Guy Lafleur	560	793	1353	1126	1971-92
Paul Coffey	358	978	1336	1078	1980-95
Gilbert Perreault	512	814	1326	1191	1970-87
Dale Hawerchuk	489	825	1314	1009	1981-95
Jari Kurri	565	731	1296	1028	1980-95
Alex Delvecchio	456	825	1281	1549	1951-74
Jean Ratelle	491	776	1267	1281	1960-81
Other players with more than 550 goals					
Mike Gartner	629	562	1191	1208	1979-95
Bobby Hull	610	560	1170	1063	1957-80
Mike Bossy	573	553	1126	752	1980-89

Most playoff points
346 Wayne Gretzky (record 110 goals, 236 assists)
259 Mark Messier (99G, 160A)
222 Jari Kurri (102G, 120A)
207 Glenn Anderson (91G, 116A)
184 Bryan Trottier (71G, 113A)

National League Season Scoring Records

Goals	92	Wayne Gretzky (Edmonton Oilers) 1981/2
Assists	163	Wayne Gretzky (Edmonton Oilers) 1985/6
Points	215	Wayne Gretzky (Edmonton Oilers) 1985/6
NHL points	132	Montreal Canadiens 1976/7 (80 games, won 60, lost 8, tied 12)
Team goals	446	Edmonton Oilers 1983/4
Team assists	737	Edmonton Oilers 1985/6
Team points	1182	Edmonton Oilers 1983/4

National League Scoring Records in a Game

Goals	7	Joe Malone for Québec Bulldogs v Toronto St Patrick's, 31 Jan 1920
Assists	7	Billy Taylor for Detroit Red Wings v Chicago Black Hawks, 16 Mar 1947
	7	Wayne Gretzky for Edmonton Oilers v Washington, 15 Feb 1980
	7	Wayne Gretzky for Edmonton Oilers v Chicago, 11 Dec 1985
	7	Wayne Gretzky for Edmonton Oilers v Québec, 14 Feb 1986
Points	10	Darryl Sittler (6 goals 4 assists) for Toronto Maple Leafs v Boston Bruins, 7 Feb 1976

Most points in a playoff game

	8	(3g/5a) Patrik Sundström for New Jersey Devils v Washington 22 Apr 1988
	8	(5g/3a) Mario Lemieux for Pittsburgh v Philadelphia 25 Apr 1989.

Team Goals

16 Montreal Canadiens beat Québec Bulldogs 16-3, Québec City, 3 Nov 1920

Team Aggregate

21 Montreal Canadiens beat Toronto St Patrick's 14-7, Montreal, 10 Jan 1930

21 Edmonton Oilers beat Chicago Black Hawks 12-9, Chicago 11 Dec 1985

Wayne Gretzky

The phenomenal Gretzky has been scoring at a record pace since he entered the NHL. On 15 Oct 1989 he passed Gordie Howe's NHL scoring record of 1850 points in 10 years to Howe's 26 and on 23 Mar 1994 Howe's career record of 801 goals. Gretzky's season by season record in regular season games - for Edmonton Oilers until 1987/8 and subsequently the Los Angeles Kings:

Season	Goals	Assists	Points
1979/80	51	86	137
1980/1	55	109	164
1981/2	92	120	212
1982/3	71	125	196
1983/4	87	118	205
1984/5	73	135	208
1985/6	52	163	215
1986/7	62	121	183
1987/8	40	109	149
1988/9	54	114	168
1989/90	40	102	142
1990/1	41	122	163
1991/2	31	90	121
1992/3	16	49	65
1993/4	38	92	130
1994/5	11	37	48

Hart Trophy

Awarded annually from the 1923/4 season by the Professional Hockey Writers Association as the Most Valuable Player award of the NHL. Named after Cecil Hart, former manager-coach of the Montreal Canadiens.

Most wins: 9 Wayne Gretzky (Edmonton) 1980-7, 1989; 6 Gordie Howe (Detroit) 1952-3, 1957-8, 1960, 1963; 3 Eddie Shore (Boston) 1933, 1936, 1938; 3 Bobby Orr (Boston) 1970-2; 3 Bobby Clarke (Philadelphia) 1973, 1975-6.

Other winners since 1970: 1974 Phil Esposito (Boston), 1977-8 Guy Lafleur (Montreal), 1979 Bryan Trottier (NY Islanders), 1988 Mario Lemieux (Pittsburgh), 1990 Mark Messier (Edmonton), 1991 Brett Hull (St Louis), 1992 Mark Messier (New York), 1993 Mario Lemieux (Pittsburgh), 1994 Sergey Fedorov (Detroit Red Wings), 1995 Eric Lindros (Philadelphia)

Art Ross Trophy

For the NHL season's leading scorer annually from 1947/8..

Most wins: 10 Wayne Gretzky (Edmonton) 1981-7, 1990-1, 1994; 6 Gordie Howe (Detroit) 1951-4, 1957, 1963; 5 Phil Esposito (Boston) 1969, 1971-4; 4 Stan Mikita (Chicago) 1964-5, 1967-8; 4 Mario Lemieux (Pittsburgh) 1988-9, 1992-3; 3 Bobby Hull (Chicago) 1960, 1962, 1966; Guy Lafleur (Montreal Can) 1976-8.
Other winners since 1970: 1970 & 1975 Bobby Orr (Boston), 1979 Bryan Trottier (NY Islanders), 1980 Marcel Dionne (Los Angeles), 1995 Jaromir Jagr (Pittsburgh).

James Norris Memorial Trophy

Awarded annually from the 1953/4 season to the league's leading defenseman.
Most wins: 8 Bobby Orr (Boston) 1968-75, 7 Doug Harvey (Montreal/NY Rangers) 1955-8, 1960-2; 4 Ray Bourque (Boston) 1987-8, 1990-1; 3 Pierre Pilote (Chicago) 1963-5, 3 Denis Potvin (NY Islanders) 1976,

Wayne Gretzky

1978-9; 3 Paul Coffey (Edmonton/Detroit) 1985-6, 1995.
Other winners from 1980: 1980 Larry Robinson
(Montreal), 1981 Randy Carlyle (Pittsburgh), 1982
Doug Wilson (Chicago), 1983-4 Rod Langway
(Washington), 1985-6 Paul Coffey (Edmonton), 1989
Chris Chelios (Montreal), 1992 Brian Leetch (New
York), 1993 Chris Chelios (Chicago), 1994 Ray
Bourque (Boston).

World Hockey Association

Contested for seven seasons from 1972/3 to 1978/9 as a 12-team rival of the NHL. *Winners*

1973	NE Whalers
1974-5	Houston Aeros
1976	Winnipeg Jets
1977	Québec Nordiques
1978-9	Winnipeg Jets

Adding WHA points to NHL points the leading
scorers have been:
2568 Wayne Gretzky (849G/1719A), 2358 Gordie
Howe (975/1383), 1808 Bobby Hull (913/895)

Ice Skating

Skating in a primitive form is over 2000 years old, but probably first became popular on frozen canals in the Netherlands some 300 years ago. The Dutch were the main exponents of speed skating over the next two hundred years. Figure skating originated in Britain and the first known skating club was the Edinburgh Skating Club, formed c.1742. The first recorded race was in the Fens in 1763 and the earliest artificial rink was opened in Baker Street, London, in 1842, although the surface was not of ice. The first artificial ice rink was opened at the Glaciarium, London, in 1876, three years before the foundation of the National Skating Association of Great Britain.

Ice skating may be divided into two: figure skating, on rinks of 60m x 30m, and speed skating. The world governing body for both is the International Skating Union (ISU), founded in 1892, and which now has its headquarters in Switzerland.

Figure Skating

Note that in pairs and ice dance competitions the woman's name is conventionally listed first.

Olympic Games

Ice skating was first included at the Olympic Games in 1908 in London, where events were held at Prince's Rink. The sport was included again in 1920 and at all Winter Games from 1924. *Winners:*

Men

1908	Ulrich Salchow (Swe)
1908*	Nikolay Panin (USSR)
1920	Gillis Grafström (Swe)
1924	Gillis Grafström (Swe)
1928	Gillis Grafström (Swe)
1932	Karl Schäfer (Aut)
1936	Karl Schäfer (Aut)
1948	Richard Button (USA)
1952	Richard Button (USA)
1956	Hayes Alan Jenkins (USA)
1960	David Jenkins (USA)
1964	Manfred Schnelldorfer (FRG)
1968	Wolfgang Schwarz (Aut)
1972	Ondrej Nepela (Cs)
1976	John Curry (UK)
1980	Robin Cousins (UK)
1984	Scott Hamilton (USA)
1988	Brian Boitano (USA)
1992	Viktor Petrenko (CIS/Ukr)
1994	Aleksey Urmanov (Rus)

*special figures competition

Women

1908	Madge Syers (née Cave) (UK)
1920	Magda Julin-Mauroy (Swe)
1924	Herma Planck-Szabó (Aut)
1928	Sonja Henie (Nor)
1932	Sonja Henie (Nor)
1936	Sonja Henie (Nor)
1948	Barbara Ann Scott (Can)
1952	Jeannette Altwegg (UK)
1956	Tenley Albright (USA)
1960	Carol Heiss (USA)
1964	Sjoukje Dijkstra (Hol)
1968	Peggy Fleming (USA)
1972	Beatrix Schuba (Aut)
1976	Dorothy Hamill (USA)
1980	Anett Pötzsch (GDR)
1984	Katarina Witt (GDR)
1988	Katarina Witt (GDR)
1992	Kristi Yamaguchi (USA)
1994	Oksana Bayul (Ukr)

Pairs

1908	Anna Hübler/Heinrich Burger (Ger)
1920	Ludowika Jakobsson/Walter Jakobsson (Fin)
1924	Helene Engelmann/Alfred Berger (Aut)
1928	Andrée Joly/Pierre Brunet (Fra)
1932	Andrée Brunet (née Joly)/Pierre Brunet (Fra)
1936	Maxi Herber/Ernst Baier (Ger)
1948	Micheline Lannoy/Pierre Baugniet (Bel)
1952	Ria Falk/Paul Falk (FRG)
1956	Elisabeth Schwarz/Kurt Oppelt (Aut)
1960	Barbara Wagner/Robert Paul (Can)
1964	Lyudmila Belousova/Oleg Protopopov (USSR)
1968	Lyudmila Belousova/Oleg Protopopov (USSR)
1972	Irina Rodnina/Aleksey Ulanov (USSR)
1976	Irina Rodnina/Aleksandr Zaitsev (USSR)
1980	Irina Rodnina/Aleksandr Zaitsev (USSR)
1984	Yelena Valova/Oleg Vasilyev (USSR)
1988	Yekaterina Gordeyeva/Sergey Grinkov (USSR)
1992	Natalya Mishkutienok/Artur Dmitriyev (CIS)
1994	Yekaterina Gordeyeva/Sergey Grinkov (Rus)

Ice Dance

1976	Lyudmila Pakhomova/Aleksandr Gorshkov (USSR)
1980	Natalya Linichuk/Gennadiy Karponosov (USSR)
1984	Jayne Torvill/Christopher Dean (UK)

1988	Natalya Bestemianova/Andrey Bukin (USSR)
1992	Marina Klimova/Sergey Ponomarenko (CIS)
1994	Oksana Gritschuk/Yevgeniy Platov (Rus)

Medals

Most gold medals: 3 Gillis Grafström, Sonja Henie, Irina Rodnina

Most medals: 4 Gillis Grafström, who also won a silver in 1932.

Oldest gold medallist: 38 yr 80 days Walter Jakobsson, pairs 1920

Youngest gold medallist: 15 yr 128 days Maxi Herber, pairs 1936

Best marks: Jayne Torvill and Christopher Dean were awarded a maximum nine sixes for artistic impression, as well as a further three sixes for technical merit, in the 1984 ice dancing free dance section.

World Championships

Held annually, first in St Petersburg (now Leningrad) in 1896. The 1961 championships were cancelled after all the US team were killed in a plane crash. *Winners:*

Men

1896	Gilbert Fuchs (Ger)
1897	Gustav Hügel (Aut)
1898	Henning Grenander (Swe)
1899-1900	Gustav Hügel (Aut)
1901-5	Ulrich Salchow (Swe)
1906	Gilbert Fuchs (Ger)
1907-11	Ulrich Salchow (Swe)
1912-3	Fritz Kachler (Aut)
1914	Gösta Sandahl (Swe)
1922	Gillis Grafström (Swe)
1923	Fritz Kachler (Aut)
1924	Gillis Grafström (Swe)
1925-8	Willy Böckl (Aut)
1929	Gillis Grafström (Swe)
1930-6	Karl Schäfer (Aut)
1937-8	Felix Kaspar (Aut)
1939	Graham Sharp (UK)
1947	Hans Gerschwiler (Swi)
1948-52	Richard Button (USA)
1953-6	Hayes Alan Jenkins (USA)
1957-9	David Jenkins (USA)
1960	Alain Giletti (Fra)
1962	Donald Jackson (Can)
1963	Donald McPherson (Can)
1964	Manfred Schnelldorfer (FRG)
1965	Alain Calmat (Fra)
1966-8	Emmerich Danzer (Aut)
1969-70	Tim Wood (USA)
1971-3	Ondrej Nepela (Cs)
1974	Jan Hoffmann (GDR)
1975	Sergey Volkov (USSR)
1976	John Curry (UK)
1977	Vladimir Kovalyev (USSR)
1978	Charles Tickner (USA)
1979	Vladimir Kovalyev (USSR)
1980	Jan Hoffmann (GDR)
1981-4	Scott Hamilton (USA)
1985	Aleksandr Fadeyev (USSR)
1986	Brian Boitano (USA)
1987	Brian Orser (Can)
1988	Brian Boitano (USA)
1989-91	Kurt Browning (Can)
1992	Viktor Petrenko (CIS/Ukr)
1993	Kurt Browning (Can)
1994-5	Elvis Stojko (Canada)

Most wins: 10 Ulrich Salchow, 7 Karl Schäfer, 5 Richard Button

Women

1906-7	Madge Syers (née Cave) (UK)
1908-11	Lily Kronberger (Hun)
1912-4	Opika von Méray Horvath (Hun)
1922-4	Herma Planck (née Szabó) (Aut)
1925-6	Herma Jaross (was Planck-Szabó) (Aut)
1927-36	Sonja Henie (Nor)
1937	Cecilia Colledge (UK)
1938-9	Megan Taylor (UK)
1947-8	Barbara Ann Scott (Can)
1949-50	Alena Vrzánová (Cs)
1951	Jeannette Altwegg (UK)
1952	Jacqueline du Bief (Fra)
1953	Tenley Albright (USA)
1954	Gundi Busch (FRG)
1955	Tenley Albright (USA)
1956-60	Carol Heiss (USA)
1962-4	Sjoukje Dijkstra (Hol)
1965	Petra Burka (Can)
1966-8	Peggy Fleming (USA)
1969-70	Gabriele Seyfert (GDR)
1971-2	Beatrix Schuba (Aut)
1973	Karen Magnussen (Can)
1974	Christine Errath (GDR)
1975	Dianne De Leeuw (Hol)
1976	Dorothy Hamill (USA)
1977	Linda Fratianne (USA)
1978	Anett Pötzsch (GDR)
1979	Linda Fratianne (USA)
1980	Anett Pötzsch (GDR)
1981	Denise Biellmann (Swi)
1982	Elaine Zayak (USA)
1983	Rosalynn Sumners (USA)
1984-5	Katarina Witt (GDR)
1986	Debbie Thomas (USA)
1987-8	Katarina Witt (GDR)
1989	Midori Ito (Jap)
1990	Jill Trenary (USA)
1991-2	Kristi Yamaguchi (USA)
1993	Oksana Bayul (Ukr)
1994	Yuka Sato (Japan)
1995	Lu Chen (Chn

Most wins: 10 Sonja Henie, 5 Carol Heiss

Pairs

1908	Anna Hübler/Heinrich Burger (Ger)
1909	Phyllis Johnson/James Johnson (UK)
1910	Anna Hübler/Heinrich Burger (Ger)
1911	Ludowika Eilers/Walter Jakobsson (Fin)
1912	Phyllis Johnson/James Johnson (UK)
1913	Helene Engelmann/Karl Mejstrick (Aut)

1914	Ludowika Eilers/Walter Jakobsson (Fin)
1922	Helene Engelmann/Alfred Berger (Aut)
1923	Ludowika Jakobsson (née Eilers)/Walter Jakobsson (Fin)
1924	Helene Engelmann/Alfred Berger (Aut)
1925	Herma Jaross/Ludwig Wrede (Aut)
1926	Andrée Joly/Pierre Brunet (Fra)
1927	Herma Jaross/Ludwig Wrede (Aut)
1928	Andrée Joly/Pierre Brunet (Fra)
1929	Lilly Scholz/Otto Kaiser (Aut)
1930	Andrée Brunet (née Joly)/Pierre Brunet (Fra)
1931	Emilia Rotter/László Szollás (Hun)
1932	Andrée Brunet/Pierre Brunet (Fra)
1933-5	Emilie Rotter/László Szollás (Hun)
1936-9	Maxi Herber/Ernst Baier (Ger)
1947-8	Micheline Lannoy/Pierre Baugniet (Bel)
1949	Andrea Kékesy/Ede Király (Hun)
1950	Karol Kennedy/Peter Kennedy (USA)
1951-2	Ria Falk (née Baran)/Paul Falk (FRG)
1953	Jennifer Nicks/John Nicks (UK)
1954-5	Frances Dafoe/Norris Bowden (Can)
1956	Elisabeth Schwarz/Kurt Oppelt (Aut)
1957-60	Barbara Wagner/Robert Paul (Can)
1962	Maria Jelinek/Otto Jelinek (Can)
1963-4	Marika Kilius/Hans-Jürgen Bäumler (FRG)
1965-8	Lyudmila Belousova/Oleg Protopopov (USSR)
1969-72	Irina Rodnina/Aleksey Ulanov (USSR)
1973-8	Irina Rodnina/Aleksandr Zaitsev (USSR)
1979	Tai Babilonia/Randy Gardner (USA)
1980	Marina Tcherkasova/Sergey Shakrai (USSR)
1981	Irina Vorobyeva/Igor Lissovsky (USSR)
1982	Sabine Baess/Tassilo Thierbach (GDR)
1983	Yelena Valova/Oleg Vasilyev (USSR)
1984	Barbara Underhill/Paul Martini (Can)
1985	Yelena Valova/Oleg Vasilyev (USSR)
1986-7	Yekaterina Gordeyeva/Sergey Grinkov (USSR)
1988	Yelena Valova/Oleg Vasilyev (USSR)
1989-90	Yekaterina Gordeyeva/Sergey Grinkov (USSR)
1991-2	Natalya Mishkutienok/Artur Dmitriyev (CIS)
1993	Isabelle Braseur/Lloyd Eisler (Can)
1994	Yevgeniya Shishkova & Vadim Naumov (Rus)
1995	Radka Kovács & Rene Novotny (Cze)

Most wins: 10 Irina Rodnina, 6 Aleksandr Zaitsev
The only skater to win both singles and pairs world titles in the same year was Herma Jaross (née Stark, then Planck, then Jaross, then Stark) in 1925.

Ice Dance

Although the first official world ice dance championships were in 1952, unofficial championships were staged in 1950 and 1951.

1950	Lois Waring/Michael McGean (USA)
1951	Jean Westwood/Lawrence Demmy (UK)
1952-5	Jean Westwood/Lawrence Demmy (UK)
1956	Pamela Weight/Paul Thomas (UK)
1957-8	June Markham/Courtney Jones (UK)

1959-60	Doreen Denny/Courtney Jones (UK)
1962-5	Eva Romániová/Pavel Roman (Cs)
1966-9	Diana Towler/Bernard Ford (UK)
1970-4	Lyudmila Pakhomova/Aleksandr Gorshkov (USSR)
1975	Irina Moiseyeva/Andrey Minenkov (USSR)
1976	Lyudmila Pakhomova/Aleksandr Gorshkov (USSR)
1977	Irina Moiseyeva/Andrey Minenkov (USSR)
1978-9	Natalya Linichuk/Gennadiy Karponosov (USSR)
1980	Krisztina Regoczy/András Sallay (Hun)
1981-4	Jayne Torvill/Christopher Dean (UK)
1985-8	Natalya Bestemianova/Andrey Bukin (USSR)
1989-90	Marina Klimova/Sergey Ponomarenko (USSR)
1991	Isabelle & Paul Duchesnay (Fra)
1992	Marina Klimova/Sergey Ponomarenko (CIS)
1993	Maia Usova/Aleksandr Zhulin (Rus)
1994-5	Oksana Gritschuk/Yevgeniy Platov (Rus)

Most wins: 6 Lyudmila Pakhomova & Aleksandr Gorshkov

Best marks

Jayne Torvill and Christopher Dean were awarded 29 maximum sixes for ice dancing at the 1984 World Championships. This comprised seven in the compulsory dances, a perfect set of nine for artistic impression in both the set pattern and free dance sections and a further four sixes for technical merit in the latter

Speed Skating

A standard outdoor speed skating circuit is 400 metres, with two lanes. The speed skaters race in pairs, the lanes crossing on the straights on either side of the track.

Indoor speed skating is conducted on short tracks, the standard length being 111.12 metres, which can be laid out on a 60m x 30m skating or ice hockey rink.

Olympic Games

Held at each Olympic Games from 1924 (for men) and 1960 (for women). Women's races had also been staged as demonstration events in 1932. *Winners:*

Men's 500 metres

1924	Charles Jewtraw (USA)	44.0
1928	Bernt Evensen (Nor) &	
	Clas Thunberg (Fin)	43.4
1932	John Shea (USA)	43.4
1936	Ivar Ballangrud (Nor)	43.4
1948	Finn Helgesen (Nor)	43.1
1952	Kenneth Henry (USA)	43.2
1956	Yevgeniy Grischin (USSR)	40.2
1960	Yevgeniy Grischin (USSR)	40.2
1964	Terry McDermott (USA)	40.1
1968	Erhard Keller (FRG)	40.3
1972	Erhard Keller (FRG)	39.44
1976	Yevgeniy Kulikov (USSR)	39.17
1980	Eric Heiden (USA)	38.03
1984	Sergey Fokichev (USSR)	38.19

1988	Uwe-Jens Mey (GDR) 36.45
1992	Uwe-Jens Mey (Ger) 37.14
1994	Aleksandr Golubev (Rus) 36.33

Men's 1000 metres

1976	Peter Mueller (USA) 1:19.32
1980	Eric Heiden (USA) 1:15.18
1984	Gaetan Boucher (Can) 1:15.80
1988	Nikolay Gulyayev (USSR) 1:13.03
1992	Olaf Zinke (Ger) 1:14.85
1994	Dan Jansen (USA) 1:12.43

Men's 1500 metres

1924	Clas Thunberg (Fin) 2:20.8
1928	Clas Thunberg (Fin) 2:21.1
1932	John Shea (USA) 2:57.5
1936	Charles Mathiesen (Nor) 2:19.2
1948	Sverre Farstad (Nor) 2:17.6
1952	Hjalmar Andersen (Nor) 2:20.4
1956	Yevgeniy Grischin (USSR) & Yuriy Mikhailov (USSR) 2:08.6
1960	Roald Aas (Nor) & Yevgeniy Grischin (USSR) 2:10.4
1964	Ants Antson (USSR) 2:10.3
1968	Cornelis Verkerk (Hol) 2:03.4
1972	Ard Schenk (Hol) 2:02.96
1976	Jan Egil Storholt (Nor) 1:59.38
1980	Eric Heiden (USA) 1:55.44
1984	Gaetan Boucher (Can) 1:58.36
1988	André Hoffmann (GDR) 1:52.06
1992	Johann Olav Koss (Nor) 1:54.81
1994	Johann Olav Koss (Nor) 1:51.29

Men's 5000 metres

1924	Clas Thunberg (Fin) 8:39.0
1928	Ivar Ballangrud (Nor) 8:50.5
1932	Irving Jaffee (USA) 9:40.8
1936	Ivar Ballangrud (Nor) 8:19.6
1948	Reidar Liaklev (Nor) 8:29.4
1952	Hjalmar Andersen (Nor) 8:10.6
1956	Boris Schilkov (USSR) 7:48.7
1960	Viktor Kositschkin (USSR) 7:51.3
1964	Knut Johannesen (Nor) 7:38.4
1968	Anton Maier (Nor) 7.22.4
1972	Ard Schenk (Hol) 7:23.61
1976	Sten Stensen (Nor) 7:24.48
1980	Eric Heiden (USA) 7:02.29
1984	Tomas Gustafsson (Swe) 7:12.28
1988	Tomas Gustafsson (Swe) 6:44.63
1992	Geir Karlstad (Nor) 6:59.97
1994	Johann Olav Koss (Nor) 6:34.96

Men's 10,000 metres

1924	Julius Skutnabb (Fin) 18:04.8
1928	event cancelled after five races
1932	Irving Jaffee (USA) 19:13.6
1936	Ivar Ballangrud (Nor) 17:24.3
1948	Äke Seyffarth (Swe) 17:26.3
1952	Hjalmar Andersen (Nor) 16:45.8
1956	Sigvard Ericsson (Swe) 16:35.9
1960	Knut Johannesen (Nor) 15:46.6
1964	Jonny Nilsson (Swe) 15:50.1

Johann-Olav Koss – the star of the 1994 Olympic Games at Lillehammer

1968	Johnny Höglin (Swe) 15:23.6
1972	Ard Schenk (Hol) 15:01.35
1976	Piet Kleine (Hol) 14:50.59
1980	Eric Heiden (USA) 14:28.13
1984	Igor Malkov (USSR) 14:39.90
1988	Tomas Gustafsson (Swe) 13:48.20
1992	Bart Veldkamp (Hol) 14:12.12
1994	Johann Olav Koss (Nor) 13:30.55

Men's all-round (aggregate)
1924   Clas Thunberg (Fin)

Women's 500 metres
1960	Helga Haase (GDR) 45.9
1964	Lidiya Skoblikova (USSR) 45.0
1968	Lyudmila Titova (USSR) 46.1
1972	Anne Henning (USA) 43.33
1976	Sheila Young (USA) 42.76
1980	Karin Enke (GDR) 41.78
1984	Christa Rothenburger (GDR) 41.02
1988	Bonnie Blair (USA) 39.10
1992	Bonnie Blair (USA) 40.33
1994	Bonnie Blair (USA) 39.25

Women's 1000 metres
1960	Klara Guseva (USSR) 1:34.1
1964	Lidiya Skoblikova (USSR) 1:33.2
1968	Carolina Geijssen (Hol) 1:32.6
1972	Monika Pflug (FRG) 1:31.40
1976	Tatyana Averina (USSR) 1:28.43
1980	Natalya Petruseva (USSR) 1:24.10
1984	Karin Enke (GDR) 1:21.61
1988	Christa Rothenburger (GDR) 1:17.65
1992	Bonnie Blair (USA) 1:21.90
1994	Bonnie Blair (USA) 1:18.74

Women's 1500 metres
1960	Lidiya Skoblikova (USSR) 2:25.2
1964	Lidiya Skoblikova (USSR) 2:22.6
1968	Kaija Mustonen (Fin) 2:22.4
1972	Dianne Holum (USA) 2:20.85
1976	Galina Stepanskaya (USSR) 2:16.58
1980	Annie Borckink (Hol) 2:10.95
1984	Karin Enke (GDR) 2:03.42
1988	Yvonne van Gennip (Hol) 2:00.68
1992	Jacqueline Börner (Ger) 2:05.87
1994	Emese Hunyady (Aut) 2:02.19

Women's 3000 metres
1960	Lidiya Skoblikova (USSR) 5:14.3
1964	Lidiya Skoblikova (USSR) 5:14.9
1968	Johanna Schut (Hol) 4:56.2
1972	Christina Baas-Kaiser (Hol) 4:52.14
1976	Tatyana Averina (USSR) 4:45.19
1980	Björg Eva Jensen (Nor) 4:32.13
1984	Andrea Schöne (GDR) 4:27.79
1988	Yvonne van Gennip (Hol) 4:11.94
1992	Gunda Niemann (Ger) 4:19.90
1994	Svetlana Bazhanova (Rus) 4:17.43

Women's 5000 metres
1988	Yvonne van Gennip (Hol) 7:14.13
1992	Gunda Niemann (Ger) 7:31.57
1994	Claudia Pechstein (Ger) 7:14.37

Most Olympic Medals (G - Gold, S - Silver, B - Bronze)

Men		G	S	B
7	Clas Thunberg (Nor)	5	1	1
7	Ivar Ballangrud (Nor)	4	2	1
6	Roald Larsen (Nor)	-	2	4
5	Eric Heiden (USA)	5	-	-
5	Yevgeniy Grischin (USSR)	4	1	-
5	Johann Olav Koss (Nor)	4	1	-
5	Knut Johannesen (Nor)	2	2	1
Women				
8	Karin Enke/Kania (GDR)	3	4	1
7	Andrea Schöne/Ehrig (GDR)	1	5	1
6	Lidiya Skoblikova (USSR)	6	-	-
6	Bonnie Blair(USA)	5	-	1

Eric Heiden, uniquely, won all five gold medals at one Games (1980).

World Championships

Held annually, first at Amsterdam in 1889. Officially recognised by the ISU from 1893. *Overall champions:*

Men - Overall
Contested over four distances: 500m, 1000m, 5000m and 10,000m. Titles not awarded 1889-90, 1894, 1902-3, 1906-7.

1891	Joseph Donoghue (USA)
1893	Jaap Eden (Hol)
1895-6	Jaap Eden (Hol)
1897	Jack McCulloch (Can)
1898-9	Peder Østlund (Nor)
1900	Edvard Engelsaas (Nor)
1901	Franz Frederik Wathen (Fin)
1904	Sigurd Mathisen (Nor)
1905	Coen de Koning (Hol)
1908-9	Oscar Mathisen (Nor)
1910-1	Nikolay Strunnikov (Rus)
1912-4	Oscar Mathisen (Nor)
1922	Harald Ström (Nor)
1923	Clas Thunberg (Fin)
1924	Roald Larsen (Nor)
1925	Clas Thunberg (Fin)
1926	Ivar Ballangrud (Nor)
1927	Bernt Evensen (Nor)
1928-9	Clas Thunberg (Fin)
1930	Michael Staksrud (Nor)
1931	Clas Thunberg (Fin)
1932	Ivar Ballangrud (Nor)
1933	Hans Engnestangen (Nor)
1934	Bernt Evensen (Nor)
1935	Michael Staksrud (Nor)
1936	Ivar Ballangrud (Nor)
1937	Michael Staksrud (Nor)
1938	Ivar Ballangrud (Nor)
1939	Birger Wasenius (Fin)
1947	Lauri Parkkinen (Fin)
1948	Odd Lundberg (Nor)
1949	Kornel Pajor (Hun)
1950-2	Hjalmar Andersen (Nor)
1953	Oleg Goncharenko (USSR)
1954	Boris Schilkov (USSR)

1955	Sigvard Ericsson (Swe)
1956	Oleg Goncharenko (USSR)
1957	Knut Johannesen (Nor)
1958	Oleg Goncharenko (USSR)
1959	Juhani Järvinen (Fin)
1960	Boris Stenin (USSR)
1961	Henk van der Grift (Hol)
1962	Viktor Kosichkin (USSR)
1963	Jonny Nilsson (Swe)
1964	Knut Johannesen (Nor)
1965	Per Ivar Moe (Nor)
1966-7	Cornelis Verkerk (Hol)
1968	Anton Maier (Nor)
1969	Dag Fornaess (Nor)
1970-2	Ard Schenk (Hol)
1973	Göran Claesen (Swe)
1974	Sten Stensen (Nor)
1975	Harm Kuipers (Hol)
1976	Piet Kleine (Hol)
1977-9	Eric Heiden (USA)
1980	Hilbert van der Duim (Hol)
1981	Amund Sjøbrend (Nor)
1982	Hilbert van der Duim (Hol)
1983	Rolf Falk-Larssen (Nor)
1984	Oleg Bozyiev (USSR)
1985-6	Hein Vergeer (Hol)
1987	Nikolay Gulyayev (USSR)
1988	Eric Flaim (USA)
1989	Leo Visser (Hol)
1990-1	Johann Olav Koss (Nor)
1992	Roberto Sighel (Ita)
1993	Falko Zandstra (Hol)
1994	Johann Olav Koss (Nor)
1995	Rintje Ritsma (Hol)

Most wins: 5 Mathisen, Thunberg

Women - Overall

Contested over four distances: 500m, 1000m, 1500m and 3000m.

1936	Kit Klein (USA)
1937-8	Laila Schou Nilsen (Nor)
1939	Vernä Lesche (Fin)
1947	Vernä Lesche (Fin)
1948-50	Maria Isakova (USSR)
1951	Eevi Huttunen (Fin)
1952	Lidiya Selikhova (USSR)
1953	Khalida Schegoleyeva (USSR)
1954	Lidiya Selikhova (USSR)
1955	Rimma Zhukova (USSR)
1956	Sofiya Kondakova (USSR)
1957-8	Inga Artamonova (USSR)
1959	Tamara Rylova (USSR)
1960-1	Valentina Stenina (USSR)
1962	Inga Artamonova (USSR)
1963-4	Lidiya Skoblikova (USSR)
1965	Inga Artamonova (USSR)
1966	Valentina Stenina (USSR)
1967-8	Christina Kaiser (Hol)
1969	Lasma Kauniste (USSR)
1970	Atje Keulen-Deelstra (Hol)
1971	Nina Statkevich (USSR)
1972-4	Atje Keulen-Deelstra (Hol)

1975	Karin Kessow (GDR)
1976	Sylvia Burka (Can)
1977	Vera Bryndzey (USSR)
1978	Tatyana Averina (USSR)
1979	Beth Heiden (USA)
1980-1	Natalya Petruseva (USSR)
1982	Karin Enke (then Busch) (GDR)
1983	Andrea Schöne (GDR)
1984	Karin Enke (GDR)
1985	Andrea Schöne (GDR)
1986-8	Karin Kania (née Enke) (GDR)
1989	Constanze Moser (GDR)
1990	Jacqueline Börner (GDR)
1991-3	Gunda Niemann (née Kleeman) (Ger)
1994	Emese Hunyady (Aut)
1995	Gunda Niemann (Ger)

Most wins: 5 Kania, 4 Artamonova, Keulen-Deelstra, Niemann

World Sprint Championships

First held in 1970. Both men's and women's championships are contested over two distances: 500m and 1000m.

Men - Overall

1970	Valeriy Muratov (USSR)
1971	Erhard Keller (FRG)
1972	Leo Linkovesi (Fin)
1973	Valeriy Muratov (USSR)
1974	Per Bjørang (Nor)
1975	Aleksandr Safranov (USSR)
1976	Johan Granath (Swe)
1977-80	Eric Heiden (USA)
1981	Frode Rømming (Nor)
1982	Sergey Khlebnikov (USSR)
1983	Akira Kuroiwa (Jap)
1984	Gaetan Boucher (Can)
1985-6	Igor Zhelezovskiy (USSR)
1987	Akira Kuroiwa (Jap)
1988	Dan Jansen (USA)
1989	Igor Zhelezovskiy (USSR)
1990	Ki Tae-bae (SKo)
1991-3	Igor Zhelezovskiy (USSR/Bls)
1994	Dan Jansen (USA)
1995	Kim Yoon-man (SKo)

Most wins: 6 Zhelezovskiy, 4 Heiden

Women - Overall

1970	Lyudmila Titova (USSR)
1971	Ruth Schleiermacher (GDR)
1972	Monika Pflug (FRG)
1973	Sheila Young (USA)
1974	Leah Poulos (USA)
1975-6	Sheila Young (USA)
1977	Sylvia Burka (Can)
1978	Lyubov Sadchikova (USSR)
1979	Leah Muller (née Poulos) (USA)
1980-1	Karin Enke (GDR)
1982	Natalya Petruseva (USSR)
1983-4	Karin Enke (GDR)
1985	Christa Rothenburger (GDR)
1986-7	Karin Kania (née Enke) (GDR)
1988	Christa Rothenburger (GDR)

1989   Bonnie Blair (USA)
1990   Angela Hauck (GDR)
1991   Monique Garbrecht (Ger)
1992-3 Ye Qiaobo (Chn)
1994-5 Bonnie Blair (USA)
Most wins: 6 Kania

World Cup

Contested over a series of events during the winter, annually from the 1985/6 season. *Winners:*

Men - 500 metres
1986   Dan Jansen (USA)
1987   Nick Thometz (USA)
1988-91 Uwe-Jens Mey (GDR)
1992-4 Dan Jansen (USA)
1995   Hiroyasu Shimizu (Jap)

Men - 1000 metres
1986   Dan Jansen (USA)
1987   Nick Thometz (USA)
1988   Dan Jansen (USA)
1989-90 Uwe-Jens Mey (GDR)
1991-3 Igor Zhelezovskiy (USSR/Bls)
1994   Dan Jansen (USA)

Men - 1500 metres
1986   Michael Hadschieff (Aut)
1987   Hans Magnusson (Swe)
1988   André Hoffmann (GDR)
1989   Eric Flaim (USA)
1990-1 Johann Olav Koss (Nor)
1992   Falko Zandstra (Hol)
1993   Rintje Ritsma (Hol)
1994   Falko Zandstra (Hol)
1995   Neal Marshal (Can)

Men - 5000 & 10000 metres
1986   Dave Silk (USA)
1987   Geir Karlstad (Nor)
1988   Tomas Gustafsson (Swe)
1989   Gerard Kemkers (Hol)
1990   Bart Veldkamp (Hol)

1991   Johann Olav Koss (Nor)
1992   Geir Karlstad (Nor)
1993   Bart Veldkamp (Hol)
1994   Johann Olav Koss (Nor)
1995   Rintje Ritsma (Hol)

Women - 500 metres
1986   Christa Rothenburger (GDR)
1987   Bonnie Blair (USA)
1988   Christa Rothenburger (GDR)
1989   Christa Luding (née Rothenburger) (GDR)
1990   Angela Hauck (GDR) and Bonnie Blair (USA)
1991   Kyoko Shimazaki (Jap)
1992   Bonnie Blair (USA)
1993   Ye Qiaobo (Chn)
1994-5 Bonnie Blair (USA)

Women - 1000 metres
1986   Karin Kania (GDR)
1987   Bonnie Blair (USA)
1988   Christa Rothenburger (GDR)
1989-90 Angela Hauck (GDR)
1991   Monique Garbrecht (Ger)
1992-4 Bonnie Blair (USA)

Women - 1500 metres
1986   Annette Carlén (Swe)
1987   Yvonne van Gennip (Hol)
1988   Bonnie Blair (USA)
1989   Constanze Moser (GDR)
1990   Jacqueline Börner (GDR)
1991-3 Gunda Kleeman/Niemann (Ger)
1994   Emese Hunyady (Aut)
1995   Gunda Niemann (Ger)

Women - 3000 metres (and 5000m from 1989)
1986   Andrea Ehrig (GDR)
1987   Yvonne van Gennip (Hol)
1988   Gabi Zange (GDR)
1989   Heike Schalling (GDR)
1990   Gunda Kleeman (GDR)
1991   Heike Warnicke (née Schalling) (Ger)
1992-5 Gunda Niemann (Ger)

Speed Skating World Records

Men

	min:sec	Name	Venue	Date
500m	35.76	Dan Jansen (USA)	Calgary	30 Jan 1994
1000m	1:12.37	Yasunori Miyabe (Jap)	Calgary	26 Mar 1994
	1:12.05Au	Nick Thometz (USA)	Medeo	26 Mar 1987
1500m	1:51.29	Johann Olav Koss (Nor)	Hamar	16 Feb 1994
3000m	3:56.16	Thomas Bos (Hol)	Calgary	3 Mar 1992
5000m	6:34.96	Johann Olav Koss (Nor)	Hamar	13 Feb 1994
10,000m	13:30.55	Johann Olav Koss (Nor)	Hamar	20 Feb 1994
Sprint points (500m, 1000m, 500m, 1000m)	144.445	Yasunori Miyabe (Jap)	Calgary	26 Mar 1994
Points (500m, 3000m, 1500m, 5000m)	156.059	Falko Zandstra (Hol)	Calgary	1-3 Mar 1993
Overall points (500m, 5000m, 1500m, 10,000m)	156.201	Rintje Ritsma (Hol)	Hamar	7-9 Jan 1994

The Olympic 1000m final of 1992, with Kim Ki-hoon of South Korea in the lead

Women

	min:sec	Name	Venue	Date
500m	38.69	Bonnie Blair (USA)	Calgary	12 Feb 1995
1000m	1:17.65	Christa Rothenburger (GDR)	Calgary	26 Feb 1988
1500m	1:59.30A	Karin Kania (née Enke) (GDR)	Medeo	22 Mar 1986
3000m	4:09.32	Gunda Kleeman (Ger)	Calgary	25 Mar 1994
5000m	7:03.26	Gunda Niemann (Ger) (née Kleeman)	Calgary	26 Mar 1994
10,000m (u)	15:25.25	Yvonne van Gennip (Hol)	Heerenveen	19 Mar 1988
Sprint points (500m, 1000m, 500m, 1000m)	156.505	Bonnie Blair (USA)	Calgary	26 Mar 1994
Points (500m, 1500m, 1000m, 3000m)	162.058u	Karen Kania (GDR)	Calgary	4/5 Dec 1987
Overall points (500m, 3000m, 1500m, 5000m)	164.658	Emese Hunyady (Aut)	Calgary	26-27 Mar 1994

u = unofficial marks not ratified, A = marks set at Medeo (USSR) assisted by high altitude (1691m above sea level)

Short Track Speed Skating

Short-track speed skating is held indoors on a 111.12m circumference oval track, with four to six skaters in a race. Championships are contested over four distances: 500m, 1000m, 1500m and 3000m.

Olympic Games

After being a demonstration sport at the 1988 Olympic Games, short track racing was added to the 1992 programme with the programme expanded in 1994. *Winners:*

Men - 500m
1994   Chae Ji-hoon (SKo) 43.45

Men - 1000m
1992   Kim Ki-hoon (SKo) 1:30.76
1994   Kim Ki-hoon (SKo) 1:34.57

Men - 5000m relay
1992   South Korea 7:14.02
1994   Italy 7:11.74

Women - 500m
1992   Cathy Turner (USA) 47.04
1994   Cathy Turner (USA) 45.98

Women - 1000m
1994   Chun Lee-kyung (SKo) 1:36.87

Women - 3000m relay
1992   Canada 4:36.62
1994   South Korea 4:26.64

Most gold medals
3 Kim Kee-hoon (SKo) 1000m 1992 & 1994, relay 1992

World Championships

World Championships held unofficially 1978-80 and officially recognised by the ISU from 1981. *Winners:*

Men
1978   Jim Lynch (Aus)
1979   Hiroshi Toda (Jap)

1980	Gaetan Boucher (Can)
1981	Benoit Baril (Can)
1982	Guy Daigneault (Can)
1983	Louis Grenier (Can)
1984	Guy Daigneault (Can)
1985	Toshinobu Kawai (Jap)
1986	Tatsuyoshi Isihara (Jap)
1987	Michel Daignault (Can) & Toshinobu Kawai (Jap)
1988	Paul van der Velde (Hol)
1989	Michel Daignault (Can)
1990	Lee Joon-ho (SKo)
1991	Wilfred O'Reilly (UK)
1992	Kim Ki-hoon (SKo)
1993-4	Marc Gagnon (Can)
1995	Chae Ji-hoon (Sko)

Women

1978	Sarah Docter (Can)
1979	Sylvie Daigle (Can)
1980	Miyoshi Kato (Jap)
1981	Miyoshi Kato (Jap)
1982	Maryse Perreault (Can)
1983	Sylvie Daigle (Can)
1984	Mariko Kinoshita (Jap)
1985	Eiko Shishii (Jap)
1986	Bonnie Blair (USA)
1987	Eiko Shishii (Jap)
1988-90	Sylvie Daigle (Can)
1991	Nathalie Lambert (Can)
1992	Kim So-hee (SKo)
1993-4	Nathalie Lambert (Can)
1995	Chun Lee-kyung (SKo)

Most wins: 4 Daigle

World Short Track Speed Skating World Records

	min:sec	Name	Venue	Date
Men				
500m	42.99	Mirko Vuillermin (Ita)	Graz	21 Jan 1995
1000m	1:28.47	Mike McMillen (NZ)	Denver	4 Apr 1992
1500m	2:22.36	Eric Flaim (USA)	Beijing	21 Mar 1993
3000m	5:00.83	Chae Ji-hoon (SKo)	Lake Placid	16 Jan 1993
5000m relay	7:10.95	New Zealand	Beijing	28 Mar 1993
Women				
500m	45.60	Zhang Yanmei (Chn)	Beijing	27 Mar 1993
1000m	1:34.07	Nathalie Lambert (Can)	Hamar	7 Nov 1993
1500m	2:27.38	Chun Lee-kyung (SKo)	Jaca	23 Feb 1995
3000m	5:17.75	Won Hye-kyung (SKo)	Sapporo	6 Dec 1993
3000m relay	4:26.56	Canada	Beijing	28 Mar 1993

Judo

The combat sport of judo developed from Japanese martial arts, especially from several different schools of ju-jitsu. Dr Jigoro Kano devised the modern sport from these and founded the Kodokan Judo, a training school, in 1882 at Shitaya. Efficiency classes in judo are divided into pupil (kyu) and master (dan) grades. The highest possible grade is 12th dan, awarded only to Jigoro Kano, the only Shihan (or doctor). Apart from him, the highest is the red belt awarded for 10th Dan to thirteen men.

Belt colours for Dan grades: 1st-5th Dan - black, 6th-8th Dan - red and white, 9th-11th Dan - red, 12th Dan - white.

The first judo club in Europe was The Budokwai, founded in London in 1918. The first All-Japan Championships were held in 1930. The International Judo Federation (IJF), which had 154 member nations in 1994, was formed in 1951, in which year the first European championships were held. World championships were first held in 1956. Competitions are held at various weight limits; note that these changed in 1979.

Olympic Games

When the Olympic Games were held in Tokyo in 1964 judo was added to the Olympic programme, initially at three weight categories. Judo was not included in 1968, but from 1972 has been on the programme at all Games. Women's judo was staged as a demonstration sport at Seoul in 1988 and became a medal sport in 1992. *Winners:*

Men - Open

1964	Anton Geesink (Hol)
1972	Willem Ruska (Hol)
1976	Haruki Uemura (Jap)
1980	Dietmar Lorenz (GDR)
1984	Yasuhiro Yamashita (Jap)
1988-92	*Not Held*

Men - Over 95kg

1980	Angelo Parisi (Fra)
1984	Hitoshi Saito (Jap)
1988	Hitoshi Saito (Jap)
1992	David Khakkaleichvili (CIS/Geo)

Men - Over 93kg
1964   Isao Inokuma (Jap)
1972   Willem Ruska (Hol)
1976   Sergey Novikov (USSR)

Men - Under 95kg
1980   Robert Van de Walle (Bel)
1984   Ha Hyoung-zoo (SKo)
1988   Aurelio Miguel (Bra)
1992   Antal Kovács (Hun)

Men - Under 93kg
1972   Shota Chochoshvili (USSR)
1976   Kazuhiro Ninomiya (Jap)

Men - Under 86kg
1980   Jürg Röthlisberger (Swi)
1984   Peter Seisenbacher (Aut)
1988   Peter Seisenbacher (Aut)
1992   Waldemar Legien (Pol)

Men - Under 80kg
1964   Isao Okano (Jap)
1972   Shinobu Sekine (Jap)
1976   Isamu Sonoda (Jap)

Men - Under 78kg
1980   Shota Khabareli (USSR)
1984   Frank Weineke (FRG)
1988   Waldemar Legien (Pol)
1992   Hidehiko Yoshida (Jap)

Men - Under 71kg
1980   Ezio Gamba (Ita)
1984   Ahn Byeong-kuen (SKo)
1988   Marc Alexandre (Fra)
1992   Toshihiko Koga (Jap)

Men - Under 70kg
1964   Takehide Nakatani (Jap)
1972   Toyokazu Nomura (Jap)
1976   Vladimir Nevzorov (USSR)

Men - Under 65kg
1980   Nikolay Solodukhin (USSR)
1984   Yoshiyuki Matsuoka (Jap)
1988   Lee Kyung-keun (SKo)
1992   Rogerio Sampalo (Bra)

Men - Under 63kg
1972   Takao Kawaguchi (Jap)
1976   Héctor Rodriguez (Cub)

Men - Under 60kg
1980   Thierry Rey (Fra)
1984   Shinji Hosokawa (Jap)
1988   Kim Jae-yup (SKo)
1992   Nazim Gusseinov (CIS/Aze)

Men - Most titles
2 Ruska, Saito, Seisenbacher, Legien

Women - Under 48kg
1988   Li Zhongyun (Chn)
1992   Cécile Nowak (Fra)

Women - Under 52kg
1988   Sharon Rendle (UK)
1992   Almudena Munoz (Spa)

Women - Under 56kg
1988   Suzanne Williams (Aus)
1992   Miriam Blasco (Spa)

Women - Under 61kg
1988   Diane Bell (UK)
1992   Catherine Fleury (Fra)

Women - Under 66kg
1988   Hikari Sasaki (Jap)
1992   Odalis Reve (Cub)

Women - Under 72kg
1988   Ingrid Berghmans (Hol)
1992   Kim Mi-jung (SKo)

Women - Over 72kg
1988   Angelique Seriese (Hol)
1992   Zhuang Xiaoyan (Chn)

World Champions

World Championships were first held in 1956, and split into weight categories from 1965. Women's World Championships were first held in 1980. Championships are now biennial.

Men - Open
1956   Shokichi Natsui (Jap)
1958   Koji Sone (Jap)
1961   Anton Geesink (Hol)
1965   Isao Inokuma (Jap)
1967   Matsuo Matsunaga (Jap)
1969   Masatoshi Shinomaki (Jap)
1971   Masatoshi Shinomaki (Jap)
1973   Kazuhiro Ninomiya (Jap)
1975   Haruki Uemura (Jap)
1979   Sumio Endo (Jap)
1981   Yasuhiro Yamashita (Jap)
1983   Hitoshi Saito (Jap)
1985   Yoshimi Masaki (Jap)
1987   Naoya Ogawa (Jap)
1989   Naoya Ogawa (Jap)
1991   Naoya Ogawa (Jap)
1993   Rafael Kubacki (Pol)

Men - Over 95kg
1979   Yasuhiro Yamashita (Jap)
1981   Yasuhiro Yamashita (Jap)
1983   Yasuhiro Yamashita (Jap)
1985   Cho Yong-chul (SKo)
1987   Grigoriy Vertichev (USSR)
1989   Naoya Ogawa (Jap)
1991   Sergey Kosorotov (USSR)
1993   David Douillet (Fra)

Men - Over 93kg
1965   Anton Geesink (Hol)
1967   Willem Ruska (Hol)
1969   Shuji Suma (Jap)
1971   Willem Ruska (Hol)
1973   Chonufuhe Tagaki (Jap)
1975   Sumio Endo (Jap)

Men - Under 95kg
1979   Tengiz Khubuluri (USSR)
1981   Tengiz Khubuluri (USSR)
1983   Valeriy Divisenko (USSR)

1985	Hitoshi Sugai (Jap)
1987	Hitoshi Sugai (Jap)
1989	Koba Kurtanidze (USSR)
1991	Stéphane Traineau (Fra)
1993	Antal Kovács (Hun)

Men - Under 93kg
1967	Nobuyuki Sato (Jap)
1969	Fumio Sasahara (Jap)
1971	Fumio Sasahara (Jap)
1973	Nobuyuki Sato (Jap)
1975	Jean-Luc Rouge (Fra)

Men - Under 86kg
1979	Detlef Ultsch (GDR)
1981	Bernard Tchoullouyan (Fra)
1983	Detlef Ultsch (GDR)
1985	Peter Seisenbacher (Aut)
1987	Fabien Canu (Fra)
1989	Fabien Canu (Fra)
1991	Hirotaka Okada (Jap)
1993	Yoshiro Nakamura (Jap)

Men - Under 80kg
1965	Isao Okano (Jap)
1967	Eiji Maruki (Jap)
1969	Isamu Sonoda (Jap)
1971	Shozo Fujii (Jap)
1973	Shozo Fujii (Jap)
1975	Shozo Fujii (Jap)

Men - Under 78kg
1979	Shozo Fujii (Jap)
1981	Neil Adams (UK)
1983	Nobutoshi Hikage (Jap)
1985	Nobutoshi Hikage (Jap)
1987	Hirotaka Okada (Jap)
1989	Kim Byung-ju (SKo)
1991	Daniel Lascau (Ger)
1993	Chun Ki-young (SKo)

Men - Under 71kg
1979	Kyoto Katsuki (Jap)
1981	Park Chong-hak (SKo)
1983	Hidetoshi Nakanishi (Jap)
1985	Ahn Byeong-kuen (SKo)
1987	Mike Swain (USA)
1989	Toshihiko Koga (Jap)
1991	Toshihiko Koga (Jap)
1993	Yung Chung-hoon (SKo)

Men - Under 70kg
1967	Hiroshi Minatoya (Jap)
1969	Hiroshi Minatoya (Jap)
1971	Hizashi Tsuzawa (Jap)
1973	Kazutoyo Nomura (Jap)
1975	Vladimir Nevzorov (USSR)

Men - Under 65kg
1979	Nikolay Soludukhin (USSR)
1981	Katsuhiko Kashiwazaki (Jap)
1983	Nikolay Soludukhin (USSR)
1985	Yuriy Sokolov (USSR)
1987	Yosuke Yamamoto (Jap)
1989	Drago Becanovic (Yug)

1991	Udo Quellmalz (Ger)
1993	Yukimasa Nakamura (Jap)

Men - Under 63kg
1965	Hirofumi Matsuda (Jap)
1967	Takosumi Shigeoka (Jap)
1969	Yoshio Sonoda (Jap)
1971	Takao Kawaguchi (Jap)
1973	Yoshiharu Minami (Jap)
1975	Yoshiharu Minami (Jap)

Men - Under 60kg
1979	Thierry Ray (Fra)
1981	Yasuhiko Moriwaki (Jap)
1983	Khazret Tletseri (USSR)
1985	Shinji Hosokawa (Jap)
1987	Kim Jae-yup (SKo)
1989	Amiran Totikashvilli (USSR)
1991	Tadanori Koshino (Jap)
1993	Ryuji Sonoda (Jap)

Most men's titles
4 Yashiro Yamashita, Shozo Fujii, Naoya Ogawa

Women - Open
1980	Ingrid Berghmans (Bel)
1982	Ingrid Berghmans (Bel)
1984	Ingrid Berghmans (Bel)
1986	Ingrid Berghmans (Bel)
1987	Gao Fengliang (Chn)
1989	Estella Rodriguez (Cub)
1991	Zhuang Xiaoyan (Chn)
1993	Beata Maksymow (Pol)

Women - Over 72kg
1980	Margarita de Cal (Ita)
1982	Natalina Lupino (Fra)
1984	Maria-Teresa Motta (Ita)
1986	Gao Fengliang (Chn)
1987	Gao Fengliang (Chn)
1989	Gao Fengliang (Chn)
1991	Moon Ji-yoon (SKo)
1993	Johanna Hagn (Ger)

Women - Under 72kg
1980	Jocelyne Triadou (Fra)
1982	Barbara Classen (FRG)
1984	Ingrid Berghmans (Bel)
1986	Irene de Kok (Hol)
1987	Irene de Kok (Hol)
1989	Ingrid Berghmans (Bel)
1991	Kim Mi-jung (SKo)
1993	Leng Chunhui (Chn)

Women - Under 66kg
1980	Edith Simon (Aut)
1982	Brigitte Deydier (Fra)
1984	Brigitte Deydier (Fra)
1986	Brigitte Deydier (Fra)
1987	Alexandra Schreiber (FRG)
1989	Emanuela Pierantozzi (Ita)
1991	Emanuela Pierantozzi (Ita)
1993	Cho Min-sun (SKo)

Women - Under 61kg
1980	Anita Staps (Hol)

1982	Martine Rothier (Fra)
1984	Natasha Hernandez (Ven)
1986	Diane Bell (UK)
1987	Diane Bell (UK)
1989	Catherine Fleury (Fra)
1991	Fraucke Eickoff (Ger)
1993	Gella van de Cavaye (Bel)

Women - Under 56kg

1980	Gerda Winklbauer (Aut)
1982	Béatrice Rodriguez (Fra)
1984	Ann-Maria Burns (USA)
1986	Ann Hughes (UK)
1987	Catherine Arnaud (Fra)
1989	Catherine Arnaud (Fra)
1991	Miriam Blasco (Spa)
1993	Nicola Fairbrother (UK)

Women - Under 52kg

1980	Edith Hrovat (Aut)
1982	Loretta Doyle (UK)
1984	Kaori Yamaguchi (Jap)
1986	Dominique Brun (Fra)
1987	Sharon Rendle (UK)
1989	Sharon Rendle (UK)
1991	Alessandra Giungi (Ita)
1993	Legna Verdecia (Cub)

Women - Under 48kg

1980	Jane Bridge (UK)
1982	Karen Briggs (UK)
1984	Karen Briggs (UK)
1986	Karen Briggs (UK)
1987	Zhangyun Li (Chn)
1989	Karen Briggs (UK)
1991	Cécile Nowak (Fra)
1993	Ryoko Tamura (Jap)

Most women's titles

6 Berghmans, 4 Briggs, Gao Fengliang; 3 Deydier

Men's World Cup

A team event, first held in 1994, when the winners were France.

Nicola Fairbrother on her way to victory in 1993

Jiu-Jitsu

Jiu-jitsu incorporates the martial arts skills of both body throws and kicking and punching techniques. The World Council of Jiu-Jitsu Organisations have staged biennial world championships from 1984. Canada won the team event on each occasion: 1984, 1986 and 1988.

Karate

Karate is a martial art developed in Japan, the name originating as recently as the 1930s. The techniques used, however, were devised from the sixth century Chinese art of Shaolin boxing 'kempo' and its development in Okinawa c.1500 into 'Tang Hand', whereby the island's inhabitants fought bare handed against armed Japanese oppressors. Tang Hand was introduced to Japan in the 1920s by Funakoshi Gichin, who adopted the word karate, meaning empty hand. The style he practised became known as Shotokan, now one of five major styles in Japan, the others being Wado-ryu, Gojo-ryu, Shito-ryu and Kyokushinkai, each placing different emphasis on technique, speed and power. Karate spread to the Western world from the 1950s, and the All-Japan Karate-do Organization (FAJKO), founded in 1964, staged the first multi-style world championships in 1970. Following this the World Union of Karate-do Organizations was created.

World Championships

First held in Tokyo in 1970, when there were team and individual championships. Women first competed in 1980. Kumite championships are now staged at different weight categories and there are also Kata (or sequence) events, whereby contestants do not fight each other but are marked for their routines. *Winners:*

Men's Team

1970	Japan
1972	France
1975	Great Britain
1977	Netherlands
1980	Spain
1982	Great Britain
1984	Great Britain
1986	Great Britain
1988	Great Britain
1990	Great Britain
1992	Spain
1994	France

Men Kumite - No weight limit

1970	Kouji Wada (Jap)
1972	L.Watanabe-Taske (Bra)
1975	Kazusada Murakami (Jap)
1977	Otti Roethoff (Hol)

Men Kumite - Under 60kg

1980	Ricardo Abad (Spa)
1982	Jukka-Pekka Väyrinen (Fin)

1984   Dirk Betzien (FRG)
1986   Hideto Nakano (Jap)
1988   Abdu Shaher (UK)
1990   Stewin Widar Rönning (Nor)
1992   Veysel Bugur (Tur)
1994   Damien Dovy (Fra)

Men Kumite - Under 65kg
1980   Toshiaki Maeda (Jap)
1982   Yuichi Suzuki (Jap)
1984   Ramon Malavé (Swe)
1986   Eizou Kondo (Jap)
1988   Tim Stephens (UK)
1990   Toshikatsu Azumi (Jap)
1992   Jesús Juan Rubio (Spa)
1994   Teruchika Ito (Jap)

Men Kumite - Under 70kg
1980   Damian Gonzales (Spa)
1982   Seiji Nishimura (Jap)
1984   Jim Collins (UK)
1986   Thierry Masci (Fra)
1988   Thierry Masci (Fra)
1990   Haldun Alagas (Tur)
1992   Willie Thomas (UK)
1994   Shisua Shiina (Jap)

Men Kumite - Under 75kg
1980   Sadao Tajima (Jap)
1982   Javier Gomez (Swi)
1984   Toon Stelling (Hol)
1986   Kenneth Leeuwin (Hol)
1988   Kyo Hayashi (Jap)
1990   Hideo Tamaru (Jap)
1992   Wayne Otto (UK)
1994   Daniel Devigli (Aut)

Men Kumite - Under 80kg
1980   Tokey Hill (USA)
1982   Pat McKay (UK)
1984   Pat McKay (UK)
1986   Jacques Tapol (Fra)
1988   Dudley Josepa (Hol)
1990   José Manuel Egea (Spa)
1992   José Manuel Egea (Spa)
1994   David Benetello (Ita)

Men Kumite - Over 80kg
1980   Jean-Luc Montana (Fra)
1982   Jeff Thompson (UK)
1984   Jerome Atkinson (UK)
1986   Vic Charles (UK)
1988   Emmanuel Pinda (Fra)
1990   Marc Pyrée (Fra)
1992   B Peakall (Aus)
1994   Alain Le Hetet (Fra)

Men Kumite - Open
1980   Ricciardi (Ita)
1982   Hsiao Murase (Jap)
1984   Emmanuel Pinda (Fra)
1986   Karl Daggfeldt (Swe)
1992   Hiroshi Hayashi (Jap)
1994   Manabu Takanouchi (Jap)
Sanbon shobu
1988   José Manuel Egea (Spa)

1990   Wayne Otto (UK)
Ippon shobu
1988   Claudio Guazzaroni (Ita)
1990   Giovanni Tramontini (Fra)

Men's Individual Kata
1977   Keiji Okada (Jap)
1980   Keiji Okada (Jap)
1982   Masashi Koyama (Jap)
1984   Tsuguo Sakumoto (Jap)
1986   Tsuguo Sakumoto (Jap)
1988   Tsuguo Sakumoto (Jap)
1990   Tomojuki Aihara (Jap)
1992   Luis-Maria Sanz (Spa)
1994   Michaël Milan (Fra)

Men's Team Kata
1986   Japan
1988   Japan
1990   Italy
1992   Japan
1994   Japan

Women Kumite - Under 53kg
1982   Sophie Berger (Fra)
1984   Sophie Berger (Fra)
1986   Johanna Kauri (Fin)
1988   Yuko Hasama (Jap)
1990   Yuko Hasama (Jap)
1992   C Machin (Aus)
1994   Sari Laine (Fin)

Women Kumite - Under 60kg
1982   Yukari Yamakawa (Jap)
1984   Tomoko Kinishi (Jap)
1986   Ritva Virelius (Fin)
1988   Akimi Kimura (Jap)
1990   Monique Amghar (Fra)
1992   Mollie Samuels (UK)
1994   Mayumi Baba (Jap)

Women Kumite - Over 60kg
1982   Guus van Mourik (Hol)
1984   Guus van Mourik (Hol)
1986   Guus van Mourik (Hol)
1988   Guus van Mourik (Hol)
1990   Catherine Belrhiti (Fra)
1992   Catherine Belrhiti (Fra)
1994   Sandra Louw (SAf)

Women's Individual Kata
1980   Suzuko Okamura (Jap)
1982   Mie Nakayama (Jap)
1984   Mie Nakayama (Jap)
1986   Mie Nakayama (Jap)
1988   Yuki Mimura (Jap)
1990   Yuki Mimura (Jap)
1992   Yuki Mimura (Jap)
1994   Hisami Yokoyama (Jap)

Women's Team Kata
1986   Taiwan
1988   Japan
1990   Japan
1992   Japan
1994   Japan

Kendo

The Japanese martial art of swordsmanship, which was practised by the warrior class, the samurai. The earliest known reference to such arts in Japan was in 789 AD. Kendo is now practised with shiani, or bamboo swords.

World Championships

First held in 1970. *Winners:*

Men

1970	Mitsuru Kobayashi (Jap)
1973	Tatsushi Sakuragi (Jap)
1976	Eijo Yoko (Jap)
1979	Hironori Yamada (Jap)
1982	Minoru Makita (Jap)
1985	Kunishide Koda (Jap)
1988	Isawu Okido (Jap)
1991	S Muto (Jap)
1994	H Takahashi (Jap)

Japan has won the team title at all nine championships.

Women
1994   A Horibe (HK)

Team
1994   S Korea

Korfball

Korfball is played indoors on a pitch of 40 x 20 metres (or outdoors up to 60 x 30 metres) by mixed teams of four men and four women. Its origins can be traced back to the game developed in 1902 in Amsterdam, Netherlands by school-teacher Nico Broekhuysen, who was inspired by a game that he had played in Nääs, Sweden. The sport was demonstrated at the Olympic Games of 1920 and 1928.

The sport has grown during this century from an Amsterdam school activity into an international sport. The Fédération Internationale de Korfball (FIK) was founded in 1933 by the Dutch and Belgian Associations. Its name was changed to the International Korfball Federation (IKF) in 1982. From just four member nations in 1970, the membership reached 29 in 1992.

World Championships

The first World Championships were held in 1978 to celebrate the 75th anniversary of the founding of the Royal Netherlands Korfball Association (KNKV). Eight nations took part at the first two championships, with 12 subsequently. *Winners:*

Netherlands	1978, 1984, 1987
Belgium	1991

Lacrosse

The name 'La Crosse', the French word for a crozier or staff, was given by French settlers in North America to the game played by Indians, and known by them as 'baggataway'. The Indians played on a very large pitch, some 500m long, their crosse or racket being a staff curved at one end into a rough circle, into which was fitted a net. The first non-Indian club was the Montreal Lacrosse Club, founded in 1839. The sport was introduced to Britain in 1867 by a party of Caughnawaga Indians.

The first national body was the National Lacrosse Association, formed in Canada in 1867. The International Federation of Amateur Lacrosse (IFAL) was founded in 1928. Women were first reported to have played lacrosse in 1886 and the All-England Women's Lacrosse Association was formed in 1912. The women's game has evolved from the men's game and there are now considerable differences in the rules. Men's lacrosse is played by teams of 10-a-side and women's principally by 12-a-side, although a major variant is the 6-a-side game.

Men's Lacrosse

World Championships
First held in 1967 in Toronto, winners have been:
USA   1967, 1974, 1982, 1986, 1990, 1994
Canada   1978
The USA also won the pre-Olympic tournament in 1984. Their only loss at this level was by 16-17 to Canada in the 1978 final, after extra time, the only drawn game at this level.

Olympic Games
Lacrosse was played at two Olympics, when the winners were: 1904 Shamrock (Can), 1908 Canada. It was also a demonstration sport in 1928, 1932 and 1948.

English Club Championships
Contested annually for the Iroquois Cup from 1890. *Most wins:*

17	Stockport	1897-1901, 1903, 1905, 1911-3, 1923-4, 1926, 1928, 1934, 1987, 1989
11	South Manchester	1890, 1895, 1904, 1906, 1909, 1933, 1966, 1971-3, 1980
11	Mellor	1935-7, 1948, 1963, 1965-7, 1969, 1988, 1994
10	Old Hulmeians	1907-8, 1910, 1914, 1932, 1949-50, 1962, 1964, 1968
8	Cheadle	1978-9, 1981, 1984-5, 1990-2
7	Old Waconians	1938-9, 1947, 1951-3, 1955
7	Heaton Mersey	1927, 1954, 1958-60, 1986, 1993
3	Boardman & Eccles	1922, 1929, 1961
3	Sheffield University	1977, 1982-3

Women's Lacrosse

World Championships
First held in 1969. *Winners:*
1969 GB   1978 Canada
1974 USA

World Cup

First held 1982, replacing the World Championships. *Winners:*
1982 USA
1986 Australia
1989 USA
1993 USA

Modern Pentathlon

This is the five sport discipline of cross-country riding, épée fencing, pistol shooting (at 25m), swimming (300m) and cross-country running (4000m). It has been included at every Olympic Games from 1912, and has been known as the military pentathlon. For many years the sport was dominated by members of the armed forces, who were best able to pursue such diverse activities. Military lore explains the origin of the sport: a messenger has to travel across country on horseback, fighting his way through with sword and pistol; he then has to swim across a river, before finishing his journey on foot.

Each event is scored on points, determined either against the other competitors or against scoring tables. Note that the points scores given in the lists of champions are not necessarily comparable. Prior to 1954 the scoring was on the basis of places at each event.

The sport's governing body is L'Union Internationale de Pentathlon Moderne (UIPM), founded in 1948. In 1960 Biathlon (cross-country skiing and shooting) joined the Union to form an umbrella organisation of the UIPMB. In 1995 the UIPM had 60 member nations affiliated to it.

Olympic Games

Held as a five-day event 1912-80, over 3-4 days 1984-92. For Atlanta 1996 the competition will be a one-day event for 32 men to have qualified from pre-Olympic events. *Winners:*

Individual
1912 Gösta Lilliehöök (Swe) 27
1920 Gustaf Dyrssen (Swe) 18
1924 Bo Lindman (Swe) 18
1928 Sven Thofelt (Swe) 47
1932 Johan Oxenstierna (Swe) 32
1936 Gotthard Handrick (Ger) 31.5
1948 Willie Grut (Swe) 16
1952 Lars Hall (Swe) 32
1956 Lars Hall (Swe) 4843
1960 Ferenc Németh (Hun) 5024
1964 Ferenc Török (Hun) 5116
1968 Björn Ferm (Swe) 4964
1972 András Balczó (Hun) 5412
1976 Janusz Pyciak-Peciak (Pol) 5520
1980 Anatoliy Starostin (USSR) 5568
1984 Daniele Masala (Ita) 5469
1988 János Martinek (Hun) 5404
1992 Arkadiusz Skrzypaszek (Pol) 5559

Team (first held 1952)
Hungary 1952, 1960, 1968, 1988
USSR 1956, 1964, 1972, 1980
Great Britain 1976
Italy 1984
Poland 1992

Most gold medals: 3 András Balczó (Hun) individual 1972, team 1960 and 1968.
Most medals: 7 Pavel Lednev (USSR): individual 2nd 1976, 3rd 1968, 1972, 1980; team 1st 1972, 1980, 2nd 1968.
Greatest margin of victory: probably by Willie Grut in 1948 as he won three events and was placed fifth and eighth in the other two. On the present scoring system: 77 points András Balczó in 1972 over Boris Onischenko (USSR), who four years later was disqualified for using an illegal fencing weapon, which registered hits when no contact had occured with his opponent.

World Championships

Held annually from 1949 with the exception of Olympic years. *Winners:*

Individual
1949 Tage Bjurefelt (Swe) 19
1950 Lars Hall (Swe) 19
1951 Lars Hall (Swe) 22
1953 Gábor Benedek (Hun) 22
1954 Björn Thofelt (Swe) 4634.5
1955 Konstantin Salnikov (USSR) 4453.5
1957 Igor Novikov (USSR) 4769
1958 Igor Novikov (USSR) 4924
1959 Igor Novikov (USSR) 4847
1961 Igor Novikov (USSR) 5217
1962 Eduards Dobnikov (USSR) 4647
1963 András Balczó (Hun) 5267
1965 András Balczó (Hun) 5302
1966 András Balczó (Hun) 5217
1967 András Balczó (Hun) 5056
1969 András Balczó (Hun) 5515
1970 Péter Kelemen (Hun) 5220
1971 Boris Onischenko (USSR) 5206
1973 Pavel Lednev (USSR) 5413
1974 Pavel Lednev (USSR) 5302
1975 Pavel Lednev (USSR) 5056
1977 Janusz Pyciak-Peciak (Pol) 5485
1978 Pavel Lednev (USSR) 5498
1979 Robert Nieman (USA) 5483
1981 Janusz Pyciak-Peciak (Pol) 5662
1982 Daniele Masala (Ita) 5680
1983 Anatoliy Starostin (USSR) 5506
1985 Attila Mizsér (Hun) 5525
1986 Carlo Massullo (Ita) 5463*
1987 Joël Bouzou (Fra) 5462
1989 László Fábián (Hun) 5654
1990 Gianluca Tiberti (Ita) 5441
1991 Arkadiusz Skrzypaszek (Pol) 5498
1993 Richard Phelps (UK) 5755
1994 Dmitriy Svatkovskiy (Rus) 5543
1995 Dmitriy Svatovskiy (Rus) 5583

* *original winner was Anatoliy Starostin (USSR) 5563, but he and 14 others were subsequently disqualified for illegal drugs use. The USSR also lost their women's team title.*

Poland's Arkadiusz Skrzypaszek show-jumping

Team

14	USSR	1957-9, 1961-2, 1969, 1971, 1973-4, 1982-3, 1985, 1990-1
11	Hungary	1954-5, 1963, 1965-7, 1970, 1975, 1987, 1989, 1995
4	Sweden	1949-51, 1953
3	Poland	1977-8, 1981
1	USA 1979, Italy 1986, France 1994	

Relay

First held as a one-day event for three-man teams, in 1989.

1989	Hungary
1990	USSR
1991	Hungary
1992	Poland
1993	Hungary
1994	Hungary

Most titles: 13 András Balczó (Hun) six individual, seven team including Olympics 1960-72.

Women's World Championships

First held in London in 1981. *Winners:*

Individual

1981	Anne Ahlgren (Swe) 4975
1982	Wendy Norman (UK) 5311
1983	Lynn Chernobrywy (Can) 5328
1984	Svetlana Yakovleva (USSR) 5481
1985	Barbara Kotowska (Pol) 5336
1986	Irina Kiselyeva (USSR) 5323
1987	Irina Kiselyeva (USSR) 5406
1988	Dorota Idzi (Pol) 5308
1989	Lori Norwood (USA) 5315
1990	Eva Fjellerup (Den) 5478
1991	Eva Fjellerup (Den) 5286
1992	Iwona Kowalewska (Pol)
1993	Eva Fjellerup (Den) 5543
1994	Eva Fjellerup (Den) 5590
1995	Kerstin Danielsson (Swe) 5524

Team

7	Poland	1985, 1988-92, 1995
3	Great Britain	1981-3
2	USSR	1984, 1987
1	France 1986, Italy 1994	

Team relay

1991	Poland
1992	Poland
1993	Russia
1994	Poland

Women's World Cup

This event preceded the world championships. *Winners:*

1978	Wendy Skipwith (UK)
1979	Kathy Taylor (UK)
1980	Wendy Norman (UK)

Team: Great Britain 1978-80

Motor Cycling

The first known motor cycle race was on 20 September 1896 when eight competitors took part in a race from Paris to Nantes and back. The course covered 152 km (139 miles) and was won by M.Chevalier on a Michelin-Dion tricycle in 4 hr 10 min 37 sec. The first race for two-wheeled motor cycles was held over one mile (1.6 km) of an oval track at Sheen House, Richmond, Surrey on 29 Nov, 1897. The race was won by Charles Jarrott, riding a Fournier, in a time of 2 min 8 sec. The Auto-Cycle Union (ACU), founded in 1903, is the governing body of the sport in Britain. The world governing body, the Fédération Internationale Motorcycliste (FIM), was formed in 1904 under the title Fédération Internationale des Clubs Motorcyclistes.

World Championships

World Championships were instituted by the FIM in 1949 for 125, 250, 350 and 500 cc classes, as well as for sidecars. The 50 cc class was introduced in 1962 but was discontinued in 1983 to make way for the larger 80 cc class. In 1977-8 a Formula 750 class was contested. The 350cc class was discontinued at the end of the 1982 season. *Winners with make of bike ridden:*

50 cc

1962	Ernst Degner (FRG)	Suzuki
1963-4	Hugh Anderson (NZ)	Suzuki
1965	Ralph Bryans (Ire)	Honda
1966-8	Hans-Georg Anscheidt (FRG)	Suzuki
1969-70	Angel Nieto (Spa)	Derbi

1971	Jan de Vries (Hol)	Kreidler
1972	Angel Nieto (Spa)	Derbi
1973	Jan de Vries (Hol)	Kreidler
1974	Henk van Kessel (Hol)	Kreidler
1975	Angel Nieto (Spa)	Kreidler
1976-7	Angel Nieto (Spa)	Bultaco
1978	Ricardo Tormo (Spa)	Bultaco
1979-80	Eugenio Lazzarini (Ita)	Kreidler
1981	Ricardo Tormo (Spa)	Bultaco
1982	Stefan Dörflinger (Swi)	MBA
1983	Stefan Dörflinger (Swi)	Krauser Kreidler

80cc

1984	Stefan Dörflinger (Swi)	Zundapp
1985	Stefan Dörflinger (Swi)	Krauser
1986-8	Jorge Martinez (Spa)	Derbi
1989	Manuel Herreros (Spa)	Derbi

125cc

1949	Nello Pagani (Ita)	Mondial
1950	Bruno Ruffo (Ita)	Mondial
1951	Carlo Ubbiali (Ita)	Mondial
1952	Cecil Sandford (UK)	MV
1953	Werner Haas (FRG)	NSU
1954	Rupert Hollaus (Aut)	NSU
1955-6	Carlo Ubbiali (Ita)	MV
1957	Tarquinio Provini (Ita)	Mondial
1958-60	Carlo Ubbiali (Ita)	MV
1961	Tom Phillis (Aus)	Honda
1962	Luigi Taveri (Swi)	Honda
1963	Hugh Anderson (NZ)	Suzuki
1964	Luigi Taveri (Swi)	Honda
1965	Hugh Anderson (NZ)	Suzuki
1966	Luigi Taveri (Swi)	Honda
1967	Bill Ivy (UK)	Yamaha
1968	Phil Read (UK)	Yamaha
1969	Dave Simmonds (UK)	Kawasaki
1970	Dieter Braun (FRG)	Suzuki
1971-2	Angel Nieto (Spa)	Derbi
1973-4	Kent Andersson (Swe)	Yamaha
1975	Paolo Pileri (Ita)	Morbidelli
1976-7	Pier-Paolo Bianchi (Ita)	Morbidelli
1978	Eugenio Lazzarini (Ita)	MBA
1979	Angel Nieto (Spa)	Morbidelli
1980	Pier-Paolo Bianchi (Ita)	MBA
1981	Angel Nieto (Spa)	Minarelli
1982-4	Angel Nieto (Spa)	Garelli
1985	Fausto Gresini (Ita)	Garelli
1986	Luca Cadalora (Ita)	Garelli
1987	Fausto Gresini (Ita)	Garelli
1988	Jorge Martinez (Spa)	Derbi
1989	Alex Criville (Spa)	Cobas
1990-1	Loris Capirossi (Ita)	Honda
1992	Alessandro Gramigni (Ita)	Aprilia
1993	Dirk Raudies (Ger)	Honda
1994	Kazuto Sakata (Jap)	Aprilia

250cc

1949	Bruno Ruffo (Ita)	Guzzi
1950	Dario Ambrosini (Ita)	Benelli
1951	Bruno Ruffo (Ita)	Guzzi
1952	Enrico Lorenzetti (Ita)	Guzzi
1953-4	Werner Haas (FRG)	NSU
1955	Herman Müller (FRG)	NSU
1956	Carlo Ubbiali (Ita)	MV
1957	Cecil Sandford (UK)	Mondial
1958	Tarquinio Provini (Ita)	MV
1959-60	Carlo Ubbiali (Ita)	MV
1961	Mike Hailwood (UK)	Honda
1962-3	Jim Redman (Rho)	Honda
1964-5	Phil Read (UK)	Yamaha
1966-7	Mike Hailwood (UK)	Honda
1968	Phil Read (UK)	Yamaha
1969	Kel Caruthers (Aus)	Benelli
1970	Rod Gould (UK)	Yamaha
1971	Phil Read (UK)	Yamaha
1972	Jarno Saarinen (Fin)	Yamaha
1973	Dieter Braun (FRG)	Yamaha
1974-6	Walter Villa (Ita)	Harley-Davidson
1977	Mario Lega (Ita)	Morbidelli
1978-9	Kork Ballington (SAf)	Kawasaki
1980-1	Anton Mang (FRG)	Kawasaki
1982	Jean-Louis Tournadre (Fra)	Yamaha
1983	Carlos Lavado (Ven)	Yamaha
1984	Christian Sarron (Fra)	Yamaha
1985	Freddie Spencer (USA)	Honda
1986	Carlos Lavado (Ven)	Yamaha
1987	Anton Mang (FRG)	Honda
1988-9	Sito Pons (Spa)	Honda
1990	John Kocinski (USA)	Yamaha
1991-2	Luca Cadalora (Ita)	Honda
1993	Tetsuya Harada (Jap)	Yamaha
1994	Massimiliano Biaggi (Ita)	Aprilia

350cc

1949	Freddie Frith (UK)	Velocette
1950	Bob Foster (UK)	Velocette
1951-2	Geoff Duke (UK)	Norton
1953-4	Fergus Anderson (UK)	Guzzi
1955-6	Bill Lomas (UK)	Guzzi
1957	Keith Campbell (Aus)	Guzzi
1958-60	John Surtees (UK)	MV
1961	Gary Hocking (Rho)	MV
1962-5	Jim Redman (Rho)	Honda
1966-7	Mike Hailwood (UK)	Honda
1968-73	Giacomo Agostini (Ita)	MV
1974	Giacomo Agostini (Ita)	Yamaha
1975	Johnny Cecotto (Ven)	Yamaha
1976	Walter Villa (Ita)	Harley-Davidson
1977	Takazumi Katayama (Jap)	Yamaha
1978-9	Kork Ballington (SAf)	Kawasaki
1980	Jon Ekerold (SAf)	Yamaha
1981-2	Anton Mang (FRG)	Kawasaki

500cc

1949	Leslie Graham (UK)	AJS
1950	Umberto Masetti (Ita)	Gilera
1951	Geoff Duke (UK)	Norton
1952	Umberto Masetti (Ita)	Gilera
1953-55	Geoff Duke (UK)	Gilera
1956	John Surtees (UK)	MV
1957	Libero Liberati (Ita)	Gilera

Michael Doohan – by July 1995 he had taken his number of 500cc Grand Prix victories to 25

1958-60	John Surtees (UK)	MV
1961	Gary Hocking (Rho)	MV
1962-65	Mike Hailwood (UK)	MV
1966-72	Giacomo Agostini (Ita)	MV
1973-4	Phil Read (UK)	MV
1975	Giacomo Agostini (Ita)	Yamaha
1976-7	Barry Sheene (UK)	Suzuki
1978-80	Kenny Roberts (USA)	Yamaha
1981	Marco Lucchinelli (Ita)	Suzuki
1982	Franco Uncini (Ita)	Suzuki
1983	Freddie Spencer (USA)	Honda
1984	Eddie Lawson (USA)	Yamaha
1985	Freddie Spencer (USA)	Honda
1986	Eddie Lawson (USA)	Yamaha
1987	Wayne Gardner (Aus)	Honda
1988	Eddie Lawson (USA)	Yamaha
1989	Eddie Lawson (USA)	Honda
1990-2	Wayne Rainey (USA)	Yamaha
1993	Kevin Schwantz (USA)	Suzuki
1994	Michael Doohan (Aus)	Honda

750cc

1977	Steve Baker (USA)	Yamaha
1978	Johnny Cecotto (Ven)	Yamaha
1979	Patrick Pons (Fra)	Yamaha

Sidecar

1949-51	Eric Oliver (UK)	Norton
1952	Cyril Smith (UK)	Norton
1953	Eric Oliver (UK)	Norton
1954	Wilhelm Noll (FRG)	BMW

1955	Wilhelm Faust (FRG)	BMW
1956	Wilhelm Noll (FRG)	BMW
1957	Fritz Hillebrand (FRG)	BMW
1958-9	Walter Schneider (FRG)	BMW
1960	Helmut Fath (FRG)	BMW
1961-4	Max Deubel (FRG)	BMW
1965-6	Fritz Scheidegger (Swi)	BMW
1967	Klaus Enders (FRG)	BMW
1968	Helmut Fath (FRG)	URS
1969-70	Klaus Enders (FRG)	BMW
1971	Horst Owesle (FRG)	Munch
1972-3	Klaus Enders (FRG)	BMW
1974	Klaus Enders (FRG)	Busch BMW
1975	Rolf Steinhausen (FRG)	Konig
1976	Rolf Steinhausen (FRG)	Busch Konig
1977	George O'Dell (UK)	Yamaha
1978-9	Rolf Biland (Swi)	Yamaha
1980	Jock Taylor (UK)	Yamaha
1981	Rolf Biland (Swi)	Yamaha
1982	Werner Schwärzel (FRG)	Yamaha
1983	Rolf Biland (Swi)	Yamaha
1984-6	Egbert Streuer (Hol)	Yamaha
1987-9	Steve Webster (UK)	Yamaha
1990	Alain Michel (Fra)	Krauser
1991	Steve Webster (UK)	Krauser
1992-3	Rolf Biland (Swi)	Krauser
1994	Rolf Biland (Swi)	Swiss Auto

Most titles (Solo)

Total	Rider	50cc	80	125	250	350	500	750	F1	Years
15	Giacomo Agostini (Ita)	-	-	-	-	7	8	-	-	1966-75
13	Angel Nieto (Spa)	6	-	7	-	-	-	-	-	1969-84
10	Mike Hailwood (UK)	-	-	-	3	2	4	-	1	1961-78
9	Carlo Ubbiali (Ita)	-	-	6	3	-	-	-	-	1951-60
8	Phil Read (UK)	-	-	1	4	-	2	-	1	1964-77
7	John Surtees (UK)	-	-		-	3	4	-	-	1956-60
6	Geoff Duke (UK)	-	-	-	-	2	4	-	-	1951-5
6	Jim Redman (Rho)	-	-	-	2	4	-	-	-	1962-5

Mike Hailwood and Phil Read are the only riders to have won world titles in four classes.

Most titles in each class

50cc 6 Angel Nieto, 3 Hans-Georg Anscheidt (FRG)
80cc 3 Jorge Martinez (Spa), 2 Stefan Dörflinger (Swi)
125cc 7 Angel Nieto, 6 Carlo Ubbiali (Ita)
250cc 4 Phil Read, 3 Mike Hailwood, Carlo Ubbiali, Walter Villa (Ita), Anton Mang (FRG)
350cc 7 Giacomo Agostini, 4 Jim Redman
500cc 8 Giacomo Agostini, 4 Geoff Duke, Mike Hailwood, John Surtees, Eddie Lawson (USA); 3 Kenny Roberts (USA)
750cc 1 Steve Baker (USA), Johnny Cecotto (Ven), Patrick Pons (Fra)
F1 5 Joey Dunlop (Ire), 2 Graeme Crosby (NZ)
Sidecar 7 Rolf Biland (Swi), 6 Klaus Enders (FRG); 4 Max Deubel (FRG), Eric Oliver (UK), Steve Webster (UK); 3 Egbert Streuer (Hol)

Most Grand Prix wins

122 Giacomo Agostini (350cc- 54, 500cc- 68)
90 Angel Nieto (50cc 27, 80cc- 1, 125cc- 62)
76 Mike Hailwood (125cc- 2, 250cc 21, 350cc 16, 500cc- 37)
77 Rolf Biland (sidecar 77)
52 Phil Read (125cc- 10, 250cc- 27, 350cc- 4, 500cc- 11)

Hailwood, Read, Jim Redman (Rho) and Charles Mortimer (UK) are the only riders to have won Grands Prix in four different classes.

Most wins at 500cc

68 Agostini, 37 Hailwood, 32 Eddie Lawson (USA), 25 Kevin Schwantz (USA), Michael Doohan (Aus); 24 Wayne Rainey (Aus), 22 Geoff Duke (UK), Kenny Roberts (USA), John Surtees (UK); 20 Freddie Spencer (USA), 19 Barry Sheene (UK), 18 Wayne Gardner (Aus). To end July 1995.

Most wins in other class

50cc 27 Angel Nieto (Spa)
80cc 21 Jorge Martinez (Spa)
125cc 62 Angel Nieto (Spa)
250cc 33 Anton Mang (FRG)
350cc 54 Giacomo Agostini (Ita)
Sidecar 77 Rolf Biland (Swi)

Fastest race: 1977 Belgian GP at Spa-Francorchamps, won by Barry Sheene (UK) on a 495cc Suzuki at an average speed of 217.37 km/h (135.07 mph)

World Manufacturers Championships

Most wins:

37 MV Augusta 125cc: 1952-3, 1955-6, 1958-60
250cc: 1955-6, 1958-60
350cc: 1958-61, 1968-72,
500cc: 1956, 1958-65, 1967-73
34 Honda 50cc: 1965-6
125cc: 1961-2, 1964, 1966, 1990-1, 1993
250cc: 1961-3, 1966-7, 1985-9, 1991-2
350cc: 1962-7
500cc: 1966, 1983-5, 1987, 1989, 1994
31 Yamaha 125cc: 1967-8, 1973-4
250cc: 1964-5, 1968, 1970-4, 1977, 1982-4, 1990, 1993
350cc: 1973-7, 1980
500cc: 1974-5, 1986, 1988, 1990-2
16 Suzuki 50cc: 1962-4, 1967-8
125cc: 1963, 1965, 1970
500cc: 1976-82, 1993

Most wins - Sidecar

19 BMW 1955 73
11 Yamaha/LCR Yamaha 1977-87
6 LCR Krauser 1988-93
5 Norton 1949-53

World Endurance Championship

Inaugurated in 1980, it replaced the FIM Coupe d'Endurance. *Winners:*

1980	Marc Fontan & Hervé Moineau (Fra)	Honda
1981	Jean Lafond & Raymond Roche (Fra)	Kawasaki
1982	Jean-Claude Chemarin (Fra) & Jacques Cornu (Swi)	Kawasaki
1983	Richard Hubin (Bel) & Hervé Moineau (Fra)	Suzuki
1984-5	Gérard Coudray & Patrick Igoa (Fra)	Honda
1986	Patrick Igoa (Fra)	Honda
1987	Hervé Moineau (Fra)	Suzuki
1988	Hervé Moineau (Fra) & Thierry Crine (Fra)	Suzuki
1989-90	Alex Vieira (Fra)	Honda
1991	Alex Vieira (Fra)	Kawasaki
1992	Carl Fogarty & Terry Rymer (UK)	Kawasaki
1993	Douglas Toland (USA)	Kawasaki
1994	Adrien Morillas (Fra))	Kawasaki

TT Formula One World Championship

Formula One, Two and Three World Championships were introduced in 1977. Formula Three was discontinued at the end of 1981, and Formula Two in 1986. The Formula One race at the Isle of Man TT formed a round in the Formula One Championship, but the series stopped after 1990. *Formula One winners:*

1977	Phil Read (UK)	Honda
1978	Mike Hailwood (UK)	Ducati
1979	Ron Haslam (UK)	Honda
1980-1	Graeme Crosby (NZ)	Suzuki
1982-6	Joey Dunlop (UK)	Honda
1987	Virginio Ferrari (Ita)	Yamaha
1988-90	Carl Fogarty (UK)	Honda

World Superbike Championships

Contested over a series of races annually from 1988. *Winners:*

1988-9	Fred Merkel (USA)	Honda
1990	Raymond Roche (Fra)	Ducati
1991-2	Doug Polen (USA)	Ducati
1993	Scott Russell (USA)	Kawasaki
1994	Carl Fogarty (UK)	Ducati

Isle of Man TT

In 1905 the Auto Cycle Club of the RAC held rehearsals for the 1906 International Cup Race on the Isle of Man, because road racing on the mainland was banned. It was so popular that it led to the first Tourist Trophy race being staged on 28 May 1907, won by Charlie Collier on a single-cylinder Matchless. The 15.8-mile St. John's course was used until 1911 when the 37 -mile Mountain course was used for the first time. The exact distance of the current Mountain circuit is 37.73 miles 60.72 km. The shorter Clypse course (10.79 miles 17.36 km) was introduced in 1954 to accomodate the return of sidecar racing, but it was unpopular with riders, and was abandoned at the end of 1959.

Senior TT

The most prestigious of all TT races. *Winners (all UK riders unless otherwise stated):*

1911	Oscar Godfrey	Indian
1912	Frank Applebee	Scott
1913	Tim Wood	Scott
1914	Cyril Pullin	Rudge
1920	Tommy de la Hay	Sunbeam
1921	Howard Davies	AJS
1922	Alec Bennett	Sunbeam
1923	Tom Sheard	Douglas
1924	Alec Bennett	Norton
1925	Howard Davies	HRD
1926	Stanley Woods	Norton
1927	Alec Bennett	Norton
1928-9	Charlie Dodson	Sunbeam
1930	Wal Handley	Rudge Whitworth
1931	Tim Hunt	Norton
1932-3	Stanley Woods	Norton
1934	Jimmy Guthrie	Norton
1935	Stanley Woods	Moto Guzzi
1936	Jimmy Guthrie	Norton
1937	Freddie Frith	Norton
1938	Harold Daniell	Norton
1939	Georg Meier (FRG)	BMW
1947	Harold Daniell	Norton
1948	Artie Bell	Norton
1949	Harold Daniell	Norton
1950-1	Geoff Duke	Norton
1952	Reg Armstrong (Ire)	Norton
1953-4	Ray Amm (S Rho)	Norton
1955	Geoff Duke	Gilera
1956	John Surtees	MV
1957	Bob McIntyre	Gilera
1958-60	John Surtees	MV
1961	Mike Hailwood	Norton
1962	Gary Hocking (S Rho)	MV
1963-5	Mike Hailwood	MV
1966-7	Mike Hailwood	Honda
1968-72	Giacomo Agostini (Ita)	MV
1973	Jack Findlay (Aus)	Suzuki
1974	Phil Carpenter	Yamaha
1975	Mick Grant	Kawasaki
1976	Tom Herron (Ire)	Yamaha
1977	Phil Read	Suzuki
1978	Tom Herron (Ire)	Suzuki
1979	Mike Hailwood	Suzuki
1980	Graeme Crosby (NZ)	Suzuki
1981	Mick Grant	Suzuki
1982	Norman Brown	Suzuki
1983-4	Rob McElnea	Suzuki
1985	Joey Dunlop	Honda
1986	Roger Burnett	Honda
1987-8	Joey Dunlop	Honda
1989	Steve Hislop	Honda
1990	Carl Fogarty	Honda
1991-2	Steve Hislop	Honda
1993	Phil McCallen	Honda
1994	Steve Hislop	Honda
1995	Joey Dunlop	Honda

Winners of other major classes, since 1977

Junior (formerly 250cc, now 600 Supersport)

1977	Charlie Williams	Yamaha
1978	Charles Mortimer	Yamaha
1979-80	Charlie Williams	Yamaha
1981	Steve Tonkin	Armstrong CCM
1982	Con Law	Waddon
1983	Con Law	EMC
1984	Graeme McGregor (Aus)	Yamaha
1985	Joey Dunlop	Honda
1986	Steve Cull (Ire)	Honda
1987	Eddie Laycock (Ire)	EMC
1988	Joey Dunlop	Honda
1989	Johnny Rea	Yamaha
1990	Ian Lougher	Yamaha
1991	Robert Dunlop	Honda
1992	Brian Reid	Honda
1993-4	Joey Dunlop	Honda
1995	Iain Duffus	Honda

Formula I

1977	Phil Read	Honda
1978	Mike Hailwood	Ducati
1979	Alex George	Honda
1980	Mick Grant	Honda
1981	Graeme Crosby (NZ)	Suzuki
1982	Ron Haslam	Honda
1983-8	Joey Dunlop	Honda
1989	Steve Hislop	Honda
1990	Carl Fogarty	Honda
1991	Steve Hislop	Honda
1992	Phillip McCallen	Honda
1993	Nick Jefferies	Honda
1994	Steve Hislop	Honda
1995	Phillip McCallen	Honda

Most TT wins
19 Joey Dunlop 1977-95, 14 Mike Hailwood 1961-79, 11 Steve Hislop 1987-94, 10 Stan Woods 1923-39, Giacomo Agostini (Ita) 1966-75, 8 Phil Read 1961-77, Charles Mortimer 1970-78, Charlie Williams 1973-80
Sidecar: 9 Siegfried Schauzu (FRG) 1967- 75, Mike Boddice 1983- 91, Dave Saville 1988-92.
TT lap record: 198.92 kmh/123.61 mph Carl Fogarty (Honda) 12 Jun 1992
Three TT wins in one week: Mike Hailwood 1961 Senior, Lightweight 125, Lightweight 250
Mike Hailwood 1967 Senior, Junior, Lightweight 250
Joey Dunlop 1985 Senior, Junior, Formula One
Joey Dunlop 1987 Senior, Junior, Formula One
Steve Hislop 1989 Senior, Formula One, Supersport 600
Steve Hislop 1991 Senior, Formula One, 600cc
Dual Senior/Junior TT winners in one year:
Tim Hunt 1931, Stan Woods 1932-3, Jimmy Guthrie 1934, Geoff Duke 1951, Ray Amm 1953, Bob McIntyre 1957, John Surtees 1958-9, Mike Hailwood 1967, Giacomo Agostini 1968-70, 1972, Joey Dunlop 1985, 1988

World Superbike champion Carl Fogarty

Moto-Cross

Also known as Scrambling, Moto-Cross is a specialised branch of Motor Cycling. The first moto-cross race, over an undulating course, with many climbs, drops, bends, and on a dirt circuit, was at Camberley, Surrey in 1924. While primarily a British sport, it went international in 1947 with the introduction of the Moto-Cross des Nations, an annual team event for 500cc machines. The Trophée des Nations, a team event for 250cc machines, was introduced in 1961. A European Championship for 500cc machines was introduced in 1952 and for 250cc machines in 1957. The 500cc class became the World Championship in 1957 and the 250cc event acquired World Championship status in 1962. A 125cc event was added in 1975, and a sidecar championship in 1980.

World Champions

500cc

1957	Bill Nilsson (Swe)	AJS
1958	René Baeten (Bel)	FN
1959	Sten Lundin (Swe)	Monark
1960	Bill Nilsson (Swe)	Husqvarna
1961	Sten Lundin (Swe)	Monark
1962-3	Rolf Tibblin (Swe)	Husqvarna
1964-5	Jeff Smith (UK)	BSA
1966-8	Paul Friedrichs (GDR)	CZ
1969-70	Bengt Aberg (Swe)	Husqvarna
1971-3	Roger de Coster (Bel)	Suzuki
1974	Heikki Mikkola (Fin)	Husqvarna
1975-6	Roger de Coster (Bel)	Suzuki
1977-8	Heikki Mikkola (Fin)	Yamaha
1979	Graham Noyce (UK)	Honda
1980-1	André Malherbe (Bel)	Honda
1982	Brad Lackey (USA)	Suzuki
1983	Håkan Carlqvist (Swe)	Yamaha
1984	André Malherbe (Bel)	Honda
1985-6	Dave Thorpe (UK)	Honda
1987	Georges Jobé (Bel)	Honda
1988	Eric Geboers (Bel)	Honda
1989	Dave Thorpe (UK)	Honda
1990	Eric Geboers (Bel)	Honda
1991-2	Georges Jobé (Bel)	Honda
1993	Jacky Martens (Bel)	Husqvarna
1994	Marcus Hansson (Swe)	Honda

250cc

1962-3	Torsten Hallman (Swe)	Husqvarna
1964	Joël Robert (Bel)	CZ
1965	Viktor Arbekov (USSR)	CZ
1966-7	Torsten Hallman (Swe)	Husqvarna

1968-9	Joël Robert (Bel)	CZ
1970-2	Joël Robert (Bel)	Suzuki
1973	Håkan Andersson (Swe)	Yamaha
1974	Gennadiy Moisseyev (USSR)	KTM
1975	Harry Everts (Bel)	Puch
1976	Heikki Mikkola (Fin)	Husqvarna
1977-8	Gennadiy Moisseyev (USSR)	KTM
1979	Håkan Carlqvist (Swe)	Husqvarna
1980	Georges Jobe (Bel)	Suzuki
1981	Neil Hudson (UK)	Yamaha
1982	Danny la Porte (USA)	Yamaha
1983	Georges Jobé (Bel)	Suzuki
1984-5	Heinz Kinigadner (Aut)	KTM
1986	Jacky Vimond (Fra)	Yamaha
1987	Eric Geboers (Bel)	Honda
1988-9	Jean-Michel Bayle (Fra)	Honda
1990	Alessandro Puzar (Ita)	Suzuki
1991	Trampas Parker (USA)	Honda
1992	Donny Schmit (USA)	Yamaha
1993	Greg Albertyn (SAf)	Honda
1994	Greg Albertyn (SAf)	Suzuki

125cc

1975-7	Gaston Rahier (Bel)	Suzuki
1978	Akira Watanabe (Jap)	Suzuki
1979-81	Harry Everts (Bel)	Suzuki
1982-3	Eric Geboers (Bel)	Suzuki
1984	Michèle Rinaldi (Ita)	Suzuki
1985	Pekka Vehkonen (Fin)	Cagira
1986	Dave Strijbos (Hol)	Cagira
1987-8	John Van Den Berg (Hol)	Yamaha
1989	Trampas Parker (USA)	KTM
1990	Donny Schmit (USA)	Suzuki
1991	Stefan Everts (Bel)	Suzuki
1992	Greg Albertyn (SAf)	Honda
1993	Pedro Tragter (Hol)	Suzuki
1994	Bobby Moore (USA)	Yamaha

Sidecar

1980	Reinhardt Bohler (FRG)	Yamaha
1981	Tom van Heugten (Hol)	Yamaha Wasp
1982-3	Erik Bollhalder (Swi)	Yamaha
1984-7	Hans Bachtöld (Swi)	EML Jumbo
1988	Christoph Hüsser (Lie)	KTM
1989	Christoph Hüsser (Lie)	KU 71
1990	Benny Janssen (Hol)	EML Honda
1991-2	Eimbert Timmermans (Hol)	Kawasaki
1993-4	Andreas Fuhrer (Swi)	VMC

Most world titles

6 (all 250cc) Joël Robert (Bel) 1964, 1968-72

Moto-Cross Des Nations

1947-75 for five-man teams (best three to score). 1976-84 four man teams, at 500 cc. From 1985 the Coupe des Nations, Trophée des Nations, and Moto Cross des Nations have been merged into one three class (500, 250 and 125cc) competition. *Wins:*

16	Great Britain	1947, 1949-50, 1952-4, 1956-7, 1959-60, 1963-7, 1994
13	USA	1981-93
9	Belgium	1948, 1951, 1969, 1972-3, 1976-7, 1979-80
7	Sweden	1955, 1958, 1961-2, 1970-1, 1974
2	USSR	1968, 1978
1	Czechoslovakia	1975

Trophée des Nations

1961-75 for five-man teams (best three to score). From 1976-84 four-man teams, at 250cc. Merged with the above event in 1985. *Wins:*

11	Belgium	1969-78, 1980
5	Sweden	1963-4, 1966-8
4	USA	1981-4
3	Great Britain	1961-2, 1965
1	USSR	1979

1965 – no result, meeting declared null and void

Coupe des Nations

At 125 cc *Winners:*
Italy 1982, Belgium 1983, Netherlands 1984

Trials

Trials riding – manipulating the cycle around a pre-determined course containing many obstacles and natural hazards – has been undertaken since the early days of motor cycling. The famous Scottish Six Days Trial, based around Edinburgh, was introduced in 1909, and the first International Six Days Trial took place in 1913. A World Championship was introduced in 1975.

World Champions		
1975	Martin Lampkin (UK)	Bultaco
1976-8	Yrjö Vesterinen (Fin)	Bultaco
1979	Bernie Schreiber (USA)	Bultaco
1980	Ulf Karlsson (Swe)	Montesa
1981	Gilles Burgat (Fra)	SWM
1982-4	Eddy Lejeune (Bel)	Honda
1985-6	Thierry Michaud (Fra)	Fantic
1987	Jordi Tarrès (Spa)	Beta
1988	Thierry Michaud (Fra)	Fantic
1989-91	Jordi Tarrès (Spa)	Beta
1992	Tommi Ahvala (Fin)	Aprilia
1993-4	Jordi Tarrès (Spa)	Gas-Gas

Most titles: 6 Tarrès, 3 Vesterinen, Lejeune, Michaud

Motor Racing

Following the birth of the motor car in the 19th century, it was inevitable that man would soon start racing. The first race involving motorised vehicles was believed to be the La Vélocipède race of 531km (19.3 miles) in Paris on 20 April 1887, won by Count Jules Felix Philippe Albert de Dion de Malfiance driving a De Dion steam quadricycle. There is a claim, however, that a race took place in the United States in 1878, from Green Bay to Madison, Wisconsin, won by an Oshkosk steamer. The first 'real' motor car race was on 11-14 June 1895, a 1178 km (732 miles) race from Paris to Bordeaux and back. Grand Prix racing started with the 1906 French Grand Prix, and the World Drivers' Championship was instituted in 1950. The sport's international controlling body is the Fédération Internationale de l'Automobile (FIA), whose headquarters are in Paris.

World Championship Grand Prix Races

The FIA took a decision in 1949 to inaugurate a World Championship for Drivers in 1950 and the first race was at Silverstone on 13 May 1950 when the Italian Giuseppe Farina won the British Grand Prix. A Constructors' Championship was instituted in 1958. From 1950 to 1960 the Indianapolis 500 formed part of the Championship. The following is a list of winners of all World Championship Grand Prix races, with notes on the origins of the Grand Prix races in pre-World Championhip days.

Argentine Grand Prix

The inaugural Buenos Aires Grand Prix was run in 1947.
At Buenos Aires:

1953	Alberto Ascari (Ita)	Ferrari
1954	Juan Manuel Fangio (Arg)	Maserati
1955	Juan Manuel Fangio (Arg)	Mercedes-Benz
1956	Juan Manuel Fangio (Arg)	Ferrari
	& Luigi Musso (Arg) *(shared drive)*	
1957	Juan Manuel Fangio (Arg)	Maserati
1958	Stirling Moss (UK)	Cooper
1960	Bruce McLaren (NZ)	Cooper
1972	Jackie Stewart (UK)	Tyrrell
1973	Emerson Fittipaldi (Bra)	Lotus
1974	Denny Hulme (NZ)	McLaren
1975	Emerson Fittipaldi (Bra)	McLaren
1977	Jody Scheckter (SAf)	Wolf
1978	Mario Andretti (USA)	Lotus
1979	Jacques Laffite (Fra)	Ligier
1980	Alan Jones (Aus)	Williams
1981	Nelson Piquet (Bra)	Brabham
1995	Damon Hill (UK)	Williams

Australian Grand Prix

The first Australian Grand Prix was held at Phillip Island, Victoria in 1928. *At Adelaide:*

1985	Keke Rosberg (Fin)	Williams
1986	Alain Prost (Fra)	McLaren
1987	Gerhard Berger (Aut)	Ferrari
1988	Alain Prost (Fra)	McLaren
1989	Thierry Boutsen (Fra)	Williams
1990	Nelson Piquet (Bra)	Benetton
1991	Ayrton Senna (Bra)	McLaren
1992	Gerhard Berger (Aut)	McLaren
1993	Ayrton Senna (Bra)	McLaren
1994	Nigel Mansell (UK)	Williams

Austrian Grand Prix

At Zeltweg 1964, Österreichring 1970-87:

1964	Lorenzo Bandini (Ita)	Ferrari
1970	Jacky Ickx (Bel)	Ferrari
1971	Jo Siffert (Swi)	BRM
1972	Emerson Fittipaldi (Bra)	Lotus
1973	Ronnie Peterson (Swe)	Lotus
1974	Carlos Reutemann (Arg)	Brabham
1975	Vittorio Brambilla (Ita)	March
1976	John Watson (UK)	Penske
1977	Alan Jones (Aus)	Shadow
1978	Ronnie Peterson (Swe)	Lotus

1979	Alan Jones (Aus)	Williams
1980	Jean-Pierre Jabouille (Fra)	Renault
1981	Jacques Laffite (Fra)	Ligier
1982	Elio de Angelis (Ita)	Lotus
1983	Alain Prost (Fra)	Renault
1984	Niki Lauda (Aut)	McLaren
1985-6	Alain Prost (Fra)	McLaren
1987	Nigel Mansell (UK)	Williams

Belgian Grand Prix

The Belgian GP was first raced in 1925. *At Spa-Francorchamps 1950-6, 1958, 1960 8, 1970, 1983, 1985-94; Nivelles 1972, 1974; Zolder 1973, 1975-82, 1984:*

1950	Juan Mauel Fangio (Arg)	Alfa-Romeo
1951	Giuseppe Farina (Ita)	Alfa-Romeo
1952-3	Alberto Ascari (Ita)	Ferrari
1954	Juan Manuel Fangio (Arg)	Maserati
1955	Juan Manuel Fangio (Arg)	Mercedes-Benz
1956	Peter Collins (UK)	Ferrari
1958	Tony Brooks (UK)	Vanwall
1960	Jack Brabham (Aus)	Cooper
1961	Phil Hill (USA)	Ferrari
1962-5	Jim Clark (UK)	Lotus
1966	John Surtees (UK)	Ferrari
1967	Dan Gurney (USA)	Eagle
1968	Bruce McLaren (NZ)	McLaren
1970	Pedro Rodriguez (Mex)	BRM
1972	Emerson Fittipaldi (Bra)	Lotus
1973	Jackie Stewart (UK)	Tyrrell
1974	Emerson Fittipaldi (Bra)	McLaren
1975-6	Niki Lauda (Aut)	Ferrari
1977	Gunnar Nilsson (Swe)	Lotus
1978	Mario Andretti (USA)	Lotus
1979	Jody Scheckter (SAf)	Ferrari
1980	Didier Pironi (Fra)	Ligier
1981	Carlos Reutemann (Arg)	Williams
1982	John Watson (UK)	McLaren
1983	Alain Prost (Fra)	Renault
1984	Michele Alboreto (Ita)	Ferrari
1985	Ayrton Senna (Bra)	Lotus
1986	Nigel Mansell (UK)	Williams
1987	Alain Prost (Fra)	McLaren
1988-91	Ayrton Senna (Bra)	McLaren
1992	Michael Schumacher (Ger)	Benetton
1993-4	Damon Hill (UK)	Williams

Damon Hill celebrates his Argentine victory in 1995

Brazilian Grand Prix

At Interlagos, São Paulo 1973-7, 1979-80, 1990-5; Rio de Janeiro 1978, 1981-9:

1973	Emerson Fittipaldi (Bra)	Lotus
1974	Emerson Fittipaldi (Bra)	McLaren
1975	Carlos Pace (Bra)	Brabham
1976	Niki Lauda (Aut)	Ferrari
1977-8	Carlos Reutemann (Arg)	Ferrari
1979	Jacques Laffite (Fra)	Ligier
1980	René Arnoux (Fra)	Renault
1981	Carlos Reutemann (Arg)	Williams
1982	Alain Prost (Fra)	Renault
1983	Nelson Piquet (Bra)	Brabham
1984-5	Alain Prost (Fra)	McLaren
1986	Nelson Piquet (Bra)	Williams
1987-8	Alain Prost (Fra)	McLaren
1989	Nigel Mansell (UK)	Ferrari
1990	Alain Prost (Fra)	Ferrari
1991	Ayrton Senna (Bra)	McLaren
1992	Nigel Mansell (UK)	Williams
1993	Ayrton Senna (Bra)	McLaren
1994-5	Michael Schumacher (Ger)	Benetton

Michael Schumacher – disqualified and reinstated in the Brazilian Grand Prix at São Paulo in 1995

British Grand Prix

The RAC Grand Prix was raced at Brooklands in 1926-7 and at Donington 1935-9, with the name Britsih Grand Prix first used at Silverstone in 1948. *At Silverstone 1950-4, 1956, 1958, 1960 and uneven years from 1963-87, then annually from 1988. Aintree 1955, 1957, 1959, 1961-2; Brands Hatch, even years from 1964-86:*

1950	Giuseppe Farina (Ita)	Alfa-Romeo
1951	José Froilan González (Arg)	Ferrari
1952-3	Alberto Ascari (Ita)	Ferrari
1954	José Froilan González (Arg)	Ferrari
1955	Stirling Moss (UK)	Mercedes-Benz
1956	Juan Manuel Fangio (Arg)	Ferrari
1957	Stirling Moss (UK) & Tony Brooks (UK)	Vanwall
1958	Peter Collins (UK)	Ferrari
1959-60	Jack Brabham (Aus)	Cooper
1961	Wolfgang von Trips (FRG)	Ferrari
1962-5	Jim Clark (UK)	Lotus
1966	Jack Brabham (Aus)	Brabham
1967	Jim Clark (UK)	Lotus
1968	Jo Siffert (Swi)	Lotus
1969	Jackie Stewart (UK)	Matra
1970	Jochen Rindt (Aut)	Lotus
1971	Jackie Stewart (UK)	Tyrrell
1972	Emerson Fittipaldi (Bra)	Lotus
1973	Peter Revson (USA)	McLaren
1974	Jody Scheckter (SAf)	Tyrrell
1975	Emerson Fittipaldi (Bra)	McLaren
1976	Niki Lauda (Aut)	Ferrari
1977	James Hunt (UK)	McLaren
1978	Carlos Reutemann (Arg)	Ferrari
1979	Clay Regazzoni (Swi)	Williams
1980	Alan Jones (Aus)	Williams
1981	John Watson (UK)	McLaren
1982	Niki Lauda (Aut)	McLaren
1983	Alain Prost (Fra)	Renault
1984	Niki Lauda (Aut)	McLaren
1985	Alain Prost (Fra)	McLaren
1986-7	Nigel Mansell (UK)	Williams
1988	Ayrton Senna (Bra)	McLaren
1989	Alain Prost (Fra)	McLaren
1990	Alain Prost (Fra)	Ferrari
1991-2	Nigel Mansell (UK)	Williams
1993	Alain Prost (Fra)	Williams
1994	Damon Hill (UK)	Williams
1995	Johnny Herbert	Benetton

Canadian Grand Prix

At Mosport 1967, 1969, 1971-7; Mont Tremblant 1968, 1970; Montreal 1978-86, 1988-95::

1967	Jack Brabham (Aus)	Brabham
1968	Denny Hulme (NZ)	McLaren
1969	Jacky Ickx (Bel)	Brabham
1970	Jacky Ickx (Bel)	Ferrari
1971-2	Jackie Stewart (UK)	Tyrrell
1973	Peter Revson (USA)	McLaren
1974	Emerson Fittipaldi (Bra)	McLaren
1976	James Hunt (UK)	McLaren
1977	Jody Scheckter (SAf)	Wolf
1978	Gilles Villeneuve (Can)	Ferrari
1979-80	Alan Jones (Aus)	Williams
1981	Jacques Laffite (Fra)	Ligier
1982	Nelson Piquet (Bra)	Brabham
1983	René Arnoux (Fra)	Ferrari
1984	Nelson Piquet (Bra)	Brabham
1985	Michele Alboreto (Ita)	Ferrari
1986	Nigel Mansell (UK)	Williams
1988	Ayrton Senna (Bra)	McLaren
1989	Thierry Boutsen (Bel)	Williams
1990	Ayrton Senna (Bra)	McLaren
1991	Nelson Piquet (Bra)	Benetton
1992	Gerhard Berger (Aut)	McLaren
1993	Alain Prost (Fra)	Williams
1994	Michael Schumacher (Ger)	Benetton
1995	Jean Alesi	Ferrari

Dutch Grand Prix

First held in 1948. *At Zandvoort:*

1952-3	Alberto Ascari (Ita)	Ferrari
1955	Juan Manuel Fangio (Arg)	Mercedes-Benz

1958	Stirling Moss (UK)	Vanwall
1959	Jo Bonnier (Swe)	BRM
1960	Jack Brabham (Aus)	Cooper
1961	Wolfgang von Trips (FRG)	Ferrari
1962	Graham Hill (UK)	BRM
1963-5	Jim Clark (UK)	Lotus
1966	Jack Brabham (Aus)	Brabham
1967	Jim Clark (UK)	Lotus
1968-9	Jackie Stewart (UK)	Matra
1970	Jochen Rindt (Aut)	Lotus
1971	Jacky Ickx (Bel)	Ferrari
1973	Jackie Stewart (UK)	Tyrrell
1974	Niki Lauda (Aut)	Ferrari
1975	James Hunt (UK)	Hesketh
1976	James Hunt (UK)	McLaren
1977	Niki Lauda (Aut)	Ferrari
1978	Mario Andretti (USA)	Lotus
1979	Alan Jones (Aus)	Williams
1980	Nelson Piquet (Bra)	Brabham
1981	Alain Prost (Fra)	Renault
1982	Didier Pironi (Fra)	Ferrari
1983	René Arnoux (Fra)	Ferrari
1984	Alain Prost (Fra)	McLaren
1985	Niki Lauda (Aut)	McLaren

European Grand Prix

In the early years of the World Championships one Grand Prix each year was designated 'European Grand Prix', from the British Grand Prix of 1950, but in 1983-5 and 1993-4 it was held as a separate race. *At Brands Hatch 1983, 1985; New Nürburgring 1984; Donington Park 1993. Jerez 1994:*

1983	Nelson Piquet (Bra)	Brabham
1984	Alain Prost (Fra)	McLaren
1985	Nigel Mansell (UK)	Williams
1993	Ayrton Senna (Bra)	McLaren
1994	Michael Schumacher (Ger)	Benetton

French Grand Prix

The oldest Grand Prix, the French dates from 1906 at Le Mans. *At Rheims 1950-1, 1953-4, 1956, 1958-61, 1963, 1966; Rouen-les Essarts 1952, 1957, 1962, 1964, 1968; Clermont-Ferrand 1965, 1969-70, 1972; Le Mans 1967, Paul Ricard 1971, 1973, 1975-6, 1978, 1980, 1982-3, 1985-9; Dijon Prenois 1974, 1977, 1979, 1981, 1984; Magny Cours 1991-5:*

1950	Juan Manuel Fangio (Arg)	Alfa-Romeo
1951	Juan Manuel Fangio (Arg) & Luigi Fagioli (Ita)	Alfa-Romeo
1952	Alberto Ascari (Ita)	Ferrari
1953	Mike Hawthorn (UK)	Ferrari
1954	Juan Manuel Fangio (Arg)	Mercedes-Benz
1956	Peter Collins (UK)	Ferrari
1957	Juan Manuel Fangio (Arg)	Maserati
1958	Mike Hawthorn (UK)	Ferrari
1959	Tony Brooks (UK)	Ferrari
1960	Jack Brabham (Aus)	Cooper
1961	Giancarlo Baghetti (Ita)	Ferrari
1962	Dan Gurney (USA)	Porsche
1963	Jim Clark (UK)	Lotus
1964	Dan Gurney (USA)	Brabham
1965	Jim Clark (UK)	Lotus

1966-7	Jack Brabham (Aus)	Brabham
1968	Jacky Ickx (Bel)	Ferrari
1969	Jackie Stewart (UK)	Matra
1970	Jochen Rindt (Aut)	Lotus
1971-2	Jackie Stewart (UK)	Tyrrell
1973-4	Ronnie Peterson (Swe)	Lotus
1975	Niki Lauda (Aut)	Ferrari
1976	James Hunt (UK)	McLaren
1977-8	Mario Andretti (USA)	Lotus
1979	Jean-Pierre Jabouille (Fra)	Renault
1980	Alan Jones (Aus)	Williams
1981	Alain Prost (Fra)	Renault
1982	René Arnoux (Fra)	Renault
1983	Alain Prost (Fra)	Renault
1984	Niki Lauda (Aut)	McLaren
1985	Nelson Piquet (Bra)	Brabham
1986-7	Nigel Mansell (UK)	Williams
1988-9	Alain Prost (Fra)	McLaren
1990	Alain Prost (Fra)	Ferrari
1991-2	Nigel Mansell (UK)	Williams
1993	Alain Prost (Fra)	Williams
1994-5	Michael Schumacher (Ger)	Benetton

German Grand Prix

The first German Grand Prix was held at Avus in 1926. *At Nürburgring 1951-4, 1956-8, 1961-9, 1971-6; Avus 1959, Hockenheim 1970, 1977-84, 1986-94; New Nürburgring 1985:*

1951-2	Alberto Ascari (Ita)	Ferrari
1953	Giuseppe Farina (Ita)	Ferrari
1954	Juan Manuel Fangio (Arg)	Mercedes-Benz
1956	Juan Manuel Fangio (Arg)	Ferrari
1957	Juan Manuel Fangio (Arg)	Maserati
1958	Tony Brooks (UK)	Vanwall
1959	Tony Brooks (UK)	Ferrari
1961	Stirling Moss (UK)	Lotus
1962	Graham Hill (UK)	BRM
1963-4	John Surtees (UK)	Ferrari
1965	Jim Clark (UK)	Lotus
1966	Jack Brabham (Aus)	Brabham
1967	Denny Hulme (NZ)	Brabham
1968	Jackie Stewart (UK)	Matra
1969	Jacky Ickx (Bel)	Brabham
1970	Jochen Rindt (Aut)	Lotus
1971	Jackie Stewart (UK)	Tyrrell
1972	Jacky Ickx (Bel)	Ferrari
1973	Jackie Stewart (UK)	Tyrrell
1974	Clay Regazzoni (Swi)	Ferrari
1975	Carlos Reutemann (Arg)	Brabham
1976	James Hunt (UK)	McLaren
1977	Niki Lauda (Aut)	Ferrari
1978	Mario Andretti (USA)	Lotus
1979	Alan Jones (Aus)	Williams
1980	Jacques Laffite (Fra)	Ligier
1981	Nelson Piquet (Bra)	Brabham
1982	Patrick Tambay (Fra)	Ferrari
1983	René Arnoux (Fra)	Ferrari
1984	Alain Prost (Fra)	McLaren
1985	Michele Alboreto (Ita)	Ferrari
1986-7	Nelson Piquet (Bra)	Williams
1988-90	Ayrton Senna (Bra)	McLaren

1991-2	Nigel Mansell (UK)	Williams
1993	Alain Prost (Fra)	Williams
1994	Gerhard Berger (Aut)	Ferrari
1995	Michael Schumacher (Ger)	Benetton

Hungarian Grand Prix
At Budapest:

1986-7	Nelson Piquet (Bra)	Williams
1988	Ayrton Senna (Bra)	McLaren
1989	Nigel Mansell (UK)	Ferrari
1990	Thierry Boutsen (Bel)	Williams
1991-2	Ayrton Senna (Bra)	McLaren
1993	Damon Hill (UK)	Williams
1994	Michael Schumacher (Ger)	Benetton

Italian Grand Prix

The first Italian Grand Prix was raced at Brescia in 1921, with Monza staging the race from 1922 *At Monza 1950-79, 1981-9, 1991-4, Imola 1980:*

1950	Giuseppe Farina (Ita)	Alfa-Romeo
1951-2	Alberto Ascari (Ita)	Ferrari
1953	Juan Manuel Fangio (Arg)	Maserati
1954-5	Juan Manuel Fangio (Arg)	Mercedes-Benz
1956	Stirling Moss (UK)	Maserati
1957	Stirling Moss (UK)	Vanwall
1958	Tony Brooks (UK)	Vanwall
1959	Stirling Moss (UK)	Cooper
1960-1	Phil Hill (USA)	Ferrari
1962	Graham Hill (UK)	BRM
1963	Jim Clark (UK)	Lotus
1964	John Surtees (UK)	Ferrari
1965	Jackie Stewart (UK)	BRM
1966	Lodovico Scarfiotti (Ita)	Ferrari
1967	John Surtees (UK)	Honda
1968	Denny Hulme (NZ)	McLaren
1969	Jackie Stewart (UK)	Matra
1970	Clay Regazzoni (Swi)	Ferrari
1971	Peter Gethin (UK)	BRM
1972	Emerson Fittipaldi (Bra)	Lotus
1973-4	Ronnie Peterson (Swe)	Lotus
1975	Clay Regazzoni (Swi)	Ferrari
1976	Ronnie Peterson (Swe)	March
1977	Mario Andretti (USA)	Lotus
1978	Niki Lauda (Aut)	Brabham
1979	Jody Scheckter (SAf)	Ferrari
1980	Nelson Piquet (Bra)	Brabham
1981	Alain Prost (Fra)	Renault
1982	René Arnoux (Fra)	Renault
1983	Nelson Piquet (Bra)	Brabham
1984	Niki Lauda (Aut)	McLaren
1985	Alain Prost (Fra)	McLaren
1986-7	Nelson Piquet (Bra)	Williams
1988	Gerhard Berger (Aut)	Ferrari
1989	Alain Prost (Fra)	McLaren
1990	Ayrton Senna (Bra)	McLaren
1991	Nigel Mansell (UK)	Williams
1992	Ayrton Senna (Bra)	McLaren
1993-4	Damon Hill (UK)	Williams

Japanese Grand Prix
At Fuji 1976-7, Suzuka 1987-94:

1976	Mario Andretti (USA)	Lotus
1977	James Hunt (UK)	McLaren
1987	Gerhard Berger (Aut)	Ferrari
1988	Ayrton Senna (Bra)	McLaren
1989	Alessandro Nannini (Ita)	Benetton
1990	Nelson Piquet (Bra)	Benetton
1991	Gerhard Berger (Aut)	McLaren
1992	Riccardo Patrese (Ita)	Williams
1993	Ayrton Senna (Bra)	McLaren
1994	Damon Hill (UK)	Williams

Las Vegas Grand Prix
At Caesar's Palace:

| 1981 | Alan Jones (Aus) | Williams |
| 1982 | Michele Alboreto (Ita) | Tyrrell |

Mexican Grand Prix

First held in 1962 and granted World Championhip status a year later. *At Mexico City:*

1963	Jim Clark (UK)	Lotus
1964	Dan Gurney (USA)	Brabham
1965	Richie Ginther (USA)	Honda
1966	John Surtees (UK)	Cooper
1967	Jim Clark (UK)	Lotus
1968	Graham Hill (UK)	Lotus
1969	Denny Hulme (NZ)	McLaren
1970	Jacky Ickx (Bel)	Ferrari
1986	Gerhard Berger (Aut)	Benetton
1987	Nigel Mansell (UK)	Williams
1988	Alain Prost (Fra)	McLaren
1989	Ayrton Senna (Bra)	McLaren
1990	Alain Prost (Fra)	Ferrari
1991	Riccardo Patrese (Ita)	Williams
1992	Nigel Mansell (UK)	Williams

Monaco Grand Prix

First held in 1929. *At Monte Carlo:*

1950	Juan Manuel Fangio (Arg)	Alfa-Romeo
1955	Maurice Trintignant (Fra)	Ferrari
1956	Stirling Moss (UK)	Maserati
1957	Juan Manuel Fangio (Arg)	Maserati
1958	Maurice Trintignant (Fra)	Cooper
1959	Jack Brabham (Aus)	Cooper
1960-1	Stirling Moss (UK)	Lotus
1962	Bruce McLaren (NZ)	Cooper
1963-5	Graham Hill (UK)	BRM
1966	Jackie Stewart (UK)	BRM
1967	Denny Hulme (NZ)	Brabham
1968-9	Graham Hill (UK)	Lotus
1970	Jochen Rindt (Aut)	Lotus
1971	Jackie Stewart (UK)	Tyrrell
1972	Jean-Pierre Beltoise (Fra)	BRM
1973	Jackie Stewart (UK)	Tyrrell
1974	Ronnie Peterson (Swe)	Lotus
1975-6	Niki Lauda (Aut)	Ferrari
1977	Jody Scheckter (SAf)	Wolf
1978	Patrick Depailler (Fra)	Tyrrell
1979	Jody Scheckter (SAf)	Ferrari
1980	Carlos Reutemann (Arg)	Williams

1981	Gilles Villeneuve (Can)	Ferrari
1982	Riccardo Patrese (Ita)	Brabham
1983	Keke Rosberg (Fin)	Williams
1984-6	Alain Prost (Fra)	McLaren
1987	Ayrton Senna (Bra)	Lotus
1988	Alain Prost (Fra)	McLaren
1989-93	Ayrton Senna (Bra)	McLaren
1994-5	Michael Schumacher (Ger)	Benetton

Moroccan Grand Prix
First held in 1925. *At Ain Diab, Casablanca:*

1958	Stirling Moss (UK)	Vanwall

Pacific Grand Prix
First held 1994. *At Aida, Japan:*

1994	Michael Schumacher (Ger)	Benetton

Pescara Grand Prix
First held in 1924. *At Circuit Pescara:*

1957	Stirling Moss (UK)	Vanwall

Portuguese Grand Prix
First held for sports cars in 1951. *At Oporto 1958, 1960; Monsanto 1959; Estoril 1984-94*

1958	Stirling Moss (UK)	Vanwall
1959	Stirling Moss (UK)	Cooper
1960	Jack Brabham (Aus)	Cooper
1984	Alain Prost (Fra)	McLaren
1985	Ayrton Senna (Bra)	Lotus
1986	Nigel Mansell (UK)	Williams
1987-8	Alain Prost (Fra)	McLaren
1989	Gerhard Berger (Aut)	Ferrari
1990	Nigel Mansell (UK)	Ferrari
1991	Riccardo Patrese (Ita)	Williams
1992	Nigel Mansell (UK)	Williams
1993	Michael Schumacher (Ger)	Benetton
1994	Damon Hill (UK)	Williams

San Marino Grand Prix
At Imola (where the 1980 Italian GP was run):

1981	Nelson Piquet (Bra)	Brabham
1982	Didier Pironi (Fra)	Ferrari
1983	Patrick Tambay (Fra)	Ferrari
1984	Alain Prost (Fra)	McLaren
1985	Elio de Angelis (Ita)	Lotus
1986	Alain Prost (Fra)	McLaren
1987	Nigel Mansell (UK)	Williams
1988-9	Ayrton Senna (Bra)	McLaren
1990	Riccardo Patrese (Ita)	Williams
1991	Ayrton Senna (Bra)	McLaren
1992	Nigel Mansell (UK)	Williams
1993	Alain Prost (Fra)	Williams
1994	Michael Schumacher (Ger)	Benetton
1995	Damon Hill (UK)	Williams

South African Grand Prix
First raced at East London in 1934. *At East London 1962-3, 1965; Kyalami 1967-80, 1982-5, 1991-3:*

1962	Graham Hill (UK)	BRM
1963	Jim Clark (UK)	Lotus
1965	Jim Clark (UK)	Lotus
1967	Pedro Rodriguez (Mex)	Cooper
1968	Jim Clark (UK)	Lotus

1969	Jackie Stewart (UK)	Matra
1970	Jack Brabham (Aus)	Brabham
1971	Mario Andretti (USA)	Ferrari
1972	Denny Hulme (NZ)	McLaren
1973	Jackie Stewart (UK)	Tyrrell
1974	Carlos Reutemann (Arg)	Brabham
1975	Jody Scheckter (SAf)	Tyrrell
1976-7	Niki Lauda (Aut)	Ferrari
1978	Ronnie Peterson (Swe)	Lotus
1979	Gilles Villeneuve (Can)	Ferrari
1980	René Arnoux (Fra)	Renault
1982	Alain Prost (Fra)	Renault
1983	Riccardo Patrese (Ita)	Brabham
1984	Niki Lauda (Aut)	McLaren
1985	Nigel Mansell (UK)	Williams
1992	Nigel Mansell (UK)	Williams
1993	Alain Prost (Fra)	Williams

Spanish Grand Prix
The first Spanish Grand Prix was at Guadarrama in 1913. *At Pedralbes 1951, 1954; Jarama 1968, 1970, 1972, 1974, 1976-9, 1981; Montjuich Park 1969, 1971, 1973, 1975; Jerez de la Frontera 1986-90; Catalunya, Barcelona 1991-5:*

1951	Juan Manuel Fangio (Arg)	Alfa-Romeo
1954	Mike Hawthorn (UK)	Ferrari
1968	Graham Hill (UK)	Lotus
1969	Jackie Stewart (UK)	Matra
1970	Jackie Stewart (UK)	March
1971	Jackie Stewart (UK)	Tyrrell
1972-3	Emerson Fittipaldi (Bra)	Lotus
1974	Niki Lauda (Aut)	Ferrari
1975	Jochen Mass (FRG)	McLaren
1976	James Hunt (UK)	McLaren
1977-8	Mario Andretti (USA)	Lotus
1979	Patrick Depailler (Fra)	Ligier
1981	Gilles Villeneuve (Can)	Ferrari
1986	Ayrton Senna (Bra)	Lotus
1987	Nigel Mansell (UK)	Williams
1988	Alain Prost (Fra)	McLaren
1989	Ayrton Senna (Bra)	McLaren
1990	Alain Prost (Fra)	Ferrari
1991-2	Nigel Mansell (UK)	Williams
1993	Alain Prost (Fra)	Williams
1994	Damon Hill (UK)	Williams
1995	Michael Schumacher (Ger)	Benetton

Swedish Grand Prix
First held in 1955-7 for sports cars. *At Anderstorp:*

1973	Denny Hulme (NZ)	McLaren
1974	Jody Scheckter (SAf)	Tyrrell
1975	Niki Lauda (Aut)	Ferrari
1976	Jody Scheckter (SAf)	Tyrrell
1977	Jacques Lafitte (Fra)	Ligier
1978	Niki Lauda (Aut)	Brabham

Swiss Grand Prix
First held at Bremgarten, Berne in 1934. *At Bremgarten 1950-4, Dijon (France) 1982:*

1950	Giuseppe Farina (Ita)	Alfa-Romeo
1951	Juan Manuel Fangio (Arg)	Alfa-Romeo
1952	Piero Taruffi (Ita)	Ferrari

1953	Alberto Ascari (Ita)	Ferrari
1954	Juan Manuel Fangio (Arg)	Mercedes-Benz
1982	Keke Rosberg (Fin)	Williams

United States Grand Prix

The first US Grand Prix was a sports car race in 1958. *At Sebring 1959, Riverside 1960, Watkins Glen 1961-80, Detroit 1987-8, Phoenix 1989-91:*

1959	Bruce McLaren (NZ)	Cooper
1960	Stirling Moss (UK)	Lotus
1961	Innes Ireland (UK)	Lotus
1962	Jim Clark (UK)	Lotus
1963-5	Graham Hill (UK)	BRM
1966-7	Jim Clark (UK)	Lotus
1968	Jackie Stewart (UK)	Matra
1969	Jochen Rindt (Aut)	Lotus
1970	Emerson Fittipaldi (Bra)	Lotus
1971	François Cevert (Fra)	Tyrrell
1972	Jackie Stewart (UK)	Tyrrell
1973	Ronnie Peterson (Swe)	Lotus
1974	Carlos Reutemann (Arg)	Brabham
1975	Niki Lauda (Aut)	Ferrari
1976-7	James Hunt (UK)	McLaren
1978	Carlos Reutemann (Arg)	Ferrari
1979	Gilles Villeneuve (Can)	Ferrari

1980	Alan Jones (Aus)	Williams
1987	Ayrton Senna (Bra)	Lotus
1988	Ayrton Senna (Bra)	McLaren
1989	Alain Prost (Fra)	McLaren
1990-1	Ayrton Senna (Bra)	McLaren

United States Grand Prix (East)

At Detroit:

1982	John Watson (UK)	McLaren
1983	Michele Alboreto (Ita)	Tyrrell
1984	Nelson Piquet (Bra)	Brabham
1985	Keke Rosberg (Fin)	Williams
1986	Ayrton Senna (Bra)	Lotus

United States Grand Prix (West)

At Long Beach 1976-8, Fir Park , Dallas1984:

1976	Clay Regazzoni (Swi)	Ferrari
1977	Mario Andretti (USA)	Lotus
1978	Carlos Reutemann (Arg)	Ferrari
1979	Gilles Villeneuve (Can)	Ferrari
1980	Nelson Piquet (Fra)	Brabham
1981	Alan Jones (Aus)	Williams
1982	Niki Lauda (Aut)	McLaren
1983	John Watson (UK)	McLaren
1984	Keke Rosberg (Fin)	Williams

World Champions and Runners-up

Points allocated: 1950-9: 1st 8, 2nd 6, 3rd 4, 4th 3, 5th 2; fastest lap 1; 1960: 8-6-4-3-2-1 for 1st to 6th; 1961-90: 9-6-4-3-2-1 for 1st to 6th; 1992- 10-6-4-3-2-1 for 1st to 6th.

Year	Winner	Points	Runner-up	Points
1950	Giuseppe Farina (Ita)	30	Juan Manuel Fangio (Arg)	27
1951	Juan Manuel Fangio (Arg)	31	Alberto Ascari (Ita)	25
1952	Alberto Ascari (Ita)	36	Giuseppe Farina (Ita)	24
1953	Alberto Ascari (Ita)	34.5	Juan Manuel Fangio (Arg)	28
1954	Juan Manuel Fangio (Arg)	42	José Froilán González (Arg)	25.14
1955	Juan Manuel Fangio (Arg)	40	Stirling Moss (UK)	23
1956	Juan Manuel Fangio (Arg)	30	Stirling Moss (UK)	27
1957	Juan Manuel Fangio (Arg)	40	Stirling Moss (UK)	25
1958	Mike Hawthorn (UK)	42	Stirling Moss (UK)	41
1959	Jack Brabham (Aus)	31	Tony Brooks (UK)	27
1960	Jack Brabham (Aus)	43	Bruce McLaren (NZ)	34
1961	Phil Hill (USA)	34	Wolfgang von Trips (FRG)	33
1962	Graham Hill (UK)	42	Jim Clark (UK)	30
1963	Jim Clark (UK)	54	Graham Hill (UK) & Richie Ginther (USA)	29 29
1964	John Surtees (UK)	40	Graham Hill (UK)	39
1965	Jim Clark (UK)	54	Graham Hill (UK)	40
1966	Jack Brabham (Aus)	42	John Surtees (UK)	28
1967	Denny Hulme (NZ)	51	Jack Brabham (Aus)	46
1968	Graham Hill (UK)	48	Jackie Stewart (UK)	36
1969	Jackie Stewart (UK)	63	Jacky Ickx (Bel)	37
1970	Jochen Rindt (Aut)	45	Jacky Ickx (Bel)	40
1971	Jackie Stewart (UK)	62	Ronnie Peterson (Swe)	33
1972	Emerson Fittipaldi (Bra)	61	Jackie Stewart (UK)	45
1973	Jackie Stewart (UK)	71	Emerson Fittipaldi (Bra)	55
1974	Emerson Fittipaldi (Bra)	55	Clay Regazzoni (Swi)	52
1975	Niki Lauda (Aut)	64.5	Emerson Fittipaldi (Bra)	45
1976	James Hunt (UK)	69	Niki Lauda (Aut)	68
1977	Niki Lauda (Aut)	72	Jody Scheckter (SAf)	55

1978	Mario Andretti (USA)	64	Ronnie Peterson (Swe)	51
1979	Jody Scheckter (SAf)	51	Gilles Villeneuve (Can)	47
1980	Alan Jones (Aus)	67	Nelson Piquet (Bra)	54
1981	Nelson Piquet (Bra)	50	Carlos Reutemann (Arg)	49
1982	Keke Rosberg (Fin)	44	John Watson (UK) &	39
			Didier Pironi (Fra)	39
1983	Nelson Piquet (Bra)	59	Alain Prost (Fra)	57
1984	Niki Lauda (Aut)	72	Alain Prost (Fra)	71.5
1985	Alain Prost (Fra)	73	Michele Alboreto (Ita)	53
1986	Alain Prost (Fra)	72	Nigel Mansell (UK)	70
1987	Nelson Piquet (Bra)	73	Nigel Mansell (UK)	61
1988	Ayrton Senna (Bra)	90	Alain Prost (Fra)	87
1989	Alain Prost (Fra)	76	Ayrton Senna (Bra)	60
1990	Ayrton Senna (Bra)	78	Alain Prost (Fra)	71
1991	Ayrton Senna (Bra)	96	Nigel Mansell (UK)	72
1992	Nigel Mansell (UK)	108	Riccardo Patrese (Ita)	56
1993	Alain Prost (Fra)	99	Ayrton Senna (Bra)	73
1994	Michael Schumacher (Ger)	92	Damon Hill (UK)	91

Most Grand Prix wins in a career   *to the end of 1994*

Wins	Driver	Career	Races	Points	Av.pts	Poles	Champs
51	Alain Prost (Fra)	1980-93	199	798.5	4.0	33	4
41	Ayrton Senna (Bra)	1985-94	161	614	3.9	65	3
31	Nigel Mansell (UK)	1980-94	185	482	2.6	32	1
27	Jackie Stewart (UK)	1965-73	99	360	3.6	17	3
25	Jim Clark (UK)	1960-8	72	274	3.8	33	2
25	Niki Lauda (Aut)	1971-85	171	420.5	2.5	24	3
24	Juan Manuel Fangio (Arg)	1950-8	51	277.14	5.4	28	5
23	Nelson Piquet (Bra)	1978-91	204	485.5	2.4	24	3
16	Stirling Moss (UK)	1951-61	66	186.64	2.8	16	-
14	Graham Hill (UK)	1958-75	176	289	1.6	13	2
14	Jack Brabham (Aus)	1955-70	126	261	2.1	13	3
14	Emerson Fittipaldi (Bra)	1970-80	144	281	2.0	6	2
13	Alberto Ascari (Ita)	1951-5	31	140.64	4.5	14	2
12	Mario Andretti (USA)	1968-82	128	180	1.4	18	1
12	Carlos Reutemann (Arg)	1972-82	146	310	2.1	6	-
12	Alan Jones (Aus)	1975-86	116	206	1.8	6	1
10	Michael Schumacher (Ger)	1991-4	51	201	3.7	6	1
10	James Hunt (UK)	1973-9	92	179	1.9	14	1
10	Ronnie Peterson (Swe)	1970-8	123	206	1.7	14	-
10	Jody Scheckter (SAf)	1972-80	112	255	2.3	3	1
9	Damon Hill (UK)	1992-4	34	160	4.7	4	-
9	Gerhard Berger (Aut)	1984-94	163	306	1.9	10	-
8	Denny Hulme (NZ)	1965-74	112	248	2.2	1	1
7	Jackie Ickx (Bel)	1966-79	116	181	1.6	13	-
7	René Arnoux (Fra)	1978-89	149	179	1,2	18	-
Others to average more than 2.8 points per drive							
5	Giuseppe Farina (Ita)	1950-5	33	127.33	3.9	5	1
3	Mike Hawthorn (UK)	1953-8	45	127.64	2.8	4	1
Most Grand Prix starts or over 200 points							
6	Riccardo Patrese (Ita)	1977-93	256	281	1.1	8	-
6	Jacques Laffite (Fra)	1974-86	176	228	1.3	7	-
5	Clay Regazzoni (Chl)	1970-80	132	212	1.6	6	-

Points – 9 for 1st (10 from 1991), 6 for 2nd, 4 for 3rd, 3 for 4th, 2 for 5th, 1 for 6th – include those that were deducted in some years, when a driver had more qualifying races than those counted.

Most wins in a season: 9 Mansell 1992, 8 Senna 1988, Schumacher 1994; 7 Clark 1963, Prost 1984, 1988, Senna 1991, Prost 1993; 6 Ascari 1952, Fangio 1954, Clark 1965, Stewart 1969 & 1971, Hunt 1976, Andretti 1978, Mansell 1987, Senna 1989 & 1990, Hill 1994

Most successive wins: 9 Ascari 1952-3, 5 Brabham 1960, Clark 1965, Mansell 1992

Most pole positions in a season: 14 Mansell 1992
Oldest GP driver: 55 yr 292 days Louis Chiron (Mon) 1955 Monaco GP
Oldest GP winner: 53 yr 22 days Luigi Fagioli (Ita) 1951 French GP
Oldest GP points scorer: 53 yr 248 days Phillipe Etancelin (Fra) 1950 Italian GP (5th)
Oldest world champion: 46 yr 41 days Juan Manuel Fangio (Arg) 1957
Youngest GP driver: 19 yr 182 days Mike Thackwell (NZ) 1980 Canadian GP
Youngest GP winner: 22yr 80 days Troy Ruttman (USA) 1952 Indianapolis 500 (a championship race that year), 22yr 104 days Bruce McLaren (NZ) 1959 US GP
Youngest GP points scorer: 20 yr 113 days Ricardo Rodriguez (Mex) 1962 Belgian GP (4th)
Youngest world champion: 25 yr 273 days Emerson Fittipaldi (Bra) 1972

Constructors' Championship

Year	Constructor	Points
1958	Vanwall	48
1959	Cooper-Climax	40
1960	Cooper-Climax	48
1961	Ferrari	45
1962	BRM	42
1963	Lotus-Climax	54
1964	Ferrari	45
1965	Lotus-Climax	54
1966	Brabham-Repco	42
1967	Brabham-Repco	63
1968	Lotus-Ford	62
1969	Matra-Ford	66
1970	Lotus-Ford	59
1971	Tyrrell-Ford	73
1972	Lotus-Ford	61
1973	Lotus-Ford	92
1974	McLaren-Ford	73
1975	Ferrari	72
1976	Ferrari	83
1977	Ferrari	95
1978	Lotus-Ford	86
1979	Ferrari	113
1980	Williams-Ford	120
1981	Williams-Ford	95
1982	Ferrari	74
1983	Ferrari	89
1984	McLaren-Porsche	143
1985	McLaren-TAG	90
1986	Williams-Honda	141
1987	Williams-Honda	137
1988	McLaren-Honda	199
1989	McLaren-Honda	141
1990	McLaren-Honda	110
1991	McLaren-Honda	139
1992	Williams-Remault	164
1993	Williams-Renault	168
1994	Williams-Renault	118

Most wins: 8 Ferrari, 7 Lotus, McLaren; 6 Williams

Most Grand Prix wins

104	McLaren	1968-93
104	Ferrari	1951-94
79	Lotus	1960-87
78	Williams	1979-94
35	Brabham	1964-85
23	Tyrrell	1971-83
17	BRM	1959-72
16	Cooper	1958-67
15	Renault	1979-83
15	Benetton	1986-94
10	Alfa Romeo	1950-51

Most wins in a season: 15 McLaren 1988; 12 McLaren 1984; 10 McLaren 1989, Williams 1992; 9 Williams 1987 & 1993; 8 Lotus 1978; 8 McLaren 1991, Benetton 1994; 7 Ferrari 1952-3, Lotus-Climax 1963, Tyrrell 1971, Lotus 1973, Williams 1991 & 1994
Most successive wins: 14 Ferrari 1952-3; 11 McLaren-Honda 1988; 9 Alfa Romeo 1950-1; 8 McLaren-Porsche 1984-5
Fastest average speed: 242.62 km/h *150.75 mph* 1971 Italian GP at Monza, won by Peter Gethin (UK) in a BRM. **The fastest for a circuit in current use** is 235.421 km/h *146.284 mph* by Nigel Mansell in a Williams-Honda at Zeltweg in the 1987 Austrian GP.
Slowest winning average speed: 98.68 km/h *61.33 mph* 1950 Monaco GP, Monte Carlo, won by Juan Manuel Fangio (Arg) in an Alfa Romeo.
Fastest lap: 247.02 km/h *153.49 mph* Henri Pescarolo (Fra) March-Ford, 1971 Italian GP at Monza.
Qualifying lap record: 258.803 km/h *160.817 mph* Keke Rosberg (Fin) Williams-Honda, 1985 British GP at Silverstone.
Longest circuit: 25.57 km *15.89 miles* Pescara, Italy (1957 Pescara GP)
Shortest circuit: 3.14 km *1.95 miles* Monte Carlo, France (1955-72 Monaco GP)

Indianapolis 500

The Indianapolis 500 forms part of the Memorial Day celebrations at the end of May each year. The race is held at the Indianapolis Raceway, Indiana, over 200 laps of the 2.5-mile oval shaped circuit. The first race, on 30 May 1911, was won by Ray Harroun in a Marmon Wasp. From 1950 to 1960 the race formed part of the World Driver's Championship, but very few European drivers competed in it.

Alain Prost – world champion for Williams in 1993

The Borg-Warner Trophy has been awarded to the winner annually from 1936. It was introduced by Captain Eddie Rickenbacker, then owner of the Indianapolis Motor Speedway, and replaced the Wheeler-Shebler Trophy, presented from 1911 to 1935. The trophy, made of 80 lbs of sterling silver cost $10,000 originally and is now priceless. It displays the faces of all winners of the race from 1911. Winners personally keep a sterling silver miniature of the trophy, which is 5ft 9 in high plus a new base 1ft 6in high. *Winners since 1950 (all US unless otherwise stated):*

Year	Winner	Manufacturer	Av. speed (mph)
1950	Johnny Parsons	Kurtis Kraft-Offenhauser	124.002
1951	Lee Wallard	Kurtis Kraft-Offenhauser	126.244
1952	Troy Ruttmann	Kuzna-Offenhauser	128.922
1953	Bill Vukovich	Kurtis Kraft 500A-Offenhauser	128.740
1954	Bill Vukovich	Kurtis Kraft 500A-Offenhauser	130.840
1955	Bob Sweikert	Kurtis Kraft 500C-Offenhauser	128.209
1956	Pat Flaherty	Watson-Offenhauser	128.490
1957	Sam Hanks	Epperly-Offenhauser	135.601
1958	Jimmy Bryan	Epperly-Offenhauser	133.791
1959	Rodger Ward	Watson-Offenhauser	135.857
1960	Jim Rathmann	Watson-Offenhauser	138.767
1961	A J Foyt	Watson-Offenhauser	139.130
1962	Rodger Ward	Watson-Offenhauser	140.293
1963	Parnelli Jones	Watson-Offenhauser	143.137
1964	A J Foyt	Watson-Offenhauser	147.350
1965	Jim Clark (UK)	Lotus-Ford	150.686
1966	Graham Hill (UK)	Lola-Ford	144.317
1967	A J Foyt	Coyote-Ford	151.207
1968	Bobby Unser	Eagle-Offenhauser	152.882
1969	Mario Andretti	Hawk-Ford	156.867
1970	Al Unser	P.J.Colt-Ford	155.749
1971	Al Unser	P.J.Colt-Ford	157.735
1972	Mark Donohue	McLaren-Offenhauser	162.962
1973	Gordon Johncock	Eagle-Offenhauser	159.036
1974	Johnny Rutherford	McLaren-Offenhauser	158.589
1975	Bobby Unser	Eagle-Offenhauser	149.213
1976	Johnny Rutherford	McLaren-Offenhauser	148.725
1977	A J Foyt	Coyote-Ford	161.331
1978	Al Unser	Lola-Cosworth	161.363
1979	Rick Mears	Penske-Cosworth	158.899
1980	Johnny Rutherford	Chaparral-Cosworth	142.862
1981	Bobby Unser	Penske-Cosworth	139.085
1982	Gordon Johncock	Wildcat-Cosworth	162.062
1983	Tom Sneva	March-Cosworth	162.117
1984	Rick Mears	March-Cosworth	163.621
1985	Danny Sullivan	March-Cosworth	152.982
1986	Bobby Rahal	March-Cosworth	170.722
1987	Al Unser	March-Cosworth	162.175
1988	Rick Mears	Penske-Chevrolet	144.809
1989	Emerson Fittipaldi (Bra)	Penske-Chevrolet	167.581
1990	Arie Luyendyk (Hol)	Lola-Chevrolet	185.981
1991	Rick Mears	Penske-Chevrolet	176.457
1992	Al Unser Jr	Penske-Chevrolet	134.477
1993	Emerson Fittipaldi (Bra)	Penske-Chevrolet	157.207
1994	Al Unser Jr	Penske-Mercedes	160.872
1995	Jacques Villeneuve (Can)	Reynard-Ford	153.616

Most wins: 4 A J Foyt, Al Unser, Rick Mears; 3 Louis Meyer 1928, 1933, 1936; Mauri Rose 1941, 1947, 1948; Bobby Unser, Johnny Rutherford.

Fastest winning speed: 185.981 mph *299.299 km/h* Arie Luyendyk in a Lola-Chevrolet, 1990

Qualifying record speed for four laps: 232.482 mph *374,133 km/h* Roberto Guerrero (Col) in a Lola-Buick, 1992. including single lap qualifying record: 232.618mph *374.352km/h*

Most starts: 35 A J Foyt 1958-92

Closest finish: 0.043 sec Al Unser Jr over Scott Goodyear 1992

Al Unser Jr

Record career earnings to 1995

$4,299,392	Rick Mears
$4,262,690	Al Unser Jr.
$4,042,767	Emerson Fittipaldi (Bra)
$3,378,018	Al Unser
$3,180,666	Arie Luyendyk (Hol)
$3,001,146	Bobby Rahal

Indy Car Racing

Indy-car racing (on oval speedways) has been in existence since 1909. Between 1909-55 the season-long championship was known as the AAA National Championship. It then became the United States Auto Club (USAC) National Championship.

CART (Championship Auto Racing Teams, Inc.) was founded in 1978 by Roger Penske and U E 'Pat' Patrick, in a break away from the USAC. CART had its own series of races in 1979, and after a short-lived joint venture between CART and USAC in 1980, CART produced its own National Championship series and now sanctions all Indy car racing (the PPG IndyCar World Series), except the Indianapolis 500, still governed by the USAC.

National ChampionshipWinners:

AAA National Championship

1909	George Robertson
1910	Ray Harroun
1911	Ralph Mulford
1912	Ralph DePalma
1913	Earl Cooper
1914	Ralph DePalma
1915	Earl Cooper
1916	Dario Resta
1917	Earl Cooper
1918	Ralph Mulford
1919	Howard Wilcox
1920-1	Tommy Milton
1922	Jimmy Murphy
1923	Eddie Hearne
1924	Jimmy Murphy
1925	Peter DePaolo
1926	Harry Hartz
1927	Peter DePaolo
1928	Louie Meyer
1929	Louie Meyer
1930	Billy Arnold
1931	Louis Schneider
1932	Bob Carey
1933	Louie Meyer
1934	Bill Cummings
1935	Kelly Petillo
1936	Mauri Rose
1937	Wilbur Shaw
1938	Floyd Roberts
1939	Wilbur Shaw
1940-1	Rex Mays
1942-5	*No racing*
1946-8	Ted Horn
1949	Johnny Parsons
1950	Henry Banks
1951	Tony Bettenhausen, Sr
1952	Chuck Stevenson
1953	Sam Hanks
1954	Jimmy Bryan
1955	Bob Swikert

USAC National Championship

1956-7	Jimmy Bryan
1958	Tony Bettenhausen, Sr
1959	Rodger Ward
1960-1	A J Foyt
1962	Rodger Ward
1963-4	A J Foyt
1965-6	Mario Andretti
1967	A J Foyt
1968	Bobby Unser
1969	Mario Andretti
1970	Al Unser
1971-2	Joe Leonard
1973	Roger McCluskey
1974	Bobby Unser
1975	A J Foyt
1976	Gordon Johncock
1977-8	Tom Sneva
1979	A J Foyt

PPG Indy Car World Series

1979	Rick Mears
1980	Johnny Rutherford
1981-2	Rick Mears

1983	Al Unser
1984	Mario Andretti
1985	Al Unser
1986-7	Bobby Rahal
1988	Danny Sullivan
1989	Emerson Fittipaldi
1990	Al Unser Jr
1991	Michael Andretti
1992	Bobby Rahal
1993	Nigel Mansell (UK)
1994	Al Unser Jr

Most championships: 7 A J Foyt Jr, 4 Mario Andretti, 3 Cooper, Meyer, Horn, Bryan, Al Unser, Mears, Rahal

Most wins in a season: 10 A J Foyt Jr 1964, Al Unser 1970

Most wins in career: 67 A J Foyt Jr 1960-81 (whole career 1957-93), 52 Mario Andretti, 39 Al Unser, 35 Bobby Unser, 29 Rick Mears, Michael Andretti

Season's money record: $2,575,554 Emerson Fittipaldi 1993

Indy Car Career Earnings Leaders
as at end 1994

Al Unser Jr	$15,379,906
Emerson Fittipaldi (Bra)	13,272,875
Bobby Rahal	13,003,241
Mario Andretti	11,552,154
Michael Andretti	11,332,566
Rick Mears	11,050,807
Danny Sullivan	8,254,673
Arie Luyendyk (Hol)	7,124,771
Al Unser Sr	6,740,843
A J Foyt Jr	5,357,589

NASCAR Championship - Winston Cup

The National Association for Stock Car Auto Racing, Inc. (NASCAR) was the brainchild of Virginian Bill France who formed the association in 1947. The first race sanctioned by NASCAR was over the Daytona Beach course on 15 February 1948. Early races were either over dirt tracks or beach circuits. Today they are run over enclosed circuits and NASCAR races are now among the most popular in the United States. The Winston Cup series was started in 1949 and was known as the Grand National series. It became the Winston Cup in 1970 following sponsorship by the R.J.Reynolds Tobacco Company. *Winners:*

1949	Red Byron
1950	Bill Rexford
1951	Herb Thomas
1952	Tim Flock
1953	Herb Thomas
1954	Lee Petty
1955	Tim Flock
1956-7	Buck Baker
1958-9	Lee Petty
1960	Rex White
1961	Ned Jarrett
1962-3	Joe Weatherley
1964	Richard Petty
1965	Ned Jarrett
1966	David Pearson
1967	Richard Petty
1968-9	David Pearson
1970	Bobby Isaac
1971-2	Richard Petty
1973	Benny Parsons
1974-5	Richard Petty
1976-8	Cale Yarborough
1979	Richard Petty
1980	Dale Earnhardt
1981-2	Darrell Waltrip
1983	Bobby Allison
1984	Terry Labonte
1985	Darrell Waltrip
1986-7	Dale Earnhardt
1988	Bill Elliott
1989	Rusty Wallace
1990-1	Dale Earnhardt
1992	Alan Kulwicki
1993-4	Dale Earnhardt

Most titles: 7 Richard Petty, Dale Earnhardt; 3 Lee Petty, David Pearson, Cale Yarborough, Darrell Waltrip

NASCAR all-time leading money winners
As at 19 June 1995

Dale Earnhardt	$23,791,114
Bill Elliott	14,803,518
Darrell Waltrip	13,988,369
Rusty Wallace	11,637,223
Terry Labonte	9,529,621
Ricky Rudd	9,186,995
Geoff Bodine	8,824,948
Mark Martin	8,819,629
Harry Gant	8,438,094
Richard Petty	7,757,964

Season's money record: $3,353,789 Dale Earnhardt 1993

Most Winston Cup race wins: 200 Richard Petty, 105 David Pearson, 84 Bobby Allison, Darrell Waltrip; 83 Cale Yarborough, 64 Dale Earnhardt.

Daytona 500

The Daytona 500, held at the Daytona International Speedway every February, is one of NASCAR's top events. *Winners:*

Year	Winner	Car	Average speed
1959	Lee Petty	Oldsmobile	218.05 km/h *135.52mph*
1960	Junior Johnson	Chevrolet	200.71 km/h *124.74mph*
1961	Marvin Panch	Pontiac	240.71 km/h *149.60mph*
1962	Fireball Roberts	Pontiac	245.42 km/h *152.53mph*
1963	Tiny Lund	Ford	243.88 km/h *151.57mph*

1964	Richard Petty	Plymouth	248.32 km/h *154.33mph*
1965	Fred Lorenzen	Ford	227.74 km/h *141.54mph*
1966	Richard Petty	Plymouth	258.45 km/h *160.63mph*
1967	Mario Andretti	Ford	236.41 km/h *146.93mph*
1968	Cale Yarborough	Mercury	230.49 km/h *143.25mph*
1969	LeeRoy Yarborough	Ford	254.14 km/h *157.95mph*
1970	Pete Hamilton	Plymouth	240.71 km/h *149.60mph*
1971	Richard Petty	Plymouth	232.44 km/h *144.46mph*
1972	A J Foyt	Mercury	259.93 km/h *161.55mph*
1973	Richard Petty	Dodge	252.95 km/h *157.21mph*
1974	Richard Petty	Dodge	226.69 km/h *140.89mph*
1975	Benny Parsons	Chevrolet	247.22 km/h *153.65mph*
1976	David Pearson	Mercury	244.86 km/h *152.18mph*
1977	Cale Yarborough	Chevrolet	246.53 km/h *153.22mph*
1978	Bobby Allison	Ford	257.01 km/h *159.73mph*
1979	Richard Petty	Oldsmobile	231.66 km/h *143.98mph*
1980	Buddy Baker	Oldsmobile	285.76 km/h *177.60mph*
1981	Richard Petty	Buick	272.97 km/h *169.65mph*
1982	Bobby Allison	Buick	247.77 km/h *153.99mph*
1983	Cale Yarborough	Pontiac	250.97 km/h *155.98mph*
1984	Cale Yarborough	Chevrolet	242.94 km/h *150.99mph*
1985	Bill Elliott	Ford	277.18 km/h *172.27mph*
1986	Geoff Bodine	Chevrolet	238.33 km/h *148.12mph*
1987	Bill Elliott	Ford	283.60 km/h *176.26mph*
1988	Bobby Allison	Buick	221.29 km/h *137.53mph*
1989	Darrell Waltrip	Chevrolet	238.88 km/h *148.47mph*
1990	Derrike Cope	Chevrolet	266.76 km/h *165.76mph*
1991	Ernie Irvan	Chevrolet	238.42 km/h *148.15mph*
1992	Davey Allison	Ford	257.90 km/h *160.256 mph*
1993	Dale Jarrett	Chevrolet	252.993 km/h *157.207 mph*
1994	Sterling Marlin	Chevrolet	252.556 km/h *156.931 mph*
1995	Sterling Marlin	Chevrolet	228.054 km/h *141.710 mph*

Most Wins: 7 Richard Petty, 4 Cale Yarborough, 3 Bobby Allison

Le Mans

The most famous of all sports car races, the Le Mans 24 Hour race was inaugurated on 26-27 May 1923, and won by André Lagache and René Leonard in a 3-litre Chenard & Walcker. The original Le Mans circuit at Sarthe, France, measured 17.26 km 10.73 miles but the present circuit is 13.64km 8.48 miles. *Post-war winners:*

Year	Drivers	Car	Av speed km/h
1949	Luigi Chinetti (Ita), Lord Peter Selsdon (UK)	Ferrari	132.418
1950	Louis Rosier, Jean-Louis Rosier (Fra)	Talbot-Lago	144.379
1951	Peter Walker, Peter Whitehead (UK)	Jaguar	150.466
1952	Hermann Lang, Karl Riess (FRG)	Mercedes-Benz	155.574
1953	Tony Rolt, Duncan Hamilton (UK)	Jaguar	170.335
1954	Froilan Gonzalez (Arg), Maurice Trintignant (Fra)	Ferrari	164.386
1955	Mike Hawthorn, Ivor Bueb (UK)	Jaguar	172.308
1956	Ron Flockhart, Ninian Sanderson (UK)	Jaguar	168.120
1957	Ron Flockhart, Ivor Bueb (UK)	Jaguar	183.216
1958	Olivier Gendebien (Bel), Phil Hill (USA)	Ferrari	170.912
1959	Carroll Shelby, Roy Salvadori (UK)	Aston Martin	181.162
1960	Olivier Gendebien, Paul Frère (Bel)	Ferrari	175.729
1961	Olivier Gendebien (Bel), Phil Hill (USA)	Ferrari	186.526
1962	Olivier Gendebien (Bel), Phil Hill (USA)	Ferrari	185.467
1963	Ludovico Scarfiotti, Lorenzo Bandini (Ita)	Ferrari	190.071
1964	Jean Guichet (Fra), Nino Vaccarella (Ita)	Ferrari	195.638
1965	Jochen Rindt (Aut), Masten Gregory (USA)	Ferrari	194.879
1966	Chris Amon, Bruce McLaren (NZ)	Ford	201.795
1967	Dan Gurney, A J Foyt (USA)	Ford	218.033
1968	Pedro Rodriguez (Mex), Lucien Bianchi (Bel)	Ford	185.536
1969	Jacky Ickx (Bel), Jackie Oliver (UK)	Ford	208.250
1970	Hans Herrmann (FRG), Richard Attwood (UK)	Porsche	191.992

1971	Helmut Marko (Aut), Gijs van Lennep (Hol)	Porsche	222.304
1972	Henri Pescarolo (Fra), Graham Hill (UK)	Matra-Simca	195.472
1973	Henri Pescarolo, Gérard Larrousse (Fra)	Matra-Simca	202.250
1974	Henri Pescarolo, Gérard Larrousse (Fra)	Matra-Simca	191.940
1975	Jacky Ickx (Bel), Derek Bell (UK)	Mirage-Ford	191.480
1976	Jacky Ickx (Bel), Gijs van Lennep (Hol)	Porsche	198.750
1977	Jacky Ickx (Bel), Jürgen Barth (FRG), Hurley Haywood (USA)	Porsche	194.802
1978	Jean-Pierre Jaussaud, Didier Pironi (Fra)	Renault Alpine	210.190
1979	Klaus Ludwig (FRG), Bill Whittington (USA), Don Whittington (USA)	Porsche	173.900
1980	Jean-Pierre Jaussaud, Jean Rondeau (Fra)	Rondeau-Ford	192.000
1981	Jacky Ickx (Bel), Derek Bell (UK)	Porsche	201.060
1982	Jacky Ickx (Bel), Derek Bell (UK)	Porsche	204.128
1983	Vern Schuppan (Aut), Hurley Haywood (USA), Al Holbert (USA)	Porsche	210.330
1984	Klaus Ludwig (FRG), Henri Pescarolo (Fra)	Porsche	204.180
1985	Klaus Ludwig (FRG), Paulo Barillo (Ita), 'John Winter' (FRG)	Porsche	212.021
1986	Hans Stück (FRG), Derek Bell (UK), Al Holbert (USA)	Porsche	203.197
1987	Hans Stück (FRG), Derek Bell (UK), Al Holbert (USA)	Porsche	199.657
1988	Jan Lammers (Hol), Johnny Dumfries (UK), Andy Wallace (UK)	Jaguar	221.630
1989	Jochen Mass (FRG), Manuel Reuter (FRG), Stanley Dickens (Swe)	Mercedes	219.991
1990	John Nielsen (Den), Martin Brundle (UK), Price Cobb (USA)	Jaguar	204.07
1991	Johnny Herbert (UK), Bertrand Gachot (Bel), Volker Wendler (Ger)	Mazda	206.53
1992	Derek Warwick (UK), Mark Blundell (UK), Yannick Dalmas (Fra)	Peugeot	199.342
1993	Geoff Brabham (Aus), Cristophe Bouchut (Fra), Éric Hélary (Fra)	Peugeot	213.358
1994	Yannick Dalmas (Fra), Hurley Haywood (USA), Mauro Baldi (Ita)	Dauer Porsche	195.265
1995	Yannick Dalmas (Fra), J J Lehto (Fin), Masanori Sekiya (Jap)	McLaren	168.992

Most wins: 6 Ickx, 5 Bell, 4 Gendebien, Pescarolo; 3 Woolf Barnato (UK) 1928-30, Luigi Chinetti (Ita/USA) 1932, 1934, 1949, Hill, Holbert, Ludwig

Most successful combinations: 3 wins Olivier Gendebien/Phil Hill, and Jacky Ickx/Derek Bell

Fastest winning speed: 222.304 kph Helmut Marko/Gijs van Lennep 1971

Greatest distance covered: 5333.72 km *3314.22 miles* Helmut Marko/Gijs van Lennep 1971

Record for current circuit: 5332 km *3313.24 miles* Jan Lammers/Johnny Dumfries/Andy Wallace 1988

Most successful cars: 13 wins Porsche, 9 Ferrari, 7 Jaguar

World Sports Car Championship

The format, and car specification, has changed many times since its introduction in 1953. Between 1953-61 it was known as the Sports Car World Championship, with the title going to the leading manufacturer. A Speed World Challenge was contested in 1962-3 and an International Championship for Makes from 1964-71, with new regulations from 1968; a championship for competition sports cars and prototypes. With the distinction between competition and prototypes disappearing, a new World Championship for Makes was introduced in 1972, with a separate World Championship for Sports Cars in 1976-7. In 1981, a championship for drivers was introduced for the first time, and it was known as the World Endurance Championship from 1982 to 1985. The name was changed again in 1986, to the World Sports-Prototype Championship, for both cars and drivers, and back to World Sports Car Championship in 1991-2. From 1985 the constructors' championship was for teams. FISA declared that the series would be terminated after the 1992 season. *Winners*

Drivers

1981	Bob Garretson (USA)
1982-3	Jacky Ickx (Bel)
1984	Stefan Bellof (FRG)
1985-6	Derek Bell (UK) & Hans-Joachim Stück (FRG)
1987	Raul Boesel (Bra)
1988	Martin Brundle (UK)
1989	Jean-Louis Schlesser (Fra)
1990	Mauro Baldi (Ita) & Jean-Louis Schlesser (Fra)
1991	Teo Fabi (Ita)
1992	Derek Warwick (UK) & Yannick Dalmas (Fra)

Cars

1953-4	Ferrari
1955	Mercedes-Benz
1956-8	Ferrari
1959	Aston Martin
1960-5	Ferrari
1966	Ford
1967	Ferrari
1968	Ford
1969-71	Porsche
1972	Ferrari
1973-4	Matra-Simca
1975	Alfa Romeo
1976-9	Porsche
1980	Lancia
1981-4	Porsche
1985	Rothmans-Porsche
1986	Brun Motorsport
1987-8	Silk Cut Jaguar
1989-90	Sauber Mercedes
1991	Silk Cut Jaguar
1992	Peugeot Talbot Special

Sports Cars

1976	Porsche
1977	Alfa Romeo

Formula Two, Formula Three and Formula 3000

Formula Two was introduced in 1947 to enable young drivers to gain experience for the step up to Formula One. Formula Three was created in the early 1950s for much the same reason. A European Formula Two championship was introduced in 1967 and a Formula Three championship followed in 1975. Both were discontinued in 1984, making way for the new European Formula 3000 Championship, later re-named the FIA Formula 3000 International Championship. Formula Three remains popular in Britain and championships have existed in various forms since 1966 when Harry Stiller won the Les Leston Championship. It was not until the introduction of the Vandervell British Formula Three Championship in 1979 that the event became unified. In 1992 the British Formula 3000 Championship was renamed F2.

European Formula Two champions
1967   Jacky Ickx (Bel)
1968   Jean-Pierre Beltoise (Fra)
1969   Johnny Servoz-Gavin (Fra)
1970   Clay Regazzoni (Swi)
1971   Ronnie Peterson (Swe)
1972   Mike Hailwood (UK)
1973   Jean-Pierre Jarier (Fra)
1974   Patrick Depailler (Fra)
1975   Jacques Laffite (Fra)
1976   Jean-Pierre Jabouille (Fra)
1977   René Arnoux (Fra)
1978   Bruno Giacomelli (Ita)
1979   Marc Surer (Swi)
1980   Brian Henton (UK)
1981   Geoff Lees (UK)
1982   Corrado Fabi (Ita)
1983   Jonathan Palmer (UK)
1984   Mike Thackwell (NZ)
Most race wins: 12 Jochen Rindt (Aut), 11 Bruno Giacomelli (Ita), 9 Mike Thackwell (NZ), 7 Jean-Pierre Jarier (Fra), Jacques Laffite (Fra)

European Formula Three champions
1975   Larry Perkins (Aus)
1976   Riccardo Patrese (Ita)
1977   Piercarlo Ghinzani (Ita)
1978   Jan Lammers (Hol)
1979   Alain Prost (Fra)
1980   Michele Alboreto (Ita)
1981   Mauro Baldi (Ita)
1982   Oscar Larrauri (Arg)
1983   Pierluigi Martini (Ita)
1984   Ivan Capelli (Ita)
Most race wins: 11 Mauro Baldi (Ita), 8 Oscar Larrauri (Arg), Alain Prost (Fra); 7 Anders Olofsson (Swe), 6 John Nielsen (Den), Emanuele Pirro (Ita)

British Formula Three champions since 1979
1979   Chico Serra (Bra)
1980   Stefan Johansson (Swe)
1981   Jonathan Palmer (UK)
1982   Tommy Byrne (Ire)
1983   Ayrton Senna (Bra)
1984   Johnny Dumfries (UK)
1985   Mauricio Gugelmin (Bra)
1986   Andy Wallace (UK)
1987   Johnny Herbert (UK)
1988   Jyrki Järvilehto (J J Lehto) (Fin)
1989   David Brabham (Aus)
1990   Mike Hakkinen (Fin)
1991   Rubens Barricello (Bra)
1992   Gil De Ferran (Bra)
1993   Kelvin Burt (UK)
1994   Jan Magnussen (Den)
Most race wins in a year: 14 Jan Magnussen 1994, 12 Ayrton Senna 1983

FIA Formula 3000 Champions
1985   Christian Danner (FRG)
1986   Ivan Capelli (Ita)
1987   Stefano Modena (Ita)
1988   Roberto Moreno (Bra)
1989   Jean Alesi (Fra)
1990   Eric Comas (Fra)
1991   Christian Fittipaldi (Bra)
1992   Luca Badoer (Ita)
1993   Olivier Panis (Fra)
1994   Jules Boullion (Fra)
Most race wins: 6 Eric Comas

Rallying

The first long-distance rally was from Peking, China, to Paris between 10 June-10 August 1907. It was won by Prince Scipione Borghese (Ita) driving an Itala. Since then many famous rallies have been staged, the most famous being the Monte Carlo Rally, instituted in 1911, when it was won by Henri Rougier (Fra) in a Tyrcat-Mery. The RAC International Rally of Great Britain (now known as the Lombard-RAC Rally) was first held in 1927 but it did not gain recognition as an international event by the FIA until 1951.

Monte Carlo Rally
Winners:

Year	Winner	Car
1911	Henri Rougier (Fra)	Turcat-Mery
1912	Julius Beutler (Ger)	Berliet
1924	Jean Ledure (Fra)	Bignan
1925	François Repusseau (Fra)	Renault 40 CV
1926	Hon. Victor Bruce/W J Brunell (UK)	AC Bristol
1927	Lefebvre & Despeux (Fra)	Amilcar
1928	Jacques Bignan (Fra)	Fiat
1929	Dr Sprenger van Eijk (Hol)	Graham-Paige
1930	Hector Petit (Fra)	Licorne
1931	Donald Healey (UK)	Invicta
1932-3	M Vasselle (Fra)	Hotchkiss
1934	Gas/Jean Trevoux (Fra)	Hotchkiss
1935	Christian Lahaye/R Quatresous (Fra)	Renault Nervasport
1936	I Zamfirescu/Christea (Rom)	Ford
1937	René le Begue/J Quinlin (Fra)	Delahaye
1938	G Bakker Schut/Karel Ton (Hol)	Ford
1939	Jean Trevoux/M Lesurque (Fra)	Hotchkiss
1949	Jean Trevoux/M Lesurque (Fra)	Hotchkiss
1950	Marcel Becquart/H Secret (Fra)	Hotchkiss
1951	Jean Trevoux/Roger Crovetto (Fra)	Delahaye
1952	Sidney Allard/Guy Warburton (UK)	Allard P2
1953	Maurice Gatsonides (Hol)/P Worledge (UK)	Ford Zephyr

Didier Auriol, world champion of 1994, in his Toyota

1954	Louis Chiron (Fra)/	
	Giro Basadonna (Spa)	Lancia-Aurelia
1955	Per Malling/	
	Gunnar Fadum (Nor)	Sunbeam-Talbot
1956	Ronnie Adams/Frank Bigger (Ire)	Jaguar Mk VII
1957	*No race due to Suez crisis*	
1958	Guy Monraisse/	
	Jacques Feret (Fra)	Renault Dauphine
1959	Paul Coltelloni/	
	Pierre Alexandre (Fra)	Citroen ID19
1960	Walter Schock/Ralf Moll (Ger)	Mercedes 220SE
1961	Maurice Martin/	
	Roger Bateau (Fra)	Panhard PL17
1962	Erik Carlsson/Gunnar Häggbom (Swe)	Saab 96
1963	Erik Carlsson/Gunnar Palm (Swe)	Saab 96
1964	Paddy Hopkirk/Henry Liddon (UK)	Mini-Cooper 'S'
1965	Timo Mäkinen (Fin)/	
	Paul Easter (UK)	Mini-Cooper 'S'
1966	Pauli Toivonen/Ensio Mikander (Fin)	Citroen DS21
1967	Rauno Aaltonen (Fin)/	
	Henry Liddon (UK)	Mini-Cooper 'S'
1968	Vic Elford/David Stone (UK)	Porsche 911T
1969-70	Björn Waldegård/Lars Helmer (Swe)	Porsche 911
1971	Ove Andersson (Swe)/	
	avid Stone (UK)	Alpine Renault A110
1972	Sandro Munari/Mario Manucci (Ita)	Lancia Fulvia
1973	Jean-Claude Andruet (Fra)/	
	'Biche' (Michèle Petit)	Alpine Renault A110

1974	*No race due to fuel crisis*	
1975	Sandro Munari/	
	Mario Manucci (Ita)	Lancia Stratos
1976	Sandro Munari/Silvio Maiga (Ita)	Lancia Stratos
1977	Sandro Munari/	
	Mario Manucci (Ita)	Lancia Stratos
1978	Jean-Pierre Nicolas/	
	Vincent Laverne (Fra)	Porsche Carrera 911
1979	Bernard Darniche/	
	lain Mahe (Fra)	Lancia Stratos
1980	Walter Röhrl/	
	Christian Geistdörfer (FRG)	Fiat Abarth 131
1981	Jean Ragnotti/	
	Jean-Marc André (Fra)	Renault 5 Turbo
1982-3	Walter Röhrl/	
	Christian Geistdörfer (FRG)	Opel Ascona
1984	Walter Röhrl/	
	Christian Geistdörfer (FRG)	Audi Quattro
1985	Ari Vatanen (Fin)/	
	erry Harryman (UK)	Peugeot 205 Turbo 16
1986	Henri Toivonen (Fin)/	
	Sergio Cresto (Ita)	Lancia Delta S4
1987	Massimo Biasion/	
	Tiziano Siviero (Ita)	Lancia Delta HF4
1988	Bruno Saby/	
	ean-Francois Fauchille (Fra)	Lancia Delta HF4
1989	Massimo Biasion/	
	Tiziano Siviero (Ita)	Lancia Delta Integrale
1990	Didier Auriol/	
	Bernard Occelli (Fra)	Lancia Delta Integrale 16

1991   Carlos Sainz/Luis Moya (Spa) Toyoya Celica GT4
1992   Didier Auriol/
        Bernard Occelli (Fra)   Lancia HF Integrale
1993   Didier Auriol/Bernard Occelli (Fra) Toyota Celica
1994   François Delecour/
        Daniel Grataloup (Fra)   Ford Escort
1995   Carlos Sainz/Luis Moya (Spa)   Subaru Impreza
Most wins: 4 Munari, Röhrl; 3 Trevoux
Most successful co-driver: 4 wins Geistdörfer

Lombard RAC Rally

Winners since 1951:
1951   Ian Appleyard/Pat Appleyard (UK)Jaguar XK120
1952   Godfrey Imhof/
        Mrs B Fleming (UK)   Allard Cadillac J2
1953   Ian Appleyard/Pat Appleyard (UK)Jaguar XK120
1954   Johnny Wallwork/J H Brooks (UK) Triumph TR2
1955   James Ray/Brian Horrocks (UK)   Standard Ten
1956   Lyndon Sims, R Jones/
        Tony Ambrose (UK)   Aston Martin DB2
1957   *Not held due to Suez crisis*
1958   Peter Harper/Bill Deane (UK) Sunbeam Rapier II
1959   Gerald Burgess/
        Sam Croft-Pearson(UK)   Ford Zephyr
1960   Erik Carlsson (Swe)/Stuart Turner (UK)   Saab 96
1961   Erik Carlsson (Swe)/John Brown (UK)   Saab 96
1962   Erik Carlsson (Swe)/David Stone (UK)   Saab 96
1963   Tom Trana/Sune Lindström (Swe)   Volvo PV544
1964   Tom Trana/Gunnar Thermaenius (Swe) Volvo 122S
1965   Rauno Aaltonen (Fin)/
        Tony Ambrose (UK)   BMC Mini-Cooper 'S'
1966   Bengt Soderström/
        Gunnar Palm (Swe)   Ford Cortina Lotus
1967   *Not held due to foot and mouth outbreak*
1968   Simo Lampinen (Fin)/
        John Davenport (UK)   Saab 96 V4
1969-70 Harry Kallström (Fin)/
        Gunnar Häggbom (Swe)   Lancia Fulvia HF
1971   Stig Blomqvist/Arne Hertz (Swe)   Saab 96 V4
1972   Roger Clark/Tony Mason (UK)   Ford Escort RS
1973-5 Timo Mäkinen (Fin)/
        Henry Liddon (UK)   Ford Escort RS
1976   Roger Clark/Stuart Pegg (UK)   Ford Escort RS
1977   Björn Waldegård/
        Hans Thorszelius (Swe)   Ford Escort RS
1978-9 Hannu Mikkola (Fin)/
        Arne Hertz (Swe)   Ford Escort RS
1980   Henri Toivonen (Fin)/
        Paul White (UK)   Talbot Sunbeam Lotus
1981-2 Hannu Mikkola (Fin)/
        Arne Hertz (Swe)   Audi Quattro A1/A2
1983   Stig Blomqvist/
        Björn Cederberg (Swe)   Audi Quattro A2
1984   Ari Vatanen (Fin)/
        Terry Harryman (UK)   Peugeot 205 Turbo 16
1985   Henri Toivonen (Fin)/
        Neil Wilson (UK)   Lancia Delta S4
1986   Timo Salonen (Fin)/Seppo Harjanne (Fin)
                            Peugeot 205 Turbo 16E2
1987   Juha Kankkunen/
        Jiro Piironen (Fin)   Lancia Delta 4WD

Carlos Sainz en route to victory in Monte Carlo, 1995

1988   Markku Alén/
        Ilkka Kivimäki (Fin)   Lancia Delta HF Integrale
1989   Pentti Airikkala (Fin)/
        Ronan McNamee (Ire   Mitsibushi Galant VR-4
1990   Carlos Sainz/Luis Moya (Spa) Toyoya Celica GT4
1991   Juha Kankkunen/
        Juha Piironen (Fin)   Lancia Delta HF Integrale
1992   Carlos Sainz/
        Luis Moya (Spa)   Toyoya Celica GT-Four
1993   Juha Kankkunen (Fin)/
        Nicky Grist (UK)   Toyota Celica Turbo
1994   Colin McRae/Derek Ringer (UK) Subaru Impreza
Most wins:
4 Mikkola, 3 Carlsson, Mäkinen, Kankkunen
Most successful co-drivers:
5 wins Hertz (Swe), 3 Liddon

Safari Rally

The longest rally held annually is the Safari Rally, first raced
in 1953 as the Coronation Safari in Kenya, Tanzania and
Uganda but now restricted to Kenya. The race has covered
up to 6234 km 3874 miles, as it did in 1971, but was at its
shortest ever, 2992 km 1859 miles in 1995. No overall winner
was declared in 1953, but the Class A prize went to Alan Dix
and Jerry Larsen in their Volkswagen 1200. *Winners:*
1954   D Marwaha/Vic Preston   Volkswagen 1200
1955   D Marwaha/Vic Preston   Ford Zephyr
1956   Eric Cecil/Tony Vickers   D.K.W.
1957   Arthur Burton/Angus Hofmann Volkswagen 1200
1958   *No outright winner declared*
1959-60 Bill Fritschy/Jack Ellis   Mercedes 219
1961   John Manussis/Bill Coleridge/
        David Beckett   Mercedes 220
1962   Tommy Fjastad/
        Bernhard Schneider   Volkswagen 1200
1963   Nick Nowicki/Paddy Cliff   Peugeot 404
1964   Peter Hughes/Billy Young   Ford Cortina GT
1965   Joginder Singh/Jaswant Singh (Ken) Volvo PV544
1966-7 Bert Shankland/Chris Rothwell   Peugeot 404
1968   Nick Nowicki/Paddy Cliff   Peugeot 404
1969   Robin Hillyar/
        Jock Aird (UK)   Ford Taunus 20MRS
1970   Edgar Herrmann/
        Hans Schüller (FRG)   Datsun 1600SSS
1971   Edgar Herrmann/Hans Schüller (FRG) Datsun 240Z

1972	Hannu Mikkola (Fin)/	
	Gunnar Palm (Swe)	Ford Escort RS1600
1973	Shekhar Mehta/Lofty Drews (Ken)	Datsun 250Z
1974	Joginder Singh (Ken)/	
	David Doig	Colt Galant 1600
1975	Ove Andersson/Arne Hertz (Swe)	Peugeot 504
1976	Joginder Singh (Ken)/	
	David Doig	Mitsubishi Colt Lancer
1977	Björn Waldegård (Swe)/	
	Hans Thorszelius	Ford Escort RS 1800
1978	Jean-Pierre Nicolas/Jean-Claude Lefebvre (Fra)	
		Peugeot 504 Coupe V6
1979-80	Shekhar Mehta/Mike Doughty (Ken)	Datsun 160J
1981-2	Shekhar Mehta/	
	Mike Doughty (Ken)	Datsun Violet GT
1983	Ari Vartanen (Fin)/	
	Terry Harryman (UK)	Opel Ascona 400
1984	Björn Waldegård/	
	Hans Thorszelius (Swe)	Toyota Celica TCT
1985	Juha Kankkunen (Fin)/	
	Fred Gallagher (UK)	Toyota Celica TCT
1986	Björn Waldegård (Swe)/	
	Fred Gallagher (UK)	Toyota Celica Turbo
1987	Hannu Mikkola (Fin)/	
	Arne Hertz (Swe)	Audi 200 Quattro
1988-9	Mikki Biasion/Tiziano Siviero (Ita)	Lancia Delta
1990	Björn Waldegård (Swe)/	
	Fred Gallagher (UK)	Toyota Celica GT4
1991	Juha Kankkunen/	
	Juha Piironen (Fin)	Lancia Integrale
1992	Carlos Sainz/Luis Moya (Spa)	Toyota Celica
1993	Juha Kankkunen/	
	Juha Piironen (Fin)	Toyota Celica
1994	Ian Duncan/	
	Dave Williamson (Ken)	Toyota Celica
1995	Yoshio Fujimoto (Jap)/	
	Arne Hertz (Swe)	Toyota Celica

Most wins: 5 Mehta, 4 Waldegård, 3 Joginder Singh, Kankkunen

Most wins as co-driver: 4 Mike Doughty

World Rally Championships

A World Championship for makes of car was inaugurated in 1968 and a driver's championship, known as the FIA Cup for Drivers was instituted in 1977; it became the official World Drivers' Championship in 1979. A championship for co-drivers was introduced in 1981. *Winners:*

Makes

1968	Ford (GB)
1969	Ford (Europe)
1970	Porsche
1971	Alpine-Renault
1972	Lancia
1973	Alpine-Renault
1974-6	Lancia
1977-8	Fiat
1979	Ford
1980	Fiat
1981	Talbot
1982	Audi
1983	Lancia
1984	Audi
1985-6	Peugeot
1987-92	Lancia
1993-4	Toyota

Drivers

1977	Sandro Munari (Ita)
1978	Markku Alén (Fin)
1979	Björn Waldegård (Swe)
1980	Walter Röhrl (FRG)
1981	Ari Vatanen (Fin)
1982	Walter Röhrl (FRG)
1983	Hannu Mikkola (Fin)
1984	Stig Blomqvist (Swe)
1985	Timo Salonen (Fin)
1986-7	Juha Kankkunen (Fin)
1988-9	Mikki Biasion (Ita)
1990	Carlos Sainz (Spa)
1991	Juha Kankkunen (Fin)
1992	Carlos Sainz (Spa)
1993	Juha Kankkunen (Fin)
1994	Didier Auriol (Fra)

Most event wins from 1970 to end 1994: 21 Kankkunen, 19 Alén, Mikkola, Waldegård; 17 Biasion, 16 Auriol, 14 Blomqvist, Röhrl, Sainz; 11 Salonen; 10 Vatanen

Most wins in a season: 6 Auriol 1992

DRAG RACING

In this form of motor racing two cars (or bikes) race each other over a distance of a quarter of a mile (402.3m). The sport was developed in the 1930s in the USA. The sport's governing body in the USA, the National Hot Rod Association (NHRA), was founded in 1950.

Records

The lowest elapsed time recorded by a piston engined dragster from a standing start to 440 yards is 4.665 seconds by Larry Dixon (USA) at Englishtown, New Jersey on 19 May 1995 and the highest terminal velocity reached at the end of a 440 yards run is 314.46 mph *506.07 km/h* by Kenny Bernstein (USA) at the NHRA Finals at Pomona, California on 30 Oct 1994.

NHRA Winston Series

Each year drivers collect points in a series of races throughout North America, culminating in the annual Winston Finals. The élite competition is the Top Fuel class, at which recent winners have been:

1980	Shirley Muldowney
1981	Jeb Allen
1982	Shirley Muldowney
1983	Gary Beck
1984	Joe Amato
1985-6	Don Garlits
1987	Dick LaHaie
1988	Joe Amato
1989	Gary Ormsby
1990-2	Joe Amato
1993	Eddie Hill
1994	Scott Kalita

Pro Stock: Most titles: 10 Bob Glidden 1974-5, 1978-80, 1985-9.
Funny Car: Most titles: 4 Don Prudhomme 1975-8, Kenny Bernstein 1985-8.

NHRA Winston Finals

Top Fuel winners, with (ET) and terminal speed (mph) reached from the inaugural Finals in 1965 have been:

Year	Driver	ET	mph
1965	Maynard Rupp	7.82	200.00
1966	Pete Robinson	7.27	203.16
1967	Bennie Osborn	7.03	223.88
1968	Bennie Osborn	7.05	211.76
1969	Steve Carbone	6.71	207.85
1970	Ronnie Martin	6.65	223.88
1971	Gerry Glynn	6.59	227.27
1972	Jim Walther	7.32	152.80
1973	Jerry Ruth	6.11	232.55
1974	Don Garlits	6.11	237.46
1975	Don Garlits	5.74	247.93
1976	Shirley Muldowney	5.94	248.61
1977	Dennis Baca	5.97	234.98
1978	Rob Bruins	5.98	247.58
1979	Don Garlits	6.36	237.46
1980	Shirley Muldowney	5.95	241.28
1981	Gary Beck	5.57	245.23
1982	Jim Barnard	5.92	233.16
1983	Shirley Muldowney	5.63	246.57
1984	Don Garlits	5.509	261.62
1985	Gary Beck	5.537	247.66
1986	Darryl Gwynn	5.361	269.21
1987	Darryl Gwynn	5.138	276.32
1988	Joe Amato	6.818	202.79
1989	Gary Ormsby	4.919	291.26
1990	Joe Amato	4.935	282.39
1991	Pat Austin	5.018	284.57
1992	Joe Amato	4.861	292.68
1993	Rance McDaniel	4.875	295.37
1994	Kenny Bernstein	4.72	314.46

Netball

Invented in the USA in 1891, netball is a women's 7-a-side game, developed from basketball. The first national association was that of New Zealand in 1924, followed by England in 1926. The International Federation of Women's Basketball and Netball Associations (IFWBNA) was formed in 1960.

World Championships

First held in 1963. *Winners:*
1963 Australia
1967 New Zealand
1971 Australia
1975 Australia
1979 Australia, New Zealand, Trinidad & Tobago
1983 Australia
1987 New Zealand
1991 Australia
1995 Australia

Olympic Games

The first Olympic Games of the modern era were staged in Athens, Greece from the 6th to 15th April 1896. The driving force behind their revival was Pierre de Fredi, Baron de Coubertin, who was born in Paris in 1863. He believed in the Greek athletic ideal of perfection of mind and body, and his energies were devoted to achieving his dream of reintroducing the Olympic Games, which had been staged for more than a thousand years before their prohibition in AD 394. In 1889 de Coubertin was commissioned by the French government to form a universal sports association and he visited other European nations to gather information. He made public his views on 25 Nov 1892 at the Sorbonne in Paris. These led to the formation of the International Olympic Committee in 1894 and thence to the staging of the Olympic Games, which were opened in Athens on Easter Monday 1896.
Membership of the IOC reached 196 nations in 1994.

Venues of Summer Games

1896 Athens
1900 Paris
1904 St Louis
1906 Athens*
1908 London
1912 Stockholm
1920 Antwerp
1924 Paris
1928 Amsterdam
1932 Los Angeles
1936 Berlin
1948 London
1952 Helsinki
1956 Melbourne
1960 Rome
1964 Tokyo
1968 Mexico City
1972 Munich
1976 Montreal
1980 Moscow
1984 Los Angeles
1988 Seoul
1992 Barcelona
1996 Atlanta
2000 Sydney

Intercalated Games held as the tenth anniversary celebration of the 1896 Games. Results from these 1906 Games have been included in the records in this book.
The record participation was in 1992 when there were 9369 competitors (6659 men, 2710 women) from a record 169 nations.

Venues of Winter Games

1924 Chamonix
1928 St Moritz
1932 Lake Placid
1936 Garmisch-Partenkirchen
1948 St Moritz1952 Oslo
1956 Cortina d'Ampezzo
1960 Squaw Valley

1964 Innsbruck
1968 Grenoble
1972 Sapporo
1976 Innsbruck
1980 Lake Placid
1984 Sarajevo
1988 Calgary
1992 Albertville
1994 Lillehammer
1998 Nagano
2002 Salt Lake City

From 1994 the Winter Games are being held in the middle of the four-year cycle of the Summer Games. The record participation was 1737 (1216 men and 521 women) in 1994 with a record 67 nations.

Olympic Records

See individual sports for champions at all events.

Most medals
18 Larissa Latynina (USSR) Gymnastics 1956-64
15 Nikolay Andrianov (USSR) Gymnastics 1972-80
13 Eduardo Mangaiorotti (Ita) Fencing 1936-60
13 Takashi Ono (Jap) Gymnastics 1952-64
13 Boris Shakhlin (USSR) Gymnastics 1956-64
12 Sawao Kato (Jap) Gymnastics 1968-76
12 Paavo Nurmi (Fin) Athletics 1920-28

Most gold medals
10 Ray Ewry (USA) Athletics 1900-08
9 Larissa Latynina (USSR) Gymnastics 1956-64
9 Paavo Nurmi (Fin) Athletics 1920-28
9 Mark Spitz (USA) Swimming 1968-72
8 Sawao Kato (Jap) Gymnastics 1968-76
8 Carl Lewis (USA) Athletics 1984-92
8 Matt Biondi (USA) Swimming 1984-92

Most silver medals
6 Shirley Babashoff (USA) Swimming 1972-76
6 Aleksandr Dityatin (USSR) Gymnastics 1976-80
6 Mikhail Voronin (USSR) Gymnastics 1968-72

Most bronze medals
6 Heikki Savolainen (Fin) Gymnastics 1928-52

Most Games winning medals
6 Aladár Gerevich (Hun) Fencing 1932-60

Most Games

Men
8 Raimondo d'Inzeo (Ita) Equestrian 1948-76
8 Piero d'Inzeo (Ita) Equestrian 1948-76
8 Paul Elvstrøm (Den) Yachting 1948-60, 1968-72, 1984-8
8 Durwood Knowles (UK/Bah) Yachting 1948-72, 1988
8 Hubert Raudaschl (Aut) Yachting 1964-92
7 Ivan Ossier (Den) Fencing 1908-32, 1948
7 Rainer Klimke (FRG) Equestrian 1960-76, 1984-8
7 Michael Plumb (USA) Equestrian 1960-76, 1984, 1992

Women
7 Kerstin Palm (Swe) Fencing 1964-88
6 Janice Lee Romary (née York) (USA) Fencing 1948-68
6 Lia Manoliu (Rom) Athletics 1952-72
6 Christilot Hanson-Boylen (Can) Equestrian 1964-76, 1984, 1992

Longest span of appearances
40 years Ivan Ossier (Den) Fencing 1908-48
40 years Magnus Konow (Nor) Yachting 1908-48
40 years Durwood Knowles (UK/Bah) Yachting 1948-88
40 years Paul Elvstrøm (Den) Yachting 1948-88

Youngest medallists:
The unknown French boy who coxed the winning Netherlands rowing pair in 1900 was aged 7-10 years.
Next youngest medallists:
10y 215d Dimitrios Loundras (Gre) M bronze Gymnastics 1896
11y 302d Luigina Giavotti (Ita) W silver Gymnastics1928
12y 24d Inge Sörensen (Den) W bronze Swimming 1936

Next youngest gold medallists:
13y 83 d Kim Yoon-mi (SKo) W short-track speed skating1994 (youngest at Winter Games)
13y 267d Marjorie Gestring (USA) Diving 1936
14y 12d Giorgio Cesana (Ita) Rowing 1906

Oldest medallists
72y 279d Oscar Swahn (Swe) silver Shooting 1920
68y 194d Samuel Duvall (USA) silver Archery 1904
66y 154d Louis Noverraz (Swi) silver Yachting 1968

Oldest gold medallists
64y 257d Oscar Swahn (Swe) Shooting 1912
64y 2d Galen Spencer (USA) Archery 1904
63y 244d Robert Williams (USA) Archery 1904

Oldest at Winter Games
47yr 218d Giacomo Conti (Ita) Bobsleigh 1956
The only man to win gold medals in both Summer and Winter Games in Edward Eagan (USA), Boxing 1920 and Bobsleigh 1932.

The first woman to win a medal at both Summer and Winter Games was Christa Luding (née Rothenburger). She won speed skating gold at 500m in 1984 and 1000m in 1988 as well as the silver for 500m in 1988; in the 1988 summer Games she won the silver medal at sprint cycling.

Olympic medal winners at the Summer Games 1896-1992
(including 1906)

Nation	Gold	Silver	Bronze	Total
USA	789	603	518	1910
USSR/CIS	442	361	333	1136
Germany *	186	227	236	649
United Kingdom	177	224	218	619
France	161	175	191	527
Sweden	133	149	171	453

Nation	Gold	Silver	Bronze	Total
GDR	154	131	126	411
Italy	153	126	131	410
Hungary	136	124	144	404
Finland	98	77	112	287
Japan	90	83	93	266
Australia	78	76	98	252
Romania	59	70	90	219
Poland	43	62	105	210
Canada	45	67	80	192
Netherlands	45	52	72	169
Switzerland	42	63	58	163
Bulgaria	38	69	55	162
Czechoslovakia	49	50	49	148
Denmark	26	51	53	130
Belgium	35	47	44	126
Norway	43	37	34	114
China	36	41	37	114
Greece	24	40	39	103
South Korea	31	27	41	99
Yugoslavia	26	30	30	86
Cuba	36	25	23	84
Austria	19	29	33	81
New Zealand	27	10	28	65
Turkey	26	15	12	53
South Africa	16	17	20	53
Argentina	13	19	15	47
Spain	17	19	10	46
Mexico	9	13	18	40
Brazil	9	10	21	40
Kenya	13	13	13	39
Iran	4	12	17	33
Jamaica	4	13	9	26
Estonia	7	6	10	23
North Korea	6	5	10	21
Egypt	6	6	6	18
Ireland	5	5	5	15
India	8	3	3	14
Ethiopia	6	1	6	13
Portugal	2	4	7	13
Mongolia	-	5	8	13
Pakistan	3	3	4	10
Morocco	4	2	3	9
Uruguay	2	1	6	9
Venezuela	1	2	5	8
Chile	-	6	2	8
Nigeria	-	4	4	8
Philippines	-	1	7	8
Trinidad & Tobago	1	2	4	7
Indonesia	2	3	1	6
Latvia	-	4	2	6
Colombia	-	2	4	6
Uganda	1	3	1	5
Tunisia	1	2	2	5
Puerto Rico	-	1	4	5
Peru	1	3	-	4
Algeria	1	-	3	4
Lebanon	-	2	2	4
Taiwan	-	2	2	4
Ghana	-	1	3	4
Thailand	-	1	3	4

Nation	Gold	Silver	Bronze	Total
Bahamas	1	-	2	3
Croatia	-	1	2	3
Luxembourg	1	1	-	2
Lithuania	1	-	1	2
Surinam	1	-	1	2
Namibia	-	2	-	2
Tanzania	-	2	-	2
Cameroon	-	1	1	2
Haiti	-	1	1	2
Iceland	-	1	1	2
Israel	-	1	1	2
Panama	-	-	2	2
Slovenia	-	-	2	2

1 gold: Zimbabwe
1 silver: Costa Rica, Ivory Coast, Netherlands Antilles, Sénegal, Singapore, Sri Lanka, Syria, Virgin Islands
1 bronze: Barbados, Bermuda, Djibouti, Dominican Republic, Guyana, Iraq, Malaysia, Niger Republic, Qatar, Zambia

* *Germany 1896-1952 and 1992, Federal Republic of Germany 1956-88. Medals won by the combined German teams of 1956, 1960 and 1964 have been allocated to FRG or GDR according to the athlete's origin.*

Czechoslovakia includes Bohemia.

In all 98 nations have won medals at the Summer Olympics, with Croatia, Israel, Lithuania, Malaysia, Namibia, Qatar, Slovenia added to the list in 1992. Medals won in 1896, 1900 and 1904 by mixed teams from two countries have been included for both.

Olympic medal winners at the Winter Games to 1994

Nation	Gold	Silver	Bronze	Total
USSR/CIS #	88	63	67	218
Norway	73	77	64	214
USA	53	55	39	147
Austria	36	48	44	128
Germany *	45	43	37	125
Finland	36	45	42	123
GDR *	39	36	35	110
Sweden	39	26	34	99
Switzerland	27	29	29	85
Italy	25	21	21	67
Canada	19	21	24	64
France	16	16	21	53
Netherlands	14	19	17	50
Czechoslovakia	2	8	16	26
Russia	11	8	4	23
United Kingdom	7	4	12	23
Japan	3	8	8	19
Liechtenstein	2	2	5	9
South Korea	6	2	2	8
China	-	4	2	6
Hungary	-	2	4	6
Poland	1	1	2	4
Belgium	1	1	2	4
Yugoslavia	-	3	1	4

Kazakhstan	1	2	-	3
Slovenia	-	-	3	3
Spain	1	-	1	2
Ukraine	1	-	1	2
Luxembourg	-	2	-	2
Belarus	-	2	-	2
North Korea	-	1	1	2
Uzbekistan	1	-	-	1
New Zealand	-	1	-	1
Romania	-	-	1	1
Bulgaria	-	-	1	1
Australia	-	-	1	1

separate republics from 1994
* *Germany to 1952 and 1992, Federal Republic of Germany 1956-88. GDR 1956-88 tallied separately. Medals won by the combined German teams of 1956, 1960 and 1964 have been allocated to FRG or GDR according to the athlete's origin.*

Liechtenstein is the only nation to have won medals at the Winter Games but not the Summer.

Orienteering

Cross-country running with the aid of map and compass, orienteering was invented by Major Ernst Killander in 1918 in Sweden. Their national federation, the Svenska Orienterings-förbundet, was formed in 1938. The International Orienteering Federation was established in 1961.

World Championships

First held in 1966 and staged biennially. Short event titles were added in 1991 (when the long event was at 17.5km, short at 5.8km for men; women 10.5km and 5.5km). *Winners:*

Men
1966	Åge Hadler (Nor)
1968	Karl Johansson (Swe)
1970	Stig Berge (Nor)
1972	Åge Hadler (Nor)
1974	Bernt Frilen (Swe)
1976	Egil Johansen (Nor)
1978	Egil Johansen (Nor)
1979	Øyvin Thon (Nor)
1981	Øyvin Thon (Nor)
1983	Morten Berglia (Nor)
1985	Kari Sallinen (Fin)
1987	Kent Olsson (Swe)
1989	Petter Thoresen (Nor)
1991	Jörgen Mårtensson (Swe)
1993	Allan Mogensen (Den)

Men's short distance
1991	Petr Kazak (Cs)
1993	Petter Thoresen (Nor)

Women
1966	Ulla Lindkvist (Swe)
1968	Ulla Lindkvist (Swe)
1970	Ingrid Hadler (Nor)
1972	Sarolta Monspart (Hun)
1974	Mona Norgaard (Den)
1976	Liisa Veijalainen (Fin)
1978	Anne Berit Eid (Nor)
1979	Outi Borgenstrom (Fin)
1981	Annichen Kringstad (Swe)
1983	Annichen Kringstad (Swe)
1985	Annichen Kringstad (Swe)
1987	Arja Hannus (Swe)
1989	Marita Skogum (Swe)
1991	Katalin Olah (Hun)
1993	Marita Skogum (Swe)

Women's short distance
1991	Jana Cieslarová (Cs)
1993	Anna Bogren (Swe)

Men's Relay
Norway	1970, 1978, 1981, 1983, 1985, 1987, 1989
Sweden	1966, 1968, 1972, 1974, 1976, 1979
Switzerland	1991, 1993

Women's Relay
Sweden	1966, 1970, 1974, 1976, 1981, 1983, 1985, 1989, 1991, 1993
Finland	1972, 1978, 1979
Norway	1968, 1987

World Cups

A biennial event introduced in 1988 and held over a series of races. *Overall winners:*

Men
1988	Øyvin Thon (Nor)
1990	Havard Tveite (Nor)
1992	Joakim Ingelssen (Swe)
1994	Petter Thorsen (Nor)

Women
1988	Ragnhild Bratberg (Nor)
1990	Ragnhild Bente-Andersen (Nor)
1992	Marita Skogum (Swe)
1994	Marlena Jansson (Swe

Ski Orienteering World Championships

First held in 1975 and now contested bienially at the classic distance (c.20 km) and (from 1988) a short distance or sprint event (7-9 km) as well. *Winners:*

Men - Classic
1975	Olavi Svanberg (Fin)
1977	Örjan Svahn (Swe)
1980	Pertti Tikka (Fin)
1982	Olavi Svanberg (Fin)
1984	Anssi Juutilainen (Fin)
1986	Claes Berglund (Swe)
1988	Anssi Juutilainen (Fin)
1990	Anders Björkman (Swe)
1992	Vidar Benjaminsen (Nor)
1994	Nicolo Corradini (Ita)

Men - Sprint
1988	Hannu Koponen (Fin)
1990	Anssi Juutilainen (Fin)
1992	Vidar Benjaminsen (Nor)
1994	Nicolo Corradini (Ita) & Ivan Kuzmin (Rus)

Men's Relay
Sweden	1977. 1980, 1982, 1984, 1990
Finland	1975, 1988, 1992
Norway	1986, 1994

Women - Classic
1975	Sinikka Kukkonen (Fin)
1977	Marianne Bogestedt (Swe)
1980	Mirja Puhakka (Fin)
1982	Arja Hannus (Swe)
1984	Mirja Puhakka (Fin)
1986	Ragnhild Bratberg (Nor)
1988	Virpi Juutilainen (Fin)
1990	Ragnhild Bratberg (Nor)
1992	Annika Zell (Swi)
1994	Pepa Miloucheva (Bul)

Women - Sprint
1988	Ragnhild Bratberg (Nor)
1990	Ragnhild Bratberg (Nor)
1992	Arja Hannus (Swe)
1994	Virpi Juutilainen (Fin)

Women's Relay
Sweden	1982, 1984, 1992, 1994
Finland	1975, 1977, 1980, 1988, 1990
Norway	1986

Pelota

Pelota is the generic name for a number of court games that are played, usually with gloves or baskets, although originally with the hands. Longue paume was played in France, having been introduced from Italy in the 13th century, and this developed into Real Tennis (qv), which was for long the French national game. When the game languished in the 17th century, it survived in the Basque country, straddling France and Spain, where the current game of Pelote Basque was developed. The Fédération Française de Pelote Basque was formed in 1921 and the Federacion Internacional de Pelota Vasca (FIPV) was founded in 1929 in Spain, where the sport is known as Pelota.

In the Basque country the traditional courts are known as trinquete, while usual in Latin America and Spain are courts of the fronton (enclosed stadium) variety, known in Basque as jai-alai, the name of the game in the USA and Latin America.

The chistera, used to propel the ball at great speed, was developed from a wicker fruit-basket in the 1860s. Claims for the game to be the fastest of all ball games are reinforced by the highest ball velocity speed measured electronically at 302 km/h by José Ramon Areitio at Newport, Rhode Island in 1979.

World Championships

The FIVP stage world championships every four years, the first of which was in 1952 for a variety of events, including long and short court and trinquete court games. The most successful pair have been Roberto Elias and Juan Labat (Arg), who won the Trinquete Share in 1952, 1958, 1962 and 1966. Labat won seven world titles in all.

The most wins in the long court game of Cesta Punta is three by Hamuy (Mex), with different partners, 1958, 1962 and 1966.

Olympic Games

Pelota was played as a demonstration sport at the Olympic Games in 1924, 1968 and 1992.

Petanque

Also known as 'boules', pétanque is derived from the ancient French game of Jeu Provençal, now differing from that game in that in the latter the bowls are delivered from a short run-up, whereas in pétanque they are delivered from a stationary position. The steel bowls (or boules) have a diameter of 7-8 cm and weigh 620-800 gm.

The Fédération Français de Pétanque et Jeu Provençal (FFPJP) was formed in 1945 and subsequently the Fédération Internationale (FIPJP). The British Pétanque Association was founded in 1974.

World Championships
First held in 1959. *Wins:*
14	France	1959, 1961, 1963, 1972, 1974, 1976-7, 1985, 1988-9, 1991-4
4	Switzerland	1965-6, 1973, 1980
3	Italy	1975, 1978-9
3	Morocco	1984, 1987, 1990
2	Tunisia	1983, 1986
1	Algeria 1964, Spain 1971, Belgium 1981, Monaco 1982

Women's World Championships
First held in 1988. *Winners:*
2	Thailand	1988, 1990
2	France	1992, 1994

Polo

A four-a-side stick and ball game played on horseback, polo originated in Central Asia. It can be traced to origins in Manipur state, India c. 3100 BC when it was played as Sagol Kangjei. It is also claimed to be of Persian origin, having been played as Pulu c. 525BC. The British learnt of the game in India in the 1850s, and the earliest polo club of the modern era was the Cachar Club, founded in Assam in 1859. The game was first played in England in 1869 by the 10th Hussars, and in the USA in 1876.

The game's governing body is the Hurlingham Polo Association. Hurlingham, in London, first staged a match in 1874 and the club committee drew up the first set of English rules a year later.

Polo is played on the largest pitch of any game, with maximum length of 300 yards (274m) and width of 200 yards (182m) without boards, or 160 yards (146m with boards).

High goal players

Polo games are often contested on a handicap basis, each player being awarded a handicap measured in goals up to a maximum of ten, attained by the world's best players. In the history of the game 55 players have been awarded this handicap. A high goal player is one with a handicap of five, so a high goal team rates at 20 or more. Two matches have been played between two 40-goal teams, that is all players on the maximum: first at Palermo, Buenos Aires, Argentina between El Trébol and Venado Tuerto in 1975, and the second, contested by Mexican and Argentinian players at the Empire Polo Club, Indio, California, USA on 16 December 1990, with Westbury beating River Plate 8-7.

The highest handicap ever attained by a woman is five by Claire Tomlinson in 1986.

World Championships

Contested in 1989 in West Berlin, when the USA beat Great Britain 7-6 in the final. 3rd Argentina, 4th Chile.

WestchesterCup

The first international match was between Great Britain and the United States at Newport, Rhode Island in 1886 for an international trophy given by the Westchester Club. Last contested in 1939, the winners in this series were:

Great Britain 1886, 1900, 1902, 1914
United States 1909, 1911, 1913, 1921, 1924, 1927, 1930, 1936, 1939

Contest for the Cup was revived in 1988, when the USA beat Australasia by goal average in two games at Lexington, Kentucky and in 1992 when the USA beat GB 8-7 in a series contested by 30-goal teams.

Cup of the Americas

Contested by Argentina and the USA. The US won the first two matches in 1928 and 1932, and the Argentinians have won all subsequent contests: 1936, 1950, 1966, 1969, 1979, 1980 and 1988.

Olympic Games

Polo has been included at five Olympic Games. *Winners:*
1900   Foxhunters (UK/USA)
1908   Roehampton (UK)
1920   Great Britain
1924 and 1936 Argentina

Champion Cup

Britain's premier tournament from its inception in 1876 to 1939, when it was last played at Hurlingham, London. The teams with most wins were Freebooters 9, and Sussex 8

British Open Championship

Played annually for the Cowdray Park Gold Cup (now the Veuve Clicquot Gold Cup) at Cowdray Park, Midhurst, Sussex; this competition replaced the Champion Cup. *Winners:*

1956	Los Indios
1957	Windsor Park
1958	Cowdray Park
1959-60	Casarejo
1961-2	Cowdray Park
1963	La Vulci
1964-5	Jersey Lilies
1966	Windsor Park
1967	Woolmer's Park
1968	Pimms
1969	Windsor Park
1970	Boca Raton
1971-2	Pimms
1973-4	Stowell Park
1975	Greenhill Farm
1976	Stowell Park
1977	Foxcote
1978	Stowell Park
1979	Songhai
1980	Stowell Park
1981	Falcons
1982	Southfield
1983	Falcons
1984	Southfield
1985	Maple Leafs
1986-9	Tramontana
1990	Hildon
1991	Tramontana
1992	Black Bears
1993	Alcatel
1994	Ellerston Black
1995	Ellerston White

Most wins: 5 Stowell Park, Tramontana
Most wins by Individual: 9 Carlos Gracida (Mex)

Powerboating

Powerboat racing started in about 1900, and there are now a large number of categories of boats that race on either inland waters or offshore. A petrol engine had first been fitted in a boat by Jean Lenoir on the River Seine in 1865.

Harmsworth Trophy

This perpetual trophy was presented by Sir Alfred Harmsworth (later Lord Northcliffe) in 1903. The race for the trophy was for many years the world's most prestigious powerboating event. *Winners:*

Year	Boat	Driver	Speed km/h
1903	Napier I (Eng)	Dorothy Levitt	31.43
1904	Trefle-A-Quatre (Fra)	Emile Thubron	42.86
1905	Napier II (Eng)	Lord Montague	41.89
1906	Yarrow-Napier (Eng)	Lionel de Rothschild	24.91
1907	Dixie I (USA)	E J Schroeder	51.14
1908	Dixie II (USA)	E J Schroeder	50.45
1910	Dixie III (USA)	F K Burnham	58.00
1911	Dixie IV (USA)	F K Burnham	64.82
1912	Maple Leaf IV (Eng)	Tommy Sopwith	69.49
1913	Maple Leaf IV (Eng)	Tommy Sopwith	92.46
1920	Miss America I (USA)	Garfield Wood	98.99
1921	Miss America II (USA)	Garfield Wood	96.16
1926	Miss America V (USA)	Garfield Wood	98.359
1928	Miss America VII (USA)	Garfield Wood	95.474

1929	Miss America VIII (USA)	Garfield Wood	121.163
1930	Miss America IX (USA)	Garfield Wood	124.294
1932	Miss America X (USA)	Garfield Wood	126.315
1933	Miss America X (USA)	Garfield Wood	139.915
1949	Skip-A-Long (USA)	Stanley Dollar	151.737
1950	Slo-Mo-Shun IV (USA)	Stanley Sayres	162.029
1956	Shanty I (USA)	William Waggoner Jr	144.439
1959	Miss Supertest III (Can)	Bob Hayward	160.595
1960	Miss Supertest III (Can)	Bob Hayward	185.852
1961	Miss Supertest III (Can)	Bob Hayward	158.066

The series then lapsed, but was revised under a new formula in 1977 as the Harmsworth British & Commonwealth Trophy for Motorboats. *Winners:*

Year	Boat	Driver
1977-8	Limit-Up (Eng)	Michael Doxford & Tim Powell
1979	Uno-Mint-Jewellery (Eng)	Derek Pobjoy.

From 1980 to 1983 the Harmsworth Trophy was awarded on points for a series of offshore races. *Winning drivers:*

1980	Bill Elswick & Paul Clauser (USA)
1981	Paul Clauser (USA)
1982	Al Copeland & B Sirios (USA)
1983	George Morales (USA)

In 1985 the Harmsworth trophy was contested by two-boat national teams at Formula Two for outboard engines:

1985	Jonathan Jones, Mark Wilson & John Hill (UK)
1986	Bill Seebold Jr (USA)

Not contested in 1987 and 1988, in 1989 the trophy was returned to world offshore competition and won by Stefano Casiraghi (Ita).

American Power Boat Association Gold Cup

The American Power Boat Association was formed in 1903, and held its first Gold Cup race on the Hudson River in 1904, when the winner was Standard, piloted by C C Riotto at an average speed of 39 km/h. *Winners (with average speed) from 1970:*

Year	Boat	Driver	km/h	mp/h
1970	Miss Budweiser	Dean Chenoweth	101.848	163.908
1971	Miss Madison	Jim McCormick	101.522	163.384
1972	Atlas Van Lines	Bill Muncey	103.547	166.643
1973	Miss Budweiser	Dean Chenoweth	104.046	167.446
1974	Pay'N Pak	George Henley	112.056	180.337
1975	Pay'N Pak	George Henley	113.350	182.419
1976	Miss US	Tom d'Eath	108.021	173.843
1977	Atlas Van Lines	Bill Muncey	114.849	184.832
1978	Atlas Van Lines	Bill Muncey	104.448	167.330
1979	Atlas Van Lines	Bill Muncey	107.892	173.631
1980	Miss Budweiser	Dean Chenoweth	108.459	174.543
1981	Miss Budweiser	Dean Chenoweth	117.815	189.600
1982	Atlas Van Lines	Chip Hanauer	120.081	193.246
1983	Atlas Van Lines	Chip Hanauer	118.506	190.712
1984	Atlas Van Lines	Chip Hanauer	130.866	210.603
1985	Miller American	Chip Hanauer	121.612	195.710
1986	Miller American	Chip Hanauer	116.886	188.105
1987	Miller American	Chip Hanauer	127.745	205.580
1988	Circus Circus	Chip Hanauer	128.406	206.644
1989	Miss Budweiser	Tom D'Eath	131.388	211.443
1990	Miss Budweiser	Tom D'Eath	143.176	230.413
1991	Winston Eagle	Mark Tate	137.771	221.715
1992	Miss Budweiser	Chip Hanauer	136.282	219.319
1993	Miss Budweiser	Chip Hanauer	141.296	227.388
1994	Smokin' Joe Camel	Mark Tate	145.260	233.773
1995	Miss Budweiser	Chip Hanauer	149.160	240.050

Most wins: (pilot) 10 Chip Hanauer as above
8 Bill Muncey 1956-7, 1961-2, 1972, 1977-9
5 Garfield Wood 1917-21.

Olympic Games

Motor boating was included in the 1908 Olympic Games. *Winners:* Emile Thubron (Fra) won Class A in *Camille*; Thomas Thornycroft, Bernard Redwood and Captain Field-Richards won Classes B and C in *Gyrinus*.

World Champions

Formula One

1982	Roger Jenkins (UK)
1983	Renato Molinari (Ita)
1984	Renato Molinari (Ita)
1985	Bob Spalding (UK)
1986	Gene Thibodaux (USA)
1987	Ben Robertson (USA) (just one race)

Formula Two (Formula Grand Prix) World Champions

Inland circuit championships.

1982-3	Michael Werner (FRG)
1984-5	John Hill (UK)
1986	Jonathan Jones (UK) and Buck Thornton (USA)
1987	Bill Seebold (USA)
1988	Chris Bush (USA)
1989	Jonathan Jones (UK)

Formula One World Champions

1990	John Hill (UK)
1991	Jonathan Jones (UK)
1992	Fabricio Bocca (Ita)
1993-4	Guido Cappellini (Ita)

Offshore Class 1 World Champions

First held 1961. For 16 litre engines.

1966	Jim Wynne (USA)
1967	Don Aronow (USA)
1968	Vincenzo Balestrieri (Ita)
1969	Don Aronow (USA)
1970	Vincenzo Balestrieri (Ita)
1971	William Wishnick (USA)
1972	Bobby Rautboard (USA)
1973-4	Carlo Bonomi (Ita)
1975	Franz Wallace (Bra)
1976	Tom Gentry (USA)
1977	Betty Cook (USA)
1978	Francesco Cosentino (Ita)
1979	Betty Cook (USA)

1980	Michael Maynard (USA)
1981	Jerry Jacoby (USA)
1982	Renato della Valle (Ita)
1983	Tony Garcia (USA)
1984	Alberto Petri (Ita)
1985	Anthony Roberts (USA)
1986	Antonio Giofredi (Ita)
1987	Steve Curtis (UK)
1988	Fabio Buzzi (Ita)
1989	Stefano Casiraghi (Ita)

Speed records

The Union Internationale Motonautique (UIM) recognise a large number of speed records for different categories of boats. The fastest recognised for an outboard powered boat is 285.83 km/h in class (e) by P R Knight in a Lauterbach hull powered by a Chevrolet engine on Lake Ruataniwha, New Zealand, 1986.

The fastest speed recorded for a diesel (compression ignition) boat is 218.248 km/h by the hydroplane Iveco World Leader powered by an Aifo-Fiat engine, driven by Carlo Bonomi at Venice, Italy on 4 Apr 1985.

Powerlifting

From the many different lifts that have been practised by weightlifters and incorporated in tests of strength, powerlifting now recognises the squat, bench press and dead lift, all performed two-handed. The competitor is allowed three attempts at each lift and the best successful attempt on each lift is totalled. There are eleven weight categories for men and ten for women.

The sport of powerlifting was first contested at national level in Great Britain in 1958. The first US Championships were held in 1964. The International Powerlifting Federation (IPF) was founded in 1972.

World Championships

First held for men as unofficial championships in 1971 and officially in 1973, and for women in 1980.
Champions from 1980 (totals given are the total of the three lifts in kilograms):

Men - 52kg
1980	Hideaki Inaba (Jap) 567.5
1981	Hideaki Inaba (Jap) 560
1982	Hideaki Inaba (Jap) 552.5
1983	Hideaki Inaba (Jap) 565
1984	Chuck Dunbar (USA) 532.5
1985	Hideaki Inaba (Jap) 562.5
1986	Hideaki Inaba (Jap) 577.5
1987	Hideaki Inaba (Jap) 587.5
1988	Hideaki Inaba (Jap) 560
1989	Hideaki Inaba (Jap) 560
1990	Hideaki Inaba (Jap) 560
1991	Hideaki Inaba (Jap) 545
1992	Sergey Zhuravlev (Rus) 550
1993	Andrzej Stanaszek (Pol) 567.5
1994	Andrzej Stanaszek (Pol) 577.5

Men - 56kg
1980	Precious McKenzie (NZ) 587.5
1981	Hiroyuki Isagawa (Jap) 577.5
1982	Lamar Gant (USA) 590
1983	Lamar Gant (USA) 575
1984	Lamar Gant (USA) 580
1985	Hiroyuki Isagawa (Jap) 562.5
1986	Hiroyuki Isagawa (Jap) 572.5
1987	Gerrard McNamara (Ire) 550
1988	Hiroyuki Isagawa (Jap) 585
1989	Hiroyuki Isagawa (Jap) 600
1990	Gary Simes (UK) 567.5
1991	Hiroyuki Isagawa (Jap) 602.5
1992	Denis Thios (Ina) 580
1993	Denis Thios (Ina) 605
1994	Hiroyuki Isagawa (Jap) 592.5

Men - 60kg
1980	Lamar Gant (USA) 705
1981	Lamar Gant (USA) 625
1982	Kullervo Lampela (Fin) 582.5
1983	Göran Henrysson (Swe) 605
1984	Göran Henrysson (Swe) 600
1985	Göran Henrysson (Swe) 605
1986	Lamar Gant (USA) 647.5
1987	Lamar Gant (USA) 677.5
1988	Lamar Gant (USA) 675
1989	Lamar Gant (USA) 650
1990	Lamar Gant (USA) 647.5
1991	Gerard Tromp (Hol) 615
1992	Gerald McNamara (Ire) 650
1993	Talambanua Nanda (Ina) 630
1994	Wim Elyn (Bel) 645

Men - 67.5kg
1980	Rickey Crain (USA) 730
1981	Joe Bradley (USA) 702.5
1982	Stefan Nentis (Swe) 697.5
1983	Bob Wahl (USA) 705
1984	Dan Austin (USA) 722.5
1985	Eddie Pengelly (UK) 667.5
1986	Dan Austin (USA) 712.5
1987	Dan Austin (USA) 717.5
1988	Dan Austin (USA) 717.5
1989	Dan Austin (USA) 690
1990	Dan Austin (USA) 730
1991	Dan Austin (USA) 742.5
1992	Dan Austin (USA) 695
1993	Aleksey Sivokon (Kzk) 750
1994	Aleksey Sivokon (Kzk) 765

Men - 75kg
1980	Rick Gaugler (USA) 787.5
1981	Steve Alexander (USA) 752.5
1982	Rickey Crain (USA) 772.5
1983	Rickey Crain (USA) 762.5
1984	Gene Bell (USA) 762.5
1985	Eric Coppin (Bel) 765
1986	Rick Crilly (Can) 732.5
1987	Jarmo Virtanen (Fin) 802.5
1988	Jarmo Virtanen (Fin) 792.5
1989	Ausby Alexander (USA) 752.5
1990	Ausby Alexander (USA) 770

1991	Dave Ricks (USA) 782.5
1992	Dave Ricks (USA) 755
1993	Dave Ricks (USA) 750
1994	Dave Ricks (USA) 807.5

Men - 82.5kg

1980	Bill West (UK) 777.5
1981	Mike Bridges (USA) 945
1982	Mike Bridges (USA) 845
1983	Mike Bridges (USA) 807.5
1984	Ed Coan (USA) 875
1985	Jarmo Virtanen (Fin) 842.5
1986	Jarmo Virtanen (Fin) 850
1987	Gene Bell (USA) 822.5
1988	Hannu Malinen (Fin) 750
1989	Jarmo Virtanen (Fin) 827.5
1990	Jarmo Virtanen (Fin) 832.5
1991	Aleksandr Lekomtyev (USSR) 790
1992	Jarmo Virtanen (Fin) 832.5
1993	Jarmo Virtanen (Fin) 850
1994	Walter Thomas 807.5

Men - 90kg

1980	Vince Anello (USA) 867.5
1981	Walter Thomas (USA) 930
1982	Walter Thomas (USA) 857.5
1983	Kenneth Mattsson (Swe) 872.5
1984	Dennis Wright (USA) 840
1985	David Caldwell (UK) 832.5
1986	Jari Tahtinen (Fin) 822.5
1987	Sly Anderson (USA) 830
1988	Gene Bell (USA) 860
1989	George Herring (USA) 855
1990	George Herring (USA) 835
1991	Sly Anderson (USA) 835
1992	Sly Anderson (USA) 862.5
1993	Gene Bell (USA) 870
1994	Frank Schramm (Ger) 882.5

Men - 100kg

1980	Mark Dimiduk (USA) 922.5
1981	Jim Cash (USA) 922.5
1982	Kenneth Mattsson (Swe) 880
1983	Fred Hatfield (USA) 920
1984	Tony Stevens (UK) 915
1985	Tony Stevens (UK) 907.5
1986	Tony Stevens (UK) 882.5
1987	Conny Nilsson (Swe) 847.5
1988	Ed Coan (USA) 972.5
1989	Ed Coan (USA) 1015
1990	Juha Hyttinen (Fin) 887.5
1991	George Harring (USA) 905
1992	Brian Reynolds (UK) 872.5
1993	Ed Coan (USA) 1017.5
1994	Ed Coan (USA) 1035

Men -110kg

1980	John Kuc (USA) 1000
1981	Reijo Kiviranta (Fin) 920
1982	Hannu Saarelainen (Fin) 887.5
1983	Steve Wilson (USA) 910
1984	Dave Jacoby (USA) 935
1985	Dave Jacoby (USA) 907.5

1986	Fred Hatfield (USA) 902.5
1987	Dave Jacoby (USA) 910
1988	Dave Jacoby (USA) 902.5
1989	John Neighbour (UK) 925
1990	Aarre Käpypä (Fin) 920
1991	Guon Sigurjonsson (Ice) 907.5
1992	Dave Jacoby (USA) 935
1993	Philip Farmer (USA) 962.5
	Andrey Mustrikov (Rus) 912.5
1994	Kirk Karwoski (USA) 980

Men - 125kg

1981	Ernie Hackett (USA) 962.5
1982	John Gamble (USA) 907.5
1983	Lars Norén (Swe) 890
1984	Ab Wolders (Hol) 945
1985	Tom Henderson (USA) 935
1986	Lars Norén (Swe) 942.5
1987	John Neighbour (UK) 922.5
1988	Kyösti Vilmi (Fin) 930
1989	Kyösti Vilmi (Fin) 930
1990	Kyösti Vilmi (Fin) 970
1991	Kirk Karwoski (USA) 942.5
1992	Kirk Karwoski (USA) 980
1993	Kirk Karwoski (USA) 977.5
1994	Viktor Naleykin (Ukr) 960

Men - over 125kg

1980	(over 110kg) Doyle Kenady (USA) 1000
1981	Paul Wrenn (USA) 1027.5
1982	Tom Maggee (Can) 942.5
1983	Bill Kazmaier (USA) 975
1984	Lee Moran (USA) 977.5
1985	George Hechter (USA) 947.5
1986	Mike Hall (USA) 980
1987	Lars Norén (Swe) 1077.5
1988	Oders Wilson (USA) 1012.5
1989	Mike Hall (USA) 952.5
1990	Jean-Pierre Brulois (Fra) 972.5
1991	Hjalti Arnason (Ice) 957.5
1992	Luiz Farnettani (Bra) 975
1993	Hans Zerhoch (Ger) 985
1994	Karl Saliger (Aut) 1000

Women - 44kg

1980	Joan Fruth (USA) 275
1981	Donna Wicker (USA) 287.5
1982	Ginger Lord (USA) 300
1983	Cheryl Jones (USA) 317.5
1984	Cheryl Jones (USA) 347.5
1985	Cheryl Jones (USA) 350
1986	Judy Gedney (USA) 322.5
1987	Anna-Liisa Prinkkala (Fin) 332.5
1988	Hisako Yoshida (Jap) 335
1989	Anna-Liisa Prinkkala (Fin) 340
1990	Anna-Liisa Prinkkala (Fin) 347.5
1991	Helen Wolsey (UK) 350
1992	Helen Wolsey (UK) 337.5
1993	Nathalie Janot (Fra) 365
1994	Anna-Liisa Prinkkala (Fin) 362.5

Women - 48kg
1980 Sue Roberts (Aus) 330
1981 Terry Dillard (USA) 340
1982 Terry Dillard (USA) 347.5
1983 Diana Rowell (USA) 355
1984 Majik Jones (USA) 390
1985 Bernadette Plouviez (Bel) 345
1986 Marie Vassart (Bel) 350
1987 Vuokko Viitasaari (Fin) 352.5
1988 Irma Ruler (Hol) 360
1989 Claudine Cognac (Fra) 352.5
1990 Claudine Cognac (Fra) 372.5
1991 Malou Thill (Lux) 357.5
1992 Claudine Cognac (Fra) 375
1993 Claudine Cognac (Fra) 382.5
1994 Vuokko Viitasaari (Fin) 370

Women - 52kg
1980 Terry Dillard (USA) 347.5
1981 Sue Roberts (Aus) 370
1982 Sue Jordan (Aus) 365
1983 Kali Bogias (Can) 390
1984 Kali Bogias (Can) 392.5
1985 Sisi Dolman (Hol) 400
1986 Sisi Dolman (Hol) 400
1987 Mary Jeffrey (USA) 420
1988 Sisi Dolman (Hol) 410
1989 Sisi Dolman (Hol) 422.5
1990 Sisi Dolman (Hol) 400
1991 Sisi Dolman (Hol) 415
1992 Mary Jeffrey (USA) 435
1993 Gema Cristóbal (Spa) 405
1994 Ingeborg Marx (Bel) 410

Women - 56kg
1980 Sue Elwyn (USA) 330
1981 Gayla Crain (USA) 395
1982 Julie Thomas (USA) 365
1983 Juli Thomas (USA) 440
1984 Vicky Steenrod (USA) 475
1985 Tina van Duyn-Woodley (Hol) 415
1986 Felecia Johnson (USA) 407.5
1987 Joy Burt (Can) 427.5
1988 Mary Jeffrey (USA) 440
1989 Mary Jeffrey (USA) 445
1989 Mary Jeffrey (USA) 447.5
1991 Carrie Graffam (USA) 442.5
1992 Joy Burt (Can) 470
1993 Carrie Graffam-Boudreau (USA) 500
1994 Nadezhda Mir (Kaz) 427.5

Women - 60kg
1980 Karen Gajda (USA) 405
1981 Eileen Todaro (USA) 387.5
1982 Ruth Shafer (USA) 450
1983 Ruth Shafer (USA) 500
1984 Diane Frantz (USA) 435
1985 Vicky Steenrod (USA) 502.5
1986 Rita Bass (UK) 420
1987 Vicky Steenrod (USA) 487.5
1988 Silvana Bollmann (FRG) 445
1989 Judith Auerbach (USA) 427.5
1990 Rachel Mathias (USA) 417.5

1991 Ingjerd Pytte (Nor) 420
1992 Marion Hammang (Lux) 440
1993 Beate Amdahl (Nor) 482.5
1994 Beate Amdahl (Nor) 492.5

Women - 67.5kg
1980 Jennifer Reid (USA) 405
1981 Jennifer Weyland (USA) 467.5
1982 Angie Ross (USA) 435
1983 Linda Miller (Aus) 435
1984 Ruth Shafer (USA) 552.5
1985 Ruth Shafer (USA) 427.5
1986 Heidi Wittesch (Aus) 470
1987 Deborah McElroy (USA) 490
1988 Jackie Pierce (USA) 497.5
1989 Silvana Bollmann (FRG) 502.5
1990 Jackie Pierce (USA) 515
1991 Yekaterina Tanakova (USSR) 490
1992 Yekaterina Tanakova (Rus) 497.5
1993 Yekaterina Tanakova (Rus) 535
1994 Yekaterina Tanakova (Rus) 535

Women - 75kg
1980 Beverley Francis (Aus) 460
1981 Judith Oakes (UK) 462.5
1982 Beverley Francis (Aus) 497.5
1983 Pamela Matthews (Aus) 487.5
1984 Deborah McElroy-Patton (USA) 475
1985 Heidi Wittesch (Aus) 470
1986 Deborah Patton (USA) 462.5
1987 Terry Byland (USA) 477.5
1988 Heidi Wittesch (Aus) 522.5
1989 Liz Odendaal (Hol) 577.5
1990 Liz Odendaal (Hol) 552.5
1991 Cathy Millen (NZ) 602.5
1992 Sara Robertson (USA) 512.5
1993 Tammy Dainde (USA) 540
1994 Yelena Suchoruk (Ukr) 577.5

Women - 82.5kg
1980 Vicky Gagne (USA) 450
1981 Beverley Francis (Aus) 575
1982 Judith Oakes (UK) 502.5
1983 Beverley Francis (Aus) 577.5
1984 Beverley Francis (Aus) 557.5
1985 Beverley Francis (Aus) 565
1986 Juanita Trujillo (USA) 537.5
1987 Maggie Sandoval (USA) 522.5
1988 Judith Oakes (UK) 542.5
1989 Heidi Wittesch (Aus) 520
1990 Cathy Millen (NZ) 562.5
1991 Shelby Corson (USA) 477.5
1992 Monika Norberg (Swe) 465
1993 Natalya Rumyantseva (Rus) 532.5
1994 Natalya Rumyantseva (Rus) 575

Women - Over 82.5kg
1980 Ann Turbyne (USA) 502.5
1981 Wanda Sander (USA) 550

Women - 90kg
1982 Rebecca Waibler (FRG) 475
1983 Gael Mulhall (Aus) 525
1984 Annette Bohach (USA) 500

1985	Tore Eriksen (Nor) 465
1986	Lorraine Costango (USA) 550
1987	Jacqueline Pepper (UK) 462.5
1988	Lorraine Costanzo (USA) 605
1989	Heike Buch (FRG) 555
1990	Ulrike Herchenhein (FRG) 532.5
1991	Susanne Tjernell-Formgren (Swe) 485
1992	Cathy Millen (NZ) 622.5
1993	Cathy Millen (NZ) 655
1994	Cathy Millen (NZ) 682.5

Women - Over 90kg

1982	Annie McElroy (USA) 502.5
1983	Wanda Sander (USA) 522.5
1984	Annie McElroy (USA) 485
1985	Annie McElroy (USA) 527.5
1986	Annie McElroy (USA) 527.5
1987	Lorraine Costanzo (USA) 622.5
1988	Myrtle Augee (UK) 557.5
1989	Ulrike Herchenhein (FRG) 555
1900	Sylvia Iskin (Fra) 510
1991	Sylvia Iskin (Fra) 552.5
1992	Juanita Trujillo (USA) 560
1993	Ulrike Herchenhein (Ger) 610
1994	Ulrike Herchenhein (Ger) 630

Most world titles:

Men

17	Hideaki Inaba (Jap) 52kg 1974-83, 1985-91
15	Lamar Gant (USA) 56kg 1975-7, 1979, 1982-4; 60kg 1978, 1980-1, 1986-90
8	Larry Pacifico (USA) 90kg 1976; 100kg 1974-5, 1977-9; 110kg 1972-3
8	Dan Austin (USA) 67.5kg 1984, 1986-92
8	Jarmo Virtanen (Fin) 75kg 1987-8, 82.5kg 1985-6, 1989-90, 1992-3

Women

6	Beverley Francis (Aus) 75kg 1980, 1982; 82.5kg 1981, 1983-5
6	Sisi Dolman (Hol) 52kg 1985-6, 1988-91

World Records

All weights in kilograms

Men

Class	Squat	
52kg	270	Andrzej Stanashek (Pol) 1994
56kg	260	Magnus Karlsson (Swe) 1994
60kg	295.5	Magnus Karlsson (Swe) 1994
67.5kg	300	Jessie Jackson (USA) 1987
75kg	328	Ausby Alexander (USA) 1989
82.5kg	379.5	Mike Bridges (USA) 1982
90kg	375	Fred Hatfield (USA) 1980
100kg	423	Ed Coan (USA) 1994
110kg	415	Kirk Karwoski (USA) 1994
125kg	440	Kirk Karwoski (USA) 1993
125+kg	447.5	Shane Hamman (USA) 1994

Class	Bench Press	
52kg	177.5	Andrzej Stanashek (Pol) 1994
56kg	175	Magnus Karlsson (Swe) 1993
60kg	180.5	Magnus Karlsson (Swe) 1993
67.5kg	200	Kristoffer Hulecki (Swi) 1985
75kg	217.5	James Rouse (USA) 1980
82.5kg	240	Mike Bridges (USA) 1981
90kg	255	Mike McDonald (USA) 1980
100kg	261.5	Mike McDonald (USA) 1977
110kg	270	Jeffrey Magruder (USA) 1982
125kg	278.5	Tom Hardman (USA) 1982
125+kg	310	Antony Clark (USA) 1994

Class	Dead Lift	
52kg	256	Sajeeva Bhaskaran (Ind) 1993
56kg	289.5	Lamar Gant (USA) 1982
60kg	310	Lamar Gant (USA) 1988
67.5kg	316	Daniel Austin (USA) 1991
75kg	337.5	Daniel Austin (USA) 1994
82.5kg	357.5	Veli Kumpuniemi (Fin) 1980
90kg	372.5	Walter Thomas (USA) 1982
100kg	390	Ed Coan (USA) 1993
110kg	395	John Kuc (USA) 1980
125kg	387.5	Lars Norén (Swe) 1987
125+kg	406	Lars Norén (Swe) 1988

Class	Total	
52kg	587.5	Hideaki Inaba (Jap) 1987
56kg	625	Lamar Gant (USA) 1982
60kg	707.5	Joe Bradley (USA) 1982
67.5kg	762.5	Daniel Austin (USA) 1989
75kg	850	Rick Gaugler (USA) 1982
82.5kg	952.5	Mike Bridges (USA) 1982
90kg	937.5	Mike Bridges (USA) 1980
100kg	1035	Ed Coan (USA) 1994
110kg	1000	John Kuc (USA) 1980
125kg	1005	Ernie Hackett (USA) 1982
125+kg	1100	Bill Kazmaier (USA) 1981

Women

Class	Squat	
44kg	156	Raija Koskinen (Fin) 1995
48kg	160.5	Raija Koskinen (Fin) 1994
52kg	175.5	Mary Jeffrey (USA) 1991
56kg	191	Mary Jeffrey (USA) 1989
60kg	210	Beate Amdahl (Nor) 1994
67.5kg	230	Ruth Shafer (USA) 1984
75kg	240.5	Yelena Sukhoruk (Ukr) 1995
82.5kg	240	Cathy Millen (NZ) 1991
90kg	260	Cathy Millen (NZ) 1994
90+kg	277.5	Juanita Trujillo (USA) 1994

Class	Bench Press	
44kg	82.5	Irina Krylova (Rus) 1993
48kg	93	Isako Watanabe (Jap) 1994
52kg	105	Mary Jeffrey (USA) 1991
56kg	115	Mary Jeffrey (née Ryan) (USA) 1988
60kg	110.5	Emiko Himeno (Jap) 1994
67.5kg	120	Vicky Steenrod (USA) 1990
75kg	142.5	Liz Odendaal (Hol) 1989
82.5kg	150.5	Cathy Millen (NZ) 1993
90kg	160	Cathy Millen (NZ) 1994
90+kg	157.5	Ulrike Herchenhein (Ger) 1994

Class	Dead Lift	
44kg	165	Nancy Belliveau (Can) 1985
48kg	182.5	Majik Jones (USA) 1984

52kg	197.5	Diana Rowell (USA) 1984
56kg	220.5	Carrie Boudreau (USA) 1995
60kg	213	Ruth Shafer (USA) 1983
67.5kg	244	Ruth Shafer (USA) 1984
75kg	240	Cathy Millen (NZ) 1991
82.5kg	252.5	Yelena Sukhoruk (Ukr) 1995
90kg	260	Cathy Millen (NZ) 1994
90+kg	240	Ulrike Herchenhein (Ger) 1994

Class	Total	
44kg	365	Jacqueline Janot (Fra) 1993
48kg	400	Yelena Yamskich (Rus) 1994
52kg	452.5	Mary Jeffrey (USA) 1991
56kg	517.5	Carrie Boudreau (USA) 1995
60kg	502.5	Vicky Steenrod (USA) 1985
67.5kg	565	Ruth Shafer (USA) 1984
75kg	605	Yelena Sukhoruk (Ukr) 1995
82.5kg	637.5	Cathy Millen (NZ) 1993
90kg	682.5	Cathy Millen (NZ) 1994
90+kg	640	Juanita Trujillo (USA) 1994

Racquetball

Two versions of the game exist. The initial game of Racquetball (US spelling), using handball courts 40ft by 20ft (12.2m by 6.1m), was invented in 1949 by Joe Sobek at the Greenwich YMCA, Connecticut, USA, originally as Paddle Rackets; he sawed half the handle off a tennis racquet. In the USA the International Racquetball Association was founded in 1968 by Bob Kendler (USA). Its name was changed in 1980 to the American Amateur Racquetball Association (AARA). The sport now has more than ten million players in the USA. The international governing body is The International Racquetball Federation (IRF), originally founded in 1979

World Records

The IRF has staged world championships biennially since 1982 at men's and women's singles and doubles and mixed doubles. Competitors from a record 32 nations contested the 1992 events. *Singles winners:*

Men
1982	Ed Andrews (USA)
1984	Ross Horney (Can)
1986	Egan Inoue (USA)
1988	Andy Roberts (USA)
1990	Egan Inoue (USA)
1992	Chris Cole (USA)
1994	Sherman Greenfeld (Can)

Women
1982	Cindy Baxter (USA)
1984	Mary Dee (USA)
1986	Cindy Baxter (USA)
1988	Heather Stupp (Can)
1990	Heather Stupp (Can)
1992	Michelle Gould (USA)
1994	Michelle Gould (USA)

Most titles: 3 Doug Ganim (USA) men's doubles 1988, 1990, 1992

Team winners
The USA have been overall team champions at all seven championships, except 1986 when they tied with Canada. Canada won the men's team title in 1986 and 1988, but the other five men's and all seven women's team titles went to the USA.

Racketball
Racketball (British spelling), using squash courts 32ft by 21ft (9.75m by 6.4m) was introduced in 1976, by Ian Wright, at Bexley SRC, Kent using a less bouncy ball than that used in the larger American courts. The British Racketball Association (BRA) was formed and staged inaugural British National Championships in 1984.
(Years relate to first part of winter season)*Winners:*

British Racketball Championships

Men
1984	Denis Secher
1985	John Hakes
1986	Murray Scott
1987	Matthew Parker
1988-9	Eric Sommers
1990-1	Simon Martin
1992	Steve Bateman
1993-5	Nathan Dugan

Women
1984	Greer Batty
1985-7	Bett Dryhurst
1988	Kim Kelly & Bett Dryhurst
1989	Bett Dryhurst
1990	Kim Kelly
1991	Bett Dryhurst
1992-5	Mary Newell

Rackets

A racket and ball game for two or four players, derived as with other such games from various forms of hand ball games played in the Middle Ages. In England it was often played against walls of buildings, especially those of the Fleet Prison, London in the 18th century. An inmate Robert Mackay claimed the first world title in 1820.

The first closed court was built in 1853 at the Prince's Club, Hans Place, London. The English governing body, the Tennis and Rackets Association was formed in 1907.

World Champions
Determined on a challenge basis, world champions have been:
1820	Robert Mackay (UK)
1825-34	Thomas Pittman (UK)
1834-8	John Pittman (UK)
1838-40	John Lamb (UK)
1840-6	*vacant*
1846-60	L C Mitchell (UK)
1860	Francis Erwood (UK)
1862-3	Sir William Hart-Dyke (UK)
1863-6	Henry Gray (UK)

1866-75	William Gray (UK)
1876-8	H B Fairs (UK)
1878-87	Joseph Gray (UK)
1887-1902	Peter Latham (UK)
1903-11	J Jamsetji (Ind)
1911-3	Charles Williams (UK)
1913-28	Jock Soutar (USA)
1929-35	Charles Williams (UK)
1937-47	David Milford (UK)
1947-54	James Dear (UK)
1954-71	Geoffrey Atkins (UK)
1972-3	William Surtees (USA)
1973-4	Howard Angus (UK)
1975-81	William Surtees (USA)
1981-4	John Prenn (UK)
1984-6	William Boone (UK)
1986-8	John Prenn (UK)
1988-	James Male (UK)

World Doubles Championships

Held over two legs, first in 1990.

1990	James Male and John Prenn (UK) beat Neil Smith and Shannon Hazell (UK)
1992	Neil Smith and Shannon Hazell (UK) beat William Boone and John Prenn (UK)
1993	Neil Smith and Shannon Hazell (UK) beat James Male and John Prenn (UK)

British Amateur Championships

Held annually, first in 1888 at singles and in 1890 at doubles.

Singles Winners from 1969

1969	Charles Swallow
1970-1	Martin Smith
1972-5	Howard Angus
1976	William Boone
1977	Charles Hue Williams
1978	William Boone
1979-80	John Prenn
1981	William Boone
1982-3	John Prenn
1984-5	William Boone
1986	James Male*
1987	William Boone
1988	James Male (Jan)
1989-90	William Boone
1991	James Male*
1992	John Prenn*
1993	James Male*
1994	William Boone *
1995	James Male*

* *December the previous year*

Most wins

9	Edgar M Baerlein 1903, 1905, 1908-11, 1920-1, 1923
9	William Boone
8	Henry K Foster 1894-1900, 1904
7	David Milford 1930, 1935-8, 1950-1
5	John Thompson 1954-5, 1957-9
5	John Prenn
5	James Male

Doubles Winners from 1969

1969-71	Richard Gracey & Martin Smith
1972-3	Howard Angus & Charles Hue Williams
1974	Geofrey Atkins & Charles Hue Williams
1975-7	William Boone & Tom Pugh
1978-9	Howard Angus & Andrew Milne
1980-4	William Boone & Randall Crawley (6 wins)
1985	John Prenn & Charles Hue Williams
1986	William Boone & Randall Crawley
1987	James Male & Rupert Owen-Browne
1988-91	James Male & John Prenn
1992	William Boone & Tim Cockroft
1993	James Male & John Prenn
1994	William Boone & Tim Cockroft
1995	James Male & John Prenn

Most wins
by the same pair:
10 David Milford & John Thompson 1948, 1950-2, 1954-9

by individuals with various partners:

12	William Boone
11	David Milford also in 1938
11	John Thompson also in 1966
8	Harry Foster 1893-4, 1896-1900, 1903
8	Lord Aberdare (formerly the Hon. C N Bruce) 1921, 1924-8, 1930, 1934

British Open Championships

Held irregularly for the Sheppard Cup 1929-71 on a challenge basis. From 1971 there has been an annual championship, held first as the Louis Roederer Open Invitation Tournament. From 1981 Celestion Loudspeakers have sponsored the sport and the event is now the Celestion Open Championship.

Sheppard Cup champions

1929-30	Cyril Simpson
1932	Lord Aberdare
1933	Ian Akers-Douglas
1934	Albert Cooper
1936	David Milford
1946	James Dear
1951	James Dear
1954	Geoffrey Atkins
1959	John Thompson
1960	James Dear
1961	Geoffrey Atkins
1964	Geoffrey Atkins
1967	James Leonard
1970	Charles Swallow
1971	Martin Smith
1971	Howard Angus

Open Singles Champions

1971-3	Howard Angus
1974	William Surtees
1975-6	Howard Angus
1977	John Prenn
1978	Howard Angus
1979	William Boone
1980-3	John Prenn
1984	William Boone

1985	John Prenn
1986	William Boone
1987-9	James Male
1990	Neil Smith
1991	James Male
1992	Shannon Hazell
1993-4	Neil Smith
1995	William Boone

Open Doubles winners
First held 1981

1981-5	William Boone & Randall Crawley
1986-90	John Prenn & James Male
1991-2	Neil Smith & Shannon Hazell
1993	John Prenn & James Male
1994	William Boone & Tim Cockroft

Olympic Games

Rackets was included in the 1908 Olympics, when gold medals were won at singles by Evan Noel (UK) and doubles by Vane Pennel and John Jacob Astor (UK).

Real Tennis

An indoor racket and ball game, which was first played as Jeu de paume in France in monastery cloisters in the 11th century. From the Middle Ages it was played by royalty, particularly by several Kings of France, where the game was extremely popular around 1600. It spread to other parts of Europe and was played by Henry VII and Henry VIII of England, but declined considerably in popularity in the 17th and 18th centuries.

The English governing body, the Tennis and Rackets Association was formed in 1907.

World Champions

The first recorded world champion is the oldest for any sport, the Frenchman Clergé from 1740.
Determined on a challenge basis, world champions have been:

Men's singles

c.1740-50	Clergé (Fra)
1765-85	Raymond Masson (Fra)
1785-1816	Joseph Barcellon (Fra)
1816-9	Marchesio (Ita)
1819-29	Philip Cox (UK)
1829-62	Edmond Barre (Fra)
1862-71	Edmund Tomkins (UK)
1871-85	George Lambert (UK)
1885-90	Tom Pettitt (USA)
1890-95	Charles Saunders (UK)
1895-1905	Peter Latham (UK)
1905-7	Cecil Fairs (UK)
1907-8	Peter Latham (UK)
1908-12	Cecil Fairs (UK)
1912-4	Fred Covey (UK)
1914-6	Jay Gould (USA)
1916-28	Fred Covey (UK)
1928-54	Pierre Etchebaster (Fra)
1955-7	James Dear (UK)
1957-9	Albert Johnson (UK)
1959-69	Northrup Knox (USA)
1969-72	G.H.'Pete' Bostwick (USA)
1972-5	Jimmy Bostwick (USA)
1976-81	Howard Angus (UK)
1981-7	Chris Ronaldson (UK)
1987-94	Wayne Davies (Aus)
1994	Robert Fahey (Aus)

Women's singles
First played in 1985.

1985	Judy Clarke (Aus)
1987	Judy Clarke (Aus)
1989	Penny Fellows (UK)
1991	Penny Lumley (née Fellows) (UK)
1993	Sally Jones (UK)
1995	Penny Lumley (UK)

Women's doubles
First played in 1985.

1985	Judy Clarke & Annie Link (Aus)
1987	Lesley Ronaldson & Katrina Allen (UK)
1989	Alex Warren-Piper & Melissa Briggs (UK)
1991	Sally Jones & Alex Garside (née Warren-Piper) (UK)
1993	Charlotte Cornwallis & Penny Lumley (UK

World Invitation Tournament

Men's singles

1987-8	Lachlan Deuchar (Aus)
1990	Lachlan Deuchar (Aus)

Men's Doubles

1988	Wayne Davies & Lachlan Deuchar (Aus)
1990	Wayne Davies & Lachlan Deuchar (Aus)

Women's Singles

1988	Sally Jones (UK)
1990	Alex Warren-Piper (UK)

Women's Doubles

1988	D Barrabé & Penny Fellows (UK)
1990	Sally Jones & Alex Warren-Piper (UK)

Olympic Games

The sport was included once in the Olympic Games, in 1908, when the title was won by Jay Gould (USA).

British Amateur Championships

Held annually, first in 1888 at singles and in 1920 at doubles. All winners from UK unless stated.

Singles Winners from 1965

1965	David Warburg
1966-80	Howard Angus
1981	Alan Lovell
1982	Howard Angus
1983-6	Alan Lovell
1987-9	Julian Snow
1990	James Male
1991-5	Julian Snow

Most wins
16 Howard Angus 1966-80, 1982
13 Edgar M.Baerlein 1912, 1914, 1919-27, 1929-30
9 Eustace Miles 1899-1903, 1905-6, 1909-10

Doubles Winners from 1967
1967-70 Howard Angus & David Warburg
1972-4 Howard Angus & David Warburg
1975 John Clench & Alan Lovell
1976 Howard Angus & David Warburg
1977-9 Alan Lovell & Andrew Windham
1980 Howard Angus & Richard Cooper
1981 Alan Lovell & Michael Dean
1982 Peter Seabrook & John Ward
1983-6 Alan Lovell & Michael Dean
1987 Julian Snow & James Male
1988 Alan Lovell & Michael Dean
1989-90 James Male (UK) & Michael Happell (Aus)
1991-3 Julian Snow & Michael McMurragh
1994 James Acheson-Gray & Nigel Pendrigh

Most wins
by the same pair
8 Howard Angus & David Warburg 1967-70,
1972-4, 1976
7 Edgar M Baerlein & Lowther Lees 1929-31, 1934-7

by individuals with various partners
11 Edgar M Baerlein 1920-2, 1925, 1929-31, 1934-7
10 Lowther Lees 1926, 1928-31, 1934-7, 1946
10 Alan Lovell 1975, 1977-9, 1981, 1983-6, 1988

British Open Championships
The Open championship on a challenge basis for the Prince's Club Shield (to 1976), has been won as follows: (all winners from UK unless stated)

1931 Edgar Baerlein
1931 E Ratcliffe
1932 W A Groom
1934-5 Lowther Lees
1938 James Dear
1950 Ronald Hughes
1951 James Dear
1956 James Dear
1962 Ronald Hughes
1967-8 Frank Willis
1970 Howard Angus
1972 Howard Angus
1975-6 Howard Angus

The Open Invitation tournament was contested annually for the Field Trophy 1965-73; it was sponsored by Cutty Sark, 1974-8, then by Unigate, Rank Xerox and George Wimpey.

Open Singles
1965 Ronald Hughes
1966-7 Frank Willis
1968 Howard Angus
1969 Frank Willis
1970 Howard Angus
1970 (Nov) Frank Willis
1971 Norwood Cripps
1972 Frank Willis
1973 Norwood Cripps
1974 Howard Angus
1975 Chris Ennis
1976-7 Howard Angus
1978 Chris Ronaldson
1979 Howard Angus
1980-5 Chris Ronaldson (two in 1980)
1986-91 Lachlan Deuchar (Aus)
1992-4 Julian Snow
Most wins: 8 Ronaldson, Angus; 6 Deuchar

Open Doubles
First held 1971
1971 Ronald Hughes & Norwood Cripps
1972 Frank Willis & Chris Ennis
1973-5 Charles Swallow & Norwood Cripps
1976 Frank Willis & David Cull
1977-80 Norwood Cripps & Alan Lovell
(5 wins, two in 1977)
1981 Chris Ronaldson & Michael Dean
1982 Norwood Cripps & Alan Lovell
1983 Chris Ronaldson & Michael Dean
1984-90 Wayne Davies & Lachlan Deuchar (Aus)
1991 Chris Bray & Mike Gooding
1992 Lachlan Deuchar & Wayne Davies (Aus)
1993 Chris Bray & Mike Gooding
1994 Lachlan Deuchar & Robert Fahey (Aus)
1995 Chris Bray & Mike Gooding

Women's Open Singles
First held 1978
1978 Anna Moore
1979-81 Lesley Ronaldson
1982 Judy Clarke (Aus)
1983-6 Katrina Allen
1986 (Nov) Lesley Ronaldson
1987 Sally Jones
1988 Penny Fellows
1989 Sally Jones
1990 Alex Warren-Piper
1991 Penny Fellows
1992 Charlotte Cornwallis
1993 Penny Lumley (née Fellows)
1994 Alex Garside
1995 Penny Lumley

Women's Open Doubles
1989 Sally Jones & Alex Warren-Piper
1990 Alex Warren-Piper & Melissa Briggs
1991 Penny Fellows & Alex Garside
(née Warren-Piper)
1992-3 Sally Grant (née Jones) & Alex Garside
1994 Fiona Deuchar & Mandy Happell (Aus)
1995 Sally Jones & Sue Haswell

Rodeo

Rodeo was developed from the 18th century fiestas of the early days of the North American cattle industry. Ranching skills, such as bronc busting, bull riding, steer wrestling and calf roping have become highly competitive activities in the professional rodeos held throughout the USA, Canada and Mexico. A bronc riding competition for prize money was held in Deer Trail, Colorado, USA in 1869, while claims to the first rodeo held before paying spectators are many. The earliest documented, organised competition was the West of the Pecos Rodeo at Pecos, Texas, first held in 1883.

The governing body is the Professional Rodeo Cowboys Association (PRCA), the name taken in 1974 by the Rodeo Cowboys Association, originally formed in 1936, and known as the Cowboys Turtles Association until 1945.

Standard rodeo events are: bareback riding, saddle bronc riding, bull riding, calf roping and steer wrestling with three additional events also often contested: team roping, barrel racing and single-steer roping. In the first three riding events the object is to stay on for a minimum of eight seconds; in the others the object is to complete the task in the minimum time.

National Finals Rodeo

Each December the PRCA and Women's Professional Rodeo Association (WPRA) stage the National Finals Rodeo (NFR), which is the culmination of the season's rodeo events. The top 15 money-earning cowboys in each of six PRCA events and the top 15 WPRA barrel racers compete at the Finals. The first NFR was in 1959 in Dallas, Texas. Oklahoma City, Oklahoma hosted the Finals for 20 years before the event was moved to Las Vegas, Nevada in 1985. *Most wins at each event:*

Saddle bronc riding	6 Casey Tibbs 1949, 1951-4, 1959
Bareback bronc riding	5 Joe Alexander 1971-5; 5 Bruce Ford 1979-80, 1982-3, 1987
Bull riding	8 Donnie Gay 1974-7, 1979-81, 1984; 7 Jim Shoulders 1951, 1954-9
Calf roping	8 Dean Oliver 1955, 1958, 1960-4, 1969; 8 Roy Cooper 1976-8, 1980-4
Steer wrestling	6 Homer Pettigrew 1940, 1942-5, 1948
Team roping	7 Jake Barnes & Clay O'Brien Cooper 1985-9, 1992, 1994
Steer roping	9 Guy Allen 1977, 1980, 1982, 1984, 1989, 1991-4
Women's barrel racing	10 Charmayne Rodman 1984-93
All events	16 Jim Shoulders 1949-59

All-Around Cowboy World Champions

Won annually by the cowboy who has won the most money in two or more different events. *Winners, with money won:*

1947	Todd Whatley	-
1948	Gerald Roberts	21,766
1949	Jim Shoulders	21,496
1950	Bill Linderman	30,715
1951	Casey Tibbs	29,104
1952	Harry Tompkins	30,934
1953	Bill Linderman	33,674
1954	Buck Rutherford	40,404
1955	Casey Tibbs	42,065
1956	Jim Shoulders	43,381
1957	Jim Shoulders	33,299
1958	Jim Shoulders	33,212
1959	Jim Shoulders	32,905
1960	Harry Tompkins	32,522
1961	Benny Reynolds	31,309
1962	Tom Nesmith	32,611
1963	Dean Oliver	31,329
1964	Dean Oliver	31,150
1965	Dean Oliver	33,163
1966	Larry Mahan	40,358
1967	Larry Mahan	51,996
1968	Larry Mahan	49,129
1969	Larry Mahan	57,726
1970	Larry Mahan	41,493
1971	Phil Lyne	49,245
1972	Phil Lyne	60,852
1973	Larry Mahan	64,447
1974	Tom Ferguson	66,929
1975	Leo Camarillo & Tom Ferguson	50,300
1976	Tom Ferguson	87,908
1977	Tom Ferguson	76,730
1978	Tom Ferguson	103,734
1979	Tom Ferguson	96,272
1980	Paul Tierney	105,568
1981	Jimmie Cooper	105,862
1982	Chris Lybbert	123,709
1983	Roy Cooper	153,391
1984	Dee Pickett	122,618
1985	Lewis Feild	130,347
1986	Lewis Feild	166,042
1987	Lewis Feild	144,334
1988	Dave Appleton	121,546
1989	Ty Murray	134,806
1990	Ty Murray	213,772
1991	Ty Murray	244,231
1992	Ty Murray	225,992
1993	Ty Murray	297,896
1994	Ty Murray	246,170

Most wins: 6 Mahan, Ferguson, Murray

The leading career earnings winners
$1,510,795 Roy Cooper
$1,441,877 Ty Murray

Roller Hockey

An adaptation of hockey and ice hockey, played as a five-a-side game on roller skates. It was first known in Europe as Rink Hockey. The Amateur Rink Hockey Association was formed in Britain, originally c.1898, taking this name in 1908. The NHRA is affiliated to the Fédération Internationale de Roller Skating. The first European Championships were held at Herne Bay, England in 1926.

World Championships

First held in 1936. A biennial tournament, the World Group A Championship was transferred to odd years from 1989. *Wins:*

14	Portugal	1947-50, 1952, 1956, 1958, 1960, 1962, 1968, 1974, 1982, 1991, 1993
10	Spain	1951, 1954-5, 1964, 1966, 1970, 1972, 1976, 1980, 1989
3	Italy	1953, 1986, 1988
2	England	1936, 1939
2	Argentina	1978, 1984

Women's World Championships

First held in October 1992. *Winners:*

1992 Canada
1994 Spain

Olympic Games

Roller Hockey was staged as a demonstration sport at the 1992 Olympic Games. Gold medallists were Argentina.

European Championships

Preceded the world championships, with which it was amalgamated from 1936 to 1957. *Wins:*

18	Portugal	1947-50, 1952, 1956, 1959, 1961, 1963, 1965, 1967, 1971, 1973, 1975, 1977, 1987, 1992, 1994
12	England	1926-32, 1934, 1936-9
9	Spain	1951, 1954-5, 1957, 1969, 1979, 1981, 1983, 1985
3	Italy	1953, 1990-1

A women's European championship was held unofficially in 1989, and officially from 1991. *Winners:*

Netherlands	1989
Italy	1991, 1993

Roller Skating

The first ever roller skate had been invented by Joseph Merlin of Belgium. He demonstrated it in 1760, but it was not a success. The modern four-wheeled roller skate was introduced by James Plympton in the USA in 1863. At first it was used by ice skaters for practice, but soon developed into a sport in its own right. The first roller rink in the USA was opened by Plympton in 1866 at Newport, Rhode Island. In Britain the National Skating Association assumed control of roller skating in 1893 and staged the first national championships the following year. The International Roller Skating Federation (Fédération Internationale de Patinage à Roulettes) was founded in 1924; it now has its headquarters in Lincoln, Nebraska.

In 1937 the first world championships were held for speed skating (at Monza) and in the same year European championships for figure skating were introduced (at Stuttgart).

World Figure Skating Championships

First held in 1947. *Winners:*

Men - Combined figures and free skating

1947	Donald Mounce (USA)
1949	Karl Peter (Swi)
1951-2	Freimut Stein (FRG)
1955-6	Franz Ningel (FRG)
1958-9	Karl-Heinz Losch (FRG)
1961-2	Karl-Heinz Losch (FRG)
1965	Hans Dahmen (FRG)
1966	Karl-Heinz Losch (FRG)
1967	Hans Dahmen (FRG)
1968	Jack Courtney (USA)
1970-2	Michael Obrecht (FRG)
1973	Randy Dayney (USA)
1974	Michael Obrecht (FRG)
1975	Leonardo Lienhard (Swi)
1976-8	Thomas Nieder (FRG)
1979-82	Michael Butzke (GDR)
1983	Joachim Helmle (FRG)
1984-5	Michele Biserni (Ita)
1986	Michele Tolomini (Ita)
1987-9	Sandro Guerra (Ita)
1990	Samo Kokorovec (Ita)
1991-2	Sandro Guerra (Ita)
1993	Samo Kokorovec (Ita)
1994	Lee Taylor (UK)

Most wins: 5 Losch, Guerra

Women - Combined figures and free skating

1947	Ursula Wehrli (Swi)
1949	Franca Rio (Ita)
1951	Franca Rio (Ita)
1952	Lotte Cadenbach (FRG)
1955	Helene Kienzle (FRG)
1956	Rita Blumenberg (FRG)
1958	Marika Kilius (FRG)
1959	Ute Kitz (FRG)
1961	Marlies Fahse (FRG)
1962	Fränzi Schmidt (Swi)
1965-8	Astrid Bader (FRG)
1970	Christine Kreutzfeldt (FRG)
1971-2	Petra Häusler (FRG)
1973-5	Sigrid Mullenbach (FRG)
1976-8	Natalie Dunn (USA)
1979-81	Petra Schneider (née Ernert) (FRG)
1982-4	Claudia Bruppacher (FRG)
1985-7	Chiara Sartori (Ita)
1988-92	Rafaella Del Vinaccio (Ita)
1993-4	Letizia Tinghi (Ita)

Most wins: 5 Del Vinaccio, 4 Bader

Pairs

1947	Fernand Leemans & Elvire Collin (Bel)
1949	Ken Byrne & Jean Phethean (UK)

1951	Paul Falk & Ria Baran (FRG)
1952	Günther Koch & Sigrid Knake (FRG)
1955-6	Günther Koch & Sigrid Knake (FRG)
1958	Werner Mensching & Rita Blumenberg (FRG)
1959	Dieter Fingerle & Susu Schneider (FRG)
1961-2	Walther Hoffman & Maria Ludolph (FRG)
1965-7	Dieter Fingerle & Uta Keller (FRG)
1968	Jack Courtney & Sheryl Trueman (USA)
1970-2	Ronald Robovitsky & Gail Robovitsky (USA)
1973	Louis Stovel & Vicki Handyside (USA)
1974	Ron Sabo & Susan McDonald (USA)
1975-6	Ron Sabo & Darlene Waters (USA)
1977	Ray Chapatta & Karen Mejia (USA)
1978	Pat Jones & Rooie Coleman (USA)
1979	Ray Chapatta & Karen Mejia (USA)
1980-2	Paul Price & Tina Kniesley (USA)
1983-6	John Arishita & Tammy Jeru (USA)
1987-8	Fabio Trevisani & Monica Mezzadri (Ita)
1989	David DeMotte & Nicky Armstrong (USA)
1990-1	Larry McGrew & Tammy Jeru (USA)
1992-3	Patrick Venerucci & Maura Ferri (Ita)
1994	Patrick Venerucci & Beatrice Palazzi-Rossi (Ita)

Most wins: 6 Tammy Jeru, 4 Dieter Fingerle, John Arishtita

The following skaters won world titles on both ice and rollers:
Ria and Paul Falk - roller pairs 1951, ice pairs 1951-2
Marika Kilius - roller 1958, ice pairs 1963-4

Dance

1947	Fred Ludwig & Barbara Gallagher (USA)
1949	Ken Byrne & Jean Phethean (UK)
1952	Ted Ellis & Marion Mercer (UK)
1955	Karl-Heinz Beyer & Marga Schäfer (FRG)
1956	Günther Koch & Sigrid Knake (FRG)
1958	Sydney Cooper & Patricia Cooper (UK)
1959	Peter Kwiet & Rita Paucka (FRG)
1961	Peter Kwiet & Rita Kwiet (née Paucka) (FRG)
1962	Brian Colclough & Patricia Colclough (UK)
1965	Brian Colclough & Patricia Colclough (UK)
1966-7	Hans-Jürgen Schamberger & Martha Schamberger (FRG)
1968	Donald Rudalawicz & Rita Smith (USA)
1970-1	Richard Horne & Jane Pankey (USA)
1972	Tom Straker & Bonnie Lambert (USA)
1973	James Stephens & Jane Puracchio (USA)
1974	Udo Donsdorf & Christine Henke (FRG)
1975-6	Kerry Cavazzi & Jane Puracchio (USA)
1977-9	Dan Littel & Florence Arsenault (USA)
1980	Torsten Carels & Gabriele Achenbach (GDR)
1981-2	Mark Howard & Cindy Smith (USA)
1983-4	David Golub & Angela Famiano (USA)
1985	Martin Hauss & Andrea Steudte (FRG)
1986	Scott Myers & Anna Danks (USA)
1987	Rolf Ferando & Lori Walsh (USA)
1988	Peter Wulf & Michaela Mitzlaff (FRG)
1989-91	Greg Goody & Jodee Viola (USA)
1992-3	Doug Wait & Deanna Monahan (USA)
1994	Timothy Patten & Lisa Friday (USA)

World Speed Skating Championships

First contested in 1937 for men and 1953 for women. Held on track or road, men's and women's events at distances from 300m to 10000m.

Most titles won (Track/Road)

Men: 15 Giuseppe Cantarella (Ita) 7/8 1964-80, Giuseppe Cruciani (Ita) 8/7 1978-83
Women: 18 Alberta Vianello (Ita) 8/10 1953-65, Annie Lambrechts (Bel) 1/17 1964-81

World Speed Skating Records

Men - Track

	min:sec	
300m	25.248	Oscar Galliazzo (Ita) 1987
500m	41.233	Giuseppe De Persio (Ita) 1980
1000m	1:23.09	G.L.Botero (Col) 1988
1500m	2:07.770	Giuseppe De Persio (Ita) 1980
2000m	2:54.56	Roland Klöss (FRG) 1988
3000m	4:21.764	Giuseppe De Persio (Ita) 1980
5000m	7:34.938	Marco Giupponi (Ita) 1987
10,000m	15:14.876	Oscar Galliazzo (Ita) 1987
15,000m	23:07.868	Oscar Galliazzo (Ita) 1987
20,000m	30:52.792	P.Bomben (Ita) 1987
30,000m	47:42.820	Tommaso Rossi (Ita) 1987
50,000m	1hr 20:17.736	Tommaso Rossi (Ita) 1987

Road - where superior to track times

300m	24.547	Tony Muse (USA) 1994
500m	40.910	Patrizio Sarto (Ita) 1987
1000m	1:22.124	Patrizio Sarto (Ita) 1987
2000m	2:51.333	Giuseppe De Persio (Ita) 1987
5000m	7:32.462	Giuseppe De Persio (Ita) 1987
10,000m	14:55.64	Giuseppe De Persio (Ita) 1988

Women - Track

	min:sec	
300m	26.986	S.De Cesaris (Ita) 1987
500m	44.404	S.De Cesaris (Ita) 1987
1000m	1:27.60	Barbara Fischer (FRG) 1988
1500m	2:14.644	Marisa Canafoglia (Ita) 1987
2000m	3:02.25	Nicola Malmström (FRG) 1988
3000m	4:38.464	Marisa Canafoglia (Ita) 1987
5000m	7:48.508	Marisa Canafoglia (Ita) 1987
10,000m	15:58.022	Marisa Canafoglia (Ita) 1987
15,000m	26:18.290	Francesca Monteverde (Ita) 1987
20,000m	32:53.970	Annie Lambrechts (Bel) 1985
30,000m	49:15.906	Annie Lambrechts (Bel) 1985
50.000m	1hr 21:26.942	Annie Lambrechts (Bel) 1985

Road - where superior to track times

300m	26.794	Marisa Canafoglia (Ita) 1987
1500m	2:14.122	Marisa Canafoglia (Ita) 1987
15,000m	26:02.624	Patrizia Biagini (Ita) 1987

Rowing

Rowing originates from ancient times but the sport in its present form dates to 1715 when Irish comedian Thomas Doggett instituted his famous race for scullers. There were many races at Walton in 1768, but the first known regatta was on the Thames at Ranelagh Gardens, Putney in 1775. The international governing body is the Fédération Internationale des Sociétés d'Aviron (FISA), founded in 1892, two years after the Belgian Federation of Rowing Clubs had staged a 'European Championship', with just one category of boat, the sculling outrigger. The winner over the 2800m course was Edouard Lescrauwaet (Bel). FISA held their first official European Championships in 1893.

Olympic Games

The first Olympic rowing competition was on the River Seine over a 1750m course in 1900, but in more recent times rowing courses have been on still waters. The standard length is now 2000m, but the course measured 2 miles (3219m) in 1904, 1.5 miles (2414m) in 1908 and 1883m in 1948. Weather and water conditions affect the times recorded. *Winners:*

Men

Single Sculls
1900 Henri Barrelet (Fra) 7:35.6
1904 Frank Greer (USA) 10:08.5
1906 Gaston Delaplane (Fra) 5:53.4
1908 Harry Blackstaffe (UK) 9:26.0
1912 William Kinnear (UK) 7:47.6
1920 John Kelly Snr (USA) 7:35.0
1924 Jack Beresford Jr (UK) 7:49.2
1928 Henry Pearce (Aus) 7:11.0
1932 Henry Pearce (Aus) 7:44.4
1936 Gustav Schäfer (Ger) 8:21.5
1948 Mervyn Wood (Aus) 7:24.4
1952 Yuriy Tyukalov (USSR) 8:12.8
1956 Vyacheslav Ivanov (USSR) 8:02.5
1960 Vyacheslav Ivanov (USSR) 7:13.96
1964 Vyacheslav Ivanov (USSR) 8:22.51
1968 Henri Jan Wienese (Hol) 7:47.80
1972 Yuriy Malishev (USSR) 7:10.12
1976 Pertti Karppinen (Fin) 7:29.03
1980 Pertti Karppinen (Fin) 7:09.61
1984 Pertti Karpinnen (Fin) 7:00.24
1988 Thomas Lange (GDR) 6:49.86
1992 Thomas Lange (Ger) 6:51.40

Double Sculls
1904 John Mulcahy/William Varley (USA) 10:03.2
1920 Paul Costello/John Kelly Snr (USA) 7:09.0
1924 Paul Costello/John Kelly Snr (USA) 7:45.0
1928 Paul Costello/Charles McIlvaine (USA) 6:41.4
1932 William Garrett Gilmore/Kenneth Myers (USA) 7:17.4
1936 Jack Beresford/Leslie Southwood (UK) 7:20.8
1948 Richard Burnell/Herbert Bushnell (UK) 6:51.3
1952 Tranquilo Capozzo/Eduardo Guerrero (Arg) 7:32.2

1956 Aleksandr Berkutov/Yuriy Tyukalov (USSR) 7:24.0
1960 Václav Kozák/Pavel Schmidt (Cs) 6:47.50
1964 Boris Dubrovsky/Oleg Tyurin (USSR) 7:10.66
1968 Anatoliy Sass/Aleksandr Timoshinin (USSR) 6:51.82
1972 Gennadiy Korshikov/Aleksandr Timoshinin (USSR) 7:01.77
1976 Alf Hansen/Frank Hansen (Nor) 7:13.20
1980 Joachim Dreifke/Klaus Kröppelien (GDR) 6:24.33
1984 Bradley Lewis/Paul Enquist (USA) 6:36.87
1988 Ronald Florjin/Nicolaas Rienks (Hol) 6:21.13
1992 Peter Antonie/Mark Hawkins (Aus) 6:17.72

Coxless Pairs
1904 Robert Farnam/Joseph Ryan (USA) 10:57.0
1908 John Fenning/Gordon Thomson (UK) 9:41.0
1924 Antonie Beijnen/Wilhelm Rösingh (Hol) 8:19.4
1928 Kurt Moeschter/Bruno Müller (Ger) 7:06.4
1932 Lewis Clive/Arthur Edwards (UK) 8:00.0
1936 Willie Eichorn/Hugo Strauss (Ger) 8:16.1
1948 George Laurie/John Wilson (UK) 7:21.1
1952 Charles Logg/Thomas Price (USA) 8:20.7
1956 James Fifer/Duvall Hecht (USA) 7:55.4
1960 Valentin Boreyko/Oleg Golovanov (USSR) 7:02.01
1964 George Hungerford/Roger Jackson (Can) 7:32.94
1968 Heinz-Jürgen Bothe/Jörg Lucke (GDR) 7:26.56
1972 Siegfried Brietzke/Wolfgang Mager (GDR) 6:53.16
1976 Bernd Landvoigt/Jörg Landvoigt (GDR) 7:23.31
1980 Bernd Landvoigt/Jörg Landvoigt (GDR) 6:48.01
1984 Petru Iosub/Valer Toma (Rom) 6:45.39
1988 Andrew Holmes/Steven Redgrave (UK) 6:36.84
1992 Matthew Pinsent/Steven Redgrave (UK) 6:27.72

Coxed Pairs (Coxes names omitted)
1900 François Brandt/Roelof Klein (Hol) 7:34.2
1906 Enrico Bruna/Emilio Fontanella (Ita) 4:23.0 *(1000m)*
1906 Enrico Bruna/Emilio Fontanella (Ita) 7:32.4 *(1609m)*
1920 Ercole Olgeni/Giovanni Scatturin (Ita) 7:56.0
1924 Edouard Candeveau/Alfred Felber (Swi) 8:39.0
1928 Hans Schöchlin/Karl Schöchlin (Swi) 7:42.6
1932 Joseph Schauers/ Charles Kieffer (USA) 8:25.8
1936 Gerhard Gustmann/Herbert Adamski (Ger) 8:36.9
1948 Finn Pedersen/Tage Henriksen (Den) 8:00.5
1952 Raymond Salles/Gaston Mercier (Fra) 8:28.6
1956 Arthur Ayrault/Conn Findlay (USA) 8:26.1
1960 Bernhard Knubel/Heinz Renneberg (FRG) 7:29.14
1964 Edward Ferry/Conn Findlay (USA) 8:21.23
1968 Primo Baran/Renzo Sambo (Ita) 8:04.81
1972 Wolfgamg Gunkel/Jörg Lucke (GDR) 7:17.25
1976 Harald Jährling/Freidrich-Wilhlem Ulrich (GDR) 7:58.99
1980 Harald Jährling/Freidrich-Wilhlem Ulrich (GDR) 7:02.54
1984 Carmine & Giuseppe Abbagnale (Ita) 7:05.99
1988 Carmine & Giuseppe Abbagnale (Ita) 6:58.79
1992 Greg & Jonny Searle (UK) 6:49.83

Quadruple Sculls
1976 GDR 6:18.65
1980 GDR 5:49.81
1984 FR Germany 5:57.55
1988 Italy 5:53.37
1992 Germany 5:45.17

Coxless Fours
1904 Century BC, St.Louis (USA) 9:53.8
1908 Magdalen College, Oxford (UK) 8:34.0
1924 Great Britain 7:08.6
1928 Great Britain 6:36.0
1932 Great Britain 6:58.2
1936 Germany 7:01.8
1948 Italy 6:39.0
1952 Yugoslavia 7:16.0
1956 Canada 7:08.8
1960 USA 6:26.26
1964 Denmark 6:59.30
1968 GDR 6:39.18
1972 GDR 6:24.27
1976 GDR 6:37.42
1980 GDR 6:08.17
1984 New Zealand 6:03.48
1988 GDR 6:03.11
1992 Australia 5:55.04

Coxed Fours
1900 Germania RC, Hamburg (Ger) 5:59.0*
1900 Cercle de l'Aviron (Fra) 7:11.0*
1906 Italy 8:13.0
1912 Germany 6:59.4
1920 Switzerland 6:54.0
1924 Switzerland 7:18.4
1928 Italy 6:47.8
1932 Germany 7:19.0
1936 Germany 7:16.2
1948 USA 6:50.3
1952 Czechoslovakia 7:33.4
1956 Italy 7:19.4
1960 FR Germany 6:39.12
1964 FR Germany 7:00.44
1968 New Zealand 6:45.62
1972 FR Germany 6:31.85
1976 USSR 6:40.22
1980 GDR 6:14.51
1984 Great Britain 6:18.64
1988 GDR 6:10.74
1992 Romania 5:59.37
Two finals were held in 1900

Eights
1900 Vesper BC (USA) 6:09.8
1904 Vesper BC (USA) 7:50.0
1908 Leander Club (UK) 7:52.0
1912 Leander Club (UK) 6:15.0
1920 USA 6:02.6
1924 USA 6:33.4
1928 USA 6:03.2
1932 USA 6:37.6
1936 USA 6:25.4
1948 USA 5:56.7
1952 USA 6:25.9

Steven Redgrave (right) and Matthew Pinsent

1956 USA 6:35.2
1960 Germany 5:57.18
1964 USA 6:18.23
1968 FR Germany 6:07.00
1972 New Zealand 6:08.94
1976 GDR 5:58.29
1980 GDR 5:49.05
1984 Canada 5:41.32
1988 FR Germany 5:46.05
1992 Canada 5:29.53

Discontinued Events
76-Man Naval rowing boats (2000m)
1906 Varese (Ita) 10:45.0
17-Man Naval Rowing (3000m)
1906 Poros (Gre) 16:35.0
Coxed Fours Inriggers
1912 Denmark 7:47.0

Women
Women rowed over 1000m 1976-84, and over 2000m from 1988

Single Sculls
1976 Christine Scheiblich (GDR) 4:05.56
1980 Sanda Toma (Rom) 3:40.69
1984 Valeria Racila (Rom) 3:40.68
1988 Jutta Behrendt (GDR) 7:47.19
1992 Elisabeta Lipa (Rom) 7:25.54

Double Sculls
1976 Svetla Otzetova/Zdravka Yordanova (Bul)
       3:44.36
1980 Yelena Khlopsteva/Larisa Popova (USSR)
       3:16.27
1984 Marioara Popescu/Elisabeta Oleniuc (Rom)
       3:26.75
1988 Brigit Peter/Martina Schröter (GDR) 7:00.48
1992 Kerstin Köppen/Kathrin Boron (Ger) 6:49.00

Coxless Pairs
1976 Stoyanka Grouitcheva/Siika Kelbetcheva (Bul)
       4:01.22
1980 Cornelia Klier/Ute Steindorf (GDR) 3:30.49
1984 Rodica Arba/Elena Horvat (Rom) 3:32.60
1988 Rodica Arba/Olga Homeghi (Rom) 7:28.13
1992 Marnie McBean/Kathleen Heddle (Can) 7:06.22

Quadruple Sculls
1976 GDR 3:29.99
1980 GDR 3:15.32
1984 Romania 3:14.11
1988 GDR 6:21.06
1992 Germany 6:20.18

Coxed Fours
1976 GDR 3:45.08
1980 GDR 3:19.27
1984 Romania 3:19.30
1988 GDR 6:56.00

Coxless Fours
1992 Canada 6:30.85

Eights
1976 GDR 3:33.32
1980 GDR 3:03.32
1984 USA 2:59.80
1988 GDR 6:15.17
1992 Canada 6:02.62

In the summaries that follow, the following abbreviations are used: 1x single sculls, 2x double sculls, 4x quadruple sculls, 4x+ quadruple sculls with coxswain, 2- coxless pairs, 2+ coxed pairs, 4- coxless fours, 4+ coxed fours, 8+ eights.

Most gold medals
3   John B.Kelly (USA) 1x 1920; 2x 1920, 1924
3   Paul Costello (USA) 2x 1920, 1924, 1928
3   Jack Beresford Jr (UK) 1x 1924; 4+ 1932; 2x 1936
3   Vyacheslav Ivanov (USSR) 1x 1956, 1960, 1964
3   Siegfried Brietzke (GDR) 2- 1972; 4- 1976, 1980
3   Pertti Karpinnen (Fin) 1x 1976, 1980, 1984
3   Steven Redgrave (UK) 4+ 1984, 2- 1988, 2+ 1992

Most medals: (gold/silver/bronze)
5 (3/2/-) Jack Beresford Jr 1920-36 (at five different Games)

The youngest Olympic medallist at any sport is an unknown French boy who coxed the winning Dutch pair in 1900; he was believed to have been between seven and ten years of age. The oldest Olympic medallist, also a winner, was Robert Zimonyi who coxed the US eights in 1964 at 46 yr 180 days. The oldest oarsman to win a gold medal was Guy Nickalls (UK) at 42 yr 170 days in the eights in 1908.

World Championships

The first World Championships were held at Lucerne in 1962. Women's events were first included in 1974. *Winners:*

Men

Single Sculls
1962   Vyacheslav Ivanov (USSR)
1966   Don Spero (USA)
1970   Alberto Demiddi (Arg)
1974   Wolfgang Hönig (GDR)
1975   Peter-Michael.Kolbe (FRG)
1977   Joachim Dreifke (GDR)
1978   Peter-Michael Kolbe (FRG)
1979   Pertti Karppinen (Fin)
1981   Peter-Michael Kolbe (FRG)

1982   Rüdiger Reiche (GDR)
1983   Peter-Michael Kolbe (FRG)
1985   Pertti Karppinen (Fin)
1986   Peter-Michael Kolbe (FRG)
1987   Thomas Lange (GDR)
1989   Thomas Lange (GDR)
1990   Yuriy Yaanson (USSR)
1991   Thomas Lange (Ger)
1993   Derek Porter (Can)
1994   André Willms (Ger)

Double Sculls
1962   René Duhamel/Bernard Monnereau (Fra)
1966   Melchior Bürgin/Martin Studach (Swi)
1970   Jörgen Engelbrecht/Niels Secher (Den)
1974   Christof Kreuziger/Hans-Ulrich Schmied (GDR)
1975   Alf Hansen/Frank Hansen (Nor)
1977   Chris Baillieu/Michael Hart (UK)
1978-9 Alf Hansen/Frank Hansen (Nor)
1981   Klaus Kröppelien/Joachim Dreifke (GDR)
1982   Alf Hansen/Rolf Thorsen (Nor)
1983   Thomas Lange/Uwe Heppner (GDR)
1985   Thomas Lange/Uwe Heppner (GDR)
1986   Alberto Belgori/Igor Pescialli (Ita)
1987   Vasil Radeyev/Danatyl Yordanov (Bul)
1989   Lars Bjønness/Rol Bent Thorsen (Nor)
1990   Christophe Zerbst/Arnold Jonke (Aut)
1991   Henk-Jan Zwolle/Nicolaas Rienks (Hol)
1993   Yves Lamarque/Samuel Barathay (Fra)
1994   Ralf Thorsen/Lars Bjønness (Nor)

Coxless Pairs
1962   Dieter Bender/Günther Zumkeller (FRG)
1966   Peter Gorny/Werner Klatt (GDR)
1970   Peter Gorny/Werner Klatt (GDR)
1974-5 Bernd Landvoigt/Jörg Landvoigt (GDR)
1977   Vitaliy Yeliseyev/Aleksandr Kulagin (USSR)
1978-9 Bernd Landvoigt/Jörg Landvoigt (GDR)
1981   Yuriy Pimenov/Nikolay Pimenov (USSR)
1982   Magnus Grepperud/Sverre Loken (Nor)
1983   Carl Ertel/Ulf Sauerbrey (GDR)
1985-6 Nikolay Pimenov/Yuriy Pimenov (USSR)
1987   Andrew Holmes/Steven Redgrave (UK)
1989-90 Thomas Jung/Uwe Kellner (GDR)
1991   Steven Redgrave/Matthew Pinsett (UK)
1993-4 Steven Redgrave/Matthew Pinsett (UK)

Coxed Pairs
1962   FR Germany
1966   Netherlands
1970   Romania
1974   USSR
1975   GDR
1977   Bulgaria
1978   GDR
1979   GDR
1981   Italy
1982   Italy
1983   GDR
1985   Italy
1986   Great Britain
1987   Italy

1989-91	Italy
1993	Great Britain
1994	Croatia

Coxless Fours

1962	FR Germany
1966	GDR
1970	GDR
1974-5	GDR
1977	GDR
1978	USSR
1979	GDR
1981	USSR
1982	Switzerland
1983	FR Germany
1985	FR Germany
1986	USA

1987	GDR
1989	GDR
1990-1	Australia
1993	France
1994	Italy

Coxed Fours

1962	FR Germany
1966	GDR
1970	FR Germany
1974	GDR
1975	USSR
1977-9	GDR
1981-2	GDR
1983	New Zealand
1985	USSR
1986-7	GDR

1989	Romania
1990	GDR
1991	Germany
1993-4	Romania

Quadruple Sculls

1974-5	GDR
1977-9	GDR
1981-2	GDR
1983	FR Germany
1985	Canada
1986-7	USSR
1989	Romania
1990	USSR
1991	USSR
1993	Germany
1994	Italy

Eights

1962	FR Germany
1966	FR Germany
1970	GDR
1974	USA
1975	GDR
1977-9	GDR
1981	USSR
1982-3	New Zealand
1985	USSR
1986	Australia
1987	USA
1989-90	FR Germany
1991	Germany
1993	Germany
1994	USA

Women

Single Sculls

1974-5	Christine Scheiblich (GDR)
1977	Christine Scheiblich (GDR)
1978	Christine Hahn (née Scheiblich) (GDR)
1979	Sanda Toma (Rom)
1981	Sanda Toma (Rom)
1982	Irina Fetissova (USSR)
1983	Jutta Hampe (GDR)
1985	Cornelia Linse (GDR)
1986	Jutta Hampe (GDR)
1987	Magdalena Georgeyeva (Bul)
1989	Elisabeta Lipa (Rom)
1990	Birgit Peter (GDR)
1991	Silken Laumann (Can)
1993	Jana Thieme (Ger)
1994	Trine Hansen (Den)

Double Sculls

1974-5	Yelena Antonova/Galina Yermoleyeva (USSR)
1977	Anke Borchmann/Roswietha Zobelt (GDR)
1978	Svetla Otzetova/Zdravka Yordanova (Bul)
1979	Cornelia Linse/Heidi Westphal (GDR)
1981	Margarita Kokarevitha/Antonina Makhina (USSR)
1982	Yelena Braticko/Antonina Makhina (USSR)
1983	Jutta Scheck/Martina Schröter (GDR)
1985	Sylvia Schurabe/Martina Schröter (GDR)
1986	Sylvia Schurabe/Beate Schramm (GDR)
1987	Steska Madina/Violeta Ninova (Bul)
1989	Jana Sorgers/Beate Schramm (GDR)
1990-1	Kathrin Boron/Beate Schramm (GDR/Ger)
1993-4	Philippa Baker/Brenda Lawson (NZ)

Coxless Pairs

1974	Marilena Ghita/Cornelia Neascu (Rom)
1975	Sabine Dähne/Angelika Noack (GDR)
1977	Sabine Dähne/Angelika Noack (GDR)
1978-9	Cornelia Bugel/Ute Steindorf (GDR)
1981	Sigrid Anders/Iris Rudolph (GDR)
1982-3	Silvia Frohlich/Marita Sandig (GDR)
1985	Rodica Arba/Elena Florea (Rom)
1986-7	Rodica Arba/Olga Homeghi (Rom)
1989	Kathrin Haaker/Judith Zeidler (GDR)
1990	Stefanie Werremeier/Ingeburg Althoff (FRG)
1991	Marnie McBean/Kathleen Heddle (Can)
1993-4	Héléne Cortin/Christine Gossé (Fra)

Quadruple Sculls

1974-5	GDR
1977	GDR
1978	Bulgaria
1979	GDR
1981-2	USSR
1983	USSR
1985-7	GDR
1989-90	GDR
1991	Germany
1993	China
1994	Germany

Coxed Fours

1974-5	GDR
1977-8	GDR
1979	USSR
1981-2	USSR
1983	GDR
1985	GDR
1986-7	Romania

Coxless Fours

1986	USA
1989	GDR
1990	Romania
1991	Canada
1993	China
1994	Netherlands

Eights

1974-5	GDR
1977	GDR
1978-9	USSR
1981-3	USSR
1985-6	USSR
1987	Romania
1989-90	Romania
1991	Canada
1993	Romania
1994	Germany

Lightweight World Champions - Men

Single Sculls

1974	William Belden (USA)
1975	Reto Wyss (Swi)
1976	Raimund Haberl (Aut)
1977	Reto Wyss (Swi)
1978	José Antonio Montosa (Spa)
1979	William Belden (USA)
1980	Christian Georg Wahrlich (FRG)
1981	Scott Roop (USA)
1982	Raimund Haberl (Aut)
1983-4	Bjarne Eltang (Den)

1985	Ruggero Verroca (Ita)
1986	Peter Antonie (Aus)
1987	Willem Van Belleghem (Bel)
1988	Alwin Otten (FRG)
1989-90	Frans Goebel (Hol)
1991	Niall O'Toole (Ire)
1992	Jens Mohr Ernst (Den)
1993-4	Peter Haining (UK)

Double Sculls

1978-9	Pal Bornick/Arne Gilje (Nor)
1980-4	Francesco Esposito/Ruggero Verroca (Ita)
1985	Luc Crispon/Thierry Renault (Fra)
1986	Carl Smith/Allan Whitwell (UK)
1987	Enrico Gandola/Giovanni Calabrese (Ita)
1988	Enrico Gandola/Francesco Esposito (Ita)
1989	Christoph Schmölzer/Walter Rantasa (Aut)
1990	Steve Peterson/Robert Dreher (USA)
1991	Kai Von Warburg/Michael Buchheit (Ger)
1992-3	Gary Lynagh/Bruce Hick (Aus)
1994	Francesco Esposito/Michelangelo Crispi (Ita)

Coxless Pairs

1993	Fernando Climent & Fernando Molina (Spa)
1994	Leonardo Pettinari/Carlo Gaddi (Ita)

Coxless Fours

1974	Australia
1975-7	France
1978	Switzerland
1979	United Kingdom
1980-1	Australia
1982	Italy
1983	Spain
1984	Spain
1985	FR Germany
1986	Italy
1987	FR Germany
1988	Italy
1989-90	FR Germany
1991-2	United Kingdom
1993	USA
1994	Denmark

Quadruple Sculls

1989	FR Germany
1990	Italy
1991	Australia
1992	Italy
1993-4	Austria

Eights

1974	USA
1975-6	FR Germany
1977-8	United Kingdom
1979	Spain
1980	United Kingdom
1981	Denmark
1982	Italy
1983	Spain
1984	Denmark
1985-91	Italy
1992	Denmark
1993	Canada

1994	United Kingdom

Lightweight Women

Single Sculls

1985	Adair Ferguson (Aus)
1986	Maria Sava (Rom)
1987	Magdalena Georgieva (Bul)
1988-9	Kris Karlson (USA)
1990	Mette Bloch Jensen (Den)
1991	Philippa Baker (NZ)
1992	Mette Bloch Jensen (Den)
1993	Michele Darvill (Can)
1994	Constanta Pipota (Rom)

Coxless Pairs

1987	Rodica Arba/Olga Homeghi (Rom)

Double Sculls

1985	Lin Clark/Beryl Crockford (UK)
1986	Chris Ernst/Cary Beth Sands (USA)
1987	Stefka Madina/Violeta Ninova (Bul)
1988	Laurien Vermuist/Ellen Meliesie (Hol)
1989	Cary Beth Sands/Kris Karlson (USA)
1990	Ulla Jensen/Regitze Siggaard (Den)
1991-2	Christiane Weber/Claudia Waldi (Ger)
1993-4	Colleen Miller/Wendy Wiebe (Can)

Coxed Fours

1985	FR Germany
1986	USA
1987	Romania

Coxless Fours

1988	China
1989	China
1990	Canada
1991	China
1992	Australia
1993	United Kingdom
1994	USA

Most gold medals overall - World Championships and Olympic Games

Men

9	Giuseppe & Carmine Abbagnale (Ita) 2+ 1981-2, 1984-5, 1987-91
8	Steven Redgrave (UK) 4+ 1984, 2- 1987-8, 1991, 1992-4; 2+ 1986
7	Thomas Lange (GDR) 1x 1987-9, 1991-2; 2x 1983, 1985
6	Bernd & Jörg Landvoigt (GDR) 2- 1974-80
6	Joachim Dreifke (GDR) 1x 1977; 2x 1980-1, 4x 1974, 1978-9
6	Karl-Heinz Bussert (GDR) 4x 1976-9, 1981-2
6	Ulrich Diessner (GDR) 4+ 1977-80, 1982; 2+ 1983
6	Siegfried Brietzke & Wolfgang Mager (GDR) 2- 1972; 4- 1974-7, 1979
5	Pertti Karppinen (Fin) 1x 1976, 1979-80, 1984-5
5	Peter-Michael Kolbe (FRG) 1x 1975, 1978, 1981, 1983, 1986
5	Andreas Decker & Stefan Sempler (GDR) 4- 1974-7, 1979
5	Ulrich Karnatz (GDR) 8+ 1975-9
5	Gottfried Döhn (GDR) 4+ 1977-8, 1980; 8+ 1975-6

5   Alf Hansen (Nor) 2x 1975-6, 1978-9, 1982
    (first four with his brother Frank)
5   Martin Winter (GDR) 4x 1977-8, 1980-2
5   Uwe Heppner (GDR) 2x 1983, 1985; 4x 1980-2
5   Andreas Gregor (GDR) cox 2+ 1983; 4+ 1977-8,
    1980, 1982
5   Thomas Greiner (GDR) 4+ 1982, 2+ 1983, 4- 1987-9

Lightweight men
9   Francesco Esposito (Ita) 2x 1980-4 (all with
    Verroca), 1988 (with Enrico Gandola), 1994 (with
    Michelangelo Crispi), 4x 1990, 1992
7   Andrea Re and Fabrizio Ravasi (Ita) 8+ 1985-91
6   Ruggero Verroca (Ita) 1x 1985; 2x 1980-4

Women
7   Yelena Tereshina (USSR) 8+ 1978-9, 1981-3, 1985-6
6   Jutta Behrendt (née Hampe) 1x 1983, 1986, 1988;
    4x 1985, 1987, 1989
6   Birgit Peter (GDR/Ger) 1x 1990; 4x 1985-8, 1992
5   Christine Hahn (née Schieblich) 1x 1974-8
5   Angelika Noack (GDR) 2- 1975, 1977; 4+ 1974,
    1978, 1980
5   Beate Schramm (GDR/Ger) 2x 1986, 1988-91

World Cup

Introduced for men's and women's single sculls over a series
of races during a season in 1990. *Winners:*

Men
1990-1 Vaclav Chalupa (Cs)
1992   Thomas Lange (Ger)
1993   Vaclav Chalupa (Cze)
1994   Xeno Müller (Swi)

Women
1990   Birgit Peter (GDR)
1991   Silken Laumann (Can)
1992   Beate Schramm (Ger)
1993   Annelies Bredael (Bel)
1994   Marnie McBean (Can)

University Boat Race

The Boat race between the Universities of Oxford and
Cambridge is rowed annually on the River Thames from
Putney to Mortlake over a distance of 6779km (4 miles 374
yards). It was first contested on 10 June 1829 from Hambledon
Lock to Henley Bridge. From 1836 to 1842 it was rowed from
Westminster to Putney, and in 1846, 1856 and 1863 from
Mortlake to Putney; on all other occasions the present course
has been used. Outrigged eights were first used in 1846.
To 1995 Cambridge lead in the series of 141 races with 72
wins to Oxford's 68. There were two races in 1849 and on 24
Mar 1877 there was the only dead-heat in the race's history.

Cambridge wins: 1836, 1839-41, 1845-6, 1849, 1856,
    1858, 1860, 1870-4, 1876, 1879, 1884, 1886-9, 1899-
    1900, 1902-4, 1906-8, 1914, 1920-2, 1924-36, 1939,
    1947-51, 1953, 1955-8, 1961-2, 1964, 1968-73, 1975,
    1986, 1993-5
Oxford wins: 1829, 1842, 1849, 1852, 1854, 1857, 1859,
    1861-9, 1875, 1878, 1880-3, 1885, 1890-8, 1901, 1905,
    1909-13, 1923, 1937-8, 1946, 1952, 1954, 1959-60,

1963, 1965-7, 1974, 1976-85, 1987-92
Race record time: 16 min 45 sec Oxford 18 Mar
1984, an average speed of 24.28 km/h (15.09 mph)
Greatest margin: 20 lengths Cambridge 1900, apart
from sinkings
Most successful individual: Boris Rankov
(Oxford) rowed in six winning boats 1978-83
Most successful coach: Daniel Topolski of Oxford's
ten successive wins 1976-85
Heaviest competitor: Chris Heathcote (Oxford,
1990) 110kg (243 lb)
Heaviest crew: Oxford (1990) average weight:
94.5kg (208 lb)
Tallest competitor: Gavin Stewart (Oxford, 1987)
204.5cm (6 ft 8 in)
Youngest competitor: Matthew Brittin (Cambridge,
1987) 18yr 208 days
Oldest rower: Donald McDonald (Oxford, 1987)
31yr *cox*: Andy Probert (Cambridge) 38 yrs 1992
The first woman to take part was Susan Brown,
who coxed the winning Oxford boats of 1981-2

Henley Royal Regatta

Inaugurated in 1839. The course has varied slightly, but has
been about 1 mile 550 yards (2112m).

Diamond Sculls
Instituted in 1884 the Diamond Challenge Sculls at Henley is
regarded as the Blue Riband of amateur sculling. *Winners
since 1970:*

1970   Jochen Meissner (FRG)
1971   Alberto Demiddi (Arg)
1972   Aleksandr Timoshin (USSR)
1973-5 Sean Drea (Ire)
1976   Edward Hale (Aus)
1977-8 Tim Crooks (UK)
1979   Hugh Matheson (UK)
1980   Riccardo Ibarra (Arg)
1981-2 Chris Baillieu (UK)
1983   Steven Redgrave (UK)
1984   Chris Baillieu (UK)
1985   Steven Redgrave (UK)
1986   Bjarne Eltang (Den)
1987   Peter Michael Kolbe (FRG)
1988   Hamish McGlashan (Aus)
1989   Vaclav Chalupa (Cs)
1990   Eric Verdonk (NZ)
1991   Win Van Belleghem (Bel)
1992   Rorie Henderson (UK)
1993   Thomas Lange (Ger)
1994   Xeno Müller (Swi)
1995   Juri Jaanson (Est)
Most wins: 6 Stuart Mackenzie 1957-62, Guy
Nickalls (1888-91, 1893-4); 5 A.A.Casamajor 1855-8,
1861, J Lowndes 1879-83; 4 Jack Beresford Jr 1920,
1924-6; 3 A C Dicker 1873-5, Frederick Kelly 1902-3,
1905, Sean Drea, as above, Chris Baillieu, as above
Record time: 7 min 23 sec Vaclav Chalupa, 2 Jul
1989

Grand Challenge Cup

The oldest of all the Henley races, it dates to the first Regatta in 1839. It is the world's premier open event for eights. *Winners since 1970:*

1970 ASK Rostock (GDR)
1971 Tideway Scullers (UK)
1972 WMF Moscow (USSR)
1973-4 Trud Kolomna (USSR)
1975 Leander/Thames Tradesmen (UK)
1976 Thames Tradesmen (UK)
1977 University of Washington (USA)
1978 Trakia Club (Bul)
1979 Thames Tradesmen (UK)
1980 Charles River RA (USA)
1981 Oxford University/Thames Tradesmen (UK)
1982 Leander/London RC(UK)
1983 London RC/University of London (UK)
1984 Leander/London RC (UK)
1985 Harvard University (USA)
1986 Nautilus (UK)
1987 Soviet Army (USSR)
1988 Leander/Univeristy of London RC (UK)
1989-90 Hansa Dortmund RC (FRG)
1991 Leander/Star (UK)
1992 University of London (UK)
1993 Dortmund (Ger)
1994 Charles River and San Diego (USA)
1995 San Diego (USA)

Most wins: 27 Leander Club 1840, 1875, 1880, 1891-4, 1896, 1898-1901,1903-5, 1913, 1922, 1924-6, 1929, 1932, 1934, 1946, 1949, 1952-3

Most winning teams: 7 Guy Nickalls 1920-2, 1924-6, 1929

Record time: 5min 58sec Hansa Dortmund RC 2 Jul 1989

The Nickalls family, Guy, his brother Vivian, and Guy's son, Guy Oliver, had 43 Henley wins between them.

Rugby League

When the Rugby Union refused permission for players of northern clubs to receive broken time for loss of wages, 22 clubs formed their own breakaway union and, following a meeting at the George Hotel, Huddersfield, Yorkshire, in 1895, the Northern Union was formed. The number of players per side was reduced from 15 to 13 in 1906 and the union's name was changed to the Northern Rugby League in 1922. The word 'Northern' was dropped in 1980.

World Cup/International Championship

Inaugurated in France in 1954, when Great Britain, France, New Zealand and Australia played each other on a round-robin basis. In 1975, when the competition was renamed the International Championship, England and Wales replaced Great Britain and the competition was played world wide. The World Cup was discontinued after the 1977 championship but was revived in 1985 when one match from each test series was designated a World Cup game, with the leading two nations playing off in the final in 1988.

	Winners	Venue
1954	Great Britain	France
1957	Australia	Australia
1960	Great Britain	England
1968	Australia	Australia/New Zealand
1970	Australia	England
1972	Great Britain	France
1975	Australia	Worldwide
1977	Australia	Australia/New Zealand
1988	Australia	New Zealand (final)
1992	Australia	Great Britain (final)

Most wins: 7 Australia

Highest score: Papua New Guinea 12 Australia 62, at Port Moresby 4 Oct 1986

Challenge Cup

Rugby League's premier knockout tournament in England, the first final was at Leeds in 1897. The first Wembley final was in 1929 and since 1933 the London stadium has been the final's permanent venue, with the exception of the war years. Now the Silk Cut Challenge Cup. *Results of finals:*

1897	Batley	10	St Helens	3
1898	Batley	7	Bradford	0
1899	Oldham	19	Hunslet	9
1900	Swinton	16	Salford	8
1901	Batley	6	Warrington	0
1902	Broughton Rangers	25	Salford	0
1903	Halifax	7	Salford	0
1904	Halifax	8	Warrington	3
1905	Warrington	6	Hull K R	0
1906	Bradford	5	Salford	0
1907	Warrington	17	Oldham	3
1908	Hunslet	14	Hull	0
1909	Wakefield Trinity	17	Hull	0

Ellery Hanley can find no way through the Australian defence in the 1992 World Cup final

Year	Winner	Score	Runner-up	Score
1910	Leeds	7	Hull	7
replay	Leeds	26	Hull	12
1911	Broughton Rangers	4	Wigan	0
1912	Dewsbury	8	Oldham	5
1913	Huddersfield	9	Warrington	5
1914	Hull	6	Wakefield Trinity	0
1915	Huddersfield	37	St Helens	3
1920	Huddersfield	21	Wigan	10
1921	Leigh	13	Halifax	0
1922	Rochdale Hornets	10	Hull	9
1923	Leeds	28	Hull	3
1924	Wigan	21	Oldham	4
1925	Oldham	16	Hull K R	3
1926	Swinton	9	Oldham	3
1927	Oldham	26	Swinton	7
1928	Swinton	5	Warrington	3
1929	Wigan	13	Dewsbury	2
1930	Widnes	10	St Helens	3
1931	Halifax	22	York	8
1932	Leeds	11	Swinton	8
1933	Huddersfield	21	Warrington	17
1934	Hunslet	11	Widnes	5
1935	Castleford	11	Huddersfield	8
1936	Leeds	18	Warrington	2
1937	Widnes	18	Keighley	5
1938	Salford	7	Barrow	4
1939	Halifax	20	Salford	3
1940	*Not held*			
1941	Leeds	19	Halifax	2
1942	Leeds	15	Halifax	10
1943*	Dewsbury	16	Leeds	9
	Dewsbury	0	Leeds	6
1944*	Bradford Northern	0	Wigan	3
	Bradford Northern	8	Wigan	0
1945*	Huddersfield	7	Bradford Northern	4
	Huddersfield	6	Bradford Northern	5
1946	Wakefield Trinity	13	Wigan	12
1947	Bradford Northern	8	Leeds	4
1948	Wigan	8	Bradford Northern	3
1949	Bradford Northern	12	Halifax	0
1950	Warrington	19	Widnes	0
1951	Wigan	10	Barrow	0
1952	Workington Town	18	Featherstone Rovers	10
1953	Huddersfield	15	St Helens	10
1954	Warrington	4	Halifax	4
Replay	Warrington	8	Halifax	4
1955	Barrow	21	Workington Town	12
1956	St Helens	13	Halifax	2
1957	Leeds	9	Barrow	7
1958	Wigan	13	Workington Town	9
1959	Wigan	30	Hull	13
1960	Wakefield Trinity	38	Hull	5
1961	St Helens	12	Wigan	6
1962	Wakefield Trinity	12	Huddersfield	6
1963	Wakefield Trinity	25	Wigan	10
1964	Widnes	13	Hull K R	5
1965	Wigan	20	Hunslet	16
1966	St Helens	21	Wigan	2
1967	Featherstone Rovers	17	Barrow	12
1968	Leeds	11	Wakefield Trinity	10
1969	Castleford	11	Salford	6
1970	Castleford	7	Wigan	2
1971	Leigh	24	Leeds	7
1972	St Helens	16	Leeds	13
1973	Featherstone Rovers	33	Bradford Northern	14
1974	Warrington	24	Featherstone Rovers	9
1975	Widnes	14	Warrington	7
1976	St Helens	20	Widnes	5
1977	Leeds	16	Widnes	7
1978	Leeds	14	St Helens	12
1979	Widnes	12	Wakefield Trinity	3
1980	Hull Kingston Rovers	10	Hull	5
1981	Widnes	18	Hull K R	9
1982	Hull	14	Widnes	14
replay	Hull	18	Widnes	9
1983	Featherstone Rovers	14	Hull	12
1984	Widnes	19	Wigan	6
1985	Wigan	28	Hull	24
1986	Castleford	15	Hull K R	14
1987	Halifax	19	St Helens	18
1988	Wigan	32	Halifax	12
1989	Wigan	27	St Helens	0
1990	Wigan	36	Warrington	14
1991	Wigan	13	St Helens	8
1992	Wigan	28	Castleford	12
1993	Wigan	20	Widnes	14
1994	Wigan	26	Leeds	16
1995	Wigan	30	Leeds	10

* In 1943-5 it was held over two legs, with the winner determined on aggregate.

Most wins: 16 Wigan, 10 Leeds, 7 Widnes, 6 Huddersfield; 5 St Helens, Wakefield Trinity, Warrington, Halifax

Most finals: 26 Wigan, 17 Leeds, 13 St Helens, Warrington, Widnes

Highest score (final): Wakefield Trinity 38 Hull 5 on 14 May 1960

Record aggregate (final): 52 pts Wigan 28 Hull 24 on 4 May 1985

Most wins by a player: 9 Shaun Edwards 1985, 1988-95 (all for Wigan, also played on losing side in 1984); 7 Andy Gregory 1981, 1984, 1988-92 (for Wigan, from 8 finals, also played 1982 for Widnes), 7 Denis Betts (Wigan) 1989-95

Most points in a final: 20 Neil Fox, Wakefield 1960

Lance Todd Award

The Lance Todd Award goes to the Man of the Match in the Challenge Cup Final as decided by a panel of rugby league writers. The trophy is named after former New Zealand international Lance Todd who played for Wigan and later managed Salford. The first award was made in 1946. *Recent winners:*

1976	Geoff Pimblett (St Helens)
1977	Steve Pitchford (Leeds)
1978	George Nicholls (St Helens)
1979	Dave Topliss (Wakefield Trinity)
1980	Brian Lockwood (Hull Kingston Rovers)

1981	Mick Burke (Widnes)
1982	Eddie Cunningham (Widnes)
1983	David Hobbs (Featherstone Rovers)
1984	Joe Lydon (Widnes)
1985	Brett Kenny (Wigan)
1986	Bob Beardmore (Castleford)
1987	Graham Eadie (Halifax)
1988	Andy Gregory (Wigan)
1989	Ellery Hanley (Wigan)
1990	Andy Gregory (Wigan)
1991	Dennis Betts (Wigan)
1992	Martin Offiah (Wigan)
1993	Dean Bell (Wigan)
1994	Martin Offiah (Wigan)
1995	Jason Robinson (Wigan)

Warrington's Gerry Helme (1950 and 1954), Andy Gregory and Martin Offiah are the only dual winners

Premiership Trophy

The Premiership competition replaced the Championship Play-off, and was first contested at the end of the 1974/5 season. It is a knockout competition involving the top eight clubs in the first division with the champions playing the 8th club, 2nd club playing the 7th, and so on. The highest placed club has home advantage, and the final is played at a neutral venue. A 2nd Division Premiership was launched in 1987. Both Premiership finals are now played at Old Trafford, Manchester United FC.

Winners - Premiership Trophy
Figures in brackets indicates final league positions:

1975	Leeds (3)
1976	St Helens (5)
1977	St Helens (2)
1978	Bradford Northern (2)
1979	Leeds (4)
1980	Widnes (2)
1981	Hull Kingston Rovers (3)
1982	Widnes (3)
1983	Widnes (5)
1984	Hull Kingston Rovers (1)
1985	St Helens (2)
1986	Warrington (4)
1987	Wigan (1)
1988	Widnes (1)
1989	Widnes (1)
1990	Widnes (3)
1991	Hull (3)
1992	Wigan (1)
1993	St Helens (2)
1994	Wigan (1)
1995	Wigan (1)

Most wins: 6 Widnes, 4 St Helens, Wigan
Highest score (final): Wigan 69 Leeds 12, 21 May 1995
Most appearances (final): 8 (6 wins, 2 losses) Martin Offiah (Widnes 1988-91, Wigan 1992-5), 6 (all wins) Mike O'Neill (Widnes 1980,1982-3, 1988-90)

Harry Sunderland Trophy

Named after former Australian team manager, broadcaster and journalist Harry Sunderland, the award is made to the Man of the Match in the Premiership Final (formerly the

Wigan celebrate a 6th successive championship in 1995

Championship Play-off). It was first awarded in 1965. *Recent winners:*

1976	George Nicholls (St Helens)
1977	Geoff Pimblett (St Helens)
1978	Bob Haigh (Bradford Northern)
1979	Kevin Dick (Leeds)
1980	Mal Aspey (Widnes)
1981	Len Casey (Hull Kingston Rovers)
1982	Mick Burke (Widnes)
1983	Tony Myler (Widnes)
1984	John Dorahy (Hull Kingston Rovers)
1985	Harry Pinner (St Helens)
1986	Les Boyd (Warrington)
1987	Joe Lydon (Wigan)
1988	David Hulme (Widnes)
1989	Alan Tait (Widnes)
1990	Alan Tait (Widnes)
1991	Greg Mackey (Hull)
1992	Allan Platt (Wigan)
1993	Chris Joynt (St Helens)
1994	Sam Panapa (Wigan)
1995	Kris Radlinski (Wigan)

Until Alan Tait in 1989-90, no player had won the trophy more than once.

Divisional Premiership

Winners. Positions in 2nd Division in brackets:

1987	Swinton (2)
1988	Oldham (1)
1989	Sheffield Eagles (3)
1990	Oldham (3)
1991	Salford (1)
1992	Sheffield Eagles (1)
1993	Featherstone Rovers (1)
1994	Workington Town (1)
1995	Keighley Cougars (1)

League Championship

Twenty-two clubs formed the original Northern Union in 1895/6, won by Manningham. The 'league' then split into Yorkshire and Lancashire Senior Competitions until 1901/2 when 14 clubs broke away to form the Northern Rugby League. Two divisions were formed the following season. In 1905/6 the two divisions were merged into one and that is how they stayed (excepting the war years) until 1962/3 when two divisions were re-introduced. That lasted just two years, but returned in 1973/4. In 1991/2 and 1992/3 there were three divisions and from1993/4 two divisions of 16 clubs.

The title 'Rugby Football League' was adopted in 1922. Because not all clubs played each other twice, or at all in some cases, a Championship Play-off, involving the top four teams, was introduced in 1906/7. This remained unaltered (except during the war years) until 1962 when two divisions were re-introduced. On the return to one division in 1964/5 the play-off involved the top 16 teams. It was scrapped at the end of the 1972/3 season.

Championship play-off wins

9	Wigan	1909, 1922, 1926, 1934, 1946-7, 1950, 1952, 1960
7	Huddersfield	1912-3, 1915, 1929-30, 1949, 1962
6	St Helens	1932, 1953, 1959, 1966, 1970-1
5	Hull	1920-1, 1936, 1956, 1958
4	Salford	1914, 1933, 1937, 1939
4	Swinton	1927-8, 1931, 1935
3	Leeds	1961, 1969, 1972
3	Oldham	1910-1, 1957
3	Warrington	1948, 1954-5
2	Halifax	1907, 1965
2	Hull KR	1923, 1925
2	Hunslet	1908, 1938
2	Wakefield Trinity	1967-8
1	Batley 1924, Dewsbury 1973, Leigh 1906, Workington Town 1951	

Division One Champions *since 1974*

1973/4 Salford
1974/5 St Helens
1975/6 Salford
1976/7 Featherstone Rovers
1977/8 Widnes
1978/9 Hull Kingston Rovers
1979/80 Bradford Northern
1980/1 Bradford Northern
1981/2 Leigh
1982/3 Hull
1983/4 Hull Kingston Rovers
1984/5 Hull Kingston Rovers
1985/6 Halifax
1986/7 Wigan
1987/8 Widnes
1988/9 Widnes
1989/90 Wigan
1990/1 Wigan
1991/2 Wigan
1992/3 Wigan
1993/4 Wigan
1994/5 Wigan

Division Two

1973/4 Bradford Northern
1974/5 Huddersfield
1975/6 Barrow
1976/7 Hull
1977/8 Leigh
1978/9 Hull
1979/80 Featherstone Rovers
1980/1 York
1981/2 Oldham
1982/3 Fulham
1983/4 Barrow
1984/5 Swinton
1985/6 Leigh
1986/7 Hunslet
1987/8 Oldham
1988/9 Leigh
1989/90 Hull Kingston Rovers
1990/1 Salford
1991/2 Sheffield
1992/3 Featherstone Rovers
1993/4 Workington Town
1994/5 Keighley Cougars

Division Three

1991/2 Huddersfield
1992/3 Keighley Cougars

Knockout trophy

The knockout competition was first held in 1971/2. It was originally known as the Player's No.6 Trophy, and then the John Player Trophy until 1983, when it was renamed the John Player Special Trophy. It became the **Regal Trophy** in 1989. *Winners:*

1972	Halifax
1973	Leeds
1974	Warrington
1975	Bradford Northern
1976	Widnes
1977	Castleford
1978	Warrington
1979	Widnes
1980	Bradford Northern
1981	Warrington
1982	Hull
1983	Wigan
1984	Leeds
1985	Hull Kingston Rovers
1986-7	Wigan
1988	St Helens
1989-90	Wigan
1991	Warrington
1992	Widnes
1993	Wigan
1994	Castleford
1995	Wigan

Wins: 7 Wigan, 4 Warrington, 3 Widnes, 2 Bradford Northern, Leeds
Highest aggregate (final): Wigan 40, Warrington 10 at Huddersfield on 28 Jan 1995
Most appearances (final): 6 Mick Adams, Keith Elwell, Eric Hughes (all Widnes) 1975-6, 1978-80, 1984

County Cups

Both the Lancashire and Yorkshire County Challenge Cup competitions were first held in 1905/6 and became early-season knock-out competitions. Discontinued in 1993/4. *Years indicate first half of season, although in a few cases the final was played early in the following year. Wins:*

Lancashire Cup

21	Wigan	1905, 1908-09, 1912, 1922, 1928, 1938, 1946-51, 1966, 1971, 1973, 1985-8, 1992
11	St Helens	1926, 1953, 1960-4, 1967-8, 1984, 1991
9	Oldham	1907, 1910, 1913, 1919, 1924, 1933, 1956-8
9	Warrington	1921, 1929, 1932, 1937, 1959, 1965, 1980, 1982, 1989
7	Widnes	1945, 1974-6, 1978-9, 1990
5	Salford	1931, 1934-6, 1972
4	Swinton	1925, 1927, 1939, 1969
4	Leigh	1952, 1955, 1970, 1981
3	Rochdale Hornets	1911, 1914, 1918

2	Broughton Rangers	1906, 1920
2	St Helens Recs	1923, 1930
2	Barrow	1954, 1983
1	Workington Town	1977

Yorkshire Cup

17	Leeds	1921, 1928, 1930, 1932, 1934-5, 1937, 1958, 1968, 1970, 1972-3, 1975-6, 1979-80, 1988
12	Huddersfield	1909, 1911, 1913-4, 1918-9, 1926, 1931, 1938, 1950, 1952, 1957
11	Bradford Northern	1940-1, 1943, 1945, 1948-9, 1953, 1965, 1978, 1987, 1989
10	Wakefield Trinity	1910, 1924, 1946-7, 1951, 1956, 1960-1, 1964, 1992
7	Hull Kingston R	1920, 1929, 1966-7, 1971, 1974, 1985
5	Halifax	1908, 1944, 1954-5, 1963
5	Hull	1923, 1969, 1982-4

5	Castleford	1977, 1981, 1986, 1990-1
3	Hunslet	1905, 1907, 1962
3	York	1922, 1933, 1936
3	Dewsbury	1925, 1927, 1942
2	Featherstone R	1939, 1959
1	Bradford	1906
1	Batley	1912

County Leagues

With the introduction of two divisions in 1902/3 the Lancashire and Yorkshire Senior competitions were scrapped, but they re-appeared in 1907/8 as the Lancashire and Yorkshire Leagues. Club's results in the normal league, against teams from their own county, counted towards the appropriate County League. Both leagues were abandoned in 1970. *Most wins:*

Lancashire League: 18 Wigan 1909, 1911-5, 1921, 1923-4, 1926, 1941, 1946-7, 1950, 1952, 1959, 1962, 1970
Yorkshire League: 15 Leeds 1902, 1928, 1931, 1934-5, 1937-8, 1951, 1955, 1957, 1961, 1967-70

The Top Teams

Wins in major competitions by teams currently playing in the League.
In the final column is a points system: Challenge Cup 5, Premiership/Championship 4, Regal/John Player Trophy 4, Division One title 2, Lancashire or Yorkshire Cup 1.

	Chall Cup	Champ P-off	Prem Trphy	Div.2 Prem	KO Trophy	Floodlit Final	C'ty Cup	C'ty Lge.	Div 1	Div 2	Points
Wigan	16	9	4	-	7	1	21	18	7	-	195
Leeds	10	3	2	-	2	1	17	15	-	-	95
Widnes	7	-	6	-	3	1	7	1	3	-	84
St Helens	5	6	4	-	1	2	11	8	1	1	82
Huddersfield Barracudas	6	7	-	-	-	-	12	11	-	1	70
Warrington	5	3	1	-	4	-	9	8	-	-	66
Bradford Northern	4	-	1	-	2	-	12	5	3	1	50
Halifax	5	2	-	-	1	-	5	6	2	-	46
Hull	2	5	1	-	1	1	5	4	1	2	45
Wakefield Trinity	5	2	-	-	-	-	10	7	-	1	43
Swinton	3	4	-	1	-	-	4	5	2	1	39
Hull Kingston Rovers	1	2	2	-	1	1	7	2	3	1	38
Oldham	3	3	-	2	-	-	9	7	1	3	38
Castleford	4	-	-	-	2	4	5	3	-	-	33
Salford	1	4	-	1	-	1	5	5	2	-	30
Hunslet	2	2	-	-	-	-	3	3	-	2	21
Batley	3	1	-	-	-	-	1	2	-	-	20
Leigh	2	1	-	-	-	2	4	-	1	3	20
Featherstone Rovers	3	-	-	1	-	-	2	-	1	2	19
Dewsbury	2	1	-	-	-	-	3	1	-	1	17
Workington Town	1	1	-	1	-	-	1	-	-	1	10
Rochdale Hornets	1	-	-	-	-	-	3	1	-	-	8
Barrow	1	-	-	-	-	-	2	-	-	2	7
Ryedale York	-	-	-	-	-	-	3	-	-	1	3

Man of Steel

The RFL personality judged to have made the greatest impact on the season. Sponsored by Trumans Steel 1977-83, Greenall Whitley 1984-9, Stones Bitter 1990-. *Winners:*

1977 David Ward (Leeds)
1978 George Nicholls (St Helens)
1979 Doug Laughton (Widnes)
1980 George Fairbairn (Wigan)
1981 Ken Kelly (Warrington)
1982 Mick Morgan (Carlisle)
1983 Allan Agar (Featherstone R)
1984 Joe Lydon (Widnes)
1985 Ellery Hanley (Bradford N)
1986 Gavin Miller (Hull KR)
1987 Ellery Hanley (Wigan)
1988 Martin Offiah (Widmes)
1989 Ellery Hanley (Wigan)
1990 Shaun Edwards (Wigan)
1991 Garry Schofield (Leeds)

1992 Dean Bell (Wigan)
1993 Andy Platt (Wigan)
1994 Jonathan Davies (Warrington)
1995 Denis Betts (Wigan)

Sydney Premiership

The principal competition in Australia is the Sydney Premiership (sometimes referred to as the New South Wales Premiership), which culminates in the Grand Final each year. The winning team receives the Winfield Cup. The first Grand Final was in 1908. *Most wins:*

20	South Sydney	1908-9, 1914, 1918, 1925-9, 1931-2, 1950-1, 1953-5, 1967-8, 1970-1
15	St.George	1941, 1949, 1956-66, 1977, 1979
11	Balmain	1915-7, 1919-20, 1924, 1939, 1944, 1946-7, 1969
11	Eastern Suburbs	1911-3, 1923, 1935-7, 1940, 1945, 1974-5

Recent Winners

1980	Canterbury-Bankstown
1981-3	Parramatta
1984-5	Canterbury-Bankstown
1986	Parramatta
1987	Manly-Warringah
1988	Canterbury-Bankstown
1989-90	Canberra
1991	Penrith
1992-3	Brisbane Broncos
1994	Canberra

State of Origin Series

The annual series of matches between New South Wales and Queensland began in 1980, taking the current format of a 3-match series from 1982.
The series score in the current format to 1995 is Queensland 8, New South Wales 6.

World Club Challenge

Contested by the winners of the Challenge Cup Final and thre Australian Grand Final winners. Sponsored by Fosters Lager.

1987	Wigan 8	Manly-Warringah ?	
1989	Widnes 30	Canberra 18	
1991	Wigan 21	Penrith 4	
1992	Brisbane Broncos 22	Wigan 8	
1994	Wigan 20	Brisbane Broncos 14	

Records

All Matches

Biggest win: 142-4 Huddersfield v Blackpool Gladiators (Regal Trophy first round) 26 Nov 1994
Most tries in a match: 11 George West (Hull Kingston Rovers) v Brookland Rovers (Challenge Cup) 4 Mar 1905
Most goals in a match: 22 Jim Sullivan (Wigan) v Flimby & Fothergill (Challenge Cup) 14 Feb 1925
Most points in a match: 53 (10 goals, 11 tries) George West (Hull Kingston Rovers) - as above

Internationals

Most appearances: 60 Jim Sullivan (Wigan) Wales, GB & Other Nationalities, 1921-39

Most tries: 45 Mick Sullivan (Huddersfield, Wigan, St Helens, York) GB & England 1954-63
Most goals: 160 Jim Sullivan
Most points: 329 Jim Sullivan
Biggest win: Australia 74 France 0 at Béziers 4 Dec 1994

Season

Most tries: 80 Albert Rosenfeld (Huddersfield) 1913/4
Most goals: 221 David Watkins (Salford) 1972/3
Most points: 496 (194 goals, 36 tries) Lewis Jones (Leeds) 1956/7

Career

Most tries: 796 Brian Bevan (Warrington & Blackpool Borough) 1946-64
Most goals: 2,867 Jim Sullivan (Wigan) 1921-46
Most points: 6,220 (2575 goals, 358 tries, 4 drop goals) Neil Fox (Wakefield Trinity, Bradford Northern, Hull Kingston Rovers, York, Bramley, Huddersfield) 1956-79
Most senior appearances: 928 Jim Sullivan (Wigan) 1921-46
Most consecutive club appearances: 239 Keith Elwell (Widnes) May 1977- Sep 1982
Most consecutive games scoring points: 92 David Watkins (Salford) Aug 1972-Apr 1974

Test Match Records as at July 1995			
Great Britain	P	W	D	L
v Australia	111	53	4	4
v France	60	43	3	14
v New Zealand	82	51	3	28
v Papua New Guinea	7	6	0	1
Australia				
v France	43	28	3	12
v New Zealand	74	51	1	22
France				
v New Zealand	37	10	4	23
v Papua New Guinea	1	0	0	1
New Zealand				
v Papua New Guinea	9	8	0	1

World Sevens

Held at Sydney in 1994, when the winners were Manly-Warringah (Aus).

Rugby Union

The game of Rugby Union is traditionally said to have had its beginnings at Rugby School, when William Webb Ellis picked up the ball during a game of football in November 1823, and ran with it. The new 'handling' code of football developed and was played at Cambridge University in 1839. The first rugby club was formed at Guy's Hospital in 1843 and the Rugby Football Union (RFU) was founded in January 1871.

The International Rugby Football Board (IRFB) was founded in 1886. Members are: Australia, England, France, Ireland, New Zealand, Scotland, South Africa and Wales. The Fédération Internationalede Rugby Amateur (FIRA) held its first meeting in 1934, and membership reached 49 nations in 1992.

Changing values of points scored:

From year	Try	conversion	penalty goal	drop goal	goal from mark
1890	1	2	2	3	3
1892	2	3	3	4	4
1894	3	2	3	4	4
1905	3	2	3	4	3
1948	3	2	3	3	3
1971	4	2	3	3	3
1978	4	2	3	3	-
1992	5	2	3	3	-

World Cup

The inaugural World Cup was contested in Australia and New Zealand in 1987 by 16 national teams. The second was played in Britain and France in 1991 and the third in South Africas in 1995. *Results of finals:*

1987	New Zealand 29	France 9
1991	Australia 12	England 6
1995	South Africa 15	New Zealand 12

Highest team score: New Zealand 145 v Japan 17 at Bloemfontein on 4 Jun 1995.

Most points in a match by an individual

45 Simon Culhane (1 try, 20 conversions), New Zealand 145 Japan 17, Bloemfontein 4 Jun 1995

44 Gavin Hastings (4 tries, 2 penalty goals, 9 conversions), Scotland 89 Ivory Coast 0, Rustenberg 26 May 1995

31 Gavin Hastings (1 try, 8 penalties, 1 conversion), Scotland 41 Tonga 5, Pretoria 30 May 1995

30 Didier Camberabero (3 tries, 9 conversions), France 70 Zimbabwe 12, Auckland 2 June 1987.

Most tries in a match: 6 Marc Ellis, New Zealand v Japan at Bloemfontein on 4 Jun 1995

Highest points scorers

1987 Grant Fox (MZ) 126 points in 6 games
1991 Roger Keyes (Ire) 68 points in 4 games
1995 Thierry Lacroix (Fra) 112 points in 6 games
    Gavin Hastings (Sco) 104 points in 4 games
1987-95: 227 Hastings, 195 Michael Lynagh (Aus), 170 Fox

Scorers of most tries

1987 Craig Green (NZ) and John Kirwan (NZ) 6
1991 David Campese (Aus), Jean-Baptiste Lafond (Fra) 6
1995 Marc Ellis & Jonah Lomu (NZ) 7
1987-95: 11 Rory Underwood (Eng), 10 Campese

Most appearances: Sean Fitzptarick (New Zealand) 17

International Championship

First contested by England, Ireland, Scotland and Wales in 1884. France made it a 'Five Nations' tournament when they joined in 1910. Each country plays each other once during each season's championship. The championships of 1885, 1888-9, 1897-8 and 1972 were not completed for various reasons. *Winners (outright/shared wins):*

22/11	Wales	1893, 1900, 1902, 1905, 1906*, 1908-9, 1911, 1920*, 1922, 1931, 1932*, 1936, 1939*, 1947*, 1950, 1952, 1954*-5*, 1956, 1964*, 1965-6, 1969, 1970*, 1971, 1973*, 1975-6, 1978-9, 1988*, 1994
21/9	England	1883-4, 1886*, 1890*, 1892, 1910, 1912*, 1913-4, 1921, 1923-4, 1928, 1930, 1932*, 1934, 1937, 1939*, 1947*, 1953, 1954*, 1957-8, 1960*, 1963, 1973*, 1980, 1991-2, 1995
13/8	Scotland	1886*, 1887, 1890*, 1891, 1895, 1901, 1903-4, 1907, 1920*, 1925, 1926*-7*, 1929, 1933, 1938, 1964*, 1973*, 1984, 1986*, 1990
10/8	Ireland	1894, 1896, 1899, 1906*, 1912*, 1926*-7*, 1932*, 1935, 1939*, 1948-9, 1951, 1973*, 1974, 1982, 1983*, 1985
10/8	France	1954*, 1955*, 1959, 1960*, 1961-2, 1967-8, 1970*, 1973*, 1977, 1981, 1983*, 1986*, 1987, 1988*, 1989, 1993

* denotes shared win (note: there was a quintuple tie in 1973)

Grand Slam

The beating of all other four countries during one season's championship has been achieved as follows:

11	England	1913-4, 1921, 1923-4, 1928, 1957, 1980, 1991-2, 1995
8	Wales	1908-9*, 1911, 1950, 1952, 1971, 1976, 1978
4	France	1968, 1977, 1981, 1987
3	Scotland	1925, 1984, 1990
1	Ireland	1948

* not including France, yet to enter

Triple Crown

The beating of the other three 'Home Countries' in one season's championship has been achieved as follows:

18	England	1883-4, 1892, 1913-4, 1921, 1923-4, 1928, 1934, 1937, 1954, 1957, 1960, 1980, 1991-2, 1995
17	Wales	1893, 1900, 1902, 1905, 1908-9, 1911, 1950, 1952, 1965, 1969, 1971, 1976, 1977-9, 1988
10	Scotland	1891, 1895, 1901, 1903, 1907, 1925, 1933, 1938, 1984, 1990
6	Ireland	1894, 1899, 1948-9, 1982, 1985

International Championship Records

Team

Highest score: Wales 49 France 14 at Swansea, 1 Jan 1910 (on present day scoring it would have been 59-16)

Most points in a season: 118 England 1992

Most tries in a season: 21 Wales 1909-10

Individual

Most points in a season:

67 (3 tries, 3 pen, 11 con) Jonathan Webb (Eng) 1992
60 (18 pen, 3 con) Simon Hodgkinson (Eng) 1991
56 (13 pen, 6 con, 1 try) Gavin Hastings (Sco) 1995
54 (10 pen, 4 con, 4 dg) Jean-Patrick Lescarboura (Fra) 1984

Most tries in a season: 8 Cyril Lowe (Eng) 1913-14; Ian Smith (Sco) 1924-5

Most conversions in a season: 11 Jonathan Webb (Eng) 1992

Most penalty goals in a season: 18 Simon Hodgkinson (Eng) 1991

Most points in a match: 24 Sébastien Viers (Fra) v Ireland, Paris 21 Mar 1992 (2 tries, 2 PG, 5 con); 24 Rob Andrew (Eng) v Scotland, Twickenham 18 Mar 1995 (7 PG, 1 G)

Most goals in a match: 9 (8 con, 1 pen) William Bancroft (Wales) v France 1 Jan 1910
Most tries in a match: 5 George Lindsay (Sco) v Wales 26 Feb 1887, Douglas 'Daniel' Lambert (Eng) v France 5 Jan 1907   (con - conversion, pen - penalty goal, dg - drop goal)

International Records

The playing records between major Rugby-playing nations at 1 August 1995.

	ARG	AUS	BI	ENG	FIJ	FRA	IRE	NZ	ROM	SCO	SAF	WAL
Argentina	-	3/1	-	1/2	0/0	4/1	0/0	0/1	1/0	3/0	0/0	1/1
Australia	7/1	-	2/-	12/-	12/1	9/3	10/0	27/5	-	7/0	10/0	8/0
British Isles	-	8/0	-	-	0/0	-	-	6/5	-	-	14/6	-
England	4/2	6/0	-	-	5/1	40/7	62/8	4/0	2/0	56/17	4/1	41/12
Fiji	1/0	2/1	1/0	0/1	-	0/0	0/0	0/0	0/0	0/0		0/0
France	21/1	13/3	-	25/7	3/0	-	39/5	7/0	33/2	33/3	5/5	29/3
Ireland	2/0	6/0	-	38/8	2/0	25/5	-	0/1	2/1	45/6	1/1	35/6
New Zealand	10/1	68/5	24/5	14/0	3/0	23/0	11/1	-	1/0	16/2	18/3	13/0
Romania	0/0	-	-	0/0	1/0	8/2	0/1	0/0	-	2/0	-	2/0
Scotland	3/0	7/0	-	39/17	3/0	31/3	56/6	0/2	6/0	-	3/0	43/2
South Africa	2/0	23/0	20/6	7/1		13/5	8/1	21/3	1/0	6/0	-	7/1
Wales	2/1	8/0	-	48/12	4/0	37/3	58/6	3/0	3/0	54/2	0/1	-

Calcutta Cup: The annual England - Scotland games (results above) are played for the Calcutta Cup, so named because it was made in India from the rupees left in the bank by the disbanded Calcutta Club in 1876.

Bledisloe Cup: Contested by New Zealand and Australia, it was instigated in 1931 by Lord Bledisloe, the Governer-General of New Zealand. To August 1995 New Zealand had 57 wins, Australia 21, and 4 matches were drawn.

Individual Records

Leading cap winners
Figures in brackets indicates number of British Lions appearances. As at 1 August 1995:

111	Philippe Sella (Fra) 1982-95
93	Serge Blanco (France) 1980-91
92	David Campese (Aus) 1982-95
85 (6)	Rory Underwood (Eng) 1984-95
81 (12)	Mike Gibson (Ire) 1964-79
80 (17)	Willie John McBride (Ire) 1962-75
75 (5)	Rob Andrew (Eng) 1985-94
70	Sean Fitzpatrick (NZ) 1986-95
69	Roland Bertranne (Fra) 1971-81
69	Michael Lynagh (Aus) 1984-95
69 (5)	Brian Moore (Eng) 1987-94
68 (6)	Gavin Hastings (Sco) 1986-95
65 (4)	Fergus Slattery (Ire) 1970-84
65 (7)	Peter Winterbottom (Eng) 1982-93
63	Michel Crauste (Fra) 1957-66
63	Benoit Dauga (Fra) 1964-72
63 (10)	Gareth Edwards (Wal) 1967-78
63 (8)	John P R Williams (Wal) 1969-81
63	Nick Farr-Jones (Aus) 1984-93
63	John Kirwan (NZ) 1984-94
61	Jean Condom (Fra) 1982-90
61 (1)	Will Carling (Eng) 1988-95
60 (6)	Ieuan Evans (Wal) 1987-95
60 (9)	Andy Irvine (Sco) 1972-82

Leading Points Scorers
Points, matches, and average per match

Michael Lynagh (Aus)	911	72	12.7	1984-95
Gavin Hastings (Sco/BL)	755	68	11.1	1986-95
Grant Fox (NZ)	645	46	14.0	1985-93
Hugo Porta (Arg)	530	33	10.0	1972-90

Gavin Hastings – Scotland's record points scorer

Michael Lynagh prepares to add to his record

Rob Andrew (Eng/BL)	407	75	5.4	1985-95
Neil Jenkins (Wal)	399	36	11.1	1991-5
Didier Camberabero (Fra)	354	36	9.8	1985-93
Thierry Lacroix (Fra)	339	35	9.7	1989-95
Naas Botha (SAf)	312	28	11.1	1980-92
Michael Kiernan (Ire)	308	43	7.2	1982-91
Paul Thorburn (Wal)	301	37	8.1	1985-91
Andy Irvine (Sco/BL)	301	60	5.0	1972-82

More than 200 points and average over 10

Simon Hodgkinson (Eng)	203	14	14.5	1989-91
Paul McLean (Aus)	260	22	11.8	1979-82

Also note 483 Stefano Bettarolo (Ita) 1979-91

Most points in a major international match
See World Cup and:
30 Rob Andrew, England v Canada at Twickenham 10 Dec 1994

Leading Try Scorers

Tries		*Matches*	
63	David Campese (Aus)	92	1982-95
47	Rory Underwood (Eng/BL)	86	1984-95
38	Serge Blanco (Fra)	93	1980-91
35	John Kirwan (NZ)	63	1984-94
29	Philippe Sella (Fra)	111	1982-95
24	Ian Smith (Sco)	32	1924-33
24	Ieuan Evans (Wal/BL)	61	1987-95

23	Christian Darrouy (Fra)	40	1957-67
23	Gerald Davies (Wal/BL)	51	1966-78

Most for the other nations
Ireland: 15 George Stephenson 1920-30
South Africa: 15 Danie Gerber 1980-6

Most dropped goals
24 Hugo Porta (Arg) 1972-90
23 Rob Andrew (Eng/BL) 1985-95
18 Naas Botha (SAf) 1980-92
17 Stefano Betterello (Ita) 1979-91
15 Jean-Patrick Lescarboura (Fra) 1982-90

Most successful captains
40 wins in 53 games Will Carling (Eng) 1988-95
23 wins in 36 games Nick Farr-Jones (Aus) 1984-92
22 wins in 30 games Wilson Whineray (NZ) 1958-65

Other Records (All matches)

Hong Kong beat Singapore 154-13 at Kuala Lumpur on 27 Oct 1994 in the Asian Championships, with Ashley Billington scoring a record 10 tries and James McKee kicking a record 17 conversions.
International Tour match score: 128-0 Western Samoa v Marlborough at Blenheim, New Zealand, 8 Jul 1993
Most team points scored in a season: 1917 by Neath (Wales) in 1988/9
Most team tries in a season: 345 by Neath (Wales) also in 1988/9
Individual career points: 7337 Dusty Hare (Nottingham, Leicester, England, British Lions, and other representative matches) 1971-89

Hong Kong Sevens

Now sponsored by Cathay Pacific and the Hong Kong Bank, the first Hong Kong International sevens was held in 1976, with 12 teams taking part. Now, it is regarded as the most prestigious sevens tournament in the world. *Wins:*

7	Fiji	1977-8, 1980, 1984, 1990-2
5	Australia	1979, 1982-3, 1985, 1988
5	New Zealand	1986-7, 1989, 1994-5
1	Cantabrians 1976, Barbarians 1981, Western Samoa 1993	

British Lions

The British Lions went on their first Tour in 1888, when they played a total of 35 matches in Australia and New Zealand. Since then there have been a further 21 Lions tours. *Complete record of all matches on each tour:*

Year	Country	P	W	D	L	F	A	Tour captain
1888	Australia	16	14	2	0	210	65	Robert Seddon (Eng)*
	New Zealand	19	13	4	2	82	33	
1891	South Africa	19	19	0	0	224	3	Bill MacLagan (Sco)
1896	South Africa	21	19	1	1	310	45	John Hammond (Eng)#
1899	Australia	21	18	0	3	333	90	Rev Matthew Mullineaux (Eng)#
1903	South Africa	22	11	3	8	231	138	Mark Morrison (Sco)
1904	Australia	14	14	0	0	265	51	Darky Bedell-Sivright (Sco)
	New Zealand	5	2	1	2	22	33	
1908	Australia	9	7	0	2	139	48	Arthur Harding (Wal)
	New Zealand	17	9	1	7	184	153	
1910	South Africa	24	13	3	8	290	236	Dr Tom Smyth (Ire)
1924	South Africa	21	9	3	9	175	155	Dr Ronald Cove-Smith (Eng)

1930	New Zealand	21	15	0	6	420	205	Doug Prentice (Eng)
	Australia	7	5	0	2	204	113	
1938	South Africa	23	17	0	6	407	272	Sam Walker (Ire)
1950	New Zealand	23	17	1	5	420	162	
	Australia	6	5	0	1	150	52	Karl Mullen (Ire)
1955	South Africa	24	18	1	5	418	271	Robin Thompson (Ire)
1959	Australia	6	5	0	1	174	70	Ronnie Dawson (Ire)
	New Zealand	25	20	0	5	582	266	
1962	South Africa	24	15	4	5	351	208	Arthur Smith (Sco)
1966	Australia	8	7	1	0	202	48	Michael Campbell-Lamerton (Sco)
	New Zealand	25	15	2	8	300	281	
1968	South Africa	20	15	1	4	377	181	Tom Kiernan (Ire)
1971	Australia	2	1	0	1	25	27	John Dawes (Wal)
	New Zealand	24	22	1	1	555	204	
1974	South Africa	22	21	1	0	729	207	Wilie John McBride (Ire)
1977	New Zealand	25	21	0	4	596	295	Phil Bennett (Wal)
	Fiji	1	0	0	1	21	25	
1980	South Africa	18	15	0	3	401	244	Billy Beaumont (Eng)
1983	New Zealand	18	12	0	6	478	276	Cieran Fitzgerald (Ire)
1989	Australia	12	11	0	1	360	192	Finlay Calder (Sco)
1993	New Zealand	13	7	0	6	314	285	Gavin Hastings (Sco)

Seddon lost his life in a drowning accident hile sculling on the Hunter River, NSW, during the tour and was replaced by Andrew Stoddart (Eng), who also went on to captain England at cricket, the only man to achieve this double distinction.

 # Mullineaux and Hammond never played international rugby for one of the home countries.

Test Summaries

British Lions	P	W	D	L
v Australia	17	14	0	3
v New Zealand	35	25	3	7
v South Africa	40	14	6	20

British Lions Records

Biggest test win: 31-0 v Australia at Brisbane, 4 Jun 1966

Biggest test defeat: 6-38 by New Zealand at Auckland, 16 Jul 1983

Most caps: 17 Willie John McBride (Ire) 1962-74

Most internationals as captain: 6 Ronnie Dawson (Ire) 1959

Most points in internationals: 66 Gavin Hastings (Sco) 1989-93 (7 games)

Most points in one international: 18 Tony Ward (Ire) v South Africa at Cape Town 31 May 1980; 18 Gavin Hastings (Sco) v New Zealand at Christchurch 12 Jun 1993

Most tries in internationals: 6 Tony O'Reilly (Ire) 1955-9

Most tries in one international: 8 players have each score two tries, the most recent being Gavin Hastings (Sco) against Australia in 1989

Most points on a tour: 188 Barry John (Wal) 1971 to Australia and New Zealand

Most tries on a tour: 22 Tony O'Reilly (Ire) 1959 to Australia and New Zealand

Most points in a tour match: 37 Alan Old (Eng) v South Western Districts at Mossel Bay, SAf 29 May 1974

Most tries in a tour match: 6 David Duckham (Eng) v West Coast-Buller at Greymouth, NZ 17 Jun 1971; 6 J.J.Williams (Wal) v South Western Districts at Mossel Bay, SAf 29 May 1974

University Match

The first match between the Universities of Oxford and Cambridge took place at The Parks, Oxford on 10 Feb 1872. It has been contested annually ever since, with the exception of the First World War years. During the second World War, a special series of matches was played. Cambridge staged the second match in 1873, the Oval 1874-80, Blackheath 1881-7, Queen's Club 1888-1921, and Twickenham thereafter. The years quoted are for the second half of the season, although the match is now played annually in December. *Wins:*

51 Cambridge 1873, 1877, 1880, 1886-9, 1892, 1896,1899-1900, 1905-6, 1913-14, 1920, 1923, 1926-9, 1935, 1937, 1939, 1946, 1948, 1953, 1955, 1957, 1959, 1961-4, 1968-9, 1973-7, 1979, 1981-5, 1988, 1990, 1992-3

48 Oxford 1872, 1876, 1878, 1882-5, 1890, 1894, 1897-8, 1901-2, 1904, 1907-8, 1910-2, 1921-2, 1924-5, 1930, 1932-4, 1938, 1947, 1949-52, 1956, 1958, 1960, 1965, 1967, 1970-2, 1978, 1980, 1986-7, 1989, 1991, 1994

13 Drawn 1874-5, 1879, 1881, 1891, 1893, 1895, 1903, 1909, 1931, 1936, 1954, 1966

War-time series: Between 1940-5 a total of 12 matches were played and the winners were:

9 Cambridge 1941 (2), 1942 (2), 1943 (3), 1944, 1944, 1945; 2 Oxford 1940, 1944; 1 Drawn 1945

County Championship

The English County Championship was introduced in 1889, when, after an unbeaten season, Yorkshire were declared the champions by the Rugby Union. The current system, the fifth, divides the counties into Northern Midland, London and South-Western divisions, with a promotion and relegation system, before the leading four counties play-off in semi-finals to decide which two meet in the final. In 1994 the event was downgraded with the exclusion of players from the 1st and 2nd Divisions of the Courage Clubs Championship. Not held 1915-9, 1945-6. *Winners:*

16	Lancashire	1891, 1935, 1938, 1947-9, 1955, 1969, 1973, 1977, 1980, 1982, 1988, 1990, 1992-3
15	Gloucestershire	1910, 1913, 1920-2, 1930-2, 1937, 1972, 1974-6, 1983-4
12	Yorkshire	1889-90, 1892-6, 1926, 1928, 1953, 1987, 1994
10	Warwickshire	1939, 1958-60, 1962-5, 1986, 1995
8	Durham	1900, 1902-3, 1905, 1907*, 1909, 1967*, 1989
8	Middlesex	1929, 1952, 1954, 1956, 1966, 1968, 1979, 1985
7	Devon	1899, 1901, 1906, 1907*, 1911-2, 1957
3	Kent	1897, 1904, 1927
2	Cornwall	1908, 1991
2	Northumberland	1898, 1981
2	Hampshire	1933, 1936
2	East Midlands	1934, 1951
2	Cheshire	1950, 1961
2	Surrey	1967*, 1971

1 Midlands 1914, Cumberland 1924, Leicestershire 1925, Staffordshire 1970, North Midlands 1978

* *shared title*

John Player Special/Pilkington Cup

The RFU Knockout Competition for English club sides was inaugurated in the 1971/2 season and has been held annually since then. Sponsored by John Player 1971/2 to 1987/8 and by Pilkington from 1988/9. The final is at Twickenham. *Finals:*

1972	Gloucester 17	Moseley 6
1973	Coventry 27	Bristol 15
1974	Coventry 26	London Scottish 6
1975	Bedford 28	Rosslyn Park 12
1976	Gosforth 23	Rosslyn Park 14
1977	Gosforth 27	Waterloo 11
1978	Gloucester 6	Leicester 3
1979	Leicester 15	Moseley 12
1980	Leicester 21	London Irish 9
1981	Leicester 22	Gosforth 15
1982	Gloucester 12 shared with Moseley 12 *	
1983	Bristol 28	Leicester 22
1984	Bath 10	Bristol 9
1985	Bath 24	London Welsh 15
1986	Bath 25	Wasps 17
1987	Bath 19	Wasps 12
1988	Harlequins 28	Bristol 22
1989	Bath 10	Leicester 6
1990	Bath 48	Gloucester 6
1991	Harlequins 25	Northampton 13 *
1992	Bath 15	Harlequins 12 *
1993	Leicester 23	Harlequins 16
1994	Bath 21	Leicester 9
1995	Bath 36	Wasps 16

Most wins: 9 Bath, 3 Leicester and Gloucester

* *after extra time*

Most successful clubs on a points system of 3 for a win, 2 for losing in the final and 1 for losing in the semi-finals:
27 Bath, 25 Leicester, 16 Harlequins, 13.5 Gloucester, 12 Coventry, 9 Bristol, 8.5 Moseley, 7 Gosforth

National Merit Tables - Courage Clubs Championship

The RFU approved a plan in 1985 for the leading English clubs to form into two divisions known as Merit Tables 'A' and 'B'. Selected matches throughout the season were designated Merit Table matches, and an end-of-season league table was drawn up. A third Merit Table, C was added in 1986/7. Now the extensive series of Leagues are numbered and sponsored by Courage. *Winners of Merit Table A 1985/6 and 1986/7 and of Division One of the Courage League:*

1985/6	Gloucester
1986/7	Bath
1987/8	Leicester
1988/9	Bath
1989/90	Wasps
1990/1	Bath
1991/2	Bath
1992/3	Bath
1993/4	Bath
1994/5	Leicester

Welsh Cup

The Welsh Rugby Union Challenge Cup has been contested annually since the 1971/2 season. All finals have been in Cardiff, at Arms Park, now the National Stadium. Formerly the Schweppes Cup, the competition was renamed the Swalec Cup from 1992/3. *Finals:*

1972	Neath 15	Llanelli 9
1973	Llanelli 30	Cardiff 7
1974	Llanelli 12	Aberavon 10
1975	Llanelli 15	Aberavon 6
1976	Llanelli 15	Swansea 4
1977	Newport 16	Cardiff 15
1978	Swansea 13	Newport 9
1979	Bridgend 18	Pontypridd 12
1980	Bridgend 15	Swansea 9
1981	Cardiff 14	Bridgend 6
1982	Cardiff 12*	Bridgend 12
1983	Pontypool 18	Swansea 6
1984	Cardiff 24	Neath 19
1985	Llanelli 15	Cardiff 14
1986	Cardiff 28	Newport 21
1987	Cardiff 16	Swansea 15 (et)
1988	Llanelli 28	Neath 13
1989	Neath 14	Llanelli 13
1990	Neath 16	Bridgend 10
1991	Llanelli 24	Pontypool 9
1992	Llanelli 16	Swansea 7
1993	Llanelli 21	Neath 18
1994	Cardiff 15	Llanelli 8
1995	Swansea 17	Pontypridd 12

* *won on most tries*

Most wins: 9 Llanelli, 6 Cardiff

Most successful clubs on a points system for 3 for a win, 2 for losing in the final and 1 for losing in the semi-finals:
38 Llanelli, 29 Cardiff, 16 Bridgend, 18 Neath, 21 Swansea, 12 Aberavon, 9 Pontypool, Newport

Welsh League

Sponsored by Heineken and introduced in 1990/1. *Premier Division winners:*

1990/1 Neath
1991/2 Swansea
1992/3 Llanelli
1993/4 Swansea
1994/5 Cardiff

Scottish Club Championship

The premier club competition in Scotland is the McEwans League, instituted 1974. There are currently seven divisions.
Division One winners:

1974-8 Hawick
1979 Heriot's FP
1980 Gala
1982 Hawick
1983 Gala
1984-7 Hawick
1988-9 Kelso
1990 Melrose
1991 Boroughmuir
1992-4 Melrose
1995 Stirling County
Most wins: 10 Hawick

All-Ireland Championship

Inaugurated in 1990. Prior to that league competitions were organised by the four Irish provinces: Connacht, Leinster, Munster and Ulster. *Winners:*

1991 Cork Constitution
1992 Garryowen
1993 Young Munster
1994 Garryowen
1995 Shannon

Middlesex Sevens

This leading Sevens tournament was inaugurated in 1926. The final of the knockout tournament is played at Twickenham and regularly attracts crowds in excess of 50,000. The winners receive the Russell Cargill Trophy. *Winners:*

1926	Harlequins 25	St Mary's Hospital 3
1927	Harlequins 28	Blackheath 6
1928	Harlequins 19	Blackheath 8
1929	Harlequins 16	Rosslyn Park 9
1930	London Welsh 6	Blackheath 0
1931	London Welsh 9	Harlequins 5
1932	Blackheath 18	Harlequins 10
1933	Harlequins 23	Wasps 0
1934	Barbarians 6	Richmond 3*
1935	Harlequins 10	London Welsh 3
1936	Sale 18	Blackheath 6
1937	London Scottish 19	Old Merchant Taylors 3
1938	Metropolitan Police 13	London Scottish 3
1939	Cardiff 11	London Scottish 6
1940	St Mary's Hospital 14	OCTU Sandhurst 10
1941	Cambridge University 6	Welsh Guards 0
1942	St Mary's Hospital 8	RAF 6
1943	St Mary's Hospital 8	Middlesex Hospital 3
1944	St Mary's Hospital 15	RAF Jurby 5
1945	Nottingham 6	St Mary's Hospital 3
1946	St Mary's Hospital 13	Cardiff 3
1947	Rosslyn Park 12	Richmond 6
1948	Wasps 14	Harlequins 5
1949	Heriot's FP 16	London Scottish 6
1950	Rosslyn Park 16	Heriot's FP 0
1951	Richmond II 13	Wasps 10
1952	Wasps 12	St Thomas's Hospital 10
1953	Richmond 10	London Welsh 3
1954	Rosslyn Park 16	London Scottish 0
1955	Richmond 5	St Luke's College 0
1956	London Welsh 24	Emmanuel College, Cambridge 10
1957	St Luke's College 18	London Welsh 5
1958	Blackheath 16	Harlequins 3
1959	Loughborough Colls 3	London Welsh 0
1960	London Scottish 16	London Welsh 5
1961	London Scottish 20	Stewart's College FP 6
1962	London Scottish 18	Rosslyn Park 6
1963	London Scottish 15	Hawick 11
1964	Loughborough Colls 18	London Scottish 16
1965	London Scottish 15	Loughborough Colleges 8
1966	Loughborough Colls 29	Northampton 10
1967	Harlequins 14	Richmond 11
1968	London Welsh 16	Richmond 3
1969	St Luke's College 21	Edinburgh Wanderers 16
1970	Loughborough Colls 26	Edinburgh Wanderers 11
1971	London Welsh 18	Harlequins 9
1972	London Welsh 22	Public School Wanderers 18
1973	London Welsh 24	Public School Wanderers 22
1974	Richmond 34	London Welsh 16
1975	Richmond 24	Loughborough Colleges 8
1976	Loughborough Colls 21	Harlequins 20
1977	Richmond 26	Gosforth 16
1978	Harlequins 40	Rosslyn Park 12
1979	Richmond 24	London Scottish 10
1980	Richmond 34	Rosslyn Park 18
1981	Rosslyn Park 16	London Welsh 14
1982	Stewart's Melville FP 34	Richmond 12
1983	Richmond I 20	London Welsh 13
1984	London Welsh 34	Heriot's FP 18
1985	Wasps 25	Nottingham 6
1986	Harlequins 18	Nottingham 10
1987	Harlequins 22	Rosslyn Park 6
1988	Harlequins 20	Bristol 18
1989	Harlequins 18	Rosslyn Park 12

1990	Harlequins 26	Rosslyn Park 10
1991	London Scottish 20	Harlequins 16
1992	Western Samoa 30	London Scottish 6
1993	Wasps 26	Northampton 24
1994	Bath 19	Orrell 12
1995	Leicester 38	Ithuba (SAf) 19

* after extra time

Most wins: 13 Harlequins, 9 Richmond, 8 London Welsh, 7 London Scottish, 5 St Mary's Hospital, Loughborough Colleges, 4 Rosslyn Park, Wasps

French Championship

First contested in 1892.

Most titles

12	Toulouse	1912, 1922-4, 1926-7, 1947, 1985-6, 1989, 1994-5 (and wartime 1916)
11	AS Béziers	1961, 1971-2, 1974-5, 1977-8, 1980-1, 1983-4
8	Stade Français	1893-5, 1897-8, 1901, 1903, 1908,
8	SU Agen	1930, 1945, 1962, 1965-6, 1976, 1982, 1988
8	FC Lourdes	1948, 1952-3, 1956-8, 1960, 1968
7	Bordeaux	1899, 1904-7, 1909, 1911
5	Racing Club de France	1892, 1900, 1902, 1959, 1990 (and wartime 1918)
5	USA Perpignan	1921, 1925, 1938, 1944, 1955

Olympic Games

Rugby has been included in four Olympic celebrations, the first at Paris in 1900. Three teams took part in 1900 and 1924, and played on a round-robin basis, while just two teams entered in 1908 and 1920 with the one match deciding the gold medallists. *Winners:*

1900	France	1920	USA
1908	Australia	1924	USA

Australia

Rugby was first played in Australia in 1829 and the first administrative body, the Southern Union, was formed in 1874. It was renamed the NSW Rugby Union in 1892. The first Australian rugby club was that of Sydney University, formed in 1864. New South Wales and Queensland are the predominant states for the game.

Sydney First Grade Premiership

First played in 1900. *Wins (* shared)*

25	Randwick	1930, 1934, 1938, 1940, 1948, 1959, 1965-7, 1971, 1973-4, 1978-82, 1984, 1987-92, 1994
21	University	1901*, 1904, 1919-20, 1923-4, 1926-8, 1937, 1939, 1945, 1951, 1953-5, 1961-2, 1968, 1970, 1972
9	Eastern Suburb	1903, 1913, 1921, 1931, 1941, 1944, 1946-7, 1969
8	Glebe	1900, 1901*, 1906-7, 1909, 1912, 1914, 1925*
6	Northern Suburbs	1933, 1935, 1960, 1963-4, 1975
6	Manly	1922, 1932, 1942-3, 1950, 1983
6	Gordon	1949, 1952, 1956, 1958, 1976, 1993
3	Newtown	1908, 1910-1
3	Parramatta	1977, 1985-6
2	Western Suburbs	1902, 1929
1	South Sydney	1905
1	Balmain	1925*
1	Drummoyne	1936
1	St.George	1957

New Zealand

Rugby was introduced into New Zealand in 1870. The first provincial union was that of Canterbury in 1879, and the New Zealand Rugby Football Union was founded in 1892.

Ranfurly Shield

The inter-provincial championship, first held in 1904. It is not a knockout competition, but one in which the champion state puts its title up for a challenge. *Winner and years when the title changed hands:*

1904 Wellington	1956 Wellington
1905 Auckland	1957 Otago
1913 Taranki	1957 Taranaki
1914 Wellington	1959 Southland
1920 Southland	1959 Auckland
1921 Wellington	1960 North Auckland
1922 Hawke's Bay	1960 Auckland
1927 Wairarapa	1963 Wellington
1927 Manawhenua	1963 Taranaki
1927 Canterbury	1965 Auckland
1928 Wairarapa	1966 Waikato
1929 Southland	1966 Hawke's Bay
1930 Wellington	1969 Canterbury
1931 Canterbury	1971 Auckland
1934 Hawke's Bay	1971 North Auckland
1934 Auckland	1972 Auckland
1935 Canterbury	1972 Canterbury
1935 Otago	1973 Marlborough
1937 Southland	1974 South Canterbury
1938 Otago	1974 Wellington
1938 Southland	1974 Auckland
1947 Otago	1976 Manawatu
1950 Canterbury	1978 North Auckland
1950 Wairarapa	1979 Auckland
1950 South Canterbury	1980 Waikato
1950 North Auckland	1981 Wellington
1951 Waikato	1982 Canterbury
1952 Auckland	1985 Auckland
1952 Waikato	1993 Waikato
1953 Wellington	1994 Canterbury
1953 Canterbury	

Most successive defences: 61 Auckland 1985-93, 25 Auckland 1960-3, 25 Canterbury 1982-5
Record attendance: 52,000 Auckland v Canterbury at Lancaster Park 1985

New Zealand National Championship

A season-long league championship was inaugurated in 1976 involving 11 states in the first division, with each team playing every other once. There were also supplementary divisions enabling promotion to the first division. The format was changed in 1992 to 27 teams divided into three groups of nine, with the top four from each section playing semi-finals and a final. *Winners of first division:*

1976	Bay of Plenty
1977	Canterbury
1978	Wellington
1979	Counties
1980	Manawatu
1981	Wellington
1982	Auckland
1983	Canterbury
1984-5	Auckland
1986	Wellington
1987-90	Auckland
1991	Otago
1992	Waikato
1993-4	Auckland

South Africa

Rugby in South Africa, developed from a form of football known as 'Gog's game', was first played between civilian and military teams at Green Point Common, Cape Town, in 1862. The first union to be formed was Western Province in 1883 and the South African Rugby Board was founded in 1889.

Currie Cup

Inter-provincial tournament, first held 1889. Annual from 1968, prior to that it was mostly biennial, avoiding international tours. *Wins (* shared):*

29	Western Province	1889, 1892, 1894-5, 1897-8, 1904, 1906, 1908, 1914, 1920, 1925, 1927, 1929, 1932*, 1934*, 1936, 1947, 1954, 1959, 1964, 1966, 1979*, 1982-6, 1989*
18	Northern Transvaal	1946, 1956, 1968-9, 1971*, 1973-8, 1979*, 1980-1, 1987-8, 1989*, 1991
8	Transvaal	1922, 1939, 1950, 1952, 1971*, 1972, 1993-4
3	Griqualand West	1899, 1911, 1970
2	Border	1932*, 1934*
2	Natal	1990, 1992

Note 1934 competition was unfinished.

Highest score: Transvaal beat Far North 99-9 at Ellis Park, Johannesburg 7 Jul 1973

Women's World Cup

Contested for the first time in 1991, when 12 national teams played in Cardiff, Wales, where the final was won the USA who beat England 19-6. England beat USA 38-23 in the final to win the second championship in 1994.

Shinty

This 12-a-side curved stick (the caman) and ball game is played almost exclusively in the Scottish Highlands. The pitch is up to 170 yards *155m* long and 80 yards *73m* wide, and the goals 10ft by 12ft *3.0 - 3.65m*. The ball is about the size of a tennis ball and has a thick leather covering over a cork and worsted core.

The game's antecedents date back more than 2000 years to the ancient game of camanachd, meaning 'the sport of the curved stick', and was brought to Scotland from Ireland with the Celtic immigration about 1400 years ago. The sport provided effective battle tr aining, indeed it was probably a crude substitute for battle between clans. The present ruling body, the Camanachd Association was founded in 1893.

Camanachd Cup

The Camanachd Association Challenge Cup, instituted in 1896, is shinty's premier competition. *Most wins:*

28	Newtonmore	1907-10, 1929, 1931-2, 1936, 1947-8, 1950-1, 1955, 1957-9, 1967, 1970-2, 1975, 1977-9, 1981-2, 1985-6
20	Kyles Athletic	1904-6, 1920, 1922, 1924, 1927-8, 1935, 1956, 1962, 1965-6, 1968-9, 1974, 1976, 1980, 1983, 1994
14	Kingussie	1896, 1900, 1902-3, 1914, 1921, 1961, 1984, 1987-9, 1991, 1993, 1995

Other recent winners: 1990 Skye, 1992 Fort William A record 11 winner's medals have been won by the Newtonmore players Johnnie Campbell, David Ritchie and Hugh Chisholm.

Highest score: 11-3 Newtonmore v Furnace 1909

Shooting

The first shooting club, the Lucerne Shooting Guild (Switzerland) was formed around 1466 and the first recorded shooting match was at Zürich in 1472. The National Rifle Association of Great Britain was formed in 1860 and the Clay Bird Shooting Association was founded in 1903. The American National Rifle Association was formed in 1871. The international governing body for the sport, the Union Internationale de Tir (UIT), was formed in Zürich in 1907.

Olympic Games

Shooting has been part of the Olympic programme since the first Games in 1896; its inclusion possibly being as a result of the Games' founder, Baron Pierre de Coubertain, being an excellent shot. Separate events for women were first held in 1984, although they had competed alongside their male counterparts since 1968. In 1986 the ISU introduced new regulations for determining major championships and world records. The leading eight competitors at the end of the designated number of rounds take part in a final shoot-out round with the target sub-divided into tenths of a point for rifle and pistol shooting. For trap and skeet shooting each of the leading competitors has 25 extra shots. This new scoring system was introduced into the Olympic programme for the first time in 1988. *Winners:*

Free Pistol
60 shots from 50 metres

1896	Sumner Paine (USA)	442
1900	Conrad Röderer (Swi)	503
1906	Georgios Orphanidis (Gre)	221
1912	Alfred Lane (USA)	499
1920	Karl Frederick (USA)	496

1936   Torsten Ullmann (Swe) 559
1948   Edwin Vazquez Cam (Per) 545
1952   Huelet Benner (USA) 553
1956   Pentti Linnosvuo (Fin) 556
1960   Aleksey Gushchin (USSR) 560
1964   Väinö Markkanen (Fin) 560
1968   Grigoriy Kossykh (USSR) 562
1972   Ragnar Skanåkar (Swe) 567
1976   Uwe Potteck (GDR) 573
1980   Aleksandr Melentyev (USSR) 581
1984   Xu Haifeng (Chn) 566
1988   Sorin Babii (Rom) 660 (566 + 94)
1992   Konstantin Loukachik (CIS/Bls) 658 (567 + 91)

Rapid Fire Pistol

Since 1948; 30 shots at five targets each at 25 metres. The shooter has 8 secs at each target in the first round, then 6 secs and then 4 secs. The set of 15 shots is then repeated.

1896   Jean Phrangoudis (Gre) 344
1900   Maurice Larrouy (Fra) 58
1906   Maurice Lecoq (Fra) 250
1908   Paul van Asbroeck (Bel) 490
1912   Alfred Lane (USA) 287
1920   Guilherme Paraense (Bra) 274
1924   Henry Bailey (USA) 18
1932   Renzo Morigi (Ita) 36
1936   Cornelius van Oyen (Ger) 36
1948   Károly Takács (Hun) 580
1952   Károly Takács (Hun) 579
1956   Stefan Petrescu (Rom) 587
1960   William McMillan (USA) 587
1964   Pentti Linnosvuo (Fin) 592
1968   Józef Zapedzki (Pol) 593
1972   Józef Zapedzki (Pol) 595
1976   Norbert Klaar (GDR) 597
1980   Corneliu Ion (Rom) 596
1984   Takeo Kamachi (Jap) 595
1988   Afanasi Kuzmin (USSR) 698 (598+100)
1992   Ralf Schumann (Ger) 885 (594 + 105 + 96)

Small Bore Rifle - Prone

60 shots within two hours at a target with a bullseye diameter of a mere 0.487in, and 50 metres away

1908   A A Carnell (UK) 387
1912   Frederick Hird (USA) 194
1920   Lawrence Nuesslein (USA) 391
1924   Pierre Coquelin de Lisle (Fra) 398
1932   Bertil Rönnmark (Swe) 294
1936   Willy Rögeberg (Nor) 300
1948   Arthur Cook (USA) 599
1952   Iosif Sarbu (Rom) 400
1956   Gerald Ouellette (Can) 600*
1960   Peter Kohnke (FRG) 590
1964   László Hammerl (Hun) 597
1968   Jan Kurka (Cs) 598
1972   Li Ho-jun (NKo) 599
1976   Karlheinz Smieszek (FRG) 599
1980   Károly Varga (Hun) 599
1984   Edward Etzel (USA) 599
1988   Miroslav Varga (Cs) 703.9 (600+103.9)
1992   Lee Eun-chul (SKo) 702.5 (597 + 105.5)

Record not allowed, range marginally short.

Small Bore Rifle - Three Positions

40 shots each from kneeling, standing and prone positions at a target 50 metres away

1952   Erling Kongshaug (Nor) 1164
1956   Anatoliy Bogdanov (USSR) 1172
1960   Viktor Shamburkin (USSR) 1149
1964   Lones Wigger (USA) 1164
1968   Bernd Klingner (FRG) 1157
1972   John Writer (USA) 1166
1976   Lanny Bassham (USA) 1162
1980   Viktor Vlasov (USSR) 1173
1984   Malcolm Cooper (UK) 1173
1988   Malcolm Cooper (UK) 1279.3 (1180+99.3)
1992   Grachya Petikian (CIS/Arm) 1267.4 (1169 + 98.4)

Running Game Target

30 shots at a 2in 10-ring target on a simulated boar that does two runs across a 10-metre gap; one at 2.5 secs and one at 5 secs

1900   Louis Debray (Fra) 20
1972   Yakov Zhelezniak (USSR) 569
1976   Aleksandr Gazov (USSR) 579
1980   Igor Sokolov (USSR) 589
1984   Li Yuwei (Chn) 587
1988   Tor Heiestad (Nor) 689 (591+98)
1992   Michael Jakosits (Ger) 673 (580 + 93)

Air Rifle

60 shots at 10 metres

1984   Philippe Heberle (Fra) 589
1988   Goran Maksimovic (Yug) 695.6 (594+101.6)
1992   Yuriy Fedkin (CIS/Rus) 695.3 (593 + 102.3)

Air Pistol

60 shots at 10 metres

1988   Taniou Kiriakov (Bul) 687.9 (585+102.9)
1992   Wang Yifu (Chn) 684.8 (585 + 99.8)

Open to men and women

Trap

200 clay birds are released, one at a time, and at varying angles. The shooter is allowed two shots at each clay.

1900   Roger de Barbarin (Fra) 17
1906   Gerald Merlin (UK)* 24
       Sidney Merlin (UK)** 15
1908   Walter Ewing (Can) 72
1912   James Graham (USA) 96
1920   Mark Arie (USA) 95
1924   Gyula Halasy (Hun) 98
1952   George Généreux (Can) 192
1956   Galliano Rossini (Ita) 195
1960   Ion Dumitrescu (Rom) 192
1964   Ennio Mattarelli (Ita) 198
1968   Bob Braithwaite (UK) 198
1972   Angelo Scalzone (Ita) 199
1976   Don Haldeman (USA) 190
1980   Luciano Giovanetti (Ita) 198
1984   Luciano Giovanetti (Ita) 192
1988   Dmitriy Monakov (USSR) 222 (197+25)
1992   Petr Hrdlicka (Cs) 219 (195 + 24)

*single shot, ** double shot*

Skeet

The shooter attempts to hit 200 clay targets which are released either one or two at a time. Unlike trap shooting he/she fires from eight different 'stations' and the birds are released from towers as opposed to ground level.

1968	Yevgeniy Petrov (USSR)	198
1972	Konrad Wirnhier (FRG)	195
1976	Josef Panácek (Cs)	198
1980	Hans Kjeld Rasmussen (Den)	196
1984	Matthew Dryke (USA)	198
1988	Axel Wegner (GDR) 222 (198+24)	
1992	Zhang Shan (Chn) 223 (200 + 23) (woman)	

Women - Sport Pistol

60 shots at 10 metres

1984	Linda Thom (Can)	585
1988	Nino Salukvadze (USSR)	690 (591+99)
1992	Marina Logvinenko (CIS/Rus)	684 (587 + 97)

Women - Air Rifle

40 shots at 10 metres

1984	Pat Spurgin (USA)	393
1988	Irina Chilova (USSR)	498.5 (395+103.5)
1992	Yeo Kab-soon (SKo)	498.2 (396 + 102.2)

Women - Air Pistol

40 shots at 10 metres

1988	Jasna Sekaric (Yug)	489.5 (389+100.5)
1992	Marina Logvinenko (CIS/Rus)	486.4 (387 + 99.4)

Women - Small Bore Standard Rifle

60 shots at 10 metres

1984	Wu Xiaoxuan (Chn)	581
1988	Silvia Sperber (FRG)	685.6 (590+95.6)
1992	Launi Melli (USA)	684.3 (587 + 97.3)

Discontinued events

Free Rifle - three postions

120 shots from 300 metres

1896	Georgis Orphanidis (Gre)	1583
1906	Gudbrand Skatteboe (Nor)	973
1908	Albert Helgerud (Nor)	909
1912	Paul Colas (Fra)	987
1920	Morris Fisher (USA)	996
1924	Morris Fisher (USA)	95
1948	Emil Grüning (Swi)	1120
1952	Anatoliy Bogdanov (USSR)	1123
1956	Vasiliy Borissov (USSR)	1138
1960	Hubert Hammerer (Aut)	1129
1964	Gary Anderson (USA)	1153
1968	Gary Anderson (USA)	1157
1972	Lones Wigger (USA)	1155

Free Rifle

1896	Pantelis Karasevdas (Gre) 2320: over 200m
1906	Marcel de Stadelhofen (Swi) 243: any position (300m)
1906	Gudbrand Skatteboe (Nor) prone (300m)
1906	Konrad Stäheli (Swi) kneeling (300m)
1906	Gudbrand Skatteboe (Nor) standing (300m)
1908	Jerry Millner (UK) 98: over 1000y

Free Rifle - Team

1906	Switzerland 4596
1908	Norway 5055

Yeo Kab-soon, 1992 Olympic champion

1912	Sweden 5655
1920	USA 4876
1924	USA 676

Military Rifle

1900	Emil Kellenberger (Swi) 930: three pos. (300m)
1900	Lars Madsen (Den) 305: standing (300m)
1900	Konrad Stäheli (Swi) 324: kneeling (300m)
1900	Achille Paroche (Fra) 332: prone (300m)
1906	Léon Moreaux (Fra) 187: stand or kneel (200m)
1906	Louis Richardet (Swi) 238: stand or kneel (300m)
1912	Sándor Prokopp (Hun) 97: three positions (300m)
1912	Paul Colas (Fra) 94: any position (600m)
1920	Otto Olsen (Nor) 60: prone (300m)
1920	Carl Osburn (USA) 56: standing (300m)
1920	Hugo Johansson (Swe) 59: prone (600m)

Military Rifle - Team

1900	Switzerland 4399: (300m)
1908	USA 2531: (200, 500, 600, 800, 900, 1000yd)
1912	USA 1687: (200, 400, 500, 600m)
1920	Denmark 266: standing (300m)
1920	USA 289: prone (300m)
1920	USA 287: prone (600m)
1920	USA 573: prone (300m & 600m)

Small Bore Rifle

1908	John Fleming (UK) 24: moving target
1908	William Styles (UK) 45: disappearing target
1912	Wilhelm Carlberg (Swe) 242: disappearing target

Small Bore Rifle - Team

1908	United Kingdom 771: (50 & 100yd)
1912	Sweden 925: (25m)
1912	United Kingdom 762: (50m)
1920	USA 1899: (50m)

Live Pigeon Shooting

1900	Léon de Lunden (Bel) 21

Clay Pigeons - Team

1908	United Kingdom 407
1912	USA 532
1920	USA 547
1924	USA 363

Running Deer

1908	Oscar Swahn (Swe)	25 *
1908	Walter Winans (USA)	46 **
1912	Alfred Swahn (Swe)	41 *
1912	Åke Lundeberg (Swe)	79 **
1920	Otto Olsen (Nor)	43 *
1920	Ole Lilloe-Olsen (Nor)	82 **
1924	John Boles (USA)	40 *
1924	Ole Lilloe-Olsen (Nor)	76 **

* single shot, ** double shot

Running Deer - Team

1908	Sweden	86
1912	Sweden	151
1920	Norway	178 *
1920	Norway	343 **
1924	Norway	160 *
1924	United Kingdom	263 **

* single shot, **double shot

Running Deer - Single and double shot

1952	John Larsen (Nor)	413
1956	Vitaliy Romanenko (USSR)	441

Military Revolver

1896	John Paine (USA)	442: (25m)
1906	Louis Richardet (Swi)	253: (20m)
1906	Jean Fouconnier (Fra)	219 (model 1873)

Duelling Pistol

1906	Léon Moreaux (Fra)	242: Over 20m
1906	Konstantinos Skarlatos (Gre)	133: Over 25m

Team Event

1900	Switzerland	2271
1908	USA	1914
1912	USA	1916 *
1912	Sweden	1145 **
1920	USA	2372 *
1920	USA	1310 **

* over 50m, **over 30m

Most Olympic medals (G gold, S silver, B bronze)

Shooters to have won four or more gold medals:

Total	Name	G	S	B	Years
11	Carl Osburn (USA)	5	4	2	1912-24
8	Konrad Stäheli (Swi)	5	2	1	1900
8	Otto Olsen (Nor)	4	3	1	1920-4
7	Gudbrand Skatteboe (Nor)	4	3	-	1906-20
7	Willis Lee (USA)	5	1	1	1920
7	Lloyd Spooner (USA)	4	1	2	1920
7	Einer Liberg (Nor)	4	2	1	1908-24
6	Louis Richardet (Swi)	5	1	-	1900
6	Ole Lilloe-Olsen (Nor)	5	1	-	1920-4
6	Alfred Lane (USA)	5	-	1	1912-20
5	Morris Fisher (USA)	5	-	-	1920-4

Most by women

3	Jasna Sekaric (Yug)	1	1	1	1988-92
2	Marina Logvinenko (CIS/Rus)	2	-	-	1992

Three other women have one gold and one other medal

Most individual gold medals: 3 Gudbrand Skatteboe (Nor) 1906

Oscar Swahn (Swe) was aged 64 years 258 days when he won a gold medal in the team running deer event in 1912 to become the oldest gold medallist in Olympic history. He became the oldest ever Olympic competitor, and indeed medallist, in 1920 when he appeared in Sweden's silver medal winning team, again in the running deer event. He qualified for the 1924 Games, but illness prevented him competing. Ragnar Skanåker (Swe) won the gold medal at free pistol in 1972, he took the silver in 1984 and 1988 and the bronze in 1992 for a record 20-year medal span.

<hr>

World Records

World records, as recognised by the UIT can only be set in certain major championships, such as the Olympic Games, World and Continental Championships and the World Cup events.

Figures in brackets indicates score at end of regular competition + final shoot-out round score:

Men

Free Rifle (Three positions, 3 x 40 shots at 50m)
1287.9 (1186 + 101.9) Rajmond Debevec (Slo)   1992
Free Rifle (Prone, 60 shots at 50m)
703.5 (599 +104.5)   Jens Harskov (Den)   1991
Free Pistol (60 shots at 50m)
672.5 (575 + 97.5)   Sergey Pyzhyanov (Rus)   1993
Rapid Fire Pistol (60 shots at 25m)
699.7 (596 + 103.7)   Ralf Schumann (FRG)   1994
Running Game Target (60 shots at 50m with small bore rifle)
678.8 (579 + 99.8)   Jens Zimmermann (Ger)   1994
Air Rifle (60 shots at 10m)
699.4 (596+ 103.4)   Rajmond Debevec (Slo)   1990
Air Pistol (60 shots at 10m)
695.1 (593 + 102.1)   Sergey Pyzhyanov (USSR) 1989

Women

Standard Rifle (Three positions, 3 x 20 shots at 50m)
689.3 (590 + 99.3)   Vessela Letcheva (Bul)   1991
Sport Pistol (60 shots at 25m)
696.2 (594 + 102.2)   Diana Jorgova (Bul)   1994
Air Rifle (40 shots at 10m)
500.8 (399 + 101.8)   Valentina Cherkasova (USSR)
                                   1991
Air Pistol (40 shots at 10m)
492.4 (392 + 100.4)   Lieselotte Breker (FRG)   1989

Open

Trap (125 targets + 25)
149 (125 + 24)   Giovanni Pellielo (Ita)   1994
149 (125 + 24)   Marco Venturini (Ita)   1994
Skeet (125 targets + 25)
149 (124 + 25)   Dean Clark (USA)   1993
149 (124 + 25)   Andrea Benelli (Ita) (twice) 1994

<hr>

Skiing

The word *ski* was the Norwegian word for snow-shoe. The earliest ski, recovered from a peat bog in Sweden, has been dated as c.2500 BC. It is 1.1m long and c.20cm wide. Long skis, over 2m in length, were used in Norway about 4000 years ago, and both long and short skis have been widely used in Scandinavian countries.

In modern times two main categories of skiing have evolved, Nordic, which encompasses cross-country and ski-jumping, and Alpine, which has down-hill and slalom events. The first ski races were held in Norway and Australia in the 1850s and 1860s, after Søndre Nordheim had developed techniques and skis in the province of Telemark in Norway. The first national governing body was that of Norway, formed in 1883, public imagination being caught by the epic Greenland trek using skis of the great Norwegian explorer Fridtjof Nansen in 1888.

The technique of Alpine skiing was pioneered by the Austrian Mathias Zdarsky at the end of the 19th century and British enthusiasts developed winter sports and races, notably in Switzerland at the turn of the century. Sir Henry Lunn pioneered skiing holidays and his son Sir Arnold Lunn introduced the modern slalom event. The International Ski Federation (FIS) was founded in 1924 to succeed the International Skiing Commission, founded in Oslo in 1910.

See also *Biathlon* for the results of combined skiing and shooting.

ALPINE SKIING

Olympic Games

Alpine skiing events were first included at the Olympic Games in 1936. *Winners:*

Men's Alpine Combination
Downhill and slalom
1936 Franz Pfnür (Ger)
1948 Henri Oreiller (Fra)
1988 Hubert Strolz (Aut)
1992 Josef Polig (Ita)
1994 Lasse Kjus (Nor)

Men's Downhill
1948 Henri Oreiller (Fra)
1952 Zeno Colò (Ita)
1956 Toni Sailer (Aut)
1960 Jean Vuarnet (Fra)
1964 Egon Zimmermann (Aut)
1968 Jean-Claude Killy (Fra)
1972 Bernhard Russi (Swi)
1976 Franz Klammer (Aut)
1980 Leonhard Stock (Aut)
1984 William Johnson (USA)
1988 Pirmin Zurbriggen (Swi)
1992 Patrick Ortlieb (Aut)
1994 Tommy Moe (USA)

Men's Giant Slalom
1952 Stein Eriksen (Nor)
1956 Toni Sailer (Aut)
1960 Roger Staub (Swi)
1964 François Bonlieu (Fra)
1968 Jean-Claude Killy (Fra)
1972 Gustavo Thoeni (Ita)
1976 Heini Hemmi (Swi)
1980 Ingemar Stenmark (Swe)
1984 Max Julen (Swi)
1988 Alberto Tomba (Ita)
1992 Alberto Tomba (Ita)
1994 Markus Wasmeier (Ger)

Men's Slalom
1948 Edy Reinalter (Swi)
1952 Othmar Schneider (Aut)
1956 Toni Sailer (Aut)
1960 Ernst Hinterseer (Aut)
1964 Josef Stiegler (Aut)
1968 Jean-Claude Killy (Fra)
1972 Francisco Fernandez Ochoa (Spa)
1976 Piero Gros (Ita)
1980 Ingemar Stenmark (Swe)
1984 Phil Mahre (USA)
1988 Alberto Tomba (Ita)
1992 Finn-Christian Jagge (Nor)
1994 Thomas Stangassinger (Aut)

Men's Super Giant Slalom
1988 Franck Riccard (Fra)
1992 Kjetil Andre Aamodt (Nor)
1994 Markus Wasmeier (Ger)

Women's Alpine Combination
Downhill and slalom
1936 Christl Cranz (Ger)
1948 Trude Beiser (Aut)
1988 Anita Wachter (Aut)
1992 Petra Kronberger (Aut)
1994 Pernilla Wiberg (Swe)

Women's Downhill
1948 Hedy Schlunegger (Swi)
1952 Trude Jochum (née Beiser) (Aut)
1956 Madeleine Berthod (Swi)
1960 Heidi Biebl (FRG)
1964 Christl Haas (Aut)
1968 Olga Pall (Aut)
1972 Marie-Thérèse Nadig (Swi)
1976 Rosi Mittermaier (FRG)
1980 Annemarie Moser-Pröll (Aut)
1984 Michela Figini (Swi)
1988 Marina Kiehl (FRG)
1992 Kerrin Lee-Gartner (Can)
1994 Katja Seizinger (Ger)

Women's Giant Slalom
1952 Andrea Mead-Lawrence (USA)
1956 Ossi Reichert (FRG)
1960 Yvonne Rüegg (Swi)
1964 Marielle Goitschel (Fra)
1968 Nancy Greene (Can)
1972 Marie-Thérèse Nadig (Swi)
1976 Kathy Kreiner (Can)
1980 Hanni Wenzel (Lie)
1984 Debbie Armstrong (USA)
1988 Vreni Schneider (Swi)
1992 Pernilla Wiberg (Swe)
1994 Deborah Compagnoni (Ita)

Women's Slalom
1948 Gretchen Fraser (USA)
1952 Andrea Mead-Lawrence (USA)
1956 Renée Colliard (Swi)
1960 Anne Heggtveit (Can)
1964 Christine Goitschel (Fra)
1968 Marielle Goitschel (Fra)
1972 Barbara Cochran (USA)

Alberto Tomba

1976 Rosi Mittermaier (FRG)
1980 Hanni Wenzel (Lie)
1984 Paoletta Magoni (Ita)
1988 Vreni Schneider (Swi)
1992 Petra Kronberger (Aut)
1994 Vreni Schneider (Swi)

Women's Super Giant Slalom
1988 Sigrid Wolf (Aut)
1992 Deborah Compagnoni (Ita)
1994 Diann Roffe-Steinrotter
      (USA)

Most Olympic gold medals
Men
3 Toni Sailer (Aut) 1956
3 Jean-Claude Killy (Fra) 1968
3 Alberto Tomba (Aut) 1988-92
Women
3 Vreni Schneider (Swi) 1988-94

Most Olympic medals
Men
5 Alberto Tomba - 3 gold, silver
   slalom 1992, 1994
5 Kjetil André Aamodt (Nor)
   gold - super G 1992; silver -
   combined, downhill 1994;
   bronze - giant slalom 1992,
   super G 1994
Women
5 Vreni Schneider (Swi) 3 gold,
   silver - combined 1994, bronze
   - giant slalom 1994

World Championships

First held at downhill in 1931 at
Mürren. Held annually 1931-9 and
biennially post-war. Up to 1980 the
Olympic Champions were also world
champions, except in 1936 when separate championships were held. The
1995 championships were cancelled
due to lack of snow.

Winners additional to those shown
earlier as Olympic Champions, and
those to have won most titles (including Olympics shown by *):

Men's Alpine Combination
1932   Otto Furrer (Swi)
1933   Anton Seelos (Aut)
1934   David Zogg (Swi)
1935   Anton Seelos (Aut)
1936   Rudolf Rominger (Swi)
1937-8 Emile Allais (Fra)
1939   Josef Jennewein (Ger)
1954   Stein Eriksen (Nor)
1956   Toni Sailer (Aut)
1958   Toni Sailer (Aut)
1960   Guy Périllat (Fra)
1962   Karl Schranz (Aut)
1964   Ludwig Leitner (FRG)
1966   Jean-Claude Killy (Fra)

1968 Jean-Claude Killy (Fra)
1970 Bill Kidd (USA)
1972 Gustavo Thoeni (Ita)
1974 Franz Klammer (Aut)
1976 Gustavo Thoeni (Ita)
1978 Andreas Wenzel (Lie)
1980 Phil Mahre (USA)
1982 Michel Vion (Fra)
1985 Pirmin Zurbriggen (Swi)
1987 Marc Girardelli (Lux)
1989 Marc Girardelli (Lux)
1991 Stefan Eberharter (Aut)
1993 Lasse Kjus (Nor)
Most wins: 2 Seelos, Allais,
Sailer, Killy, Thoeni, Girardelli.

Men's Downhill
1931 Walter Prager (Swi)
1932 Guzzi Lantschner (Aut)
1933 Walter Prager (Swi)
1934 David Zogg (Swi)
1935 Franz Zingerle (Aut)
1936 Rudolf Rominger (Swi)
1937 Emile Allais (Fra)
1938 James Couttet (Fra)
1939 Helmut Lantschner (Ger)
1950 Zeno Colò (Ita)
1954 Christian Pravda (Aut)
1958 Toni Sailer (Aut)
1962 Karl Schranz (Aut)
1966 Jean-Claude Killy (Fra)
1970 Bernhard Russi (Swi)
1974 David Zwilling (Aut)
1978 Josef Walcher (Aut)
1982 Harti Weirather (Aut)
1985 Pirmin Zurbriggen (Swi)
1987 Peter Müller (Swi)
1989 Hansjörg Tauscher (FRG)
1991 Franz Heinzer (Swi)
1993 Urs Lehmann (Swi)
Most wins: 2 Prager (Swi); each
also one *: Colò, Sailer, Killy,
Russi.

Men's Giant Slalom
1950 Zeno Colò (Ita)
1954 Stein Eriksen (Nor)
1958 Toni Sailer (Aut)
1962 Egon Zimmermann (Aut)
1966 Guy Périllat (Fra)
1970 Karl Schranz (Aut)
1974 Gustavo Thoeni (Ita)
1978 Ingemar Stenmark (Swe)
1982 Steve Mahre (USA)
1985 Markus Wasmaier (FRG)
1987 Pirmin Zurbriggen (Swi)
1989 Rudolf Nierlich (Aut)
1991 Rudolf Nierlich (Aut)
1993 Kjetil Andre Aamodt (Nor)
Most wins: 2 Eriksen, Sailer,
Thoeni, Stenmark (each also
one *), Nierlich

Men's Slalom
1931   David Zogg (Swi)
1932   Friedrich Daüber (Ger)
1933   Anton Seelos (Aut)
1934   Franz Pfnür (Ger)
1935   Anton Seelos (Aut)
1936   Rudi Matt (Ger)
1937   Emile Allais (Fra)
1938-9   Rudolf Rominger (Ger)
1950   Georges Schneider (Swi)
1954   Stein Eriksen (Nor)
1958   Josef Rieder (Aut)
1962   Charles Bozon (Fra)
1966   Carlo Senoner (Ita)
1970   Jean-Noël Augert (Fra)
1974   Gustavo Thoeni (Ita)
1978   Ingemar Stenmark (Swe)
1982   Ingemar Stenmark (Swe)
1985   Jonas Nilsson (Swe)
1987   Frank Wörndl (FRG)
1989   Rudolf Nierlich (Aut)
1991   Marc Girardelli (Lux)
1993   Kjetil Andre Aamodt (Nor)
Most wins: 3 Stenmark also 1980*

Men's Super Giant Slalom
1987 Pirmin Zurbriggen (Swi)
1989 Martin Hangl (Swi)
1991 Stefan Eberharter (Aut)
1993 *not held*

Women's Alpine Combination
1954 Ida Schöpfer (Swi)
1956 Madeleine Berthod (Swi)
1958 Frieda Dänzer (Swi)
1960 Anne Heggtveit (Can)
1962 Marielle Goitschel (Fra)
1964 Marielle Goitschel (Fra)
1966 Marielle Goitschel (Fra)
1968 Nancy Greene (Can)
1970 Michèle Jacot (Fra)
1972 Annemarie Pröll (Aut)
1974 Fabienne Serrat (Fra)
1976 Rosi Mittermaier (FRG)
1978 Annemarie Moser-Pröll
      (Aut)
1980 Hanni Wenzel (Lie)
1982 Erika Hess (Swi)
1985 Erika Hess (Swi)
1987 Erika Hess (Swi)
1989 Tamara McKinney (USA)
1991 Chantal Bournissen (Swi)
1993 Miriam Vogt (Ger)
Most wins: 5 Cranz, 3 M
Goitschel, Hess.

Women's Downhill
1950 Trude Beiser-Jochum (Aut)
1954 Ida Schöpfer (Swi)
1958 Lucille Wheeler (Can)
1962 Christl Haas (Aut)
1966 Erika Schinegger (Aut) #

1970	Annerösli Zyrd (Swi)
1974	Annemarie Moser-Pröll (Aut)
1978	Annemarie Moser-Pröll (Aut)
1982	Gerry Sorensen (Can)
1985	Michela Figini (Swi)
1987	Maria Walliser (Swi)
1989	Maria Walliser (Swi)
1991	Petra Kronberger (Aut)
1993	Kate Pace (Can)

Most wins: 3 Cranz, Moser-Pröll also 1980*

 # later declared as a man and gold went to Marielle Goitschel (Fra)

Women's Giant Slalom
1950	Dagmar Rom (Aut)
1954	Lucienne Schmitt (Fra)
1958	Lucille Wheeler (Can)
1962	Marianne Jahn (Aut)
1966	Marielle Goitschel (Fra)
1970	Betsy Clifford (Can)
1974	Fabienne Serrat (Fra)
1978	Maria Epple (FRG)
1982	Erika Hess (Swi)
1985	Diann Roffe (USA)
1987	Vreni Schneider (Swi)
1989	Vreni Schneider (Swi)
1991	Pernilla Wiberg (Swe)
1993	Carole Merle (Fra)

Most wins: 3 Schneider also 1988*

Women's Slalom
1950	Dagmar Rom (Aut)
1954	Trude Klecker (Aut)
1958	Inger Bjørnbakken (Nor)
1962	Marianne Jahn (Aut)
1966	Annie Famose (Fra)
1970	Ingrid Lafforgue (Fra)
1974	Hanni Wenzel (Lie)
1978	Lea Sölkner (Aut)
1982	Erika Hess (Swi)
1985	Perrine Pelen (Fra)
1987	Erika Hess (Swi)
1989	Mateja Svet (Yug)
1991	Vreni Schneider (Swi)
1993	Karin Buder (Aut)

Most wins: 4 Cranz

Women's Super-giant Slalom
1987	Maria Walliser (FRG)
1989	Ulrike Maier (Aut)
1991	Ulrike Maier (Aut)
1993	Katja Seizinger (Ger)

Most wins at all events
Men 7 Toni Sailer (Aut), 6 Jean-Claude Killy (Fra)
Women 12 Christl Cranz (Ger) - and the 1936 Olympic combined; 7 Marielle Goitschel, 6 Erika Hess

Vreni Schneider

All four titles have been won in one year by Sailer 1956 and Killy 1968.

World Cup

Contested annually from 1967 over a series of events during the winter season. The year given is that of the second half of the season. *Winners:*

Men's Overall
1967-8	Jean-Claude Killy (Fra)
1969-70	Karl Schranz (Aut)
1971-3	Gustavo Thoeni (Ita)
1974	Piero Gros (Ita)
1975	Gustavo Thoeni (Ita)
1976-8	Ingemar Stenmark (Swe)
1979	Peter Lüscher (Swi)
1980	Andreas Wenzel (Lie)
1981-3	Phil Mahre (USA)
1984	Pirmin Zurbriggen (Swi)
1985-6	Marc Girardelli (Lux)
1987-8	Pirmin Zurbriggen (Swi)
1989	Marc Girardelli (Lux)
1990	Pirmin Zurbriggen (Swi)
1991	Marc Girardelli (Lux)
1992	Paul Accola (Swi)
1993	Marc Girardelli (Lux)
1994	Kjetil Andre Aamodt (Nor)
1995	Alberto Tomba (Ita)

Most: 5 Girardelli, 4 Thoeni, Zurbriggen; 3 Stenmark, Mahre, Zurbriggen

Men's Downhill
1967	Jean-Claude Killy (Fra)
1968	Gerhard Nenning (Aut)
1969	Karl Schranz (Aut)
1970	Karl Schranz (Aut) & Karl Cordin (Aut)
1971-2	Bernhard Russi (Swi)
1973-4	Roland Collombin (Swi)
1975-8	Franz Klammer (Aut)
1979-80	Peter Müller (Swi)
1981	Harti Weirather (Aut)
1982	Steve Podborski (Can) & Peter Müller (Swi)
1983	Franz Klammer (Aut)
1984	Urs Räber (Swi)
1985	Helmut Höhflehner (Aut)
1986	Peter Wirnsberger (Aut)
1987-8	Pirmin Zurbriggen (Swi)
1989	Marc Girardelli (Lux)
1990	Helmut Höhflehner (Aut)
1991-3	Franz Heinzer (Swi)
1994	Marc Girardelli (Lux)
1995	Luc Alphand (Fra)

Most: 5 Klammer

Men's Giant Slalom
1967-8	Jean-Claude Killy (Fra)
1969	Karl Schranz (Aut)
1970	Gustavo Thoeni (Ita)
1971	Gustavo Thoeni (Ita) & Patrick Russel (Fra)
1972	Gustavo Thoeni (Ita)
1973	Hans Hinterseer (Aut)
1974	Piero Gros (Aut)
1975-6	Ingemar Stenmark (Swe)
1977	Heini Hemmi (Swi)
1978-81	Ingemar Stenmark (Swe)
1982-3	Phil Mahre (USA)
1984	Ingemar Stenmark (Swe) & Pirmin Zurbriggen (Swi)
1985	Marc Girardelli (Lux)
1986	Joel Gaspoz (Swi)

1987	Joel Gaspoz (Swi) & Pirmin Zurbriggen (Swi)
1988	Alberto Tomba (Ita)
1989	Ole Christian Furuseth (Nor) & Pirmin Zurbriggen (Swi)
1990	Ole Christian Furuseth (Nor)
1991-2	Alberto Tomba (Ita)
1993	Kjetil Andre Aamodt (Nor)
1994	Christian Mayer (Aut)
1995	Alberto Tomba (Ita)

Most: 7 Stenmark, 4 Tomba

Men's Slalom

1967	Jean-Claude Killy (Fra)
1968	Domeng Giovanoli (Swi)
1969	Jean-Noël Augert (Fra), Alfred Matt (Aut), Alain Penz (Fra), Patrick Russel (Fra)
1970	Patrick Russel & Alain Penz (Fra)
1971-2	Jean-Noël Augert (Fra)
1973-4	Gustavo Thoeni (Ita)
1975-81	Ingemar Stenmark (Swe)
1982	Phil Mahre (USA)
1983	Ingemar Stenmark (Swe)
1984-5	Marc Girardelli (Lux)
1986	Rok Petrovic (Yug)
1987	Bojan Krizaj (Yug)
1988	Alberto Tomba (Ita)
1989-90	Armin Bittner (FRG)
1991	Marc Girardelli (Lux)
1992	Alberto Tomba (Ita)
1993	Tomas Fogdö (Swe)
1994-5	Alberto Tomba (Ita)

Most: 8 Stenmark

Men's Super Giant Slalom

1986	Markus Wasmeier (FRG)
1987-90	Pirmin Zurbriggen (Swi)
1991	Franz Heinzer (Swi)
1992	Paul Accola (Swi)
1993	Kjetil Andre Aamodt (Nor)
1994	Jan Einar Thorsen (Nor)
1995	Peter Runggaldier (Ita)

Most: 4 Zurbriggen

Women's Overall

1967-8	Nancy Greene (Can)
1969	Gertrud Gabl (Aut)
1970	Michèle Jacot (Fra)
1971-5	Annemarie Moser-Pröll (Aut)
1976	Rosi Mittermaier (FRG)
1977	Lise-Marie Morerod (Swi)
1978	Hanni Wenzel (Lie)
1979	Annemarie Moser-Pröll (Aut)
1980	Hanni Wenzel (Lie)
1981	Marie-Thérèse Nadig (Swi)
1982	Erika Hess (Swi)

1983	Tamara McKinney (USA)
1984	Erika Hess (Swi)
1985	Michela Figini (Swi)
1986-7	Maria Walliser (Swi)
1988	Michela Figini (Swi)
1989	Vreni Schneider (Swi)
1990-2	Petra Kronberger (Aut)
1993	Anita Wachter (Aut)
1994-5	Vreni Schneider (Swi)

Most: 6 Moser-Pröll

Women's Downhill

1967	Marielle Goitschel (Fra)
1968	Isabelle Mir (Fra) & Olga Pall (Aut)
1969	Wiltrud Drexel (Aut)
1970	Isabelle Mir (Fra)
1971-5	Annemarie Moser-Pröll (Aut)
1976-7	Brigittte Habersatter-Totschnig (Aut)
1978-9	Annemarie Moser-Pröll (Aut)
1980-1	Marie-Thérèse Nadig (Swi)
1982	Cécile Gros-Gaudenier (Fra)
1983	Doris De Agostini (Swi)
1984	Maria Walliser (Swi)
1985	Michela Figini (Swi)
1986	Maria Walliser (Swi)
1987-9	Michela Figini (Swi)
1990	Katrin Gütensohn-Knopl (FRG)
1991	Chantal Bournissen (Swi)
1992-4	Katja Seizinger (Ger)
1995	Picabo Street (USA)

Most: 7 Moser-Pröll (Aut), 4 Figini

Women's Giant Slalom

1967-8	Nancy Greene (Can)
1969	Marilyn Cochran (USA)
1970	Michèle Jacot & Françoise Macchi (Fra)
1971-2	Annemarie Moser-Pröll (Aut)
1973	Monika Kaserer (Aut)
1974	Hanni Wenzel (Lie)
1975	Annemarie Moser-Pröll (Aut)
1976-8	Lise-Marie Morerod (Swi)
1979	Christa Kinshoffer (Aut)
1980	Hanni Wenzel (Lie)
1981	Tamara McKinney (USA)
1982	Irene Epple (FRG)
1983	Tamara McKinney (USA)
1984	Erika Hess (Swi)
1985	Marina Kiehl (FRG)
1986	Vreni Schneider (Swi)
1987	Vreni Schneider (Swi)
1988	Mateja Svet (Yug)
1989	Vreni Schneider (Swi)

1990	Anita Wachter (Aut)
1991	Vreni Schneider (Swi)
1992-3	Carole Merle (Fra)
1994	Anita Wachter (Aut)
1995	Vreni Schneider (Swi)

Most: 5 Schneider

Women's Slalom

1967	Marielle Goitschel (Fra) & Annie Famose (Fra)
1968	Marielle Goitschel (Fra)
1969	Gertrud Gabl (Aut)
1970	Ingrid Lafforgue (Fra)
1971	Britt Laforgue (Fra) & Betsy Clifford (Can)
1972	Britt Laforgue (Fra)
1973	Patricia Emonet (Fra)
1974	Christa Zechmeister (FRG)
1975	Lise-Marie Morerod (Swi)
1976	Rosi Mittermaier (FRG)
1977	Lise-Marie Morerod (Swi)
1978	Hanni Wenzel (Lie)
1979	Regina Sackl (Aut)
1980	Perrine Pelen (Fra)
1981-3	Erika Hess (Swi)
1984	Tamara McKinney (USA)
1985	Erika Hess (Swi)
1986	Erika Hess (Swi) & Roswitha Steiner (Aut)
1987	Corinne Schmidhauser (Swi)
1988	Roswitha Steiner (Aut)
1989-90	Vreni Schneider (Swi)
1991	Petra Kronberger (Aut)
1992-5	Vreni Schneider (Swi)

Most: 6 Schneider, 5 Hess

Women's Super Giant Slalom

1986	Marina Kiehl (FRG)
1987	Maria Walliser (Swi)
1988	Michela Figini (Swi)
1989-92	Carole Merle (Fra)
1993-5	Katja Seizinger (Ger)

Most: 4 Merle

Most individual event wins

Men

86	Ingemar Stenmark (Swe) 1974-89
44	Alberto Tomba (Ita) 1984-95
43	Marc Girardelli (Lux) 1983-94
40	Pirmin Zurbriggen (Swi) 1982-90
27	Phil Mahre (USA) 1977-84

Franz Klammer (Aut) won a record 25 downhill races, 1974-85.

Women

62	Annemarie Moser (Aut), 1970-9
55	Vreni Schneider (Sui) 1986-95

Vreni Schneider won a record 14 World Cup races in a season, including all seven slalom, in 1988/9.

Ingemar Stenmark won a men's record 13 World Cup races in a season, 1978/9, including a record at one discipline, 10 giant slalom. The next bests: 12 Jean-Claude Killy (Fra) 1966/7, 11 Marc Girardelli (Lux) 1984/5, Stenmark 1979/80, Pirmin Zurbriggen 1986/7, Alberto Tomba 1994/5.

Nations' Cup
Awarded on the overall results for men and women obtained in the World Cup. *Wins:*

16	Austria	1969, 1973-80, 1982, 1990-5
8	Switzerland	1981, 1983-9
5	France	1967-8, 1970-2

NORDIC SKIING

Skiing events
Until 1985 there was just one skiing technique, classical, but now the faster skating technique, known as freetsyle is also recognised, and there are events for both disciplines. At the 1992 Winter Olympics the pursuit was introduced; this consists of a classical race on the first day, 10km for men and 5km for women, with a freestyle race on the second day over 15km and 10km respectively, with the competitors starting by their time difference from the first day.

Olympic Games

The first Winter Olympic Games, held at Chamonix in 1924, included Nordic skiing events, and they have been included on the programme ever since. Winners:

Men's 10km Cross-country (Classical style)
1992 Vegard Ulvang (Nor) 27:36.0
1994 Bjørn Daehlie (Nor) 24:20.1

Men's 15km Cross-country
Held at 18km 1924, 1936-52, 19.7km 1928, 18.214km 1932. Changed from classical style to freestyle 1992.
1924 Thorleif Haug (Nor) 1:14:31
1928 Johan Grøttumsbraaten (Nor) 1:37:01
1932 Sven Utterström (Swe) 1.23.07
1936 Erik-August Larsson (Swe) 1:14:38
1948 Martin Lundström (Swe) 1:13:50
1952 Hallgeir Brenden (Nor) 1:01:34
1956 Hallgeir Brenden (Nor) 49:39.0
1960 Haakon Brusveen (Nor) 51:55.5
1964 Eero Mäntyranta (Fin) 50:54.1
1968 Harald Grönningen (Nor) 47:54.2
1972 Sven-Åke Lundback (Swe) 45:28.24
1976 Nikolay Bayukov (USSR) 43:58.47
1980 Thomas Wassberg (Swe) 41:57.63
1984 Gunde Svan (Swe) 41:25.6
1988 Mikhail Devyatyarov (USSR) 41:18.9

Men 10+15 km Cross-country pursuit
1992 Bjørn Daehlie (Nor)
1994 Bjørn Daehlie (Nor)

Men's 30km Cross-country (Classical)
1956 Veikko Hakulinen (Fin) 1:44:06.0
1960 Sixten Jernberg (Swe) 1:51:03.9
1964 Eero Mäntyranta (Fin) 1:30:50.7
1968 Franco Nones (Ita) 1:35:39.2
1972 Vyacheslav Vedenin (USSR) 1:36:31.2
1976 Sergey Savelyev (USSR) 1:30:29.38

1980 Nikolay Zimyatov (USSR) 1:27:02.80
1984 Nikolay Zimyatov (USSR) 1:28:56.3
1988 Aleksey Prokurakov (USSR) 1:24:26.3
1992 Vegard Ulvang (Nor) 1:22:27.8
1994 Thomas Alsgaard (Nor) 1:12:26.4

Men's 50km Cross-country (Freestyle)
1924 Thorleif Haug (Nor) 3:44:32
1928 Per-Erik Hedlund (Swe) 4:52:03
1932 Veli Saarinen (Fin) 4:28:00
1936 Elis Wiklund (Swe) 3:30:11
1948 Nils Karlsson (Swe) 3:47:48
1952 Veikko Hakulinen (Fin) 3:33:33
1956 Sixten Jernberg (Swe) 2:50:27
1960 Kalevi Hämäläinen (Fin) 2:59:06.3
1964 Sixten Jernberg (Swe) 2:43:52.6
1968 Ole Ellefsaeter (Nor) 2:28:45.8
1972 Pål Tyldum (Nor) 2:43:14.75
1976 Ivar Formo (Nor) 2:37:30.50
1980 Nikolay Zimyatov (USSR) 2:27:24.60
1984 Thomas Wassberg (Swe) 2:15:55.8
1988 Gunde Svan (Swe) 2:04:30.9
1992 Bjørn Daehlie (Nor) 2:03:41.5
1994 Vladimir Smirnov (Kaz) 2:07:20.3

Men's 4 x 10km Cross-country Relay
1936 Finland 2:41:33
1948 Sweden 2:32:08

Vladimir Smirnov

1952 Finland 2:20:16
1956 USSR 2:15:30
1960 Finland 2:18:45.6
1964 Sweden 2:18:34.6
1968 Norway 2:08:33.5
1972 USSR 2:04:47.94
1976 Finland 2:07:59.72
1980 USSR 1:57:03.46
1984 Sweden 1:55:06.30
1988 Sweden 1:43:58.6
1992 Norway 1:39:26.0
1994 Italy 1:41:15.0

Men's Ski Jumping - Normal hill
90m hill 1992-4
1924 Jacob Tullin Thams (Nor)
1928 Alf Andersen (Nor)
1932 Birger Ruud (Nor)
1936 Birger Ruud (Nor)
1948 Petter Hugstedt (Nor)
1952 Arnfinn Bergmann (Nor)
1956 Anti Hyvärinen (Fin)
1960 Helmut Recknagel (GDR)
1964 Viekko Kankkänen (Fin)
1968 Jiri Raska (Cs)

1972 Yukio Kasaya (Jap)
1976 Hans-Georg Aschenbach (GDR)
1980 Toni Innauer (Aut)
1984 Jens Weissflog (GDR)
1988 Matti Nykänen (Fin)
1992 Ernst Vettori (Aut)
1994 Espen Bredesen (Nor)

Men's Ski Jumping - Large hill
120m hill 1992-4
1964 Toralf Engan (Nor)
1968 Vladimir Byeloussov (USSR)
1972 Wojciech Fortuna (Pol)
1976 Karl Schnabl (Aut)
1980 Jouko Törmänen (Fin)
1984 Matti Nykänen (Fin)
1988 Matti Nykänen (Fin)
1992 Toni Nieminen (Fin)
1994 Jens Weissflog (Ger)

Men's Team Ski Jumping
1988 Finland
1992 Finland
1994 Germany

Men's Nordic Combined - Skiing and Jumping
1924 Thorleif Haug (Nor)
1928 Johan Grøttumsbraaten (Nor)
1932 Johan Grøttumsbraaten (Nor)
1936 Oddbjørn Hagen (Nor)
1948 Heikki Hasu (Fin)
1952 Simon Slätvik (Nor)
1956 Sverre Stenersen (Nor)
1960 Georg Thoma (FRG)
1964 Tormod Knutsen (Nor)
1968 Franz Keller (FRG)
1972 Ulrich Wehling (GDR)
1976 Ulrich Wehling (GDR)
1980 Ulrich Wehling (GDR)
1984 Tom Sandberg (Nor)
1988 Hippolyt Kempf (Swi)
1992 Fabrice Guy (Fra)
1994 Fred Borre Lundberg (Nor)

Men's Team Nordic Combined
1988 FR Germany
1992 Japan
1994 Japan

Women's 5km Cross-country (Classical)
1964 Klaudia Boyarskikh (USSR) 17:50.5
1968 Toini Gustafsson (Swe) 16:45.2
1972 Galina Kulakova (USSR) 17:00.50
1976 Helena Takalo (Fin) 15:48.69
1980 Raisa Smetanina (USSR) 15:06.92

Most Olympic medals (G -Gold, S - Silver, B - Bronze)

Men

	G	S	B	Years
9 Sixten Jernberg (Swe)	4	3	2	1956-64
8 Bjørn Daelie (Nor)	5	1	1	1992-4
7 Veikko Hakulinen (Fin)	3	3	1	1952-60
7 Eero Mäntyranta (Fin)	3	2	2	1960-8
6 Gunde Svan (Swe)	4	1	1	1984-8
6 Johan Grøttumsbraaten (Nor)	3	1	2	1924-32
6 Vegard Ullvang (Nor)	3	2	1	1988-94
6 Vladimir Smirnov (USSR/Kaz)	1	4	1	1988-94

Also four gold medals: Matti Nykänen (Fin) 1984-8, and a silver at 70m ski jumping 1984; Thomas Wassberg (Swe) 1980-8

Also three gold medals: Ulrich Wehling (GDR) 1972-80,Nikolay Zimyatov (USSR) 1984-8, Jens Weissflog (GDR/Ger) 1984-94.

Women

	G	S	B	Years
10 Raisa Smetanina (USSR)	4	5	1	1976-92
9 Lyubov Yegorova (Rus)	6	3	-	1992-4
8 Galina Kulakova (USSR)	4	2	2	1968-80
7 Marja-Liisa Hämäläinen/ Kirvesniemi (Fin)	3	-	4	1984-92

1984 Marja-Liisa Hämäläinen (Fin) 17:04.0
1988 Marjo Matikainen (Fin) 15:04.0
1992 Marjat Lukkarinen (Fin) 14:13.8
1994 Lyubov Yegorova (Rus) 14:08.8

Women's 10km Cross-country
Changed from classical style to freestyle 1992.
1952 Lydia Wideman (Fin) 41:40.0
1956 Lyubov Kozyryeva (USSR) 38:11.0
1960 Maria Gusakova (USSR) 39:46.6
1964 Klaudia Boyarskikh (USSR) 40:24.3
1968 Toini Gustafsson (Swe) 36:46.5
1972 Galina Kulakova (USSR) 34:17.8
1976 Raisa Smetanina (USSR) 30:13.41
1980 Barbara Petzold (GDR) 30:31.54
1984 Marja-Liisa Hämäläinen (Fin) 31:44.2
1988 Vida Ventsene (USSR) 30:08.3

Women 5+10 km Cross-country combined Pursuit
1992 Lyubov Yegorova (CIS) 40:07.7
1994 Lyubov Yegorova (Rus) 41:38.9

Women's 15km Cross-country (Classical)
1992 Lyubov Yegorova (CIS) 42:20.8
1994 Manuela Di Centa (Ita) 39:44.5

Women's 20km Cross-country (Freestyle)
1984 Marja-Liisa Hämäläinen (Fin) 1:01:45.0
1988 Tamara Tikhonova (USSR) 55:53.6

Women's 30km Cross-country (Freestyle)
1992 Stefania Belmondo (Ita) 1:22:30.1
1994 Manuela Di Centa (Ita) 1:25:41.6

Women's 4 x 5km Cross-country Relay
1956 Finland 1:09:01.0

1960 Sweden 1:04:21.4
1964 USSR 59:20.2
1968 Norway 57:30.0
1972 USSR 48:46.15
1976 USSR 1:07:49.75
1980 GDR 1:02:11.10
1984 Norway 1:06:49.70
1988 USSR 59:51.1
1992 CIS 59:34.8
1994 Russia 57:12.5

World Championships

After Nordic events had been included in the 1924 Olympics, the FIS organised annual competitions until 1937, when for the first time they were given official world championship status. Held annually until 1939, but biennially post-war. Up to 1980 the Olympic Champions were also world champions. Winners additional to those shown earlier as Olympic Champions and those to have won most titles (including Olympics shown by *):

Men's 10km Cross-country (classical)
1991 Terje Langli (Nor)
1993 Sture Sivertsen (Nor)
1995 Vladimir Smirnov (Kaz)

Men's 18km Cross-country
1925 Otokar Nemecky (Cs)
1927 John Lindgren (Swe)
1929 Veli Saarinen (Fin)
1930 Arne Rudstadstuen (Nor)
1931 Johan Gröttumsbraaten (Nor)
1933 Nils-Joel Englund (Swe)
1934 Sulo Nurmela (Fin)
1935 Klaes Karppinen (Fin)
1937 Lauritz Bergendahl (Nor)
1938 Pauli Pitkänen (Fin)
1939 Juho Kurikkala (Fin)
1950 Karl Erik Åström (Swe)

Men's 15km Cross-country
1954 Veikko Hakulinen (Fin)
1958 Veikko Hakulinen (Fin)
1962 Assar Rönnlund (Swe)
1966 Gjermund Eggen (Nor)
1970 Lars-Göran Åslund (Swe)
1974 Magne Myrmo (Nor)
1978 Josef Luszczek (Pol)
1982 Oddvar Brå (Nor)
1985 Kari Härkänen (Fin)
1987 Marco Albarello (Ita)
1989 Gunde Svan (Swe)
 Classical: Harri Kirvesniemi (Fin)

Freestyle
1991 Björn Daehli (Nor)
1993 Björn Daehli (Nor)
1995 Vladimir Smirnov (Kzk)

Most wins: 2 Johan Gröttumsbraaten (Nor) 1928*, 1931
2 Hallgeir Brendan 1952*, 1956*
2 Hakulinen; 2 Svan 1984*

Men's 30km Cross-country
Now classical
1926 Matti Raivo (Fin)
1954 Vladimir Kusin (USSR)
1958 Kalevi Hämäläinen (Fin)
1962 Eero Mäntyranta (Fin)
1966 Eero Mäntyranta (Fin)
1970 Vyacheslav Vedenin (USSR)
1974 Thomas Magnusson (Swe)
1978 Sergey Savelyev (USSR)
1982 Thomas Eriksson (Swe)
1985 Gunde Svan (Swe)
1987 Thomas Wassberg (Swe)
1989 Vladimir Smirnov (USSR)
1991 Gunde Svan (Swe)
1993 Björn Daehli (Nor)
1995 Vladimir Smirnov (Kaz)
Most wins: 3 Mäntyranta also 1964*

Men's 50km Cross-country
1925 Frantisek Donth (Cs)
1926 Matti Raivo (Fin)
1927 John Lindgren (Swe)
1929 Anselm Knuttila (Fin)
1930 Sven Utterström (Swe)
1931 Ole Stenen (Nor)
1933 Veli Saarinen (Fin)
1934 Elis Wiklund (Swe)
1935 Nils-Joel Englund (Swe)
1937 Pekka Niemi (Fin)
1938 Kalle Jalkanen (Fin)
1939 Lauritz Bergendahl (Nor)
1950 Gunnar Eriksson (Swe)
1954 Vladimir Kusin (USSR)
1958 Sixten Jernberg (Swe)
1962 Sixten Jernberg (Swe)
1966 Gjermund Eggen (Nor)
1970 Kalevi Oikarainen (Fin)
1974 Gerhard Grimmer (GDR)
1978 Sven-Åke Lundbäck (Swe)
1982 Thomas Wassberg (Swe)
1985 Gunde Svan (Swe)
1987 Maurilio De Zolt (Ita)
1989 Gunde Svan (Swe)
1991 Torgny Mogren (Swe)
1993 Torgny Mogren (Swe)
1995 Silvio Fauner (Ita)
Most wins: 4 Jernberg also 1956*, 1964*

Men's pursuit - 10km classical and 15km freestyle
1993 Björn Daehli (Nor)
1995 Vladimir Smirnov (Kaz)

Men's 4 x 10km Cross-country Relay
Wins including Olympics (*):
10 Sweden 1933, 1950, 1958, 1962, 1978, 1987, 1989 and 3*
9 Finland 1934-5, 1938-9, 1954 and 4*
8 Norway 1937, 1966, 1982 tie, 1985, 1991, 1993, 1995 and 1*
5 USSR 1970, 1982 tie and 3*
1 GDR 1974

Men's Ski Jumping - Normal hill (70m, now 90m)
1925 Willi Dick (Cs)
1926 Jacob Thullin Thams (Nor)
1927 Tore Edman (Swe)
1929 Sigmund Ruud (Nor)
1930 Reidar Andersen (Nor)
1931 Birger Ruud (Nor)
1933 Marcel Reymond (Swi)
1934 Kristian Johanson (Nor)
1935 Birger Ruud (Nor)
1937 Birger Ruud (Nor)
1938 Asbjörn Ruud (Nor)
1939 Joseph Bradl (Ger)
1950 Hans Bjornstad (Nor)
1954 Matti Pietikäinen (Fin)
1958 Juhanni Kärkänen (Fin)
1962 Toralf Engan (Nor)
1966 Björn Wirkola (Nor)
1970 Gariy Napalkov (USSR)
1974 Hans-Georg Aschenbach (GDR)
1978 Mathias Buse (GDR)
1982 Armin Kogler (Aut)
1985 Jens Weissflog (GDR)
1987 Jiri Parma (Cs)
1989 Jens Weissflog (GDR)
1991 Heinz Kuttin (Aut)
1993 Masahiko Harada (Jap)
1995 Takanobu Okabe (Jap).
Most wins: 5 Birger Ruud also 2*

Men's Ski Jumping - Large hill (90m, to 115m and now 120m)
1962 Helmut Recknagel (GDR)
1966 Björn Wirkola (Nor)
1970 Gariy Napalkov (USSR)
1974 Hans-Georg Aschenbach (GDR)
1978 Tapio Räisänen (Fin)
1982 Matti Nykänen (Fin)
1985 Per Bergerud (Nor)
1987 Andreas Felder (Aut)
1989 Jari Puikkonen (Fin)
1991 Franci Petek (Yug)
1993 Espen Bredesen (Nor)
1995 Tommy Ingebrigtsen (Nor)
Most wins: 3 Nykänen 1982, 1984*, 1988*

Men's Team Ski Jumping

1982 Norway
1984 Finland
1985 Finland
1987 Finland
1989 Finland
1991 Austria
1993 Norway
1995 Finland

Men's Nordic Combined

1925 Otokar Nemecky (Cs)
1926 Johan Gröttumsbraaten (Nor)
1927 Rudolf Purkert (Cs)
1929-30 Hans Vinjarengen (Nor)
1931 Johan Gröttumsbraaten (Nor)
1933 Sven Eriksson (Swe)
1934-5 Oddbjörn Hagen (Nor)
1937 Sigurd Röen (Nor)
1938 Olaf Hoffsbakken (Nor)
1939 Gustaf Berauer (Ger)
1950 Heikki Hasu (Fin)
1954 Sverre Stenersen (Nor)
1958 Paavo Korhonen (Fin)
1962 Arne Larsen (Nor)
1966 Georg Thoma (FRG)
1970 Ladislav Rygel (Cs)
1974 Ulrich Wehling (GDR)
1978 Konrad Winkler (GDR)
1982 Tom Sandberg (Nor)
1985 Hermann Weinbuch (FRG)
1987 Torbjørn Løkken (Nor)
1989 Einar Elden (Nor)
1991 Fred-Børre Lundberg (Nor)
1993 Kenji Ogiwara (Jap)
1995 Fred Børre Lundberg (Nor)

Most wins:
4 Johan Grøttumsbraaten (Nor)
1926, 1928*, 1931, 1932*;
4 Wehling with 3*; 3 Oddbjørn
Hagen (Nor) 1934-5, 1936*

Men's Team Nordic Combined

1982 GDR
1984 Norway
1985 FR Germany
1987 FR Germany
1989 Norway
1991 Austria
1993 Japan
1995 Japan

Women's 5km Cross-country

now classical
1962 Alevtina Kolchina (USSR)
1966 Alevtina Kolchina (USSR)
1970 Galina Kulakova (USSR)
1974 Galina Kulakova (USSR)
1978 Helena Takalo (Fin)
1982 Berit Aunli (Nor)

Larisa Lazutina won four gold medals at the 1995 World Championships

1985 Anette Bøe (Nor)
1987 Marjo Matikainen (Fin)
1991 Trude Dybendahl (Nor)
1993 Larisa Lazutina (Rus)
1995 Larisa Lazutina (Rus

Most wins: 3 Kulakova also 1972*

Women's 10km Cross-country

1954 Lyubov Kozyryeva (USSR)
1958 Alevtina Kolchina (USSR)
1962 Alevtina Kolchina (USSR)
1966 Klaudia Boyarskikh (USSR)
1970 Alevtina Olyunina (USSR)
1974 Galina Kulakova (USSR)

1978 Zinaida Amosova (USSR)
1982 Berit Aunli (Nor)
1985 Anette Bøe (Nor)
1987 Anne Jahren (Nor)
1989 Yelena Välbe (USSR)
  Classical: Marja-Liisa Kirvesniemi (Fin)

Freestyle
1991 Yelena Välbe (USSR)
1993 Stefania Belmondo (Ita)
1995 Larisa Lazutina (Rus

Most wins:
2 Kozyryeva also 1956*,
Koltschina, Kulakova also 1972*,
Välbe

Women's 15km Cross-country
(Classical)

1989 Marjo Matikainen (Fin)
1991 Yelena Välbe (USSR)
1993 Yelena Välbe (Rus)
1995 Larisa Lazutina (Rus

Women's 20km Cross-country

1978 Zinaida Amosova (USSR)
1980 Veronika Hesse (GDR)
1982 Raisa Smetanina (USSR)
1985 Grete Nykkelmo (Nor)
1987 Maria-Elena Westin (Swe)

Women's 30km Cross-country
(freestyle)

1989 Yelena Välbe (USSR)
1991 Lyubov Yegorova (USSR)
1993 Stefania Belmondo (Ita)
1995 Yelena Välbe (USSR)

Women's Cross-country Relay 3
x 5km 1954-72, 4 x 5km from 1974

Wins including Olympics (*):

12   USSR 1954, 1958, 1962, 1966,
     1970, 1974, 1985, 1987 and 4*
3   Finland 1978, 1989 and 1*
2   Russia 1993, 1995
1   Sweden, Norway, GDR all *

Most wins at all events
(individual/relay)

Men

11   (7/4) Gunde Svan (Swe) 1984-
     91
8   (5/3) Sixten Jernberg (Swe)
     1956-64
7   (4/3) Thomas Wassberg (Swe)
     1980-8
6   (6/-) Johan Grøttumsbraaten
     (Nor) 1926 32
6   (4/2) Veikko Hakulinen (Fin)
     1952-60
6   (1/5) Klaes Karppinen (Fin)
     1934-9

Women

11   (6/5) Yelena Välbe
     (USSR/Rus) 1989-95
9   (5/4) Galina Kulakova (USSR)
     1970-80
8   (4/4) Alevtina Kolchina
     (USSR) 1958-66
8   (4/4) Larisa Lazutina
     (USSR/Rus) 1992-5
7   (3/4) Raisa Smetanina (USSR)
     1974-91

Most medals: 23 Raisa
Smetanina, 18 Galina Kulakova

Most at one Championships: 5
Marjo Matikainen 1988

World Ski-flying Championships

Held separately from the Nordic
World Championships in 1972 and
biennially from 1973. *Winners:*

1972 Walter Steiner (Swi)
1973 Hans-Georg Aschenbach
      (GDR)
1975 Karel Kodejska (Cs)
1977 Walter Steiner (Swi)
1979 Armin Kogler (Aut)
1981 Jarri Puikkonen (Fin)
1983 Klaus Ostwald (GDR)
1985 Matti Nykänen (Fin)
1986 Andreas Felder (Aut)
1988 Gunnar Fidjestøl (Nor)
1990 Dieter Thoma (FRG)
1992 Noriaki Kasai (Jap)
1994 Jaroslav Sakala (Cze)

World Cup

Contested over a series of events during the winter season. *Winners:*

Men's Cross-country World Cup

1979 Oddvar Brå (Nor)
1980 Juha Mieto (Fin)
1981 Aleksandr Zavialov (USSR)
1982 Bill Koch (USA)
1983 Aleksandr Zavialov (USSR)
1984 Gunde Svan (Swe)
1985 Gunde Svan (Swe)
1986 Gunde Svan (Swe)
1987 Torgny Mogren (Swe)
1988 Gunde Svan (Swe)
1989 Gunde Svan (Swe)
1990 Vegard Ulvang (Nor)
1991 Vladimir Smirnov (USSR)
1992-3 Bjørn Daehli (Nor)
1994 Vladimir Smirnov (Kaz)
1995 Bjørn Daehli (Nor)

Women's Cross-country World
Cup

1979 Galina Kulakova (USSR)
1980 *Not held*
1981 Raisa Smetanina (USSR)
1982 Berit Aunli (Nor)
1983 Marja-Liisa Hämäläinen (Fin)
1984 Marja-Liisa Hämäläinen (Fin)
1985 Anette Bøe (Nor)
1986 Marjo Matikainen (Fin)
1987 Marjo Matikainen (Fin)
1988 Marjo Matikainen (Fin)
1989 Yelena Välbe (USSR)
1990 Larisa Lasutina (USSR)
1991-2 Yelena Välbe (USSR/Rus)
1993 Lyubov Yegorova (Rus)
1994 Manuela Di Centa (Ita)
1995 Yelena Välbe (Rus)

Cross-country Nation's Cup
(men and women)

Norway   1982-7, 1992-3
USSR   1981, 1989-91
Sweden   1988
Russia   1994-5

Ski Jumping Nations Cup

Austria 1981-2, 1986, 1990-3
Norway   1983, 1987, 1989, 1994
Finland 1984-5, 1988, 1995

Ski Jumping World Cup

1980 Hubert Neuper (Aut)
1981 Armin Kogler (Aut)
1982 Armin Kogler (Aut)
1983 Matti Nykänen (Fin)
1984 Jens Weissflog (GDR)
1985 Matti Nykänen (Fin)
1986 Matti Nykänen (Fin)
1987 Vegard Opaas (Nor)
1988 Matti Nykänen (Fin)
1989 Jan Boklöv (Swe)
1990 Ari-Pekka Nikkola (Fin)
1991 Andreas Felder (Aut)
1992 Toni Nieminen (Fin)
1993 Andreas Goldberger (Aut)
1994 Espen Bredesen (Nor)
1995 Andreas Goldberger (Aut)

Nordic Combination World Cup

1983 Espen Andersen (Nor)
1984 Tom Sandberg (Nor)
1985 Geir Andersen (Nor)
1986 Hermann Weinbuch (FRG)
1987 Torbjørn Løkken (Nor)
1988 Klaus Sulzenbacher (Aut)
1989 Trond Arne Bredesen (Nor)
1990 Klaus Sulzenbacher (Aut)
1991 Fred-Børre Lundberg (Nor)
1992 Fabrice Guy (Fra)
1993-5 Kenji Ogiwara (Jap)

Vasalopp

The world's most famous long distance
skiing race is the Vasalopp, contested
annually since 1922 over a distance of
90km. This race commemorates the
flight in 1521 of Gustav Vasa, later King
Gustavus Eriksson, from Mora to Sälen
in Sweden (85.8km). He was overtaken
by speedy, loyal scouts on skis and per-
suaded to return and lead a rebellion and
become king of Sweden. This famous
race is always run on the first Sunday in
March from Sälen to Mora, and about
12,000 men and women now contest the
Vasalopp annually. The fastest recorded
time is 3 hr 48 min 55 sec by Bengt
Hassis (Swe) in 1986. *Most wins:*

8 Nils Karlsson (Swe) 1945-51, 1953
7 Janne Stefansson (Swe) 1962-6,
   1968-9

4   Arthur Häggblad (Swe)   1933, 1935, 1937, 1940

Worldloppet Cup

The Vasalopp is the longest of a series of great long distance (42-90km) races staged in various parts of the world which annually form the Worldloppet (11 races scheduled 1990-2). *Champions:*

1979-80 Matti Kuosku (Swe)
1981   Sven-Åke Lundbäck (Swe)
1982-3 Lars Frykberg (Swe)
1984   Bengt Hassis (Swe)
1985   Örjan Blomqvist (Swe)
1986   Konrad Hallenbarter (Swi)
1987-8 Anders Blomqvist (Swe)
1989   Örjan Blomqvist (Swe)
1990   Konrad Hallenbarter (Swi)
1991   Håkan Westin (Swe)
1992   Erik Hansson (Swe)
1993   Håkan Westin (Swe)
1994   Alec Vanek (Cze)

Women (from 1989)

1989   Ellen Holcomb (USA)
1990- Dorota Dziadkowiec (Pol)
1993   Beatrice Grünenfelder (Swi)
1994   Maria Theuri (Aut)

Freestyle Skiing

Freestyle skiing is comprised of three activities: aerials, ballet and moguls.
erials, incorporating two different jumps take place on a small jumping hill at c. 30° angle. In the moguls event competitors have timed and judged runs incorporating two jumps, down a 250m 30° slope covered with moguls, or hard-packed mounds of snow.
Competition originated in New Hampshire, USA in 1973, and after coming under the wing of the FIS a World Cup circuit began in 1980.

Olympic Games

Introduced in 1992 as a medal sport for moguls and with ballet and aerials as demonstration events. Medals were awarded for both moguls and aerials in 1994. *Winners:*

Moguls Men

1992 Edgar Grospiron (Fra)
1994 Jean-Luc Brassard (Can)

Aerials Men

1994 Andreas Schönbächler (Swi)

Moguls Women

1992 Donna Weinbrecht (USA)
1994 Stine Lise Hattestad (Nor)

Aerials Women

1994 Lina Cheryazova (Uzb)

World Champions

Men's Ballet

1986 Richard Schabel (FRG)
1989 Hermann Reitberger (FRG)
1991 Lane Spina (USA)
1993 Fabrice Becker (Fra)
1995 Rune Kristiansen (Nor)

Men's Moguls

1986 Eric Berthon (Fra)
1989 Edgar Grospiron (Fra)
1991 Edgar Grospiron (Fra)
1993 Jean-Luc Brassard (Can)
1995 Edgar Grospiron (Fra)

Men's Aerials

1986 Lloyd Langlois (Can)
1989 Lloyd Langlois (Can)
1991 Philippe Laroche (Can)
1993 Philippe Laroche (Can)
1995 Trace Worthington (USA)

Men's Combined

1986 Alain Laroche (Can)
1989 Chris Simboli (Can)
1991 Sergey Shupletsov (USSR)
1993 Sergey Shupletsov (Rus)

Women's Ballet

1986 Jan Bucher (USA)
1989 Jan Bucher (USA)
1991 Ellen Breen (USA)
1993 Ellen Breen (USA)
1995 Yelena Batalova (Rus)

Women's Moguls

1986 Mary Jo Tiampo (USA)
1989 Raphaëlle Monod (Fra)
1991 Donna Weinbrecht (USA)
1993 Stine Lise Hattestad (Nor)
1995 Candice Gilg (Fra)

Women's Aerials

1986 Maria Quintana (Cub)
1989 Catherine Lombard (Fra)
1991 Vasselisa Semenchuk (USSR)
1993 Lina Cheryazova (Uzb)
1995 Nikki Stone (USA)

Women's Combined

1986 Connie Kissling (Swz)
1989 Melanie Palenik (USA)
1991 Maja Schmid (Swz)
1993 Katherina Kubenk (Can)

World Cup

First held in 1980.

Men Overall

1982   Frank Beddor (USA)
1983-5 Alain Laroche (Can)
1986-8 Eric Laboureix (Fra)
1989   Chris Simboli (Can)
1990-1 Eric Laboureix (Fra)
1992-3 Trace Worthington (USA)

1994   Sergey Shupletsov (Rus)
1995   Trace Worthington (USA)

Women Overall

1982   Marie-Claude Asselin (Can)
1983-92 Conny Kissling (Swi)
1993   Katherina Kubenk (Can)
1994-5 Kristean Porter (USA)

Speed Skiing

Olympic games

Staged at Albertville in 1992 as a demonstration sport. World records were set by the winners:
men - Michaël Prüfer (Fra) 229.299 km/h; women - Tarja Mulari (Fin) 219.245 km/h.

World Records subsequently:
Men
233.615 km/h Philippe Goitschel (Fra), Les Arcs 21 Apr 1993
241.448 km/h Jeffrey Hamilton (USA), Vars, Hautes-Alpes 14 Apr 1995
Women
225.000 km/h Karine Dubouchet (Fra), Vars, Hautes-Alpes 14 Apr 1995

Grass Skiing

World Champions

World Championships for grass skiing were first held in 1979 in the USA. Combined titles awarded on the giant slalom and slalom. *Champions:*

Men's Giant Slalom

1979 Vincent Riewe (FRG)
1981 Erwin Gansner (Swz)
1983 Marcus Dejori (Ita)
1985 Rainer Grossmann (FRG)
1987 Erwin Gansner (Swz)
1989 Marcus Peschek (Aut)
1991 Rainer Grossman (Ger)
1993 Rainer Grossman (Ger)

Men's Slalom

1979 Vincent Riewe (FRG)
1981 Richi Christen (Swz)
1983 Erwin Gansner (Swz)
1985 Richi Christen (Swz)
1987 Klaus Spinka (Aut)
1989 Klaus Spinka (Aut)
1991 Rainer Grossman (Ger)
1993 Klaus Spinka (Aut)

Men's Super Giant Slalom

1987 Erwin Gansner (Swz)
1989 Oscar Bazzi (Ita)
1991 Rainer Grossman (Ger)
1993 Rainer Grossman (Ger)

Men's Combined
1979 Vincent Riewe (FRG)
1981 Erwin Gansner (Swz)
1983 Erwin Gansner (Swz)
1985 Richi Christen (Swz)
1987 Erwin Gansner (Swz)
1989 Marcus Peschek (Aut)
1991 Rainer Grossman (Ger)
1993 Klaus Spinka (Aut)

Women's Giant Slalom
1979 Brigitte Single (FRG)
1981 Ingrid Hirschhofer (Aut)
1983 Ingrid Hirschhofer (Aut)
1985 Claudia Otratowitz (Aut)
1987 Cinzia Valt (Ita)
1989 Katja Krey (FRG)

1991 Cristina Mauri (Ita)
1993 Ingrid Hirschhofer (Aut)

Women's Slalom
1979 Ingrid Hirschhofer (Aut)
1981 Carole Petitjean (Fra)
1983 Bettina Dongue (FRG)
1985 Ingrid Hirschhofer (Aut)
1987 Ingrid Hirschhofer (Aut)
1989 Martina Bauknecht (FRG)
1991 Katja Krey (Ger)
1993 Ingrid Hirschhofer (Aut)

Women's Super Giant Slalom
1987 Cinzia Valt (Ita)
1989 Ingrid Hirschhofer (Aut)
1991 Katja Krey (Ger)
1993 Ingrid Hirschhofer (Aut)

Women's Combined
1979 Ingrid Hirschhofer (Aut)
1981 Carole Petitjean (Fra)
1983 Ingrid Hirschhofer (Aut)
1985 Ingrid Hirschhofer (Aut)
1987 Ingrid Hirschhofer (Aut)
1989 Martina Bauknecht (FRG)
1991 Katja Krey (Ger)
1993 Ingrid Hirschhofer (Aut)

Most world titles: men - 7 Gansner, Grossman women - 14 Hirschhofer.

Speed record
Grass skiing record: 92.07 km/h Kluas Spinka (Aut) at Waldsassen, Germany on 24 Sep 1989

Sled Dog Racing

Racing between harnessed dog teams (usually huskies) had been practised by the Inuit people of the north of the North American continent and in Scandinavia, but the first formal record of a race was in 1908 when the All-Alaskan Sweepstakes were contested on a run of 408 miles (657 km) from Nome to Candle and back.

Sled dog racing was a demonstration sport at the 1932 Olympic Games, with two races for twelve sled teams, seven dogs to a sled; winner on aggregate was Emile St Goddard (Can).

The International Sled Dog Racing Association was formed in 1966, with most races held at comparatively short distances, such as the World Championship races, first held in 1936 at 18 miles (29 km). Undoubtedly, however, the Iditarod now captures the greatest worldwide interest.

Iditarod trail

Raced annually since 1973 by dog teams, 1158 miles (1864 km) from Anchorage to Nome, Alaska. The inaugural winner Dick Wilmarth took 20 days 49 minutes and 41 seconds to complete the course, beating 33 other racers.

In 1985 Libby Riddles became the first woman ever to win the race and she was followed by Susan Butcher the first to win in three successive years. *Winners (all USA except where shown)*

with times in days hr:min:sec:
1973 Dick Wilmarth 20d 00:49:41
1974 Carl Huntington 20d 15:02:07
1975 Emmitt Peters 14d 14:43:45
1976 Gerald Riley 18d 22:58:17
1977 Rick Swenson 16d 17:27.13
1978 Rick Mackey 14d 18:52:24
1979 Rick Swenson 15d 10:37:47
1980 Joe May 14d 07:11:51
1981 Rick Swenson 12:08:45:02
1982 Rick Swenson 12d 14:10:44
1984 Dean Osmar 12d 15:07:33
1985 Libby Riddles 18d 00.20.17
1986 Susan Butcher 11d 15:06:00
1987 Susan Butcher 11d 02:05:13
1988 Susan Butcher 11d 11:41:40
1989 Joe Runyan 11d 05:24:34
1990 Susan Butcher 11d 01:53:23
1991 Rick Swenson 12d 16:34:39
1992 Martin Buser (Swi) 10d 19:36:15
1993 Jeff King 10d 15:38
1994 Martin Buser (Swi) 10d 13:02:39
1995 Doug Swingley 9d 2:42:19
Most wins: 5 Swenson, 4 Butcher

Snooker

Snooker was first played at Jubbulpore, India in 1875 when Colonel Neville Chamberlain (not to be confused wth the Prime Minister of the same name) insulted a fellow officer in the Devonshire Regiment by calling him a 'snooker' after missing an easy shot during a game of Black Pool which they were playing, but with extra coloured balls added. A 'snooker' was the name given to a new recruit at the Woolwich Military Academy at the time. The name stuck and their new game was called snooker. The Billiards Association was formed in 1885 and they recognised the sport's first set of rules in 1900.

Embassy World Professional

The first world professional championship was organised in 1926-7 and was held continuously (except for the war years) until 1952 when the professional players and the governing body, the Billiards Association & Control Club, had a disagreement. A match between Horace Lindrum (Aus) and Clark McConachy (NZ) in 1952 was accorded world championship status. The professional players, however, did

Stephen Hendry

not recognise this as the official championship and broke away to organise their own championship, known as the professional match-play championship. This ended in 1957 and it was not until its revival, albeit on a challenge basis, in 1964 that the world championship was held again. It became a knockout event, similar to today's competition, in 1969.

Current sponsors Embassy started their association with the championship in 1976 and all finals since 1977 have been played at the Crucible Theatre in Sheffield. *Winners:*

1927-40 Joe Davis (Eng)
1946   Joe Davis (Eng)
1947   Walter Donaldson (Sco)
1948-9 Fred Davis (Eng)
1950   Walter Donaldson (Sco)
1951   Fred Davis (Eng)
1952   Horace Lindrum(Aus)
1952-6# Fred Davis (Eng)
1957 # John Pulman (Eng)
1964-8* John Pulman (Eng)
1969   John Spencer (Eng)
1970   Ray Reardon (Wal)
1971   John Spencer (Eng)
1972   Alex Higgins (NI)
1973-6 Ray Reardon (Wal)
1977   John Spencer (Eng)
1978   Ray Reardon (Wal)
1979   Terry Griffiths (Wal)
1980   Cliff Thorburn (Can)
1981   Steve Davis (Eng)
1982   Alex Higgins (NI)
1983-4 Steve Davis (Eng)
1985   Dennis Taylor (NI)
1986   Joe Johnson (Eng)
1987-9 Steve Davis (Eng)
1990   Stephen Hendry (Sco)
1991   John Parrott (Eng)
1992-5 Stephen Hendry (Sco)

 # Professional match-play championship
* between 1964 and 1968 John Pulman met, and beat, seven challengers: Fred Davis (3), Rex Williams (2), Freddie Van Rensburg, Eddie Charlton

World Rankings

The World Professional Billiards & Snooker Association, representing the top players, published its first set of world rankings in 1976. Players gather world ranking points at leading events around the world. A revised list is produced after the World Championship each year. *Top ranked players:*

1976-80 Ray Reardon (Wal)
1981   Cliff Thorburn (Can)
1982   Ray Reardon (Wal)

1983-9 Steve Davis (Eng)
1990-5 Stephen Hendry (Sco)

Grand Prix

Previously known as the Professional Players Tournament, it was the Rothmans Grand Prix 1984-92 and the Skoda Grand Prix in 1993-4. *Winners:*

1982   Ray Reardon (Wal)
1983   Tony Knowles (Eng)
1984   Dennis Taylor (NI)
1985   Steve Davis (Eng)
1986   Jimmy White (Eng)
1987   Stephen Hendry (Sco)
1988-9 Steve Davis (Eng)
1990-1 Stephen Hendry (Sco)
1992   Jimmy White (Eng)
1993   Peter Ebdon (Eng)
1994   John Higgins (Eng)

Mercentile Credit Classic

Mercentile succeeded Lada as sponsors of the Classic in 1985. Lada had, in turn, succeeded the event's first sponsors, Wilsons Brewery, in 1981 and it has been a ranking tournament from 1984. *Winners:*

1980 (Jan) John Spencer (Eng)
1980 (Dec) Steve Davis (Eng)
1982   Terry Griffiths (Wal)
1984   Steve Davis (Eng)
1985   Willie Thorne (Eng)
1986   Jimmy White (Eng)
1987-8 Steve Davis (Eng)
1989   Doug Mountjoy (Wal)
1990   Steve James (Eng)
1991   Jimmy White (Eng)
1992   Steve Davis (Eng)

United Kingdom Open/Championship

First held at Blackpool in 1977 it was known as the United Kingdom Professional Championship until 1984 when it became open to overseas players. All finals since 1978 have been at the Preston Guildhall. It became the Royal Liver Assurance **UK Championship** 1992-4. *Winners (ranking from 1984):*

1977   Patsy Fagan (Ire)
1978   Doug Mountjoy (Wal)
1979   John Virgo (Eng)
1980-1 Steve Davis (Eng)
1982   Terry Griffiths (Wal)
1983   Alex Higgins (NI)
1984-7 Steve Davis (Eng)
1988   Doug Mountjoy (Wal)
1989-90 Stephen Hendry (Sco)
1991   John Parrott (Eng)
1992   Jimmy White (Eng)
1993   Ronnie O'Sullivan (Eng)
1994   Stephen Hendry (Sco)

British Open

The British Open started as the British Gold Cup in 1980. Between 1981-4 it was known as the Yamaha International, and from 1985 it has been a ranking tournament with various sponsors. *Winners:*

1980   Alex Higgins (NI)
1981-2 Steve Davis (Eng)
1983   Ray Reardon (Wal)
1984   Steve Davis (Eng)
1985   Silvino Francisco (SAf)
1986   Steve Davis (Eng)
1987   Jimmy White (Eng)
1988   Stephen Hendry (Sco)
1989   Tony Meo (Eng)
1990   Bob Chaperon (Can)
1991   Stephen Hendry (Sco)
1992   Jimmy White (Eng)
1993   Steve Davis (Eng)
1994   Ronnie O'Sullivan (Eng)

European Open

First held in 1989 at Deauville and subsequently in various countries. *Winners:*

1989-90 John Parrott (Eng)
1991   Tony Jones (Eng)
1992   Jimmy White (Eng)
1993   Steve Davis (Eng)
1993-4* Stephen Hendry (Sco)
* held in December

Benson & Hedges Masters

One of the most prestigious events after the World Professional Championship, and the leading non-ranking tournament. Entry is by invitation only to 16 leading players. *Winners:*

1975   John Spencer (Eng)
1976   Ray Reardon (Wal)
1977   Doug Mountjoy (Wal)
1978   Alex Higgins (NI)
1979   Perrie Mans (SAf)
1980   Terry Griffiths (Wal)
1981   Alex Higgins (NI)
1982   Steve Davis (Eng)
1983   Cliff Thorburn (Can)
1984   Jimmy White (Eng)
1985-6 Cliff Thorburn (Can)
1987   Dennis Taylor (NI)
1988   Steve Davis (Eng)
1989-93 Stephen Hendry (Sco)
1994   Alan McManus (Sco)

Benson & Hedges Irish Masters

Held annually at the Goff's Sales Ring in County Kildare as the last major event before the World Championships.

Winners:

1978	John Spencer (Eng)
1979	Doug Mountjoy (Wal)
1980-2	Terry Griffiths (Wal)
1983-4	Steve Davis (Eng)
1985-6	Jimmy White (Eng)
1987-8	Steve Davis (Eng)
1989	Alex Higgins (NI)
1990-1	Steve Davis (Eng)
1992	Stephen Hendry (Sco)
1993-4	Steve Davis (Eng)
1995	Peter Ebdon (Eng)

World Cup

First staged in 1979, the event was moved to the second half of the season in 1984/5 and held annually until 1990. *Winners:*

1979-80	Wales
1981	England
1982	Canada
1983	England
1985	All-Ireland
1986-7	All-Ireland 'A'
1988-9	England
1990	Canada

Scottish Masters

This early-season competition carries no ranking points as the field is limited to invited professionals only. *Winners:*

1981	Jimmy White (Eng)
1982-4	Steve Davis (Eng)
1985-6	Cliff Thorburn (Can)
1987	Joe Johnson (Eng)
1989-90	Stephen Hendry (Sco)
1991	Mike Hallett (Eng)
1992	Neal Foulds (Eng)
1993-4	Ken Doherty (Ire)

World Match-play Championship

An invitation-only event restricted to the world's top 12 players based on the previous season's performances only. It was the first snooker competition, in 1988, to offer a £100,000 first prize. *Winners:*

1988	Steve Davis (Eng)
1989-90	Jimmy White (Eng)
1991	Gary Wilkinson (Eng)
1992	James Wattana (Tha)

IBSF World Amateur Championship

First held in Calcutta, India in 1963 it was a biennial event until 1984 when it became an annual competition. The championships are run by the International Billiards & Snooker Federation which became the non-professional game's governing body in 1985.

Winners:

1963	Gary Owen (Eng)
1966	Gary Owen (Eng)
1968	David Taylor (Eng)
1970	Jonathan Barron (Eng)
1972	Ray Edmonds (Eng)
1974	Ray Edmonds (Eng)
1976	Doug Mountjoy (Wal)
1978	Cliff Wilson (Wal)
1980	Jimmy White (Eng)
1982	Terry Parsons (Wal)
1984	O B Agrawal (Ind)
1985-6	Paul Mifsud (Malta)
1987	Darren Morgan (Wal)
1988	James Wattana (Tha)
1989	Ken Doherty (Ire)
1990	Stephen O'Connor (Ire)
1991	Noppodol Noppachorn (Tha)
1992	Neil Mosley (Eng)
1993	Tai Pichit (Tha)
1994	Mohamed Yusuf (Pak)

Most wins: 2 Owen, Edmonds, Mifsud

Highest break: 135 Brady Gollan (Can) 1988

Breaks

In recent years the compiling of a maximum 147 break under official conditions has become more common. The first man to compile a maximum was 'Murt' O'Donoghue (NZ) at Griffiths, New South Wales, Australia in 1934 and the first officially ratified maximum was by Joe Davis in 1955. The first achieved in major tournaments were by John Spencer at Slough in 1979, when the table had oversized pockets, and by Steve Davis in the 1982 Lada Classic.

The first official maximum break by an amateur was by Geet Sethi (Ind) during his national championships on 21 February 1988.

Maximum breaks in ranking tournaments:

147 Cliff Thorburn (1983 Embassy World Championship)
147 Willie Thorne (1987 Tennents UK Open)
147 Alain Robidoux (1989 ICI European Open)
147 Jimmy White (1992 World Championship)
147 Peter Ebdon (1992 UK Championships)
147 Stephen Hendry (1995 World Championships)

Women's World Open Championships

The Women's Billiards Association. later the Billiards and Snooker Association, was founded in 1931, running the Women's Amateur Billiards Championship from 1931 and the Women's Amateur Snooker Championship from 1933. The first snooker world championship was held in 1976, in conjunction with the men's event at Middlesbrough. Women's world championships have subsequently been staged annually from 1980, except for 1982 and 1992. The 1985-6 events were entitled Amateur Championship, the rest Open. *Winners:*

1976	Vera Selby (Eng)
1980	Lesley McIlraith (Aus)
1981	Vera Selby (Eng)
1983	Sue Foster (Eng)
1984	Stacey Hillyard (Eng)
1985-6	Allison Fisher (Eng)
1987	Ann-Marie Farren (Eng)
1988-9	Allison Fisher (Eng)
1990	Karen Corr (Eng)
1991	Allison Fisher (Eng)
1993-4	Allison Fisher (Eng)

UK Women's Championship

The UK Women's Open Championship was first held in 1986. *Winners:*

1986-90	Allison Fisher
1991-2	Tessa Davidson
1993	Stacey Hillyard
1994	Karen Corr

The Women's Amateur Snooker Championship was first held in 1933. The most wins is eight by Maureen Baynton (née Barrett) 1954-6, 1961-2, 1964, 1966, 1968 and five by Vera Selby 1972-5, 1979.

Softball

Softball, invented by George Hancock of the Farragut Boat Club, Chicago in 1887, began as an indoor version of baseball. The game was originally known as 'kitten-ball' or 'mush-ball', the name softball being introduced by Walter Hakanson in 1926. The sport gained appeal rapidly in the 1920s and 1930s and the Amateur Softball Association of America (ASA) was formed in 1933 after a national tournament contested by 55 teams was staged as part of the Century of Progress Exposition in Chicago. The ASA introduced US Championships for both men's and women's teams that year. Played by nine-a-side teams, the game developed internationally following the formation in 1950 of the International Softball Federation (ISF). There are slow pitch and fast pitch varieties.

World Championships

World championships (fast pitch) for women were introduced in 1965 and for men a year later. *Winners (men's title shared in 1976):*

Men
USA	1966, 1968, 1976 (=), 1980, 1988
Canada	1972, 1976 (=), 1992
New Zealand	1976 (=), 1984

Women
USA	1974, 1978, 1986, 1994
Australia	1965
Japan	1970
New Zealand	1982

World Championship tournament records:
Men
Most runs: 19 Marty Kernaghan(Can) 1988
Best average: .647 Clark Bosch (Can) 1988
Most strikeouts: 99 Kevin Herlihy (NZ) 1972
Women
Most runs: 13 Kathy Elliott (USA) 1974
Best average: .550 Tamara Bryce (Pan) 1978
Most strikeouts: 76 Joan Joyce (USA) 1974

ISF slow pitch championships
First held in 1987 – men's winners USA

European Championships
Women's winners: 1979-84 Netherlands, 1986-7 Italy, 1988 Netherlands, 1990 Netherlands, 1992 Italy

US National Fast Pitch Champions
Most annual Championships won:

Men
10 Clearwater (Florida) Bombers 1950, 1954, 1956-7, 1960, 1962-3, 1966, 1968, 1973
7 Raybestos (Franklin) Cardinals, Stratford, Ct. 1955, 1958, 1969-70, 1972, 1976, 1983

Women
23 Raybestos (Hi Ho) Brakettes, Stratford, Ct. 1958-60, 1963, 1966-8, 1971-8, 1980, 1982-3, 1985, 1988, 1990-2
9 Orange (Cal.) Lionettes 1950-2, 1955-6, 1962, 1965, 1969-70

US National Slow Pitch Champions
Slow pitch championships were first held in 1953 for men and 1962 for women. *Most championships won:*

Men
3 Skip Hogan A.C., Pittsburgh 1962, 1964-5
3 Joe Gatliff Auto Sales, Newport, Ky. 1956-7, 1963

Super slow pitch - Men:
4 Steele's Sports/Silver Bullets, Grafton, Ohio 1985-7, 1990

Women
5 Dots, Miami, Fla as Converse Dots 1969, Marks Brothers, N.Miami Dots 1974-5, Bob Hoffman Dots 1978-9

Speedway

Dirt track racing on motorcycles in the United States has been traced back to 1902, and in England the first fully documented motorcycle track races were held at the Portman Road Ground in Ipswich in 1904. Modern speedway has developed from the 'short track' races held at the West Maitland Agricultural Show, New South Wales in 1923. The organiser of that meeting, Johnnie Hoskins, brought the sport to Britain, where it evolved with small diameter track racing at Droylsden, Greater Manchester in 1927. The first meeting on a cinder track took place at High Beech, Essex the following year.

World Championships

The first World Championships, for individual riders, was held at Wembley, London in 1936. The team competition was introduced in 1960, and the Pairs in 1970. Two Pairs championships, in 1968 and 1969, had claimed the status of 'World' championship, but the governing body does not recognise these two events for record purposes. The Long Track championship was inaugurated in 1971. *Winners:*

Individual
1936	Lionel Van Praag (Aus)
1937	Jack Milne (USA)
1938	Bluey Wilkinson (Aus)
1949	Tommy Price (Eng)
1950	Freddie Williams (Wal)
1951-2	Jack Young (Aus)
1953	Freddie Williams (Wal)
1954	Ronnie Moore (NZ)
1955	Peter Craven (Eng)
1956	Ove Fundin (Swe)
1957-8	Barry Briggs (NZ)
1959	Ronnie Moore (NZ)
1960-1	Ove Fundin (Swe)
1962	Peter Craven (Eng)
1963	Ove Fundin (Swe)
1964	Barry Briggs (NZ)
1965	Björn Knutsson (Swe)
1966	Barry Briggs (NZ)
1967	Ove Fundin (Swe)
1968-70	Ivan Mauger (NZ)
1971	Ole Olsen (Den)
1972	Ivan Mauger (NZ)
1973	Jerzy Szczakiel (Pol)
1974	Anders Michanek (Swe)
1975	Ole Olsen (Den)
1976	Peter Collins (Eng)
1977	Ivan Mauger (NZ)
1978	Ole Olsen (Den)
1979	Ivan Mauger (NZ)
1980	Michael Lee (Eng)
1981-2	Bruce Penhall (USA)
1983	Egon Müller (FRG)
1984-5	Erik Gundersen (Den)
1986-7	Hans Nielsen (Den)
1988	Erik Gundersen (Den)
1989	Hans Nielsen (Den)

1990	Per Jonsson (Swe)		
1991	Jan O Pedersen (Den)		
1992	Gary Havelock (Eng)		
1993	Sam Ermolenko (USA)		
1994	Tony Rickardsson (Swe)		

Most successful riders

Name	1st	2nd	3rd
Ivan Mauger	6	3	1
Ove Fundin	5	3	3
Barry Briggs	4	3	3
Hans Nielsen	3	4	-
Ole Olsen	3	1	2
Erik Gundersen	3	1	-

Most appearances in finals: 18 Briggs 1954-70 and 1972

Pairs

Unofficial 1968-9

1968	Sweden (Ove Fundin/Torbjörn Harryson)
1969	New Zealand (Ivan Mauger/Bob Andrews)
1970	New Zealand (Ronnie Moore/Ivan Mauger)
1971	Poland (Jerzy Szczakiel/Andrzej Wyglenda)
1972	England (Ray Wilson/Terry Betts)
1973	Sweden (Anders Michanek/Tommy Jansson)
1974	Sweden (Anders Michanek/Soren Sjösten)
1975	Sweden (Anders Michanek/Tommy Jansson)
1976	England (John Louis/Malcolm Simmons)
1977	England (Peter Collins/Malcolm Simmons)
1978	England (Malcolm Simmons/Gordon Kennett)
1979	Denmark (Ole Olsen/Hans Nielsen)
1980	England (David Jessup/Peter Collins)
1981	USA (Bruce Penhall/Bobby Schwartz)
1982	USA (Dennis Sigalos/Bobby Schwartz)
1983	England (Kenny Carter/Peter Collins)
1984	England (Peter Collins/Chris Morton)
1985	Denmark (Erik Gundersen/Tommy Knudsen)
1986-9	Denmark (Hans Nielsen/Erik Gundersen)
1990-1	Denmark (Hans Nielsen/Jan O.Pedersen)
1992	USA (Greg Hancock, Sam Ermolenko, Ronnie Correy)
1993	Sweden (Tony Rickardsson, Henrik Gustafsson, Per Jonsson)

Renamed as team event 1994

1994	Sweden (Tony Rickardsson, Henrik Gustafsson)

Most wins (Team):
8 Denmark, 7 England, 6 Sweden

Most wins (Individual): 7 Nielsen, 5 Gundersen, 4 Collins; 3 Michanek, Simmons

Maximum points (then 30/30) were scored by the winners in 1971 and 1982.

Team

Discontinued 1994. Wins:

9	Great Britain/ England	1968, 1971-3 1974-5, 1977, 1980, 1989
9	Denmark	1978, 1981, 1983-8, 1991
6	Sweden	1960, 1962-4, 1967, 1970
4	Poland	1961, 1965-6, 1969
4	USA	1982, 1990, 1992-3
1	Australia	1976
1	New Zealand	1979

Most wins by individual team members

9	Hans Nielsen (Den) 1978, 1981, 1983-8, 1991
7	Erik Gundersen (Den) 1981, 1983-8
6	Ove Fundin (Swe) 1960, 1962-4, 1967, 1970
5	Peter Collins (GB/Eng) 1973-5, 1977, 1980
4	Malcolm Simmons (GB/Eng) 1973-5, 1977
4	Ivan Mauger (GB/NZ) 1968, 1971-2, 1979
4	Rune Sormander (Swe) 1960, 1962-4
4	Björn Knutsson (Swe) 1960, 1962-4
4	Gote Nordin (Swe) 1962-4, 1967

Long Track

1971-2	Ivan Mauger (NZ)
1973	Ole Olsen (Den)
1974-5	Egon Müller (FRG)
1976	Ivan Mauger (NZ)
1977	Anders Michanek (Swe)
1978	Egon Müller (FRG)
1979	Alois Weisbock (FRG)
1980	Karl Maier (FRG)
1981	Michael Lee (Eng)
1982	Karl Maier (FRG)
1983	Shawn Moran (USA)
1984	Erik Gundersen (Den)
1985	Simon Wigg (Eng)
1986	Erik Gundersen (Den)
1987-8	Karl Maier (FRG)
1989-90	Simon Wigg (Eng)
1991	Gerd Riss (Ger)
1992	Marcel Gerhard (Swi)
1993-4	Simon Wigg (Eng)

Most wins: 5 Wigg, 4 Maier, 3 Müller
Most placings in first three: 7 Müller and Maier

British Speedway League

League racing was introduced to Britain in 1929, with a Southern League and a Northern Dirt Track League. The National League was founded in 1932. A second division was added in 1936 and there was a third division in 1947-51. From 1957 there was again only one division. A rival league, the Provincial League came into being in 1960 and the two leagues merged in 1965 to form the British League. A second division was created in 1968. The new division was renamed the New National League in 1975, and from 1976 was known as the National League. In 1994 there were three divisions of the British League. *Winners:*

National League

	Division 1	Division 2	Division 3
1932	Wembley		
1933	Belle Vue		
1934	Belle Vue		
1935	Belle Vue		
1936	Belle Vue	Southampton	
1937	West Ham	Bristol	
1938	New Cross	Hackney Wick	
1939	Belle Vue	Newcastle	
1946	Wembley	-	
1947	Wembley	Middlesbrough	Eastbourne

	Division 1	Division 2	Division 3
1948	New Cross	Bristol	Exeter
1949	Wembley	Bristol	Stoke
1950	Wembley	Norwich	Oxford
1951	Wembley	Norwich	Poole
1952	Wembley	Poole	
1953	Wembley	Coventry	
1954	Wimbledon	Bristol	
1955	Wimbledon	Poole	
1956	Wimbledon	Swindon	
1957	Swindon		
1958	Wimbledon		
1959	Wimbledon		

National League / Provincial League

1960	Wimbledon	Rayleigh
1961	Wimbledon	Poole
1962	Southampton	Poole
1963	Belle Vue	Wolverhampton
1964	Oxford	Newcastle

British League

1965	West Ham
1966	Halifax
1967	Swindon

	Division 1	Division 2
1968	Coventry	Belle Vue Colts
1969	Poole	Belle Vue Colts
1970	Belle Vue	Canterbury
1971	Belle Vue	Eastbourne
1972	Belle Vue	Crewe
1973	Reading	Boston
1974	Exeter	Birmingham

	British League	National League
1975	Ipswich	Birmingham
1976	Ipswich	Newcastle
1977	White City	Eastbourne
1978	Coventry	Canterbury
1979	Coventry	Mildenhall
1980	Reading	Rye House
1981	Cradley Heath	Middlesbrough
1982	Belle Vue	Newcastle
1983	Cradley Heath	Newcastle
1984	Ipswich	Long Eaton
1985	Oxford	Ellesmere Port
1986	Oxford	Eastbourne
1987	Coventry	Eastbourne
1988	Coventry	Hackney
1989	Oxford	Poole
1990	Reading	Poole
1991	Wolverhampton	Arena Essex (Div 2)
1992	Reading	Peterborough
1993	Belle Vue	Glasgow
1994	Poole	Glasgow

Most wins (Div.1): 11 Belle Vue, 8 Wembley, 7 Wimbledon, 5 Coventry

British League Riders' Championship

1965-70	Barry Briggs (Swindon)
1971	Ivan Mauger (Belle Vue)
1972	Ole Olsen (Wolverhampton)
1973	Ivan Mauger (Exeter)

1974-5	Peter Collins (Belle Vue)
1976-8	Ole Olsen (Coventry)
1979	John Louis (Ipswich)
1980	Les Collins (Leicester)
1981-2	Kenny Carter (Halifax)
1983	Erik Gundersen (Cradley Heath)
1984	Chris Morton (Belle Vue)
1985	Erik Gundersen (Cradley Heath)
1986-7	Hans Nielsen (Oxford)
1988	Jan Pedersen (Cradley Heath)
1989	Shawn Moran (Belle Vue)
1990	Hans Nielsen (Oxford)
1991	Sam Ermolenko (Wolverhampton)
1992	Joe Screen (Belle Vue)
1993	Per Jonsson (Reading)
1994	Sam Ermolenko (Wolverhampton)

Most world titles overall

	Total	Ind	Pairs	Team	L/T
Hans Nielsen (Den)	19	3	7	9	-
Erik Gundersen (Den)	17	3	5	7	2
Ivan Mauger (NZ)	15	6	2*	4	3
Ove Fundin (Swe)	12	5	1*	6	-
Peter Collins (Eng)	10	1	4	5	-
Ole Olsen (Den)	8	3	1	3	1
Malcolm Simmons (Eng)	7	-	3	4	-
Jan O Pedersen (Den)	7	1	2	4	-
Barry Briggs (NZ)	6	4	-	2	-
Tommy Knudsen (Den)	6	-	1	5	-

* including one unofficial pairs win

World Ice Speedway Championship

Ice Speedway world championships were instituted in 1966 with an individual competition; a team competition was added in 1979.

Individual winners

1966	Gabdrahman Kadirov (USSR)
1967	Boris Samorodov (USSR)
1968-9	Gabdrahman Kadirov (USSR)
1970	Antonin Svaab (Cs)
1971-3	Gabdrahman Kadirov (USSR)
1974	Milan Spinka (Cs)
1975-8	Sergey Tarabanko (USSR)
1979-80	Anatoliy Bondarenko (USSR)
1981	Vladimir Lyubich (USSR)
1982-3	Sergey Kosakov (USSR)
1984	Erik Stenlund (Swe)
1985	Vladimir Suchov (USSR)
1986-7	Yuriy Ivanov (USSR)
1988	Erik Stenlund (Swe)
1989	Nikolay Nischenko (USSR)
1990	Jarmo Hirvasoija (Fin)
1991	Sergey Ivanov (USSR)
1992	Yuriy Ivanov (Rus)
1993	Vladimir Fadeyev (Rus)
1994	Aleksandr Balashchov (Rus)

Team wins

13	USSR	1979-84, 1986-92
2	Russia	1993-4
1	Sweden	1985

Squash

Squash rackets developed from rackets, being played with a softer ball, first at Harrow School in 1817, but it was not until the formation of the Squash Rackets Association in 1928 that the game grew in popularity world-wide.

The first recognised champion was John Miskey, who won the US Amateur Championship in 1907, the year that the United States Squash Racquets Association was founded. The Women's Squash Rackets Association was founded in 1934, the International Squash Rackets Federation (ISRF) in 1967 and the Women's International Squash Rackets Federation in 1976.

In 1992 the ISRF abandoned the name of rackets and reconstituted as the World Squash Federation (WSF).

Jansher Khan displays the British Open Championship Cup

World Open Championship

First held in 1976. There were no championships in 1978 but since 1979 it has been an annual event for men, and a biennial (annual from 1990) event for women. *Winners:*

Men
1976-7	Geoff Hunt (Aus)
1979-80	Geoff Hunt (Aus)
1981-5	Jahangir Khan (Pak)
1986	Ross Norman (NZ)
1987	Jansher Khan (Pak)
1988	Jahangir Khan (Pak)
1989-90	Jansher Khan (Pak)
1991	Rodney Martin (Aus)
1992-4	Jansher Khan (Pak)

Most wins: 6 Jahangir Khan, Jansher Khan, 4 Hunt

Women
1976	Heather McKay (Aus)
1979	Heather McKay (Aus)
1981	Rhonda Thorne (Aus)
1983	Vicki Cardwell (Aus)
1985	Susan Devoy (NZ)
1987	Susan Devoy (NZ)
1989	Martine Le Moignan (UK)
1990-2	Susan Devoy (NZ)
1993-5	Michelle Martin (Aus)

Most wins: 5 Devoy

Women's Team
Great Britain	1979
Australia	1981, 1983, 1992, 1994
England	1985, 1987, 1989, 1990

World Amateur / ISRF Championship

First held in 1967 the championship became known as the ISRF World Championship in 1979 after the sport went open. Held every two years until 1985. *Winners:*
1967	Geoff Hunt (Aus)
1969	Geoff Hunt (Aus)
1971	Geoff Hunt (Aus)
1973	Cameron Nancarrow (Aus)
1975	Kevin Shawcross (Aus)
1977	Maqsood Ahmed (Pak)
1979	Jahangir Khan (Pak)
1981	Steve Bowditch (Aus)
1983	Jahangir Khan (Pak)
1985	Jahangir Khan (Pak)

Most wins: 3 Hunt, Jahangir Khan

Men's team
Held with the World Amateur/ISRF until 1985 and now separately.
Australia	1967, 1969, 1971, 1973, 1989, 1991
Pakistan	1977, 1981, 1983, 1985, 1987, 1993
Great Britain	1975, 1979

World Masters

First held in 1979, it has not been held since 1984.

Men
1979	Qamar Zaman (Pak)
1980	Mohibullah Khan (Pak)
1981-4	Jahangir Khan (Pak)

Women
1984	Lucy Soutter (UK)

World Cup

Held in 1984, when the mens winners were:
Singles: Jahangir Khan (Pak)
Pairs: Ross Thorne & Dean Williams (Aus)

British Open Championship

First held in 1922 for women, and in 1930 for men, the British Open was regarded as the unofficial World Championship until the creation of the World Amateur Championship in 1967.

Men
1930-1	Don Butcher (UK)
1932-7	Abdelfattah Amr Bey (Egy)
1938	James Dear (UK)
1946-9	Mahmoud Karim (Egy)
1950-5	Hashim Khan (Pak)
1956	Roshan Khan (Pak)
1957	Hashim Khan (Pak)
1958-61	Azam Khan (Pak)
1962	Mohibullah Khan (Pak)
1963-6	Abdelfattah AbouTaleb (Egy)
1967-8	Jonah Barrington (UK)
1969	Geoff Hunt (Aus)
1970-3	Jonah Barrington (UK)
1974	Geoff Hunt (Aus)
1975	Qamar Zaman (Pak)
1976-81	Geoff Hunt (Aus)
1982-91	Jahangir Khan (Pak)
1992-5	Jansher Khan (Pak)

Most wins: 10 Jahangir Khan, 8 Hunt, 7 Hashim Khan, 6 Amr Bey, Barrington

Women
1922	Joyce Cave (UK)
1922	Sylvia Huntsman (UK)

1923	Nancy Cave (UK)
1924	Joyce Cave (UK)
1925-6	Cecily Fenwick (UK)
1928	Joyce Cave (UK)
1929-30	Nancy Cave (UK)
1931	Cecily Fenwick (UK)
1932-4	Susan Noel (UK)
1934-9	Margot Lumb (UK)
1947-9	Joan Curry (UK)
1950-8	Janet Morgan (ten wins) (UK)
1960	Sheila Macintosh (UK)
1961	Fran Marshall (UK)
1962-5	Heather Blundell (Aus)
1966-77	Heather McKay (née Blundell) (Aus)
1978	Susan Newman (Aus)
1979	Barbara Wall (Aus)
1980-1	Vicki Hoffman (Aus)
1982-3	Vicki Cardwell (née Hoffman) (Aus)
1984-90	Susan Devoy (NZ)
1991	Lisa Opie (UK)
1992	Susan Devoy (NZ)
1993-5	Michelle Martin (Aus)

Most wins: 16 Blundell/McKay, 10 Morgan, 8 Devoy, 6 Lumb, 4 Hoffmann/Cardwell

British Amateur Championship

Instituted in 1922. With the distinction between amateurs and professionals disappearing in 1979, the tournament came to an end. *Winners, all UK unless otherwise stated:*

1922-3	Tommy Jameson
1924	Dugald Macpherson
1925	Victor Cazalet
1926	Jimmy Tomkinson
1927	Victor Cazalet
1928	Dugald McPherson
1929-30	Victor Cazalet
1931-3	Abdelfattah Amr Bey (Egy)
1934	Cyril Hamilton
1935-7	Abdelfattah Amr Bey (Egy)
1938	Kenneth Gandar Dower
1946-50	Norman Borrett
1951	Gavin Hildick-Smith
1952-3	Alan Fairbairn
1954	Roy Wilson
1955	Ibrahim Amin (Egy)
1956	Roy Wilson
1957-8	Nigel Broomfield
1959	Ibrahim Amin (Egy)
1960-1	Michael Oddy
1962	Ken Hiscoe (Aus)
1963-5	Aftab Jawaid (Pak)
1966-8	Jonah Barrington
1969	Geoff Hunt (Aus)
1970-1	Gogi Alauddin (Pak)
1972	Cameron Nancarrow (Aus)
1973-4	Mohibullah Khan (Pak)
1975	Kevin Shawcross (Aus)
1976	Bruce Brownlee (NZ)
1977-8	Gamal Awad (Egy)
1979	Jonathan Leslie

Most wins: 6 Amr Bey, 5 Borrett, 4 Cazalet, 3 Aftab Jawaid

Unbeaten Champions

Heather McKay (née Blundell) was unbeaten in women's squash from 1962 to 1980. She won 16 British Open titles and 14 consecutive Australian amateur titles 1960-73 before turning professional. After winning her second world title in 1979 she concentrated on a new sport - racquetball, and became the best player in Canada (to where she had moved in 1975) within a year. When Jahangir Khan lost to Ross Norman in the World Championship final at Toulouse, France, in November 1986, it was his first defeat since April 1981 when Geoff Hunt had beaten him in the final of the British Open.

Surfing

Surfing was a traditional Polynesian activity, which has long been popular on suitable coast lines, such as off California, Hawaii or Australia. It was developed as a sporting activity in the 1950s and 1960s, with the first professional event for women held in 1969.

World Professional Championships

First held in 1970. The Grand Prix circuit is held throughout the year at venues worldwide. It is now organised by the Association of Surfing Professionals (ASP). *Winners (year given 1983-7 is the first half of each May-April season):*

Men

1970	Robert Young (Aus)
1971	Paul Neilsen (Aus)
1972	Jonathan Paarman (SAf)
1973	Ian Cairns (Aus)
1974	Reno Abellira (USA/Haw)
1975	Mark Richards (Aus)
1976	Peter Townend (Aus)
1977	Shaun Tomson (SAf)
1978	Wayne Bartholomew (Aus)
1979-82	Mark Richards (Aus)
1983-4	Tom Carroll (Aus)
1985-6	Tommy Curren (USA)
1987	Damien Hardman (Aus)
1988	Barton Lynch (Aus)
1989	Martin Potter (UK)
1990	Tommy Curren (USA)
1991	Damien Hardman (Aus)
1992	Kelly Slater (USA)
1993	Derek Ho (USA/Haw)
1994	Kelly Slater (USA)

Women

1977	Margo Oberg (Haw)
1978-9	Lyne Boyer (Haw)
1980-1	Margo Oberg (Haw)
1982	Debbie Beacham (USA)
1983	Kim Mearig (USA)
1984-6	Frieda Zamba (USA)
1987	Wendy Botha (SAf)
1988	Frieda Zamba (USA)
1989	Wendy Botha (SAf)
1990	Pam Burridge (Aus)
1991-2	Wendy Botha (Aus, ex SAf))
1993	Pauline Menczer (Aus)
1994	Lisa Andersen (USA)

World Amateur Championships

First held in 1964. The only triple winner is Michael Novokov (Aus), who won men's Kneeboard titles in 1982, 1984 and 1986. *Open winners:*

Men

1964	Bernard Farrelly (Aus)
1965	Felipe Pomar (Per)

1966	Robert 'Nat' Young (USA)
1968	Fred Hemmings (USA/Haw)
1970	Ralph Arness (USA)
1972	Jimmy Blears (USA/Haw)
1980	Mark Scott (Aus)
1982	Tommy Curren (USA)
1984	Scott Farnsworth (USA)
1986	Mark Sainsbury (Aus)
1988	Fabio Gouveia (Bra)
1990	Heifara Tahutini (Tahiti)
1992	Grant Foster (Aus)
1994	Sasha Stocker (Aus)

Swimming

Although swimming may have been popular in ancient times, it was not included in the Greek Olympic Games. The earliest references to swimming races were in Japan in 36 BC. In modern times competitive swimming was popularised in Britian from at least 1791. The first national swimming association was the Metropolitan Swimming Clubs Association, later to become the Amateur Swimming Association (ASA), founded in London in 1869. The first national champion was Tom Morris, who won a mile race in the Thames that year. Swimming has been held at every Olympic Games from the first in 1896.

The international governing body for swimming, diving and water polo, the Fédération International de Natation Amateur (FINA) was founded in 1908 and in 1994 had 149 member nations.

World Records

World records for swimming were first recognised by FINA in 1908. At that time records for distances under 800m could be set in pools of any length over 25 yards, and it was possible for times to be taken in mid-course, and not just at the end of the pool. The range of distances proliferated, but was cut back in 1948 and in 1952, when, also, records for the breast-stroke and butterfly were separated. In 1957 FINA decreed that henceforth only times set in 50m or 55y pools would be accepted and no mid-pool times would be recognised. As short-course times are quicker (by c. 0.7 sec. per turn), due to more turns, at some events it took a few years before the old records were surpassed. In 1968 Imperial distances were cut from the lists.

Records are shown for each of the currently recognised events, with the records at 15-year intervals from 1915 to 1990, with all records since then. Also listed are those swimmers to have set most records at each distance.

 # records set in short-course pools (up to 1957), y mark made at the longer equivalent Imperial distance.

Men

50 metres freestyle

	min sec	name	date
1990	21.98	Tom Jager (USA)	24 Mar 1990
	21.81	Tom Jager (USA)	24 Mar 1990
Most	5 Tom Jager (USA) 22.32 - 21.81 1987-90		
	3 Matt Biondi (USA) 22.33 - 22.14 1986-8		

Women

1964	Phyllis O'Donnell (Aus)
1965	Joyce Hoffmann (USA)
1966	Joyce Hoffmann (USA)
1968	Margo Godfrey (USA)
1970	Sharon Weber (USA/Haw)
1972	Sharon Weber (USA/Haw)
1980	Alisa Schwarzstein (USA)
1982	Jenny Gill (Aus)
1984	Janice Aragon (USA)
1986	Connie Nixon (Aus)
1988	Pauline Menczer (Aus)
1990	Kathy Newman (Aus)

100 metres freestyle

1915	1:01.6	Duke Kahanamoku (USA)	17 Feb 1924
1930	57.4 #	Johnny Weissmuller (USA)	17 Feb 1924
1945	55.9 #	Alan Ford (USA)	13 Apr 1944
1960	54.6	John Devitt (Aus)	28 Jan 1957
1975	50.59	Jim Montgomery (USA)	23 Aug 1975
1990	48.42	Matt Biondi (USA)	10 Aug 1988
	48.21	Aleksandr Popov (Rus)	18 Jun 1994
Most:	4 Jim Montgomery (USA) 51.12 - 49.99 1975-6		
	4 Matt Biondi (USA) 49.24 - 48.42 1985-8		
	3 Duke Kahanamoku (USA) 61.6 - 60.4 1912-20		
	3 Mark Spitz (USA) 51.9 - 51.22 1970-2		

200 metres freestyle (y = 220 yards)

1915	2:25.4y#	Charles Daniels (USA)	26 Mar 1909
1930	2:08.0 #	Johnny Weissmuller (USA)	5 Apr 1927
1945	2:06.2 #	Bill Smith (USA)	12 Feb 1944
1960	2:01.5	Tsuyoshi Yamanaka (Jap)	26 Jul 1959
1975	1:50.32	Bruce Furniss (USA)	21 Aug 1975
1990	1:46.69	Giorgio Lamberti (Ita)	15 Aug 1989
Most:	9 Don Schollander (USA) 1:58.8 - 1:54.3 1963-8		
	5 Tsuyoshi Yamanaka (Jap) 2:03.0 - 2:00.4 1958-61		
	4 Mark Spitz (USA) 1:54.3 - 1:52.78 1969-72		
	4 Bruce Furniss (USA) 1:51.41 - 1:50.29 1975-6		
	4 Michael Gross (FRG) 1:48.28 - 1:47.44 1983-4		

400 metres freestyle (y = 440 yards)

1915	5:21.6 #	Jack Hatfield (UK)	26 Sep 1912
1930	4:50.3 #	Arne Borg (Swe)	11 Sep 1925
1945	4:38.5 #	Bill Smith (USA)	13 May 1941
1960	4:15.9y	John Konrads (Aus)	23 Feb 1960
1975	3:53.31	Tim Shaw (USA)	20 Aug 1975
1990	3:46.95	Uwe Dassler (GDR)	23 Sep 1988
	3:46.47	Kieren Perkins (Aus)	3 Apr 1992
	3:45.00	Yevgeniy Sadoviy (CIS/Rus)	29 Jul 1992
	3:43.80	Kieren Perkins (Aus)	9 Sep 1994
Most:	6 Vladimir Salnikov (USSR) 3:51.41 - 3:48.32 1979-83		
	4 John Konrads (Aus) 4:25.9y - 4:15.9y 1958-60		
	4 Tim Shaw (USA) 3:56.96 - 3:53.31 1974-5		

800 metres freestyle
(y = 880 yards)

1915	11:25.4y	Henry Taylor (UK)	21 Jul 1906
1930	10:19.6	Jean Taris (Fra)	30 May 1930
1945	9:50.9	Bill Smith (USA)	24 Jul 1941
1960	8:59.6y	John Konrads (Aus)	10 Jan 1959
1975	8:09.60	Tim Shaw (USA)	12 Jul 1975
1990	7:50.64	Vladimir Salnikov (USSR)	4 Jul 1986
	7:47.85	Kieren Perkins (Aus)	25 Aug 1991
	7:46.60	Kieren Perkins (Aus)	16 Feb 1992
	7:46.00	Kieren Perkins (Aus)	24 Aug 1994

Most: 7 Steve Holland (Aus) 8:17.6 - 8:02.91 1973-6
4 Shozo Makino (Jap) 10:16.6 - 9:55.8 1931-5
4 Vladimir Salnikov (USSR) 7:56.43 - 7:50.64 1979-86

1500 metres freestyle

1915	22:00.0	George Hodgson (Can)	10 Jul 1912
1930	19:07.2	Arne Borg (Swe)	2 Sep 1927
1945	18:58.8	Tomikatsu Amano (Jap)	10 Aug 1938
1960	17:11.0y	John Konrads (Aus)	27 Feb 1960
1975	15:20.91	Tim Shaw (USA)	21 Jun 1975
1990	14:54.76	Vladimir Salnikov (USSR)	22 Feb 1983
	14:53.6	Glen Housman (Aus)	13 Dec 1989

(unratified due to timing malfunction)

	14:50.36	Jörg Hoffmann (Ger)	13 Jan 1991
	14:48.40	Kieren Perkins (Aus)	3 Apr 1992
	14:43.48	Kieren Perkins (Aus)	31 Jul 1992
	14:41.66	Kieren Perkins (Aus)	24 Aug 1994

Most: 5 Arne Borg (Swe) 21:35.3 - 19:07.2 1923-7
5 Mike Burton (USA) 16:41.6 - 15:52.58 1966-72
4 Steve Holland (Aus) 15:37.8 - 15:10.59 1973-6

4 x 100 metres freestyle

1945	3:50.8 #	Yale University (USA)	18 Mar 1942
1960	3:44.4	USA	21 Jul 1959
1975	3:24.85	USA	23 Jul 1975
1990	3:16.53	USA	23 Sep 1988

(Chris Jacobs, Troy Dalbey, Tom Jager, Matt Biondi)

4 x 200 metres freestyle relay

1945	8:51.5	Japan	11 Aug 1936
1960	8:10.2	USA	1 Sep 1960
1975	7:30.54	Long Beach SC (USA)	22 Aug 1975

evinen – gold medal and world record in 1994

1990	7:12.51	USA	21 Sep 1988
	7:11.95	CIS	27 Jul 1992

(Dmitriy Lepikov, Vladimir Pychnenko, Venyamin Tayanovich, Yevgeniy Sadoviy)

100 metres backstroke

1915	1:15.6 #	Otto Fahr (Ger)	29 May 1912
1930	1:08.2	George Kojac (USA)	9 Aug 1928
1945	1:04.8 #	Adolph Kiefer (USA)	18 Jan 1936
1960	1:01.5y	John Monckton (Aus)	15 Feb 1958
1975	56.30	Roland Matthes (GDR)	4 Sep 1972
1990	54.51	David Berkoff (USA)	24 Sep 1988
	53.93	Jeff Rouse (USA)	25 Aug 1991
	53.86	Jeff Rouse (USA)	31 Jul 1992

Most: 8 Roland Matthes (GDR) 58.4 - 56.30 1967-72
4 Warren Kealoha (USA) 1:14.8 - 1:11.4 # 1920-6
4 Adolph Kiefer (USA) 1:07.0 #- 1:04.8 # 1935-6

200 metres backstroke

1915	2:48.4 #	Otto Fahr (Ger)	3 Apr 1912
1930	2:32.2 #	George Kojac (USA)	16 Jun 1930
1945	2:19.3 #	Adolph Kiefer (USA)	4 Mar 1944
1960	2:13.2	Tom Stock (USA)	24 Jul 1960
1975	2:01.87	Roland Matthes (GDR)	7 Sep 1973
1990	1:58.14	Igor Polyanskiy (USSR)	3 Mar 1985
	1:57.30	Martin López-Zubero (Spa)	13 Aug 1991
	1:56.57	Martin López-Zubero (Spa)	23 Nov 1991

Most: 9 Roland Matthes (GDR) 2:07.9 - 2:01.87 1967-73
4 Tom Stock (USA) 2:16.0 - 2:10.9 1960-2

100 metres breaststroke
(* with butterfly stroke)

1915	1:17.8	Walther Bathe (Ger)	18 Dec 1910
1930	1:14.0 #	Walter Spence (USA)	28 Oct 1927
1945	1:07.3*#	Dick Hough (USA)	15 Apr 1939
1960	1:11.5	Vladimir Minashkin (USSR)	15 Sep 1957
1975	1:03.88	John Hencken (USA)	31 Aug 1974
1990	1:01.49	Adrian Moorhouse (UK)	15 Aug 1989
	1:01.49	Adrian Moorhouse (UK)	25 Jan 1990
	1:01.49	Adrian Moorhouse (UK)	26 Jul 1990
	1:01.49	Norbert Rózsa (Hun)	7 Jan 1991
	1:01.45	Norbert Rózsa (Hun)	7 Jan 1991
	1:01.29	Norbert Rózsa (Hun)	20 Aug 1991
	1:00.95	Karoly Guttler (Hun)	3 Aug 1993

Most: 7 John Hencken (USA) 1:05.68 - 1:03.11 1972-6
6 Chet Jastremski (USA) 1:11.1 - 1:07.5 1961
5 Leonid Meshkov (USSR) 1:07.2*#- 1:06.5*# 1949-51
5 Steven Lundquist (USA) 1:02.62 - 1:01.65 1982-4

200 metres breaststroke
(* with butterfly stroke)

(u under-water swimming, permitted at breaststroke until 1957)

1915	2:56.6 #	Percy Courtman (UK)	28 Jul 1914
1930	2:45.0 #	Yoshiyuki Tsuruta (Jap)	27 Jul 1929
1945	2:36.8*#	Alfred Nakache (Fra)	6 Jul 1941
1960	2:36.5y	Terry Gathercole (Aus)	28 Jun 1958
1975	2:18.21	John Hencken (USA)	1 Sep 1974
1990	2:11.53	Mike Barrowman (USA)	21 Jul 1990

	2:11.23	Mike Barrowman (USA)	11 Jan 1991
	2:10.60	Mike Barrowman (USA)	13 Aug 1991
	2:10.16	Mike Barrowman (USA)	29 Jul 1992

Most: 6 Joe Verdeur (USA) 2:35.6*#- 2:28.3*# 1946-50
6 Mike Barrowman (USA) 2:12.90 - 2:10.16 1989-92
5 John Hencken (USA) 2:22.79 - 2:18.21 1972-4
4 Masaru Furukawa (Jap) 2:36.6u#- 2:31.0u# 1954-5

100 metres butterfly

1960	58.7	Lance Larson (USA)	24 Jul 1960
1975	54.27	Mark Spitz (USA)	31 Aug 1972
1990	52.84	Pablo Morales (USA)	24 Jun 1986

Most: 7 Mark Spitz (USA) 56.3 - 54.27 1967-72
6 György Tumpek (Hun) 1:04.3# - 1:03.4 1953-7
5 Takashi Ishimoto (Jap) 1:01.5 - 1:00.1 1957-8

200 metres butterfly (y = 220 yards)

1960	2:12.8	Mike Troy (USA)	2 Sep 1960
1975	2:00.70	Mark Spitz (USA)	28 Aug 1972
1990	1:56.24	Michael Gross (FRG)	28 Jun 1986
	1:55.69	Melvin Stewart (USA)	12 Jan 1991
	1:55.22	Dennis Pankratov (Rus)	14 Jun 1995

Most: 9 Mark Spitz (USA) 2:06.4 - 2:00.70 1967-72
6 Mike Troy (USA) 2:19.0 - 2:12.8 1959-60
5 Kevin Berry (Aus) 2:12.5y - 2:06.6 1962-4

200 metres individual medley

1975	2:06.08	Bruce Furniss (USA)	23 Aug 1975
1990	2:00.11	David Wharton (USA)	20 Aug 1989
	1:59.36	Tamás Darnyi (Hun)	13 Jan 1991
	1:58.16	Jani Sievinen (Fin)	11 Sep 1994

Most: 4 Alex Baumann (Can) 2:02.78 - 2:01.42 1981-6

400 metres individual medley (y = 440 yards)

1960	5:04.5	Dennis Rounsavelle (USA)	22 Jul 1960
1975	4:28.89	András Hargitay (Hun)	20 Aug 1974
1990	4:14.75	Tamás Darnyi (Hun)	21 Sep 1988
	4:12.36	Tamás Darnyi (Hun)	8 Jan 1991
	4:12.30	Tom Dolan (USA)	9 Sep 1994

Most: 5 Gary Hall (USA) 4:43.3 - 4:30.81 1968-72
4 Ted Stickles (USA) 5:04.3 - 4:51.0y 1961-2

4 x 100 metres medley relay

1960	4:05.4	USA	1 Sep 1960
1975	3:48.16	USA	4 Sep 1972
1990	3:36.93	USA	25 Sep 1988

(David Berkoff, Richard Schroeder, Matt Biondi, Chris Jacobs)

	3:36.93	USA	31 Jul 1992

(Jeff Rouse, Nelson Diebel, Pablo Morales, Jon Olsen)

Women

50 metres freestyle

1990	24.98	Yang Wenyi (Chn)	11 Apr 1988
	24.79	Yang Wenyi (Chn)	31 Jul 1992
	24.51	Le Jingyi (Chn)	11 Sep 1994

Most: 4 Tamara Costache (Rom) 25.50 - 25.28 1986

100 metres freestyle

1915	1:16.2	Fanny Durack (Aus)	6 Feb 1915
1930	1:08.0 #	Helene Madison (USA)	14 Mar 1930
1945	1:04.6 #	Willy den Ouden (Hol)	27 Feb 1936
1960	1:00.2y	Dawn Fraser (Aus)	23 Feb 1960
1975	56.22	Kornelia Ender (GDR)	26 Jul 1975
1990	54.73	Kristin Otto (GDR)	19 Aug 1986
	54.48	Jenny Thompson (USA)	1 Mar 1992
	54.01	Le Jingyi (Chn)	5 Sep 1994

Most: 11 Dawn Fraser (Aus) 1:04.5 - 58.9 1956-64
10 Kornelia Ender (GDR) 58.25 - 55.65 1973-6

200 metres freestyle (y = 220 yards)

1915	2:56.0y#	Fanny Durack (Aus)	4 Mar 1915
1930	2:34.6 #	Helene Madison (USA)	6 Mar 1930
1945	2:21.7 #	Ragnhild Hveger (Den)	11 Sep 1938
1960	2:11.6y	Dawn Fraser (Aus)	27 Feb 1960
1975	2:02.27	Kornelia Ender (GDR)	15 Mar 1975
1990	1:57.55	Heike Friedrich (GDR)	18 Jun 1986
	1:56.78	Franziska van Almsick (Ger)	6 Sep 1994

Most: 4 Dawn Fraser (Aus) 2:20.7 - 2:11.6y 1956-60
4 Kornelia Ender (GDR) 2:03.22 - 1:59.26 1974-6

400 metres freestyle (y = 440 yards)

1930	5:39.2 #	Martha Norelius (USA)	27 Aug 1928
1945	5:00.1 #	Ragnhild Hveger (Den)	15 Sep 1940
1960	4:44.5	Chris von Saltza (USA)	5 Aug 1960
1975	4:14.76	Shirley Babashoff (USA)	20 Jun 1975
1990	4:03.85	Janet Evans (USA)	22 Sep 1988

Most: 8 Ragnhild Hveger (Den) 5:14.2# - 5:00.1# 1937-40
5 Debbie Meyer (USA) 4:32.6 - 4:24.3 1967-70
4 Martha Norelius (USA) 5:51.4y - 5:39.2# 1927-8

800 metres freestyle (y = 880 yards)

1930	11:41.2y#	Helene Madison (USA)	6 Jul 1930
1945	10:52.5	Ragnhild Hveger (Den)	13 Aug 1941
1960	9:55.6	Jane Cederqvist (Swe)	17 Aug 1960
1975	8:43.48	Jenny Turrall (Aus)	31 Mar 1975
1990	8:16.22	Janet Evans (USA)	20 Aug 1989

Most: 5 Debbie Meyer (USA) 9:35.8 - 9:10.4 1967-8
4 Ilsa Konrads (Aus) 10:17.7y -10:11.4y 1958-9
4 Petra Thümer (GDR) 8:40.68 - 8:35.04 1976-7

1500 metres freestyle

1930	23:44.6	Martha Norelius (USA)	28 Jul 1927
1945	20:57.0	Ragnhild Hveger (Den)	20 Aug 1941
1960	19:23.6	Jane Cederqvist (Swe)	8 Sep 1960
1975	16:33.94	Jenny Turrall (Aus)	25 Aug 1974
1990	15:52.10	Janet Evans (USA)	26 Mar 1988

Most: 5 Jenny Turrall (Aus) 16:49.9 - 16:33.94 1973-4
4 Debbie Meyer (USA) 18:11.1 - 17:19.9 1967-9

4 x 100 metres freestyle

1945	4:27.6	Denmark	7 Aug 1938
1960	4:08.9	USA	3 Sep 1960
1975	3:49.37	GDR	26 Jul 1975
1990	3:40.57	GDR	19 Aug 1986
	3:39.46	USA	28 Jul 1992
	3:37.91	China	7 Sep 1994

(Le Jingyi, Shan Ying, Le Ying, Lu Bin)

4 x 200 metres freestyle relay

1990	7:55.47	GDR	18 Aug 1987

(Manuela Stellmach, Astrid Strauss, Anke Möhring, Heike Friedrich)

100 metres backstroke

1930	1:20.6 #	Bonnie Mealing (Aus)	27 Feb 1930
1945	1:10.9 #	Cor Kint (Hol)	22 Sep 1939
1960	1:09.0	Lynn Burke (USA)	2 Sep 1960
1975	1:02.98	Ulrike Richter (GDR)	1 Sep 1974
1990	1:00.59	Ina Kleber (GDR)	24 Aug 1984
	1:00.31	Krisztina Egerszegi (Hun)	22 Aug 1991
	1:00.16	He Cihong (Chn)	10 Sep 1994

Most: 9 Ulrike Richter (GDR) 1:05.39 - 1:01.51 1973-6
4 Ria van Velsen (Hol) 1:12.3 - 1:10.9 1958-60
4 Lynn Burke (USA) 1:10.1 - 1:09.0 1960

200 metres backstroke   (y = 220 yards)

1930	2:58.2 #	Eleanor Holm (USA)	1 Mar 1930
1945	2:38.8 #	Cor Kint (Hol)	29 Nov 1939
1960	2:33.3	Satoko Tanaka (Jap)	23 Jul 1960
1975	2:15.46	Birgit Treiber (GDR)	25 Jul 1975
1990	2:08.60	Betsy Mitchell (USA)	27 Jun 1986
	2:06.62	Krisztina Egerszegi (Hun)	25 Aug 1991

Most: 10 Satoko Tanaka (Jap) 2:37.1 - 2:28.2 1959-63
4 Karen Muir (SAf) 2:27.1 - 2:23.8 1966-8

100 metres breaststroke

1930	1:26.3 #	Lotte Mühe (Ger)	9 Jun 1928
1945	1:19.8 #	Gisela Grass (Ger)	9 May 1943
1960	1:19.0	Ursula Küper (GDR)	14 Jul 1960
1975	1:12.28	Renate Vogel (GDR)	1 Sep 1974
1990	1:07.91	Silke Hörner (GDR)	21 Aug 1987
	1:07.69	Samantha Riley (Aus)	9 Sep 1994

Most: 6 Ute Geweniger (GDR) 1:10.20 - 1:08.51 1980-3
5 Catie Ball (USA) 1:15.6 - 1:14.2 1966-8

200 metres breaststroke   (y = 220 yards)

1930	3:11.2	Lotte Mühe (Ger)	15 Jul 1928
1945	2:56.0 #	Maria Lenk (Bra)	8 Nov 1939
1960	2:49.5	Anita Lonsbrough (UK)	27 Aug 1960
1975	2:34.99	Karla Linke (GDR)	19 Aug 1974
1990	2:26.71	Silke Hörner (GDR)	21 Sep 1988
	2:25.92	Anita Nall (USA)	2 Mar 1992
	2:25.35	Anita Nall	2 Mar 1992
	2:24.76	Rebecca Brown (Aus)	16 Mar 1994

Most: 4 Ada den Haan (Hol) 2:46.4# - 2:51.3 1956-7
4 Galina Prozumenshikova (USSR) 2:47.7y- 2:40.8 1964-6

100 metres butterfly

1960	1:09.1	Nancy Ramey (USA)	2 Sep 1959
1975	1:01.24	Kornelia Ender (GDR)	24 Jul 1975
1990	57.93	Mary T Meagher (USA)	16 Aug 1981

Most: 6 Atie Voorbij (Hol) 1:13.7# - 1:10.5 1955-7
6 Kornelia Ender (GDR) 1:03.05 - 1:00.13 1973-6

200 metres butterfly   (y = 220 yards)

1960	2:34.4	Marianne Heemskerk (Hol)	12 Jun 1960
1975	2:13.76	Rosemarie Kother (GDR)	8 Sep 1973
1990	2:05.96	Mary T Meagher (USA)	13 Aug 1981

Most: 5 Rosemarie Kother (GDR) 2:15.45 - 2:11.22 1973-6
5 Mary T Meagher (USA) 2:09.77 - 2:05.96 1979-81

	4 Ada Kok (Hol)	2:25.8 - 2:21.0y 1965-7
	4 Karen Moe (USA)	2:20.7 - 2:15.27 1970-2

200 metres individual medley

1975	2:18.83	Ulrike Tauber (GDR)	10 Jun 1975
1990	2:11.73	Ute Geweniger (GDR)	4 Jul 1981
	2:11.65	Li Lin (Chn)	30 Jul 1992
	(2:11.57	Lu Bin (Chn) drugs dq	7 Oct 1994)

Most: 6 Ulrike Tauber (GDR) 2:18.97 - 2:15.85 1974-7
5 Claudia Kolb (USA) 2:27.8 - 2:23.5 1966-8

400 metres individual medley

1960	5:36.5	Donna de Varona (USA)	15 Jul 1960
1975	4:52.20	Ulrike Tauber (GDR)	7 Jun 1975
1990	4:36.10	Petra Schneider (GDR)	1 Aug 1982

Most: 6 Donna de Varona (USA) 5:36.5 - 5:14.9 1960-4
5 Claudia Kolb (USA) 5:11.7 - 5:04.7 1967-8
4 Sylvia Ruuska (USSR) 5:46.6 - 5:40.2y 1958-9
4 Petra Schneider (GDR) 4:39.96 - 4:36.10 1980-2

4 x 100 metres medley relay

1960	4:41.1	USA	2 Sep 1960
1975	4:13.78	GDR	24 Aug 1974
1990	4:03.69	GDR	24 Aug 1984
	4:02.54	USA	30 Jul 1992
	4:01.67	China	10 Sep 1994

(He Cihong, Dai Guohong, Liu Limin, Li Yingyi)

Most world records at individual events

Including now obsolete distances the most world records set is:
Men 32 Arne Borg (Swe) 1921-9; **Women** 42 Ragnhild Hveger (Den) 1936-42.
The most for the currently recognised events:
(fr = freestyle, ba = backstroke, br = breaststroke, bu = butterfly, im = individual medley)

Men

26 Mark Spitz (USA) 3 100fr, 4 200fr, 3 400fr, 7 100bu, 9 200bu 1967-72
17 Roland Matthes (GDR) 8 100ba, 9 200ba 1967-73
13 Vladimir Salnikov (USSR) 6 400fr, 4 800fr, 3 1500fr
12 John Konrads (Aus) 3 200fr, 4 400fr, 3 800fr,) 9 200fr, 3 400fr 1963-8
12 John Hencken (USA) 7 100br, 5 200br 1972-6
10 Arne Borg (Swe) 3 400fr, 2 800fr, 5 1500fr 1922-7
10 Gary Hall (USA) 1 200ba, 1 200bu, 3 200im, 5 400im 1968-72
10 Steve Holland (Aus) 6 800fr, 4 1500fr 1973-6
10 Michael Gross (FRG) 4 200fr, 1 400fr, 1 100bu, 4 200bu 1983-6

Women

23 Kornelia Ender (GDR) 10 100fr, 4 200fr, 1 100ba, 6 100bu, 2 200im 1973-6
15 Ragnhild Hveger (Den) 1 200fr, 8 400fr, 2 800fr, 3 1500fr, 1 200ba 1937-41
15 Dawn Fraser (Aus) 11 100fr, 4 200fr 1956-64
15 Debbie Meyer (USA) 1 200fr, 5 400fr, 5 800fr, 4 1500fr 1967-70
11 Claudia Kolb (USA) 5 200im, 5 400im, 1 100br 1964-8
11 Shane Gould (Aus) 2 100fr, 3 200fr, 2 400fr, 1

800fr, 2 1500fr, 1 200im 1971-2
11 Ulrike Richter (GDR) 9 100ba,
2 200ba 1973-6
Helene Madison (USA) 1930-2
and Shane Gould (Aus) 1971-2
set records at each freestyle
distance: 100m, 200m, 400m,
800m and 1500m.

Olympic Games

Olympic records are indicated by OR.
Events on the current programme are
listed, followed by discontinued events.

Men

50 metres freestyle
1988 Matt Biondi (USA) 22.14
1992 Aleksandr Popov (Rus) 21.90
OR

100 metres freestyle
1896 Alfréd Hajós (Hun) 1:22.2
1904 Zoltán von Halmay (Hun)
1:02.08 (100y)
1906 Charles Daniels (USA) 1:13.4
1908 Charles Daniels (USA) 1:05.6
1912 Duke Kahanamoku (USA)
1:03.4
1920 Duke Kahanamoku (USA)
1:01.4
1924 Johnny Weissmuller (USA) 59.0
1928 Johnny Weissmuller (USA)
58.6
1932 Yasuji Miyazaki (Jap) 58.2
1936 Ferenc Csik (Hun) 57.6
1948 Walter Ris (USA) 57.3
1952 Clarke Scholes (USA) 57.4
1956 Jon Henricks (Aus) 55.4
1960 John Devitt (Aus) 55.2
1964 Don Schollander (USA) 53.4
1968 Mike Wenden (Aus) 52.2
1972 Mark Spitz (USA) 51.22
1976 Jim Montgomery (USA) 49.99
1980 Jörg Woithe (GDR) 50.40
1984 Rowdy Gaines (USA) 49.80
1988 Matt Biondi (USA) 48.63 OR
1992 Aleksandr Popov (CIS/Rus)
49.02

200 metres freestyle
1900 Frederick Lane (Aus) 2:25.2
1904 Charles Daniels (USA) 2:44.2
(220y)
1968 Mike Wenden (Aus) 1:55.2
1972 Mark Spitz (USA) 1:52.78
1976 Bruce Furniss (USA) 1:50.29
1980 Sergey Koplyakov (USSR)
1:49.81
1984 Michael Gross (FRG) 1:47.44
1988 Duncan Armstrong (Aus)
1:47.25
1992 Yevgeniy Sadoviy (CIS/Rus)
1:46.70 OR

Aleksandr Popov – Olympic, World and European sprint champion

400 metres freestyle
1896 Paul Neumann (Aut) 8:12.6
(500m)
1904 Charles Daniels (USA) 6:16.2
(440y)
1906 Otto Scheff (Aut) 6:23.8
1908 Henry Taylor (UK) 5:36.8
1912 George Hodgson (Can) 5:24.4
1920 Norman Ross (USA) 5:26.8
1924 Johnny Weissmuller (USA)
5:04.2
1928 Albeto Zorilla (Arg) 5:01.6
1932 Buster Crabbe (USA) 4:48.4
1936 Jack Medica (USA) 4:44.5
1948 William Smith (USA) 4:41.0
1952 Jean Boiteux (Fra) 4:30.7
1956 Murray Rose (Aus) 4:27.3
1960 Murray Rose (Aus) 4:18.3
1964 Don Schollander (USA) 4:12.2
1968 Mike Burton (USA) 4:09.0
1972 Brad Cooper (Aus) 4:00.27
1976 Brian Goodell (USA) 3:51.93
1980 Vladimir Salnikov (USSR)
3:51.31
1984 George DiCarlo (USA) 3:51.23
1988 Uwe Dassler (GDR) 3:46.95
1992 Yevgeniy Sadoviy (CIS/Rus)
3:45.00

1500 metres freestyle
1896 Alfréd Hajós (Hun) 18:22.2
(1200m)
1900 John Jarvis (UK) 13:40.2
(1000m)
1904 Emil Rausch (Ger) 27:18.2
(1 Mile)
1906 Henry Taylor (UK) 28:28.0
1908 Henry Taylor (UK) 22:48.4
1912 George Hodgson (Can)
22:00.0

1920 Norman Ross (USA) 22:23.2
1924 Andrew Charlton (Aus)
20:06.6
1928 Arne Borg (Swe) 19:51.8
1932 Kusuo Kitamura (Jap) 19:12.4
1936 Noboru Terada (Jap) 19:13.7
1948 James McLane (USA) 19:18.5
1952 Ford Konno (USA) 18:30.0
1956 Murray Rose (Aus) 17:58.9
1960 John Konrads (Aus) 17:19.6
1964 Bob Windle (Aus) 17:01.7
1968 Mike Burton (USA) 16:38.9
1972 Mike Burton (USA) 15:52.58
1976 Brian Goodell (USA) 15:02.40
1980 Vladimir Salnikov (USSR)
14:58.27
1984 Michael O'Brien (USA)
15:05.20
1988 Vladimir Salnikov (USSR)
15:00.40
1992 Kieren Perkins (Aus) 14:43.48
OR

100 metres backstroke
1904 Walter Brack (Ger) 1:16.8
(100y)
1908 Arno Bieberstein (Ger) 1:24.6
1912 Harry Hebner (USA) 1:21.2
1920 Warren Kealoha (USA) 1:15.2
1924 Warren Kealoha (USA) 1:13.2
1928 George Kojac (USA) 1:08.2
1932 Masaji Kiyokawa (Jap) 1:08.6
1936 Adolf Kiefer (USA) 1:05.9
1948 Allen Stack (USA) 1:06.4
1952 Yoshinobu Oyakawa (USA)
1:05.4
1956 David Theile (Aus) 1:02.2
1960 David Theile (Aus) 1:01.9
1968 Roland Matthes (GDR) 58.7
1972 Roland Matthes (GDR) 56.58

1976 John Naber (USA) 55.49
1980 Bengt Baron (Swe) 56.53
1984 Rick Carey (USA) 55.79
1988 Daichi Suzuki (Jap) 55.05
1992 Mark Tewksbury (Can) 53.98

200 metres backstroke
1900 Ernst Hoppenberg (Ger)
  2:47.0
1964 Jed Graef (USA) 2:10.3
1968 Roland Matthes (GDR) 2:09.6
1972 Roland Matthes (GDR)
  2.02.82
1976 John Naber (USA) 1:59.19
1980 Sándor Wladár (Hun) 2:01.93
1984 Rick Carey (USA) 2:00.23
1988 Igor Polyanskiy (USSR)
  1:59.37
1992 Martin López-Zubero (Spa)
  1:58.47 OR

100 metres breaststroke
1968 Don McKenzie (USA) 1:07.7
1972 Nobutaka Taguchi (Jap)
  1:04.94
1976 John Hencken (USA) 1:03.11
1980 Duncan Goodhew (UK)
  1:03.34
1984 Steve Lundquist (USA)
  1:01.65
1988 Adrian Moorhouse (UK)
  1:02.04
1992 Nelson Diebel (USA) 1:01.50
  OR

200 metres breaststroke
1908 Frederick Holman (UK)
  3:09.2
1912 Walter Bathe (Ger) 3:01.8
1920 Håken Malmroth (Swe) 3:04.4
1924 Robert Skelton (USA) 2:56.5
1928 Yoshiyuki Tsuruta (Jap) 2:48.8
1932 Yoshiyuki Tsuruta (Jap) 2:45.4
1936 Tetsuo Hamuro (Jap) 2:41.5
1948 Joseph Verdeur (USA) 2:39.3
1952 John Davies (Aus) 2:34.4
1956 Masaru Furukawa (Jap) 2:34.7
1960 William Mulliken (USA)
  2:37.4
1964 Ian O'Brien (Aus) 2:27.8
1968 Felipe Munoz (Mex) 2:28.7
1972 John Hencken (USA) 2:21.55
1976 David Wilkie (UK) 2:15.11
1980 Robertas Zhulpa (USSR)
  2:15.85
1984 Victor Davis (Can) 2:13.34
1988 József Szabó (Hun) 2:13.52
1992 Mike Barrowman (USA)
  2:10.16 OR

100 metres butterfly
1968 Doug Russell (USA) 55.9
1972 Mark Spitz (USA) 54.27

1976 Matt Vogel (USA) 54.35
1980 Pär Arvidsson (Swe) 54.92
1984 Michael Gross (FRG) 53.08
1988 Anthony Nesty (Sur) 53.00
  OR
1992 Pablo Morales (USA) 53.32

200 metres butterfly
1956 William Yorzyk (USA) 2:19.3
1960 Mike Troy (USA) 2:12.8
1964 Kevin Berry (Aus) 2:06.6
1968 Carl Robie (USA) 2:08.7
1972 Mark Spitz (USA) 2:00.70
1976 Mike Bruner (USA) 1:59.23
1980 Sergey Fesenko (USSR)
  1:59.76
1984 Jon Sieben (Aus) 1:57.04
1988 Michael Gross (FRG) 1:56.94
1992 Melvin Stewart (USA) 1:56.26
  OR

200 metres individual medley
1968 Charles Hickcox (USA) 2:12.0
1972 Gunnar Larsson (Swe) 2:07.17
1984 Alex Baumann (Can) 2:01.42
1988 Tamás Darnyi (Hun) 2:00.17
  OR
1992 Tamás Darnyi (Hun) 2:00.76

400 metres individual medley
1964 Richard Roth (USA) 4:45.4
1968 Charles Hickcox (USA) 4:48.4
1972 Gunnar Larsson (Swe) 4:31.98
1976 Rod Strachan (USA) 4:23.68
1980 Aleksandr Sidorenko (USSR)
  4:22.89
1984 Alex Baumann (Can) 4:17.41
1988 Tamás Darnyi (Hun) 4:14.75
1992 Tamás Darnyi (Hun) 4:14.23
  OR

4 x 100 metres freestyle relay
1964 USA 3:33.2
1968 USA 3:31.7
1972 USA 3:26.42
1984 USA 3:19.03
1988 USA 3:16.53 OR
1992 USA 3:16.74

4 x 200 metres freestyle relay
1906 Hungary 16:52.4
1908 United Kingdom 10:55.6
1912 Australasia 10:11.6
1920 USA 10:04.4
1924 USA 9:53.4
1928 USA 9:36.2
1932 Japan 8:58.4
1936 Japan 8:51.5
1948 USA 8:46.0
1952 USA 8:31.1
1956 Australia 8:23.6
1960 USA 8:10.2
1964 USA 7:52.1
1968 USA 7:52.3

1972 USA 7:35.78
1976 USA 7:23.22
1980 USSR 7:23.50
1984 USA 7:15.69
1988 USA 7:12.51
1992 CIS 7:11.95 OR

4 x 100 metres medley relay
1960 USA 4:05.4
1964 USA 3:58.4
1968 USA 3:54.9
1972 USA 3:48.16
1976 USA 3:42.22
1980 Australia 3:45.70
1984 USA 3:39.30
1988 USA 3:36.93 OR
1992 USA 3:36.93 OR

Springboard diving
1908 Albert Zürner (Ger)
1912 Paul Günther (Ger)
1920 Louis Kuehn (USA)
1924 Albert White (USA)
1928 Peter Desjardins (USA)
1932 Michael Galitzen (USA)
1936 Richard Degener (USA)
1948 Bruce Harlan (USA)
1952 David Browning (USA)
1956 Robert Clotworthy (USA)
1960 Gary Tobian (USA)
1964 Kenneth Sitzberger (USA)
1968 Bernard Wrightson (USA)
1972 Vladimir Vasin (USSR)
1976 Philip Boggs (USA)
1980 Aleksandr Portnov (USSR)
1984 Greg Louganis (USA)
1988 Greg Louganis (USA)
1992 Mark Lenzi (USA)

Highboard platform diving
1904 George Sheldon (USA)
1906 Gottlob Walz (Ger)
1908 Hjalmar Johansson (Swe)
1912 Erik Adlerz (Swe)
1920 Clarence Pinkston (USA)
1924 Albert White (USA)
1928 Peter Desjardins (USA)
1932 Harold Smith (USA)
1936 Marshall Wayne (USA)
1948 Samuel Lee (USA)
1952 Samuel Lee (USA)
1956 Joaquin Capilla (Mex)
1960 Robert Webster (USA)
1964 Robert Webster (USA)
1968 Klaus Dibiasi (Ita)
1972 Klaus Dibiasi (Ita)
1976 Klaus Dibiasi (Ita)
1980 Falk Hoffmann (GDR)
1984 Greg Louganis (USA)
1988 Greg Louganis (USA)
1992 Sun Shuwei (Chn)

Women

50 metres freestyle
1988 Kristin Otto (GDR) 25.49
1992 Yang Wenyi (Chn) 24.79 OR

100 metres freestyle
1912 Fanny Durack (Aus) 1:22.2
1920 Ethelda Bleibtrey (USA) 1:13.6
1924 Ethel Lackie (USA) 1:12.4
1928 Albina Osipowich (USA) 1:11.0
1932 Helene Madison (USA) 1:06.8
1936 Hendrika Mastenbroek (Hol) 1:05.9
1948 Greta Andersen (Den) 1:06.3
1952 Katalin Szöke (Hun) 1:06.8
1956 Dawn Fraser (Aus) 1:02.0
1960 Dawn Fraser (Aus) 1:01.2
1964 Dawn Fraser (Aus) 59.5
1968 Jan Henne (USA) 1:00.0
1972 Sandra Neilson (USA) 58.59
1976 Kornelia Ender (GDR) 55.65
1980 Barbara Krause (GDR) 54.79
1984 Nancy Hogshead (USA) & Carrie Steinseifer (USA) 55.92
1988 Kristin Otto (GDR) 54.93
1992 Zhuang Yong (Chn) 54.64 OR

200 metres freestyle
1968 Debbie Meyer (USA) 2:10.5
1972 Shane Gould (Aus) 2:03.56
1976 Kornelia Ender (GDR) 1:59.26
1980 Barbara Krause (GDR) 1:58.33
1984 Mary Wayte (USA) 1:59.23
1988 Heike Friedrich (GDR) 1:57.65 OR
1992 Nicole Haislett (USA) 1:57.90

400 metres freestyle
1920 Ethelda Bleibtrey (USA) 4:34.0 (300m)
1924 Martha Norelius (USA) 6:02.2
1928 Martha Norelius (USA) 5:42.8
1932 Helene Madison (USA) 5:28.5
1936 Hendrika Mastenbroek (Hol) 5:26.4
1948 Ann Curtis (USA) 5:17.8
1952 Valéria Gyenge (Hun) 5:12.1
1956 Lorraine Crapp (Aus) 4:54.6
1960 Chris Von Saltza (USA) 4:50.6
1964 Virginia Duenkel (USA) 4:43.3
1968 Debbie Meyer (USA) 4:31.8
1972 Shane Gould (Aus) 4:19.04
1976 Petra Thümer (GDR) 4:09.89
1980 Ines Diers (GDR) 4:08.76
1984 Tiffany Cohen (USA) 4:07.10
1988 Janet Evans (USA) 4:03.85 OR
1992 Dagmar Hase (Ger) 4:07.18

800 metres freestyle
1968 Debbie Meyer (USA) 9:24.0
1972 Keena Rothhammer (USA) 8:53.68
1976 Petra Thümer (GDR) 8:37.14
1980 Michelle Ford (Aus) 8:28.90
1984 Tiffany Cohen (USA) 8:24.95
1988 Janet Evans (USA) 8:20.20 OR
1992 Janet Evans (USA) 8:25.52

100 metres backstroke
1924 Sybil Bauer (USA) 1:23.2
1928 Maria Braun (Hol) 1:22.0
1932 Eleanor Holm (USA) 1:19.4
1936 Nida Senff (Hol) 1:18.9
1948 Karen Harup (Den) 1:14.4
1952 Joan Harrison (SAf) 1:14.3
1956 Judy Grinham (UK) 1:12.9
1960 Lynn Burke (USA) 1:09.3
1964 Cathy Ferguson (USA) 1:07.7
1968 Kaye Hall (USA) 1:06.2
1972 Melissa Belote (USA) 1:05.78
1976 Ulrike Richter (GDR) 1:01.83
1980 Rica Reinisch (GDR) 1:00.86
1984 Theresa Andrews (USA) 1:02.55
1988 Kristin Otto (GDR) 1:00.89
1992 Krisztina Egerszegi (Hun) 1:00.68 OR

200 metres backstroke
1968 Pokey Watson (USA) 2:24.8
1972 Melissa Belote (USA) 2:19.19
1976 Ulrike Richter (GDR) 2:13.43
1980 Rica Reinisch (GDR) 2:11.77
1984 Jolanda de Rover (Hol) 2:12.38
1988 Krisztina Egerszegi (Hun) 2:09.29
1992 Krisztina Egerszegi (Hun) 2:07.06 OR

100 metres breaststroke
1968 Djurdjica Bjedov (Yug) 1:15.8
1972 Catherine Carr (USA) 1:13.58
1976 Hannelore Anke (GDR) 1:11.16
1980 Ute Geweniger (GDR) 1:10.22
1984 Petra Van Staveren (Hol) 1:09.88
1988 Tania Dangalakova (Bul) 1:07.95 OR
1992 Yelena Rudkovskaya (CIS/Bls) 1:08.00

200 metres breaststroke
1924 Lucy Morton (UK) 3:33.2
1928 Hilde Schrader (Ger) 3:12.6
1932 Claire Dennis (Aus) 3:06.3
1936 Hideko Maehata (Jap) 3:03.6
1948 Petronella van Vliet (Hol) 2:57.2
1952 Eva Székely (Hun) 2:51.7

1956 Ursula Happe (FRG) 2:53.1
1960 Anita Lonsbrough (UK) 2:49.5
1964 Galina Prozumenshchikova (USSR) 2:46.4
1968 Sharon Wichman (USA) 2:44.4
1972 Beverley Whitfield (Aus) 2:41.71
1976 Marina Koshevaya (USSR) 2:33.35
1980 Lina Kachushite (USSR) 2:29.54
1984 Anne Ottenbrite (Can) 2:30.38
1988 Silke Hörner (GDR) 2:26.71
1992 Kyoko Iwasaki (Jap) 2:26.65 OR

100 metres butterfly
1956 Shelley Mann (USA) 1:11.0
1960 Carolyn Schuler (USA) 1:09.5
1964 Sharon Stouder (USA) 1:04.7
1968 Lynette McClements (Aus) 1:05.0
1972 Mayumi Aoki (Jap) 1:03.34
1976 Kornelia Ender (GDR) 1:00.13
1980 Caren Metschuck (GDR) 1:00.42
1984 Mary T Meagher (USA) 59.26
1988 Kristin Otto (GDR) 59.00
1992 Qian Hong (Chn) 58.62 OR

200 metres butterfly
1968 Ada Kok (Hol) 2:24.7
1972 Karen Moe (USA) 2:15.57
1976 Andrea Pollack (GDR) 2:11.41
1980 Ines Geissler (GDR) 2:10.44
1984 Mary T Meagher (USA) 2:06.90 OR
1988 Kathleen Nord (GDR) 2:09.51
1992 Summer Sanders (USA) 2:08.67

200 metres individual medley
1968 Claudia Kolb (USA) 2:24.7
1972 Sharon Gould (Aus) 2:23.07
1984 Tracy Caulkins (USA) 2:12.64
1988 Daniela Hunger (GDR) 2:12.59
1992 Lin Li (Chn) 2:11.65 OR

400 metres individual medley
1964 Donna De Varona (USA) 5:18.7
1968 Claudia Kolb (USA) 5:08.5
1972 Gail Neall (Aus) 5:02.97
1976 Ulrike Tauber (GDR) 4:42.77
1980 Petra Schneider (GDR) 4:36.29 OR
1984 Tracy Caulkins (USA) 4:39.24
1988 Janet Evans (USA) 4:37.76
1992 Krisztina Egerszegi (Hun) 4:36.54

4 x 100 metres freestyle medley
1912 United Kingdom 5:52.8
1920 USA 5:11.6
1924 USA 4:58.8
1928 USA 4:47.6
1932 USA 4:38.0
1936 Netherlands 4:36.0
1948 USA 4:29.2
1952 Hungary 4:24.4
1956 Australia 4:17.1
1960 USA 4:08.9
1964 USA 4:03.8
1968 USA 4:02.5
1972 USA 3:55.19
1976 USA 3:44.82
1980 GDR 3:42.71
1984 USA 3:43.43
1988 GDR 3:40.63
1992 USA 3:39.46 OR

4 x 100 metres medley relay
1960 USA 4:41.1
1964 USA 4:33.9
1968 USA 4:28.3
1972 USA 4:20.75
1976 GDR 4:07.95
1980 GDR 4:06.67
1984 USA 4:08.34
1988 GDR 4:03.74
1992 USA 4:02.54 OR

Springboard diving
1920 Aileen Riggin (USA)
1924 Elizabeth Becker (USA)
1928 Helen Meany (USA)
1932 Georgia Coleman (USA)
1936 Marjorie Gestring (USA)
1948 Victoria Draves (USA)
1952 Pat McCormick (USA)
1956 Pat McCormick (USA)
1960 Ingrid Krämer (GDR)
1964 Ingrid Engel (née Krämer)
  (GDR)
1968 Sue Gossick (USA)
1972 Micki King (USA)
1976 Jennifer Chandler (USA)
1980 Irina Kalinina (USSR)
1984 Sylvie Bernier (Can)
1988 Gao Min (Chn)
1992 Gao Min (Chn)

Highboard platform diving
1912 Greta Johansson (Swe)
1920 Stefani Fryland-Clausen
  (Den)
1924 Caroline Smith (USA)
1928 Elizabeth Pinkston (USA)
1932 Dorothy Poynton (USA)
1936 Dorothy Hill (née Poynton)
  (USA)

1948 Victoria Draves (USA)
1952 Pat McCormick (USA)
1956 Pat McCormick (USA)
1960 Ingrid Krämer (GDR)
1964 Lesley Bush (USA)
1968 Milena Duchková (Cs)
1972 Ulrika Knape (Swe)
1976 Elena Vaytsekhovskaya
  (USSR)
1980 Martina Jäschke (GDR)
1984 Zhou Jihong (Chn)
1988 Xu Yanmei (Chn)
1992 Fu Mingxia (Chn)

Synchronised Swimming Solo
1984 Tracie Ruiz (USA)
1988 Carolyn Waldo (Can)
1992 Sylvie Frechette (*Can)*

* Frechette was awarded the gold medal over a year later, after a judge had admitted to pressing the wrong scoring button. Her total then exceeded that of Kristen Babb-Sprague (USA), originally declared the winner, who was allowed to keep her gold medal.

Synchronised Swimming Duet
1984 Candy Costie & Tracie Ruiz
  (USA)
1988 Michelle Cameron & Carolyn
  Waldo (Can)
1992 Karen & Sarah Josephson
  (USA)

Discontinued events - Men

50 yards freestyle
1904 Zoltán Halmay (Hun) 28.0

100 metres freestyle for sailors
1896 Ioannis Maiokinis (Gre) 2:20.4

200 metres obstacle event
1900 Frederick Lane (Aus) 2:38.4

400 metres breaststroke
1904 Georg Zacharias (Ger) 7:23.6
1912 Walter Bathe (Ger) 6:29.6
1920 Håkan Malmroth (Swe) 6:31.8

880 yards freestyle
1904 Emil Rausch (Ger) 13:11.4

4000 metres freestyle
1900 John Jarvis (UK) 58:24.0

Underwater swimming
1900 Charles de Vendeville (Fra)

Plunge for distance
1904 Paul Dickey (USA) 19.05m

200 metres team swimming
1900 Germany

4 x 50 yards relay
1904 New York AC (USA)

Plain high diving
1912 Erik Adlerz (Swe)
1920 Arvid Wallman (Swe)
1924 Richmond Eve (USA)

Most Olympic gold medals
(individual/relay)
Men
9 (4/5) Mark Spitz (USA) 1968-72
8 (3/5) Matt Biondi (USA) 1984-92
5 (4/1) Charles Daniels (USA)
  1904-08
5 (3/2) Johnny Weissmuller
  (USA) 1924-8
5 (2/3) Don Schollander (USA)
  1964-8
4 (4/-) Roland Matthes (GDR)
  1968-72
4 (3/1) Henry Taylor (UK) 1906-08
4 (3/1) Murray Rose (Aus) 1956-60
4 (2/2) John Naber (USA) 1976
4 (3/1) Vladimir Salnikov (USSR)
  1980-8
4 (4/-) Greg Louganis (USA)
  1984-8

Women
6 (4/2) Kristin Otto (GDR) 1988
4 (4/-) Krisztina Egerszegi (Hun)
  1988-92
4 (4/-) Pat McCormick (USA)
  1952-6
4 (3/1) Dawn Fraser (Aus) 1956-64
4 (3/1) Kornelia Ender (GDR)
  1976
Spitz won a record seven gold medals at one Games, in 1972.

Most Olympic medals
(gold/silver/bronze)
Men
11 (9/1/1) Mark Spitz (USA)
  1968-72
11 (8/2/1) Matt Biondi (USA)
  1984-92
8 (5/1/2) Charles Daniels (USA)
  1904-08
8 (4/2/2) Roland Matthes (GDR)
  1968-72
8 (4/1/3) Henry Taylor (UK)
  1906-20

Women
8 (4/4/-) Dawn Fraser (Aut)
  1956-64
8 (4/4/-) Kornelia Ender (GDR)
  1972-6
8 (2/6/-) Shirley Babashoff
  (USA) 1972-6

Youngest gold medallist
Men   14yr 309d   Kusuo Kitamura (Jap) 1500m freestyle 1932
Women   13yr 268d   Marjorie Gestring (USA) springboard diving 1936

Oldest gold medallist
Men   34yr 186d   Hjalmar Johansson (Swe) highboard diving 1908
Women   30yr 41d   Ursula Happe (FRG) 200m breaststroke 1956

Youngest medallist
Men   14yr 10d   Nils Skoglund (Swe) 2nd highboard diving 1928
Women   12yr 24d   Inge Sørensen (Den) 3rd 200m breaststroke 1936

World Championships

World Championships separate from the Olympic Games were first held in 1973, and are now staged every four years. Venues have been: 1973 Belgrade; 1975 Cali, Colombia; 1978 West Berlin; 1982 Guayaquil, Ecuador; 1986 Madrid; 1991 (January) Perth, Australia; 1994 Rome (Italy). Long distance events, over 25 kilometres, were introduced in 1991. *Champions have been:*

Men

50 metres freestyle
1986 Tom Jager (USA) 22.49
1991 Tom Jager (USA) 22.16
1994 Aleksandr Popov (Rus) 22.17

100 metres freestyle
1973 Jim Montgomery (USA) 51.70
1975 Andrew Coan (USA) 51.25
1978 David McCagg (USA) 50.24
1982 Jörg Woithe (GDR) 50.18
1986 Matt Biondi (USA) 48.94
1991 Matt Biondi (USA) 49.18
1994 Aleksandr Popov (Rus) 49.12

200 metres freestyle
1973 Jim Montgomery (USA) 1:53.02
1975 Tim Shaw (USA) 1:51.04
1978 William Forrester (USA) 1:51.02
1982 Michael Gross (FRG) 1:49.84
1986 Michael Gross (FRG) 1:47.92
1991 Giorgio Lamberti (Ita) 1:47.27
1994 Antti Kasvio (Fin) 1:47.32

400 metres freestyle
1973 Rick DeMont (USA) 3:58.18
1975 Tim Shaw (USA) 3:54.88
1978 Vladimir Salnikov (USSR) 3:51.94
1982 Vladimir Salnikov (USSR) 3:51.30
1986 Rainer Henkel (FRG) 3:50.05
1991 Jörg Hoffmann (Ger) 3:48.04
1994 Kieren Perkins (Aus) 3:43.80

1500 metres freestyle
1973 Steve Holland (Aus) 15:31.85
1975 Tim Shaw (USA) 15:28.92
1978 Vladimir Salnikov (USSR) 15:03.99
1982 Vladimir Salnikov (USSR) 15:01.77
1986 Rainer Henkel (FRG) 15:05.31
1991 Jörg Hoffmann (Ger) 14:50.36
1994 Kieren Perkins (Aus) 14:50.52

4 x 100 metres freestyle
1973 USA 3:27.18
1975 USA 3:24.85
1978 USA 3:19.74
1982 USA 3:19.26
1986 USA 3:19.89
1991 USA 3:17.15
1994 USA 3:16.90

4 x 200 metres freestyle relay
1973 USA 7:33.22
1975 FRG 7:39.44
1978 USA 7:20.82
1982 USA 7:21.09
1986 GDR 7:15.91
1991 GER 7:13.50
1994 SWE 7:17.70

100 metres backstroke
1973 Roland Matthes (GDR) 57.47
1975 Roland Matthes (GDR) 58.15
1978 Robert Jackson (USA) 56.36
1982 Dirk Richter (GDR) 55.95
1986 Igor Polyanski (USSR) 55.58
1991 Jeff Rouse (USA) 55.23
1994 Martin López Zubero (Spa) 55.17

200 metres backstroke
1973 Roland Matthes (GDR) 2:01.87
1975 Zoltan Verraszto (Hun) 2:05.05
1978 Jesse Vassallo (USA) 2:02.16
1982 Rick Carey (USA) 2:00.82
1986 Igor Polyanski (USSR) 1:58.78
1991 Martin López Zubero (Spa) 1:59.52
1994 Vladimir Selkov (Rus) 1:57.42

100 metres breaststroke
1973 John Hencken (USA) 1:04.02
1975 David Wilkie (UK) 1:04.26
1978 Walter Kusch (GDR) 1:03.56
1982 Steve Lundquist (USA) 1:02.75
1986 Victor Davis (Can) 1:02.71
1991 Norbert Rózsa (Hun) 1:01.45
1994 Norbert Rózsa (Hun) 1:01.24

200 metres breaststroke
1973 David Wilkie (UK) 2:19.28
1975 David Wilkie (UK) 2:18.23
1978 Nick Nevid (USA) 2:18.37
1982 Victor Davis (Can) 2:14.77
1986 József Szabó (Hun) 2:14.27
1991 Mike Barrowman (USA) 2:11.23
1994 Norbert Rózsa (Hun) 2:12.81

100 metres butterfly
1973 Bruce Robertson (Can) 55.69
1975 Greg Jagenburg (USA) 55.63
1978 Joe Bottom (USA) 54.30
1982 Matt Gribble (USA) 53.88
1986 Pablo Morales (USA) 53.54
1991 Anthony Nesty (Sur) 53.29
1994 Rafal Szukala (Pol) 53.51

200 metres butterfly
1973 Robin Backhaus (USA) 2:03.32
1975 William Forrester (USA) 2:01.95
1978 Michael Bruner (USA) 1:59.38
1982 Michael Gross (FRG) 1:58.85
1986 Michael Gross (FRG) 1:56.53
1991 Melvin Stewart (USA) 1:55.69
1994 Denis Pankratov (Rus) 1:56.54

200 metres individual medley
1973 Gunnar Larsson (Swe) 2:08.36
1975 András Hargitay (Hun) 2:07.72
1978 Graham Smith (Can) 2:03.65
1982 Aleksey Sidorenko (USSR) 2:03.30
1986 Tamás Darnyi (Hun) 2:01.57
1991 Tamás Darnyi (Hun) 1:59.36
1994 Jani Sievinen (Fin) 1:58.16

400 metres individual medley
1973 András Hargitay (Hun) 4:31.11
1975 András Hargitay (Hun) 4:32.57
1978 Jesse Vassallo (USA) 4:20.05
1982 Ricardo Prado (Bra) 4:19.78
1986 Tamás Darnyi (Hun) 4:18.98
1991 Tamás Darnyi (Hun) 4:12.36
1994 Tom Dolan (USA) 4:12.30

4 x 100 metres medley relay
1973 USA 3:49.49
1975 USA 3:49.00
1978 USA 3:44.63
1982 USA 3:40.84
1986 USA 3:41.25

1991 USA 3:39.66
1994 USA 3:37.74

25km river/sea swim
1991 Chad Hundeby (USA)
5:01:45.78
1994 Greg Steppel (Can) 5:35:25.56

1m Springboard diving
1991 Edwin Jongejans (Hol)
1994 Evan Stewart (Zim)

Springboard diving (3m from 1991)
1973 Phil Boggs (USA)
1975 Phil Boggs (USA)
1978 Phil Boggs (USA)
1982 Greg Louganis (USA)
1986 Greg Louganis (USA)
1991 Kent Ferguson (USA)
1994 Yu Zhuocheng (Chn)

Highboard (platform) diving
1973 Klaus Dibiasi (Ita)
1975 Klaus Dibiasi (Ita)
1978 Greg Louganis (USA)
1982 Greg Louganis (USA)
1986 Greg Louganis (USA)
1991 Sun Shuwei (Chn)
1994 Dmitriy Sautin (Rus)

Women

50 metres freestyle
1986 Tamara Costache (Rom) 25.28
1991 Zuang Yong (Chn) 25.47
1994 Le Jingyi (Chn) 24.51

100 metres freestyle
1973 Kornelia Ender (GDR) 57.54
1975 Kornelia Ender (GDR) 56.50
1978 Barbara Krause (GDR) 55.68
1982 Birgit Meineke (GDR) 55.79
1986 Kristin Otto (GDR) 55.05
1991 Nicole Haislett (USA) 55.17
1994 Le Jingyi (Chn) 54.01

200 metres freestyle
1973 Keena Rothhammer (USA)
2:04.99
1975 Shirley Babashoff (USA)
2:02.50
1978 Cynthia Woodhead (USA)
1:58.53
1982 Annemarie Verstappen (Hol)
1:59.53
1986 Heike Friedrich (GDR) 1:58.26
1991 Hayley Lewis (Aus) 2:00.48
1994 Franziska van Almsick (Ger)
1:56.78

400 metres freestyle
1973 Heather Greenwood (USA)
4:20.28
1975 Shirley Babashoff (USA)
4:16.87

1978 Tracey Wickham (Aus) 4:06.28
1982 Carmela Schmidt (GDR)
4:08.98
1986 Heike Friedrich (GDR) 4:07.45
1991 Janet Evans (USA) 4:08.63
1994 Yang Aihua (Chn) 4:09.64

800 metres freestyle
1973 Novella Calligaris (Ita) 8:52.97
1975 Jenny Turrall (Aus) 8:44.75
1978 Tracey Wickham (Aus) 8:24.94
1982 Kim Lineham (USA) 8:27.48
1986 Astrid Strauss (GDR) 8:28.24
1991 Janet Evans (USA) 8:24.05
1994 Janet Evans (USA) 8:29.85

4 x 100 metres freestyle
1973 GDR 3:52.45
1975 GDR 3:49.37
1978 USA 3:43.43
1982 GDR 3:43.97
1986 GDR 3:40.57
1991 USA 3:43.26
1994 China 3:37.91

4 x 200 metres freestyle relay
1986 GDR 7:59.33
1991 Germany 8:02.56
1994 China 7:57.96

100 metres backstroke
1973 Ulrike Richter (GDR) 1:05.42
1975 Ulrike Richter (GDR) 1:03.30
1978 Linda Jezek (USA) 1:02.55
1982 Kristin Otto (GDR) 1:01.30
1986 Betsy Mitchell (USA) 1:01.74
1991 Krisztina Egerszegi (Hun)
1:01.78
1994 He Cihong (Chn) 1:00.57

200 metres backstroke
1973 Melissa Belote (USA) 2:20.52
1975 Birgit Treiber (GDR) 2:15.46
1978 Linda Jezek (USA) 2:11.93
1982 Cornelia Sirch (GDR) 2:09.91
1986 Cornelia Sirch (GDR) 2:11.37
1991 Krisztina Egerszegi (Hun)
2:09.15
1994 He Cihong (Chn) 2:07.40

100 metres breaststroke
1973 Renate Vogel (GDR) 1:13.74
1975 Hannelore Anke (GDR)
1:12.72
1978 Yulia Bogdanova (USSR)
1:10.31
1982 Ute Geweniger (GDR) 1:09.14
1986 Sylvia Gerasch (GDR) 1:08.11
1991 Linley Frame (Aus) 1:08.81
1994 Samantha Riley (Aus) 1:07.69

200 metres breaststroke
1973 Renate Vogel (GDR) 2:40.01
1975 Hannelore Anke (GDR)
2:37.25

1978 Lina Kachushite (USSR)
2:31.42
1982 Svetlana Varganova (USSR)
2:28.82
1986 Silke Horner (GDR) 2:27.40
1991 Yelena Volkova (USSR)
2:29,53
1994 Samantha Riley (Aus) 2:26.87

100 metres butterfly
1973 Kornelia Ender (GDR) 1:02.53
1975 Kornelia Ender (GDR) 1:01.24
1978 Mary-Joan Pennington (USA)
1:00.20
1982 Mary T.Meagher (USA) 59.41
1986 Kornelia Gressler (GDR) 59.51
1991 Qian Hong (Chn) 59.68
1994 Liu Limin (Chn) 58.98

200 metres butterfly
1973 Rosemarie Kother (GDR)
2:13.76
1975 Rosemarie Kother (GDR)
2:13.82
1978 Tracy Caulkins (USA) 2:09.87
1982 Ines Geissler (GDR) 2:08.66
1986 Mary T.Meagher (USA)
2:08.41
1991 Summer Sanders (USA)
2:09.24
1994 Liu Limin (Chn) 2:07.25

200 metres individual medley
1973 Angela Hübner (GDR) 2:20.51
1975 Kathy Heddy (USA) 2:19.80
1978 Tracy Caulkins (USA) 2:14.07
1982 Petra Schneider (GDR) 2:11.79
1986 Kristin Otto (GDR) 2:15.56
1991 Lin Li (Chn) 2:13.40
1994 Lu Bin (Chn) 2:12.34

400 metres individual medley
1973 Gudrun Wegner (GDR) 4:57.31
1975 Ulrike Tauber (GDR) 4:52.76
1978 Tracy Caulkins (USA) 4:40.83
1982 Petra Schneider (GDR) 4:36.10
1986 Kathleen Nord (GDR) 4:43.75
1991 Lin Li (Chn) 4:41.45
1994 Dai Guohong (Chn) 4:39.14

4 x 100 metres medley relay
1973 GDR 4:16.84
1975 GDR 4:14.74
1978 USA 4:08.21
1982 GDR 4:05.88
1986 GDR 4:04.82
1991 USA 4:06.51
1994 China 4:01.67

25km river/sea swim
1991 Shelley Taylor-Smith (Aus)
5:21:05.53
1994 Melissa Cunningham (Aus)
5:48:25.04

1m Springboard diving
1991 Gao Min (Chn)
1994 Chen Lixia (Chn)

Springboard diving
(3m from 1991)
1973 Christine Kohler (GDR)
1975 Irina Kalinina (USSR)
1978 Irina Kalinina (USSR)
1982 Megan Neyer (USA)
1986 Gao Min (Chn)
1991 Gao Min (Chn)
1994 Tan Shuping (Chn)

Highboard (platform) diving
1973 Ulrike Knape (Swe)
1975 Janet Ely (USA)
1978 Irina Kalinina (USSR)
1982 Wendy Wyland (USA)
1986 Lin Chen (Chn)
1991 Fu Mingxia (Chn)
1994 Fu Mingxia (Chn)

Synchronised swimming solo
1973 Teresa Andersen (USA)
1975 Gail Buzonas (USA)
1978 Helen Vanderburg (Can)
1982 Tracie Ruiz (USA)
1986 Carolyn Waldo (Can)
1991 Sylvie Frechette (Can)
1994 Becky Dyroen Lancer (USA)

Synchronised swimming duet
1973 Teresa Andersen & Gail
Johnson (USA)
1975 Robin Curren & Amanda
Norrish (USA)
1978 Michele Calkins & Helen
Vanderburg (Can)
1982 Kelly Kryczka & Sharon
Hambrook (Can)
1986 Carolyn Waldo & Michelle
Cameron (Can)
1991 Karen & Sarah Josephson
(USA)
1994 Becky Dyroen Lancer & Jill
Sudduth (USA)

Synchronised swimming team
1973 USA
1975 USA
1978 USA
1982 Canada
1986 Canada
1991 USA
1994 USA

Most gold medals
(individual/relay)
Men
6 (2/4) Jim Montgomery (USA)
1973-5
5 (5/0) Greg Louganis (USA)
1978-86

5 (4/1) Michael Gross (FRG)
1982-90
5 (0/5) Rowdy Gaines (USA)
1978-82
Women
8 (4/4) Kornelia Ender (GDR)
1973-5
7 (3/4) Kristin Otto (GDR) 1982-6

Most medals (gold/silver/bronze)
Men
13 (5/5/3) Michael Gross (FRG)
1982-90
11 (5/3/3) Matt Biondi (USA)
1986-90
8 (5/3/0) Rowdy Gaines (USA)
1978-82
Women
10 (8/2/0) Kornelia Ender (GDR)
1973-5
9 (7/2/0) Kristin Otto (GDR)
1982-6
9 (2/5/2) Mary T Meagher
(USA) 1982-6

Most medals at one Championships
(gold/silver/bronze)
Men
7 (3/1/3) Matt Biondi (USA) 1986
Women
6 (5/1/0) Tracy Caulkins (USA)
1978
6 (4/2/0) Kristin Otto (GDR) 1986
6 (1/3/2) Mary T.Meagher (USA)
1986

World Cup
Held as a team competition in 1979 only, when the USA won both men's and women's events.

World Cup - Diving
First held in 1979, it has been a biennial team competition. *Winners:*
1981 China
1983 China
1985 China
1987 USA
1989 China
1991 China

European Cup
The European inter-nation competitions for men and women were first held in 1969. Staged biennially at first, then annually in the winter in a 25m pool. *Winners:*
Men
10 USSR 1971, 1975 6, 1979-83, 1987-8
4 FRG/GER 1985-6, 1989, 1991
3 GDR 1969, 1973, 1984

Women
15 GDR 1969, 1971, 1973, 1975, 1979-89
2 USSR 1976, 1991

European Championships
First held in Budapest in 1926, and subsequently in 1927, 1931, 1934, 1938, 1947, at four-yearly intervals 1950-74, in 1977 and biennially from 1981. Winners since 1983 and swimmers to have won a particular event twice:

Men

50 metres freestyle
1987 Jörg Woithe (GDR) 22.66
1989 Vladimir Tkachenko (USSR) 22.64
1991 Nils Rudolph (Ger) 22.73
1993 Aleksandr Popov (Rus) 22.27

100 metres freestyle
1983 Per Johansson (Swe) 50.20
1985 Stéphane Caron (Fra) 50.20
1987 Sven Lodziewski (GDR) 49.79
1989 Giorgio Lamberti (Ita) 49.24
1991 Aleksandr Popov (USSR) 49.18
1993 Aleksandr Popov (Rus) 49.15
Most: 2 Istvan Barany (Hun) 1926, 1931; Alex Jany (Fra) 1947, 1950; Peter Nocke (FRG) 1974, 1977; Per Johansson (Swe) 1981, 1983; Popov

200 metres freestyle
1983 Michael Gross (FRG) 1:47.87
1985 Michael Gross (FRG) 1:47.95
1987 Anders Holmertz (Swe) 1:48.44
1989 Giorgio Lamberti (Ita) 1:46.69
1991 Artur Wojdat (Pol) 1:48.10
1993 Antti Kasvio (Fin) 1:47.11
Most: 2 Peter Nocke (FRG) 1974, 1977; Gross

400 metres freestyle
1983 Vladimir Salnikov (USSR) 3:49.80
1985 Uwe Dassler (GDR) 3:51.52
1987 Uwe Dassler (GDR) 3:48.95
1989 Artur Wojdat (Pol) 3:47.78
1991 Yevgeniy Sadovyi (USSR) 3:49.02
1993 Antti Kasvio (Fin) 3:47.81
Most: 2 Arne Borg (Swe) 1926-7, Alex Jany (Fra) 1947, 1950; Dassler

1500 metres freestyle
1983 Vladimir Salnikov (USSR) 15:08.84
1985 Uwe Dassler (GDR) 15:08.56
1987 Rainer Henkel (FRG) 15:02.23
1989 Jörg Hoffmann (GDR) 15:01.52

1991 Jörg Hoffmann (Ger) 15:02.57
1993 Jörg Hoffmann (Ger) 15:13.31
Most: 3 Vladimir Salnikov (USSR)
1977, 1981, 1983; Hoffmann; 2
Arne Borg (Swe) 1926-7

4 x 100 metres freestyle relay
1983 USSR 3:20.88
1985 FRG 3:22.18
1987 GDR 3:19.17
1989 FRG 3:19.68
1991 USSR 3:17.11
1993 Russia 3:18.80

4 x 200 metres freestyle relay
1983 FRG 7:20.40
1985 FRG 7:19.23
1987 FRG 7:13.10
1989 Italy 7:15.39
1991 USSR 7:15.96
1993 Russia 7:15.84

100 metres backstroke
1983 Dirk Richter (GDR) 56.10
1985 Igor Polyanskiy (USSR) 55.24
1987 Sergey Zabolotnov (USSR)
56.06
1989 Martin López-Zubero (Spa)
56.44
1991 Martin López-Zubero (Spa)
55.30
1993 Martin López-Zubero (Spa)
55.03
Most: 3 Lopez-Zubero, 2 Roland
Matthes (GDR) 1970, 1974

200 metres backstroke
1983 Sergey Zabolotnov (USSR)
2:01.00
1985 Igor Polyanskiy (USSR) 1:58.50
1987 Sergey Zabolotnov (USSR)
1:59.35
1989 Stefano Battistelli (Ita) 1:59.96
1991 Martin López-Zubero (Spa)
1:58.66
1993 Vladimir Selkov (Rus) 1:58.09
Most: 2 Roland Matthes (GDR)
1970, 1974; Zabolotnov

100 metres breaststroke
1983 Robertas Zhulpa (USSR)
1:03.32
1985 Adrian Moorhouse (UK)
1:02.99
1987 Adrian Moorhouse (UK)
1:02.13
1989 Adrian Moorhouse (UK)
1:01.71 (1:01.49 ht)
1991 Norbert Rózsa (Hun) 1:01.49
(1:01.29 ht)
1993 Karoly Guttler (Hun) 1:01.04
(1:00.95 ht)
Most: 3 Moorhouse, 2 Nikolay
Pankin (USSR) 1970, 1974

200 metres breaststroke
1983 Adrian Moorhouse (UK)
2:17.49
1985 Dmitriy Volkov (USSR)
2:19.53
1987 József Szabó (Hun) 2:13.87
1989 Nick Gillingham (UK) 2:12.90
1991 Nick Gillingham (UK) 2:12.55
1993 Nick Gillingham (UK) 2:12.49
Most: 3 Gillingham, 2 Erich
Rademacher (Ger) 1926-7, Georgiy
Prokopenko (USSR) 1962, 1966

100 metres butterfly
1983 Michael Gross (FRG) 54.00
1985 Michael Gross (FRG) 54.02
1987 Andrew Jameson (UK) 53.62
1989 Rafal Szukala (Pol) 54.47
1991 Vladislav Kulikov (USSR)
54.22
1993 Rafal Szukala (Pol) 53.41
Most: 2 Roger Pyttel (GDR) 1974,
1977; Gross

200 metres butterfly
1983 Michael Gross (FRG) 1:57.05
1985 Michael Gross (FRG) 1:56.65
1987 Michael Gross (FRG) 1:57.59
1989 Tamás Darnyi (Hun) 1:58.87
1991 Franck Esposito (Fra) 1:59.59
1993 Denis Pankratov (Rus) 1:56.25
Most: 4 Gross 1981 and above; 2
Valentin Kuzmin (USSR) 1962, 1966

200 metres individual medley
1983 Giovanni Franceshi (Ita)
2:02.48
1985 Tamás Darnyi (Hun) 2:03.23
1987 Tamás Darnyi (Hun) 2:00.56
1989 Tamás Darnyi (Hun) 2:01.03
1991 Lars Sørensen (Den) 2:02.63
1993 Jani Sievinen (Fin) 1:59.50
Most: 3 Darnyi

400 metres individual medley
1983 Giovanni Franceshi (Ita)
4:20.41
1985 Tamás Darnyi (Hun) 4:20.70
1987 Tamás Darnyi (Hun) 4:15.42
1989 Tamás Darnyi (Hun) 4:15.25
1991 Luca Sacchi (Ita) 4:17.81
1993 Tamás Darnyi (Hun) 4:15.24
Most: 4 Darnyi, 2 Sergey Fesenko
(USSR) 1977, 1981

4 x 100 metres medley relay
1983 USSR 3:43.99
1985 FRG 3:43.59
1987 USSR 3:41.51
1989 USSR 3:41.44
1991 USSR 3:40.68
1993 Russia 3:38.90

Springboard diving (3m)
1983 Petar Georgiev (Bul)
1985 Nikolay Droschin (USSR)
1987 Albin Killat (FRG)
1989 Albin Killat (FRG)
1991 Albin Killat (FRG)
1993 Jan Hempel (Ger)
Most: 3 Killiat, 2 Ewald
Riebschlager (Ger) 1927, 1932

1m Springboard diving
1989 Edwin Jongejans (Hol)
1991 Andrey Semeniyk (USSR)
1993 Peter Böhler (Ger)

Highboard diving
1983 David Ambarzumyan (USSR)
1985 Thomas Knuths (GDR)
1987 Georgiy Chogovadze (USSR)
1989 Georgiy Chogovadze (USSR)
1991 Vladimir Timoshinin (USSR)
1993 Dmitriy Sautin (Rus)
Most: 2 Hans Luber (Ger) 1926-7,
Brian Phelps (UK) 1958, 1962;
Klaus Dibiasi (Ita) 1966, 1974;
Chogovadze

Women

50 metres freestyle
1987 Tamara Costache (Rom) 25.50
1989 Catherine Plewinski (Fra)
25.63
1991 Simone Osygus (Ger) 25.80
1993 Franziska van Almsick (Ger)
25.23

100 metres freestyle
1983 Birgit Meineke (GDR) 55.18
1985 Heike Friedrich (GDR) 55.71
1987 Kristin Otto (GDR) 55.38
1989 Katrin Meissner (GDR) 55.38
1991 Catherine Plewinski (Fra) 56.20
1993 Franziska van Almsick (Ger)
54.57

200 metres freestyle
1983 Birgit Meineke (GDR) 1:59.45
1985 Heike Friedrich (GDR) 1:59.55
1987 Heike Friedrich (GDR) 1:58.95
1989 Manuela Stellmach (GDR)
1:58.93
1991 Mette Jacobsen (Den) 2:00.29
1993 Franziska van Almsick (Ger)
1:57.97
Most: 2 Friedrich

400 metres freestyle
1983 Astrid Strauss (GDR) 4:08.07
1985 Astrid Strauss (GDR) 4:09.22
1987 Heike Friedrich (GDR) 4:06.39
1989 Anke Möhring (GDR) 4:05.84
1991 Irene Dalby (Nor) 4:11.63
1993 Dagmar Hase (Ger) 4:10.47

Most: 2 Marie Braun (Hol) 1927, 1931; Strauss

800 metres freestyle
1983 Astrid Strauss (GDR) 8:32.12
1985 Astrid Strauss (GDR) 8:32.45
1987 Anke Möhring (GDR) 8:19.53
1989 Anke Möhring (GDR) 8:23.99
1991 Irene Dalby (Nor) 8:32.08
1993 Jana Henke (Ger) 8:32.47
Most: 2 Strauss, Möhring

4 x 100 metres freestyle
1983 GDR 3:44.72
1985 GDR 3:44.48
1987 GDR 3:42.58
1989 GDR 3:42.46
1991 Netherlands 3:45.36
1993 Germany 3:41.69

4 x 200 metres freestyle relay
1983 GDR 8:02.27
1985 GDR 8:03.82
1987 GDR 7:55.47
1989 GDR 7:58.54
1991 Denmark 8:05.90
1993 Germany 8:03.13

100 metres backstroke
1982 Ina Kleber (GDR) 1:01.79
1985 Birte Weigang (GDR) 1:02.16
1987 Kristin Otto (GDR) 1:01.86
1989 Kristin Otto (GDR) 1:01.86
1991 Krisztina Egerszegi (Hun) 1:00.31
1993 Krisztina Egerszegi (Hun) 1:00.83
Most: 2 Kleber 1981, 1983; Otto, Egerszegi

200 metres backstroke
1983 Cornelia Sirch (GDR) 2:12.05
1985 Cornelia Sirch (GDR) 2:10.89
1987 Cornelia Sirch (GDR) 2:10.20
1989 Dagmar Hase (GDR) 2:12.46
1991 Krisztina Egerszegi (Hun) 2:06.62
1993 Krisztina Egerszegi (Hun) 2:09.12
Most: 3 Sirch; 2 Egerszegi

100 metres breaststroke
1983 Ute Geweniger (GDR) 1:08.51
1985 Sylvia Gerasch (GDR) 1:08.62
1987 Silke Hörner (GDR) 1:07.91
1989 Susanne Börnicke (GDR) 1:09.55
1991 Yelena Rudkovskaya (USSR) 1:09.05
1993 Sylvia Gerasch (Ger) 1:10.65
Most: 2 Geweniger 1981, 1983; Gerasch

200 metres breaststroke
1983 Ute Geweniger (GDR) 2:30.64

1985 Tamara Bogomilova (Bul) 2:28.57
1987 Silke Hörner (GDR) 2:27.49
1989 Susanne Börnicke (GDR) 2:27.77
1991 Yelena Rudkovskaya (USSR) 2:29.50
1993 Brigitte Bécue (Bel) 2:31.18
Most: 2 Galina Prozumeshikova/Stepanova (USSR) 1966, 1970; Geweniger 1981, 1983

100 metres butterfly
1983 Ines Geissler (GDR) 1:00.31
1985 Kornelia Gressler (GDR) 59.46
1987 Kristin Otto (GDR) 59.52
1989 Catherine Plewinski (Fra) 59.08
1991 Catherine Plewinski (Fra) 1:00.32
1993 Catherine Plewinski (Fra) 1:00.13
Most: 3 Plewinski, 2 Ada Kok (Hol) 1962, 1966

200 metres butterfly
1983 Cornelia Polit (GDR) 2:07.82
1985 Jacqueline Alex (GDR) 2:11.78
1987 Kathleen Nord (GDR) 2:08.85
1989 Kathleen Nord (GDR) 2:09.33
1991 Mette Jacobsen (Den) 2:12.87
1993 Krisztina Egerszegi (Hun) 2:10.71
Most: 2 Nord

200 metres Individual medley
1983 Ute Geweniger (GDR) 2:13.07
1985 Kathleen Nord (GDR) 2:16.07
1987 Cornelia Sirch (GDR) 2:15.04
1989 Daniela Hunger (GDR) 2:13.26
1991 Daniela Hunger (Ger) 2:15.53
1993 Daniela Hunger (Ger) 2:15.33
Most: 3 Hunger, 2 Ulrike Tauber (GDR) 1974, 1977; Geweniger 1981 (2:12.64 rec), 1983

400 metres individual medley
1983 Kathleen Nord (GDR) 4:39.95
1985 Kathleen Nord (GDR) 4:47.08
1987 Noemi Lung (Rom) 4:40.21
1989 Daniela Hunger (GDR) 4:41.82
1991 Krisztina Egerszegi (Hun) 4:39.78
1993 Krisztina Egerszegi (Hun) 4:39.55
Rec: 1981 Petra Schneider (GDR) 4:39.30
Most: 2 Ulrike Tauber (GDR) 1974, 1977; Nord, Egerszegi

4 x 100 metres medley relay
1983 GDR 4:05.79
1985 GDR 4:06.93
1987 GDR 4:04.05

1989 GDR 4:07.40
1991 USSR 4:08.55
1993 Germany 4:06.91

Springboard diving (3m)
1983 Brita Baldus (GDR)
1985 Zhanna Tsirulnikova (USSR)
1987 Daphne Jongejans (Hol)
1989 Marina Babkova (USSR)
1991 Irina Lashko (USSR)
1993 Brita Baldus (Ger)
Most: 2 Olga Jensch (née Jordan) (Ger) 1931, 1934; Mady Moreau (Fra) 1947, 1950; Baldus

1m Springboard diving
1989 Irina Lashko (USSR)
1991 Brita Baldus (Ger)
1993 Simona Koch (Ger)

Highboard diving
1983 Alla Lobankina (USSR)
1985 Anzyela Stasyulevich (USSR)
1987 Yelena Miroshina (USSR)
1989 Ute Wetzig (GDR)
1991 Yelena Miroshina (USSR)
1993 Svetlana Khokhlova (Rus)
Most: 2 Nicole Pelissard (Fra) 1947, 1950

Synchronised swimming solo
1983 Carolyn Wilson (UK)
1985 Carolyn Wilson (UK)
1987 Muriel Hermine (Fra)
1989 Khristina Falashidi (USSR)
1991 Olga Sedakova (USSR)
1993 Olga Sedakova (Rus)
Most: 2 Wilson, Sedakova

Synchronised swimming duet
1983 Carolyn Wilson & Amanda Dodd (UK)
1985 Eva-Maria Edinger & Alexandra Worisch (Aut)
1987 Muriel Hermine & Karine Schuler (Fra)
1989 Karine Schuler & Marianne Aeschbacher (Fra)
1991 Anna Kozlova & Olga Sedakova (USSR)
1993 Anna Kozlova & Olga Sedakova (Rus

Synchronised swimming team
1983 UK
1985 France
1987 France
1989 France
1991 USSR
1993 Russia

Most gold medals (individual/relay)
Men
13 (8/5) Michael Gross (FRG) 1981-5
Women
11 (4/7) Heike Friedrich (GDR) 1985-9
9 (4/5) Kristin Otto (GDR) 1983-9
8 (7/1) Ute Geweniger (GDR) 1981-3
Krisztina Egerszegi won a record four individual events in 1993.
Michael Gross won three individual events in both 1983 and 1985; in the latter he also swam on three winning FRG relay teams, for a record six golds at one Championships. With 13 gold medals, four silvers and a bronze he had a record 18 medals in the four Championships 1981-7.
A women's record six gold medals at one Championships was won by Franziska van Almsick (Ger) in 1993 (three individual, three relay). Five have been won by three women: two individual and three relay for the GDR by Birgit Meineke in 1983 and Heike Friedrich in 1985; three individual and two relay for GDR by Kristin Otto in 1987.
Others to have won three individual events at one Championships: Arne Borg (Swe) 1927, Ian Black (UK) 1958, Gunnar Larsson (Swe) 1970, Ute Geweniger (GDR) 1981, Tamás Darnyi (Hun) 1987.

Short Course Swimming

World Short-Course Championships

The first championships, in a 25m pool, were staged at Palma de Mallorca, Spain in December 1993. *Winners:*

Men

50m freestyle	Mark Foster (UK) 21.84
100m freestyle	Fernando Scherer (Bra) 48.38
200m freestyle	Antti Kasvio (Fin) 1:45.21
400m freestyle	Daniel Kowalski (Aus) 3:42.95
1500m freestyle	Daniel Kowalski (Aus) 14:42.04
4 x 100m freestyle relay	Brazil 3:12.11
4 x 200m freestyle relay	Sweden 7:05.92
100m backstroke	Tripp Schwenk (USA) 52.98
200m backstroke	Tripp Schwenk (USA) 1:54.19
100m breaststroke	Philip Rogers (Aus) 59.56
200m breaststroke	Nick Gillingham (UK) 2:07.91
100m butterfly	Milos Milosevic (Cro) 52.79
200m butterfly	Franck Esposito (Fra) 1:55.42
200m individual medley	Christian Keller (Ger) 1:56.80
400m individual medley	Curtis Myden (Can) 4:10.41
4 x 100m medley relay	USA 3:32.57

Women

50m freestyle	Le Jingyi (Chn) 24.23
100m freestyle	Le Jingyi (Chn) 53.01
200m freestyle	Karen Pickering (UK) 1:56.25
400m freestyle	Janet Evans (UA) 4:05.64
800m freestyle	Janet Evans (UA) 8:22.43
4 x 100m freestyle relay	China 3:35.97
4 x 200m freestyle relay	China 7:52.45
100m backstroke	Angel Martino (USA) 58.50
200m backstroke	He Cihong (Chn) 2:06.09
100m breaststroke	Dai Guohong (Chn) 1:06.58
200m breaststroke	Dai Guohong (Chn) 2:21.99
100m butterfly	Susan O'Neill (Aus) 59.19
200m butterfly	Liu Limin (Chn) 2:08.51
200m individual medley	Allison Wagner (USA) 2:07.79
400m individual medley	Dai Guohong (Chn) 4:29.00
4 x 100m medley relay	China 3:57.73

The most successful individual was Dai Guohong, who won four gold medals, setting world records in each, including the medley relay, and one silver (200m individual medley).

World Short-Course Records - in 25m pools

Men

event	min:sec	name	date
50m freestyle	21.50	Aleksandr Popov (Rus)	13 Mar 1994
100m freestyle	46.74	Aleksandr Popov (Rus)	19 Mar 1994
200m freestyle	1:43.64	Giorgio Lamberti (Ita)	11 Feb 1990
400m freestyle	3:40.46	Danyon Loader (NZ)	11 Feb 1995
800m freestyle	7:34.90	Kieren Perkins (Aus)	25 Jul 1993
1500m freestyle	14:26.52	Kieren Perkins (Aus)	14 Jul 1993
4 x 50m freestyle	1:27.62	Sweden	3 Dec 1994
4 x 100m freestyle	3:12.11	Brazil	5 Dec 1993
4 x 200m freestyle	7:05.17	FR Germany	9 Feb 1986
50m backstroke	24.37	Jeff Rouse (USA)	12 Feb 1995
100m backstroke	51.43	Jeff Rouse (USA)	12 Apr 1993
200m backstroke	1:56.57	Martin López-Zubero (Spa)	8 Feb 1987
50m breaststroke	27.00	Mark Warnecke (Ger)	18 Feb 1995
100m breaststroke	59.07	Philip Rogers (Aus)	29 Aug 1993
200m breaststroke	2:07.80	Philip Rogers (Aus)	28 Aug 1993
50m butterfly	23.55	Mark Foster (UK)	11 Feb 1995
100m butterfly	52.07	Marcel Gery (Can)	23 Feb 1990

event	min:sec	name	date
200m butterfly	1:53.05	Franck Esposito (Fra)	26 Mar 1994
100m individual medley	53.78	Jani Sievinen (Fin)	21 Nov 1992
200m individual medley	1:54.65	Jani Sievinen (Fin)	21 Jan 1994
400m individual medley	4:07.10	Jani Sievinen (Fin)	9 Feb 1993
4 x 50m medley	1:38.01	Germany	4 Dec 1994
4 x 100m medley	3:32.57	USA	2 Dec 1993
Women			
50m freestyle	24.23	Le Jingyi (Chn)	3 Dec 1993
100m freestyle	53.01	Le Jingyi (Chn)	2 Dec 1993
200m freestyle	1:55.84	Franziska van Almsick (Ger)	9 Jan 1993
400m freestyle	4:02.05	Astrid Strauss (GDR)	8 Feb 1987
800m freestyle	8:15.34	Astrid Strauss (GDR)	6 Feb 1987
1500m freestyle	15:43.31	Petra Schneider (GDR)	10 Jan 1982
4 x 50m freestyle	1:40.63	Germany	22 Nov 1992
4 x 100m freestyle	3:35.97	China	4 Dec 1993
4 x 200m freestyle	7:52.45	China	2 Dec 1993
50m backstroke	27.64	Bai Xiunju (Chn)	12 Mar 1994
100m backstroke	58.50	Angel Martino (USA)	3 Dec 1993
200m backstroke	2:06.09	He Cihong (Chn)	5 Dec 1993
50m breaststroke	31.19	Louise Karlsson (Sweden)	21 Nov 1992
100m breaststroke	1:06.58	Dai Guohong (Chn)	4 Dec 1993
200m breaststroke	2:21.99	Dai Guohong (Chn)	3 Dec 1993
50m butterfly	26.56	Angela Kennedy (Aus)	12 Feb 1995
100m butterfly	58.91	Mary T Meagher (USA)	3 Jan 1981
200m butterfly	2:05.65	Mary T Meagher (USA)	2 Jan 1981
100m individual medley	1:01.03	Louise Karlsson (Swe)	22 Nov 1992
200m individual medley	2:07.79	Allison Wagner (USA)	5 Dec 1993
400m individual medley	4:29.00	Dai Guohong (Chn)	2 Dec 1993
4 x 50m medley	1:52.44	Germany	21 Nov 1992
4 x 100m medley	3:57.73	China	5 Dec 1993

on relay first leg

Note: Zhong Weiyua (Chn) set new marks at 50m and 100m butterfly of 26.44 and 58.71 on 6 and 5 Jan 1994 respectively, but these were not ratified as records as she failed a drugs test.

Table Tennis

The origins of table tennis are uncertain, but sports goods manufacturers were selling equipment for the game in England in the 1880s. The use of a celluloid table tennis ball was pioneered by James Gibb. This ball, called 'Gossima', was manufactured by J.Jacques & Son, and it was probably Jacques who conceived the onomatopoeic name 'Ping Pong', by which the game was popularly known in the early part of this century. The use of pimpled rubber stuck on to a wooden bat was introduced around this time. A Ping Pong Association was formed in 1902, when the craze for the game was at a peak. This organisation was re-named the Table Tennis Association, but became defunct, before being re-constituted as the English Table Tennis Association in 1927.

The world governing body is the International Table Tennis Federation (ITTF), which was founded in 1926, with over 160 member nations in 1995.

World Championships

European Championships were contested in December 1926, when the ITTF was formed, and the event was retrospectively designated as the World Championships. Subsequent championships were contested annually until 1957, except for the war years, and biennially from 1959.

Note that two events are shown for 1933, and none for 1934, as the 1933/4 tournament was held in December 1933.

Swaythling Cup

The trophy for the **men's team** championship was given in 1926 by Lady Swaythling, mother of the Hon. Ivor Montagu, the first President of the ITTF. Matches are played over the best of nine singles, by teams of three. Wins:

12	Hungary	1926, 1928-31, 1933 (2), 1935, 1938, 1949, 1952, 1979
11	China	1961, 1963, 1965, 1971, 1975, 1977, 1981, 1983, 1985, 1987, 1995
7	Japan	1954-7, 1959, 1967, 1969
6	Czechoslovakia	1932, 1939, 1947-8, 1950-1
4	Sweden	1973, 1989, 1991, 1993
1	Austria 1936, USA 1937, England 1953	

Corbillon Cup

The Marcel Corbillon Cup was presented in 1934 by M.Corbillon, President of the French Table Tennis Association, for the winners of the **women's team** event. Matches are contested as the best of four singles and a doubles. *Wins:*

11	China	1965, 1975, 1977, 1979, 1981, 1983, 1985, 1987, 1989, 1993, 1995
8	Japan	1952, 1954, 1957, 1959, 1961, 1963, 1967, 1971
5	Romania	1950-1, 1953, 1955-6
3	Czechoslovakia	1935-6, 1938
2	Germany	1933, 1939
2	USA	1937, 1949
2	England	1947-8
2	Korea	1973 (South), 1991 (North & South)
1	USSR	1969

Men's singles

Contested for the St Bride Vase, presented in 1929 by the St Bride Institute Table Tennis Club, London in recognition of the title won in 1929 by Fred Perry, later triple Wimbledon champion at lawn tennis. *Winners:*

1926	Roland Jacobi (Hun)
1928	Zoltán Mechlovits (Hun)
1929	Fred Perry (Eng)
1930	Viktor Barna (Hun)
1931	Miklós Szabados (Hun)
1932-5	Viktor Barna (Hun)
1936	Stanislav Kolár (Cs)
1937	Richard Bergmann (Aut)
1938	Bohumil Vána (Cs)
1939	Richard Bergmann (Aut)
1947	Bohumil Vána (Cs)
1948	Richard Bergmann (Eng)
1949	Johnny Leach (Eng)
1950	Richard Bergmann (Eng)
1951	Johnny Leach (Eng)
1952	Hiroji Satoh (Jap)
1953	Ferenc Sidó (Hun)
1954	Ichiro Ogimura (Jap)
1955	Toshiaki Tanaka (Jap)
1956	Ichiro Ogimura (Jap)
1957	Toshiaki Tanaka (Jap)
1959	Jung Kuo-tuan (Chn)
1961	Chuang Tse-tung (Chn)
1963	Chuang Tse-tung (Chn)
1965	Chuang Tse-tung (Chn)
1967	Nobuhiko Hasegawa (Jap)
1969	Shigeo Ito (Jap)
1971	Stellan Bengtsson (Swe)
1973	Hsi En-ting (Chn)
1975	István Jónyer (Hun)
1977	Mitsuru Kohno (Jap)
1979	Seiji Ono (Jap)
1981	Guo Yuehua (Chn)
1983	Guo Yuehua (Chn)
1985	Jiang Jialiang (Chn)
1987	Jiang Jialiang (Chn)
1989	Jan-Ove Waldner (Swe)
1991	Jörgen Persson (Swe)
1993	Jean-Philippe Gatien (Fra)
1995	Kong Linghui (Chn)

Most wins: 5 Viktor Barna, 4 Richard Bergmann

Women's singles:

Contested for the G.Geist Prize, donated in 1931 by Dr Gaspar Geist, President of the Hungarian Association. *Winners:*

1926	Mária Mednyánszky (Hun)
1928-31	Mária Mednyánszky (Hun)
1932-3	Anna Sipos (Hun)
1933	Marie Kettnerová (Cs)
1935	Marie Kettnerová (Cs)
1936	Ruth Aarons (USA)
1937	Ruth Aarons (USA) and Trudi Pritzi (Aut) *
1938	Trudi Pritzi (Aut)
1939	Vlasta Depetrisová (Cs)
1947-9	Gizi Farkas (Hun)
1950-5	Angelica Rozeanu (Rom)
1956	Tomi Okawa (Jap)
1957	Fujie Eguchi (Jap)
1959	Kimiyo Matsuzaki (Jap)
1961	Chiu Chung-hui (Chn)
1963	Kimiyo Matsuzaki (Jap)
1965	Naoko Fukazu (Jap)
1967	Sachiko Morisawa (Jap)
1969	Toshiko Kowada (Jap)
1971	Lin Hui-ching (Chn)
1973	Hu Yu-lan (Chn)
1975	Pak Yung-sun (NKo)
1977	Pak Yung-sun (NKo)
1979	Ge Xinai (Chn)
1981	Tong Ling (Chn)
1983	Cao Yanhua (Chn)
1985	Cao Yanhua (Chn)
1987	He Zhili (Chn)
1989	Qiao Hong (Chn)
1991	Deng Yaping (Chn)
1993	Hyun Jung-hwa (SKo)
1995	Deng Yaping (Chn)

* *title left vacant, these were the finalists*

Most wins: 6 Angelica Rozeanu, 5 Mária Mednyánszky

Men's doubles

Contested for the Iran Cup, presented by the Shah of Iran in Paris in 1947. *Winners:*

1926	Roland Jacobi & Daniel Pécsi (Hun)
1928	Alfred Liebster & Robert Thum (Aut)
1929-32	Viktor Barna & Miklós Szabados (Hun)
1933	Viktor Barna & Sándor Glancz (Hun)
1933	Viktor Barna & Miklós Szabados (Hun)
1935	Viktor Barna & Miklós Szabados (Hun)
1936-7	Robert Blattner & James McClure (USA)
1938	James McClure & Sol Schiff (USA)
1939	Viktor Barna & Richard Bergmann (Eng)
1947	Adolf Slár & Bohumil Vána (Cs)
1948	Ladislav Stipek & Bohumil Vána (Cs)
1949	Ivan Andreadis & Frantisek Tokár (Cs)
1950	Ferenc Sidó & Ferenc Soós (Hun)
1951	Ivan Andreadis & Bohumil Vána (Cs)
1952	Norikazu Fujii & Tadaski Hayashi (Jap)
1953	József Kóczián & Ferenc Sidó (Hun)
1954	Zarko Dolinar & Vilim Harangozo (Yug)
1955	Ivan Andreadis & Ladislav Stipek (Cs)

1956	Ichiro Ogimura & Yoshio Tomita (Jap)
1957	Ivan Andreadis & Ladislav Stipek (Cs)
1959	Teruo Murakami & Ichiro Ogimura (Jap)
1961	Nobuyo Hoshino & Koji Kimura (Jap)
1963	Chang Shih-lin & Wang Chih-liang (Chn)
1965	Chuang Tse-tung & Hsu Yin-sheng (Chn)
1967	Hans Alser & Kjell Johansson (Swe)
1969	Hans Alser & Kjell Johansson (Swe)
1971	István Jonyer & Tibor Klampar (Hun)
1973	Stellan Bengtsson & Kjell Johansson (Swe)
1975	Gábor Gergely & István Jónyer (Hun)
1977	Li Zhenshi & Liang Geliang (Chn)
1979	Dragutin Surbek & Anton Stipancic (Yug)
1981	Cai Zhenhua & Li Zhenshi (Chn)
1983	Dragutin Surbek & Zoran Kalinic (Yug)
1985	Mikael Applegren & Ulf Carlsson (Swe)
1987	Chen Longcan & Wei Qinguang (Chn)
1989	Jörg Rosskopf & Steffen Fetzner (FRG)
1991	Peter Karlsson & Thomas von Scheele (Swe)
1993	Wang Tao & Lu Lin (Chn)
1995	Wang Tao & Lu Lin (Chn)

Most wins: 8 Viktor Barna, 6 Miklós Szabados

Women's doubles

Contested for the W J Pope Trophy. Mr Pope, Honorary Secretary of the ITTF 1947-50, presented the trophy in 1948. *Winners:*

1928	Erika Flamm (Aut) & Mária Mednyánszky (Hun)
1929	Erika Metzger & Mona Küster (Ger)
1930-5	Mária Mednyánszky & Anna Sipos (Hun)
1936	Marie Kettnerová & Marie Smídová (Cs)
1937-8	Vlasta Depetrisová & Vera Votrubcová (Cs)
1939	Hilde Bussmann & Trudi Pritzi (Ger)
1947	Gizi Farkas (Hun) & Trudi Pritzi (Aut)
1948	Margaret Franks & Vera Thomas (Eng)
1949	Helen Elliot (Sco) & Gizi Farkas (Hun)
1950	Dora Beregi (Eng) & Helen Elliot (Sco)
1951	Diane Rowe & Rosalind Rowe (Eng)
1952	Shizuki Narahara & Tomi Nishimura (Jap)
1953	Gizi Farkas (Hun) & Angelica Rozeanu (Rom)
1954	Diane Rowe & Rosalind Rowe (Eng)
1955-6	Angelica Rozeanu & Ella Zeller (Rom)
1957	Livia Mosoczy & Agnes Simon (Hun)
1959	Taeko Namba & Kazuko Yamaizumi (Jap)
1961	Maria Alexandru & Geta Pitica (Rom)
1963	Kimiyo Matsuzaki & Masako Seki (Jap)
1965	Cheng Min-chih & Lin Hui-ching (Chn)
1967	Saeko Hirota & Sachiko Morisawa (Jap)
1969	Svetlana Grinberg & Zoya Rudnova (USSR)
1971	Cheng Min-chih & Lin Hui-ching (Chn)
1973	Maria Alexandru (Rom) & Miho Hamada (Jap)
1975	Maria Alexandru (Rom) & Shoko Takashima (Jap)
1977	Pak Yong-ok (NKo) & Yang Yin (Chn)
1979	Zhang Li & Zhang Deying (Chn)
1981	Zhang Deying & Cao Yanhua (Chn)
1983	Shen Jianping & Dai Lili (Chn)
1985	Dai Lili & Geng Lijuan (Chn)
1987	Yang Young-Ja & Hyun Jung-hwa (SKo)
1989	Deng Yaping & Qiao Hong (Chn)

1991	Chen Zhie & Gao Jun (Chn)
1993	Liu Wei & Qiao Yunping (Chn)
1995	Deng Yaping & Qiao Hong (Chn)

Most wins: 7 Mária Mednyánszky, 6 Anna Sipos

Mixed doubles

Contested for the Heydusek Prize, presented in 1948 by Zdenek Heydusek, Secretary of the Czechoslovak Association. *Winners:*

1927-8	Zoltán Mechlovits & Mária Mednyánszky (Hun)
1929	István Kelen & Anna Sipos (Hun)
1930-1	Miklós Szabados & Mária Mednyánszky (Hun)
1932	Viktor Barna & Anna Sipos (Hun)
1933	István Kelen & Mária Mednyánszky (Hun)
1933	Miklós Szabados & Mária Mednyánszky (Hun)
1935	Viktor Barna & Anna Sipos (Hun)
1936	Miloslav Hamr & Trude Kleinová (Cs)
1937	Bohumil Vána & Vera Votrubcová (Cs)
1938	Lászlo Béllak (Hun) & Wendy Woodhead (Eng)
1939	Bohumil Vána & Vera Votrubcová (Cs)
1947	Ferenc Soós & Gizi Farkas (Hun)
1948	Richard Miles & Thelma Thall (USA)
1949-50	Ferenc Sidó & Gizi Farkas (Hun)
1951	Bohumil Vána (Cs) & Angelica Rozeanu (Rom)
1952-3	Ferenc Sidó (Hun) & Angelica Rozeanu (Rom)
1954	Ivan Andreadis (Cs) & Gizi Farkas (Hun)
1955	Kálmán Szepesi & Eva Kóczián (Hun)
1956	Erwin Klein & Leah Neuberger (USA)
1957	Ichiro Ogimura & Fujie Eguchi (Jap)
1959	Ichiro Ogimura & Fujie Eguchi (Jap)
1961	Ichiro Ogimura & Kimiyo Matsuzaki (Jap)
1963	Koji Kimura & Kazuko Ito (Jap)
1965	Koji Kimura & Masako Seki (Jap)
1967	Nobuhiko Hasegawa & Noriko Yamanaka (Jap)
1969	Nobuhiko Hasegawa & Yasuka Kono (Jap)
1971	Chang Shih-ling & Lin Hui-ching (Chn)
1973	Liang Geliang & Li Li (Chn)
1975	Stanislav Gomozkov & Tatyana Ferdman (USSR)
1977	Jacques Secretin & Claude Bergeret (Fra)
1979	Liang Geliang & Ge Xinai (Chn)
1981	Xie Saike & Huang Junqun (Chn)
1983	Guo Yuehua & Ni Xialian (Chn)
1985	Cai Zhenhua & Cao Yanhua (Chn)
1987	Hui Jun & Geng Lijuan (Chn)
1989	Yoo Nam-kyu & Hyun Jung-hwa (SKo)
1991	Wang Tao & Liu Wei (Chn)
1993	Wang Tao & Liu Wei (Chn)
1995	Wang Tao & Liu Wei (Chn)

Most wins: 6 Mária Mednyánszky

Most individual world titles overall:

Men: 15 Viktor Barna (Hun/Eng), 10 Miklós Szabados (Hun)

Women: 18 Mária Mednyánszky (- Klucsik) (Hun), 12 Angelica Rozeanu (Rom), 11 Anna Sipos, (Hun), 10 Gizi Farkas (Hun)

Olympic Games

Table Tennis was added to the Olympic programme for the first time in 1988. *Winners:*

Men's singles
1988 Yoo Nam-kyu (SKo)
1992 Jan-Ove Waldner (Swe)

Men's doubles
1988 Chen Longcan & Wei Qingguang (Chn)
1992 Lu Lin & Wang Tao (Chn)

Women's singles
1988 Chen Jing (Chn)
1992 Deng Yaping (Chn)

Women's doubles
1988 Hyun Jung-hwa & Yang Young-ja (SKo)
1992 Deng Yaping & Qiao Hong (Chn)

World Cup

Held annually from 1980. *Winners:*

Men's singles
1980 Guo Yuehua (Chn)
1981 Tibor Klampar (Hun)
1982 Guo Yuehua (Chn)
1983 Mikael Appelgren (Swe)
1984 Jiang Jialiang (Chn)
1985 Chen Xinhua (Chn)
1986 Chen Longcan (Chn)
1987 Yi Teng (Chn)
1988 Andrzej Grubba (Pol)
1989 Ma Wenge (Chn)
1990 Jan-Ove Waldner (Swe)
1991 Jörgen Persson (Swe)
1992 Ma Wenge (Chn)
1993 Zoran Primorac (Cro)
1994 Jean-Philippe Gatien (Fra)

Men's doubles
1990 Yoo Nam-kyu & Kim Taek-soo (SKo)
1992 Kim Taek-soo & Yoo Nam-kyu (SKo)

Women's doubles
1990 Hyun J ung-hwa & Hong Cha-ok (SKo)

1992 Deng Yaping & Qiao Hong (Chn)

World Team Cup

	Men	Women
1990	Sweden	China
1991	China	China
1994	China	Russia

European Championships

Held biennially from 1958. *Singles champions:*

Men's singles
1958 Zoltán Berczik (Hun)
1960 Zoltán Berczik (Hun)
1962 Hans Alser (Swe)
1964 Kjell Johansson (Swe)
1966 Kjell Johansson (Swe)
1968 Dragutin Surbek (Yug)
1970 Hans Alser (Swe)
1974 Milan Orlowski (Cs)
1976 Jacques Secretin (Fra)
1978 Gábor Gergely (Hun)
1980 John Hilton (UK)
1982 Mikael Appelgren (Swe)
1984 Ulf Bengtsson (Swe)
1986 Jörgen Persson (Swe)
1988 Mikael Appelgren (Swe)
1990 Mikael Appelgren (Swe)
1992 Jörg Rosskopf (Ger)
1994 Jean-Michel Saive (Bel)

Women's singles
1958 Eva Kóczián (Hun)
1960 Eva Kóczián (Hun)
1962 Agnes Simon (FRG)
1964 Eva Földi (née Kóczián) (Hun)
1966 Maria Alexandru (Rom)
1968 Ilona Vostová (Cs)
1970 Zoya Rudnova (USSR)
1972 Zoya Rudnova (USSR)
1974 Judit Magos (Hun)
1976 Jull Hammersley (UK)
1978 Judit Magos (Hun)
1980 Valentina Popova (USSR)
1982 Bettina Vriesekoop (Hol)
1984 Valentina Popova (USSR)
1986 Csilla Bátorfi (Hun)

1988 Flyura Bulatova (USSR)
1990 Daniela Guergelcheva (Bul)
1992 Bettine Vriesekoop (Hol)
1994 Marie Svensson (Swe)

Men's team
11 Sweden 1964, 1966, 1968, 1970, 1972, 1974, 1980, 1986, 1988, 1990, 1992
4 Hungary 1958, 1960, 1978, 1982
2 Yugoslavia 1962, 1976
2 France 1984, 1994

Women's team
7 Hungary 1960, 1966, 1972, 1978, 1982, 1986, 1990
6 USSR 1970, 1974, 1976, 1980, 1984, 1988
2 England 1958, 1964
2 F.R.Germany 1962, 1968
1 Romania 1992
1 Russia 1994

English Open Championships

Instituted in 1921 this is the longest established national championship and has attracted many of the world's best players. Held annually to 1980, but biennially since then. *Most titles:*

Men's singles: 6 Richard Bergmann (Aut/Eng) 1939-40, 1948, 1950, 1952, 1954; 5 Viktor Barna (Hun) 1933-5, 1937-8
Women's singles: 6 Maria Alexandru (Rom) 1963-4, 1970-2, 1974
Men's doubles: 7 Viktor Barna 1931, 1933-5, 1938-9, 1949
Women's doubles: 12 Diane Rowe (Eng) 1950-6, 1960, 1962-5 (first 6 with her twin Rosalind)
Mixed doubles: 8 Viktor Barna 1933-6, 1938, 1940, 1951, 1953
All events
Men: 20 Viktor Barna (as above)
Women: 17 Diane Rowe (& singles 1962, mixed 1952, 1954, 1956, 1960)

Taekwondo

Taekwondo is a martial art and all its activities are based on a defensive spirit. Developed over 20 centuries in Korea and was officially recognised as part of Korean tradition and culture in 1955. Thereafter the sport spread internationally to an estimated 22 million practitioners in the 144 member-states of the World Taekwondo Federation. This governing body was inaugurated following the first world championships in 1973 and recognised by the IOC in 1980. Taekwondo was played as an official sport at the 1983 Pan-American Games and at the 1984 Asian Games. It was a demonstration sport at the 1988 and 1992 Olympic Games. There are eight weight categories ranging from fin to heavyweight.

World Championships

These biennial championships were first held in Seoul in 1973, when they were organised by the Korea Taekwondo Association. Women's events were first staged unofficially in 1983, and have been included on the official programme from 1987. A record 82 nations contested the men's events and 54 nations the women's in 1993. *Champions at each weight category:*

Men

Fin (50 kg)
1975 Whang Soo-yong (SKo)
1977 Song Ki-yul (SKo)
1979 Lee Seung-kyung (SKo)
1982 José Cedeno (Ecu)
1983 Kwang Yeon-wang (SKo)
1985 Lee Sun-jang (SKo)
1987 Lim Sung-wook (SKo)
1989 Kwon Tae-ho (SKo)
1991 Salim Gergely (Den)
1993 Jin Seung-tae (SKo)

Fly (54 kg)
1975 Han You-keun (SKo)
1977 Ha Suk-kwang (SKo)
1979 Yang Ki-mo (SKo)
1982 Jeon Woong-hwan (SKo)
1983 Ko Jeong-ho (SKo)
1985 Kim Yeong-sik (SKo)
1987 Kang Chang-mo (SKo)
1989 Kim Chul-ho (SKo)
1991 Kim Chul-ho (SKo)
1993 Javier Argudo (Spa)

Bantam (58 kg)
1975 Son Tae-whan (SKo)
1977 Kim Chong-ki (SKo)
1979 Kim Chong-ki (SKo)
1982 Kim Chong-ki (SKo)
1983 Han Hong-sik (SKo)
1985 Yoo Myung-sik (SKo)
1987 Yoo Myung-sik (SKo)
1989 Ham Jun (SKo)
1991 Angel Alonso (Spa)
1993 Kim In-kyoung (SKo)

Feather (64 kg)
1975 Lee Gyeo-sung (SKo)
1977 Park Chung-ho (SKo)
1979 Yim Dai-taik (SKo)
1982 Jang Myeong-sam (SKo)
1983 Lee Jae-bong (SKo)
1985 Han Jae-koo (SKo)
1987 Lee Chian-hsiang (Tai)
1989 Jang Hyuk (SKo)
1991 Jang Hyuk (SKo)
1993 Kim Byong-cheol (SKo)

Light (70 kg)
1973 Lee Ki-hyung (SKo)
1975 You Young-hab (SKo)
1977 Hwang Ming Der (Tai)
1979 Park Oh-sung (SKo)
1982 Park Oh-sung (SKo)
1983 Han Jae-ku (SKo)
1985 Park Bong-kwon (SKo)
1987 Yang Dae-seung (SKo)
1989 Yang Dae-seung (SKo)
1991 Yang Dae-seung (SKo)
1993 Park Se-jin (SKo)

Welter (76 kg)
1975 Song Hur (SKo)
1977 You Young-hab (SKo)
1979 Oscar Mendiola (Mex)
1982 Park Cheon-jae (SKo)
1983 Yilmaz Helvacioglu (Tur)
1985 Chung Kook-hyun (SKo)
1987 Chung Kook-hyun (SKo)
1989 Lee Hyun-suk (SKo)
1991 Park Yong-woong (SKo)
1993 Lim Young-ho (SKo)

Light-middle
1979 Rainer Müller (FRG)
1982 Chung Kook-hyun (SKo)
1983 Chung Kook-hyun (SKo)

Middle (83 kg)
1975 Yang Young-kwan (SKo)
1977 Song Hur (SKo)
1979 Kim Sang-chun (SKo)
1982 Kim Sang-chun (SKo)
1983 Lee Dong-joon (SKo)
1985 Lee Dong-joon (SKo)
1987 Lee Kye-haeng (SKo)
1989 Jeong Yong-suk (SKo)
1991 Yoon Soon-cheul (SKo)
1993 Michael Meloui (Fra)

Light-heavy
1979 Chung Chan (SKo)
1982 Ha Yong-seong (SKo)
1983 Fargas Inreno (Spa)

Heavy (over 83 kg)
1973 Kim Jeong-tae (SKo)
1975 Choi Jeong-do (SKo)
1977 Ahn Jang-shik (SKo)
1979 Sjef Vos (Hol)
1982 Dirk Jung (FRG)
1983 Jang Seung-hwa (SKo)
1985 Hendrik Meijer (Hol)
1987 Michael Arndt (FRG)
1989 Amr Khairy Mahmoud (Egy)
1991 Tonny Sorensen (Den)
1993 Kim Je-kyoung (SKo)
Most wins: 4 Chung Kook-hyun,
3 Kim Chong-ki, Yang Dae-seung

Women

Fin (43 kg)
1987 Jang Ei-suk (SKo)
1989 Chin Yu-fang (Tai)
1991 Elisabeth Delgado (Spa)
1993 Isabel Cruzado (Spa)

Fly (47 kg)
1987 Pai Yun-yao (Tai)
1989 Weon Sun-jin (SKo)
1991 Tan Arzu (Tur)
1993 You Su-mi (SKo)

Bantam (51 kg)
1987 Tennur Yerlhsu (Tur)
1989 Jung Nam-suk (SKo)
1991 Park Dong-seon (SKo)
1993 Tang Hui-wen (Tai)

Feather (55 kg)
1987 Kim So-young (SKo)
1989 Kim So-young (SKo)
1991 Tung Ya-ling (Tai)
1993 Lee Seung-min (SKo)

Light (60 kg)
1987 Lee Eun-young (SKo)
1989 Lee Eun-young (SKo)
1991 Jeong Eun-ok (Kor)
1993 Jesús Santolaria (Spa)

Welter (65 kg)
1987 Coral Bistuer (Spa)
1989 Anita Silsby (USA)
1991 Arlene Limas (USA)
1993 Kim Mi-young (SKo)

Middle (70kg)
1987 Margaretha de Jongh (Hol)
1989 Lydia Zele (USA)
1991 Yang In-deok (SKo)
1993 Park Eun-sun (SKo)

Heavy (over 70 kg)
1987 Lynette Love (USA)
1989 Jung Wan-sook (SKo)
1991 Lynette Love (USA)
1993 Jung Myung-suk (SKo)

Olympic Games

Included on the Olympic programme as a demonstration sport in 1988 and 1992. *Winners:*

Men	1988	1992
50kg	Kwon Tae-ho (SKo)	Gergely Salim (Den)
54kg	Ha Tae-kyung (SKo)	Arlindo Couvela (Ven)
58kg	Ji Young-suk (SKo)	William Cordova (Mex)
64kg	Chang Myung-sam (SKo)	Kim Byong-cheol (SKo)
70kg	Park Bong-kwon (SKo)	José Santolaria (Spa)
76kg	Chung Kook-hyun (SKo)	Ha Tae-kyoung (SKo)
83kg	Lee Kye-haeng (SKo)	Herbert Perez (USA)
83kg +	Jimmy Kim (USA)	Kim Je-kyoung (SKo)
Women		
43kg	Chin Yu-fang (Tai)	Lo Yueh-ying (Tai)
47kg	Choo Nan-yool (SKo)	Elisabet Delgado (Spa)
51kg	Chen Yi-an (Tai)	Hwang Eun-suk (SKo)
55kg	Annemette Christensen (Den)	Tung Ya-ling (Tai)
60kg	Dana Hee (USA)	Chen Yi-an (Tai)
65kg	Arlene Limas (USA)	Elena Benitez (Spa)
70kg	Kim Hyun-hee (SKo)	Lee Sun-hee (SKo)
70kg +	Lynette Love (USA)	Coral Astrid Bistuer (Spa)

Tennis

Lawn Tennis evolved from Real Tennis and while accounts of various forms of 'Field Tennis' were recorded in the 18th century, the real 'father' of lawn tennis is regarded as Major Wingfield who showed off his new game, which he called Sphairistike, at a Christmas party at a country house at Nantcwlyd, Wales, in 1873. He patented the game in 1874. The Marylebone Cricket Club were responsible in revising Wingfield's initial rules and in 1877 the All England Croquet Club added the name Lawn Tennis to their title.

The sport's governing body is the International Tennis Federation. It was founded as the International Lawn Tennis Federation in Paris in 1913 with 12 founding member nations. Membership reached 176 nations in 1993.

Wimbledon Championships

The All-England Championships at Wimbledon are regarded as the most prestigious championships in the world. They were first held in 1877 and, until 1922, were organised on a challenge round basis, in which the defending champion met the winner of an all comers tournament in the final. The tournament became Open in 1968, when, with a prize money total of £26,150, the men's singles champion received £2000. In 1994 the corresponding figures were £5,682,170 and £345,000. *Winners:*

Men's singles

1877	Spencer Gore (UK)
1878	Frank Hadow (UK)
1879-80	Rev. John Hartley (UK)
1881-6	William Renshaw (UK)
1887	Herbert Lawford (UK)
1888	Ernest Renshaw (UK)
1889	William Renshaw (UK)
1890	Willoughby Hamilton (UK)
1891-2	Wilfred Baddeley (UK)
1893-4	Joshua Pim (UK)
1895	Wilfred Baddeley (UK)
1896	Harold Mahoney (UK)
1897-1900	Reginald Doherty (UK)
1901	Arthur Gore (UK)
1902-6	Laurence Doherty (UK)
1907	Norman Brookes (Aus)
1908-9	Arthur Gore (UK)
1910-3	Tony Wilding (NZ)
1914	Norman Brookes (Aus)
1919	Gerald Patterson (Aus)
1920-1	Bill Tilden (USA)
1922	Gerald Patterson (Aus)
1923	William Johnston (USA)
1924	Jean Borotra (Fra)
1925	René Lacoste (Fra)
1926	Jean Borotra (Fra)
1927	Henri Cochet (Fra)
1928	René Lacoste (Fra)
1929	Henri Cochet (Fra)
1930	Bill Tilden (USA)
1932	Ellsworth Vines (USA)
1933	Jack Crawford (Aus)
1934-6	Fred Perry (UK)
1937-8	Donald Budge (USA)
1939	Bobby Riggs (USA)
1946	Yvon Petra (Fra)
1947	Jack Kramer (USA)
1948	Bob Falkenburg (USA)
1949	Ted Schroeder (USA)
1950	Budge Patty (USA)
1951	Dick Savitt (USA)
1952	Frank Sedgman (Aus)
1953	Vic Seixas (USA)
1954	Jaroslav Drobny (Egy)
1955	Tony Trabert (USA)
1956-7	Lew Hoad (Aus)
1958	Ashley Cooper (Aus)
1959	Alex Olmedo (USA)
1960	Neale Fraser (Aus)
1963	Chuck McKinley (USA)
1964-5	Roy Emerson (Aus)
1966	Manuel Santana (Spa)
1967	John Newcombe (Aus)
1968-9	Rod Laver (Aus)
1970-1	John Newcombe (Aus)
1972	Stan Smith (USA)
1973	Jan Kodes (Cs)
1974	Jimmy Connors (USA)
1975	Arthur Ashe (USA)
1976-80	Björn Borg (Swe)
1981	John McEnroe (USA)
1982	Jimmy Connors (USA)
1983-4	John McEnroe (USA)
1985-6	Boris Becker (FRG)
1987	Pat Cash (Aus)
1988	Stefan Edberg (Swe)
1989	Boris Becker (FRG)
1990	Stefan Edberg (Swe)
1991	Michael Stich (Ger)
1992	Andre Agassi (USA)
1993-5	Pete Sampras (USA)

Most wins
(pre-1922): 7 William Renshaw; (post-1922): 5 Borg

Women's singles

Note: see end of Tennis section for cross-reference list of women's maiden and married names.

1884-5	Maud Watson (UK)
1886	Blanche Bingley (UK)
1887-8	Lottie Dod (UK)
1889	Blanche Hillyard (UK)
1890	Helena Rice (UK)
1891-3	Lottie Dod (UK)
1894	Blanche Hillyard (UK)
1895-6	Charlotte Cooper (UK)
1897	Blanche Hillyard (UK)
1898	Charlotte Cooper (UK)
1899-1900	Blanche Hillyard (UK)
1901	Charlotte Sterry (UK)
1902	Muriel Robb (UK)
1903-4	Dorothea Douglass (UK)
1905	May Sutton (USA)
1906	Dorothea Douglass (UK)
1907	May Sutton (USA)
1908	Charlotte Sterry (UK)
1909	Dora Boothby (UK)
1910-1	Dorothea Lambert Chambers (UK)
1912	Ethel Larcombe (UK)
1913-4	Dorothea Lambert Chambers (UK)
1919-23	Suzanne Lenglen (Fra)
1924	Kathleen McKane (UK)
1925	Suzanne Lenglen (Fra)
1926	Kathleen Godfree (UK)
1927-9	Helen Wills (USA)
1930	Helen Moody (USA)
1931	Cilly Aussem (Ger)
1932-3	Helen Moody (USA)
1934	Dorothy Round (UK)
1935	Helen Moody (USA)
1936	Helen Jacobs (USA)
1937	Dorothy Round (UK)
1938	Helen Moody (USA)
1939	Alice Marble (USA)
1946	Pauline Betz (USA)
1947	Margaret Osborne (USA)
1948-50	Louise Brough (USA)

Pete Sampras

1951	Doris Hart (USA)
1952-4	Maureen Connolly (USA)
1955	Louise Brough (USA)
1956	Shirley Fry (USA)
1957-8	Althea Gibson (USA)
1959-60	Maria Bueno (Bra)
1961	Angela Mortimer (UK)
1962	Karen Susman (USA)
1963	Margaret Smith (Aus)
1964	Maria Bueno (Bra)
1965	Margaret Smith (Aus)
1966-8	Billie Jean King (USA)
1969	Ann Jones (UK)
1970	Margaret Court (Aus)
1971	Evonne Goolagong (Aus)
1972-3	Billie Jean King (USA)
1974	Chris Evert (USA)
1975	Billy Jean King (USA)
1976	Chris Evert (USA)
1977	Virginia Wade (UK)
1978-9	Martina Navrátilová (Cs)
1980	Evonne Cawley (Aus)
1981	Chris Evert Lloyd (USA)
1982-7	Martina Navrátilová (USA)
1988-9	Steffi Graf (FRG)
1990	Martina Navrátilová (USA)
1991-3	Steffi Graf (Ger)
1994	Conchita Martinez (Spa)
1995	Steffi Graf (Ger)

Most wins (pre-1922): 7 Dorothea Lambert Chambers (née Douglass); (post-1922): 9 Navrátilová, 8 Moody (née Wills)

Men's doubles

1879	L R Erskine & Herbert Lawford (UK)
1880-1	Ernest Renshaw & William Renshaw (UK)
1882	Rev. John Hartley & R T Richardson (UK)
1883	C W Grinstead & C E Welldon (UK)
1884-6	Ernest Renshaw & William Renshaw (UK)
1887	Patrick Bowes-Lyon & Herbert Wilberforce (UK)
1888-9	Ernest Renshaw & William Renshaw (UK)
1890	Joshua Pim & Frank Stoker (UK)
1891	Herbert Baddeley & Wilfred Baddeley (UK)
1892	Harry Barlow & Ernest Lewis (UK)
1893	Joshua Pim & Frank Stoker (UK)
1894-6	Herbert Baddeley & Wilfred Baddeley (UK)
1897-1901	Laurence Doherty & Reginald Doherty (UK)
1902	Frank Riseley & Sidney Smith (UK)
1903-5	Laurence Doherty & Reginald Doherty (UK)
1906	Frank Riseley & Sidney Smith (UK)
1907	Norman Brookes (Aus) & Anthony Wilding (NZ)
1908	Major Ritchie (UK) & Anthony Wilding (NZ)
1909	Arthur Gore & Roper Barrett (UK)
1910	Major Ritchie (UK) & Anthony Wilding (NZ)
1911	Max Decugis & André Gobert (Fra)
1912-3	Charles Dixon & Roper Barrett (UK)
1914	Norman Brookes (Aus) & Anthony Wilding (NZ)
1919	Pat O'Hara Wood & Ronald Thomas (Aus)
1920	Charles Garland & Richard Williams (USA)

Steffi Graf after the fifth of her six Wimbledon wins

1921	Randolph Lycett & Max Woosnam (UK)
1922	James Anderson (Aus) & Randolph Lycett (UK)
1923	Leslie Godfree & Randolph Lycett (UK)
1924	Frank Hunter & Vincent Richards (USA)
1925	Jean Borotra & René Lacoste (Fra)
1926	Jacques Brugnon & Henri Cochet (Fra)
1927	Frank Hunter & William Tilden (USA)
1928	Jacques Brugnon & Henri Cochet (Fra)
1929 30	William Allison & John Van Ryn (USA)
1931	George Lott & John Van Ryn (USA)
1932-3	Jean Borotra & Jacques Brugnon (Fra)
1934	George Lott & Lester Stoefen (USA)
1935	Jack Crawford & Adrian Quist (Aus)
1936	Pat Hughes & Raymond Tuckey (UK)
1937-8	Don Budge & Gene Mako (USA)
1939	Ellwood Cooke & Bobby Riggs (USA)
1946	Tom Brown & Jack Kramer (USA)
1947	Bob Falkenburg & Jack Kramer (USA)
1948	John Bromwich & Frank Sedgman (Aus)
1949	Ricardo Gonzales & Frank Parker (USA)
1950	John Bromwich & Adrian Quist (Aus)
1951-2	Ken McGregor & Frank Sedgman (Aus)
1953	Lew Hoad & Ken Rosewall (Aus)
1954	Rex Hartwig & Mervyn Rose (Aus))
1955	Rex Hartwig & Lew Hoad (Aus)
1956	Lew Hoad & Ken Rosewall (Aus)
1957	Gardnar Mulloy & Budge Patty (USA)
1958	Sven Davidson & Ulf Schmidt (Swe)
1959	Roy Emerson & Neale Fraser (Aus)
1960	Rafael Osuna (Mex) & Dennis Ralston (USA)
1961	Roy Emerson & Neale Fraser (Aus)
1962	Bob Hewitt & Fred Stolle (Aus)
1963	Rafael Osuna & Antonio Palafox (Mex)
1964	Bob Hewitt & Fred Stolle (Aus)
1965	John Newcombe & Tony Roche (Aus)
1966	Ken Fletcher & John Newcombe (Aus)
1967	Bob Hewitt & Frew McMillan (SAf)
1968-70	John Newcombe & Tony Roche (Aus)
1971	Roy Emerson & Rod Laver (Aus)
1972	Bob Hewitt & Frew McMillan (SAf)
1973	Jimmy Connors (USA) & Ilie Nastase (Rom)
1974	John Newcombe & Tony Roche (Aus)
1975	Vitas Gerulaitis & Sandy Mayer (USA)

1976	Brian Gottfried (USA) & Raúl Ramirez (Mex)
1977	Ross Case & Geoff Masters (Aus)
1978	Bob Hewitt & Frew McMillan (SAf)
1979	Peter Fleming & John McEnroe (USA)
1980	Pete McNamara & Paul McNamee (Aus)
1981	Peter Fleming & John McEnroe (USA)
1982	Peter McNamara & Paul McNamee (Aus)
1983-4	Peter Fleming & John McEnroe (USA)
1985	Heinz Günthardt (Swi) & Balázs Taróczy (Hun)
1986	Joakim Nyström & Mats Wilander (Swe)
1987-8	Ken Flach & Robert Seguso (USA)
1989	John Fitzgerald (Aus) & Anders Järryd (Swe)
1990	Rick Leach & Jim Pugh (USA)
1991	John Fitzgerald (Aus) & Anders Järryd (Swe)
1992	John McEnroe (USA) & Michael Stich (Ger)
1993-5	Todd Woodbridge & Mark Woodforde (Aus)

Most wins: 8 Laurence & Reginald Doherty

Women's doubles

1913	Winifred McNair & Dora Boothby (UK)
1914	Agnes Morton (UK) & Elizabeth Ryan (USA)
1919-23	Suzanne Lenglen (Fra) & Elizabeth Ryan (USA)
1924	Hazel Wightman & Helen Wills (USA)
1925	Suzanne Lenglen (Fra) & Elizabeth Ryan (USA)
1926	Mary Browne & Elizabeth Ryan (USA)
1927	Helen Wills & Elizabeth Ryan (USA)
1928	Peggy Saunders & Phyllis Watson (UK)
1929	Peggy Michell & Phyllis Watson (UK)
1930	Helen Moody (née Wills) & Elizabeth Ryan (USA)
1931	Dorothy Barron & Phyllis Mudford (UK)
1932	Doris Metaxa (Fra) & Josane Sigart (Bel)
1933-4	Simone Mathieu (Fra) & Elizabeth Ryan (USA)
1935-6	Freda James & Kay Stammers (UK)
1937	Simone Mathieu (Fra) & Billie Yorke (UK)
1938-9	Sarah Fabyan & Alice Marble (USA)
1946	Louise Brough & Margaret Osborne (USA)
1947	Doris Hart & Pat Todd (USA)
1948-50	Louise Brough & Margaret Du Pont (USA)
1951-3	Shirley Fry & Doris Hart (USA)
1954	Louise Brough & Margaret Du Pont (USA)
1955	Angela Mortimer & Anne Shilcock (UK)
1956	Angela Buxton (UK) & Althea Gibson (USA)
1957	Althea Gibson & Darlene Hard (USA)
1958	Maria Bueno (Bra) & Althea Gibson (USA)
1959	Jean Arth & Darlene Hard (USA)
1960	Maria Bueno (Bra) & Darlene Hard (USA)
1961	Karen Hantze & Billie Jean Moffitt (USA)
1962	Billie Jean Moffit & Karen Susman (USA)
1963	Maria Bueno (Bra) & Darlene Hard (USA)
1964	Margaret Smith & Lesley Turner (Aus)
1965	Maria Bueno (Bra) & Billie Jean Moffitt (USA)
1966	Maria Bueno (Bra) & Nancy Richey (USA)
1967-8	Rosemary Casals & Billie Jean King (USA)
1969	Margaret Court & Judy Tegart (Aus)
1970-1	Rosemary Casals & Billie Jean King (USA)
1972	Billie Jean King (USA) & Betty Stove (Hol)
1973	Rosemary Casals & Billie Jean King (USA)

1974	Evonne Goolagong (Aus) & Peggy Michel (USA)
1975	Ann Kiyomura (USA) & Kazuko Sawamatsu (Jap)
1976	Chris Evert (USA) & Martina Navrátilová (Cs)
1977	Helen Cawley (Aus) & Joanne Russell (USA)
1978	Kerry Reid & Wendy Turnbull (Aus)
1979	Billie Jean King (USA) & Martina Navrátilová (Cs)
1980	Kathy Jordan & Anne Smith (USA)
1981-4	Martina Navrátilová & Pam Shriver (USA)
1985	Kathy Jordan (USA) & Elizabeth Smylie (Aus)
1986	Martina Navrátilová & Pam Shriver (USA)
1987	Claudia Kohde-Kilsch (FRG) & Helena Sukova (Cs)
1988	Steffi Graf (FRG) & Gabriela Sabatini (Arg)
1989-90	Jana Novotná & Helena Suková (Cs)
1991	Larisa Savchenko & Natalya Zvereva (USSR)
1992-4	Gigi Fernandez (USA) & Natalya Zvereva (Bls)
1995	Jana Novotná & Arantxa Sánchez (Spa)

Most wins: 12 Ryan

Mixed doubles

1913	Hope Crisp & Agnes Tuckey (UK)
1914	Cecil Parke & Ethel Larcombe (UK)
1919	Randolph Lycett (UK) & Elizabeth Ryan (USA)
1920	Gerald Patterson (Aus) & Suzanne Lenglen (Fra)
1921	Randolph Lycett (UK) & Elizabeth Ryan (USA)
1922	Pat O'Hara Wood (USA) & Suzanne Lenglen (Fra)
1923	Randolph Lycett (UK) & Elizabeth Ryan (USA)
1924	Brian Gilbert & Kathleen McKane (UK)
1925	Jean Borotra & Suzanne Lenglen (Fra)
1926	Leslie Godfree & Kathleen Godfree (UK)
1927	Frank Hunter & Elizabeth Ryan (USA)
1928	Pat Spence (SAf) & Elizabeth Ryan (USA)
1929	Frank Hunter & Helen Wills (USA)
1930	Jack Crawford (Aus) & Elizabeth Ryan (USA)
1931	George Lott & Anna Harper (USA)
1932	Enrique Maier (Spa) & Elizabeth Ryan (USA)
1933	Gottfried von Cramm & Hilda Krahwinkel (Ger)
1934	Ryuki Miki (Jap) & Dorothy Round (UK)
1935-6	Fred Perry & Dorothy Round (UK)
1937-8	Don Budge & Alice Marble (USA)
1939	Bobby Riggs & Alice Marble (USA)
1946	Tom Brown & Louise Brough (USA)
1947-8	John Bromwich (Aus) & Louise Brough (USA)
1949	Eric Sturgess & Sheila Summers (SAf)
1950	Eric Sturgess (SAf) & Louise Brough (USA)
1951-2	Frank Sedgman (Aus) & Doris Hart (USA)
1953-5	Vic Seixas & Doris Hart (USA)
1956	Vic Seixas & Shirley Fry (USA)
1957	Mervyn Rose (Aus) & Darlene Hard (USA)
1958	Bob Howe & Lorraine Coghlan (Aus)
1959-60	Rod Laver (Aus) & Darlene Hard (USA)
1961	Fred Stolle & Lesley Turner (Aus)
1962	Neale Fraser (Aus) & Margaret Du Pont (USA)
1963	Ken Fletcher & Margaret Smith (Aus)
1964	Fred Stolle & Lesley Turner (Aus)

1965-6	Ken Fletcher & Margaret Smith (Aus)
1967	Owen Davidson (Aus) & Billie Jean King (USA)
1968	Ken Fletcher & Margaret Court (Aus)
1969	Fred Stolle (Aus) & Ann Jones (UK)
1970	Ilie Nastase (Rom) & Rosemary Casals (USA)
1971	Owen Davidson (Aus) & Billie Jean King (USA)
1972	Ilie Nastase (Rom) & Rosemary Casals (USA)
1973-4	Owen Davidson (Aus) & Billie Jean King (USA)
1975	Marty Riessen (USA) & Margaret Court (Aus)
1976	Tony Roche (Aus) & Françoise Durr (Fra)
1977	Bob Hewitt & Greer Stevens (SAf)
1978	Frew McMillan (SAf) & Betty Stove (Hol)
1979	Bob Hewitt & Greer Stevens (SAf)
1980	John Austin & Tracy Austin (USA)
1981	Frew McMillan (SAf) & Betty Stove (Hol)
1982	Kevin Curren (SAf) & Anne Smith (USA)
1983-4	John Lloyd (UK) & Wendy Turnbull (Aus)
1985	Paul McNamee (Aus) & Martina Navrátilová (USA)
1986	Ken Flach & Kathy Jordan (USA)
1987	Jeremy Bates & Jo Durie (UK)
1988	Sherwood Stewart & Zina Garrison (USA)
1989	Jim Pugh (USA) & Jana Novotná (Cs)
1990	Rick Leach & Zina Garrison (USA)
1991	John Fitzgerald & Elizabeth Smylie (Aus)
1992	Cyril Suk (CS) & Larisa Savchenko (Lat)
1993	Mark Woodforde (Aus) & Martina Navrátilová (USA)
1994	Todd Woodbridge (Aus) & Helena Suková (Cs)
1995	Jonathan Stark & Martina Navrátilová (USA)

Most wins (Men): 4 Seixas, Davidson, Fletcher; (Women): 7 Ryan

Most Wimbledon titles

	Total	Singles	Doubles	Mixed	Years
Billie Jean King (USA)	20	6	10	4	1961-79
Elizabeth Ryan (USA)	19	-	12	7	1914-34
Martina Navrátilová	19	9	7	3	1976-95
Suzanne Lenglen (Fra)	15	6	6	3	1919-25
Laurence Doherty (UK)	13	5	8	-	1897-1905
Louise Brough (USA)	13	4	5	4	1946-55

Most successful singles players

From the abolition of the challenge round in 1922, the leading players on the following points basis: 8 for winning the tournament, 4 for losing in the final, 2 for losing semi-finalists and 1 for losing quarter finalists have been:

Men

Points	Name	Won	F	SF	QF	Years
46	Björn Borg	5	1	-	2	1973-81
45	Jimmy Connors	2	4	5	3	1972-87
45	Boris Becker	3	4	2	1	1985-94
41	Rod Laver	4	2	-	1	1959-71
39	John McEnroe	3	2	3	1	1977-92
33	Jean Borotra	2	3	2	1	1924-31
29	John Newcombe	3	1	-	1	1966-74
27	Henri Cochet	2	1	3	1	1925-33
27	Fred Perry	3	-	1	1	1931-6
27	Stefan Edberg	2	1	3	1	1987-93
26	Pete Sampras	3	-	1	-	1992-5
24	Jaroslav Drobny	1	2	3	2	1946-55
23	Roy Emerson	2	-	1	5	1959-70
20	Don Budge	2	-	2	-	1935-8

Note: Bill Tilden had two wins 1920-1 in challenge round days plus 14 points (1 win, 2 sf) 1927-30.

Women

Points	Name	Won	F	SF	QF	Years
97	Martina Navrátilová	9	3	5	3	1975-94
75	Billie Jean King	6	3	5	5	1962-83
68	Helen Wills/Moody	8	1	-	-	1924-38
66	Chris Evert	3	7	7	-	1972-89
54	Steffi Graf	6	1	1	-	1987-95
51	Louise Brough	4	3	3	1	1946-57
41	Margaret Smith/Court	3	2	4	1	1961-75
36	Maria Bueno	3	2	-	4	1958-68
35	Helen Jacobs	1	5	2	3	1929-39
28	Doris Hart	1	3	3	2	1946-55
27	Evonne Goolagong/Cawley	2	3	3	1	1971-80
26*	Suzanne Lenglen	3	-	1	-	1922-5
26	Ann Haydon/Jones	1	1	6	2	1958-69
24	Dorothy Round	2	1	-	4	1931-7
24	Maureen Connolly	3	-	-	-	1952-4
23	Kitty McKane/Godfree	2	1	1	1	1923-7
23	Margaret Osborne/Du Pont	1	2	2	3	1946-58
20	Virginia Wade	1	-	3	6	1967-83

* also three wins 1919-21

Most appearances in finals: 12 Navratilova, 10 Evert, 9 King

Most semi-finals: 17 Evert, Navratlilova; 14 King, 11 Connors (men's record)

Prior to 1922, there was a challenge round in which the defending champion played against the winner of the all-comers tournament. The most successful players were as follows: *(W = winner, RU = runner-up, losing in challenge round final, AC = winning all-comers tournament)*

Name	W	RU	AC
Men			
William Renshaw	7	1	2
Laurence Doherty	5	1	2
Reginald Doherty	4	1	1
Tony Wilding	4	1	1
Arthur Wentworth Gore	3	3	4
Wilfred Baddeley	3	3	3
Herbert Lawford	1	5	5
Women			
Dorothea Douglass/ Lambert Chambers	7	4	4
Blanche Bingley/Hillyard	6	6	8
Charlotte Cooper/Sterry	5	5	6
Lottie Dod	5	-	2

United States Championships

An American championship, open to all comers, was held at Staten Island in September 1880 and won by Englishman O E Woodhouse. The first official US Championships were in 1881, following the formation of the US National Lawn Tennis Association. These were contested annually by amateurs until 1969, the year after the sport went open. In 1968 and 1969, however, there were two Championships, Amateur and Open events. Since 1970 there has only been an Open competition. Played at Flushing Meadow, New York since 1978, previously at various venues, notably the West Side Club, Forest Hills, New York for the singles 1915-6 and 1924-77. *Winners:*

Men's singles
Challenge Round basis 1884-1911

1881-7	Richard Sears (USA)
1888-9	Henry Slocum Jr (USA)
1890-2	Oliver Campbell (USA)
1893-4	Robert Wrenn (USA)
1895	Fred Hovey (USA)
1896-7	Robert Wrenn (USA)
1898-1900	Malcolm Whitman (USA)
1901-2	William Larned (USA)
1903	Laurence Doherty (UK)
1904	Holcombe Ward (USA)
1905	Beals Wright (USA)
1906	William Clothier (USA)
1907-11	William Larned (USA)
1912-3	Maurice McLoughlin (USA)
1914	Norris Williams (USA)
1915	William Johnston (USA)
1916	Norris Williams (USA)
1917-8	Lindley Murray (USA)
1919	William Johnston (USA)
1920-5	Bill Tilden (USA)
1926-7	René Lacoste (Fra)
1928	Henri Cochet (Fra)
1929	Bill Tilden (USA)
1930	John Doeg (USA)
1931-2	Ellsworth Vines (USA)
1933-4	Fred Perry (UK)
1935	Wilmer Allison (USA)
1936	Fred Perry (UK)
1937-8	Donald Budge (USA)
1939	Bobby Riggs (USA)
1940	Donald McNeil (USA)
1941	Bobby Riggs (USA)
1942	Ted Schroeder (USA
1943	Joseph Hunt (USA)
1944-5	Frank Parker (USA)
1946-7	Jack Kramer (USA)
1948-9	Ricardo Gonzales (USA)
1950	Arthur Larsen (USA)
1951-2	Frank Sedgman (Aus)
1953	Tony Trabert (USA)
1954	Vic Seixas (USA)
1955	Tony Trabert (USA)
1956	Ken Rosewall (Aus)
1957	Malcolm Anderson (Aus)
1958	Ashley Cooper (Aus)
1959-60	Neale Fraser (Aus)
1961	Roy Emerson (Aus)
1962	Rod Laver (Aus)
1963	Raphael Osuna (Mex)
1964	Roy Emerson (Aus)
1965	Manuel Santana (Spa)
1966	Fred Stolle (Aus)
1967	John Newcombe (Aus)
1968	Arthur Ashe (USA)
Open	Arthur Ashe (USA)
1969	Stan Smith (USA)
Open	Rod Laver (Aus)
1970	Ken Rosewall (Aus)
1971	Stan Smith (USA)
1972	Ilie Nastase (Rom)
1973	John Newcombe (Aus)
1974	Jimmy Connors (USA)
1975	Manuel Orantes (Spa)
1976	Jimmy Connors (USA)
1977	Guillermo Vilas (Arg)
1978	Jimmy Connors (USA)
1979-81	John McEnroe (USA)
1982-3	Jimmy Connors (USA)
1984	John McEnroe (USA)
1985-7	Ivan Lendl (Cs)
1988	Mats Wilander (Swe)
1989	Boris Becker (FRG)
1990	Pete Sampras (USA)
1991-2	Stefan Edberg (Swe)
1993	Pete Sampras (USA)
1994	Andre Agassi (USA)

Most wins: 7 Sears, Larned, Tilden

Women's singles
Challenge Round basis 1887-1918

1887	Ellen Hansell (USA)
1888-9	Bertha Townsend (USA)
1890	Ellen Roosevelt (USA)
1891-2	Mabel Cahill (USA)
1893	Aline Terry (USA)
1894	Helen Helwig (USA)
1895	Juliette Atkinson (USA)
1896	Elisabeth Moore (USA)
1897-8	Juliette Atkinson (USA)
1899	Marion Jones (USA)
1900	Myrtle McAteer (USA)
1901	Elisabeth Moore (USA)
1902	Marion Jones (USA)
1903	Elisabeth Moore (USA)
1904	May Sutton (USA)
1905	Elisabeth Moore (USA)
1906	Helen Homans (USA)
1907	Evelyn Sears (USA)
1908	Maud Bargar-Wallach (USA)
1909-11	Hazel Hotchkiss (USA)
1912-4	Mary Browne (USA)
1915-8	Molla Bjurstedt (USA)
1919	Hazel Wightman (née Hotchkiss)
1920-2	Molla Mallory (née Bjurstedt)
1923-5	Helen Wills (USA)
1926	Molla Mallory (USA)
1927-9	Helen Wills (USA)
1930	Betty Nuthall (UK)

1931	Helen Moody (née Wills)	1959	Maria Bueno (Bra)	1979	Tracy Austin (USA)
		1960-1	Darlene Hard (USA)	1980	Chris Evert Lloyd (USA)
1932-5	Helen Jacobs (USA)	1962	Margaret Smith (Aus)	1981	Tracy Austin (USA)
1936	Alice Marble (USA)	1963-4	Maria Bueno (Bra)	1982	Chris Evert Lloyd (USA)
1937	Anita Lizana (Chl)	1965	Margaret Smith (Aus)	1983-4	Martina Navrátilová (USA)
1938-40	Alice Marble (USA)	1966	Maria Bueno (Bra)		
1941	Sarah Cooke (USA)	1967	Billie Jean King (USA)	1985	Hanna Mandlíková (Cs)
1942-4	Pauline Betz (USA)	1968	Margaret Court (Aus)	1986-7	Martina Navrátilová (USA)
1945	Sarah Cooke (USA)	Open	Virginia Wade (UK)		
1946	Pauline Betz (USA)	1969	Margaret Court (Aus)	1988-9	Steffi Graf (FRG)
1947	Louise Brough (USA)	Open	Margaret Court (Aus)	1990	Gabriela Sabatini (Arg)
1948-50	Margaret Du Pont (USA)	1970	Margaret Court (Aus)	1991-2	Monica Seles (Yug)
1951-3	Maureen Connolly (USA)	1971-2	Billie Jean King (USA)	1993	Steffi Graf (Ger)
1954-5	Doris Hart (USA)	1973	Margaret Court (Aus)	1994	Arantxa Sánchez (Spa)
1956	Shirley Fry (USA)	1974	Billie Jean King (USA)	**Most wins:** 7 Bjurstedt/Mallory, Helen Wills/Moody	
1957-8	Althea Gibson (USA)	1975-8	Chris Evert (USA)		

Men's doubles (Winners from 1946)

1946	Gardnar Mulloy & William Talbert (USA)
1947	Jack Kramer & Ted Schroeder (USA)
1948	Gardnar Mulloy & William Talbert (USA)
1949	John Bromwich & William Sidwell (Aus)
1950	John Bromwich & Frank Sedgman (Aus)
1951	Ken McGregor & Frank Sedgman (Aus)
1952	Mervin Rose (Aus) & Vic Seixas (USA)
1953	Rex Hartwig & Mervyn Rose (Aus)
1954	Vic Seixas & Tony Trabert (USA)
1955	Kosei Kano & Atsushi Miyagi (Jap)
1956	Lew Hoad & Ken Rosewall (Aus)
1957	Ashley Cooper & Neale Fraser (Aus)
1958	Alex Olmedo & Ham Richardson (USA)
1959-60	Roy Emerson & Neale Fraser (Aus)
1961	Charles McKinley & Dennis Ralston (USA)
1962	Antonio Palafox & Rafael Osuna (Mex)
1963-4	Charles McKinley & Dennis Ralston (USA)
1965-6	Roy Emerson & Fred Stolle (Aus)
1967	John Newcombe & Tony Roche (Aus)
1968	Bob Lutz & Stan Smith (USA)
Open	Bob Lutz & Stan Smith (USA)
1969	Dick Crealy & Allan Stone (Aus)
Open	Ken Rosewall & Fred Stolle (Aus)
1970	Pierre Barthes (Fra) & Nikki Pilic (Yug)
1971	John Newcombe (Aus) & Roger Taylor (UK)
1972	Cliff Drysdale (SAf) & Roger Taylor (UK)
1973	Owen Davidson & John Newcombe (Aus)
1974	Bob Lutz & Stan Smith (USA)
1975	Jimmy Connors (USA) & Ilie Nastase (Rom)
1976	Tom Okker (Hol) & Marty Riessen (USA)
1977	Bob Hewitt & Frew McMillan (SAf)
1978	Bob Lutz & Stan Smith (USA)
1979	Peter Fleming & John McEnroe (USA)
1980	Bob Lutz & Stan Smith (USA)
1981	Peter Fleming & John McEnroe (USA)
1982	Kevin Curren (SAf) & Steve Denton (USA)
1983	Peter Fleming & John McEnroe (USA)
1984	John Fitzgerald (Aus) & Tomás Smid (Cs)
1985	Ken Flach & Robert Seguso (USA)
1986	Andrés Gómez (Ecu) & Slobodan Zivojinovic (Yug)
1987	Stefan Edberg & Anders Järryd (Swe)
1988	Sergio Casal & Emilio Sánchez (Spa)
1989	John McEnroe (USA) & Mark Woodforde (Aus)
1990	Pieter Aldrich & Danie Visser (SAf)
1991	John Fitzgerald (Aus) & Anders Järryd (Swe)
1992	Jim Grabb & Richey Reneberg (USA)
1993	Ken Flach & Rick Leach (USA)
1994	Jacco Eltingh & Paul Haarhuis (Hol)

Most wins by one pair: 5 Richard Sears & James Dwight 1882-4, 1886-7

By player: 6 Richard Sears (also won with Joseph Clark 1885), 6 Holcombe Ward 1899-1901 (with Dwight Davis), 1904-6 (with Beals Wright); 5 Bill Tilden 1918, 1921-2 (with Vincent Richards), 1923 (with Brian Norton), 1927 (with Francis Hunter); 5 Vincent Richards, also with Norris Williams 1925-6; 5 George Lott Jr 1928 (with John Hennessy), 1929-30 (with John Doeg), 1933-4 (with Lester Stoefen)

Women's doubles (Winners from 1946)

1942-50	Louise Brough & Margaret Osborne (USA)
1951-4	Shirley Fry & Doris Hart (USA)
1955-7	Louise Brough & Margaret Du Pont (USA)
1958-9	Jean Arth & Darlene Hard (USA)
1960	Maria Bueno (Bra) & Darlene Hard (USA)
1961	Darlene Hard (USA) & Lesley Turner (Aus)
1962	Maria Bueno (Bra) & Darlene Hard (USA)
1963	Robyn Ebbern & Margaret Smith (Aus)
1964	Karen Susman & Billie Jean Moffitt (USA)
1965	Nancy Richey & Carole Graebner (USA)
1966	Maria Bueno (Bra) & Nancy Richey (USA)
1967	Rosemary Casals & Billie Jean King (USA)
1968	Maria Bueno (Bra) & Margaret Court (Aus)
Open	Maria Bueno (Bra) & Margaret Court (Aus)
1969	Margaret Court (Aus) & Virginia Wade (UK)
Open	Françoise Durr (Fra) & Darlene Hard (USA)
1970	Margaret Court & Judy Dalton (Aus)
1971	Rosemary Casals (USA) & Judy Dalton (Aus)
1972	Françoise Durr (Fra) & Betty Stove (Hol)
1973	Margaret Court (Aus) & Virginia Wade (UK)
1974	Rosemary Casals & Billie Jean King (USA)
1975	Margaret Court (Aus) & Virginia Wade (UK)
1976	Linda Boshoff & Ilana Kloss (SAf)

1977	Martina Navrátilová (Cs) & Betty Stove (Hol)	1964	John Newcombe & Margaret Smith (Aus)
1978	Billie Jean King (USA) & Martina Navrátilová (Cs)	1965	Fred Stolle & Margaret Smith (Aus)
1979	Betty Stove (Hol) & Wendy Turnbull (Aus)	1966	Owen Davidson (Aus) & Donna Fales (USA)

1977   Martina Navrátilová (Cs) & Betty Stove (Hol)

1978   Billie Jean King (USA) & Martina Navrátilová (Cs)

1979   Betty Stove (Hol) & Wendy Turnbull (Aus)

1980   Billie Jean King (USA) & Martina Navrátilová (Cs)

1981   Kathy Jordan & Anne Smith (USA)

1982   Rosemary Casals (USA) & Wendy Turnbull (Aus)

1983-4   Martina Navrátilová & Pam Shriver (USA)

1985   Claudia Kohde-Kilsch (FRG) & Helena Suková (Cs)

1986-7   Martina Navrátilová & Pam Shriver (USA)

1988   Gigi Fernandez & Robin White (USA)

1989   Martina Navrátilová (USA) & Hana Mandlíková (Aus)

1990   Martina Navrátilová & Gigi Fernandez (USA)

1991   Pam Shriver (USA) & Natalya Zvereva (USSR)

1992   Jana Novotná (Cs) & Larisa Savchenko (Lat)

1993   Arantxa Sánchez (Spa) & Helena Suková (Cze)

1994   Arantxa Sánchez (Spa) & Jana Novotná (Cze)

Most wins by one pair: 12 Louise Brough & Margaret Du Pont (née Osborne), as above

By player: 13 Margaret Du Pont also 1941 (with Sarah Cooke), 12 Louise Brough, 9 Navrátilová, 7 Juliette Atkinson 1894-5 (with Helen Helwig), 1896 (with Elisabeth Moore), 1897-8 (with Kathleen Atkinson), 1901 (with Myrtle McAteer), 1902 (with Marion Jones); 7 Smith/Court, 6 Hazel Wightman (née Hotchkiss) 1909-10 (with Edith Rotch), 1911, 1915 (with Eleonora Sears), 1924, 1928 (with Helen Wills)

Mixed doubles (Winners from 1946)

1943-6   William Talbert & Margaret Osborne (USA)

1947   John Bromwich (Aus) & Louise Brough (USA)

1948   Tom Brown & Louise Brough (USA)

1949   Eric Sturgess (SAf) & Louise Brough (USA)

1950   Ken McGregor (Aus) & Margaret Du Pont (USA)

1951-2   Frank Sedgman (Aus) & Doris Hart (USA)

1953-5   Vic Seixas & Doris Hart (USA)

1956   Ken Rosewall (Aus) & Margaret Du Pont (USA)

1957   Kurt Nielsen (Den) & Althea Gibson (USA)

1958-60   Neale Fraser (Aus) & Margaret Du Pont (USA)

1961   Robert Mark & Margaret Smith (Aus)

1962   Fred Stolle & Margaret Smith (Aus)

1963   Ken Fletcher & Margaret Smith (Aus)

1964   John Newcombe & Margaret Smith (Aus)

1965   Fred Stolle & Margaret Smith (Aus)

1966   Owen Davidson (Aus) & Donna Fales (USA)

1967   Owen Davidson (Aus) & Billie Jean King (USA)

1968   Peter Curtis (UK) & Mary-Ann Eisel (USA)

1969   Paul Sullivan & Patty Hogan (USA)

Open   Marty Riessen (USA) & Margaret Court (née Smith) (Aus)

1970   Marty Riessen (USA) & Margaret Court (Aus)

1971   Owen Davidson (Aus) & Billie Jean King (USA)

1972   Marty Riessen (USA) & Margaret Court (Aus)

1973   Owen Davidson (Aus) & Billie Jean King (USA)

1974   Geoff Masters (Aus) & Pam Teeguarden (USA)

1975   Dick Stockton & Rosemary Casals (USA)

1976   Phil Dent (Aus) & Billie Jean King (USA)

1977-8   Frew McMillan (SAf) & Betty Stove (Hol)

1979   Bob Hewitt & Greer Stevens (SAf)

1980   Marty Riessen & Wendy Turnbull (USA)

1981-2   Kevin Curren (SAf) & Anne Smith (USA)

1983   John Fitzgerald & Elizabeth Sayers (Aus)

1984   Tom Gullikson (USA) & Manuela Maleeva (Bul)

1985   Heinz Günthardt (Swi) & Martina Navrátilová (USA)

1986   Sergio Casal (Spa) & Raffaella Reggi (Ita)

1987   Emilio Sánchez (Spa) & Martina Navrátilová (USA)

1988   Jim Pugh (USA) & Jana Novotná (Cs)

1989   Shelby Cannon & Robin White (USA)

1990   Todd Woodbridge & Elizabeth Smylie (Aus)

1991   Tom Hussen & Manon Bollegraf (Hol)

1992   Mark Woodforde & Nicole Provis (Aus)

1992   Todd Woodbridge (Aus) & Helena Suková (Cze)

1994   Patrick Galbraith (USA) & Elna Reinach (SAf)

Most wins by one pair: 4 William Talbert & Margaret Osborne 1943-6

By woman: 9 Osborne/Du Pont as above, 8 Smith/Court, 6 Hazel Wightman (née Hotchkiss) 1909, 1911, 1920 (with Wallace Johnson), 1910 (with Joseph Carpenter), 1915 (with Harry Johnson), 1918 (with Irving Wright)

By man: 4 Edwin Fischer 1894-6, 1898; Wallace Johnson 1907, 1909, 1911, 1920; Bill Tilden 1913-4, 1922-3; William Talbert 1943-6; Davidson, Riessen

Most United States titles

	Total	Singles	Doubles	Mixed	Years
Margaret Du Pont (USA)	25	3	13	9	1941-60
Margaret Smith/Court (Aus)	22	7	7	8	1961-75*
Louise Brough (USA)	17	1	12	4	1942-57
Bill Tilden (Aus)	16	7	5	4	1913-29
Hazel Wightman (USA)	16	4	6	6	1909-28
Martina Navrátilová (Cs/USA)	15	4	9	2	1977-90
Sarah Cooke (USA)	15	2	9	4	1930-45

* including both Amateur and Open Championships 1968-9

French Championships

The French Championships were first held in 1891 but they remained 'closed', open only to members of French clubs, until 1925 when they became a fully international event. They have always been held on hard courts, and at the Stade Roland Garros since 1928. Prize money totalled 51 million francs in 1995. *All champions from 1925 for singles and from 1946 for doubles:*

Men's singles

1925	René Lacoste (Fra)
1926	Henri Cochet (Fra)
1927	René Lacoste (Fra)
1928	Henri Cochet (Fra)
1929	René Lacoste (Fra)
1930	Henri Cochet (Fra)
1931	Jean Borotra (Fra)
1932	Henri Cochet (Fra)
1933	Jack Crawford (Aus)
1934	Gottfried Von Cramm (Ger)
1935	Fred Perry (UK)
1936	Gottfried Von Cramm (Ger)
1937	Henner Henkel (Ger)
1938	Donald Budge (USA)
1939	Donald McNeill (USA)
1946	Marcel Bernard (Fra)
1947	József Asboth (Hun)
1948-9	Frank Parker (USA)
1950	Budge Patty (USA)
1951-2	Jaroslav Drobny (Egy)
1953	Ken Rosewall (Aus)
1954-5	Tony Trabert (USA)
1956	Lew Hoad (Aus)
1957	Sven Davidson (Swe)
1958	Mervyn Rose (Aus)
1959-60	Nicola Pietrangeli (Ita)
1961	Manuel Santana (Spa)
1962	Rod Laver (Aus)
1963	Roy Emerson(Aus)
1964	Manuel Santana (Spa)
1965	Fred Stolle (Aus)
1966	Tony Roche (Aus)
1967	Roy Emerson (Aus)
1968	Ken Rosewall (Aus)
1969	Rod Laver (Aus)
1970-1	Jan Kodes (Cs)
1972	Andrés Gimeno (Spa)
1973	Ilie Nastase (Rom)
1974-5	Björn Borg (Swe)
1976	Adriano Panatta (Ita)
1977	Guillermo Vilas (Arg)
1978-81	Björn Borg (Swe)
1982	Mats Wilander (Swe)
1983	Yannick Noah (Fra)
1984	Ivan Lendl (Cs)
1985	Mats Wilander (Swe)
1986-7	Ivan Lendl (Cs)
1988	Mats Wilander (Swe)
1989	Michael Chang (USA)
1990	Andrés Gómez (Ecu)
1991-2	Jim Courier (USA)
1993-4	Sergi Bruguera (Spa)
1995	Thomas Muster (Aut)

Most wins: 6 Borg

Women's singles

1925-6	Suzanne Lenglen (Fra)
1927	Kea Bouman (Hol)
1928-30	Helen Wills Moody (USA)
1931	Cilly Aussem (Ger)
1932	Helen Moody (USA)
1933-4	Margaret Scriven (UK)
1935-7	Hilde Sperling (Ger)
1938-9	Simone Mathieu (Fra)
1946	Margaret Osborne (USA)
1947	Pat Todd (USA)
1948	Nelly Landry (Fra)
1949	Margaret Du Pont (née Osborne) (USA)
1950	Doris Hart (USA)
1951	Shirley Fry (USA)
1952	Doris Hart (USA)
1953-4	Maureen Connolly (USA)
1955	Angela Mortimer (UK)
1956	Althea Gibson (USA)
1957	Shirley Bloomer (UK)
1958	Zsuzsi Körmöczy (Hun)
1959	Christine Truman (UK)
1960	Darlene Hard (USA)
1961	Ann Haydon (UK)
1962	Margaret Smith (Aus)
1963	Lesley Turner (Aus)
1964	Margaret Smith (Aus)
1965	Lesley Turner (Aus)
1966	Ann Jones (UK)
1967	Françoise Durr (Fra)
1968	Nancy Richey (USA)
1969	Margaret Court (née Smith) (Aus)
1970	Margaret Court (Aus)
1971	Evonne Goolagong (Aus)
1972	Billie Jean King (USA)
1973	Margaret Court (Aus)
1974-5	Chris Evert (USA)
1976	Sue Barker (UK)
1977	Mimi Jausovec (Yug)
1978	Virginia Ruzici (Rom)
1979-80	Chris Evert Lloyd (USA)
1981	Hana Mandlíková (Cs)
1982	Martina Navrátilová (USA)
1983	Chris Evert Lloyd (USA)
1984	Martina Navrátilová (USA)
1985-6	Chris Evert Lloyd (USA)
1987-8	Steffi Graf (FRG)
1989	Arantxa Sánchez (Spa)
1990-2	Monica Seles (Yug)
1993	Steffi Graf (Ger)
1994	Arantxa Sánchez (Spa)
1995	Steffi Graf (Ger)

Most win: 7 Evert Lloyd

Men's doubles

1946	Marcel Bernard & Yvon Petra (Fra)
1947	Eustace Fannin & Eric Sturgess (SAf)
1948	Lennart Bergelin (Swe) & Jaroslav Drobny (Cs)
1949	Richard Gonzales & Frank Parker (USA)
1950	William Talbert & Tony Trabert (USA)
1951-2	Ken McGregor & Frank Sedgman (Aus)
1953	Lew Hoad & Ken Rosewall (Aus)
1954-5	Vic Seixas & Tony Trabert (USA)
1956	Don Candy (Aus) & Robert Perry (USA)
1957	Mal Anderson & Ashley Cooper (Aus)
1958	Ashley Cooper & Neale Fraser (Aus)
1959	Nicola Pietrangeli & Orlando Sirola (Ita)
1960	Roy Emerson & Neale Fraser (Aus)
1961	Roy Emerson & Rod Laver (Aus)
1962	Roy Emerson & Neale Fraser (Aus)
1963	Roy Emerson (Aus) & Manuel Santana (Spa)
1964	Roy Emerson & Ken Fletcher (Aus)
1965	Roy Emerson & Fred Stolle (Aus)
1966	Clark Graebner & Dennis Ralston (USA)
1967	John Newcombe & Tony Roche (Aus)
1968	Ken Rosewall & Fred Stolle (Aus)
1969	John Newcombe & Tony Roche (Aus)
1970	Ilie Nastase & Ion Tiriac (Rom)
1971	Arthur Ashe & Marty Riessen (USA)
1972	Bob Hewitt & Frew McMillan (SAf)
1973	John Newcombe (Aus) & Tom Okker (Hol)
1974	Dick Crealy (Aus) & Onny Parun (NZ)
1975	Brian Gottfried (USA) & Raúl Ramirez (Mex)
1976	Fred McNair & Sherwood Stewart (USA)
1977	Brian Gottfried (USA) & Raúl Ramirez (Mex)
1978	Gene Mayer & Hank Pfister (USA)
1979	Sandy Mayer & Gene Mayer (USA)
1980	Victor Amaya & Hank Pfister (USA)
1981	Heinz Günthardt (Swi) & Balázs Taróczy (Hun)

1982	Sherwood Stewart & Ferdi Taygan (USA)
1983	Anders Järryd & Hans Simonsson (Swe)
1984	Henri Leconte & Yannick Noah (Fra)
1985	Mark Edmondson & Kim Warwick (Aus)
1986	John Fitzgerald (Aus) & Tomás Smid (Cs)
1987	Anders Järryd (Swe) & Robert Seguso (USA)
1988	Andrés Gómez (Ecu) & Emilio Sánchez (Spa)
1989	Jim Grabb & Patrick McEnroe (USA)
1990	Sergio Casal & Emilio Sánchez (Spa)
1991	John Fitzgerald (Aus) & Anders Järryd (Swe)
1992	Jakob Hlasek & Marc Rosset (Swi)
1993	Luke Jensen & Murphy Jensen (USA)
1994	Byron Black (Zim) & Jonathan Stark (USA)
1995	Jacco Eltingh & Paul Haarhuis (Hol)

Most wins: 6 Emerson, 5 Jean Borotra, 1925, 1929 (with René Lacoste), 1928, 1934 (with Jacques Brugnon), 1936 (with Marcel Bernard); 5 Jacques Brugnon 1927, 1930, 1932 (with Henri Cochet), 1928, 1934 (with Borotra)

Women's doubles

1946-7	Louise Brough & Margaret Osborne (USA)
1948	Doris Hart & Pat Todd (USA)
1949	Louise Brough & Margaret Du Pont (née Osborne) (USA)
1950-3	Shirley Fry & Doris Hart (USA)
1954	Maureen Connolly (USA) & Nell Hopman (Aus)
1955	Beverley Fleitz & Darlene Hard (USA)
1956	Angela Buxton (UK) & Althea Gibson (USA)
1957	Shirley Bloomer (UK) & Darlene Hard (USA)
1958	Yola Ramirez & Rosa Reyes (Mex)
1959	Sandra Reynolds & Renée Schuurman (SAf)
1960	Maria Bueno (Bra) & Darlene Hard (USA)
1961	Sandra Reynolds & Renée Schuurman (SAf)
1962	Sandra Price (née Reynolds) & Renée Schuurman (SAf)
1963	Ann Jones (UK) & Renée Schuurman (SAf)
1964-5	Margaret Smith & Lesley Turner (Aus)
1966	Margaret Smith & Judy Tegart (Aus)
1967	Françoise Durr (Fra) & Gail Sheriff (Aus)
1968-9	Françoise Durr (Fra) & Ann Jones (UK)
1970-1	Françoise Durr & Gail Chanfreau (Fra)
1972	Billie Jean King (USA) & Betty Stove (Hol)
1973	Margaret Court (Aus) & Virginia Wade (UK)
1974	Chris Evert (USA) & Olga Morozova (USSR)
1975	Chris Evert (USA) & Martina Navrátilová (Cs)
1976	Fiorella Bonicelli (Uru) & Gail Lovera (Fra)
1977	Regina Marsikova (Cs) & Pam Teeguarden (USA)
1978	Mimi Jausovec (Yug) & Virginia Ruzici (Rom)
1979	Betty Stove (Hol) & Wendy Turnbull (Aus)
1980	Kathy Jordan & Anne Smith (USA)
1981	Ros Fairbank & Tanya Harford (SAf)
1982	Martina Navrátilová & Anne Smith (USA)
1983	Ros Fairbank (SAf) & Candy Reynolds (USA)
1984-5	Martina Navrátilová & Pam Shriver (USA)
1986	Martina Navrátilová (USA) & Andrea Temesvári (Hun)
1987-8	Martina Navrátilová & Pam Shriver (USA)
1989	Larissa Savchenko & Natalya Zvereva (USSR)
1990	Jana Novotná & Helena Suková (Cs)
1991	Gigi Fernandez (USA) & Jana Novotná (Cs)
1992	Conchita Martinez & Arantxa Sánchez (Spa)
1993-4	Gigi Fernandez (USA) & Natalya Zvereva (Bls)
1995	Gigi Fernandez (USA) & Natalya Zvereva (Bls)

Most wins: 7 Navrátilová, 6 Simone Mathieu (Fra) 1933-4 (with Elizabeth Ryan), 1936-8 (with Billie Yorke)

Mixed doubles

1946	Budge Patty & Pauline Betz (USA)
1947	Eric Sturgess & Sheila Summers (SAf)
1948	Jaroslav Drobny (Cs) & Pat Todd (USA)
1949	Eric Sturgess & Sheila Summers (SAf)
1950	Enrique Morea (Arg) & Barbara Scofield (USA)
1951-2	Frank Sedgman (Aus) & Doris Hart (USA)
1953	Vic Seixas & Doris Hart (USA)
1954	Lew Hoad (Aus) & Maureen Connolly (USA)
1955	Gordon Forbes (SAf) & Darlene Hard (USA)
1956	Luis Ayala (Chl) & Thelma Long (Aus)
1957	Jan Javorsky & Vera Puzejová (Cs)
1958	Nicola Pietrangeli (Ita) & Shirley Bloomer (UK)
1959	Billy Knight (UK) & Yola Ramirez (Mex)
1960	Bob Howe (Aus) & Maria Bueno (Bra)
1961	Rod Laver (Aus) & Darlene Hard (USA)
1962	Bob Howe (Aus) & Renée Schuurman (SAf)
1963-5	Ken Fletcher & Margaret Smith (Aus)
1966	Frew McMillan & Annette Van Zyl (SAf)
1967	Owen Davidson (Aus) & Billie Jean King (USA)
1968	Jean-Claude Barclay & Françoise Durr (Fra)
1969	Marty Riessen (USA) & Margaret Court (née Smith) (Aus)
1970	Bob Hewitt (SAf) & Billie Jean King (USA)
1971	Jean-Claude Barclay & Françoise Durr (Fra)
1972	Kim Warwick & Evonne Goolagong (Aus)
1973	Jean-Claude Barclay & Françoise Durr (Fra)
1974	Ivan Molina (Col) & Martina Navrátilová (Cs)
1975	Thomaz Koch (Bra) & Fiorella Bonicelli Uru)
1976	Kim Warwick (Aus) & Ilana Kloss (SAf)
1977	John McEnroe & Mary Carillo (USA)
1978	Pavel Slozil & Renata Tomanova (Cs)
1979	Bob Hewitt (SAf) & Wendy Turnbull (Aus)
1980	Bill Martin & Anne Smith (USA)
1981	Jimmy Arias & Andrea Jaeger (USA)
1982	John Lloyd (UK) & Wendy Turnbull (Aus)
1983	Eliot Teltscher & Barbara Jordan (USA)
1984	Dick Stockton & Anne Smith (USA)
1985	Heinz Günthardt (Swi) & Martina Navrátilová (USA)
1986	Ken Flach & Kathy Jordan (USA)
1987	Emilio Sánchez (Spa) & Pam Shriver (USA)
1988	Jorge Lozano (Mex) & Lori McNeill (USA)
1989	Tom Nijssen & Manon Bollegraf (Hol)
1990	Jorge Lozano (Mex) & Arantxa Sánchez (Spa)
1991	Cyril Suk & Helena Suková (Cs)
1992	Todd Woodbridge (Aus) & Arantxa Sánchez (Spa)
1993	Andrey Olkhovskiy & Yevgeniya Manyokova (Rus)
1994	Menno Oosting & Kristie Boogert (Hol)
1995	Mark Woodforde (Aus) & Larisa Neiland (Lat)

Most wins (Men): 3 Fletcher, Barclay; (Women): 4 Smith/Court

Most French titles

	Total	Singles	Doubles	Mixed	Years
Margaret Smith/Court (Aus)	13	5	4	4	1962-73
Martina Navrátilová (Cs/USA)	11	2	7	2	1974-88
Simone Mathieu (Fra)	10	2	6	2	1933-9
Doris Hart (USA)	10	2	5	3	1948-53
Henri Cochet (Fra)	9	4	3	2	1926-30
Françoise Durr (Fra)	9	1	5	3	1967-73
Chris Evert Lloyd (USA)	9	7	2	-	1974-86

Australian Championships

The first Australasian championships were held in 1905, and it was not until 1925 that the title changed to its present style. New Zealand twice hosted the championship, in 1906 and 1912. There were two championships in 1977 because the event was moved from early-season (January) to December. It reverted to a January date in 1987, which meant there was no championship in 1986. *Post-war winners:*

Men's singles

1946	John Bromwich (Aus)
1947	Dinny Pails (Aus)
1948	Adrian Quist (Aus)
1949-50	Frank Sedgman (Aus)
1951	Dick Savitt (USA)
1952	Ken McGregor (Aus)
1953	Ken Rosewall (Aus)
1954	Mervyn Rose (Aus)
1955	Ken Rosewall (Aus)
1956	Lew Hoad (Aus)
1957-8	Ashley Cooper (Aus)
1959	Alex Olmedo (USA)
1960	Rod Laver (Aus)
1961	Roy Emerson (Aus)
1962	Rod Laver (Aus)
1963-7	Roy Emerson (Aus)
1968	Bill Bowrey (Aus)
1969	Rod Laver (Aus)
1970	Arthur Ashe (USA)
1971-2	Ken Rosewall (Aus)
1973	John Newcombe (Aus)
1974	Jimmy Connors (USA)
1975	John Newcombe (Aus)
1976	Mark Edmondson (Aus)
1977	Roscoe Tanner (USA)
1977	Vitas Gerulaitis (USA)
1978-9	Guillermo Vilas (Arg)
1980	Brian Teacher (USA)
1981-2	Johan Kriek (SAf)
1983-4	Mats Wilander (Swe)
1985	Stefan Edberg (Swe)
1987	Stefan Edberg (Swe)
1988	Mats Wilander (Swe)
1989-90	Ivan Lendl (Cs)
1991	Boris Becker (Ger)
1992-3	Jim Courier (USA)
1994	Pete Sampras (USA)
1995	Andre Agassi (USA)

Most wins: 6 Emerson, 4 Jack Crawford (Aus) 1931-3, 1935; Rosewall

Women's singles

1946-8	Nancye Bolton (Aus)
1949	Doris Hart (USA)
1950	Louise Brough (USA)
1951	Nancye Bolton (Aus)
1952	Thelma Long (Aus)
1953	Maureen Connolly (USA)
1954	Thelma Long (Aus)
1955	Beryl Penrose (Aus)
1956	Mary Carter (Aus)
1957	Shirley Fry (USA)
1958	Angela Mortimer (UK)
1959	Mary Reitano (Aus)
1960-6	Margaret Smith (Aus)
1967	Nancy Richey (USA)
1968	Billie Jean King (USA)
1969	Margaret Court (née Smith) (Aus)
1970-1	Margaret Court (Aus)
1972	Virginia Wade (UK)
1973	Margaret Court (Aus)
1974-5	Evonne Goolagong (Aus)
1976	Evonne Cawley (née Goolagong) (Aus)
1977	Kerry Reid (Aus)
1977	Evonne Cawley (Aus)
1978	Christine O'Neill (Aus)
1979	Barbara Jordan (USA)
1980	Hana Mandlíková (Cs)
1981	Martina Navrátilová (USA)
1982	Chris Evert Lloyd (USA)
1983	Martina Navrátilová (USA)
1984	Chris Evert Lloyd (USA)
1985	Martina Navrátilová (USA)
1987	Hana Mandlíková (Cs)
1988-90	Steffi Graf (FRG)
1991-3	Monica Seles (Yug)
1994	Steffi Graf (Ger)
1995	Mary Pierce (Fra)

Most wins: 11 Smith/Court, 6 Nancye Bolton (née Wynne) 1937, 1940, 1946-8, 1951; 5 Daphne Akhurst 1925-6, 1928-30

Men's doubles

1946-50	John Bromwich & Adrian Quist (Aus)
1951-2	Ken McGregor & Frank Sedgman (Aus)
1953	Lew Hoad & Ken Rosewall (Aus)
1954	Rex Hartwig & Mervyn Rose (Aus)
1955	Vic Seixas & Tony Trabert (USA)
1956	Lew Hoad & Ken Rosewall (Aus)
1957	Neale Fraser & Lew Hoad (Aus)
1958	Ashley Cooper & Neale Fraser (Aus)
1959-61	Rod Laver & Robert Mark (Aus)
1962	Roy Emerson & Neale Fraser (Aus)
1963-4	Bob Hewitt & Fred Stolle (Aus)
1965	John Newcombe & Tony Roche (Aus)
1966	Roy Emerson & Fred Stolle (Aus)
1967	John Newcombe & Tony Roche (Aus)

Andre Agassi at the 1995 Australian Open

1968	Dick Crealy & Allan Stone (Aus)
1969	Roy Emerson & Rod Laver (Aus)
1970	Bob Lutz & Stan Smith (USA)
1971	John Newcombe & Tony Roche (Aus)
1972	Owen Davidson & Ken Rosewall (Aus)
1973	Mal Anderson & John Newcombe (Aus)
1974	Ross Case & Geoff Masters (Aus)
1975	John Alexander & Phil Dent (Aus)
1976	John Newcombe & Tony Roche (Aus)
1977	Arthur Ashe (USA) & Tony Roche (Aus)
1977	Ray Ruffels & Allan Stone (Aus)
1978	Wojtek Fibak (Pol) & Kim Warwick (Aus)
1979	Peter McNamara & Paul McNamee (Aus)
1980-1	Mark Edmondson & Kim Warwick (Aus)
1982	John Alexander & John Fitzgerald (Aus)
1983	Mark Edmonson & Paul McNamee (Aus)
1984	Mark Edmondson (Aus) & Sherwood Stewart (USA)
1985	Paul Annacone (USA) & Christo Van Rensburg (SAf)
1987	Stefan Edberg & Anders Järryd (Swe)
1988-9	Rick Leach & Jim Pugh (USA)
1990	Pieter Aldrich & Dannie Visser (SAf)
1991	Scott Davis & David Pate (Aus)
1992	Todd Woodbridge & Mark Woodforde (Aus)
1993	Dannie Visser (SAf) & Laurie Warder (Aus)
1994	Jacco Eltingh & Paul Haarhuis (Hol)
1995	Richey Reneburg & Jared Palmer (USA)

Most wins by one pair: 8 John Bromwich & Adrian Quist 1938-40, 1946-50

By player: 10 Adrian Quist 1936-7 (with Don Turnbull), and 8 with John Bromwich.

Women's doubles

1946	Mary Bevis & Joyce Fitch (Aus)
1947-9	Nancye Bolton & Thelma Long (Aus)
1950	Louise Brough & Doris Hart (USA)
1951-2	Nancye Bolton & Thelma Long (Aus)
1953	Maureen Connolly & Julie Sampson (USA)
1954	Mary Hawton (née Bevis) & Beryl Penrose (Aus)
1955	Mary Hawton & Beryl Penrose (Aus)
1956	Mary Hawton & Thelma Long (Aus)
1957	Shirley Fry & Althea Gibson (USA)
1958	Mary Hawton & Thelma Long (Aus)
1959	Sandra Reynolds & Renée Schuurman (SAf)
1960	Maria Bueno (Bra) & Christine Truman (UK)
1961	Mary Reitano & Margaret Smith (Aus)
1962-3	Robyn Ebbern & Margaret Smith (Aus)
1964	Judy Tegart & Lesley Turner (Aus)
1965	Margaret Smith & Lesley Turner (Aus)
1966	Carole Graebner & Nancy Richey (USA)
1967	Judy Tegart & Lesley Turner (Aus)
1968	Karen Krantzcke & Kerry Melville (Aus)
1969	Margaret Court (née Smith) & Judy Tegart (Aus)
1970	Margaret Court & Judy Dalton (née Tegart) (Aus)
1971	Margaret Court & Evonne Goolagong (Aus)
1972	Helen Gourlay & Kerry Harris (Aus)
1973	Margaret Court (Aus) & Virginia Wade (UK)
1974-5	Evonne Goolagong (Aus) & Peggy Michel (USA)
1976	Evonne Cawley (née Goolagong) & Helen Gourlay (Aus)

1977	Diane Fromholtz & Helen Gourlay (Aus)
1977	Evonne Cawley & Helen Cawley (Aus) & Ramona Guerrant (USA) & Kerry Reid (née Melville) (Aus) *shared title, final not played*
1978	Betsy Nagelsen (USA) & Renata Tomanova (Cs)
1979	Judith Chaloner (NZ) & Dianne Evers (Aus)
1980	Betsy Nagelsen (USA) & Martina Navrátilová (Cs)
1981	Kathy Jordan & Anne Smith (USA)
1982-5	Martina Navrátilová & Pam Shriver (USA)
1987-9	Martina Navrátilová & Pam Shriver (USA)
1990	Helena Suková & Jana Novotná (Cs)
1991	Patti Fendick & Mary Jo Fernandez (USA)
1992	Arancha Sánchez (Spa) & Helena Suková (Cs)
1993-4	Gigi Fernandez (USA) & Natalya Zvereva (Bls)
1995	Jana Novotná (Cze) & Arantxa Sánchez (Spa)

Most wins by one pair: 10 Nancye Bolton (née Wynne) & Thelma Long (née Coyne) 1936-40, 1947-9, 1951-2; 7 Navrátilová & Shriver

By player: 12 Thelma Long, also 1956, 1958 (with Mary Hawton); 10 Bolton, 8 Smith/ Court, Navrátilová; 7 Shriver

Mixed doubles

1946-8	Colin Long & Nancye Bolton (Aus)
1949-50	Frank Sedgman (Aus) & Doris Hart (USA)
1951-2	George Worthington & Thelma Long (Aus)
1953	Rex Hartwig (Aus) & Julie Sampson (USA)
1954	Rex Hartwig & Thelma Long (Aus)
1955	George Worthington & Thelma Long (Aus)
1956	Neale Fraser & Beryl Penrose (Aus)
1957	Mal Anderson & Fay Muller (Aus)
1958	Bob Howe & Mary Hawton (Aus)
1959	Robert Mark (Aus) & Sandra Reynolds (SAf)
1960	Trevor Fancutt (SAf) & Jan Lehane (Aus)
1961	Bob Hewitt & Jan Lehane (Aus)
1962	Fred Stolle & Lesley Turner (Aus)
1963-4	Ken Fletcher & Margaret Smith (Aus)
1965	John Newcombe & Margaret Smith (Aus) Owen Davidson & Robyn Ebbern (Aus) *shared title, final not played*
1966	Tony Roche & Judy Tegart (Aus)
1967	Owen Davidson & Lesley Turner (Aus)
1968	Dick Crealy (Aus) & Billie Jean King (USA)
1969	Marty Riessen (USA) & Margaret Court (née Smith) (Aus) Fred Stolle (Aus) & Ann Jones (UK *shared title, final not played*
1970-85	*not held*
1987	Sherwood Stewart & Zina Garrison (USA)
1988-90	Jim Pugh (USA) & Jana Novotná (Cs)
1991	Jeremy Bates & Jo Durie (UK)
1992	Mark Woodforde & Nicole Provis (Aus)
1993	Todd Woodbridge (Aus) & Arantxa Sánchez (Spa)
1994	Andrey Olkhovskiy (Rus) & Larisa Neiland (Lat)
1995	Rick Leach (USA) & Natalya Zvereva (Bls)

Most wins by one pair: 4 Harry Hopman & Nell Hopman (née Hall) 1930, 1936-7, 1939; 4 Colin Long & Nancye Bolton (née Wynne) 1940, 1946-8

Most Australian titles

	Total	Singles	Doubles	Mixed	Years
Margaret Court (Aus)	21	11	8	2	1960-73
Nancye Bolton (Aus)	20	6	10	4	1936-51
Thelma Long (Aus)	18	2	12	4	1936-58
Daphne Akhurst (Aus)	13	5	4	4	1924-30
Adrian Quist (Aus)	13	3	10	-	1936-50
Best record by a non-Australian:					
Martina Navrátilová	11	3	8	-	1980-89

The All-Time Greats

A summary of the most titles won by players in the four Grand Slam events - Wimbledon, US Open, French Championship, and Australian Championship, first for each tournament and then analysed by singles and doubles.

	Total	Wimb.	US	French	Aus	Singles	Doubles	Mixed
Margaret Court (Aus) *	66	10	22	13	21	26	21	19
Martina Navrátilová (Cs/USA)	56	19	15	11	11	18	31	7
Billie Jean King (USA)	39	20	13	4	2	12	16	11
Margaret Du Pont (USA)	37	7	25	5	-	6	21	10
Louis Brough (USA)	35	13	17	3	2	6	21	8
Doris Hart (USA)	35	10	11	10	4	6	14	15
Helen Wills-Moody (USA)	31	12	13	6	-	19	9	3
Roy Emerson (Aus)	28	5	6	8	9	12	16	-
Elizabeth Ryan (USA)	26	19	3	4	-	-	17	9
John Newcombe (Aus) *	25	9	6	3	7	7	17	1
Steffi Graf (Ger)	18	7	3	4	4	17	1	-

* Court's totals include both US Amateur and Open Championships 1968-9. Not included are the undecided Australian mixed doubles finals: two for Court, one for Newcombe.

The most Grand Slam tournament doubles wins by one pair

20 Louise Brough & Margaret Du Pont 1942-57
20 Martina Navrátilová & Pam Shriver 1981-9

Grand Slam

To achieve the Grand Slam is to simultaneously hold the titles of the four major tournaments as above. Most precisely the Grand Slam is for all four titles in one calendar year. The following players have held all four at once: *(Single years indicates all four titles won in one year)*

Men's singles
Donald Budge (USA) 1937/8, 1938
Rod Laver (Aus) 1962 and 1969

Women's singles
Maureen Connolly (USA) 1952/3, 1953
Margaret Court (Aus) 1969/70, 1970, 1970/1
Martina Navrátilová (USA) 1983/4
Steffi Graf (FRG/Ger) 1988, 1988/9 and 1993/4
The first three each won six successive Grand Slam tournaments, Graf won five in 1988/9.

Men's doubles
Frank Sedgman (Aus) 1950/1, 1951, 1951/2
Ken McGregor (Aus) 1951, 1951/2

Women's doubles
Louise Brough (USA) 1949/50
Maria Bueno (Bra) 1960
Martina Navrátilová (USA) 1983/4, 1984, 1984/5, 1985/6, 1986/7
Pam Shriver (USA) 1983/4, 1984, 1984/5, 1986/7
Navrátilová and Shriver won a record eight successive Grand Slam tournaments together 1983-5

Mixed doubles
Margaret Smith (Aus) 1962/3, 1963, 1963/4
Ken Fletcher (Aus) 1963, 1963/4
Owen Davidson (Aus) 1966/7, 1967
Billie Jean King (USA) 1967/8

Davis Cup

The American player Dwight F Davis donated a cup in 1900 to be contested by national teams. Up to 1971 the winning nation accepted a challenge from the country winning a knockout competition. Since 1972 the entire competition has been on a knockout basis with countries divided into zonal groups with a promotion and relegation system into the World Group of 16 nations who play-off for the Cup. There was no competition in 1901 and 1910, or during the war years. Each match is contested over two pairs of singles and a doubles.

Finals	Winners	Runners-Up	Score
1900	USA	British Isles	3-0
1902	USA	British Isles	3-2
1903	British Isles	USA	4-1
1904	British Isles	Belgium	5-0
1905	British Isles	USA	5-0
1906	British Isles	USA	5-0
1907	Australasia	British Isles	3-2
1908	Australasia	USA	3-2
1909	Australasia	USA	5-0
1911	Australasia	USA	5-0
1912	British Isles	Australasia	3-2
1913	USA	British Isles	3-2
1914	Australasia	USA	3-2

Year	Winner	Runner-up	Score	Year	Winner	Runner-up	Score
1919	Australasia	British Isles	4-1	1963	USA	Australia	3-2
1920	USA	Australasia	5-0	1964	Australia	USA	3-2
1921	USA	Japan	5-0	1965	Australia	Spain	4-1
1922	USA	Australasia	4-1	1966	Australia	India	4-1
1923	USA	Australia	4-1	1967	Australia	Spain	4-1
1924	USA	Australia	5-0	1968	USA	Australia	4-1
1925	USA	France	5-0	1969	USA	Romania	5-0
1926	USA	France	4-1	1970	USA	F R Germany	5-0
1927	France	USA	3-2	1971	USA	Romania	3-2
1928	France	USA	4-1	1972	USA	Romania	3-2
1929	France	USA	3-2	1973	Australia	USA	5-0
1930	France	USA	4-1	1974	South Africa	India	w/o
1931	France	Great Britain	3-2	1975	Sweden	Czechoslovakia	3-2
1932	France	USA	3-2	1976	Italy	Chile	4-1
1933	Great Britain	France	3-2	1977	Australia	Italy	3-1
1934	Great Britain	USA	4-1	1978	USA	Great Britain	4-1
1935	Great Britain	USA	5-0	1979	USA	Italy	5-0
1936	Great Britain	Australia	3-2	1980	Czechoslovakia	Italy	4-1
1937	USA	Great Britain	4-1	1981	USA	Argentina	3-1
1938	USA	Australia	3-2	1982	USA	France	4-1
1939	Australia	USA	3-2	1983	Australia	Sweden	3-2
1946	USA	Australia	5-0	1984	Sweden	USA	4-1
1947	USA	Australia	4-1	1985	Sweden	F R Germany	3-2
1948	USA	Australia	5-0	1986	Australia	Sweden	3-2
1949	USA	Australia	4-1	1987	Sweden	India	5-0
1950	Australia	USA	4-1	1988	F R Germany	Sweden	4-1
1951	Australia	USA	3-2	1989	F R Germany	Sweden	3-2
1952	Australia	USA	4-1	1990	USA	Australia	3-2
1953	Australia	USA	3-2	1991	France	USA	3-1
1954	USA	Australia	3-2	1992	USA	Switzerland	3-1
1955	Australia	USA	5-0	1993	Germany	Australia	4-1
1956	Australia	USA	5-0	1994	Sweden	Russia	4-1
1957	Australia	USA	3-2				
1958	USA	Australia	3-2				
1959	Australia	USA	3-2				
1960	Australia	Italy	4-1				
1961	Australia	Italy	5-0				
1962	Australia	Mexico	5-0				

Wins: 30 USA, 26 Australia/Australasia, 9 British Isles/Great Britain, 7 France, 5 Sweden, 3 Germany, 1 Czechoslovakia, Italy, South Africa

Most times played for winning team: 8 Roy Emerson (Aus) 1959-62, 1964-7; 7 Bill Tilden (USA) 1920-6

Most Davis Cup Appearances

	Rubbers	Wins	Singles	Doubles	Win%	Years
Nicola Pietrangeli (Ita)	164	120	78/110	42/54	73.1	1954-72
Ilie Nastase (Rom)	146	109	74/96	35/50	74.7	1966-85
Manuel Santana (Spa)	120	92	69/86	23/34	76.7	1958-73
Jacques Brichant (Bel)	120	71	52/79	19/41	59.2	1949-65
Thomaz Koch (Bra)	118	74	46/78	28/40	62.7	1962-81

Best win percentage of those to have played more than 100 matches

	Rubbers	Wins	Singles	Doubles	Win%	Years
Gottfried von Cramm (Ger)	101	82	58/68	24/33	81.2	1932-53

Most appearances and most wins for Great Britain

	Rubbers	Wins	Singles	Doubles	Win%	Years
Mike Sangster	65	43	29/48	14/17	66.2	1960-8
Bobby Wilson	61	41	16/28	25/33	67.9	1955-68
Fred Perry	52	45	34/38	11/14	86.5	1931-6

Singles and doubles figures show wins/matches played

Best records in Davis Cup Finals/Challenge Rounds (10 or more wins)

Bill Tilden (USA)	28	21	17/22	4/6	75.0	1920-30
Roy Emerson (Aus)	18	15	11/12	4/6	83.3	1959-62, 1964-7
Norman Brookes (Aus)	22	15	9/14	6/8	68.2	1907-09, 1911-12, 1914, 1919-20
Henri Cochet (Fra)	20	14	11/14	3/6	70.0	1926-33
Stan Smith (USA)	16	12	6/8	6/8	75.0	1968-73, 1978-9

William Johnston (USA)	16	13	11/14	2/2	81.2	1920-7
Laurence Doherty (UK)	12	12*	7/7	4/4	100.0	1902-06
John McEnroe (USA)	14	12	9/10	3/4	85.7	1978-9, 1981-2, 1984, 1992
Rod Laver (Aus)	12	10	8/10	2/2	83.3	1959-62, 1973

* including a walk-over

Wightman Cup

The former American player Hazel Wightman (née Hotchkiss) donated the trophy in 1920 to be contested by national female teams. However, none showed any interest until 1923 when the USA and Great Britain played for the trophy. Since then all Wightman Cup matches have been between the two nations. The format was five singles and two doubles. In 1990, with the decline in British tennis standards and after four 7-0 US wins in the previous five matches, a decision was taken to suspend the event. Wins:

51 USA 1923, 1926-7, 1929, 1931-9, 1946-57, 1959, 1961-7, 1969-73, 1976-7, 1979-89

10 Great Britain 1924-5, 1928, 1930, 1958, 1960, 1968, 1974-5, 1978

The United States 'whitewashed' Great Britain 14 times by inflicting a 7-0 defeat upon them: 1923, 1946-7, 1949-50, 1952-4*, 1977, 1979, 1981, 1985-6, 1988-9.
* In 1954 the USA won all six matches played.
Great Britain's best results were 6-1 wins in 1924 and 1974.

Most Wightman Cup appearances

	Rubbers	Wins	Years
Virginia Wade (UK)	56	19	1965-85
Chris Evert Lloyd (USA)	38	34*	1971-85
Ann Jones (UK)	32	16	1957-75
Helen Moody (USA)	30	21	1923-38
Helen Jacobs (USA)	30	19	1927-39

* won all her 26 singles
Others with 20 or more wins:

Billie Jean King (USA)	26	21	1961-78
Doris Hart (USA)	24	22	1946-55
Louise Brough (USA)	22	22	1946-57

Federation Cup/Fed Cup

An international women's team competition played on a knockout basis at one venue each year. The Federation Cup was held from 1963 to 1994 as a knock-out competition at one venue, with a record number of 74 nations competing in 1993, all the contests having two singles and a doubles. From 1995 the competition, renamed the Fed Cup, had a new format, with a record 87 nations competing in groups: eight in each of the World Group and Group 1 followed by teams split into continental zones. The group matches (quarter-finals) are followed by semi-finals and finals at different dates and venues. Wins:

Most Federation Cup Appearances

	Rubbers	Wins	Singles	Doubles	Win%	Years
Virginia Wade (UK)	100*	66	36/56	30/44*	66.0	1967-83
Wendy Turnbull (Aus)	62	46	17/25	29/37	74.2	1977-88
Chris Evert (USA)	60	56	40/42	16/18	93.3	1977-89
Billie Jean King (USA)	58*	52	25/29	27/29*	89.7	1963-79
Betty Stove (Hol)	55	41	21/26	20/29	74.5	1964-83
Helga Masthoff (FRG)	55	37	23/33	14/22	67.2	1965-77
Hana Mandlikova (Cs)	54	42	31/37	11/17	77.8	1978-87

* including one unfinished rubber

14 USA 1963, 1966-7, 1969, 1976-82, 1986, 1989-90
7 Australia 1964-5, 1968, 1970-1, 1973-4
5 Czechoslovakia 1975, 1983-5, 1988
3 Spain 1991, 1993-4

2 Germany 1987 (FRG), 1992
1 South Africa 1972
Chris Evert Lloyd won her first 29 singles in the competition 1977-86. Margaret Court won all her 20 singles matches (and 15/20 in doubles) for Australia 1963-71.

1 Argentina 1980
1 France 1986
1 Yugoslavia 1990

World Team Cup

Formerly known as the Nations Cup, it is an eight-nation men's team event. First held in Kingston, Jamaica, in 1975 it was not held the next two years but was revived in 1977. Winners:

5	USA	1975, 1982, 1984-5, 1993
4	Sweden	1988, 1991-2, 1995
2	Spain	1978, 1983
2	Czechoslovakia	1981, 1987
2	Germany	1989 (FRG), 1994
1	Australia	1979

Men's Grand Prix Masters - ATP Championships

Throughout the season various tournaments count towards the Masters and points are gained according to performances. The value of points available per tournament is geared to the stature of the tournament. At the end of the season the leading 16 players play-off for the Masters singles title, and eight pairs play-off for the doubles title. There was no event in 1977 because the date of the final was switched from December to the following January. There were two tournaments in 1986 because it reverted to a December final.

From 1990 the event was replaced by the ATP Tour World Championship (see below). Winners:

Singles

1970	Stan Smith (USA)
1971-3	Ilie Nastase (Rom)
1974	Guillermo Vilas (Arg)

1975	Ilie Nastase (Rom)
1976	Manuel Orantes (Spa)
1978	Jimmy Connors (USA)
1979	John McEnroe (USA)
1980-1	Björn Borg (Swe)
1982-3	Ivan Lendl (Cs)
1984-5	John McEnroe (USA)
1986-7	Ivan Lendl (Cs)
1988	Boris Becker (FRG)
1989	Stefan Edberg (Swe)

Most wins: 4 Nastase, Lendl
Jimmy Connors qualified for the play-offs for a record 14 years 1972-85.

Doubles

1970	Arthur Ashe & Stan Smith (USA)
1971-4	*Not held*
1975	Juan Gisbert & Manuel Orantes (Spa)
1976	Fred McNair & Sherwood Stewart (USA)
1978	Bob Hewitt & Frew McMillan (SAf)
1979-85	Peter Fleming & John McEnroe (USA)
1986	Stefan Edberg & Anders Järryd (Swe) (2 wins)
1987	Miloslav Mecir & Tomás Smid (Cs)
1988	Rick Leach & Jim Pugh (USA)
1989	Patrick McEnroe & Jim Grabb (USA)

Most wins: 7 John McEnroe & Peter Fleming

ATP Tour World Championships Final

Contested annually at Frankfurt, Germany each November from 1990. *Winners:*

1990	Andre Agassi (USA)
1991	Pete Sampras (USA)
1992	Boris Becker (Ger)
1993	Michael Stich (Ger)
1994	Pete Sampras (USA)

ATP World Doubles

1990	Guy Forget (Fra) & Jakob Hlasek (Swi)
1991	John Fitzgerald (Aus) & Anders Järryd (Swe)
1992	Todd Woodbridge & Mark Woodforde (Aus)
1993	Jacco Eltingh & Paul Haarhuis (Hol)
1994	Jan Apell & Jonas Bjorkman (Swe)

Women's International Series

As with the men, so women have had an International championship played after a season-long series of tournaments. *Winners: (see also Virginia Slims/ Avon Series below)*

Singles

1977-8	Chris Evert (USA)
1979*	Martina Navrátilová (Cs)
1980*	Tracy Austin (USA)
1981	Tracy Austin (USA)
1982	Martina Navrátilová (USA)
1983*	Martina Navrátilová (USA)
1984*	Martina Navrátilová (USA)

Doubles

1977	Françoise Durr (Fra) & Virginia Wade (UK)
1978	Billie Jean King (USA) & Martina Navrátilová (Cs)
1979*	Billie Jean King (USA) & Martina Navrátilová (Cs)
1980*	Rosemary Casals (USA) & Wendy Turnbull (Aus)

1981	Martina Navrátilová (Cs) & Pam Shriver (USA)
1982	Martina Navrátilová & Pam Shriver (USA)
1983*	Martina Navrátilová & Pam Shriver (USA)
1984*	Martina Navrátilová & Pam Shriver (USA)

* *played the following year*

Virginia Slims/Avon Series

From 1971 there was an annual series of Virginia Slims tournaments, with a Championships as the climax. Avon Products took over the sponsorship 1979-82, with Virginia Slims back again in 1983 when their initial series ran for 15 months to March 1984. From 1983 the Virginia Slims final has been the one women's match played over the best of five sets. *Championship winners (the Doubles event has not been staged each year):*

Singles

1971	Billie Jean King (USA)
1972-3	Chris Evert (USA)
1974	Evonne Goolagong (Aus)
1975	Chris Evert (USA)
1976	Evonne Cawley (née Goolagong) (Aus)
1977	Chris Evert (USA)
1978-9	Martina Navrátilová (Cs)
1980	Tracy Austin (USA)
1981	Martina Navrátilová (Cs)
1982	Sylvia Hanika (FRG)
1983-5*	Martina Navrátilová (USA)
1986	Martina Navrátilová (USA)
1987	Steffi Graf (FRG)
1988	Gabriela Sabatini (Arg)
1989	Steffi Graf (FRG)
1990-2	Monica Seles (Yug)
1993	Steffi Graf (Ger)
1994	Gabriela Sabatini (Arg)

Doubles

1971	Rosemary Casals & Bille Jean King (USA)
1973	Rosemary Casals (USA) & Margaret Court (Aus)
1974	Rosemary Casals & Billlie Jean King (USA)
1979	Françoise Durr (Fra) & Betty Stove (Hol)
1980	Billie Jean King (USA) & Martina Navrátilová (Cs)
1981	Martina Navrátilová (Cs) & Pam Shriver (USA)
1982	Martina Navrátilová & Pam Shriver (USA)
1984*	Martina Navrátilová & Pam Shriver (USA)
1985*	Hana Mandlíková (Cs) & Wendy Turnbull (Aus)
1986-9	Martina Navrátilová & Pam Shriver (USA)
1990	Kathy Jordan (USA) & Liz Smylie (Aus)
1991	Martina Navrátilová & Pam Shriver (USA)
1992	Arantxa Sánchez (Spa) & Helena Suková (Cs)
1993-4	Gigi Fernandez (USA) & Natalya Zvereva (Bls)

* *played the following year*

World Championship Tennis

World Championship Tennis Incorporated (WCT) was founded in 1967 to promote professional tennis. Following a series of qualifying tournaments a finals tournament was held annually for men from 1971. *Winners:*

1971-2	Ken Rosewall (Aus)
1973	Stan Smith (USA)
1974	John Newcombe (Aus)
1975	Arthur Ashe (USA)
1976	Björn Borg (Swe)
1977	Jimmy Connors (USA)
1978	Vitas Gerulaitas (USA)
1979	John McEnroe (USA)
1980	Jimmy Connors (USA)
1981	John McEnroe (USA)
1982	Ivan Lendl (Cs)
1983-4	John McEnroe (USA)
1985	Ivan Lendl (Cs)
1986	Anders Järryd (Swe)
1987	Miloslav Mecir (Cs)
1988	Boris Becker (FRG)
1989	John McEnroe (USA)

WCT Doubles

Introduced in 1973, winners were:

1973	Bob Lutz & Stan Smith (USA)
1974	Bob Hewitt & Frew McMillan (SAf)
1975	Brian Gottfried (USA) & Raúl Ramirez (Mex)
1976	Wojtek Fibak (Pol) & Tom Okker (Hol)
1977	Vijay Amritraj (Ind) & Dick Stockton (USA)
1978	Wojtek Fibak (Pol) & Tom Okker (Hol)
1979	Peter Fleming & John McEnroe (USA)
1980	Brian Gottfried (USA) & Raúl Ramirez (Mex)
1981	Peter McNamara & Paul McNamee (Aus)
1982-3	Heinz Günthardt (Swi) & Balázs Taróczy (Hun)
1984	Pavel Slozil & Tomás Smid (Cs)
1985	Ken Flach & Robert Seguso (USA)
1986	Heinz Günthardt (Swi) & Balázs Taróczy (Hun)
1986#	Stefan Edberg & Anders Järryd (Swe)
1990	Rick Leach & Jim Pugh (USA)

 # brought forward from January to December

Grand Slam Cup

Introduced in 1990, when it was played in Munich, and contested by the leading players in the Grand Slam events of the previous year. The winner received $2 million, by far the biggest prize ever given to a tennis player, and the runner-up took $1 million. *Winners:*

1990	Pete Sampras (USA)
1991	David Wheaton (USA)
1992	Michael Stich (Ger)
1993	Petr Korda (Cze)
1994	Magnus Larsson (Swe)

ITF World Champions

A panel of former champions decide annually who are the International Tennis Federation's World Champions. *Winners since the inauguration of the award in 1978 have been:*

Men

1978-80	Björn Borg (Swe)
1981	John McEnroe (USA)
1982	Jimmy Connors (USA)
1983-4	John McEnroe (USA)
1985-7	Ivan Lendl (Cs)

1988	Mats Wilander (Swe)
1989	Boris Becker (FRG)
1990	Ivan Lendl (Cs)
1991	Stefan Edberg (Swe)
1992	Jim Courier (USA)
1993-4	Pete Sampras (USA)

Women

1978	Chris Evert (USA)
1979	Martina Navrátilová (Cs)
1980-1	Chris Evert Lloyd (USA)
1982-6	Martina Navrátilová (USA)
1987-90	Steffi Graf (FRG)
1991-2	Monica Seles (Yug)
1993	Steffi Graf (Ger)
1994	Arantxa Sánchez (Spa)

Top Money Winners

Players to have won the most prize money - as at 1 Jun 1995

Men

Ivan Lendl	$20,512,417
Stefan Edberg	18,561,932
Boris Becker	15,997,530
Pete Sampras	12,548,992
John McEnroe	12,239,622
Jim Courier	10,712,263
Andre Agassi	8,723,765
Jimmy Connors	8,513,840
Michael Stich	7,799,555
Mats Wilander	7,687,251
Goran Ivanisovic	7,412,391
Michael Chang	6,598,070

Women - *as at 19 June 1995*

Martina Navrátilová	$20,283,727
Steffi Graf	15,558,230
Arantxa Sánchez Vicario	9,253,498
Chris Evert	8,896,195
Gabriela Sabatini	8,179,202
Monica Seles	7,408,981
Helena Suková	5,343,186
Pam Shriver	5,316,614
Jana Novotná	4,780,455
Conchita Martínez	4,736,131
Natalya Zvereva	4,592,310
Zina Garrison-Jackson	4,385,857

ATP Number One Players

The ATP has produced ranking lists of male tennis players weekly from 23 Aug 1973. Players to have made the number one ranking, with number of weeks there in total as at 1 Jun 1995:

Name	Weeks	Years
Ilie Nastase (Rom)	40	1973-4
John Newcombe (Aus)	8	1974
Jimmy Connors (USA)	268	1974-83
Bjorn Borg (Swe)	109	1977-81
John McEnroe (USA)	170	1980-5
Ivan Lendl (Cs)	270	1983-90
Mats Wilander (Swe)	20	1988-9
Stefan Edberg (Swe)	72	1990-2
Boris Becker (Ger)	12	1991
Jim Courier (USA)	58	1992-3

| Pete Sampras (USA) | 101 | 1993-5 |
| Andre Agassi (USA) | 8+ | 1995 |

Longest span continously at number one

| 29 Jul 74 - 16 Aug 77 | Jimmy Connors (160 weeks) |
| 9 Sep 85 - 5 Sep 88 | Ivan Lendl (157 weeks) |

Professional Tour Records

Men

Most singles titles in career : 109 Jimmy Connors (USA) 1972-89, 94 Ivan Lendl (Cs/USA)

Most singles titles in season: 15 Jimmy Connors 1977, Guillermo Vilas (Arg) 1977, Ivan Lendl (Cs) 1982

Most consecutive match wins: 46 Guillermo Vilas 1977-8

Most doubles titles in career: 78 Tom Okker (Hol) 1968-79, 77 John McEnroe (USA) 1976-92

Most doubles titles in season: 17 John McEnroe 1979

Most career titles (singles & doubles): 154 John McEnroe 1976-92

Highest winnings in a season: $4,857,812 Pete Sampras (USA) 1994

Women

Most singles titles in career: 167 Martina Navratílová (Cs/USA) 1975-94, 157 Chris Evert (USA) 1972-88, 89 Steffi Graf (Ger), 88 Evonne Cawley (Aus)

Most singles titles in year: 16 Martina Navratílová 1983, Chris Evert 1974 and 1975

Most consecutive match wins: 74 Martina Navratílová 1984

Most doubles titles in career: 165 Martina Navratílová (Cs/USA) 1975-94

Most doubles titles by one partnership: 79 Martina Navratílová & Pam Shriver (USA)

Most weeks ranked at no.1: 332 Martina Navratílová

Most consecutive weeks at no.1: 186 Steffi Graf (Ger) 17 Aug 1987 - 10 Mar 1991

Highest winnings in a season: $2,943,665 Arantxa Sánchez (Spa) 1994

Olympic Games

Lawn tennis was included in the Olympic Games from 1896 to 1924 and as a demonstration sport in 1968. Following the staging of an international tournament at the 1984 Games, at which the singles winners were Stefan Edberg (Swe) and Steffi Graf (FRG), tennis was re-introduced to the Olympics in 1988. *Champions:*

Men's singles

1896	John Boland (UK/Ire)
1900	Hugh Doherty (UK)
1904	Beals Wright (USA)
1906	Max Decugis (Fra)
1908 (a)	Josiah Ritchie (UK)
1908 (b)	Arthur Gore (UK)
1912 (a)	Charles Winslow (SAf)
1912 (b)	André Gobert (Fra)
1920	Louis Raymond (SAf)
1924	Vince Richards (USA)
1988	Miloslav Mecir (Cs)
1992	Marc Rosset (Swi)

Men's doubles

1896	John Boland (Ire) & Fritz Traun (Ger)
1900	Reginald & Hugh Doherty (UK)
1904	Beals Wright & Edgar Leonard (USA)
1906	Max Decugis & Maurice Germot (Fra)
1908 (a)	George Hillyard & Reginald Doherty (UK)
1908 (b)	Arthur Gore & Herbert Roper Barrett (UK)
1912 (a)	Charles Winslow & Harold Kitson (SAf)
1912 (b)	André Gobert & Maurice Germot (Fra)
1920	Oswald Turnbull & Max Woosnam (UK)
1924	Vince Richards & Frank Hunter (UK)
1988	Ken Flach & Robert Seguso (USA)
1992	Boris Becker & Michael Stich (Ger)

Women's singles

1900	Charlotte Cooper (UK)
1906	Esmée Simiriotou (Gre)
1908 (a)	Dorothea Lambert Chambers (UK)
1908 (b)	Gwendoline Eastlake-Smith (UK)
1912 (a)	Marguerite Broquedis (Fra)
1912 (b)	Edith Hannam (UK)
1920	Suzanne Lenglen (Fra)
1924	Helen Wills (USA)
1988	Steffi Graf (FRG)
1992	Jennifer Capriatti (USA)

Women's doubles

1920	Winifred McNair & Kathleen McKane (UK)
1924	Hazel Wightman & Helen Wills (USA)
1988	Pam Shriver & Zina Garrison (USA)
1992	Gigi Fernandez & Mary Joe Fernandez (USA)

Mixed doubles

1900	Reginald Doherty & Charlotte Cooper (UK)
1906	Max and Marie Decugis (Fra)
1912 (a)	Heinrich Schomburgk & Dora König (Ger)
1912 (b)	Percy Dixon & Edith Hannam (UK)
1920	Max Decugis & Suzanne Lenglen (Fra)
1924	Norris Williams & Hazel Wightman (USA)

(a) outdoor (b) indoor

Most medals: 6 Max Decugis (Fra) a record 4 gold, 1 silver and 1 bronze 1900-20; 5 Kathleen McKane (UK) 1 gold, 2 silver, 2 bronze, 1920-4

Maiden Names/Married names

	Maiden Name	Married Name
Chris	Evert	Lloyd, now Mill
Mary	Bevis	Hawton
Blanche	Bingley	Hillyard
Molly	Bjurstedt	Mallory
Mary	Carter	Reitano
Charlotte	Cooper	Sterry
Thelma	Coyne	Long
Evonne	Goolagong	Cawley
Helen	Gourlay	Cawley
Karen	Hantze	Susman
Ann	Haydon	Jones
Hazel	Hotchkiss	Wightman
Dorothea	Lambert-Chambers	Douglass
Kathleen	McKane	Godfree
Kerry	Melville	Reid
Billie Jean	Moffitt	King
Sarah	Palfrey	Fabyan, then Cooke

Margaret	Osborne	Du Pont
Vera	Puzejová	Suková
Peggy	Saunders	Michel
Larisa	Savchenko	Neiland
Elizabeth	Sayers	Smyllie
Gail	Sherriff	Chanfreau, then Lovera
Margaret	Smith	Court
Judy	Tegart	Dalton
Helen	Wills	Moody
Nancye	Wynne	Bolton

Trampolining

Trampolining has formed part of circus acts for many years but it only started to attract interest as a sport after the design of trampolines similar to modern day ones, by George Nissen in the United States in 1936. The first official trampolining tournament took place in the United States in 1947. The International Trampoline Federation (FIT) was founded in 1964.

World Championships

Instituted in 1964 they have been held biennially since 1968. *Winners:*

Men's Individual
1964 Danny Millman (USA)
1965 George Irwin (USA)
1966 Wayne Miller (USA)
1967-8 Dave Jacobs (USA)
1970 Wayne Miller (USA)
1972 Paul Luxon (UK)
1974 Richard Tisson (Fra)
1976 Richard Tisson (Fra) & Yevgeniy Yanes (USSR)
1978 Yevgeniy Yanes (USSR)
1980 Stewart Matthews (UK)
1982 Carl Furrer (UK)
1984 Lionel Pioline (Fra)
1986 Lionel Pioline (Fra)
1988 Vadim Krasnochapka (USSR)
1990 Aleksandr Moskalenko (USSR)
1992 Aleksandr Moskalenko (Rus)
1994 Aleksandr Moskalenko (Rus)

Men's synchronised pairs
1965 Gary Irwin & Frank Smith (USA)
1966 Wayne Miller & David Jacobs (USA)
1967 Hartmut Riehler & Kurt Treiter (FRG)
1968 Klaus Forster & Michael Budenberg (FRG)
1970 Don Waters & Gary Smith (USA)
1972 Paul Luxon & Robert Hughes (UK)
1974 Robet Nealy & Jim Cartledge (USA)
1976 Yevgeniy Yakovenko & Yevgeniy Yanes (USSR)
1978 Yevgeniy Yanes & Vladimir Zhadoyev (USSR)
1980 Stewart Matthews & Carl Furrer (UK)
1982 Stuart Ransom & Mark Calderon (USA)
1984 Igor Bogachev & Vadim Krasnochapka (USSR)
1986 Igor Bogachev & Vadim Krasnochapka (USSR)
1988 Igor Bogachev & Vadim Krasnochapka (USSR)
1990 Dmitriy Polyarush & Sergey Nestrelyai (USSR)
1992 Aleksandr Danilchenko & Aleksandr Moskalenko (Rus)
1994 Aleksandr Danilchenko & Aleksandr Moskalenko (Rus)

Men's Team
USSR	1984, 1988, 1990, 1992
France	1982
FR Germany	1986
Belarus	1994

Men's tumbling
1965 Frank Schmitz (USA)
1966 Frank Fortier (USA)
1976 Jim Bertz (USA)
1978 Jim Bertz (USA)
1980 Kevin Eckberg (USA)
1982 Steve Elliott (USA)
1984 Steve Elliott (USA)
1986 Jerry Hardy (USA)
1988 Pascal Eouzan (Fra)
1990 Pascal Eouzan (Fra)
1992 Jon Beck (USA)
1994 Adrian Sienkiewicz (Pol)

Men's double mini trampoline
1976 Ron Merriott (USA)
1978 Stuart Ransom (USA)
1980 Derrick Lotz (SAf)
1982 Brett Austine (Aus)
1984 Brett Austine (Aus)
1986 Brett Austine (Aus)
1988 Adrian Wareham (Aus)
1990 Adrian Wareham (Aus)
1992 Jorge Pereira (Por)
1994 Jorge Pereira (Por)

Men's team tumbling
1990 France
1992 USA
1994 USA

Women's individual
1964-8 Judy Wills (USA)
1970 Renee Ransom (USA)
1972 Alexandra Nicholson (USA)
1974 Alexandra Nicholson (USA)
1976 Svetlana Levina (USSR)
1978 Tatyana Anisimova (USSR)
1980 Ruth Keller (Swi)
1982 Ruth Keller (Swi)
1984 Sue Shotton (UK)
1986 Tatyana Lushina (USSR)
1988 Rusadan Khoperia (USSR)
1990 Yelena Merkulova (USSR)
1992 Yelena Merkulova (Rus)
1994 Irina Karaveyeva (Rus)
Most wins: 5 Wills

Women's synchronised pairs
1966-7 Judy Wills & Nancy Smith (USA)
1968 Ute Czech & Agathe Jarosch (FRG)
1970 Jennifer Liebenberg & Lucia Odendaal (SAf)

1972 Marilyn Stieg & Bobby Grant (USA)
1974 Ute Scheile & Petra Wenzel (FRG)
1976 Svetlana Levina & Olga Starikova (USSR)
1978 Ute Luxon & Ute Scheile (FRG)
1980 Gabriele Bahr & Beate Kruswicki (FRG)
1982 Jacqueline de Ruiter & Marjo van Dierman (Hol)
1984 Kirsty McDonald & Sue Shotton (UK)
1986 Tatyana Lushina & Yelena Merkulova (USSR)
1988 Yelena Kolomeets & Rusadan Khoperia (USSR)
1990 Tatyana Lushina & Yelena Merkulova (USSR)
1992 Andrea Holmes & Lorraine Lyon (UK)
1994 Hiltrud Roewe & Tina Ludwig (Ger)

Women's Team

USSR	1986, 1988, 1990
Great Britain	1984, 1992
FR Germany	1982
Russia	1994

Women's tumbling

1965-6 Judy Wills (USA)
1976   Tracey Long (USA)
1978   Nancy Quattrochi (USA)
1980   Tracy Contour (USA)
1982   Jill Hollembeak (USA)
1984   Jill Hollembeak (USA)
1986   Jill Hollembeak (USA)
1988   Megan Cunningham (USA)
1990   Chrystel Robert (Fra)
1992   Chrystel Robert (Fra)
1994   Chrystel Robert (Fra)

Women's double mini trampoline

1976 Leigh Hennessy (USA)
1978 Leigh Hennessy (USA)
1980 Beth Fairchild (USA)
1982 Christine Tough (Can)
1984 Gabi Dreier (FRG)
1986 Bettina Lehmann (FRG)
1988 Elizabeth Jensen (Aus)
1990 Lisa Neuman-Morris (Aus)
1992 Kylie Walker (NZ)
1994 Kylie Walker (NZ)

Women's team tumbling

1990 Chrystel & Corinne Robert (Fra)
1992 France
1994 France

World Cup

Held annually from 1980, except 1988. *Most titles at each discipline:*

Men's Individual: 3 Carl Furrer (UK) 1980-1, 1983
Women's Individual: 5 Andrea Holmes (UK) 1984-5, 1987, 1991, 1994; 3 Sue Shotton (UK) 1981, 1983, 1986
Men's Synchro: 2 John Hansen & Anders Christiansen (Den) 1982, 1985; Lionel Pioline & Daniel Pean (Fra) 1983-4
Women's Synchro: 3 Gabriel Bahr & Beate Kruswicki (FRG) 1983-5

Triathlon

The triathlon combines long distance swimming, cycling and running. A group of Americans first established the sport in 1974. Their efforts led to the first Hawaii 'Ironman', which was contested by 15 intrepid sportsmen, of whom 12 finished, on 18 Feb 1978. The growth in popularity of the event can be seen from the numbers of contestants in the 'Ironman', from 15 in its first two years to 108 in 1980, 326 in 1981, 580 and 850 in the two held in 1982, to reach 1000 in 1984. After earlier abortive attempts to found a worldwide governing body, L'Union Internationale de Triathlon (UIT) was founded and staged the first official World Championships at Avignon, France on 6 Aug 1989.

World Championships

The first official championships were contested by national teams of five men and five women over the internationally regulated 'Olympic' distances of 1.5km swim (actually the event was held in the river Rhône, and the distance extended to compensate for the flow, but at 2.2km it was overestimated), 40km cycle ride and 10km run. *Winners:*

Men	Individual		Team
1989	Mark Allen (USA)	1:58:46	USA
1990	Greg Welch (Aus)	1:51:37	AUS
1991	Miles Stewart (Aus)	1:48:20	USA
1992	Simon Lessing (UK)	1:49:04	CAN
1993	Spencer Smith (UK)	1:51.20	UK
1994	Spencer Smith (UK)	1:51.04	AUS
Women	*Individual*		*Team*
1989	Erin Baker (NZ)	2:10:01	USA
1990	Karen Smyers (USA)	2:03:33	USA
1991	Jo-Anne Richie (Can)	2:02:04	CAN
1992	Michellie Jones (Aus)	2:02:07	AUS
1993	Michellie Jones (Aus)	2:07:41	AUS
1994	Emma Carney (Aus)	2:03:19	AUS

World Long Distance Championships

First held in 1994.
Distances: 4 km swim, 120km cycle, 32km run

Men

1994	Rob Barel (Hol) 5:59:47	GER

Women

1994	Isabelle Mouthon (Fra) 6:41:50	FRA

Hawaii Ironman

Contestants first swim 2.4 miles (3.8km), then cycle 112 miles (180km) and finally run a full marathon of 26 miles 385 yards (42.195km). The 1978-80 course was in Oahu, from 1981 it has been in Kona, Hawaii. *Winners:*

Men

1978   Gordon Haller (USA) 11:46:58
1979   Tom Warren (USA) 11:15:56
1980   Dave Scott (USA) 9:24:33
1981   John Howard (USA) 9:38:29
1982 (Feb) Scott Tinley (USA) 9:19:41

1982 (Oct) Dave Scott (USA) 9:08:23
1983   Dave Scott (USA) 9:05:57
1984   Dave Scott (USA) 8:54:30
1985   Scott Tinley (USA) 8:50:54
1986   Dave Scott (USA) 8:28:37
1987   Dave Scott (USA) 8:34:13
1988   Scott Molina (USA) 8:31:00
1989   Mark Allen (USA) 8:09:16
1990   Mark Allen (USA) 8:28:17
1991   Mark Allen (USA) 8:18:32
1992   Mark Allen (USA) 8:09:08
1993   Mark Allen (USA) 8:07:45
1994   Greg Welch (Aus) 8:20:27

Women

1979   Lyn Lemaire (USA) 12:55:38
1980   Robin Beck (USA) 11:21:24
1981   Linda Sweeney (USA) 12:00:32
1982 (Feb) Kathleen McCartney (USA) 11:09:40
1982 (Oct) Julie Leach (USA) 10:54:08
1983   Sylviane Puntous (Can) 10:43:36
1984   Sylviane Puntous (Can) 10:25:13
1985   Joanne Ernst (USA) 10:25:22
1986   Paula Newby-Fraser (Zim) 9:49:14*
1987   Erin Baker (NZ) 9:35:25
1988   Paula Newby-Fraser (Zim) 9:01:01
1989   Paula Newby-Fraser (Zim) 9:00:56
1990   Erin Baker (NZ) 9:13:42
1991   Paula Newby-Fraser (Zim) 9:07:52
1992   Paula Newby-Fraser (Zim) 8:55:28
1993   Paula Newby-Fraser (Zim) 8:58:23
1994   Paula Newby-Fraser (Zim) 9:20:14

* *Sylviane Puntous was disqualified after finishing in 9:47:49.*
The fastest times ever recorded over the Ironman distances:
Men: 8:01:32 by Dave Scott (USA) at Lake Biwa, Japan on 30 Jul 1989.
Women: 8:55:00 Paula Newby-Fraser (Zim) at Roth, Germany on 12 Jul 1992.

European Championships

Contested from 1985 over the same distances as in Hawaii. European Championships have subsequently been held at shorter distance categories as well - middle distance: - 2.5km swim, 80km cycle, 20km run; Olympic distance (as for World Championship above).

Men – long distance

1984   Klaus Klaeren (FRG) 6:03:04
1985   Gregor Stam (Hol) 8:56:55
1986   Scott Tinley (USA) 8:27:46
European Magnus Lönnqvist (Fin) 8:40:11
1987   Axel Keonders (Hol) 8:36:22
1988   *Not held*
1989   Axel Koenders (Hol) 8:26:58
1991   Ben van Zelst (Hol) 8:25:30
1992   Jos Everts (Hol) 8:06:12
1993   Philippe Lie (Fra) 10:08:01

Women – long distance

1984   Sarah Springman (UK) 6:56:34
1985   Erin Baker (NZ) 9:26:30

European Sarah Springman (UK) 10:18:53
1986   Erin Baker (NZ) 9:27:36
European Sarah Springman (UK) 9:59:49
1987   Sarah Coope (UK) 9:48:17
1989   Sarah Coope (UK) 9:33:20
1991   Thea Sybesma (Hol) 9:18:04
1992   Paula Newby-Fraser (Zim) 8:55:00
1993   Anne-Marie Rouchon (Fra) 11:37:51

Men – middle distance

1985   Peter Zijerveld (Hol) 4:10:05
1986   Rob Barel (Hol) 3:54:31
1987   Glenn Cook (UK) 3:57:19
1988   Rob Barel (Hol) 3:44:50
1990   Karl Blondeel (Bel) 4:02:25
1992   Glen Cook (UK) 3:37:58
1994   Rob Barel (Hol) 3:48:19

Women – middle distance

1985   Lieve Paulus (Bel) 4:45:19
1986   Sarah Coope (UK) 4:32:13
1987   Sarah Coope (UK) 4:28:38
1988   Sarah Coope (UK) 4:15:42
1990   Isabelle Mouthon (Fra) 4:29:04
1992   Jeannine de Ruysscher (Bel) 4:05:19
1994   Isabelle Mouthon (Fra) 4:17:45

Men – Olympic distance

1985   Rob Barel (Hol) 2:37:42
1986   Rob Barel (Hol) 1:59:50
1987   Rob Barel (Hol) 1:58:12
1988   Rob Barel (Hol) 1:50:23
1989   Yves Cordier (Fra) 2:02:08
1990   Fons Hamblock (Bel) 1:50.29
1991   Simon Lessing (UK) 1:53:25
1992   Spencer Smith (UK) 1:48:37
1993   Simon Lessing (UK) 1:54:04
1994   Simon Lessing (UK) 1:50:38

Women – Olympic distance

1985   Erin Baker (NZ) 2:51.18
European Alexandra Kremer (FRG) 3:06:02
1986   Lieve Paulus (Bel) 2:17:10
1987   Sarah Coope (UK) 2:17:03
1988   Sarah Springman (UK) 2:04:53
1989   Simone Mortier (Fra) 2:16:59
1990   Thea Sybesma (Hol) 2:04:01
1991   Isabelle Mouthon (Fra) 2:07:53
1992   Sonja Krolik (Ger) 2:02:47
1993   Sabine Westhoff (Ger) 2:08:59
1994   Sonja Krolik (Ger) 2:02:51

'World Championship' Triathlon at Nice

Contested annually from 1982 over shorter distances than the 'Ironman': 3.2km swim, 120km cycle, 32km run from 1982-7. In 1988 the swim distance was changed to 4000m. *Winners:*

Men

1982   Mark Allen (USA) 6:33:52
1983   Mark Allen (USA) 6:04:51
1984   Mark Allen (USA) 6:05:23
1985   Mark Allen (USA) 5:53:13
1986   Mark Allen (USA) 5:46:10

1987	Richard Wells (NZ) 5:59:53

1987 Richard Wells (NZ) 5:59:53
1988 Rob Barel (Hol) 6:05:06
1989 Mark Allen (USA) 5:54:31
1990 Mark Allen (USA) 5:50:52
1991 Mark Allen (USA) 5:54:12
1992 Mark Allen (USA) 5:59:43
1993 Mark Allen (USA) 6:05:59

Women
1982 Lyn Brooks (USA) 7:40:44
1983 Linda Buchanan (USA) 7:06:03
1984 Colleen Cannon (USA) 7:05:15
1985 Erin Baker (NZ) 6:37:21
1986 Linda Buchanan (USA) 6:50:56*
1987 Kirsten Hanssen (USA) 6:54:27
1988 Erin Baker (NZ) 6:27:06
1989 Paula Newby-Fraser (Zim) 6:49:43
1990 Paula Newby-Fraser (Zim) 6:36:19
1991 Paula Newby-Fraser (Zim) 6:40:33
1992 Paula Newby-Fraser (Zim) 6:43:41
1993 Isabelle Mouthon (Fra) 6:44:36
* Erin Baker was disqualified after finishing in 6:40:26

World Cup

A worldwide series was first held over 11 events in 1991. *Winners:*

Men
1991 Leandro Macedo BRA
1993 Brad Beven (Aus)

Women
1991 Karen Smyers (USA)
1993 Jo-Anne Richie (Can)

Tug-of-War

The term 'Tug-of-War' is thought to have originated in England in the 19th century. Such a trial of strength and skill, involving two teams of eight pulling against each other on opposite ends of a long, thick rope is believed to be of great antiquity.

The first rules were framed by the New York AC in 1879 and the sport was included in the Olympic Games from 1900 until 1920. In Britain tug-of-war was administered by the Amateur Athletic Association, and championships held in conjunction with the AAAs until 1970, but a separate organisation, the Tug-of-War Association was formed in 1958. The world governing body is the International Tug-of-War Federation.

Olympic Games

Winners:
1900 Sweden/Denmark
1904 Milwaukee AC (USA)
1906 Germany
1908 City Police (UK)
1912 Sweden
1920 Great Britain

World Championships

European Championships for men were first held in 1965, and these were followed by World Championships for men in 1975 and for women in 1986. World Championships are now held biennially. There are categories depending on the total weight of the team. *World champions:*

Men 720 kg
Englan   1975-8, 1980, 1982
Ireland   1984, 1986, 1988, 1990
Switzerland 1985, 1992
Netherlands 1994

Men 680 kg
Switzerland 1990, 1994
Men 640 kg
England   1975-6, 1978, 1980, 1986, 1988
Ireland   1982, 1984, 1990
Switzerland 1985, 1992, 1994

Men 560 kg
Switzerland 1982, 1985, 1990
England   1984, 1988, 1993
Ireland   1986
Spain   1992, 1994

Men Catchweight (no weight specification)
England   1984

Women 520 kg
Sweden   1986, 1988, 1994
Switzerland 1990
Netherlands 1992

Women 560 kg
Sweden   1986, 1988, 1990, 1992, 1994

World Indoor Championships

First held in 1991. *Winners:*

Men 560 kg
England   1991, 1993

Men 600 kg
Spain   1991
Ireland   1993

Men 640 kg
England   1991, 1993

Men 680 kg
England   1991, 1993

Women 480 kg
Spain   1991
Netherlands 1993

Women 520 kg
Netherlands 1991, 1993

Volleyball

The game was invented, originally as 'Mintonette' in 1895 by William G Morgan, director of physical training at the YMCA, Holyoke, Massachussets, USA. His aim was to provide a more recreational, non-contact game than basketball, which had been invented just four years earlier by James Naismith, whom Morgan had met while a student at Springfield YMCA. The number of players per side was fixed at six in 1918.

Volleyball was first played at an international games, at the 1913 Far Eastern Games in Manila, Philippines. The International Volleyball Federation (FIVB) was formed in 1947 and world championships first held in 1949, with the game introduced to the Olympics in 1964. It is now one of the most widely practised game in the world, with 210 members of the FIVB in 1994.

Olympic Games

Held for men and women at all Olympics from 1964.

	Men	**Women**
1964	USSR	Japan
1968	USSR	USSR
1972	Japan	USSR
1976	Poland	Japan
1980	USSR	USSR
1984	USA	China
1988	USA	USSR
1992	Brazil	Cuba

Most medals
Men: 2 gold, 1 bronze Yuriy Poyarkov (USSR) 1964-72 1 gold, 1 silver, 1 bronze Katsutoshi Nekoda (Jap) 1964-72
Women: 2 gold, 2 silver Inna Ryskal (USSR) 1964-76

World Champions

First held 1949, then every four years from 1952.

Men
6	USSR	1949, 1952, 1960, 1962, 1978, 1982
2	Czechoslovakia	1956, 1966
2	Italy	1990, 1994
1	GDR 1970, Poland 1974, USA 1986	

Brian Ivie in action for 1992 bronze medallists USA

Women
5	USSR	1952, 1956, 1960, 1970, 1990
3	Japan	1962, 1967, 1974
2	China	1982, 1986
2	Cuba	1978, 1994

World Cup

Held every four years from 1965 (men) and 1973 (women). *Wins:*

Men
4	USSR	1965, 1977, 1981, 1991
1	GDR 1969, USA 1985, Cuba 1989	

Women
2	China	1981, 1985
2	Cuba	1989, 1991
1	USSR 1973, Japan 1977	

World League

First held in 1990, as an eight-team, two-division, 12-match per team series, culminating in a final. Expanded to 10 countries in 1991. *Winners.*

1990-2	Italy
1993	Brazil
1994	Italy

Women's World Grand Prix

Contested by the world's top eight teams; introduced in 1993. *Winners:*

1993	Cuba
1994	Brazil

European Championships

First held in 1948 for men and 1949 for women. Now held biennially. *Wins:*

Men
12	USSR	1950-1, 1967, 1971, 1975, 1977, 1979, 1981, 1983, 1985, 1987, 1991
3	Czechoslovakia	1948, 1955, 1958
2	Italy	1989, 1993
1	Romania	1963

Women
13	USSR	1949-51, 1958, 1963, 1967, 1971, 1975, 1977, 1979, 1983, 1985, 1989, 1991
1	Czechoslovakia 1955, Bulgaria 1981, GDR 1987	
1	Russia 1993	

Beach Volleyball

In professional beach volleyball teams play two-a-side on the same size court as that used for indoor volleyball. The sport originated in California in the 1940s and grew rapidly in the 1960s. The Association of Volleyball Professionals (AVP) was formed in 1981 and the AVP/Miller Lite tour started that year. Beach volleyball has been added to the Olympic programme for 1996.

Top ranked players on the Miller Lite/AVP Tpur
1990-1 Sinjin Smith and Randy Stoklos (USA)
1992 Karch Kiraly (USA)
1993-4: Karch Kiraly & Kent Steffes (USA)
On the AVP/Miller Lite tour, Sinjin Smith has won a record 139 events 1977-95 and Karch Kiraly has earned a career record $1,784,974 to June 1995.

Water Polo

Played by teams of 7-a-side (from squads of 11). Originally known as 'football in the water' it was developed in Britain from 1869. The first rules were drafted in 1876 and the sport was first given official recognition by the Amateur Swimming Association in Great Britain in 1885. It has been an Olympic event since 1900, and came under the aegis of FINA after swimming's governing body was founded in 1908. The first women's international competition was in 1978. Governed by FINA (see swimming).

Olympic Games

The first two winning teams were club sides: Osborne Swimming Club, Manchester, representing Great Britain in 1900 and New York AC in 1904. *Wins:*

6	Hungary	1932, 1936, 1952, 1956, 1964, 1976
4	Great Britain	1900, 1908, 1912, 1920
3	Yugoslavia	1968, 1984, 1988
3	Italy	1948, 1960, 1992
2	USSR	1972, 1980
1	USA (New York AC) 1904, France 1924	
1	Germany	1928

Individuals to have won three gold medals

George Wilkinson (UK) 1900-12, Paul Radmilovic & Charles Smith (UK) 1908-20, Deszö Gyarmati & György Kárpáti (Hun) 1952-64. Gyarmati won most medals, adding silver in 1948 and bronze in 1960.

World Championships

First held at the world swimming championships in 1973. Held separately in 1991. *Winners:*

Men
1973 Hungary
1975 USSR
1978 Italy
1982 USSR
1986 Yugoslavia
1991 Yugoslavia
1994 Italy

Women
1986 Australia
1991 Netherlands
1994 Hungary

FINA World Cup

First held in 1979. *Winners:*

Men
1979 Hungary
1981 USSR
1983 USSR
1985 FR Germany
1987 Yugoslavia
1989 Yugoslavia
1991 USA
1993 Italy

Women (unofficial until 1989)
1979 USA
1981 Canada
1988 Netherlands
1989 Netherlands
1991 Netherlands
1993 Netherlands

European Champions

Men
10	Hungary	1926-7, 1931, 1934, 1938, 1954, 1958, 1962, 1974, 1977
5	USSR	1966, 1970, 1983, 1985, 1987
2	FR Germany	1981, 1989
2	Italy	1947, 1993
1	Netherlands	1950
1	Yugoslavia	1991

Women
3	Netherlands	1985, 1987, 1989, 1993
1	Hungary	1991

Water Skiing

Water-skiing, as practised today, was pioneered in the 1920s, particularly by Ralph Samuelson on Lake Pepin, Minnesota, USA. The sport's origins, however, can be traced back hundreds of years through people walking on planks and aquaplaning. The development of the motor boat to tow skiers was clearly the key factor in the sport's growth.

The world governing body is the International Water Ski Federation (IWSF), formerly the World Water Ski Union (WWSU), first formed as the Union Internationale de Ski Nautique in Geneva in 1946. World championships were instituted in 1949. Membership of the IWSF reached 76 nations in 1992.

World Championships

First held at Juan Les Pins, France in 1949 and now staged biennially. *Winners:*

Men's Overall
1949 Christian Jourdan (Fra) &
      Guy de Clercq (Bel)
1950 Dick Pope Jr (USA)
1953 Alfredo Mendoza (USA)
1955 Alfredo Mendoza (USA)
1957 Joe Cash (USA)
1959 Chuck Stearns (USA)
1961 Bruno Zaccardi (Ita)
1963 Billy Spencer (USA)
1965 Roland Hillier (USA)
1967 Mike Suyderhoud (USA)
1969 Mike Suyderhoud (USA)
1971 George Athans (Can)
1973 George Athans (Can)
1975 Carlos Suarez (Ven)
1977 Mike Hazelwood (UK)
1979 Joel McClintock (Can)
1981 Sammy Duvall (USA)

1983 Sammy Duvall (USA)   1987 Sammy Duvall (USA)   1991 Patrice Martin (Fra)
1985 Sammy Duvall (USA)   1989 Patrice Martin (Fra)   1993 Patrice Martin (Fra)

	Men's Slalom	Men's Tricks	Men's Jumping
1949	Christian Jourdan (Fra)	Pierre Gouin (Fra)	Guy de Clercq (Bel)
1950	Dick Pope Jr (USA)	Jack Andresen (USA)	Guy de Clercq (Bel)
1953	Charles Blackwell (Can)	Warren Witherall (USA)	Alfredo Mendoza (USA)
1955	Alfredo Mendoza (USA)	Scotty Scott (USA)	Alfredo Mendoza (USA)
1957	Joe Cash (USA)	Mike Amsbury (USA)	Joe Mueller (USA)
1959	Chuck Stearns (USA)	Philippe Logut (Fra)	Buster McCalla (USA)
1961	Jimmy Jackson (USA)	Jean Marie Muller (Fra)	Larry Penacho (USA)
1963	Billy Spencer (USA)	Billy Spencer (USA)	Jimmy Jackson (USA)
1965	Roland Hillier (USA)	Ken White (USA)	Larry Penacho (USA)
1967	Tito Antunano (Mex)	Alan Kempton (USA)	Alan Kempton (USA)
1969	Victor Palomo (Spa)	Bruce Cockburn (Aus)	Wayne Grimditch (USA)
1971	Mike Suyderhoud (USA)	Ricky McCormick (USA)	Mike Suyderhoud (USA)
1973	George Athans (Can)	Wayne Grimditch (USA)	Ricky McCormick (USA)
1975	Roby Zucchi (Ita)	Wayne Grimditch (USA)	Ricky McCormick (USA)
1977	Bob LaPoint (USA)	Carlos Suarez (Ven)	Mike Suyderhoud (USA)
1979	Bob LaPoint (USA)	Patrice Martin (Fra)	Mike Hazelwood (UK)
1981	Andy Mapple (UK)	Cory Pickos (USA)	Mike Hazelwood (UK)
1983	Bob LaPoint (USA)	Cory Pickos (USA)	Sammy Duvall (USA)
1985	Bob LaPoint (USA)	Patrice Martin (Fra)	Geoff Carrington (Aus)
1987	Bob LaPoint (USA)	Patrice Martin (Fra)	Sammy Duvall (USA)
1989	Andy Mapple (UK)	Aymeric Benet (Fra)	Geoff Carrington (USA)
1991	Lucky Lowe (USA)	Patrice Martin (Fra)	Bruce Neville (Aus)
1993	Glen Thurley (Aus)	Tory Baggiano (USA)	Andrea Alessi (Ita)

Women's Overall

1949 Willa Worthington (USA)	1963 Jeanette Brown (USA)	1981 Karin Roberge (USA)	
1950 Willa McGuire* (USA)	1965 Liz Allan (USA)	1983 Ana Maria Carrasco (Ven)	
1953 Leah Marie Rawls (USA)	1967 Jeanette Stewart-Wood (UK)	1985 Karen Neville (Aus)	
1955 Willa McGuire (USA)	1969 Liz Allan (USA)	1987 Deena Brush (USA)	
1957 Marina Doria (Swi)	1971 Christy Weir (USA)	1989 Deena Mapple (née Brush) (USA)	
1959 Vickie Van Hook (USA)	1973 Lisa St John (USA)	1991 Karen Neville (Aus)	
1961 Sylvie Hulsemann (Lux)	1975 Liz Shetter (née Allan) (USA)	1993 Natalya Rumyantseva (Rus)	
	1977 Cindy Todd (USA)		
	1979 Cindy Todd (USA)		

	Women's Slalom	Women's Tricks	Women's Jumping
1949	Willa Worthington (USA)	Madeleine Boutellier (Fra)	Willa Worthington (USA)
1950	Evie Wolford (USA)	Willa McGuire* (USA)	Johnette Kirkpatrick (USA)
1953	Evie Wolford (USA)	Leah Marie Rawls (USA)	Sandra Swaney (USA)
1955	Willa McGuire (USA)	Marina Doria (Swi)	Willa McGuire (USA)
1957	Marina Doria (Swi)	Marina Doria (Swi)	Nancie Rideout (USA)
1959	Vickie Van Hook (USA)	Piera Castelvetri (Ita)	Nancie Rideout (USA)
1961	Janelle Kirkley (USA)	Sylvie Hulsemann (Lux)	Renate Hansluvka (Aut)
1963	Jeanette Brown (USA)	Guyonne Dalle (Fra)	Renate Hansluvka (Aut)
1965	Barbara Cooper-Clack (USA)	Dany Duflot (Fra)	Liz Allan (USA)
1967	Liz Allan (USA)	Dany Duflot (Fra)	Jeanette Stewart-Wood (UK)
1969	Liz Allan (USA)	Liz Allan (USA)	Liz Allan (USA)
1971	Christy Freeman (USA)	Willi Stahle (Hol)	Christy Weir (USA)
1973	Sylvie Maurial (Fra)	Maria Victoria Carrasco (Ven)	Liz Shetter (née Allan) (USA)
1975	Liz Shetter (USA)	Maria Victoria Carrasco (Ven)	Liz Shetter (USA)
1977	Cindy Todd (USA)	Maria Victoria Carrasco (Ven)	Linda Giddens (USA)
1979	Pattsie Messner (USA)	Natalya Rumyantseva (USSR)	Cindy Todd (USA)
1981	Cindy Todd (USA)	Ana Maria Carrasco (Ven)	Deena Brush (USA)
1983	Cindy Todd (USA)	Natalya Ponomaryeva (USSR)*	Cindy Todd (USA)
1985	Camille Duvall (USA)	Judy McClintock (Can)	Deena Brush (USA)

1987	Kim Laskoff (USA)	Natalya Rumyantseva (USSR)	Deena Brush (USA)
1989	Kim Laskoff (USA)	Tawn Larsen (USA)	Deena Mapple (née Brush) (USA)
1991	Helena Kjellander (Swe)	Tawn Larsen (USA)	Sheri Stone (USA)
1993	Helena Kjellander (Swe)	Britt Larsen (USA)	Kim De Macedo (Can)

* McGuire née Worthington, Ponomaryeva née Rumyantseva

Most wins

Overall: Men: 4 Duvall; Women 3 Willa Worthington/McGuire, Allan/ Shetter
Individual and overall: Men: 7 Martin, 6 Duvall, 5 LaPoint, Suyderhoud; Women: 11 Allan/ Shetter, 8 Worthington/McGuire, 7 Todd, 6 Brush/Mapple
Liz Allan is the only water skier to win all four titles in one year, 1969.
Team: Title won by the USA at all 17 championships 1957-89, Canada 1991, 1993

European Champions

Held annually since 1947. *Overall champions:*

Men

1947	Claude de Clercq (Bel)
1948	Jean-Pierre Mussat (Fra)
1949	Christian Jourdan (Fra) & Guy de Clercq (Bel)
1950-2	Claude de Clercq (Bel)
1953	Guy Vermeersch (Bel)
1954	Marc Flachard (Fra)
1955	Simon Khoury (Leb)
1956	Franco Carraro (Ita)
1957-8	Jean Marie Muller (Fra)
1959-61	Bruno Zaccardi (Ita)
1962-3	Maxime Vazeille (Fra)
1964	Mario Pozzini (Ita)
1965	Jean-Jacques Pottier (Fra)
1966	Bruno Zaccardi (Ita)
1967	Jean Michel Jamin (Fra)
1968	Roby Zucchi (Ita)
1969	Jean-Yves Parpette
1970-1	Roby Zucchi (Ita)
1972	Paul Seaton (UK)
1973	Lars Björk (Swe)
1974-5	Paul Seaton (UK)
1976-7	Mike Hazelwood (UK)
1978-83	Mike Hazelwood (UK)
1984-5	Patrice Martin (Fra)
1986	Mike Hazelwood (UK)
1987-91	Andrea Alessi (Ita)
1992-3	Patrice Martin (Fra)
1994	Patrick Wehner (Ger)

Deena Brush, now married to Andy Mapple

Women

1947	Maggy Savard (Fra)
1950	Monique Girod (Swz)
1951-2	Jacqueline Marcour (Fra)
1953-6	Marina Doria (Swi)
1957	Jacqueline Keller (Fra)
1958-60	Piera Castelvetri (Ita)
1961	Sylvie Hulsemann (Lux)
1962-3	Renate Hansluvka (Aut)
1964	Dany Duflot (Fra)]
1965	Renate Hansluvka (Aut)
1966	Sylvie Hulsemann (Lux)
1967	Jeanette Stewart-Wood (UK)
1968	Sylvie Hulsemann (Lux)
1969	Eliane Borter (Swz)
1970-1	Sylvie Maurial (Fra)
1972	Willi Stahle (Hol)
1973	Sylvie Maurial (Fra)
1974-5	Willi Stahle (Hol)
1976-7	Chantal Escot-Amade (Fra)
1978-9	Anita Carlman (Swe)
1980	Marlon van Dijk (Hol)
1981	Anita Carlman (Swe)
1982	Natalya Rumyantseva (USSR)
1983	Anita Carlman (Swe)
1984	Natalya Ponomaryeva (née Rumyantseva) (USSR)

1985	Helena Kjellander (Swe)
1986	Philippa Roberts (UK)
1987	Natalya Rumyantseva (USSR)
1988	Helena Kjellander (Swe)
1989	Natalya Rumyantseva (USSR)
1990	Philippa Roberts (UK)
1991	Olga Pavlova (USSR)
1992-3	Natalya Rumyantseva (Rus)
1994	Jacqueline Pfeiffer (Swi)

Most wins
Men: 9 Hazelwood, 5 Alessi, 4 de Clercq, Zaccardi
Women: 6 Rumyantseva, 4 Doria, Carlman

World Cup

For men's teams, first held 1980. *Wins:*

2	Great Britain	1980, 1984
2	USA	1982, 1986
1	France	1988

European Cup

For men's teams, first held 1980. *Wins:*

4	Great Britain	1983, 1987-9, 1991
2	Italy	1980, 1986
2	Sweden	1984-5
1	France	1982
1	USSR	1991

World Records

Men

Slalom	4 buoys on a 10.25m line Andy Mapple (UK), Charleston, South Carolina, USA 4 Sep 1994
Tricks	11,590 Aymeric Benet (Fra), West Palm Baech, Florida 30 Oct 1994
Jump	63.3m Sammy Duval (USA) Shreveport, Louisiana, USA 24 Jul 1992

Women

Slalom	2.25 buoys on a 10.75m line Susi Graham (Can), Santa Rosa, Florida, 25 Sep 1994
Tricks	8580 points Tawn Larsen (USA), Groveland, Florida, USA 4 Jul 1992
Jump	47.5m Deena Mapple (USA) Charlotte, N Carolina, USA 9 Jul 1988

World Barefoot Water Skiing Championships

The first person reported to water ski barefoot was Dick Pope Jr in Florida in 1947. World barefoot championships, which have been dominated by Australians, were first held in 1978; events are wake slalom, tricks, start methods (not in 1988) and jump. *Overall winners:*

Year	Men	Women
1978	Brett Wing (Aus)	Colleen Wilkinson (Aus)
1980	Brett Wing (Aus)	Kim Lampard (Aus)
1982	Brett Wing (Aus)	Kim Lampard (Aus)
1985	Mike Seipel (USA)	Kim Lampard (Aus)
1986	Mike Seipel (USA)	Kim Lampard (Aus)
1988	Rick Powell (USA)	Lori Powell (USA)
1990	Rick Powell (USA)	Jennifer Calleri (USA)
1992	Ron Scarpa (USA)	Jennifer Calleri (USA)
1994	John Penney (Aus)	Jennifer Calleri (USA)

Brett Wing won all five titles in 1980.
Team: Championship won by Australia on all five occasions 1978-86 and USA four times 1988-94.

Barefoot world jump records
Men   27.5m Richard Mainwaring (UK) 1994
Women 16.6m Sharon Stekelenburg (Aus) 1991

World Ski Racing championships

Individual winners

Year	Men	Women
1979	Wayne Ritchie (Aus)	Bronwyn Wright (Aus)
1981	Danny Bartels (Bel)	Liz Hobbs (UK)
1984	Danny Bartels (Bel)	Liz Hobbs (UK)
1985	Mark Pickering (Aus)	Debbie Nordblad (USA)
1988	Stephen Moore (UK)	Tanya Williams (Aus)
1989	Ian Dipple (Aus)	Marsha Fitzgerald (USA)
1991	Paul Robertson (Aus)	Debbie Nordblad (USA)
1993	Kirk Book (USA)	Leanne Brown (Aus)

Team

5	USA	1979, 1984, 1988, 1989, 1993
4	Australia	1979, 1981, 1985, 1991

In 1986 Stephen Moore (UK) won the inaugural ski racing World Cup, winning all three races. The World Cup and the World Championships now take place in alternate years.

Speed Records

The fastest speed recorded on water skis is 230.26 km/h by Christopher Massey (Aus) on the Hawkesbury River, New South Wales, Australia in 1983.
The official barefoot speed record over a quarter-mile course is 192.08 km/h by Scott Pelaton (USA) at Chowchilla, California, USA in 1983. The fastest by a woman is 118.56 km/h by Karen Toms (Aus) on the Hawkesbury River, Salisbury, New South Wales in 1984.

Weightlifting

Strength testing by lifting heavy weights is an ancient sport and competitions for lifting weights of stone were included in the ancient Olympic Games. Just five years after a world championship competition was held in 1891, weightlifting was included in the first of the modern Olympic Games. The events were for one-arm and two-arm lifts. During the couple of centuries preceding that, professional strongmen had demonstrated awesome feats of strength, but some of the advertised weights may be doubted.

Modern weightlifting, as included on the Olympic programme, is a combination of strength and skill. There are two standard lifts: the snatch, which is a one-movement lift from the floor to an extended arm position above the head; and the jerk, which is a two movement lift, the clean from floor to shoulders, and then the jerk itself from the shoulders to a fully extended arm position above the head. Competitors have up to three attempts at each weight, and three referees determine whether lifts are correct. Until 1972 the press was also included as a standard lift, but it was then dropped due to the difficulties involved in judging it. There are ten bodyweight categories for lifters.

The world governing body, the International Weightlifting Federation (IWF), with 157 member nations in 1994, was formed in 1920 as the Fédération Haltérophile Internationale.

World and Olympic Champions

Although the IWF first ran world championships at Tallinn, Estonia in 1922, they have subsequently recognised 18 championships held from those in Vienna, Austria in 1898 to 1920. Championships were held again in 1923, but not again until 1937 and 1938. They have been held annually from 1946 (except for 1967), with the Olympic Games recognised as the official championships during those years.

Olympic Games weightlifting was contested at one-hand jerk and two-hand jerk with no weight categories in 1896, 1904 and 1906. Weight categories were introduced at the 1920 Olympic Games and have expanded over the years. From 1920 to 1946 there were five: 60kg, 67.5kg, 75kg, 82.5kg, over 82.5kg. Further additions were: 56kg 1947, 90kg 1951, 52kg and 110kg 1969, 100kg 1977, with the super-heavyweights now over 110kg. The heavyweight class was thus over 82.5kg until 1950, over 90kg until 1968, and at the 110kg limit when the super-heavyweight class was introduced in 1969.

New weight categories were introduced on 1 Jan 1993, and a fresh start made for world records - felt to be appropriate in order to distance the sport from accusations of drug taking by participants in the past. These are:

Men - 54kg,, 59kg, 64kg, 70kg, 76kg, 83kg, 91kg, 99kg, 108kg, over 108kg
Women - 46kg, 50kg, 54kg, 59kg, 64kg, 70kg, 76kg, 83kg, over 83kg

At the 1920 Olympics three lifts were totalled, with one-hand snatch added to the one- and two-handed jerk. In 1924 two additional lifts were added, two-hands press and snatch. From 1928 to 1972 the results were decided on the aggregate of press, snatch and jerk, and from the 1973 World Championships on snatch and jerk.

Most World and Olympic (*) titles 1896-1924
6 Josef Grafl (Aut) 67.5+kg 1910; 80+kg 1908-11, 1913
4 Josef Steinbach (Aut) overall 1904, 1905, 80kg+ 1905; one-hand jerk 1906*
4 Leopold Hennermüller (Aut) 67.5kg 1910, 80kg 1911 (twice), 1913
4 Emil Kliment (Aut) 60kg 1910, 1911 (twice), 1913

World and Olympic Champions (*) from 1928
Olympic Games 1964 to 1984 also recognised as World Championships; 1988 was not.
Totals are shown in kilograms; 1928-72 three lifts, since 1973 two lifts.

52kg Formerly Flyweight
1969 Vladimir Krishchisin (USSR) 337.5
1970 Sandor Holczreiter (Hun) 342.5
1971 Zygmunt Smalcerz (Pol) 340
1972* Zygmunt Smalcerz (Pol) 337.5

1973 Mohammed Nassiri (Irn) 240
1974 Mohammed Nassiri (Irn) 232.5
1975 Zygmunt Smalcerz (Pol) 237.5
1976* Aleksandr Voronin (USSR) 242.5
1977 Aleksandr Voronin (USSR) 247.5
1978 Kanybek Osmonalyev (USSR) 240
1979 Kanybek Osmonalyev (USSR) 242.5
1980* Kanybek Osmonalyev (USSR) 245
1981 Kanybek Osmonalyev (USSR) 247.5
1982 Stefan Leletko (Pol) 250
1983 Neno Terziiski (Bul) 260
1984* Zeng Guoqiang (Chn) 235
1985 Sevdalin Marinov (Bul) 252.5
1986 Sevdalin Marinov (Bul) 257.5
1987 Sevdalin Marinov (Bul) 262.5
1988* Sevdalin Marinov (Bul) 270
1989 Ivan Ivanov (Bul) 272.5
1990 Ivan Ivanov (Bul) 265
1991 Ivan Ivanov (Bul) 272.5
1992* Ivan Ivanov (Bul) 265

54kg
1993 Ivan Ivanov (Bul) 277.5
1994 Halil Mutlu (Tur) 290

56kg Formerly Bantamweight
1947 Joseph de Pietro (USA) 300
1948* Joseph de Pietro (USA) 307.5
1949 Mahmoud Namdjou (Irn) 315
1950 Mahmoud Namdjou (Irn) 310
1951 Mahmoud Namdjou (Irn) 317.5
1952* Ivan Udodov (USSR) 315
1953 Ivan Udodov (USSR) 315
1954 Bakir Farhutdinov (USSR) 315
1955 Vladimir Stogov (USSR) 335
1956* Charles Vinci (USA) 342.5
1957 Vladimir Stogov (USSR) 345
1958 Vladimir Stogov (USSR) 342.5
1959 Vladimir Stogov (USSR) 332.5
1960* Charles Vinci (USA) 345
1961 Vladimir Stogov (USSR) 345
1962 Yoshinobu Miyake (Jap) 352.5
1963 Aleksey Vakhonin (USSR) 345
1964* Aleksey Vakhonin (USSR) 357.5
1965 Imre Földi (Hun) 360
1966 Aleksey Vakhonin (USSR) 362.5
1968* Mohammad Nassiri (Irn) 367.5
1969 Mohammed Nassiri (Irn) 360
1970 Mohammed Nassiri (Irn) 362.5
1971 Gennadiy Chetin (USSR) 370
1972* Imre Földi (Hun) 377.5
1973 Atanas Kirov (USSR) 257.5
1974 Atanas Kirov (USSR) 255
1975 Atanas Kirov (USSR) 255
1976* Norair Nurikyan (Bul) 262.5
1977 Jiro Hosotani (Jap) 252.5
1978 Daniel Nunez (Cub) 260
1979 Anton Kodiabashev (Bul) 267.5
1980* Daniel Nunez (Cub) 275
1981 Anton Kodiabashev (Bul) 272.5
1982 Anton Kodiabashev (Bul) 280
1983 Oksen Mirzoyan (USSR) 292.5

1984* Wu Shude (Chn) 267.5
1985 Neno Terziiski (Bul) 280
1986 Mitko Grablev (Bul) 290
1987 Neno Terziiski (Bul) 287.5
1988* Oksen Mirzoyan (USSR) 292.5
(Mitko Grablev (Bul) 297.5 disqualified after positive drugs test)
1989 Hafiz Suleimanov (USSR) 287.5
1990 Liu Shoubin (Chn) 285
1991 Chun Byung-kwan (SKo) 295
1992* Chun Byung-kwan (SKo) 287.5

54kg
1993 Nikolay Peshalov (Bul) 305
1994 Nikolay Peshalov (Bul) 302.5

60kg Formerly featherweight
1928* Franz Andrysek (Aut) 287.5
1932* Raymond Suvigny (Fra) 287.5
1936* Anthony Terlazzo (USA) 312.5
1937 Georg Liebsch (Ger) 297.5
1938 Georg Liebsch (Ger) 305
1946 Arvid Andersson (Swe) 320
1947 Robert Higgins (USA) 310
1948* Mahmoud Fayad (Egy) 332.5
1949 Mahmoud Fayad (Egy) 332.5
1950 Mahmoud Fayad (Egy) 327.5
1951 Sayed Gouda (Egy) 310
1952* Rafael Chimiskyan (USSR) 337.5
1953 Nikolay Saksonov (USSR) 337.5
1954 Rafael Chimiskyan (USSR) 350
1955 Rafael Chimiskyan (USSR) 350
1956* Isaac Berger (USA) 352.5
1957 Yevgeniy Minayev (USSR) 362.5
1958 Isaac Berger (USA) 372.5
1959 Marian Zielinski (Pol) 365
1960* Yevgeniy Minayev (USSR) 372.5
1961 Isaac Berger (USA) 367.5
1962 Yevgeniy Minayev (USSR) 362.5
1963 Yoshinobu Miyake (Jap) 375
1964* Yoshinobu Miyake (Jap) 397.5
1965 Yoshinobu Miyake (Jap) 385
1966 Yoshinobu Miyake (Jap) 387.5
1968* Yoshinobu Miyake (Jap) 392.5
1969 Yoshiyuki Miyake (Jap) 385
1970 Mieczyslaw Nowak (Pol) 392.5
1971 Yoshiyuki Miyake (Jap) 387.5
1972* Norair Nurikyan (Bul) 402.5
1973 Dito Shanidze (USSR) 272.5
1974 Georgi Todorov (Bul) 280
1975 Georgi Todorov (Bul) 285
1976* Nikolay Kolesnikov (USSR) 285
1977 Nikolay Kolesnikov (USSR) 280
1978 Nikolay Kolesnikov (USSR) 270
1979 Marek Severyn (USSR) 290
1980* Viktor Mazin (USSR) 290
1981 Beloslav Manolov (Bul) 302.5
1982 Yurik Sarkisyan (USSR) 302.5
1983 Yurik Sarkisyan (USSR) 312.5
1984* Chen Weiqiang (Chn) 282.5
1985 Neum Shalamanov (Bul) 322.5
1986 Neum Shalamanov (Bul) 335

1987 Stefan Topurov (Bul) 315
1988* Naim Suleymanoglü # (Tur) 342.5
1989 Naim Suleymanoglü (Tur) 317.5
1990 Nikolai Peshalov (Bul) 297.5
1991 Naim Suleymanoglü (Tur) 310
1992* Naim Suleymanoglü (Tur) 320
 # formerly Naim Suleimanov or Neum Shalamanov

64kg
1993 Naim Suleymanoglü (Tur) 322.5
1994 Naim Suleymanoglü (Tur) 330

67.5kg Formerly Lightweight
1928* Kurt Helbig (Ger) 322.5
    & Hans Haas (Aut) 322.5
1932* René Duverger (Fra) 325
1936* Anwar Mohammed Mesbah (Egy) 342.5
    & Robert Fein (Aut) 342.5
1937 Anthony Terlazzo (USA) 357.5
1938 Anthony Terlazzo (USA) 350
1946 Stanley Stanczyk (USA) 367.5
1947 Peter George (USA) 352.5
1948* Ibrahim Shams (Egy) 360
1949 Ibrahim Shams (Egy) 352.5
1950 Joseph Pitman (USA) 352.5
1951 Ibrahim Shams (Egy) 342.5
1952* Tommy Kono (USA) 362.5
1953 Peter George (USA) 370
1954 Dmitriy Ivanov (USSR) 367.5
1955 Nikolay Kostilyev (USSR) 382.5
1956* Igor Rybak (USSR) 380
1957 Viktor Bushuyev (USSR) 380
1958 Viktor Bushuyev (USSR) 390
1959 Viktor Bushuyev (USSR) 385
1960* Viktor Bushuyev (USSR) 397.5
1961 Waldemar Baszanowski (Pol) 402.5
1962 Vladimir Kaplunov (USSR) 415
1963 Marian Zielinski (Pol) 417.5
1964* Waldemar Baszanowski (Pol) 432.5
1965 Waldemar Baszanowski (Pol) 427.5
1966 Yevgeniy Katsura (USSR) 437.5
1968* Waldemar Baszanowski (Pol) 437.5
1969 Waldemar Baszanowski (Pol) 445
1970 Zbigniew Kaczmarek (Pol) 440
1971 Zbigniew Kaczmarek (Pol) 440
1972* Mukharbi Kirzhinov (USSR) 460
1973 Mukharbi Kirzhinov (USSR) 305
1974 Pyotr Korol (USSR) 305
1975 Pyotr Korol (USSR) 312.5
1976* Pyotr Korol (USSR) 305
1977 Roberto Urrutia (Cub) 315
1978 Yanko Rusev (Bul) 310
1979 Yanko Rusev (Bul) 332.5
1980* Yanko Rusev (Bul) 342.5
1981 Joachim Kunz (GDR) 340
1982 Piotr Mandra (Pol) 325
1983 Joachim Kunz (GDR) 340
1984* Yao Jingyuan (Chn) 320
1985 Mikhail Petrov (Bul) 335
1986 Mikhail Petrov (Bul) 342.5
1987 Mikhail Petrov (Bul) 350

1988* Joachim Kunz (GDR) 340
  (Angel Guenchev (Bul) 362.5 disqualified after positive drugs test)
1989 Israil Militosian (USSR) 347.5
1990 Kim Myong-nam (NKo) 342.5
1991 Yoto Yotov (Bul) 345
1992* Israil Militosian (CIS/Arm) 337.5

70kg
1993 Yoto Yotov (Bul) 342.5
1994 Fedail Guler (Tur) 350

75kg Formerly Middleweight
1928* Roger Francois (Fra) 335
1932* Rudolf Ismayr (Ger) 345
1936* Khadr El Touni (Egy) 387.5
1937 John Terpak (USA) 352.5
1938 Adolf Wagner (Ger) 367.5
1946 Khadr El Touni (Egy) 377.5
1947 Stanley Stanczyk (USA) 405
1948* Frank Spellman (USA) 390
1949 Khadr El Touni (Egy) 397.5
1950 Khadr El Touni (Egy) 400
1951 Peter George (USA) 395
1952* Peter George (USA) 400
1953 Tommy Kono (USA) 407.5
1954 Peter George (USA) 405
1955 Peter George (USA) 405
1956* Fyodor Bogdanovskiy (USSR) 420
1957 Tommy Kono (USA) 420
1958 Tommy Kono (USA) 430
1959 Tommy Kono (USA) 425
1960* Aleksandr Kurinov (USSR) 437.5
1961 Aleksandr Kurinov (USSR) 435
1962 Aleksandr Kurinov (USSR) 422.5
1963 Aleksandr Kurinov (USSR) 437.5
1964* Hans Zdrazila (Cs) 445
1965 Viktor Kurentsov (USSR) 437.5
1966 Viktor Kurentsov (USSR) 450
1968* Viktor Kurentsov (USSR) 475
1969 Viktor Kurentsov (USSR) 467.5
1970 Viktor Kurentsov (USSR) 462.5
1971 Vladimir Kanygin (USSR) 477.5
1972* Yordan Bikov (Bul) 485
1973 Nedelcho Kolev (Bul) 337.5
1974 Nedelcho Kolev (Bul) 335
1975 Peter Wenzel (GDR) 335
1976* Yordan Mitkov (Bul) 335
1977 Yurik Vardanyan (USSR) 345
1978 Roberto Urrutia (Cub) 347.5
1979 Roberto Urrutia (Cub) 345
1980* Asen Zlatev (Bul) 360
1981 Yanko Rusev (Bul) 360
1982 Yanko Rusev (Bul) 365
1983 Alexander Varbanov (Bul) 370
1984* Karl-Heinz Radschinsky (FRG) 340
1985 Alexander Varbanov (Bul) 370
1986 Alexander Varbanov (Bul) 377.5
1987 Borislav Guidikov (Bul) 375
1988* Borislav Guidikov (Bul) 375
1989 Altjamurat Orazdurdyev (USSR) 362.5
1990 Fyodor Kassapu (USSR) 360

1991 Pablo Lara (Cub) 355
1992* Fyodor Kassapu (CIS/Mol) 357.5

76kg
1993 Altjamurat Orazdurdyev (Tkm) 362.5
1994 Pablo Lara (Cub) 365

82.5kg Formerly Light-Heavyweight
1928* Said Nosseir (Egy) 355
1932* Louis Hostin (Fra) 372.5
1936* Louis Hostin (Fra) 372.5
1937 Fritz Haller (Aut) 375
1938 John Davis (USA) 387.5
1946 Grigoriy Novak (USSR) 425
1947 John Terpak (USA) 387.5
1948* Stanley Stanczyk (USA) 417.5
1949 Stanley Stanczyk (USA) 412.5
1950 Stanley Stanczyk (USA) 420
1951 Stanley Stanczyk (USA) 402.5
1952* Trofim Lomakin (USSR) 417.5
1953 Arkadiy Vorobyev (USSR) 430
1954 Tommy Kono (USA) 435
1955 Tommy Kono (USA) 435
1956* Tommy Kono (USA) 447.5
1957 Trofim Lomakin (USSR) 450
1958 Trofim Lomakin (USSR) 440
1959 Rudolf Plyukfelder (USSR) 457.5
1960* Ireneusz Palinski (Pol) 442.5
1961 Rudolf Plyukfelder (USSR) 450
1962 Gyözö Veres (Hun) 460
1963 Gyözö Veres (Hun) 477.5
1964* Rudolf Plyukfelder (USSR) 475
1965 Norbert Osimek (Pol) 472.5
1966 Vladimir Belyayev (USSR) 485
1968* Boris Syelitskiy (USSR) 485
1969 Masashi Ohuchi (Jap) 487.5
1970 Gennadiy Ivanchenko (USSR) 505
1971 Boris Pavlov (USSR) 495
1972* Leif Jensen (Nor) 507.5
1973 Vladimir Rizhenkov (USSR) 350
1974 Trendafil Stoychev (Bul) 350
1975 Valeriy Shariy (USSR) 357.5
1976* Valeriy Shariy (USSR) 365
1977 Gennadiy Bessonov (USSR) 352.5
1978 Yurik Vardanyan (USSR) 377.5
1979 Yurik Vardanyan (USSR) 370
1980* Yurik Vardanyan (USSR) 400
1981 Yurik Vardanyan (USSR) 392.5
1982 Asen Zlatev (Bul) 400
1983 Yurik Vardanyan (USSR) 392.5
1984* Petre Becheru (Rom) 355
1985 Yurik Vardanyan (USSR) 397.5
1986 Asen Zlatev (Bul) 405
1987 László Barsi (Hun) 390
1988* Israil Arsamakov (USSR) 377.5
1989 Kiril Kounev (Bul) 385
1990 Altjamurat Orazdurdyev (USSR) 377.5
1991 Ivan Samadov (USSR) 367.5
1992* Pyrros Dimas (Gre) 370

83kg
1993 Pyrros Dimas (Gre) 377.5
1994 Marc Huster (Ger) 382.5

90kg Formerly Middle-heavyweight
1951 Norbert Schemansky (USA) 427.5
1952* Norbert Schemansky (USA) 445
1953 Norbert Schemansky (USA) 442.5
1954 Arkadiy Vorobyev (USSR) 460
1955 Arkadiy Vorobyev (USSR) 455
1956* Arkadiy Vorobyev (USSR) 462.5
1957 Arkadiy Vorobyev (USSR) 470
1958 Arkadiy Vorobyev (USSR) 465
1959 Louis Martin (UK) 445
1960* Arkadiy Vorobyev (USSR) 472.5
1961 Ireneusz Palinski (Pol) 475
1962 Louis Martin (UK) 480
1963 Louis Martin (UK) 480
1964* Vladimir Golovanov (USSR) 487.5
1965 Louis Martin (UK) 487.5
1966 Geza Toth (Hun) 487.5
1968* Kaarlo Kangasniemi (Fin) 517.5
1969 Kaarlo Kangasniemi (Fin) 515
1970 Vasiliy Kolotov (USSR) 537.5
1971 David Rigert (USSR) 542.5
1972* Andon Nikolov (Bul) 525
1973 David Rigert (USSR) 365
1974 David Rigert (USSR) 387.5
1975 David Rigert (USSR) 377.5
1976* David Rigert (USSR) 382.5
1977 Sergey Poltoratskiy (USSR) 375
1978 Rolf Milser (FRG) 377.5
1979 Gennadiy Bessonov (USSR) 380
1980* Peter Baczako (Hun) 377.5
1981 Blagoi Blagoyev (Bul) 405
1982 Blagoi Blagoyev (Bul) 415
1983 Blagoi Blagoyev (Bul) 417.5
1984* Nicu Vlad (Rom) 392.5
1985 Anatoliy Khrapatiy (USSR) 395
    & Viktor Solodov (USSR) 395
1986 Anatoliy Khrapatiy (USSR) 412.5
1987 Anatoliy Khrapatiy (USSR) 417.5
1988* Anatoliy Khrapatiy (USSR) 412.5
1989 Anatoliy Khrapatiy (USSR) 415
1990 Anatoliy Khrapatiy (USSR) 397.5
1991 Sergey Syrtsov (USSR) 410
1992* Kakhi Kakhiashvili (CIS/Geo) 412.5

91kg
1993 Ivan Chakarov (Bul) 407.5
1994 Aleksey Petrov (Rus) 412.5

99kg
1993 Viktor Tregubov (Rus) 407.5
1994 Sergey Syrtsov (Rus) 417.5

100kg
1977 Anatoliy Kozlov (USSR) 367.5
1978 David Rigert (USSR) 390
1979 Pavel Sirchin (USSR) 385
1980* Otto Zaremba (Cs) 395
1981 Viktor Sots (USSR) 407.5
1982 Viktor Sots (USSR) 422.5
1983 Pavel Kuznyetsov (USSR) 422.5
1984* Rolf Milser (FRG) 385
1985 Sandor Szanyi (Hun) 415
1986 Nicu Vlad (Rom) 437.5

1987 Pavel Kuznyetsov (USSR) 422.5
1988* Pavel Kuznyetsov (USSR) 425
1989 Petar Stefanov (Bul) 415
1990 Nicu Vlad (Rom) 412.5
1991 Igor Sadykov (USSR) 415
1992* Viktor Tregubov (CIS/Rus) 420

108kg
1993 Timur Taimazov (Ukr) 420
1994 Timur Taimazov (Ukr) 435

110kg Formerly Heavyweight
1969 Robert Bednarski (USA) 555
1970 Jan Talts (USSR) 565
1971 Yuriy Kozin (USSR) 552.5
1972* Jan Talts (USSR) 580
1973 Pavel Pervushin (USSR) 385
1974 Valeriy Ustyuzhin (USSR) 380
1975 Valentin Khristov (Bul) 417.5
1976* Yuriy Zaitsev (USSR) 385
1977 Valentin Khristov (Bul) 405
1978 Yuriy Zaitsev (USSR) 402.5
1979 Sergey Arakelov (USSR) 410
1980* Leonid Taranenko (USSR) 422.5
1981 Valeriy Kravchuk (USSR) 415
1982 Sergey Arakelov (USSR) 427.5
1983 Vyacheslav Klokov (USSR) 440
1984* Norberto Oberburger (Ita) 390
1985 Yuriy Zakharevich (USSR) 422.5
1986 Yuriy Zakharevich (USSR) 447.5
1987 Yuriy Zakharevich (USSR) 445
1988* Yuriy Zakharevich (USSR) 455
1989 Stefan Botev (Bul) 427.5
1990 Stefan Botev (Bul) 440
1991 Artur Akoyev (USSR) 427.5
1992* Ronny Weller (Ger) 432.5

82.5+kg Heavyweight
1928* Josef Strassberger (Ger) 372.5
1932* Jaroslav Skobla (Cs) 380
1936* Josef Manger (Aut) 410
1937 Josef Manger (Ger) 420
1938 Josef Manger (Ger) 410
1946 John Davis (USA) 435
1947 John Davis (USA) 455
1948* John Davis (USA) 452.5
1949 John Davis (USA) 442.5
1950 John Davis (USA) 462.5

90kg+ Heavyweight
1951 John Davis (USA) 432.5
1952* John Davis (USA) 460
1953 Douglas Hepburn (Can) 467.5
1954 Norbert Schemansky (USA) 487.5
1955 Paul Anderson (USA) 512.5
1956* Paul Anderson (USA) 500
1957 Aleksey Medvedev (USSR) 500
1958 Aleksey Medvedev (USSR) 485
1959 Yuriy Vlasov (USSR) 500
1960* Yuriy Vlasov (USSR) 537.5
1961 Yuriy Vlasov (USSR) 525
1962 Yuriy Vlasov (USSR) 540
1963 Yuriy Vlasov (USSR) 557.5

1964* Leonid Zhabotinskiy (USSR) 572.5
1965 Leonid Zhabotinskiy (USSR) 552.5
1966 Leonid Zhabotinskiy (USSR) 567.5
1968* Leonid Zhabotinskiy (USSR) 572.5

110kg+ Formerly Super-heavyweight
1969 Joseph Dube (USA) 577.5
1970 Vasiliy Alekseyev (USSR) 612.5
1971 Vasiliy Alekseyev (USSR) 635
1972* Vasiliy Alekseyev (USSR) 640
1973 Vasiliy Alekseyev (USSR) 402.5
1974 Vasiliy Alekseyev (USSR) 425
1975 Vasiliy Alekseyev (USSR) 427.5
1976* Vasiliy Alekseyev (USSR) 440
1977 Vasiliy Alekseyev (USSR) 430
1978 Jürgen Heuser (GDR) 417.5
1979 Sultan Rakhmanov (USSR) 430
1980* Sultan Rakhmanov (USSR) 440
1981 Anatoliy Pisarenko (USSR) 425
1982 Anatoliy Pisarenko (USSR) 445
1983 Anatoliy Pisarenko (USSR) 450
1984* Dean Lukin (Aus) 412.5
1985 Antonio Krastev (Bul) 437.5
1986 Antonio Krastev (Bul) 460
1987 Aleksandr Kurlovich (USSR) 472.5
1988* Aleksandr Kurlovich (USSR) 462.5
1989 Aleksandr Kurlovich (USSR) 460
1990 Leonid Taranenko (USSR) 450
1991 Aleksandr Kurlovich (USSR) 455
1992* Aleksandr Kurlovich (CIS/Bls) 450

108kg+
1993 Ronny Weller (Ger) 442.5
1994 Aleksandr Kurlovich (Bls) 457.5

Most Titles
Olympic Games
Eleven men have won two gold medals. The most
medals is four by Norbert Schemansky (USA) gold
90kg 1952, silver 82+kg 1948, bronze 90+kg 1960, 1964.
World and Olympic:
8 John Davis (USA) 1938-52
8 Tommy Kono (USA) 1952-9
8 Vasiliy Alekseyev (USSR) 1970-7
8 Naim Suleymanoglü (Bul/Tur) 1985-94
7 Arkadiy Vorobyev (USSR) 1953-60
7 Yurik Vardanyan (USSR) 1977-85
6 Stanley Stanczyk (Pol) 1946-51
6 Peter George (USA) 1947-55
6 Yoshinobu Miyake (Jap) 1962-8
6 David Rigert (USSR) 1971-8
6 Anatoliy Khrapatiy (USSR) 1985-90
6 Aleksandr Kurlovich (USSR/Bls) 1987-94
Gold medals are also awarded at World
Championships for each lift. The lifters to have won
the most gold medals overall have been: P - press, S -
snatch, J - jerk, T - Total

No	Name	P	S	J	T
22	Vasiliy Alekseyev (USSR)	2	5	7	8
20	Yurik Vardanyan (USSR)	-	6	7	7
19	Naim Suleymanoglü (Bul/Tur)	-	7	6	6
17	David Rigert (USSR)	1	5	5	6
15	Yanko Rusev (Bul)	-	5	5	5

World Cup

Awarded on a points basis to the best lifter from a worldwide
series of events, who formerly attended an annual gala

Year	World Cup winner	Gala winner
1980	György Szalai (Hun)	János Sólyomvári (Hun)
1981	Yanko Rusev (Bul)	Blagoi Blagoyev (Bul)
1982	Blagoi Blagoyev (Bul)	Blagoi Blagoyev (Bul)
1983	Blagoi Blagoyev (Bul)	Yurik Sarkisian (USSR)
1984	Naim Suleimanov	Naim Suleimanov (Bul)
1985	Neum Shalamanov* (Bul)	Neum Shalamanov (Bul)
1986	Neum Shalamanov	Asen Zlatev (Bul)
1987	Mikhail Petrov (Bul)	Mikhail Petrov (Bul)
1988	Stefan Botev (Bul)	Stefan Botev (Bul)
1989	Liu Shoubin (Chn)	Liu Shoubin (Chn)
1990	Ivan Ivanov (Bul)	Ivan Ivanov (Bul)
1991	Yoto Yotov (Bul)	Ivan Ivanov (Bul)
1992	Kakhi Kakhiashvili (Geo)	Liu Weiguo (Chn)
1993	not held	
1994	Aleksandr Kurlovich (Bls)	

* *Change of name from Naim Suleimanov*

World Weightlifting Records

*The final list when the bodyweight categories changed on 1 Jan
1993:*

Bodyweight Class	Lift	kg	Name and country	Date
52kg	Snatch	121	He Zhouqiang (Chn)	1992
	Jerk	155.5	Ivan Ivanov (Bul)	1991
	Total	272.5	Ivan Ivanov (Bul)	1989
56kg	Snatch	135	Liu Shoubin (China)	1991
	Jerk	171	Neno Terziiski (Bul)	1987
	Total	300	Neum Shalamanov (Bul)	1984
60kg	Snatch	152.5	Naim Suleymanoglü (Tur) #	1988
	Jerk	190	Naim Suleymanoglü (Tur) #	1988
	Total	342.5	Naim Suleymanoglü (Tur) #	1988
67.5kg	Snatch	160 162.5u	Israil Militosyan (USSR) Kim Men-nam (NKo)	1989 1990
	Jerk	200.5	Mikhail Petrov (Bul)	1987
	Total	355	Mikhail Petrov (Bul)	1987
75kg	Snatch	170	Angel Guenchev (Bul)	1987
	Jerk	215.5	Alexander Varbanov (Bul)	1987
	Total	382.5	Alexander Varbanov (Bul)	1988
82.5kg	Snatch	183	Asen Zlatev (Bul)	1986
	Jerk	225	Asen Zlatev (Bul)	1986
	Total	405	Yurik Vardanyan (USSR)	1984
90kg	Snatch	195.5	Blagoi Blagoyev (Bul)	1983
	Jerk	235	Anatoliy Khrapatiy (USSR)	1988
	Total	422.5	Viktor Solodov (USSR)	1984
100kg	Snatch	200.5	Nicu Vlad (Rom)	1986
	Jerk	242.5	Aleksandr Popov (USSR)	1988
	Total	440	Yuriy Zakharevich (USSR)	1983
110kg	Snatch	210	Yuriy Zakharevich (USSR)	1988
	Jerk	250.5	Yuriy Zakharevich (USSR)	1988
	Total	455	Yuriy Zakharevich (USSR)	1988
110kg+	Snatch	216	Antonio Krastev (Bul)	1987
	Jerk	266	Leonid Taranenko (USSR)	1988
	Total	475	Leonid Taranenko (USSR)	1988

formerly Suleimanov/Shalanov of Bulgaria

World records at new weight categories

(from 1 Jan 1993)

World records can be set only at events pre-elected by the IWF and at which anti-doping controls are carried out.

Bodyweight

Class	Lift	kg	Name and country	Date
54kg	Snatch	130.5	Halil Mutlu (Tur)	1995
	Jerk	160	Halil Mutlu (Tur)	1994
	Total	290	Halil Mutlu (Tur)	1994
59kg	Snatch	140	Hafiz Suleymanoglü (Tur)	1995
	Jerk	170	Nikolai Peshalov (Bul)	1995
	Total	305	Nikolai Peshalov (Bul)	1993
64kg	Snatch	147.5	Naim Suleymanoglü (Tur)	1994
	Jerk	183	Valerios Leonidis (Gre)	1995
	Total	330	Naim Suleymanoglü (Tur)	1994
70kg	Snatch	160	Fedail Guler (Tur)	1994
	Jerk	193	Fedail Guler (Tur)	1995
	Total	350	Fedail Guler (Tur)	1994
76kg	Snatch	170	Ruslan Savchenko (Ukr)	1993
	Jerk	207.5	Pablo Lara (Cub)	1995
	Total	370	Ruslan Savchenko (Ukr)	1993
83kg	Snatch	177.5	Pyrros Dimas (Gre)	1995
	Jerk	211	Pyrros Dimas (Gre)	1995
	Total	387.5	Pyrros Dimas (Gre)	1995
91kg	Snatch	186	Aleksey Petrov (Rus)	1994
	Jerk	228.5	Khaki Kakiasvilis (Gre)	1995
	Total	412.5	Aleksey Petrov (Rus)	1994
99kg	Snatch	192.5	Sergey Syrtsov (Rus)	1994
	Jerk	227.5	Khaki Kakiasvilis (Gre)	1995
	Total	417.5	Sergey Syrtsov (Rus)	1994
108kg	Snatch	200	Timur Taimazov (Ukr)	1994
	Jerk	235.5	Timur Taimazov (Ukr)	1994
	Total	435	Timur Taimazov (Ukr)	1994
108kg+	Snatch	205	Aleksandr Kurlovich (Bls)	1994
	Jerk	253.5	Andrey Chemerkin (Rus)	1995
	Total	457.5	Aleksandr Kurlovich (Bls)	1994

How the super-heavyweight jerk record has progressed. The record at the end of each decade:

161.5	Charles Rigoulet (Fra)	1925
167.5	Arnold Luhäär (Estonia)	1937
177.5	John Davis (USA)	1948
197.5	Juri Vlasov (USSR)	1959
220.5	Robert Bednarski (USA)	1968
256	Vasiliy Alekseyev (USSR)	1977
266	Leonid Taranenko (USSR)	1988

Most improvements

31 Vasiliy Alexeyev (USSR) 221.5kg 1970 - 256kg 1977

9 Juri Vlasov (USSR) 197.5kg 1959 - 215.5kg 1964

6 Norbert Schemansky (USA) 185kg 1952 - 192.5kg 1954

6 Leonid Zhabotinsky (USSR) 213kg 1964 - 220kg 1968

Women's Weightlifting

World Records

The final list when the bodyweight categories changed on 1 Jan 1993

Class	Lift	kg	Name and country	Date
44kg	Snatch	77.5	Xing Fen (Chn)	1992
	Jerk	102.5	Xing Fen (Chn)	1992
	Total	180	Xing Fen (Chn)	1992
48kg	Snatch	83	Liao Suping (Chn)	1992
	Jerk	105.5	Liao Suping (Chn)	1992
	Total	187.5	Liu Xiuhua (Chn)	1992
52kg	Snatch	87.5	Peng Liping (Chn)	1992
	Jerk	115	Peng Liping (Chn)	1992
	Total	202.5	Peng Liping (Chn)	1992
56kg	Snatch	95	Zhang Juhua (Chn)	1992
	Jerk	120	Zhang Juhua (Chn)	1992
	Total	215	Zhang Juhua (Chn)	1992
60kg	Snatch	100	Su Yuanghong (Chn)	1992
	Jerk	125	Li Hongyun (Chn)	1992
	Total	222.5	Li Hongyun (Chn)	1992
67.5kg	Snatch	105	Lei Li (Chn)	1992
	Jerk	132.5	Lei Li (Chn)	1992
	Total	237.5	Lei Li (Chn)	1992
75kg	Snatch	107.5	Hua Ju (Chn)	1992
	Jerk	140	Xing Shuwen (Chn)	1992
	Total	242.5	Zhang Xiaoli (Chn)	1991
82.5kg	Snatch	110.5	Zang Lina (Chn)	1992
	Jerk	145	Zang Lina (Chn)	1992
	Total	255	Zang Lina (Chn)	1992
82.5kg+				
	Snatch	115	Li Yajuan (Chn)	1992
	Jerk	150	Li Yajuan (Chn)	1992
	Total	265	Li Yajuan (Chn)	1992

* unratified mark made at 1990 Asian Games

World records at new weight categories

(from 1 Jan 1993)

Class	Lift	kg	Name and country	Date
46kg	Snatch	80.5	Yun Yanhong (Chn)	1994
	Jerk	102.5	Guan Hong (Chn)	1994
	Total	182.5	Guan Hong (Chn)	1994
50kg	Snatch	87.5	Liu Xiuhua (Chn)	1994
	Jerk	110.5	Liu Xiuhua (Chn)	1994
	Total	197.5	Liu Xiuhua (Chn)	1994
54kg	Snatch	92.5	Zhang Juhua (Chn)	1994
	Jerk	112.5	Long Yuiling (Chn)	1993
	Total	202.5	Zhang Juhua (Chn)	1994
59kg	Snatch	98.5	Zou Feic (Chn)	1994
	Jerk	123.5	Zou Feie (Chn)	1994
	Total	220	Chen Xiaomin (Chn)	1994
		220	Zou Feie (Chn)	1994
64kg	Snatch	105	Li Hongyun (Chn)	1994
	Jerk	130	Li Hongyun (Chn)	1994
	Total	235	Li Hongyun (Chn)	1994
70kg	Snatch	102.5	Tan Weifang (Chn)	1994
	Jerk	128.5	Zhou Meihong (Chn)	1994
	Total	230	Tan Weifang (Chn)	1994
76kg	Snatch	105.5	Hua Ju (Chn)	1993
	Jerk	140	Zhang Guomei (Chn)	1993
	Total	235	Zhang Guomei (Chn)	1993
83kg	Snatch	108	Zhang Xiaoli (Chn)	1994
	Jerk	132.5	Maria Urrutia (Col)	1994
	Total	240	Xing Shuwen (Chn)	1994
83kg+	Snatch	105.5	Li Yajuan (Chn)	1994
	Jerk	155	Li Yajuan (Chn)	1993
	Total	260	Li Yajuan (Chn)	1993

World Champions

World Championships have been held annually from the first in 1987 at Daytona Beach, Florida, USA. *Winners:*

44kg
1987 Cai Jun (Chn) 145
1988 Xing Fen (Chn) 147.5
1989 Xing Fen (Chn) 165
1990 Wu Xiangmei (Chn) 152.5
1991 Xing Fen (Chn) 162.5
1992 Guan Hong (Chn) 175

46kg
1993 Chu Nan-mei (Tai) 152.5
1994 Yun Yanhong (Chn) 180

48kg
1987 Huang Xiaoyu (Chn) 170
1988 Huang Xiaoyu (Chn) 165
1989 Huang Xiaoyu (Chn) 172.5
1990 Cai Jun (Chn) 165
1991 Izabela Rifatova (Bul) 170
1992 Liu Xiuhua (Chn) 187.5

50kg
1993 Liu Xiuhua (Chn) 187.5
1994 Robin Byrd (USA) 175

52kg
1987 Yan Zangqun (Chn) 157.5
1988 Peng Liping (Chn) 175
1989 Peng Liping (Chn) 185
1990 Liao Shuping (Chn) 177.5
1991 Peng Liping (Chn) 187.5
1992 Peng Liping (Chn) 202.5

54kg
1993 Chen Xiaoming (Chn) 200
1994 Kamami Maleswari (Ind) 197.5
(Original winner Wang Shen (Chn) 197.5 disqualified for drugs)

56kg
1987 Cui Aihong (Chn) 160
1988 Ma Na (Chn) 180

1989 Xing Liwei (Chn) 180
1990 Wu Haiqing (Chn) 190
1991 Sun Caiyan (Chn) 192.5
1992 Sun Caiyan (Chn) 210

59kg
1993 Sun Caiyan (Chn) 217.5
1994 Zou Feie (Chn) 220

60kg
1987 Zeng Xinling (Chn) 180
1988 Jing Yang (Chn) 195
1989 Ma Na (Chn) 202.5
1990 Maria Christoforidi (Gre) 197.5
1991 Han Lixia (Chn) 197.5
1992 Li Hongyun (Chn) 222.5

64kg
1993 Li Hongyun (Chn) 220
1994 Li Hongyun (Chn) 235

67.5kg
1987 Gao Lijuan (Chn) 180
1988 Guo Qiuxiang (Chn) 210
1989 Guo Qiuxiang (Chn) 220
1990 Wang Genying (Chn) 212.5
1991 Lei Li (Chn) 210
1992 Gao Lijuan (Chn) 222.5

70kg
1993 Milena Trendafilova (Bul) 220
1994 Zhou Meihong (Chn) 222.5

75kg
1987 Li Hongling (Chn) 210
1988 Li Hongling (Chn) 212.5
1989 Milena Trendafilova (Bul) 220
1990 Milena Trendafilova (Bul) 237.5
1991 Zhang Xiaoli (Chn) 242.5
1992 Hua Ju (Chn) 237.5

76kg
1993 Hua Ju (Chn) 230
1994 Panagiota Antonopoulou (Gre) 220

82.5kg
1987 Karyn Marshall (USA) 220
1988 Li Yanxia (Chn) 215
1989 Li Hongling (Chn) 240
1990 Maria Urrutia (Col) 230
1991 Li Hongling (Chn) 240
1992 Zhang Xiaoli (Chn) 252.5

83kg
1993 Chen Shu-chih (Tai) 230
1994 Maria Urrutia (Col) 237.5

82.5+kg
1987 Han Changmei (Chn) 210
1988 Han Changmei (Chn) 232.5
1989 Han Changmei (Chn) 242.5
1990 Li Yajuan (Chn) 245
1991 Li Yajuan (Chn) 255
1992 Li Yajuan (Chn) 265

83+ kg
1993 Li Yajuan (Chn) 260
1994 Karolina Lundahl (Fin) 230
(Original winner Li Dan (Chn) 242.5 disqualified for drugs)
Most overall titles: 4 Peng Liping, Li Hingling, Li Yajuan
Most gold medals (snatch, jerk and total): 12 Milena Trendafilova, Peng Liping
An extraordinary total of 59 world records were set at the 6th World Championships in Varna, Bulgaria in 1992, 55 of them by Chinese lifters.

World Cup Gala

Women were first invited to take part in 1991.
1991 Sun Caiyun (Chn) (also won World Cup)
1992 Milena Trendafilova (Bul)
1993 *not held*
1994 Xing Shuwen (Chn)

Wrestling

Wrestling was part of the Ancient Olympics, and wall drawings from nearly 6000 years ago depict it as taking place long before then. Wrestling was included in the first Modern Olympics in 1896, sixteen years before the formation of the International Amateur Wrestling Association (FILA). The two forms of wrestling at international level are Freestyle and Greco-Roman. The principle difference between the two is that use of the legs is completely prohibited in the Greco-Roman style. Holds below the waist are also prohibited in this style of wrestling.

Olympic Games

A heavyweight division of Greco-Roman wrestling was included in the first modern Olympics. Freestyle wrestling was introduced in 1904. *Winners:*

Freestyle

48kg - Light-flyweight
1904 Robert Curry (USA)
1972 Roman Dmitriyev (USSR)
1976 Hasan Isaev (Bul)
1980 Claudio Pollio (Ita)
1984 Robert Weaver (USA)
1988 Takashi Kobayashi (Jap)
1992 Kim Il (NKo)

52kg - Flyweight
Limit 115lb/52.16kg in 1904
1904 George Mehnert (USA)
1948 Lennart Viitala (Fin)
1952 Hasan Gemici (Tur)
1956 Mirian Tsalkalamanidze (USSR)
1960 Ahmet Bilek (Tur)
1964 Yoshikatsu Yoshida (Jap)
1968 Shigeo Nakata (Jap)

1972 Kiyomi Kato (Jap)
1976 Yuji Takada (Jap)
1980 Anatoliy Beloglazov (USSR)
1984 Saban Trstena (Yug)
1988 Mitsuru Sato (Jap)
1992 Li Hak-son (NKo)

57kg - Bantamweight
Limits: 125lb/56.70kg 1904,
119lb/54kg 1908, 56kg 1924-36
1904 Isidor Niflot (USA)
1908 George Mehnert (USA)
1924 Kustaa Pihlajamäki (Fin)
1928 Kaarlo Mäkinen (Fin)
1932 Robert Pearce (USA)
1936 Odön Zombori (Hun)
1948 Nasuh Akar (Tur)
1952 Shohachi Ishii (Jap)
1956 Mustafa Dagistanli (Tur)
1960 Terrence McCann (USA)
1964 Yojiro Uetake (Jap)
1968 Yojiro Uetake (Jap)
1972 Hideaki Yanagida (Jap)
1976 Vladimir Yumin (USSR)
1980 Sergey Beloglazov (USSR)
1984 Hideaki Tomiyama (Jap)
1988 Sergey Beloglazov (USSR)
1992 Alejandro Puerto (Cub)

62kg - Featherweight
Limits: 135lb/61.24kg 1904,
133lb/60.3kg 1908, 60kg 1920, 61kg
1924-36, 63kg 1964-8
1904 Benjamin Bradshaw (USA)
1908 George Dole (USA)
1920 Charles Ackerly (USA)
1924 Robin Reed (USA)
1928 Allie Morrison (USA)
1932 Hermanni Pihlajamäki (Fin)
1936 Kustaa Pihlajamäki (Fin)
1948 Gazanfer Bilge (Tur)
1952 Bayram Sit (Tur)
1956 Shozo Sasahara (Jap)
1960 Mustafa Dagistanli (Tur)
1964 Osamu Watanabe (Jap)
1968 Masaaki Kaneko (Jap)
1972 Zagalav Abdulbekov (USSR)
1976 Yang Jung-mo (SKo)
1980 Magomedgasan Abushev (USSR)
1984 Randy Lewis (USA)
1988 John Smith (USA)
1992 John Smith (USA)

68kg - Lightweight
Limits: 145lb/65.77kg 1904, 146.75
lb/66.6kg 1908, 67.5kg 1920, 66kg
1924-36, 67kg 1948-60, 70kg 1964-8
1904 Otto Roehm (USA)
1908 George de Relwyskow (UK)
1920 Kalle Anttila (Fin)
1924 Russell Vis (USA)
1928 Osväld Käpp (Est)

1932 Charles Pacôme (Fra)
1936 Károly Kárpáti (Hun)
1948 Celál Atik (Tur)
1952 Olle Anderberg (Swe)
1956 Emamali Habibi (Irn))
1960 Shelby Wilson (USA)
1964 Enyu Valtschev (Bul) *
1968 Abdollah Movahed Ardabili (Irn)
1972 Dan Gable (USA)
1976 Pavel Pinigin (USSR)
1980 Saipulla Absaidov (USSR)
1984 You In-tak (SKo)
1988 Arsen Fadzeyev (USSR)
1992 Arsen Fadzeyev (CIS/Rus)
* *competed as Dimov in 1960*

74kg - Welterweight
Limits: 158lb/71.67kg 1904; 72kg
1924-36, 73kg 1948-60, 78kg 1964-8
1904 Charles Erickson (USA)
1924 Hermann Gehri (Swi)
1928 Arvo Haavisto (Fin)
1932 Jack Van Bebber (USA)
1936 Frank Lewis (USA)
1948 Yasar Dogu (Tur)
1952 William Smith (USA)
1956 Mitsuo Ikeda (Jap)
1960 Douglas Blubaugh (USA)
1964 Ismail Ogan (Tur)
1968 Mahmut Atalay (Tur)
1972 Wayne Wells (USA)
1976 Jiichiro Date (Jap)
1980 Valentin Raitchev (Bul)
1984 David Schultz (USA)
1988 Ken Monday (USA)
1992 Park Jang-soon (SKo)

82kg - Middleweight
Limits: 161lb/73kg 1908, 165 lb/75kg
1920, 79kg 1924-60, 87kg 1964-8
1908 Stanley Bacon (UK)
1920 Eino Leino (Fin)
1924 Fritz Hagmann (Swi)
1928 Ernst Kyburz (Swi)
1932 Ivar Johansson (Swe)
1936 Emile Poilvé (Fra)
1948 Glen Brand (USA)
1952 David Tsimakuridze (USSR)
1956 Nikolai Stanchev (Bul)
1960 Hasan Güngör (Tur)
1964 Prodan Gardschev (Bul)
1968 Boris Gurevich (USSR)
1972 Levan Tediashvili (USSR)
1976 John Peterson (USA)
1980 Ismail Abilov (Bul)
1984 Mark Schultz (USA)
1988 Han Myung-woo (SKo)
1992 Kevin Jackson (USA)

90kg - Light-heavyweight
Limits: 82.5kg, 1920, 87kg 1924-60,
97kg 1964-8

1920 Anders Larsson (Swe)
1924 John Spellman (USA)
1928 Thure Sjöstedt (Swe)
1932 Peter Mehringer (USA)
1936 Knut Fridell (Swe)
1948 Henry Wittenberg (USA)
1952 Wiking Palm (Swe)
1956 Gholam Reza Takhti (Irn)
1960 Ismet Atli (Tur)
1964 Aleksandr Medved (USSR)
1968 Ahmet Ayik (Tur)
1972 Ben Peterson (USA)
1976 Levan Tediashvili (USSR)
1980 Sanasar Oganesyan (USSR)
1984 Ed Banach (USA)
1988 Makharbek Khadartsev (USSR)
1992 Makharbek Khadartsev (CIS/Rus)

100kg - Heavyweight
Limits: over 158lb/71.60kg 1904, over
73kg, 1908, over 82.5kg 1920, over
87kg 1924-60, over 97kg 1964-8
1904 Bernhuff Hansen (USA)
1908 George O'Kelly (UK)
1920 Robert Roth (Swi)
1924 Harry Steel (USA)
1928 Johan Richthoff (Swe)
1932 Johan Richthoff (Swe)
1936 Kristjan Palusalu (Est)
1948 Gyula Bóbis (Hun)
1952 Arsen Mekokishvili (USSR)
1956 Hamit Kaplan (Tur)
1960 Wilfried Dietrich (FRG)
1964 Aleksandr Ivanitskiy (USSR)
1968 Aleksandr Medved (USSR)
1972 Ivan Yarygin (USSR)
1976 Ivan Yarygin (USSR)
1980 Ilya Mate (USSR)
1984 Lou Banach (USA)
1988 Vasile Puscasu (Rom)
1992 Leri Khabelov (CIS/Geo)

Over 100kg - Super-heavyweight
1972 Aleksandr Medved (USSR)
1976 Soslan Andiyev (USSR)
1980 Soslan Andiyev (USSR)
1984 Bruce Baumgartner (USA)
1988 David Gobedzhishviliy (USSR)
1992 Bruce Baumgartner (USA)

Greco-Roman

48kg - Light-flyweight
1972 Gheorghe Berceanu (Rom)
1976 Aleksey Schumakov (USSR)
1980 Zaksylik Ushkempirov (USSR)
1984 Vincenzo Maenza (Ita)
1988 Vincenzo Maenza (Ita)
1992 Oleg Kucherenko (CIS/Ukr)

52kg - Flyweight
1948 Pietro Lombardi (Ita)

1952 Boris Gurevich (USSR)
1956 Nikolay Solovyov (USSR)
1960 Dumitru Pirvulescu (Rom)
1964 Tsutomu Hanahara (Jap)
1968 Petar Kirov (Bul)
1972 Petar Kirov (Bul)
1976 Vitaliy Konstantinov (USSR)
1980 Vakhtang Blagidze (USSR)
1984 Atsuji Miyahara (Jap)
1988 Jon Rønningen (Nor)
1992 Jon Rønningen (Nor)

57kg - Bantamweight
Limits: 58kg 1924-8, 56kg 1932-6
1924 Eduard Pütsep (Est)
1928 Kurt Leucht (Ger)
1932 Jakob Brendel (Ger)
1936 Márton Lörincz (Hun)
1948 Kurt Pettersén (Swe)
1952 Imre Hódos (Hun)
1956 Konstantin Vyrupayev
     (USSR)
1960 Oleg Karavayev (USSR)
1964 Masamitsu Ichiguchi (Jap)
1968 János Varga (Hun)
1972 Rustem Kazakov (USSR)
1976 Pertti Ukkola (Fin)
1980 Shamil Serikov (USSR)
1984 Pasquale Passarelli (FRG)
1988 András Sike (Hun)
1992 An Han-bong (SKo)

62kg - Featherweight
Limits: 60kg 1912-20, 62kg 1924-8,
1948-60, 61kg 1932-6, 63kg 1964-8
1912 Kaarlo Koskelo (Fin)
1920 Oskari Friman (Fin)
1924 Kalle Antila (Fin)
1928 Voldemar Väli (Est)
1932 Giovanni Gozzi (Ita)
1936 Yasar Erkan (Tur)
1948 Mehmet Oktav (Tur)
1952 Yakov Punkin (USSR)
1956 Rauno Mäkinen (Fin)
1960 Müzahir Sille (Tur)
1964 Imre Polyák (Hun)
1968 Roman Rurua (USSR)
1972 Georgi Markov (Bul)
1976 Kazimierz Lipién (Pol)
1980 Stylianos Migiakis (Gre)
1984 Kim Weon-kee (SKo)
1988 Kamandar Madzhidov
     (USSR)
1992 Akif Pirim (Tur)

68kg - Lightweight
Limits: 75kg 1906, 66.6kg 1908,
67.5kg 1912-28, 66kg 1932-6, 67kg
1948-60, 70kg 1964-8
1906 Rudolf Watzl (Aut)
1908 Enrico Porro (Ita)
1912 Eemil Väre (Fin)
1920 Eemil Väre (Fin)

1924 Oskari Friman (Fin)
1928 Lajos Keresztes (Hun)
1932 Erik Malmberg (Swe)
1936 Lauri Koskela (Fin)
1948 Gustaf Freij (Swe)
1952 Schazam Safin (USSR)
1956 Kyösti Lehtonen (Fin)
1960 Avtandil Koridze (USSR)
1964 Kazim Ayvaz (Tur)
1968 Munji Mumemura (Jap)
1972 Shamil Khisamutdinov
     (USSR)
1976 Suren Nalbandyan (USSR)
1980 Stefan Rusu (Rom)
1984 Vlado Lisjak (Yug)
1988 Levon Dzhulfalakyan (USSR)
1992 Attila Repka (Hun)

74kg - Welterweight
Limits: 72kg 1932-36, 73kg 1948-60,
78kg 1964-8
1932 Ivar Johansson (Swe)
1936 Rudolf Svedberg (Swe)
1948 Gösta Andersson (Swe)
1952 Miklós Szilvási (Hun)
1956 Mithat Bayrak (Tur)
1960 Mithat Bayrak (Tur)
1964 Anatoliy Kolesov (USSR)
1968 Rudolf Vesper (GDR)
1970 Vitezslav Mácha (Cs)
1976 Anatoliy Bykov (USSR)
1980 Ferenc Kocsis (Hun)
1984 Jouko Salomaki (Fin)
1988 Kim Young-nam (SKo)
1992 Mnatsakan Iskandarian
     (CIS/Arm)

82kg - Middleweight
Limits: 85kg 1906, 73kg 1908, 75kg
1912-28, 79kg 1932-60, 87kg 1964-8
1906 Verner Weckman (Fin)
1908 Frithiof Mårtensson (Fin)
1912 Claes Johansson (Swe)
1920 Carl Westergren (Swe)
1924 Edvard Westerlund (Fin)
1928 Väinö Kokkinen (Fin)
1932 Väinö Kokkinen (Fin)
1936 Ivar Johansson (Swe)
1948 Axel Grönberg (Swe)
1952 Axel Grönberg (Swe)
1956 Givy Kartoziya (USSR)
1960 Dimiter Dobrev (Bul)
1964 Branislav Simic (Yug)
1968 Lothar Metz (GDR)
1972 Csaba Hegedüs (Hun)
1976 Momir Petkovic (Yug)
1980 Gennadiy Korban (USSR)
1984 Ion Draica (Rom)
1988 Mikhail Mamiashvili (USSR)
1992 Péter Farkas (Hun)

90kg - Light-heavyweight
Limits: 93kg 1908, 82.5kg 1912-28,

87kg 1932-60, 97kg 1964-8
1908 Verner Weckman (Fin)
1912 No winner - Anders Ahlgren
     (Swe) and Ivan Böhling (Fin)
     fought out a draw after nine hours
1920 Claes Johansson (Swe)
1924 Carl Westergren (Swe)
1928 Ibrahim Moustafa (Egy)
1932 Rudolf Svensson (Swe)
1936 Axel Cadier (Swe)
1948 Karl-Eric Nilsson (Swe)
1952 Kelpo Gröndahl (Fin)
1956 Valentin Nikolayev (USSR)
1960 Tevfik Kis (Tur)
1964 Boyan Radev (Bul)
1968 Boyan Radev (Bul)
1972 Valeriy Rezantsev (USSR)
1976 Valeriy Rezantsev (USSR)
1980 Norbert Növényi (Hun)
1984 Steven Fraser (USA)
1988 Atanas Komchev (Bul)
1992 Maik Bullmann (Ger)

100kg - Heavyweight
Limits: open 1896,over 85kg 1906,
over 93kg, 1908, over 82.5kg 1912-28,
over 81kg 1932-60, over 91kg 1964-8
1896 Carl Schuhmann (Ger)
1906 Søren Jensen (Den)
1908 Richárd Weisz (Hun)
1912 Yrjö Saarela (Fin)
1920 Adolf Lindfors (Fin)
1924 Henri Deglane (Fra)
1928 Rudolf Svensson (Swe)
1932 Carl Westergren (Swe)
1936 Kristjan Palusalu (Est)
1948 Ahmet Kirecci (Tur)
1952 Johannes Kotkas (USSR)
1956 Anatoliy Parfenov (USSR)
1960 Ivan Bogdan (USSR)
1964 István Kozma (Hun)
1968 István Kozma (Hun)
1972 Nicolae Martinescu (Rom)
1976 Nikolay Balboshin (USSR)
1980 Georgi Raikov (Bul)
1984 Vasile Andrei (Rom)
1988 Andrzej Wronski (Pol)
1992 Héctor Milian (Cub

Over 100kg - Super-heavyweight
1972 Anatoliy Roschin (USSR)
1976 Aleksandr Kolchinsky
     (USSR)
1980 Aleksandr Kolchinsky
     (USSR)
1984 Jeffrey Blatnick (USA)
1988 Aleksandr Karelin (USSR)
1992 Aleksandr Karelin (CIS/Rus)

Discontinued event - 3-class winner
1906 Søren Marinus Jensen (Den)

World Championships

Unofficial world championships for Greco-Roman wrestling were held at Vienna in 1904, with further such championships held on 14 occasions (including five in 1911!) prior to the first official world championships, held in Helsinki in 1921. There was a further Greco-Roman world championship in 1922 but no more until 1950, since when they have been held regularly, and now annually in non-Olympic years. The first Freestyle championships were held at Helsinki in 1951. Olympic champions are automatically world champions in Olympic years. The current weight limits have been standard since 1969, variations are shown for each category. Note that those shown for 1953 were unofficial. *Winners since 1950:*

Freestyle

48kg - Light-flyweight

1969-71	Ebrahim Javadi (Irn)
1973	Roman Dmitriyev (USSR)
1974-5	Hasan Isaev (Murselov) (Bul)
1977	Anatoliy Beloglazov (USSR)
1978-9	Sergey Kornilayev (USSR)
1981-2	Sergey Kornilayev (USSR)
1983	Kim Chol-hwan (SKo)
1985	Kim Chol-hwan (SKo)
1986-7	Li Yae-sik (NKo)
1989	Kim Jong-shin (SKo)
1990	Aldo Martinez (Cub)
1991	Vugar Orudzhev (USSR)
1993-4	Alexis Vila (Cub)

52kg - Flyweight

1951	Ali Yücel (Tur)
1953	Georgiy Saydov (USSR)
1954	Hüseyin Akbas (Tur)
1957	Mehmet Kartal (Tur)
1959	Ali Aliyev (USSR)
1961-2	Ali Aliyev (USSR)
1963	Kemal Yanilmaz (Tur)
1965	Yoshikatsu Yoshida (Jap)
1966	Jang Chang-sun (SKo)
1967	Shigeo Nakata (Jap)
1969	Richard Sanders (USA)
1970	Ali Riza (Tur)
1971	Mohamad Ghorbani (Irn)
1973	Ebrahim Javadi (Irn)
1974-5	Yuji Takada (Jap)
1977	Yuji Takada (Jap)
1978	Anatoliy Beloglazov (USSR)
1979	Yuji Takada (Jap)
1981	Toshio Asakura (Jap)

1982	Hartmut Reich (GDR)
1983	Valentin Jordanov (Bul)
1985	Valentin Jordanov (Bul)
1986	Kim Yong-sik (NKo)
1987	Valentin Jordanov (Bul)
1989	Valentin Jordanov (Bul)
1990	Majid Torkan (Irn)
1991	Larry 'Zeke' Jones (USA)
1993-4	Valentin Jordanov (Bul)

57kg - Bantamweight

1951	Nasuh Akar (Tur)
1953	Hüseyin Akbas (Tur)
1954	Mustafa Dagistanli (Tur)
1957	Hüseyin Akbas (Tur)
1959	Hüseyin Akbas (Tur)
1961	Mohamad Saifpour Sabadi (Irn)
1962	Hüseyin Akbas (Tur)
1963	Aidyn Ibragimov (USSR)
1965	Tomiaki Fukada (Jap)
1966-7	Ali Aliyev (USSR)
1969	Tamadichi Tanaka (Jap)
1970-1	Hideaki Yanagida (Jap)
1973	Mohsen Farahvashi (Irn)
1974	Vladimir Yumin (USSR)
1975	Masao Arai (Jap)
1977	Tadashi Sasaki (Jap)
1978-9	Hideaki Tomiyama (Jap)
1981	Sergey Beloglazov (USSR)
1982	Anatoliy Beloglazov (USSR)
1983	Sergey Beloglazov (USSR)
1985-7	Sergey Beloglazov (USSR)
1989	Kim Sik-seung (NKo)
1990	Alejandro Puerto (Cub)
1991	Sergey Smal (USSR)
1993	Terry Brands (USA)
1994	Alejandro Puerto (Cub)

62kg - Featherweight
Limit: 63kg 1962-7

1951	Haydar Zafer (Tur)
1953	Norair Musyegyan (USSR)
1954	Shozo Sasahara (Jap)
1957	Mustafa Dagistanli (Tur)
1959	Mustafa Dagistanli (Tur)
1961	Vladimir Rubashvili (USSR)
1962-3	Osamu Watanabe (Jap)
1965	Mohamad Saifpour Sabadi (Irn)
1966-7	Masaki Kaneko (Jap)
1969	Takeo Morita (Jap)
1970	Shamseddin Seyed-Abassy (Irn)
1971	Zagalav Abdulbekov (USSR)
1973	Zagalav Abdulbekov (USSR)
1974-5	Zeveg Oidov (Mgl)

1977-9	Vladimir Yumin (USSR)
1981	Simeon Sjeterev (Bul)
1982	Sergeiy Beloglazov (USSR)
1983	Viktor Alekseyev (USSR)
1985	Viktor Alekseyev (USSR)
1986	Hasar Isayev (USSR)
1987	John Smith (USA)
1989-91	John Smith (USA)
1993	Tom Brands (USA)
1994	Abdulaziz Azizov (Rus)

68kg - Lightweight
Limits: 67kg 1951-61, 70kg 1962-7

1951	Olle Anderberg (Swe)
1953	Viktor Sinyavskiy (USSR)
1954	Djahanbakte Tovfighe (Irn)
1957	Alimbek Bestayev (USSR)
1959	Viktor Sinyavskiy (USSR)
1961	Mohamad-Ali Sanatkaram (Irn)
1962	Enyu Valtschev (Bul)
1963	Iwao Horiuchi (Jap)
1965-7	Abdollah Movahed (Irn)
1969-70	Abdollah Movahed (Irn)
1971	Dan Gable (USA)
1973	Lloyd Keaser (USA)
1974	Nasrulla Nasrullayev (USSR)
1975	Pavel Pinigin (USSR)
1977-8	Pavel Pinigin (USSR)
1979	Mikhail Kharachura (USSR)
1981	Saipulla Absaidov (USSR)
1982	Mikhail Kharachura (USSR)
1983	Arsen Fadzeyev (USSR)
1985-7	Arsen Fadzeyev (USSR)
1989	Boris Budayev (USSR)
1990-1	Arsen Fadzeyev (USSR)
1993	Akbar Fallah (Iran)
1994	Alexander Leipold (Ger)

74kg - Welterweight
Limits: 73kg 1951-61, 78kg 1962-7

1951	Celál Atik (Tur)
1953	Ismail Ogan (Tur)
1954	Vakhtang Balavadze (USSR)
1957	Vakhtang Balavadze (USSR)
1959	Emamali Habibi (Irn)
1961-2	Emamali Habibi (Irn)
1963	Guliko Sagaradze (USSR)
1965	Guliko Sagaradze (USSR)
1966	Mahmut Atalay (Tur)
1967	Daniel Robin (Fra)
1969	Zarbeg Beriashvili (USSR)
1970	Wayne Wells (USA)
1971	Yuriy Gusov (USSR)

1973	Mansour Barzegar (Irn)
1974-5	Ruslan Ashuraliyev (USSR)
1977	Stan Dziedzic (USA)
1978-9	Leroy Kemp (USA)
1981	Martin Knosp (FRG)
1982	Leroy Kemp (USA)
1983	Dave Schultz (USA)
1985-6	Raúl Cascaret (Cub)
1987	Adlan Vareyev (USSR)
1989	Ken Monday (USA)
1990	Rahmat Sofiyadi (Bul)
1991	Amir Khadem (Irn)
1993	Park Jang-soon (SKo)
1994	Turan Ceylan (Tur)

82kg - Middleweight
Limits: 79kg 1951-61, 87kg 1962-7

1951	Haydar Zafer (Tur)
1953	Hasan Güngör (Tur)
1954	Abbas Zandi (Irn)
1957	Nabi Sorouri (Irn)
1959	Georgiy Chirtladze (USSR)
1961-2	Mansour Mehdizadeh (Irn)
1963	Prodan Gardschev (Bul)
1965	Mansour Mehdizadeh (Irn)
1966	Prodan Gardschev (Bul)
1967	Boris Gurevich (USSR)
1969	Fred Fozzard (USA)
1970	Yuriy Shakhmuradov (USSR)
1971	Levan Tediashvili (USSR)
1973	Vasiliy Sulzhin (USSR)
1974	Viktor Novozhilov (USSR)
1975	Adolf Seger (FRG)
1977	Adolf Seger (FRG)
1978	Magomed Aratsilov (USSR)
1979	István Kovács (Hun)
1981	Chris Campbell (USA)
1982-3	Tejmuraj Dzogolyev (USSR)
1985	Mark Schultz (USA)
1986	Vladimir Modosyan (USSR)
1987	Mark Schultz (USA)
1989	Elmadi Zhabraylov (USSR)
1990	Jozef Lohyna (Cs)
1991	Kevin Jackson (USA)
1993	Sabahattin Öztürk (Tur)
1994	Elmadi Zhabraylov (Mol)

90kg - Light-heavyweight
Limits: 87kg 1951-61, 97kg 1962-7

1951	Yasar Dogu (Tur)
1953	Anatoliy Albul (USSR)
1954	August Englas (USSR)

1957	Petro Sirakov (Bul)
1959	Golam Reza Takhti (Irn)
1961	Golam Reza Takhti (Irn)
1962-3	Aleksandr Medved (USSR)
1965	Ahmet Ayik (Tur)
1966	Aleksandr Medved (USSR)
1967	Ahmet Ayik (Tur)
1969	Boris Gurevich (USSR)
1970	Gennadiy Strakhov (USSR)
1971	Rusi Petrov (Bul)
1973-5	Levan Tediashvili (USSR)
1977	Anatoliy Prokopchuk (USSR)
1978	Uwe Neupert (GDR)
1979	Khasan Ortsyev (USSR)
1981	Sanasar Oganesyan (USSR)
1982	Uwe Neupert (GDR)
1983	Piotr Nanev (USSR)
1985	Bill Sherr (USA)
1986-7	Makharbek Khadartsev (USSR)
1989-91	Makharbek Khadartsev (USSR)
1993	Abbas Jadidi (Iran)
1994	Rasoul Khadem (Iran)

100kg - Heavyweight
Limits: over 87kg 1951-61, over 97kg 1962-7

1951	Bertil Antonsson (Swe)
1953	Lyutvi Akhmedov (Bul)
1954	Arsen Mekokishvili (USSR)
1957	Hamit Kaplan (Tur)
1959	Lyutvi Ahmedov (Bul)
1961	Wilfried Dietrich (FRG)
1962-3	Aleksandr Ivanitskiy (USSR)
1965-6	Aleksandr Ivanitskiy (USSR)
1967	Aleksandr Medved (USSR)
1969	Shota Lomidze (USSR)
1970	Vladimir Gulyutkin (USSR)
1971	Shota Lomidze (USSR)
1973	Ivan Yarygin (USSR)
1974	Vladimir Gulyutkin (USSR)
1975	Khorloo Baianmunkh (Mgl)
1977	Aslanbek Bisultanov (USSR)
1978	Harald Büttner (GDR)
1979	Ilya Mate (USSR)
1981	Roland Gehrke (GDR)
1982	Ilya Mate (USSR)
1983	Aslan Khadartsev (USSR)

1985	Leri Khabelov (USSR)
1986	Aslan Khadartsev (USSR)
1987	Leri Khabelov (USSR)
1989	Akhmed Atanov (USSR)
1990-1	Leri Khabelov (USSR)
1993	Leri Khabelov (Rus)
1994	Aravat Sabejev (Ger)

Over 100kg - Super-heavyweight (now 130kg)

1969-71	Aleksandr Medved (USSR)
1973	Soslan Andiyev (USSR)
1974	Ladislav Simon (Rom)
1975	Soslan Andiyev (USSR)
1977	Soslan Andiyev (USSR)
1979	Salman Khasimikov (USSR)
1981-3	Salman Khasimikov (USSR)
1985	David Gobedzhishviliy (USSR)
1986	Bruce Baumgartner (USA)
1987	Aslan Khadartsev (USSR)
1989	Ali Reza Soleimani (Ira)
1990	David Gobedzhishviliy (USSR)
1991	Andreas Schröder (Ger)
1993	Bruce Baumgartner (USA)
1994	Mahmut Demir (Tur)

Greco-Roman

48kg - Light-flyweight

1969-70	Gheorghe Berceanu (Rom)
1971	Vladimir Zubkov (USSR)
1973-5	Vladimir Zubkov (USSR)
1977	Aleksey Shumakov (USSR)
1978	Constantin Alexandru (Rom)
1981	Zaksylik Ushkempirov (USSR)
1982	Temur Kazarashvili (USSR)
1983	Bratan Tsenov (Bul)
1985-7	Magyatdin Allakhverdyev (USSR)
1989-90	Oleg Kucherenko (USSR)
1991	Goon Duk-young (SKo)
1993-4	Wilber Sánchez (Cub)

52kg - Flyweight

1950	Bengt Johansson (Swe)
1953	Boris Gurevich (USSR)
1955	Ignazio Fabra (Ita)
1958	Boris Gurevich (USSR)
1961	Armais Sayadov (USSR)
1962	Sergey Rybalko (USSR)
1963	Borivoje Vukov (Yug)
1965	Sergey Rybalko (USSR)
1966	Angel Kerezov (Bul)
1967	Vladimir Bakulin (USSR)

1969	Aluzadeh Firuz (Irn)
1970-1	Petar Kirov (Bul)
1973	Nicu Ginga (Rom)
1974	Peter Kirov (USSR)
1975	Vitaliy Konstantinov (USSR)
1977	Nicu Ginga (Rom)
1978	Vakhtang Blagidze (USSR)
1979	Lajos Rácz (Hun)
1981	Vakhtang Blagidze (USSR)
1982-3	Benyur Pashayan (USSR)
1985	Jan Rønningen (Nor)
1986	Sergey Dyudyayev (USSR)
1987	Pedro Roque (Cuba)
1989-90	Aleksandr Ignatenko (USSR)
1991	Raúl Martínez (Cub)
1993	Raúl Martínez (Cub)
1994	Alfred Ter-Mkrtchyan (Ger)

57kg - Bantamweight

1950	Ali Mahmoud Hannan (Egy)
1953	Artyem Teryan (USSR)
1955	Vladimir Stashevich (USSR)
1958	Oleg Karavayev (USSR)
1961	Oleg Karavayev (USSR)
1962	Masamitsu Ichiguchi (Jap)
1963	János Varga (Hun)
1965	Ion Cernea (Rom)
1966	Fritz Stange (FRG)
1967	Ion Baciu (Rom)
1969	Rustem Kazakov (USSR)
1970	János Varga (Hun)
1971	Rustem Kazakov (USSR)
1973	Jozef Lipien (Pol)
1974-5	Farhat Mustafin (USSR)
1977	Pertti Ukkola (Fin)
1978-9	Shamil Serikov (USSR)
1981	Pasquale Passarelli (FRG)
1982	Piotr Michalik (Pol)
1983	Masaki Eto (Jap)
1985	Stojan Balov (Bul)
1986	Emil Ivanov (Bul)
1987	Patrice Mourier (Fra)
1989	Emil Ivanov (Bul)
1990-1	Rifat Yildiz (Ger)
1993	Agazi Manukjan (Arm)
1994	Yuriy Melnichenko (Kzk)

62kg - Featherweight
Limit: 63kg 1962-7

1950	Olle Anderberg (Swe)
1953	Olle Anderberg (Swe)
1955	Imre Polyák (Hun)
1958	Imre Polyák (Hun)
1961	Hamid Mustafa (Egy)

1962	Imre Polyák (Hun)
1963	Gennadiy Sapunov (USSR)
1965	Yuriy Grigoryev (USSR)
1966-7	Roman Rurua (USSR)
1969	Roman Rurua (USSR)
1970	Hideo Fujimoto (Jap)
1971	Georgi Markov (Bul)
1973-4	Kazimierz Lipien (Pol)
1975	Nelson Davidyan (USSR)
1977	Lászlo Réczi (Hun)
1978	Boris Kramarenko (USSR)
1979	István Tóth (Hun)
1981	István Tóth (Hun)
1982	Ryszard Swierad (Pol)
1983	Hannu Lahtinen (Fin)
1985	Zhivko Vangelov (Bul)
1986	Kamandar Madzhidov (USSR)
1987	Zhivko Vangelov (Bul)
1989	Kamandar Madzhidov (USSR)
1990	Mario Oliveras (Cub)
1991	Sergey Martynov (USSR)
1993-4	Sergey Martynov (Rus)

68kg - Lightweight
Limit: 67kg 1950-61, 70kg 1962-7

1950	József Gál (Hun)
1953	Gustav Freij (Swe)
1955	Grigoriy Gamarnik (USSR)
1958	Riza Dogan (Tur)
1961	Avtandil Koridze (USSR)
1962	Kazim Ayvaz (Tur)
1963	Stevan Horvat (Yug)
1965	Gennadiy Supanov (USSR)
1966	Stevan Horvat (Yug)
1967	Eero Tapio (Fin)
1969	Simion Popescu (Rom)
1970	Roman Rurua (USSR)
1971	Sreten Damjanovic (Yug)
1973	Shamil Khisamutdinov (USSR)
1974	Nelson Davidyan (USSR)
1975	Shamil Khisamutdinov (USSR)
1977	Heinz-Helmut Wehling (GDR)
1978	Stefan Rusu (Rom)
1979	Andrzej Supron (Pol)
1981-2	Gennadiy Yermilov (USSR)
1983	Tapio Sipilä (Fin)
1985	Stefan Negrisan (Rom)
1986	Levon Dzhulfalakyan (USSR)
1987	Aslautdin Abeyev (USSR)
1989	Claudio Passarelli (GDR)
1990-1	Islam Duguchiyev (USSR)
1993-4	Islam Duguchiyev (Rus)

74kg - Welterweight
Limit: 73kg 1950-61, 78kg 1962-7

1950	Matti Simanainen (Fin)
1953	Gurgen Chatvorjan (USSR)
1955	Vladimir Maneyev (USSR)
1958	Kazim Ayvaz (Tur)
1961	Valeriu Bularca (Rom)
1962-3	Anatoliy Kolesov (USSR)
1965	Anatoliy Kolesov (USSR)
1966-7	Viktor Igumenov (USSR)
1969-71	Viktor Igumenov (USSR)
1973	Ivan Kolev (Bul)
1974	Viteslav Mácha (Cs)
1975	Anatoliy Bykov (USSR)
1977	Viteslav Mácha (Cs)
1978	Arif Niftulayev (USSR)
1979	Ferenc Kocsis (Hun)
1981	Aleksandr Kudryavtsev (USSR)
1982	Stefan Rusu (Rom)
1983	Mikhail Mamiashvili (USSR)
1985-6	Mikhail Mamiashvili (USSR)
1987	Jouko Salomaki (Fin)
1989	Daulet Turlykhanov (USSR)
1990-1	Mnatsakan Iskamdarian (USSR)
1993	Nestor Almanza (Cub)
1994	Mnatsakan Iskamdarian (Rus)

82kg - Middleweight
Limit: 79kg 1950-61, 97kg 1962-7

1950	Axel Grönberg (Swe)
1953	Givy Kartoziya (USSR)
1955	Givy Kartoziya (USSR)
1958	Riza Dogan (Tur)
1961	Vasiliy Zenin (USSR)
1962-3	Tevfik Kis (Tur)
1965	Roman Bogdanov (USSR)
1966	Valentin Olenik (USSR)
1967	László Sillai (Hun)
1969	Petar Krumov (Bul)
1970	Anatoliy Nazarenko (USSR)
1971	Csaba Hegedüs (Hun)
1973	Leonid Liberman (USSR)
1974-5	Anatoliy Nazarenko (USSR)
1977	Vlademir Cheboskarov (USSR)
1978	Ion Draica (Rom)
1979	Gennadiy Korban (USSR)
1981	Gennadiy Korban (USSR)
1982-3	Temur Abkhasava (USSR)
1985	Bogdan Daras (Pol)

1986	No medal awarded - both Bogdan Karas (Pol) & Tibor Komaromi (Hun) disqualified
1987	Tibor Komaromi (Hun)
1989	Tibor Komaromi (Hun)
1990-1	Péter Farkas (Hun)
1993	Hamza Yerlikaya (Tur)
1994	Thomas Zander (Ger)

90kg - Light-heavyweight
Limit: 87kg 1950-61, 97kg 1962-7

1950	Muharrem Candas (Tur)
1953	August Englas (USSR)
1955	Valentin Nikolayev (USSR)
1958	Rostom Abashidze (USSR)
1961	György Gurics (Hun)
1962-3	Rostom Abashidze (USSR)
1965	Valeriy Anisimov (USSR)
1966	Boyan Radev (Bul)
1967	Nikolay Yakovenko (USSR)
1969	Aleksandr Yurkevich (USSR)
1970-1	Valeriy Rezantsev (USSR)
1973-5	Valeriy Rezantsev (USSR)
1977	Frank Andersson (Swe)
1978	Stojan Nikolov (Bul)
1979	Frank Andersson (Swe)
1981	Igor Kanygin (USSR)
1982	Frank Andersson (Swe)
1983	Igor Kanygin (USSR)
1985	Michael Houk (USA)
1986	Andrzej Malina (Pol)
1987	Vladimir Popov (USSR)
1989-91	Maik Bullmann (GDR)
1993-4	Gogi Koguashvili (Rus)

100kg - Heavyweight
Limits: over 87kg 1950-61, over 97kg 1962-7

1950	Bertil Antonsson (Swe)
1953	Bertil Antonsson (Swe)
1955	Aleksandr Mazur (USSR)
1958	Ivan Bogdan (USSR)
1961	Ivan Bogdan (USSR)
1962	István Kozma (Hun)
1963	Anatoliy Rochin (USSR)
1965	Nikolay Shmakov (USSR)
1966-7	István Kozma (Hun)
1969	Nikolay Yakovenko (USSR)
1970-1	Per Svensson (Swe)
1973-4	Nikolay Balboshin (USSR)
1975	Kamen Lozanov (Bul)
1977-9	Nikolay Balboshin (USSR)
1981	Mikhail Saladze (USSR)
1982	Roman Wroclawski (Pol)
1983	Andrej Dmitrov (Bul)
1985	Andrej Dmitrov (Bul)
1986	Tamás Gáspár (Hun)
1987	Guram Gedekhauri (USSR)
1989	Gerhard Himmel (FRG)
1990	Sergey Demiashkyevich (USSR)
1991	Héctor Milian (Cub)
1993	Mikael Ljungberg (Swe)
1994	Andrzej Wronski (Pol)

Over 100kg - Super-heavyweight (now 130kg)

1969-70	Anatoliy Roshin (USSR)
1971	Alexandr Tomov (Bul)
1973-5	Alexandr Tomov (Bul)
1977	Nikolai Dinev (Bul)
1978	Aleksandr Kolinchskiy (USSR)
1979	Alexandr Tomov (Bul)
1981	Refik Memisevic (Yug)
1982	Nikolai Dinev (Bul)
1983	Yevgeniy Artioshin (USSR)
1985	Igor Rostozotskiy (USSR)
1986	Tomas Johansson (Swe)
1987	Igor Rostorotskiy (USSR)
1989-91	Aleksandr Karelin (USSR)
1993-4	Aleksandr Karelin (Rus)

Most World and Olympic Titles

10	Aleksandr Medved (USSR) Freestyle: 97kg 1962-4, 1966; over 97kg 1967-8, over 100kg 1969-72
8	Sergey Beloglazov (USSR) Freestyle: 57kg 1980-1, 1983, 1985-8; 62kg 1982
8	Arsen Fadzeyev (USSR) Freestyle 68kg 1983, 1985-8, 1990-2
7	Valeriy Rezantsev (USSR) Greco Roman: 90kg 1970-6
7	Makharbek Khadartsev (USSR) Freestyle 90kg 1986-92
7	Aleksandr Karelin (Rus) Greco-Roman: over 100kg 1988-94
6	Abdollah Movahed (Irn) Freestyle: 70/68kg 1965-70
6	Levan Tediashvili (USSR) Freestyle: 82kg 1971-2; 90kg 1973-6
6	Nikolay Balboshin (USSR) Greco Roman: 100kg 1973-4, 1976, 1977-9
6	Soslan Andiyev (USSR) Freestyle: over 100kg 1973, 1975-8, 1980
6	John Smith (USA) Freestyle 62kg 1987-92
6	Leri Khabelov (USSR) Freestyle: 100kg 1985, 1987, 1990-3
6	Valentin Jordanov (Bul) Freestyle: 52kg 1983, 1985, 1987, 1989, 1993-4
5	Ali Aliev (USSR) Freestyle: 52kg 1959, 1961-2; 57kg 1966-7
5	Aleksandr Ivanitskiy (USSR) Freestyle: over 97kg 1962-6
5	István Kozma (Hun) Greco-Roman: over 97kg 1962, 1964, 1966-8
5	Viktor Igumenov (USSR) Greco Roman: 78kg 1966-7, 74kg 1969-71
5	Roman Rurua (USSR) Greco Roman: 63/62kg 1966-69, 68kg 1970
5	Petar Kirov (Bul) Greco-Roman: 52kg 1968, 1970-2, 1974
5	Alexandr Tomov (Bul) Greco-Roman over 100kg 1971, 1973-5, 1979
5	Yuji Takada (Jap) Freestyle: 52kg 1974-7, 1979

Yachting

Yachting originated in the 16th and 17th centuries in the Netherlands, then the world's greatest maritime power. The first known yacht race for pleasure was in September 1661 when Charles II challenged the Duke of York to a race over a 23-mile stretch of the River Thames from Greenwich to Gravesend. The sport became popular towards the end of the 19th century, nearly 150 years after the formation of the world's first yacht club, the Water Club of Cork, Ireland in 1720.

America's Cup

One of the most famous of all sporting trophies, the Cup was donated by the Royal Yacht Squadron for a race around the Isle of Wight in 1851. The American schooner America won the race and took the trophy to the United States. The New York Yacht club then offered it as a challenge trophy but, despite many challenges over the years, the cup stayed in American hands until 1983 when it temporarily became Australian property, and again in 1995 when it was taken to New Zealand.

Year	Winning boat	Winning skipper	Score	Challenger
1870	Magic	Andrew Comstock	-	Cambria (Eng)
1871	Columbia & Sappho	Nelson Comstock Sam Greenwood	4-1	Livonia (Eng)
1876	Madeleine	Josephus Williams	2-0	Countess of Dufferin (Can)
1881	Mischief	Nathaniel Clock	2-0	Atalanta (Can)
1885	Puritan	Aubrey Crocker	2-0	Genesta (Eng)
1886	Mayflower	Martin Stone	2-0	Galatea (Eng)
1887	Volunteer	Henry Haff	2-0	Thistle (Sco)
1893	Vigilant	William Hansen	3-0	Valkyrie II (Eng)
1895	Defender	Henry Haff	3-0	Valkyrie III (Eng)
1899	Columbia	James Barr	3-0	Shamrock (Eng)
1901	Columbia	James Barr	3-0	Shamrock II (Eng)
1903	Reliance	James Barr	3-0	Shamrock III (Eng)
1920	Resolute	Charles Adams	3-2	Shamrock IV (Eng)
1930	Enterprise	Harold Vanderbilt	4-0	Shamrock V (Eng)
1934	Rainbow	Harold Vanderbilt	4-2	Endeavour (Eng)

The 1995 America's Cup winners – New Zealand's Black Magic

1937	Ranger	Harold Vanderbilt	4-0	Endeavour II (Eng)
1958	Columbia	Briggs Cunningham	4-0	Sceptre (Eng)
1962	Weatherly	Emil Mosbacher Jr	4-1	Gretel (Aus)
1964	Constellation	Bob Bavier Jr	4-0	Sovereign (Eng)
1967	Intrepid	Emil Mosbacher Jr	4-0	Dame Pattie (Aus)
1970	Intrepid	Bill Ficker	4-1	Gretel II (Aus)
1974	Courageous	Ted Hood	4-0	Southern Cross (Aus)
1977	Courageous	Ted Turner	4-0	Australia (Aus)
1980	Freedom	Dennis Conner	4-1	Australia (Aus)
1983	Australia II (Aus)	John Bertrand	4-3	Liberty (USA)
1987	Stars & Stripes	Dennis Conner	4-0	Kookaburra III (Aus)
1988	Stars & Stripes	Dennis Conner	2-0	New Zealand (NZ)
1992	America³	Bill Koch	4-1	Il Moro di Venezia (Ita)
1995	Black Magic (NZ)	Russell Coutts	5-0	Young America (USA)

* *Stars and Stripes* accepted a special challenge from *New Zealand* (skippered by David Barnes) in a best-of-three series in 1988. After a successful defence the American Supreme Court ruled that Conner's use of the catamaran against the New Zealand monohull had violated the Deed of Gift governing the race. However this decision was reversed by the New York Appeals Court in 1989, and the legal battle ended in 1990 in favour of Conner.

Most times winning skipper:
3 Charlie Barr, Harold Vanderbilt, Dennis Conner; 2 Henry Haff, Emil Mosbacher Jr
Most times skippered challenger: 3 Jim Hardy 1970, 1974, 1980

Admiral's Cup

The Royal Ocean Racing Club donated the trophy in 1957 to encourage yachtsmen from abroad to race in English waters. National three-boats teams contest the Cup, and in 1975, 1977 and 1979, a record 19 nations competed. The biennial series of six races (five until 1987), combining inshore and offshore racing , take place in the English Channel, at Cowes, in the Solent, and culminating with the Fastnet Race (established in 1925), 605 miles (975 km) from Cowes, round the Fastnet Rock off the south-west coast of Ireland and back. The points system is weighted towards the offshore races.
Winners:

9	UK	1957, 1959, 1963, 1965, 1971, 1975, 1977, 1981, 1989
3	Germany	1973, 1983, 1985 (FRG); 1993
2	USA	1961, 1969
2	Australia	1967, 1979
1	New Zealand	1987
1	France	1991

Olympic Games

Yachting did not make its Olympic debut until 1900. It should have been included in the first modern Olympics programme four years earlier, but bad weather prevented any competition. The classes of competition have varied over the years, with the champions at current classes shown first, followed by winning teams at the discontinued events.

Soling
1972 USA (Harry Melges, William Bentsen, William Allen)
1976 Denmark (Poul Jensen, Valdemar Bandolowski, Erik H Hansen)
1980 Denmark (Poul Jensen, Valdemar Bandolowski, Erik H Hansen)
1984 USA (Robert Haines Jr, Edward Trevelyan, Roderick Davis)
1988 GDR (Jochen Schümann, Thomas Flach, Bernd Jäkel)
1992 Denmark (Jesper Bonk, Steen Secher, Jesper Seier)

Finn - Olympic monotype
Classes: 12-foot and 18-foot (2-handed) dinghies in 1920, Meulan 1924, International 12-foot 1928, Snowbird 1932, International Olympia 1936, Firefly 1948. Finn from 1952.
1920 Franciscus Hin/Johannes Hin (Hol) *12-foot*
1920 Francis Richards/T Hedburg(UK) *18-foot*
1924 Léon Huybrechts (Bel)
1928 Sven Thorell (Swe)
1932 Jacques Lebrun (Fra)
1936 Daniel Kagchelland (Hol)
1948 Paul Elvstrøm (Den)
1952 Paul Elvstrøm (Den)
1956 Paul Elvstrøm (Den)
1960 Paul Elvstrøm (Den)
1964 Willi Kuhweide (FRG)
1968 Valentin Mankin (USSR)
1972 Serge Maury (Fra)
1976 Jochen Schümann (GDR)
1980 Esko Rechardt (Fin)
1984 Russell Coutts (NZ)
1988 José-Luis Doreste (Spa)
1992 José Maria van der Ploeg (Spa)

470 class
1976 Frank Hübner/Harro Bode (FRG)
1980 Marcos Soares/Eduardo Penido (Bra)
1984 Luis Doreste/Roberto Molina (Spa)
1988 Thierry Peponnet/Luc Pillot (Fra)
1992 Jorge Calafat/Francisco Sánchez (Spa)

Flying Dutchman
Sharpie class in 1956
1956 Peter Mander/John Cropp (NZ)
1960 Peder Lunde Jr/Björn Bergvall (Nor)

1964 Helmer Pedersen/Earle Wells (NZ)
1968 Rodney Pattisson/Iain Macdonald-Smith (UK)
1972 Rodney Pattisson/Christopher Davies (UK)
1976 Jörg Diesch/Eckert Diesch (FRG)
1980 Alejandro Abascal/Miguel Noguer (Spa)
1984 Jonathan McKee/William Carl Buchan (USA)
1988 Jørgen Bojsen-Møller/Christian Grønberg (Den)
1992 Luis Doreste/Domingo Manrique (Spa)

Star
1932 Gilbert Gray/Andrew Libano Jr (USA)
1936 Peter Bischoff/Hans-Joachim Weise (Ger)
1948 Hilary Smart/Paul Smart (USA)
1952 Agostino Straulino/Nicolo Rode (Ita)
1956 Herbert Williams/Lawrence Low (USA)
1960 Timir Pinegin/Fyodor Shutkov (USSR)
1964 Durward Knowles/Cecil Cooke (Bah)
1968 Lowell North/Peter Barrett (USA)
1972 David Forbes/John Anderson (Aus)
1980 Valentin Mankin/Aleksandr Muzychenko (USSR)
1984 Bill Buchan/Stephen Erickson (USA)
1988 Michael McIntyre/Bryn Vaile (UK)

1992 Mark Reynolds/Hal Haenel (USA)

Tornado
1976 Reg White/John Osborn (UK)
1980 Alexandre Welter/Lars Björkström (Bra)
1984 Rex Sellers/Christopher Timms (NZ)
1988 Jean-Yves Le Deroff/Nicolas Henard (Fra)
1992 Yves Loday/Nicolas Hénard (Fra)

Boardsailing (Windglider)
1984 Stephan van den Berg (Hol)
1988 Bruce Kendall (NZ)
1992 Franck David (Fra)

Women's Boardsailing
1992 Barbara-Anne Kendall (NZ)

Women's 470 class
1988 Allison Jolly/Lynne Jewell (USA)
1992 Theresa Zabell/Patricia Guerra (Spa)

Women's Europe class
1992 Linda Andersen (Nor)

Most individual gold medals: 4 Paul Elvstrøm

Discontinued Events

Swallow
1948 Stewart Morris/David Bond (UK)

Tempest
1972 Valentin Mankin/Vitaliy Dyrdyra (USSR)
1976 John Albrechtson/Ingvar Hansson (Swe)

Dragon
1948 Norway
1952 Norway
1956 Sweden
1960 Greece
1964 Denmark
1968 USA
1972 Australia

5.5 metres
1952 USA
1956 Sweden
1960 USA
1964 Australia
1968 Sweden

6 metres
1908 Great Britain

1912 France
1920 Norway
1924 Norway
1928 Norway
1932 Sweden
1936 Great Britain
1948 USA
1952 USA

6 metres (1907 rating)
1920 Belgium

6.5 metres
1920 Netherlands

7 metres
1908 Great Britain
1920 Great Britain

8 metres
1908 Great Britain
1912 Norway
1920 Norway
1924 Norway
1928 France
1932 USA
1936 Italy

8 metres (1907 rating)
1920 Norway

10 metres
1912 Sweden
1920 Norway (1907 rating)
     Norway (1919 rating)

12 metres
1908 Great Britain
1912 Norway
1920 Norway (1907 rating)
     Norway (1919 rating)

30 square metres
1920 Sweden

40 square metres
1920 Sweden

Tonnage categories in 1900
$1/2$ Ton France
$1/2$-1 Ton France
1-2 Ton Switzerland
2-3 Ton Great Britain
3-10 Ton France
10-20 Ton France
Open Great Britain

The Whitbread Round the World Race

The longest race in the world, it was inaugurated in August 1973, and is organised by the Royal Naval Sailing Association. Held quadrennially, the distance has been 26,180 nautical miles (increaseed to 32,000 in 1990), starting and finishing at Portsmouth, England and rounding the Cape of Good Hope and Cape Horn. Conducted as a handicap race, with various classes. In the following list the handicap winner is shown first, followed by the fastest yacht that year; Flyer II and Steinlager 2 won on both actual and corrected time.

Year	Winning skipper	Yacht	Time
1974	Ramon Carlin (Mex)	Sayula II	152d 9h 00m
	Chay Blyth (UK)	Great Britain II	144d 10 hr

Year	Winning skipper	Yacht	Time
1978	Cornelis van Rietschoten (Hol)	Flyer	136d 5hr
	Rob James (UK)	Great Britain II	134d 12hr
1982	Cornelis van Rietschoten (Hol)	Flyer II	120d 6h 35m
1986	Lionel Pean (Fra)	L'Esprit d'Equipe	132d 0h 16m
	Pierre Fehlmann (Swi)	UBS Switzerland	117d 14h 32m
1990	Peter Blake (NZ)	Steinlager 2	128d 9h 40m
1994	Grant Dalton (NZ)	New Zealand Endeavour	120d 5h 9m

A world record for single-handed non-stop sailing around the world was set in the Vendée Globe Challenge, 109 days 8 hrs, 48 mins 50 secs by Titouan Lamazou (Fra) in the 60-ft sloop *Ecureuil d'Aquitaine* from Les Sables d'Olonne, France and back, 26 Nov 1989 to 15 Mar 1990.

Single-handed Transatlantic Race

Held every four years from Plymouth to Newport, Rhode Island, approximately 3000 miles 4825 km, the race was named the Observer Single-Handed Transatlantic Race (OSTAR) 1960-84. When The Observer were succeeded as sponsors by the Carlsberg brewing company the 1988 race was known as C-STAR. The race was the idea of Colonel 'Blondie' Hasler, who finished second in the inaugural race.

There is now a size limit for the boats of 18.3m 60 ft, but the largest contestant was the 71.9m four-master Club Mediterranée, sailed to second place in 1976 by Alain Colas (Fra). Monohulls won the first three races and in 1976, trimarans all the others, as the average speed of the winner has risen from 3.09 knots in 1960 to 11.23 knots in 1988.

Year	Winner	Yacht	Time
1960	Francis Chichester (UK)	Gypsy Moth III	40d 12hr 30min
1964	Éric Tabarly (Fra)	Pen Duick II	27d 3hr 56min
1968	Geoffrey Williams (UK)	Sir Thomas Lipton	25d 20hr 33min
1972	Alain Colas (Fra)	Pen Duick IV	20d 13hr 15min
1976	Éric Tabarly (Fra)	Pen Duick VI	23d 20hr 12min
1980	Phil Weld (USA)	Moxie	17d 23hr 12min
1984	Yvon Fauconnier (Fra)	Umupro Jardin V	16d 6hr 00min
1988	Philippe Poupon (Fra)	Fleury Michon	10d 9hr 15min

Boardsailing

Boardsailing (often called Windsurfing, which is a trade name) was pioneered as a sport by Henry Hoyle Schweitzer and Jim Drake in California, USA, in 1968, but the origin of boardsailing dates back to 1958 when 12-year-old Peter Chilvers of England devised the first prototype sailboard. The sport became popular in the 1970s and a world championship was instituted in 1973. Boardsailing was included in the Olympic Games for the first time in 1984.

Speed Records

The highest speed reached under sail on water by any craft over a 500m timed run is 46.52 knots (86.21 km/h) by Simon McKeon and Tim Daddo (Aus) in Yellow Pages Endeavour, a wing-mastedtri-foiler at Shallow Inlet, Melbourne, Australia on 26 Oct 1993.

The boardsailing record was set by Thierry Bielak (Fra) at 45.34 knots (83.95 km/h) at Saintes Maries de-le-Mer, Camargue, France on 24 Apr 1993. The women's record was set by Babethe Coquelle (Fra) who achieved a speed of 40.36 knots (74.79 km/h) at Tarifa, Spainon 8 Jul 1995.

Commonwealth Games

The Commonwealth Games are multi-sport competitions, held every four years and contested by representatives of the nations of the British Commonwealth. They were first staged as the British Empire Games at Hamilton, Canada, opening on 16 August 1930. The eleven nations participating were Australia, Bermuda, British Guiana, Canada, England, Ireland, Newfoundland, New Zealand, Scotland, South Africa and Wales. Six sports were included, but there were women's events only in swimming. Women first competed in athletics in 1934.

The idea of staging such an event was first put forward by a Yorkshireman, Rev. J Astley Cooper in the magazine Greater Britain in 1891. The first Inter-Empire Sports meeting was held at Crystal Palace, London in 1911, forming part of the celebrations for the Coronation of King George V. Competitors from Britain, Canada, Australia and New Zealand contested four sports - athletics (five events), heavyweight boxing, swimming (two events) and middleweight wrestling. Canadians won four gold medals, Britain three, and Australia two.

The Games became the British Empire and Commonwealth Games in 1954, and simply the British Commonwealth Games in 1970, in which year the Games went metric for distances and weights.

Ten sports are held at each Games - athletics and swimming are obligatory, and the others are selected from 15 recognised sports, with additionally two demonstration sports. The recognised sports yet to be included officially at any Games are canoeing, table tennis and yachting. Judo was included for the first time in 1990.

Venues
1930 Hamilton, Canada
1934 London, England
1938 Sydney, Australia
1950 Auckland, New Zealand
1954 Vancouver, Canada
1958 Cardiff, Wales
1962 Perth, Australia
1966 Kingston, Jamaica
1970 Edinburgh, Scotland
1974 Christchurch, New Zealand
1978 Edmonton, Canada
1982 Brisbane, Australia
1986 Edinburgh, Scotland
1990 Auckland, New Zealand
1994 Victoria, Canada
1998 Kuala Lumpur, Malaysia

Commonwealth Games Winners

Archery
Held in 1982 only, when the winners were:
Men: Mark Blenkarne (Eng) 2446
Women: Neroli Fairhall (NZ) 2373

Athletics
Imperial distances run 1930 to 1966. Note that where known fully-automatic times are given as per the current regulations (original official hand times may well have differed).
w = wind assisted performance.

Men

100 yards (91.4m)
1930 Percy Williams (Can) 9.9
1934 Arthur Sweeney (Eng) 10.0
1938 Cyril Holmes (Eng) 9.7
1950 John Treloar (Aus) 9.7
1954 Mike Agostini (Tri) 9.6
1958 Keith Gardner (Jam) 9.66
1962 Seraphino Antao (Ken) 9.50
1966 Harry Jerome (Can) 9.41

100 metres
1970 Don Quarrie (Jam) 10.24w
1974 Don Quarrie (Jam) 10.38
1978 Don Quarrie (Jam) 10.03w
1982 Allan Wells (Sco) 10.05w
1986 Ben Johnson (Can) 10.07
1990 Linford Christie (Eng) 9.93w
1994 Linford Christie (Eng) 9.91

220 yards (201.17m)
1930 Stanley Engelhart (Eng) 21.8
1934 Arthur Sweeney (Eng) 21.9
1938 Cyril Holmes (Eng) 21.2
1950 John Treloar (Aus) 21.5
1954 Donald Jowett (NZ) 21.5
1958 Tom Robinson (Bah) 21.08
1962 Seraphino Antao (Ken) 21.28
1966 Stanley Allotey (Gha) 20.65

200 metres
1970 Don Quarrie (Jam) 20.56
1974 Don Quarrie (Jam) 20.73
1978 Allan Wells (Sco) 20.12w
1982 Allan Wells (Sco) &
  Mike McFarlane (Eng) 20.43
1986 Atlee Mahorn (Can) 20.31w
1990 Marcus Adam (Eng) 20.10w
1994 Frank Fredericks (Nam) 19.97

440 yards (402.34m)
1930 Alex Wilson (Can) 48.8
1934 Godfrey Rampling (Eng) 48.0
1938 Bill Roberts (Eng) 47.9
1950 Edwin Carr (Aus) 47.9
1954 Kevan Gosper (Aus) 47.2
1958 Milkha Singh (Ind) 46.71
1962 George Kerr (Jam) 46.74
1966 Wendell Mottley (Tri) 45.08

400 metres
1970 Charles Asati (Ken) 45.01
1974 Charles Asati (Ken) 46.04
1978 Rick Mitchell (Aus) 46.34
1982 Bert Cameron (Jam) 45.89
1986 Roger Black (Eng) 45.57
1990 Darren Clark (Aus) 44.60
1994 Charles Gitonga (Ken) 45.00

880 yards (804.67m)
1930 Thomas Hampson (Eng) 1:52.4
1934 Phil Edwards (Guy) 1:54.2
1938 Vernon Boot (NZ) 1:51.2
1950 John Parlett (Eng) 1:53.1
1954 Derek Johnson (Eng) 1:50.7
1958 Herb Elliott (Aus) 1:49.32
1962 Peter Snell (NZ) 1:47.64
1966 Noel Clough (Aus) 1:46.9

800 metres
1970 Robert Ouko (Ken) 1:46.89
1974 John Kipkurgat (Ken) 1:43.85
1978 Mike Boit (Ken) 1:46.39
1982 Peter Bourke (Aus) 1:45.18
1986 Steve Cram (Eng) 1:43.22
1990 Sammy Tirop (Ken) 1:45.98
1994 Patrick Konchellah
  (Ken) 1:45.18

1 mile (1609.35m)
1930 Reg Thomas (Eng) 4:14.0
1934 Jack Lovelock (NZ) 4:12.8
1938 Jim Alford (Wal) 4:11.6
1950 William Parnell (Can) 4:11.0
1954 Roger Bannister (Eng) 3:58.8
1958 Herb Elliott (Aus) 3:59.03
1962 Peter Snell (NZ) 4:04.58
1966 Kipchoge Keino (Ken) 3:55.34

1500 metres
1970 Kipchoge Keino (Ken) 3:36.6
1974 Filbert Bayi (Tan) 3:32.16

1978 David Moorcroft (Eng)
3:35.48
1982 Steve Cram (Eng) 3:42.37
1986 Steve Cram (Eng) 3:50.87
1990 Peter Elliott (Eng) 3:33.39
1994 Reuben Chesang (Ken)
3:36.70

3 miles (4820.04m)
1930 Stan Tomlin (Eng) 14:27.4
1934 Walter Beavers (Eng) 14:32.6
1938 Cecil Matthews (NZ) 13:59.6
1950 Len Eyre (Eng) 14:23.6
1954 Chris Chataway (Eng) 13:35.2
1958 Murray Halberg (NZ)
13:14.96
1962 Murray Halberg (NZ)
13:34.15
1966 Kipchoge Keino (Ken) 12:57.4

5000 metres
1970 Ian Stewart (Sco) 13:22.8
1974 Ben Jipcho (Ken) 13:14.4
1978 Henry Rono (Ken) 13:23.04
1982 David Moorcroft (Eng)
13:33.00
1986 Steve Ovett (Eng) 13:24.11
1990 Andrew Lloyd (Aus) 13:24.86
1994 Rob Denmark (Eng) 13:23.00

6 miles (9656.07m)
1930 John Savidan (NZ) 30:49.6
1934 Arthur Penny (Eng) 31:00.6
1938 Cecil Matthews (NZ) 30:14.5
1950 Harold Nelson (NZ) 30:29.6
1954 Peter Driver (Eng) 29:09.4
1958 David Power (Aus) 28:48.16
1962 Bruce Kidd (Can) 28:26.13
1966 Naftali Temu (Ken) 27:14.21

10 000 metres
1970 Lachie Stewart (Sco) 28:11.71
1974 Richard Tayler (NZ) 27:46.4
1978 Brendan Foster (Eng) 28:13.65
1982 Gidamis Shahanga (Tan)
28:10.15
1986 Jonathan Solly (Eng) 27:57.42
1990 Eamonn Martin (Eng)
28:08.57
1994 Lameck Aguta (Ken) 28:38.22

Marathon (26 miles 385 yards or
42.195km)
1930 Duncan McL.Wright (Sco)
2:43:43
1934 Harold Webster (Can) 2:40:36
1938 Johannes Coleman (SAf)
2:30:49.8
1950 Jack Holden (Eng) 2:32:57
1954 Joseph McGhee (Sco) 2:39:36
1958 David Power (Aus) 2:22:45.6
1962 Brian Kilby (Eng) 2:21:17
1966 Jim Alder (Sco) 2:22:07.8
1970 Ron Hill (Eng) 2:09:28

1974 Ian Thompson (Eng) 2:09:12
1978 Gidamis Shahanga (Tan)
2:15:39.8
1982 Rob de Castella (Aus) 2:09:18
1986 Rob de Castella (Aus) 2:10:15
1990 Douglas Wakiihuri (Ken)
2:10:27
1994 Steve Moneghetti (Aus)
2:11:49

3000 metres steeplechase
*Held over 8 laps in 1930 and at 2 miles
(3218.7m) in 1934.*
1930 George Bailey (Eng) 9:52.0
1934 Stanley Scarsbrook (Eng)
10:23.4
1962 Trevor Vincent (Aus) 8:43.4
1966 Peter Welsh (NZ) 8:29.44
1970 Tony Manning (Aus) 8:26.2
1974 Ben Jipcho (Ken) 8:20.8
1978 Henry Rono (Ken) 8:26.54
1982 Julius Korir (Ken) 8:23.94
1986 Graeme Fell (Can) 8:24.49
1990 Julius Kariuki (Ken) 8:20.64
1994 Johnstone Kipkoech (Ken)
8:14.72

120 yards hurdles (109.73m)
1930 Lord Burghley (Eng) 14.6
1934 Don Finlay (Eng) 15.2
1938 Tom Lavery (SAf) 14.0w
1950 Peter Gardner (Aus) 14.3
1954 Keith Gardner (Jam) 14.2
1958 Keith Gardner (Jam) 14.20w
1962 Ghulam Raziq (Pak) 14.34
1966 David Hemery (Eng) 14.1

110 metres hurdles
1970 David Hemery (Eng) 13.66w
1974 Fatwel Kimaiyo (Ken) 13.69
1978 Berwyn Price (Wal) 13.70w
1982 Mark McKoy (Can) 13.37
1986 Mark McKoy (Can) 13.31w
1990 Colin Jackson (Wal) 13.08
1994 Colin Jackson (Wal) 13.08

440 yards hurdles (402.34m)
1930 Lord Burghley (Eng) 54.4
1934 Alan Hunter (Sco) 55.2
1938 John Loaring (Can) 52.9
1950 Duncan White (Sri) 52.5
1954 David Lean (Aus) 52.4
1958 Gerhardus Potgieter (SAf)
49.73
1962 Ken Roche (Aus) 51.5
1966 Ken Roche (Aus) 50.95

400 metres hurdles
1970 John Sherwood (Eng) 50.03
1974 Alan Pascoe (Eng) 48.83
1978 Daniel Kimaiyo (Ken) 49.48
1982 Garry Brown (Aus) 49.37
1986 Phil Beattie (NI) 49.60
1990 Kriss Akabusi (Eng) 48.89

1994 Samuel Matete (Zim) 48.67

4 x 110 yards relay (4 x 100.54m)
1930 Canada 42.2
1934 England 42.2
1938 Canada 41.6
1950 Australia 42.2
1954 Canada 41.3
1958 England 40.72
1962 England 40.62
1966 Ghana 39.8

4 x 100 metres relay
1970 Jamaica 39.46
1974 Australia 39.31
1978 Scotland 39.24
1982 Nigeria 39.15
1986 Canada 39.15
1990 England 38.67
1994 Canada 38.39

4 x 440 yards relay
1930 England 3:19.4
1934 England 3:16.8
1938 Canada 3:16.9
1950 Australia 3:17.8
1954 England 3:11.2
1958 South Africa 3:08.21
1962 Jamaica 3:10.2
1966 Trinidad & Tobago 3:02.8

4 x 400 metres relay
1970 Kenya 3:03.63
1974 Kenya 3:04.4
1978 Kenya 3:03.54
1982 England 3:05.45
1986 England 3:07.19
1990 Kenya 3:02.48
1994 England 3:02.14

High jump
1930 Johannes Viljoen (SAf) 1.90
1934 Edwin Thacker (SAf) 1.90
1938 Edwin Thacker (SAf) 1.96
1950 John Winter (Aus) 1.98
1954 Emmanuel Ifeajuna (Nig)
2.03
1958 Ernest Haisley (Jam) 2.06
1962 Percy Hobson (Aus) 2.11
1966 Lawrie Peckham (Aus) 2.08
1970 Lawrie Peckham (Aus) 2.14
1974 Gordon Windeyer (Aus) 2.16
1978 Claude Ferragne (Can) 2.20
1982 Milt Ottey (Can) 2.31
1986 Milt Ottey (Can) 2.30
1990 Nick Saunders (Ber) 2.36
1994 Tim Forsyth (Aus) 2.32

Pole vault
1930 Victor Pickard (Can) 3.73
1934 Sylvanus Apps (Can) 3.81
(3.88 jump-off)
1938 Andries du Plessis (SAf) 4.11
1950 Tim Anderson (Eng) 3.97

1954 Geoff Elliott (Eng) 4.26
1958 Geoff Elliott (Eng) 4.16
1962 Trevor Bickle (Aus) 4.49
1966 Trevor Bickle (Aus) 4.80
1970 Mike Bull (NI) 5.10
1974 Don Baird (Aus) 5.05
1978 Bruce Simpson (Can) 5.10
1982 Ray Boyd (Aus) 5.20
1986 Andrew Ashurst (Eng) 5.20
1990 Simon Arkell (Aus) 5.35
1994 Nick Winter (Wal) 5.40

Long jump
1930 Leonard Hutton (Can) 7.20
1934 Sam Richardson (Can) 7.17
1938 Harold Brown (Can) 7.43
1950 Neville Price (SAf) 7.31
1954 Ken Wilmshurst (Eng) 7.54
1958 Paul Foreman (Jam) 7.47
1962 Michael Ahey (Gha) 8.05w
1966 Lynn Davies (Wal) 7.99
1970 Lynn Davies (Wal) 8.06w
1974 Alan Lerwill (Eng) 7.94
1978 Roy Mitchell (Eng) 8.06
1982 Gary Honey (Aus) 8.13
1986 Gary Honey (Aus) 8.08
1990 Yusuf Alli (Nig) 8.39w
1994 Obinna Eregbu (Nig) 8.05w
   (8.22q)

Triple jump
1930 Gordon Smallacombe (Can)
   14.76
1934 Jack Metcalfe (Aus) 15.63
1938 Jack Metcalfe (Aus) 15.49
1950 Brian Oliver (Aus) 15.61
1954 Ken Wilmshurst (Eng) 15.28
1958 Ian Tomlinson (Aus) 15.74
1962 Ian Tomlinson (Aus) 16.20
1966 Samuel Igun (Nig) 16.40
1970 Phil May (Aus) 16.72
1974 Joshua Owusu (Gha) 16.50
1978 Keith Connor (Eng) 17.21
1982 Keith Connor (Eng) 17.81w
1986 John Herbert (Eng) 17.27w
1990 Marios Hadjiandreou (Cyp)
   16.95
1994 Julian Golley (Eng) 17.03

Shot
1930 Hendrik Hart (SAf) 14.58
1934 Hendrik Hart (SAf) 14.67
1938 Louis Fouche (SAf) 14.48
1950 Maitaika Tuicakau (Fiji) 14.64
1954 John Savidge (Eng) 16.77
1958 Arthur Rowe (Eng) 17.57
1962 Martyn Lucking (Eng) 18.08
1966 David Steen (Can) 18.79
1970 David Steen (Can) 19.21
1974 Geoff Capes (Eng) 20.74
1978 Geoff Capes (Eng) 19.77
1982 Bruno Pauletto (Can) 19.55
1986 Billy Cole (Eng) 18.16

1990 Simon Williams (Eng) 18.54
1994 Matthew Simson (Eng) 19.49

Discus
1930 Hendrik Hart (SAf) 41.44
1934 Hendrik Hart (SAf) 41.54
1938 Eric Coy (Can) 44.76
1950 Ian Reed (Aus) 47.72
1954 Stephanus du Plessis (SAf)
   51.70
1958 Stephanus du Plessis (SAf)
   55.94
1962 Warwick Selvey (Aus) 56.48
1966 Les Mills (NZ) 56.18
1970 George Puce (Can) 59.02
1974 Robin Tait (NZ) 63.08
1978 Borys Chambul (Can) 59.70
1982 Brad Cooper (Bah) 64.04
1986 Raymond Lazdins (Can)
   58.86
1990 Adewale Olokoju (Nig) 62.62
1994 Werner Reiterer (Aus) 62.76

Hammer
1930 Malcolm Nokes (Eng) 47.12
1934 Malcolm Nokes (Eng) 48.24
1938 George Sutherland (Can)
   48.70
1950 Duncan Clark (Sco) 49.94
1954 Muhammad Iqbal (Pak) 55.38
1958 Mike Ellis (Eng) 62.90
1962 Howard Payne (Eng) 61.64
1966 Howard Payne (Eng) 61.98
1970 Howard Payne (Eng) 67.80
1974 Ian Chipchase (Eng) 69.56
1978 Peter Farmer (Aus) 71.10
1982 Robert Weir (Eng) 75.08
1986 David Smith (Eng) 74.06
1990 Sean Carlin (Aus) 75.66
1994 Sean Carlin (Aus) 73.48

Javelin
1930 Stanley Lay (NZ) 63.12
1934 Robert Dixon (Can) 60.02
1938 James Courtwright (Can)
   62.80
1950 Leo Roininen (Can) 57.10
1954 James Achurch (Aus) 68.52
1958 Colin Smith (Eng) 71.28
1962 Alfred Mitchell (Aus) 78.10
1966 John FitzSimons (Eng) 79.78
1970 David Travis (Eng) 79.50
1974 Charles Clover (Eng) 84.92
1978 Phil Olsen (Can) 84.00
1982 Michael O'Rourke (NZ) 89.48
1986 David Ottley (Eng) 80.62
1990 Steve Backley (Eng) 86.02
1994 Steve Backley (Eng) 82.74

Decathlon
All scored on the 1984 Scoring Tables.
1966 Roy Williams (NZ) 7133
1970 Geoff Smith (Aus) 7420

1974 Mike Bull (NI) 7363
1978 Daley Thompson (Eng)
   8470w
1982 Daley Thompson (Eng) 8424
1986 Daley Thompson (Eng) 8663
1990 Mike Smith (Can) 8525
1994 Mike Smith (Can) 8326

20 miles road walk
1966 Ron Wallwork (Eng) 2:44:42.8
1970 Noel Freeman (Aus) 2:33:33
1974 John Warhurst (Eng) 2:35:23.0

30 kilometres road walk
1978 Ollie Flynn (Eng) 2:22:03.7
1982 Steve Barry (Wal) 2:10:16
1986 Simon Baker (Aus) 2:07:47
1990 Guillaume LeBlanc (Can)
   2:08:28
1994 Nick A'Hern (Aus) 2:07:53

Women

100 yards
1934 Eileen Hiscock (Eng) 11.3
1938 Decima Norman (Aus) 11.1
1950 Marjorie Jackson (Aus) 10.8
1954 Marjorie Jackson (Aus) 10.7
1958 Marlene Willard (Aus) 10.70
1962 Dorothy Hyman (Eng) 11.2
1966 Dianne Burge (Aus) 10.6

100 metres
1970 Raelene Boyle (Aus) 11.26w
1974 Raelene Boyle (Aus) 11.27
1978 Sonia Lannaman (Eng)
   11.27w
1982 Angella Taylor (Can) 11.00
1986 Heather Oakes (Eng) 11.20w
1990 Merlene Ottey (Jam) 11.02w
1994 Mary Onyali (Nig) 11.06

220 yards
1934 Eileen Hiscock (Eng) 25.0
1938 Decima Norman (Aus) 24.7
1950 Marjorie Jackson (Aus) 24.3
1954 Marjorie Nelson (née
   Jackson) (Aus) 24.0
1958 Marlene Willard (Aus) 23.65
1962 Dorothy Hyman (Eng) 24.00
1966 Dianne Burge (Aus) 23.73

200 metres
1970 Raelene Boyle (Aus) 22.75w
1974 Raelene Boyle (Aus) 22.50
1978 Denise Boyd (Aus) 22.82w
1982 Merlene Ottey (Jam) 22.19w
1986 Angella Issajenko (Can)
   22.91w
1990 Merlene Ottey (Jam) 22.76
1994 Cathy Freeman (Aus) 22.25

440 yards
1966 Judy Pollock (Aus) 53.0

400 metres
1970 Marilyn Neufville (Jam) 51.02
1974 Yvonne Saunders (Can) 51.67
1978 Donna Hartley (Eng) 51.69
1982 Raelene Boyle (Aus) 51.26
1986 Debbie Flintoff (Aus) 51.29
1990 Fatima Yusuf (Nig) 51.08
1994 Cathy Freeman (Aus) 50.38

880 yards
1934 Gladys Lunn (Eng) 2:19.4
1962 Dixie Willis (Aus) 2:03.85
1966 Abigail Hoffman (Can) 2:04.3

800 metres
1970 Rosemary Stirling (Sco) 2:06.24
1974 Charlene Rendina (Aus) 2:01.1
1978 Judy Peckham (Aus) 2:02.82
1982 Kirsty McDermott (Wal) 2:01.31
1986 Kirsty Wade (née McDermott) (Wal) 2:00.94
1990 Diane Edwards (Eng) 2:00.25
1994 Inez Turner (Jam) 2:01.74

1500 metres
1970 Rita Ridley (Eng) 4:18.8
1974 Glenda Reiser (Can) 4:07.8
1978 Mary Stewart (Eng) 4:06.34
1982 Christina Boxer (Eng) 4:08.28
1986 Kirsty Wade (Wal) 4:10.91
1990 Angela Chalmers (Can) 4:08.41
1994 Kelly Holmes (Eng) 4:08.86

3000 metres
1978 Paula Fudge (Eng) 9:12.95
1982 Anne Audain (NZ) 8:45.53
1986 Lynn Williams (Can) 8:54.29
1990 Angela Chalmers (Can) 8:38.38
1994 Angela Chalmers (Can) 8:32.17

10 000 metres
1986 Liz Lynch (Sco) 31:41.42
1990 Liz McColgan (née Lynch) (Sco) 32:23.56
1994 Yvonne Murray (Sco) 31:56.97

Marathon
1986 Lisa Martin (Aus) 2:26:07
1990 Lisa Martin (Aus) 2:25:28
1994 Carole Rouillard (Can) 2:30:41

80 metres hurdles
1934 Marjorie Clark (SAf) 11.8
1938 Barbara Burke (SAf) 11.7
1950 Shirley Strickland (Aus) 11.6
1954 Edna Maskell (Zam) 10.9
1958 Norma Thrower (Aus) 10.72w

1962 Pam Kilborn (Aus) 11.07
1966 Pam Kilborn (Aus) 10.9

100 metres hurdles
1970 Pam Kilborn (Aus) 13.27
1974 Judy Vernon (Eng) 13.45
1978 Lorna Boothe (Eng) 12.98w
1982 Shirley Strong (Eng) 12.78w
1986 Sally Gunnell (Eng) 13.29
1990 Kay Morley (Wal) 12.91
1994 Michelle Freeman (Jam) 13.12

400 metres hurdles
1982 Debbie Flintoff (Aus) 55.89
1986 Debbie Flintoff (Aus) 54.94
1990 Sally Gunnell (Eng) 55.38
1994 Sally Gunnell (Eng) 54.51

Sprint Relay - 2 x 220 yards, 2 x 110 yards
1934 Canada 1:14.4
1938 Australia 1:15.2
1950 Australia 1:13.4

4 x 110 yards relay
1954 Australia 46.8
1958 England 45.37
1962 Australia 46.71
1966 Australia 45.3

4 x 100 metres relay
1970 Australia 44.14
1974 Australia 43.51
1978 England 43.70
1982 England 43.15
1986 England 43.39
1990 Australia 43.87
1994 Nigeria 42.99

4 x 400 metres relay
1974 England 3:29.2
1978 England 3:27.19
1982 Canada 3:27.70
1986 Canada 3:28.92
1990 England 3:28.08
1994 England 3:27.06

High jump
1934 Marjorie Clark (SAf) 1.60
1938 Dorothy Odam (Eng) 1.60
1950 Dorothy Tyler (née Odam) (Eng) 1.60
1954 Thelma Hopkins (NI) 1.67
1958 Michele Mason (Aus) 1.70
1962 Robyn Woodhouse (Aus) 1.78
1966 Michele Brown (née Mason) (Aus) 1.73
1970 Debbie Brill (Can) 1.78
1974 Barbara Lawton (Eng) 1.84
1978 Katrina Gibbs (Aus) 1.93
1982 Debbie Brill (Can) 1.88
1986 Christine Stanton (Aus) 1.92
1990 Tania Murray (NZ) 1.88
1994 Alison Inverarity (Aus) 1.94

Long jump
1934 Phyllis Bartholomew (Eng) 5.47
1938 Decima Norman (Aus) 5.80
1950 Yvette Williams (NZ) 5.90
1954 Yvette Williams (NZ) 6.08
1958 Sheila Hoskin (Eng) 6.02
1962 Pam Kilborn (Aus) 6.27
1966 Mary Rand (Eng) 6.36
1970 Sheila Sherwood (Eng) 6.73
1974 Modupe Oshikoya (Nig) 6.46
1978 Sue Reeve (Eng) 6.59
1982 Shonel Ferguson (Bah) 6.91w
1986 Joyce Oladapo (Eng) 6.43
1990 Jane Flemming (Aus) 6.78
1994 Nicole Boegman (Aus) 6.82w

Shot
1954 Yvette Williams (NZ) 13.96
1958 Valerie Sloper (NZ) 15.54
1962 Valerie Young (née Sloper) (NZ) 15.23
1966 Valerie Young (NZ) 16.50
1970 Mary Peters (NI) 15.93
1974 Jane Haist (Can) 16.12
1978 Gael Mulhall (Aus) 17.31
1982 Judy Oakes (Eng) 17.92
1986 Gael Martin (Aus) 19.00
1990 Myrtle Augee (Eng) 18.48
1994 Judy Oakes (Eng) 18.16

Discus
1954 Yvette Williams (NZ) 45.02
1958 Suzanne Allday (Eng) 45.91
1962 Valerie Young (NZ) 50.20
1966 Valerie Young (NZ) 49.78
1970 Rosemary Payne (Sco) 54.46
1974 Jane Haist (Can) 55.52
1978 Carmen Ionescu (Can) 62.16
1982 Margaret Ritchie (Sco) 62.98
1986 Gael Martin (Aus) 56.42
1990 Lisa-Marie Vizaniari (Aus) 56.38
1994 Daniela Costian (Aus) 63.72

Javelin
1934 Gladys Lunn (Eng) 32.18
1938 Robina Higgins (Can) 38.28
1950 Charlotte MacGibbon-Weeks (Aus) 38.84
1954 Magdalena Swanepoel (SAf) 43.82
1958 Anna Pazera (Aus) 57.40
1962 Susan Platt (Eng) 50.24
1966 Margaret Parker (Aus) 51.38
1970 Petra Rivers (Aus) 52.00
1974 Petra Rivers (Aus) 55.48
1978 Tessa Sanderson (Eng) 61.34
1982 Suzanne Howland (Aus) 64.46
1986 Tessa Sanderson (Eng) 69.80
1990 Tessa Sanderson (Eng) 65.72
1994 Louise McPaul (Aus) 63.76

Pentathlon (Scored on 1971 tables)
1970 Mary Peters (NI) 4515 (5148 on tables used)
1974 Mary Peters (NI) 4455
1978 Diane Konihowski (Can) 4768

Heptathlon (Scored on 1984 tables)
1982 Glynis Nunn (Aus) 6254
1986 Judy Simpson (Eng) 6282w
1990 Jane Flemming (Aus) 6695
1994 Denise Lewis (Eng) 6325

10 kilometres walk
1990 Kerry Saxby (Aus) 45:03
1994 Kerry Junna-Saxby (Aus) 44:25

Badminton

Men's singles
1966 Tan Aik Huang (Mal)
1970 Jamie Paulson (Can)
1974 Punch Gunalan (Mal)
1978 Padukone Prakash (Ind)
1982 Syed Modi (Ind)
1986 Steve Baddeley (Eng)
1990 Rashid Sidek (Mal)
1994 Rashid Sidek (Mal)

Men's doubles
1966 Tan Aik Huang & Yew Cheng Hoe (Mal)
1970 Ng Boon Bee & Punch Gunalam (Mal)
1974 Derek Talbot & Elliot Stuart (Eng)
1978 Ray Stevens & Michael Tredgett (Eng)
1982 Razif Sidek & Beng Teong Ong (Mal)
1986 Billy Gilliland & Dan Travers (Sco)
1990 Jalani Sidek & Razif Sidek (Mal)
1994 Cheah Soon Kit & Ong Ewe Hock (Mal)

Women's singles
1966 Angela Bairstow (Eng)
1970 Margaret Beck (Eng)
1974 Gillian Gilks (Eng)
1978 Sylvia Ng (Mal)
1982 Helen Troke (Eng)
1986 Helen Troke (Eng)
1990 Fiona Smith (Eng)
1994 Lisa Campbell (Aus)

Women's doubles
1966 Helen Horton & Ursula Smith (Eng)
1970 Margaret Boxall & Susan Whetnall (Eng)
1974 Margaret Beck & Gillian Gilks (Eng)
1978 Nora Perry & Anne Statt (Eng)
1982 Claire Backhouse & Johanne Falardeau (Can)
1986 Gillian Clark & Gillian Gowers (Eng)
1990 Fiona Smith & Sara Sankey (Eng)
1994 Joanne Muggeridge & Joanne Wright (Eng)

Mixed doubles
1966 Roger Mills & Angela Bairstow (Eng)
1970 Derek Talbot & Margaret Boxall (Eng)
1974 Derek Talbot & Gillian Gilks (Eng)
1978 Michael Tredgett & Nora Perry (Eng)
1982 Martin Dew & Karen Chapman (Eng)
1986 Mike Scandolera & Audrey Tuckey (Aus)
1990 Chan Chi Choi & Amy Chan (HK)
1994 Chris Hunt & Gillian Clark (Eng)

Team
1978 England
1982 England
1986 England
1990 England
1994 England

Bowls

Men's Singles
1930 Robert Colquhoun (Eng)
1934 Robert Sprot (Sco)
1938 Horace Harvey (SAf)
1950 James Pirret (NZ)
1954 Ralph Hodges (Zim)
1958 Phineas Danilowitz (SAf)
1962 David Bryant (Eng)
1970 David Bryant (Eng)
1974 David Bryant (Eng)
1978 David Bryant (Eng)
1982 William Wood (Sco)
1986 Ian Dickison (NZ)
1990 Rob Parella (Aus)
1994 Richard Corsie (Sco)

Men's Pairs
1930 Tommy Hills & George Wright (Eng)
1934 Tommy Hills & George Wright (Eng)
1938 Lance Macey & William Denison (NZ)
1950 Robert Henry & Phil Exelby (NZ)
1954 William Rosbotham & Percy Watson (NI)
1958 John Morris & Richard Pilkington (NZ)
1962 Robert McDonald & Hugh Robson (NZ)
1970 Norman King & Peter Line (Eng)
1974 John Christie & Alex McIntosh (Sco)
1978 Eric Liddell & Clementi Delgado (HK)
1982 John Watson & David Gourlay (Sco)
1986 George Adrain & Grant Knox (Sco)
1990 Trevor Morris & Ian Schuback (Aus)
1994 Rex Johnson & Cameron Curtis (Aus)

Men's Fours
1930 England
1934 England
1938 New Zealand
1950 South Africa
1954 South Africa
1958 England
1962 England
1970 Hong Kong
1974 New Zealand
1978 Hong Kong
1982 Australia
1986 Wales
1990 Scotland
1994 South Africa

Women's singles
1986 Wendy Line (Eng)
1990 Geua Vada Tau (PNG)
1994 Margaret Johnstone (NI)

Women's pairs
1986 Freda Elliott & Margaret Johnstone (NI)
1990 Marie Watson & Judy Howat (NZ)
1994 Sarah Gourlay & FrancesWhite (Sco)

Women's triples
1982 Zimbabwe

Women's fours
1986 Wales
1990 Australia
1994 South Africa

Boxing

48kg - Light Flyweight
1970 James Odwori (Uga)
1974 Stephen Muchoki (Ken)
1978 Stephen Muchoki (Ken)
1982 Abraham Wachire (Ken)
1986 Scott Olson (Can)
1990 Justin Juko (Uga)
1994 Abdurahaman Ramadhani (Ken)

51kg - Flyweight
1930 Jacob Smith (SAf)
1934 Patrick Palmer (Eng)
1938 Johannes Joubert (SAf)
1950 Hugh Riley (Sco)
1954 Richard Currie (Sco)
1958 Jackie Brown (Sco)
1962 Robert Mallon (Sco)
1966 Sulley Shittu (Gha)
1970 David Needham (Eng)
1974 David Larmour (NI)
1978 Michael Irungu (Ken)
1982 Michael Mutua (Ken)
1986 John Lyon (Eng)
1990 Wayne McCullough (NI)
1994 Paul Shepherd (Sco)

54kg - Bantamweight
1930 Hyman Mizler (Eng)
1934 Freddy Ryan (Eng)
1938 William Butler (Eng)
1950 Johannes van Rensburg (SAf)
1954 John Smillie (Sco)
1958 Howard Winstone (Wal)
1962 Jeffery Dynevor (Aus)
1966 Edward Ndukwu (Nig)
1970 Sulley Shittu (Gha)
1974 Pat Cowdell (Eng)
1978 Barry McGuigan (NI)
1982 Joe Orewa (Nig)
1986 Sean Murphy (Eng)
1990 Sabo Mohammed (Nig)
1994 Robert Peden (Aus)

57kg - Featherweight
1930 F R Meachem (Eng)
1934 Charles Catterall (SAf)
1938 Anadale Henricus (Sri)
1950 Henry Gilliland (Sco)
1954 Leonard Leisching (SAf)
1958 Wally Taylor (Aus)
1962 John McDermott (Sco)
1966 Philip Waruinge (Ken)
1970 Philip Waruinge (Ken)
1974 Edward Ndukwa (Nig)
1978 Azumah Nelson (Gha)
1982 Peter Konyegwachie (Nig)
1986 Billy Downey (Can)
1990 John Irwin (Eng)
1994 Casey Patton (Can)

60kg - Lightweight
1930 James Rolland (Sco)
1934 Leslie Cook (Aus)
1938 Harry Groves (Eng)
1950 Ronald Latham (Eng)
1954 Piet van Staden (Zim)
1958 Dick McTaggart (Sco)
1962 Eddie Blay (Gha)
1966 Anthony Andeh (Nig)
1970 Abayomi Adeyemi (Nig)
1974 Ayub Kalule (Uga)
1978 Gerard Hamil (NI)

1982 Hussein Khalili (Ken)
1986 Asif Dar (Can)
1990 Godfrey Nyakana (Uga)
1994 Mike Strange (Can)

63.5kg Light-Welterweight
1954 Mickey Bergin (Can)
1958 Henry Loubscher (SAf)
1962 Clement Quartey (Gha)
1966 James McCourt (NI)
1970 Muhamad Muruli (Uga)
1974 Obisia Nwakpa (Nig)
1978 Winfield Braithwaite (Guy)
1982 Christopher Ossai (Nig)
1986 Howard Grant (Can)
1990 Charlie Kane (Sco)
1994 Peter Richardson (Eng)

67kg - Welterweight
1930 Leonard Hall (SAf)
1934 David McCleave (Eng)
1938 Bill Smith (Aus)
1950 Terence Ratcliffe (Eng)
1954 Nicholas Gargano (Eng)
1958 Joseph Greyling (SAf)
1962 Wallace Coe (NZ)
1966 Eddie Blay (Gha)
1970 Emma Ankudey (Gha)
1974 Muhamad Muruli (Uga)
1978 Michael McCallum (Jam)
1982 Christopher Pyatt (Eng)
1986 Darren Dyer (Eng)
1990 David Defiagbon (Nig)
1994 Neil Sinclair (NI)

71kg - Light-Middleweight
1954 Wilfred Greaves (Can)
1958 Grant Webster (SAf)
1962 Harold Mann (Can)
1966 Mark Rowe (Eng)
1970 Tom Imrie (Sco)
1974 Lotti Mwale (Zam)
1978 Kelly Perlette (Can)
1982 Shawn O'Sullivan (Can)
1986 Dan Sherry (Can)
1990 Richie Woodhall (Eng)
1994 Jim Webb (NI)

75kg - Middleweight
1930 Frederick Mallin (Eng)
1934 Alf Shawyer (Eng)
1938 Denis Reardon (Wal)
1950 Theunis van Schalkwyk (SAf)
1954 Johannes van der Kolff (SAf)
1958 Terry Milligan (NI)
1962 Cephas Colquhoun (Jam)
1966 Joe Darkey (Gha)
1970 John Conteh (Eng)
1974 Frankie Lucas (SVI)
1978 Philip McElwaine (Aus)
1982 Jimmy Price (Eng)
1986 Rod Douglas (Eng)
1990 Christopher Johnson (Can)

1994 Ron Donaldson (Can)

81kg - Light-Heavyweight
1930 Joe Goyder (Eng)
1934 George Brennan (Eng)
1938 Nicholaas Wolmarans (SAf)
1950 Donald Scott (Eng)
1954 Piet Van Vuuren (SAf)
1958 Tony Madigan (Aus)
1962 Tony Madigan (Aus)
1966 Roger Tighe (Eng)
1970 Fatai Ayinla (Nig)
1974 William Knight (Eng)
1978 Roger Fortin (Can)
1982 Fine Sani (Fiji)
1986 James Moran (Eng)
1990 Joseph Akhasamba (Nig)
1994 Dale Brown (Can)

Over 81kg - Heavyweight
1930 Victor Stuart (Eng)
1934 Pat Floyd (Eng)
1938 Thomas Osborne (Can)
1950 Frank Creagh (NZ)
1954 Brian Harper (Eng)
1958 Daniel Bekker (SAf)
1962 George Oywello (Uga)
1966 William Kini (NZ)
1970 Benson Masanda (Uga)
1974 Neville Meade (Eng)
1978 Julius Awome (Eng)
1982 Willie DeWit (Can)

91kg - Heavyweight
1986 James Peau (NZ)
1990 George Onyango (Ken)
1994 Omaar Ahmed (Ken)

Over 91kg - Super-Heavyweight
1986 Lennox Lewis (Can)
1990 Michael Kenny (NZ)
1994 Duncan Dokiwari (Nig)

Cycling

Sprint
1934 Ernest Higgins (Eng)
1938 Edgar Gray (Aus)
1950 Russell Mockridge (Aus)
1954 Cyril Peacock (Eng)
1958 Dick Ploog (Aus)
1962 Thomas Harrison (Aus)
1966 Roger Gibbon (Tri) and
1970 John Nicholson (Aus)
1974 John Nicholson (Aus)
1978 Kenrick Tucker (Aus)
1982 Kenrick Tucker (Aus)
1986 Gary Neiwand (Aus)
1990 Gary Neiwand (Aus)
1994 Gary Neiwand (Aus)

1000 metres time trial
1934 Edgar Gray (Aus) 1:16.4
1938 Robert Porter (Aus) 1:15.2
1950 Russell Mockridge (Aus) 1:13.4

1954 Dick Ploog (Aus) &
   Alfred Swift (SAf) 1:12.5
1958 Neville Tong (Eng) 1:12.1
1962 Peter Bartels (Aus) 1:12.9
1966 Roger Gibbon (Tri) 1:09.6
1970 Harry Kent (NZ) 1:08.69
1974 Dick Paris (Aus) 1:11.85
1978 Jocelyn Lovell (Can) 1:06.00
1982 Craig Adair (NZ) 1:06.954
1986 Martin Vinnicombe (Aus)
   1:06.23
1990 Martin Vinnicombe (Aus)
   1:05.572
1994 Shane Kelly (Aus) 1:05.386

4000 metres individual pursuit
1950 Cyril Cartwright (Eng) 5:16.3
1954 Norman Sheil (Eng) 5:03.5
1958 Norman Sheil (Eng) 5:10.2
1962 Maxwell Langshaw (Aus)
   5:08.2
1966 Hugh Porter (Eng) 4:56.6
1970 Ian Hallam (Eng) 5:01.41
1974 Ian Hallam (Eng) 5:05.46
1978 Michael Richards (NZ)
   4:49.74
1982 Michael Turtur (Aus) 4:50.990
1986 Dean Woods (Aus) 4:43.92
1990 Garry Anderson (NZ)
   4:44.610
1994 Rodney McGee (Aus)
   4:31.371

4000 metres team pursuit
1974 England 4:40.50
1978 Australia 4:29.43
1982 Australia 4:26.090
1986 Australia 4:26.94
1990 New Zealand 4:22.76
1994 Australia 4:10.485

Tandem sprint
1970 Gordon Johnson & Ron
   Jonker (Aus) 11.43
1974 Geoffrey Cooke & Ernest
   Crutchlow (Eng) 10.74
1978 Jocelyn Lovell & Gordon
   Singleton (Can) 15.52

10 miles track
1934 Robert McLeod (Can) 24:26.2
1938 William Maxfield (Eng)
   24:44.0
1950 William Heseltine (Aus)
   23:23.4
1954 Lindsay Cocks (Aus) 21:59.5
1958 Ian Browne (Aus) 21:40.2
1962 Douglas Adams (Aus) 22:10.8
1966 Ian Alsop (Eng) 21:46.0
1970 Jocelyn Lovell (Can) 20:46.72
1974 Stephen Heffernan (Eng)
   20:51.25
1978 Jocelyn Lovell (Can) 20:05.81

1982 Kevin Nichols (Aus)
   19:56.559
1986 Wayne McCarney (Aus)
   19:40.61
1990 Gary Anderson (NZ) 19:44.20
1994 Stuart O'Grady (Aus)
   18:50.520

Points
1990 Robert Burns (Aus)
1994 Brett Aitken (Aus)

**100 kilometres road team time
trial**
1982 England 2:09:27
1986 England 2:13:16
1990 New Zealand 2:06:46.5
1994 Australia 1:53:19.133

Road race
*Raced over 100km 1938-54, 120 miles 193
km 1958-66, 164.6 km 1970, 183km 1974,
188 km 1978, 184km 1982, 169 km 1986,
173km 1990, 182 km 1994.*
1938 Hendrik Binneman (SAf)
   2:53:29.6
1950 Hector Sutherland (Aus)
   3:13.06.4
1954 Eric Thompson (Eng)
   2:44:08.1
1958 Ray Booty (Eng) 5:16:33.7
1962 Wesley Mason (Eng) 5:20:26.2
1966 Peter Buckley (IOM) 5:07:52.5
1970 Bruce Biddle (NZ) 4:38:05.8
1974 Clyde Sefton (Aus) 5:07.16.87
1978 Philip Anderson (Aus)
   4:22:34.41
1982 Malcolm Elliott (Eng)
   4:34:40.06
1986 Paul Curran (Eng) 4:08:50
1990 Graeme Miller (NZ) 4:34:00.19
1994 Mark Rendell (N) 4:46:07

Women's sprint
1990 Louise Jones (Wal)
1994 Tanya Dubnicoff (Can)

**Women's 3000m individual
pursuit**
1990 Madonna Harris (NZ)
   3:54.670
1994 Kathy Watt (Aus) 3:48:52.2

Women's road race
1990 Kathy Watt (Aus) 1:55:11.60
1994 Kathy Watt (Aus) 2:48:04.73

Women's points
1994 Yvonne McGregor (Eng)

Women's 50km team time trial
1994 Australia 1:04:03.20

Fencing

Men's foil
1950 René Paul (Eng)

1954 René Paul (Eng)
1958 Raymond Paul (Eng)
1962 Alexander Leckie (Sco)
1966 Allan Jay (Eng)
1970 Mike Breckin (Eng)

Men's epée
1950 Charles-Louis de Beaumont
   (Eng)
1954 Ivan Lund (Aus)
1958 William Hoskyns (Eng)
1962 Ivan Lund (Aus)
1966 William Hoskyns (Eng)
1970 William Hoskyns (Eng)

Men's sabre
1950 Arthur Pilbrow (Eng)
1954 Michael Amberg (Eng)
1958 William Hoskyns (Eng)
1962 Ralph Cooperman (Eng)
1966 Ralph Cooperman (Eng)
1970 Alexander Leckie (Sco)

Women's foil - individual
1950 Mary Glen-Haig (Eng)
1954 Mary Glen-Haig (Eng)
1958 Gillian Sheen (Eng)
1962 Melody Coleman (NZ)
1966 Janet Wardell-Yerburgh (Eng)
1970 Janet Wardell-Yerburgh (Eng)

Men's team foil
1950 England
1954 England
1958 England
1962 England
1966 England
1970 England

Men's team epée
1950 Australia
1954 England
1958 England
1962 England
1966 England
1970 England

Men's team sabre
1950 England
1954 Canada
1958 England
1962 England
1966 England
1970 England

Women's team foil
1966 England
1970 England

Gymnastics

Men's all-round
1978 Philip Delesalle(Can)
1990 Curtis Hibbert (Can)
1994 Neil Thomas (Eng)

Men's rings
1990 Curtis Hibbert (Can)
1994 Lee McDermott (Eng)

Men's parallel bars
1990 Curtis Hibbert (Can)
1994 Peter Hogan (Aus)

Men's horizontal bars
1990 Curtis Hibbert (Can) & Alan
  Nolet (Can)
1994 Alan Nolet (Can)

Men's floor exercises
1990 Neil Thomas (Eng)
1994 Neil Thomas (Eng)

Men's pommel horse
1990 Brennon Dowrick (Aus)
1994 Brennon Dowrick (Aus)

Men's vault
1990 James May (Eng)
1994 Bret Hudson (Aus)

Men's team
1978 Canada
1990 Canada
1994 Canada

Women's all-round
1978 Elfi Schlegel (Can)
1990 Lori Strong (Can)
1994 Stella Umeh (Can)

Women's beam
1990 Lori String (Can)
1994 Salli Willis (Aus)

Women's floor exercises
1990 Lori String (Can)
1994 Annika Reeder (Eng)

Women's vault
1990 Nicky Jenkins (NZ)
1994 Stella Umeh (Can)

Women's asymmetrical Bars
1990 Monique Allen (Aus)
1994 Rebecca Stoyal (Aus)

Women's team
1978 Canada
1990 Canada
1994 England

Rhythmic Gymnastics - Individual
1990 Mary Fuzesi (Can) won
  overall, ribbon and hoop;
  Angela Walker (NZ) won rope
1994 Kasumi Takahashi (Aus) won
  all five gold medals: all-
  around, hoops, ball, clubs
  and ribbon

Rhythmic Gymnastics - Team
1994 Canada

Judo

Held in 1990 only when the winners were:

Men
60kg: Carl Finney (Eng)
65kg: Brent Cooper (NZ)
71kg: Roy Stone (Eng)
78kg: David Southby (Eng)
86kg: Densign White (Eng)
95kg: Ray Stevens (Eng)
Over 95kg: Elvis Gordon (Eng)
Open: Elvis Gordon (Eng)

Women
48kg: Karen Briggs (Eng)
52kg: Sharon Rendle (Eng)
56kg: Loretta Cusack (Sco)
61kg: Diane Bell (Eng)
66kg: Sharon Mills (Eng)
72kg: Jane Morris (Eng)
Over 72kg: Sharon Lee (Eng)
Open: Sharon Lee (Eng)

Rowing

Single sculls
1930 Bobby Pearce (Aus) 8:03.6
1938 Herbert Turner (Aus) 8:24.0
1950 Mervyn Wood (Aus) 7:46.8
1954 Donald Rowlands (NZ) 8:28.2
1958 Stuart Mackenzie (Aus) 7:20.1
1962 James Hill (NZ) 7:39.7
1986 Steven Redgrave (Eng)
  7:28.29

Double sculls
1930 Elswood Bole & Bob Richards
  (Can) 7:48.0
1938* William Bradley & Cecil
  Pearce (Aus) 7:29.4
1950 Mervyn Wood & Murray
  Riley (Aus) 7:22.0
1954 Mervyn Wood & Murray
  Riley (Aus) 7:54.5
1958 Michael Spracklen &
  Geoffrey Baker (Eng) 6:54.4
1962 George Justice & Nicholas
  Birkmyre (Eng) 6:52.4
1986 Pat Walter & Bruce Ford
  (Can) 6:19.43
* *no medals awarded*

Coxless pairs
1950 Walter Lambert & Jack
  Webster (Aus) 7:58.0
1954 Robert Parker & Reginald
  Douglas (NZ) 8:23.9
1958 Robert Parker & Reginald
  Douglas (NZ) 7:11.1
1962 Stewart Farquharson & James
  Lee-Nicholson (Eng) 7:03.7
1986 Steven Redgrave & Andrew
  Holmes (Eng) 6:40.48

Coxless fours
1930 England 7:04.6
1958 England 6:34.4
1962 England 6:31.1
1986 Canada 6:00.56

Coxed fours
1930 New Zealand 8:02.0
1938 Australia 7:16.8
1950 New Zealand 7:17.2
1954 Australia 7:58.3
1958 England 6:46.5
1962 New Zealand 6:48.2
1986 England 6:08.13

Eights
1930 England 6:37.0
1938 England 6:29.0
1950 Australia 6:27.0
1954 Canada 6:59.0
1958 Canada 5:51.1
1962 Australia 5:53.4
1986 Australia 5:44.42

Lightweight single sculls
1986 Peter Antonie (Aus) 7:16.43

Lightweight coxless fours
1986 England 6:25.86

Women's single sculls
1986 Stephanie Foster (NZ) 7:43.22

Women's double sculls
1986 Stephanie Foster & Robin
  Clarke (NZ) 7:21.52

Women's coxless pairs
1986 Kathryn Barr & Andrea
  Schreiner (Can) 7:34.51

Women's coxed fours
1986 Canada 6:50.13

Women's eights
1986 Australia 6:43.69

Women's lightweight single sculls
1986 Adair Ferguson (Aus) 7:45.49

Women's lightweight coxless Fours
1986 England 6:54.70

Shooting

Small bore rifle (.22 rifle)
1966 Gilmour Boa (Can) 587
1974 Yvonne Gowland (Aus) 594
1978 Alister Allan (Sco) 1194

Small bore rifle - prone
1982 Alan Smith (Aus) 1184
1986 Alan Smith (Aus) 599
1990 Roger Harvey (NZ) 591
1994 Stephen Petterson (NZ) 698.4

Small bore rifle - prone - pairs
1982 Malcolm Cooper & Mike
  Sullivan (Eng) 1187

1986 Michael Ashcroft & Gale Stewart (Can) 1175
1990 Stephen Pettersson & Roger Harvey (NZ) 1185
1994 Stephen Pettersson & Lindsay Arthur (NZ) 1181

Small bore rifle- three positions
1982 Alister Allan (Sco) 1146
1986 Malcolm Cooper (Eng) 1170
1990 Mart Klepp (Can) 1157
1994 Michel Dion (Can) 1234.2

Small bore rifle - three positions - pairs
1982 Malcolm Cooper & Barry Dagger (Eng) 2301
1986 Malcolm Cooper & Sarah Cooper (Eng) 2278
1990 Jean-François Senecal & Mart Klepp (Can) 2272
1994 Wayne Sorensen & Michel Dion (Can) 2300

Full bore rifle
.303 rifle 1966, 7.62mm rifle from 1974.
1966 Lord (John) Swansea (Wal) 394
1974 Maurice Gordon (NZ) 387.26
1978 Desmond Vamplew (Can) 391
1982 Arthur Clarke (Sco) 387
1986 Stan Golinski (Aus) 396
1990 Colin Mallett (Jersey) 394
1994 David Calvert (NI) 398

Full bore rifle - pairs
1982 Keith Affleck & Geoffrey Ayling (Aus) 572
1986 Alain Marion & William Baldwin (Can) 583
1990 Simon Belither & Andrew Tucker (Eng) 580
1994 Albert Bowden & Geoffrey Grenfell (Aus) 593

Free pistol (.22 single shot)
1966 Charles Sexton (Eng) 544
1974 Jules Sobrian (Can) 549
1978 Yvon Trempe (Can) 543
1982 Tom Guinn (Can) 553
1986 Greg Yelavich (NZ) 551
1990 Phillip Adams (Aus) 554
1994 Michael Gault (Eng) 654.1

Free pistol - pairs
1982 Phillip Adams & John Tremelling (Aus) 1077
1986 Tom Guinn & Claude Beaulieu (Can) 1099
1990 Phillip Adams & Bengt Sandström (Aus) 1106
1994 Phillip Adams & Bengt Sandström (Aus) 1104

Centre fire pistol
1966 James Lee (Can) 576
1982 John Cooke (Eng) 580
1986 Robert Northover (Eng) 583
1990 Ashok Pandit (Ind) 583
1994 Jaspal Rana (Ind) 581

Centre fire pistol - pairs
1982 Noel Ryan & Alexander Taransky (Aus) 1151
1986 Phillip Adams & Roderick Hack (Aus) 1165
1990 Phillip Adams & Bruce Quick (Aus) 1155
1994 Jaspal Rana & Ashok Pandit (Ind) 1168

Rapid fire pistol (.22 semi automatic)
1966 Anthony Clark (Eng) 585
1974 William Hare (Can) 586
1978 Jules Sobrian (Can) 587
1982 Solomon Lee (HK) 583
1986 Pat Murray (Aus) 591

1990 Adrian Breton (Guernsey) 583
1994 Michael Jay (Wal) 670.2

Rapid fire pistol - pairs
1982 Peter Heuke & Alexander Taransky (Aus) 1160
1986 Brian Girling & Terry Turner (Eng) 1169
1990 Bruce Farrell & Patrick Murray (Aus) 1153
1994 Patrick Murray & Robert Dowling (Aus) 1148

Air pistol
1982 George Darling (Eng) 576
1986 Greg Yelavich (NZ) 575
1990 Bengt Sandström (Aus) 580
1994 Jean-Pierre Huot (Can) 672.4

Air pistol - pairs
1982 Phillip Adams & Gregory Colbert (Aus) 1128
1986 Paul Leatherdale & Ian Reid (Eng) 1143
1990 Atteequr Rahman & Abdus Sattar (Ban) 1138
1994 Michelangelo Giustiniano & Bengt Sandstrom(Aus) 1137

Air rifle
1982 Jean-François Senecal (Can) 574
1986 Guy Lorion (Can) 588
1990 Guy Lorion (Can) 583
1994 Chris Hector (Eng) 685.9

Air rifle - pairs
1982 Alister Allan & Bill McNeil (Sco) 1137
1986 Guy Lorion & Sharon Bowes (Can) 1167
1990 Guy Lorion & Mart Klepp (Can) 1163
1994 Jean-François Senecal & Wayne Sorensen (Can) 1166

Open Olympic trap (Clay pigeon)
1974 John Primrose (Can) 196
1978 John Primrose (Can) 186
1982 Peter Boden (Eng) 191
1986 Ian Peel (Eng) 195
1990 John Maxwell (Aus) 184
1994 Manaher Singh (Ind) 141

Open Olympic trap - pairs
1982 Jim Ellis & Terry Rumbel (Aus) 190
1986 Ian Peel & Peter Boden (Eng) 185
1990 Kevin Gill & Ian Peel (Eng) 181
1994 Thomas Hewitt & Samuel Allen (NI) 188

Open skeet
1974 Harry Willsie (Can) 194
1978 John Woolley (NZ) 193
1982 John Woolley (NZ) 197
1986 Nigel Kelly (IOM) 196
1990 Kenneth Harman (Eng) 187
1994 Ian Hale (Aus) 144

Open skeet - pairs
1982 Brian Gabriel & Fred Altmann (Can) 191
1986 Joe Neville & Kenneth Harman (Eng) 195
1990 Ian Marsden & James Dunlop (Sco) 189
1994 Antonis Andreou & Christos Kourtellas (Cyp) 189

Running target
1990 Colin Robertson (Aus) 539
1994 Bryan Wilson (Aus) 657.9

Running target - pairs
1990 Paul Carmine & Tony Clarke (NZ) 1091
1994 Mark Bedlington & Matthew Bedlington (Can) 1088

Women small bore rifle- prone
1994 Shirley McIntosh (Sco) 586

Women small bore rifle- prone- pairs
1994 Kim Frazer & Sylvia Purdie (Aus)

Women small bore rifle- three positions
1994 Sharon Bowes (Can) 666.4

Women small bore rifle- three positions - pairs
1994 Sharon Bowes & Christina Ashcroft (Can) 1143

Women air rifle
1994 Fotini Theofanous (Cyp) 488.7

Women air rifle - pairs
1994 Pushpannali Ramanayake & Mali Wickremasinghe (Sri) 771

Women air pistol
1994 Helen Smith (Can) 474.2

Women air pistol - pairs
1994 Annette Woodward & Christine Treffrey (Aus) 747

Women sport pistol
1994 Christine Trefry (Aus) 679.4

Women sport pistol - pairs
1994 Annette Woodward & Christine Trefrey (Aus)

Swimming

Men

50 metres freestyle
1990 Andrew Baildon (Aus) 22.76
1994 Mark Foster (Eng) 23.12

100 yards freestyle (91.44m)
1930 Munroe Bourne (Can) 56.0
1934 George Burleigh (Can) 55.0

110 yards freestyle (100.58m)
1938 Bob Pirie (Can) 59.6
1950 Peter Salmon (Can) 1:00.4
1954 Jon Henricks (Aus) 56.5
1958 John Devitt (Aus) 56.6
1962 Richard Pound (Can) 55.8
1966 Mike Wenden (Aus) 54.0

100 metres freestyle
1970 Mike Wenden (Aus) 53.06
1974 Mike Wenden (Aus) 52.73
1978 Mark Morgan (Aus) 52.70
1982 Neil Brooks (Aus) 51.14
1986 Greg Fasala (Aus) 50.95
1990 Andrew Baildon (Aus) 49.80
1994 Stephen Clarke (Can) 50.21

200 metres freestyle
1970 Mike Wenden (Aus) 1:56.69
1974 Stephen Badger (Aus) 1:56.72
1978 Ron McKeon (Aus) 1:52.06
1982 Andrew Astbury (Eng) 1:51.52
1986 Robert Gleria (Aus) 1:50.57
1990 Martin Roberts (Aus) 1:49.58
1994 Kieren Perkins (Aus) 1:49.31

400 yards freestyle (365.76m)
1930 Noel Ryan (Aus) 4:39.8

440 yards freestyle (402.34m)
1934 Noel Ryan (Aus) 5:03.0
1938 Bob Pirie (Can) 4:54.6
1950 Garrick Agnew (Aus) 4:49.4
1954 Gary Chapman (Aus) 4:39.8
1958 John Konrads (Aus) 4:25.9
1962 Murray Rose (Aus) 4:20.0
1966 Robert Windle (Aus) 4:15.0

400 metres freestyle
1970 Graham White (Aus) 4:08.48
1974 John Kulasalu (Aus) 4:01.44
1978 Ron McKeon (Aus) 3:54.43
1982 Andrew Astbury (Eng) 3:53.29
1986 Duncan Armstrong (Aus) 3:52.25
1990 Ian Brown (Aus) 3:49.91
1994 Kieren Perkins (Aus) 3:45.77

1500 yards freestyle (1371.6m)
1930 Noel Ryan (Aus) 18:55.4
1934 Noel Ryan (Aus) 18:25.4

1650 yards freestyle (1508.76m)
1938 Robert Leivers (Eng) 19:46.4
1950 Graham Johnston (SAf) 19:55.7
1954 Graham Johnston (SAf) 19:01.4
1958 John Konrads (Aus) 17:45.4
1962 Murray Rose (Aus) 17:18.1
1966 Ron Jackson (Aus) 17:25.9

1500 metres freestyle
1970 Graham Windeatt (Aus) 16:23.82
1974 Steve Holland (Aus) 15:34.73
1978 Max Metzker (Aus) 15:31.92
1982 Max Metzker (Aus) 15:23.94
1986 Jason Plummer (Aus) 15:12.62
1990 Glen Housman (Aus) 14:55.25
1994 Kieren Perkins (Aus) 14:41.66

4 x 110 yards freestyle relay
1962 Australia 3:43.9
1966 Australia 3:35.6

4 x 100 metres freestyle relay
1970 Australia 3:36.02
1974 Canada 3:33.79
1978 Canada 3:27.94
1982 Australia 3:24.17
1986 Australia 3:21.58
1990 Australia 3:20.05
1994 Australia 3:20.89

4 x 200 yards freestyle relay
1930 Canada 8:42.4
1934 Canada 8:40.6

4 x 220 yards freestyle relay
1938 England 9:19.0
1950 New Zealand 9:27.7
1954 Australia 8:47.6
1958 Australia 8:33.4
1962 Australia 8:13.4
1966 Australia 7:59.5

4 x 200 metres freestyle relay
1970 Australia 7:50.77
1974 Australia 7:50.13
1978 Australia 7:34.83
1982 Australia 7:28.81
1986 Australia 7:23.49
1990 Australia 7:21.17
1994 Australia 7:20.80

100 yards backstroke
1930 John Trippett (Eng) 1:05.4
1934 Willie Francis (Sco) 1:05.2

110 yards backstroke
1938 Percy Oliver (Aus) 1:07.9
1950 Jacobus Wiid (SAf) 1:07.7
1954 John Brockway (Wal) 1:06.5
1958 John Monckton (Aus) 1:01.7
1962 Graham Sykes (Eng) 1:04.5
1966 Peter Reynolds (Aus) 1:02.4

100 metres backstroke
1970 Bill Kennedy (Can) 1:01.65
1974 Mark Tonelli (Aus) 59.65
1978 Glenn Patching (Aus) 57.90
1982 Michael West (Can) 57.12
1986 Mark Tewksbury (Can) 56.45
1990 Mark Tewksbury (Can) 56.07
1994 Martin Harris (Eng) 55.77

220 yards backstroke (201.17m)
1962 Julian Carroll (Aus) 2:20.9
1966 Peter Reynolds (Aus) 2:12.0

200 metres backstroke
1970 Mike Richards (Wal) 2:14.53
1974 Brad Cooper (Aus) 2:06.31
1978 Gary Hurring (NZ) 2:04.37
1982 Cameron Henning (Can) 2:02.88
1986 Sandy Goss (Can) 2:02.55
1990 Gary Anderson (Can) 2:01.69
1994 Adam Ruckwood (Eng) 2:00.79

110 yards breaststroke
1962 Ian O'Brien (Aus) 1:11.4
1966 Ian O'Brien (Aus) 1:08.2

100 metres breaststroke
1970 Bill Mahony (Can) 1:09.0
1974 David Leigh (Eng) 1:06.52
1978 Graham Smith (Can) 1:03.81
1982 Adrian Moorhouse (Eng) 1:02.93
1986 Victor Davis (Can) 1:03.01
1990 Adrian Moorhouse (Eng) 1:01.49
1994 Phil Rogers (Aus) 1:02.62

200 yards breaststroke
1930 Jack Aubin (Can) 2.38.4
1934 Norman Hamilton (Sco) 2:41.4

220 yards breaststroke
1938 John Davies (Eng) 2:51.9
1950 David Hawkins (Aus) 2:54.1
1954 John Doms (NZ) 2:52.6
1958 Terry Gathercole (Aus) 2:41.6
1962 Ian O'Brien (Aus) 2:38.2
1966 Ian O'Brien (Aus) 2:29.3

200 metres breaststroke
1970 Bill Mahony (Can) 2:30.29
1974 David Wilkie (Sco) 2:24.42
1978 Graham Smith (Can) 2:20.86
1982 Victor Davis (Can) 2:16.25
1986 Adrian Moorhouse (Eng) 2:16.35
1990 John Cleveland (Can) 2:14.96
1994 Nick Gillingham (Eng) 2:12.54

110 yards butterfly
1962 Kevin Berry (Aus) 59.5
1966 Ron Jacks (Can) 1:00.3

100 metres butterfly
1970 Byron MacDonald (Can) 58.44
1974 Neil Rogers (Aus) 56.58
1978 Dan Thompson (Can) 55.04
1982 Dan Thompson (Can) 54.71
1986 Andrew Jameson (Eng) 54.07
1990 Andrew Baildon (Aus) 53.98
1994 Scott Miller (Aus) 54.39

220 yards butterfly
1958 Ian Black (Sco) 2:22.6
1962 Kevin Berry (Aus) 2:10.8
1966 David Gerrard (NZ) 2:12.7

200 metres butterfly
1970 Tom Arusoo (Can) 2:08.97
1974 Brian Brinkley (Eng) 2:04.51
1978 George Nagy (Can) 2:01.99
1982 Phil Hubble (Eng) 2:00.98
1986 Anthony Mosse (NZ) 1:57.27
1990 Anthony Mosse (NZ) 1:57.33
1994 Danyon Loader (NZ) 1:59.54

200 metres Individual medley
1970 George Smith (Can) 2:13.72
1974 David Wilkie (Sco) 2:10.11
1978 Graham Smith (Can) 2:05.25
1982 Alex Baumann (Can) 2:02.25
1986 Alex Baumann (Can) 2:01.80
1990 Gary Anderson (Can) 2:02.94
1994 Matthew Dunn (Aus) 2:02.28

440 yards individual medley
1962 Alex Alexander (Aus) 5:15.3
1966 Peter Reynolds (Aus) 4:50.8

400 metres individual medley
1970 George Smith (Can) 4:48.87
1974 Mark Treffers (NZ) 4:35.90
1978 Graham Smith (Can) 4:27.34
1982 Alex Baumann (Can) 4:23.53
1986 Alex Baumann (Can) 4:18.29
1990 Rob Bruce (Aus) 4:20.26
1994 Matthew Dunn (Aus) 4:17.01

3 x 100 yards medley relay
1934 Canada 3:11.2

3 x 110 yards medley relay
1938 England 3:28.2
1950 England 3:26.6
1954 Australia 3:22.0

4 x 110 yards medley relay
Butterfly leg added.
1958 Australia 4:14.2
1962 Australia 4:12.4
1966 Canada 4:10.5

4 x 100 metres medley relay
1970 Canada 4:01.10
1974 Canada 3:52.93
1978 Canada 3:49.76
1982 Australia 3:47.34
1986 Canada 3:44.00
1990 Canada 3:42.45
1994 Australia 3:40.41

Springboard diving
1930 Alfred Phillips (Can)
1934 J.Briscoe Ray (Eng)
1938 Ron Masters (Aus)
1950 George Athans (Can)
1954 Peter Heatly (Sco)
1958 Keith Collin (Eng)
1962 Brian Phelps (Eng)

1966 Brian Phelps (Eng)
1970 Donald Wagstaff (Aus)
1974 Donald Wagstaff (Aus)
1978 Chris Snode (Eng)
1982 Chris Snode (Eng)
1986 Shaun Panayi (Aus)
1990 **3m** Craig Rogerson (Aus)
      1m Russell Butler (Aus)
1994 **3m** Michael Murphy (Aus)
      1m Jason Napper (Can)

Highboard diving
1930 Alfred Phillips (Can)
1934 Tommy Mather (Eng)
1938 Doug Tomalin (Eng)
1950 Peter Heatly (Sco)
1954 William Patrick (Can)
1958 Peter Heatly (Sco)
1962 Brian Phelps (Eng)
1966 Brian Phelps (Eng)
1970 Donald Wagstaff (Aus)
1974 Donald Wagstaff (Aus)
1978 Chris Snode (Eng)
1982 Chris Snode (Eng)
1986 Craig Rogerson (Aus)
1990 Robert Morgan (Wal)
1994 Michael Murphy (Aus)

Water Polo
1950 Australia

Women

50 metres freestyle
1990 Lisa Curry-Kenny (Aus) 25.80
1994 Karen Van Wirdum (Aus) 25.90

100 yards freestyle
1930 Joyce Cooper (Eng) 1:07.0
1934 Phyllis Dewar (Can) 1:03.0

110 yards freestyle
1938 Evelyn de Lacy (Aus) 1:10.1
1950 Marjorie McQuade (Aus) 1:09.0
1954 Lorraine Crapp (Aus) 1:05.8
1958 Dawn Fraser (Aus) 1:01.4
1962 Dawn Fraser (Aus) 59.5
1966 Marion Lay (Can) 1:02.3

100 metres freestyle
1970 Angela Coughlan (Can) 1:01.22
1974 Sonya Gray (Aus) 59.13
1978 Carol Klimpel (Can) 57.78
1982 June Croft (Eng) 56.97
1986 Jane Kerr (Can) 57.62
1990 Karen Van Wirdum (Aus) 56.48
1994 Karen Pickering (Eng) 56.20

200 metres freestyle
1970 Karen Moras (Aus) 2:09.78
1974 Sonya Gray (Aus) 2:04.27

1978 Rebecca Perrott (NZ) 2:00.63
1982 June Croft (Eng) 1:59.74
1986 Susie Baumer (Aus) 2:00.61
1990 Hayley Lewis (Aus) 2:00.79
1994 Susan O'Neill (Aus) 2:00.86

400 yards freestyle
1930 Joyce Cooper (Eng) 5:25.4

440 yards freestyle
1934 Phyllis Dewar (Can) 5:45.6
1938 Dorothy Green (Aus) 5:39.7
1950 Joan Harrison (SAf) 5:26.4
1954 Lorraine Crapp (Aus) 5:11.4
1958 Ilsa Konrads (Aus) 4:49.4
1962 Dawn Fraser (Aus) 4:51.4
1966 Kathy Wainwright (Aus)
    4:38.8

400 metres freestyle
1970 Karen Moras (Aus) 4:27.38
1974 Jenny Turrall (Aus) 4:22.09
1978 Tracey Wickham (Aus)
    4:08.45
1982 Tracey Wickham (Aus)
    4:08.82
1986 Sarah Hardcastle (Eng)
    4:07.68
1990 Hayley Lewis (Aus) 4:08.89
1994 Hayley Lewis (Aus) 4:12.56

800 metres freestyle
1970 Karen Moras (Aus) 9:02.45
1974 Jaynie Parkhouse (NZ)
    8:58.49
1978 Tracey Wickham (Aus)
    8:24.62
1982 Tracey Wickham (Aus)
    8:29.05
1986 Sarah Hardcastle (Eng)
    8:24.77
1990 Julie McDonald (Aus) 8:30.27
1994 Stacey Gartrell (Aus) 8:30.18

4 x 100 yards freestyle relay
1930 England 4:32.8
1934 Canada 4:21.8

4 x 110 yards freestyle relay
1938 Canada 4:48.3
1950 Australia 4:44.9
1954 South Africa 4:33.9
1958 Australia 4:17.4
1962 Australia 4:11.0
1966 Canada 4:10.8

4 x 100 metres freestyle relay
1970 Australia 4:06.41
1974 Canada 3:57.14
1978 Canada 3:50.28
1982 England 3:54.23
1986 Canada 3:48.45
1990 Australia 3:46.85
1994 England 3:46.23

4 x 200 metres freestyle relay
1986 Australia 8:12.09
1990 Australia 8:08.95
1994 Australia 8:08.06

100 yards backstroke
1930 Joyce Cooper (Eng) 1:15.0
1934 Phyllis Harding (Eng) 1:13.8

110 yards backstroke
1938 Pat Norton (Aus) 1:19.5
1950 Judy-Joy Davies (Aus) 1:18.6
1954 Joan Harrison (SAf) 1:15.2
1958 Judy Grinham (Eng) 1:11.9
1962 Linda Ludgrove (Eng) 1:11.1
1966 Linda Ludgrove (Eng) 1:09.2

100 metres backstroke
1970 Lynne Watson (Aus) 1:07.10
1974 Wendy Cook (Can) 1:06.37
1978 Debra Forster (Aus) 1:03.97
1982 Lisa Forrest (Aus) 1:03.48
1986 Sylvia Hume (NZ) 1:04.00
1990 Nicole Livingstone (Aus)
    1:02.46
1994 Nicola Stevenson (Aus)
    1:02.68 (née Livingstone)

220 yards backstroke
1962 Linda Ludgrove (Eng) 2:35.2
1966 Linda Ludgrove (Eng) 2:28.5

200 metres backstroke
1970 Lynne Watson (Aus) 2:22.86
1974 Wendy Cook (Can) 2:20.37
1978 Cheryl Gibson (Can) 2:16.57
1982 Lisa Forrest (Aus) 2:13.36
1986 Georgina Parkes (Aus)
    2:14.88
1990 Anna Simcic (NZ) 2:12.32
1994 Nicola Stevenson (Aus)
    2:12.73

110 yards breaststroke
1962 Anita Lonsbrough (Eng)
    1:21.3
1966 Diana Harris (Eng) 1:19.7

100 metres breaststroke
1970 Beverley Whitfield (Aus)
    1:17.40
1974 Catherine Gaskell (Eng)
    1:16.42
1978 Robin Corsiglia (Can) 1:13.56
1982 Kathy Bald (Can) 1:11.89
1986 Allison Higson (Can) 1:10.84
1990 Keltie Duggan (Can) 1:10.74
1994 Samantha Riley (Aus) 1:08.02

200 yards breaststroke
1930 Celia Wolstenholme (Eng)
    2:54.8
1934 Claire Dennis (Aus) 2:50.2

220 yards breaststroke
1938 Doris Storey (Eng) 3:06.3

1950 Elenor Gordon (Sco) 3:01.7
1954 Elenor Gordon (Sco) 2:59.2
1958 Anita Lonsbrough (Eng)
    2:53.5
1962 Anita Lonsbrough (Eng)
    2:51.7
1966 Jill Slattery (Eng) 2:50.3

200 metres breaststroke
1970 Beverley Whitfield (Aus)
    2:44.12
1974 Pat Beavan (Wal) 2:43.11
1978 Lisa Borsholt (Can) 2:37.70
1982 Anne Ottenbrite (Can) 2:32.07
1986 Allison Higson (Can) 2:31.20
1990 Nathalia Giguere (Can)
    2:32.16
1994 Samantha Riley (Aus) 2:25.53

110 yards butterfly
1958 Beverley Bainbridge (Aus)
    1:13.5
1962 Mary Stewart (Can) 1:10.1
1966 Elaine Tanner (Can) 1:06.8

100 metres butterfly
1970 Diane Lansley (Eng) 1:07.90
1974 Patti Stenhouse (Can) 1:05.38
1978 Wendy Quirk (Can) 1:01.92
1982 Lisa Curry (Aus) 1:01.22
1986 Caroline Cooper (Eng)
    1:02.12
1990 Lisa Curry-Kenny (Aus)
    1:00.66
1994 Petra Thomas (Aus) 1:00.21

220 yards butterfly
1966 Elaine Tanner (Can) 2:29.9

200 metres butterfly
1970 Maree Robinson (Aus)
    2:24.67
1974 Sandra Yost (Aus) 2:20.57
1978 Michelle Ford (Aus) 2:11.29
1982 Michelle Ford (Aus) 2:11.89
1986 Donna McGinnis (Can)
    2:11.97
1990 Hayley Lewis (Aus) 2:11.15
1994 Susan O'Neill (Aus) 2:09.96

200 metres individual medley
1970 Denise Langford (Aus)
    2:28.89
1974 Leslie Cliff (Can) 2:24.13
1978 Sharron Davies (Eng) 2:18.37
1982 Lisa Curry (Aus) 2:16.94
1986 Suzanne Landells (Aus)
    2:17.02
1990 Nancy Sweetnam (Can)
    2:15.61
1994 Elli Overton (Aus) 2:15.59

---

440 yards individual medley
1962 Anita Lonsbrough (Eng) 5:38.6
1966 Elaine Tanner (Can) 5:26.3

400 metres individual medley
1970 Denise Langford (Aus) 5:10.74
1974 Leslie Cliff (Can) 5:01.35
1978 Sharron Davies (Eng) 4:52.44
1982 Lisa Curry (Aus) 4:51.95
1986 Suzanne Landells (Aus) 4:45.82
1990 Hayley Lewis (Aus) 4:42.65
1994 Elli Overton (Aus) 4:44.01

3 x 100 yards medley relay
1934 Canada 3:42.0

3 x 110 yards medley relay
1938 England 3:57.7
1950 Australia 3:53.8
1954 Scotland 3:51.0

4 x 110 yards medley relay
Butterfly leg added
1958 England 4:54.0
1962 Australia 4:45.9
1966 England 4:40.6

4 x 100 metres medley relay
1970 Australia 4:30.66
1974 Canada 4:24.77
1978 Canada 4:15.26
1982 Canada 4:14.33
1986 England 4:13.48
1990 Australia 4:10.87
1994 Australia 4:07.89

Springboard diving
1930 Oonagh Whitsett (SAf)
1934 Judy Moss (Can)
1938 Irene Donnett (Aus)
1950 Edna Child (Eng)
1954 Ann Long (Eng)
1958 Charmian Welsh (Eng)
1962 Susan Knight (Aus)
1966 Kathy Rowlatt (Eng)
1970 Beverley Boys (Can)
1974 Cindy Shatto (Can)
1978 Janet Nutter (Can)
1982 Jenny Donnet (Aus)
1986 Debbie Fuller (Can)
1990 **3m** Jenny Donnet (Aus)
1m Mary De Piero (Can)
1994 **3m** Annie Pelletier (Can)
1m Annie Pelletier (Can)

Highboard diving
1930 Pearl Stoneham (Can)
1934 Elizabeth Macready (Eng)
1938 Lurline Hook (Aus)
1950 Edna Child (Eng)
1954 Barbara McAulay (Aus)
1958 Charmian Welsh (Eng)
1962 Susan Knight (Aus)

1966 Joy Newman (Eng)
1970 Beverley Boys (Can)
1974 Beverley Boys (Can)
1978 Linda Cuthbert (Can)
1982 Valerie Beddoe (Aus)
1986 Debbie Fuller (Can)
1990 Anna Dacyshyn (Can)
1994 Anne Montminy (Can)

Synchronised swimming - solo
1986 Sylvie Frechette (Can)
1990 Sylvie Frechette (Can)
1994 Lisa Alexander (Can)

Synchronised swimming - duet
1986 Carolyn Waldo & Michelle Cameron (Can)
1990 Katherine Glen & Christine Larsen (Can)
1994 Lisa Alexander & Erin Woodley (Can)

Synchronised swimming - team
1986 Canada

Weightlifting

Three lifts 1950-70, two from 1974. Separate medals also awarded for each lift - snatch, clean and jerk from 1990. All weights are for totals in kilograms (originally measured in pounds 1950-66). The weight categories changed in 1994.

Flyweight - up to 52kg
1970 George Vasiliades (Aus) 290
1974 Precious McKenzie (Eng) 215
1978 Ekambaram Karunakaran (Ind) 205
1982 Nick Voukelatos (Aus) 207.5
1986 Greg Hayman (Aus) 212.5
1990 Chandersekaran Raghavan (Ind) 232.5

54kg
1994 Badathala Adisekhar (Ind) 237.5

Bantamweight - up to 56kg
1950 Tho Fook Hung (Mal) 297
1954 Maurice Megennis (Eng) 281
1958 Reginald Gaffley (SAf) 299
1962 Chua Phung Kim (Sin) 322
1966 Precious McKenzie (Eng) 319.5
1970 Precious McKenzie (Eng) 335
1974 Michael Adams (Aus) 222.5
1978 Precious McKenzie (NZ) 220
1982 Geoffrey Laws (Eng) 235
1986 Nick Voukelatos (Aus) 245
1990 Rangaswamy Punnuswamy (Ind) 247.5

59kg
1994 Marcus Stephen (Nauru) 262.5

Featherweight - up to 60kg
1950 Koh Eng Tong (Mal) 310.5
1954 Rodney Wilkes (Tri) 313
1958 Tan Ser Cher (Sin) 310.5
1962 George Newton (Eng) 326.5
1966 Kum Weng Chung (Wal) 337
1970 George Perrin (Eng) 342.5
1974 George Vasiliades (Aus) 237.5
1978 Michel Mercier (Can) 237.5
1982 Dean Willey (Eng) 267.5
1986 Raymond Williams (Wal) 252.5
1990 Chandra Sharma (Ind) 257.5

64kg
1994 Sevdalin Marinov (Aus) 277.5

Lightweight - up to 67.5kg
1950 James Halliday (Eng) 344.5
1954 Verdi Barberis (Aus) 347
1958 Tan Howe Liang (Sin) 358
1962 Carlton Goring (Eng) 351.5
1966 Hugo Gittens (Tri) 367
1970 George Newton (Eng) 372.5
1974 George Newton (Eng) 260
1978 Bill Stellios (Aus) 272.5
1982 David Morgan (Wal) 295
1986 Dean Willey (Eng) 315
1990 Paramjit Sharma (Ind) 295

70kg
1994 Moji Oluwa (Nig) 295

Middleweight - up to 75kg
1950 Gerard Gratton (Can) 360.5
1954 James Halliday (Eng) 362.5
1958 Blair Blenman (Bar) 360.5
1962 Tan Howe Laing (Sin) 390
1966 Pierre St Jean (Can) 404.5
1970 Russell Perry (Aus) 412.5
1974 Tony Ebert (NZ) 275
1978 Sam Castiglione (Aus) 300
1982 Stephen Pinsent (Eng) 312.5
1986 Bill Stellios (Aus) 302.5
1990 Ron Laycock (Aus) 310

76kg
1994 David Morgan (Wal) 327.5

Light-Heavyweight - up to 82.5kg
1950 James Varaleau (Can) 369.5
1954 Gerry Gratton (Can) 403.5
1958 Phil Caira (Sco) 396.5
1962 Phil Caira (Sco) 408
1966 George Vakakis (Aus) 419.5
1970 Nicolo Ciancio (Aus) 447.5
1974 Tony Ford (Eng) 302.5
1978 Robert Kabbas (Aus) 322.5
1982 Newton Burrowes (Eng) 325
1986 David Morgan (Wal) 350
1990 David Morgan (Wal) 347.5

83kg
1994 Kiril Kounev (Aus) 352.5

Middle-Heavyweight - up to 90kg
1954 Keevil Daly (Can) 399
1958 Manoel Santos (Aus) 403.5
1962 Louis Martin (Eng) 469.5
1966 Louis Martin (Eng) 462
1970 Louis Martin (Eng) 457.5
1974 Nicolo Ciancio (Aus) 330
1978 Gary Langford (Eng) 335
1982 Robert Kabbas (Aus) 337.5
1986 Keith Boxell (Eng) 350
1990 Duncan Dawkins (Eng) 357.5

91kg
1994 Harvey Goodman (Aus) 362.5

Sub-Heavyweight - up to 100kg
1978 John Burns (Wal) 340
1982 Oliver Orok (Nig) 350
1986 Denis Garon (Can) 360
1990 Andrew Saxton (Eng) 362.5

99kg
1994 Andrew Callard (Eng) 347.5

Heavyweight - up to 110kg
1950 Harold Cleghorn (NZ) 408
1954 Doug Hepburn (Can) 471.5
1958 Ken McDonald (Eng) 455.5
1962 Arthur Shannos (Aus) 465
1966 Donald Oliver (NZ) 497
1970 Russell Prior (Can) 490
1974 Russell Prior (Can) 352.5
1978 Russell Prior (Can) 347.5
1982 John Burns (Wal) 347.5
1986 Kevin Roy (Can) 375
1990 Mark Thomas (Eng) 357.5

108kg
1994 Nicu Vlad (Aus) 405

Super Heavyweight - over 110kg
1970 Ray Rigby (Aus) 500
1974 Graham May (NZ) 342.5
1978 Jean-Marc Cardinal (Can) 365
1982 Dean Lukin (Aus) 377.5
1986 Dean Lukin (Aus) 392.5
1990 Andrew Davies (Wal) 402.5

Over 108kg
1994 Stefan Botev (Aus) 360

Wrestling

48kg - Light-Flyweight
1970 Ved Prakash (Ind)
1974 Mitchell Kawasaki (Can)
1978 Ashok Kumar (Ind)
1982 Ram Chander Sarang (Ind)
1986 Ron Moncur (Can)
1994 Jacob Isaac (Nig)

52kg - Flyweight
1950 Bert Harris (Aus)
1954 Louis Baise (SAf)
1958 Ian Epton (SAf)
1962 Mohammad Niaz (Pak)
1966 Mohammad Nazir (Pak)

1970 Sudesh Kumar (Ind)
1974 Sudesh Kumar (Ind)
1978 Ray Takahashi (Can)
1982 Mahabir Singh (Ind)
1986 Chris Woodcroft (Can)
1994 Selwyn Tam (Can)

57kg - Bantamweight
1930 James Trifunov (Can)
1934 Edward Melrose (Sco)
1938 Ted Purcell (Aus)
1950 Douglas Mudgeway (NZ)
1954 Geoffrey Jameson (Aus)
1958 Muhammad Akhtar (Pak)
1962 Siraj-ud-Din (Pak)
1966 Bishambar Singh (Ind)
1970 Sadar Mohd (Pak)
1974 Premnath (Ind)
1978 Satbir Singh (Ind)
1982 Brian Aspen (Eng)
1986 Mitch Ostberg (Can)
1994 Robert Dawson (Can)

62kg - Featherweight
1930 Clifford Chilcott (Can)
1934 Robert McNab (Can)
1938 Roy Purchase (Aus)
1950 John Armitt (NZ)
1954 Abraham Geldenhuys (SAf)
1958 Abraham Geldenhuys (SAf)
1962 Ala-ud-Din (Pak)
1966 Mohammad Akhtar (Pak)
1970 Mohammad Saeed (Pak)
1974 Egon Beiler (Can)
1978 Egon Beiler (Can)
1982 Bob Robinson (Can)
1986 Paul Hughes (Can)
1994 Marty Calder (Can)

68kg - Lightweight
1930 Howard Thomas (Can)
1934 Richard Garrard (Aus)
1938 Richard Garrard (Aus)
1950 Richard Garrard (Aus)
1954 Godfrey Pienaar (SAf)
1958 Muhammad Ashraf (Pak)
1962 Muhammad Akhtar (Pak)
1966 Mukhtiar Singh (Ind)
1970 Udey Chand (Ind)
1974 Jagrup Singh (Ind)
1978 Zsigmund Kelevitz (Aus)
1982 Jagminder Singh (Ind)
1986 David McKay (Can)
1994 Chris Wilson (Can)

74kg - Welterweight
1930 Reg Priestley (Can)
1934 Joseph Schleimer (Can)
1938 Thomas Trevaskis (Aus)
1950 Henry Hudson (Can)
1954 Nicholas Laubscher (SAf)
1958 Muhammad Bashir (Pak)
1962 Muhammad Bashir (Pak)

1966 Muhammad Bashir (Pak)
1970 Mukhtiar Singh (Ind)
1974 Raghunath Pawar (Ind)
1978 Rajinder Singh (Ind)
1982 Rajinder Singh (Ind)
1986 Gary Holmes (Can)
1994 David Hohl (Can)

82kg - Middleweight
1930 Mike Chepwick (Can)
1934 Terry Evans (Can)
1938 Terry Evans (Can)
1950 Maurice Vachon (Can)
1954 Hermanus van Zyl (SAf)
1958 Hermanus van Zyl (SAf)
1962 Muhammad Faiz (Pak)
1966 Muhammad Faiz (Pak)
1970 Harish Rajindra (Ind)
1974 David Aspin (NZ)
1978 Richard Deschatelets (Can)
1982 Chris Rinke (Can)
1986 Chris Rinke (Can)
1994 Justin Abdou (Can)

90kg - Light-Heavyweight
1930 Bill McIntyre (Can)
1934 Mick Cubbin (SAf)
1938 Edward Scarf (Aus)
1950 Patrick Morton (SAf)
1954 Jacob Theron (SAf)
1958 Jacob Theron (SAf)
1962 Anthony Buck (Eng)
1966 Robert Chamberot (Can)
1970 Muhammad Faiz (Pak)
1974 Terry Paice (Can)
1978 Stephen Danier (Can)
1982 Clark Davis (Can)
1986 Noel Loban (Eng)
1994 Scott Bianco (Can)

100kg - Heavyweight
1930 Earl McCready (Can)
1934 Jack Knight (Aus)
1938 Jack Knight (Aus)
1950 James Armstrong (Aus)
1954 Kenneth Richmond (Eng)
1958 Lila Ram (Ind)
1962 Muhammad Niaz (Pak)
1966 Bhim Singh (Ind)
1970 Edward Millard (Can)
1974 Claude Pilon (Can)
1978 Wyatt Wishart (Can)
1982 Richard Deschatelets (Can)
1986 Clark Davis (Can)
1994 Greg Edgelow (Can)

Over 100kg - Super-Heavyweight
Limit 130kg from 1986.
1970 Ikram Ilahi (Pak)
1974 Bill Benko (Can)
1978 Robert Gibbons (Can)
1982 Wyatt Wishart (Can)
1986 Wayne Brightwell (Can)
1994 Andrew Borodow (Can)

Commonwealth Games Medals by Nation 1930 to 1994

Gold - G, Silver - S, Bronze - B

Nation	G	S	B	Total
England	451	413	417	1281
Australia	484	426	365	1275
Canada	327	343	345	1015
New Zealand	99	137	181	417
Scotland	62	77	120	259
South Africa *	62	48	52	162
Wales	37	47	66	150
India	43	47	38	128
Kenya	42	29	41	112
Nigeria	30	38	39	107
Northern Ireland #	20	22	37	79
Jamaica	22	18	20	60
Pakistan	20	13	13	46
Ghana	12	16	13	41
Malaysia	12	13	11	36
Uganda	8	13	15	36
Zambia	3	11	18	32
Trinidad & Tobago	7	11	13	31
Zimbabwe	3	10	17	30
Hong Kong	5	2	9	17
Tanzania	3	5	6	14
Bahamas	3	6	4	13
Guyana	2	5	6	13
Singapore	4	1	4	9
Fiji	2	2	5	9
Sri Lanka	3	4	1	8
Western Samoa	-	2	6	8
Cyprus	3	2	2	7
Nauru	4	2	-	6
Barbados	1	3	2	6
Guernsey	1	3	2	6
Isle of Man	2	-	3	5
Papua New Guinea	1	3	1	5
Bermuda	1	1	2	4
Jersey	1	-	3	4
Malawi	-	-	3	3
Swaziland	-	1	2	3
St. Vincent	1	-	1	2
Bangladesh	1	-	1	2
Namibia	1	-	1	2
Botswana	-	-	2	2
Gambia	-	-	1	1
Malta	-	-	1	1
Norfolk Island	-	-	1	1
Seychelles	-	-	1	1
Tonga	-	1	-	1
TOTAL	1566	1558	1650	4774

Commonwealth Games Medals by Nation 1994

Nation	G	S	B	Total
Australia	87	52	43	182
Canada	40	42	46	128
England	31	45	49	125
New Zealand	5	16	20	41
Nigeria	11	13	13	37
India	6	11	7	24
Scotland	6	3	11	20
Kenya	7	4	8	19
Wales	5	8	6	19
South Africa	2	4	5	11
Northern Ireland	5	2	3	10
Jamaica	2	4	2	8
Malaysia	2	3	2	7
Zimbabwe	-	-	3	6
Cyprus	2	1	2	5
Zambia	1	1	2	4
Hong Kong	-	-	4	4
Nauru	3	-	-	3
Sri Lanka	1	2	-	3
Pakistan	-	-	3	3
Namibia	1	-	1	2
Trinidad & Tobago	-	-	2	2
Uganda	-	-	2	2
Papua New Guinea	-	1	-	1
Western Samoa	-	1	-	1
Bermuda	-	-	1	1
Botswana	-	-	1	1
Ghana	-	-	1	1
Guernsey	-	-	1	1
Norfolk Island	-	-	1	1
Seychelles	-	-	1	1
Tanzania	-	-	1	1
Tonga	-	1	-	1

no longer a member of the Commonwealth

 # Ireland in 1930

Most gold medals

9 Bill Hoskyns (Eng) fencing - 3 individual épée and 6 team golds 1958-70

9 Michael Wenden (Aus) swimming - 4 individual and 5 relay golds 1966-74

Women's record

7 Marjorie Jackson (Aus) athletics - 4 individual and 3 relay 1950-4

7 Raelene Boyle (Aus) athletics - 5 individual and 2 relay 1970-82

Most gold medals won at one Games

6 Graham Smith (Can) swimming - 4 individual and 2 relay 1978

5 Decima Norman (Aus) athletics - 3 individual and 2 relay 1938

5 Hayley Lewis (Aus) swimming - 4 individual and 1 relay 1990

Most medals

14 Phillip Adams (Aus) shooting - 6 gold, 7 silver, 1 bronze 1982-90

13 Michael Wenden (Aus) swimming - 9 gold, 3 silver, 1 bronze 1966-74

13 Ivan Lund (Aus) fencing - 3 gold, 6 silver, 4 bronze 1950-62

Women's record

9 Raelene Boyle (Aus) athletics - 7 gold, 2 silver 1970-82

8 Dawn Fraser (Aus) swimming - 6 gold, 2 silver 1958-62

Most medals won at one Games

8 Ralph Hutton (Can) swimming - 1 gold, 5 silver, 2 bronze 1966

7 Elaine Tanner (Can) swimming - 4 gold, 3 silver 1966

Other Major International Games and Championships

All-African Games

The first African Games, at ten sports, were contested in Brazzaville, Congo in 1965. Subsequent Games were staged at Lagos, Nigeria in 1973, at Algiers in 1978, Nairobi, Kenya in 1987 and at Cairo, Egypt in 1991, when 42 nations took part. The 1995 Games have been awarded to Zimbabwe.

Asian Games

The first Asian Games were held at New Delhi, India on 8-11 Mar 1951, when ten nations took part. These multi-sport Games have since 1954 been held at four-yearly intervals. In 1990 new records were set with some 6000 competitors at 29 sports, including two demonstration ones, from 36 nations, of which 25 won medals. Those figures were exceeded in 1994, when there were about 6800 competitors from 43 nations, of which 32 won medals.

Venues: 1951 New Delhi, 1954 Manila, 1958 Tokyo, 1962 Djakarta, 1966 Bangkok, 1970 Bangkok, 1974 Teheran, 1978 Bangkok, 1982 New Delhi, 1986 Seoul, 1990 Beijing, 1994 Hiroshima.

A precursor of the Asian Games were the Far Eastern Games, first held in 1913 in Manila, with China, the Phillipines and two Japanese athletes taking part. These Games were held every two years to 1927 and then in 1930 and 1934.

Medal table of leading nations in 1994

Nation	Gold	Silver	Bronze
China	137	92	60
South Korea	63	53	63
Japan	59	68	80
Kazkhstan	25	26	26

Central American and Caribbean Games

First held in 1926 in Mexico City, and at four-yearly intervals ever since except for 1942. The 16th Games were staged a year early in Puerto Rico in 1993.

Goodwill Games

First staged in 1986 Games in Moscow and run by the Turner Broadcast System not only as an important televised sports meeting, but also to promote goodwill between the USA and the USSR following the boycotts by the USA of the 1980 Olympic Games and by the USSR of the 1984 Olympic Games. The second Goodwill Games were staged in Seattle in 1990 at 21 sports and the third Games in St Petersburg and Moscow at 24 sports in 1994. The 1998 Games are scheduled for New York.

Pan-Arab Games

These Games were instituted by decree of the Arab League in 1951, and first held in 1953. Thereafter they were staged every four years until 1965, but then a gap until 1985 (at 18 sports).

South East Asia Games

First held in Bangkok, Thailand in 1959, they have subsequently been held bienially except for 1963. At the 15th Games in 1989 in Kuala Lumpur, Malaysia 24 sports were contested, including, amongst more familiar ones, the regional sports of sepak takrwa and silat olahraga, a martial art. The 16th Games were held in 1991 in Manila, Philippines and the 17th in Singapore in 1993.

World Games

A four-yearly international championship for sports not on the Olympic programme, the World Games were first held at Santa Clara, USA in 1981. Subsequent festivals were held in London (UK) 1985, Karlruhe (FRG) in 1989 and Amsterdam (Hol) in 1993.

World Student Games

The 'Universiade' or World Student Games, organised by the Féderation Internationale du Sport Universitaire (FISU), is well established as one of the world's most important sports meetings, although it has been somewhat under-regarded in the UK and perhaps in the USA.

The first 'International Universities' Games was held in Warsaw, organised by the Confédération Internationale des Étudiants (CIE). From 1951 to 1962 rival Games were staged by FISU and the UIE. The latter, Communist inspired, were known as the World Youth Games from 1954 and these had the higher standards. From 1963, however, the Games merged and are now held biennially.

Ten sports are usually included at the summer Games: association football, athletics, basketball, fencing, gymnastics, judo, swimming, tennis, volleyball and water polo.

Venues (from 1951-61: U - UIE, F - FISU)
1924 Warsaw, 1927 Rome, 1928 Paris, 1930 Darmstadt, 1933 Turin, 1935 Budapest, 1937 Paris, 1939 Monaco, 1947 Paris, 1949 Budapest, 1951 Berlin (U) & Luxembourg (F), 1953 Bucharest (U) & Dortmund (F), 1954 Budapest (U), 1955 Warsaw (U) & San Sebastián (F), 1957 Moscow (U) & Paris (F), 1959 Vienna (U) & Turin (F), 1961 Sofia (F), 1962 Helsinki (U), 1963 Porto Alegre, 1965 Budapest, 1967 Tokyo, 1970 Turin, 1973 Moscow, 1975 Rome (unofficial), 1977 Sofia, 1979 Mexico City, 1981 Bucharest, 1983 Edmonton, 1985 Kobe, 1987 Zagreb, 1989 Duisberg (restricted schdeule of athletics, men's basketball, fencing and rowing after São Paulo withdrew). 1991 Sheffield, 1993 Buffalo, 1995 Fukuoka.

Winter sports are staged at the Winter Universiade, of which the 17th was at Jaca, Spain in 1995. There are also separate World University Championships at various other sports.

Pan American Games

The Pan-American Games are multi-sport competitions open to athletes from North, Central and South American nations. They have been held every four years from 1951, when the Games were opened in Buenos Aires by the Argentinian President, Juan Perón, in front of a 100,000 crowd. They were originally planned for 1942, but delayed due to the outbreak of war.

A record 37 sports were contested at the Games in 1995, when there were over 5000 competitors from a record 42 nations affiliated to the controlling body, the Pan-American Sports Organization.

Venues
1951 Buenos Aires, ARG; 1955 Mexico City, MEX; 1959 Chicago, USA; 1963 São Paulo, BRA; 1967 Winnipeg, CAN; 1971 Cali, COL; 1975 Mexico City, MEX; 1979 San Juan, PR; 1983 Caracas, VEN; 1987 Indianapolis, USA; 1991 Havana, CUB; 1995 Mar del Plata, ARG

Athletics - Games best performances

Men	min: sec	Name	Year
100 metres	10.06	Leandro Peñalver (Cub)	1983
200 metres	19.86	Don Quarrie (Jam)	1971
400 metres	44.45	Ronnie Ray (USA)	1975
800 metres	1:46.02	José Luiz Barbosa (Bra)	1995
1500 metres	3:40.5	Don Paige (USA)	1979
5000 metres	13:31.40	Arturo Barrios (Mex)	1987
10000 metres	28:20.37	Bruce Bickford (USA)	1987
Marathon	2hr 12:42	Jorge González (PR)	1983
3000m steeple	8:14.41	Wander Moura (Bra)	1995
110m hurdles	13.20	Renaldo Nehemiah (USA)	1979
400m hurdles	48.49	Winthrop Graham (Jam)	1987
4x100m relay	38.31	USA	1975
4x400m relay	2:59.54	USA	1987
20km walk	1hr 22:53	Jefferson Pérez (Ecu)	1995
50km walk	3hr 47:55	Carlos Mercenario (Mex)	1995

	Metres	Name	Year
High jump	2.40	Javier Sotomayor (Cub)	1995
Pole vault	5.75	Pat Manson (USA)	1995
Long jump	8.75	Carl Lewis (USA)	1987
Triple Jump	17.89	João Carlos de Oliveira (Bra)	1975
Shot	20.52	C J Hunter (USA)	1995
Discus	67.32	Luis M Delis (Cub)	1983
Hammer	77.24	Jud Logan (USA)	1987
Javelin (old)	84 16	Duncan Atwood (USA)	1979
(new)	79.28	Emeterio González (Cub)	1995
Decathlon	8024 pts	Bruce Jenner (USA)	1975

Women	min: sec	Name	Year
100 metres	11.05	Evelyn Ashford (USA) (semi)	1979
	11.05	Chryste Gaines (USA)	1995
200 metres	22.24w	Evelyn Ashford (USA)	1979
	22.45	Ashford (in semi)	1979
400 metres	49.61	Ana F Quirot (Cub)	1991
800 metres	1:58.71	Ana F Quirot (Cub)	1991
1500 metres	4:05.7	Mary Decker (USA)	1979
3000 metres	8:53.6	Jan Merrill (USA)	1979
10000 metres	33:00.00	Marty Cooksey (USA)	1987
Marathon	2hr 43:36	Olga Avalos (Mex)	1991
100m hurdles	12.81	LaVonna Martin (USA)	1987
	12.68w	Aliuska López (Cub)	1995
400m hurdles	54.23	Judi Brown King (USA)	1987
4x100m relay	42.90	USA	1975
4x400m relay	3:23.35	USA	1987
10km walk	46:31.93	Graciela Mendoza (Mex)	1995

	Metres	Name	Year
High Jump	1.96	Coleen Sommer (USA)	1987
Long jump	7.45	Jackie Joyner (USA)	1987
Triple jump	14.09	Laiza Carrillo (Cub)	1995
Shot	19.34	María Sarria (Cub)	1983
Discus	65.58	Maritza Martén (Cub)	1987
Hammer	58.92	Alexandra Givan (USA)	1995
Javelin	64.78	Dulce M Garcia (Cub)	1983
Heptathlon	6266 pts	Jamie McNeair (USA)	1995

w = wind assisted mark

Most individual event wins
4 Osvaldo Suárez (Arg) 5000m 1955, 1963; 10000m 1955, 1959

4 João Carlos de Oliveira (Bra) long jump and triple jump 1975 and 1979

4 Ana Quirot (Cub) 400m & 800m 1987, 1991

Swimming - Games best performances

Event	min:sec	Name	Year
Men			
50m freestyle	22.55	Tom Williams (USA)	1987
100m freestyle	49.31	Gustavo Borges (Bra)	1995
200m freestyle	1:48.49	Gustavo Borges (Bra)	1995
400m freestyle	3:50.38	Sean Killion (USA)	1991
1500m freestyle	15:20.90	Alex Kostich (USA)	1987
4 x 100m free	3:18.68	USA	1995
4 x 200m free	7:21.61	USA	1995
100m back	54.74	Jeff Rouse (USA)	1995
200m back	1:59.34	Rick Carey (USA)	1983
100m breast	1:02.28	Steve Lundquist (USA)	1983
200m breast	2:15.50	Marion González (Cub)	1991
100m butterfly	53.45	Anthony Nesty (Sur)	1991
200m butterfly	1:58.85	Craig Beardsley (USA)	1983
200m IM	2:00.92	Ronald Karnaugh (USA)	1991
400m IM	4:18.55	Curtis Myden (Can)	1995
4x100m medley	3:40.42	USA	1983
Women			
50m freestyle	26.01	Kristen Tropham (Can)	1991
100m freestyle	55.62	Angel Martino (USA)	1995
200m freestyle	1:58.43	Cynthia Woodhead (USA)	1979
400m freestyle	4:10.56	Cynthia Woodhead (USA)	1979
800m freestyle	8:34.72	Tami Bruce (USA)	1987
4 x 100m free	3:44.71	USA	1995
4 x 200m free	8:07.30	USA	1995
100m back	1:01.71	Barbara Bedford (USA)	1995
200m back	2:13.65	Katie Welch (USA	1987
100m breast	1:10.36	Lisa Flood (Can)	1995
200m breast	2:28.69	Dorsey Tierney (USA)	1991
100m butterfly	1:00.53	Jill Sterkel (USA)	1979
200m butterfly	2:09.77	Mary T Meagher (USA)	1983
200m IM	2:15.66	Joanne Malar (Can)	1995
400m IM	4:43.64	Joanne Malar (Can)	1995
4x100m medley	4:08.17	USA	1995

Most individual event wins
Men: 4 Steve Furniss (USA) 200m and 400m ind. medley 1971 and 1975

Women: 4 Cynthia Woodhead (USA) 100m, 200m and 400m freestyle 1979, 200m freestyle 1983; 4 Tracy Caulkins (USA) 200m and 400m ind. medley 1979 and 1983

Leading nations at all sports 1951-95

Nation	Gold	Silver	Bronze	Total
USA	1426	1016	670	3012

					1995 Games - leading nations at all sports			
					Nation	*Gold*	*Silver*	*Bronze*
Cuba	580	415	354	1349	USA	169	146	109
Canada	217	394	505	1116	Cuba	112	66	60
Argentina	206	224	275	705	Canada	48	60	69
Brazil	134	171	236	541	Argentina	40	45	74
Mexico	108	150	318	576	Mexico	23	20	37
Venezuela	38	104	145	287	Brazil	18	27	37
Chile	28	51	82	161				
Colombia	25	64	107	196	*31 nations won medals (15 golds).*			
Puerto Rico	14	57	84	155				

Sportsmen and Women of the Year

Sports Illustrated Sportsman of the Year

The great American magazine has awarded this title annually since 1954 to the sports man or woman who 'symbolizes in character and performance the ideals of sportsmanship'. Nationality US unless shown. *Winners:*
1954 Roger Bannister (UK, T & F, miler)
1955 Johnny Podres (baseball)
1956 Bobby Joe Morrow (T & F, sprinter)
1957 Stan Musial (baseball)
1958 Rafer Johnson (T & F, decathlon)
1959 Ingemar Johansson (Swe, boxing)
1960 Arnold Palmer (golf)
1961 Jerry Lucas (basketball)
1962 Terry Baker (football)
1963 Pete Rozelle (NFL commissioner)
1964 Ken Venturi (golf)
1965 Sanford Koufax (baseball)
1966 Jim Ryun (T & F, miler)
1967 Carl Yastrzemski (basketball)
1968 Bill Russell (basketball)
1969 Tommy Seaver (baseball)
1970 Bobby Orr (Can, ice hockey)
1971 Lee Trevino (golf)
1972 Billie Jean King (tennis) &
  John Wooden (basketball coach)
1973 Jackie Stewart (UK, motor racing)
1974 Muhammad Ali (boxing)
1975 Pete Rose (baseball)
1976 Chris Evert (tennis)
1977 Steve Cauthen (horse racing)
1978 Jack Nicklaus (golf)
1979 Willie Stargell (baseball) &
  Terry Bradshaw (football)
1980 US Olympic ice hockey team
1981 Ray Leonard (boxing)
1982 Wayne Gretzky (Can, ice hockey)
1983 Mary Decker (T & F, distance)
1984 Edwin Moses (T & F, 400m hurdler) &
  Mary Lou Retton (gymnastics)
1985 Kareem Abdul-Jabbar (basketball)
1986 Joe Paterno (football coach)
1987 'Athletes who care'
1988 Orel Hershiser (baseball)
1989 Greg LeMond (cycling)
1990 Joe Montana (football)
1991 Michael Jordan (basketball)
1992 Arthur Ashe (tennis)
1993 Don Shula (football coach)
1994 Johan Olav Koss (Nor) &
  Bonnie Blair (USA) (ice skating)
T & F = track and field athletics

Jesse Owens International Award

Presented annually in February following the year of achievement to the international athlete (in Olympic sports) who best personifies the qualities of the great Olympian, who won four gold medals in 1936. *Winners:*
1981 Eric Heiden (USA, speed skating)
1982 Sebastian Coe (UK, athletics)
1983 Mary Slaney (USA, athletics)
1984 Edwin Moses (USA, athletics)
1985 Carl Lewis (USA, athletics)
1986 Saïd Aouita (Mor, athletics)
1987 Greg Louganis (USA, diving)
1988 Ben Johnson (Can, athletics)
1989 Florence Griffith-Joyner (USA, athletics)
1990 Roger Kingdom (USA, athletics)
1991 Greg LeMond (USA, cycling)
1992 Mike Powell (USA, athletics)
1993 Wang Junxia (Chn, athletics)
1994 Johan Olav Koss (Nor, ice skating)

L'Equipe Champion des Champions

The French sports daily newspaper L'Equipe has selected the following as its world sports man or woman of the year:
1976 Alberto Juantorena (Cub, athletics)
1977 Rosemarie Ackermann (GDR, athletics)
1978 Henry Rono (Ken, athletics)
1979 Sebastian Coe (UK, athletics)
1980 Eric Heiden (USA, ice skating)
1981 Sebastian Coe (UK, athletics)
1982 Paolo Rossi (Ita, football)
1983 Carl Lewis (USA, athletics)
1984 Carl Lewis (USA, athletics)
1985 Sergey Bubka (USSR, athletics)
1986 Diego Maradona (Arg, football)
1987 Ben Johnson (Can, athletics)
1988 Florence Griffith-Joyner (USA, athletics)
1989 Greg LeMond (USA, cycling)
1990 Ayrton Senna (Bra, motor racing)
1991 Carl Lewis (USA, athletics)
1992 Michael Jordan (USA, basketball)
1993 Noureddine Morceli (Mor, athletics)
1994 Romario (Bra, football)

Index

This index contains the sports included in this book, with cross-references to alternative names. It also includes various competitions, but not many of those that are, by their name, obviously included in their respective sports.

ILLUSTRATIONS

The publishers would like to acknowledge the work
of the following Allsport photographers:

Al Bello pp 236, 393
Shaun Botterill pp 15 (left), 145, 240, 300, 308, 339
Howard Boylan pp 72, 74
Clive Brunskill pp 151, 160, 363
Simon Bruty pp 87, 295, 336
David Cannon pp 18, 177, 182 (both), 187, 188, 307
Graham Chadwick pp 106, 173
Chris Cole pp 131, 196, 207, 212, 231, 235
Phil Cole p 327
Michael Cooper pp 57, 82, 254, 333
Jonathan Daniel pp 65, 67, 70, 147
Tony Duffy pp 21, 30 (left), 38
John Gichigi p 135
Otto Greule p 66
Mike Hewitt pp 23, 199, 259
David Leah pp 35, 375
Bob Martin p 47, 192
Gray Mortimore pp 28, 30 (right), 31, 33, 248, 252, 315
Adrian Murrell p 104
Gary Newkirk p 179
Tertius Pickard p 113
Mike Powell pp 10, 24, 40,
Duncan Raban p 378
Ben Radford pp 105, 112
David Rogers p 225
Pascal Rondeau pp 76, 260, 273, 274
Dan Smith pp 100, 224
Holly Stein p 85
Steve Swope p 268
Anton Want pp 257, 302

Agence Vandystadt pp 15 (right), 132, 317, 319, 321,
324
Allsport Historical Collection p 84
Allsport USA p 69
International Olympic Committee p 19

POSTSCRIPT

I believe in packing as much as possible into my
books, and even with 416 pages in this volume, I have
not been able to include everything that enthusiasts
might regard as being of international significance.
With just a little more space to spare, however, here
are some details on one of the world's newest sports:

Snowboarding

World Championships

First held in 1993 *Winners:*

Men slalom
1993   Alexis Parmentier (Fra)
1995   Martin Freinademetz (Aut)

Men slalom parallel
1993   Mosa Cla (Swi)
1995   Martin Freinademetz (Aut)

Men halfpipe
1993   Terje Haakonsen (Nor)
1995   Terje Haakonsen (Nor)

Men combined
1993   Kevin Delany (USA)
1995   Bertrand Denervaud (Swi)

Women slalom
1993   Ashild Loftus (Nor)
1995   Christine Rauter (Aut)

Women slalom parallel
1993   Ashild Loftus (Nor)
1995   Michelle Taggart (USA)

Women halfpipe
1993   Nicole Angelrath (Swi)
1995   Satu Jarvela (Fin)

Women combined
1993   Michelle Taggart (USA)
1995   Sandra Farmand (Ger)